Index to Characters in the Performing Arts

Part IV:
Radio and Television

by

Harold S. Sharp

and

Marjorie Z. Sharp

The Scarecrow Press, Inc.
Metuchen, N.J.   1973

Library of Congress Cataloging in Publication Data

Sharp, Harold S   comp.
    Index to characters in the performing arts.

    Parts 2-   have imprint Metuchen, N. J., Scarecrow
Press.
    CONTENTS: pt. 1. Non-musical plays; an alphabetical
listing of 30,000 characters. 2 v.--pt. 2. Operas,
and musical productions. 2 v.--pt. 3. Ballets A-Z and
symbols.--pt. 4. Radio and television.
    1. Performing arts--Dictionaries. 2. Characters
and characteristics in literature--Dictionaries.
I. Sharp, Marjorie Z., joint comp. II. Title.
PN1579.S45   808.8292703   66-13744
ISBN 0-8108-0436-7 (pt. 3) 0-8108-0605-3 (pt. 4)

FOREWORD

Radio and television are comparatively modern media. Drama as such dates back more than 2000 years. Opera, as it is known today, originated, according to some authorities, in the year 1594; others contend that it was first performed in 1597. Ballet originated sometime during the late 16th century. The broadcasting of radio programs to the general public, however, commenced in the early 1920s and commercial television broadcasts followed approximately 25 years later. In spite of the comparatively short time that radio and television have been available to the public, audience coverage far exceeds that of the older types of performing arts. It has been estimated that a single broadcast of a popular Western, variety, detective, comedy or quiz television program is viewed by more people than have seen a live performance of "Hamlet" since it was first produced over 370 years ago.

With this, Part IV of the Index to Characters in the Performing Arts series, started almost nine years ago, the series is at last complete. Part I (1966) identifies characters of the non-musical plays in which they appear; Part II (1969) covers opera and musical productions; Part III (1972) deals with ballet, and this part is concerned with radio and television characters. Like the other books in the series, the object of this one is to identify characters with the productions in which they appear. It also gives a little information concerning each character, shows whether such characters were real people (Jack Benny, Bob Hope, Walter Winchell) or fictitious characters (Michael Shayne, Archie Bunker, Paladin), and indicates whether the production(s) in which they appeared were broadcast by radio, television, or both. It also designates the type of each program, as "detective drama," "variety," "quiz," "Western," "situation comedy," and the like.

This is in no sense a book of criticism. No attempt is made to evaluate the merits of any program or performer. It is intended essentially as a finding list.

The compilers of this book have sought to analyze the major national radio and television broadcasts since these first started. Local programs, "specials" and most minor, short-lived programs are not included. In all, approximately 2,500 programs are covered, and about 20,000 characters, actors and actresses are identified. Guest celebrities and persons and/or characters who appeared on programs only occasionally are not indicated by name. In terms of time, coverage extends from the inception of these broadcasting media to about 1955 in the case of radio and to the Fall, 1972, season for television.

This book consists of a single alphabetical listing of characters and of the productions in which they appear. A representative entry is shown below:

> BUNKER, ARCHIE, bigoted, opinionated
> head of the family
> EDITH ("Dingbat"), his wife
> GLORIA STIVIC, his daughter
> MIKE STIVIC ("Meathead"), Gloria's
> Polish husband, college student
> living with the Bunkers
> LIONEL, Negro friend of the Stivics
> All In the Family (TV) (Family situation
> comedy)

Cross references are made to the main entry, as follows:

> ARCHIE. See: Bunker, Archie
> EDITH. See: Bunker, Archie
> "DINGBAT." See: Bunker, Archie
> GLORIA STIVIC. See: Bunker, Archie
> STIVIC, GLORIA. See: Bunker, Archie
> MIKE STIVIC. See: Bunker, Archie
> STIVIC, MIKE. See: Bunker, Archie
> "MEATHEAD." See: Bunker, Archie
> LIONEL. See: Bunker, Archie
> All In the Family. See: Bunker, Archie
> Family, All In the. See: Bunker, Archie

Names of characters are shown in CAPITAL LETTERS and the titles of the programs in lower case and underlined. The broadcast medium is indicated, as (R) for radio, (TV) for television, and (R) (TV) for such programs as The Thin Man and Michael Shayne, Private Detective when a production was broadcast in both. Following this identification the type of program is shown, as "Family situation comedy."

When appropriate, titles are shown in several forms in "see" entries, as Broadway Open House, Open House, Broadway, and House, Broadway Open. Names, such as ABBEY, ABBIE, ABBY and ABIE are cross-referenced in "see also" entries. This should assist the user who is not sure of the title of a production or the exact spelling of a particular name.

Some performers, such as Jack Barry, Arthur Godfrey, Tom Kennedy, Xavier Cugat and Walter Winchell, appear as heading more than one program. When this is the case the main entries covering each specific program are numbered, and cross references refer to these numbers. This makes the locating of items cross-referenced to the main entries easier than if such numbering were not used. An example follows:

CUGAT, XAVIER (1)
    BENNY GOODMAN
    KEL MURRAY, orchestra leaders
    (themselves)
    THEIR ORCHESTRAS
    Let's Dance (R) (Dance music)

CUGAT, XAVIER (2), tango/rhumba
    orchestra leader (himself)
    HIS ORCHESTRA
    ABBE LANE, featured vocalist
    on the program (herself)
    Xavier Cugat (TV) (Dance music)

For the first main entry, cross references read as follows:

GOODMAN, BENNY. See: Cugat, Xavier (1)
BENNY GOODMAN. See: Cugat, Xavier (1)
MURRAY, KEL. See: Cugat, Xavier (1)
KEL MURRAY. See: Cugat, Xavier (1)
Let's Dance. See: Cugat, Xavier (1)
Dance, Let's. See: Cugat, Xavier (1)

For the second main entry we have as cross references:

LANE, ABBE. See: Cugat, Xavier (2)
ABBE LANE. See: Cugat, Xavier (2)
Xavier Cugat. See: Cugat, Xavier (2)

For both main entries the cross references read:

XAVIER CUGAT. See:
    Cugat, Xavier (1) (2)
    Durante, Jimmy
    Whiteman, Paul

As Cugat appeared on programs headed by other people as well as by himself, further cross references appear, as follows:

CUGAT, XAVIER. See also:
    Durante, Jimmy
    Whiteman, Paul

These cross references to Durante and Whiteman also appear in the "XAVIER CUGAT. See:" entry, above.

In the BUNKER, ARCHIE entry the words "himself," "herself," or "themselves" do not appear. This is because Bunker and the other characters mentioned are characters, not real people. When real people appear on programs as themselves, as in the CUGAT, XAVIER entries, the word "himself," "herself," or "themselves," as applicable, indicates this, as above: CUGAT, XAVIER; BENNY GOODMAN; KEL MURRAY; and ABBE LANE.

No attempt has been made to identify real persons with the characters they portray, with a very few exceptions. Carroll O'Connor, the actor, plays Archie Bunker, the character, on television, but this is not shown in the BUNKER, ARCHIE, entry. The compilers of this book felt that such information, if desired, could be found elsewhere in the voluminous periodical, newspaper and book literature of radio and television.

While this volume was being compiled many people gave willing and valuable assistance. Markita Patrick was especially helpful, assisting with typing, alphabetizing and checking the entries. O. Gene Norman, head of general reference at the Cunningham Memorial Library, Indiana State University, Terre Haute, and his staff assisted in locating source materials and in other ways, as did Linda Fagg and Jane Covert, members of the staff of the Emeline Fairbanks Memorial Library, Terre Haute. Ed Howard, Fairbanks head librarian, was also helpful in many ways.

Susan Peters, Pegi Ritchie, Ken Lauer, Dick Seagley and other members of the staff of Fred Reynolds, head librarian of the Fort Wayne and Allen County Library, were obliging and cooperative.

Alan Jones, regional manager of T. V. Guide Magazine for Central Indiana, Indianapolis, and Cindi Gordon, his secretary, made available certain otherwise difficult to locate source materials. E. Alice Peters and Jean Sharp assisted in assembling data concerning certain television programs not available to the compilers.

We wish to express our gratitude and appreciation to all these willing helpers at this time.

Harold S. Sharp
Marjorie Z. Sharp

December 1, 1972

Index to Radio and TV Characters

A. A. F., Roosty of the. See: Roosty

A. & P. Bandwagon, The. See: Smith, Kate (2)

A. & P. Gypsies, The. See: Parker, Frank

A. B. C. Comedy Hour, The (The Kopykats). See: Little, Rich

A. B. C. Evening News, The. See: Smith, Howard K. (1)

A. B. C. Scope. See: Smith, Howard K. (2)

A. B. C. 's Wide World of Sports. See: McKay, Jim (1)

A-Go-Go, Hollywood. See: Riddle, Sam (2)

A. L. See: Alexander, A. L. (1) (2) (3)

A. L. Alexander and His Mediation Board. See: Alexander, A. L. (1)

A. L. Alexander's Good Will Court. See: Alexander, A. L. (2)

AARON. See: Peppertag, Aaron

AARON SILVERMAN. See: Barrett, David

AARON STEMPEL. See: Bolt, Jason

AARONSON, IRVING. See: Winchell, Walter (1)

ABBE. See also:
Abbey
Abbie
Abby

Abie

ABBE LANE. See: Cugat, Xavier (2)

ABBEY. See also:
Abbe
Abbie
Abby
Abie

ABBEY TROWBRIDGE. See: Hargrave-Scott, Joan

ABBIE. See also:
Abbe
Abbey
Abby
Abie

Abbie, Dear. See: Van Buren, Abigail

Abbott and Costello. See: Abbott, Bud (1)

Abbott and Costello Program, The. See: Abbott, Bud (2)

ABBOTT, BUD (1)
LOU COSTELLO, comedians
(themselves)
Abbott and Costello (TV) (Situation comedy)

ABBOTT, BUD (2)
LOU COSTELLO, comedians
(themselves)
The Abbott and Costello Program (R) (Comedy)

ABBOTT, BUD. See also: Martin, Dean (1)

ABBOTT, CHARLOTTE. See: Sunday

ABBOTT, CHRISTINE. See: Barbour, Henry Wilson

1

ABBOTT, JOHN
  EMILY ABBOTT
  LINDA ABBOTT
  BARBARA ABBOTT
  JACK ABBOTT
  ISABEL KENYON
  HILDA, maid
  MADELYN, characters appearing
  in the drama
  We, The Abbotts (R) (Serial
  drama)

ABBOTT, MR.
  MRS. ABBOTT, his wife, ama-
  teur detectives
  Abbott Mysteries (R) (Drama)

Abbott Mysteries. See: Abbott,
  Mr.

ABBOTT, PHILIP, plays part of
  court probation officer (himself)
  JUDGES, PSYCHIATRISTS, AT-
  TORNEYS (themselves)
  MANY ACTORS AND ACTRESSES
  The House on High Street (TV)
  (Courtroom dramas dealing with
  probation)

Abbotts, We the. See: Abbott,
  John

ABBRUZIO, JULIUS. See: Harris,
  Phil

ABBY. See:
  Abbe
  Abbey
  Abbie
  Abie
  Hudson, Nancy Smith

ABBY ADAMS. See: Major, Bob

ABBY BRADFORD. See: Chandler,
  Dr. Susan

ABBY GRAHAM. See: Banyon,
  Miles C.

ABBY MATSON. See: Jones,
  Lorenzo

ABE. See: Uncle Abe

Abe and David, Uncle. See: Uncle
  Abe

ABE FINKELSTEIN. See: O'Leary,
  Hannah

ABE LYMAN. See:
  Munn, Frank (2)
  Winchell, Walter (1)

ABEL, WALTER, host of the pro-
  gram (himself)
  MANY ACTORS AND ACTRESSES
  Suspicion (TV) (Suspense drama)

ABENDROTH, DR. See: Hargrave-
  Scott, Joan

ABERNATHY, DR. See: Hackett,
  Doc

ABIE. See:
  Abbe
  Abbey
  Abbie
  Abby
  Levy, Abie

Abie's Irish Rose. See: Levy, Abie

ABIGAIL. See:
  Barbour, Henry Wilson
  Churchill, John
  Van Buren, Abigail

ABNER. See:
  Marshall, John
  Yokum, Li'l Abner

ABNER KRAVITZ. See: Stephens,
  Samantha

Abner, L'il. See: Yokum, Li'l
  Abner

Abner, Lum and. See: Edwards,
  Lum

ABNER PEABODY. See:
  Edwards, Lum
  Marlin, Mary

Aboard the Century, Bob Elson.
  See: Elson, Bob

About Faces. See: Alexander, Ben
  (1)

About Hollywood, Man. See: Mc-
  Call, George

About Time, It's. See: Mac

ABRAHAM. See: Jones, Abraham
Lincoln

ABRAHAM LINCOLN WATTS. See:
Peters, Bill

ABRAMS, SERGEANT SOL. See:
Muldoon, Francis

Academy Awards, The. See:
Hope, Bob (1)

Accent. See: Ciardi, John

Accidental Family. See: Webster,
Jerry

ACCOUNT, CHARGE. See: Murray, Jan (2)

ACE, GOODMAN, comedian (him-
self)
JANE ACE, his wife, comedi-
enne (herself)
MISS THOMAS
MRS. MARSH
MARGE
JOHNNY
LAURA, maid
COKEY
BETTY, characters appearing
on the program
Easy Aces (R) (Comedy) (later
known as Mr. Ace and Jane) (R)

ACE, GOODMAN. See also: Kaye,
Danny

Ace of the Airways, Hop Harrigan,
America's. See: Harrigan, Hop

Aces, Easy. See: Ace, Goodman

ACHMED. See: Ross, David (1)

ACKROYD, DAVID. See: Ames,
Peter

Acres, Green. See: Douglas,
Oliver

ACROPOLOUS, CHRIS. See: Mix,
Tom

Action, Deadline For. See: Evans,
Dean

ACTION SINGERS, THE WORLD.
See: Roberts, Oral

Action, Treasury Men in. See:
Chief, The

ACTOR. See: Garrison, Lieut.
Craig

ADA. See: Noble, Mary

ADA DOWNS. See: Randolph, Alice

ADA JACKS. See: Peyton, Martin

ADA MANION. See: Jordan, Joyce

ADA, SISTER. See: Rutledge, Dr.
John

ADAIR, DAVID. See: Marshall,
John

ADAIR, JEAN. See: Johnson, Bess

ADAIR, JERRY. See: Johnson,
Bess

ADAM. See:
Cartwright, Ben
Collins, Barnabas
McLean, Adam
Shepherd, Adam
Strange, Adam
Troy, Adam
Waring, Evelyn

ADAM BASSETT. See: Nielson,
Torwald

ADAM DRAKE. See: Karr, Mike

ADAM FLINT, DETECTIVE. See:
Parker, Lieut. Mike

ADAM GARNER. See: Horwitz,
Hans

ADAM GREER, CAPTAIN. See:
Hayes, Linc

ADAM HUDSON, Dr. See: Hudson,
Nancy Smith

ADAM LLOYD. See: Driggs,
Karleton King

ADAM THORPE. See: Bauer, Bertha

Adam-12. See: Malloy, Officer
  Pete

ADAMIK, STAN. See: James,
  Nancy

ADAMS. See also: Addams

ADAMS, ABBY. See: Major, Bob

ADAMS, ARTHUR. See: Marlin,
  Mary

ADAMS, BETTY. See: Harding,
  Karen Adams

ADAMS, BILL. See:
  Halop, Billy
  Welles, Orson (2)

ADAMS, CAPTAIN, Arizona caval-
  ryman of the 1870s
  Boots and Saddles (TV) (Western)

ADAMS, CHUCK. See: Sherwood,
  Ruth

ADAMS, CRUNCH, captain of the
  fishing cruiser "Poseidon"
  SARI, his wife
  DESPERATE SMITH (Des), his
  mate
  Crunch Adams and Desperate
  Smith (TV) (Fishing adventure)
  (Also called Crunch and Des)
  (TV)

ADAMS, CYNTHIA. See: Marlin,
  Mary

ADAMS, DANNY. See: Burns,
  George (3)

ADAMS, DOC. See: Dillon,
  Marshal Matt

ADAMS, Don, agent
  Coronado 9 (TV) (Adventure)

ADAMS, DON. See also: Crosby,
  Bing (2)

ADAMS, DOUG, Centerville editor,
  employed by Consolidated Syndicate
  PERRY "QUIZ" QUISINBERRY,
  news photographer, also employee of Consolidated Syndicate

Passport for Adams (R) (Drama)

ADAMS, EDIE. See:
  Blair, Janet
  Kovacs, Ernie (1)

ADAMS, FRANKLIN. See: Marlin,
  Mary

ADAMS, FRANKLIN P., featured
  on the program (himself)
  MANY ACTORS AND ACTRESSES
  Davey Adams, Son of the Sea
  (R) (Drama)

ADAMS, FRANKLIN P. See also:
  Fadiman, Clifton (1)

ADAMS, FUFFY. See: Graves,
  Harry

ADAMS, HOWARD
  EVE DRAKE, his wife, motion
  picture star team
  Mr. Adams and Eve (TV)
  (Comedy)

ADAMS, ICHABOD. See: Major,
  Bob

ADAMS, JANET MUNSON. See:
  Harding, Karen Adams

ADAMS, JOEY, host of the program
  (himself) (1)
  PANEL OF COMEDIANS
  Gags to Riches (TV) (Humor)

ADAMS, JOEY, moderator of the
  program (himself) (2)
  MARRIED AND ENGAGED
  COUPLES
  Rate Your Mate (R) (Interview/
  quiz)

ADAMS, JOHN. See: Harding,
  Karen Adams

ADAMS, JUDITH. See: Brown,
  Ellen

ADAMS, LIEUT. PRICE, police
  officer; member of the Metro-
  politan Squad
  JOE HUDDLESTON
  PETE GARCIA, patrolman
  SERGEANT VINCE CAVELLI
  CAPTAIN KEITH GREGORY,

police officers
The New Breed (TV) (Police
drama)

ADAMS, LORRAINE. See: Hillman, India

ADAMS, MAJOR SETH, commander
of wagon train
FLINT McCULLOUGH, scout
COOPER SMITH, scout
FLINT HALE, wagonmaster
Wagon Train (TV) (Western ad-
venture) (later reissued in part
under the title Trailmaster) (TV)
(also known as Major Adams)
(TV)

ADAMS, MARCIA. See: Ames,
Peter

ADAMS, MARGE. See: Marlin,
Mary

ADAMS, MISS. See: Perkins, Ma

Adams, Passport for. See: Adams,
Doug

Adams, Red. See: Davis, Red

ADAMS, STEVE. See: Straight
Arrow

ADAMS, TEMBER. See: Trent,
Helen

ADDAMS. See also: Adams

Addams Family, The. See: Addams,
Gomez

ADDAMS, GOMEZ, head of the
family
MORTICIA, his wife
PUGSLEY, their son
WEDNESDAY, their daughter
OPHELIA, Morticia's sister
UNCLE FESTER, Morticia's uncle
GRANDMAMA, Gomez's mother
COUSIN ITT, Morticia's half-
human cousin
LURCH, the Addams's butler
THING, mysterious hand, per-
forms services for the family
KITTY KAT, the Addams's pet
lion
The Addams Family (TV) (Situa-
tion comedy/horror satire)

ADDIE. See also:
Eddie
Eddy
Edie
Eydie

ADDIE PRICE. See: Wayne,
Ruth Evans

ADDISON, KAY. See: Post, Wilbur

ADDISON, ROGER. See: Post,
Wilbur

ADELAIDE DE LOCA. See: Roxy

ADELE CARMODY. See: Nelson,
Carolyn Kramer

ADELE CORLIS. See: Brent, Dr.
Jim

ADELE KINGMAN. See: Sloan,
Holly

ADELE LANG. See: Warren,
Wendy

ADELINA THOMASON. See:
Weems, Ambrose J.

ADELINE, SWEET. See: Uncle
Walter

ADELLA WINSTON. See: Fairchild, Kay

ADLER, BILL, moderator of the
program (himself)
FOUR JUVENILE PANELISTS
GUEST CELEBRITIES
Kid Talk (TV) (Discussion/
interview)

ADMIRAL. See:
Nelson, Admiral Harriman
Zacharias, Rear Admiral Ellis
M.

Admiral Broadway Revue, Your
Show of Shows. See: Caesar,
Sid (3)

ADOLF HITLER. See: Husing,
Ted

ADOLPHE. See: Menjou, Adolphe

ADRIAN, COMMANDER. See:
Morgan, Lieut. Anne

ADRIENNE. See: Peyton, Martin

ADRIENNE HARRIS, DR. See:
Prescott, Kate Hathaway

Adventure. See: Collingwood,
Charles (1)

Adventure at Scott Island. See:
Scott, David

Adventure, High. See: Thomas,
Lowell (2)

Adventure Hour, Kellogg's Presents
the Banana Splits. See: Fleegle

Adventure, I Search for. See:
Douglas, Jack (1)

Adventure, The Great. See: Heflin,
Van

Adventure Theater, The N.B.C. See:
Hope, Bob (3)
McMahon, Ed (1)

Adventurer, The. See: Bradley,
Gene

Adventures, Bobby Benson's. See:
Benson, Bobby

Adventures, Count Von Luckner's.
See: Von Luckner, Count Felix

Adventures, Dick Daring's. See:
Daring, Dick

Adventures in Paradise. See: Troy,
Adam

Adventures of Bullwinkle and Rocky,
The. See: Bullwinkle

Adventures of Captain Diamond, The.
See: Diamond, Captain

Adventures of Christopher Wells, The.
See: Wells, Christopher

Adventures of Helen and Mary, The.
See: Halop, Billy

Adventures of Hiram Holliday, The.

See: Holliday, Hiram

Adventures of Huck Finn, The New.
See: Finn, Huck

Adventures of Huckleberry Finn,
The. See: Finn, Huckleberry

Adventures of Jim Bowie, The.
See: Bowie, Jim

Adventures of Jimmie Allen, The
Air. See: Allen, Jimmie

Adventures of Martin Kane, The
New. See: Kane, Martin

Adventures of Mr. Magoo, The
Famous. See: Magoo, Mr.

Adventures of Mr. Meek, The.
See: Meek, Mortimer

Adventures of Nero Wolfe, The.
See: Wolfe, Nero

Adventures of Ozzie and Harriet,
The. See: Nelson, Ozzie

Adventures of Philip Marlowe, The.
See: Marlowe, Philip

Adventures of Rin-Tin-Tin, The.
See: Rin-Tin-Tin

Adventures of Robin Hood, The.
See: Hood, Robin

Adventures of Sam Spade, The.
See: Spade, Sam

Adventures of Sherlock Holmes,
The. See: Holmes, Sherlock

Adventures of Sir Lancelot, The.
See: Sir Lancelot

Adventures of Superman, The.
See: Kent, Clark

Adventures of Tom Mix, The. See:
Mix, Tom

Adventures of Topper, The. See:
Topper, Cosmo

Advocates, The. See: Palmieri,
Victor

AERNE, ANDRE. See: Kelly,
Joe (2)

Affair, Family. See: Davis, Uncle
Bill

Affairs of Anthony, The. See:
Anthony

Affairs of Dr. Gentry, The. See:
Gentry, Dr. Anne

Affairs of Peter Salem, The. See:
Salem Peter

Affairs of Tom, Dick and Harry, The.
See: Tom

Africa, Cowboy in. See: Hayes,
Wing Commander

African Patrol. See: Derek, Inspector

African Trek. See: Marais, Josef

After Dark, America. See: Lescoulie, Jack (4)

After Dark, Playboy. See: Hefner,
Hugh

Against the Storm. See: Cameron,
Christy Allen

AGAMEMNON. See: Baines, Scattergood

AGAR, CYNTHIA. See: Sterling,
Vanessa Dale

AGARN, CORPORAL. See: Parmenter, Captain Wilton

AGATHA. See: Meek, Mortimer

AGATHA ANTHONY. See: Trent,
Helen

AGATHA, AUNT. See: Higby,
Mary Jane

AGATHA FOLSOM. See: Myrt

AGATHA GRISWOLD. See: Dallas,
Stella

AGE. See also: Ages

Age, Youth Vs. See: Tinney, Cal

AGENT. See:
Sheppard, F.B.I. Field Agent
Treasury Agent

Agent, Amos Burke, Secret. See:
Burke, Amos

AGENT 86. See: Smart, Maxwell

Agent, Ned Jordan, Secret. See:
Jordan, Ned

AGENT 99. See: Smart, Maxwell

AGENT PETERS, SPECIAL. See:
Harding, David

Agent, Secret. See: Drake, John

Agent 7, Special. See: Conroy,
Phil

Agent, Special. See: Drake, Alan

Agent, Treasury. See: Lincoln,
Joe

AGES. See also: Age

Ages, Key to the. See: Low,
Theodore

AGGIE. See: Horn, Aggie

AGGIE, AUNT. See: Canova,
Judy

Aggie Horn, In Care of. See:
Horn, Aggie

AGGIE RILEY. See: Dugan,
Jimmie

AGNES. See:
Barkley, Arnie
Montague, Edwin
Trent, Helen
Varner, Will

AGNES FOY. See: Randolph,
Ellen

AGNES LAWSON. See: Aldrich,
Henry

AGNES MOORHEAD. See:

Frees, Paul
Welles, Orson (1) (2)

AGNES WESTCOTT. See: Har-
grave-Scott, Joan

AGRONSKY, MARTIN, interviewer
of the program (himself)
MANY PROMINENT INTERVIEWEES
Look Here! (TV) (Interviews)

AHA. See: Little Orphan Annie

AIMI. See also: Amy

AIMI MACDONALD. See: Davidson, John (2)

Air Adventures of Jimmie Allen,
The. See: Allen, Jimmie

Air, America's Town Meeting of
the. See: Denny, George V.,
Jr.

Air, Dorothy Dix on the. See: Dix,
Dorothy (2)

Air, Mystery in the. See: Lorre,
Peter

Air of the Americas, School of the.
See: Bryson, Dr. Lyman (2)

Air Power. See: Cronkite, Walter
(1)

Air, The American Forum of the.
See: Granik, Theodore (1)

Air, The American School of the.
See: Bryson, Dr. Lyman (2)

Air, The Fishing and Hunting Club
of the. See: Begley, Martin

Air, The Folies Bergere of the.
See: Howard, Willie

Air, The Heinz Magazine of the.
See: Edmondson, Delmar

Air, The Mickey Mouse Theater of
the. See: Mouse, Mickey

Air, The National Church of the.
See: Fosdick, Rev. Harry
Emerson

Air, The Theater Guild of the.
See: Langner, Lawrence

Airport, San Francisco International.
See: Conrad, Jim

Airways, Hop Harrigan, America's
Ace of the. See: Harrigan,
Hop

AJAX CASSIDY. See: Allen, Fred

AKEMAN, DAVE. See: Owens,
Buck

AL. See:
Binford, Al
Hirt, Al (1) (2)
Jolson, Al
Lohman, Al
Peterson, Irma

AL BONACORSI. See: Shannon

AL BROWN. See: Butler, Jerry

AL BUTLER. See: Karr, Mike

AL CAPONE. See: Winchell,
Walter (2)

AL DOUGLAS. See: Solomon,
David

AL GOERING. See: Bernie, Ben

AL GOODMAN. See:
Allen, Fred
Ross, Lanny
Taylor, Deems

Al Hirt. See: Hirt, Al (1)

AL JOLSON. See:
Crosby, Bing (3)
Jolson, Al

AL McBURNEY. See: Driggs,
Karleton King

AL MANN. See: Shadel, Bill

AL MURRAY. See: MacLennon,
Jeannie

Al Pearce and His Gang. See:
Blurt, Elmer

AL PRESTON. See: Garrison,
Spencer

AL WEEKS. See: Hardy, Dr.
Steven

ALABAMA RANDALL. See: Arden,
Jane

ALADDIN. See: Welk, Lawrence

ALAN. See:
Allan
Allen
Allyn
Drake, Alan
Ellen
Harris, Alan
Josie
MacKenzie, Colonel Alan
Reed, Alan
Sterling, Vanessa Dale
Young, Alan

ALAN BISHOP. See: Drake, Betty

ALAN BRADY. See: Petrie, Rob

ALAN BUNCE. See: Soule, Olan
(1)

ALAN COPELAND. See:
Lanson, Snooky
Nye, Louis

ALAN DALE. See: Seymour, Dan

ALAN, DON, sleight-of-hand artist;
host of the program (himself)
GUEST PROFESSIONAL MAGI-
CIANS
GUEST FLEDGLING MAGICIANS
Magic Ranch (TV) (Children's
magic program)

ALAN GREEN. See: Perry, John

ALAN HALE. See: Featherstone,
Mrs.

ALAN SIMMS, DR. See: Dallas,
Stella

ALAN SUES. See: Rowan, Dan

ALAN WEBSTER, DR. See:
Jordan, Joyce

Alan Young Show, The. See:
Young, Alan

Alaskans, The. See: Harris, Silky

ALBA, ROBERT, quizmaster of the
program (himself)
MANY CONTESTANTS
Can Do (TV) (Quiz)

ALBATROSS, THE SILVER. See:
Armstrong, Jack

ALBERT. See:
Elbert
Ethel
Miller, Albert
Nipper

ALBERT ALEY. See: Halop,
Billy

Albert and the Cosby Kids, Fat.
See: Cosby, Bill (3)

Albert, Ethel and. See: Ethel

ALBERT, FAT. See: Cosby,
Bill (3)

ALBERT SACK. See: Morgan,
Frank (1)

ALBERT VANE. See: Novak, John

ALBRIGHT, MARGIE, young girl
VERN ALBRIGHT, her father,
lawyer
My Little Margie (TV) (Comedy)

Album of Familiar Music, The
American. See: Munn, Frank
(1)

ALCALA, THOMAS JEFFERSON,
mayor of southwestern American
town for sixteen years
ANDY HAYS, his aide
MARIAN CRANE, his secretary
The Man and the City (TV)
(Crime fighting/adventure)

Alcoa Premiere. See: Astaire,
Fred (1)

ALDEN, GREGORY. See: O'Farrell, Packy

ALDEN, MICHAEL, amnesia victim
seeking his identity; known as
Coronet Blue
ANTHONY, monk, his friend
Coronet Blue (TV) (Adventure)

ALDIS, GUY. See: Cameron,
Christy Allen

ALDRICH, DR. STEVE. See:
Davis, Dr. Althea

Aldrich Family, The. See: Aldrich,
Henry

ALDRICH, HENRY, teen-age Ameri-
can boy
SAM, his father
ALICE, his mother
MARY, his elder sister
HOMER BROWN, his teen-age
friend
WILL BROWN, Homer's father
MRS. BROWN, Homer's mother
KATHLEEN ANDERSON, Henry's
girl friend
MRS. ANDERSON, Kathleen's
mother
AGNES LAWSON
STRINGBEAN KITTINGER
WILLIE MARSHALL
DIZZY STEVENS
AUNT HARRIET
GEORGE BIGELOW
TOBY SMITH
GERALDINE, characters appearing
on the program
The Aldrich Family (R) (TV) (Sit-
uation comedy) (also known as
Henry Aldrich) (R)

ALDRIDGE, MOTHER. See: Horton,
Dot

ALEC. See:
Fleming, Tony
Josie
Templeton, Alec

ALEC FERGUSON. See: O'Leary,
Hannah

ALEC GORDON, DR. See: Hargrave-Scott, Joan

ALEC HOUSTON. See: Hamilton,
George

Alec Templeton Time. See: Templeton, Alec

ALEX. See:
Stockton, Sandy (2)
Stone, Dr. Alex

ALEX CALDWELL. See: Sterling,
Vanessa Dale

ALEX DELAVAN. See: Nelson,
Carolyn Kramer

ALEX DREIER. See:
Arnold, Eddy
Goren, Charles
Jones, Dean

ALEX PRATT. See: Worthington,
Nora

ALEXANDER. See:
Bell, Alexander Graham
Mundy, Alexander
Scott, Alexander
Woollcott, Alexander

ALEXANDER, A. L. (1), purveyor
of advice (himself)
A. L. Alexander and His Mediation Board (R) (Advice)

ALEXANDER, A. L. (2), purveyor
of advice (himself)
A. L. Alexander's Good Will
Court (R) (Advice)

ALEXANDER, A. L. (3), moderator
of the program (himself)
MARRIED COUPLES WITH PROB-
LEMS
PANEL OF MEDIATORS who judge
the issues
The Court of Human Relations
(TV) (Counseling)

ALEXANDER (BABY DUMPLING).
See: Bumstead, Blondie

ALEXANDER, BEN (1), moderator
of the program (himself)
AUDIENCE PARTICIPANTS
GUEST STARS
About Faces (TV) (Game)

ALEXANDER, BEN (2), master of
ceremonies of the program (himself)

MANY AUDIENCE PARTICIPANTS
Anniversary Club (R) (Audience
participation)

ALEXANDER, BEN (3), moderator
of the program (himself)
MANY AUDIENCE PARTICIPANTS
Heart's Desire (R) (Game)

ALEXANDER, BEN (4), master of
ceremonies of the program (himself)
Little Ol' Hollywood (R) (Hollywood gossip)

ALEXANDER GREY, DR. See:
Jordan, Joyce

ALEXANDER, JOAN. See:
James, Dennis (3)
Roberts, Ken

ALEXANDER KENDRICK. See:
Ciardi, John

ALEXANDER, LYNNE. See:
Bennett, Nita

ALEXANDER, NICK, reporter on
New York newspaper
MARK GRAINGER, city editor
KLUGIE, staff photographer
DAVE TABAK, copy editor
LIZZIE HOGAN, Washington cor-
respondent
Saints and Sinners (TV) (Drama)

ALEXANDER, ROD. See: Caesar,
Sid (3)

ALEXANDER SAS-JAWORSKY, DR.
See: March, Hal

ALEXANDER, VAN. See: Arthur,
Jack (1)

ALEXANDER WAVERLY. See:
Dancer, April
Solo, Napoleon

ALEXANDRIA. See: Josie

ALEY, ALBERT. See: Halop, Billy

ALFRED. See:
Batman
Bronson, Millie
Hitchcock, Alfred

ALFRED DRAKE. See: Barlow,
Howard

Alfred Hitchcock Hour, The. See:
Hitchcock, Alfred

Alfred Hitchcock Presents. See:
Hitchcock, Alfred

ALFRED KIDDER, DR. See:
Rainey, Dr. Froelich

ALFRED WALLENSTEIN. See:
Barlow, Howard

ALFREDO ANTONINI. See: Froman, Jane (2)

Alias Jimmy Valentine. See:
Valentine, Jimmy

Alias Smith and Jones. See:
Heyes, Hannibal

ALICE. See:
Aldrich, Henry
Alyce
Brady, Mike
Gobel, George
Holliday, Alice
Horton, Dr. Tom
Jackson, Jarrin' Jack
Kramden, Ralph
Mitchell, Dennis
Randolph, Alice
Stockton, Sandy (1)
Trimble, Jonathan

ALICE AMES WARNER. See:
Rogers, Patricia

ALICE, AUNT. See: Sunday

ALICE CARROLL. See: Trent,
Helen

ALICE CORNETT. See: Carlisle,
Kitty

ALICE, COUSIN. See: Jones,
Sam

ALICE CRAIG. See: Harding,
Karen Adams

ALICE DARLING. See: McGee,
Fibber

ALICE DAY. See: Harding, Karen
Adams

ALICE DUFFY. See: Noble, Mary

ALICE FAYE. See: Crosby, Bing
(2)

ALICE FAYE HARRIS. See: Harris, Phil

ALICE GHOSTLEY. See: Andrews,
Julie

ALICE HENDERSON. See: Beulah

ALICE HENDRICKS. See: Harding,
Karen Adams

ALICE HUGHES. See: Malone, Dr.
Jerry

ALICE JAMISON. See: Brent, Dr.
Jim

ALICE JOHNSON. See: Kaufman,
Seymour

ALICE, LITTLE. See: Harris, Phil

ALICE LON. See: Welk, Lawrence

ALICE MacROBERTS. See: Higgins

ALICE PORTNOY. See: Burnett,
Carol

ALICE RANDALL. See: Brent,
Dr. Jim

ALICE ROGERS. See: Allen,
Frederick Lewis

ALICE SANDERS. See: Sothern,
Mary

Alice, This Is. See: Holliday,
Alice

ALISON. See:
Allison
Allyson
Carr, Alison
Endicott, Professor Mike

ALISON, HOPE. See: Jordan,
Joyce

ALISON RADCLIFFE. See:
Graham, Dr. Bob

ALISTAIRE. See: Cooke, Alistaire (1) (2)

ALISTER. See: Mundy, Alexander

Alive, Bring'em Back. See: Buck,
Frank

Alka Seltzer Time. See: Shriner,
Herb (1)

All-American Boy, Jack Armstrong,
The. See: Armstrong, Jack

All In the Family. See: Bunker,
Archie

All My Children. See: Davis,
Ann Tyler

All Star Revue, The. See: Raye,
Martha (1)

All, Winner Take. See: Cullen,
Bill (5)

Allakazam. See: Wilson, Mark

Allakazam, The Magic Land of.
See: Wilson, Mark

ALLAN. See also:
Alan
Allen
Allyn
Ellen

ALLAN MacRAE. See: Marshall,
John

ALLEN. See:
Alan
Allan
Allyn
Ellen
Funt, Allen
Ludden, Allen
Prescott, Allen (1) (2)

ALLEN, BOB. See: Kemp, Hal

ALLEN, BRET. See: Dyke,
Charity Amanda

Allen, Burns and. See: Burns,
George (1)

ALLEN, DAVE. See: Berman,
Shelley

ALLEN, DENNIS. See: Jones,
Dean

ALLEN, DR. KATE, physician
DR. FRED CROWLEY, physician
SARAH TUTTLE
JACK HALSEY, characters appear-
ing in the drama
Dr. Kate (R) (Serial drama)

ALLEN DUNBAR. See: Ames,
Peter

ALLEN, ED, physical culturist,
host of the program (himself)
Ed Allen (TV) (Exercise)

ALLEN, FRED, comedian, star of
the program (himself)
PORTLAND HOFFA (Mrs. Fred
Allen), comedienne (herself)
ONE LONG PAN, Chinese detec-
tive, portrayed by Allen
MRS. PANSY NUSSBAUM
PIERRE NUSSBAUM, her husband
SOCRATES MULLIGAN
MR. PINKBAUM
FALSTAFF OPENSHAW
SENATOR BLOAT
TITUS MOODY
SENATOR BEAUREGARD CLAG-
HORN
JOHN DOE
AJAX CASSIDY
DOTTIE MAHONEY, characters
appearing on the program
PETER VAN STEEDEN
LENNIE HAYTON
FERDE GROFE
AL GOODMAN
LOU KATZMAN, orchestra lead-
ers appearing on the program
(themselves)
THEIR ORCHESTRAS
THE TOWN HALL QUARTET,
vocal group
THE DEMARCO SISTERS, vocal
group
MANY GUEST STARS
The Fred Allen Show (R) (Comedy/
variety) (also known as The Salad
Bowl Revue (R), The Sal Hepatica

Revue (R), The Hour of Smiles
(R), Town Hall Tonight (R), and
The Texaco Theater) (R)

ALLEN, FRED. See also:
Daly, John (3)
Martin, Dean (1)

ALLEN, FREDERICK LEWIS
CAROL LYNN GILLMER
EDWARD HILL
WALTER KIERNAN
ALICE ROGERS, panel members
of the program (themselves)
Cliche Club (R) (Panel quiz)

ALLEN FUNT. See:
Funt, Allen (1) (2)
Moore, Garry (3)

ALLEN, GRACIE. See: Burns,
George (1) (2)

ALLEN, IDA BAILEY, hostess of
the program (herself)
Ida Bailey Allen (R) (Cooking
instruction)

ALLEN, JANE. See: Williams,
Emily

ALLEN, JASON. See: Kaufman,
Seymour

ALLEN, JERRY. See: Novak,
John

ALLEN, JIMMIE, boy pilot of the
racing aeroplane the Blue Bird
Special
SPEED ROBERTSON, his com-
panion and idol; veteran pilot and
World War I ace
BARBARA CROFT, his girl
friend
FLASH, aeroplane mechanic; his
friend
PROFESSOR PARTENON PRO-
TEUS, enemy scientist and in-
ventor
The Air Adventures of Jimmie
Allen (R) (Aviation drama)

ALLEN, JOAN HOUSTON
DAVID ALLEN
FLORA LITTLE
ROBERT HOUSTON
DOT HOUSTON

ALLEN, LORETTA   14

BILLY HOUSTON
DICK MARTIN
JOHNNY WARD
DR. ROBERT GARDNER, physician
MICHAEL DENBY
SANDRA HALL
HARRIET BROOKS
BEULAH
SALLY, characters appearing in
the drama
A Tale of Today (R) (Serial
drama)

ALLEN, LORETTA. See: Sterling,
Vanessa Dale

ALLEN, MEL. See: Cowan, Thomas

ALLEN, MRS. MARGARET. See:
Cameron, Christy Allen

ALLEN, PROFESSOR JASON Mc-
KINLEY. See: Cameron,
Christy Allen

ALLEN, ROGER. See: Wayne,
Ruth Evans

ALLEN ROTH. See: Berle,
Milton

ALLEN, SIRI. See: Cameron,
Christy Allen

ALLEN, STEVE (1), host of the
program (himself)
TOM POSTON
LOUIS NYE
DON KNOTTS, comedians ap-
pearing on the program (them-
selves)
GORDON HATHAWAY, character
portrayed by Nye
MR. NERVOUS, character por-
trayed by Knotts
MANY GUEST STARS
The Steve Allen Show (TV)
(Variety)

ALLEN, STEVE (2), host of the
program (himself)
JUNIE
MANUEL LABOR
CLAUDE HORRIBLY, characters
appearing on the program
Smile Time (R) (Comedy)

ALLEN, STEVE (3), host of the

program (himself)
MANY GUEST HOSTS
TOM POSTON
LOUIS NYE
DON KNOTTS
STEVE LAWRENCE
EYDIE GORME, performers
appearing on the program (them-
selves)
MANY GUEST STARS
SKITCH HENDERSON, orchestra
leader (himself)
HIS ORCHESTRA
The Tonight Show (TV) (Talk/
interview)

ALLEN, STEVE. See also:
Berman, Shelley
Daly, John (3)
Moore, Garry (4)
Steinberg, David (2)

ALLEN, WOODY. See: Worley,
Jo Anne

Alley, Gasoline. See: Wallet,
Skeezix

Alley, Jazz. See: Hodes, Art

ALLIE. See: Miles, Allie Lowe

ALLISON. See also:
Alison
Allyson

ALLISON, CAM. See: Winchell,
Walter (2)

ALLISON, CATHERINE. See:
MacDonald, Eleanor

ALLISON, DAN. See: Davis, Dr.
Althea

ALLISON, DR. CLEM. See:
Booth, Martha

ALLISON, FRAN
JIM BISHOP, interviewers on
the program (themselves)
MANY INTERVIEWEES "from
all walks of life"
For Your Information (TV)
(Interviews)

ALLISON, FRAN. See also:
Kukla

ALLISON, FRANK. See: Mac-
Donald, Eleanor

ALLISON HATHAWAY JESSUP. See:
Prescott, Kate Hathaway

ALLISON HOPEWELL. See: Ames,
Peter

ALLISON, LIZ. See: Davis, Dr.
Althea

ALLISON MACKENZIE. See: Peyton, Martin

ALLISON MILLS. See: Uggams,
Leslie

ALLISON, SYLVIA. See: Goldberg,
Molly

ALLMAN, ELVIA. See: Bolger,
Ray

ALLYN. See:
Alan
Allan
Allen
Edwards, Allyn
Ellen

ALLYSON. See also:
Alison
Allison

ALLYSON, JUNE, actress; hostess
of the program (herself)
MANY ACTORS AND ACTRESSES
The June Allyson Show (TV)
(Drama anthology) (also called
The DuPont Show With June
Allyson) (TV)

ALMA. See: Elma

Alone, Girl. See: Rogers,
Patricia

ALONZO. See: Cole, Alonzo Dean

ALTHEA. See:
Davis, Dr. Althea
Dennis, Liz

ALTMAN, DR. BERNARD. See:
Whitman, Dr. James

ALTMAN, JULIAN. See: Halop,
Billy

Alumni Fun. See: Hayes, Peter
Lind (1)

ALVA BOMBERGER. See: Roxy

ALVIN. See:
Elizabeth
Saville, David

Alvin Cartoon Show, The. See:
Saville, David

ALVIN CRAIG. See: Webster,
Martha

ALVIN FUDDLE. See: Bumstead,
Blondie

ALVINO REY. See: Driggs,
Karleton King

ALVY WEST. See: Williams,
Andy (1)

Always Jan, It's. See: Stewart,
Jan

ALYCE. See also: Alice

ALYCE DRIGGS CLARKE. See:
Driggs, Karleton King

AMAH, THE. See: Higby, Mary
Jane

Amanda of Honeymoon Hill. See:
Dyke, Charity Amanda

Amateur Hour, Major Bowes and
His Original. See: Bowes,
Major Edward (2)

Amateur Hour, Ted Mack's. See:
Mack, Ted

Amateur Night, National. See:
Perkins, Ray

Amateur's Guide to Love, The.
See: Rayburn, Gene (1)

AMATO, TONY. See: Darin,
Bobby

Amazing Chan and the Chan Clan,
The. See: Chan

Amazing Mr. Malone, The. See:
Malone, Mr.

Amazing Mr. Smith, The. See:
  Smith, Gregory

Amazing World of Kreskin, The.
  See: Kreskin

AMBER HOLLISTER. See: Cord

AMBROSE. See: Weems, Ambrose
  J.

Amby, Scramby. See: Ward,
  Perry

AMECHE, DON (1), host of the
  program (himself)
  EDGAR BERGEN, ventriloquist
  (himself)
  CHARLIE McCARTHY
  MORTIMER SNERD
  EFFIE KLINKER, dummies used
  by Bergen
  DOROTHY LAMOUR, vocalist
  NELSON EDDY, singer
  W.C. FIELDS, comedian (them-
  selves)
  ROBERT ARMBRUSTER
  RAY NOBLE, orchestra leaders
  (themselves)
  THEIR ORCHESTRAS
  MANY GUEST STARS
  The Chase and Sanborn Hour (R)
  (Variety)

AMECHE, DON (2), host of the
  program (himself)
  MANY ACTORS AND ACTRESSES
  Don Ameche's Playhouse (TV)
  (Drama)

AMECHE, DON (3)
  RAYMOND EDWARD JOHNSON
  BETTY WINKLER
  ANNE SEYMOUR
  DON BRIGGS
  PHIL LORD
  BARBARA LUDDY
  JIM AMECHE
  OLAN SOULE, actors and
  actresses featured on the pro-
  gram (themselves)
  Grand Hotel (R) (Drama)

AMECHE, DON (4), host of the
  program (himself)
  MANY CIRCUS ACTS
  MANY SKATING ACTS
  International Show Time (TV)

(Circus/ice show)

AMECHE, DON. See also:
  Detective
  First Nighter, Mr.

AMECHE, JIM
  CHARLES BOYER
  GALE PAGE, masters of cere-
  mony of the program (themselves)
  MANY ACTORS AND ACTRESSES
  Hollywood Playhouse (R) (Drama)

AMECHE, JIM. See also:
  Ameche, Don (3)
  Arthur, Jack (2)

AMELIA BLAKE. See: Manning,
  Portia Blake

AMELIA COLE. See: Fuller,
  Ward

AMELIA JAMESON. See: Harding,
  Karen Adams

America, A Woman of. See:
  Dane, Prudence

America After Dark. See: Lescoulie, Jack (4)

AMERICA, CAPTAIN, crime
  fighter; cartoon character
  Captain America (TV) (Cartoon)

America, Cavalcade of. See:
  Welles, Orson (2)

America Contest, The Miss. See:
  Parks, Bert (4)

AMERICA, MR. See: James,
  Dennis (4)

America, R.F.D. See: Bottcher,
  Ed

America, Speak Up. See: Wordmaster, The

American Album of Familiar
  Music, The. See: Munn,
  Frank (1)

American Bandstand. See: Clark,
  Dick (1)

American Boy, Jack Armstrong,
   The All. See: Armstrong, Jack

American Dream Machine, The Great.
   See: Efron, Marshall

American Forum of the Air, The.
   See: Granik, Theodore (1)

American Scene Magazine, Jackie
   Gleason's. See: Gleason,
   Jackie (2)

American School of the Air, The.
   See: Bryson, Dr. Lyman (2)

American West, The. See: Smith,
   Jack

American Woman's Jury. See:
   Williams, Emily

American Women. See: Kummer,
   Eloise

Americans, The. See: Canfield,
   Ben

America's Ace of the Airways, Hop
   Harrigan. See: Harrigan, Hop

America's Greatest Bands. See:
   Whiteman, Paul

America's Hour. See: Welles,
   Orson (1)

Americas, School of the Air of the.
   See: Bryson, Dr. Lyman (2)

America's Town Meeting. See:
   Murrow, Edward R. (1)

America's Town Meeting of the Air.
   See: Denny, George V., Jr.

Ames Brothers, The. See: Ames,
   Joe

AMES, FRASER. See: Dyke,
   Charity Amanda

AMES, JOE
   GENE AMES
   ED AMES
   VIC AMES, brothers; vocal group
   (themselves)
   The Ames Brothers (TV) (Music)

AMES, NANCY
   ELLIOT REED
   ELAINE MAY
   MIKE NICHOLS
   DAVID FROST, actors and enter-
   tainers appearing on the program
   (themselves)
   That Was the Week That Was (TV)
   (Satire) (also known as T.W. 3)
   (TV)

AMES, PETER, widower
   DAN KINCAID
   KEVIN KINCAID
   AMY BRITTON
   BELLE BRITTON
   PHIL FORRESTER
   MARTHA ANN ASHLEY
   REILLY
   LISA BRITTON
   ANDREA WINTHROP BROWNING
   MITCH BROWNING
   CHARLOTTE MENCKEN
   FRANK CARVER
   SUSAN CARVER
   JOE SULLIVAN
   PAULINE HARRIS
   BRYAN FULLER
   CALEB ANDERSON
   KIP RYSDALE
   HUGH CLAYBORN
   JILL CLAYBORN
   MR. MALONE
   JOE MULHOLLAND
   JOANNA MORRISON
   MRS. TYRRELL
   DOUGLAS WINTHROP
   URSULA WINTHROP
   VIC CORELLI
   MARCIA ADAMS
   DAVID ACKROYD
   MYRA LAKE
   MR. GREGORY
   ALLISON HOPEWELL
   ALLEN DUNBAR
   TEX
   MR. MURPHY
   BRANNIGAN
   WALKER
   JIM
   RENICH
   NANCY
   ANDY, characters appearing in
   the drama
   The Secret Storm (TV) (Serial
   Drama)

AMES, TOM. See: Dyke, Charity
   Amanda

AMICUS CURIAE. See: Kegg,
Jonathan

AMODEO, ORIE. See: Welk,
Lawrence

AMOROSO, JOHNNY. See:
Kaye, Sammy (1)
Lopez, Vincent

AMOS. See:
Bickerson, John
Burke, Amos
Hoople, Major Amos
Jones, Amos

Amos Burke, Secret Agent. See:
Burke, Amos

AMOS, JOHN. See: Kelly, Gene

Amos 'n' Andy. See: Jones, Amos

AMOS Q. SNOOD. See: Mix, Tom

AMSTERDAM, MOREY, comedian,
moderator of the program (himself)
MANY GUEST PANELISTS
Can You Top This? (TV) (Comedy
panel)

AMSTERDAM, MOREY. See also:
Lester, Jerry
Reiner, Carl

Amusement Company, Dean Martin
Presents the Bobby Darin. See:
Darin, Bobby

AMY. See:
Aimi
Fitzgerald, Bridget Theresa Mary
Coleen
March, Mrs.
Monroe, Clayt
Morgan, Mrs. Amy

AMY BINGHAM. See: Hargrave-
Scott, Joan

AMY BRITTON. See: Ames, Peter

AMY BROWN. See: Randolph,
Ellen

AMY FOSTER. See: Marshall,
John

AMY GORDON BARTLETT. See:
Meredith, Charles

AMY JENNINGS. See: Collins,
Barnabas

AMY SNOWDEN. See: Prescott,
Kate Hathaway

ANA, SR. See: Bertrille, Sr.

ANDAMO. See: Lucky, Mr.

ANDERS. See also: Andrews

ANDERS, ARNE. See: Nielson,
Torwald

ANDERS, HARVE. See: Varner,
Will

ANDERS, LAURIE. See: Murray,
Ken (3)

ANDERS, MATT, free lance writer
Crusader (TV) (Adventure)

ANDERS, MRS. ARNE. See:
Nielson, Torwald

ANDERSON, ARTHUR. See: Halop,
Billy

ANDERSON, CALEB. See: Ames,
Peter

ANDERSON, CAROL. See: Silver,
Captain

ANDERSON, DOUGLAS ("MR.
DOCUS"). See: Kirchner,
Claude (1)

ANDERSON, ELSIE. See: Harum,
David

ANDERSON, JIM (Father), head of
the house
MARGARET ANDERSON (Mother),
his wife
BETTY ANDERSON
KATHY ANDERSON, their
daughters
BUD ANDERSON, their son
ELIZABETH SMITH
HECTOR SMITH, Elizabeth's
husband
BILLY SMITH, son of Elizabeth

and Hector; neighbors of the
Andersons
Father Knows Best (R) (TV)
(Situation comedy)

ANDERSON, JIM. See also: Burton,
Terry

ANDERSON, JULIE. See: Peyton,
Martin

ANDERSON, KATHLEEN. See:
Aldrich, Henry

ANDERSON, LIEUT. See: Pyle,
Gomer

ANDERSON, LIEUT. JAMES. See:
Mason, Perry

ANDERSON, LILLIAN. See: Burton,
Terry

ANDERSON, LYNN. See: Welk,
Lawrence

ANDERSON, MARIAN. See: Bell,
Alexander Graham

ANDERSON, MICKEY. See: Hutton,
Ina Ray

ANDERSON, MILDRED. See: Day,
Dennis

ANDERSON, MILLY. See: Stockdale, Will

ANDERSON, MR. See: Day, Dennis

ANDERSON, MRS. See:
Aldrich, Henry
Day, Dennis
West, Michael

ANDERSON, SERGEANT NICK, law
enforcement officer
JOHN EGAN, lawyer
MILLER
PINE
KIRBY
SNYDER, characters appearing
in the drama
Arrest and Trial (TV) (Crime ad-
venture/courtroom drama)

ANDRA WILLIS. See: Welk,
Lawrence

ANDRE AERNE. See: Kelly, Joe
(2)

ANDRE, JEAN-GASTON. See:
Sheppard, Franklin

ANDRE KOSTELANETZ. See:
Martin, Tony (2)

ANDREA. See: Nuvo, Arnie

ANDREA REYNOLDS. See:
Peters, Bill

ANDREA WHITING. See: Tate,
Joanne

ANDREA WINTHROP BROWNING.
See: Ames, Peter

ANDREW DUNCAN. See: Caesar,
Sid (1)

ANDREW H. BROWN. See: Jones,
Amos

ANDREW HUMMEL. See: Hollister, Dick

ANDREW KING. See: Drake,
Nora

ANDREW SELLERS, DR. See:
Locke, Dr. Simon (1)

ANDREW "SKIPPER" BARBOUR.
See: Barbour, Henry Wilson

ANDREW WHITE, DR. See:
Perkins, Ma

ANDREW WINTERS. See: Davis,
Dr. Althea

ANDREWS. See also: Anders

ANDREWS, ARCHIE, high school
student
FRED ANDREWS, his father
MARY ANDREWS, his mother
JUGHEAD JONES, his friend;
high school student
BETTY COOPER, his girl friend
VERONICA LODGE, his friend
MR. LODGE, Veronica's
wealthy father
REGGIE MANTLE, high school
student, his rival

PRINCIPAL of the high school
Archie Andrews (R) (Situation
comedy)

ANDREWS, BETTY. See: Van
Dyke, Dick (2)

ANDREWS, CAPTAIN. See: Crooke,
Lennie

ANDREWS, CAROLINE. See: Roxy

ANDREWS, CECILY. See: Bennett,
Nita

ANDREWS, CULLEN. See: Bennett,
Nita

ANDREWS, DR. See: Jordan, Joyce

ANDREWS, DRAKE
LARRY LAHR
MIKE MADISON, professional
snorkel divers
The Aquanauts (TV) (Underwater
adventure) (also known as Malibu
Run) (TV)

ANDREWS, ISABEL. See: Kelly,
Kitty

ANDREWS, JACK. See: Sterling,
Vanessa Dale

ANDREWS, JULIE, singer, actress
and entertainer; star of the pro-
gram (herself)
RICH LITTLE, featured impres-
sionist (himself)
ALICE GHOSTLEY, comedienne
(herself)
THE TONY CHARMOLI DANCERS
THE DICK WILLIAMS SINGERS
MANY GUEST STARS
NELSON RIDDLE, orchestra
leader (himself)
HIS ORCHESTRA
The Julie Andrews Hour (TV)
(Variety)

ANDREWS, LIZ. See: Slattery, Jim

ANDREWS, MARY. See: Horton,
Dr. Tom

ANDREWS, MEG DALE. See:
Sterling, Vanessa Dale

ANDREWS, NORMAN. See: Reed,
Jerry

ANDREWS, RUSS
STEVE BANKS, insurance in-
vestigators
MAGGIE PETERS, their girl
Friday
BILL DAVIS, member of in-
surance firm's staff
POLLY WALTERS, secretary
The Investigators (TV) (Crime
drama)

ANDREWS, RUTH. See: Meredith,
Charles

ANDREWS SISTERS, THE. See:
Baker, Phil (1)
Crosby, Bob (2)

ANDREWS, WALTER, eccentric
millionaire tycoon; chairman of
the board of Thunder Holding
Corporation
MARTHA KEANE, his grand-
daughter
UNA FIELDS, his housekeeper
BETTY FRANKLIN, his secretary
PAT BURNS, his young executive
aide
HERBERT WILSON, corporation
president
The Tycoon (TV) (Drama)

ANDY. See:
Ames, Peter
Devine, Andy
Gump, Andy
Guthrie, Mitch
Hardy, Andy
Jones, Amos
Sawyer, Andy
Taylor, Andy
Thompson, Andy
Williams, Andy (1) (2)

Andy, Amos 'n'. See: Jones,
Amos

ANDY BARRETT. See: Randolph,
Ellen

ANDY BOONE. See: Dugan,
Queenie

ANDY CLAYTON. See: Fairchild,
Kay

ANDY DEVINE. See:
Benny, Jack
Devine, Andy

ANDY GILBREATH. See: Wizard,
Mr.

ANDY GRIFFITH. See:
Sawyer, Andy
Taylor, Andy
Thompson, Andy

Andy Griffith Show, The. See: Taylor, Andy

Andy Griffith Show, The New. See:
Sawyer, Andy

ANDY HAYS. See: Alcala, Thomas
Jefferson

ANDY HOYT. See: Young, Larry
"Pepper"

ANDY LOVE'S VOCAL GROUP.
See: Dunninger, Joseph

Andy of Mayberry. See: Taylor,
Andy

ANDY PRUITT, GRANDPA. See:
Endicott, Professor Mike

ANDY RUSSELL. See: Ross,
Lanny

Andy Williams and June Valli. See:
Williams, Andy (1)

Andy Williams Show, The. See:
Williams, Andy (2)

Andy's Gang. See: Devine, Andy

Angel. See: Smith, Angel

ANGEL. See: Smith, Angel

ANGEL CHERNAK. See: Garrison,
Spencer

ANGEL GOOD. See: Rowan, Dan

ANGEL, GUS, insurance salesman
VICKIE, his wife
WILMA CLEMSON, neighbor of
the Angels
GEORGE CLEMSON, Wilma's

husband
Date With the Angels (TV) (Situation comedy)

Angel of Mercy, Kate Hopkins.
See: Hopkins, Kate

ANGEL, THE RED-HEADED. See:
Wilbur, Judy

ANGEL, THE SWEDISH. See:
James, Dennis (4)

ANGELIQUE. See: Collins,
Barnabas

Angels, Blue. See: Scott, Captain

Angels, Date With the. See:
Angel, Gus

ANGIE. See: Davis, Joan Field

ANGIE DOW. See: Lane, Hondo

ANGIE PALLUCCI. See: Martin,
Doris

ANGUS. See: Jones, Lorenzo

ANGUS MacDONALD. See: Lawton,
Lora

Animal News Club. See: Straight,
Clarence

Animal Secrets. See: Eiseley,
Loren C.

Animal World. See: Burrud, Bill
(1)

ANITA. See also: Nita

ANITA ELLIS. See: Bergen,
Edgar (2)

ANITA GORDON. See: Bergen,
Edgar (2)

ANITA KURT. See: Riggs, Tommy

ANKA, PAUL. See: Jones, Jack

ANN, character appearing in the
drama
Crossroads (R) (Serial drama)

ANN. See also:
Anne
Cooper, Ann
Davis, Ann Tyler
Gidget
Lincoln, Dr. Matt
Weston, Sam

ANN BLYTH. See: Cross, Milton
(2)

ANN ELDER. See: Rowan, Dan

ANN HELM. See: Hardy, Dr.
Steven

ANN HOWARD. See: Peyton,
Martin

ANN HOWE. See: Palooka, Joe

ANN LOWERY. See: Booth, Martha

ANN MARIE. See: Hollinger, Don

ANN, MARY. See: Gilligan

ANN RICHARDS MALONE. See:
Malone, Dr. Jerry

ANN SHEPHERD. See: Johnson,
Raymond Edward (1)

Ann Sothern Show, The New. See:
O'Connor, Katy

ANN SWENK, DR. See: Newman,
Tony

ANN THOMAS. See: Parker, Lou

ANN WAITE BARBOUR. See: Barbour, Henry Wilson

ANN WILLIAMS. See: Casey

ANNA. See:
Cameron, Barry
Harding, Karen Adams
Owens, Anna
Rose, George
Sunday
Young, Larry "Pepper"

Anna and the King. See: Owens,
Anna

ANNA CAMERON. See: Kidder,
Margot

ANNA HEJAK. See: Keene, Kitty

ANNA NIELSON, MRS. See: Nielson, Torwald

ANNALEE. See: Cannon, John

ANNE. See:
Ann
Gentry, Dr. Anne
Jamison, Dr. Sean
Lee, Jim
Morgan, Lieut. Anne
Morrison, Mother

ANNE BENEDICT. See: Bauer,
Bertha

ANNE BOLEYN. See: Henry VIII,
King of England

ANNE BONNY. See: Tempest,
Dan

ANNE DAVIS (MOTHER DAVIS).
See: Davis, Joan Field

ANNE GOODWIN. See: Grimm,
Arnold

ANNE HILL. See: Jordan, Joyce

ANNE OF CLEVES. See: Henry
VIII, King of England

ANNE, PRINCESS. See: Churchill,
John

ANNE, QUEEN. See: Churchill,
John

ANNE SEYMOUR. See: Ameche,
Don (3)

ANNETTE. See:
Dodd, Jimmie
Forsyte, Soames

ANNETTE FUNICELLO. See:
Jones, Jack

ANNETTE HANSHAW. See: Henry,
Captain

ANNETTE ROGERS SULLIVAN.
See: Perry, John

ANNIE. See:

Brennan, Tugboat Annie
Campanelli, Dr.
Little Orphan Annie
Marlin, Mary
Oakley, Annie
Preston, Dick
Worthington, Nora

Annie, Little Orphan. See: Little
Orphan Annie

ANNIE MARIE TEMPLETON. See:
Harding, Karen Adams

Annie Oakley. See: Oakley, Annie

Annie, Tugboat. See: Brennan,
Tugboat Annie

Anniversary Club. See: Alexander,
Ben (2)

ANNOUNCER, MARATHON DANCE.
See: Nye, Louis

ANNOUNCERS, RADIO. See:
Welles, Orson (3)

Annual Thanksgiving Day Parade,
Macy's. See: Myerson, Bess

Another World. See: Randolph,
Alice

ANSON FOSTER. See: Grindl

ANSON WEEKS. See:
Medbury, John P.
Winchell, Walter (1)

Answer Man, The. See: Answer
Man, The

ANSWER MAN, THE, provided
answers to questions submitted
by listeners
The Answer Man (R) (Information)

ANSWERING SERVICE, MR. JONES'.
See: Pam

Answers, Issues and. See: Peterson, Roger

ANT. See: Atom Ant

ANTAEUS RIAKOS. See: Carlyle,
Baylor

ANTHONY, cub reporter
SUSAN
JANE DALY, characters appear-
in the drama
The Affairs of Anthony (R) (Serial
drama)

ANTHONY. See also:
Alden, Michael
Antony
Girelli, Joe
Smith, Anthony

ANTHONY, AGATHA. See: Trent,
Helen

ANTHONY HALE. See: James,
Nancy

ANTHONY, JOHN J., host of the
program (himself)
MANY ACTORS AND ACTRESSES
Helping Hand (R) (Dramatizations)

ANTHONY, JOHN J. See also:
Anthony, Mr.

ANTHONY LINK. See: Myrt

ANTHONY LORING, DR. See:
Brown, Ellen

ANTHONY, MICHAEL, executive
secretary of the Millionaire who
gives million dollar gifts to
strangers
JOHN BERRESFORD TIPTON, the
Millionaire
The Millionaire (TV) (Drama)
(also called If You Had a Million)
(TV)

ANTHONY, MR. (John J. Anthony),
moderator of the program (himself)
MANY INTERVIEWEES
The Goodwill Hour (R) (Advice)

ANTHONY, MR. See also:
Anthony, John J.

ANTHONY, RAY, trumpeter and
orchestra leader; host of the
program (himself)
HIS ORCHESTRA
DON DURANT
MED FLORY, entertainers appearing on the program (themselves)

FRANK LEAHY, football coach,
appearing on the program (him-
self)
THE FOUR FRESHMEN, vocal
group
MANY GUEST STARS
The Ray Anthony Show (TV)
(Music/variety)

ANTHONY, RAY. See also: Whiteman, Paul

Anthony, The Affairs of. See:
Anthony

ANTOINE, JOSEPHINE. See: Faith,
Percy

ANTON JULIKAK. See: Perkins,
Ma

ANTONINI, ALFREDO. See:
Froman, Jane (2)

ANTONINO ROCCA. See: James,
Dennis (4)

ANTONY. See also: Anthony

ANTONY, PAULINE. See: Chidsey, Jackie

Anybody Can Play. See: Fenneman,
George

APPLE, MR. See: Meek, Mortimer

APPLEBY, GEORGE. See: Junior

APPLEBY, THE. See: O'Toole,
Ensign

APPLEGATE, PROFESSOR
ULYSSES S. See: Kaltenmeyer,
Professor August, D.U.N.

APPLEGATE, RORY. See: Farrell,
David

APPOPOLOUS. See: Sherwood,
Ruth

APRIL. See:
Dancer, April
Muggsy

Aquanauts, The. See: Andrews,
Drake

ARABELLA DONN. See: Cooke,
Alistaire (1)

Arabesque. See: Ross, David (1)

ARAGON, CATHERINE OF. See:
Henry VIII, King of England

ARAM. See: Speaker, The

ARBADELLA. See: Jones, Amos

ARCANE, MR. See: Croft,
Jonathan

ARCARO, DETECTIVE FRANK.
See: Parker, Lieut. Mike

ARCH FENSTER. See: Dickens,
Harry

ARCH HADLEY. See: Wilbur,
Judy

ARCHBISHOP THOMAS CRANMER.
See: Henry VIII, King of
England

ARCHER ARMSTEAD, DEAN. See:
Ballew, Wally

ARCHER, CORLISS, 15 1/2 year
old girl
MR. ARCHER, her father
MRS. ARCHER, her mother
LITTLE RAYMOND, her brother
DEXTER FRANKLIN, her boy
friend
Meet Corliss Archer (R) (TV)
(Situation comedy)

ARCHER, KITTY. See: McGarry,
Dan

ARCHER, MOM. See: McGarry,
Dan

ARCHER, THE. See: Batman

ARCHER, WARD. See: Bernie,
Ben

ARCHIE (The Manager) of Duffy's
Tavern
MISS DUFFY, Duffy's daughter
CLIFTON FINNEGAN, habitue
of the Tavern
WILFRED, Finnegan's younger

brother
CLANCY, policeman
EDDIE, waiter at the Tavern
DOLLY SNAFFLE, habitue of the
Tavern
TITO GUIZAR
BENAY VENUTA
HELEN WARD
BOB GRAHAM, featured vocalists
on the program (themselves)
JOE VENUTI
REET VEET REEVES, orchestra
leaders (themselves)
THEIR ORCHESTRAS
MANY GUEST STARS
Duffy's Tavern (R) (Comedy)
(Many of these characters also
appeared on Duffy's Tavern) (TV)

ARCHIE. See also:
Andrews, Archie
Bunker, Archie

Archie Andrews. See: Andrews,
Archie

ARCHIE BLEYER. See: Godfrey,
Arthur (1) (2)

ARCHIE BUNKER. See:
Bunker, Archie
Findlay, Maude

ARCHIE CAMPBELL. See: Owens,
Buck

ARCHIE GOODWIN. See: Wolfe,
Nero

ARDALA VALMAR. See: Rogers,
Buck

ARDEN, DALE. See: Gordon,
Flash

ARDEN, EVE. See:
Kaye, Danny
Owner

ARDEN, JANE
MR. ARDEN
MRS. ARDEN
BOB BRANDON
BETTY HARRISON
ALABAMA RANDALL
LOUISE WEST
JACK FRASER
DR. STEVE, physician

E.J. WALKER
JACK GALLOWAY, characters
appearing in the drama
Jane Arden (R) (Serial drama)

Are You a Genius? See: Chappell,
Ernest (1)

ARGYLE, INSPECTOR. See:
West, Jim (1)

Ark, Noah's. See: McCann, Dr.
Noah

ARKANSAS TRAVELER, THE,
singer and bazooka player
SHARON O'SHAUGHNESSEY, his
friend
The Bob Burns Show (R) (Comedy)

ARKANSAS WOODCHOPPER, ARKIE
THE. See: Kelly, Joe (1)

ARKIE, THE ARKANSAS WOOD-
CHOPPER. See: Kelly, Joe (1)

ARLEN, MARGARET, hostess of
the program (herself)
MANY GUESTS
Margaret Arlen (R) (Interviews)

ARLENE. See:
Arline
Dahl, Arlene
Francis, Arlene (1) (2) (3) (4)

Arlene Francis. See: Francis,
Arlene (1)

ARLENE FRANCIS. See:
Daly, John (3)
Francis, Arlene (1) (2) (3) (4)
Hulick, Wilbur Budd
Myerson, Bess

ARLINE. See also: Arlene

ARLINE HARRISON. See: Manning,
Portia Blake

ARLINE MANNING. See: Manning,
Portia Blake

ARLO PRITCHARD. See: Cade,
Sam

ARMBRUSTER, ROBERT. See:

Ameche, Don (1)
Bergen, Edgar (2)
Eddy, Nelson (1)
Marx, Groucho (1)
Weems, Ambrose J.

ARMEN, KAY. See: Parks, Bert
(6)

ARMOUR, CHARLOTTA LAGORRO.
See: Carter, Kathryn

ARMOUR, KEITH. See: Carter,
Kathryn

ARMS, RUSSELL. See: Lanson,
Snooky

ARMSTEAD, DEAN ARCHER. See:
Ballew, Wally

ARMSTEAD, POLLY. See: Benson, Bobby

ARMSTRONG, JACK, teen-age ad-
venturer; sometime student at
Hudson High School
BILLY FAIRFIELD, his best
friend
BETTY FAIRFIELD, Billy's sister
UNCLE JIM FAIRFIELD, uncle of
Billy and Betty; army intelligence
officer, aircraft manufacturing
executive and owner of the Silver
Albatross, amphibian aeroplane
MONTE DEVOL, Jack's enemy;
school bully
GWENDOLYN DEVOL, Monte's
sister
COACH HARDY, athletic coach at
Hudson High School
CAPTAIN HUGHES, officer
BABU
BLACKBEARD FLINT
SULLIVAN LODGE
MICHAEL
WEISSOUL
PETE
DICKIE, characters appearing on
the program
Jack Armstrong, The All-Ameri-
can Boy (R) (Adventure)

ARMSTRONG, LOUIS. See: Whiteman, Paul

ARMSTRONG, MRS. See: Myrt

ARMSTRONG QUAKER GIRL, THE,
featured on the program
MANY ACTORS AND ACTRESSES
The Armstrong Theater of Today
(R) (Drama)

Armstrong Theater of Today, The.
See: Armstrong Quaker Girl,
The

Army Hour, The. See: Herlihy,
Ed

Army, The Wackiest Ship in the.
See: Butcher, Major Simon

ARNE ANDERS. See: Nielson,
Torwald

ARNE ANDERS, MRS. See: Nielson, Torwald

ARNHEIM, GUS. See: Medbury,
John P.

Arnie. See: Nuvo, Arnie

ARNIE. See:
Arny
Barkley, Arnie
Nuvo, Arnie
Smith, Eugene

ARNIE TOPPER. See: Harding,
Mrs. Rhoda

ARNOLD. See:
Douglas, Oliver
Grimm, Arnold
Marlin, Mary

ARNOLD CAREY. See: Noble,
Mary

ARNOLD, EDDY
ALEX DREIER
MAL HANSON
CARMELITA POPE, singers,
entertainers and newscasters
featured on the program (themselves)
Today On the Farm (TV) (Music/
news/farm information)

ARNOLD, EDDY. See also: Berman, Shelley

ARNOLD, GENE
GUS VAN, interlocutors on the
program (themselves)
THE SINCLAIR MINSTREL MEN
THE SINCLAIR QUARTET
SPARE RIBS, featured on the
program
The Sinclair Minstrel Show (R)
(Music/comedy)

Arnold Grimm's Daughter. See:
Grimm, Arnold

ARNOLD, JACK. See: Myrt

ARNOLD, LIZA. See: Hansen,
Dean Eric

ARNOLD, MARY. See: Rogers,
Kenny

ARNOLD, MR. See: Myrt

ARNOLD, MRS. See: Myrt

ARNOLD MOSS. See: Arthur,
Jack (2)

ARNOLD STANG. See: Edwards,
Ralph (1)

ARNOLD, UNCLE. See: Muir,
Carolyn

ARNY. See also: Arnie

ARNY LOGAN. See: Brooks,
Cameron

ARQUETTE, CLIFF. See:
Haymes, Dick
Marshall, Peter
Winters, Jonathan

Arrest and Trial. See: Anderson,
Sergeant Nick

Arrest, Under. See: Drake, Captain

ARROW. See: Straight Arrow

Arrow, Broken. See: Jeffords,
Tom

Arrow, Straight. See: Straight
Arrow

ART. See:
Baker, Art (1) (2)
Fleming, Art
Hodes, Art
James, Art
Linkletter, Art (1) (2) (3) (4)

ART BUCHWALD. See: DeLuise,
Dom (2)

ART FORD. See: Shaw, Stan

ART GENTRY. See: Lewis, Welcome (2)

ART METRANO. See: Conway,
Tim

ART MOONEY. See:
Basie, Count
Whiteman, Paul

ART VAN DAMME QUINTET, THE
See: Garroway, Dave (3)

ARTE. See also: Artie

ARTE JOHNSON. See: Rowan,
Dan

ARTEMUS GORDON. See: West,
Jim (2)

ARTHUR. See:
Drake, Nora
Elmer, Arthur
Fiedler, Arthur
Fields, Arthur
Godfrey, Arthur (1) (2) (3) (4)
Hale, Arthur
Murray, Arthur
Murray, Kathryn
Ross, Arthur
Tate, Joanne
Tracy, Arthur

ARTHUR ADAMS. See: Marlin,
Mary

ARTHUR ANDERSON. See: Halop,
Billy

ARTHUR BLAINE. See: Webster,
Nancy

ARTHUR, CAROL. See: DeLuise,
Dom (1)

ARTHUR COOK. See: Rogers,
Patricia

ARTHUR DONNELLY. See: Carter,
Kathryn

ARTHUR DUNCAN. See: Welk,
Lawrence

ARTHUR GODFREY. See:
Funt, Allen (1)
Godfrey, Arthur (1) (2) (3) (4)

Arthur Godfrey and His Friends.
See: Godfrey, Arthur (1)

Arthur Godfrey Time. See: Godfrey, Arthur (1)

Arthur Godfrey's Talent Scouts.
See: Godfrey, Arthur (2)

ARTHUR HALL. See: Grimm,
Arnold

ARTHUR HARMON. See: Findlay,
Maude

ARTHUR, JACK (1)
ETHEL OWEN, featured on the
program (themselves)
VAN ALEXANDER, orchestra
leader (himself)
HIS ORCHESTRA
The Callahans (R) (Music)

ARTHUR, JACK (2), narrator of the
program (himself)
BEVERLY BAYNE
JIM AMECHE
MARY MASON
HUME CRONYN
NANCY COLEMAN
ARNOLD MOSS
McKAY MORRIS
OTHERS, actors and actresses
appearing on the program (them-
selves)
Grand Central Station (R) (Drama)

ARTHUR, JACK (3), master of
ceremonies of the program (him-
self)
MANY MUSICIANS, ACTORS AND
ACTRESSES
Little Old New York (R) (Variety)

ARTHUR, JACK. See also: Weems,

Ambrose J.

ARTHUR, KING. See: Sir Lancelot

ARTHUR, MAUREEN. See:
Jones, Dean
Kovacs, Ernie (1)

Arthur Murray Party, The. See:
Murray, Kathryn

ARTHUR Q. BRYAN. See:
Coogan, Jackie
Lescoulie, Jack (2)

ARTHUR Q. LEWIS. See: Ed-
wards, Ralph (1)

ARTHUR READS. See: Brent,
Dr. Jim

ARTHUR TRAGG, LIEUT. See:
Mason, Perry

ARTHUR TREACHER. See: Griffin, Merv (1)

ARTHUR, UNCLE. See: Stephens,
Samantha

ARTHUR WARD. See: Erskine,
Inspector Louis

ARTIE. See also: Arte

ARTIE BURNS. See: Taylor,
Danny

Arts, The Seven Lively. See:
Crosby, John

As Caesar Sees It. See: Caesar,
Sid (1)

As Others See Us. See: Michaels,
Joe

As the Twig Is Bent. See: Peters,
Bill

As the World Turns. See: Hughes,
Chris

ASA GRIFFIN. See: Wayne, Ruth
Evans

ASHBY, ELLA. See: Davis, Joan
Field

ASHER, INSPECTOR FRED. See:
Guthrie, Lieut. Ben

ASHLEY, MARTHA ANN. See:
Ames, Peter

ASHWORTH, MARY. See: Como,
Perry (1)

Ask, Funny You Should. See:
Thaxton, Lloyd (2)

Ask-it Basket, The. See: Mc-
Williams, Jim (1)

Ask Your Doctor. See: Edman,
Karl

ASP. See: Little Orphan Annie

Asphalt Jungle, The. See: Gower,
Matthew

Assignment, Dangerous. See:
Mitchell, Steve

Assignment, Foreign. See: Foreign
Correspondent, The

Assignment Foreign Legion. See:
Oberon, Merle

Assignment: Vienna. See: Webster, Jake

ASTA. See: Charles, Nick

ASTAIRE, FRED (1), host of the
program (himself)
MANY ACTORS AND ACTRESSES
Alcoa Premiere (TV) (Dramas)

ASTAIRE, FRED (2), dancer; star
of the program (himself)
BARRIE CHASE, his dancing partner; co-star of the program (herself)
An Evening With Fred Astaire
(TV) (Dancing)

ASTAIRE, FRED. See also: Ross,
Lanny

ASTRAKHAN, MR. See: Kelly,
Kitty

ASTRO. See:
Corbett, Tom (2)

Jetson, George

Astro Boy. See: Astro Boy

ASTRO BOY, super-boy robot; cartoon character
Astro Boy (TV) (Cartoon)

At the Village Store. See: Owner

ATCHER, BOB. See: Kelly,
Joe (1)

ATHELNEY, SALLY. See: Carey,
Dr. Philip

ATHLETE, THE. See: Morgan,
Henry

ATKINS, REVEREND C.E., moderator of the program (himself)
MANY JUVENILE ACTORS
Breakthru (TV) (Dramatizations
of solutions to young people's
moral problems)

Atom Ant. See: Atom Ant

ATOM ANT, "super ant; The World's
Mightiest Insect"
Atom Ant (TV) (Cartoon)

ATTERBURY, RUDOLPH. See:
Cooper, Liz

ATTIRED, NATTILY. See: Ballew, Wally

ATTORNEY. See: District Attorney, Mr.

Attorney at Law. See: Regan,
Terry

Attorney at Law, Ben Jerrod. See:
Jerrod, Ben

Attorney at Law: Terry Regan.
See: Regan, Terry

Attorney, Mr. District. See:
District Attorney, Mr.

ATWATER, MRS. VAN. See:
Canova, Judy

ATWOOD, JESSIE. See: Hopkins,
Kate

ATWOOD, ROBERT. See: Hopkins,
Kate

AUBRY, GEORGE. See: Welk,
Lawrence

Auction Gallery. See: Elman,
Dave (1)

AUDRA. See: Barkley, Victoria

AUDREY BALDWIN. See: Hardy,
Dr. Steven

AUDREY MEADOWS. See:
Donald, Peter
James, Dennis (3)

AUDREY ROBERTS. See: Dawson,
Rosemary

AUGIE. See: Muggsy

AUGIE DOGGIE. See: McGraw,
Quick Draw

AUGUST. See: Kaltenmeyer,
Professor August, D. U. N.

AUGUST, DAN, police lieutenant;
head of homicide bureau at Santa
Luisa, California
CHARLES WILENTZ, detective
sergeant
JOE RIVERA, police sergeant
CHIEF GEORGE UNTERMEYER,
police chief
KATY GRANT, their Negro
secretary
Dan August (TV) (Crime drama)

AUGUSTUS PENDLETON. See:
Perkins, Ma

AUNT AGATHA. See: Higby,
Mary Jane

AUNT AGGIE. See: Canova, Judy

AUNT ALICE. See: Sunday

AUNT BEE. See:
Jones, Sam
Taylor, Andy

AUNT BESSIE. See: Gilman,
Gordon

AUNT CLARA. See: Stephens,
Samantha

AUNT DEBBIE. See: Hoyt,
Vikki Adams

AUNT DORRIE. See: Warren,
Wendy

AUNT DRUSILLA. See: Cooke,
Alistaire (1)

AUNT EMILY MAYFIELD. See:
Marshall, John

AUNT ETHEL. See: Webster,
Martha

AUNT FANNY. See: McNeill,
Don

AUNT GLADYS. See: Grimm,
Arnold

AUNT GUS. See: Miller, Socrates

AUNT HARRIET. See:
Aldrich, Henry
Batman
Endicott, Professor Mike

AUNT HELEN SPALDING. See:
Harding, Karen Adams

AUNT HENRIETTA. See: Everett,
Professor

Aunt Jennie's True Life Stories.
See: Aunt Jenny (Aunt Lucy)

AUNT JENNY (AUNT LUCY), intro-
duced story with the help of her
announcer
DANNY, her announcer
HER WHISTLING CANARY
Aunt Jennie (also known as
Aunt Jennie's True Life Stories
and, in Canada, as Aunt Lucy)
(R) (Serial drama)

AUNT KATE. See: Rogers,
Patricia

AUNT LIL. See: Peepers, Robinson J.

AUNT LIVVY. See: Major, Bob

AUNT LUCINDA SKINFLINT. See:
Peppertag, Aaron

Aunt Lucy. See: Aunt Jenny (Aunt
Lucy)

AUNT LUCY. See: Aunt Jenny
(Aunt Lucy)

AUNT MAIZIE. See: Dyke, Charity
Amanda

AUNT MARGARET. See: Fleming,
Tony

AUNT MARIA. See: Henry, Captain

AUNT MARTHA. See: Carter,
Kathryn

Aunt Mary. See: Aunt Mary

AUNT MARY
JESSIE WARD, characters appear-
ing in the drama
Aunt Mary (R) (Serial drama)

AUNT MATT. See: Waring, Evelyn

AUNT MEG. See: West, Honey

AUNT MINTA OWENS. See: Vance,
Connie

AUNT PHOEBE. See: Clayton,
Margie

AUNT POLLY BENSON. See:
Harum, David

AUNT SALLY. See: Carson, Jack

AUNT SAP AND UNCLE SIP. See:
Foley, Red

AUNTIE. See: Brent, Dr. Jim

AUSTIN, JERRY. See: Malone,
Mike

Author Meets the Critics, The.
See: Gray, Barry (1)

AUTRY, GENE, cowboy and singer,
star of the program (himself)
PAT BUTTRAM, comedian, co-
star of the program (himself)
CHAMPION, Autry's horse (himself)

Gene Autry's Melody Ranch (R)
(TV) (Western music and adventure)

AVALON, FRANKIE. See: Jones,
Jack

Avalon Time. See: Skelton, Red

Avengers, The. See: Steed, John

AVENUE HILLBILLY, THE PARK.
See: Jones, Spike (2)

AVERAGE RADIO LISTENER, MR.
See: Kaye, Danny

Awards, The Academy. See: Hope,
Bob (1)

Away We Go. See: Greco, Buddy

AWFUL. See: Gibson, Dot

AXEL STORDAHL. See:
MacKenzie, Gisele
Ross, Lanny
Sinatra, Frank

AXFORD, MICHAEL. See: Reid,
Britt

Axis Sally. See: Sisk, Mildred
Elizabeth

AXLAND, DR. See: Malone, Dr.
Jerry

AYRES, BETSY. See: Roxy

AYRES, LEW
MELVYN DOUGLAS
DICK POWELL, hosts of the pro-
gram (themselves)
MANY ACTORS AND ACTRESSES
Frontier Justice (TV) (Western
dramas; re-runs of old Zane
Grey Theater presentations)

AYRES, MITCHELL. See:
Como, Perry (1) (2) (3)
Crosby, Bing (2)
Dunninger, Joseph
La Rosa, Julius

AZEVDO, LEX DE. See: Driggs,
Karleton King

AZEVDO, RIC DE. See: Driggs,
Karleton King

B. A. ROLFE. See:
Edmondson, Delmar
Ripley, Robert L.

B-Bar-B, Songs of the. See: Benson, Bobby

B. J. CLAWSON. See: Slattery, Jim

BAAR. See also:
Paar
Parr

BAAR, BILL. See: Burton, Grandpa

BABBITT, FENWICK. See: Gleason, Jackie (1) (2)

BABBITT, HARRY. See: Kyser, Kay

"BABBY." See also: Baby

"BABBY" DENNIS, BARBARA.
See: Dennis, Liz

BABE. See: Ruth, Babe

Babe Ruth, Here's. See: Ruth, Babe

BABETTE, MADAME. See: Grimm, Arnold

BABS. See:
Hooton, Babs
Riley, Chester A.

BABS AND HER BROTHERS. See:
Waring, Fred (1)

BABU. See: Armstrong, Jack

BABY. See also "Babby"

BABY DAL. See: Grimm, Arnold

BABY DUMPLING (ALEXANDER).
See: Bumstead, Blondie

BABY, LOLLY. See: Dallas, Stella

BABY SNOOKS, precocious young child
DADDY HIGGINS, her father
MOMMY, her mother
ROBESPIERRE, her brother
ROGER
PHOEBE, her friends
The Baby Snooks Show (R)
(Comedy)

BABY SNOOKS. See also:
Dragonette, Jessica (2)
Morgan, Frank (2)

BABY SUSY. See: Ethel

BABYFACE NELSON. See: McKenzie, Captain Craig

Bachelor Father. See: Gregg, Uncle Bentley

Bachelor's Children. See:
Graham, Dr. Bob

BACKSTAGE, HARRY. See: Ballew, Wally

BACKSTAGE, MARY, NOBLE
WIFE. See: Ballew, Wally

Backstage Wife. See: Noble, Mary

Backstage Wife, Mary Noble. See:
Noble, Mary

BACKUS. See also: Bagus

BACKUS, JIM. See:
Kaye, Danny
Marshall, Peter

Bad Girl, Peck's. See: Peck, Torey

Badge 714. See: Friday, Sergeant Joe

BAEZ, JOAN, folk music singer;
star of the program (herself)
The Creative Person (TV) (Music/
discussion)

BAGUS. See also: Backus

BAGUS, SANDRA. See: Kelly, Joe (2)

BAILEY, BILL. See: Top Cat

BAILEY, BILL "BOOM BOOM."

See: Kirchener, Claude (1)

BAILEY, BOB. See: Soule, Olan (4)

BAILEY, F. LEE, criminal lawyer; star of the program (himself) MANY PROMINENT INTERVIEWEES Good Company (TV) (Interviews)

BAILEY, JACK, master of ceremonies of the program (himself) MANY CONTESTANTS Queen For a Day (R) (TV) (Audience participation)

BAILEY, JACK. See also: Edwards, Ralph (3) Elliott, Win (1)

BAILEY, MRS. TRUDY. See: O'Neill, Mrs.

BAILEY, NORMAN. See: Welk, Lawrence

BAILEY, PEARL, singer and entertainer; star of the program (herself) LOUIS BELLSON, drummer and orchestra leader (himself) HIS ORCHESTRA THE BOB SIDNEY DANCERS MANY GUEST STARS The Pearl Bailey Show (TV) (Variety)

BAILEY, SAM, skipper of the charter boat "Island Princess" JIM, his son CECIL WYNTOON, wealthy yachtsman BARBARA WYNTOON, Cecil's daughter BUCK SINGLETON, Sam Bailey's pal and shipmate The Baileys of Balboa (TV) (Comedy)

BAILEY, STUART JEFF SPENCER, private investigators GERALD LLOYD KOOKSON III (Kookie), parking lot attendant, later partner with Bailey and Spencer ROSCOE, investigator SUZANNE, secretary and telephone switchboard operator 77 Sunset Strip (TV) (Detective drama)

BAILEY, WANDA. See: Chidsey, Jackie

Baileys of Balboa, The. See: Bailey, Sam

BAIN. See also: Baines Bayn Bayne

BAIN, NOAH. See: Mundy, Alexander

BAINES. See also: Bain Bayn Bayne

BAINES, SCATTERGOOD, storekeeper and village sage JIMMY BAINES, his son PLINY PICKETT HIPPOCRATES BROWN J. WELLINGTON KEATS ERNE BAKER DR. CHANCELLOR ELOISE COMSTOCK VERNE SANDERS BARBARA CALKINS GERALDINE QUINTON AGAMEMNON CLARA POTTS ED POTTS, Clara's husband MR. MARTIN BETH REED MIRANDY LORINDA SPOTTY MRS. BLACK MARGIE BOB, characters appearing in the drama Scattergood Baines (R) (Serial drama)

BAKALYAN, DICK. See: Darin, Bobby

BAKER. See: Hogan, Colonel Robert

BAKER, ART (1), host of the program (himself)

MANY RECIPIENTS OF NEEDED
ASSISTANCE
End of the Rainbow (TV) (Human
interest)

BAKER, ART (2), host of the program (himself)
You Asked for It (TV) (Films
covering "many facets of many
things")

BAKER, BIFF, adventurer
LOUISE, his wife
Biff Baker, U.S.A. (TV) (Ad-
venture)

BAKER, BILL. See: Manning,
Portia Blake

BAKER, BONNIE. See: Ross,
Lanny

BAKER, BUFFALO. See: Lane,
Hondo

BAKER, CATHY. See: Owens,
Buck

BAKER, CLAY. See: Troy, Adam

BAKER, DEAN FRED, dean of
Channing University
JOSEPH HOWE, professor of
English at the University
Channing (TV) (Drama)

BAKER, ERNE. See: Baines,
Scattergood

BAKER, JEAN. See: Noble, Mary

BAKER, JEFF. See: Hughes, Chris

BAKER, JOE. See: Little, Rich

BAKER, JULIA, widow; Negro nurse
COREY, her 7-year-old son
WAGGEDORN, friend and neighbor
of Julia
MARIE WAGGEDORN, Waggedorn's
wife
EARL, Waggedorn's 7-year-old
son
DR. MORTON CHEGLEY, physician,
Julia's employer
MRS. CHEGLEY, Dr. Chegley's
wife
NORTON CHEGLEY, Dr. Chegley's

92-year-old uncle
STEVE BRUCE, lawyer, Julia's
boy friend
Julia (TV) (Comedy)

BAKER, KENNY, tenor, master of
ceremonies of the program (him-
self)
BARBARA
SCHLEPPERMAN
MRS. BIDDLE
MRS. WILSON
CAPTAIN BILLY
WANDA WEREWULF, characters
appearing on the program
MANY GUEST STARS
Glamour Manor (R) (Variety)

BAKER, KENNY. See also:
Benny, Jack
Marx, Groucho (1)

BAKER, PAT. See: Harris, Bill

BAKER, PHIL (1), accordionist
and comedian; star of the pro-
gram (himself)
BOTTLE, his English butler
BEETLE, stooge and heckler
THE ANDREWS SISTERS, vocal
group (themselves)
LYN MURRAY, orchestra leader
(himself)
HIS ORCHESTRA
Honolulu Bound (R) (Variety)

BAKER, PHIL (2), accordionist
and comedian, star of the show
(himself)
BOTTLE, his English butler
BEETLE, stooge and heckler
FERDINAND
MRS. SARAH HEARTBURN,
characters appearing on the show
The Phil Baker Show (R) (Comedy)

BAKER, PHIL (3)
EDDIE CANTOR
BOB HAWK
GARRY MOORE
JACK PAAR, quizmasters of the
program (themselves)
BEETLE, Baker's stooge and
heckler
BOTTLE, Baker's English butler
MANY CONTESTANTS
Take It or Leave It (R) (Quiz)
(later known as The Sixty-Four

Dollar Question) (R)

BAKER, STEVE. See: Harris, Bill

BAKER, TRACY. See: Barbour,
Henry Wilson

Baker's Broadcast, The. See:
Penner, Joe

Balboa, The Baileys of. See:
Bailey, Sam

BALDRIDGE, FANNY MAY, featured
in the drama (herself)
Miracles of Magnolia (R) (Serial
drama)

BALDWIN, AUDREY. See: Hardy,
Dr. Steven

BALDWIN, DR. Tom. See: Hardy,
Dr. Steven

BALDWIN, JUDGE. See: Walleck,
Meredith

BALDWIN, LEE. See: Hardy, Dr.
Steven

BALDY. See: Horn, Aggie

BALL, DEE DEE. See: Hutton,
Ina Ray

BALL, LUCILLE. See:
Carmichael, Lucy
Carter, Lucy
Frees, Paul
Landi, Elissa
Ricardo, Ricky

BALLANTINE, BOB. See: Kelly,
Joe (1)

BALLARD BRANDON. See: Perry,
John

BALLARD, PAT
CHARLIE HENDERSON, quiz-
masters of the program (them-
selves)
MANY CONTESTANTS
Melody Treasure Hunt (R) (Quiz)

BALLEW, SMITH. See: Jolson, Al

BALLEW, WALLY, bumbling radio

announcer and interviewer
MARY MAGOON, cooking "expert"
STEVE BOSCO
BIFF BURNS, sportscasters
MARY BACKSTAGE, NOBLE
WIFE, spoof of soap opera
character
HARRY BACKSTAGE, Mary's
matinee idol husband
WORD CARR, soap opera an-
nouncer
TEX BLAISDELL, cowboy and
Western entertainer
FATHER BUTCHER
MOTHER BUTCHER, his wife,
radio serial characters on "One
Feller's Family"
LAWRENCE FECHTENBERGER,
"Interstellar Officer Candidate,"
spoof of radio adventure serials
MUGG MELLISH, friend of
Lawrence Fechtenberger
NATTILY ATTIRED, song "sayer"
DEAN ARCHER ARMSTEAD, agri-
culture "expert"
CLAUDE
CLYDE, gourmet "experts"
Bob and Ray (R) (Satire comedy)

BALLINGER, LIEUT. FRANK
CAPTAIN GREY, police officers
in Chicago
M-Squad (TV) (Drime drama)

Ballroom, The Make-Believe. See:
Block, Martin

BAMBI LYNN. See: Caesar, Sid
(3)

Banacek. See: Banacek, Thomas

BANACEK, THOMAS, Polish-Ameri-
can free lance insurance investigator
Banacek (TV) (Crime drama)

Banana Splits Adventure Hour,
Kellogg's Presents the. See:
Fleegle

Banana Splits, The. See: Fleegle

BANCROFT, CURTIS. See: Trent,
Helen

Band, Beat the. See: Hildegarde
(1)

Band, So You Want To Lead a?
See: Kaye, Sammy (2)

BAND, THE CIRCUSEVEN JAZZ.
See: Kirchener, Claude (1)

BANDIT. See: Quest, Jonny

Bands, America's Greatest. See:
Whiteman, Paul

Bands, The Big. See: Basie,
Count

Bandstand, American. See: Clark,
Dick (1)

Bandwagon, The A. & P. See:
Smith, Kate (2)

Bandwagon, The Fitch. See:
Daley, Cass
Harris, Phil
Moore, Garry (2)

BANFORD, MRS. MYRTLE. See:
Truesdale, Sally

BANG, CAPTAIN. See: Parker,
Seth

BANG, GEORGE. See: Parker, Seth

Banjoist, Red Godfrey, The Warbling.
See: Godfrey, Arthur (4)

Bank, Break the. See: Parks,
Bert (1)

Bank, Break the $250,000. See:
Parks, Bert (1)

BANKER, THE MENTAL. See:
I.Q., Dr.

BANKHEAD, TALLULAH, actress;
star of the program (herself)
MEREDITH WILLSON, orchestra
leader (himself)
HIS ORCHESTRA
MANY GUEST STARS
The Big Show (R) (Variety)

BANKS, JOAN. See: Lovejoy,
Frank (1) (2)

BANKS, STANLEY, the "father of
the bride"

ELLIE BANKS, his wife
KAY BANKS, his daughter
BUCKLEY DUNSTAN, engaged to
Kay Banks
HERBERT DUNSTAN, Buckley's
father
DORIS DUNSTAN, Buckley's
mother
Father of the Bride (TV)
(Comedy)

BANKS, STEVE. See: Andrews,
Russ

BANNER, DEBBIE. See: Goldberg,
Molly

BANNER, WOODY, struggling play-
wright; landlord of New York
brownstone apartment house
BONNIE BANNER, his sister
CHUCK HOOKSTRATTEN,
struggling comedian; his roommate
JACK ELLENHORN, his next-
door-neighbor
Hey Landlord! (TV) (Comedy)

BANNING, BOB. See: Harding,
Karen Adams

BANNING, DR. BRUCE. See:
Bauer, Bertha

BANNING, ELSA. See: Wayne,
Ruth Evans

BANNING, ERNEST. See: Wayne,
Ruth Evans

BANNING, PEGGY. See: Benton,
Steve

BANNING, SCOTT. See: Horton,
Dr. Tom

BANNION. See also: Banyon

BANNION, REV. TOM. See:
Rutledge, Dr. John

BANNISTER, CLAY
JEAN PAGE (Mrs. Clay Bannister), his wife
TETLOW, character appearing
in the drama
Follow the Moon (R) (Serial
drama)

BANNISTER, DR. REED. See:
Wayne, Ruth Evans

BANNISTER, MR. See: Dickens,
Harry

BANNON, ROGER "RACE." See:
Quest, Jonny

BANTA, FRANK. See: Dragonette,
Jessica (1)

Banyon. See: Banyon, Miles C.

BANYON. See also: Bannion

BANYON, MILES C., private detec-
tive operating in the 1930s
PEGGY REVERE, proprietress of
secretarial school
LIEUT. PETE McNEIL, officer of
Los Angeles police department
ABBY GRAHAM, Banyon's girl
friend, pianist and singer in cock-
tail bar
Banyon (TV) (Detective drama)

Bar, The Corner. See: Grant,
Harry

BARBARA. See:
Abbott, John
Baker, Kenny
Crabtree, Dave
Douglas, Steve
Driggs, Karleton King
Erskine, Inspector Louis
Lee, Jim
Robinson, Don
Scott, Karen
Stanwyck, Barbara
Walters, Barbara
West, Michael
Whiting, Margaret
Worthington, Nora

BARBARA "BABBY" DENNIS. See:
Dennis, Liz

BARBARA BOYLAN. See: Welk,
Lawrence

BARBARA CALKINS. See: Baines,
Scattergood

BARBARA CASON. See: Klein,
Robert

BARBARA CRAYLEY. See: Marlin,
Mary

BARBARA CROFT. See: Allen,
Jimmie

BARBARA DICKERSON. See:
Simms, Paul

BARBARA FARRELL. See: Davis,
Dr. Althea

BARBARA GORDON. See: Batman

BARBARA GRAYSON. See: O'Neill,
Mrs.

BARBARA HAMILTON. See:
Sunday

BARBARA HUGHEY. See: O'Leary,
Hannah

BARBARA LATTIMER. See:
Sterling, Vanessa Dale

BARBARA LUDDY. See:
Ameche, Don (3)
First Nighter, Mr.

BARBARA NORRIS. See: Bauer,
Bertha

BARBARA PUTNAM. See: Wilbur,
Judy

BARBARA RYAN. See: Hughes,
Chris

BARBARA SHARMAN. See: Rowan,
Dan

Barbara Stanwyck Show, The. See:
Stanwyck, Barbara

BARBARA STORM. See: Brown,
Ellen

BARBARA SUE. See: Trent,
Helen

BARBARA WALTERS. See:
Downs, Hugh
Marshall, E. G.

BARBARA WINTHROP. See: Dix,
Dorothy (2)

BARBARA WYNTOON. See: Bailey,
Sam

Barbasol Man, Singin' Sam the.
   See: Singin' Sam

Barber, Bill the.   See: Davidson,
   Bill

Barber, His Honor the.   See: Fitz,
   Judge

BARBER, RED.   See: Cowan,
   Thomas

BARBOUR, HENRY WILSON (Father
   Barbour), San Francisco stock-
   broker and head of the family
FANNY MARTIN BARBOUR, his
   wife
PAUL BARBOUR, their son; army
   flyer in World War I
ELAINE HUNTER BARBOUR,
   Paul's wife
TEDDY BARBOUR GIDDINGS,
   adopted daughter of Paul and
   Elaine; army nurse
ELWOOD GIDDINGS, Teddy's hus-
   band
HAZEL BARBOUR HERBERT,
   daughter of Henry and Fanny
WILLIAM "BILL" HERBERT,
   Hazel's husband
WILLIAM MARTIN "PINKY" HER-
   BERT
HENRY BARBOUR "HANK" HER-
   BERT, twin sons of Hazel and
   William
MARGARET HERBERT, daughter
   of Hazel and William
CLIFFORD BARBOUR, son of
   Henry and Fanny; Claudia's twin
ANN WAITE BARBOUR, Clifford's
   first wife; dies
ANDREW "SKIPPER" BARBOUR,
   son of Clifford and Ann
IRENE FRANKLIN BARBOUR,
   Clifford's second wife; killed in
   auto crash
CLAUDIA BARBOUR ROBERTS
   LACEY, daughter of Henry and
   Fanny; Clifford's twin
JOHNNY ROBERTS, Claudia's
   first husband; deserts her, dies
   in China
JOAN ROBERTS FARNSWORTH,
   daughter of Claudia and Johnny
ROSS FARNSWORTH, Joan's hus-
   band
PAUL JOHN FARNSWORTH, son
   of Joan and Ross

CAPTAIN NICHOLAS "NICKY"
   LACEY, Claudia's second hus-
   band
PENNY LACEY, daughter of
   Claudia and Nicholas
NICHOLAS "NICKY" LACEY, JR.,
   son of Claudia and Nicholas
JACK BARBOUR, son of Henry
   and Fanny
BETTY CARTER BARBOUR, wife
   of Jack
ABIGAIL BARBOUR
DEBORAH BARBOUR
CONSTANCE BARBOUR, triplet
   daughters of Jack and Betty
ELIZABETH SHARON ANN
   BARBOUR
MARY LOU BARBOUR, daughters
   of Jack and Betty
BETH HOLLY, widow, friend of
   Clifford and Paul
DR. FRED THOMPSON, physician
JUDGE GLENN HUNTER, jurist
REVEREND McARTHUR, minis-
   ter
TRACY BAKER
NICOLETTE MOORE
CHRISTINE ABBOTT
WAYNE GRUBB
COUSIN CONSIDER
BEN, friends and neighbors of
   the Barbour family
One Man's Family (R) (TV)
(Serial drama)

BARCLAY, DOC, physician
CONNIE BARCLAY
MARGE BARCLAY
MIMI BARCLAY, his daughters
CLARABELLE HIGGINS
TOM CLARK, his friends
Doc Barclay's Daughters (R)
(Serial drama)

BARCLAY, LUDA.   See: Davis,
   Red

BARCLAY, MR.   See: Hargrave-
   Scott, Joan

BARCLAY, SANDRA.   See: Noble,
   Mary

BARDINE, SYLVIA.   See: Davidson, Bill

Barefoot in the Park.   See: Bratter,
   Paul

BARGY, ROY. See:
  Bolger, Ray
  Crosby, Bing (3)

BARKER, BOB, moderator of the
  program (himself)
  MANY CONTESTANTS
  The New Price Is Right (TV)
  (Game)

BARKER, BOB. See also:
  Cullen, Bill (3)
  Edwards, Ralph (3)

BARKER, COLONEL U. CHARLES.
  See: McKay, Judson

BARKER, IRMA. See: Jones,
  Lorenzo

BARKER, JEFFREY. See: Guest,
  Edgar A. (2)

BARKER, JIM. See: Jones,
  Lorenzo

BARKER, MATHILDA. See: Guest,
  Edgar A. (2)

BARKER, MR. See:
  Hardy, Dr. Steven
  Meek, Mortimer

BARKER, MRS. See: Meek,
  Mortimer

BARKLEY. See also: Berkeley

BARKLEY, ARNIE, dog; father of
  the family
  AGNES, his wife
  TERRY
  ROGER
  CHESTER, their children; all
  cartoon characters
  The Barkleys (TV) (Cartoon)

BARKLEY, ROGER. See: Lohman,
  Al

BARKLEY, VICTORIA, widowed wife
  of Tom Barkley; operates Barkley
  Sierra Mine
  JARROD
  NICK
  EUGENE, her sons
  AUDRA, her daughter
  HEATH, illegitimate half-brother
  of her legitimate children
  The Big Valley (TV) (Western)

Barkleys, The. See: Barkley,
  Arnie

BARLOW, HOWARD
  ALFRED WALLENSTEIN, sym-
  phony orchestra conductors
  (themselves)
  THEIR ORCHESTRAS
  RENATA TEBALDI
  ALFRED DRAKE
  JEROME HINES
  PATRICE MUNSEL
  RICHARD CROOKS
  MARGARET SPEAKS, opera and
  musical comedy stars (themselves)
  The Voice of Firestone (R) (TV)
  (Classical and semi-classical
  music)

BARLOW, HOWARD. See also:
  Mary
  Melton, James (2)

BARLOW, MIKE. See: Rogers,
  Patricia

Barn Dance, The National. See:
  Kelly, Joe (1)

BARNABAS. See: Collins, Barnabas

BARNABAS ROGERS. See: Calhoun, Ben

Barnacle Bill. See: Barnacle
  Bill

BARNACLE BILL, sailor
  Barnacle Bill (R) (Children's
  program)

BARNES. See also: Burns

BARNES, BINNACLE. See: Brown,
  Robinson, Jr.

BARNES, BINNIE. See: Landi,
  Elissa

BARNES, GORDON, meteorologist
  (himself)
  Weekend Weather (R) (Weather
  forecasting)

BARNES, JOEY, nightclub comedian
ELLIE, his wife
JILLSON, their landlord
FREDDIE, Joey's friend and
manager
The Joey Bishop Show (TV) (Situation comedy)

BARNES, JULIE. See: Hayes, Linc

BARNES, PHIL. See: Lambert,
Louise

BARNES, ROBERT. See: Henry
VIII, King of England

BARNES, SERGEANT. See: McKeever, Cadet Gary

BARNES, TIM. See: Harding,
Karen Adams

BARNETT, CAPTAIN BARNET.
See: Henry, Captain

BARNETT, CHARLIE. See: Whiteman, Paul

BARNETT, DR. See: Cameron

BARNETT, JIM. See: Myrt

BARNETT, KAY. See: Farrell,
David

BARNETT, MIKE, detective
Man Against Crime (TV) (Detective) (also known as Follow That
Man) (TV)

BARNETT, MRS. See: Prescott,
Kate Hathaway

BARNETT, SALLY. See: Brent,
Dr. Jim

BARNEY. See:
Dillon, Marshal Matt
Mallory, Lieut. Col. Spencer
Nelson
Phelps, Jim
Ruditsky, Barney

BARNEY BELZER. See: Myrt

BARNEY, BLACK. See: Rogers,
Buck

BARNEY CALDWELL, MAJOR. See:
Webster, Jake

BARNEY FIFE. See: Taylor,
Andy

BARNEY HOGAN. See: Cooper,
Dick

BARNEY LIDDELL. See: Welk,
Lawrence

BARNEY RUBBLE. See: Flintstone, Fred

BARNEY VERICK. See: Cavanaugh, Father Samuel Patrick

BARNHOUSE, DONALD, moderator
of the program (himself)
MANY GUESTS
Frontiers of Faith (TV) (Religious discussion)

BARON. See:
Barron
Munchausen, Baron

Baron, The. See: Mannering,
John

BARON, THE. See: Mannering,
John

BARRETT, ANDY. See: Randolph,
Ellen

BARRETT, DAVID, distinguished
lawyer, supervisor of Neighborhood Law Office
AARON SILVERMAN
PAT WALTERS, student lawyers,
practicing in Boston
The Young Lawyers (TV) (Courtroom drama)

BARRETT, JIM. See: Hargrave-Scott, Joan

BARRETT, MR. See: Randolph,
Ellen

BARRETT, MRS. See: Randolph,
Ellen

BARRETT, RICHARD. See: Stirling,
Craig

BARRETT, RONA, motion picture
commentator and Hollywood gossip
columnist, featured on the program (herself)
Rona Barrett's Hollywood Movie
(TV) (Motion picture commentary)

BARRETT, SHEILA. See: Stoopnagle, Colonel Lemuel Q. (1)

BARRETT, TIMOTHY "SPUD," pilot
for Triple A Airlines
BECKY, his girl friend
HERBERT KENWROTH, president
of Triple A Airlines
MRS. CRAWFORD, owner of
rival airline
RONNIE CRAWFORD, her son
HARRY, hamburger stand pro-
prietor
SHERMAN, operator of flight
tower
THE LUCKY LINDA, one and only
plane operated by Triple A Air-
lines
The Tim Conway Show (TV)
(Comedy)

BARRIE. See also:
Barry
Beery
Berry

BARRIE CHASE. See: Astaire,
Fred (2)

Barrier Reef. See: King

BARRINGTON, BRYN CLARK, New
York society girl
HER BROTHER
RUSS BARRINGTON
DEXTER HAYES, characters
appearing in the drama
Society Girl (R) (Serial drama)

BARRIS, MARTY. See: Klein,
Robert

BARRON. See also: Baron

BARRON, SANDY. See: Martindale, Wink (2)

BARROWS, TONIA. See: Kirk,
Captain James

BARRY, husband

PAT, his wife
The Trouble With Marriage (R)
(Serial drama)

BARRY. See also:
Barrie
Beery
Berry
Cameron, Barry
Gray, Barry (1) (2)
Lockridge, Barry
McKinley, Barry

Barry Cameron. See: Cameron,
Barry

BARRY, CAPTAIN JOHN. See:
Johnson, Bess

BARRY, GENE. See: Crosby,
Bing (2)

Barry Gray on Broadway. See:
Gray, Barry (2)

BARRY, GWEN. See: Johnson,
Bess

BARRY, JACK (1)
MIKE WALLACE, quizmasters of
the program (themselves)
LENNY ROSS
MRS. OFRA BIKEL, contestants
on the program
MANY OTHER CONTESTANTS
The Big Surprise (TV) (Quiz)

BARRY, JACK (2), host of the
program (himself)
THREE TEEN-AGE PANELISTS
THREE "OVER-THIRTY" PAN-
ELISTS
The Generation Gap (TV) (Game)

BARRY, JACK (3), quizmaster of
the program (himself)
THREE CONTESTANTS
PANEL OF THREE EXPERTS
High Low (TV) (Quiz)

BARRY, JACK (4), quizmaster of
the program (himself)
MANY CONTESTANTS
The Joker's Wild (TV) (Quiz)

BARRY, JACK (5), quizmaster of
the program (himself)
GUEST STARS

CHILDREN PANELISTS
Juvenile Jury (R) (TV) (Quiz/
discussion)

BARRY, JACK (6), quizmaster of
the program (himself)
MANY CONTESTANTS
Life Begins at Eighty (R) (Quiz)

BARRY, JACK (7), quizmaster of
the program (himself)
MANY AUDIENCE PARTICIPANTS
The Reel Game (TV) (Quiz)

BARRY, JACK (8)
BILL WENDELL
JAY JACKSON, quizmasters of
the program (themselves)
MANY CONTESTANTS
Tic-Tac-Dough (TV) (Quiz)

BARRY, JACK (9), quizmaster of
the program (himself)
CHARLES VAN DOREN
ELFRIDA VON NARDROFF
WOLFGANG WEISSLEDER
HERBERT HULSE
R. LEICESTER
J. E. SNODGRASS
HERBERT M. STEMPEL
HAROLD CRAIG
VIVIENNE NEARING, contestants
on the program (themselves)
MANY OTHER CONTESTANTS
Twenty-One (TV) (Quiz)

BARRY, JACK (10), moderator of
the program (himself)
WINKY DINK, paper cutout char-
acter
MANY CHILDREN PANELISTS
Winky Dink and You (TV)
(Children)

BARRY MARKHAM. See: Solomon,
David

BARRY, ROY. See: Johnson, Bess

BARRY, STORMY. See: Kelly,
Joe (2)

BARRY, WENDY. See: Uttal,
Fred (1)

BARRY WOOD. See: Ross, Lanny

BARRYMORE, ETHEL, actress; star

of the program (herself)
DICKIE VAN PATTEN, actor,
featured on the program (him-
self)
MANY ACTORS AND ACTRESSES
Miss Hattie (R) (Drama)

BART. See:
Bert
Burt
Grant, Bart
McClelland, Bart
Maverick, Bret
Merriwell, Frank

BARTENDER, JOE THE. See:
Gleason, Jackie (1) (2)

BARTLETT, AMY GORDON. See:
Meredith, Charles

BARTLETT, DR. See: Lochner,
Dr. Paul

BARTLETT, GEORGE. See: Larimore, Marilyn

BARTLETT, JILL
LINDA BARTLETT
PENNY BARTLETT
RUSSELL BARTLETT, charac-
ters appearing on the program
My Best Girls (R) (Situation
comedy)

BARTLETT, JOHN. See: Carter,
Kathryn

BARTLETT, MICHAEL. See:
Benny, Jack

BARTLETT, STANLEY. See:
Meredith, Charles

BARTLETT, TOMMY, host of the
program (himself)
GUEST TRAVELERS
Welcome, Traveler (R) (Audience participation)

BARTON. See: Drake, Barton

BARTON, BELLY-LAUGH. See:
Benny, Jack

BARTON, BUD
GRANDMA BARTON
BILL MURRAY

COLONEL FRANCIS WELCH,
officer
FRANCIS WELCH, JR., the
colonel's son
HERMAN BRANCH
JUDGE SUMMERFIELD, jurist
JOY WYNN
PA, characters appearing in the
drama
The Barton Family (R) (Serial
drama) (also known as The Story
of Bud Barton (R) and Those
Bartons) (R)

BARTON, CLARA
MAJOR DRUCKER, characters
appearing in the drama
Junior Nurse Corps (R) (Serial
drama)

BARTON, DR. GLENN, scientific
investigator; assigned by government to find persons willing to
undergo dangerous scientific missions
The Man and the Challenge (TV)
(Scientific drama)

BARTON, EILEEN. See: Hall,
Monte (3)

Barton Family, The. See: Barton,
Bud

BARTON J. REED. See: Beamish,
Stanley

BARTON, JEFFREY. See: Johnson, Bess

BARTON, JOE
STAR TRAVIS, characters appear-
ing in the drama
Cimarron Tavern (R) (Drama)

BARTON, PHILIP. See: Steele,
Tracy

Bartons, Those. See: Barton, Bud

BARTRAM, SYLVIA. See: Brent,
Dr. Jim

Baseball, Quizzer. See: Pitcher,
The

BASIE, COUNT
GUY LOMBARDO

RAY McKINLEY
SI ZENTNER
DUKE ELLINGTON
HARRY JAMES
STAN KENTON
VAUGHN MONROE
RALPH FLANAGAN
JAN GARBER
ART MOONEY
PEREZ PRADO
RALPH MARTIERE
SAM DONOHUE
TEX BENEKE
LEE CASTLE
SAMMY KAYE
LIONEL HAMPTON, dance
orchestra leaders (themselves)
THEIR ORCHESTRAS AND
FEATURED VOCALISTS
The Big Bands (TV) (Popular
dance music)

BASIE, COUNT. See also:
O'Connor, Father Norman
Whiteman, Paul

BASIL. See: O'Neill, Mrs.

BASIL RATHBONE. See:
Carroll, Madeleine
Rathbone, Basil

Basin Street, The Chamber Music
Society of Lower. See: Cross,
Milton (1)

Basket, The Ask-it. See: Mc-
Williams, Jim (1)

BASS, TOD. See: Rowan, Dan

BASSETT, ADAM. See: Nielson,
Torwald

BASSETT, CURTIS. See: Nielson,
Torwald

BASSETT, DR. THEODORE,
psychiatrist, expert witness in
court cases
DR. PAUL GRAHAM, psychologist, his associate
The Eleventh Hour (TV) (Court/
medical drama)

Bat Masterson. See: Masterson,
Bat

BAT MASTERSON. See:
Earp, Wyatt
Masterson, Bat

BATGIRL. See: Batman

BATMAN (Millionaire Bruce Wayne)
(with Robin also known as the
Caped Crusaders and the Dynamic
Duo), masked crime fighter of
Gotham City
ROBIN (Dick Grayson) (The Boy
Wonder), Wayne's ward and
masked assistant in crime fighting
HARRIET COOPER (Aunt Harriet),
Wayne's aunt, unaware of the
double identities of Wayne and
Grayson
ALFRED, Wayne's valet and
associate in his crime fighting
activities
POLICE COMMISSIONER GORDON
of Gotham City, unaware of Bat-
man and Robin's real identities
BATGIRL, masked associate of
Batman and Robin, actually
Barbara Gordon, daughter of
Police Commissioner Gordon who,
like Batman and Robin, is un-
aware of her dual identity
POLICE CHIEF O'HARA of Gotham
City, unaware of the true identities
of Batman, Robin and Batgirl
THE ARCHER
THE BLACK WIDOW
THE BOOKWORM
THE CAT WOMAN
CHANDELL
LORELEI CIRCE
THE CLOCK KING
COLONEL GUMM
DR. CASSANDRA
CABALA, husband of Dr. Cas-
sandra
EGGHEAD
FALSE FACE
THE JOKER
KING TUT (William Omaha Mc
Elroy)
LOLA LASAGNE
LORD MARMADUKE FFOGG
LADY PENELOPE PEASOUP,
associate of Lord Marmaduke
Ffogg
LOUIE THE LILAC
MA PARKER
MA PARKER'S THREE CHILDREN
THE MAD HATTER

MINERVA
THE MINSTREL
MR. FREEZE
ROCKET O'ROURKE
THE PENGUIN
THE PUZZLER
THE RIDDLER
THE SANDMAN
SHAME
THE SIREN
ZELDA, arch criminals, ene-
mies of Batman, Robin and their
crime fighting associates
Batman (TV) (Crime satire)

BATMAN. See also: Kent, Clark

Battle Line. See: Bishop, Jim

Battle of the Sexes, The. See:
Crumit, Frank (1)

BAUER. See also:
Bower
Burr

BAUER, BERTHA
PAPA BAUER
MICHAEL BAUER
CHARLOTTE BAUER
ED BAUER
LESLIE JACKSON BAUER
HOPE BAUER
JANET MASON NORRIS
KEN NORRIS
DR. JOHN FLETCHER
DR. PAUL FLETCHER
NEIL RAWSON
TRACY DELMAR
ROGER THORPE
ADAM THORPE
HOLLY THORPE
DAVID FARRELL
KIT FARRELL
DR. SARAH McINTYRE
PETER WEXLER
MR. WARSHAW
DR. WERNER
BARBARA NORRIS
PEGGY DILLON
DR. STEVE JACKSON
DR. JOE WARNER
MISS BRIGGS
FLIP MALONE
DEBORAH
DR. MITCHELL
HOLLY NORRIS
DR. KAZAN
DR. BRUCE BANNING

META BAUER ROBERTS
MARION WINTERS
DR. DICK GRANT
MARIE GRANT
ANNE BENEDICT
MARK HOLDEN
ROBIN
KATHY, characters appearing in
the drama
The Guiding Light (TV) (Serial
drama)

BAUER, BERTHA. See also:
Rutledge, Dr. John

BAUER, META. See: Rutledge,
Dr. John

BAUER, TRUDY. See: Rutledge,
Dr. John

BAXTER, CAPTAIN RALPH, police
officer
Harbor Command (TV) (Waterfront police drama)

BAXTER, DR. See: James,
Nancy

BAXTER, DR. BILL, physician in
the Old West
Frontier Doctor (TV) (Western)

BAXTER, DOROTHY. See: Hazel

BAXTER, FRANK. See: Nesbit,
John (2)

BAXTER, GEORGE. See: Hazel

BAXTER, HAROLD. See: Hazel

BAXTER, LUKE. See: Brown,
Ellen

BAXTER, MARION. See: Brent,
Dr. Jim

BAXTER, MILLIE. See: Brown,
Ellen

BAXTER, PHILIP. See: Dallas,
Stella

BAXTER, STEVE. See: Hazel

BAXTER, TED. See: Richards,
Mary

BAXTER, TUG. See: Brown,
Ellen

BAXTER, UNCLE. See: Riley,
Chester A.

BAYARD MACMICHAEL. See:
March, Hal
Story, Ralph

BAYLOR. See:
Carlyle, Baylor
Taylor

BAYLOS, GENE. See: Lewis,
Robert Q. (1)

BAYN. See also:
Bain
Baines
Bayne

BAYN JOHNSON. See: Jones,
Dean

BAYNE. See also:
Bain
Baines
Bayn

BAYNE, BEVERLY. See: Arthur,
Jack (2)

Be Counted, Stand Up and. See:
Russell, Bob

Be Our Guest. See: Brasselle,
Keefe

Be Seated, Ladies. See: Moore,
Tom (1)

BEA. See also:
Bee
Bees

BEA WAYNE. See:
Edwards Ralph (1)
Ross, Lanny

Beachcomber. See: Lackland,
John

Beacon Street, 21. See: Chase,
Dennis

BEALE, RACHEL. See: Sterling,
Vanessa Dale

BEAMER, JOHN, widower, living in
small college town; portrayed by
Ed Wynn
LAURIE
MIDGE, his daughters
ERNIE HINSHAW, attorney; his
friend
The Ed Wynn Show (TV) (Situa-
tion comedy)

BEAMISH, COLONEL. See: Storm,
Lieut.

BEAMISH, LIEUT. See: Tempest,
Dan

BEAMISH, STANLEY, filling station
attendant; agent for the Bureau of
Secret Projects under the name of
Mr. Terrific, caped crime fighter
HAL, his friend
BARTON J. REED, his supervisor,
head of the Bureau of Special Pro-
jects
Mr. Terrific (TV) (Crime fighting
satire)

BEAN, JUDGE ROY, Western law
enforcement agent and saloon
keeper
Judge Roy Bean (TV) (Western)

BEAN, MISS. See: Winters, Evelyn

BEAN, ORSON. See:
Moore, Garry (5)
Reiner, Carl

BEANBLOSSOM, ROBERT S., real
estate salesman
MR. THACKERAY, his boss
My Hero (TV) (Comedy)

BEANIE. See:
Horn, Aggie
Kent, Clark

BEANY, cartoon character
CECIL, seasick sea serpent
CABOOSE GOOSE, cartoon
characters
Time For Beany (TV) (Children's
cartoons) (later continued with
some amending as Beany and
Cecil) (TV)

Beany and Cecil. See: Beany

Beany, Time For. See: Beany

BEAR. See: Yogi Bear

BEAR, SMOKEY. See:
Parmenter, Captain Wilton
Smokey Bear

Bearcats! See: Brackett, Hank

Bears, The Chicago Teddy. See:
McCray, Linc

BEASEY. See:
Beezie
Hardy, Andy

BEASLEY. See:
Falvey, Hal
Gilligan

BEASLEY, GRANDPA. See: Peppertag, Aaron

BEASLEY, IRENE (1), quizmistress
of the program (herself)
MANY CONTESTANTS
Grand Slam (R) (Musical quiz)

BEASLEY, IRENE (2), singer,
featured on the program (herself)
R.F.D. #1 (R) (Farm songs and
talk)

Beat, Book. See: Cromie, Bob

Beat, Bourbon Street. See: Randolph, Rex

Beat, Night. See: Stone, Lucky

Beat, San Francisco. See: Guthrie,
Lieut. Ben

Beat the Band. See: Hildegarde
(1)

Beat the Clock. See: Narz, Jack
(1)

BEATRICE. See:
Fairfax, Beatrice
Kay, Beatrice
Meyer
Nick

BEATRICE BELKIN. See: Roxy

Beatrice Fairfax. See: Fairfax,
Beatrice

BEATRICE MARTIN. See: Dallas,
Stella

BEATTIE, BESSIE. See: Deane,
Martha

BEATTY, CLYDE, animal trainer
The Clyde Beatty Show (R)
(Drama)

BEAU. See: Maverick, Bret

BEAU McCLOUD. See: Hardie
Jim

BEAUCHAMP, MR. See: Grover,
Millie

BEAUREGARD CLAGHORN, SENA-
TOR. See: Allen, Fred

BEAUTIES, THE BEAUTIFUL DOWN-
TOWN. See: Rowan, Dan

BEAUTIFUL DOWNTOWN BEAUTIES,
THE. See: Rowan, Dan

Beautiful, Life Can Be. See: Solomon, David

Beautiful Machine, Maggie and the.
See: Lettvin, Maggie

Beautiful Phyllis Diller Show, The.
See: Diller, Phyllis

BEAUTY, BLACK. See: Reid,
Britt

Beauty Box Theater, The Palmolive.
See: Dragonette, Jessica (2)

"BEAVER" CLEAVER, THEODORE.
See: Cleaver, Ward

Beaver, Leave It to. See: Cleaver,
Ward

BEAVER, LITTLE. See: Ryder,
Red

BEBE SPODE. See: Karr, Mike

BECK. See also: Buck

BECK, JACKSON
GERTRUDE WARNER, featured
on the program (themselves)
CLAYTON HAMILTON, narrator
of the program (himself)
MANY ACTORS AND ACTRESSES
Brownstone Theater (R) (Drama)

BECK, JACKSON. See also:
Roberts, Ken

BECK, LISA DE. See: Cameron,
Christy Allen

BECKER. See: Nelson

BECKER, SANDY, quizmaster of
the program (himself)
MANY CONTESTANTS
Win With a Winner (TV) (Quiz)

BECKET. See: Churchill, John

BECKMAN, JACK. See: Kelly,
Joe (2)

BECKY. See: Barrett, Timothy
"Spud"

BECKY FINKELSTEIN. See:
O'Leary, Hannah

BECKY THATCHER. See: Finn,
Huck

BEE. See also:
Bea
Bees

BEE, AUNT. See:
Jones, Sam
Taylor, Andy

BEE, MOLLY. See:
Ford, Tennessee Ernie (4)
Lee, Pinky (1)

Bee, Singing. See: Lewis, Welcome

Bee, The National Spelling. See:
Wing, Paul

Bee, Uncle Jim's Question. See:
Uncle Jim

Beebe, Elsie. See: Solomon,
David

BEERY, WALLACE. See: Jolson,
Al

BEERY. See also:
Barrie
Barry
Berry

BEES. See also:
Bea
Bee

BEES, HONEY AND THE. See:
Waring, Fred (1)

BEETHOVEN, MRS. See: Morgan,
Henry

BEETLE. See: Baker, Phil (1) (2)

BEEZIE. See also: Beasey

BEEZIE JENKS. See: Teen,
Harold

BEGGS, LUCY. See: Farrell,
David

BEGLEY, MARTIN
JIM HURLEY
DAVE NEWELL
ROLAND WINTERS, panelists on
the program (themselves)
The Fishing and Hunting Club of
the Air (R) (Fishing and hunting
discussion)

Behind Closed Doors. See: Zacharias, Rear Admiral Ellis M.

Behind the Gun, The Man. See:
McCormick, Myron

Behind the Mike. See: McNamee,
Graham

BEHMILLER, HELEN. See: Caine,
Betty

BELCHER, JERRY. See: Johnson,
Parks

BELDING, SERGEANT FRAN. See:
Ironside, Chief Robert

Believe It or Not. See: Ripley,
Robert L.

BELINDA BOYD. See: Green,
Billy

BELKIN, BEATRICE. See: Roxy

BELL. See also:
Belle
Bill

BELL, ALEXANDER GRAHAM, in-
ventor of the telephone; portrayed
by Raymond Edward Johnson
EZIO PINZA
JOSE ITURBI
LILY PONS
ROBERT CASADESUS
NELSON EDDY
GRACE MOORE
MARIAN ANDERSON
JASCHA HEIFETZ
HELEN TRAUBEL
JAMES MELTON
MANY OTHERS, guest stars ap-
pearing on the program (them-
selves)
DONALD VORHEES, orchestra
conductor (himself)
THE BELL TELEPHONE OR-
CHESTRA
The Telephone Hour (R) (Music)

BELL, HARRY
HERBIE BELL
SYLVESTER BELL, brothers,
employed in Hollywood prop shop
MR. SLOCUM, their boss
KITTY, their friend
MRS. STANFIELD, their landlady
Oh, Those Bells! (TV) (Comedy)

BELL, JOSEPH. See: Hayes,
Helen (2)

BELL, MIKE, New York press
agent and man-about-town
TOKI, his girl Friday
HANK McCLURE, contact man
Mr. Broadway (TV) (Drama)

BELL, NIKKI. See: Longstreet,
Mike

BELL, RALPH. See: Voice of
Superstition, The

BELL, TINKER. See:
McHale, Lieut. Commander
Quinton

Pan, Peter

BELLAMY, RALPH. See: Moore, Garry (5)

BELLAND, BRUCE. See: Conway, Tim

BELLBOYS. See: Hopkins, Peggy

BELLE. See:
Bell
Bill
Carlyle, Baylor
Jones, Lorenzo

BELLE BRITTON. See: Ames, Peter

BELLE, JANE. See: Jordan, Joyce

BELLINI, DR. NICK. See: Davis, Dr. Althea

BELLOWS, DR. See: Nelson, Major Tony

BELLOWS, MRS. See: Nelson, Major Tony

Bells, Oh Those! See: Bell, Harry

BELLSON, LOUIS. See: Bailey, Pearl

BELLY-LAUGH BARTON. See: Benny, Jack

BELZER, BARNEY. See: Myrt

BELZER, PAUL. See: Massey, Christine

BEN. See:
Alexander, Ben (1) (2) (3) (4)
Barbour, Henry Wilson
Bernie, Ben
Calhoun, Ben
Canfield, Ben
Cartwright, Ben
Casey, Dr. Ben
Clark, Ben
Fraser, Ben
Grauer, Ben (1) (2) (3)
Gregory, Ben
Guthrie, Lieut. Ben
January, Dr. Ben

Jerrod, Ben
Jones, Ben
Pride, Ben
Richards, Ben
Stockton, Sandy (2)
Walton, Grandpa

Ben Bernie. See: Bernie, Ben

BEN BLUE. See: Olsen, Ole

Ben Casey. See: Casey, Dr. Ben

BEN FOSTER, CAPTAIN. See: Talbot, Commander Dan

BEN FRASER. See:
Fraser, Ben
Holden, Grey

BEN FRASER, JR. See: Fraser, Ben

Ben, Gentle. See: Wedloe, Tom

BEN, GENTLE. See: Wedloe, Tom

BEN GRANT. See: Hillman, India

Ben Jerrod: Attorney at Law. See: Jerrod, Ben

BEN KOKUA. See: McGarrett, Steve

BEN MANFRED. See: Collier, Tim

BEN MATHESON. See: Dunbar, Mike

BEN PORTER. See: Cummings, Brenda

BEN QUICK. See: Varner, Will

BEN ROMERO, SERGEANT. See: Friday, Sergeant Joe

BEN TRAVIS. See: Thompson, Colonel Casey

BEN, UNCLE. See:
Meyer
Turp, Joe

BEN WHITLEDGE. See: Stockdale, Will

BENARI, CARLA. See: Walleck,
Meredith

BENAY VENUTA. See: Archie

BENCHLEY BOTSFORD, COUNT.
See: Canova, Judy

BENEDICT, ANNE. See: Bauer,
Bertha

BENEDICT, CAPTAIN JIM. See:
Wright, Conley

BENEDICT, CEZAR. See: West,
Michael

BENEDICT GINSBURG. See: Steel,
Richard

BENEDICT, JOSEPH. See: Jackson, Martha

BENEDICT, SAM, San Francisco
attorney
Sam Benedict (TV) (Courtroom
drama)

BENEDICT, SUSAN. See: Jackson,
Martha

BENEDICT, TYLER. See: Robinson, Don

BENEKE, TEX. See:
Basie, Count
Whiteman, Paul

Bengal Lancers, Tales of the 77th.
See: Storm, Lieut.

Bengal Lancers, The. See: Storm,
Lieut.

BENITA. See: Bizarre, Benita

BENITO MUSSOLINI. See: Husing,
Ted

BENJAMIN. See:
Ordway, Dr. Benjamin
Spock, Dr. Benjamin M.

BENJAMIN CALDWELL. See:
Judd, Clinton

BENJIE. See: Major, Bob

BENKOIL, MAURY. See: Halop,
Billy

BENNETT CERF. See: Daly,
John (3)

BENNETT, CONSTANCE. See:
Landi, Elissa

BENNETT, GARY. See: Winters,
Evelyn

BENNETT, JUDGE. See: Hardy,
Dr. Steven

BENNETT, MISS. See: Graham,
Dr. Bob

BENNETT, NITA
WOLFE BENNETT
MRS. WOLFE BENNETT, SR.
KYLE KING
SYDNEY SHERWOOD McKENZIE
FRANCESCA MAGUIRE
MAL TANNER
CULLEN ANDREWS
CECILY ANDREWS
ROLLO ST. CLOUD
LANSING McKENZIE
LANCE McKENZIE
LELIA MATTHEWS
JIM MATTHEWS
MRS. JESSIE KING
LYNNE ALEXANDER
HENRY NEWMAN
TAO SMITH
JEAN, characters appearing in
the drama
Lone Journey (R) (Serial drama)

BENNETT, REESE. See: Parmalee,
Ranger Captain

BENNETT, TONY, singer and entertainer; star of the program
(himself)
MANY GUEST STARS
Tony Bennett (TV) (Variety)

BENNY. See:
Dennie
Denny
Fox, Jennie
Top Cat

BENNY FIELDS. See: Dragonette,
Jessica (2)

BENNY GOODMAN. See: Cugat,
Xavier (1)

BENNY, JACK, comedian, violinist
and host of the program (himself)
MARY LIVINGSTONE (Mrs. Jack
Benny), comedienne (herself)
DENNIS DAY
FRANK PARKER
KENNY BAKER
LARRY STEVENS
MICHAEL BARTLETT, singers
(themselves)
ROCHESTER, Benny's valet
FRANK NELSON
ANDY DEVINE
BLANCHE STEWART
SHELDON LEONARD
ETHEL SHUTTS, entertainers ap-
pearing on the program (them-
selves)
FRANK REMLEY
SCHLEPPERMAN
MR. KITZEL
GLADYS ZABISCO
DENNIS DAY'S MOTHER
VIOLIN TEACHER
JOHN L. C. SIVONEY
GERTRUDE, telephone operator
MABEL, telephone operator
BELLY-LAUGH BARTON
THE NEW YEAR
RUBY WAGNER
BUCK BENNY
DETECTIVE O'HARE, characters
appearing on the program
DON BESTOR
TED WEEMS
BOB CROSBY
PHIL HARRIS
FRANK BLACK
GEORGE OLSEN
JOHNNY GREEN, orchestra
leaders (themselves)
THEIR ORCHESTRAS
THE SPORTSMEN QUARTET,
vocal group
MANY GUEST STARS
The Jack Benny Program (R)
(Comedy/variety) (later produced
in essentially the same format)
(TV)

BENNY, JACK. See also:
Crosby, Bing (2)
Lundigan, Bill (2)

BENSON, AUNT POLLY. See:

Harum, David

BENSON, BOBBY, young adventurer
TEX MASON (originally Buck
Mason), aviator
WINDY WALES, handy man and
teller of tall tales
Bobby Benson's Adventures (R)
(Children's adventure)
Songs of the B-Bar-B (R) (Music
and comedy)
POLLY ARMSTEAD, Benson's
young friend
HARKA, Indian
Bobby Benson's Adventures (R)

BENSON, DR. JOHN. See: Sothern,
Mary

BENSON, EMILY FRASER. See:
Fraser, Ben

BENSON, JAMES. See: Harum,
David

BENSON, KATY. See: Ryan, Paul

BENSON, LYDDIE. See: Fraser,
Ben

BENSON, RED, master of ceremonies of the program (himself)
MANY AUDIENCE PARTICIPANTS
Take a Number (R) (Audience
participation)

BENSON, TIM. See: Fraser, Ben

Bent, As the Twig Is. See:
Peters, Bill

BENTI, JOSEPH
JOHN HART
BERNARD KALB
NELSON BENTON, newscasters
(themselves)
The C. B. S. Morning News (TV)
(News)

BENTINCK. See: Churchill, John

BENTLEY. See: Gregg, Uncle
Bentley

BENTON, LINDA. See: Young,
Larry "Pepper"

BENTON, NELSON. See: Benti,
Joseph

BENTON QUEST, DR. See: Quest,
Jonny

BENTON, STEVE, aviator
PEGGY BANNING, his friend
BROOKLYN, mechanic
Wings of Destiny (R) (Drama)

Berg, Gertrude. See: Green,
Sarah

BERGEN. See: Evans, Bergen
(1) (2)

BERGEN, EDGAR (1), ventriloquist
and quizmaster of the program
(himself)
CHARLIE McCARTHY
MORTIMER SNERD
EFFIE KLINKER, dummies used
by Bergen
ERIK GUDE, husband
HELENA GUDE, his wife; con-
testants on the program (them-
selves)
MANY OTHER HUSBAND AND
WIFE CONTESTANTS
Do You Trust Your Wife? (TV)
(Quiz)

BERGEN, EDGAR (2), ventriloquist,
host of the program (himself)
CHARLIE McCARTHY
MORTIMER SNERD
EFFIE KLINKER, dummies used
by Bergen on the program
PASQUALE
ERSEL TWING
CHARLIE McCARTHY'S SCHOOL
   PRINCIPAL
VERA VAGUE
PROFESSOR LEMUEL CARP
JOHN BICKERSON
BLANCHE BICKERSON, char-
acters appearing on the program
DONALD DIXON
ANITA GORDON
DALE EVANS
ANITA ELLIS, vocalists appearing
on the program (themselves)
MANY GUEST STARS
ROBERT ARMBRUSTER
RAY NOBLE, orchestra leaders
THEIR ORCHESTRAS
The Edgar Bergen and Charlie
McCarthy Show (R) (Comedy/
variety)

BERGEN, EDGAR. See also:
Ameche, Don (1)

BERGEN, POLLY, actress; hostess
of the show (herself)
MANY GUEST STARS
LUTHER HENDERSON, JR.,
orchestra leader (himself)
HIS ORCHESTRA
The Polly Bergen Show (TV)
(Variety)

BERGEN, POLLY. See also:
Moore, Garry (5)

BERGER. See also: Burger

BERGER, GORDON. See: Waring,
Fred (1)

BERGMAN, DAN. See: Tate,
Joanne

BERGMAN, KEITH. See: Tate,
Joanne

BERGMAN, MARGE. See: Tate,
Joanne

BERGMAN, STU. See: Tate,
Joanne

BERGMAN, TEDDY. See: Ryan,
Tim

BERKELEY. See also: Barkley

BERKELEY, MR. See: Mike

BERLE. See also: Beryl

BERLE, MILTON (1), comedian;
host of the program (himself)
MANY PROFESSIONAL BOWLERS
Jackpot Bowling Starring Milton
Berle (TV) (Sports)

BERLE, MILTON (2), comedian;
star of the program (himself)
MANY GUEST STARS
The Milton Berle Show (R) (TV)
(Comedy/variety)
ALLEN ROTH, orchestra leader
(himself)
HIS ORCHESTRA
The Milton Berle Show (TV)

BERLE, MILTON (3), comedian,

star of the program (himself)
MANY GUEST STARS AND ENTER-
TAINERS
The Texaco Star Theater (TV)
(Comedy/variety)

BERLE, MILTON. See also:
Bower, Roger
Crosby, Bing (2)

BERLINGER, WARREN. See:
Kelly, Gene

BERMAN, SHELLEY
LIBERACE
EDDY ARNOLD
FRANK FONTAINE
TERRY-THOMAS
DON KNOTTS
PHYLLIS DILLER
DAVE ALLEN
JULIET PROWSE
STEVE ALLEN
GEORGE GOBEL
GODFREY CAMBRIDGE, hosts of
the program (themselves)
MANY GUEST STARS
THE LONDON LINE DANCERS
THE MIKE SAMMES SINGERS
JACK PARNELL, orchestra
leader (himself)
HIS ORCHESTRA
Showtime (TV) (Variety)

BERNARD. See:
Herrmann, Bernard
Lenrow, Bernard

BERNARD ALTMAN, DR. See:
Whitman, Dr. James

BERNARD CRIBBINS. See:
Doonican, Val

BERNARD GRIESEL. See: Kelly,
Joe (2)

BERNARD KALB. See: Benti,
Joseph

BERNARD MARTIN. See: Murray,
Jan (1)

BERNARDO. See: Vega, Don
Diego

BERNICE. See:
Carter, Mr.

McGarry, Dan

BERNICE FARRADAY. See:
Grimm, Arnold

BERNICE ROBBINS. See: Randolph,
Alice

BERNIE. See: Herman, Bernie

BERNIE, BEN (The Old Maestro),
violinist, dance orchestra leader
and host of the program (him-
self)
LITTLE JACKIE HELLER
MARY SMALL
BUDDY CLARK
FRANK PRINCE
BILL WILGUS
PAT KENNEDY, vocalists (them-
selves)
DICK STABILE
COLONEL MANNY PRAEGER,
saxophonists and vocalists (them-
selves)
AL GOERING, pianist (himself)
WARD ARCHER
GILBERT GRAU, drummers
(themselves)
WHISTLIN' PULLEN, whistler
(himself)
Ben Bernie (R) (Music)

Bernie, Bridget Loves. See: Fitzgerald, Bridget Theresa Mary
Coleen

BERNIE DAVIS. See: Preston,
Dick

BERNIE GREEN. See: Morgan,
Henry

BERNIE STEINBERG. See: Fitzgerald, Bridget Theresa Mary
Coleen

BERNIE WEIL. See: Sharp, Hal

BERNSTEIN, LEONARD, symphony
orchestra conductor; host of the
program (himself)
OTHER CONDUCTORS
THE NEW YORK PHILHAR-
MONIC ORCHESTRA
Young People's Concerts (TV)
(Musical education)

BERRY. See also:
Barrie
Barry
Beery

BERRY, KEN, star of the program
(himself)
BILLY VAN
STEVE WATSON
DON WAYNE
TERI GARR, entertainers fea-
tured on the program (themselves)
THE NEW SEEKERS, vocal group
THE JAIME ROGERS DANCERS
JIMMY DALE, orchestra leader
(himself)
HIS ORCHESTRA
MANY GUEST STARS
The Ken Berry Wow Show (TV)
(Comedy/variety)

BERT. See:
Bart
Burnett, Carol
Burt
Cookie Monster, The
Gramus, Bert
Lytell, Bert (1) (2)
Parks, Bert (1) (2) (3) (4) (5)
(6) (7)

BERT COLLINS. See: McKenzie,
Captain Craig

BERT LOWN. See: Winchell,
Walter (1)

BERT METCALF. See: Slattery,
Jim

BERT QUINN. See: Stockton,
Sandy (2)

BERT SKELLY. See: Walleck,
Meredith

BERT WESTON. See: Fairchild,
Kay

BERTELLI. See: Scott, Captain

BERTHA. See:
Bauer, Bertha
Brainard, Bertha
Meredith, Charles

BERTHA BRINSKY. See: Sherwood, Ruth

BERTHA SCHULTZ. See:
Carter, Kathryn
Larimore, Marilyn

BERTIE. See: Mix, Tom

BERTRAND, MARCELLE. See:
Noble, Mary

BERTRILLE, SR., originally
named Elsie Ethrington; nun,
able to fly unassisted
REVEREND MOTHER, head of
convent San Tunco
CAPTAIN GASPAR FORMENTO,
chief of police
CARLOS RAMIREZ, proprietor of
Casino Carlos; friend of Sr.
Bertrille and the other nuns
SR. JACQUELINE
SR. SIXTO
SR. ANA, nuns
The Flying Nun (TV) (Comedy)

BERYL. See also: Berle

BERYL VAUGHN. See:
Elders, Harry
Soule, Olan (2)

BESS. See:
Johnson, Bess
Myerson, Bess

BESS JOHNSON. See:
Johnson, Bess
Lady Esther

Bess Johnson, The Story of. See:
Johnson, Bess

BESS LINDSTROM. See: Richards,
Mary

BESS MYERSON. See:
James, Dennis (3)
Moore, Garry (4)
Myerson, Bess
Paige, Bob

BESSIE. See:
Davidson, Bill
Glass, Bessie

BESSIE, AUNT. See: Gilman,
Gordon

BESSIE BEATTIE. See: Deane,
Martha

BESSIE FLOUNCE. See: Perkins,
Ma

Best Girls, My. See: Bartlett, Jill

Best, Look Your. See: Charm
Expert

Best of Bowling, The. See: Jackson, Keith (1)

Best of Groucho, The. See: Marx,
Groucho (3)

Best Seller. See: Morrison, Bret

Best Years, The. See: Randolph,
Walt

BESTOR, DON. See: Benny, Jack

Bet, I'll. See: Narz, Jack (3)

Bet, It's Your. See: Waggoner,
Lyle

Bet Your Life, You. See: Marx,
Groucho (3)

BETH. See: March, Mrs.

BETH HOLLY. See: Barbour,
Henry Wilson

BETH PURCELL. See: Rockford,
Matthew

BETH REED. See: Baines, Scattergood

BETH WILSON. See: Lescoulie,
Jack (2)

BETSEY GARTH. See: Virginian,
The

BETSY. See: Nebb, Rudolph

BETSY AYRES. See: Roxy

BETSY CHERNAK. See: Garrison,
Spencer

BETSY PALMER. See:
Donald, Peter
Moore, Garry (4)

BETSY ROSS GIRL, THE LITTLE.

See: Loveridge, Marion

Betsy Ross Girl Variety Program,
The Little. See: Loveridge,
Marion

BETSY STUART. See: Hughes,
Chris

Better or Worse, For. See: Peterson, Dr. James

BETTY. See:
Ace, Goodman
Anderson, Jim
Boop, Betty
Caine, Betty
Craine, Betty
Crane, Betty
Crocker, Betty
Drake, Betty
Furness, Betty
Moore, Betty
Smith, Chad
White, Betty (1) (2)
White, Billy
Winkler, Betty
Young, Alan

BETTY ADAMS. See: Harding,
Karen Adams

Betty and Bob. See: Drake, Betty

BETTY ANDERSON HARRINGTON.
See: Peyton, Martin

BETTY ANDREWS. See: Van
Dyke, Dick (2)

BETTY ANN GROVE. See: Parks,
Bert (6)

BETTY ANN SUNDOWN. See:
Cade, Sam

Betty, Billy and. See: White,
Billy

Betty Boop Fables. See: Boop,
Betty

BETTY BURNS. See: Noble, Mary

BETTY CAINE. See:
Caine, Betty
Johnson, Raymond Edward (1)
(2)

BETTY CARTER BARBOUR. See:
Barbour, Henry Wilson

BETTY COLBY. See: Blanc, Mel

BETTY COOPER. See: Andrews,
Archie

BETTY CORCORAN (CORKY). See:
Karr, Mike

Betty Crocker, Time For. See:
Crocker, Betty

BETTY FAIRFIELD. See: Armstrong, Jack

BETTY FRANKLIN. See: Andrews,
Walter

BETTY GARDE. See:
Morgan, Henry
Welles, Orson (1)

BETTY HAMILTON. See: Lockridge,
Barry

BETTY HARRISON. See: Arden,
Jane

Betty Hutton Show, The. See:
Strickland, Goldie

BETTY JANE RHODES. See:
Parkyakarkas, Nick

BETTY JO BRADLEY ELLIOTT.
See: Carson, Uncle Joe

BETTY LOU. See:
Gooch, Mortimer
Riggs, Tommy

BETTY LOU GERSON. See: First
Nighter, Mr.

Betty Lou, Tommy Riggs and. See:
Riggs, Tommy

BETTY McDONALD. See: Davis,
Joan Field

BETTY MAHONEY. See: Bracken,
Eddie

Betty Moore. See: Moore, Betty

BETTY RANDALL. See: Steele,
Ted

BETTY RUBBLE. See: Flintstone,
Fred

BETTY SKIDMORE. See: Davis,
Joan Field

BETTY SWANSON. See: Kelly,
Joe (2)

Betty White Show, The. See:
White, Betty (1)

Betty White's Pet Set. See: White,
Betty (2)

BETTY WINKLER. See:
Ameche, Don (3)
Winkler, Betty

Between the Bookends. See: Malone,
Ted (1)

BEULAH, Negro maid
BILL JACKSON, her boy friend
HARRY HENDERSON, her em-
ployer
ALICE HENDERSON, Harry's
wife
DONNIE HENDERSON, son of
Harry and Alice
ORIOLE, Beulah's friend
MR. JENKINS, neighbor of the
Henderson family
Beulah (R) (TV) (Comedy)

BEULAH. See also:
Allen, Joan Houston
McGee, Fibber

BEULAH THE WITCH. See: Kukla

BEVERLY BAYNE. See: Arthur,
Jack (2)

BEVERLY GARLAND. See: Harrington, Pat, Jr.

Beverly Hillbillies, The. See:
Clampett, Jed

Bewitched. See: Stephens, Samantha

Beyond, One Step. See: Newland,
John

Beyond These Valleys. See: Lane,
Rebecca

BIANCO, NICK. See: Cameron

BICKART, SANFORD, host of the
program (himself)
The Fish and Hunt Club (R) (Fishing and hunting)

BICKERSON, BLANCHE. See:
Bergen, Edgar (2)
Bickerson, John

BICKERSON, JOHN
BLANCHE, his wife, quarreling
couple
AMOS, John's brother
The Bickersons (R) (Comedy)

BICKERSON, JOHN. See also:
Bergen, Edgar (2)

BIDDIE CLOOM. See: Bolt, Jason

BIDDLE, MRS. See: Baker, Kenny

BIDDY. See:
Buddy
Myrt

BIDEAUX, JOE. See: West, Jim
(1)

BIFF. See:
Baker, Biff
Dante, Willy

Biff Baker, U.S.A. See: Baker,
Biff

BIFF BRADLEY. See: Young,
Larry "Pepper"

BIFF BURNS. See: Ballew, Wally

Big Bands, The. See: Basie, Count

BIG BIRD. See: Cookie Monster,
The

Big Game, The. See: Kennedy,
Tom (1)

BIG JOE. See: Rosenfield, Joe, Jr.

BIG JON
SPARKY, characters appearing on
the program
GIL HOOLEY, orchestra leader
(himself)

HIS LEPRECHAUN MARCHING
BAND
Big Jon and Sparky (R) (Chil-
dren's program)

Big Jon and Sparky. See: Big Jon

Big Moment. See: Palmer, Bud

BIG NICK MARR. See: McCray,
Linc

Big Payoff, The. See: Paige, Bob

Big Record, The. See: Page,
Patti (1)

Big Sister. See: Wayne, Ruth
Evans

BIG SISTER, THE. See: Wayne,
Ruth Evans

Big Show, The. See: Bankhead,
Tallulah

Big Story, The. See:
Grauer, Ben (1)
Sloane, Robert

Big Surprise, The. See: Barry,
Jack (1)

BIG TIM CHAMPION. See: Corky

BIG TINY LITTLE. See: Welk,
Lawrence

BIG TOOTH. See: Og

Big Top, The. See: Sterling, Jack

Big Town. See: Wilson, Steve

BIG TWIN. See: Monroe, Clayt

Big Valley, The. See: Barkley,
Victoria

BIGELOW, GEORGE. See: Aldrich,
Henry

Bigelow Show, The. See: Winchell,
Paul (1)

BIKEL, MRS. OFRA. See: Barry,
Jack (1)

BILGEWATER, LORD. See: Blurt,
  Elmer

BILKO, SERGEANT ERNEST, con-
  niving non-commissioned army
  officer
  COLONEL HALL, his commanding
  officer
  MRS. HALL, Colonel Hall's wife
  SERGEANT GROVER
  PRIVATE PAPARELLI
  PRIVATE ZIMMERMAN
  PRIVATE NAGY
  PRIVATE DOBERMAN, soldiers in
  his army unit
  SERGEANT RUPERT RITZIK, mess
  sergeant
  EMMA RITZIK, Sergeant Ritzik's
  wife
  SERGEANT JOAN HOGAN, Bilko's
  WAC girl friend
  You'll Never Get Rich (TV) (Situ-
  ation comedy) (also known as
  The Phil Silvers Show (TV) and
  The Sergeant Bilko Show) (TV)

BILL, police captain
  HIS GIRL ASSISTANT
  THE POLICE SERGEANT, officer
  Call the Police (R) (Crime ad-
  venture)

BILL. See also:
  Adler, Bill
  Barnacle Bill
  Baxter, Dr. Bill
  Bell
  Belle
  Buffalo Bill, Jr.
  Burrud, Bill (1) (2) (3) (4)
  Cosby, Bill (1) (2) (3)
  Cullen, Bill (1) (2) (3) (4) (5)
  Cummings, Brenda
  Davidson, Bill
  Davis, Uncle Bill
  Driggs, Karleton King
  Goodwin, Bill
  Grimes, Bill
  Harris, Bill
  Hastings, Bill
  Hayes, Bill
  Hickock, Wild Bill
  Hillman, India
  Hooton, Babs
  Leonard, Bill
  Leyden, Bill (1) (2)
  Longley, Bill
  Lundigan, Bill (1) (2)

  Maisie
  Martin, Doris
  Maud
  Moyers, Bill
  Nimmo, Bill
  Peters, Bill
  Rice, Lieut. Bill
  Shadel, Bill
  Slater, Bill (1) (2)
  Stern, Bill

BILL ADAMS. See:
  Halop, Billy
  Welles, Orson (2)

BILL BAAR. See: Burton, Grandpa

BILL BAILEY. See: Top Cat

BILL BAILEY, "BOOM BOOM."
  See: Kirchener, Claude (1)

BILL BAKER. See: Manning,
  Portia Blake

BILL "BOOM BOOM" BAILEY.
  See: Kirchener, Claude (1)

BILL BOYLE. See: Myrt

BILL BURCH. See: Driggs,
  Karleton King

BILL BURNETTA. See: Jackson, Keith (1)

BILL, CECIL. See: Kukla

BILL COCHRAN. See: Shannon,
  Joe

BILL COSBY. See:
  Cookie Monster, The
  Cosby, Bill (1) (2) (3)

Bill Cosby Show, The. See: Kincaid, Chet

Bill Cosby Show, The New. See:
  Cosby, Bill (2)

BILL CULLEN. See:
  Blyden, Larry (2)
  Cullen, Bill (1) (2) (3) (4) (5)
  DeWitt, George
  Moore, Garry (4) (5)
  Roberts, Ken

Bill Cullen Show, The. See: Cullen,
  Bill (1)

BILL DANA. See: Jones, Spike (2)

Bill Dana Show, The. See: Jiménez,
  José

BILL DAVIS. See: Andrews, Russ

BILL EGAN. See: March, Hal

BILL EVANS, DR. See: Brent, Dr.
  Jim

BILL FINEGAN. See: Whiteman,
  Paul

BILL FLEMMING. See: McKay,
  Jim (1)

BILL FLOOD. See: Warren, Wendy

BILL FOSTER DANCERS, THE.
  See: King, Dave (2)

BILL GANNON, OFFICER. See:
  Friday, Sergeant Joe

BILL GREY. See: Johnson, Bess

BILL GWINN. See: Williamson,
  Dud

BILL HARRINGTON. See: Ross,
  Lanny

BILL HARTLEY. See: Grimm,
  Arnold

BILL HAYES. See:
  Caesar, Sid (3)
  Hayes, Bill

"BILL" HERBERT, WILLIAM. See:
  Barbour, Henry Wilson

BILL JACKSON. See: Beulah

BILL JENKINS. See: Sunday

BILL JOHNSTONE. See: Welles,
  Orson (2)

Bill, Just Plain. See: Davidson,
  Bill

BILL LAWRENCE. See:

Como, Perry (1)
Godfrey, Arthur (1)

BILL LIPTON. See:
  Halop, Billy
  Johnson, Raymond Edward (1)

BILL McCUTCHEON. See: De-
  Luise, Dom (1)

BILL MARCEAU. See: Karr,
  Mike

Bill, Maud and Cousin. See:
  Maud

BILL MURRAY. See: Barton, Bud

BILL O'CONNOR. See: Kelly,
  Joe (1)

BILL PAGE. See: Welk,
  Lawrence

BILL PERRY. See: Dragonette,
  Jessica (3)

BILL ROBERTS. See: Dawson,
  Rosemary

BILL SHORT. See: Moore,
  Garry (1)

BILL SLATER. See:
  Cowan, Thomas
  Dunninger, Joseph
  Hagen, Dr. Harry
  Slater, Bill (1) (2)

Bill Stern, The Colgate Sports
Newsreel Starring. See: Stern,
  Bill

Bill Stern's Colgate Sports Newsreel. See: Stern, Bill

BILL STOUT. See: McKay, Jim
  (2)

BILL SUTTER. See: Guest,
  Edgar A. (2)

BILL TAYLOR. See:
  Carter, Kathryn
  Marlin, Mary

Bill the Barber. See: Davidson,
  Bill

BILL THOMPSON. See: Sherman,
Ransom (2)

BILL, UNCLE. See:
Davis, Dr. Althea
Davis, Uncle Bill
Halop, Billy
Harding, Karen Adams

BILL WALKER. See: Nelson,
Carolyn Kramer

BILL WEIGAND. See: North,
Jerry

BILL WENDELL. See: Barry,
Jack (8)

BILL WILGUS. See: Bernie, Ben

BILL WINTERS. See:
Hunter, Mel
Jordan, Joyce

BILLIE. See:
Billy
Burke, Billie (1) (2)
Dodd, Jimmie

BILLIE BURKE. See:
Burke, Billie (1) (2)
Featherstone, Mrs.

Billie Burke Show, The. See:
Burke, Billie (1)

BILLIE DE VERE. See: Myrt

BILLIE JO BRADLEY. See:
Carson, Uncle Joe

BILLIE McDANIELS. See: Sothern,
Mary

BILLINGS, JOE. See: Waring,
Evelyn

BILLINGSLEY, MRS. See: Burns,
George (1)

BILLINGSLEY, SHERMAN. See:
Hayes, Peter Lind (4)

BILLY. See:
Billie
Brains
Fairchild, Kay
Garrison, Spencer

Graham, Billy
Green, Billy
Halop, Billy
Hargrave-Scott, Joan
Harris, Alan
Jones, Billy
Red Lantern
White, Billy
Wiggs, Mrs.

Billy and Betty. See: White,
Billy

BILLY, CAPTAIN. See: Baker,
Kenny

BILLY DANIELS. See:
Edwards, Ralph (1)
Loveridge, Marion

BILLY FAIRFIELD. See: Armstrong, Jack

Billy Graham Crusade, The. See:
Graham, Billy

BILLY HALOP. See:
Cross, Milton (2)
Halop, Billy

BILLY HOUSTON. See: Allen,
Joan Houston

BILLY JONES. See:
Happiness Boys, The
Jones, Billy

BILLY M. GREENE. See: Kay,
Beatrice

BILLY MAUCH. See:
Cross, Milton (2)
Halop, Billy

BILLY MAY. See:
Coogan, Jackie
Whiteman, Paul

BILLY MILLS. See:
Borge, Victor
McGee, Fibber

BILLY MOOREHEAD. See:
Hackett, Doc

BILLY PEARSON. See:
March, Hal
Story, Ralph

BILLY SMITH. See: Anderson, Jim

BILLY THE KID, Western gunfighter
PAT GARRETT, sheriff
The Tall Man (TV) (Western)

BILLY URCHIN. See: Cord

BILLY VAN. See:
Berry, Ken
Stevens, Ray

BILLY WILLIAMS QUARTET, THE.
See: Caesar, Sid (3)

BINFORD, AL, host of the program
(himself)
GUEST EDUCATORS
What's New (TV) (Children's education program)

BING. See:
Collins, Bing
Crosby, Bing (1) (2) (3)

Bing Crosby Show, The. See:
Collins, Bing
Crosby, Bing (1)

BINGHAM, AMY. See: Hargrave-
Scott, Joan

BINGHAMPTON, CAPTAIN WALLACE.
See: McHale, Lieut. Commander
Quinton

BINGO. See: Fleegle

BINKIE. See: Massey, Christine

BINNACLE BARNES. See: Brown,
Robinson, Jr.

BINNEY, JOE. See: Noble, Mary

BINNEY, WALDO. See: Riley,
Chester A.

BINNIE BARNES. See: Landi,
Elissa

Biography. See: Wallace, Mike (1)

BIRD, BIG. See: Cookie Monster,
The

BIRD, HAZEL. See: Rogers,
Patricia

BIRD SPECIAL, THE BLUE. See:
Allen, Jimmie

BIRD, TWEETY THE. See: Bunny,
Bugs

BIRDIE LEE COGGINS. See:
Gildersleeve, Throckmorton P.

Birdman. See: Birdman

BIRDMAN, crime fighter; cartoon
character
Birdman (TV) (Cartoon)

Bird's Eye View, From a. See:
Grover, Millie

BIRTHDAY MAN, THE, quizmaster
of the program, portrayed by
Edmund "Tiny" Ruffner
HELEN O'CONNELL, featured
vocalist (herself)
MANY CONTESTANTS
JIMMY DORSEY, orchestra
leader (himself)
HIS ORCHESTRA
Your Happy Birthday (R) (Music/
quiz)

Birthday, Your Happy. See: Birthday Man, The

BISHOP. See: Sheen, Bishop
Fulton J.

BISHOP, ALAN. See: Drake,
Betty

BISHOP GARDINER. See: Henry
VIII, King of England

BISHOP, JENIFER. See: Owens,
Buck

BISHOP, JIM, narrator of the
program (himself)
Battle Line (TV) (World War II
documentary)

BISHOP, JIM. See also: Allison,
Fran

BISHOP, JOAN. See: Kelly,
Joe (2)

BISHOP, JOEY, comedian and
actor; host of the program

(himself)
REGIS PHILBIN, his assistant
(himself)
JOHNNY MANN, orchestra leader
(himself)
HIS ORCHESTRA
MANY GUEST STARS
The Joey Bishop Show (TV) (Talk/
interview)

BISHOP, JOEY. See also: Reiner,
Carl

BISHOP, NEIL, soldier in World
War II France
MARTHA, his wife
This Changing World (R) (Serial
drama)

BISHOP, THE, crime fighter;
former member of Sing Sing
prison parole board
THE GARGOYLE, former convict;
Bishop's aide in crime fighting
The Bishop and the Gargoyle (R)
(Crime adventure)

Bits of Hits. See: King, Jean Paul

BIZARRE, BENITA, rock witch,
portrayed by Martha Raye
SPARKY
BUGALOO I.Q.
HARMONY
COURAGE
JOY, characters appearing on the
program
Bugaloos (TV) (Children's pro-
gram)

BLABBER. See: McGraw, Quick
Draw

BLACK BARNEY. See: Rogers,
Buck

BLACK BEAUTY. See: Reid,
Britt

Black Chamber, Stories of the.
See: Drake, Bradley

BLACK COUPLE, THE. See:
Kelly, Gene

BLACK CROWS, THE TWO. See:
Drew, John
Two Black Crows, The (1) (2)

BLACK, DR. See: Davis, Ann
Tyler

BLACK, FRANK. See:
Benny, Jack
Melton, James (2)

BLACK HAWK, Indian
Black Hawk (R) (Adventure)

BLACK HAWK. See also: Blackhawk

Black Hood, The. See: Cop, The

Black Journal. See: Brown, Tony

BLACK, MRS. See: Baines,
Scattergood

BLACK, PETER, Chief Inspector
of Scotland Yard
Pursuit (R) (Adventure)

Black Saddle. See: Culhane, Clay

BLACK, THE MAN IN. See:
Frees, Paul

BLACK TOOTH. See: Sales,
Soupy

BLACK WIDOW, THE. See: Batman

BLACKBEARD FLINT. See: Armstrong, Jack

BLACKBURN, HARRIET. See:
Hutton, Ina Ray

BLACKHAWK. See also: Black
Hawk

Blackhawk, The Man From. See:
Logan, Sam

BLACKIE. See:
Boston Blackie
Preston, Sergeant

Blackie, Boston. See: Boston
Blackie

BLACKMAN, STEVE. See: Marshall, John

BLACKSTONE, HARRY, magician

and detective
Blackstone, The Magic Detective
(R) (Crime adventure)

Blackstone Plantation. See: Crumit,
Frank (2)

Blackstone, The Magic Detective.
See: Blackstone, Harry

BLACKSTONE TWINS, THE. See:
Edwards, Ralph (1)

BLACKWELL, COLONEL HARVEY.
See: McKeever, Cadet Gary

BLADE, SHEILA. See: Dale,
Linda

BLADES, TED. See: Winters,
Evelyn

BLAINE, ARTHUR. See: Webster,
Nancy

BLAINE, GLORIA. See: Jordan,
Joyce

BLAINE, LIEUT. See: Karr,
Mike

BLAINE, VIVIAN. See: Lee,
Pinky (2)

BLAIR. See also: Blore

BLAIR, CHUCK. See: Trent,
Helen

BLAIR, JANET
EDIE ADAMS
JOHN RAITT, singers and enter-
tainers; stars of the program
(themselves)
MANY GUEST STARS
The Chevy Show (TV) (Variety)

BLAIR, JANET. See also: Caesar,
Sid (2)

BLAIR, LEE. See: Marshall,
E. G.

BLAIR, MORTON. See: Brent,
Dr. Jim

BLAIR, TIMOTHY, masquerades as
girl fashion model under the name

of Timmy Blair
GENE, his brother, photographer
JULIE, English starlet, his girl
friend
The Ugliest Girl in Town (TV)
(Situation comedy)

BLAISDELL, TEX. See: Ballew,
Wally

BLAKE. See: Holden, Grey

BLAKE, AMELIA. See: Manning,
Portia Blake

BLAKE, CLARA. See: Trent,
Helen

BLAKE, CRICKET. See: Steele,
Tracy

BLAKE, HARRY. See: Falvey,
Hal

BLAKE, LIEUT. COL. HENRY.
See: Pierce, Captain Hawkeye

BLAKE, ROD, state trooper
State Trooper (TV) (Police
drama)

BLAKE, TED. See: Dennis, Liz

BLAKE, TOM, head of the family
MARY, his wife
PAM, their 15-year-old daughter
JOHNNY, their 17-year-old son
Too Young to Go Steady (TV)
(Family situation comedy)

BLAKE, TOM. See also: Noble,
Mary

BLAKELY, DAWSON. See: Jordan,
Joyce

BLAKELY, IRIS. See: Jordan,
Joyce

BLAKENEY, SIR PERCY, outwardly
a fop, actually the "Scarlet
Pimpernel," rescuer of victims
of the French Revolutionists
The Scarlet Pimpernel (R) (TV)
(Adventure)

BLANC, MEL, comedian, star of
the program (himself)

BETTY COLBY
MR. COLBY
MR. CUSHING, characters ap-
pearing on the program
The Mel Blanc Show (R) (Comedy)
(also known as Mel Blanc's Fix-
it Shop (R) and The Fix-it Shop)
(R)

BLANCHARD, RED. See: Kelly,
Joe (1)

BLANCHE. See:
Bickerson, John
Ungar, Felix

BLANCHE BICKERSON. See:
Bergen, Edgar (2)
Bickerson, John

BLANCHE MORTON. See: Burns,
George (1)

BLANCHE STEWART. See: Benny,
Jack

BLASSINGAME, DAVE, cowboy of the
1890s
BROWN, his mongrel dog
The Westerner (TV) (Western)

Blazers, Sky. See: Turner, Colonel
Roscoe

BLEDSOE, JULES. See: Henry,
Captain

BLEYER, ARCHIE. See: Godfrey,
Arthur (1) (2)

BLIMP, BLOSSOM. See: Owner

Blind Date. See: Francis, Arlene
(2)

BLINKY, DR. See: Pufnstuf, H. R.

BLIVENS, PERCY. See: Davidson,
Bill

BLOAT, SENATOR. See: Allen,
Fred

BLOCH, RAY. See:
Gleason, Jackie (2)
Howard, Tom (2)
Kay, Beatrice
Seymour, Dan

BLOCK, CAPTAIN. See: Muldoon,
Francis

BLOCK, HAL. See: Daly, John
(3)

BLOCK, MARTIN, host of the
program (himself)
The Make-Believe Ballroom (R)
(Recorded music)

BLOCK, VIVIAN. See: Halop,
Billy

BLOCKER, DAN. See: Cookie
Monster, The

BLOMFIELD, EDDIE. See:
Malone, Dr. Jerry

Blondie. See: Bumstead, Blondie

BLONDIE. See: Bumstead, Blondie

BLOOM, MICKEY. See: Goldberg,
Molly

BLOOMGARDEN, HANK. See:
Narz, Jack (2)

BLORE. See also: Blair

BLORE, ERIC. See: Morgan,
Frank (1)

BLOSSOM BLIMP. See: Owner

BLUE. See: Cannon, John

Blue Angels. See: Scott, Captain

BLUE, BEN. See: Olsen, Ole

BLUE BIRD SPECIAL, THE. See:
Allen, Jimmie

BLUE-COLLAR COUPLE, THE.
See: Kelly, Gene

Blue, Coronet. See: Alden,
Michael

BLUE, CORONET. See: Alden,
Michael

Blue Light, The. See: March,
David

BLUE, MISS GENEVIEVE. See: Jones, Amos

Blue Monday Jamboree. See: Holloway, Harrison

Blue Playhouse. See: Lovejoy, Frank (1)

Blue Ribbon Town. See: Marx, Groucho (1)

BLUE-TOOTH JOHNSON. See: Gook, Vic

Blues, Pete Kelly's. See: Kelly, Pete

BLURT, ELMER, door-to-door sales-
man
TIZZIE LISH, cooking "expert"
REGINALD CHEERILY, travel
lecturer
YAHBUT, his sound effects man
and "effervescent assistant"
LORD BILGEWATER, nobleman
THE HUMAN CHATTERBOX
EB
ZEB
MR. KITZEL
THE LAUGHING LADY
YOGI YORGESON, comedians
featured on the program
Al Pearce and His Gang (R)
(Comedy) (also known as Watch
the Fords Go By) (R)

BLUSTER, PHINEAS T. See:
Doody, Howdy

BLYDEN, LARRY (1), moderator
of the program (himself)
MANY GUEST CELEBRITIES
ON-FILM PERSONALITIES
Personality (TV) (Game)

BLYDEN, LARRY (2)
GARY OWENS, hosts of the pro-
gram (themselves)
PEGGY CASS
BILL CULLEN, panelists (them-
selves)
MANY GUEST STARS
You're Putting Me On (TV)
(Game)

BLYDEN, LARRY. See also: Fox,
Sonny

BLYTH, ANN. See: Cross, Milton (2)

Board, A. L. Alexander and His
Mediation. See: Alexander,
A. L. (1)

BOARDMAN, TRUE. See: Judge,
The

BOB. See:
Baines, Scattergood
Barker, Bob
Brannagan, Mike
Carson, Bob
Clayton, Bob (1) (2)
Collins, Bob
Cookie Monster, The
Cromie, Bob
Crosby, Bob (1) (2) (3)
Drake, Betty
Elson, Bob
Emery, Bob
Eubanks, Bob
Graham, Dr. Bob
Hastings, Bob
Hawk, Bob (1) (2)
Hope, Bob (1) (2) (3)
Hughes, Chris
Kennedy, Bob (1) (2)
Lassie
Lewandowski, Bob
McDonald, Bob
Major, Bob
Mary
Morgan, Jaye P.
Newhart, Bob
Nolan, Bob
Paige, Bob
Ralston, Bob
Russell, Bob
Smith, Chad
Sweeney, Bob
Thompson, Jim
Walsh, Bob

BOB ALLEN. See: Kemp, Hal

Bob and Ray. See: Ballew, Wally

BOB AND RAY. See:
James, Dennis (3)
Nye, Louis

BOB ATCHER. See: Kelly, Joe
(1)

BOB BAILEY. See: Soule, Olan
(4)

BOB BALLANTINE. See: Kelly,
Joe (1)

BOB BANNING. See: Harding,
Karen Adams

BOB BARKER. See:
Barker, Bob
Cullen, Bill (3)
Edwards, Ralph (3)

Bob, Betty and. See: Drake, Betty

BOB BOUCHER. See: Desmond,
Johnny

BOB BRANDON. See: Arden,
Jane

BOB BREWER. See: Carter,
Kathryn

BOB BROWN. See: Sherman,
Ransom (1)

BOB BURNS. See: Crosby, Bing
(3)

Bob Burns Show, The. See:
Arkansas Traveler, The

BOB CARTER. See: Sharp, Hal

BOB CLARKE. See: Driggs,
Karleton King

BOB CONSIDINE. See:
Daly, John (4)
Lescoulie, Jack (4)

BOB CRANE. See: Carter, Kathryn

BOB CROSBY. See:
Benny, Jack
Crosby, Bob (1) (2) (3)
Whiteman, Paul

Bob Crosby Show, The. See:
Crosby, Bob (1)

BOB CROSBY'S BOBCATS. See:
Crosby, Bob (1) (2)

Bob Cummings Show, The. See:
Carson, Bob
Collins, Bob

BOB DRAINARD. See: Guest,

Edgar A. (2)

BOB EINSTEIN. See: Paulsen,
Pat

BOB ELSON. See:
Cowan, Thomas
Elson, Bob

Bob Elson Aboard the Century.
See: Elson, Bob

BOB GRAHAM. See: Archie

BOB HASTINGS. See:
Hastings, Bob
Kelly, Joe (1)

BOB HATTEN. See: Conrad, Jim

BOB HAVEN. See: Welk, Lawrence

BOB HAWK. See:
Baker, Phil (3)
Hawk, Bob (1) (2)

Bob Hawk Show, The. See: Hawk,
Bob (1)

BOB HOPE. See:
Hope, Bob (1) (2) (3)
Martin, Dean (1)

Bob Hope Presents the Chrysler
Theater. See: Hope, Bob (3)

Bob Hope Show, The. See: Hope,
Bob (2)

Bob Hope Theater. See:
Hope, Bob (3)
McMahon, Ed (1)

BOB HOWARD. See: Seymour, Dan

BOB HUGHES, DR. See: Hughes,
Lisa

BOB JAMES. See: Dallas, Stella

BOB, JIM. See: Walton, Grandpa

BOB JONES. See: Keene, Kitty

BOB KEESHAN. See:
Doody, Howdy
Kangaroo, Captain

BOB LEE. See: Susan (1)

BOB LIDO. See: Welk, Lawrence

Bob, Love That. See: Collins, Bob

BOB MALONE, POLICE LIEUT.
See: Dante, Willy

BOB, MR. See: Wiggs, Mrs.

BOB NEWHART. See:
DeLuise, Dom (2)
Newhart, Bob (1) (2)

Bob Newhart Show, The. See:
Hartley, Dr. Robert
Newhart, Bob

BOB RALSTON. See:
Ralston, Bob
Welk, Lawrence

Bob Ralston's Music Box. See:
Ralston, Bob

BOB RAMIREZ. See: Ryan, Paul

BOB RANDALL. See: Burnley,
Walter

BOB READICK. See: Halop, Billy

BOB ROGERS, DR. See: Tate,
Joanne

BOB ROSENGARDEN. See:
Cavett, Dick (1) (3)

BOB SIDNEY DANCERS, THE.
See: Bailey, Pearl

BOB SMALE. See: Welk, Lawrence

BOB SMITH, BUFFALO. See:
Doody, Howdy

BOB STRONG. See:
Skelton, Red
Uncle Walter

Bob, The True Story Hour With
Mary and. See: Mary

BOB TODD. See: Doonican, Val

BOB WAGNER. See: Sharp, Hal

BOB WHITE. See:
Detective
Lovejoy, Frank (2)

BOB WILSON. See: Driggs,
Karleton King

BOB WINTON. See: O'Neill, Mrs.

BOBBE MARSH. See: Goldstone,
Dr. Peter

BOBBIE GENTRY. See: Crosby,
Bing (2)

BOBBIE JO BRADLEY. See:
Carson, Uncle Joe

BOBBY. See:
Benson, Bobby
Brady, Mike
Breneman, Tom (1)
Conway, Bobby
Darin, Bobby
Dixon, Bobby
Dodd, Jimmie
Gibson, Dot
Robby
West, Michael

Bobby Benson's Adventures. See:
Benson, Bobby

BOBBY BREEN. See: Cantor,
Eddie (2)

BOBBY BURGESS. See: Welk,
Lawrence

BOBBY BURNS. See: Kelly, Joe
(2)

Bobby Darin Amusement Company,
Dean Martin Presents the. See:
Darin, Bobby

BOBBY HOOKEY. See:
Edwards, Ralph (1)
Loveridge, Marion

BOBBY KEEN. See: Old Ranger,
The

BOBBY MAUCH. See:
Cross, Milton (2)
Halop, Billy

BOBBY MILLETTE. See: Welles,
Orson (3)

BOBBY MORAN. See: Carter,
Kathryn

BOBBY SHERMAN. See: Steinberg, David (2)

BOBBY SHERWOOD. See: Donald,
Peter

BOBBY VANDERVENTER. See:
Slater, Bill (2)

BOBBY VINTON. See: Jones, Jack

BOBBY VINTOR. See: Griffin,
Merv (3)

BOBCATS, BOB CROSBY'S. See:
Crosby, Bob (1) (2)

BOBO. See: Mulligan, Mickey

BODIE, CHEYENNE, cowboy
Cheyenne (TV) (Western)

BODKIN, MR. See: Dillon,
Marshal Matt

BOGGS, DARIUS. See: Brown,
Ellen

BOGUE, MERVYN. See: Kyser,
Kay

Boing-Boing Show, The. See: Mc-
Boing-Boing, Gerald

BOLAND, BONNIE. See: Conway,
Tim

Bold Journey. See: Stephenson,
John

Bold Ones, The (The Doctors).
See: Hunter, Dr. Paul

Bold Ones, The (The Lawyers).
See: Nichols, Walter

Bold Ones, The (The Protectors).
See: Washburn, William

Bold Ones, The (The Senator). See:
Stowe, Senator Hays

Bold Venture. See: Shannon, Slate

BOLES, JIM. See: Morrison, Bret

BOLEYN, ANNE. See: Henry VIII,
King of England

BOLGAR. See: Lockridge, Barry

BOLGER, RAY, dancer and actor;
host of the program (himself)
The Ray Bolger Show (R) (TV)
(Variety)
HARRY LANG
JERI SULLAVAN
ELVIA ALLMAN
VERNA FELTON, entertainers
appearing on the program (them-
selves)
ROY BARGY, orchestra leader
(himself)
HIS ORCHESTRA
The Ray Bolger Show (R)
MANY GUEST STARS
The Ray Bolger Show (TV)

BOLGER, RAY. See also:
Crosby, Bing (2)
Rogers, Ginger

BOLIVAR SHAGNASTY. See:
Junior

BOLT, JASON
JEREMY BOLT
JOSHUA BOLT, brothers; engaged
in logging business in Seattle
AARON STEMPEL, business rival
of the Bolts
BIDDIE CLOOM
CANDY PRUITT
LOTTIE
CLANCEY, characters appearing
on the program
Here Come the Brides (TV)
(Situation comedy)

BOLT, SAM. See: West, Honey

BOLTON, PATSY. See: Sweeney,
Bob

BOLTON, PATTY. See: Parkyakarkas, Nick

BOMBERGER, ALVA. See: Roxy

BONACORSI, AL. See: Shannon

Bonanza. See: Cartwright, Ben

BOND, J. BLASINGAME. See:

Kaye, Sammy (1)

Bondage, Of Human. See: Carey, Dr. Philip

BONI. See also:
Bonnie
Bonny

BONI ENTEN. See: Klein, Robert

BONNER, VINT, cowboy roaming the West in the late 1860s
Restless Gun (TV) (Western)

BONNIE. See:
Banner, Woody
Boni
Bonny
West, Michael

BONNIE BAKER. See: Ross, Lanny

BONNIE BOLAND. See: Conway, Tim

BONNIE LEE. See: Kirchener, Claude (1)

BONNY. See also:
Boni
Bonnie

BONNY, ANNE. See: Tempest, Dan

BONO, SALVATORE (Sonny)
CHERILYN BONO (Cher), his wife; singers and entertainers, co-hosts of the program (themselves)
CHASTITY, their daughter (herself)
THE EARL BROWN SINGERS
THE TONY MORDENTE DANCERS
JIMMY DALE, orchestra leader (himself)
HIS ORCHESTRA
MANY GUEST STARS
The Sonny and Cher Show (TV) (Variety) (later called The Sonny and Cher Comedy Hour) (TV)

BONOMO, puppeteer, magician and clown
The Magic Clown (TV) (Children)

BOO. See: Muggsy

BOO-BOO. See: Yogi Bear

Book Beat. See: Cromie, Bob

Bookends, Between the. See: Malone, Ted (1)

BOOKER, GERRY. See: Packard, Jack

BOOKWORM, THE. See: Batman

"BOOM BOOM" BAILEY, BILL. See: Kirchener, Claude (1)

BOOMER, HORATIO K. See: McGee, Fibber

BOOMHAUER. See: Wedloe, Tom

BOONE, ANDY. See: Dugan, Queenie

BOONE, CRANDALL. See: Harding, Karen Adams

BOONE, DANIEL, American frontiersman
REBECCA, his wife
ISRAEL, his 10-year-old son
MINGO, Indian friend of Boone
CINCINNATUS, storekeeper
GIDEON, trapper, Negro friend of Boone
GABE COOPER, runaway Negro slave, now Chief Canawahcha- quaoo of the Tuscarora Indians
Daniel Boone (TV) (Frontier drama)

BOONE, FRANK. See: Miller, Johnny

BOONE, JOHNNY, JR. See: Bronson, Millie

BOONE, JOHNNY, SR. See: Bronson, Millie

BOONE, MRS. See: Bronson, Millie

BOONE, PAT, singer and entertainer; star of the program (himself)
MANY GUEST STARS
The Pat Boone Show (TV) (Music/variety)

BOONE, RICHARD, actor; star of

the program (himself)
MANY GUEST ACTORS AND
ACTRESSES
The Richard Boone Show (TV)
(Play anthology)

BOOP, BETTY, motion picture cartoon character
FERDIE FROG, also cartoon character
Betty Boop Fables (R) (Children's
program)

BOOTH, MARTHA
NANCY BOOTH
TED BOOTH
DR. CLEM ALLISON, physician
ANN LOWERY
HARVEY, hired man
PHOEBE
JOHN, characters appearing in
the drama
Trouble House (R) (Serial drama)

Boots and Saddles. See: Adams,
Captain

Boots, Seven League. See: Douglas,
Jack (3)

BORDEN. See also: Bordon

BORDEN, HOWARD. See: Hartley,
Dr. Robert

Borden Show, The. See: Waters,
Ethel

Border Patrol. See: Jagger, Don

Border Patrol, U.S. See: Jagger,
Don

BORDON. See also: Borden

BORDON, ROSARIO. See: Dragonette, Jessica (1)

BORDONI, IRENE, singer, featured
on the program (herself)
EUGENE ORMANDY, orchestra
leader
HIS ORCHESTRA
The Coty Playgirl (R) (Music)

BORGE, VICTOR, pianist-comedian;
star of the program (himself)
GUEST MUSICIANS AND ENTER-

TAINERS
The Victor Borge Show (R) (TV)
(Music/variety)
THE PAT FRIDAY SINGERS
THE HENRY RUSSELL CHORUS,
featured on the program
BILLY MILLS, orchestra leader
(himself)
HIS ORCHESTRA
The Victor Borge Show (R)

BORGE, VICTOR. See also:
Crosby, Bing (3)

BORIS KARLOFF. See:
Karloff, Boris (1) (2)
Munster, Herman

Boris Karloff Presents Thriller.
See: Karloff, Boris (1)

Boris Karloff, Starring. See:
Karloff, Boris (2)

BORIS NATASHA. See: Bullwinkle

BOROS, DR. See: Johnson, Bess

BOROS, GILDA. See: Johnson,
Bess

BOSCO, STEVE. See: Ballew,
Wally

BOSINNEY, PHILIP. See: Forsyte, Soames

BOSLEY, TOM. See: Martin,
Dean (2)

BOSS. See: Mac

BOSS HUGHEY. See: O'Leary,
Hannah

BOSS McKINNEY. See: Fairchild,
Kay

BOSTON BLACKIE, detective
MARY
SHORTY, his friends
INSPECTOR FARADAY, police
officer
Boston Blackie (R) (TV) (De-
tective adventure)

BOSTON POPS ORCHESTRA, THE.
See: Fiedler, Arthur

BOSWELL, CONNEE. See: Crosby, Bing (3)

BOSWELL, THOMAS. See: Ferguson, Martha

BOSWELL, WILLIAM. See: Canova, Judy

BOTAK, Javanese adventurer
The Orange Lantern (R) (Mystery)

BOTNIK, MARION. See: Morgan, Lieut. Anne

BOTSFORD, COUNT BENCHLEY. See: Canova, Judy

BOTTCHER, ED, master of ceremonies of the program (himself)
R. F. D. America (R) (Farm)

BOTTLE. See: Baker, Phil (1) (2)

Bottom of the Sea, Voyage to the. See: Nelson, Admiral Harriman

BOTTS, HEYWOOD. See: Clayton, Margie

BOUCHER, BOB. See: Desmond, Johnny

BOULTON, MILO. See: Heatter, Gabriel

Bourbon Street Beat. See: Randolph, Rex

BOWEN, PATSY. See: Carter, Nick

BOWEN, TERRY, American boy in India, searching for his father
RAJI, Indian elephant boy
MAYA, elephant, being taken back to jungle by Raji
Maya (TV) (Adventure)

BOWER. See also:
Bauer
Burr

BOWER, MARY. See: Wincholl, John

BOWER, ROGER, host of the program (himself)
JAY C. FLIPPEN
MILTON BERLE
HARRY HERSHFIELD, comedians featured on the program (themselves)
HORACE HEIDT, orchestra leader (himself)
HIS ORCHESTRA
Stop Me If You've Heard This One (R) (Comedy)

BOWERS, BRAINY, comic character portrayed by Jimmy Durante
GLORIA GRAFTON
DONALD NOVIS, featured vocalists (themselves)
MANY GUEST STARS
Jumbo (R) (Circus/variety)

BOWES, MAJOR EDWARD (1)
TED MACK, moderators of the program (themselves)
MANY AMATEUR CONTESTANTS
The Family Hour (R) (Amateur talent contest) (also known as The Capitol Family Hour (R), The Major Bowes Family Hour (R), and The Ted Mack Family Hour) (R)

BOWES, MAJOR EDWARD (2)
TED MACK
JAY C. FLIPPEN, moderators of the program (themselves)
MANY AMATEUR CONTESTANTS
Major Bowes and His Original Amateur Hour (R) (Amateur talent contest)

BOWIE, JIM, American soldier and adventurer
The Adventures of Jim Bowie (TV) (Adventure) (also known as Jim Bowie) (TV)

Bowl, College. See: Earle, Robert

Bowl, The G. E. College. See: Earle, Robert

Bowling Starring Milton Berle, Jackpot. See: Berle, Milton (1)

Bowling, The Best of. See: Jackson, Keith (1)

BOWMAN, LEE. See: Donald,
Peter

BOWMAN, PATRICIA. See: Roxy

BOWSER. See: Hanks, Henrietta

BOX, HARVEY
GILMORE BOX, his brother;
bachelor brothers; operate San
Francisco photography studio
The Brothers (TV) (Situation
comedy)

Box Theater, The Palmolive Beauty.
See: Dragonette, Jessica (2)

Box 13. See: Holiday, Dan

BOY. See:
Astro Boy
Boys

Boy, Circus. See: Corky

Boy Detective, Chick Carter. See:
Carter, Chick

BOY, HEY. See: Paladin

Boy, Jack Armstrong, The All-
American. See: Armstrong,
Jack

BOY, JOHN. See: Walton, Grandpa

Boy Reporter, Dick Steele. See:
Steele, Dick

Boy, That Brewster. See: Brewster, Joey

Boy, That's My. See: Jackson,
Jarrin' Jack

BOY, THE SHOESHINE. See:
Lewis, Jerry

BOY WONDER, THE. See: Batman

BOYD, BELINDA. See: Green,
Billy

BOYD, TOM
LARRY CRANDALL, hosts of the
program (themselves)
MANY GUEST STARS

THE HEADLINERS ORCHESTRA
Look Who's Here (TV) (Variety)

BOYD, WILLIAM. See: Cassidy,
Hopalong

BOYER, CHARLES
DAVID NIVEN
DICK POWELL
ROSALIND RUSSELL
JOEL McCREA
IDA LUPINO, actors and
actresses featured on the pro-
gram (themselves)
Four Star Playhouse (TV)
(Drama)

BOYER, CHARLES. See also:
Ameche, Jim
Ryan, Robert (1)

BOYLAN, BARBARA. See: Welk,
Lawrence

BOYLE, BILL. See: Myrt

BOYLE, JORDAN. See: Stowe,
Senator Hays

BOYLE, MISS. See: Brent, Dr.
Jim

BOYLE, PETER. See: Klein,
Robert

BOYNTON, PHILIP. See: Brooks,
Connie

BOYS. See:
Boy
Happiness Boys, The
Simpson Boys, The

Boys of Sprucehead Bay, The Simpson. See: Simpson Boys, The

BOYS, THE ETON. See: Howard,
Tom (2)

Boys, The Happiness. See: Happiness Boys, The

BOYS, THE LECUONA CUBAN.
See: Whiteman, Paul

BOYS, THE RANCH. See: Mix,
Tom

BRACKEN, DENNIS. See: Roy,
Mike

BRACKEN, EDDIE, comedian, star
of the program (himself)
MRS. PRINGLE
BETTY MAHONEY, characters
appearing on the program
The Eddie Bracken Show (R)
(Situation comedy)

BRACKEN, EDDIE. See also:
Donald, Peter

BRACKEN, JOHN, motion picture
producer at Century Studios
SYLVIA CALDWELL, his secre-
tary and "field marshal"
LAURA DEANE, studio talent
school executive and teacher
KEVIN GRANT, motion picture
director
MARJORIE GRANT, his alcoholic
wife
TOM HUTSON
DAVEY EVANS, actors
RACHEL HOLT
DIANE WARING
PAULETTE DOUGLAS, starlets
Bracken's World (TV) (Drama)

BRACKEN, PHIL. See: Grant,
Harry

Bracken's World. See: Bracken,
John

BRACKETT, DR. KELLY. See:
Gage, John

BRACKETT, HANK, trouble-shooter
JOHNNY REACH, his partner and
fellow trouble-shooter, "roaming
the Southwest in 1914 in a Stutz
Bearcat"
Bearcats! (TV) (Adventure)

BRAD. See:
Burton, Terry
Myrt
Runyon, Brad
Stevens, Joan

BRAD FORBES. See: Lambert,
Louise

BRAD ROBINSON. See: Hughes,
Lisa

BRADDOCK, CAPTAIN, police
officer, active in prosecuting
confidence games
Racket Squad (TV) (Police drama)
(also known as Captain Braddock)
(TV)

BRADDOCK, JORDAN. See:
Richards, Ben

BRADDOCK, PRIVATE. See:
Hanley, Lieut. Gil

BRADFORD, ABBY. See: Chandler,
Dr. Susan

BRADLEY. See: Drake, Bradley

BRADLEY, BIFF. See: Young,
Larry "Pepper"

BRADLEY, BILLIE JO. See: Carson, Uncle Joe

BRADLEY, BOBBIE JO. See: Carson, Uncle Joe

BRADLEY, CURT. See: Young,
Larry "Pepper"

BRADLEY, DR. See: Harding,
Karen Adams

BRADLEY ELLIOTT, BETTY JO.
See: Carson, Uncle Joe

BRADLEY, GENE, international
film star involved in espionage
The Adventurer (TV) (Adventure)

BRADLEY, HELEN. See: Harding,
Karen Adams

BRADLEY, JUDITH
DON BRADLEY
JAKE BRADLEY
SUSAN BRADLEY
DR. RALPH STEVENS, physician
MADGE HARRINGTON
LILLIAN, maid
MRS. GORDON, characters ap-
pearing in the drama
Glorious One (R) (Serial drama)

BRADLEY, KATE. See: Carson,
Uncle Joe

BRADLEY, MISS. See: Brent, Dr.
Jim

BRADLEY, MRS. CURT. See:
Young, Larry "Pepper"

BRADLEY, OSCAR. See:
Heatter, Gabriel
Pryor, Roger

BRADLEY, TRUMAN, host of the
program (himself)
MANY ACTORS AND ACTRESSES
Science Fiction Theater (TV)
(Drama)

BRADY. See also: Grady

BRADY, ALAN. See: Petrie, Rob

Brady Bunch, The. See: Brady,
Mike

BRADY, IRENE. See: Potter, Tom

BRADY, JEFF. See: Trent, Helen

BRADY, MIKE, architect; widower,
remarried
PETER
GREG
BOBBY, his sons by his first
marriage
CAROL BRADY, his wife, widow,
remarried
CINDY
MARCIA
JAN, her daughters by her first
marriage
ALICE, their housekeeper
TIGER, their dog
The Brady Bunch (TV) (Family
situation comedy)

BRADY, PAT. See:
Nolan, Bob
Nona
Rogers, Roy

BRADY, PETER, British scientist,
discovers secret of making himself invisible
The Invisible Man (TV) (Science
fiction/drama)

BRAGONIER, DR. J. ROBERT,
physician
LETA POWELL DRAKE, co-hosts
of the program (themselves)
Nine To Get Ready (TV) (Pre-
natal health care)

BRAHMS. See: Christopher, Peter

BRAHMS, MRS. See: Christopher,
Peter

BRAIN, THE. See: Top Cat

BRAINARD, BERTHA, hostess of
the program (herself)
Broadcasting Broadway (R) (Play
reviews and theater information)

BRAINFEEBLE, CHUCK. See:
Gook, Vic

BRAINFEEBLE, DOTTIE. See:
Gook, Vic

BRAINS
DOUGHNUTS
SCOOPER
SPRING
BILLY
BRICKS
TIGER, English children, come-
dians
The Double Deckers (TV) (Chil-
dren's comedy program) (also
called Here Come the Double
Deckers) (TV)

Brains and Brawn. See: Davis,
Fred

BRAINY. See: Bowers, Brainy

BRANCH, HERMAN. See: Barton,
Bud

BRANCH, MISS. See: Keene,
Kitty

BRAND, OSCAR, host of the pro-
gram (himself)
MANY GUEST ENTERTAINERS
Fanfare (TV) (Folk series)

BRAND, SHEILA. See: Jordan,
Joyce

Branded. See: McCord, Jason

BRANDON, BALLARD. See:
Perry, John

BRANDON, BOB. See: Arden,
Jane

BRANDON, CHARLOTTE. See: Rutledge, Dr. John

BRANDON, CHIEF. See: Tracy, Dick

BRANDON, JESS. See: Marshall, Owen

BRANNAGAN, MIKE, detective
BOB BRANNAGAN, his brother, also a detective
The Brothers Brannagan (TV) (Detective)

BRANNIGAN. See: Ames, Peter

BRANNUM, LUMPY. See: Waring, Fred (1)

BRASSELLE, KEEFE, host of the program (himself)
MANY GUEST STARS
BURT FARBER, orchestra leader (himself)
HIS ORCHESTRA
Be Our Guest (TV) (Variety)

BRASUHN, TUFFY
JOAN WESTON
MARY GARDNER
MANY OTHERS, professional roller skaters (themselves)
The Roller Derby (TV) (Sports)

BRATTER, PAUL, newly married Negro lawyer, employed by the Wall Street law firm of Kendricks, Keen and Klein
CORIE, his wife
MABEL (MAMA), Corie's mother
HONEY ROBINSON, neighbor of the Bratters; pool hall owner, fond of Mabel
KENDRICKS, Paul Bratter's boss; Wall Street attorney
Barefoot in the Park (TV) (Comedy)

BRATTON, CHARLIE. See: Gleason, Jackie (1) (2)

Brave Eagle. See: Brave Eagle

BRAVE EAGLE, Indian
KEENA, his son
MORNING STAR, Indian maiden
Brave Eagle (TV) (Western)

Brave, Home of the. See: Joe (1)

Brave Stallion. See: Newton, Jim

Brave Tomorrow. See: Lambert, Louise

Brawn, Brains and. See: Davis, Fred

Break the Bank. See: Parks, Bert (1)

Break the $250,000 Bank. See: Parks, Bert (1)

Breakfast at Sardi's. See: Breneman, Tom (1)

Breakfast Club, Don McNeill's. See: McNeill, Don

Breakfast Club, The. See: McNeill, Don

Breakfast in Hollywood. See: Breneman, Tom (2)

Breakfast With Dorothy and Dick. See: Kilgallen, Dorothy (1)

Breaking Point. See: Thompson, Dr. McKinley

Breakthru. See: Atkins, Reverend C. E.

Breed, The New. See: Adams, Lieut. Price

Breen and DeRose. See: Breen, May Singhi

BREEN, BOBBY. See: Cantor, Eddie (2)

BREEN, MAY SINGHI, singer
PETER DeROSE, her husband, composer (themselves)
Breen and DeRose (R) (Music and conversation)

BREER. See: Mac

BREESON, CHALK. See: Caine, Frank

BREGMAN, BUDDY, orchestra

leader and disc jockey; host of
the program (himself)
MANY GUESTS
Music Shop (TV)(Recorded and
live music)

BRELLERTON WHITE. See: Myrt

BRENDA. See:
Canova, Judy
Cummings, Brenda
Curtis, Brenda
Hope, Bob (2)

Brenda Curtis. See: Curtis, Brenda

BRENEMAN, TOM (1), master of
ceremonies of the program (himself)
BOBBY, Filipino busboy, his
assistant
MANY AUDIENCE PARTICIPANTS
Breakfast at Sardi's (R) (Audience
participation)

BRENEMAN, TOM (2)
JACK McELROY, masters of
ceremonies of the program (themselves)
MANY AUDIENCE PARTICIPANTS
Breakfast in Hollywood (R) (Audience participation)

BRENNAN, EILEEN. See: Rowan,
Dan

BRENNAN, JACK, investigator and
trouble shooter, working out of
the U.S. Consulate in Paris
MAURIOS, French investigator
STEVENS, associate
Paris 7000 (TV) (Crime drama)

BRENNAN, LESTER. See: Hargrave-Scott, Joan

BRENNAN, TUGBOAT ANNIE, captain of towing tug in the Harbor
of Secoma
HORATIO BULLWINKLE, her
rival, also a tugboat captain
PINTO, crew member employed
by Tugboat Annie
Tugboat Annie (TV) (Comedy)

Brenner. See: Brenner, Roy

BRENNER, CLAUDE. See: Kelly,

Joe (2)

BRENNER, ROY, police detective
lieutenant
ERNIE BRENNER, his son, plain
clothes policeman
Brenner (TV) (Detective drama)

BRENT. See: Maverick, Bret

BRENT, DR. JIM, physician
FRANCIE BRENT, his wife
MR. BRENT, his father
MRS. BRENT, his mother
DR. REGINALD PARSONS
DR. BILL EVANS
DR. GRANT FRASIER
DR. CARSON McVICKER
DR. MILLER
DR. WINSLOW
DR. YATES
DR. RALPH THOMPSON
DR. BURKE, physicians
DUTCH BRENT
ARTHUR READS
MARY HOT
HELEN GOWAN STEPHENSON
ISOBEL DALEY
TOM STEPHENSON
ADELE CORLIS
DOROTHY READS
MARY HOLT
GEORGE HURLEY
MRS. HURLEY
FRANK ROBERTS
FRANCES BRENT
CLIFFORD FOSTER
ELOISE CUMMINGS
HARTLEY KNOWLTON
MR. OVERTON
MRS. OVERTON
LINDEN WAKE
JUNIOR STEPHENSON
CAROL EVANS MARTIN
ALICE JAMISON
VERNA ROBERTS
DALE HUMPHREY
MAGGIE LOWELL
RAY SAWYER
JANET MERCER
PAULA HARWOOD
SYLVIA BARTRAM
MORTON BLAIR
JOE BUCKLEY
JACK FELZER
SALLY BARNETT
CLAUDIA WILSON
MRS. CHAPMAN

MARION BAXTER
GRANDPA SUTTER
FAITH RICHARDS
MISS TODD
FRANK DANA
DALEY
ALICE RANDALL
MISS BOYLE
MISS BRADLEY
MISS RADCLIFF
FRED
JULIA
AUNTIE
JOCELYN
NURSE LANIER
ELIZABETH, characters appearing
in the drama
Road of Life (R) (TV) (Serial
drama)

BRENT, JOHN. See: Tammy

BRENT, PHILIP. See: Davis, Ann
Tyler

BRENT, PORTIA
MARTHA YOUNG DUDLEY
DR. NORFOLK, physician
JOE EDWARDS
NORA MAWSON
DAPHNE ROYCE
PHILIP WEST
GABRIELLE FAURE
DRIZ GUMP
STEVE DIRK
LANCE DUDLEY
JANE
JAY
PETER
NANCY
MICHAEL, characters appearing
in the drama
Brenthouse (R) (Serial drama)

Brenthouse. See: Brent, Portia

BRESSLER, BRIAN. See: Rowan,
Dan

BRET. See:
Maverick, Bret
Morrison, Bret

BRET ALLEN. See: Dyke, Charity
Amanda

BRETT SINCLAIR, LORD. See:
Wilde, Danny

BREWER, BOB. See: Carter,
Kathryn

BREWER, DR. PHIL. See: Hardy,
Dr. Steven

BREWER, JESSIE. See: Hardy,
Dr. Steven

Brewster Boy, That. See: Brewster, Joey

BREWSTER, DAVID. See: Wayne,
Ruth Evans

BREWSTER, GAIL
DAN GENTRY
THE PARSON, characters appear-
ing in the drama
Dangerous Paradise (R) (Serial
drama)

BREWSTER, JOEY, young boy
JIM BREWSTER, his father
JANE BREWSTER, his mother
NANCY BREWSTER
MARK BROWN
JANEY BROWN
LEFTIE HARPER
PHIL HAYWORTH
ENGLISH TEACHER
HERBERT CLARK
MINERVA
PEE WEE
CHUCK, characters appearing
on the program
That Brewster Boy (R) (Situa-
tion comedy)

BREWSTER, MONICA. See: Hargrave-Scott, Joan

BREWSTER, TOM, nicknamed
Sugarfoot; cowboy
Sugarfoot (TV) (Western)

BRIAN. See:
Bryan
Byron
Chase, Dennis
Kincaid, Chet
Sir Lancelot
Smith, Chad

BRIAN BRESSLER. See: Rowan,
Dan

BRIAN DARRELL. See: Nichols,
Walter

BRIAN DONLEVY. See: Frees,
Paul

BRIAN WELLS. See: Harum,
David

BRICE, POINDEXTER. See: Chandler, Faith

BRICK MUSH MAN, THE. See:
Gook, Vic

BRICKERT, CARLTON. See:
Thurston, Howard

BRICKS. See: Brains

Bride and Groom. See: Nelson,
John

Bride, December. See: Ruskin,
Lily

Bride, Father of the. See: Banks,
Stanley

BRIDEHEAD, SUE. See: Cooke,
Alistaire (1)

Brides, Here Come the. See: Bolt,
Jason

Bridge With Charles Goren, Championship. See: Goren, Charles

BRIDGES, CARA, formerly Miss
Wilson, secretly married
FRANK BRIDGES, her husband,
efficiency expert
BURKHARDT, their employer,
does not believe in employing
married couples
The Cara Williams Show (TV)
(Comedy)

BRIDGET. See: Fitzgerald, Bridget
Theresa Mary Coleen

Bridget Loves Bernie. See: Fitzgerald, Bridget Theresa Mary
Coleen

BRIERLY, JIMMY. See: Reser,
Harry

BRIGADIER GENERAL. See:
Savage, Brigadier General Frank

BRIGADIER GENERAL HAMMOND.
See: Pierce, Captain Hawkeye

BRIGADIER GENERAL MONT-
GOMERY SMITH. See: Welles,
Orson (3)

BRIGGS. See also: Driggs

BRIGGS, DAN. See:
Phelps, Jim
Stone, Sam

BRIGGS, DON. See: Ameche,
Don (3)

BRIGGS, JIM. See: Stone, Sam

BRIGGS, MARY. See: Hardy,
Dr. Steven

BRIGGS, MISS. See: Bauer,
Bertha

BRIGGS, STEVE. See: Edman,
Karl

BRIGGS, WALDO. See: Wayne,
Ruth Evans

Bright Horizon. See: West,
Michael

Bright Promise. See: Ferguson,
Martha

Brighter Day, The. See: Dennis,
Liz

Bring 'em Back Alive. See: Buck,
Frank

Bringing Up Buddy. See: Buddy

Bringing up Father. See: Jiggs

BRINK. See: Grafton, Harry

BRINKLEY, DAVID, host of the
program (himself)
David Brinkley's Journal (TV)
(Human interest)

BRINKLEY, DAVID. See also:
Huntley, Chet (1)

BRINKLEY, JACK. See: Soule,
Olan (1)

Brinkley Report, The Huntley. See:
Huntley, Chet (1)

BRINSKY, BERTHA. See: Sherwood, Ruth

BRINTHROPE, LORD HENRY. See:
Sunday

BRISTOL, CODY. See: Burke,
Stoney

BRISTOW, HANK. See: Solomon,
David

BRITAIN. See also: Britton

BRITAIN, KING OF. See: Sir
Lancelot

BRITAIN, QUEEN OF. See: Sir
Lancelot

BRITT. See: Reid, Britt

BRITT, DAN, detective
POLICE SERGEANT, officer
Official Detective (R) (Detective
adventure)

BRITT, JIM. See: Cowan, Thomas

BRITTON. See also: Britain

BRITTON, AMY. See: Ames,
Peter

BRITTON, BELLE. See: Ames,
Peter

BRITTON, JOHN. See: Davidson,
Bill

BRITTON, LISA. See: Ames,
Peter

BRITTON, REBA. See: Davidson,
Bill

Broadcast, The Baker's. See: Penner, Joe

Broadcasting Broadway. See:
Brainard, Bertha

Broadcasts, Metropolitan Opera.
See: Cross, Milton (3)

BROADHURST, DETECTIVE. See:
McCloud, Sam

Broadside. See: Morgan, Lieut.
Anne

Broadway, Barry Gray on. See:
Gray, Barry (2)

Broadway, Broadcasting. See:
Brainard, Bertha

BROADWAY HARRY. See: Kay,
Beatrice

Broadway, Mr. See: Bell, Mike

Broadway Open House. See: Lester,
Jerry

Broadway Revue, Your Show of
Shows, Admiral. See: Caesar,
Sid (3)

Broadway, The Voice of. See:
Kilgallen, Dorothy (2)

Broadway Tonight, On. See:
Vallee, Rudy (1)

BROCK SPENCER. See: McKenzie,
Captain Craig

BRODER, DAVID S. See: Schoumacher, David

BRODIE, LEE. See: Kirkwood,
Jack

BROEKMAN, DAVID. See: Cross,
Mason

Broken Arrow. See: Jeffords,
Tom

BRONCATO, ROSEMARIE. See:
Twin Stars, The

Bronco. See: Layne, Bronco

BRONCO. See:
Gildersleeve, Throckmorton P.
Layne, Bronco

BRONSKY, MAX. See: Hennessey,
Lieut. Chick

BRONSON, JIM, motorcyclist, rides

about the country seeking adventure
Then Came Bronson (TV) (Adventure)

BRONSON, MILLIE, working girl;
New York secretary
MAMA, her mother, widow
ALFRED, her neighbor
JOHNNY BOONE, SR., her boss
MRS. BOONE, wife of Johnny
Boone, Sr.
JOHNNY BOONE, JR., son of
Johnny Boone, Sr. and Mrs.
Boone; Millie's boy friend
Meet Millie (TV) (Comedy)

Bronson, Then Came. See: Bronson, Jim

BROOK. See: Hooton, Babs

BROOK FORRESTER. See: Trent,
Helen

BROOK LEWIS. See: Cameron,
Christy Allen

BROOKLYN. See: Benton, Steve

BROOKS. See: Waring, Evelyn

BROOKS, CAMERON, novelist, comes
home to Millburg to write
LLOYD RAMSEY, newspaper editor
CHRIS LOGAN, widower, resident
of Millburg
ARNY LOGAN, Chris' teenage son
HARRY McGIL, desk clerk in
local hotel
Window on Main Street (TV)
(Comedy)

BROOKS, CONNIE, English teacher
at Madison High School
OSGOOD CONKLIN, principal of
the school
HARRIET CONKLIN, Osgood's
daughter
WALTER DENTON, student at the
school
PHILIP BOYNTON, biology
teacher at the school
MRS. DAVIS, Connie Brooks'
landlady
Our Miss Brooks (R) (TV) (Situation comedy)

BROOKS, DR. MARK. See: Horton, Dr. Tom

BROOKS, FOSTER. See: Cosby,
Bill (2)

BROOKS, HARRIET. See: Allen,
Joan Houston

BROOKS, JEROME. See: Randolph,
Ellen

BROOKS, JOAN. See: Marlowe,
Sylvia

BROOKS, NED. See: Rountree,
Martha

Brooks, Our Miss. See: Brooks,
Connie

BROTHERS. See: Osmond Brothers,
The

BROTHERS, BABS AND HER. See:
Waring, Fred (1)

Brothers Brannagan, The. See:
Brannagan, Mike

Brothers Comedy Hour, The
Smothers. See: Smothers, Tom
(1)

BROTHERS, DR. JOYCE, psychologist, hostess of the program (herself)
Dr. Joyce Brothers (TV) (Advice)

BROTHERS, DR. JOYCE. See also:
March, Hal
Story, Ralph
Walleck, Meredith

Brothers, Johnny Cash Presents
the Everly. See: Everly, Don

Brothers Show, The Smothers. See:
Smothers, Tom (2)

Brothers Show, The Wilburn. See:
Wilburn, Doyle

Brothers Summer Show, The
Smothers. See: Smothers,
Tom (3)

Brothers, The. See: Box, Harvey

Brothers, The Ames. See: Ames,
Joe

BROTHERS, THE DEAN. See:
Kelly, Joe (1)

BROTHERS, THE GENTRY. See:
DeLuise, Dom (1)

BROTHERS, THE NICHOLAS. See:
Edwards, Ralph (1)

Brothers, The Osmond. See: Osmond Brothers, The

BROTHERS, THE STATLER. See:
Cash, Johnny

BROWN. See: Blassingame, Dave

BROWN, AL. See: Butler, Jerry

BROWN, AMY. See: Randolph,
Ellen

BROWN, ANDREW H. See: Jones,
Amos

BROWN, BOB. See: Sherman,
Ransom (1)

BROWN, BUSTER, small boy, had
many adventures
TIGE, his dog
Buster Brown (R) (Children's
program)

BROWN, CHARLEY. See: Perkins,
Ma

BROWN, CHELSEA. See: Rowan,
Dan

BROWN, CLAY. See: Sloan, Holly

BROWN, DAVID. See: Drake, Nora

BROWN, DICK. See: Parks, Bert
(6)

BROWN, ELLEN (Young Widder
Brown), widow; proprietress of
tea room in the town of Simpson-
ville
JANE BROWN
MARK BROWN
DR. ANTHONY LORING, intern
DR. DOUGLASS, physician

MILLIE BAXTER
MARJORIE WILLIAMS
NORINE TEMPLE
JUDITH ADAMS
MARIA HAWKINS
WAYNE GARDNER
TUG BAXTER
ROGER POWER
UNCLE JOSH
JIMMY DAVIS
VICTORIA LORING
DARIUS BOGGS
MRS. CHARLOTTE BROWN
LUKE BAXTER
OLIVIA McEVOY
FREDERICK NELSON
BARBARA STORM
JOYCE TURNER
MAGGIE SPRAGUE
HERBERT TEMPLE
HOPE WAYNE MUNKS
PETER TURNER
MRS. GARVIN
MISS TODD
NELSON DAVIS
MRS. TYSON
MARK
MARTHA
YVONNE
EVELYN
PETER
HULDA, characters appearing in
the drama
Young Widder Brown (R) (Serial
drama)

BROWN, HIPPOCRATES. See:
Baines, Scattergood

BROWN, HOMER. See: Aldrich,
Henry

BROWN, JANE. See: Goldberg,
Molly

BROWN, JANEY. See: Brewster,
Joey

BROWN, JOE E. (1), comedian,
star of the program (himself)
MARGARET McCREA
GILL AND DEMLING, enter-
tainers appearing on the pro-
gram (themselves)
MANY GUEST STARS
HARRY SOSNIK, orchestra
leader (himself)
HIS ORCHESTRA

Joe E. Brown (R) (Comedy/
music)

BROWN, JOE E. (2), comedian;
quizmaster of the program (himself)
MANY CONTESTANTS
Stop and Go (R) (Quiz)

BROWN, JOHN. See: Cantor,
Eddie (2)

BROWN, JOHN MASON. See:
Evans, Bergen (2)

BROWN, JOHNNY. See:
Rowan, Dan
Uggams, Leslie

BROWN, LES. See:
Damone, Vic (2)
Hope, Bob (2)
Martin, Dean (2)
Whiteman, Paul

BROWN, LOU. See: Lewis, Jerry

BROWN, MARK. See: Brewster,
Joey

BROWN, MARY KAY. See:
Packard, Jack

BROWN, MAURICE. See: Halop,
Billy

BROWN, MRS. See:
Aldrich, Henry
Levy, Abie
Naughton, Claudia
Uncle Martin

BROWN, R.G. See: Byner, John
(1)

BROWN, ROBINSON, JR. , rich boy,
shipwrecked on island
JULIE
JINKY
FRIDAY
THE TWINS, his playmates, ship-
wrecked
KATIE, the maid, also ship-
wrecked
BINNACLE BARNES, sailor, also
shipwrecked
Robinson Crusoe, Jr. (R) (Chil-
dren's adventure)

BROWN, SAVANNAH. See: Kelly,
Pete

BROWN, SEDLEY. See: Miles,
Allie Lowe

BROWN, SERGEANT ED. See:
Ironside, Chief Robert

BROWN SINGERS, THE EARL.
See: Bono, Salvatore

BROWN, TONY, host of the pro-
gram (himself)
GUEST PANELISTS
Black Journal (TV) (Discussion)

BROWN, VANESSA. See: Kelly,
Joe (2)

BROWN, VELVET, 12-year-old
girl, extremely interested in
horses
MR. BROWN, her father, farmer
MRS. BROWN, her mother
EDWINA BROWN, her sister
DONALD BROWN, her brother
MI, hired man
KING, chestnut gelding
National Velvet (TV) (Drama)

BROWN, WILL. See: Aldrich,
Henry

BROWNELL, JERRY. See:
Thompson, Andy

BROWNING, ANDREA WINTHROP.
See: Ames, Peter

BROWNING, JANE. See: Nelson,
Carolyn Kramer

BROWNING, MITCH. See: Ames,
Peter

BROWNSPUN, MILTON. See:
Cummings, Brenda

Brownstone Theater. See: Beck,
Jackson

BRUBECK, DAVE. See: O'Connor, Father Norman

BRUCE. See:
Sterling, Vanessa Dale
Thompson, Jim

West, Honey

BRUCE BANNING, DR. See:
Bauer, Bertha

BRUCE BELLAND. See: Conway,
Tim

BRUCE, CAROL. See: Edwards,
Ralph (1)

BRUCE CRAWFORD. See: Fraser,
Ben

BRUCE DOUGLAS. See: Dyke,
Charity Amanda

BRUCE EVANS. See: Roseleigh,
Jack

BRUCE KINGSLEY, DR. See:
O'Neill, Mrs.

BRUCE, MR. See: Dallas, Stella

BRUCE PORTER, DR. See:
Dale, Linda
Graham, Dr. Bob

BRUCE, STEVE. See: Baker, Julia

BRUCE WAYNE, MILLIONAIRE. See:
Batman
Kent, Clark

BRUISER, DICK THE. See: James,
Dennis (4)

BRUNER, WALLY (1)
NATALIE BRUNER, co-hosts of the
program (themselves)
JACK PAAR, host of the program
(himself)
MANY GUESTS
The Morning Show (TV) (Human
interest/variety)

BRUNER, WALLY (2)
NATALIE BRUNER, co-hosts of the
program (themselves)
Wally's Workshop (TV) (Do-it-
yourself carpentry)

BRUNER, WALLY. See also:
Daly, John (3)
Moore, Garry (5)

BRUTUS. See:

Holiday, Laurel
Popeye

BRYAN. See:
Brian
Byron
Prescott, Kate Hathaway

BRYAN, ARTHUR Q. See:
Coogan, Jackie
Lescoulie, Jack (2)

BRYAN FULLER. See: Ames,
Peter

BRYAN, PAUL, lawyer, incurably
ill, "racing to spend his last
days in meaningful living"
Run for Your Life (TV) (Drama)

BRYANT CHANDLER. See:
Harding, Karen Adams

BRYN. See: Barrington, Bryn
Clark

BRYNNER, YUL
VIRGINIA GILMORE, featured performers on the program (themselves)
Mr. and Mrs. (TV) (Situation
comedy)

BRYSON, DR. LYMAN (1), moderator of the program (himself)
CHEF, prepared dinner prior to
the discussion
MANY GUEST PANELISTS
People's Platform (R) (Dinner
discussion)

BRYSON, DR. LYMAN (2), moderator of the program (himself)
THE HAMILTON FAMILY, pre-
sented geography lessons by
touring the world (themselves)
School of the Air of the Americas (R) (Education) (later known
as The American School of the
Air) (R)

BRYSON, TOM. See: Noble,
Mary

BUB. See:
Bud
Douglas, Steve

BUBBA McCOY. See: Huddles, Ed

BUBBLES, KING, comic character,
portrayed by Ed Wynn
Happy Island (R) (Comedy)

BUCCANEERS, CAPTAIN STUBBY
AND THE. See: Kelly, Joe (1)

Buccaneers, The. See: Tempest,
Dan

BUCHANAN, RANDOLPH. See:
Hillman, India

BUCHET, PAUL. See: Rule,
Harry

BUCHWALD, ART. See: DeLuise,
Dom (2)

BUCK. See:
Beck
Benny, Jack
Cannon, John
Manning, Portia Blake
Martin, Doris
Owens, Buck
Rogers, Buck

BUCK, FRANK, trapper of wild
animals, featured on the program
(himself)
Bring 'em Back Alive (R) (Jungle
adventure) (also known as The
Frank Buck Show) (R)

BUCK MASON. See: Benson, Bobby

Buck Rogers in the Twenty-Fifth
Century A.D. See: Rogers, Buck

BUCK SINCLAIR, SERGEANT. See:
Flagg, Captain Jim

BUCK SINGLETON. See: Bailey,
Sam

BUCKHART, SAM, Indian deputy
marshal
The Law of the Plainsman (TV)
(Western) (also known as The
Plainsman) (TV)

BUCKLEY DUNSTAN. See: Banks,
Stanley

BUCKLEY, JIM. See: McKeever,
Ted

BUCKLEY, JOE. See: Brent,
Dr. Jim

BUCKLEY, UNCLE. See: Riley,
Chester A.

BUCKLEY, WILLIAM F., JR.,
host of the program (himself)
MANY GUESTS
Firing Line (TV) (Political /
economic interview)

Buckskin. See: O'Connell, Jody

BUD. See:
Abbott, Bud (1) (2)
Anderson, Jim
Barton, Bud
Bub
Budd
Dud
Fairchild, Kay
Palmer, Bud
Trent, Helen

BUD ABBOTT. See:
Abbott, Bud (1) (2)
Martin, Dean (1)

Bud Barton, The Story of. See:
Barton, Bud

"BUD" COLLYER, CLAYTON. See:
Collyer, Clayton "Bud"
Cullen, Bill (5)
Moore, Garry (5)
Narz, Jack (1)
Parks, Bert (1)

BUD DANT. See: Canova, Judy

BUD GARDNER. See: Tate,
Joanne

BUD RICKS. See: Flipper

BUDD. See also:
Bud
Dud

Budd, Stoopnagle and. See: Stoopnagle, Colonel Lemuel Q. (2)

BUDD HULICK, WILBUR. See:
Hulick, Wilbur Budd
Pitcher, The
Stoopnagle, Colonel Lemuel Q.
(2)

BUDDY, young bachelor
  VIOLET FLOWER
  IRIS FLOWER, his maiden aunts
  Bringing Up Buddy (TV) (Situation comedy)

BUDDY. See also:
  Biddy
  Bregman, Buddy
  Grady, Mickey
  Greco, Buddy
  McGovern, Dan
  Overstreet, Buddy

Buddy, Bringing Up. See: Buddy

BUDDY CLARK. See:
  Bernie, Ben
  Faith, Percy
  Ross, Lanny

BUDDY (FREDDY) DOUGLAS. See:
  Johnny

BUDDY HAYES. See: Welk,
  Lawrence

BUDDY LESTER. See: Lewis,
  Robert Q. (1)

BUDDY MERRILL. See: Welk,
  Lawrence

BUDDY MORROW. See: Rodgers,
  Jimmie

BUDDY RICH. See: Greco, Buddy

BUDDY ROGERS. See: Whiteman,
  Paul

BUDDY SORRELL. See: Petrie,
  Rob

BUDDY WATSON. See: Vance,
  Connie

BUELL, MRS. HAROLD C., narrator of the program (herself)
  Red Cross Course (TV) (First aid instruction)

BUELL, ROGER
  KAYE, his wife; neighbors of the Hubbards
  JERRY, their son
  SUZIE, Jerry's wife
  HERB HUBBARD, Suzie's father

EVE HUBBARD, Herb's wife,
  Suzie's mother
  The Mothers-in-Law (TV)
  (Family situation comedy)

BUFF COBB. See: Donald, Peter

BUFF MacKNIGHT. See: Sawyer,
  Andy

BUFFALO BAKER. See: Lane,
  Hondo

Buffalo Bill, Jr. See: Buffalo
  Bill, Jr.

BUFFALO BILL, JR., teenage
  Westerner
  CALAMITY JANE, his sister
  JUDGE WILEY, their guardian
  Buffalo Bill, Jr. (TV) (Western)

BUFFALO BOB SMITH. See:
  Doody, Howdy

BUFFY. See: Davis, Uncle Bill

BUGALOO I.Q. See: Bizarre,
  Benita

Bugaloos. See: Bizarre, Benita

BUGGSY O'TOOLE. See: Trent,
  Helen

BUGS. See: Bunny, Bugs

Bugs Bunny. See: Bunny, Bugs

BULL RIGHT, GENERAL. See:
  Rowan, Dan

BULLARD, CRAIG. See: Gildersleeve, Throckmorton P.

BULLDOG. See: Drummond, Captain Hugh

Bulldog Drummond. See: Drummond, Captain Hugh

BULLER, MR. See: Gook, Vic

BULLWINKLE
  ROCKY SQUIRREL
  BORIS NATASHA, cartoon characters
  The Adventures of Bullwinkle

and Rocky (TV) (Cartoon)

Bullwinkle and Rocky, The Adventures of. See: Bullwinkle

BULLWINKLE, HORATIO. See: Brennan, Tugboat Annie

BUMP. See: Hansen, David

BUMSTEAD, BLONDIE, housewife and mother
DAGWOOD BUMSTEAD, her husband
ALEXANDER (BABY DUMPLING), their son
COOKIE, their daughter
J.C. DITHERS, Dagwood's boss
CORA DITHERS, J.C. Dithers' wife, Blondie's friend
HERB WOODLEY
TOOTSIE WOODLEY, neighbors of the Bumstead family
Blondie (R) (TV) (Family situation comedy)
FUDDLE, neighbor of the Bumstead family
ALVIN FUDDLE, Fuddle's young son
HARRIET McGONIGLE
DIMPLES WILSON, friends of the Bumstead family
Blondie (R)
DAISY, Dagwood's pet dog
DAISY'S FIVE PUPS
Blondie (TV)

BUN DAWSON. See: Malone, Dr. Jerry

BUNCE, ALAN. See: Soule, Olan (1)

Bunch, The Brady. See: Brady, Mike

BUNDY, MR. See: Burns, George (3)

BUNKER, ARCHIE, bigoted, opinionated head of the family
EDITH ("Dingbat"), his wife
GLORIA STIVIC, his daughter
MIKE STIVIC ("Meathead"), Gloria's Polish husband, college student, living with the Bunkers
LIONEL, Negro friend of the

Stivics
All In the Family (TV) (Family situation comedy)

BUNKER, ARCHIE. See also: Findlay, Maude

BUNKER, EDITH. See: Bunker, Archie
Findlay, Maude

BUNNY, BUGS
ELMER FUDD
PORKY PIG
SYLVESTER THE CAT
TWEETY THE BIRD
ROADRUNNER
HIPPITY HOPPER
HENRY HAWK, cartoon characters
Bugs Bunny (TV) (Cartoon)

BUNNY MITCHELL. See: Marlin, Mary

BUNNY RABBIT. See: Kangaroo, Captain

BUNNY SHAPIRO. See: Grimm, Arnold

BUNNY WILSON. See: Kelly, Kitty

BURBANK QUICKIES, THE. See: Rowan, Dan

BURBIG, HENRY, host of the program (himself)
Burbig's Syncopated History (R) (Comedy)

Burbig's Syncopated History. See: Burbig, Henry

BURCH. See also: Butch

BURCH, BILL. See: Driggs, Karleton King

BURCH, YVONNE DRIGGS. See: Driggs, Karleton King

BURDETTE, WINSTON. See: Ciardi, John

Bureau, The Delphi. See: Gregory, Glenn Garth

BURFORD HAMPDEN. See:
Marais, Josef

BURGER. See also: Berger

BURGER, HAMILTON. See: Mason,
Perry

BURGESS, BOBBY. See: Welk,
Lawrence

BURGESS, DICK. See: Wilbur,
Judy

BURGESS MEREDITH. See:
Heatter, Gabriel
Meredith, Burgess

BURKE, AMOS, wealthy police cap-
tain on homicide squad of Los
Angeles police department; owns
Rolls Royce automobile
Burke's Law (TV) (Crime drama)
Amos Burke, Secret Agent (TV)
(Crime drama)
HENRY, his Japanese valet and
chauffeur
TIM TILSON
LES HART, detectives, subordinate
to Burke
MANY GUEST STARS
Burke's Law (TV)

BURKE, BILLIE (1), actress, star
of the program (herself)
The Billie Burke Show (R) (Comedy)

BURKE, BILLIE (2), actress; star
of the program (herself)
Chicken Every Sunday (R) (Situation comedy)

BURKE, BILLIE. See also: Featherstone, Mrs.

BURKE, CLYDE. See: Cranston,
Lamont

BURKE, DANIEL. See: Marlin,
Mary

BURKE, DR. See: Brent, Dr. Jim

BURKE, INSPECTOR, Scotland Yard
detective
Scotland Yard's Inspector Burke
(R) (Detective)

BURKE, JERRY. See: Welk,
Lawrence

BURKE, LILLIAN. See: Jackson,
Martha

BURKE, NATHAN. See: Dillon,
Marshal Matt

BURKE, SERGEANT. See: Raven,
Dan

BURKE, SERGEANT FRANK. See:
Narz, Jack (2)

BURKE, STEVEN. See: Walleck,
Meredith

BURKE, STONEY, cowboy and
rodeo rider
VES PAINTER
CODY BRISTOL
E. J. STOCKER, rodeo per-
formers; friends of Burke
Stoney Burke (TV) (Western)

BURKE, TERRY. See:
Nelson, Carolyn Kramer
Packard, Jack

Burke's Law. See: Burke, Amos

BURKHALTER, GENERAL. See:
Hogan, Colonel Robert

BURKHARDT. See: Bridges, Cara

BURKHART, MARGOT. See: Trent,
Helen

BURL. See: Ives, Burl (1) (2)

Burl Ives Show, The. See: Ives,
Burl (1)

BURMA. See: Lee, Terry

BURNETT, CAROL, singer, come-
dienne and entertainer; hostess
of the program (herself)
ALICE PORTNOY, Fireside Girl
THE CHARWOMAN
MARIAN, resident of Canoga
Falls
MOLLY, characters portrayed
by Carol Burnett
HARVEY KORMAN, comedian
and entertainer (himself)

ROGER
BERT, characters portrayed by
Harvey Korman
VICKI LAWRENCE, comedienne
and dancer (herself)
CHRIS, character portrayed by
Vicki Lawrence
LYLE WAGGONER, announcer
and entertainer (himself)
MANY GUEST STARS
THE ERNEST FLATT DANCERS
PETER MATZ, orchestra leader
(himself)
HIS ORCHESTRA
The Carol Burnett Show (TV)
(Comedy/variety)

BURNETT, CAROL. See also:
Cookie Monster, The
DeLuise, Dom (2)
Moore, Garry (3)
Stokey, Mike

BURNETT HENDRIX. See: Sharp,
Hal

BURNETTA, BILL. See: Jackson,
Keith (1)

BURNETTE, SMILEY. See: Ritter,
Tex (1)

BURNLEY, WALTER, head of com-
plaint department at Krockmeyer's
Department Store in Los Angeles
JOAN RANDALL, his daughter
BOB RANDALL, his son-in-law
LAURIE RANDALL, daughter of
Joan and Bob
J.L. FOX, store manager,
Walter's boss
WILMA FRITTER
LYNN HALL
JOE FOLEY
HARRY PRICE, members of
Walter's staff
Many Happy Returns (TV) (Comedy)

BURNS. See also: Barnes

Burns and Allen. See: Burns,
George (1)

BURNS, ARTIE. See: Taylor,
Danny

BURNS, BETTY. See: Noble,
Mary

BURNS, BIFF. See: Ballew,
Wally

BURNS, BOB. See: Crosby, Bing
(3)

BURNS, BOBBY. See: Kelly,
Joe (2)

BURNS, CELIA. See: Karr, Mike

BURNS, FRED. See: Karr, Mike

Burns, George. See: Burns,
George (1)

BURNS, GEORGE (1)
GRACIE ALLEN, husband and
wife comedy team (themselves)
Burns and Allen (R) (Comedy/
variety) (TV) (Situation comedy)
THE HAPPY POSTMAN
MRS. BILLINGSLEY
TOOTSIE STAGWELL
MURIEL
WALDO
HERMAN THE DUCK, characters
appearing on the program
RAY NOBLE
PAUL WHITEMAN, orchestra
leaders (themselves)
THEIR ORCHESTRAS
Burns and Allen (R)
RONNIE BURNS, son of George
and Gracie (himself)
HARRY MORTON
BLANCHE MORTON, Harry's
wife; next door neighbors of
the Burnses
HARRY VON ZELL, friend of
the Burns (himself)
Burns and Allen (TV) (later
called George Burns (TV) after
Gracie Allen left the cast)

BURNS, GEORGE (2)
GRACIE ALLEN, husband and
wife comedy team (themselves)
GUY LOMBARDO, orchestra
leader (himself)
HIS ROYAL CANADIANS OR-
CHESTRA
MANY GUEST STARS
The Robert Burns Panatela Pro-
gram (R) (Music/variety)

BURNS, GEORGE (3), owner of
apartment building and com-

mentator of the program (himself)
JEFF CONWAY, airline pilot
WENDY CONWAY, Jeff's wife
DANNY ADAMS, Jeff's co-pilot
MR. BUNDY, superintendent of
the apartment building
Wendy and Me (TV) (Comedy)

BURNS, JACK. See:
DeLuise, Dom (2)
Nye, Louis

BURNS, MAJOR FRANK. See:
Pierce, Captain Hawkeye

BURNS, MARGARET. See: Davidson, Bill

BURNS, MISS. See: Malone, Dr.
Jerry

BURNS, MR. See: Uncle Martin

Burns Panatela Program, The
Robert. See: Burns, George (2)

BURNS, PAT. See: Andrews,
Walter

BURR. See also:
Bauer
Bower

BURR, DR. See: Myrt

BURR, HENRY. See: Kelly, Joe
(1)

BURR TILLSTROM. See: Kukla

BURRUD, BILL (1), narrator of
the program (himself)
Animal World (TV) (Wild life/
conservation)

BURRUD, BILL (2), narrator of the
program (himself)
Islands in the Sun (TV) (Travel)

BURRUD, BILL (3), narrator of the
program (himself)
Treasure (TV) (Films of expedi-
tions in search of lost treasures)

BURRUD, BILL (4), narrator of the
program (himself)
Vagabond (TV) (Travel)

BURT. See also:
Bart
Bert

BURT CARLON. See: Perkins,
Ma

BURT FARBER. See:
Brasselle, Keefe
Clark, Dick (3)

BURT MUSTIN. See: Kelly, Gene

BURTON, CAPTAIN STEVE. See:
Lockridge, Barry

BURTON, DR. PAUL. See:
Carter, Kathryn
Harding, Karen Adams

BURTON GILMAN. See: Garrett,
Sam

BURTON, GRANDPA, character
created by Bill Baar, who played
all other characters on the program
Grandpa Burton (R) (Drama)

BURTON, JEN. See: Carter,
Kathryn

BURTON, LARRY. See: Carter,
Hope

BURTON, NURSE. See: Wayne,
Ruth Evans

BURTON, TERRY, the second Mrs.
Burton
MRS. BURTON, her mother-in-
law, the first Mrs. Burton
STAN BURTON, Terry's husband
JUDGE WATSON, jurist
VAN VLIET, lawyer
MARIAN SULLIVAN
DON CORNWELL
GREG MARTIN
JIM ANDERSON
LILLIAN ANDERSON
MRS. MILLER
LOUISE
BRAD
STANLEY
MARION, characters appearing in
the drama
The Second Mrs. Burton (R)
(Serial drama) (also known as
Second Wife) (R)

BURTON WILEY. See: Perkins,
Ma

BURTON YORK. See: Wing, Howie

Bus, Coast to Coast on a. See:
Conductor, The

Bus Stop. See: Sherwood, Grace

Business, Inc., Show. See:
Winchell, Paul (5)

Business, Today in. See: Shepherd,
Gary

BUSTARD, SERGEANT JAMES. See:
Custer, George Armstrong

BUSTER. See: Brown, Buster

Buster Brown. See: Brown, Buster

Busy Knitter, The. See: Zimmerman, Elizabeth

BUTCH. See:
Burch
Dutch
Everett, Professor
Russell, Mayor
Young, Larry "Pepper"

BUTCHER, FATHER. See: Ballew, Wally

BUTCHER, MAJOR SIMON, Ameri-
can army officer, stationed
aboard the "Kiwi"
RICHARD C. RIDDLE, American
naval officer, commander of the
"Kiwi"
CHIEF MILLER
DAWSON
NAGURSKI, crew members
TYLER, ship's cook
The Wackiest Ship in the Army
(TV) Adventure/comedy)

BUTCHER, MOTHER. See: Ballew,
Wally

BUTLER. See: Prisoner, The

BUTLER, AL. See: Karr, Mike

BUTLER, JERRY
WILSON PICKETT

CURTIS MAYFIELD
JOE TEX
ELLIS HAIZLIP
CARLA THOMAS
AL BROWN, singers and enter-
tainers, hosts of the program
(themselves)
OTHER GUEST HOSTS
MANY GUEST STARS AND
ENTERTAINERS
Soul! (TV) (Variety "produced
by and for the black community")

BUTLER, THE. See:
Carson, Jack
Pruitt, Mrs. Phyllis Poindexter

BUTTERFLY McQUEEN. See:
Kaye, Danny

BUTTERNUT, LITTLE DOUGLAS.
See: Peppertag, Aaron

BUTTERNUT, UNCLE EZRA. See:
Peppertag, Aaron

BUTTERWORTH, RUFUS. See:
Gramus, Bert

BUTTERWORTH, WALLY, quiz-
master on the program (himself)
MARGARET "HONEY" JOHNSON,
quizmistress on the program
(herself)
MANY CONTESTANTS
Take a Card (R) (Quiz)

BUTTERWORTH, WALLY. See
also: Johnson, Parks

BUTTONS. See: Reynolds, Dr.
Mike

BUTTRAM, PAT. See:
Autry, Gene
Kelly, Joe (1)
Rogers, Roy

BUXTON, FRANK
VIRGINIA GIBSON, host and
hostess of the program (themselves)
Discovery (TV) (Children's
educational program)

Buyer, Meyer the. See: Meyer

BUZ. See: Murdock, Buz

BUZZER WILLIAMS. See: Keene,
    Kitty

BUZZI, RUTH. See: Rowan, Dan

By Kathleen Norris. See: Norris,
    Kathleen

BYNER, JOHN (1), comedian; star
    of the program (himself)
    PATTI DEUTSCH
    R. G. BROWN
    LINDA SUBLETTE, entertainers
    featured on the program (them-
    selves)
    MANY GUEST STARS
    The John Byner Comedy Hour (TV)
    (Variety)

BYNER, JOHN (2), host of the pro-
    gram (himself)
    MANY GUEST STARS
    Something Else (TV) (Variety)

BYRON. See:
    Brian
    Bryan
    Kyron
    Palmer, Byron

BYRON, DR. See: Manning,
    Portia Blake

BYRON GILLIAM. See: Rowan,
    Dan

BYRON KANE. See: Judge, The

C. B. S. Evening News With Walter Cronkite, The. See: Cronkite, Walter (2)

C. B. S. Is There. See: Sorel, Guy

C. B. S. Morning News, The. See: Benti, Joseph

C. B. S. Newcomers, The. See: Garroway, Dave (1)

C. E. See: Atkins, Reverend C. E.

C. E. CARRUTHERS. See: Jones, Abraham Lincoln

C. PEMBERTON TOOHEY. See: Perkins, Ma

CABALA. See: Batman

Cabbage Patch, Mrs. Wiggs of the. See: Wiggs, Mrs.

CABOOSE GOOSE. See: Beany

CABOT, SEBASTIAN. See: Harrington, Pat, Jr.

CADE, SAM, sheriff of Madrid County
J. J. JACKSON
ARLO PRITCHARD
RUDY
PEPE, his four deputies
JOANIE
BETTY ANN SUNDOWN, radio dispatchers
Cade's County (TV) (Contemporary Western)

Cade's County. See: Cade, Sam

CADET. See: McKeever, Cadet Gary

Cadet, Space. See: Corbett, Tom (2)

Cadet, Tom Corbett, Space. See: Corbett, Tom (2)

CADMAN, REV. S. PARKES, minister; host of the program (himself)
The National Radio Pulpit (R) (Religion)

CAESAR. See also:
Cesar
Cezar

CAESAR P. PENGUIN. See: Susan (2)

CAESAR PETRILLO. See: First Nighter, Mr.

Caesar Sees It, As. See: Caesar, Sid (1)

CAESAR, SID (1), comedian; star of the program (himself)
JANE CONNELL
ANDREW DUNCAN
PAUL SAND
NORMA DOUGLAS
JIM DOOLEY, actors and actresses appearing on the program (themselves)
As Caesar Sees It (TV) (Comedy sketches)

CAESAR, SID (2), comedian; star of the program (himself)
CARL REINER
HOWARD MORRIS, comedians (themselves)
PAT CARROLL
NANETTE FABRAY
JANET BLAIR
ELLEN PARKER
VIRGINIA CURTIS, comediennes (themselves)
Caesar's Hour (TV) (Comedy)

CAESAR, SID (3), comedian; star of the program (himself)
IMOGENE COCA, comedienne and entertainer; co-star of the program (herself)
CARL REINER
HOWARD MORRIS, comedians (themselves)
MARGUERITE PIAZZA
BILL HAYES
JUDY JOHNSON, singers featured on the program (themselves)
MATA AND HARI, dance team (themselves)
BAMBI LYNN
ROD ALEXANDER, dancers (themselves)
THE HAMILTON TRIO, dancers
THE BILLY WILLIAMS QUARTET, vocal group

Your Show of Shows (TV) (Comedy/
variety) (originally called Admiral
Broadway Revue; Your Show of
Shows (TV)

CAESAR, SID. See also: Crosby,
Bing (2)

Caesar's Hour. See: Caesar, Sid
(2)

CAHILL, KATHY. See: Darin,
Bobby

CAIN. See also:
Caine
Cane
Kane

CAIN DANCERS, THE. See:
Lewandowski, Bob

CAIN, NICHOLAS, former criminal
lawyer, now representing U.S.
Government against the top 100
criminals
Cain's Hundred (TV) (Crime
fighting)

CAINE, Chinese/American Shaolin
priest; master of Kung Fu, self-
defense technique
Kung Fu (TV) (Adventure)

CAINE. See also:
Cain
Cane
Kane

CAINE, BETTY
KATHRYN CARD
HELEN BEHMILLER, featured on
the program (themselves)
Just Neighbors (R) (Comedy)
(originally called The Three
Flats) (R)

CAINE, BETTY. See also: Johnson, Raymond Edward (1) (2)

CAINE, FRANK, U.S. Marshal
WILL FOREMAN, Chief U.S.
Marshal
HECK MARTIN
CHALK BREESON, deputies
CONSTANCE, Foreman's girl
friend
SLIM, town character

The Outlaws (TV) (Western)

Cain's Hundred. See: Cain,
Nicholas

CAJE, PRIVATE. See: Hanley,
Lieut. Gil

CAL. See: Tinney, Cal

CAL CALHOUN. See: Randolph,
Rex

CAL WILSON. See: Reed, Jerry

CALABASH, MRS. See: Durante,
Jimmy

CALAMITY. See: Mix, Tom

CALAMITY JANE. See: Buffalo
Bill, Jr.

CALDWELL. See also: Colwell

CALDWELL, ALEX. See: Sterling,
Vanessa Dale

CALDWELL, BENJAMIN. See:
Judd, Clinton

CALDWELL, CLIFF. See: Noble,
Mary

CALDWELL, MAJOR BARNEY.
See: Webster, Jake

CALDWELL, SYLVIA. See:
Bracken, John

CALEB ANDERSON. See: Ames,
Peter

CALEB JACKSON. See: Dane,
Prudence

Calendar. See: Reasoner, Harry

CALHOUN, BEN, wins bankrupt
railroad in poker game, assets of
which include "The Iron Horse,"
steam locomotive
DAVE TARRANT, locomotive
engineer
NILS TORVALD
BARNABAS ROGERS, employees
of Calhoun
ROYAL McCLINTOCK, cattle
baron

GAGE, employee of McClintock
HANNIBAL, horse
ULYSSES, raccoon
The Iron Horse (TV) (Railroad/
Western adventure)

CALHOUN, CAL. See: Randolph,
Rex

CALIFORNIA. See: Cassidy,
Hopalong

CALIFORNIA JOE MILNER. See:
Custer, George Armstrong

Californians, The. See:
Patrick, Dion
Wayne, Marshal Matt

CALKINS, BARBARA. See: Baines,
Scattergood

Call Me Charlie, Don't. See:
McKay, Judson

Call the Police. See: Bill

CALLAHAN. See: Noble, Mary

CALLAHAN, INSPECTOR. See:
Wilson, Steve

CALLAHAN, TOUGH GUY CORNELI-
US. See: Kaltenmeyer, Professor August, D.U.N.

Callahans, The. See: Arthur, Jack
(1)

CALLAS, CHARLIE. See:
Little, Rich
Williams, Andy (2)

Calling All Detectives. See: Robin

Calling, Carle Comes. See: Carle,
Frankie (1)

Calling, Hollywood. See: Murphy,
George

Calls, Hawaii. See: Edwards,
Webley

CALVERT, ROY. See: Dyke,
Charity Amanda

CALVIN. See:

Colonel, The
Kelvin
Kevin

Calvin and the Colonel. See:
Colonel, The

CAM. See: Driggs, Karleton
King

CAM ALLISON. See: Winchell,
Walter (2)

CAMARTHEN. See: Churchill,
John

CAMBRIDGE, GODFREY. See:
Berman, Shelley

CAMEL. See also: Campbell

Camel Caravan, The. See: Monroe, Vaughn

Camera, Candid. See: Funt,
Allen (1)

Camera, The Man With a. See:
Kovacs, Mike

Camera Three. See: Macandrew,
James

CAMERON, supervisor of electronic
control unit monitoring actions of
World Securities Corporation in-
vestigators in space age
DR. BARNETT, his superior
LOCKWOOD
CHRISTOPHER ROBIN GROVER
NICK BIANCO, investigators for
the Corporation
GLORIA HARDING
KUODA, Cameron's technical
assistants
Search (TV) (Scientific crime
fighting adventure) (originally
called Probe) (TV)

CAMERON. See also: Brooks,
Cameron

CAMERON, ANNA. See: Kidder,
Margot

CAMERON, BARRY
ANNA CAMERON
GLORIA MULVANEY

JOSEPHINE WHITFIELD
MARAINE CLARK
VINNIE, maid
WILL STEVENSON
MARTHA STEVENSON
JOHN NELSON
MRS. MITCHELL
FRANCES, characters appearing
in the drama
Barry Cameron (R) (Serial drama)
(also known as The Soldier Who
Came Home) (R)

CAMERON, CHRISTY ALLEN, edu-
cator
PHILIP CAMERON
MR. CAMERON
SIRI ALLEN
MRS. MARGARET ALLEN
PROFESSOR JASON McKINLEY
  ALLEN
DR. REIMER
KIP TYLER
PASCAL TYLER
EBBA FIELDING
LUCRETIA HALE
KATHY REIMER
MARK SCOTT
NICOLE SCOTT
TORBEN REIMER
BROOK LEWIS
MR. FULLERTON
MRS. SCOTT
MANUEL SANDOVAL
REID WILSON
GUY ALDIS
NURSE MADELEINE
LISA DE BECK
PENNY
NATHAN
NANNY
PETER, characters appearing in
the drama
Against the Storm (R) (Serial
drama)

CAMERON, DORIS. See: Nelson,
Carolyn Kramer

CAMERON, IRMA. See: Davis,
Joan Field

CAMERON, KATHY. See: Davis,
Joan Field

CAMERON, LITTLE RUDY. See:
Davis, Joan Field

CAMERON, MR. See:
Cameron, Christy Allen
Davis, Joan Field

CAMERON, MRS. See: Winters,
Jack

Camouflage. See: Morrow, Don

CAMP, HAMILTON. See: Martindale, Wink (2)

Camp Runamuck. See: Wivenhoe,
Commander

Campana Serenade, The. See:
Powell, Dick (1)

CAMPANELLI, DR. VINCENT, chief
surgeon at Capitol General Hos-
pital, Washington, D.C.
DR. JERRY NOLAND, intern at
the hospital
ANNIE CARLISLE, head nurse
MILDRED MACINERNEY,
assistant to head nurse
ELLEN TURNER, student nurse
Temperatures Rising (TV)
(Comedy)

CAMPBELL. See also: Camel

CAMPBELL, ARCHIE. See:
Owens, Buck

CAMPBELL, DR. RICHARD. See:
Nelson, Carolyn Kramer

CAMPBELL E. CAMPBELL. See:
Marlin, Mary

CAMPBELL, GLEN, singer,
guitarist and star of the program
(himself)
MANY GUEST STARS
The Glen Campbell Goodtime
Hour (TV) (Music/variety)

CAMPBELL, NEIL. See: Evans,
Glenn

CAMPEGGIO, CARDINAL. See:
Henry VIII, King of England

CAMPO, PUPI. See: Whiteman,
Paul

CAMPO, TONY. See: Hardy,
Dr. Steven

Can Do. See: Alba, Robert

Can You Top This? See:
Amsterdam, Morey
Wilson, Ward

CANADIANS ORCHESTRA, THE
ROYAL. See:
Burns, George (2)
Lombardo, Guy

CANARD, TIBBS. See: McKenzie,
Captain Craig

CANARY, HER WHISTLING. See:
Aunt Jenny (Aunt Lucy)

CANAWAHCHAQUAOO, CHIEF.
See: Boone, Daniel

CANDICE DRAKE. See: Carter,
Kathryn

Candid Camera. See: Funt, Allen
(1)

Candid Microphone. See: Funt,
Allen (2)

CANDY. See:
Cartwright, Ben
Hathaway, Elinor
Muir, Carolyn

CANDY CONKLING WILSON. See:
Driggs, Karleton King

CANDY KANE. See: Nash,
Carter

CANDY PRUITT. See: Bolt, Jason

CANE. See also:
Cain
Caine
Kane

CANE, VIC, American undercover
agent fighting Communism in the
Far East
O'HARA, his associate
Counterthrust (TV) (Mystery)

CANFIELD, BEN, Union loyalist
JEFF CANFIELD, his brother,
Confederate loyalist
PA CANFIELD, their father
The Americans (TV) (Drama)

CANFIELD, MAX. See: Dennis,
Liz

Cannon. See: Cannon, Frank

CANNON. See also: Gannon

CANNON, FRANK, private detective
Cannon (TV) (Crime adventure)

CANNON, JOHN, Arizona rancher
ANNALEE, his first wife
VICTORIA, his second wife
BLUE, his son
BUCK, his brother
MANOLITO, Victoria's brother
DON SEBASTIAN, father of
Victoria and Manolito
SAM, ranch hand
The High Chaparral (TV)
(Western)

Cannonball. See: Malone, Mike

CANNONBALL, THE WABASH. See:
Jones, Casey

CANOVA, JUDY, comedienne and
singer; star of the program (her-
self)
JOE CRUNCHMILLER, taxi
driver
GERANIUM, maid
AUNT AGGIE
COUNT BENCHLEY BOTSFORD
BRENDA
PEDRO
PATSY PIERCE
MRS. VAN ATWATER
ROSCOE WORTLE
MR. HEMINGWAY
WILLIAM BOSWELL
NEIGHBOR, characters appearing
on the program
THE SPORTSMEN QUARTET,
vocal group
BUD DANT, orchestra leader
(himself)
HIS ORCHESTRA
The Judy Canova Show (R)
(Comedy)

Canteen Show, The U.S. See:
Froman, Jane (1)

Canteen, Stage Door. See: Lytell,
Bert (2)

CANTOR, EDDIE (1), comedian and
singer; star of the program (him-
self)
MANY GUEST STARS
The Eddie Cantor Comedy Theater
(TV) (Variety)

CANTOR, EDDIE (2), comedian and
singer, star of the program (him-
self)
PARKYAKARKAS
THE MAD RUSSIAN
MR. GUFFY
MADEMOISELLE FIFI, characters
appearing on the program
DAVE RUBINOFF (and his magic
violin), musician and orchestra
leader (himself)
GEORGIE STOLL
COOKIE FAIRCHILD
LOUIS GRESS
JACQUES RENARD, orchestra
leaders (themselves)
THEIR ORCHESTRAS
SHIRLEY DINSDALE, ventriloquist
(herself)
JUDY SPLINTERS, her dummy
NAN RAE
MAUDE DAVIS
JOHN BROWN, entertainers (them-
selves)
BOBBY BREEN
DEANNA DURBIN
DINAH SHORE
MARGARET WHITING
NORA MARTIN, featured vocalists
(themselves)
MANY GUEST STARS
The Eddie Cantor Show (R) (Com-
edy/variety) (also known as The
Chase and Sanborn Hour (R) and
Learn to Smile) (R)

CANTOR, EDDIE. See also:
Baker, Phil (3)
Drew, John
Martin, Dean (1)

CANYON. See also: Kenyon

CANYON, STEVENSON B., Lieutenant Colonel, Air Force
Steve Canyon (TV) (Adventure)

CAPED CRUSADERS, THE. See:
Batman

CAPELL, PETER. See: Higby,

Mary Jane

CAPERS. See: Kapers

Capitol Family Hour, The. See:
Bowes, Major Edward (1)

CAP'N. See also: Captain

CAP'N JOHN. See: Herrick,
Cap'n John

CAPONE, AL. See: Winchell,
Walter (2)

CAPP, SERGEANT HORACE. See:
Rice, Lieut. Bill

CAPPS, KEN. See: Jones, Spike
(1)

CAPRICE YEUDLEMAN. See:
Wivenhoe, Commander

CAPTAIN. See:
Adams, Captain
America, Captain
Baxter, Captain Ralph
Braddock, Captain
Cap'n
Diamond, Captain
Drake, Captain
Drummond, Captain Hugh
Flagg, Captain
Flagg, Captain Jim
Gallant, Captain
Grief, Captain David
Hawthorn, Captain
Henry, Captain
Holbrook, Captain Matt
Kangaroo, Captain
Kirk, Captain James
McKenzie, Captain Craig
Midnight, Captain
O'Flynn, Captain Flynn
Parmalee, Ranger Captain
Parmenter, Captain Wilton
Pierce, Captain Hawkeye
Scott, Captain
Silver, Captain
Video, Captain
Walt, Captain
Young, Captain David

CAPTAIN ADAM GREER. See:
Hayes, Linc

Captain America. See: America,
Captain

CAPTAIN ANDREWS. See: Crooke, Lennie

CAPTAIN BANG. See: Parker, Seth

CAPTAIN BARNET BARNETT. See: Henry, Captain

CAPTAIN BEN FOSTER. See: Talbot, Commander Dan

CAPTAIN BILLY. See: Baker, Kenny

CAPTAIN BLOCK. See: Muldoon, Francis

Captain Braddock. See: Braddock, Captain

CAPTAIN CLAYTON. See: Jordan, Joyce

Captain David Grief. See: Grief, Captain David

Captain Diamond, The Adventures of. See: Diamond, Captain

CAPTAIN EDWARD McCUTCHEON. See: March, Hal Story, Ralph

Captain Flagg and Sergeant Quirt. See: Flagg, Captain

Captain Gallant of the Foreign Legion. See: Gallant, Captain

CAPTAIN GASPAR FORMENTO. See: Bertrille, Sr.

CAPTAIN GOODHUE. See: Lee, Terry

CAPTAIN GREGG. See: Muir, Carolyn

CAPTAIN GREY. See: Ballinger, Lieut. Frank

CAPTAIN GUS HONOCHECK. See: Gower, Matthew

CAPTAIN HANS DIETRICH. See: Troy, Sergeant Sam

CAPTAIN HARVEY. See: Wing, Howie

CAPTAIN HOOK. See: Pan, Peter

CAPTAIN HORTON. See: Rango

CAPTAIN HUGHES. See: Armstrong, Jack

CAPTAIN HUXLEY. See: Pomeroy, Susanna

CAPTAIN JACK. See: Story Lady, The

CAPTAIN JIM BENEDICT. See: Wright, Conley

CAPTAIN JOHN BARRY. See: Johnson, Bess

Captain Kangaroo. See: Kangaroo, Captain

CAPTAIN KEITH GREGORY. See: Adams, Lieut. Price

CAPTAIN LANSING. See: Welles, Orson (3)

CAPTAIN LOGAN, POLICE. See: Casey

CAPTAIN McCALLISTER. See: Cat, Thomas Hewitt Edward

CAPTAIN MANZINI. See: Crabtree, Dave

CAPTAIN MARTINSON. See: Stockdale, Will

Captain Midnight. See: Midnight, Captain

CAPTAIN MONASTARIO. See: Vega, Don Diego

CAPTAIN MORTON. See: Roberts, Doug

CAPTAIN MYLES KEOGH. See: Custer, George Armstrong

Captain Nice. See: Nash, Carter

CAPTAIN NICE. See: Nash, Carter

CAPTAIN NICHOLAS "NICKY" LACEY.
See: Barbour, Henry Wilson

CAPTAIN RAYMOND RAMBRIDGE.
See: Rice, Lieut. Bill

CAPTAIN RUSS. See: Falvey, Hal

CAPTAIN SHAFER. See: Hennesey,
Lieut. Chick

CAPTAIN SPARKS. See: Little
Orphan Annie

CAPTAIN STEVE BURTON. See:
Lockridge, Barry

CAPTAIN STUBBY AND THE BUC-
CANEERS. See: Kelly, Joe (1)

CAPTAIN, THE. See: Ross,
David (1)

Captain Video. See: Video, Captain

CAPTAIN WALLACE BINGHAMPTON.
See: McHale, Lieut. Commander
Quinton

CAPTAIN ZACHARY WINGATE. See:
Cord

Car 54, Where Are You? See:
Muldoon, Francis

Car, My Mother the. See: Crabtree, Dave

CAR, THE. See: Crabtree, Dave

CARA. See:
Bridges, Cara
Clara

Cara Williams Show, The. See:
Bridges, Cara

Caravan, The Camel. See: Monroe,
Vaughn

CARD. See also: Cord

CARD, KATHRYN. See: Caine,
Betty

Card, Take a. See: Butterworth,
Wally

CARDINAL CAMPEGGIO. See:
Henry VIII, King of England

CARDINAL WOLSEY. See: Henry
VIII, King of England

CARDONNEL. See: Churchill,
John

Care of Aggie Horn, In. See:
Horn, Aggie

CARELLA
HAVILLAND
MEYER
KLING, New York police officers
Eighty-Seventh Precinct (TV)
(Police/crime drama)

CAREY. See also: Cary

CAREY, ARNOLD. See: Noble,
Mary

CAREY, DR. PHILIP, physician;
marries Sally Athelney
SALLY ATHELNEY, becomes
his wife
STEPHEN, his father
HELEN, his mother
WILLIAM
LOUISA, his uncle and aunt and
his guardians
MILDRED ROGERS, alias Mrs.
Miller
Of Human Bondage (R) (Serial
drama)

CAREY, MACDONALD. See:
First Nighter, Mr.

CAREY, RON. See: Moore,
Melba

CAREY, SANDRA. See: Noble,
Mary

CARL. See:
Carle
Cordell, Carl
Darl
Karl
Reiner, Carl

CARL FORTINA. See: Jones, Spike (1)

CARL GRAINGER. See: Drake,
Betty

CARL GRAYSON. See: Jones,
Spike (1)

CARL HOFF. See: Crosby, Bob
(1)

CARL HYATT, PROFESSOR. See:
Corey, Don

CARL MARITZ. See: Webster,
Nancy

CARL MATTHEWS. See: Weems,
Ambrose J.

CARL OXFORD. See: Murray,
Arthur

CARL PERKINS. See:
Cash, Johnny
Ritter, Tex (1)

CARL PHILLIPS. See: Welles,
Orson (3)

CARL REINER. See:
Caesar, Sid (2) (3)
Reiner, Carl

CARL RICHMOND. See: Randolph,
Ellen

CARL WARD. See: Malone, Dr.
Jerry

CARLA. See also: Carlo

CARLA BENARI. See: Walleck,
Meredith

CARLA SCOTT. See: Hargrave-
Scott, Joan

CARLA THOMAS. See: Butler,
Jerry

CARLAY, RACHEL. See: Thomas,
Thomas L.

CARLE. See also:
Carl
Darl
Karl

Carle Comes Calling. See: Carle,
Frankie (1)

CARLE, FRANKIE (1), pianist and
orchestra leader, star of the
program (himself)
HIS ORCHESTRA
Carle Comes Calling (R) (Popular music)

CARLE, FRANKIE (2), pianist and
orchestra leader; host of the
program (himself)
HIS ORCHESTRA
MANY GUEST STARS
The Frankie Carle Show (TV)
(Music/variety)

CARLETON. See also:
Carlton
Karleton
Tarlton

CARLETON COON, DR. See:
Rainey, Dr. Froelich

CARLIN, GEORGE. See:
Greco, Buddy
Shawn, Dick

CARLIN, WALTER. See: Dane,
Prudence

CARLISLE. See also:
Carlyle
Carlysle

CARLISLE, ANNIE. See: CAMPA-
NELLI, DR. VINCENT

CARLISLE, KITTY
ALICE CORNETT, vocalists appearing on the program (themselves)
The Song Shop (R) (Music)

CARLISLE, KITTY. See also:
Moore, Garry (4) (5)

CARLO. See also: Carla

CARLO, UNCLE. See: Goldberg,
Molly

CARLON, BURT. See: Perkins, Ma

CARLOS RAMIREZ. See:
Bertrille, Sr.
Morgan, Frank (1)

CARLOTTA. See: Charlotta

CARLSHORN, JULES. See:
Chandler, Faith

CARLSON. See: Williams, Dr.

CARLTON. See:
  Carleton
  Fredericks, Carlton
  Karleton
  Tarlton

CARLTON BRICKERT. See: Thurston, Howard

CARLYLE. See also:
  Carlisle
  Carlysle

CARLYLE, BAYLOR, banker, dying
  DUNCAN CARLYLE, his son
  TRACY CARLYLE HASTINGS, his
  daughter, Duncan's half-sister
  PHILIP HASTINGS, his son-in-law
  JEFFREY HASTINGS, his illegiti-
  mate grandson
  JONATHAN CARLYLE, his brother
  BELLE, his secretary
  ANTAEUS RIAKOS, Greek shipping
  magnate
  SENATOR JENNINGS, politician
  MIGUEL SANTERRA, revolutionary
  The Survivors (TV) (Drama)

CARLYSLE. See also:
  Carlisle
  Carlyle

CARLYSLE, FANNY. See: Dane,
  Prudence

CARMELITA POPE. See: Arnold,
  Eddy

CARMEN LE FAVE TRIO, THE.
  See: Edwards, Frank

CARMICHAEL, LUCY, widow, por-
  trayed by Lucille Ball
  JERRY, her son
  SHERMAN, her nephew
  VIV, her friend
  THEODORE MOONEY, banker
  The Lucille Ball Show (TV) (Situ-
  ation comedy) (also called The
  Lucy Show) (TV)

CARMICHAEL, RALPH. See:
  Driggs, Karleton King
  Rogers, Roy

CARMODY, ADELE. See: Nelson,

Carolyn Kramer

Carnation Contented Hour, The.
  See: Faith, Percy

CARNE, JUDY. See: Rowan, Dan

CARNEY. See: Holden, Grey

CARNEY, KATHLEEN. See:
  Graham, Dr. Bob

CAROL. See:
  Brady, Mike
  Burnett, Carol
  Carole
  Carroll
  Chandler, Faith
  Findlay, Maude
  Kennedy, Carol
  Post, Wilbur
  Potter, Tom
  West, Michael

CAROL ANDERSON. See: Silver,
  Captain

CAROL ARTHUR. See: DeLuise,
  Dom (1)

CAROL BRUCE. See: Edwards,
  Ralph (1)

CAROL BURNETT. See:
  Burnett, Carol
  Cookie Monster, The
  DeLuise, Dom (2)
  Moore, Garry (3)
  Stokey, Mike

Carol Burnett Show, The. See:
  Burnett, Carol

CAROL "CHICHI" CONRAD. See:
  Solomon, David

CAROL DAVIS. See: Preston,
  Dick

CAROL DENNING. See: Hughes,
  Chris

CAROL EVANS MARTIN. See:
  Brent, Dr. Jim

CAROL GAULT. See: Prescott,
  Kate Hathaway

CAROL GIRARD. See: Renfrew,
Inspector Douglas

Carol Kennedy's Romance. See:
Kennedy, Carol

CAROL KESTER. See: Hartley,
Dr. Robert

CAROL LAWRENCE. See:
Damone, Vic (2)
Davidson, John (1)

CAROL LYNN GILLMER. See:
Allen, Frederick Lewis

CAROL PARKER. See: Willis,
David

CAROL PETERS. See: Farrell,
David

CAROL RICHARDS. See: Crosby,
Bob (1)

CAROL ROBINSON. See: Stevens,
Ray

CAROLE. See also:
Carol
Carroll

CAROLE LOMBARD. See: Carroll,
Madeleine

CAROLINE, small-town merchant
Caroline's Golden Store (R)
(Serial drama)

CAROLINE. See also:
Carolyn
Randolph, Alice

CAROLINE ANDREWS. See: Roxy

CAROLINE, CONTESSA DI CONTINI.
See: Rule, Harry

Caroline's Golden Store. See:
Caroline

CAROLYN. See:
Caroline
Driggs, Karleton King
Muir, Carolyn
Nelson, Carolyn Kramer

CAROLYN DeZURIK. See:

Lewandowski, Bob

CAROLYN PRINCE. See: Perry,
John

CAROLYN RUSSELL. See: Peyton, Martin

CAROLYN STODDARD. See:
Collins, Barnabas

CARP, PROFESSOR LEMUEL.
See: Bergen, Edgar (2)

CARPENTER, DONALD. See:
O'Connor, Katy

CARPENTER, LIEUT. See: Farrell, David

CARPENTER, LIEUT. ELROY.
See: McHale, Lieut. Commander
Quinton

CARPENTER, LUKE, frozen in
Alaska glacier in 1900; rescued
in 1967; 100 years old chrono-
logically, 33 in mind and body
EDWIN, his son, 67 years old
KEN, his look-alike grandson
The Second Hundred Years (TV)
(Comedy)

CARPENTERS, THE. See: Hirt,
Al (2)

Carpet, The Lucky Strike Magic.
See: Winchell, Walter (1)

CARR. See also: Karr

CARR, ALISON
JACQUES
JEAN PAUL DESMOND
DAN FORREST
MATT DAWSON
VANGIE
ERICA
HOLLY
ELIZABETH MARSHALL
RAXL
QUITO
TIM, characters appearing in
the drama
Strange Paradise (TV) (Serial
drama)

CARR, SOLARI AND. See:

Stevens, Ray

CARR, VIKKI. See: Davidson,
John (1)

CARR, WORD. See: Ballew, Wally

CARRAWAY, JOYCE. See: Drake,
Bradley

CARRIE. See: Dickey, Dan'l

CARRIE DEAN. See: James, Nancy

CARRIE, LEN. See: Jones, Spike
(1)

CARROLL. See also:
Carol
Carole

CARROLL, ALICE. See: Trent,
Helen

CARROLL, DIAHANN. See: Crosby,
Bing (2)

CARROLL, GEORGIA. See: Kyser,
Kay

CARROLL, JIM. See: Webster,
Martha

CARROLL, MADELEINE
RONALD COLMAN
CARY GRANT
CAROLE LOMBARD
CHICO MARX
GROUCHO MARX
BASIL RATHBONE, masters of
ceremony on the program (them-
selves)
The Circle (R) (Variety/discussion)

CARROLL, MARJORY. See:
Graham, Dr. Bob

CARROLL, PAT. See:
Caesar, Sid (2)
Daly, John (4)
Reiner, Carl

CARRUTHERS, C.E. See: Jones,
Abraham Lincoln

CARSON. See also: Cason

CARSON, BOB, adventurer, pilot and

playboy
LIONEL, his sidekick
HANK GOGERTY, teenage tomboy
The Bob Cummings Show (TV)
(Situation comedy)

CARSON, CONSTANCE MAC-
KENZIE. See: Peyton, Martin

CARSON, ELI. See: Peyton,
Martin

CARSON, ELLIOTT. See: Peyton,
Martin

CARSON, INSPECTOR. See:
Jordan, Joyce

CARSON, JACK, comedian (him-
self)
TUGWELL, his nephew
JACK'S PRESS AGENT
MRS. FOSTER
HERBERT PEABODY
THE BUTLER
AUNT SALLY
THE LITTLE GIRL NEXT DOOR,
comedians and characters appear-
ing on the program
The Jack Carson Show (R)
(Comedy)

CARSON, JOHNNY (1), host of
the program (himself)
MANY GUEST HOSTS
ED McMAHON, announcer (him-
self)
SKITCH HENDERSON
DOC SEVERINSEN, orchestra
leaders (themselves)
THEIR ORCHESTRAS
MANY GUEST CELEBRITIES
The Tonight Show (TV) (Talk/
interview)

CARSON, JOHNNY (2), host of the
program (himself)
MANY INTERVIEWEES
Who Do You Trust? (TV) (Inter-
view/quiz)

CARSON, KIT, frontier scout
EL TORO, his friend
Kit Carson (TV) (Western)

CARSON McVICKER, DR. See:
Brent, Dr. Jim

CARSON, MR. See: Hargrave-
Scott, Joan

CARSON, MRS. See: O'Neill, Mrs.

CARSON, UNCLE JOE, operates
Shady Rest Hotel at Hooterville
KATE BRADLEY, his widowed
sister
BOBBIE JO BRADLEY
BILLIE JO BRADLEY
BETTY JO BRADLEY ELLIOTT,
her daughters
STEVE ELLIOTT, Betty Jo's
husband, crop duster
CATHY JO ELLIOTT, infant
daughter of Betty Jo and Steve
DR. JANET CRAIG, physician
SAM DRUCKER, Hooterville
druggist, postmaster and news-
paper publisher
MAYOR POTTS of Hooterville
Petticoat Junction (TV) (Situation
comedy)

CARTER. See:
Hogan, Colonel Robert
Nash, Carter
Primus, Carter

CARTER BARBOUR, BETTY. See:
Barbour, Henry Wilson

CARTER, BOB. See: Sharp, Hal

CARTER, CHICK, adopted son of
Nick Carter; boy detective
SUE
TEX, his friends
THE RATTLER
RUFUS LASH, his enemies
Chick Carter, Boy Detective (R)
(Detective/adventure)

CARTER, CINNAMON. See: Phelps,
Jim

CARTER COLBY, JUDGE. See:
Larimore, Marilyn

CARTER COLBY, MRS. See: Larimore, Marilyn

CARTER, CYNTHIA. See: Trent,
Helen

CARTER FAMILY, THE. See:
Cash, Johnny

CARTER, HOPE
JIMMY GALE
LARRY BURTON, characters
appearing in the drama
Modern Cinderella (R) (Serial
drama)

CARTER, JAMES
JESSIE CARTER
JEFF
VIRGINIA
CLAY, characters appearing in
the drama
Woman in My House (R) (Serial
drama)

CARTER, JEAN. See: Hutchinson, Ma

CARTER, JUNE. See: Cash,
Johnny

CARTER, KATHRYN
DON CARTER
DICK CRANE
JEN BURTON
JUNIOR MATTHEWS
HELEN MARSHALL
DOROTHY MORAN
MOTHER MORAN
BOB CRANE
KAY CRANE
ROBERT MARSHALL
JERRY RYAN
KATHERINE NORTON
BILL TAYLOR
DR. PAUL BURTON
MICHAEL GREGORY
HENRY MATTHEWS
CHARLOTTA LAGORRO ARMOUR
RICHARD COLES
PATTY MORAN
GLORIA MARSH
BOB BREWER
JULIE JOHNSON
DAVID LAGORRO
ITALO LAGORRO
JACK MARSH
FRANCES MORAN MATTHEWS
JUDGE COLBY
CATHERINE COLBY
JOHN MURRAY
NAOMI
BOBBY MORAN
JOHN BARTLETT
EILEEN MORAN
JOAN YOUNG
KEITH ARMOUR

CANDICE DRAKE
ARTHUR DONNELLY
TERRY MORAN
LUCY MORAN
MR. SCHULTZ
BERTHA SCHULTZ
AUNT MARTHA
TONY
RALPH SANTO
WALTER DRAKE
LIZA
MARILYN
THERESE
MARY
PETER PIPER, characters appearing in the drama
Today's Children (R) (Serial drama)

CARTER, LUCY, career girl, portrayed by Lucille Ball
KIM, her daughter
CRAIG, her son
UNCLE HARRY (Harrison Carter), her uncle and employer, proprietor of the "Unique Employment Agency"
Here's Lucy (TV) (Situation comedy)

CARTER, MADELINE. See: Dallas, Stella

CARTER, MARK. See: Harum, David

CARTER, MR., head of the house
MRS. CARTER, his wife
JESS CARTER, their son
BERNICE CARTER, their daughter
MILDRED CARTER RANDOLPH, their daughter
SID RANDOLPH, Mildred's husband
RANDY, friend of the family
The Carters of Elm Street (R) (Serial drama)

CARTER, NICK, detective
PATSY BOWEN, his friend
SERGEANT MATHISON (MATTY), police officer
SCUBBY, reporter
Nick Carter, Master Detective (R) (Detective adventure)

CARTER, RAY. See: Murray, Kathryn

CARTER, ROBERTA. See: Peyton, Martin

CARTER, SERGEANT. See: Pyle, Gomer

CARTER TRENT. See: Young, Larry "Pepper"

Carters of Elm Street, The. See: Carter, Mr.

Cartoon Show, The Alvin. See: Saville, David

CARTWRIGHT, BEN, cattle rancher at Ponderosa Ranch
HOSS
ADAM
LITTLE JOE, his sons
JAIMIE, his adopted son
CANDY
GRIFF KING, ranch hands employed by the Cartwrights
HOP SING, Chinese cook employed by the Cartwrights
Bonanza (TV) (Western) (also known as Ponderosa) (TV)

CARTWRIGHT, PENELOPE "PENNY." See: Owner

CARUSO. See: Winters, Jack

CARVELL, DR. DUNCAN. See: Wayne, Ruth Evans

CARVELL, MRS. See: Wayne, Ruth Evans

CARVER, FRANK. See: Ames, Peter

CARVER, GAIL. See: Lawton, Lora

CARVER, MARGO, 79-year-old matriarch of the Carver family
Margo of Castlewood (R) (Serial drama)

CARVER, P. WALLACE. See: O'Leary, Hannah

CARVER, PETER. See: Lawton, Lora

CARVER, SUSAN. See: Ames, Peter

CARY. See also: Carey

CARY GRANT. See:
Carroll, Madeleine
Frees, Paul

CARY, MRS. See: Drake, Betty

CASADESUS, ROBERT. See:
Bell, Alexander Graham

Case Book of Gregory Hood, The.
See: Hood, Gregory

CASE, LENORE. See: Reid, Britt

CASE, LINC. See: Murdock, Buz

CASE, MAY. See: Lawton, Lora

Cases, National Surety's Secret.
See: Harkness, Detective

Cases of Eddie Drake, The. See:
Drake, Eddie

CASEY, photographer for the
"Morning Express"
ANN WILLIAMS, his friend; re-
porter
ETHELBERT, bartender
POLICE CAPTAIN LOGAN, police
officer
Casey, Crime Photographer (R)
(Adventure)

CASEY. See also:
Cassie
Jones, Casey (1) (2)
Levy, Abie
Phelps, Jim
Reid, Britt
Thompson, Colonel Casey

Casey, Crime Photographer. See:
Casey

CASEY, DR. BEN, resident neuro-
surgeon at County General Hos-
pital
DR. DAVID ZORBA, his friend
and mentor
DR. TED HOFFMAN
MAGGIE GRAHAM, his friends
and associates
NICK KANAVARAS, orderly
NURSE WILLS, nurse at County
General Hospital

Ben Casey (TV) (Medical drama)

CASEY FLANNIGAN. See: Sharp,
Hal

CASEY, GIL. See: Kaufman,
Seymour

Casey Jones. See: Jones, Casey
(1)

CASEY, JR. See: Jones, Casey
(1)

CASH, JOHNNY, singer, guitarist
and composer, host of the pro-
gram (himself)
JUNE CARTER
THE CARTER FAMILY
CARL PERKINS
THE STATLER BROTHERS
THE TENNESSEE THREE, enter-
tainers and singers appearing on
the program (themselves)
The Johnny Cash Show (TV)
(Country/Western music)

CASH, JOHNNY. See also: Ritter,
Tex (1)

CASHIER. See: Parkyakarkas,
Nick

CASINO. See:
Garrison, Lieut. Craig
Joe (1)

CASON. See also: Carson

CASON, BARBARA. See: Klein,
Robert

CASPER, "the friendly ghost,"
cartoon character
Casper, The Friendly Ghost (TV)
(Cartoon)

CASPER. See also:
Gaspar
Milquetoast, Casper

Casper, The Friendly Ghost. See:
Casper

CASS DALEY. See:
Daley, Cass
Morgan, Frank (1)

CASS ELLIOT, MAMMA. See:
  Riddle, Sam (1)
  Stevens, Ray

CASS, PEGGY. See:
  Blyden, Larry (2)
  Moore, Garry (5)
  Reiner, Carl

CASSANDRA, DR. See: Batman

CASSANDRA DRINKWATER. See:
  Old Ranger, The

CASSEN, DR. DOUGLAS. See:
  Hughes, Chris

CASSIDY, AJAX. See: Allen,
  Fred

CASSIDY, DAN. See: Dean,
  Spencer

CASSIDY, HOPALONG, Western
  cowboy
  Hopalong Cassidy (R) (Western
  adventure) (TV) (Reruns of old
  Western motion pictures featuring
  William Boyd)
  CALIFORNIA, his sidekick
  Hopalong Cassidy (R)
  RED, his sidekick
  Hopalong Cassidy (TV)

CASSIE. See also: Casey

CASSIE, COUSIN. See: Old Ranger,
  The

CASTLE DANCERS, THE NICK.
  See: Lewis, Jerry

CASTLE, JO ANN. See: Welk,
  Lawrence

CASTLE, LEE. See: Basie, Count

CASTLE, MARY. See: Davis, Jim

CASTLEBURY, MELVIN. See:
  White, Billy

CASTLESON, FRED. See: Sunday

Castlewood, Margo of. See:
  Carver, Margo

CAT. See:

Kat
Top Cat

CAT, CRAZY. See: Parmenter,
  Captain Wilton

CAT, SYLVESTER THE. See:
  Bunny, Bugs

CAT, THOMAS HEWITT EDWARD
  (T. H. E. Cat), cat burglar and
  jewel thief
  CAPTAIN McCALLISTER, officer
  PEPE, Cat's gypsy friend;
  owner of the café Casa del Gato
  T. H. E. Cat (TV) (Mystery/
  adventure)

CAT WOMAN, THE. See: Batman

CATERINA. See also:
  Catherine
  Katharine
  Katherine
  Kathryn
  Katrin

CATERINA VALENTE. See: De-
  Luise, Dom (2)

CATES, OPIE. See: Parkyakarkas,
  Nick

CATHCART, DICK. See: Welk,
  Lawrence

CATHERINE. See:
  Caterina
  Katharine
  Katherine
  Kathryn
  Katryn
  Peyton, Martin

CATHERINE ALLISON. See: Mac-
  Donald, Eleanor

CATHERINE COLBY. See: Carter,
  Kathryn

CATHERINE HOWARD. See:
  Henry VIII, King of England

CATHERINE KREITZER, MRS.
  See: March, Hal

CATHERINE OF ARAGON. See:
  Henry VIII, King of England

CATHERINE PARR. See: Henry
VIII, King of England

CATHERINE SHAUGHNESSEY.
See: Perkins, Ma

CATHIE. See also:
Cathy
Kathy

CATHIE RYKER. See: Davis, Dr.
Althea

CATHY. See:
Cathie
Driggs, Carleton King
Kathy
Lane, Patty

CATHY BAKER. See: Owens, Buck

CATHY JO ELLIOTT. See: Carson,
Uncle Joe

CATUSI, JIM. See: Frost, David
(2)

CAULIFLOWER McPUGG. See:
Junior

Cavalcade of America. See:
Welles, Orson (2)

Cavalcade of Fashions, Paris. See:
Emerson, Faye (2)

Cavalcade of Stars, The. See:
Gleason, Jackie (1)
Kramden, Ralph

CAVALIERS QUARTET, THE. See:
Dragonette, Jessica (1)

CAVANAUGH, DON. See: Webster,
Martha

CAVANAUGH, FATHER SAMUEL
PATRICK (Sarge), former San
Diego, California, police detec-
tive sergeant; now parish priest
VALERIE, his secretary
KENJI TAKICHI, Japanese police-
man
BARNEY VERICK, police officer
Sarge (TV) (Detective adventure)

Cave, The Hermit's. See: Hermit,
The

CAVELLI, SERGEANT VINCE. See:
Adams, Lieut. Price

CAVENDISH, DONNA. See: Wing,
Howie

CAVETT, DICK (1), host of the
program (himself)
MANY GUEST STARS AND HOSTS
BOB ROSENGARDEN, orchestra
leader (himself)
HIS ORCHESTRA
The Dick Cavett Show (TV) (In-
terview/variety)

CAVETT, DICK (2), narrator of
the program (himself)
OLD MOTION PICTURES
Hollywood: The Dream Factory
(TV) (Filmmaking history)

CAVETT, DICK (3), host of the
program (himself)
MANY GUEST STARS
BOB ROSENGARDEN, orchestra
leader (himself)
HIS ORCHESTRA
This Morning (TV) (Interview/
variety)

CAVETT, DICK. See also: Shawn,
Dick

CECIL. See:
Beany
DeMille, Cecil B.

CECIL BILL. See: Kukla

CECIL, WINIFRED. See: Henry,
Captain

CECIL WYNTOON. See: Bailey,
Sam

CECILY. See: Ungar, Felix

CECILY ANDREWS. See: Bennett,
Nita

CEDERQUIST, DENA, dietician;
hostess of the program (herself)
Food For Life (TV) (Nutrition)

CEDRIC HARDWICKE, SIR. See:
Wallace, Mike (5)

CEDRIC WEHUNT. See: Edwards,
Lum

CEFUS PETERS. See: Parker, Seth

Celebrity Talent Scouts. See: Levenson, Sam

CELESE. See: Koster, David

CELESTE CUNNINGHAM. See: Rutledge, Dr. John

CELESTE HOLM. See: Wallace, Mike (5)

CELIA. See:
Garrison, Spencer
Jordan, Joyce
Stanley

CELIA BURNS. See: Karr, Mike

Center, Medical. See: Lochner, Dr. Paul

Central City. See: Olson, Emily

Central Station, Grand. See: Arthur, Jack (2)

Century A.D., Buck Rogers in the Twenty-Fifth. See: Rogers, Buck

Century, Bob Elson Aboard the. See: Elson, Bob

Century, Sale of the. See: Garagiola, Joe (3)

Century, Stories of the. See: Davis, Jim

Century, The Twentieth. See: Cronkite, Walter (3)

Century, The 21st. See: Cronkite, Walter (4)

CERF, BENNETT. See: Daly, John (3)

CESAR. See also:
Caesar
Cezar

CESAR ROMERO. See: Kovacs, Ernie (1)

CEZAR. See also:
Caesar
Cesar

CEZAR BENEDICT. See: West, Michael

CHA-CHA O'BRIEN. See: Madison, Kenny

CHAD. See: Smith, Chad

CHAD COOPER. See: Parmalee, Ranger Captain

CHALK BREESON. See: Caine, Frank

Challenge of the Yukon, The. See: Preston, Sergeant

Challenge, The Man and the. See: Barton, Dr. Glenn

Challenge, The $64,000. See: Story, Ralph

CHALMERS, DR. TONY. See: Perry, John

CHAMBER. See also: Chambers

Chamber Music Society of Lower Basin Street, The. See: Cross, Milton (1)

Chamber, Stories of the Black. See: Drake, Bradley

CHAMBERLAIN, NEVILLE. See: Husing, Ted

CHAMBERLIN, LEE. See: Cosby, Bill (1)

CHAMBERS. See also: Chamber

CHAMBERS, ENID. See: Fraser, Ben

CHAMELEON, MR., master of disguise; used this mastery to track down criminals
HIS ASSISTANT
Mr. Chameleon (R) (Detective adventure)

CHAMPION. See: Autry, Gene

CHAMPION, BIG TIM. See:
Corky

CHAMPION, MARGE
GOWER CHAMPION, her husband;
dance team, stars of the pro-
gram (themselves)
JACK WHITING, dancer (himself)
MANY GUEST STARS
The Marge and Gower Champion
Show (TV) (Music/dancing) (also
called The Champion Show) (TV)

Champion Show, The. See:
Champion, Marge

Champions, Studebaker. See:
Himber, Richard

Champions, The. See: Stirling,
Craig

Championship Bridge With Charles
Goren. See: Goren, Charles

Championship Golf, World. See:
Crosby, Bob (3)

CHAN, "Chinese honorable private
eye and father of ten"; cartoon
character
HIS TEN CHILDREN
The Amazing Chan and the Chan
Clan (TV) (Cartoon)

Chan and the Chan Clan, The
Amazing. See: Chan

CHAN, CHARLIE, Chinese-American
detective
NUMBER ONE SON, his son and
assistant in detecting
Charlie Chan (R) (Mystery)

Chance for Romance. See: Swayze,
John Cameron

Chance of a Lifetime. See: King,
John Reed (1)

CHANCE REYNOLDS. See: Pride,
Ben

CHANCELLOR, DR. See: Baines,
Scattergood

CHANCELLOR, JOHN
FRANK McGEE, newscasters;

narrators of the program (them-
selves)
The N.B.C. Evening News (TV)
(News)

CHANCELLOR, JOHN. See also:
Downs, Hugh

CHANDELL. See: Batman

CHANDLER, BRYANT. See:
Harding, Karen Adams

CHANDLER, DICK. See: Walleck,
Meredith

CHANDLER, DR. HOWARD. See:
Chandler, Dr. Susan

CHANDLER, DR. SUSAN, physician
DR. HOWARD CHANDLER, her
husband, physician
MARILYN CHANDLER
DICKIE CHANDLER
MIRANDA CHANDLER
NANCY CHANDLER, their
children
DR. HALLIDAY, physician
ABBY BRADFORD, their friend
The Life and Loves of Dr.
Susan (R) (Serial drama)

CHANDLER, FAITH
CAROL CHANDLER
NOEL CHANDLER
JOSH CHANDLER
JULES CARSHORN
LYNN REED
POINDEXTER BRICE
MICHAEL MURRY
VIOLET SHANE
MILES NOVAK
PAMELA, characters appearing
in the drama
Dear John (R) (Serial drama)

CHANDLER, FRANK. See: Chandu
the Magician

CHANDLER, JACK. See: Peyton,
Martin

CHANDLER, JIM, portrays part
of the Tracer, seeking to locate
missing persons owed inheritances
and forgotten stocks and bonds
The Tracer (TV) (Searches for
missing persons)

CHANDLER, ROBIN. See: Landi,
Elissa

CHANDU THE MAGICIAN, actually
Frank Chandler, American secret
agent who used "supernatural
powers based on the ancient arts
of the occult" to fight crime
Chandu the Magician (R) (Adventure)

CHANG, KAM. See: Garlund,
Frank

CHANG, PETER. See: Randolph,
Ellen

CHANG, PO. See: Garlund, Frank

Changing World, This. See: Bishop,
Neil

Channing. See: Baker, Dean Fred

Chaparral, The High. See: Cannon, John

CHAPIN, TOM, host of the program
(himself)
Make a Wish (TV) (Children's
program)

CHAPLAIN JIM, World War II army
chaplain
Chaplain Jim, U.S.A. (R) (Army
drama)

CHAPMAN, MRS. See: Brent, Dr.
Jim

CHAPPELL, ERNEST (1), quizmaster of the program (himself)
MANY JUVENILE CONTESTANTS
Are You a Genius? (R) (Children's quiz)

CHAPPELL, ERNEST (2), narrator
of the program (himself)
Quiet, Please (R) (Adventure)

CHAPUYS. See: Henry VIII, King
of England

CHARGE ACCOUNT. See: Murray,
Jan (2)

CHARISSE, CYD. See: Crosby,
Bing (2)

CHARITY. See: Dyke, Charity
Amanda

CHARLES. See:
Boyer, Charles
Collingwood, Charles (1) (2)
Coughlin, Father Charles Edward
Fuller, Rev. Charles E.
Goren, Charles
Meredith, Charles
Osgood, Charles

CHARLES II. See: Churchill,
John

CHARLES BOYER. See:
Ameche, Jim
Boyer, Charles
Ryan, Robert (1)

CHARLES "CHUCK" PARKER,
ENSIGN. See: McHale, Lieut.
Commander Quinton

CHARLES COLEMAN. See:
Moore, Melba

CHARLES COLLINGWOOD. See:
Collingwood, Charles (1) (2)
Murrow, Edward R. (4)

CHARLES CORDDRY. See: Mac-
Neil, Robert

CHARLES CUNNINGHAM. See:
Rutledge, Dr. John

CHARLES DANIELS. See: Wayne,
Ruth Evans

CHARLES DANT. See: Ward,
Perry

CHARLES DELAWARE TARE. See:
Collins, Barnabas

CHARLES DUTTON. See: Miller,
Albert

Charles Goren, Championship
Bridge With. See: Goren,
Charles

CHARLES HAYDON. See: Steel,
Richard

CHARLES LANG. See: Warren,
Wendy

CHARLES McCAREY. See: West,
Michael

CHARLES MATTHEWS, DR. See:
Rutledge, Dr. John

CHARLES NELSON REILLY. See:
Chidsey, Jackie

CHARLES, NICK, private detective;
retired but takes occasional cases
NORA, his wife
ASTA, their dog
EBENEZER WILLIAMS, sheriff
of Crabtree County
The Thin Man (R) (TV) (Detective
drama)

CHARLES SCHWARTZ. See:
Kelly, Joe (2)

CHARLES SINGERS, THE RAY.
See:
Como, Perry (1) (2) (3)
Fisher, Eddie

CHARLES SPENCER. See: Churchill,
John

CHARLES TYLER, DR. See: Davis,
Ann Tyler

CHARLES VAN DOREN. See: Barry,
Jack (9)

CHARLES WEBSTER. See:
Roberts, Ken

CHARLES WILENTZ. See: August,
Dan

CHARLES WILLIAMS. See: Keene,
Kitty

CHARLES WOODS. See: Jostyn,
Jay (1)

CHARLEY. See:
Charlie
Magoo, Mr.
Sharlie
Weaver, Charley

CHARLEY BROWN. See: Perkins,
Ma

CHARLEY HACKETT. See:
Cooper, Dick

CHARLEY HALPER. See: Williams,
Danny

CHARLEY, UNCLE. See: Douglas,
Steve

CHARLEY WEAVER. See:
Marshall, Peter
Rogers, Roy
Weaver, Charley
Winters, Jonathan

Charley Weaver Show, The. See:
Weaver, Charley

CHARLIE
JESSIE, characters appearing in
the drama
Charlie and Jessie (R) (Comedy)

CHARLIE. See also:
Chan, Charlie
Charley
Farrell, Charlie
Hathaway, Elinor
Lassie
Morgan, Jaye P.
Randolph, Walt
Sharlie
Uncle Charlie
Wild, Charlie

Charlie and Jessie. See: Charlie

CHARLIE BARNETT. See: Whiteman, Paul

CHARLIE BRATTON. See: Gleason, Jackie (1) (2)

CHARLIE CALLAS. See:
Little, Rich
Williams, Andy (2)

Charlie Chan. See: Chan, Charlie

CHARLIE CULLOM. See: Harum,
David

Charlie, Don't Call Me. See:
McKay, Judson

CHARLIE DOOLEY, UNCLE. See:
Day, Chris

CHARLIE DYER. See: Hastings,
Bob

Charlie Farrell. See: Farrell,
Charlie

CHARLIE GIANNETTA. See:
Marshall, Owen

CHARLIE GLEASON. See:
Winters, Evelyn

CHARLIE HARRIS. See: Dyke,
Charity Amanda

CHARLIE HENDERSON. See:
Ballard, Pat

CHARLIE HORSE. See: Lewis,
Shari

CHARLIE, HOTSHOT. See: Lee,
Terry

CHARLIE KINGMAN. See: Primus,
Carter

CHARLIE McCARTHY. See:
Ameche, Don (1)
Bergen, Edgar (1) (2)

Charlie McCarthy Show, The Edgar
Bergen and. See: Bergen,
Edgar (2)

CHARLIE McCARTHY'S SCHOOL
PRINCIPAL. See: Bergen,
Edgar (2)

CHARLIE MACK. See: Two Black
Crows, The (1) (2)

CHARLIE MANNA. See: Martindale, Wink (2)

CHARLIE MARTIN. See: Dallas,
Stella

CHARLIE POLATTA. See: Welk,
Lawrence

CHARLIE, SLIPPERY. See:
Huddles, Ed

Charlie Wild, Private Eye. See:
Wild, Charlie

CHARLOTTA LAGORRO ARMOUR.
See: Carter, Kathryn

CHARLOTTE. See:

Bauer, Bertha
Greenwood, Charlotte
Manson, Charlotte
Thompson, Jim

CHARLOTTE ABBOTT. See:
Sunday

CHARLOTTE BRANDON. See:
Rutledge, Dr. John

CHARLOTTE BROWN, MRS. See:
Brown, Ellen

Charlotte Greenwood Show, The.
See: Greenwood, Charlotte

CHARLOTTE HALL. See: Welk,
Lawrence

CHARLOTTE MANSON. See:
Kummer, Eloise
Manson, Charlotte
Murphy, Dean

CHARLOTTE MARLEYBONE. See:
Hansen, Dean Eric

CHARLOTTE MENCKEN. See:
Ames, Peter

CHARM EXPERT, gave advice on
grooming and beauty techniques;
portrayed by Richard Willis
Look Your Best (R) (Beauty
advice)

Charm, The Hour of. See:
Spitalney, Phil

CHARMOLI DANCERS, THE TONY.
See: Andrews, Julie

CHARWOMAN, THE. See:
Burnett, Carol

Chase and Sanborn Hour, The.
See:
Ameche, Don (1)
Cantor, Eddie (2)

CHASE, BARRIE. See: Astaire,
Fred (2)

CHASE, DENNIS, private investi-
gator
LOLA
BRIAN

JIM, his assistants
21 Beacon Street (TV) (Detective
drama)

CHASE, FRANK. See: Trent,
Helen

CHASE, ILKA. See:
Donald, Peter
Glad, Gladys

CHASE MURDOCH. See: Hardy,
Dr. Steven

CHASE, SHERIFF MARK. See:
Old Ranger, The

CHASE, SYLVIA, hostess of the
program (herself)
MANY INTERVIEWEES
Today's Woman (R) (Interview)

CHASTITY. See: Bono, Salvatore

Chateau, Shell. See: Jolson, Al

Chats, Fireside. See: Roosevelt,
Franklin D.

CHATTERBOX, THE HUMAN. See:
Blurt, Elmer

CHATTERBOXES, THE. See:
Reiner, Carl

CHATTON, KATHLEEN. See:
Davidson, Bill

CHATWIN, MERLE. See: Dallas,
Stella

CHAUNCEY. See: Kaltenmeyer,
Professor August, D. U. N.

Checkmate. See: Corey, Don

Cheer, Stand Up and. See: Mann,
Johnny

Cheer, Stand Up and; Johnny Mann.
See: Mann, Johnny

CHEERILY, REGINALD. See:
Blurt, Elmer
Holloway, Harrison

CHEETAH. See: Tarzan

CHEF. See: Bryson, Dr. Lyman
(1)

Chef, The French. See: Child,
Julia

CHEGLEY, DR. MORTON. See:
Baker, Julia

CHEGLEY, MRS. See: Baker,
Julia

CHEGLEY, NORTON. See:
Baker, Julia

CHELSEA BROWN. See: Rowan,
Dan

CHER. See: Bono, Salvatore

Cher Comedy Hour, The Sonny
and. See: Bono, Salvatore

Cher Show, The Sonny and. See:
Bono, Salvatore

CHERILYN. See: Bono, Salvatore

CHERNAK, ANGEL. See: Gar-
rison, Spencer

CHERNAK, BETSY. See: Gar-
rison, Spencer

CHERNAK, DR. PETER. See:
Garrison, Spencer

CHERNAK, JOE. See: Peyton,
Martin

CHERNAK, MILLIE. See: Garrison, Spencer

CHERNAK, MR. See: Garrison,
Spencer

CHERNAK, MRS. See: Garrison,
Spencer

CHERNAK, NICOLE ALLISON.
See: Garrison, Spencer

CHERRY. See:
Sherry
Trail, Mark

CHERRY MARTIN. See: Trent,
Helen

CHERYL. See:
 Dodd, Jimmie
 Driggs, Karleton King

CHERYL ANN, THE. See: Herrick,
 Cap'n John

Chess, Koltanowski on. See: Koltanowski, George

CHESTER. See:
 Barkley, Arnie
 Gump, Andy
 Riley, Chester A.

CHESTER GOOD. See: Dillon,
 Marshal Matt

CHESTER HEDGEROW. See:
 Jordan, Joyce

CHESTER, INSPECTOR. See:
 Saber, Mark

CHESTER, JUDGE. See: Peyton,
 Martin

CHESTER MORRIS. See: Moore,
 Garry (4)

CHESTER VAN DYNE. See:
 Jones, Lorenzo

Chesterfield Supper Club, The.
 See: Como, Perry (1)

CHET. See:
 Huntley, Chet (1) (2) (3)
 Kincaid, Chet

Chevy Show Starring Dinah Shore,
 The. See: Shore, Dinah (1)

Chevy Show, The. See: Blair,
 Janet

Cheyenne. See: Bodie, Cheyenne

CHEYENNE. See: Bodie, Cheyenne

Chicago Teddy Bears, The. See:
 McCray, Linc

"CHICHI" CONRAD, CAROL. See:
 Solomon, David

CHICK. See:
 Carter, Chick

Chuck
 Hennesey, Lieut. Chick

CHICK JOHNSON. See: Olsen,
 Ole

CHICK NORRIS. See: Davis,
 Joan Field

CHICK ROGERS. See: Granville,
 Glynis

Chicken Every Sunday. See:
 Burke, Billie (2)

CHICKEN, ROARING. See: Parmenter, Captain Wilton

CHICO. See: Terry

CHICO MARX. See: Carroll,
 Madeleine

CHIDSEY, JACKIE
 MICHELLE DELLA FAVE
 PAULA CINKO
 PAULINE ANTONY
 TARA LEIGH
 WANDA BAILEY
 ROSETTA COX
 PATRICIA MICKEY
 MICKI McGLONE
 SUSAN LUND, singing and
 dancing group known as the
 Golddiggers (themselves)
 CHARLES NELSON REILLY
 MARTY FELDMAN
 TOMMY TUNE, entertainers
 appearing on the program (them-
 selves)
 MANY GUEST HOSTS AND
 GUEST STARS
 JACK PARNELL, orchestra
 leader (himself)
 HIS ORCHESTRA
 The Golddiggers (TV) (Variety)
 (also known as Dean Martin
 Presents the Golddiggers) (TV)

CHIEF. See:
 Fire Chief, The
 Garrison, Lieut. Craig
 Ironside, Chief Robert
 Smart, Maxwell

CHIEF BRANDON. See: Tracy,
 Dick

CHIEF CANAWAHCHAQUAOO. See:
Boone, Daniel

CHIEF CLIFFORD. See: McCloud,
Sam

CHIEF GEORGE UNTERMEYER.
See: August, Dan

CHIEF, INDIAN. See: Tennessee
Jed

CHIEF MILLER. See: Butcher,
Major Simon

CHIEF O'HARA, POLICE. See:
Batman

CHIEF OLIVER STAMP. See:
Ramsey, Hector "Hec"

CHIEF PETTY OFFICER HOMER
NELSON. See: O'Toole, Ensign

CHIEF SHARKEY. See: Nelson,
Admiral Harriman

CHIEF, THE, host of the program;
participates in the dramas
MANY ACTORS AND ACTRESSES
Treasury Men In Action (TV)
(Dramatizations of U. S. Treasury
Dept. cases)

CHIEF, THE. See also: Wing,
Howie

Chief, The Fire. See: Fire Chief,
The

CHIEF THUNDERTHUD. See:
Doody, Howdy

CHIESA, VIVIEN DELLA. See:
Munn, Frank (1)

CHILD. See also: Chile

CHILD, JULIA, cookery expert,
hostess of the program
(herself)
The French Chef (TV) (Cookery)

Child, Saturday's. See: Cooper,
Ann

Children, All My. See: Davis,
Ann Tyler

Children, Bachelor's. See:
Graham, Dr. Bob

Children First, Women and. See:
Joe (2)

Children, Today's. See:
Carter, Kathryn
Larimore, Marilyn

Children, Yesterday's. See:
Gordon, Dorothy

Children's Hour, The. See:
Cross, Milton

Children's Hour, The Horn and
Hardart. See: Edwards, Ralph
(1)

CHILE. See also: Child

CHILE, HONEY. See: Hope,
Bob (2)

Chimp, Lancelot Link, Secret.
See: Link, Lancelot

Chimp, Me and the. See:
Reynolds, Dr. Mike

CHIN HO KELLY. See: McGarrett, Steve

CHINA. See: Smith, China

China Smith. See: Smith, China

CHINESE HOUSEBOY. See:
Higby, Mary Jane

CHING, OSWALD. See: Marlin,
Mary

CHINGACHGOOK. See: Hawkeye

CHIP. See: Douglas, Steve

CHIP SAUNDERS, SERGEANT.
See: Hanley, Lieut. Gil

CHOATE, NURSE. See: Peyton,
Martin

Choice, The People's. See:
Miller, Socrates

CHOO CHOO. See: Top Cat

CHOP, LAMB. See: Lewis, Shari

CHOPSTICK JOE. See: Lee, Terry

CHORAL GROUP, RANDY VAN
HORN. See: Cole, Nat "King"

CHORDETTES, THE. See: Godfrey, Arthur (1)

CHORUS, THE HENRY RUSSELL.
See: Borge, Victor

CHORUS, THE KEN LANE. See:
Ross, Lanny

CHORUS, THE MANHATTAN. See:
Munn, Frank (2)

CHRIS. See:
Burnett, Carol
Day, Chris
Garrison, Pat
Hughes, Chris
Myrt
Partridge, Connie

CHRIS ACROPOLOUS. See: Mix,
Tom

CHRIS JENNINGS. See: Collins,
Barnabas

CHRIS JESSUP. See: Prescott,
Kate Hathaway

CHRIS LOGAN. See: Brooks,
Cameron

CHRIS SCHENKEL. See: McKay,
Jim (1)

CHRIS WEBBER. See: Peyton,
Martin

CHRIS WILSON. See: Trent,
Helen

CHRISTABEL. See: Monroe, John

CHRISTIAN, DR. PAUL, physician
JUDY PRICE, nurse
Dr. Christian (R) (TV) (Drama)
DR. MARK CHRISTIAN, physician;
nephew of Dr. Paul Christian
Dr. Christian (TV)

CHRISTINE. See:

Massey, Christine
Noble, Mary

CHRISTINE ABBOTT. See: Barbour, Henry Wilson

CHRISTINE TAYLOR. See:
Malone, Dr. Jerry

CHRISTOPHER. See:
Colt, Christopher
Storm, Christopher
Wells, Christopher

CHRISTOPHER, COOKIE. See:
Karr, Mike

CHRISTOPHER ELLERBE, DR.
See: Hargrave-Scott, Joan

CHRISTOPHER KEATOR. See:
Goldberg, Molly

CHRISTOPHER, PETER, theatri-
cal agent; swinging bachelor
BRAHMS, his boss, believes
his employees should be married
MRS. BRAHMS, Brahms' wife
GRETA, hatcheck girl, pretends
to be Christopher's wife
WALLY, Christopher's office
rival
Occasional Wife (TV) (Comedy)

CHRISTOPHER ROBIN GROVER.
See: Cameron

CHRISTOPHER, RON. See: Karr,
Mike

Christopher Wells, The Adventures
of. See: Wells, Christopher

CHRISTOPHER WHITING. See:
Tate, Joanne

CHRISTY. See:
Cameron, Christy Allen
McHale, Lieut. Commander
Quinton
Preston, Dick

Christy Minstrels, The New. See:
Sparks, Randy

Chronolog. See: Vanocur, Sander

Chrysler Theater, Bob Hope

Presents the. See: Hope, Bob (3)

CHUCK
P. T., helicopter pilots
Whirlybirds (TV) (Helicopter adventure)

CHUCK. See also:
Brewster, Joey
Chick
Hillman, India
O'Malley, Father Chuck

CHUCK ADAMS. See: Sherwood, Ruth

CHUCK BLAIR. See: Trent, Helen

CHUCK BRAINFEEBLE. See: Gook, Vic

CHUCK HENDERSON. See: Hughes, Chris

CHUCK HOOKSTRATTEN. See: Banner, Woody

CHUCK JONES. See: Pam

CHUCK McCANN. See: Nye, Louis

CHUCK MACDONALD. See: Collins, Bob

"CHUCK" PARKER, ENSIGN CHARLES. See: McHale, Lieut. Commander Quinton

CHUCK RAMSEY. See: Midnight, Captain

CHUCK TYLER. See: Davis, Ann Tyler

CHULALONGKORN, PRINCE. See: Owens, Anna

CHUPRIN. See: Rogers, Patricia

Church of the Air, The National.
See: Fosdick, Rev. Harry Emerson

CHURCHILL, JOHN, Duke of Marlborough
SARAH JENNINGS CHURCHILL,
his wife
LOUIS XIV, King of France
PRINCESS ANNE, later Queen Anne
ROBERT HARLEY
SHREWSBURY
ABIGAIL
HENRY ST. JOHN
CHARLES SPENCER
GEORGE OF DENMARK
SIDNEY GODOLPHIN
JAMES II, King of England
CHARLES II, King of England
LADY FITZHARDING
LORD ROCHESTER
THE DUKE OF YORK
TITUS OATES
LORD SHAFTSBURY
D'AVAUX
ST. JOHN
BECKET
SOMERS
SUNDERLAND
CARMARTHEN
BENTINCK
HEINSIUS
WRATISLAW
CARDONNEL, historical characters appearing in the drama
The First Churchills (TV) (Historical biographical drama)

CHURCHILL, STUART. See: Waring, Fred (1)

CHURCHILL, WINSTON. See: Husing, Ted

Churchills, The First. See: Churchill, John

CIARDI, JOHN
ALEXANDER KENDRICK
WINSTON BURDETTE, moderators of the program (themselves)
MANY GUEST INTERVIEWEES
Accent (TV) (Travel/education)

CICERO. See: Sweeney, Cicero P.

Cimarron City. See: Rockford, Matthew

Cimarron Strip. See: Crown, Jim

Cimarron Tavern. See: Barton, Joe

CINCINNATUS. See: Boone, Daniel

Cinderella, Modern. See: Carter, Hope

CINDY. See:
Brady, Mike
Crabtree, Dave
Pam
Smith, Chad

CINDY CLARK. See: Randolph, Alice

CINDY WILLIAMS. See: Kelly, Gene

CINKO, PAULA. See: Chidsey, Jackie

CINNAMON CARTER. See: Phelps, Jim

CIRCE, LORELEI. See: Batman

Circle, Full. See: Donovan, Gary

Circle, The. See: Carroll, Madeleine

Circus! See: Parks, Bert (2)

Circus Boy. See: Corky

Circus Days. See: Roseleigh, Jack

Circus, Frontier. See: Thompson, Colonel Casey

Circus, Mickey of the. See: Mickey

Circus Night. See: Cook, Joe

Circus, Super. See: Kirchener, Claude (2)

Circus Time. See: Winchell, Paul (2)

CIRCUSEVEN JAZZ BAND, THE. See: Kirchener, Claude (1)

Cisco Kid, The. See: Cisco Kid, The

CISCO KID, THE, Latin-American adventurer

PANCHO, his friend and fellow-adventurer
The Cisco Kid (R) (TV) (Adventure)

CISSY. See:
Davis, Uncle Bill
Potter, Tom

CISSY DRUMMOND-RANDOLPH. See: Corbett, Tom (1)

CISSY KING. See: Welk, Lawrence

Cities Service Concert, The. See: Dragonette, Jessica (1)

Cities, The Quiz of Two. See: Fitzmaurice, Michael

Citizen, Mr. See: Edwards, Allyn

CITIZENS, THE SENIOR. See: Kelly, Gene

City, Central. See: Olson, Emily

City, Cimarron. See: Rockford, Matthew

City Desk. See: Winters, Jack

City Detective. See: Grant, Bart

CITY EDITOR. See: Jones, Tom (1)

CITY FOUR, THE ELM. See: Kay, Beatrice

CITY FOUR, THE MAPLE. See: Kelly, Joe (1)

City, Naked. See: Parker, Lieut. Mike

City Playhouse, Radio. See: Collins, Fred (1)

City, Secret. See: Clark, Ben

CITY SLICKERS, THE. See: Jones, Spike (2)

City, The Heart of the. See: Wilson, Steve

City, The Man and the. See:
Alcala, Thomas Jefferson

Civilisation. See: Clark, Lord
Kenneth

CLAGHORN, SENATOR BEAURE-
GARD. See: Allen, Fred

CLAIBORNE, MARJORIE. See:
Trent, Helen

CLAIR, DICK. See:
Jones, Dean
Kelly, Gene

CLAIRE CLAYTON. See: Randolph,
Ellen

CLAIRE, HELEN. See: Twin
Stars, The

CLAIRE LOWELL. See: Hughes,
Chris

Claire, Malcolm. See: Old Witch,
The

CLAIRE, MALCOLM. See: Old
Witch, The

CLAIRE MORTON, DR. See:
Peyton, Martin

CLAIRE TREMAN. See: Dyke,
Charity Amanda

CLAIRE VAN ROON. See: O'Farrell, Packy

CLAIRE, YVONNE. See: Perry,
John

CLAMPETT, JED, newly rich hill-
billy after oil discovered on his
property; now resident of
Beverly Hills, California
GRANNY, his mother
ELLY MAY, his daughter
JETHRO, Elly May's cousin
MILBURN DRYSDALE, the
Clampetts' banker
MRS. DRYSDALE, Drysdale's wife
The Beverly Hillbillies (TV) (Sit-
uation comedy)

Clan, The Amazing Chan and the
Chan. See: Chan

CLANCEY. See: Bolt, Jason

CLANCY. See: Archie

CLANCY, MIKE. See: Keen, Mr.

CLARA
LOU
EM, gossips
Clara, Lou and Em (R) (Serial
drama)

CLARA. See also:
Barton, Clara
Cara
Mouse, Mickey
Varner, Will

CLARA, AUNT. See: Stephens,
Samantha

CLARA BLAKE. See: Trent,
Helen

CLARA GAINES. See: Mickey

CLARA, LADY. See: Noble,
Mary

Clara, Lou and Em. See: Clara

CLARA LUND. See: Keene, Kitty

CLARA POTTS. See: Baines,
Scattergood

CLARA SCHEND. See: Rogers,
Patricia

CLARABELLE HIGGINS. See:
Barclay, Doc

CLARABELL THE CLOWN. See:
Doody, Howdy

CLARENCE. See:
Day, Clarence
Straight, Clarence

CLARENCE J. MUGGINS. See:
Jones, Lorenzo

CLARENCE TIFFINGSTUFFER.
See: Myrt

CLARENCE WELLMAN. See:
Hall, Dr. William Todhunter

CLARIDGE, MISS. See: Harrigan, James, Sr.

CLARISSA CLARKE. See: Hargrave-Scott, Joan

CLARISSA OAKLEY. See: Harum, David

CLARK. See:
Clarke
Clerk
Kent, Clark
Race, Clark

CLARK, BEN, adventurer
Secret City (R) (Mystery/adventure)

CLARK, BUDDY. See:
Bernie, Ben
Faith, Percy
Ross, Lanny

CLARK, CINDY. See: Randolph, Alice

CLARK, DICK (1), moderator of the program (himself)
GUEST MUSICAL GROUPS
GUEST STARS
GUEST DANCERS
American Bandstand (TV)
(Modern music and dancing)

CLARK, DICK (2), moderator of the program (himself)
GUEST MUSICAL GROUPS
GUEST STARS
GUEST DANCERS
The Dick Clark Show (TV)
(Modern music and dancing)

CLARK, DICK (3), moderator of the program (himself)
JACK E. LEONARD, comedian, panelist (himself)
TWO GUEST PANELISTS
GUEST TALENT
BURT FARBER, orchestra leader (himself)
HIS ORCHESTRA
The World of Talent (TV) (Talent contest)

CLARK, DR. ROBBY. See: Johnson, Bess

CLARK, ELLEN. See: James, Nancy

CLARK, EMMETT. See: Jones, Sam

CLARK, EVERETT. See:
Kaye, Danny
Reser, Harry

CLARK, HERBERT. See: Brewster, Joey

CLARK, JACK, quizmaster of the program (himself)
ONE AMATEUR EXPERT
FIVE PROFESSIONAL EXPERTS
AUDIENCE PARTICIPANTS
100 Grand (TV) (Quiz)

CLARK, JEFF. See: Ross, Lanny

CLARK, JEFFREY. See: Hargrave-Scott, Joan

CLARK, JIMMY. See: Erwin, Stu

CLARK, JOYCE. See: Erwin, Stu

CLARK, JUDITH. See: Larimore, Marilyn

CLARK, LARRY. See: Lewis, Dave

CLARK, LEONARD. See: Fairchild, Kay

CLARK, LINDA. See: Johnson, Bess

CLARK, LORD KENNETH, narrator and host of the program (himself)
Civilisation (TV) (History/education)

CLARK, MAHLON. See: Welk, Lawrence

CLARK, MARAINE. See: Cameron, Barry

CLARK, MARTHA. See: Jones, Sam

CLARK, ROY. See:
Crosby, Bing (2)
Owens, Buck

CLARK, SMELLY. See: Gook,
Vic

CLARK, TED. See: Randolph,
Alice

CLARK, THOMAS R. See: Hargrave-Scott, Joan

CLARK, TOM. See: Barclay,
Doc

CLARKE. See also:
Clark
Clerk

CLARKE, ALYCE DRIGGS. See:
Driggs, Karleton King

CLARKE, BOB. See: Driggs,
Karleton King

CLARKE, CLARISSA. See: Hargrave-Scott, Joan

CLARKE, PETER. See: Kennedy,
Carol

CLAUDE. See:
Ballew, Wally
Kirchener, Claude (1) (2)

CLAUDE BRENNER. See: Kelly,
Joe (2)

CLAUDE EUSTACE TEAL, IN-
SPECTOR. See: Templar,
Simon

CLAUDE HORRIBLY. See: Allen,
Steve (2)

CLAUDE PERTWEE. See: Hud-
dles, Ed

CLAUDE THORNHILL. See:
Whiteman, Paul

Claudia. See: Naughton, Claudia

CLAUDIA. See:
Gramus, Bert
Naughton, Claudia

Claudia and David. See: Naughton, Claudia

CLAUDIA BARBOUR ROBERTS
LACEY. See: Barbour, Henry
Wilson

CLAUDIA WILSON. See: Brent,
Dr. Jim

CLAWSON, B.J. See: Slattery,
Jim

CLAY. See:
Bannister, Clay
Carter, James
Culhane, Clay
Hollister, Clay

CLAY BAKER. See: Troy, Adam

CLAY BROWN. See: Sloan, Holly

CLAY COLLIER. See: Little
Orphan Annie

CLAY GRAINGER. See: Virginian,
The

CLAY HOWARD. See: Welk,
Lawrence

CLAY HUNNICUT. See: Miller,
Socrates

CLAY McCORD. See: Fry,
Marshal Simon

CLAY MORGAN. See: Pearson,
Jace

CLAY WARNICK SINGERS, THE.
See: Crosby, Bob (1)

CLAYBORN, HUGH. See: Ames,
Peter

CLAYBORN, JILL. See: Ames,
Peter

CLAYMORE GREGG. See: Muir,
Carolyn

CLAYT. See: Monroe, Clayt

CLAYTON, ANDY. See: Fairchild,
Kay

CLAYTON, BOB (1)
HUGH DOWNS, moderators of
the program (themselves)
MANY GUEST CONTESTANTS
Concentration (TV) (Game)

CLAYTON, BOB (2), moderator of
the program (himself)
MANY CHILDREN CONTESTANTS
Make a Face (TV) (Children's
game)

CLAYTON "BUD" COLLYER. See:
Collyer, Clayton "Bud"
Cullen, Bill (5)
Moore, Garry (5)
Narz, Jack (1)
Parks, Bert (1)

CLAYTON, CAPTAIN. See: Jordan, Joyce

CLAYTON, CLAIRE. See: Randolph, Ellen

CLAYTON HAMILTON. See: Beck,
Jackson

CLAYTON, JAN. See: Harrington, Pat, Jr.

CLAYTON, JED. See: Garrett,
Sam

CLAYTON, MARGIE, teen-age girl
growing up in the 1920s
NORA CLAYTON, her mother
HARVEY CLAYTON, her father
AUNT PHOEBE, her aunt
MAYBELLE JACKSON, her friend
HEYWOOD BOTTS
JOHNNY GREEN, her boy friends
Margie (TV) (Situation comedy)

CLAYTON, PATTI. See: Seymour,
Dan

CLAYTON, PAUL. See: Crosby,
Bob (2)

CLAYTON, TED. See: Randolph,
Ellen

CLEAVER, WARD, head of the
family
JUNE CLEAVER, his wife
WALLY CLEAVER, his elder son
THEODORE "BEAVER" CLEAVER,

his younger son
Leave It to Beaver (TV) (Situation comedy)

CLEM. See: O'Leary, Hannah

CLEM ALLISON, DR. See: Booth,
Martha

CLEM KADIDDLEHOPPER. See:
Junior

CLEMENTINE. See: Johnson,
Bess

CLEMSON, GEORGE. See: Angel,
Gus

CLEMSON, WILMA. See: Angel,
Gus

CLEO. See:
Holiday, Laurel
Miller, Socrates

CLERK. See also:
Clark
Clarke

CLERK, CLIVE. See: Nye, Louis

CLETE. See: Roberts, Clete

CLEVE HARRINGTON. See:
Winters, Evelyn

CLEVES, ANNE OF. See: Henry
VIII, King of England

Cliche Club. See: Allen, Frederick Lewis

CLIFF ARQUETTE. See:
Haymes, Dick
Marshall, Peter
Winters, Jonathan

CLIFF CALDWELL. See: Noble,
Mary

CLIFF EDWARDS. See: Lane,
Richard

CLIFF NORTON. See: Garroway,
Dave (2)

CLIFF SEBASTIAN. See: Dennis,
Liz

CLIFF SOUBIER. See:
First Nighter, Mr.
Thurston, Howard

CLIFFORD. See: Barbour, Henry
Wilson

CLIFFORD, CHIEF. See: Mc-
Cloud, Sam

CLIFFORD FOSTER. See:
Brent, Dr. Jim
Rutledge, Dr. John

CLIFFORD REED, DR. See:
Jordan, Joyce

CLIFFY. See: Kirchener, Claude
(2)

CLIFTON. See: Fadiman, Clifton (1) (2) (3)

CLIFTON DAVIS. See: Moore,
Melba

Clifton Davis Show, The Melba
Moore. See: Moore, Melba

CLIFTON FINNEGAN. See: Archie

Climax. See: Lundigan, Bill (1)

CLINE. See also: Klein

CLINE, CYNTHIA. See: Kelly,
Joe (2)

CLINE, PATSY. See: Ritter, Tex
(1)

CLINE, RUSS. See: Welk,
Lawrence

CLINK. See:
Davis, Red
Klink

CLINT. See: Travis, Clint

CLINT MORLEY. See: Manning,
Portia Blake

CLINTON. See: Judd, Clinton

CLINTON, LARRY. See: Whiteman, Paul

CLIPPER. See: King, Schyler
"Sky"

CLIPPER HAMILTON. See: Ross,
Scott

Cliquot Club Eskimos, The. See:
Reser, Harry

CLIVE CLERK. See: Nye, Louis

Cloak and Dagger. See: Hungarian
Giant, The

Clock, Beat the. See: Narz, Jack
(1)

CLOCK, GRANDFATHER. See:
Kangaroo, Captain

CLOCK KING, THE. See: Batman

CLOCK, NINA. See: Wallet,
Skeezix

CLON. See: Mac

CLOOM, BIDDIE. See: Bolt,
Jason

CLOSE. See: Klose

Closed Doors, Behind. See:
Zacharias, Rear Admiral Ellis
M.

CLOUD, PINK. See: Rango

CLOWN, CLARABELL THE. See:
Doody, Howdy

CLOWN, JOEY THE. See: Corky

Clown, The Magic. See: Bonomo

Club, Animal News. See: Straight,
Clarence

Club, Anniversary. See: Alexander, Ben (2)

Club, Cliche. See: Allen, Frederick Lewis

Club, Don McNeill's Breakfast.
See: McNeill, Don

Club, Eno Crime. See: Dean,
Spencer

Club Eskimos, Cliquot. See:
    Reser, Harry

Club Fifteen. See: Crosby, Bob
    (2)

Club, Marriage. See: MacQuarrie,
    Haven (1)

Club Matinee. See: Moore, Garry
    (1)

Club Oasis. See: Jones, Spike (1)

Club of the Air, The Fishing and
    Hunting. See: Begley, Martin

Club 60. See: James, Dennis (1)

Club, T. V. Sportsman's. See:
    Wylber, Darl

Club, The Breakfast. See: Mc-
    Neill, Don

Club, The Chesterfield Supper.
    See: Como, Perry (1)

Club, The Fish and Hunt. See:
    Bickart, Sanford

Club, The Grouch. See: Les-
    coulie, Jack (2)

Club, The Mickey Mouse. See:
    Dodd, Jimmie

Club, The Saturday Night Swing.
    See: Douglas, Paul

Club, The Stork. See: Hayes,
    Peter Lind (4)

CLUBMEN, THE FOUR. See:
    Kay, Beatrice
    Kaye, Danny

Clue, Two On a. See: Spencer,
    Jeff

Clues, Crime. See: Dean,
    Spencer

CLYDE. See:
    Ballew, Wally
    Beatty, Clyde

Clyde Beatty Show, The. See:

Beatty, Clyde

CLYDE BURKE. See: Cranston,
    Lamont

CLYDE HOUSTON. See: Lawton,
    Lora

CLYDE McCOY. See: Whiteman,
    Paul

CLYDE MARSHALL. See: Harper,
    Linda Emerson

CLYDE, MR. See: Peterson,
    Irma

COACH GREATGUY. See: Daring,
    Dick

COACH HARDY. See: Armstrong,
    Jack

COACH WEISS. See: Hank

COAKLEY. See also: Cokey

COAKLEY, TOM. See: Winchell,
    Walter (1)

Coast-to-Coast On a Bus. See:
    Conductor, The

COATES, ELIZABETH. See:
    Larkin, Jeremy

COATES, PAUL, narrator of the
    program (himself)
    MANY INTERVIEWEES
    MANY ACTORS AND ACTRESSES
    Confidential File (TV) (Crime
    dramatizations)

COBB, BUFF. See: Donald,
    Peter

COBB, HANNIBAL, detective
    Hannibal Cobb (R) (Detective
    drama)

COBB, IRVIN S. See:
    Drew, John
    Old Southern Colonel, The

COBB, MAJOR JOE. See: Savage,
    Brigadier General Frank

COBINA. See:

Hope, Bob (2)
Wright, Cobina

COCA COLA GIRL, THE. See:
Vivian

COCA, IMOGENE. See:
Caesar, Sid (3)
Crosby, Bing (2)

COCHISE. See: Jeffords, Tom

Cochise, The Sheriff of. See:
Morgan, Sheriff

COCHRAN, BILL. See: Shannon,
Joe

COCHRAN, LEE, newspaper
columnist
New York Confidential (TV)
(Adventure)

COCHRAN, PETE. See: Hayes,
Linc

COCHRAN, RON, moderator of the
program (himself)
PANEL OF TEENAGERS
Youth Takes a Stand (TV) (Discussion of current issues)

CODY BRISTOL. See: Burke,
Stoney

COFFEE, DR. DANIEL, pathologist
and laboratory crime solver
DR. MOTILAL MOOKERJI, his
assistant
DORIS HUDSON, his laboratory
technician
LINK, his "rock and roll test
tube washer"
LIEUT. RITTER, captain of
detectives
Diagnosis: Unknown (TV) (Crime
mystery)

Coffee Time, Maxwell House. See:
Morgan, Frank (2)

COGGINS, BIRDIE LEE. See:
Gildersleeve, Throckmorton P.

COHEN, MR. See: Levy, Abie

COHEN, MRS. See: Levy, Abie

COKEY. See:
Ace, Goodman
Coakley

COLBERT, REGINA. See:
Wincholl, John

COLBY, BETTY. See: Blanc,
Mel

COLBY, CATHERINE. See:
Carter, Kathryn

COLBY, JED. See: Favor, Gil

COLBY, JUDGE. See: Carter,
Kathryn

COLBY, JUDGE CARTER. See:
Larimore, Marilyn

COLBY, MERCEDES. See:
Winslow, Don

COLBY, MR. See: Blanc, Mel

COLBY, MRS. CARTER. See:
Larimore, Marilyn

COLBY, TOM. See: Erskine,
Inspector Louis

COLE. See also: Coles

COLE, ALONZO DEAN, author;
host of the program (himself)
OLD NANCY, witch; character
in tale
The Witch's Tale (R) (Drama)

COLE, AMELIA. See: Fuller,
Ward

COLE, DR. TIM. See: Hughes,
Chris

COLE, LOUISE. See: Hughes,
Chris

COLE, NAT "KING," singer and
pianist; star of the program
(himself)
RANDY VAN HORN CHORAL
GROUP
MANY GUEST STARS
NELSON RIDDLE, orchestra
leader (himself)
HIS ORCHESTRA

The Nat "King" Cole Show (TV)
(Music)

COLE, STEPHANIE. See: Hansen,
Dean Eric

COLEMAN. See also: Colman

COLEMAN, CHARLES. See: Moore,
Melba

COLEMAN HAWKINS. See: O'Connor, Father Norman

COLEMAN, MR. See: O'Neill,
Mrs.

COLEMAN, NANCY. See: Arthur,
Jack (2)

COLES. See also: Cole

COLES, RICHARD. See: Carter,
Kathryn

Colgate Comedy Hour, The. See:
Martin, Dean (1)

Colgate Sports Newsreel, Bill
Stern's. See: Stern, Bill

Colgate Sports Newsreel Starring
Bill Stern, The. See: Stern,
Bill

COLIN. See also: Collins

COLIN KIRBY. See: Hargrave-
Scott, Joan

Collect, Detect and. See: Uttal,
Fred (1)

COLLEEN MOORE. See: Story
Lady, The

College Bowl. See: Earle, Robert

College Bowl, The G. E. See:
Earle, Robert

College Merry-Go-Round, The. See:
Sharp, Hal

College, Mrs. G. Goes to. See:
Green, Sarah

College of Musical Knowledge, The.

See:
Ford, Tennessee Ernie (1)
Kay Kyser's Kollege of Musical
Knowledge

College Variety Show, The. See:
Godfrey, Arthur (3)

Collie, Jeff's. See: Lassie

COLLIER. See also: Collyer

COLLIER, CLAY. See: Little
Orphan Annie

COLLIER, TIM
JEFF RYDER
BEN MANFRED
RICCO POCCARI, the Four Just
Men; banded together to correct
injustices
The Four Just Men (TV) (Ad-
venture)

COLLINGWOOD, CHARLES (1),
moderator of the program (himself)
MANY YOUNG STUDENTS
Adventure (TV) (Education)

COLLINGWOOD, CHARLES (2),
host of the program (himself)
MANY ACTORS AND ACTRESSES
Odyssey (TV) (Recreated historical events "concerning Man
and his exploits")

COLLINGWOOD, CHARLES. See
also: Murrow, Edward R. (4)

COLLINS. See also: Colin

COLLINS, BARNABAS, vampire, 2
centuries old
ROGER COLLINS
DAVID COLLINS
QUENTIN COLLINS
ELIZABETH COLLINS STODDARD
CAROLYN STODDARD
WILLIE LOOMIS
MAGGIE EVANS
CHARLES DELAWARE TARE
COUNT PETOFI
T. ELIOT STOKES
JULIA HOFFMAN
JEB HAWKES
JOE HASKELL
CHRIS JENNINGS

AMY JENNINGS
ANGELIQUE
MRS. JOHNSON
DAPHNE
GERARD
PHILIP
SABRINA
ADAM
VICTORIA WINTERS, characters
appearing in the drama
Dark Shadows (TV) (Serial Gothic
drama)

COLLINS, BERT. See: McKenzie,
Captain Craig

COLLINS, BING, onetime musician
and singer turned engineer
ELLIE, his wife
JANICE
JOYCE, his children
WILLY WALTERS, livein handy-
man
The Bing Crosby Show (TV)
(Situation comedy)

COLLINS, BOB, playboy photographer
MARGARET MACDONALD, his
widowed sister
CHUCK MACDONALD, Margaret's
son
SCHULTZIE, his secretary
SHIRLEY SWANSON, blonde model
The Bob Cummings Show (TV)
(Situation comedy) (later re-
released as Love That Bob) (TV)

COLLINS, DR. WADE. See: Tate,
Joanne

COLLINS, DOROTHY. See:
Lanson, Snooky
Ross, Lanny

COLLINS, ELLEN. See: Graham,
Dr. Bob

COLLINS, FRED (1), host of the
program (himself)
MANY GUEST ACTORS AND
ACTRESSES
Radio City Playhouse (R) (Drama)

COLLINS, FRED (2), narrator of
the program (himself)
Wanted (R) (Crime stories)

COLLINS, JANE. See: Davis,

Dr. Althea

COLLINS, JULIE. See: Rutledge,
Dr. John

COLLINS, KIT. See: Peters,
Bill

COLLINS, MR. See:
Hargrave-Scott, Joan
O'Neill, Mrs.

COLLINS, MRS. See: O'Neill,
Mrs.

COLLINS, NICK. See: Trent,
Helen

COLLINS, RAY. See: Welles,
Orson (1) (2)

COLLINS, RICHARD. See: Marie

COLLINS, ROGER. See: Rut-
ledge, Dr. John

COLLINS, TED. See: Smith,
Kate (1) (2)

COLLYER. See also: Collier

COLLYER, CLAYTON "BUD,"
moderator of the program (himself)
MANY CONTESTANTS
Number, Please (TV) (Game)

COLLYER, CLAYTON "BUD."
See also:
Cullen, Bill (5)
Moore, Garry (5)
Narz, Jack (1)
Parks, Bert (1)

COLMAN. See also: Coleman

COLMAN, RONALD. See: Car-
roll, Madeleine

COLON, DAMARIS. See: Mar-
shall, E. G.

COLONEL. See:
Craig, Colonel John B.
Flack, Colonel Humphrey
Glenn, Colonel John
Hogan, Colonel Robert
McCauley, Colonel Edward

MacKenzie, Colonel Alan
MacKenzie, Colonel Ronald S.
March, Colonel
Old Southern Colonel, The
Smith, Colonel Zachary
Stoopnagle, Colonel Lemuel Q.
  (1) (2)
Thompson, Colonel Casey
Turner, Colonel Roscoe

COLONEL BEAMISH. See: Storm,
Lieut.

Colonel, Calvin and the. See:
  Colonel, The

COLONEL CRACKLE. See: Kukla

Colonel Flack. See: Flack,
  Colonel Humphrey

COLONEL FRANCIS WELCH. See:
Barton, Bud

COLONEL GUMM. See: Batman

COLONEL H. NORMAN SCHWARTZ-
KOPF. See: Lord, Phillips H.

COLONEL HALL. See: Bilko,
Sergeant Ernest

COLONEL HARVEY BLACKWELL.
See: McKeever, Cadet Gary

COLONEL HENRY BLAKE, LIEUT.
See: Pierce, Captain Hawkeye

COLONEL LEIGHTON. See: Dyke,
Charity Amanda

Colonel, McKeever and the. See:
  McKeever, Cadet Gary

COLONEL MANNY PRAEGER. See:
Bernie, Ben

Colonel March of Scotland Yard.
  See: March, Colonel

COLONEL, THE, "a foxy fox"
CALVIN, dim-witted bear; both
cartoon characters
Calvin and the Colonel (TV)
(Cartoon)

COLONEL U. CHARLES BARKER.
See: McKay, Judson

COLONNA, JERRY. See: Olsen,
Ole

COLOSSAL MAN. See: Junior

COLT, CHRISTOPHER, gun salesman in the Old West
Colt .45 (TV) (Western)

Colt .45. See: Colt, Christopher

COLT, THATCHER, detective
Thatcher Colt (R) (Detective)

COLTON, KINGSLEY. See:
Halop, Billy

COLTON, LOIS. See: Trent,
Helen

COLTON, WILLIAM, Civil War
hero; resigns his Union commis-
sion, heads West
The Loner (TV) (Western)

COLUMBIA BROADCASTING
SYMPHONY ORCHESTRA, THE.
See: Herrmann, Bernard

Columbo. See: Columbo, Lieut.

COLUMBO, LIEUT., police officer
Columbo (TV) (Crime drama)

COLWELL. See also: Caldwell

COLWELL, TOM. See: O'Malley,
Father Chuck

COMANCHE. See: Straight
Arrow

Combat! See: Hanley, Lieut. Gil

Combat Sergeant. See: Nelson,
Sergeant

COMBS, GEORGE HAMILTON.
See: Cross, Mason

Comedy, Five Star. See: Olsen,
Ole

Comedy Hour, Pat Paulsen's Half
a. See: Paulsen, Pat

Comedy Hour, The A.B.C. (The
Kopykats). See: Little, Rich

Comedy Hour, The Colgate. See:
Martin, Dean (1)

Comedy Hour, The Flintstone. See:
Flintstone, Fred

Comedy Hour, The John Byner.
See: Byner, John (1)

Comedy Hour, The Musical. See:
Vivian

Comedy Hour, The Smothers
Brothers. See: Smothers,
Tom (1)

Comedy Hour, The Sonny and Cher.
See: Bono, Salvatore

Comedy Hour, The Tim Conway.
See: Conway, Tim

Comedy Machine, The Marty Feldman. See: Feldman, Marty

Comedy Theater, The Eddie Cantor.
See: Cantor, Eddie (1)

Comedy Tonight. See: Klein,
Robert

Command, Harbor. See: Baxter,
Captain Ralph

COMMANDER. See:
Hayes, Wing Commander
Talbot, Commander Dan
Wivenhoe, Commander

COMMANDER ADRIAN. See: Morgan, Lieut. Anne

COMMANDER FAIRFAX. See:
Welles, Orson (3)

COMMANDER LEE CRANE. See:
Nelson, Admiral Harriman

COMMANDER VIRGIL STONER,
LIEUT. See: O'Toole, Ensign

Comment! See: Newman, Edwin (1)

Comments, Paul Harvey. See:
Harvey, Paul (1)

COMMISSIONER GORDON, POLICE.
See: Batman

COMMISSIONER WESTON. See:
Cranston, Lamont

Community Sing. See: Jones,
Billy

COMO. See also: Cosmo

COMO, PERRY (1), singer and
entertainer; host of the program
(himself)
DICK EDWARDS
BILL LAWRENCE
KAY STARR
DON CORNELL
MARY ASHWORTH
JO STAFFORD
THE FONTANE SISTERS
THE PIED PIPERS
THE SATISFIERS, vocalists and
vocal groups featured on the
program (themselves)
TED STEELE
FRED WARING
SAMMY KAYE
GLENN MILLER
MITCHELL AYRES
LLOYD SCHAEFER, orchestra
leaders (themselves)
THEIR ORCHESTRAS
MANY GUEST STARS
The Chesterfield Supper Club (R)
(Variety)
THE LOUIS DA PRON DANCERS
THE RAY CHARLES SINGERS
MITCHELL AYRES, orchestra
leader (himself)
HIS ORCHESTRA
MANY GUEST STARS
The Chesterfield Supper Club (TV)
(Variety)

COMO, PERRY (2), singer and
entertainer; host of the program
(himself)
THE RAY CHARLES SINGERS
MITCHELL AYRES, orchestra
leader (himself)
HIS ORCHESTRA
MANY GUEST STARS
The Kraft Music Hall (TV)
(Variety)

COMO, PERRY (3), singer and
entertainer; host of the program
(himself)
THE LOUIS DA PRON DANCERS
THE RAY CHARLES SINGERS

MITCHELL AYRES, orchestra
leader (himself)
HIS ORCHESTRA
MANY GUEST STARS
The Perry Como Show (TV)
(Variety)

COMO, PERRY. See also: Crosby,
Bing (2)

Company, Good. See: Bailey,
F. Lee

Company, The Electric. See:
Cosby, Bill (1)

COMPTON, WALTER
JOHN REED KING
WALTER O'KEEFE
TODD RUSSELL, quizmasters of
the program (themselves)
MANY CONTESTANTS
Double or Nothing (R) (Quiz)

COMSTOCK, ELOISE. See: Baines,
Scattergood

COMSTOCK, WILTON. See:
Graham, Dr. Bob

Concentration. See: Clayton, Bob
(1)

Concerning Miss Marlowe. See:
Marlowe, Miss

Concert in Rhythm. See: Scott,
Raymond

Concert, The Cities Service.
See: Dragonette, Jessica (1)

Concerts, Young People's. See:
Bernstein, Leonard

CONCHITA SHAPIRO. See:
Vallee, Rudy (2)

CONDUCTOR, THE
THE LADY NEXT DOOR
MUMSY PIG, make trip on bus
MANY CHILD ACTORS AND
ACTRESSES
Coast-to-Coast On a Bus (R)
(Children's program)

Conference, Young People's. See:
Poling, Rev. Daniel

Confession. See: Wyatt, Jack

Confidential File. See: Coates,
Paul

Confidential, New York. See:
Cochran, Lee

Confidentially Yours. See: Hale,
Arthur

CONKLIN, HARRIET. See:
Brooks, Connie

CONKLIN, OSGOOD. See:
Brooks, Connie

CONKLING, DONNA DRIGGS. See:
Driggs, Karleton King

CONKLING, JIM. See: Driggs,
Karleton King

CONLEY. See: Wright, Conley

CONLON, PATRICK. See: Kelly,
Joe (2)

CONLON, SHEILA. See: Kelly,
Joe (2)

CONNECTICUT YANKEES OR-
CHESTRA, THE. See: Vallee,
Rudy (2) (3)

CONNEE. See also: Connie

CONNEE BOSWELL. See: Crosby,
Bing (3)

CONNELL, JANE. See: Caesar,
Sid (1)

CONNIE. See:
Barclay, Doc
Brooks, Connie
Connee
Lee, Terry
Nipper
Partridge, Connie
Vance, Connie

CONNIE FRANCIS. See:
Edwards, Ralph (1)
Rodgers, Jimmie

CONNIE GARRETT. See: Redigo,
Jim (1)

CONNIE, JANIE AND.   See: Kelly,
Joe (1)

CONNIE LOOMIS.   See: Sterling,
Vanessa Dale

CONNIE RICKARD.   See: Davis,
Red

CONNIE RUSSELL.   See: Garroway,
Dave (2) (3)

CONNOLLY.   See: Davis, Joan
Field

CONNOLLY, PEGGY.   See:
Kovacs, Ernie (1)

CONNOR, NADINE.   See:
Henry, Captain
Jolson, Al

CONNORS, MIKE (himself); portrays nameless police undercover
agent
Tightrope! (Crime drama)

CONNORS, NANCY, moderator of
the program (herself)
MANY GUEST CELEBRITY
PANELISTS
Leave It to the Girls (TV) (Panel
game)

CONOVER, DICK.   See: Rogers,
Patricia

Conquest.   See: Sevareid, Eric

CONRAD.   See:
Conried
Kenrad
Konrad
Nagel, Conrad

CONRAD, CAROL "CHICHI."   See:
Solomon, David

CONRAD, JIM, manager of San
Francisco International Airport
SUZIE, his daughter
JUNE, his secretary
BOB HATTEN, chief of airport
security
Four In One: San Francisco Inter-
national Airport (TV) (Drama)

CONRAD, NELLIE.   See: Solomon,
David

CONRAD THIBAULT.   See: Henry,
Captain

CONRIED.   See also:
Conrad
Kenrad
Konrad

CONRIED, HANS.   See: Kovacs,
Ernie (1)

CONROY, DENNIS.   See: Noble,
Mary

CONROY, PHIL, undercover intel-
ligence agent for U.S. Treasury
Department's Intelligence Bureau
Special Agent 7 (TV) (Crime
drama) (also known as S.A. 7)
(TV)

Consequences, Truth or.   See:
Edwards, Ralph (3)

CONSIDER, COUSIN.   See: Barbour, Henry Wilson

CONSIDINE, BOB.   See:
Daly, John (4)
Lescoulie, Jack (4)

CONSTABLE.   See: Scott, Constable Frank

CONSTANCE.   See:
Barbour, Henry Wilson
Caine, Frank
Grimm, Arnold

CONSTANCE BENNETT.   See:
Landi, Elissa

CONSTANCE MACKENZIE CARSON.
See: Peyton, Martin

CONSTANCE WAKEFIELD.   See:
Nelson, Carolyn Kramer

CONSUELO LOPEZ.   See: Welby,
Dr. Marcus

Contact.   See: Herman, Bernie

CONTE, JOHN.   See: Francis,
Arlene (3)

Contented Hour, The.   See: Faith,
Percy

Contented Hour, The Carnation. See:
  Faith, Percy

CONTESSA DI CONTINI, CAROLINE.
  See: Rule, Harry

Contest, The Miss America. See:
  Parks, Bert (4)

CONTINENTALS QUARTET, THE.
  See: Faith, Percy

CONTINI, CAROLINE, CONTESSA DI.
  See: Rule, Harry

Convoy. See: Talbot, Commander
  Dan

CONWAY, BOBBY, teenage song
  writer
  JENNIFER, his young sister
  LIONEL POINDEXTER, teenage
  lyric writer
  RITA SIMON, landlady
  RUDY, Rita's boy friend; police-
  man
  Getting Together (TV) (Situation
  comedy)

CONWAY, JEFF. See: Burns,
  George (3)

CONWAY, KATHLEEN. See:
  Randolph, Ellen

CONWAY, MEREDITH. See:
  Meredith, Charles

CONWAY, MICHAEL. See: Kelly,
  Kitty

CONWAY, MR. See: Larimore,
  Marilyn

CONWAY, PATRICK. See: Kelly,
  Kitty

CONWAY, TIM, comedian, star of
  the program (himself)
  ART METRANO
  BRUCE BELLAND
  DAVID SOMERVILLE
  SALLY STRUTHERS
  McLEAN STEVENSON
  BONNIE BOLAND, entertainers
  appearing on the program (them-
  selves)
  MANY GUEST STARS

The Tim Conway Comedy Hour
(TV) (Variety)

CONWAY, TIM. See also: Shawn,
  Dick

CONWAY TWITTY. See: Owens,
  Buck

CONWAY, WENDY. See: Burns,
  George (3)

"COO COO" KILEY, PHIL. See:
  Kirchener, Claude (1)

COOGAN, JACKIE
  ARTHUR Q. BRYAN
  LURENE TUTTLE, featured on
  the program (themselves)
  BILLY MAY, orchestra leader
  (himself)
  HIS ORCHESTRA
  Forever Ernest (R) (Situation
  comedy)

COOK, ARTHUR. See: Rogers,
  Patricia

COOK, JOE, comedian, star of the
  program (himself)
  TIM AND IRENE, comedy team
  PEG LA CENTRA
  LUCY MONROE, singers (them-
  selves)
  MANY GUEST STARS
  Circus Night (R) (Variety)

COOK, MARGIE. See: Hargrave-
  Scott, Joan

COOK, PHIL, singer, guitarist
  and conversationalist, featured
  on the program (himself)
  Phil Cook (R) (Music, news,
  conversation)

COOK, SKIPPER. See: Sharp,
  Hal

COOKE, ALISTAIRE (1), narrator
  of the program (himself)
  JUDE FAWLEY
  SUE BRIDEHEAD
  PHILLOTSON
  ARABELLA DONN
  AUNT DRUSILLA
  DAWLISH
  MRS. EDLIN, characters appear-

ing in the drama
Jude the Obscure (TV) (Dramatization of novel)

COOKE, ALISTAIRE (2), host of the
program (himself)
MANY DISTINGUISHED PER-
FORMERS
Omnibus (TV) (Cultural dramas,
music, ballet and similar presentations)

COOKIE. See: Bumstead, Blondie

COOKIE CHRISTOPHER. See:
Karr, Mike

COOKIE FAIRCHILD. See: Cantor,
Eddie (2)

COOKIE MONSTER, THE
BIG BIRD
SPELL-A-PHONE
WALKING LETTERS
ERNIE, muppet
BERT, muppet, characters appear-
ing on the program
CAROL BURNETT
JIM NABORS
PAT PAULSEN
BILL COSBY
JAMES EARL JONES
LORNE GREEN
MICHAEL LANDON
DAN BLOCKER
OTHERS, guests appearing on the
program (themselves)
GORDON
SUSAN
BOB
MR. HOOPER, hosts of the pro-
gram (themselves)
Sesame Street (TV) (Children's
education)

COOKIE THE SAILOR. See:
Junior

Cooking Thing, Mike Roy's. See:
Roy, Mike

COOKS, NAOMI. See: Kelly,
Joe (2)

Cool Million. See: Keyes, Jefferson

COOLEY, MEL. See: Petrie, Rob

COOLIDGE, PHILLIP. See:
Manning, Portia Blake

COON, DR. CARLETON. See:
Rainey, Dr. Froelich

COON, TY. See: Dawg, Deputy

COOPER. See also: Krupa

COOPER, ANN, character appearing in the drama
Saturday's Child (R) (Serial
drama)

COOPER, BETTY. See: Andrews,
Archie

COOPER, CHAD. See: Parmalee,
Ranger Captain

COOPER, DICK, meteorologist
PENNY COOPER, his wife; newly-
weds living with Penny's parents
BARNEY HOGAN, Penny's father
MILDRED HOGAN, Penny's
mother
CHARLEY HACKETT, Penny's
grandfather
LOVEY HACKETT, Penny's
grandmother
One Happy Family (TV) (Family
situation comedy)

COOPER, GABE. See: Boone,
Daniel

COOPER, HARRIET. See: Batman

COOPER, LAURA. See: Hillman,
India

COOPER, LIZ, wife
GEORGE, her husband
My Favorite Husband (R) (TV)
(Situation comedy)
KATIE, maid
RUDOLPH ATTERBURY, friend
of the Coopers
My Favorite Husband (R)
CORY, bachelor friend of the
Coopers
My Favorite Husband (TV)

COOPER, REX. See: Hillman,
India

COOPER SMITH. See: Adams,

Major Seth

COOPER, TONY. See: Hillman,
India

COOPERSMITH, DULCEY. See:
Crown, Jim

COOTER, UNCLE. See: Smith,
Eugene

COP. See also: Copp

COP, THE, rookie policeman,
acquired magical powers by
wearing a black hood
THE GIRL REPORTER, newspaper
woman
The Black Hood (R) (Crime adventure)

COPELAND, ALAN. See:
Lanson, Snooky
Nye, Louis

COPP. See also: Cop

COPP, DR. See: Malone, Dr.
Jerry

COPS. See: Kops

Copycats, The. See: Kopykats, The.
(The A. B. C. Comedy Hour)

CORA. See: Jackson, Martha

CORA DITHERS. See: Bumstead,
Blondie

CORA LEE SIMPSON. See: Davis,
Dr. Althea

CORBETT, JEFF. See: Grimm,
Arnold

CORBETT, TOM (1), widower;
managing director of the magazine
"Tomorrow"
EDDIE, his 8-year-old son
MRS. LIVINGSTON, his Japanese
housekeeper
TINA RICKLES, his secretary
CISSY DRUMMOND-RANDOLPH,
his employer
NORMAN, his employee; art
director on magazine
The Courtship of Eddie's Father

(TV) (Situation comedy)

CORBETT, TOM (2)
ASTRO
T. J. THISTLE, space cadets
Tom Corbett, Space Cadet (TV)
(Children) (also known as Space
Cadet) (TV)

CORCORAN, BETTY (CORKY).
See: Karr, Mike

CORD, gunslinger; undercover
agent for U. S. Cavalry
CAPTAIN ZACHARY WINGATE,
U. S. Cavalry officer
PICO McGUIRE
BILLY URCHIN
AMBER HOLLISTER, friends of
Cord
Gunslinger (TV) (Western)

CORD. See also: Card

CORD, HANNAH. See:
Hughes, Chris
Peyton, Martin

CORD, STEVEN. See: Peyton,
Martin

CORDDRY, CHARLES. See:
MacNeil, Robert

CORDELL, CARL, quizmaster of
the program (himself)
MANY AUDIENCE CONTESTANTS
Lucky Partners (TV) (Quiz)

CORDONA, INSPECTOR. See:
Cranston, Lamont

CORELLI, DR. JOE. See:
Sterling, Vanessa Dale

CORELLI, VIC. See: Ames,
Peter

COREY. See:
Baker, Julia
Corie
Cory

COREY, DAVE. See: Howard,
Glenn

COREY, DON
JED SILLS, owners and operators

of the investigating firm of Checkmate, Inc.
PROFESSOR CARL HYATT, their
consultant; former professor of
criminology
Checkmate (TV) (Detective drama)

COREY, EARL, White bounty hunter;
former slave owner
DAVID JEMAL, Negro bounty
hunter; former slave
The Outcasts (TV) (Western)

COREY, JILL. See:
Lanson, Snooky
Lewis, Robert Q. (2)

COREY LEHMAN. See: Hansen,
Dean Eric

COREY STUART. See: Lassie

CORIE. See:
Bratter, Paul
Corey
Cory

CORINNE. See: Horton, Dot

CORINNE TEMPLETON. See:
Kelly, Joe (2)

CORKIN, FLIP. See: Lee,
Terry

CORKY, twelve-year-old boy
attached to circus
BIG TIM CHAMPION, owner of
the circus
JOEY THE CLOWN, Corky's
friend
Circus Boy (TV) (Circus adventure)

CORKY (BETTY CORCORAN). See:
Karr, Mike

CORLIS, ADELE. See: Brent,
Dr. Jim

CORLISS. See: Archer, Corliss

Corliss Archer, Meet. See:
Archer, Corliss

CORNELIA SIMMONS. See: Tate,
Joanne

CORNELIUS CALLAHAN, TOUGH
GUY. See: Kaltenmeyer,
Professor August, D. U. N.

CORNELIUS PORTER. See:
Wayne, Ruth Evans

CORNELIUS TRUMBULL, SER-
GEANT. See: Spencer, Jeff

CORNELL. See also: Cornwell

CORNELL, DON. See: Como,
Perry (1)

Corner Bar, The. See: Grant,
Harry

CORNETT. See also: Coronet

CORNETT, ALICE. See: Carlisle,
Kitty

CORNFELDER, THADDEUS. See:
Myrt

CORNTASSLE, JOE. See:
Little Orphan Annie

CORNWELL. See also: Cornell

CORNWELL, DON. See: Burton,
Terry

Coronado 9. See: Adams, Don

CORONET. See also: Cornett

Coronet Blue. See: Alden,
Michael

CORONET BLUE. See: Alden,
Michael

CORPORAL. See: Taylor,
Corporal Steve

CORPORAL AGARN. See: Par-
menter, Captain Wilton

CORPORAL LEFKOWITZ. See:
McKay, Judson

CORPORAL RADAR O'REILLY.
See: Pierce, Captain Hawkeye

Correction, Please. See: Mc-
Williams, Jim

CORRESPONDENT. See: Foreign
Correspondent, The

CORSO, DETECTIVE JOHNNY.
See: Haines, Lieut. Mike

CORT. See also:
Curt
Kurt

CORT RYKER. See: Scott,
Captain

CORTLAND, STEVE. See: Johnson, Bess

CORWIN TUTTLE. See: Sharp,
Hal

CORY. See:
Cooper, Liz
Corey
Corie

COSBY. See also: Crosby

COSBY, BILL (1)
RITA MORENO
JUDY GRAUBART
LEE CHAMBERLIN
MORGAN FREEMAN
SKIP HINNANT, actors, actresses
and entertainers appearing on the
program (themselves)
JULIA GROWNUP, character por-
trayed by Judy Graubart
MADAME ROSALIE, fortune
teller
GLADYS GLOWWORM, characters
portrayed by Lee Chamberlin
EASY RIDER
MEL MOUNDS, characters por-
trayed by Morgan Freeman
FARGO NORTH, DECODER
NORMAN NEAT, MAN ON THE
STREET, characters portrayed
by Skip Hinnant
The Electric Company (TV)
(Children's educational program)

COSBY, BILL (2), comedian and
entertainer; star of the program
(himself)
QUINCY JONES, musical director
(himself)
LOLA FALANA
SUSAN TOLSKY
FOSTER BROOKS

OSCAR DeGRUY, entertainers
appearing on the program (them-
selves)
MANY GUEST STARS
THE DON McKAYLE DANCERS
The New Bill Cosby Show (TV)
(Comedy/variety)

COSBY, BILL (3), host of the pro-
gram (himself)
FAT ALBERT
HAROLD
DONALD
MUSHMOUTH
RUSSELL
BILL
ERNIE
RUDY, young Black children;
all cartoon characters
Fat Albert and the Cosby Kids
(TV) (Cartoon/education)

COSBY, BILL. See also: Cookie
Monster, The

Cosby Kids, Fat Albert and the.
See: Cosby, Bill (3)

COSELL, HOWARD. See:
Jackson, Keith (2)
McKay, Jim (1)

COSMO. See:
Como
Noble, Mary
Topper, Cosmo

Cosmopolitan, Hotel. See: Woods,
Donald

Costello, Abbott and. See: Abbott,
Bud (1)

COSTELLO, FRED. See: Grant,
Harry

COSTELLO, LOU. See:
Abbott, Bud (1) (2)
Martin, Dean (1)

Costello Program, The Abbott and.
See: Abbott, Bud (2)

COTSWORTH, STAATS. See:
Welles, Orson (2)

Cottage, The Magic. See:
Meikle, Pat

COTTEN, JOSEPH (1), narrator of
the program (himself)
FILM CLIPS OF OLD MOTION
PICTURES
Hollywood and the Stars (TV)
(Old motion picture discussion)

COTTEN, JOSEPH (2), actor; host
of the program (himself)
MANY ACTORS AND ACTRESSES
On Trial (TV) (Dramatizations
of famous trials)

COTTEN, JOSEPH. See also:
Welles, Orson (1) (2)

COTTER, DR. JIM. See: Dawson,
Rosemary

Coty Playgirl, The. See: Bordoni,
Irene

COUGHLIN, FATHER CHARLES
EDWARD, Catholic priest and
political commentator (himself)
Father Coughlin (R) (Commentary)

COULTER, ROBERT. See: Williams,
Emily

COUNCIL, ELIZABETH. See:
Roseleigh, Jack

Counselor at Law, Owen Marshall.
See: Marshall, Owen

COUNSELOR SPIFFY. See: Wivenhoe, Commander

COUNT. See:
Basie, Count
Monte Cristo, The Count of
Von Luckner, Count Felix

COUNT BASIE. See:
Basie, Count
O'Connor, Father Norman
Whiteman, Paul

COUNT BENCHLEY BOTSFORD.
See: Canova, Judy

Count of Monte Cristo, The. See:
Monte Cristo, The Count of

COUNT PETOFI. See: Collins,
Barnabas

Count Von Luckner's Adventures.
See: Von Luckner, Count
Felix

Counted, Stand Up and Be. See:
Russell, Bob

Counterspy. See: Harding, David

Counterspy, David Harding. See:
Harding, David

Counterthrust. See: Cane, Vic

COUNTESS FLORENZE. See:
Sunday

Country Doctor, The. See:
Country Doctor, The

COUNTRY DOCTOR, THE, physician
The Country Doctor (R) (Serial
drama)

COUNTRY LADS, THE. See:
Dean, Jimmy
Hamilton, George

Country Show. See: Pierce, Webb

Country, The House in the. See:
Husband

Country, The Wide. See: Guthrie,
Mitch

County, Cade's. See: Cade, Sam

County Fair. See: Elliott, Win
(1)

County Seat. See: Hackett, Doc

Couple Next Door, The. See:
Soule, Olan (1)

COUPLE, THE BLACK. See:
Kelly, Gene

COUPLE, THE BLUE-COLLAR.
See: Kelly, Gene

Couple, The Odd. See: Ungar,
Felix

COUPLES, MARRIED ON THE
PROGRAM. See: Nelson,
John

COURAGE. See: Bizarre, Benita

Courage, Woman of. See: Jackson,
Martha

Courageous, Madame. See: Craine,
Betty

Court, A. L. Alexander's Good Will.
See: Alexander, A. L. (2)

Court, Divorce. See: Judge (1)

Court, Night. See: Judge (2)

Court of Honor, Radio's. See:
Towne, Don

Court of Human Relations, The.
See: Alexander, A. L. (3)

Court of Last Resort, The. See:
Larsen, Sam

Court of Missing Heirs, The.
See: Waters, Jim

Court, Traffic. See: Jones, Edgar
Allan, Jr.

COURTLEIGH, OLIVE. See: Dyke,
Charity Amanda

COURTLEIGH, WALTER. See:
Dyke, Charity Amanda

Courtmartial. See: Young, Captain
David

COURTNEY, DIANE. See: Cross,
Milton (1)

COURTNEY, GROVER. See: Farrell, David

COURTNEY LEE. See: Jordan,
Joyce

Courtship of Eddie's Father, The.
See: Corbett, Tom (1)

COUSIN ALICE. See: Jones, Sam

Cousin Bill, Maud and. See: Maud

COUSIN CASSIE. See: Old Ranger,
The

COUSIN CONSIDER. See: Barbour,
Henry Wilson

COUSIN ITT. See: Addams,
Gomez

COUSIN MINNIE PEARL. See:
Owens, Buck
Solemn Old Judge, The

COUSTEAU, JACQUES, naturalist
and oceanographer, narrator of
the program (himself)
ROD SERLING, co-narrator of
the program (himself)
The Undersea World of Jacques
Cousteau (TV) (Science)

COWAN, THOMAS
RED BARBER
JIM BRITT
GRAHAM McNAMEE
QUIN RYAN
GRANTLAND RICE
BOB ELSON
MEL ALLEN
BILL SLATER, sports announcers
officiating at the broadcasts
(themselves)
The World Series (R) (Sports)
(Baseball)

COWBOY, DEADEYE THE. See:
Junior

Cowboy in Africa. See: Hayes,
Wing Commander

COWBOY, THE LONESOME. See:
Old Ranger, The

Cowboy Theater. See: Hall,
Monty (1)

COWBOYS, KING OF THE. See:
Rogers, Roy

COWL, JANE. See: Kaye, Danny

COX, ROSETTA. See: Chidsey,
Jackie

COX, SALLIE BELLE. See:
Weems, Ambrose J.

COX, WALLY. See: Marshall,
Peter

COY, WALTER, narrator of the
program (himself)
MANY ACTORS AND ACTRESSES
Frontier (TV) (Western drama)

CRABBE, GEORGE. See: Marlin,
Mary

CRABTREE, DAVE, lawyer, "whose
late mother returns to him in the
form of a 1928 Porter touring
car"
THE CAR, speaks only to her son
BARBARA, Dave's wife
RANDY
CINDY, his children
CAPTAIN MANZINI, collector of
old cars
My Mother the Car (TV) (Comedy)

CRACHET, STRINGBEAN. See:
Walt, Captain

CRACKER. See: Gaddis, Cracker

CRACKERBY, O. K. , Oklahoma
billionaire; "the richest man in
the world"
CYNTHIA
O. K. , JR.
HOBART, his children
ST. JOHN QUINCY, tutor to his
children
O. K. Crackerby! (TV) (Comedy)

CRACKLE, COLONEL. See: Kukla

CRAIG. See:
Carter, Lucy
Garrison, Lieut. Craig
McKenzie, Captain Craig
Stirling, Craig

CRAIG, ALICE. See: Harding,
Karen Adams

CRAIG, ALVIN. See: Webster,
Martha

CRAIG BULLARD. See: Gildersleeve, Throckmorton P.

CRAIG, COLONEL JOHN B. , host
of the program (himself)
MANY GUEST NARRATORS
Expedition (TV) (Exploration/
documentary)

CRAIG, DR. DAVID. See: Hunter,
Dr. Paul

CRAIG, DR. JAMES. See: Walleck, Meredith

CRAIG, DR. JANET. See: Carson, Uncle Joe

CRAIG, DR. JANICE. See: Walleck, Meredith

CRAIG, DR. OWEN. See: Kennedy, Carol

CRAIG EARL. See: Professor
Quiz

CRAIG, HAROLD. See: Barry,
Jack (9)

CRAIG, KENNETH. See: Harding,
Karen Adams

CRAIG, LUCY. See: Webster,
Martha

CRAIG, RICHARD. See: Webster,
Martha

CRAIG, RUTH. See:
Harding, Karen Adams
Rutledge, Dr. John

CRAIG, VIRGINIA. See: Webster,
Martha

CRAIG, WINFIELD. See: Webster, Martha

CRAINE. See also: Crane

CRAINE, BETTY, divorcée with
family to raise
HER FAMILY
Madame Courageous (R) (Serial
drama)

CRAMER. See: Kramer

CRANDALL BOONE. See: Harding,
Karen Adams

CRANDALL, EDITH. See: Larimore, Marilyn

CRANDALL, GARY. See: Kennedy,
Carol

CRANDALL, JACK. See: Larimore, Marilyn

CRANDALL, LARRY. See: Boyd,
Tom

CRANE. See also: Craine

CRANE, BETTY, newlywed
JERRY, her husband
HARRY MILLIKEN, her next door
neighbor
HELEN MILLIKEN, wife of Harry
The Imogene Coca Show (TV)
(Comedy)

CRANE, BOB. See: Carter,
Kathryn

CRANE, COMMANDER LEE. See:
Nelson, Admiral Harriman

CRANE, DICK. See: Carter,
Kathryn

CRANE, GENE. See: Sterling,
Jack

CRANE, KAY. See: Carter,
Kathryn

CRANE, LES, host of the program
(himself)
MANY GUESTS
The Les Crane Show (TV)
(Variety/discussion)

CRANE, MARIAN. See: Alcala,
Thomas Jefferson

CRANE, MATT. See: Garrett,
Susan

CRANMER, ARCHBISHOP THOMAS.
See: Henry VIII, King of England

CRANSTON, LAMONT (The Shadow),
wealthy young man about town
and crime fighter, has "the hyp-
notic power to cloud men's minds
so they cannot see him"
MARGO LANE, his friend and
companion
CLYDE BURKE, reporter
COMMISSIONER WESTON
INSPECTOR CORDONA, police
officials
MOE SHREVNITZ (Shrevie), cab

driver
The Shadow (R) (Mystery drama)

CRAVENS, DICK. See: Kelly, Joe
(2)

CRAWFORD, BRUCE. See:
Fraser, Ben

CRAWFORD, DAVID. See: Malone,
Dr. Jerry

CRAWFORD, DR. SEWALL. See:
Malone, Dr. Jerry

CRAWFORD, LUCILLE. See:
Malone, Dr. Jerry

CRAWFORD, MRS. See:
Barrett, Timothy "Spud"
Hooton, Babs

CRAWFORD, RONNIE. See: Barrett, Timothy "Spud"

CRAYLEY, BARBARA. See:
Marlin, Mary

CRAYON, PROFESSOR. See:
Green, Sarah

CRAYTHORNE, TOM. See:
Sterling, Vanessa Dale

CRAZY CAT. See: Parmenter,
Captain Wilton

CRAZY GUGGENHEIM. See:
Gleason, Jackie (2)

CRAZY HORSE. See: Custer,
George Armstrong

Creative Person, The. See:
Baez, Joan

CREED, DONNA. See: Soule,
Olan (1)

CRIBBINS, BERNARD. See:
Doonican, Val

CRICKET BLAKE. See: Steele,
Tracy

Crier, The Town. See: Woollcott,
Alexander

CRIER, THE TOWN. See: Woollcott,
Alexander

CRIERS, THE TOWN. See: Kyser,
Kay

Crime and Punishment. See:
Roberts, Clete

Crime Club, Eno. See: Dean,
Spencer

Crime Clues. See: Dean, Spencer

Crime Doctor. See: Ordway, Dr.
Benjamin

Crime, I Deal in. See: Gargan,
William (1)

Crime, Man Against. See: Barnett,
Mike

Crime Photographer, Casey. See:
Casey

CRIME, THE NAPOLEON OF. See:
Holmes, Sherlock

Crisis, Men in. See: O'Brien,
Edmond

Critics, The Author Meets the.
See: Gray, Barry (1)

CROCKER, BETTY, homemaking
and cooking expert
Time for Betty Crocker (R)
(Cooking)

CROCKER, HILDA. See: Porter,
Pete

CROCKETT, JAN. See: Hamilton,
George

CROCODILE, THE. See: Pan,
Peter

CROFT, BARBARA. See: Allen,
Jimmie

CROFT, DENNIS. See: Logan,
Shirley

CROFT, JONATHAN
MR. ARCANE
VANESSA SMITH, criminologists

The Most Deadly Game (TV)
(Crime adventure) (formerly
known as Zigzag) (TV)

CROMIE, BOB, columnist; host of
the program (himself)
MANY GUEST AUTHORS
Book Beat (TV) (Literary discussion)

CROMWELL, THOMAS. See:
Henry VIII, King of England

CRONE, GENERAL. See: Mc-
Cluskey, Mona

CRONEN. See also: Cronyn

CRONEN, LOIS. See: Hutton,
Ina Ray

CRONKITE, WALTER (1), newscaster, commentator of the
program (himself)
Air Power (TV) (World War II
documentary)

CRONKITE, WALTER (2), newscaster, narrator of the program
(himself)
ERIC SEVAREID, co-narrator
(himself)
The C.B.S. Evening News With
Walter Cronkite (TV) (News)

CRONKITE, WALTER (3), news-
caster; narrator of the program
(himself)
MANY INTERVIEWEES
The Twentieth Century (TV)
(Current events)

CRONKITE, WALTER (4), newscaster, narrator of the program
(himself)
The 21st Century (TV) (Prog-
nostications of the future)

CRONKITE, WALTER (5), newscaster featured on the program
(himself)
Walter Cronkite Reporting (R)
(News)

CRONKITE, WALTER (6), newscaster, host of the program
(himself)
VARIOUS TELEVISION

ANNOUNCERS AND INTERVIEW-
ERS
GUEST ACTORS AND ACTRESSES
You Are There (TV) (Historical
drama)

CRONYN. See also: Cronen

CRONYN, HUME. See: Arthur,
Jack (2)

CROOKE, LENNIE
GEORGE ROBINSON, bumbling
police detectives
CAPTAIN ANDREWS, their precinct captain
SERGEANT HIGGENBOTTOM,
police officer
The Partners (TV) (Crime
comedy)

CROOKS, RICHARD. See: Barlow,
Howard

CROSBY. See also: Cosby

CROSBY, BING (1), singer, actor
and star of the program (himself)
JOHN SCOTT TROTTER, orchestra
leader (himself)
HIS ORCHESTRA
MANY GUEST STARS
The Bing Crosby Show (R) (Music /
variety)

CROSBY, BING (2)
GEORGE GOBEL
PHIL HARRIS
ALICE FAYE
TONY MARTIN
CYD CHARISSE
PHYLLIS DILLER
DIAHANN CARROLL
SID CAESAR
IMOGENE COCA
DIANA ROSS
ENGELBERT HUMPERDINCK
VAN JOHNSON
DON ADAMS
RAY BOLGER
GENE BARRY
DONALD O'CONNOR
PHIL SILVERS
JACK BENNY
MILTON BERLE
PERRY COMO
STEVE LAWRENCE

EYDIE GORME
ROY ROGERS
DALE EVANS
SAMMY DAVIS, JR.
BOBBIE GENTRY
JOHN HARTFORD
ROY CLARK
MANY OTHERS, singers, dancers
and entertainers; hosts and
hostesses of the program (them-
selves)
MANY GUEST STARS
MITCHELL AYRES, orchestra
leader
HIS ORCHESTRA
The Hollywood Palace (TV)
(Variety)

CROSBY, BING (3)
BOB BURNS
GEORGE MURPHY
JERRY LESTER
VICTOR BORGE
MARY MARTIN
CONNEE BOSWELL
PEGGY LEE
THE MUSIC MAIDS AND HAL
AL JOLSON
RAMONA
JOHNNY MERCER
OSCAR LEVANT, singers,
comedians and musicians fea-
tured on the program (them-
selves)
JACK TEAGARDEN
TOMMY DORSEY
JIMMY DORSEY
JOE VENUTI
ROY BARGY, orchestra leaders
(themselves)
THEIR ORCHESTRAS
The Kraft Music Hall (R)
(Variety)

CROSBY, BOB (1), orchestra lead-
er and singer, featured on the
program (himself)
BOB CROSBY'S BOBCATS, swing
orchestra, also featured on the
program
The Bob Crosby Show (R) (TV)
CAROL RICHARDS
JOAN O'BRIEN
GRETCHEN WYLER, vocalists
(themselves)
THE CLAY WARNICK SINGERS,
vocal group
EMMETT KELLY, clown (himself)

THE MODERNAIRES, vocal group
CARL HOFF, orchestra leader
(himself)
HIS ORCHESTRA
The Bob Crosby Show (TV) (Music/
variety)

CROSBY, BOB (2), orchestra leader
and singer, featured on the pro-
gram (himself)
MARGARET WHITING
PAUL CLAYTON
JO STAFFORD
EVELYN KNIGHT
THE ANDREWS SISTERS
THE MODERNAIRES, vocalists
and vocal groups featured on the
program (themselves)
BOB CROSBY'S BOBCATS,
orchestra
JERRY GRAY, orchestra leader
(himself)
HIS ORCHESTRA
MANY GUEST STARS
Club Fifteen (R) (Music/variety)

CROSBY, BOB (3), host and com-
mentator of the program (him-
self)
MANY PROMINENT PROFES-
SIONAL GOLFERS
World Championship Golf (TV)
(Sports)

CROSBY, BOB. See also:
Benny, Jack
Whiteman, Paul

CROSBY, GARY. See: Jones,
Jack

CROSBY, JOHN, radio and tele-
vision columnist; host of the pro-
gram (himself)
PIPER LAURIE, actress, fea-
tured on the program (herself)
MANY PROMINENT ACTORS AND
ACTRESSES
The Seven Lively Arts (TV)
(Dramas pertaining to major forms
of entertainment) (later re-
released under the title of Spring
Festival) (TV)

CROSBY, NORM. See: Diller,
Phyllis

CROSS. See also: Gross

CROSS, MASON, moderator of the
program (himself)
DAVID BROEKMAN
ELOISE McELHONE
JOHN LARDNER
GEORGE HAMILTON COMBS
LEON JANNEY, panelists on the
program (themselves)
Think Fast (R) (Panel quiz)

CROSS, MILTON (1)
GENE HAMILTON, commentators
on the program (themselves)
PAUL LAVALLE
HENRY LEVINE, orchestra
leaders, featured on the pro-
gram (themselves)
THEIR ORCHESTRAS
DR. GIACOMO, character por-
trayed by Jack McCarthy
DIANE COURTNEY
LENA HORNE
JANE PICKENS
DINAH SHORE, vocalists fea-
tured on the program (them-
selves)
The Chamber Music Society of
Lower Basin Street (R) (Music
and satire)

CROSS, MILTON (2), host of the
program (himself)
ANN BLYTH
PETER DONALD
BILLY HALOP
FLORENCE HALOP
BILLY MAUCH
BOBBY MAUCH
JIMMY McCALLION
RISE STEVENS
WALTER TETLEY, featured on
the program (themselves)
The Children's Hour (R) (Chil-
dren's talent)

CROSS, MILTON (3), host of the
program (himself)
Metropolitan Opera Broadcasts
(R) (Music)

CROSS, MILTON (4), moderator of
the program (himself)
MANY JUVENILE PANELISTS
Raising Your Parents (R)
(Children's panel)

Crossroads. See: Ann

Crossword Quiz. See: Prescott, Allen (1)

CROWE, MAJOR GENERAL WILEY. See: Savage, Brigadier General Frank

CROWELL, JONAH
EBEN CROWELL
MARY CROWELL, characters appearing in the drama
Four Corners, U. S. A. (R) (Drama)

CROWLEY, DR. FRED. See: Allen, Dr. Kate

CROWLEY, ED. See: Johnson, Bess

CROWN, JIM, Oklahoma Territory marshal
FRANK McGREGOR, deputy
FRANCIS WILDE, tenderfoot photographer
DULCEY COOPERSMITH, owner of local inn
Cimarron Strip (TV) (Western adventure)

CROWS, THE TWO BLACK. See: Drew, John
Two Black Crows, The (1) (2)

CRUMIT, FRANK (1)
JULIA SANDERSON, co-quiz-masters of the program (themselves)
WALTER O'KEEFE
JAY C. FLIPPEN, quizmasters of the program (themselves)
MANY CONTESTANTS
The Battle of the Sexes (R) (Quiz)

CRUMIT, FRANK (2)
JULIA SANDERSON, singers and entertainers; featured on the program (themselves)
MANY GUEST STARS
Blackstone Plantation (R) (Variety)

CRUMIT, FRANK (3)
JULIA SANDERSON, co-hosts of the program (themselves)
Frank Crumit and Julia Sanderson (R) (Music)

CRUMIT, FRANK (4), master of ceremonies of the program (himself)
MANY GUESTS
Universal Rhythm (R) (Music/conversation)

CRUMP, PERCY. See: Dillon, Marshal Matt

CRUNCH. See: Adams, Crunch

Crunch Adams and Desperate Smith. See: Adams, Crunch

Crunch and Des. See: Adams, Crunch

CRUNCHMILLER, JOE. See: Canova, Judy

Crusade in Europe. See: Van Voorhis, Westbrook (1)

Crusade, The Billy Graham. See: Graham, Billy

Crusader. See: Anders, Matt

CRUSADERS, THE CAPED. See: Batman

Crusoe, Robinson, Jr. See: Brown, Robinson, Jr.

CUBAN BOYS, THE LECUONA. See: Whiteman, Paul

Cuckoo Hour, The. See: Weems, Ambrose J.

CUFFY SANDERS. See: Gallant, Captain

CUGAT, XAVIER (1)
BENNY GOODMAN
KEL MURRAY, orchestra leaders (themselves)
THEIR ORCHESTRAS
Let's Dance (R) (Dance music)

CUGAT, XAVIER (2), tango/rhumba orchestra leader; host of the program (himself)
HIS ORCHESTRA
ABBE LANE, featured vocalist on the program (herself)
Xavier Cugat (TV) (Dance music)

CUGAT, XAVIER. See also:
Durante, Jimmy
Whiteman, Paul

CULHANE, CLAY, former gunfighter, now lawyer
Black Saddle (TV) (Western)

Culhane, Dundee and the. See:
Dundee

CULHANE, THE. See: Dundee

CULLEN ANDREWS. See: Bennett,
Nita

CULLEN, BILL (1), host of the
program (himself)
MANY GUESTS
The Bill Cullen Show (R) (Conversation)

CULLEN, BILL (2), quizmaster of
the program (himself)
MANY CONTESTANTS
Hit the Jackpot (R) (Quiz)

CULLEN, BILL (3)
BOB BARKER, moderators of the
program (themselves)
KARIN O'BRIEN, contestant on
the program
MANY AUDIENCE CONTESTANTS
The Price Is Right (TV) (Game)

CULLEN, BILL (4), moderator of
the program (himself)
GUEST PARTICIPANTS
Three on a Match (TV) (Game)

CULLEN, BILL (5)
CLAYTON "BUD" COLLYER
WARD WILSON, quizmasters of
the program (themselves)
MANY CONTESTANTS
Winner Take All (R) (Quiz)

CULLEN, BILL. See also:
Blyden, Larry (2)
DeWitt, George
Moore, Garry (4) (5)
Roberts, Ken

CULLOM, CHARLIE. See: Harum,
David

CULPEPPER, THOMAS. See:
Henry VIII, King of England

CULVER, MISS. See: Foster,
Major John

CUMBERLAND RIDGE RUNNERS,
THE. See: Kelly, Joe (1)

CUMMINGS, BRENDA, previously
married
GRANT CUMMINGS, her second
husband
BILL CUMMINGS
DICK CUMMINGS
FRAN CUMMINGS
DR. MARK PHILLIPS, physician
EDWARDS, butler
MARION JENNINGS
LOUISE McPHERSON
IRMA WALLACE
BEN PORTER
MILTON BROWNSPUN
VALERIE WELLES
PETER
MARCIA, characters appearing
in the drama
Second Husband (R) (Serial
drama)

CUMMINGS, ELOISE. See: Brent,
Dr. Jim

CUMMINGS, ESTELLE. See:
Hargrave-Scott, Joan

CUMMINGS, IRVING. See: De-
Mille, Cecil B.

CUNNINGHAM, CELESTE. See:
Rutledge, Dr. John

CUNNINGHAM, CHARLES. See:
Rutledge, Dr. John

CUNNINGHAM, MRS. See: Rutledge, Dr. John

CURIAE, AMICUS. See: Kegg,
Jonathan

Curiosity Shop. See: Pam

CURIOSITY SHOP. See: Keeper of
the Old Curiosity Shop, The

Curiosity Shop, The Old. See:
Keeper of the Old Curiosity Shop,
The

CURRAN, EDWARD. See:

Hargrave-Scott, Joan

CURRY, JED "KID." See: Heyes,
Hannibal

CURT. See also:
Cort
Kurt

CURT BRADLEY. See: Young,
Larry "Pepper"

CURT BRADLEY, MRS. See:
Young, Larry "Pepper"

CURT GOWDY. See: Jackson,
Keith (2)

CURT LANSING. See: Perry, John

CURT MASSEY. See: Skelton, Red

CURT RAMSEY. See: Welk,
Lawrence

Curtain Time. See: Elders, Harry

CURTIN, WALTER. See: Randolph,
Alice

CURTIS BANCROFT. See: Trent,
Helen

CURTIS BASSETT. See: Nielson,
Torwald

CURTIS, BRENDA, wife
JIM CURTIS, her husband
THE MOTHER-IN-LAW, charac-
ters appearing in the drama
Brenda Curtis (R) (Serial drama)

CURTIS CURTIS. See: MacDonald,
Eleanor

CURTIS, DICK. See:
Stevens, Ray
Winters, Jonathan

CURTIS, GARY. See: Perkins, Ma

CURTIS, JEAN. See: Dyke,
Charity Amanda

CURTIS, MARTHA. See: Perry,
John

CURTIS MAYFIELD. See: Butler,

Jerry

CURTIS, PAT. See:
MacDonald, Eleanor
Mix, Tom

CURTIS, SCOOP. See: Rogers,
Patricia

CURTIS, STELLA CARLON. See:
Perkins, Ma

CURTIS, STORMY WILSON. See:
Rogers, Patricia

CURTIS, VIRGINIA. See: Caesar,
Sid (2)

CUSHING, MR. See: Blanc, Mel

Custer. See: Custer, George
Armstrong

CUSTER, GEORGE ARMSTRONG,
American general officer
CALIFORNIA JOE MILNER, U. S.
army scout
CAPTAIN MYLES KEOGH, U. S.
army officer under Custer
SERGEANT JAMES BUSTARD,
U. S. army non-commissioned
officer under Custer
CRAZY HORSE, Indian chief
Custer (TV) (Drama)

CUSTER, LIEUTENANT. See:
Rogers, Patricia

CUTLER, RICHARD. See: Fadiman, Clifton (2)

CYD. See also: Sid

CYD CHARISSE. See: Crosby,
Bing (2)

CYNTHIA. See:
Crackerby, O. K.
Teen, Harold

CYNTHIA ADAMS. See: Marlin,
Mary

CYNTHIA AGAR. See: Sterling,
Vanessa Dale

CYNTHIA CARTER. See: Trent,
Helen

CYNTHIA CLINE. See: Kelly, Joe
(2)

CYRIL. See: Worthington, Nora

D.A., The. See: Ryan, Paul

D.A.'s Man, The. See: Shannon

D., MR. See: Overstreet, Buddy

D.W. Griffith. See: Drew, John

DACK. See:
Dick
Dirk
Massey, Christine

DAD. See:
Farrell, Charlie
Mother

Dad, Mother and. See: Mother

DAD MUNSON. See: Harding,
Karen Adams

DADDY, the father
ROLLO, his son
Daddy and Rollo (R) (Dialogue)

Daddy and Rollo. See: Daddy

DADDY HIGGINS. See:
Baby Snooks
Dragonette, Jessica (2)
Morgan, Frank (2)

Daddy, Make Room for. See:
Williams, Danny

DADDY STRATFORD. See: Sothern,
Mary

"DADDY" WARBUCKS, OLIVER.
See: Little Orphan Annie

DAE. See also:
Day
Dee

DAE, DONNA. See: Waring, Fred
(1)

Dagger, Cloak and. See: Hungarian Giant, The

DAGMAR. See:
Hansen, Mama
Lester, Jerry

DAGWOOD. See: Bumstead,
Blondie

DAHL, ARLENE, hostess of the
program (herself)
MANY ACTORS AND ACTRESSES
Opening Night (TV) (Drama)

DAIN, LIEUT. FRANK, officer
assigned to the California Bureau
of Missing Persons
Jigsaw (The Men) (TV) (Crime
drama)

Daisies, Please Don't Eat the.
See: Nash, Jim

DAISY. See:
Bumstead, Blondie
Dugan, Jimmie

DAISY DEAN. See: Kaltenmeyer,
Professor August, D.U.N.

DAISY FROGG. See: Hanks,
Henrietta

DAISY MAE. See: Yokum, Li'l
Abner

DAISY MATTHEWS. See: Malone,
Dr. Jerry

DAISY, MISS. See: Manning,
Portia Blake

DAISY'S FIVE PUPS. See: Bumstead, Blondie

DAKIM. See: Randolph, Ellen

Dakotas, The. See: Marshal,
The

Daktari. See: Tracy, Dr. Marsh

DAL. See also:
Dale
Doll

DAL, BABY. See: Grimm,
Arnold

DAL TREMAINE. See: Grimm,
Arnold

DALE. See:
Dal
Doll
Robertson, Dale

DALE, ALAN. See: Seymour, Dan

DALE ARDEN. See: Gordon,
Flash

DALE, DICK. See: Welk, Lawrence

DALE EVANS. See:
Bergen, Edgar (2)
Crosby, Bing (2)
Rogers, Roy

Dale Evans Show, The Roy Rogers.
See: Rogers, Roy

DALE HUMPHREY. See: Brent,
Dr. Jim

DALE, JIMMY. See:
Berry, Ken
Bono, Salvatore
Stevens, Ray

DALE, LINDA
ERIC DALE
SHEILA BLADE
DR. BRUCE PORTER
THE JUDGE
PENNY, characters appearing in
the drama
I Love Linda Dale (R) (Serial
drama)

DALE, PEGGY. See: McKeever,
Dr. John

DALE, SARAH. See: Sterling,
Vanessa Dale

DALEY. See:
Brent, Dr. Jim
Dally
Daly

DALEY, CASS, comedienne, featured on the program (herself)
LARRY KEATING, comedian,
also featured (himself)
FREDDY MARTIN, orchestra
leader (himself)
HIS ORCHESTRA
The Fitch Bandwagon (R) (Variety/
music)

DALEY, CASS. See also: Morgan,
Frank (1)

DALEY, ISOBEL. See: Brent,

Dr. Jim

DALLAS, STELLA, seamstress
LAUREL DALLAS GROSVENOR
(Lolly Baby), her daughter
DICK GROSVENOR, Laurel's
husband
MRS. GROSVENOR, Dick's
mother
STEPHEN DALLAS
HELEN DALLAS
SAM ELLIS
NELLIE ELLIS
BOB JAMES
MADELINE CARTER
MINNIE GRADY
GUS GRADY
AGATHA GRISWOLD
MR. BRUCE
CHARLIE MARTIN
BEATRICE MARTIN
LEWIS JOHNSON
VERA JOHNSON
MADGE HARTE
MERLE CHATWIN
PHILIP BAXTER
DR. RAMEY
DR. ALAN SIMMS
ED MUNN
FLETCHER
THOMAS
JACK
JERRY, characters appearing in
the drama
Stella Dallas (R) (Serial drama)

DALLY. See also:
Daley
Daly

DALLY, DILLY. See: Doody,
Howdy

DALTON, PETER. See: Karr,
Mike

DALY. See also:
Daley
Dally

DALY, JANE. See: Anthony

DALY, JOHN (1), newscaster on
the program (himself)
John Daly and the News (TV)
(News)

DALY, JOHN (2), narrator of the

program (himself)
The Spirit of '41 (R) (World War
II news)

DALY, JOHN (3)
WALLY BRUNER, moderators of
the program (themselves)
ARLENE FRANCIS
STEVE ALLEN
FRED ALLEN
BENNETT CERF
DOROTHY KILGALLEN
SOUPY SALES
HAL BLOCK
LOUIS UNTERMEYER, panelists
on the program (themselves)
MANY GUEST PANELISTS
GUEST CONTESTANTS
MYSTERY GUEST (himself/her-
self)
What's My Line? (R) (TV) (Panel
quiz)

DALY, JOHN (4), moderator of the
program (himself)
FAYE EMERSON
BOB CONSIDINE
JAMES HAGEN
PAT CARROLL
OTHERS, panelists
Who Said That? (TV) (Panel
game)

DALY, RALPH. See: Dyke,
Charity Amanda

DAMARIS COLON. See: Marshall,
E. G.

DAME, THE DUMB. See: Medbury,
John P.

DAMONE, VIC (1), singer and entertainer; host of the program (himself)
MANY GUEST STARS
The Lively Ones (TV) (Variety)

DAMONE, VIC (2), singer and
entertainer; host of the program
(himself)
GAIL MARTIN
CAROL LAWRENCE, singers and
entertainers appearing on the
program (themselves)
THE RONALD FIELD DANCERS
LES BROWN, orchestra leader
(himself)

HIS ORCHESTRA
MANY GUEST STARS
Vic Damone (TV) (Variety)

DAMROSCH, WALTER, music com-
mentator (himself)
THE NEW YORK SYMPHONY
ORCHESTRA
The Music Appreciation Hour (R)
(Music education)

DAN. See:
August, Dan
Britt, Dan
Don
Fraser, Ben
Harding, Mrs. Rhoda
Holiday, Dan
Ingram, Dan
McGarry, Dan
McGovern, Dan
Madigan, Sergeant Dan
Matthews, Dan
Miller, Dan
O'Leary, Hannah
Palmer, Dan
Raven, Dan
Rowan, Dan
Seymour, Dan
Talbot, Commander Dan
Tempest, Dan
Troop, Marshal Dan

DAN ALLISON. See: Davis, Dr.
Althea

Dan August. See: August, Dan

DAN BERGMAN. See: Tate,
Joanne

DAN BLOCKER. See: Cookie
Monster, The

DAN BRIGGS. See:
Phelps, Jim
Stone, Sam

DAN CASSIDY. See: Dean,
Spencer

DAN ERICKSON. See: Lockridge,
Barry

DAN FARRELL. See: Howard,
Glenn

DAN FORREST. See: Carr, Alison

DAN GARRETT, DR. See: Garrett, Susan

DAN GENTRY. See: Brewster, Gail

Dan Harding's Wife. See: Harding, Mrs. Rhoda

DAN KINCAID. See: Ames, Peter

DAN MILLER. See: Evans, Dean

DAN MULDOON, DETECTIVE LIEUT. See: Parker, Lieut. Mike

DAN PALMER, LIEUT. See: Locke, Dr. Simon (2)

DAN PHILLIPS, DR. See: Sterling, Vanessa Dale

Dan Raven. See: Raven, Dan

DAN REID. See: Lone Ranger, The

DAN STUART. See: Hughes, Chris

DAN TOBIN. See: Winters, Jack

DAN WILLIAMS. See: McGarrett, Steve

DANA. See:
Dena
Phelps, Jim

DANA, BILL. See: Jones, Spike (2)

DANA, FRANK. See: Brent, Dr. Jim

DANCE ANNOUNCER, MARATHON. See: Nye, Louis

Dance, Let's. See: Cugat, Xavier (1)

Dance, The National Barn. See: Kelly, Joe (1)

DANCER, APRIL, crime fighter, opposing THRUSH
MARK SLATE, her companion in crime fighting

ALEXANDER WAVERLY, their superior
The Girl From U. N. C. L. E. (TV) (Crime fighting satire)

DANCERS, THE BILL FOSTER. See: King, Dave (2)

DANCERS, THE BOB SIDNEY. See: Bailey, Pearl

DANCERS, THE CAIN. See: Lewandowski, Bob

DANCERS, THE DON McKAYLE. See:
Cosby, Bill (2)
Hirt, Al (1)
Uggams, Leslie

DANCERS, THE ERNEST FLATT. See:
Burnett, Carol
DeLuise, Dom (2)

DANCERS, THE GAZZARI. See: Riddle, Sam (2)

DANCERS, THE HIT PARADE. See: Lanson, Snooky

DANCERS, THE JAIME ROGERS. See: Berry, Ken

DANCERS, THE JUNE TAYLOR. See:
DeLuise, Dom (1)
Dorsey, Tommy
Ford, Tennessee Ernie (2)
Gleason, Jackie (2)

DANCERS, THE LESTER WILLIAMS. See: Davis, Sammy, Jr.

DANCERS, THE LONDON LINE. See: Berman, Shelley

DANCERS, THE LOUIS DA PRON. See: Como, Perry (1) (3)

DANCERS, THE NICK CASTLE. See: Lewis, Jerry

DANCERS, THE NORMAN MAEN. See: Doonican, Val

DANCERS, THE RONALD FIELD. See: Damone, Vic (2)

DANCERS, THE SHINDIG. See:
O'Neill, Jimmy

DANCERS, THE TOM HANSEN.
See: Junior

DANCERS, THE TONY CHARMOLI.
See: Andrews, Julie

DANCERS, THE TONY MORDENTE.
See: Bono, Salvatore

DANCERS, THE WISA D'ORSO. See:
Nye, Louis

DANE, PRUDENCE, newspaper editor
JOHN DANE
WADE DOUGLAS, wagonmaster
EMMIE HATFIELD
SLIM STARK
WALTER CARLIN
PEG HALL
EMILIO PRIETO
CALEB JACKSON
FANNY CARLYSLE
LINDA
JOHNNY
TOMMY
SYLVIA
MADELEINE, characters appear-
ing in the drama
A Woman of America (R) (Serial
drama)

DANFORTH, SAM. See: Wash-
burn, William

D'ANGELO, PRIVATE. See: Wright,
Conley

Danger Man. See: Drake, John

DANGERFIELD, RODNEY. See:
Martin, Dean (2)

Dangerous Assignment. See:
Mitchell, Steve

Dangerous Paradise. See: Brewster, Gail

Dangerous Robin. See: Scott,
Robin

DANIEL. See:
Boone, Daniel
Coffee, Dr. Daniel
Dan'l

Poling, Rev. Daniel
Speaker, The

Daniel Boone. See: Boone, Daniel

DANIEL BURKE. See: Marlin,
Mary

DANIEL FINDLAY. See: Johnson,
Bess

DANIEL HATHAWAY. See: Prescott, Kate Hathaway

DANIELS, BILLY. See:
Edwards, Ralph (1)
Loveridge, Marion

DANIELS, CHARLES. See: Wayne,
Ruth Evans

DANIELS, "TERMITE." See:
Edwards, Ralph (1)
Loveridge, Marion

DANKO, JILL. See: Ryker, Lieut.
Eddie

DANKO, MIKE. See: Ryker, Lieut.
Eddie

DAN'L. See:
Daniel
Dickey, Dan'l

DANNY. See:
Aunt Jenny (Aunt Lucy)
Kaye, Danny
O'Neill, Mrs.
Partridge, Connie
Taylor, Danny
Walleck, Meredith
Wilde, Danny
Williams, Danny
Wilson, Steve

DANNY ADAMS. See: Burns,
George (3)

DANNY DAVIS. See: Lopez,
Vincent

DANNY DAYTON. See: Reiner,
Carl

DANNY DONAVAN. See: Kay,
Beatrice

DANNY DUNCAN. See: Kelly, Joe
(1)

Danny Kaye Show, The. See:
Kaye, Danny

DANNY KELLER, SERGEANT. See:
Gower, Matthew

DANNY MARTIN. See: Kelly, Joe
(2)

DANNY MORLEY. See: Holstrum,
Katy

DANNY STRATFORD. See: Sothern,
Mary

Danny Thomas Show, The. See:
Williams, Danny

DANT, BUD. See: Canova, Judy

DANT, CHARLES. See: Ward,
Perry

Dante. See: Dante, Willy

DANTE, WILLY, former gambler;
now operator of "Dante's Inferno,"
San Francisco night club
STEWART STYLES, maitre d' of
the club
BIFF, bartender at the club
POLICE LIEUTENANT BOB
MALONE, police official
Dante (TV) (Mystery)

DAPHNE. See:
Collins, Barnabas
Morgan, Henry
Scooby Doo

DAPHNE DeWITT DUTTON. See:
Madison, Kenny

DAPHNE ROYCE. See: Brent,
Portia

DA PRON DANCERS, THE LOUIS.
See: Como, Perry (1) (3)

D'AQUINO, IVA IKUKO TOGURI,
Japanese propaganda broadcaster
in World War II (herself)
Tokyo Rose (R) (Japanese war
propaganda)

DARCEL, DENISE. See: Stokey,
Mike

DARICE RICHMAN. See: Kelly,
Joe (2)

DARIN. See also: Darrin

DARIN, BOBBY, singer and enter-
tainer; star of the program (him-
self)
DICK BAKALYAN
STEVE LANDESBERG
RIP TAYLOR
KATHY CAHILL
SARAH FANKBONER
TONY AMATO, entertainers
featured on the program (them-
selves)
MANY GUEST STARS
EDDIE KARAM, orchestra leader
(himself)
HIS ORCHESTRA
Dean Martin Presents the Bobby
Darin Amusement Company (TV)
(Variety)

DARING, DICK
COACH GREATGUY, characters
appearing on the program
Dick Daring's Adventures (R)
(Adventure)

DARIUS BOGGS. See: Brown,
Ellen

Dark, America After. See: Lescoulie, Jack (4)

Dark, Playboy After. See: Hefner, Hugh

Dark Shadows. See: Collins,
Barnabas

DARL. See:
Carl
Carle
Karl
Wylber, Darl

DARLENE. See: Dodd, Jimmie

DARLING, ALICE. See: McGee,
Fibber

DARLING, JOHN. See: Pan,
Peter

DARLING, MICHAEL. See: Pan, Peter

DARLING, MR. See: Pan, Peter

DARLING, MRS. See: Pan, Peter

Darling, Rich Man's. See: O'Farrell, Packy

DARLING, WENDY. See: Pan, Peter

DARNELL, NANI. See: Wilson, Mark

DARNELL, PETER. See: Noble, Mary

DARRELL, BRIAN. See: Nichols, Walter

DARRELL MOORE. See: Myrt

DARRELL, NEIL. See: Nichols, Walter

DARRIN. See: Darin Stephens, Samantha

DARROW, GERARD. See: Kelly, Joe (2)

D'ARTEGA. See: Shields, Jimmy

DARTIE, VAL. See: Forsyte, Soames

DARTIE, MONTAGUE. See: Forsyte, Soames

DARTIE, WINIFRED. See: Forsyte, Soames

DASCOMB, ELAINE. See: Marshall, John

Date, Blind. See: Francis, Arlene (2)

Date With Judy, A. See: Foster, Judy

Date With the Angels. See: Angel, Gus

Dating Game, The. See: Lange, Jim

Daughter, Arnold Grimm's. See: Grimm, Arnold

Daughter, Editor's. See: Foster, Henry

Daughter, Mary Foster, The Editor's. See: Foster, Henry

Daughter, The Farmer's. See: Holstrum, Katy

Daughters, Doc Barclay's. See: Barclay, Doc

Daughters, Our Five. See: Lee, Jim

D'AVAUX. See: Churchill, John

DAVE. See:
Blassingame, Dave
Crabtree, Dave
Elman, Dave (1) (2)
Garroway, Dave (1) (2) (3) (4)
King, Dave (1) (2)
Lewis, Dave
Phillips, Dave

DAVE AKEMAN. See: Owens, Buck

DAVE ALLEN. See: Berman, Shelley

DAVE BRUBECK. See: O'Connor, Father Norman

DAVE COREY. See: Howard, Glenn

DAVE GARROWAY. See:
Downs, Hugh
Garroway, Dave (1) (2) (3) (4)
Myerson, Bess

Dave Garroway, Next. See: Garroway, Dave (3)

Dave King, England's. See: King, Dave (2)

Dave King Show, The. See: King, Dave (1)

DAVE NEWELL. See: Begley, Martin

DAVE PROCHASKA. See: Kelly,
Joe (2)

DAVE RUBINOFF. See: Cantor,
Eddie (2)

DAVE STREET. See:
Lester, Jerry
Owner
Parkyakarkas, Nick

DAVE TABAK. See: Alexander,
Nick

DAVE TALBOT. See: Harding,
Karen Adams

DAVE TARRANT. See: Calhoun,
Ben

DAVE THORNE. See: Madison,
Kenny

DAVEY. See:
Davie
Davy
Gillis, Dobie
Marlin, Mary

Davey Adams, Son of the Sea.
See: Adams, Franklin P.

DAVEY EVANS. See: Bracken,
John

DAVID. See:
Allen, Joan Houston
Barrett, David
Brinkley, David
Collins, Barnabas
Davidson, Bill
Farrell, David
Frost, David (1) (2)
Grief, Captain David
Hansen, David
Harding, David
Harum, David
Koster, David
Lane, Rebecca
March, David
Meredith, Charles
Naughton, Claudia
Nelson, Ozzie
Niven, David
Ross, David (1) (2) (3)
Saville, David
Schoumacher, David
Scott, David

Solomon, David
Steinberg, David (1) (2)
Susskind, David
Uncle Abe
Vincent, David
Wade, David
Willis, David
Young, Captain David

DAVID ACKROYD. See: Ames,
Peter

DAVID ADAIR. See: Marshall,
John

DAVID BREWSTER. See: Wayne,
Ruth Evans

DAVID BRINKLEY. See:
Brinkley, David
Huntley, Chet (1)

David Brinkley's Journal. See:
Brinkley, David

DAVID BROEKMAN. See: Cross,
Mason

DAVID BROWN. See: Drake, Nora

David, Claudia and. See: Naughton,
Claudia

DAVID CRAIG, DR. See: Hunter,
Dr. Paul

DAVID CRAWFORD. See: Malone,
Dr. Jerry

DAVID FARRELL. See:
Bauer, Bertha
Farrell, David

DAVID FREIFELDER. See: Kelly,
Joe (2)

DAVID FROST. See:
Ames, Nancy
Frost, David (1) (2)

David Frost Revue, The. See:
Frost, David (2)

David Frost Show, The. See:
Frost, David (1)

DAVID GRANT. See: Hillman,
India

David Grief, Captain. See: Grief,
Captain David

DAVID GUNTHER. See: Hansen,
Dean Eric

David Harding, Counterspy. See:
Harding, David

David Harum. See: Harum, David

DAVID HOUSEMAN. See: Fairchild,
Kay

DAVID JEFFERS. See: Johnson,
Bess

DAVID JEMAL. See: Corey, Earl

DAVID JENKINS. See: Kelly, Joe
(2)

DAVID JOY. See: Welk, Lawrence

DAVID KANE. See: Perry, Luke

DAVID LAGORRO. See: Carter,
Kathryn

DAVID LERNER. See: Levy,
Abie

DAVID LIPP. See: Rowan, Dan

DAVID McKENZIE, DR. See:
Grimm, Arnold

DAVID MALONE, DR. See:
Malone, Dr. Jerry

DAVID MORGAN, DR. See:
Jordan, Joyce

DAVID NIVEN. See:
Boyer, Charles
Niven, David
Ryan, Robert (1)

David Niven Show, The. See:
Niven, David

DAVID, PAPA. See: Solomon,
David

DAVID POST. See: Marlin, Mary

DAVID ROSE. See:
Junior

Martin, Tony (1)

DAVID S. BRODER. See:
Schoumacher, David

DAVID SIEGEL. See: Walleck,
Meredith

DAVID SOMERVILLE. See: Conway, Tim

David Steinberg Show, The. See:
Steinberg, David (1)

DAVID STEWART. See: Hughes,
Lisa

DAVID STUART, DR. See: Hughes,
Chris

David Susskind Show, The. See:
Susskind, David

DAVID SUTTON. See: Virginian,
The

DAVID TERRY. See: Kaye, Danny

DAVID, UNCLE. See: Gold-
berg, Molly

David, Uncle Abe and. See:
Uncle Abe

David Wade, Dining With. See:
Wade, David

DAVID ZORBA, DR. See: Casey,
Dr. Ben

DAVIDSON. See also: Davisson

DAVIDSON, BILL, barber in town
of Hartville
NANCY DONOVAN, his daughter
JONATHAN HILLERY
KERRY DONOVAN, Nancy's hus-
band
ELMER EEPS
MARGARET BURNS
SYLVIA POWERS
EDGAR HUDSON
PERCY BLIVENS
DAVID
BESSIE
JOHN BRITTON
REBA BRITTON
NED SHEPHERD

WIKI
KATHLEEN CHATTON
DOROTHY NASH
SYLVIA BARDINE, characters
appearing in the drama
Just Plain Bill (R) (Serial drama)
(originally called Bill the Barber)
(R)

DAVIDSON, DR. See: Hardy, Dr.
Steven

DAVIDSON, JOHN (1)
CAROL LAWRENCE
VIKKI CARR
LESLIE UGGAMS, hosts and
hostesses of the program (them-
selves)
OTHER HOSTS AND HOSTESSES
MANY SKATING STARS AND
ENTERTAINERS
Ice Palace (TV) (Skating/variety)

DAVIDSON, JOHN (2), singer and
entertainer; host of the program
(himself)
RICH LITTLE
MIREILLE MATHIEU
AIMI MACDONALD, entertainers
appearing on the program (them-
selves)
JACK PARNELL, orchestra
leader (himself)
HIS ORCHESTRA
MANY GUEST STARS
The John Davidson Show (TV)
(Variety)

DAVIDSON, JOHN. See also:
DeLuise, Dom (2)

DAVIE. See also:
Davey
Davy

DAVIE LANE. See: Graham, Dr.
Bob

DAVIES, GWEN. See: Halop, Billy

DAVIS, ANN TYLER
DR. CHARLES TYLER
DR. JOE MARTIN
KATE MARTIN
MARY KENNICOTT
KITTY SHEA
CHUCK TYLER
KAREN MARTIN

JEFF MARTIN
MR. MAXWELL
ERICA MARTIN
PAUL MARTIN
PHILIP BRENT
DR. BLACK
PATTY WHITE
NICK DAVIS
RUTH MARTIN
PHOEBE TYLER, characters
appearing in the drama
All My Children (TV) (Serial drama)

DAVIS, BERNIE. See: Preston,
Dick

DAVIS, BILL. See: Andrews, Russ

DAVIS, CAROL. See: Preston,
Dick

DAVIS, CLIFTON. See: Moore,
Melba

DAVIS, DANNY. See: Lopez,
Vincent

DAVIS, DIANE. See: Winters,
Jonathan

DAVIS, DR. ALTHEA
DR. MATT POWERS
DR. MAGGIE POWERS
DR. MIKE POWERS
DR. STEVE ALDRICH
DR. HANSEN
DAN ALLISON
LIZ ALLISON
DR. JOHN MORRISON
DR. VIDO McCREA
ANDREW WINTERS
BARBARA FARRELL
DR. KAREN WERNER
UNCLE BILL
GRETA POWERS
DR. GORDON MATHER
DR. NICK BELLINI
DR. IVERSON
CATHIE RYKER
WEBB SUTHERLAND
CORA LEE SIMPSON
JANE COLLINS
JESSICA MORRISON
EMMA SIMPSON, characters
appearing in the drama
The Doctors (TV) (Serial drama)

DAVIS, FRED, quizmaster of the

"Brains" team (himself)
JACK LESCOULIE, moderator of
the "Brawn" team (himself)
MANY CONTESTANTS, competing
in two teams
Brains and Brawn (TV) (Game)

DAVIS, FRED. See also: Sunday

DAVIS, GERALD. See: Randolph,
Alice

DAVIS, GLENN, former football
player; host of the program (himself)
MANY FOOTBALL PLAYERS
See the Pros (TV) (Football)

DAVIS, JAMIE. See: Randolph,
Alice

DAVIS, JANETTE. See: Godfrey,
Arthur (1)

DAVIS, JANIE. See: Hutton,
Ina Ray

DAVIS, JENNIFER. See: Noble,
Mary

DAVIS, JIM
MARY CASTLE, stars of the
program (themselves)
MANY SUPPORTING ACTORS
AND ACTRESSES
Stories of the Century (TV)
(Western biographical dramas)

DAVIS, JIMMY. See: Brown,
Ellen

DAVIS, JO. See:
Dean, Jimmy
Hamilton, George

DAVIS, JOAN, comedienne, featured
on the program (herself)
Leave It to Joan (R) (Situation
comedy)

DAVIS, JOAN. See also: Owner

DAVIS, JOHN FIELD
DR. SAMUEL TILDEN FIELD
STELLA FIELD
SYLVIA FIELD
MOTHER FIELD
KATHY CAMERON

IRMA CAMERON
BETTY SKIDMORE
STEVE SKIDMORE
ANNE DAVIS (MOTHER DAVIS)
HARRY DAVIS
TOM DAVIS
CONNOLLY, police officer
JOHN HACKETT
ELLA ASHBY
DR. WIGGINS, physician
LITTLE RUDY CAMERON
PHIL STANLEY
EVE TOPPING STANLEY
WHITEY
BETTY McDONALD
MR. CAMERON
SAMMY
LILLIE, maid
CHICK NORRIS
PROFESSOR KILPATRICK
ANGIE
MRS. STANLEY
MADISON, butler
LOLA, characters appearing in
the drama
When a Girl Marries (R)
(Serial drama)

DAVIS, JOHNNY "SCAT." See:
Waring, Fred (1)

DAVIS, KENT. See: Vance,
Connie

DAVIS, MARGERY. See: O'Leary,
Hannah

DAVIS, MAUDE. See: Cantor,
Eddie (2)

DAVIS, MIMI. See: Phelps, Jim

DAVIS, MRS. See: Brooks,
Connie

DAVIS, NELSON. See: Brown,
Ellen

DAVIS, PAMMY. See: Hillman,
India

DAVIS, PEARL. See: Keene,
Kitty

DAVIS, RACHEL CLARK. See:
Randolph, Alice

DAVIS, RED

HIS SISTER
SAM DAVIS
MOTHER
CLINK
CONNIE RICKARD
LUDA BARCLAY, characters appearing in the drama
Red Davis (R) (Serial drama)
(previously known as Red Adams;
subsequently called Forever Young
and Pepper Young's Family) (R)

DAVIS, SAMMY, JR., entertainer;
star of the program (himself)
MANY GUEST STARS
THE LESTER WILLIAMS DANCERS
GENE RHODES, orchestra leader
(himself)
HIS ORCHESTRA
The Sammy Davis, Jr., Show (TV)
(Variety)

DAVIS, SAMMY, JR. See also:
Crosby, Bing (2)
Jones, Jack

DAVIS, TED. See: Randolph, Alice

DAVIS, UNCLE BILL, guardian of
his orphaned nephew and nieces
CISSY, his 18-year-old niece
BUFFY, his 10-year-old niece
JODY, his 10-year-old nephew,
Buffy's twin
GILES FRENCH, their English
manservant
EMILY, their housekeeper
Family Affair (TV) (Comedy)

DAVIS, WHIT. See: Lambert, Louise

DAVISSON. See also: Davidson

DAVISSON, LOIS. See: Joe (1)

DAVISSON, NEIL. See: Joe (1)

DAVY. See:
Davey
Davie
Jones, Davy

DAVY DILLON. See: Mason, Maudie

DAWG. See also: Dog

DAWG, DEPUTY
THE SHERIFF
MUSKIE

VINCENT VAN GOPHER
TY COON, cartoon characters
Deputy Dawg (TV) (Cartoon)

DAWLISH. See: Cooke, Alistaire (1)

DAWSON, police officer
This Man Dawson (TV) (Crime)

DAWSON. See also: Butcher,
Major Simon

DAWSON BLAKELY. See:
Jordan, Joyce

DAWSON, BUN. See: Malone,
Dr. Jerry

DAWSON, HOWIE. See: Hardy,
Dr. Steven

DAWSON, IKE. See: Taylor, Danny

DAWSON, JANE. See: Hardy, Dr.
Steven

DAWSON, JEAN. See: Hardy, Dr.
Steven

DAWSON, MATT. See: Carr, Alison

DAWSON, MRS. See: Malone,
Dr. Jerry

DAWSON, RICHARD. See:
Martindale, Wink (2)
Rowan, Dan

DAWSON, ROSEMARY
JOYCE MILLER
PETER HARVEY
PATTI DAWSON
BILL ROBERTS
LIEUTENANT GEORGE SCHUYLER, officer
DICK PHILLIPS
DR. JIM COTTER, physician
AUDREY ROBERTS
LEFTY HIGGINS
TOMMY TAYLOR
MOTHER DAWSON
MR. DENNIS
MR. MARTIN
MRS. KENYON
JESSICA, characters appearing in
the drama
Rosemary (R) (Serial drama)

Dawson, This Man. See: Dawson

DAY. See also:
Dae
Dee

DAY, ALICE. See: Harding,
Karen Adams

DAY, CHRIS
SALLY, his wife; couple operating
the Desert Palm Hotel at Palm
Springs, California
HAPPY, their infant son
UNCLE CHARLIE DOOLEY, their
uncle
Happy (TV) (Comedy)

DAY, CLARENCE (Father), head of
the house
VINNIE (Mother), his wife
CLARENCE
JOHN
WHITNEY
HARLAN, their sons
Life With Father (TV) (Situation
comedy)

DAY, DENNIS, singer and comedian,
featured on the program (himself)
MILDRED ANDERSON, his girl
friend
MR. ANDERSON, Mildred's
father
MRS. ANDERSON, Mildred's
mother
MR. WILLOUGHBY, character
appearing on the program
A Day in the Life of Dennis Day
(R) (Situation comedy) (also
known as The Dennis Day Show)
(R)

DAY, DENNIS. See also: Benny,
Jack

DAY, DORIS. See: Ross, Lanny

DAY, GEORGIA. See: Wayne,
Johnny (2)

Day in the Life of Dennis Day, A.
See: Day, Dennis

Day Is Ours, This. See: Mac-
Donald, Eleanor

DAY, MARILYN. See: Dunninger,
Joseph

Day, Mother's. See: Van Dyke,
Dick (2)

Day, Queen For a. See: Bailey,
Jack

Day, The Brighter. See: Dennis,
Liz

Day, Valentine's. See: Farrow,
Valentine

Days, Circus. See: Roseleigh,
Jack

Days, Death Valley. See:
Old Ranger, The
Robertson, Dale

Days of Our Lives. See: Horton,
Dr. Tom

DAYTON, DANNY. See: Reiner,
Carl

DAYTON, EMMETT. See: Rogers,
Patricia

DEACON PERKINS. See: Harum,
David

Dead or Alive, Wanted. See:
Randall, Josh

DEADEYE THE COWBOY. See:
Junior

Deadline Drama. See: Lovejoy,
Frank (2)

Deadline For Action. See: Evans,
Dean

Deadly Game, The Most. See:
Croft, Jonathan

Deal in Crime, I. See: Gargan,
William (1)

Deal, Let's Make a. See: Hall,
Monty (2)

DEAN. See:
Baker, Dean Fred
Deane
Evans, Dean
Hansen, Dean Eric
Harding, Mrs. Rhoda

Jones, Dean
Martin, Dean (1) (2) (3)
Murphy, Dean
Upton, Michael

DEAN ARCHER ARMSTEAD. See:
Ballew, Wally

DEAN BROTHERS, THE. See:
Kelly, Joe (1)

DEAN, CARRIE. See: James,
Nancy

DEAN, DAISY. See: Kaltenmeyer,
Professor August, D.U.N.

DEAN, EDDIE. See: Ritter,
Tex (1)

DEAN, JIMMY, country and Western
singer; star of the program (him-
self)
JO DAVIS
MARY KLICK
JAN CROCKETT, musicians
appearing on the program (them-
selves)
THE TEXAS WILDCATS
THE COUNTRY LADS, vocal
groups
The Jimmy Dean Show (TV)
(Country/Western music)

DEAN, JIMMY. See also: Shawn,
Dick

DEAN JONES. See:
Jones, Dean
Jones, Jack
Shawn, Dick

DEAN, LARRY. See: Welk,
Lawrence

Dean Martin Presents the Bobby
Darin Amusement Company.
See: Darin, Bobby

Dean Martin Presents the Golddiggers. See: Chidsey, Jackie

Dean Martin Show, The. See:
Martin, Dean (2)

DEAN RUSSELL. See: Jordan,
Joyce

DEAN, SPENCER, detective
DAN CASSIDY
JANE ELLIOTT, his friends
Eno Crime Club (R) (Detective
adventure) (later known as
Crime Clues) (R)

DEANE. See also: Dean

DEANE, LAURA. See: Bracken,
John

DEANE, MARTHA, homemaking
expert, portrayed by Bessie
Beattie, Mary Margaret Mc-
Bride, Marion Young Taylor
and others
Martha Deane (R) (Homemaking)

DEANNA. See also:
Diana
Dianna

DEANNA DURBIN. See: Cantor,
Eddie (2)

Dear Abbie. See: Van Buren,
Abigail

Dear John. See: Chandler, Faith

Dear Phoebe. See: Hastings, Bill

Death Squad, Hearthstone of the.
See: Lenrow, Bernard

Death Valley Days. See:
Old Ranger, The
Robertson, Dale

Death Valley Sheriff. See: Old
Ranger, The

DE AZEVDO, LEX. See: Driggs,
Karleton King

DE AZEVDO, RIC. See: Driggs,
Karleton King

DEBBIE. See:
Debby
Debi
Drake, Debbie
Potter, Tom
Thompson, Jim

DEBBIE, AUNT. See: Hoyt,
Vikki Adams

DEBBIE BANNER. See: Goldberg, Molly

Debbie Drake Show, The. See: Drake, Debbie

Debbie Reynolds Show, The. See: Thompson, Jim

DEBBY. See:
Debbie
Debi
Spencer, Jeff

DE BECK, LISA. See: Cameron, Christy Allen

DEBI. See also:
Debbie
Debby

DEBI STORM. See: Winters, Jonathan

DEBORAH. See:
Barbour, Henry Wilson
Bauer, Bertha

DEBORAH MATTHEWS. See: Perkins, Ma

DEBORAH SULLIVAN. See: Hansen, David

DEBRA. See: Driggs, Karleton King

December Bride. See: Ruskin, Lily

DECKER. See also: Dekker

DECKER, GORDON. See: Trent, Helen

Deckers, Here Come the Double. See: Brains

Deckers, The Double. See: Brains

DECODER, FARGO NORTH. See: Cosby, Bill (1)

DE CORSIA, TED. See:
Reed, Alan
Welles, Orson (2)

Decoy. See: Jones, Casey (2)

DEE. See also:
Dae
Day

DEE DEE. See: Harris, Alan

DEE DEE BALL. See: Hutton, Ina Ray

DEE, DORIS. See: Noble, Mary

DEE FINCH. See: Rayburn, Gene (3)

Deed, Friend in. See: Maxwell, Richard

DEEDS, LONGFELLOW, tuba playing philanthropist and executive of business founded by his grandfather
TONY, his friend and advisor
MASTERSON, stuffy vice-president of the business
Mr. Deeds Goes to Town (TV) (Comedy)

DEEMS. See: Taylor, Deems

DEERING, WILMA. See: Rogers, Buck

Defender, Roger Kilgore, Public. See: Kilgore, Roger

Defender, The Public. See: Prentiss, Jim

Defenders, The. See: Preston, Lawrence

Defense, Judd For the. See: Judd, Clinton

DeGRUY, OSCAR. See: Cosby, Bill (2)

DeHAVEN, ROBBIE. See: Winters, Evelyn

DEKKER. See also: Decker

DEKKER, STEVE, military investigator
Not For Hire (TV) (Mystery drama)

DeKOVEN, ROGER. See: Judge,
The

DELANEY, SLIM. See: Sunday

DELAVAN, ALEX. See: Nelson,
Carolyn Kramer

DELLA CHIESA, VIVIEN. See:
Munn, Frank (1)

DELLA FAVE, MICHELLE. See:
Chidsey, Jackie

DELLA ROCCA, MICHAEL. See:
March, Hal
Story, Ralph

DELLA STREET. See: Mason,
Perry

DELMAR. See: Edmondson,
Delmar

DELMAR, KENNY, master of
ceremonies of the program (himself)
RASPUTIN X. DELMAROFF,
character portrayed by Delmar
MANY GUEST STARS
Hollywood Jackpot (R) (Variety)

DELMAR, KENNY. See also:
Kaye, Danny

DELMAR, TRACY. See: Bauer,
Bertha

DELMAROFF, RASPUTIN X. See:
Delmar, Kenny

DELO, KEN. See: Welk, Lawrence

DE LOCA, ADELAIDE. See: Roxy

Delphi Bureau, The. See:
Gregory, Glenn Garth

DeLUGG, MILTON. See:
Lester, Jerry
Winchell, Paul (3)

DeLUISE, DOM (1), comedian; host
of the program (himself)
CAROL ARTHUR
PAUL DOOLEY
BILL McCUTCHEON
MARIAN MERCER

THE GENTRY BROTHERS,
entertainers appearing on the
program (themselves)
MANY GUEST STARS
THE JUNE TAYLOR DANCERS
SAMMY SPEAR, orchestra leader
(himself)
HIS ORCHESTRA
The Dom DeLuise Show (TV)
(Variety)

DeLUISE, DOM (2)
CAROL BURNETT
BOB NEWHART
CATERINA VALENTE
TESSIE O'SHEA
ART BUCHWALD
TONY HENDRA
JACK BURNS
NIC ULLETT
JOHN DAVIDSON
OTHERS, entertainers appearing
on the program (themselves)
THE ERNEST FLATT DANCERS
MANY GUEST STARS
The Entertainers (TV) (Variety)

DeLUISE, DOM. See also: Martin,
Dean (2)

DELYS, GOGO. See: Medbury,
John P.

DEMARCO SISTERS, THE. See:
Allen, Fred

DeMILLE, CECIL B.
IRVING CUMMINGS
WILLIAM KEIGHLEY, hosts of
the program (themselves)
MANY ACTORS AND ACTRESSES
The Lux Radio Theater (R)
(Drama)

Demitasse Revue, The M. J. B.
See: Medbury, John P.

DEMLING, GILL AND. See:
Brown, Joe E. (1)

DEMPSTER. See: Randolph, Walt

DENA. See:
Cederquist, Dena
Dana

DENBY, MICHAEL. See: Allen,
Joan Houston

DENICE DARCEL. See: Stokey,
Mike

DENISE LOR. See: Paige, Bob

DENMARK, GEORGE OF. See:
Churchill, John

DENNIE. See also:
Benny
Denny

DENNIE McKENZIE. See: Marlin,
Mary

DENNIE PIERCE. See: Kelly,
Kitty

DENNING, CAROL. See: Hughes,
Chris

DENNIS. See:
Chase, Dennis
Day, Dennis
James, Dennis (1) (2) (3) (4)
Mitchell, Dennis

DENNIS ALLEN. See: Jones, Dean

DENNIS BRACKEN. See: Roy,
Mike

DENNIS CONROY. See: Noble,
Mary

DENNIS CROFT. See: Logan,
Shirley

DENNIS DAY. See:
Benny, Jack
Day, Dennis

Dennis Day, A Day in the Life of.
See: Day, Dennis

Dennis Day Show, The. See: Day,
Dennis

DENNIS DAY'S MOTHER. See:
Benny, Jack

DENNIS JAMES. See:
James, Dennis (1) (2) (3) (4)
Leyden, Bill (2)

DENNIS, LIZ, resident of Three
Rivers
RICHARD "POPPA" DENNIS
ALTHEA DENNIS
GRAYLING DENNIS
BARBARA "BABBY" DENNIS
CLIFF SEBASTIAN
SANDRA TALBOT
STEVEN MARKLEY
MAX CANFIELD
TED BLAKE
JERRY
PATSY, characters appearing in
the drama
The Brighter Day (R) (TV)
(Serial drama)

DENNIS, MR. See: Dawson,
Rosemary

Dennis O'Keefe Show, The. See:
Towne, Hal

Dennis the Menace. See: Mitchell,
Dennis

DENNIS THE MENACE. See:
Mitchell, Dennis

DENNIS, UNCLE. See: McGee,
Fibber

DENNIS WEAVER. See: Marshall,
E. G.

DENNISON, LYDIA. See: Marshall,
John

DENNY. See also:
Bennie
Benny
Drummond, Captain Hugh
Morgan, Mrs. Amy

DENNY, GEORGE V., JR., mod-
erator of the program (himself)
STUDIO AUDIENCE PARTICI-
PANTS
America's Town Meeting of the
Air (R) (Political/social discus-
sion)

DENNY, JACK. See: Winchell,
Walter (1)

DENTON, WALTER. See:
Brooks, Connie

DEPOPOLOUS, NICK. See:
McGee, Fibber

DEPUTY. See: Dawg, Deputy

Deputy Dawg. See: Dawg, Deputy

Deputy, The. See: Fry, Marshal
Simon

DEPUTY, THE. See: Tennessee
Jed

Derby, The Roller. See: Brasuhn,
Tuffy

DEREHAM, FRANCIS. See: Henry
VIII, King of England

DEREK, INSPECTOR, officer of
the African Patrol
African Patrol (TV) (Jungle adventure)

DeROSE, PETER. See: Breen,
May Singhi

DERRINGER, YANCY, ex-Confederate officer, now secret agent
in New Orleans
PAHOO-KA-TA-WHA, his Indian
friend and bodyguard
Yancy Derringer (TV) (Adventure)

DES. See:
Adams, Crunch
O'Connor, Des

Des, Crunch and. See: Adams,
Crunch

Des O'Connor Show, The. See:
O'Connor, Des

Desire, Heart's. See: Alexander,
Ben (3)

Desk, City. See: Winters, Jack

DESMOND, JEAN PAUL. See:
Carr, Alison

DESMOND, JOHNNY, singer; host
of the program (himself)
JACQUELINE DuBIEF, skater,
featured on the program (herself)
THE SKIP-JACKS, vocal group
BOB BOUCHER, orchestra leader
(himself)
HIS ORCHESTRA
Music on Ice (TV) (Music/

ice skating)

DeSOTO, ROY. See: Gage, John

DESPERATE SMITH. See: Adams,
Crunch

Desperate Smith, Crunch Adams
and. See: Adams, Crunch

Destiny, Wings of. See: Benton,
Steve

Destry. See: Destry

DESTRY, Westerner, clearing himself of trumped-up robbery
charge
Destry (TV) (Western)

Detect and Collect. See: Uttal,
Fred (1)

DETECTIVE, portrayed by Don
Ameche
HIS COMIC SIDE-KICK, por-
trayed by Bob White
Milligan and Milligan (R)
(Comedy/adventure)

DETECTIVE. See also:
Harkness, Detective
Stone, Detective Lieut. Mike

DETECTIVE ADAM FLINT. See:
Parker, Lieut. Mike

Detective, Blackstone, The Magic.
See: Blackstone, Harry

DETECTIVE BROADHURST. See:
McCloud, Sam

Detective, Chick Carter, Boy. See:
Carter, Chick

Detective, City. See: Grant,
Bart

Detective Diary. See: Saber, Mark

DETECTIVE FRANK ARCARO. See:
Parker, Lieut. Mike

Detective, House. See: Holloway,
Dick

DETECTIVE JEFF WARD. See:

Haines, Lieut. Mike

DETECTIVE JIM HALLORAN. See:
Parker, Lieut. Mike

DETECTIVE JOE SMITH. See:
Friday, Sergeant Joe

DETECTIVE JOHNNY CORSO. See:
Haines, Lieut. Mike

DETECTIVE LIEUT. DAN MULDOON.
See: Parker, Lieut. Mike

Detective, Michael Shayne, Private.
See: Shayne, Michael

Detective Mysteries, True. See:
Shuttleworth, John

Detective, Nick Carter, Master.
See: Carter, Nick

Detective, Official. See:
Britt, Dan
Sloane, Everett

DETECTIVE O'HARE. See: Benny,
Jack

Detective, Richard Diamond, Private.
See: Diamond, Richard

Detective, Sam Spade. See: Spade,
Sam

DETECTIVE STEVE KELLER.
See: Stone, Detective Lieut. Mike

Detective, The Tune. See:
Spaeth, Sigmund

Detectives, Calling All. See: Robin

Detectives, The. See: Holbrook,
Captain Matt

DEUTSCH, EMERY. See: Ross,
David (1)

DEUTSCH, PATTI. See:
Byner, John (1)
Rowan, Dan

DEVERE. See: Overstreet, Buddy

DE VERE, BILLIE. See: Myrt

DEVERE, JUNIOR. See: Overstreet, Buddy

DEVERY, MR. See: O'Connor,
Katy

DEVINE, ANDY, movie and radio
comedian; host of the program
(himself)
GUNGA RAM, elephant boy
MANY CARTOONS
Andy's Gang (TV) (Children)

DEVINE, ANDY. See also:
Benny, Jack

DEVLIN McNEIL. See: Hansen,
David

DEVLIN, PEGGY. See: Randolph,
Alice

DEVOL, GWENDOLYN. See:
Armstrong, Jack

DEVOL, MONTE. See: Armstrong,
Jack

DeWITT, GEORGE
BILL CULLEN, quizmasters of
the program (themselves)
MANY CONTESTANTS
Name That Tune (TV) (Quiz)

DeWITT McBRIDE. See: Judge,
The

DEWITT, TOM-TOM. See:
Macauley, Wes

DeWOLF. See: Hopper, DeWolf

DEXTER FRANKLIN. See:
Archer, Corliss

DEXTER HAYES. See: Barrington,
Bryn Clark

DeYOE, TY. See: Rogers,
Patricia

DeZURIK, CAROLYN. See:
Lewandowski, Bob

Diagnosis: Unknown. See: Coffee,
Dr. Daniel

DIAHANN. See also:

Diane
Dianne

DIAHANN CARROLL. See: Crosby,
Bing (2)

Dial Hot Line. See: Lincoln, Dr.
Matt

Dial M for Music. See: O'Connor,
Father Norman

DIAMOND, CAPTAIN, lighthouse
keeper and spinner of yarns
MRS. DIAMOND, his wife
The Adventures of Captain Diamond (R) (Drama)

DIAMOND, RICHARD, detective
Richard Diamond, Private Detec-
tive (R) (TV) (Detective drama)
LIEUT. LEVINSON, police officer
Richard Diamond, Private Detec-
tive (R)
SAM, Diamond's telephone operator
KAREN WELLS, his associate
Richard Diamond, Private Detec-
tive (TV)

Diamonds, King of. See: King,
John

DIANA. See also:
Deanna
Dianna

DIANA DORS. See: Harrington,
Pat, Jr.

DIANA ROSS. See: Crosby, Bing
(2)

DIANA TAYLOR. See: Hardy, Dr.
Steven

DIANA TRASK. See: Miller, Mitch

DIANE. See:
Diahann
Dianne
Norby, Pearson

DIANE CARVELL RAMSEY. See:
Wayne, Ruth Evans

DIANE COURTNEY. See: Cross,
Milton (1)

DIANE DAVIS. See: Winters,
Jonathan

DIANE OGDEN. See: Jordan,
Joyce

DIANE PERS. See: Hopkins,
Kate

DIANE WARING. See: Bracken,
John

DIANNA. See also:
Deanna
Diana

DIANNA SCOTT. See: Owens,
Buck

DIANNE. See:
Diahann
Diane
La Volta, Dianne

DIANNE LENNON. See:
Lennon, Janet
Welk, Lawrence

DIANNE MATHRE. See: Kelly,
Joe (2)

Diary, Detective. See: Saber,
Mark

Diary, Maudie's. See: Mason,
Maudie

DIBBLE. See: Top Cat

DICK. See:
Cavett, Dick (1) (2) (3)
Clark, Dick (1) (2) (3)
Cooper, Dick
Cummings, Brenda
Dack
Daring, Dick
Dirk
Gentry, Tom
Haymes, Dick
Hildreth, Dick
Hollister, Dick
Holloway, Dick
Kent, Fred
Morgan, Jaye P.
Powell, Dick (1) (2) (3) (4)
Preston, Dick
Shawn, Dick
Smothers, Tom (1) (2) (3)

Starrett, Dick
Steele, Dick
Sterling, Dick
Tom
Tracy, Dick
Van Dyke, Dick (1) (2)
Worthington, Nora

Dick and Mary, Tom. See: Gentry, Tom

Dick and the Duchess. See: Starrett, Dick

DICK BAKALYAN. See: Darin, Bobby

Dick, Breakfast With Dorothy and. See: Kilgallen, Dorothy (1)

DICK BROWN. See: Parks, Bert (6)

DICK BURGESS. See: Wilbur, Judy

DICK CATHCART. See: Welk, Lawrence

DICK CAVETT. See:
Cavett, Dick (1) (2) (3)
Shawn, Dick

Dick Cavett Show, The. See: Cavett, Dick (1)

DICK CHANDLER. See: Walleck, Meredith

DICK CLAIR. See:
Jones, Dean
Kelly, Gene

Dick Clark Show, The. See: Clark, Dick (2)

DICK CONOVER. See: Rogers, Patricia

DICK CRANE. See: Carter, Kathryn

DICK CRAVENS. See: Kelly, Joe (2)

DICK CURTIS. See:
Stevens, Ray
Winters, Jonathan

DICK DALE. See: Welk, Lawrence

Dick Daring's Adventures. See: Daring, Dick

DICK EDWARDS. See: Como, Perry (1)

DICK GRANT, DR. See: Bauer, Bertha

DICK GRAYSON. See:
Batman
Kent, Clark

DICK GROSVENOR. See: Dallas, Stella

DICK HAMILTON. See: Shayne, Michael

Dick Haymes Show, The. See: Haymes, Dick

DICK HUDDLESTON. See: Edwards, Lum

DICK KESNER. See: Welk, Lawrence

DICK KOLLMAR. See: Kilgallen, Dorothy (1)

DICK LIBERTINI. See: Moore, Melba

DICK MALOOF. See: Welk, Lawrence

DICK MARTIN. See:
Allen, Joan Houston
Rowan, Dan

DICK NORTH. See: Trent, Helen

DICK PHILLIPS. See: Dawson, Rosemary

DICK POWELL. See:
Ayres, Lew
Boyer, Charles
Powell, Dick (1) (2) (3) (4)

Dick Powell Theater, The. See: Powell, Dick (2)

Dick Powell's Zane Grey Theater. See: Powell, Dick (2)

DICK SEDLACK. See: Kelly, Joe (2)

DICK SHERIDAN. See: Rogers, Patricia

DICK SMOTHERS. See: Smothers, Tom (1) (2) (3)

DICK STABILE. See: Bernie, Ben

Dick Steele, Boy Reporter. See: Steele, Dick

DICK STUART-CLARK. See: Upton, Michael

DICK THE BRUISER. See: James, Dennis (4)

DICK TODD. See: Henry, Captain Parks, Bert (5)

Dick Tracy. See: Tracy, Dick

Dick Van Dyke Show, The. See: Petrie, Rob

Dick Van Dyke Show, The New. See: Preston, Dick

DICK WILLIAMS SINGERS, THE. See: Andrews, Julie

DICK YOUNG. See: Webster, Martha

DICKENS. See also: Dickon

DICKENS, HARRY, carpenter
KATE, his wife
ARCH FENSTER, carpenter, buddy of Dickens
MR. BANNISTER, building contractor
MEL WARSHAW
MULLIGAN, friends of Dickens and Fenster
I'm Dickens--He's Fenster (TV) (Comedy)

DICKENSON, JEAN. See: Munn, Frank (1)

DICKERSON, BARBARA. See: Simms, Paul

DICKERSON, HOWIE. See: Simms, Paul

DICKEY, DAN'L
HIRAM NEVILLE
WILBUR Z. KNOX (GRANDSIR)
HATTIE
WILBUR
MARGIE
CARRIE
GRAMMIE, residents of New England village
Snow Village (R) (Drama)

DICKIE. See:
Armstrong, Jack
Chandler, Dr. Susan
Manning, Portia Blake

DICKIE VAN PATTEN. See: Barrymore, Ethel

DICKON. See:
Dickens
Tempest, Dan

DICKSON. See also: Dixon

DICKSON, DR. JOHN. See: Hughes, Chris

DI CONTINI, CAROLINE, CONTESSA. See: Rule, Harry

DIEGO. See: Vega, Don Diego

DIETRICH, CAPTAIN HANS. See: Troy, Sergeant Sam

DIGGER O'DELL. See: Riley, Chester A.

DI JULIO, GABBY. See: O'Toole, Ensign

DILLER, PHYLLIS, comedienne; star of the program (herself)
NORM CROSBY, comedian, featured on the program (himself)
MANY CELEBRITY GUESTS
The Beautiful Phyllis Diller Show (TV) (Conversation/variety)

DILLER, PHYLLIS. See also:
Berman, Shelley
Crosby, Bing (2)

DILLON, DAVY. See: Mason, Maudie

DILLON, JEFF. See: Howard, Glenn

DILLON, MARSHAL MATT, U.S.

Marshal at Dodge City, Kansas
DOC ADAMS, his friend; physician
CHESTER GOOD, his deputy
KITTY RUSSELL, his friend;
saloon proprietress
Marshal Dillon (R) (TV) (Western)
(later known as Gunsmoke) (TV)
FESTUS HAGGEN, his deputy
LOUIS PHEETERS, town drunk
MR. JONES, general store keeper
SAM, bartender
NATHAN BURKE, freight agent
BARNEY, telegraph operator
HANK, stableman
PERCY CRUMP, undertaker
HOWIE, hotel clerk
QUINT, half-breed Indian
MA SMALLEY, boardinghouse
keeper
LATHROP, storekeeper
MR. BODKIN, banker
HALLIGAN, resident of Dodge
City
ED O'CONNOR, rancher
Gunsmoke (TV) (Western)

DILLON, PEGGY. See: Bauer,
Barbara

DILLY DALLY. See: Doody, Howdy

DIMAGGIO, JOE, professional base-
ball player (himself)
The Joe DiMaggio Show (R)
(Sports)

DIMPLES. See: Keene, Kitty

DIMPLES WILSON. See: Bumstead,
Blondie

DINAH SHORE. See:
Cantor, Eddie (2)
Cross, Milton (1)
Ross, Lanny
Shore, Dinah (1) (2) (3)

Dinah Shore Show, The. See:
Shore, Dinah (2)

Dinah Shore, The Chevy Show
Starring. See: Shore, Dinah (1)

Dinah's Place. See: Shore, Dinah
(3)

DINEEN, LYNNE. See: Malone,
Dr. Jerry

DINEEN, PHYLLIS. See: Malone,
Dr. Jerry

DINEEN, ROGER. See: Malone,
Dr. Jerry

DING-A-LINGS, THE. See:
Martin, Dean (2)

Ding Dong School. See: Horwich,
Dr. Frances

"DINGBAT." See: Bunker, Archie

DINGHY MacROBERTS. See:
Higgins

Dining With David Wade. See:
Wade, David

DINK, WINKY. See: Barry,
Jack (10)

DINKY. See: Dugan, Jimmie

DINNING SISTERS, THE. See:
Kelly, Joe (1)

DINSDALE, SHIRLEY, ventriloquist
(herself)
JUDY SPLINTERS, her dummy
Shirley Dinsdale and Judy
Splinters (R) (TV) (Ventrilo-
quism)

DINSDALE, SHIRLEY. See also:
Cantor, Eddie (2)

DINTY MOORE. See: Jiggs

DION. See: Patrick, Dion

DIONCHECK, JANET. See: Perry,
John

Directions. See: Hodges, Gilbert

DIRK. See:
Dack
Dick
Massey, Christine

DIRK, STEVE. See: Brent,
Portia

Discovery. See: Buxton, Frank

DISH, LIEUT. See: Pierce,
Captain Hawkeye

DISTRICT ATTORNEY, MR., name-
less crusading prosecutor
MISS EDITH MILLER, his secre-
tary
HARRINGTON, police officer, his
associate
MISS RAND
POLICEMAN, characters appear-
ing on the program
Mr. District Attorney (R) (TV)
(Crime drama)

DITHERS, CORA. See: Bumstead,
Blondie

DITHERS, J.C. See: Bumstead,
Blondie

DITTENFEFFER, PAPA. See:
Young, Alan

Divorce Court. See: Judge (1)

Divorce, Orphans of. See: Worthington, Nora

DIX, DOROTHY (1), advice columnist
JOHN, her nephew
ROXANNE WALLINGFORD,
heiress
SHERMAN LANE, gangster
LELA WALLINGFORD, Roxanne's
mother
Dorothy Dix at Home (R) (Serial
drama)

DIX, DOROTHY (2), advice columnist,
portrayed by Barbara Winthrop
Dorothy Dix on the Air (R) (Advice)

DIXIE. See:
Peters, Bill
Pixie
Trixie

DIXIE McCALL. See: Gage, John

DIXON. See also: Dickson

DIXON, BOBBY (Robert), newlywed
GLORIA QUIGLEY DIXON, his
wife
MR. QUIGLEY
MRS. QUIGLEY, Gloria's parents
TWO GUEST NARRATORS PER
PROGRAM
ELLIOT LAWRENCE, orchestra

leader (himself)
HIS ORCHESTRA
That's Life (TV) (Musical drama)

DIXON, DONALD. See:
Bergen, Edgar (2)
Marx, Groucho (1)

DIXON, MACINTYRE. See: Klein,
Robert

DIXON, PETE. See: Kaufman,
Seymour

DIXON, WESLEY, head of the
house
JOAN, his wife
Meet the Dixons (R) (Serial
drama)

Dixons, Meet the. See: Dixon,
Wesley

DIZZY STEVENS. See: Aldrich,
Henry

DJINN-DJINN. See: Nelson,
Major Tony

DO
RE
MI, members of female singing
trio
The Do Re Mi Program (R)
(Music)

Do It, Let George. See: Soule,
Olan

DO-RIGHT, DUDLEY, bumbling
mountie
SNIDLEY WHIPLASH, villain
NELL, "wide-eyed, innocent
girl," all cartoon characters
Dudley Do-Right (TV) (Cartoon)

Do You Trust Your Wife? See:
Bergen, Edgar (1)

DOBBS. See: Parmenter, Captain
Wilton

DOBERMAN, PRIVATE. See:
Bilko, Sergeant Ernest

DOBIE. See: Gillis, Dobie

Dobie Gillis, The Many Loves of.

See: Gillis, Dobie

DOBLEN, GRACE. See: Johnson,
Bess

DOC. See:
Barclay, Doc
Hackett, Doc
Jolly, Mr.
Roberts, Doug
West, Jim (1)

DOC ADAMS. See: Dillon, Marshal
Matt

Doc Barclay's Daughters. See:
Barclay, Doc

DOC GAMBLE. See: McGee,
Fibber

DOC GORDON. See: Joe (1)

DOC HARRISON. See: Malone, Dr.
Jerry

DOC HOLLIDAY. See: Earp,
Wyatt

"DOC" KAISER, MAJOR. See:
Savage, Brigadier General Frank

DOC LONG. See: Packard, Jack

DOC MILLER. See: Edwards, Lum

DOC SEVERINSEN. See:
Carson, Johnny (1)
Fiedler, Arthur

DOC SHARPE. See: Marlin, Mary

DR. See:
Allen, Dr. Kate
Barton, Dr. Glenn
Bassett, Dr. Theodore
Baxter, Dr. Bill
Bragonier, Dr. J. Robert
Brent, Dr. Jim
Brothers, Dr. Joyce
Bryson, Dr. Lyman (1) (2)
Campanelli, Dr. Vincent
Carey, Dr. Philip
Casey, Dr. Ben
Chandler, Dr. Susan
Christian, Dr. Paul
Coffee, Dr. Daniel
Country Doctor, The

Davis, Dr. Althea
Gentry, Dr. Anne
Goldstone, Dr. Peter
Graham, Dr. Bob
Hagen, Dr. Harry
Hall, Dr. William Todhunter
Hardy, Dr. Steven
Hartley, Dr. Robert
Hoffman, Dr. Oswald J.
Horton, Dr. Tom
Horwich, Dr. Frances
Hudson, Dr. Wayne
Hunter, Dr. Paul
I.Q., Dr.
I.Q., Jr., Dr.
Jamison, Dr. Sean
January, Dr. Ben
Karnac, Dr.
Kenrad, Dr.
Kildare, Dr. James
Kimble Dr. Richard
Lincoln, Dr. Matt
Lochner, Dr. Paul
Locke, Dr. Simon (1) (2)
McCann, Dr. Noah
McKeever, Dr. John
McPheeters, Dr. Sardinius
Malone, Dr. Jerry
Ordway, Dr. Benjamin
Peterson, Dr. James
Rainey, Dr. Froelich
Reynolds, Dr. Mike
Reynolds, Dr. Tom
Rhodes, Dr. Michael
Rutledge, Dr. John
Spock, Dr. Benjamin M.
Stone, Dr. Alex
Styner, Dr. Konrad
Thompson, Dr. McKinley
Tracy, Dr. Marsh
Weird, Dr.
Welby, Dr. Marcus
Whitman, Dr. James
Williams, Dr.
Wilson, Dr. Thomas

DR. ABENDROTH. See: Hargrave-
Scott, Joan

DR. ABERNATHY. See: Hackett,
Doc

DR. ADAM HUDSON. See: Hudson, Nancy Smith

DR. ADRIENNE HARRIS. See:
Prescott, Kate Hathaway

DR. ALAN SIMMS. See: Dallas,
Stella

DR. ALAN WEBSTER. See:
Jordan, Joyce

DR. ALEC GORDON. See: Hargrave-
Scott, Joan

DR. ALEXANDER GREY. See:
Jordan, Joyce

DR. ALEXANDER SAS-JAWORSKY.
See: March, Hal

DR. ALFRED KIDDER. See:
Rainey, Dr. Froelich

DR. ANDREW SELLERS. See:
Locke, Dr. Simon (1)

DR. ANDREW WHITE. See:
Perkins, Ma

DR. ANDREWS. See: Jordan,
Joyce

DR. ANN SWENK. See: Newman,
Tony

DR. ANTHONY LORING. See:
Brown, Ellen

Doctor, Ask Your. See: Edman,
Karl

DR. AXLAND. See: Malone, Dr.
Jerry

DR. BARNETT. See: Cameron

DR. BARTLETT. See: Lochner,
Dr. Paul

DR. BAXTER. See: James,
Nancy

DR. BELLOWS. See: Nelson,
Major Tony

DR. BENTON QUEST. See: Quest,
Jonny

DR. BERNARD ALTMAN. See:
Whitman, Dr. James

DR. BILL EVANS. See: Brent,
Dr. Jim

DR. BLACK. See: Davis, Ann
Tyler

DR. BLINKY. See: Pufnstuf,
H. R.

DR. BOB HUGHES. See: Hughes,
Lisa

DR. BOB ROGERS. See: Tate,
Joanne

DR. BOROS. See: Johnson,
Bess

DR. BRADLEY. See: Harding,
Karen Adams

DR. BRUCE BANNING. See:
Bauer, Bertha

DR. BRUCE KINGSLEY. See:
O'Neill, Mrs.

DR. BRUCE PORTER. See:
Dale, Linda
Graham, Dr. Bob

DR. BURKE. See: Brent, Dr.
Jim

DR. BURR. See: Myrt

DR. BYRON. See: Manning,
Portia Blake

DR. CARLETON COON. See:
Rainey, Dr. Froelich

DR. CARSON McVICKER. See:
Brent, Dr. Jim

DR. CASSANDRA. See: Batman

DR. CHANCELLOR. See: Baines,
Scattergood

DR. CHARLES MATTHEWS. See:
Rutledge, Dr. John

DR. CHARLES TYLER. See:
Davis, Ann Tyler

Dr. Christian. See: Christian,
Dr. Paul

DR. CHRISTOPHER ELLERBE.
See: Hargrave-Scott, Joan

DR. CLAIRE MORTON. See:
Peyton, Martin

DR. CLEM ALLISON. See:
Booth, Martha

DR. CLIFFORD REED. See:
Jordan, Joyce

DR. COPP. See: Malone, Dr.
Jerry

Doctor, Crime. See: Ordway,
Dr. Benjamin

DR. DAN GARRETT. See: Garrett, Susan

DR. DAN PHILLIPS. See:
Sterling, Vanessa Dale

DR. DAVID CRAIG. See: Hunter,
Dr. Paul

DR. DAVID McKENZIE. See:
Grimm, Arnold

DR. DAVID MALONE. See:
Malone, Dr. Jerry

DR. DAVID MORGAN. See:
Jordan, Joyce

DR. DAVID STUART. See:
Hughes, Chris

DR. DAVID ZORBA. See: Casey,
Dr. Ben

DR. DAVIDSON. See: Hardy,
Dr. Steven

DR. DICK GRANT. See: Bauer,
Bertha

DR. DOUG PRESTON. See: Garrison, Spencer

DR. DOUG WILLIAMS. See:
Horton, Dr. Tom

DR. DOUGLAS CASSEN. See:
Hughes, Chris

DR. DOUGLASS. See: Brown,
Ellen

DR. DUNCAN CARVELL. See:

Wayne, Ruth Evans

DR. DUNHAM. See: Malone, Dr.
Jerry

DR. FLEMING. See: Trent,
Helen

DR. FRED CROWLEY. See:
Allen, Dr. Kate

DR. FRED THOMPSON. See:
Barbour, Henry Wilson

Doctor, Frontier. See: Baxter,
Dr. Bill

Dr. Gentry, The Affairs of. See:
Gentry, Dr. Anne

DR. GEORGE PRIESTLEY. See:
Hackett, Doc

DR. GIACOMO. See: Cross,
Milton (1)

DR. GLASSMAN. See: Perkins,
Ma

DR. GORDON. See: Hardy, Dr.
Steven

DR. GORDON MATHER. See:
Davis, Dr. Althea

DR. GRANT FRASIER. See:
Brent, Dr. Jim

DR. GREG PETERS. See:
Horton, Dr. Tom

DR. GREGORY PETTIT. See:
Goldstone, Dr. Peter

DR. HAINES. See: Guest, Edgar
A. (2)

DR. HALLIDAY. See: Chandler,
Dr. Susan

DR. HANS SIMONS. See: Jordan,
Joyce

DR. HANSEN. See: Davis, Dr.
Althea

DR. HOWARD CHANDLER. See:
Chandler, Dr. Susan

DR. KIRK HARDING. See:
Harding, Karen Adams

DR. KURTZ. See: Hillman, India

DR. KWAN. See: Malone, Dr.
Jerry

DR. LANSON. See: Hargrave-
Scott, Joan

DR. LAURA HORTON. See:
Horton, Dr. Tom

DR. LEE MARKHAM. See:
Harding, Karen Adams

DR. LEONARD GILLESPIE. See:
Kildare, Dr. James

DR. LESLIE FOSTER. See:
Marshall, John

DR. LEWIS. See: Randolph, Ellen

DR. LEWIS ROYAL. See: Hank

DR. LILIENTHAL. See: Hargrave-
Scott, Joan

DR. LLOYD GRAY. See: Welles,
Orson (3)

DR. LONSBERRY. See: Hughes,
Chris

DR. LUND. See: Marshall, John

DR. McCOY. See: Kirk, Captain
James

DR. MacINTOSH. See: Hardy,
Dr. Steven

DR. MADELYN KELLER. See:
Graham, Dr. Bob

DR. MAGGIE POWERS. See:
Davis, Dr. Althea

Dr. Malone, Young. See: Malone,
Dr. Jerry

DR. MARION SAYLE TAYLOR.
See: Voice of Experience, The

DR. MARK BROOKS. See:
Horton, Dr. Tom

DR. MARK CHRISTIAN. See:
Christian, Dr. Paul

DR. MARK PHILLIPS. See:
Cummings, Brenda

DR. MARKHAM. See: Solomon,
David

DR. MARLOWE. See: Wayne,
Ruth Evans

DR. MASON GROSS. See:
Shriner, Herb (3)

DR. MATT POWERS. See:
Davis, Dr. Althea

DR. MICHAEL ROSSI. See:
Peyton, Martin

DR. MIGUELITO LOVELESS.
See: West, Jim (2)

DR. MIKE POWERS. See: Davis,
Dr. Althea

DR. MILBURN. See: Grimm,
Arnold

DR. MILDERMAUL. See: Jordan,
Joyce

DR. MILES. See: Peyton, Martin

DR. MILLER. See: Brent, Dr.
Jim

DR. MITCHELL. See: Bauer,
Bertha

DR. MOLLY HEDGEROW. See:
Jordan, Joyce

DR. MORTON CHEGLEY. See:
Baker, Julia

DR. MOTILAL MOOKERJI. See:
Coffee, Dr. Daniel

DR. MUELLER. See: Levy, Abie

DR. MYRON HENDERSON. See:
Solomon, David

DR. NICK BELLINI. See: Davis,
Dr. Althea

DR. NORFOLK. See: Brent, Portia

DR. ORBO. See: Kelly, Kitty

DR. OWEN CRAIG. See: Kennedy, Carol

DR. PAUL BURTON. See: Carter, Kathryn
Harding, Karen Adams

DR. PAUL FLETCHER. See: Bauer, Bertha

DR. PAUL GRAHAM. See: Bassett, Dr. Theodore

DR. PECK. See: Sterling, Vanessa Dale

Doctor, Peggy's. See: McKeever, Dr. John

DR. PETER CHERNAK. See: Garrison, Spencer

DR. PETER TAYLOR. See: Hardy, Dr. Steven

DR. PETRIE. See: Fu Manchu

DR. PHIL BREWER. See: Hardy, Dr. Steven

DR. PHILBIN. See: Randolph, Alice

DR. PHILIP HAMILTON. See: Gentry, Dr. Anne

DR. PINKHAM. See: Hardy, Dr. Steven

DR. POLK. See: Walleck, Meredith

DR. POOCH HARDIN. See: Goldstone, Dr. Peter

DR. PURDY. See: Harding, Karen Adams

DR. RALPH MUNSON. See: Malone, Dr. Jerry

DR. RALPH STEVENS. See: Bradley, Judith

DR. RALPH THOMPSON. See: Brent, Dr. Jim

DR. RAMEY. See: Dallas, Stella

DR. RAY McGREGOR. See: Newman, Tony

DR. RAYBURN. See: Prescott, Kate Hathaway

DR. REED BANNISTER. See: Wayne, Ruth Evans

DR. REGINALD PARSONS. See: Brent, Dr. Jim

DR. REIMER. See: Cameron, Christy Allen

DR. REINHARDT. See: Jordan, Joyce

DR. RICHARD CAMPBELL. See: Nelson, Carolyn Kramer

DR. ROBBY CLARK. See: Johnson, Bess

DR. ROBERT GARDNER. See: Allen, Joan Houston

DR. RUSS SCOTT. See: Randolph, Alice

DR. SALTZMAN. See: Sterling, Vanessa Dale

DR. SAM MARSH. See: Goldstone, Dr. Peter

DR. SAMUEL TILDEN FIELD. See: Davis, Joan Field

DR. SARAH McINTYRE. See: Bauer, Bertha

DR. SEABROOK. See: Wayne, Ruth Evans

DR. SERGEANT. See: Drake, Nora

DR. SEWALL CRAWFORD. See: Malone, Dr. Jerry

DR. SHADE. See: King, Schyler "Sky"

DR. SIMMONS. See: Hardy,

Dr. Steven

Dr. Simon Locke. See: Locke,
Dr. Simon (1)

DR. SIMON LOCKE. See: Locke,
Dr. Simon (1) (2)

Dr. Spock. See: Spock, Dr. Benjamin M.

DR. STANLEY HOLTON. See:
Manning, Portia Blake

DR. STEVE. See: Arden, Jane

DR. STEVE ALDRICH. See: Davis,
Dr. Althea

DR. STEVE JACKSON. See: Bauer,
Bertha

DR. STEVEN KILEY. See: Welby,
Dr. Marcus

DR. STEVENS. See: Perkins, Ma

Dr. Susan, The Life and Loves of.
See: Chandler, Dr. Susan

DR. TANNER. See: Parker, Seth

DR. TARLIFF. See: Sterling,
Vanessa Dale

DR. TED HOFFMAN. See: Casey,
Dr. Ben

DR. TED STUART. See: Hunter,
Dr. Paul

DOCTOR, THE. See: Kelly, Kitty

Doctor, The Country. See:
Country Doctor, The

DR. THOMAS WEBSTER. See:
Jordan, Joyce

DR. TIM COLE. See: Hughes,
Chris

DR. TOM BALDWIN. See: Hardy,
Dr. Steven

DR. TONY CHALMERS. See:
Perry, John

DR. TONY LARSON. See: Hughes,
Lisa

DR. TONY VINCENTE. See:
Tate, Joanne

DR. TORRANCE. See: Harding,
Karen Adams

DR. TRACY. See: Jordan, Joyce

DR. TRUMAN "TUBBY" SCOTT.
See: Hargrave-Scott, Joan

DR. VIDO McCREA. See: Davis,
Dr. Althea

DR. VINCENT MARKHAM. See:
Peyton, Martin

DR. WADE COLLINS. See: Tate,
Joanne

DR. WARREN DOUGLAS. See:
Rogers, Patricia

Dr. Weird, The Strange. See:
Weird, Dr.

DR. WERNER. See: Bauer,
Bertha

DR. WESTHEIMER. See: Sterling,
Vanessa Dale

DR. WIGGINS. See: Davis, Joan
Field

DR. WILL CONNELLY. See:
Garrison, Spencer

DR. WILLIAM HORTON. See:
Horton, Dr. Tom

DR. WILLIAM RAYMER. See:
Thompson, Dr. McKinley

DR. WILTON. See: Harding,
Karen Adams

DR. WINSLOW. See: Brent, Dr.
Jim

DR. YATES. See: Brent, Dr.
Jim

DR. ZARKOV. See: Gordon,
Flash

Doctors, Laugh.　See: Pratt,
　Russell

Doctors, The.　See: Davis, Dr.
　Althea

Doctors, The (The Bold Ones).
　See: Hunter, Dr. Paul

Doctor's Wife, The.　See: Palmer,
　Dan

"DOCUS, MR. " (DOUGLAS ANDER-
SON).　See: Kirchener, Claude
(1)

DODD, HUBIE.　See: Dugan,
　Queenie

DODD, JIMMIE, song-leader and
　host of the program (himself)
　BOBBY
　ANNETTE
　NANCY
　JODY
　LONNIE
　BILLIE
　KAREN
　DARLENE
　MOOCHIE
　LINDA
　CHERYL
　DOREEN
　SHARON, children appearing on
　the program (themselves)
　WALT DISNEY CARTOON CHAR-
　ACTERS
　The Mickey Mouse Club (TV)
　(Children) (later reissued as
　The Mouseketeers) (TV)

DODGE, MARSHALL "MIKE, " story-
　teller of the program (himself)
　Downeast Smile-In (TV) (Stories)

DODGER, WILLY, female lawyer
　PAP, her father
　EMILY, her sister
　WALTER, her brother
　FRANKLIN, her nephew
　Willy (TV) (Comedy)

DODIE.　See:
　Douglas, Steve
　Dody

DODSWORTH, SAM, retired busi-
　ness executive

FRAN, his wife
Dodsworth (R) (Serial drama)

DODY.　See also: Dodie

DODY GOODMAN.　See: Paar,
　Jack

DOE, JOHN.　See: Allen, Fred

DOG.　See also: Dawg

Dog, Hot.　See: Worley, Jo Anne

Dog House, Uncle Walter's.　See:
　Uncle Walter

DOG, THE WONDER.　See: Rin-
　Tin-Tin

DOGGIE, AUGIE.　See: McGraw,
　Quick Draw

Doin' Their Thing.　See: Les-
　coulie, Jack (1)

Doing, What Am I?　See: Phillips,
　Dave

DOLENZ, MICKY.　See: Jones,
　Davy

DOLL.　See also:
　Dal
　Dale

Doll, My Living.　See: McDonald,
　Bob

Dollar a Second.　See: Murray,
　Jan (1)

DOLLAR, JOHNNY, detective
　Yours Truly, Johnny Dollar (R)
　(Adventure)

DOLLAR, LYNN.　See: March,
　Hal

Dollar, Top.　See: Reed, Toby

DOLLY.　See: Joe (2)

DOLLY PARTON.　See: Wagoner,
　Porter

DOLLY SNAFFLE.　See: Archie

DOLORES DRAGON. See: Kukla

DOLORES DUMONT. See: Guest,
Edgar A. (2)

DOLORES KING. See: Webster,
Martha

DOLORES WINTERS. See: Perry,
John

DOM DeLUISE. See:
DeLuise, Dom (1) (2)
Martin, Dean (2)

Dom DeLuise Show, The. See:
DeLuise, Dom (1)

DON. See:
Adams, Don
Alan, Don
Ameche, Don (1) (2) (3) (4)
Bradley, Judith
Carter, Kathryn
Corey, Don
Dan
Donn
Driggs, Karleton King
Everly, Don
Goddard, Don
Hollinger, Don
Hughes, Chris
Jagger, Don
Knotts, Don
McNeill, Don
Morrow, Don
Robinson, Don
Taylor, Andy
Towne, Don
Uncle Don
Winslow, Don

DON ADAMS. See:
Adams, Don
Crosby, Bing (2)

DON AMECHE. See:
Ameche, Don (1) (2) (3) (4)
Detective
First Nighter, Mr.

Don Ameche Show, The. See:
Murgatroyd, Mr.

Don Ameche's Playhouse. See:
Ameche, Don (2)

DON BESTOR. See: Benny, Jack

DON BRIGGS. See: Ameche, Don
(3)

DON CAVANAUGH. See: Webster,
Martha

DON CORNELL. See: Como,
Perry (1)

DON CORNWELL. See: Burton,
Terry

DON DIEGO. See: Vega, Don
Diego

DON DOWD. See: Jostyn, Jay
(1)

DON DURANT. See: Anthony,
Ray

DON HARRON. See: Owens,
Buck

DON HAUSER. See: Wagoner,
Porter

DON HERBERT. See: Wizard,
Mr.

DON KNOTTS. See:
Allen, Steve (1) (3)
Berman, Shelley
Knotts, Don

Don Knotts Show, The. See:
Knotts, Don

DON McKAYLE DANCERS, THE.
See:
Cosby, Bill (2)
Hirt, Al (1)
Uggams, Leslie

Don McNeill's Breakfast Club.
See: McNeill, Don

DON MEREDITH. See: Jackson,
Keith (2)

DON REID. See: Kirkwood, Jack

Don Rickles Show, The. See:
Robinson, Don

DON SEBASTIAN. See: Cannon,
John

DON SMITH. See: Warren, Wendy

DON, TOM AND. See: Kelly, Joe
(1)

DON WALDON. See: Lee, Jim

DON WAYNE. See: Berry, Ken

Don Winslow of the Navy. See:
    Winslow, Don

DONAHUE, PHIL, host of the pro-
gram (himself)
MANY GUESTS
The Phil Donahue Show (TV)
(Interviews)

DONAL. See also: Donald

DONAL LEACE. See: Walsh, Bob

DONALD. See:
    Barnhouse, Donald
    Brown, Velvet
    Cosby, Bill (3)
    Donal
    Ludwig, Professor Donald
    O'Connor, Donald
    Woods, Donald

DONALD CARPENTER. See:
    O'Connor, Katy

DONALD DIXON. See:
    Bergen, Edgar (2)
    Marx, Groucho (1)

DONALD DUCK. See: Mouse,
    Mickey

DONALD HUGHES. See: Halop,
    Billy

DONALD NOVIS. See: Bowers,
    Brainy

DONALD O'CONNOR. See:
    Crosby, Bing (2)
    Martin, Dean (1)
    O'Connor, Donald

Donald O'Connor Show, The. See:
    O'Connor, Donald

DONALD, PETER
EDDIE BRACKEN, moderators of
the program (themselves)

BETSY PALMER
ILKA CHASE
FRANK PARKER
JOHNNY JOHNSTON
BOBBY SHERWOOD
OGDEN NASH
BUFF COBB
SAM LEVENSON
AUDREY MEADOWS
LEE BOWMAN
FAYE EMERSON
PHIL SILVERS, panelists (them-
selves)
OTHER PANELISTS
CELEBRITY GUESTS, disguised
Masquerade Party (TV) (Panel
game)

DONALD, PETER. See also:
    Cross, Milton (2)
    Wilson, Ward

DONALD PUTNAM. See: Wilbur,
    Judy

DONALD VORHEES. See:
    Bell, Alexander Graham
    Gibson, Dot
    Melton, James (1)
    Welles, Orson (2)

DONALD WEST, MAJOR. See:
    Smith, Colonel Zachary

Done, It Can Be. See: Guest,
    Edgar A. (1)

DONLEVY, BRIAN. See: Frees,
    Paul

DONN. See also: Don

DONN, ARABELLA. See: Cooke,
    Alistaire (1)

DONNA. See:
    Donnie
    Driggs, Karleton King
    Harding, Mrs. Rhoda
    Stone, Dr. Alex

DONNA CAVENDISH. See: Wing,
    Howie

DONNA CREED. See: Soule,
    Olan (1)

DONNA DAE. See: Waring, Fred
    (1)

DONNA DRIGGS CONKLING. See:
Driggs, Karleton King

DONNA JEAN YOUNG. See:
Rowan, Dan

DONNA KING. See: Driggs,
Karleton King

Donna Reed Show, The. See:
Stone, Dr. Alex

DONNELLY, ARTHUR. See:
Carter, Kathryn

DONNELLY, DR. WILL. See:
Garrison, Spencer

DONNELLY, HELEN ELLIOTT.
See: Garrison, Spencer

DONNELLY, RICKY. See: Garrison, Spencer

DONNELLY, TOM. See: Garrison,
Spencer

DONNIE. See also: Donna

DONNIE HENDERSON. See:
Beulah

DONOVAN, DANNY. See: Kay,
Beatrice

DONOVAN, GARY, young man
afflicted with wanderlust
Full Circle (TV) (Drama)

DONOVAN, KERRY. See: Davidson, Bill

DONOVAN, MICKEY. See:
Kaltenmeyer, Professor August,
D. U. N.

DONOVAN, NANCY. See: Davidson, Bill

DONOVAN, STEVE, cowboy
RUSTY, his sidekick
Steve Donovan (TV) (Western)

Don't Call Me Charlie. See:
McKay, Judson

Don't Say, You! See: Narz, Jack
(6)

DOO. See: Scooby Doo

DOODLES WEAVER. See: Jones,
Spike (1)

DOODLETOWN PIPERS, THE.
See: Miller, Roger

DOODLETOWN PIPERS, THE NEW.
See: Hirt, Al (2)

DOODY, HOWDY, puppet, dressed
as a cowboy
DOUBLE DOODY, his twin
brother
BUFFALO BOB SMITH
PHINEAS T. BLUSTER
CLARABELL THE CLOWN,
portrayed by Bob Keeshan
CHIEF THUNDERDUD
DILLY DALLY
THE FLUBADUB
PRINCESS SUMMERFALL
WINTERSPRING, characters
appearing on the program
Howdy Doody (R) (TV) (Chil-
dren's program)

DOOLEY, JIM. See: Caesar,
Sid (1)

DOOLEY, PAUL. See: DeLuise,
Dom (1)

DOOLEY, UNCLE CHARLIE. See:
Day, Chris

DOONICAN, VAL, singer; host of
the program (himself)
BERNARD CRIBBINS
BOB TODD, comedians (them-
selves)
THE MIKE SAMMES SINGERS
THE NORMAN MAEN DANCERS
KENNY WOODMAN
JACK PARNELL, orchestra
leaders (themselves)
THEIR ORCHESTRAS
MANY GUEST STARS
Val Doonican (TV) (Variety)

Door Canteen, Stage. See:
Lytell, Bert (2)

Door, The Couple Next. See:

Soule, Olan (1)

Door, The Open. See: Hansen,
Dean Eric

Door, The Squeaking. See: Raymond

Doors, Behind Closed. See:
Zacharias, Rear Admiral Ellis M.

DOPHEIDE, HAZEL. See:
Grandma

DORA. See:
Foster, Judy
Perkins, Ma

DOREEN. See: Dodd, Jimmie

DORIA VAN DORN. See: Jordan,
Joyce

DORIE. See also: Dorrie

DORIE WINTERS. See: Jordan,
Joyce

DORIS. See: Martin, Doris

DORIS CAMERON. See: Nelson,
Carolyn Kramer

DORIS DAY. See: Ross, Lanny

Doris Day Show, The. See:
Martin, Doris

DORIS DEE. See: Noble, Mary

DORIS DREW. See: Ford,
Tennessee Ernie (4)

DORIS DUNSTAN. See: Banks,
Stanley

DORIS FAIRCHILD. See: Perkins,
Ma

DORIS HUDSON. See: Coffee,
Dr. Daniel

DORIS MONET. See: Wayne,
Ruth Evans

DORIS ROYAL. See: Hank

DORNE, HENRIETTA. See:

Marlin, Mary

DORNE, MICHAEL. See: Marlin,
Mary

DOROTHY. See:
Dix, Dorothy (1) (2)
Gordon, Dorothy
Kilgallen, Dorothy (1) (2)
Lamour, Dorothy
Walker, Eddie

Dorothy and Dick, Breakfast With.
See: Kilgallen, Dorothy (1)

DOROTHY BAXTER. See: Hazel

DOROTHY COLLINS. See:
Lanson, Snooky
Ross, Lanny

Dorothy Dix at Home. See: Dix,
Dorothy (1)

Dorothy Dix on the Air. See:
Dix, Dorothy (2)

DOROTHY GISH. See: Soule,
Olan (1)

DOROTHY HART. See: Stokey,
Mike

DOROTHY JACKSON. See:
Miller, Johnny

DOROTHY KILGALLEN. See:
Daly, John (3)
Kilgallen, Dorothy (1) (2)
Landi, Elissa

DOROTHY LAMOUR. See:
Ameche, Don (1)
Lamour, Dorothy

Dorothy Lamour Program, The.
See: Lamour, Dorothy

DOROTHY LOUDON. See: Van
Dyke, Dick (1)

DOROTHY MORAN. See: Carter,
Kathryn

DOROTHY NASH. See: Davidson,
Bill

DOROTHY READS. See: Brent,
Dr. Jim

DOROTHY SHAY. See: Jones,
Spike (2)

DOROTHY STEWART. See:
Drake, Nora

DOROTHY WALLACE WEBB. See:
Regan, Terry

DORRIE. See also: Dorie

DORRIE, AUNT. See: Warren,
Wendy

DORS, DIANA. See: Harrington,
Pat, Jr.

DORSET, SERGEANT. See:
Mason, Perry

DORSEY, JIMMY. See:
Birthday Man, The
Crosby, Bing (3)
Dorsey, Tommy

DORSEY, TOMMY, trombonist and
orchestra leader (himself)
JIMMY DORSEY, saxophonist,
co-leader of orchestra (himself)
THEIR ORCHESTRA
MANY GUEST STARS
THE JUNE TAYLOR DANCERS
The Fabulous Dorseys (TV)
(Music/variety) (also known as
Stage Show) (TV)

DORSEY, TOMMY. See also:
Crosby, Bing (3)

Dorseys, The Fabulous. See:
Dorsey, Tommy

D'ORSO DANCERS, THE WISA.
See: Nye, Louis

DOT. See:
Dyke, Charity Amanda
Gibson, Dot
Horton, Dot

Dot and Will. See: Horton, Dot

DOT HOUSTON. See: Allen, Joan
Houston

DOTTIE. See also:
Dotty
Doty

DOTTIE BRAINFEEBLE. See:
Gook, Vic

DOTTIE MAHONEY. See: Allen,
Fred

DOTTIE, POLKA. See: Russell,
Todd

Dotto. See: Narz, Jack (2)

DOTTY
JOHNNY, characters appearing
on the program
Listen to This (R) (Music and
conversation)

DOTTY. See also:
Dottie
Doty

DOTTY MACK. See: Van Dyke,
Dick (2)

DOTY. See also:
Dottie
Dotty

DOTY, JACK. See: First
Nighter, Mr.

DOUBLE. See: Doody, Howdy

Double Deckers, Here Come the.
See: Brains

Double Deckers, The. See:
Brains

Double Life of Henry Phyfe, The.
See: Phyfe, Henry

Double or Nothing. See: Compton,
Walter

DOUG. See:
Adams, Doug
Pletcher, Doug
Roberts, Doug

DOUG MARTIN. See: Tate,
Joanne

DOUG PHILLIPS. See: Newman,
Tony

DOUG PRESTON, DR. See:
Garrison, Spencer

DOUG WILLIAMS, DR. See:
Horton, Dr. Tom

Dough, Tic-Tac. See: Barry, Jack
(8)

DOUGHERTY, MARGARET MARY.
See: Kelly, Joe (2)

DOUGLAS. See:
Edwards, Douglas
Fairbanks, Douglas
Renfrew, Inspector Douglas
Trent, Helen

DOUGLAS, AL. See: Solomon,
David

DOUGLAS, BRUCE. See: Dyke,
Charity Amanda

DOUGLAS BUTTERNUT, LITTLE.
See: Peppertag, Aaron

DOUGLAS CASSEN, DR. See:
Hughes, Chris

DOUGLAS, DR. WARREN. See:
Rogers, Patricia

DOUGLAS EDWARDS. See:
Edwards, Douglas
Myerson, Bess

Douglas Edwards With the News.
See: Edwards, Douglas

Douglas Fairbanks Presents.
See: Fairbanks, Douglas

DOUGLAS, FREDDY (BUDDY).
See: Johnny

DOUGLAS, JACK (1), host and
narrator of the program (himself)
I Search for Adventure (TV)
(Voyage/adventure)

DOUGLAS, JACK (2), host of the
program (himself)
MANY ACTORS AND ACTRESSES
Keyhole (TV) (Drama)

DOUGLAS, JACK (3), host and narrator of the program (himself)
Seven League Boots (TV) (Travel)

DOUGLAS, MARK. See: Warren,
Wendy

DOUGLAS, MARTIN. See: Dyke,
Charity Amanda

DOUGLAS, MELVYN. See: Ayres,
Lew

DOUGLAS, MIKE, host of the pro-
gram (himself)
VARIOUS CELEBRITIES AS CO-
HOSTS
GUEST STARS
The Mike Douglas Show (TV)
(Conversation)

DOUGLAS, MIKE. See also:
James, Dennis (1)

DOUGLAS "MR. DOCUS" ANDER-
SON. See: Kirchener, Claude
(1)

DOUGLAS, NORMA. See: Caesar,
Sid (1)

DOUGLAS NORMAN. See: Solomon, David

DOUGLAS, OLIVER, farmer, near
Hooterville
LISA, his wife
SAM DRUCKER, storekeeper
RALPH MONROE, lady carpenter
HANEY, "the pesky huckster"
EB, farmhand
ARNOLD, educated pig
ZIFFEL, Arnold's owner
MRS. ZIFFEL, Ziffel's wife
HANK KIMBALL, resident of
Hooterville
Green Acres (TV) (Situation
comedy)

DOUGLAS, PAUL, master of
ceremonies of the program
(himself)
The Saturday Night Swing Club
(R) (Music)

DOUGLAS, PAUL. See also:
Edwards, Ralph (1)

DOUGLAS, PAULETTE. See:
Bracken, John

DOUGLAS STANBURY. See: Roxy

DOUGLAS, STEVE, widower;
marries Barbara

ROBBIE, his son by his first
marriage; marries Katie
CHIP, his son by his first mar-
riage; marries Polly
ERNIE, his son by his first mar-
riage
BARBARA, his second wife; pre-
viously divorced
KATIE, her daughter by her first
marriage; marries Robbie
POLLY, her daughter by her first
marriage; marries Chip
DODIE, her daughter by her first
marriage
JOHN
HENRY
ROY, triplets; sons of Robbie and
Katie
UNCLE CHARLEY, Steve's uncle
MICHAEL FRANCIS O'CASEY
(Bub), Steve's father-in-law
My Three Sons (TV) (Family
situation comedy)

DOUGLAS, WADE. See: Dane,
Prudence

DOUGLAS WINTHROP. See:
Ames, Peter

DOUGLASS, DR. See: Brown,
Ellen

DOUGHNUTS. See: Brains

DOVETONSILS, PERCY. See:
Kovacs, Ernie (1)

DOW, ANGIE. See: Lane, Hondo

Dow Hour of Great Mysteries, The.
See: Welch, Joseph N.

DOW, JOHNNY. See: Lane, Hondo

DOWAGER DUCHESS OF NORFOLK.
See: Henry VIII, King of England

DOWD, DON. See: Jostyn, Jay
(1)

DOWLING, EDDIE. See: Heatter,
Gabriel

Down You Go. See: Evans, Bergen
(1)

Downeast Smile-In. See: Dodge,

Marshall "Mike"

DOWNS, ADA. See: Randolph,
Alice

DOWNS, ERNIE. See: Randolph,
Alice

DOWNS, HUGH
DAVE GARROWAY
JOHN CHANCELLOR
FRANK McGEE
BARBARA WALTERS, hosts of
the program (themselves)
MUGGS, chimpanzee appearing
on the program (himself)
MANY GUESTS AND GUEST
HOSTS
Today (TV) (News/variety)

DOWNS, HUGH. See also:
Clayton, Bob (1)
Paar, Jack

DOWNTOWN BEAUTIES, THE
BEAUTIFUL. See: Rowan, Dan

DOYLE. See: Wilburn, Doyle

DR. Items so prefixed are indexed
as though spelled "Doctor"

Dragnet. See: Friday, Sergeant
Joe

DRAGON, DOLORES. See: Kukla

DRAGON LADY, THE. See: Lee,
Terry

DRAGONETTE, JESSICA (1)
ROSS GRAHAM
FRANK BANTA
MILTON RETTENBERG
LUCILLE MANNERS, featured
on the program (themselves)
THE CAVALIERS QUARTET,
singing group
PAUL LAVALLE
ROSARIO BORDON, orchestra
leaders (themselves)
THEIR ORCHESTRAS
MANY GUEST STARS
The Cities Service Concert (R)
(Music)

DRAGONETTE, JESSICA (2)
BENNY FIELDS, featured on the

program (themselves)
BABY SNOOKS, precocious child
DADDY HIGGINS, her father
The Palmolive Beauty Box
Theater (R) (Music/variety)

DRAGONETTE, JESSICA (3)
BILL PERRY, singers, featured
on the program (themselves)
GUSTAVE HAENSCHEN, orchestra
leader (himself)
HIS ORCHESTRA
Saturday Night Serenade (R)
(Music)

DRAINARD, BOB. See: Guest,
Edgar A. (2)

DRAKE. See: Andrews, Drake

DRAKE, ADAM. See: Karr, Mike

DRAKE, ALAN, insurance investi-
gator
HIS ASSISTANT
Special Agent (R) (Adventure)

DRAKE, ALFRED. See: Barlow,
Howard

DRAKE, BARTON, detective
Murder Is My Hobby (R) (Detective adventure)

DRAKE, BETTY, wife
BOB DRAKE, her husband
MAE DRAKE, Bob's mother
CARL GRAINGER
ETHEL GRAINGER
TONY HARKER
PETER STANDISH
KATHY STONE
JANE HARTFORD
MARY ROSE SPENCER VANCE
ALAN BISHOP
MRS. CARY
MRS. HENDRIX
GEORGE
MARCIA
GARDENIA
MADELINE, characters appear-
ing in the drama
Betty and Bob (R) (Serial drama)

DRAKE, BRADLEY, chief of the
American Black Chamber
STEVE, his assistant
PARADINE, master spy

JOYCE CARRAWAY, Paradine's
assistant
Stories of the Black Chamber
(R) (Adventure drama)

DRAKE, CANDICE. See: Carter,
Kathryn

DRAKE, CAPTAIN, police officer
Under Arrest (R) (Adventure)

DRAKE, DEBBIE, physical culturist, hostess of the program
(herself)
The Debbie Drake Show (TV)
(Exercise)

DRAKE, EDDIE, private detective
The Cases of Eddie Drake (TV)
(Detective)

DRAKE, EVE. See: Adams,
Howard

DRAKE, GALEN, story teller and
radio personality; host of the
program (himself)
STUART FOSTER
RITA ELLIS, featured vocalists
on the program (themselves)
MANY GUEST STARS
Galen Drake (TV) (Variety)

DRAKE, JOHN, British secret
agent assigned to NATO
Secret Agent (TV) (Crime drama)
(also known as Danger Man)
(TV)

DRAKE, LETA POWELL. See:
Bragonier, Dr. J. Robert

DRAKE, LYDIA. See: Jordan,
Joyce

DRAKE, NORA
ARTHUR DRAKE
LORRAINE HARTLEY
DAVID BROWN
SUZANNE TURRIE
DOROTHY STEWART
GILLIAN GRAY
DR. KEN MARTINSON, physician
ANDREW KING
TOM MORLEY
PEG MARTINSON
ROSE FULLER
DR. SERGEANT, physician

GEORGE STEWART, characters
appearing in the drama
This Is Nora Drake (R) (Serial
drama)

DRAKE, PAUL. See: Mason,
Perry

DRAKE, SILAS. See: Wilbur, Judy

DRAKE, SIR FRANCIS, admiral in
the British navy
ELIZABETH I, Queen of England
Sir Francis Drake (TV) (Adventure)

DRAKE, WALTER. See: Carter,
Kathryn

Drama, Deadline. See: Lovejoy,
Frank (2)

Dramas, Irene Rich. See: Rich,
Irene

DRAYTON, JOHN ADAM. See:
Perkins, Ma

Dream Factory, The Hollywood.
See: Cavett, Dick (2)

Dream Has Come True, Your. See:
Keith, Ian

Dream Machine, The Great American. See: Efron, Marshall

Dream of Jeannie, I. See: Nelson,
Major Tony

Dreams Come True. See: Mc-
Kinley, Barry

Dreams, Painted. See: Moynihan,
Mother

Dreams, Rose of My. See: Rose

DREIER. See also: Drier

DREIER, ALEX. See:
Arnold, Eddy
Goren, Charles
Jones, Dean

DREW. See: Pearson, Drew

DREW, DORIS. See: Ford,

Tennessee Ernie (4)

DREW, JOHN
JULIA MARLOWE
MORAN AND MACK (The Two
Black Crows)
GEORGE GERSHWIN
WEBER AND FIELDS
EDDIE CANTOR
IRVIN S. COBB
D. W. GRIFFITH
WILL ROGERS
VAN AND SCHENCK
ELSIE JANIS
WALTER C. KELLY
MANY OTHERS
THE FLONZALEY STRING
QUARTET, actors, singers and
personalities appearing on the
program (themselves)
The Eveready Hour (R) (Variety)

Drew Pearson. See: Pearson,
Drew

DREW SINCLAIR. See: Trent,
Helen

DREXEL, THORNTON. See:
Leighton, Linda

DREXTON, OLIVER. See: Sunday

DRIER. See also: Dreier

DRIER, MOOSIE. See: Rowan,
Dan

DRIGGS. See also: Briggs

DRIGGS, KARLETON KING
HAZEL, his wife
BILL, their son
BARBARA, Bill's wife
RAY
DON, their sons
CHERYL, Don's wife
MAXINE DRIGGS THOMAS
(Maxine King), Karleton's sister
LAVARN THOMAS, Maxine's
husband
TOM, son of Maxine and Lavarn
DONNA, Tom's wife
CAROLYN, daughter of Maxine
and Lavarn
LUISE DRIGGS McBURNEY
(Luise King), sister of Karleton
AL McBURNEY (Alvino Rey),

husband of Luise
ROBI
JOHN, sons of Luise and Al
LIZA, daughter of Luise and Al
YVONNE DRIGGS BURCH (Yvonne
King), sister of Karleton
BILL BURCH, Yvonne's husband
TINA COLE HOWARD, daughter
of Yvonne by a previous marriage
CATHY, daughter of Yvonne
WILLIAM KING DRIGGS, JR.,
brother of Karleton
PHYLLIS, wife of William
STEVE
DEBRA
JONATHAN, children of William
and Phyllis
MARILYN DRIGGS LARSEN
(Marilyn King), sister of Karleton
KENT LARSEN, husband of
Marilyn
SUSANNAH LLOYD
ADAM LLOYD, children of
Marilyn by a previous marriage
JENNIFER, daughter of Marilyn
and Kent
ALYCE DRIGGS CLARKE (Alyce
King), sister of Karleton
BOB CLARKE, husband of Alyce
CAM, son of Bob and Alyce
LEX DE AZEVDO, son of Alyce
by a previous marriage
LINDA, Lex's wife
RIC DE AZEVDO, son of Alyce
by a previous marriage
DONNA DRIGGS CONKLING (Donna
King), sister of Karleton
JIM CONKLING, Donna's husband
CANDY CONKLING WILSON,
daughter of Donna and Jim
BOB WILSON, husband of Candy
JAMIE
LAURETTE
OCHRIS
XAN, children of Donna and Jim;
members of the family, singers
appearing on the program (them-
selves)
RALPH CARMICHAEL, orchestra
leader (himself)
HIS ORCHESTRA
The King Family (TV) (Vocal
music)

DRINKWATER, CASSANDRA. See:
Old Ranger, The

DRINKWATER, WILLIAM (The

Governor), politician and widower
J.J. (Jennifer Jo), his 23-year-
old daughter
MAGGIE McLEOD, his secretary
GEORGE, his political aide and
press secretary
SARA, his housekeeper
The Governor and J.J. (TV)
(Comedy)

DRIZ GUMP. See: Brent, Portia

DROOPER. See: Fleegle

Droppers, Name. See: Lohman,
Al

DRUCKER, MAJOR. See: Barton,
Clara

DRUCKER, SAM. See:
Carson, Uncle Joe
Douglas, Oliver

DRUGGIST, THE. See: Milquetoast, Casper

DRUM, JEFFERSON, crusading
newspaper editor in Western
town of Jubilee
JOEY, his son
Jefferson Drum (TV) (Western)
(originally called The Quill and
the Gun) (TV)

DRUM MAJORETTE. See: Ross,
Arthur

DRUMMOND, CAPTAIN HUGH
(Bulldog Drummond), adventurer
DENNY, his assistant
Bulldog Drummond (R) (Mystery/
adventure)

DRUMMOND-RANDOLPH, CISSY.
See: Corbett, Tom (1)

Drums, Roses and. See: Hopper,
DeWolf

DRUNK, THE. See: Junior

DRUSILLA, AUNT. See: Cooke,
Alistaire (1)

DRYSDALE, MILBURN. See:
Clampett, Jed

DRYSDALE, MRS. See: Clampett,
Jed

DUANE. See also: Dwayne

DUANE GALLOWAY. See: Varner,
Will

DuBIEF, JACQUELINE. See:
Desmond, Johnny

DUBOIS, MRS. See: Noble, Mary

Duchess, Dick and the. See:
Starrett, Dick

DUCHESS OF NORFOLK, DOWAGER.
See: Henry VIII, King of England

DUCK, DONALD. See: Mouse,
Mickey

DUCK, HERMAN THE. See:
Burns, George (1)

DUCKLES, VINCE. See: Sharp,
Hal

DUD. See:
Bud
Budd
Williamson, Dud

DUDLEY. See: Do-Right, Dudley

Dudley Do-Right. See: Do-Right,
Dudley

DUDLEY, LANCE. See: Brent,
Portia

DUDLEY, MARTHA YOUNG. See:
Brent, Portia

DUDLEY TROWBRIDGE. See:
Hargrave-Scott, Joan

DUFFY. See:
Nelson
Parmenter, Captain Wilton

DUFFY, ALICE. See: Noble, Mary

DUFFY, MISS. See: Archie

DUFFY, MR. See: Grimm,
Arnold

DUFFY, PUDDINHEAD. See:
Dugan, Jimmie

Duffy's Tavern. See: Archie

DUGAN
KODIAK, construction engineers
Troubleshooters (TV) (Adventure)

DUGAN, JIMMIE, twelve-year-old
boy
DINKY DUGAN, his brother
WASHINGTON JONES
PUDDINHEAD DUFFY
AGGIE RILEY
VICTOR
DAISY, his young friends
Reg'lar Fellers (TV) (Children's
program)

DUGAN, QUEENIE, Hollywood stunt
girl
KIM TRACY, her roommate;
aspiring actress
HUBIE DODD, her boy friend
ANDY BOONE, Kim's boy friend;
theatrical agent
So This is Hollywood (TV)
(Situation comedy)

DUKE. See:
Johnson, Bess
McCray, Linc
Morgan, Jaye P.
Pyle, Gomer

DUKE ELLINGTON. See:
Basie, Count
Whiteman, Paul

DUKE LAKALE, EDWARD. See:
McGarrett, Steve

DUKE OF MARLBOROUGH. See:
Churchill, John

DUKE OF NORFOLK. See: Henry
VIII, King of England

DUKE OF PADUCAH, THE, char-
acter portrayed by Whitey Ford
TOM, DICK AND HARRY
LOUISE MASSEY AND THE
WESTERNERS, vocal groups
Plantation Party (R) (Comedy/
music)

DUKE OF PADUCAH, THE. See

also: Solemn Old Judge, The

DUKE OF YORK, THE. See:
Churchill, John

DUKE PAIGE. See: Longstreet,
Mike

DULCEY COOPERSMITH. See:
Crown, Jim

DULCY. See: Horton, Dot

DUMB DAME, THE. See: Med-
bury, John P.

DUMKE, RALPH. See: East,
Ed (2) (3)

DUMONT, DOLORES. See:
Guest, Edgar A. (2)

DUMPLING, BABY (ALEXANDER).
See: Bumstead, Blondie

DUNBAR, ALLEN. See: Ames,
Peter

DUNBAR, MIKE, U. S. marshal in
Wichita, Kansas
BEN MATHESON, his deputy
Wichita Town (TV) (Western)

DUNCAN. See: Carlyle, Baylor

DUNCAN, ANDREW. See: Caesar,
Sid (1)

DUNCAN, ARTHUR. See: Welk,
Lawrence

DUNCAN CARVELL, DR. See:
Wayne, Ruth Evans

DUNCAN, DANNY. See: Kelly,
Joe (1)

DUNCAN ERIC TATE. See: Tate,
Joanne

DUNCAN MacROBERTS. See:
Higgins

DUNCAN, MARIE. See: Malone,
Dr. Jerry

DUNCAN WARING. See: Upton,
Michael

DUNDEE, "a trail-riding British
lawyer"
THE CULHANE, his assistant
and traveling companion
Dundee and the Culhane (TV)
(Adventure)

Dundee and the Culhane. See:
Dundee

DUNHAM, DR. See: Malone,
Dr. Jerry

DUNHAM, MIRA. See: Malone,
Dr. Jerry

DUNLAP, SALLY. See: Regan,
Terry

DUNN, EDDIE. See: Hagen, Dr.
Harry

DUNNE, STEVE, quizmaster of the
program (himself)
MANY CONTESTANTS
You're On Your Own (TV)
(Quiz)

DUNNINGER, JOSEPH (The Master
Mentalist), magician and mind
reader; host of the program
(himself)
BILL SLATER
MARILYN DAY, entertainers
appearing on the program (themselves)
ANDY LOVE'S VOCAL GROUP,
singers
MITCHELL AYRES, orchestra
leader (himself)
HIS ORCHESTRA
The Dunninger Show (R) (Mind
reading/variety) (later appeared
on TV in modified form)

DUNNINGER, JOSEPH. See also:
Winchell, Paul (1)

DUNSTAN, BUCKLEY. See:
Banks, Stanley

DUNSTAN, DORIS. See: Banks,
Stanley

DUNSTAN, HERBERT. See:
Banks, Stanley

DUO, THE DYNAMIC. See: Batman

DuPont Show With June Allyson, The.
  See: Allyson, June

DURAIN, JEFF. See: Halliday,
  Mike

DURANT, DON. See: Anthony, Ray

DURANT, HARRIET. See: Wayne,
  Ruth Evans

DURANT, WELLINGTON. See:
  Wayne, Ruth Evans

DURANTE, JIMMY, comedian,
  pianist and singer; star of the
  program (himself)
  MANY GUEST STARS
  The Jimmy Durante Show (R) (TV)
  (Comedy/variety)
  GARRY MOORE, featured on the
  program (himself)
  HOTBREATH HOULIHAN
  VERA VAGUE
  UMBRIAGO
  MRS. CALABASH, characters
  appearing on the program
  XAVIER CUGAT, orchestra
  leader (himself)
  HIS ORCHESTRA
  The Jimmy Durante Show (R)
  EDDIE JACKSON, singer and
  entertainer featured on the pro-
  gram (himself)
  The Jimmy Durante Show (TV)

DURANTE, JIMMY. See also:
  Bowers, Brainy
  Lennon, Janet
  Martin, Dean (1)
  Raye, Martha (1)

DURBIN, DEANNA. See: Cantor,
  Eddie (2)

DURWARD KIRBY. See:
  Funt, Allen (1)
  Kirby, Durward
  Moore, Garry (1) (3) (5)
  Morgan, Henry

DUSKIN, RUTHIE. See: Kelly,
  Joe (2)

DUTCH. See:
  Brent, Dr. Jim
  Butch
  McCray, Linc

DUTELL, VERNON. See: Nona

DUTTON, CHARLES. See:
  Miller, Albert

DUTTON, DAPHNE DeWITT. See:
  Madison, Kenny

DUTTON, GRACE. See: Miller,
  Albert

DUTTON, NICK. See: Miller,
  Albert

DWAYNE. See also: Duane

DWAYNE WITT. See: Tammy

DWIGHT. See: Sunday

DWIGHT EISENHOWER WONG.
  See: Jones, Kenneth Yarborough

DWIGHT KRAMER. See: Nelson,
  Carolyn Kramer

DWIGHT WEIST. See: Heatter,
  Gabriel

DYER, CHARLIE. See: Hastings,
  Bob

DYKE, CHARITY AMANDA,
  Southern girl
  JOSEPH DYKE
  COLONEL LEIGHTON
  EDWARD LEIGHTON
  MRS. LEIGHTON
  MARION LEIGHTON
  SUSAN LEIGHTON
  OLIVE COURTLEIGH
  WALTER COURTLEIGH
  CHARLIE HARRIS
  MR. LENORD
  MRS. LENORD
  AUNT MAIZIE
  JIM TOLLIVER
  FRASER AMES
  TOM AMES
  BRET ALLEN
  MRS. GILDER
  ROY CALVERT
  CLAIRE TREMAN
  MR. SCHULTZ
  IRENE MILLER
  SYLVIA MEADOWS
  ROGER MANNING
  BRUCE DOUGLAS

MARTIN DOUGLAS
JEAN CURTIS
RALPH DALY
NAT
DOT
JOB, characters appearing in
the drama
Amanda of Honeymoon Hill (R)
(Serial drama)

DYNAMIC DUO, THE. See: Batman

E. G.   See: Marshall, E. G.

E. J. STOCKER.   See: Burke,
Stoney

E. J. WALKER.   See: Arden, Jane

E. S. P.   See: Price, Vincent

EAGLE.   See: Brave Eagle

Eagle, Brave.   See: Brave Eagle

EAGLE, HARRIET.   See: Trent,
Helen

EAGLE, WILD.   See: Parmenter,
Captain Wilton

EARL.   See:
Corey, Earl
Morgan, Mrs. Amy

EARL BROWN SINGERS, THE.
See: Bono, Salvatore

EARL, CRAIG.   See: Professor
Quiz

EARL ROGERS.   See: Miller,
Mitch

EARL WAGGEDORN.   See: Baker,
Julia

EARLE, MERIE.   See: Reed,
Jerry

EARLE, ROBERT, quizmaster of
the program (himself)
PANELS OF STUDENTS FROM
COMPETING COLLEGES
College Bowl (TV) (Panel quiz)
(Also known as The G. E. College
Bowl) (TV)

EARLY, DR. JOE.   See: Gage,
John

EARP, WYATT, American sheriff
in Old West
BAT MASTERSON
DOC HOLLIDAY, his deputies
The Life and Legend of Wyatt
Earp (TV) (Western)

Earth, The Greatest Show on.   See:
Slate, Johnny

EAST, ED (1)
POLLY EAST, host and hostess
of the program (themselves)
Kitchen Quiz (R) (Homemaking)

EAST, ED (2)
RALPH DUMKE, comedians,
featured on the program (themselves)
The Quality Twins (R) (Comedy)

EAST, ED (3)
RALPH DUMKE, featured on the
program (themselves)
Sisters of the Skillet (R) (Comedy)

EAST, ED.   See also: McWilliams,
Jim (1)

East Side/West Side.   See: Scott,
George C.

Easy Aces.   See: Ace, Goodman

Easy Does It.   See: Steele, Ted

EASY RIDER.   See: Cosby, Bill
(1)

EATON.   See: Eton

EB.   See:
Blurt, Elmer
Douglas, Oliver
Ed

EB MARTIN.   See: Perkins, Ma

EBBA FIELDING.   See: Cameron,
Christy Allen

EBEN.   See: Crowell, Jonah

EBENEZER WILLIAMS.   See:
Charles, Nick

Echoes of the Orient.   See: Von
Hallberg, Gene

ECHOES, THE.   See: Fisher,
Eddie

ED.   See:
Allen, Ed
Ames, Joe
Bauer, Bertha
Bottcher, Ed
East, Ed (1) (2) (3)

Eb
Fitzgerald, Ed
Herlihy, Ed
Huddles, Ed
McConnell, Ed
McMahon, Ed (1) (2)
Sullivan, Ed
Williams, Dr.
Wynn, Ed.

Ed Allen. See: Allen, Ed

ED BROWN, SERGEANT. See:
Ironside, Chief Robert

ED CROWLEY. See: Johnson,
Bess

ED EAST. See:
East, Ed (1) (2) (3)
McWilliams, Jim (1)

ED FORD, SENATOR. See:
Wilson, Ward

ED HATHAWAY. See: Prescott,
Kate Hathaway

ED HERLIHY. See:
Edwards, Ralph (1)
Herlihy, Ed

ED JACKSON, UNCLE. See:
Noble, Mary

ED LOWRY. See: Reid, Britt

ED McMAHON. See:
Carson, Johnny (1)
McMahon, Ed (1) (2)
Sterling, Jack

ED, MR. See: Post, Wilbur

ED MUNN. See: Dallas, Stella

ED NEELY. See: Marshall, John

ED NORTON. See:
Kramden, Ralph
Nelson, Carolyn Kramer

ED O'CONNOR. See: Dillon,
Marshal Matt

ED POTTS. See: Baines, Scattergood

ED ROBBINS, SERGEANT. See:
Foster, Major John

ED SPALDING. See: Waring,
Evelyn

Ed Sullivan Show, The. See:
Sullivan, Ed

ED WYNN. See:
Beamer, John
Bubbles, King
Fire Chief, The
Wynn, Ed

Ed Wynn Show, The. See:
Beamer, John
Wynn, Ed

EDDIE. See:
Addie
Archie
Bracken, Eddie
Cantor, Eddie (1) (2)
Corbett, Tom (1)
Drake, Eddie
Eddy
Edie
Eydie
Fisher, Eddie
Jiménez, José
Munster, Herman
O'Neill, Mrs.
Ryker, Lieut. Eddie
Walker, Eddie
Wilson, Steve

EDDIE BLOMFIELD. See:
Malone, Dr. Jerry

EDDIE BRACKEN. See:
Bracken, Eddie
Donald, Peter

Eddie Bracken Show, The. See:
Bracken, Eddie

EDDIE CANTOR. See:
Baker, Phil (3)
Cantor, Eddie (1) (2)
Drew, John
Martin, Dean (1)

Eddie Cantor Comedy Theater, The.
See: Cantor, Eddie (1)

Eddie Cantor Show. The. See:
Cantor, Eddie (2)

EDDIE DEAN. See: Ritter, Tex
(1)

EDDIE DOWLING. See: Heatter,
Gabriel

Eddie Drake, The Cases of. See:
Drake, Eddie

EDDIE DUNN. See: Hagen, Dr.
Harry

EDDIE FISHER. See:
Edwards, Ralph (1)
Fisher, Eddie
Gobel, George

Eddie Fisher Show, The. See:
Fisher, Eddie

EDDIE GRADY. See: Whiteman,
Paul

EDDIE HOWARD. See: Whiteman,
Paul

EDDIE JACKS. See: Peyton,
Martin

EDDIE JACKSON. See: Durante,
Jimmy

EDDIE KARAM. See:
Darin, Bobby
Miller, Roger

EDDIE O'CONNOR. See: Lopez,
Vincent

EDDIE PEABODY. See: Kelly,
Joe (1)

EDDIE RYAN, JR. See: Halop,
Billy

EDDIE SAFRANSKI. See: Gibbs,
Georgia (1)

EDDIE SAUTER. See: Whiteman,
Paul

Eddie's Father, The Courtship of.
See: Corbett, Tom (1)

EDDY. See:
Addie
Arnold, Eddy
Eddie

Edie
Eydie

EDDY ARNOLD. See:
Arnold, Eddy
Berman, Shelley

EDDY, NELSON (1), singer and
actor, star of the program
(himself)
ROBERT ARMBRUSTER,
orchestra leader (himself)
HIS ORCHESTRA
The Electric Hour (R) (Music)

EDDY, NELSON (2), singer and
actor, star of the program
(himself)
The Nelson Eddy Show (R)
(Music)

EDDY, NELSON. See also:
Ameche, Don (1)
Bell, Alexander Graham

EDEN, ERNEST. See: Jordan,
Joyce

EDGAR. See:
Bergen, Edgar (1) (2)
Foster, Judy
Guest, Edgar A. (1) (2)
Jones, Edgar Allan, Jr.
Lustgarden, Edgar

EDGAR BERGEN. See:
Ameche, Don (1)
Bergen, Edgar (1) (2)

Edgar Bergen and Charlie Mc-
Carthy Show, The. See: Bergen,
Edgar (2)

EDGAR HUDSON. See: Davidson,
Bill

EDGAR JARVIS. See: Jordan,
Joyce

EDGAR LEE. See: Horn, Aggie

Edge of Night, The. See: Karr,
Mike

EDIE. See also:
Addie
Eddie
Eddy
Eydie

EDIE ADAMS. See:
Blair, Janet
Kovacs, Ernie (1)

EDIE GRAY. See: Young, Larry
"Pepper"

EDIE HART. See: Gunn, Peter

EDITH. See:
Bunker, Archie
Hughes, Chris

EDITH BUNKER. See:
Bunker, Archie
Findlay, Maude

EDITH CRANDALL. See: Larimore, Marilyn

EDITH MILLER, MISS. See:
District Attorney, Mr.

EDITH WINTERS ELKINS. See:
Winters, Evelyn

EDITH WOOD. See: Fairchild,
Kay

Edition, Final. See: Newspaper
Reporter

EDITION, THE FIRST. See:
Rogers, Kenny

EDITOR, CITY. See: Jones,
Tom (1)

Editor's Daughter. See: Foster,
Henry

Editor's Daughter, Mary Foster,
The. See: Foster, Henry

EDLIN, MRS. See: Cooke,
Alistaire (1)

EDMAN, KARL
STEVE BRIGGS
OTHERS, interviewers (them-
selves)
PANEL OF PHYSICIANS
Ask Your Doctor (TV) (Interviews
concerning the medical profession)

EDMOND. See:
Edmund
O'Brien, Edmond

EDMONDSON, DELMAR, "editor"
of the program; himself
MANY CELEBRITY INTERVEW-
EES
B. A. ROLFE, orchestra leader
(himself)
HIS ORCHESTRA
The Heinz Magazine of the Air
(R) (Interviews/music)

EDMONDSON, WILLIAM. See:
Peters, Lowell

EDMUND. See also: Edmond

EDMUND "TINY" RUFFNER. See:
Birthday Man, The
Henry, Captain

EDNA SEYMOUR. See: Myrt

EDSON, EDWARD. See: Horwitz,
Hans

EDWARD. See:
Bowes, Major Edward (1) (2)
McCauley, Colonel Edward
Murrow, Edward R. (1) (2) (3)
(4) (5)

EDWARD VI. See: Henry VIII,
King of England

EDWARD CURRAN. See: Har-
grave-Scott, Joan

EDWARD DUKE LAKALE. See:
McGarrett, Steve

EDWARD EDSON. See: Horwitz,
Hans

EDWARD EVERETT HORTON. See:
Jolson, Al

EDWARD GREENMAN. See: Rutledge, Dr. John

EDWARD HILGEMEIER, JR. See:
Narz, Jack (2)

EDWARD HILL. See: Allen,
Frederick Lewis

EDWARD LEIGHTON. See: Dyke,
Charity Amanda

EDWARD McCUTCHEON, CAPTAIN.

See:
March, Hal
Story, Ralph

EDWARD P. MORGAN. See:
Shadel, Bill

EDWARDS. See: Cummings, Brenda

EDWARDS, ALLYN, host of the
program (himself)
MANY ACTORS AND ACTRESSES
Mr. Citizen (TV) (Dramas based
on real life heroics)

EDWARDS, CLIFF. See: Lane,
Richard

EDWARDS, DICK. See: Como,
Perry (1)

EDWARDS, DOUGLAS, newscaster,
host of the program (himself)
Douglas Edwards With the News
(TV) (News)

EDWARDS, DOUGLAS. See also:
Myerson, Bess

EDWARDS, ELI. See: Goldberg,
Molly

EDWARDS, FRANK, news commentator; host of the program (himself)
MANY INTERVIEWEES
THE CARMEN LE FAVE TRIO,
musical group
Frank Edwards (TV) (Variety/
news)

EDWARDS, JOAN. See:
Kaye, Danny
Ross, Lanny

EDWARDS, JOE. See: Brent,
Portia

EDWARDS, LUM
ABNER PEABODY
GRANDPAPPY SPEARS
SNAKE HOGAN
CEDRIC WEHUNT
SQUIRE SKIMP
DOC MILLER
DICK HUDDLESTON, residents
of Pine Ridge, Arkansas
Lum and Abner (R) (TV) (Comedy)

EDWARDS, PEGGY. See: Marshall,
John

EDWARDS, RALPH (1)
ED HERLIHY
PAUL DOUGLAS, hosts of the
program (themselves)
ARTHUR Q. LEWIS
JOEY HEATHERTON
BILLY DANIELS
"TERMITE" DANIELS
CONNIE FRANCIS
BOBBY HOOKEY
ARNOLD STANG
CAROL BRUCE
ROY LANGER
EDDIE FISHER
BEA WAYNE
THE NICHOLAS BROTHERS
THE BLACKSTONE TWINS
MARION LOVERIDGE, child
actors and actresses featured on
the program (themselves)
The Horn and Hardart Children's
Hour (R) (Children's variety)

EDWARDS, RALPH (2), host of
the program (himself)
GUEST BIOGRAPHEES
This Is Your Life (R) (TV)
(Biography)

EDWARDS, RALPH (3), moderator
of the program (himself)
MANY CONTESTANTS
Truth or Consequences (R) (TV)
(Audience participation)
BOB BARKER
JACK BAILEY, moderators of the
program (themselves)
Truth or Consequences (TV)

EDWARDS, RALPH. See also:
Leyden, Bill (1)

EDWARDS, WEBLEY, master of
ceremonies on the program (himself)
MANY HAWAIIAN ENTERTAINERS
Hawaii Calls (R) (TV) (Hawaiian
music)

EDWIN. See:
Carpenter, Luke
Montague, Edwin
Newman, Edwin (1) (2)

EDWIN JEROME. See: Welles,
Orson (2)

EDWIN NEWMAN. See:
Newman, Edwin (1) (2)
Rountree, Martha

EDWINA. See: Brown, Velvet

EEEEK A. MOUSE. See: Pam

EEPS, ELMER. See: Davidson,
Bill

EFFIE. See: Spade, Sam

EFFIE KLINKER. See:
Ameche, Don (1)
Bergen, Edgar (1) (2)

EFRON, MARSHALL, host of the
program (himself)
STUDS TERKEL, featured on the
program (himself)
MANY GUESTS
The Great American Dream
Machine (TV) (Social comment)

EGAN, BILL. See: March, Hal

EGAN, JIM. See: March, Hal

EGAN, JOHN. See: Anderson,
Sergeant Nick

EGGHEAD. See: Batman

8, Rescue. See: Skip

Eighty, Life Begins at. See:
Barry, Jack (6)

Eighty-Seventh Precinct. See:
Carella

86, AGENT. See: Smart, Maxwell

EILEEN. See:
Elaine
Moynihan, Mother
Sherwood, Ruth

EILEEN BARTON. See: Hall,
Monte (3)

EILEEN BRENNAN. See: Rowan,
Dan

EILEEN HOLMES. See: Harding,
Karen Adams

EILEEN MARGARET SIEGEL. See:
Walleck, Meredith

EILEEN MORAN. See: Carter,
Kathryn

Eileen, My Sister. See: Sherwood, Ruth

EILEEN TURNER. See: O'Neill,
Mrs.

EILEEN WILSON. See: Ross,
Lanny

EINSTEIN, BOB. See: Paulsen,
Pat

EISELEY, LOREN C., anthropolo-
gist; host of the program (himself)
Animal Secrets (TV) (Children's
education)

EL SQUEEKO MOUSE. See:
Russell, Todd

EL TORO. See: Carson, Kit

ELAINE. See:
Eileen
Sunday

ELAINE DASCOMB. See:
Marshall, John

ELAINE ENGLER. See: Halop,
Billy

ELAINE HUNTER BARBOUR. See:
Barbour, Henry Wilson

ELAINE MAY. See:
Ames, Nancy
Van Dyke, Dick (1)

ELAINE, SISTER. See: Harding,
Karen Adams

ELAINE THE FAIR. See: Sir
Lancelot

ELBERT. See also: Albert

ELBERT GALLO. See: Manning,
Portia Blake

ELDER, ANN. See: Rowan, Dan

ELDERS, HARRY
  BERYL VAUGHN, featured on the
  program (themselves)
  MANY ACTORS AND ACTRESSES
  Curtain Time (R) (Dramas)

ELDORA WILKINS. See: Nielson,
  Torwald

ELDRIDGE, EVE. See: Hughes,
  Lisa

ELDRIDGE, HELEN. See: Hughes,
  Lisa

ELDRIDGE, JOHN. See: Hughes,
  Lisa

ELDRIDGE, TOM. See: Hughes,
  Lisa

ELEANOR. See:
  Elinor
  Howe, Eleanor
  MacDonald, Eleanor
  Roosevelt, Eleanor

Eleanor Howe's Homemaking Exchange. See: Howe, Eleanor

ELEANOR RICHARDS. See: Hargrave-Scott, Joan

ELEANOR ROOSEVELT. See:
  Husing, Ted
  Roosevelt, Eleanor

Electric Company, The. See:
  Cosby, Bill (1)

Electric Hour, The. See: Eddy,
  Nelson (1)

ELEPHANT, NOSTALGIA THE. See:
  Pam

Eleventh Hour, The. See: Bassett,
  Dr. Theodore

ELFRIDA VON NARDROFF. See:
  Barry, Jack (9)

ELGART, LES. See: Whiteman,
  Paul

ELI. See also:
  Ellie
  Elly

ELI CARSON. See: Peyton,
  Martin

ELI EDWARDS. See: Goldberg,
  Molly

ELINOR. See:
  Eleanor
  Hathaway, Elinor

ELINOR HARRIOT. See: Soule,
  Olan (1)

ELIOT. See also:
  Elliot
  Elliott

ELIOT NESS. See: Winchell,
  Walter (2)

ELISE. See: Hopkins, Kate

ELISSA. See: Landi, Elissa

ELIZABETH, wife
  ALVIN, her husband
  Life With Elizabeth (TV) (Com-
  edy)

ELIZABETH. See also:
  Brent, Dr. Jim
  Perry, John
  Walton, Grandpa
  Zimmerman, Elizabeth

ELIZABETH I, Queen of England.
  See: Drake, Sir Francis

ELIZABETH COATES. See:
  Larkin, Jeremy

ELIZABETH COLLINS STODDARD.
  See: Collins, Barnabas

ELIZABETH COUNCIL. See:
  Roseleigh, Jack

ELIZABETH LENNOX. See:
  Munn, Frank (1)

Elizabeth, Life With. See:
  Elizabeth

ELIZABETH LOVE. See: Hopper,
  DeWolf

ELIZABETH MARSHALL. See:
  Carr, Alison

ELIZABETH RAINEY. See: Prescott, Kate Hathaway

ELIZABETH RELLER. See: McCormick, Myron

ELIZABETH REYNOLDS. See: Pride, Ben

ELIZABETH SHARON ANN BARBOUR. See: Barbour, Henry Wilson

ELIZABETH SMITH. See: Anderson, Jim

ELIZABETH STUART. See: Hughes, Chris

ELKINS, EDITH WINTERS. See: Winters, Evelyn

ELLA. See: Farrell, David

ELLA ASHBY. See: Davis, Joan Field

ELLA HUNT. See: Waring, Evelyn

ELLEN. See:
Alan
Allan
Allen
Allyn
Brown, Ellen
Campanelli, Dr. Vincent
Monroe, John
Randolph, Ellen
Rutledge, Dr. John
Wedloe, Tom

ELLEN CLARK. See: James, Nancy

ELLEN COLLINS. See: Graham, Dr. Bob

ELLEN GRANT. See: Hillman, India

ELLEN LOWELL. See: Hughes, Chris

ELLEN McGUIRE. See: Horton, Dr. Tom

ELLEN, MARY. See: Walton, Grandpa

ELLEN MUDGE. See: Glass, Bessie

ELLEN PARKER. See: Caesar, Sid (2)

Ellen Randolph. See: Randolph, Ellen

ELLEN SMITH. See: O'Leary, Hannah

ELLEN STUART. See: Hughes, Chris

ELLEN WILSON. See: Manning, Laura

ELLENHORN, JACK. See: Banner, Woody

ELLERBE, DR. CHRISTOPHER. See: Hargrave-Scott, Joan

ELLERY. See: Queen, Ellery

Ellery Queen. See: Queen, Ellery

ELLIE. See:
Banks, Stanley
Barnes, Joey
Collins, Bing
Eli
Elly
Taylor, Andy

ELLIE HARPER. See: Tate, Joanne

ELLINGTON, DUKE. See:
Basie, Count
Whiteman, Paul

ELLIOT. See also:
Eliot
Elliott

ELLIOT CARSON. See: Peyton, Martin

ELLIOT LAWRENCE. See: Dixon, Bobby

ELLIOT, MAMMA CASS. See: Riddle, Sam (1)

Stevens, Ray

ELLIOT REED. See: Ames,
Nancy

ELLIOTT. See also:
Eliot
Elliot
Lewis, Elliott

ELLIOTT, BETTY JO BRADLEY.
See: Carson, Uncle Joe

ELLIOTT, CATHY JO. See:
Carson, Uncle Joe

ELLIOTT, JANE. See: Dean,
Spencer

ELLIOTT, JOHN. See: Meredith,
Charles

ELLIOTT, LAURA. See: Garrison, Spencer

ELLIOTT, MARK. See: Garrison,
Spencer

ELLIOTT, ROGER (The Mystery Man),
story teller
The House of Mystery (R) (Mystery)

ELLIOTT, STEVE. See: Carson,
Uncle Joe

ELLIOTT, WIN (1)
JACK BAILEY, masters of cere-
mony of the program (themselves)
MANY AUDIENCE PARTICIPANTS
County Fair (R) (Audience partici-
pation)

ELLIOTT, WIN (2)
JOHNNY JOHNSON, hosts of the
program (themselves)
MANY PROFESSIONAL BOWLERS
Make That Spare (TV) (Sports/
bowling)

ELLIOTT, WIN. See also:
Roberts, Ken

ELLIS. See:
Marshall, John
Zacharias, Rear Admiral Ellis M.

ELLIS, ANITA. See: Bergen,

Edgar (2)

ELLIS, GORDON. See: Rutledge,
Dr. John

ELLIS, GRANDPA. See: Rutledge,
Dr. John

ELLIS HAIZLIP. See: Butler,
Jerry

ELLIS, LARRY. See: Kaye,
Sammy (1)

ELLIS, MISS. See: Keen, Mr.

ELLIS, NELLIE. See: Dallas,
Stella

ELLIS, RITA. See: Drake, Galen

ELLIS, SAM. See: Dallas, Stella

ELLIS SMITH. See: Rutledge, Dr.
John

ELLSTROM, SIDNEY. See:
Winkler, Betty

ELLY. See:
Eli
Ellie
Parker, Richard

ELLY MAY. See: Clampett, Jed

ELM CITY FOUR, THE. See: Kay,
Beatrice

Elm Street, The Carters of. See:
Carter, Mr.

ELMA GAHRINGER. See: Sherwood, Grace

ELMAN, DAVE (1), master of
ceremonies of the program (himself)
MANY AUDIENCE PARTICIPANTS
Auction Gallery (R) (Audience
participation)

ELMAN, DAVE (2), master of
ceremonies of the program (him-
self)
CELEBRITY HOBBYISTS
GUEST HOBBYISTS
HARRY SALTER

HARRY SOSNIK, orchestra leaders
(themselves)
THEIR ORCHESTRAS
Hobby Lobby (R) (Hobbies)

ELMER. See: Blurt, Elmer

ELMER, ARTHUR, quizmaster of
the program (himself)
MANY JUVENILE CONTESTANTS
Game Parade (R) (Children's
quiz)

ELMER EEPS. See: Davidson,
Bill

ELMER FUDD. See: Bunny, Bugs

ELMO. See: Muggsy

ELMOND, WARD. See: Noble,
Mary

ELOISE. See: Kummer, Eloise

ELOISE COMSTOCK. See: Baines,
Scattergood

ELOISE CUMMINGS. See: Brent,
Dr. Jim

ELOISE McELHONE. See:
Cross, Mason
Landi, Elissa

ELONA. See: Speaker, The

ELROY. See: Jetson, George

ELROY CARPENTER, LIEUT. See:
McHale, Lieut. Commander
Quinton

ELSA BANNING. See: Wayne,
Ruth Evans

ELSIE. See: Medbury, John P.

ELSIE ANDERSON. See: Harum,
David

Elsie Beebe. See: Solomon, David

ELSIE ETHRINGTON. See:
Bertrille, Sr.

ELSIE JANIS. See: Drew, John

ELSIE JONES. See: Graham, Dr.
Bob

ELSON, BOB, interviewer of pas-
sengers aboard the Twentieth
Century Limited (himself)
MANY INTERVIEWEES
Bob Elson Aboard the Century
(R) (Interviews)

ELSON, BOB. See also: Cowan,
Thomas

ELSON, TULIP VALENTINE. See:
Johnson, Bess

ELSPETH ERIC. See: Roberts,
Ken

ELVIA ALLMAN. See: Bolger,
Ray

ELWOOD. See: Kieser, Father
Elwood

ELWOOD GIDDINGS. See: Barbour, Henry Wilson

EM. See: Clara

Emergency! See: Gage, John

EMERSON, FAYE (1), hostess of
the program (herself)
MANY GUESTS
The Faye Emerson Show (TV)
(Interviews)

EMERSON, FAYE (2), hostess of
the program (herself)
Paris Cavalcade of Fashions
(TV) (Fashions)

EMERSON, FAYE. See also:
Daly, John (4)
Donald, Peter
Moore, Garry (4)

EMERSON, GEORGE. See:
Harper, Linda Emerson

EMERSON, HOLLY. See: Harper,
Linda Emerson

EMERSON, IRENE. See: Harper,
Linda Emerson

EMERY, BOB, master of ceremonies

of the program (himself)
Rainbow House (R) (Children's
program)

EMERY DEUTSCH. See: Ross,
David (1)

EMERY PARNELL. See: Les-
coulie, Jack (2)

EMILIO. See: Hargrave-Scott,
Joan

EMILIO PRIETO. See: Dane,
Prudence

EMILIO REYES. See: Whiteman,
Paul

EMILY. See:
Abbott, John
Davis, Uncle Bill
Dodger, Willy
Hartley, Dr. Robert
Olson, Emily
Vass, Fran
Williams, Emily

EMILY FRASER BENSON. See:
Fraser, Ben

EMILY MAYFIELD, AUNT. See:
Marshall, John

EMILY NORTON. See: Nelson,
Carolyn Kramer

EMILY STUART. See: Hughes,
Chris

EMILY WILLIAMS. See:
Harris, Phil
Williams, Emily

EMMA. See: Hughes, Chris

EMMA PEEL, MRS. See: Steed,
John

EMMA RITZIK. See: Bilko,
Sergeant Ernest

EMMA SIMPSON. See: Davis,
Dr. Althea

EMMA "STEVIE" STEVENS. See:
Hargrave-Scott, Joan

EMMETT CLARK. See: Jones,
Sam

EMMETT DAYTON. See: Rogers,
Patricia

EMMETT KELLY. See: Crosby,
Bob (1)

EMMETT, MRS. See: Marshall,
John

EMMIE HATFIELD. See: Dane,
Prudence

EMMY FERGUSON. See: Guest,
Edgar A. (2)

EMMY LOU. See: Nelson, Ozzie

Empire. See: Redigo, Jim (1)

End of the Rainbow. See: Baker,
Art (1)

End, Open. See: Susskind, David

ENDEAVOR, THE. See: King

ENDICOTT, PROFESSOR MIKE,
widower; professor of American
history at school in Rome
ALISON, his 16-year-old daughter
PENNY, his 10-year-old daughter
POKEY, his 6-year-old daughter
AUNT HARRIET ENDICOTT, his
sister
GRANDPA ANDY PRUITT, his
father-in-law
GINO, Italian taxi driver
MAMA VITALE, neighbor
To Rome With Love (TV) (Family
situation comedy) (also known as
Love) (TV)

ENDICOTT, TRACEY. See:
Winters, Evelyn

ENDORA. See: Stephens, Samantha

ENGELBERT. See also: ETHEL-
BERT

ENGELBERT HUMPERDINCK. See:
Crosby, Bing (2)
Humperdinck, Engelbert

Engelbert Humperdinck Show, The.

See: Humperdinck, Engelbert

ENGLAND, KING OF. See:
Churchill, John
Henry VIII, King of England

ENGLAND, QUEEN OF. See:
Drake, Sir Francis

England's Dave King. See: King,
Dave (2)

ENGLER, ELAINE. See: Halop,
Billy

ENGLISH, GUY. See: Welk,
Lawrence

ENGLISH, RALNA. See: Welk,
Lawrence

ENGLISH TEACHER. See: Brewster, Joey

ENID CHAMBERS. See: Fraser,
Ben

Enna Jettick Melodies. See:
Shields, Jimmy

ENNIS, SKINNAY. See: Hope,
Bob (2)

Eno Crime Club. See: Dean,
Spencer

ENOCH. See: Hathaway, Elinor

ENRIC MADRIGUERA. See: Whiteman, Paul

ENRICO ROSSI. See: Winchell,
Walter (2)

ENRIGHT, SERGEANT. See:
McMillan, Stuart

ENSIGN. See: O'Toole, Ensign

ENSIGN CHARLES "CHUCK"
PARKER. See: McHale, Lieut.
Commander Quinton

Ensign O'Toole. See: O'Toole,
Ensign

ENSIGN PULVER. See: Roberts,
Doug

ENTEN, BONI. See: Klein,
Robert

ENTERPRISE, THE. See:
Holden, Grey
Kirk, Captain James

Entertainers, The. See: DeLuise,
Dom (2)

ENTERTAINMENT GIRLS, THE
OPERATION. See: Shawn,
Dick

Era, The Ragtime. See: Morath,
Max

ERIC. See:
Dale, Linda
Erik
Hansen, Dean Eric
Parmalee, Ranger Captain
Sevareid, Eric

ERIC BLORE. See: Morgan,
Frank (1)

ERIC, ELSPETH. See: Roberts,
Ken

ERIC JASON. See: Gregory,
Ben

ERIC MORGAN. See: Karr, Mike

ERIC PHILIPS. See: Tate, Joanne

ERIC RAMSEY. See: Wayne, Ruth
Evans

ERIC SAGERQUIST. See: First
Nighter, Mr.

ERIC SEVAREID. See:
Cronkite, Walter (2)
Sevareid, Eric

ERIC STOWELL. See: Trent,
Helen

ERIC WATSON. See: Manning,
Portia Blake

ERICA. See: Carr, Alison

ERICA MARTIN. See: Davis,
Ann Tyler

ERICKSON, DAN. See: Lockridge,
Barry

ERICKSON, JULIE. See: Johnson,
Bess

ERIK. See also: Eric

ERIK GUDE. See: Bergen, Edgar
(1)

ERIN. See: Walton, Grandpa

ERNE. See also: Ernie

ERNE BAKER. See: Baines,
Scattergood

ERNEST. See:
Bilko, Sergeant Ernest
Chappell, Ernest (1) (2)

ERNEST BANNING. See: Wayne,
Ruth Evans

ERNEST EDEN. See: Jordan,
Joyce

ERNEST FLATT DANCERS, THE.
See:
Burnett, Carol
DeLuise, Dom (2)

Ernest, Forever. See: Coogan,
Jackie

ERNEST HEATH, SERGEANT. See:
Vance, Philo

ERNESTINE. See: Rowan, Dan

ERNIE. See:
Brenner, Roy
Cookie Monster, The
Cosby, Bill (3)
Douglas, Steve
Erne
Ford, Tennessee Ernie (1) (2)
(3) (4)
Kovacs, Ernie (1) (2)

ERNIE DOWNS. See: Randolph,
Alice

ERNIE FREEMAN. See: Uggams,
Leslie

ERNIE HARE. See:

Happiness Boys, The
Jones, Billy

ERNIE HINSHAW. See: Beamer,
John

Ernie Kovacs Show, The. See:
Kovacs, Ernie (1)

ERNIE RUDY. See: Whiteman,
Paul

Ernie Show, The Tennessee. See:
Ford, Tennessee Ernie (4)

ERP, MR. See: Perkins, Ma

ERSEL TWING. See: Bergen,
Edgar (2)

ERSKINE, INSPECTOR LOUIS,
F. B. I. officer; widowed
BARBARA ERSKINE, his daughter
ARTHUR WARD, assistant
   F. B. I. director; his superior
JIM RHODES
TOM COLBY, his assistants
The F. B. I. (TV) (Crime detec-
tion drama)

ERSKINE, MARILYN. See:
Halop, Billy

ERWIN. See also:
Irvin
Irving

ERWIN, STU, high school teacher
JUNE ERWIN, his wife
WILLIE ERWIN, his son
JACKIE ERWIN
JOYCE CLARK, his daughters
JIMMY CLARK, Joyce Clark's
husband
MR. SELKIRK, high school
principal
Trouble With Father (TV) (Fam-
ily situation comedy)

ERWIN, TRUDY. See: Kyser, Kay

Eskimos, The Cliquot Club. See:
Reser, Harry

ESMERALDA. See: Stephens,
Samantha

Especially For You. See: Quinlan,
Roberta

ESSEX, WINSTON, host of the program; "mysterious wealthy man
who has turned his family man-
sion into an exclusive New York
hotel"
MANY ACTORS AND ACTRESSES
Ghost Story (TV) (Suspense drama)

ESTELLE CUMMINGS. See: Hargrave-Scott, Joan

ESTHER. See:
Lady Esther
Perkins, Ma

ESTHER FERGUSON. See: Guest,
Edgar A. (2)

ESTHER MILLER. See: Gold-
berg, Molly

ETHEL
ALBERT, her husband, residents
of Sandy Harbor
BABY SUSY, their child
Ethel and Albert (R) (Comedy)

ETHEL. See also:
Barrymore, Ethel
Merman, Ethel
Turp, Joe
Waters, Ethel

Ethel and Albert. See: Ethel

ETHEL, AUNT. See: Webster,
Martha

ETHEL EVERETT. See: Norris,
Kathleen

ETHEL FOSTER. See: Rutledge,
Dr. John

ETHEL GRAINGER. See: Drake,
Betty

Ethel Merman Show, The. See:
Merman, Ethel

ETHEL MERTZ. See: Ricardo,
Ricky

ETHEL OWEN. See: Arthur,
Jack (1)

ETHEL SHUTTA. See: Benny,
Jack

ETHEL SMITH. See: Ross,
Lanny

Ethel Turp, Joe and. See: Turp,
Joe

ETHELBERT. See:
Casey
Engelbert

ETHRINGTON, ELSIE. See:
Bertrille, Sr.

ETON BOYS, THE. See: Howard,
Tom (2)

EUBANKS, BOB, moderator of
the program (himself)
NEWLYWED COUPLE PANEL-
ISTS
The Newlywed Game (TV)
(Game)

EUGENE. See:
Barkley, Victoria
Howard, Willie
Kovacs, Ernie (1)
Smith, Eugene

EUGENE ORMANDY. See:
Bordoni, Irene

EUGENE SNELL. See: Mac-
Donald, Eleanor

EULA SHERMAN. See: Harding,
Mrs. Rhoda

EUNICE. See: Wayne, Ruth
Evans

EUNICE MARTIN. See: Tate,
Joanne

EUNICE WEBSTER. See: Tate,
Joanne

Europe, Crusade in. See: Van
Voorhis, Westbrook (1)

EUSTACE P. GARVEY. See:
Flack, Colonel Humphrey

EVA FOSTER. See: Harding,
Mrs. Rhoda

EVA WAINWRIGHT. See: Murphy,
Peter

EVANS, BERGEN (1), moderator of
the program (himself)
GUEST PANELISTS
Down You Go (TV) (Word usage
game)

EVANS, BERGEN (2), moderator of
the program (himself)
JOHN MASON BROWN, perma-
nent panelist (himself)
PANEL OF GUEST EXPERTS
The Last Word (TV) (Panel discussion of English language usage)

EVANS, BRUCE. See: Roseleigh,
Jack

EVANS, DALE. See:
Bergen, Edgar (2)
Crosby, Bing (2)
Rogers, Roy

EVANS, DAVEY. See: Bracken,
John

EVANS, DEAN
DAN MILLER
KATE WELLS, reporters for
wire service
Wire Service (TV) (Journalism adventure) (later re-released under
the title Deadline For Action)(TV)

EVANS, DR. BILL. See: Brent,
Dr. Jim

EVANS, FLORIDA. See: Findlay,
Maude

EVANS, GLENN, American news-
paperman, stationed in Hong
Kong
NEIL CAMPBELL, chief of Hong
Kong police
TULLY, nightclub owner
FONG, Evans' Chinese houseboy
Hong Kong (TV) (Drama/adven-
ture)

EVANS, HOPE MELTON. See:
Wayne, Ruth Evans

EVANS, JUDITH. See: Larimore,
Marilyn

EVANS, LITTLE NED "NEDDIE."
See: Wayne, Ruth Evans

EVANS, MAGGIE. See: Collins,
Barnabas

EVANS, MARION. See: O'Connell,
Helen

EVANS, MRS. See: Hargrave-
Scott, Joan

EVE ARDEN. See:
Kaye, Danny
Owner

Eve Arden Show, The. See: Hammond, Liza

EVE DRAKE. See: Adams,
Howard

EVE ELDRIDGE. See: Hughes,
Lisa

EVE HUBBARD. See: Buell,
Roger

Eve, Mr. Adams and. See:
Adams, Howard

EVE TOPPING STANLEY. See:
Davis, Joan Field

EVE UNDERWOOD. See: Marlin,
Mary

EVE WHITFIELD, SERGEANT.
See: Ironside, Chief Robert

EVELYN. See:
Brown, Ellen
Perry, John
Strange, Adam
Waring, Evelyn
Winters, Evelyn

EVELYN KAY. See: Spitalny,
Phil

EVELYN KNIGHT. See: Crosby,
Bob (2)

EVELYN LYNNE. See: Moore,
Garry (1)

EVELYN ROSE. See: Novak,
John

EVELYN WHARTON. See: James,
Nancy

Evelyn Winters. See: Winters,
Evelyn

Evelyn Winters, The Strange Romance of. See: Winters,
Evelyn

Evening News, The A. B. C. See:
Smith, Howard K. (1)

Evening News With Walter Cronkite,
The C. B. S. See: Cronkite,
Walter (2)

Evening With Fred Astaire, An.
See: Astaire, Fred (2)

Evening With Pops. See: Fiedler,
Arthur

Event, Main. See: Marciano,
Rocky

Eveready Hour, The. See: Drew,
John

EVERETT. See:
Mitchell, Everett
Sloane, Everett

EVERETT CLARK. See:
Kaye, Danny
Reser, Harry

EVERETT, ETHEL. See: Norris,
Kathleen

EVERETT PALMER. See: Wal-
leck, Meredith

EVERETT, PROFESSOR, widower;
university instructor
HAL
BUTCH, his sons
PRUDENCE, his daughter
WALDO, his dog
PHOEBE FIGALILLY (Nanny),
nurse to the Everett children
AUNT HENRIETTA, Phoebe's
eccentric aunt
Nanny and the Professor (TV)
(Family situation comedy)

EVERETT SLOANE. See:
Kaye, Danny
Sloane, Everett
Welles, Orson (2)

EVERETT, UNCLE. See: Hudson,
Nancy Smith

Everglades, The. See: Vail,
Lincoln

Everly Brothers, Johnny Cash
Presents the. See: Everly,
Don

EVERLY, DON
PHIL EVERLY, singers and
entertainers; co-hosts of the
program (themselves)
JOE HIGGINS
RUTH McDEVITT, featured
entertainers (themselves)
MANY GUEST STARS
Johnny Cash Presents the Everly
Brothers (TV) (Variety)

Everybody's Talking. See: Thaxton, Lloyd (1)

Everyman's Theater. See: Johnson, Raymond Edward (1)

EVEY PERKINS FITZ. See:
Perkins, Ma

EVICTOR. See: Holiday, Laurel

EVIE HOWETH. See: Hutton, Ina
Ray

Exchange, Eleanor Howe's Homemaker's. See: Howe, Eleanor

Exchange, Fair. See: Walker,
Eddie

Exchange, The Happiness. See:
Rosenfield, Joe, Jr.

Expedition. See: Craig, Colonel
John B.

EXPERIENCE. See: Voice of
Experience, The

Experience, The Voice of. See:
Voice of Experience, The

EXPERT. See: Charm Expert

Explorers, The. See: Nielsen,
Leslie (1)

EYDIE. See also:
  Addie
  Eddie
  Eddy
  Edie

EYDIE GORME. See:
  Allen, Steve (3)
  Crosby, Bing (2)
  Lawrence, Steve (1)

Eye, Hawaiian. See: Steele, Tracy

Eye, Charlie Wild, Private. See:
  Wild, Charlie

Eye, Martin Kane, Private. See:
  Kane, Martin

Eye on New York. See: Leonard,
  Bill

EZIO PINZA. See: Bell, Alexander Graham

EZRA BUTTERNUT, UNCLE. See:
  Peppertag, Aaron

EZRA, UNCLE. See: Kelly, Joe
  (1)

F. See: Bailey, F. Lee

F. B. I. FIELD AGENT. See:
Sheppard, F. B. I. Field Agent

F. B. I. in Peace and War, The.
Sheppard, F. B. I. Field Agent

F. B. I. , The. See: Erskine, Inspector Louis

F. B. I. , This Is Your. See:
Taylor, Jim

F Troop. See: Parmenter,
Captain Wilton

FABIAN, INSPECTOR, Scotland
Yard detective
Fabian of Scotland Yard (TV)
(Detective)

Fabian of Scotland Yard. See:
Fabian, Inspector

Fables, Betty Boop. See: Boop,
Betty

FABRAY, NANETTE. See:
Caesar, Sid (2)
Marshall, Peter

Fabulous Dorseys, The. See:
Dorsey, Tommy

FACE, FALSE. See: Batman

Face, Funny. See: Stockton,
Sandy (1)

Face, Make a. See: Clayton, Bob
(2)

Face the Nation. See: Schoumacher, David

Faces, About. See: Alexander,
Ben (1)

Faces West, Two. See: January,
Dr. Ben

Factory, Hollywood: The Dream.
See: Cavett, Dick (2)

FADIMAN, CLIFTON (1), moderator of the program (himself)
JOHN KIERAN

OSCAR LEVANT
FRANKLIN P. ADAMS, panel
members (themselves)
MANY GUEST PANELISTS
Information, Please! (R) (Panel
quiz)

FADIMAN, CLIFTON (2), moder-
ator of the program (himself)
GOODWIN SCHAEFER
ROBERT STROMM
RICHARD CUTLER
MANY MORE, panelists on the
program; all under the age of
16 (themselves)
The Quiz Kids (TV) (Quiz)

FADIMAN, CLIFTON (3), moder-
ator of the program (himself)
MANY GUESTS
Victory Volunteers (R) (World
War II war effort discussion)

FAHEY, MYRNA. See: Peyton,
Martin

Fair, County. See: Elliott, Win
(1)

FAIR, ELAINE THE. See: Sir
Lancelot

Fair Exchange. See: Walker,
Eddie

Fair, Jay Stewart's Fun. See:
Stewart, Jay (1)

Fair, Ladies. See: Moore, Tom
(2)

FAIRBANKS, DOUGLAS, actor;
host of the program (himself)
MANY ACTORS AND ACTRESSES
Douglas Fairbanks Presents (TV)
(Crime dramas)

FAIRBANKS, PEGGY. See: Hutton, Ina Ray

FAIRCHILD, COOKIE. See:
Cantor, Eddie (2)

FAIRCHILD, DORIS. See: Perkins,
Ma

FAIRCHILD, KAY, the stepmother
JOHN FAIRCHILD, her husband

PEGGY FAIRCHILD, her step-
daughter
BILLY FAIRCHILD, her stepson
GERALD LOWE
LEONARD CLARK
MOTHER FAIRCHILD
DAVID HOUSEMAN
EDITH WOOD
GENEVIEVE PORTER
MATTIE, maid
BOSS McKINNEY
BERT WESTON
PAT RORITY
ANDY CLAYTON
BUD FAIRCHILD
JAMIE O'CONNOR
GINNIE SAWYERS
ADELLA WINSTON
MRS. FLETCHER
LUELLA HAYWORTH
JIM
POP, characters appearing in
the drama
Stepmother (R) (Serial drama)

FAIRFAX, BEATRICE, dispenser
of advice
Beatrice Fairfax (R) (Counseling)

FAIRFAX, COMMANDER. See:
Welles, Orson (3)

FAIRFIELD, BETTY. See:
Armstrong, Jack

FAIRFIELD, BILLY. See: Armstrong, Jack

FAIRFIELD, PETER, III. See:
Morgan, Paul

FAIRFIELD, UNCLE JIM. See:
Armstrong, Jack

FAITH. See: Chandler, Faith

Faith, Frontiers of. See: Barnhouse, Donald

FAITH, PERCY
JOSEF PASTERNACK, orchestra
leaders (themselves)
THEIR ORCHESTRAS
BUDDY CLARK
JOSEPHINE ANTOINE
REINHOLD SCHMIDT
THE LULLABY LADY, featured
vocalists on the program (them-
selves)

THE CONTINENTALS QUARTET,
vocal group
The Carnation Contented Hour
(R) (Music) (also known as The
Contented Hour) (R)

FAITH, PERCY. See also: Whiteman, Paul

FAITH RICHARDS. See: Brent,
Dr. Jim

FALAN. See also: Folan

FALAN WELK, TANYA. See:
Welk, Lawrence

FALANA, LOLA. See: Cosby,
Bill (2)

Falcon, The. See: Waring, Mike

FALCON, THE. See: Waring,
Mike

FALKENBURG, JINX. See:
McCrary, Tex

FALSE FACE. See: Batman

False, True or. See: Hagen,
Dr. Harry

FALSTAFF OPENSHAW. See:
Allen, Fred

FALVEY, HAL
SPRAGUE
HARRY BLAKE
MAJOR FELLOWES
CAPTAIN RUSS
RUTH MORROW
BEASLEY
SUE
HALVORSEN
TONY, characters appearing in
the drama
Flying Time (R) (Drama)

Fame, Radio Hall of. See: Gibbs,
Georgia (2)

Fame, The Hallmark Radio Hall of.
See: Hilton, James

Familiar Music, The American
Album of. See: Munn, Frank
(1)

Family, Accidental. See: Webster,
Jerry

Family Affair. See: Davis, Uncle
Bill

Family, All in The. See: Bunker,
Archie

Family and Mine, Your. See:
Wilbur, Judy

Family Game, The. See: Yablonsky,
Lewis

Family Hour, The. See: Bowes,
Major Edward (1)

Family Hour, The Capitol. See:
Bowes, Major Edward (1)

Family Hour, The Major Bowes.
See: Bowes, Major Edward (1)

Family Hour, The Prudential. See:
Taylor, Deems

Family Hour, The Ted Mack. See:
Bowes, Major Edward (1)

Family, One Happy. See: Cooper,
Dick

Family, One Man's. See: Barbour,
Henry Wilson

Family, Pepper Young's. See:
Davis, Red
Young, Larry "Pepper"

Family, The Addams. See: Addams,
Gomez

Family, The Aldrich. See: Aldrich,
Henry

Family, The Barton. See: Barton,
Bud

FAMILY, THE CARTER. See:
Cash, Johnny

Family, The Gibson. See: Gibson,
Dot

FAMILY, THE HAMILTON. See:
Bryson, Dr. Lyman (2)

Family, The Hardy. See: Hardy,
Andy

Family, The Johnson. See:
Scribner, Jimmy

Family, The King. See: Driggs,
Karleton King

Family, The Nelson. See: Nelson,
Ozzie

Family, The Parker. See: Parker,
Richard

Family, The Partridge. See:
Partridge, Connie

Family, The Smith. See:
Jordan, Jim (2)
Smith, Chad

Family, The Vass. See: Vass,
Fran

Family Theater, The. See: Peyton, Father Patrick

Famous Adventures of Mr. Magoo,
The. See: Magoo, Mr.

Famous Fortunes. See: Hawley,
Mark

Famous Jury Trials. See: Judge,
The

FANCY-FANCY. See: Top Cat

Fanfare. See: Brand, Oscar

FANG. See: Midnight, Captain

FANG, WHITE. See: Sales,
Soupy

FANKBONER, SARAH. See:
Darin, Bobby

FANNY. See:
Baldridge, Fanny May
Nebb, Rudolph

FANNY, AUNT. See: McNeill,
Don

FANNY CARLYSLE. See: Dane,
Prudence

FANNY MARTIN BARBOUR. See:
Barbour, Henry Wilson

Fantastic Four, The. See: Fantastic Four, The

FANTASTIC FOUR, THE, crime
fighters; cartoon characters
The Fantastic Four (TV) (Cartoon)

FARADAY, INSPECTOR. See:
Boston Blackie

FARBER, BURT. See:
Brasselle, Keefe
Clark, Dick (3)

FARFUS, FELICIA. See: Nuvo,
Arnie

FARGO NORTH, DECODER. See:
Cosby, Bill (1)

Farm and Home Hour, The National.
See: Mitchell, Everett

Farm, Today on the. See: Arnold,
Eddy

FARMER, LOIS. See: Joe (1)

FARMER, MITCHELL. See: Hillman, India

Farmer's Daughter, The. See:
Holstrum, Katy

FARNSWORTH, JOAN ROBERTS.
See: Barbour, Henry Wilson

FARNSWORTH, MISS. See: Mac-
Donald, Eleanor

FARNSWORTH, PAUL JOHN. See:
Barbour, Henry Wilson

FARNSWORTH, ROSS. See: Barbour, Henry Wilson

FARNUM, MR. See: Perkins, Ma

FARNUM, MRS. See: Perkins, Ma

FAROUK, KING. See: Husing, Ted

FARR, HUGH. See: Nolan, Bob

FARR, KARL. See: Nolan, Bob

FARRADAY, BERNICE. See:
Grimm, Arnold

FARRELL. See also: Ferral

FARRELL, BARBARA. See:
Davis, Dr. Althea

FARRELL, CHARLIE, manager of
Raquet Club, Palm Springs,
California (himself)
DAD FARRELL, his father
SHERMAN HULL, his friend
Charlie Farrell (TV) (Comedy)

FARRELL, DAN. See: Howard,
Glenn

FARRELL, DAVID (Front Page),
star reporter
SALLY FARRELL, his wife
LUCY BEGGS
LUTHER WARREN
KAY BARNETT
SAMMY WARNER
RORY APPLEGATE
GEORGE WALKER
GROVER COURTNEY
TIM O'DONOVAN
MRS. HOWARD
LIEUT. CARPENTER
CAROL PETERS
LIZETTE
SHERRY
ELLA
NICK, characters appearing in
the drama
Front Page Farrell (R) (Ad-
venture)

FARRELL, DAVID. See also:
Bauer, Bertha

FARRELL, GAIL. See: Welk,
Lawrence

FARRELL, JIM. See: Malone,
Dr. Jerry

FARRELL, KIT. See: Bauer,
Bertha

FARRELL, MILDRED. See: Hargrave-Scott, Joan

FARRELL, PROFESSOR. See:
Welles, Orson (3)

FARRELL, SKIP. See:
Ford, Tennessee Ernie (4)
Kelly, Joe (1)

FARROW, VALENTINE, senior
editor at book publishing firm
ROCKWELL SIN, his Chinese-
American valet
LIBBY, his secretary
FIPPLE, neighborhood handyman
Valentine's Day (TV) (Comedy)

FASAIL. See: Gallant, Captain

FASCINATO, JACK. See: Ford,
Tennessee Ernie (4)

Fashions in Sewing-The Lucille
Rivers Show. See: Rivers,
Lucille

Fashions, Paris Cavalcade of. See:
Emerson, Faye (2)

FAT ALBERT. See: Cosby, Bill
(3)

Fat Albert and the Cosby Kids.
See: Cosby, Bill

Fat Man, The. See: Runyon, Brad

FAT MAN, THE. See: Runyon,
Brad

FAT, WO. See: McGarrett, Steve

Fate, Turn of. See: Ryan, Robert
(1)

FATHER. See:
Anderson, Jim
Barbour, Henry Wilson
Cavanaugh, Father Samuel Patrick
Coughlin, Father Charles Edward
Day, Clarence
Gibson, Dot
Kieser, Father Elwood
O'Connor, Father Norman
O'Malley, Father Chuck
Peyton, Father Patrick
Uncle Walter

Father, Bachelor. See: Gregg,
Uncle Bentley

Father, Bringing Up. See: Jiggs

FATHER BUTCHER. See: Ballew,
Wally

Father Coughlin. See: Coughlin,
Father Charles Edward

FATHER FITZGIBBONS. See:
O'Malley, Father Chuck

FATHER JOHN P. MULCAHY.
See: Pierce, Captain Hawkeye

Father Knows Best. See: Anderson, Jim

Father, Life With. See: Day,
Clarence

Father of the Bride. See: Banks,
Stanley

Father, Professional. See: Wilson, Dr. Thomas

Father, The Courtship of Eddie's.
See: Corbett, Tom (1)

Father, Trouble With. See:
Erwin, Stu

FATHER WHELAN. See: Levy,
Abie

FATHOM. See: Forty Fathom

Fatima, Tales of. See: Rathbone,
Basil

FATIME, MADAME. See: Mc-
Kay, Judson

FAURE, GABRIELLE. See:
Brent, Portia

FAVE, MICHELLE DELLA. See:
Chidsey, Jackie

FAVOR, GIL, cattle drover
PETE NOLAN
ROWDY YATES
JED COLBY, cowboys employed
by Favor
WISHBONE, camp cook
MUSHY, Wishbone's helper
Rawhide (TV) (Western)

Favorite Husband, My. See:
Cooper, Liz

Favorite Martian, My. See: Uncle
Martin

FAWLEY, JUDE. See: Cooke,
Alistaire (1)

FAY, FRANK, star of the program
(himself)
MANY GUEST STARS
The Frank Fay Show (R) (Variety)

FAY PERKINS HENDERSON. See:
Perkins, Ma

FAYE, ALICE. See: Crosby,
Bing (2)

FAYE EMERSON. See:
Daly, John (4)
Donald, Peter
Emerson, Faye (1) (2)
Moore, Garry (4)

Faye Emerson Show, The. See:
Emerson, Faye (1)

FAYE HARRIS, ALICE. See:
Harris, Phil

FEATHERSTONE, MRS., wealthy
widow, portrayed by Billie Burke
ALAN HALE, featured on the
program (himself)
The Gay Mrs. Featherstone (R)
(Comedy)

FEATHERSTONE, MRS. See also:
O'Malley, Father Chuck

FECHTENBERGER, LAWRENCE.
See: Ballew, Wally

FEENEY, JOE. See: Welk,
Lawrence

FEG. See: Murray, Feg

Feg Murray Show, The. See:
Murray, Feg

FELDMAN, LAWYER. See:
Meyer

FELDMAN, MARTY, comedian;
star of the program (himself)
MANY GUEST STARS
The Marty Feldman Comedy
Machine (TV) (Comedy blackouts)

FELDMAN, MARTY. See also:
Chidsey, Jackie

FELICIA FARFUS. See: Nuvo,
Arnie

FELIX. See:
Ungar, Felix
Von Luckner, Count Felix

FELIX KNIGHT. See: Marlowe,
Sylvia

FELLAS, STELLA AND THE.
See: Waring, Fred (1)

FELLOWES, MAJOR. See: Falvey, Hal

Felony Squad, The. See: Stone,
Sam

FELTON, HAPPY, quizmaster of
of the program (himself)
MANY JUVENILE CONTESTANTS,
ages 7-14 years
It's a Hit (TV) (Children's educational quiz) (also called Happy
Felton's Spotlight Gang) (TV)

FELTON, HAPPY. See also:
Parks, Bert (6)

FELTON, VERNA. See: Bolger,
Ray

FELZER, JACK. See: Brent,
Dr. Jim

FENCHER, ROY. See: Rutledge,
Dr. John

FENNEMAN, GEORGE, quizmaster
of the program (himself)
MANY CONTESTANTS
Anybody Can Play (TV) (Quiz)

FENNEMAN, GEORGE. See also:
Marx, Groucho (3)

FENSTER, ARCH. See: Dickens,
Harry

Fenster, I'm Dickens, He's. See:
Dickens, Harry

FENTON, FRANK. See:

Harding, Karen Adams
Perkins, Ma

FENWICK BABBITT. See: Gleason, Jackie (1) (2)

FERDE GROFE. See: Allen, Fred

FERDIE FROG. See: Boop, Betty

FERDINAND. See: Baker, Phil (2)

FERGUSON, ALEC. See: O'Leary, Hannah

FERGUSON, EMMY. See: Guest, Edgar A. (2)

FERGUSON, ESTHER. See: Guest, Edgar A. (2)

FERGUSON, GRACE. See: Guest, Edgar A. (2)

FERGUSON, MARTHA, marries
Tracy Graham
STUART FERGUSON, her brother
SANDRA FERGUSON, Stuart's
wife
TRACY GRAHAM, marries
Martha
THOMAS BOSWELL, widower,
president of Bancroft College
Bright Promise (TV) (Serial
drama)

FERGUSON, SHERIFF LUKE. See:
Guest, Edgar A. (2)

FERRAL. See also: Farrell

FERRAL, VERONICA. See:
Malone, Dr. Jerry

FERRANTE AND TEICHER. See:
Fiedler, Arthur

FESTER. See also: Foster

FESTER, UNCLE. See: Addams,
Gomez

Festival of Stars. See: Young,
Loretta (2)

Festival, Spring. See: Crosby,
John

FESTUS HAGGEN. See: Dillon,
Marshal Matt

FFOGG, LORD MARMADUKE.
See: Batman

FIBBER McGEE. See:
McGee, Fibber
McNeill, Don

Fibber McGee and Molly. See:
McGee, Fibber

FICKETT, MARY. See: Reasoner,.
Harry

FIDDLING KATE. See: Ritter,
Tex (1)

FIDLER, JIMMIE, Hollywood reporter (himself)
Jimmie Fidler (R) (Hollywood
gossip)

FIEDLER, ARTHUR, conductor;
host of the program (himself)
THE BOSTON POPS ORCHESTRA
DOC SEVERINSEN
FERRANTE AND TEICHER
ROBERTA FLACK
OTHERS, musicians appearing
on the program (themselves)
Evening With Pops (TV) (Music)

FIELD. See also: Fields

FIELD AGENT. See: Sheppard,
F. B. I. Field Agent

FIELD DANCERS, THE RONALD.
See: Damone, Vic (2)

FIELD, DR. JAMES. See: Karr,
Mike

FIELD, DR. SAMUEL TILDEN.
See: Davis, Joan Field

FIELD, LIZ HILLYER. See:
Karr, Mike

FIELD, MOTHER. See: Davis,
Joan Field

FIELD, STELLA. See: Davis,
Joan Field

FIELD, SYLVIA. See: Davis,
Joan Field

FIELD, TOM. See: Leighton, Linda

FIELDING, EBBA. See: Cameron, Christy Allen

FIELDING, MR. See: O'Neill, Mrs.

FIELDS. See also: Field

FIELDS, ARTHUR
WARREN HULL, masters of ceremony on the program (themselves)
JERRY SEARS, orchestra leader (himself)
HIS ORCHESTRA
Streamliner's Show (R) (Comedy)

FIELDS, BENNY. See: Dragonette, Jessica (2)

FIELDS, GRACIE, comedienne; star of the program (herself)
MANY GUEST STARS
The Gracie Fields Show (R) (Variety)

FIELDS, UNA. See: Andrews, Walter

FIELDS, W. C. See: Ameche, Don (1)

FIELDS, WEBER AND. See: Drew, John

FIFE. See also: Phyfe

FIFE, BARNEY. See: Taylor, Andy

FIFI, MADEMOISELLE. See: Cantor, Eddie (2)

Fifteen, Club. See: Crosby, Bob (2)

15, Panorama. See: Sterling, Dick

55, Music. See: Kenton, Stan

FIGALILLY, PHOEBE. See: Everett, Professor

File, Confidential. See: Coates, Paul

File, The Walter Winchell. See: Winchell, Walter (4)

Final Edition. See: Newspaper Reporter

Finance, High. See: James, Dennis (2)

FINCH. See: King

FINCH, DEE. See: Rayburn, Gene (3)

FINCH, HEATHER. See: Walker, Eddie

FINCH, NEVILLE. See: Walker, Eddie

Finch, Night Shift With Rayburn and. See: Rayburn, Gene (3)

FINCH, OSCAR. See: Solomon, David

FINCH, SYBIL. See: Walker, Eddie

FINCH, TOMMY. See: Walker, Eddie

FINCH, WILBUR. See: Taylor, Andy

FINDLAY, DANIEL. See: Johnson, Bess

FINDLAY, MAUDE, cousin of Edith Bunker; acid-tongued
WALTER, her fourth husband
CAROL, her daughter, divorcee
PHILIP, Carol's 8-year-old son
FLORIDA EVANS, Maude's Negro maid
ARTHUR HARMON, Maude's neighbor
EDITH BUNKER, Maude's cousin
ARCHIE BUNKER, Edith's husband
Maude (TV) (Family situation comedy)

FINEGAN. See also: Finnegan

FINEGAN, BILL. See: Whiteman, Paul

FINGERHOOD, SEYMOUR. See:
Goldberg, Molly

Fingers, Five. See: Sebastian,
Victor

FINKE, MR. See: Harum, David

FINKELSTEIN, ABE. See: O'Leary,
Hannah

FINKELSTEIN, BECKY. See:
O'Leary, Hannah

FINKELSTEIN, IZZY. See:
Kaltenmeyer, Professor August,
D. U. N.

FINLEY, PAT. See: Kelly, Gene

FINN. See: Leif

FINN, FRED, pianist; star and
host of the program (himself)
Mickie Finn (TV) (Music)

FINN, HUCK
TOM SAWYER
BECKY THATCHER, friends,
participate in various hair-raising
adventures
INJUN JOE, their enemy
The New Adventures of Huck Finn
(TV) (Children's adventure; com-
bination of live actors against
animated backgrounds)

FINN, HUCKLEBERRY, twelve-
year-old boy
JIM, his Negro friend
The Adventures of Huckleberry
Finn (R) (Drama)

FINNEGAN. See also: Finegan

FINNEGAN, CLIFTON. See:
Archie

FINNEGAN, WILFRED. See:
Archie

FINNEY. See: Gibbs

Finney, General Delivery, Gibbs and.
See: Gibbs

FINUCANE, LIEUT. HOWARD,
police officer

GEORGE PETERS, patrolman
Manhunt (TV) (Police drama)

FIORITO, TED. See:
Powell, Dick (3)
Medbury, John P.

FIPPLE. See: Farrow, Valentine

Fire Chief, The. See: Fire Chief,
The

FIRE CHIEF, THE, comic character, portrayed by Ed Wynn
GRAHAM McNAMEE, announcer
of the program (himself)
MANY GUEST STARS
The Fire Chief (R) (Humor /
variety)

Fire, Og, Son of. See: Og

Fireside Chats. See: Roosevelt,
Franklin D.

Firestone, The Voice of. See:
Barlow, Howard

Firing Line. See: Buckley,
William F., Jr.

First Aid. See: Ludwig, Professor Donald

First Churchills, The. See:
Churchill, John

First Edition, Rollin' on the River
With Kenny Rogers and the.
See: Rogers, Kenny

FIRST EDITION, THE. See:
Rogers, Kenny

First Impression, Your. See:
Leyden, Bill (2)

First Love, Linda's. See: Linda

FIRST MRS. BURTON, THE. See:
Burton, Terry

First Nighter. See: First Nighter,
Mr.

FIRST NIGHTER, MR., patron of
the Little Theater off Times
Square

VINCENT, usher at the theater
DON AMECHE
BARBARA LUDDY
LES TREMAYNE
JUNE MEREDITH
OLAN SOULE
BETTY LOU GERSON
MACDONALD CAREY
CLIFF SOUBIER
JACK DOTY
RAYMOND EDWARD JOHNSON
OTHERS, actors and actresses
appearing in the dramas (them-
selves)
CAESAR PETRILLO
FRANK WORTH
ERIC SAGERQUIST, orchestra
leaders (themselves)
THEIR ORCHESTRAS
First Nighter (R) (Drama)

First Piano Quartet, The. See:
Horwitz, Hans

FIRST SERGEANT WOLZNIAK.
See: McKay, Judson

First Tuesday. See: Vanocur,
Sander

FIRST TWIN. See: Pan, Peter

First, Women and Children. See:
Joe (2)

FISCHMAN, HARVE. See: Kelly,
Joe (2)

FISCHMAN, SPARKY. See: Kelly,
Joe (2)

Fish and Hunt Club, The. See:
Bickart, Sanford

FISHER, EDDIE, singer, star of
the program (himself)
GEORGE GOBEL, permanent
guest (himself)
THE RAY CHARLES SINGERS
THE ECHOES, vocal groups
MANY GUEST STARS
The Eddie Fisher Show (TV)
(Variety)

FISHER, EDDIE. See also:
Edwards, Ralph (1)
Gobel, George

FISHIGAN, ISHIGAN, OF SISHIGAN,
MICHIGAN. See: Gook, Vic

Fishing and Hunting Club of the
Air, The. See: Begley, Martin

FISK, MISS. See: Kincaid, Chet

Fitch Bandwagon, The. See:
Daley, Cass
Harris, Phil
Moore, Garry (2)

FITZ, EVEY PERKINS. See:
Perkins, Ma

FITZ, JUDGE, jurist and barber
His Honor, the Barber (R)
(Drama)

FITZ, JUNIOR. See: Perkins,
Ma

FITZ, WILLIE. See: Perkins,
Ma

FITZGERALD, BRIDGET THERESA
MARY COLEEN, Catholic school-
teacher
BERNIE STEINBERG, Jewish
taxi driver and student; in love
with, marries Bridget
WALTER FITZGERALD, Bridget's
father
AMY FITZGERALD, Bridget's
mother
MIKE FITZGERALD, Bridget's
brother; priest
SAM STEINBERG, Bernie's
father; delicatessen proprietor
SOPHIE STEINBERG, Bernie's
mother
UNCLE MOE PLOTNIK, Bernie's
uncle
OTIS FOSTER, Bernie's best
friend; Negro
Bridget Loves Bernie (TV)
(Situation comedy)

FITZGERALD, ED
PEGEEN, his wife, discussion
team (themselves)
The Fitzgeralds (R) (Conversation)

Fitzgeralds, The. See: Fitzgerald,
Ed

FITZGIBBONS, FATHER. See:

O'Malley, Father Chuck

FITZHARDING, LADY. See:
Churchill, John

FITZHUGH. See: Lockridge,
Barry

FITZMAURICE, MICHAEL, quiz-
master of the program (himself)
OTHER QUIZMASTERS
MANY CONTESTANTS
The Quiz of Two Cities (R)
(Quiz)

Five Daughters, Our. See: Lee,
Jim

Five Fingers. See: Sebastian,
Victor

Five-O, Hawaii. See: McGarrett,
Steve

FIVE PUPS, DAISY'S. See:
Bumstead, Blondie

Five Star Comedy. See: Olsen,
Ole

Five Star Jones. See: Jones,
Tom (1)

FIVE STAR JONES. See: Jones,
Tom (1)

FIX-IT, MR., lectured on repair-
ing items around the home
TYPICAL DOMESTIC COUPLE
Mr. Fix-It (R) (Home repair
dramatizations)

Fix-it Shop, Mel Blanc's. See:
Blanc, Mel

Fix-it Shop, The. See: Blanc,
Mel

FLACK, COLONEL HUMPHREY,
confidence man
EUSTACE P. GARVEY, his
accomplice
Colonel Flack (TV) (Crime
comedy)

FLACK, ROBERTA. See:
Fiedler, Arthur

FLAGG, CAPTAIN, army officer
SERGEANT QUIRT, non-com-
missioned officer
Captain Flagg and Sergeant
Quirt (R) (Situation comedy)

FLAGG, CAPTAIN JIM
LIEUT. KIRBY
SERGEANT BUCK SINCLAIR,
Civil War veterans; travel to
the West
Rough Riders (TV) (Western)

FLAHERTY, MARTIN. See:
Winchell, Walter (2)

FLANAGAN, RALPH, orchestra
leader, featured on the program
(himself)
HIS ORCHESTRA
Ralph Flanagan (TV) (Popular
music)

FLANAGAN, RALPH. See also:
Basie, Count

FLANNIGAN, CASEY. See: Sharp,
Hal

FLASH. See:
Allen, Jimmie
Gordon, Flash

Flash Gordon. See: Gordon,
Flash

Flash, Quick as a. See: Roberts,
Ken

Flatbush, The Foxes of. See:
Fox, Jennie

Flats, The Three. See: Caine,
Betty

FLATT DANCERS, THE ERNEST.
See:
Burnett, Carol
DeLuise, Dom (2)

FLEEGLE, dog
DROOPER, lion
BINGO, gorilla
SNORKY, elephant, all por-
trayed by actors dressed as
animals
Kellogg's Presents the Banana
Splits Adventure Hour (TV)

(Children's program) (also
known as The Banana Splits)
(TV)

Fleischmann's Hour, The. See:
Vallee, Rudy (2)

FLEMING, ART, moderator of the
program (himself)
GUEST CONTESTANTS
Jeopardy! (TV) (Game)

FLEMING, DR. See: Trent,
Helen

FLEMING, TONY
ALEC FLEMING
MARCEL ST. CLAIR
TIMMY ST. CLAIR, cousins
MARGARET ST. CLAIR (Aunt
Margaret), their aunt; all swind-
lers and confidence game opera-
tors
The Rogues (TV) (Crime/adven-
ture)

FLEMMING, BILL. See: Mc-
Kay, Jim (1)

FLETCHER. See:
Dallas, Stella
Pletcher
Richards, Ben
Wilson, Steve

FLETCHER, DR. JOHN. See:
Bauer, Bertha

FLETCHER, DR. PAUL. See:
Bauer, Bertha

FLETCHER, MRS. See: Fairchild, Kay

FLETCHER RABBITT. See:
Kukla

FLETCHER, RENA. See:
Randolph, Ellen

FLETCHER, UNCLE. See:
Gook, Vic

FLEUR. See:
Flower
Forsyte, Soames

FLICKA. See: McLaughlin, Ken

Flicka, My Friend. See: Mc-
Laughlin, Ken

FLINT, BLACKBEARD. See:
Armstrong, Jack

FLINT, DETECTIVE ADAM. See:
Parker, Lieut. Mike

FLINT HALE. See: Adams,
Major Seth

FLINT McCULLOUGH. See:
Adams, Major Seth

Flintstone Comedy Hour, The.
See: Flintstone, Fred

FLINTSTONE, FRED, caveman,
resident of Bedrock
WILMA FLINTSTONE, his wife
BARNEY RUBBLE, his neighbor
BETTY RUBBLE, Barney's wife;
all cartoon characters
The Flintstones (TV) (Cartoon)
(later called The Flintstone
Comedy Hour) (TV)

Flintstones, The. See: Flintstone, Fred

FLIP. See:
Rose, George
Wilson, Flip

FLIP CORKIN. See: Lee, Terry

"FLIP" FLIPPEN, FRANK. See:
Kelly, Frederick Thomas

FLIP MALONE. See: Bauer,
Bertha

FLIP THE HIPPO. See: Pam

FLIP WILSON. See:
Shawn, Dick
Wilson, Flip

Flip Wilson Show, The. See:
Wilson, Flip

FLIPPEN. See also: Flippin

FLIPPEN, FRANK "FLIP." See:
Kelly, Frederick Thomas

FLIPPEN, JAY C. See:

Bower, Roger
Bowes, Major Edward (2)
Crumit, Frank (1)

Flipper. See: Flipper

FLIPPER, pet dolphin
DR. JAMES, marine biologist
PORTER RICKS, Florida marine
ranger
SANDY RICKS
BUD RICKS, Porter's sons
PETE, pelican
SPRAY, dog
Flipper (TV) (Animal/adventure)

FLIPPIN. See also: Flippen

FLIPPIN, FRANK. See: Waring,
Evelyn

FLONZALEY STRING QUARTET,
THE. See: Drew, John

FLOOD, BILL. See: Warren,
Wendy

FLORA LITTLE. See: Allen,
Joan Houston

FLORADORA GIRLS, THE. See:
Kay, Beatrice

FLOREN. See also: Florian

FLOREN, MYRON. See: Welk,
Lawrence

FLORENCE. See:
Halop, Billy
Pritchard, Florence

FLORENCE FOLSOM. See: Kelly,
Joe (1)

FLORENCE HALOP. See:
Cross, Milton (2)
Halop, Billy

FLORENCE HENDERSON. See:
Hayes, Bill

FLORENCE MULHOLLAND. See:
Roxy

FLORENCE PRICHETT. See:
Landi, Elissa

Florence Pritchard. See:
Pritchard, Florence

FLORENCE RINARD. See:
Slater, Bill (2)

FLORENCE WESTON. See:
Waring, Evelyn

FLORENZE, COUNTESS. See:
Sunday

FLORENZE, LILE. See: Sunday

FLORIAN. See:
Floren
ZaBach, Florian

Florian ZaBach Show, The. See:
ZaBach, Florian

FLORIDA EVANS. See: Findlay,
Maude

FLORY, MED. See: Anthony,
Ray

FLOSSIE HERRINGBONE. See:
Perkins, Ma

FLOUNCE, BESSIE. See:
Perkins, Ma

FLOWER. See also: Fleur

FLOWER, IRIS. See: Buddy

FLOWER, VIOLET. See: Buddy

FLOYD. See:
Gildersleeve, Throckmorton P.
Kalber, Floyd
Prior, Jeff
Taylor, Andy

FLOYD GIBBONS. See: Thomas,
Lowell (1)

FLOYD YEOMANS. See: Story,
Ralph

FLUBADUB, THE. See: Doody,
Howdy

FLUTE, FREDDY. See: Pufnstuf,
H.R.

FLUTE, JIMMY. See: Pufnstuf,
H.R.

Flying Nun, The. See: Bertrille,
Sr.

Flying Patrol. See: Rowlands,
Hugh

Flying Time. See: Falvey, Hal

FLYNN. See: O'Flynn, Captain
Flynn

FLYNN, SALLI. See: Welk,
Lawrence

FOG. See: Ffogg

FOGHORN. See: Mix, Tom

FOLAN. See also: Falan

FOLAN, LILIAS, yoga expert;
host of the program (himself)
Lilias, Yoga and You (TV) (Yoga
demonstrations)

FOLEY, JOE. See: Burnley,
Walter

FOLEY, MR. See: Taylor, Andy

FOLEY, RED, Western music
singer; host of the program (him-
self)
AUNT SAP AND UNCLE SIP,
comedy act
SLIM WILSON, orchestra leader
(himself)
HIS JUBILEE BAND
MANY GUEST MUSICIANS AND
SINGERS
Jubilee, U.S.A. (Western/country
music)

FOLIES. See also: Follies

Folies Bergere of the Air, The.
See: Howard, Willie

Folk Guitar. See: Weber, Laura

Folk Guitar Plus. See: Weber,
Laura

Folks, Prairie. See: Nielson,
Torwald

FOLLIES. See also: Folies

Follies, Hook 'n' Ladder. See:
Walt, Captain

Follow That Man. See: Barnett,
Mike

Follow the Moon. See: Bannister,
Clay

Follow the Sun. See: Gregory,
Ben

FOLSOM, AGATHA. See: Myrt

FOLSOM, FLORENCE. See:
Kelly, Joe (1)

FONG. See: Evans, Glen

FONT, RALPH. See: Whiteman,
Paul

FONTAINE, FRANK. See:
Berman, Shelley
Gleason, Jackie (2)

FONTANE SISTERS, THE. See:
Como, Perry (1)

Food For Life. See: Cederquist,
Dena

FOODINI. See: Lucky Pup

FOOLER, OLD. See: Jones,
Ben

Football, N.F.L. Monday Night.
See: Jackson, Keith (2)

For a Song, Yours. See:
Froman, Jane (2)
Parks, Bert (7)

For Better or Worse. See:
Peterson, Dr. James

For Love or Money. See: Nimmo,
Bill

For the People. See: Koster,
David

For Your Information. See:
Allison, Fran

FORBES, BRAD. See: Lambert,
Louise

FORBES, JACK. See: Murphy,
Peter

Force, The Silent. See: Fuller,
Ward

FORD, ART. See: Shaw, Stan

FORD, MARY. See: Paul, Les

FORD, SENATOR ED. See: Wilson, Ward

Ford Show, The. See: Ford,
Tennessee Ernie (2)

Ford Summer Hour, The. See:
Melton, James (1)

FORD, TENNESSEE ERNIE (1),
singer and entertainer; host of
the program (himself)
MANY GUESTS
The College of Musical Knowledge
(TV) (Variety)

FORD, TENNESSEE ERNIE (2),
singer and entertainer; host of
the program (himself)
THE VOICES OF WALTER SCHU-
MANN, vocal group
THE JUNE TAYLOR DANCERS
MANY CELEBRITY GUEST STARS
The Ford Show (TV) (Variety)

FORD, TENNESSEE ERNIE (3),
singer and entertainer; host of
the program (himself)
MANY GUEST ENTERTAINERS
Hello, Pea Pickers (TV) (Variety)

FORD, TENNESSEE ERNIE (4),
singer and entertainer; star of
the program (himself)
MOLLY BEE
DORIS DREW
SKIP FARRELL, singers and
entertainers featured on the
program (themselves)
JACK FASCINATO, orchestra
leader (himself)
HIS ORCHESTRA
MANY GUEST STARS
The Tennessee Ernie Show (TV)
(Variety)

FORD, WHITEY. See: Duke of
Paducah, The

Fords Go By, Watch the. See:
Blurt, Elmer

Foreign Assignment. See:
Foreign Correspondent, The

FOREIGN CORRESPONDENT, THE,
newspaperman
HIS ASSISTANT
Foreign Assignment (R) (Adventure)

Foreign Intrigue. See: Storm,
Christopher

Foreign Legion, Assignment. See:
Oberon, Merle

Foreign Legion, Captain Gallant of
the. See: Gallant, Captain

FOREMAN, SKY KING'S. See:
King, Schyler "Sky"

FOREMAN, WILL. See: Caine,
Frank

FOREST. See also:
Forrest
Forrester

FOREST RANGER. See:
Mitchell, Everett

FOREST, TAMMY. See: Sterling,
Vanessa Dale

Forever Ernest. See: Coogan,
Jackie

Forever Young. See: Davis,
Red

Forget, I'll Never. See: Luther,
Frank (1)

FORMENTO, CAPTAIN GASPAR.
See: Bertrille, Sr.

FORREST. See also:
Forest
Forrester

FORREST, DAN. See: Carr,
Alison

FORREST, HELEN. See: Haymes,
Dick

FORRESTER. See also:
Fester
Forest
Forrest
Foster

FORRESTER, BROOK. See:
Trent, Helen

FORRESTER, LEROY. See:
Gildersleeve, Throckmorton P.

FORRESTER, MARJORIE. See:
Gildersleeve, Throckmorton P.

FORRESTER, PHIL. See: Ames,
Peter

Forsyte Saga, The. See: Forsyte,
Soames

FORSYTE, SOAMES, English lawyer
IRENE, his wife
OLD JOLYON FORSYTE, his
uncle
YOUNG JOLYON FORSYTE, Old
Jolyon's son
JUNE, Young Jolyon's daughter
PHILIP BOSINNEY, architect,
engaged to June
ANNETTE, Soames' second wife
FLEUR, daughter of Soames and
Annette
MICHAEL MONT, Fleur's hus-
band
JON, son of Irene and Young
Jolyon
WINIFRED DARTIE, Soames'
sister
MONTAGUE DARTIE, Winifred's
husband
HOLLY, Young Jolyon's daughter
JOLLY, Young Jolyon's son
VAL DARTIE, Holly's cousin and
husband
PROSPER FROFOND, Annette's
lover
TIMOTHY FORSYTE, "the last
of the Forstyes"
The Forsyte Saga (TV) (Bio-
graphical serial drama)

FORSYTHE, LIZ. See: Garrett,
Susan

FORTINA, CARL. See: Jones,
Spike (1)

FORTUNA, THE. See: Lucky,
Mr.

FORTUNE, PETER. See: Marlin,
Mary

Fortune, Soldiers of. See: Kelly,
Tim

Fortunes, Famous. See: Hawley,
Mark

FORTY FATHOM, old sailor, nar-
rator of the program
Forty Fathom Trawlers (R)
(Sea stories)

Forty Fathom Trawlers. See:
Forty Fathom

.45, Colt. See: Colt, Christopher

'41, The Spirit of. See: Daly,
John (2)

Forum of the Air, The American.
See: Granik, Theodore (1)

FOSDICK, MR. See: Hastings,
Bill

FOSDICK, REV. HARRY EMER-
SON, minister; host of the pro-
gram (himself)
The National Church of the Air
(R) (Religion)
National Vespers (R) (Religion)

FOSTER. See also:
Fester
Forrester

FOSTER, AMY. See: Marshall,
John

FOSTER, ANSON. See: Grindl

FOSTER BROOKS. See: Cosby,
Bill (2)

FOSTER, CAPTAIN BEN. See:
Talbot, Commander Dan

FOSTER, CLIFFORD. See:
Brent, Dr. Jim
Rutledge, Dr. John

FOSTER DANCERS, THE BILL.

See: King, Dave (2)

FOSTER, DR. LESLIE. See:
Marshall, John

FOSTER, ETHEL. See: Rutledge,
Dr. John

FOSTER, EVA. See: Harding,
Mrs. Rhoda

FOSTER, HENRY, editor
MRS. FOSTER, his wife
MARY FOSTER, his daughter
Editor's Daughter (R) (Serial
drama) (also known as Mary
Foster, The Editor's Daughter)
(R)

FOSTER, JUDY, young girl
MELVYN, her father
DORA, her mother
RANDOLPH, her brother
OOGIE PRINGLE, her boy friend
EDGAR
MITZI, characters appearing on
the program
A Date With Judy (R) (Situation
comedy)

FOSTER, MAJOR JOHN, Air Force
officer, becomes headmaster of
school for girls
SERGEANT ED ROBBINS, his
assistant
MISS CULVER, principal of the
school
MISS WILSON, teacher at the
school
JOANNA, servant at the school
The John Forsythe Show (TV)
(Comedy)

FOSTER, MISS. See: Wilson,
Steve

FOSTER, MRS. See:
Carson, Jack
Foster, Henry

FOSTER, OTIS. See: Fitzgerald,
Bridget Theresa Mary Coleen

FOSTER, SALLY. See: Kelly,
Joe (1)

FOSTER, STUART. See: Drake,
Galen

FOUNTAIN, PETE. See: Welk,
Lawrence

FOUR. See: Fantastic Four, The

FOUR CLUBMEN, THE. See:
Kay, Beatrice
Kaye, Danny

Four Corners, U.S.A. See:
Crowell, Jonah

FOUR FRESHMEN, THE. See:
Anthony, Ray

Four in One: San Francisco International Airport. See: Conrad,
Jim

Four Just Men, The. See: Collier,
Tim

Four Star Playhouse. See: Boyer,
Charles

4, Ten. See: Matthews, Dan

FOUR, THE ELM CITY. See:
Kay, Beatrice

Four, The Fantastic. See: Fantastic Four, The

FOUR, THE KIRBY STONE. See:
Rodgers, Jimmie

FOUR, THE MAPLE CITY. See:
Kelly, Joe (1)

FOUR, THE SHOW BOAT. See:
Henry, Captain

Four, We Are. See: Webster,
Nancy

Fourth Friday. See: Vanocur,
Sander

FOWLER. See: Harding, Mrs.
Rhoda

FOWLER, JIM. See: Perkins,
Marlin

FOWLER, JOHN. See: Peyton,
Martin

FOWLER, MR. See: Goldberg,
Molly

FOWLER, NEIL. See: Robin

FOWLEY, JEFFERSON. See:
Keene, Kitty

FOWLEY, LEDDY. See: Keene,
Kitty

FOX, J. L. See: Burnley, Walter

FOX, JENNIE, Flatbush housewife
BENNY, her son
The Foxes of Flatbush (R)
(Serial drama)

FOX, KAY. See: Stockton, Sandy
(2)

FOX, MEREDITH. See: Marshall,
E. G.

FOX, SONNY
LARRY BLYDEN, hosts of the
program (themselves)
MANY GUEST STARS
The Movie Game (TV) (Game)

FOX, SONNY. See also: Story,
Ralph

FOX, TEMPLETON. See:
Winkler, Betty

Foxes of Flatbush, The. See:
Fox, Jennie

FOY, AGNES. See: Randolph,
Ellen

FOYLE, KITTY, young middle-
class career girl
WYN STRAFFORD, her aristo-
cratic boy friend
Kitty Foyle (R) (TV) (Serial
drama)

FRAME, STEVEN. See: Randolph,
Alice

FRAME, WILLIS. See: Randolph,
Alice

FRAN. See:
Allison, Fran
Cummings, Brenda
Dodsworth, Sam
Vass, Fran

FRAN ALLISON. See:
Allison, Fran
Kukla

FRAN BELDING, SERGEANT. See:
Ironside, Chief Robert

FRAN McCORD. See: Fry,
Marshal Simon

FRANCE, KING OF. See:
Churchill, John

FRANCES. See:
Brent, Dr. Jim
Cameron, Barry
Francis
Horwich, Dr. Frances
Jones, Lorenzo
Nuvo, Arnie
Potter, Tom
Scott, Frances

FRANCES HUNT. See: Lane,
Richard

FRANCES MORAN MATTHEWS.
See:
Carter, Kathryn
Marlin, Mary

FRANCESCA. See: Girelli, Joe

FRANCESCA MAGUIRE. See:
Bennett, Nita

FRANCIA WHITE. See: Melton,
James (1)

FRANCIE. See: Brent, Dr. Jim

FRANCIS. See:
Drake, Sir Francis
Frances
Muldoon, Francis

FRANCIS, ARLENE (1), interviewer
and hostess of the program (herself)
MANY INTERVIEWEES
THE NORMAN PARIS TRIO,
musical group
Arlene Francis (TV) (Interviews/
variety)

FRANCIS, ARLENE (2), hostess of
the program (herself)
MANY AUDIENCE PARTICIPANTS

Blind Date (R) (Audience participation)

FRANCIS, ARLENE (3)
JOHN CONTE, featured on the
program (themselves)
My Good Wife (R) (Situation
comedy)

FRANCIS, ARLENE (4), hostess of
the program (herself)
MANY SOLDIER PERFORMERS
Soldier Parade (TV) (Army
talent)

FRANCIS, ARLENE. See also:
Daly, John (3)
Hulick, Wilbur Budd
Myerson, Bess

FRANCIS, CONNIE. See:
Edwards, Ralph (1)
Rodgers, Jimmie

FRANCIS DEREHAM. See: Henry
VIII, King of England

FRANCIS HAYFIELD. See: Myrt

FRANCIS, JOE. See: King

FRANCIS WELCH, COLONEL. See:
Barton, Bud

FRANCIS WELCH, JR. See:
Barton, Bud

FRANCIS WILDE. See: Crown,
Jim

FRANK. See:
Ballinger, Lieut. Frank
Bridges, Cara
Buck, Frank
Buxton, Frank
Caine, Frank
Cannon, Frank
Crumit, Frank (1) (2) (3) (4)
Dain, Lieut. Frank
Edwards, Frank
Fay, Frank
Garlund, Frank
Hawks, Frank
James, Jesse
Knight, Frank
Lovejoy, Frank (1) (2)
Luther, Frank (1) (2)
McGee, Frank

Merriwell, Frank
Morgan, Frank (1) (2)
Munn, Frank (1) (2)
Parker, Frank
Redigo, Jim (2)
Savage, Brigadier General Frank
Scott, Constable Frank
Sinatra, Frank
Wayne, Ruth Evans

FRANK ALLISON. See: Mac-
Donald, Eleanor

FRANK ARCARO, DETECTIVE.
See: Parker, Lieut. Mike

FRANK BANTA. See: Dragonette,
Jessica (1)

FRANK BAXTER. See: Nesbit,
John (2)

FRANK BLACK. See:
Benny, Jack
Melton, James (2)

FRANK BOONE. See: Miller,
Johnny

Frank Buck Show, The. See:
Buck, Frank

FRANK BURKE, SERGEANT. See:
Narz, Jack (2)

FRANK BURNS, MAJOR. See:
Pierce, Captain Hawkeye

FRANK CARVER. See: Ames,
Peter

FRANK CHANDLER. See: Chandu
the Magician

FRANK CHASE. See: Trent,
Helen

Frank Crumit and Julia Sanderson.
See: Crumit, Frank (3)

FRANK DANA. See: Brent, Dr.
Jim

Frank Edwards. See: Edwards,
Frank

Frank Fay Show, The. See: Fay,
Frank

FRANK FENTON. See:
Harding, Karen Adams
Perkins, Ma

FRANK "FLIP" FLIPPEN. See:
Kelly, Frederick Thomas

FRANK FLIPPIN. See: Waring,
Evelyn

FRANK FONTAINE. See:
Berman, Shelley
Gleason, Jackie (2)

FRANK GORSHIN. See: Little,
Rich

FRANK HARRISON. See: Peters,
Bill

FRANK JENKS. See: Lane,
Richard

FRANK LEAHY. See: Anthony,
Ray

FRANK LOVEJOY. See:
Lovejoy, Frank (1) (2)
McCormick, Myron

FRANK McGEE. See:
Chancellor, John
Downs, Hugh
McGee, Frank

Frank McGee Report, The. See:
McGee, Frank

FRANK McGREGOR. See:
Crown, Jim

Frank Merriwell. See: Merriwell,
Frank

FRANK MITTLER. See: Horwitz,
Hans

Frank Morgan Show, The. See:
Morgan, Frank (1)

FRANK MOULAN. See: Roxy

FRANK NELSON. See: Benny,
Jack

FRANK NITTI. See: Winchell,
Walter (2)

FRANK PALMER. See: Malone,
Dr. Jerry

FRANK PARKER. See:
Benny, Jack
Donald, Peter
Godfrey, Arthur (1)
Parker, Frank

FRANK PRINCE. See: Bernie,
Ben

FRANK RADCLIFFE. See: Slattery, Jim

FRANK READICK. See:
Judge, The
Welles, Orson (1) (2)

FRANK REMLEY. See:
Benny, Jack
Harris, Phil

FRANK REYNOLDS. See: Hodges,
Gilbert

FRANK ROBERTS. See: Brent,
Dr. Jim

FRANK SCHUSTER. See: Wayne,
Johnny (1) (2)

FRANK SCOTT. See: Welk,
Lawrence

FRANK SENRAM. See: Sharp,
Hal

FRANK SINATRA. See:
Ross, Lanny
Sinatra, Frank

FRANK SINATRA, JR. See:
Jones, Jack

Frank Sinatra Show, The. See:
Sinatra, Frank

FRANK SLOAN. See: Karr,
Mike

FRANK SUTTON. See: Nabors,
Jim

FRANK WATANABE. See:
Holloway, Harrison

FRANK WHITTAKER, MAJOR.

See: Young, Captain David

FRANK WILLOUGHBY. See:
Henry, Captain

FRANK WORTH. See: First
Nighter, Mr.

FRANKEL, HARRY. See: Singin'
Sam

FRANKENSTEIN MONSTER, THE.
See: Munster, Herman

FRANKIE. See:
Carle, Frankie (1) (2)
Girelli, Joe
Laine, Frankie

FRANKIE AVALON. See: Jones,
Jack

Frankie Carle Show, The. See:
Carle, Frankie (2)

Frankie Laine Show, The. See:
Laine, Frankie

FRANKLIN. See:
Adams, Franklin P.
Roosevelt, Franklin D.
Sheppard, Franklin
Willy

FRANKLIN ADAMS. See:
Adams, Franklin P.
Marlin, Mary

FRANKLIN BARBOUR, IRENE.
See: Barbour, Henry Wilson

FRANKLIN, BETTY. See:
Andrews, Walter

FRANKLIN D. ROOSEVELT. See:
Husing, Ted
Roosevelt, Franklin D.

FRANKLIN, DEXTER. See:
Archer, Corliss

FRANKLIN, JOE, host of the pro-
gram (himself)
MANY GUEST INTERVIEWEES
Joe Franklin's Memory Lane (R)
(TV) (Interviews) (also called
The Joe Franklin Show) (R) (TV)

FRANKLIN, MAURICE. See:
Judge, The

FRANKLIN P. ADAMS. See:
Adams, Franklin P.
Fadiman, Clifton (1)

FRASER AMES. See: Dyke,
Charity Amanda

FRASER, BEN
BEN FRASER, JR.
EMILY FRASER BENSON
LYDDIE BENSON
TIM BENSON
ROSE CORELLI FRASER
DAN FRASER
SARAH FRASER
ROBIN FRASER
BRUCE CRAWFORD
ENID CHAMBERS
LIZ, characters appearing in
the drama
From These Roots (TV) (Serial
drama)

FRASER, BEN. See also: Holden,
Grey

FRASER, JACK. See: Arden,
Jane

FRASER, RALPH. See: Harding,
Mrs. Rhoda

FRASIER, DR. GRANT. See:
Brent, Dr. Jim

FRAZIER MITCHELL. See:
Marlin, Mary

FRED. See:
Allen, Fred
Andrews, Archie
Astaire, Fred
Baker, Dean Fred
Brent, Dr. Jim
Collins, Fred (1) (2)
Davis, Fred
Finn, Fred
Flintstone, Fred
Kent, Fred
Robbins, Fred
Rogers, Fred
Sanford, Fred
Scooby Doo
Sullivan, Fred
Uttal, Fred (1) (2)
Waring, Fred (1) (2)

FRED ALLEN. See:
Allen, Fred
Daly, John (3)
Martin, Dean (1)

FRED ALLEN, MRS. See: Allen,
Fred

Fred Allen Show, The. See: Allen,
Fred

FRED ASHER, INSPECTOR. See:
Guthrie, Lieut. Ben

FRED ASTAIRE. See:
Astaire, Fred (1) (2)
Ross, Lanny

Fred Astaire, An Evening With.
See: Astaire, Fred (2)

FRED BURNS. See: Karr, Mike

FRED CASTLESON. See: Sunday

FRED COSTELLO. See: Grant,
Harry

FRED CROWLEY, DR. See:
Allen, Dr. Kate

FRED DAVIS. See:
Davis, Fred
Sunday

FRED GILMAN. See: Garrett,
Sam

FRED HOPKINS, MRS. See:
Graham, Dr. Bob

FRED MacMURRAY. See:
Powell, Dick (3)

FRED MERTZ. See: Ricardo,
Ricky

FRED MINTURN. See: Nelson,
Carolyn Kramer

FRED RUSSELL. See: Peyton,
Martin

FRED THOMPSON, DR. See:
Barbour, Henry Wilson

FRED UTTAL. See:
Hulick, Wilbur Budd

Uttal, Fred (1) (2)

FRED VANDERVENTER. See:
Slater, Bill (2)

FRED W. FRIENDLY. See:
Murrow, Edward R. (5)

FRED WARING. See:
Como, Perry (1)
Waring, Fred (1) (2)

Fred Waring Show, The. See:
Waring, Fred (1)

FREDDIE. See:
Barnes, Joey
Mulligan, Mickey

FREDDIE RICH. See: Ross,
Lanny

FREDDIE THE FREELOADER.
See: Junior

FREDDIE THE SWINGER. See:
Wilson, Flip

FREDDY (BUDDY) DOUGLAS.
See: Johnny

FREDDY FLUTE. See: Pufnstuf,
H. R.

FREDDY MARTIN. See: Daley,
Cass

FREDERIC. See: March,
Frederic

FREDERICK. See:
Allen, Frederick Lewis
Kelly, Frederick Thomas
Noad, Frederick

FREDERICK NELSON. See:
Brown, Ellen

FREDERICKA LANG. See: Rutledge, Dr. John

FREDERICKS, CARLTON, lecturer
on diet and health (himself)
Living Should Be Fun (R)
(Health)

FREDERICKS, GEORGE. See:
Malone, Dr. Jerry

FREELOADER, FREDDIE THE.
See: Junior

FREEMAN, ERNIE. See: Uggams,
Leslie

FREEMAN, MORGAN. See: Cosby,
Bill (1)

FREES, PAUL, narrator of the
program (himself)
THE MAN IN BLACK, character
appearing on the program
BRIAN DONLEVY
CARY GRANT
IDA LUPINO
AGNES MOOREHEAD
LUCILLE BALL
ORSON WELLES
OTHERS, actors and actresses
appearing on the program (them-
selves)
Suspense (R) (Drama)

FREEZE, MR. See: Batman

FREIFELDER, DAVID. See:
Kelly, Joe (2)

FREIGHT TRAIN. See: Huddles,
Ed

French Chef, The. See: Child,
Julia

FRENCH, GILES. See: Davis,
Uncle Bill

FRENCH, JACK. See: Kelly,
Joe (2)

FRENCH PRINCESS. See: Marie

French Princess, Marie the Little.
See: Marie

FRESHMEN, THE FOUR. See:
Anthony, Ray

FREUCHEN, PETER. See:
March, Hal
Story, Ralph

FRIAR TUCK. See: Hood, Robin

FRICKERT, MAUDE. See:
Winters, Jonathan

FRIDAY. See: Brown, Robinson,
Jr.

Friday, Fourth. See: Vanocur,
Sander

FRIDAY, SERGEANT JOE, Los
Angeles police detective
Dragnet (R) (TV) (Crime de-
tection drama)
SERGEANT BEN ROMERO, his
partner
Dragnet (R)
DETECTIVE JOE SMITH
OFFICER BILL GANNON, his
partners
Dragnet (TV) (also known as
Badge 714) (TV)

FRIDAY SINGERS, THE PAT. See:
Borge, Victor

FRIEDA KRAUSE. See: Marshall,
Owen

FRIEND, BUN DAWSON'S. See:
Malone, Dr. Jerry

Friend Flicka, My. See: Mc-
Laughlin, Ken

Friend in Deed. See: Maxwell,
Richard

Friend Irma, My. See: Peterson,
Irma

Friend Tony, My. See: Woodruff,
Professor

FRIENDLY, FRED W. See:
Murrow, Edward R. (5)

Friendly Ghost, Casper, The.
See: Casper

FRIENDLY UNDERTAKER, THE.
See: Riley, Chester A.

Friends, Arthur Godfrey and His.
See: Godfrey, Arthur (1)

FRIENDS, THE THREE GIRL.
See: Waring, Fred (1)

FRITTER, WILMA. See: Burnley,
Walter

235   FRITZI

FRITZI. See: Scheff, Fritzi

FROELICH. See:
  Frohlich
  Rainey, Dr. Froelich

FROG, FERDIE. See: Boop, Betty

FROGG, DAISY. See: Hanks,
  Henrietta

FROHLICH. See also: Froelich

FROHLICH, STEVEN. See: Story,
  Ralph

From a Bird's Eye View. See:
  Grover, Millie

From These Roots. See: Fraser,
  Ben

FROMAN, JANE (1), singer; star
  of the program (herself)
  MANY SOLDIER/SAILOR INTER-
  VIEWEES
  The Jane Froman Show (TV)
  (Military entertainment/interviews)
  (originally called The U.S. Can-
  teen Show) (TV)

FROMAN, JANE (2)
  ROBERT WEEDE, vocalists, fea-
  tured on the program (themselves)
  ALFREDO ANTONINI, orchestra
  leader (himself)
  HIS ORCHESTRA
  Yours For a Song (R) (Music)

Front Lawyers, The Store. See:
  Hansen, David

FRONT PAGE. See: Farrell,
  David

Front Page Farrell. See: Farrell,
  David

Frontier. See: Coy, Walter

Frontier Circus. See: Thompson,
  Colonel Casey

Frontier Doctor. See: Baxter, Dr.
  Bill

Frontier Justice. See: Ayres,
  Lew

Frontiers of Faith. See: Barnhouse, Donald

FROST, DAVID (1), host of the
  program (himself)
  MANY GUESTS
  The David Frost Show (TV)
  (Conversation)

FROST, DAVID (2), host of the
  program (himself)
  JACK GILFORD
  MARCIA RODD
  GEORGE IRVING
  JIM CATUSI
  LYNN LIPTON, entertainers
  appearing on the program (them-
  selves)
  MANY GUEST STARS
  The David Frost Revue (TV)
  (Revue)

FROST, DAVID. See also: Ames,
  Nancy

FRY, MARSHAL SIMON, law en-
  forcement officer
  HERK LAMSON, deputy
  CLAY McCORD, storekeeper
  FRAN McCORD, Clay's sister
  The Deputy (TV) (Western)

Fu Manchu. See: Fu Manchu

FU MANCHU, Chinese villain and
  chemistry wizard
  KARAMENEH, slave girl
  MALIK, French detective
  NAYLAND SMITH, English
  enemy of Fu Manchu
  DR. PETRIE, associate of
  Smith
  Fu Manchu (R) (Mystery/adven-
  ture)

FUDD, ELMER. See: Bunny,
  Bugs

FUDDLE. See: Bumstead,
  Blondie

FUDDLE, ALVIN. See: Bumstead,
  Blondie

FUFFY ADAMS. See: Graves,
  Harry

Fugitive, The. See: Kimble, Dr.
  Richard

FUJI. See: McHale, Lieut. Commander Quinton

Full Circle. See: Donovan, Gary

FULLER, BRYAN. See: Ames, Peter

FULLER, REV. CHARLES E., minister; host of the program (himself)
The Old-Fashioned Revival Hour (R) (Religion)

FULLER, ROSE. See: Drake, Nora

FULLER, WARD
AMELIA COLE
JASON HART, government agents and undercover crime fighters
The Silent Force (TV) (Crime drama)

FULLERTON, MR. See: Cameron, Christy Allen

FULTON. See: Sheen, Bishop Fulton J.

FUMBLE. See: Kangaroo, Captain

Fun, Alumni. See: Hayes, Peter Lind (1)

Fun Fair, Jay Stewart's. See: Stewart, Jay (1)

Fun, Hall of. See: Lane, Richard

Fun, Living Should Be. See: Fredericks, Carlton

Funday Funnies, Matty's. See: Matty

FUNICELLO, ANNETTE. See: Jones, Jack

Funky Phantom, The. See: Muggsy

Funnies, Matty's Funday. See: Matty

Funny Face. See: Stockton, Sandy (1)

Funny, People Are. See: Linkletter, Art (4)

Funny Side, The. See: Kelly, Gene

Funny You Should Ask. See: Thaxton, Lloyd (2)

FUNT, ALLEN (1), host of the program (himself)
ARTHUR GODFREY
DURWARD KIRBY
MARILYN VAN DERBUR, co-hosts of the program (themselves)
OTHER CO-HOSTS
Candid Camera (TV) (Audience participation) (previously a segment of The Garry Moore Show) (TV)

FUNT, ALLEN (2), host of the program (himself)
MANY INTERVIEWEES
Candid Microphone (R) (Audience participation)

FUNT, ALLEN. See also: Moore, Garry (3)

FURNESS, BETTY, hostess of the program (herself)
MANY GUESTS
Living For the Sixties (TV) (Discussion)

Fury. See: Newton, Jim

FURY. See: Newton, Jim

FURY SHARK. See: Midnight, Captain

Future, The Nation's. See: McCaffery, John K. M. (1)

FUZZY. See: Gallant, Captain

G. E. See also: General Electric

G. E. College Bowl, The. See:
Earle, Robert

G. E. True. See: Webb, Jack

G-Men. See: Lord, Phillips H.

G. , MISS. See: O'Brien, Daniel J.

G-2, The Man From. See: North,
Major Hugh

GABBERS, THE. See: Reiner,
Carl

GABBY. See: Hayes, Gabby

GABBY DI JULIO. See: O'Toole,
Ensign

Gabby Hayes Show, The. See:
Hayes, Gabby

GABE COOPER. See: Boone,
Daniel

GABLER, ROY. See: Trent,
Helen

GABRIEL. See: Heatter, Gabriel

GABRIEL KAYE. See: Hansen,
David

GABRIELLE FAURE. See:
Brent, Portia

GADDIS, CRACKER, character
appearing in the drama
Moonshine and Honeysuckle (R)
(Serial drama)

GAFF. See: Tempest, Dan

GAGE. See: Calhoun, Ben

GAGE, JOHN
ROY DeSOTO, firemen; members
of paramedical team
DR. KELLY BRACKETT
DR. JOE EARLY, physicians
DIXIE McCALL, nurse
Emergency! (TV) (Fireman/
paramedical drama)

GAGE, NICHOLAS. See: Sheppard,
Franklin

GAGNE, VERNE. See: James,
Dennis (4)

Gags to Riches. See: Adams,
Joey (1)

GAHRINGER, ELMA. See: Sherwood, Grace

GAIL. See:
Brewster, Gail
Gale
Williams, Dr.

GAIL CARVER. See: Lawton,
Lora

GAIL FARRELL. See: Welk,
Lawrence

GAIL LUCAS. See: Thorpe, Liz

GAIL MARTIN. See: Damone, Vic
(2)

GAIL NOLAN. See: Harrigan,
Hop

GAINE, JEB. See: Hardie, Jim

GAINES, CLARA. See: Mickey

Gal Sunday, Our. See: Sunday

GALA POOCHIE. See: Russell,
Todd

GALE. See also: Gail

GALE, JIMMY. See: Carter,
Hope

GALE PAGE. See: Ameche, Jim

Gale Storm Show, The. See:
Pomeroy, Susanna

GALEN. See: Drake, Galen

Galen Drake. See: Drake, Galen

GALLAGHER, TIMOTHY. See:
Perkins, Ma

GALLANT, CAPTAIN, officer of
the French Foreign Legion

CUFFY SANDERS, his orphan
ward
FUZZY
FASAIL
TALEB
NIKLOS, Legionnaires
Captain Gallant of the Foreign
Legion (TV) (Adventure)

Gallant Men, The. See: Wright,
Conley

Gallery, Auction. See: Elman,
Dave (1)

Gallery, Night. See: Serling, Rod
(1)

Gallery, Rod Serling's Night. See:
Serling, Rod (1)

Gallery, Rogue's. See: Rogue,
Richard

GALLICCHIO, JOE. See: James,
Dennis (1)

GALLO, ELBERT. See: Manning,
Portia Blake

Galloping Gourmet, The. See:
Kerr, Graham

GALLOWAY, DUANE. See: Varner,
Will

GALLOWAY, JACK. See: Arden,
Jane

GALWAY, IRENE. See: Sunday

GALWAY, PETER. See: Sunday

GAMBARELLI, MARIA. See: Roxy

GAMBARELLI, YASHA. See: Roxy

Gambit. See: Martindale, Wink (1)

GAMBLE, DOC. See: McGee,
Fibber

Game, Joe Garagiola's Memory.
See: Garagiola, Joe (2)

Game Parade. See: Elmer, Arthur

Game, The Big. See: Kennedy,

Tom (1)

Game, The Dating. See: Lange,
Jim

Game, The Family. See: Yablonsky, Lewis

Game, The Match. See: Rayburn,
Gene (2)

Game, The Most Deadly. See:
Croft, Jonathan

Game, The Movie. See: Fox,
Sonny

Game, The Name of the. See:
Howard, Glenn

Game, The Newlywed. See: Eubanks, Bob

Game, The Parent. See: Race,
Clark

Game, The Reel. See: Barry,
Jack (7)

Game, The Who, What or Where.
See: James, Art

Games, The March of. See: Ross,
Arthur

Gang, Al Pearce and His. See:
Blurt, Elmer

Gang, Andy's. See: Devine, Andy

Gang, Happy Felton's Spotlight.
See: Felton, Happy

Gang, Roxy's. See: Roxy

Gang, Smilin' Ed's. See: McConnell, Ed

Gangbusters. See: Lord, Phillips
H.

GANN MURRAY. See: Sunday

GANNON. See also: Cannon

GANNON, DR. JOSEPH. See:
Lochner, Dr. Paul

GANNON, OFFICER BILL. See:
Friday, Sergeant Joe

Gap, The Generation. See: Barry,
Jack (2)

GARAGIOLA, JOE (1), host of the
program (himself)
MANY CELEBRITY GUEST
COUPLES
He Said! She Said! (TV) (Game)

GARAGIOLA, JOE (2), host of the
program (himself)
MANY CONTESTANTS
Joe Garagiola's Memory Game
(TV) (Game)

GARAGIOLA, JOE (3), host of the
program (himself)
MANY GUEST CONTESTANTS
Sale of the Century (TV) (Quiz
game)

GARBER, JAN. See: Basie,
Count

GARCIA, PETE. See: Adams,
Lieut. Price

GARCIA, SERGEANT. See: Vega,
Don Diego

GARDE, BETTY. See:
Morgan, Henry
Welles, Orson (1)

GARDENIA. See: Drake, Betty

GARDINER. See also:
Gardner
Garner

GARDINER, BISHOP. See: Henry
VIII, King of England

GARDNER. See also:
Gardiner
Garner

GARDNER, BUD. See: Tate,
Joanne

GARDNER, DR. ROBERT. See:
Allen, Joan Houston

GARDNER, HY. See:
James, Dennis (3)

Johnson, Van
Moore, Garry (5)

GARDNER, KENNY. See: Steele,
Ted

GARDNER, MARGARET. See:
Graham, Dr. Bob

GARDNER, MARY. See: Brasuhn,
Tuffy

GARDNER, WAYNE. See: Brown,
Ellen

GARGAN, WILLIAM (1), featured
actor on the program (himself)
MANY ACTORS AND ACTRESSES
I Deal in Crime (R) (Mystery
drama)

GARGAN, WILLIAM (2), featured
actor on the program (himself)
MANY ACTORS AND ACTRESSES
Murder Will Out (R) (Mystery
drama)

GARGOYLE, THE. See: Bishop,
The

Gargoyle, The Bishop and the.
See: Bishop, The

GARLAND, BEVERLY. See:
Harrington, Pat, Jr.

GARLAND, JACK. See: Harding,
Mrs. Rhoda

GARLAND, JUDY, singer and
actress; star of the program
(herself)
MANY GUEST STARS
The Judy Garland Show (TV)
(Variety)

GARLUND, FRANK, youthful
tycoon
KAM CHANG, his friend and
foster brother
PO CHANG, his foster father
Mr. Garlund (TV) (Adventure)

GARNER. See also:
Gardiner
Gardner

GARNER, ADAM. See: Horwitz,
Hans

GARR, TERI. See: Berry, Ken

GARRETT, CONNIE. See: Redigo,
Jim (1)

GARRETT, LUCIA. See: Redigo,
Jim (1)

GARRETT, MR. See: Perkins,
Ma

GARRETT, PAT. See: Billy the
Kid

GARRETT, SAM, bumbling television
actor, plays part of Jed Clayton,
U. S. marshal
RUTH, his wife
PAUL, his son
FRED GILMAN, his neighbor
BURTON GILMAN, Fred's son
The Hero (TV) (Comedy)

GARRETT, SUSAN
DR. DAN GARRETT
LIZ FORSYTHE
MATT CRANE, characters ap-
pearing in the drama
The Young Marrieds (TV) (Serial
drama)

GARRETT, TAL. See: Redigo,
Jim (1) (2)

GARRISON, LIEUT. CRAIG, leader
of band of guerrillas assigned to
harass Nazis in World War II
France
GONIFF, thief and pickpocket
ACTOR, confidence man
CASINO, "crook of all trades"
CHIEF, "switch blade specialist,"
members of the guerrilla band
Garrison's Guerrillas (TV) (War-
time adventure)

GARRISON, PAT
SCOTT NORRIS
CHRIS, newspaper reporters in
the 1920s
PINKY PINKHAM, nightclub per-
former; sings at the Charleston
Club
The Roaring Twenties (TV)
(Drama/music)

GARRISON, SPENCER, lawyer
IRIS DONNELLY GARRISON, his

wife
BILLY, their young son
MARK ELLIOTT
LAURA ELLIOTT
JEAN GARRISON
DR. DOUG PRESTON
MRS. TAYLOR
JOE TAYLOR
MILLIE CHERNAK
MR. CHERNAK
ANGEL CHERNAK
MRS. CHERNAK
DR. PETER CHERNAK
BETSY CHERNAK
HELEN ELLIOTT DONNELLY
SAM WESTON
NICOLE ALLISON CHERNAK
TOM DONNELLY
RICKY DONNELLY
DR. WILL DONNELLY
AL PRESTON
WALTER TRAVIS
MRS. HANLEY
CELIA, characters appearing in
the drama
Love Is a Many Splendored
Thing (TV) (Serial drama)

Garrison's Guerrillas. See:
Garrison, Lieut. Craig

Garroway at Large. See: Garroway, Dave (2)

GARROWAY, DAVE (1), host of
the program (himself)
MANY YOUNG TELEVISION
PERFORMERS
The C. B. S. Newcomers (TV)
(Variety)

GARROWAY, DAVE (2), host of
the program (himself)
JACK HASKELL
CONNIE RUSSELL, vocalists
featured on the program (them-
selves)
CLIFF NORTON, comedian fea-
tured on the program (himself)
MANY GUEST STARS AND
INTERVIEWEES
Garroway at Large (TV) (Variety/
interview)

GARROWAY, DAVE (3), master of
ceremonies of the program (himself)
JACK HASKELL

CONNIE RUSSELL, vocalists featured on the program (themselves)
THE ART VAN DAMME QUINTET, musical group
Reserved for Garroway (R) (Conversation and music) (later known as Next, Dave Garroway) (R)

GARROWAY, DAVE (4), interviewer of the program (himself)
MANY PROMINENT INTERVIEWEES
Wide Wide World (TV) (Interviews)

GARROWAY, DAVE. See also:
Downs, Hugh
Myerson, Bess

Garroway, Reserved for. See:
Garroway, Dave (3)

GARRY. See also: Gary

GARRY MOORE. See:
Baker, Phil (3)
Durante, Jimmy
Moore, Garry (1) (2) (3) (4) (5)

Garry Moore Show, The. See:
Funt, Allen (1)
Moore, Garry (3)

GARRY MORFIT. See: Moore,
Garry (2)

GARTH, BETSEY. See: Virginian,
The

GARTH, JUDGE HENRY. See:
Virginian, The

GARUMPH. See: Kangaroo,
Captain

GARVEY, EUSTACE P. See:
Flack, Colonel Humphrey

GARVIN, MRS. See: Brown,
Ellen

GARY. See:
Donovan, Gary
Garry
McKeever, Cadet Gary
Owens, Gary
Shepherd, Gary

GARY BENNETT. See: Winters,
Evelyn

GARY CRANDALL. See: Kennedy,
Carol

GARY CROSBY. See: Jones, Jack

GARY CURTIS. See: Perkins, Ma

GARY OWENS. See:
Blyden, Larry (2)
Owens, Gary
Rowan, Dan

GARY ST. DENIS. See: Perkins,
Ma

GARY WALTON. See: Tate,
Joanne

Gasoline Alley. See: Wallet,
Skeezix

GASPAR. See also: Casper

GASPAR FORMENTO, CAPTAIN.
See: Bertrille, Sr.

Gateway to Music. See: Herrmann, Bernard

GAULT, CAROL. See: Prescott,
Kate Hathaway

GAWAIN, SIR. See: Sir Lancelot

Gay Mrs. Featherstone, The.
See: Featherstone, Mrs.

Gay Nineties Revue, The. See:
Kay, Beatrice

GAYLORD, PEGGY. See: Rutledge, Dr. John

GAYNE. See: Whitman, Gayne

GAZZARI DANCERS, THE. See:
Riddle, Sam (2)

GEARHART, LIVINGSTON. See:
Waring, Fred (1)

GEE, MARY. See: Hardie, Jim

GENE
GLENN, boarders at Lena's boarding house
LENA, their landlady
JAKE, handyman

Gene and Glenn With Jake and
Lena (R) (Music/comedy)

GENE. See also:
Ames, Joe
Arnold, Gene
Autry, Gene
Blair, Timothy
Bradley, Gene
Jean
Kelly, Gene
Rayburn, Gene (1) (2) (3)
Sarazen, Gene
Von Hallberg, Gene

Gene and Glenn With Jake and Lena.
See: Gene

Gene Autry's Melody Ranch. See:
Autry, Gene

GENE BARRY. See: Crosby,
Bing (2)

GENE BAYLOS. See: Lewis,
Robert Q. (1)

GENE CRANE. See: Sterling,
Jack

GENE HAMILTON. See: Cross,
Milton (1)

GENE KLAVAN. See: Wallace,
Mike (5)

GENE KRUPA. See:
O'Connor, Father Norman
Whiteman, Paul

GENE RAYBURN. See:
James, Dennis (3)
Rayburn, Gene (1) (2) (3)

GENE RHODES. See: Davis,
Sammy, Jr.

GENE WILLIAMS. See: Malone,
Dr. Jerry

GENERAL. See: Savage, Brigadier General Frank

GENERAL BULL RIGHT. See:
Rowan, Dan

GENERAL BURKHALTER. See:
Hogan, Colonel Robert

GENERAL CRONE. See: Mc-
Cluskey, Mona

General Delivery, Gibbs and Finney.
See: Gibbs

GENERAL ELECTRIC. See also:
G. E.

General Electric Theater. See:
Reagan, Ronald

GENERAL HAMMOND, BRIGADIER.
See: Pierce, Captain Hawkeye

GENERAL HARRISON. See:
Nelson, Sergeant

General Hospital. See: Hardy,
Dr. Steven

GENERAL LAFAYETTE. See:
Larkin, Jeremy

GENERAL MONTGOMERY SMITH,
BRIGADIER. See: Welles,
Orson (3)

GENERAL STEELE. See: McKay,
Judson

GENERAL WILEY CROWE, MAJOR.
See: Savage, Brigadier General
Frank

GENERAL WOODY KIRK. See:
Newman, Tony

Generation Gap, The. See: Barry,
Jack (2)

Generation, The Just. See:
Miller, Howard

GENET, SIMONE. See: Sebastian,
Victor

GENEVIEVE BLUE, MISS. See:
Jones, Amos

GENEVIEVE PORTER. See:
Fairchild, Kay

GENII. See: Hoodoo, Horatio J.

Genius, Are You a? See: Chappell, Ernest (1)

Gentle Ben. See: Wedloe, Tom

GENTLE BEN. See: Wedloe, Tom

GENTRY, ART. See: Lewis, Welcome (2)

GENTRY, BOBBIE. See: Crosby,
Bing (2)

GENTRY BROTHERS, THE. See:
DeLuise, Dom (1)

GENTRY, DAN. See: Brewster,
Gail

GENTRY, DR. ANNE
DR. PHILIP HAMILTON, char-
acters appearing in the drama
The Affairs of Dr. Gentry (R)
(Serial drama)

GENTRY, TOM, intern; living in
apartment complex in Southern
California
MARY GENTRY, his wife
DICK, their friend and boarder;
fellow-intern with Tom
Tom, Dick and Mary (TV)
(Comedy) (Segment of Ninety
Bristol Court) (TV)

GENTRY, TONY. See: Thompson,
Colonel Casey

GENTRY, WILL. See: Shayne,
Michael

GEOFFREY. See also: Jeffrey

GEOFFREY SCOTT. See: Prescott,
Kate Hathaway

GEOGHAN, RICHARD F.X., JR.
See: Steel, Richard

GEORGE. See:
Burns, George (1) (2) (3)
Cooper, Liz
Custer, George Armstrong
Denny, George V., Jr.
DeWitt, George
Drake, Betty
Drinkwater, William
Fenneman, George
Gobel, George
Georgie
Hamilton, George

Jessel, George (1) (2)
Jetson, George
Koltanowski, George
Liberace
McCall, George
Murphy, George
Nipper
Randolph, Ellen
Rose, George
Sanders, George
Scott, George C.
Smith, Angel
Susan (1)

GEORGE APPLEBY. See: Junior

GEORGE AUBRY. See: Welk,
Lawrence

GEORGE BANG. See: Parker,
Seth

GEORGE BARTLETT. See:
Larimore, Marilyn

GEORGE BAXTER. See: Hazel

GEORGE BIGELOW. See: Aldrich,
Henry

George Burns. See: Burns,
George (1)

GEORGE BURNS. See: Burns,
George (1) (2) (3)

GEORGE CARLIN. See:
Greco, Buddy
Shawn, Dick

GEORGE CLEMSON. See: Angel,
Gus

GEORGE CRABBE. See: Marlin,
Mary

George Do It, Let. See: Soule,
Olan (4)

GEORGE EMERSON. See: Harper,
Linda Emerson

GEORGE FENNEMAN. See:
Fenneman, George
Marx, Groucho (3)

GEORGE FREDERICKS. See:
Malone, Dr. Jerry

GEORGE GERSHWIN. See: Drew,
John

GEORGE GOBEL. See:
Berman, Shelley
Crosby, Bing (2)
Fisher, Eddie
Gobel, George
Kelly, Joe (1)

George Gobel Show, The. See:
Gobel, George

GEORGE, GORGEOUS. See:
James, Dennis (4)

GEORGE HAMILTON. See:
Hamilton, George
Jones, Jack

George Hamilton IV. See:
Hamilton, George

GEORGE HAMILTON COMBS. See:
Cross, Mason

GEORGE HARRISON. See: Jackson, Martha

GEORGE HERMAN. See: Schoumacher, David

GEORGE HOWELL. See: Ham-
mond, Liza

GEORGE HURLEY. See: Brent,
Dr. Jim

GEORGE IRVING. See: Frost,
David (2)

George Jessel Show, The. See:
Jessel, George (1)

GEORGE KERBY. See: Topper,
Cosmo

GEORGE KIRBY. See: Little,
Rich

GEORGE KIRGO. See: Leyden,
Bill (2)

GEORGE MORAN. See: Two
Black Crows, The (1) (2)

GEORGE MURPHY. See:
Crosby, Bing (3)

Murphy, George

GEORGE NOVACK. See: James,
Nancy

GEORGE OF DENMARK. See:
Churchill, John

GEORGE OLSEN. See:
Benny, Jack
Winchell, Walter (1)

GEORGE PARSONS. See: Prescott, Kate Hathaway

GEORGE PETERS. See:
Finucane, Lieut. Howard

GEORGE PRIESTLEY, DR. See:
Hackett, Doc

GEORGE ROBERT. See: Hor-
witz, Hans

GEORGE ROBINSON. See:
Crooke, Lennie

GEORGE ROCK. See: Jones,
Spike (1)

George Sanders Mystery Theater,
The. See: Sanders, George

GEORGE SCHUYLER, LIEUT.
See: Dawson, Rosemary

GEORGE SHELTON. See:
Howard, Tom (1) (2)

GEORGE STANLEY GIBSON. See:
Walleck, Meredith

GEORGE STEVENS. See: Jones,
Amos

GEORGE STEWART. See: Drake,
Nora

GEORGE T. PENNYFEATHER,
MRS. See: Weems, Ambrose J.

GEORGE TAGGART. See: Houston,
Temple

GEORGE THOW. See: Welk,
Lawrence

GEORGE UNTERMEYER, CHIEF.

See: August, Dan

GEORGE WALKER. See: Farrell,
David

GEORGE WILSON. See: Mitchell,
Dennis

GEORGE WYLE. See:
Reed, Jerry
Wilson, Flip

GEORGE WYLE SINGERS, THE.
See: Lewis, Jerry

GEORGIA. See: Gibbs, Georgia
(1) (2)

GEORGIA CARROLL. See:
Kyser, Kay

GEORGIA DAY. See: Wayne,
Johnny (2)

Georgia Gibbs. See: Gibbs,
Georgia (1)

GEORGIA GIBBS. See:
Gibbs, Georgia (1) (2)
Ross, Lanny

GEORGIE. See also: George

GEORGIE STOLL. See: Cantor,
Eddie (2)

GERALD. See: McBoing-Boing,
Gerald

GERALD DAVIS. See: Randolph,
Alice

GERALD LLOYD KOOKSON III.
See: Bailey, Stuart

GERALD LOWE. See: Fairchild,
Kay

GERALD MARSHALL. See: Noble,
Mary

GERALDINE. See:
Aldrich, Henry
McGee, Fibber

GERALDINE HAMBURG. See:
Kelly, Joe (2)

GERALDINE JONES. See: Wilson,
Flip

GERALDINE QUINTON. See:
Baines, Scattergood

GERALDINE WHITNEY. See:
Karr, Mike

GERANIUM. See: Canova, Judy

GERARD. See:
Collins, Barnabas
Morgan, Henry
Pam

GERARD DARROW. See: Kelly,
Joe (2)

GERARD, LIEUT. PHILIP. See:
Kimble, Dr. Richard

GEROND, PAUL. See: Wayne,
Ruth Evans

GERRI. See also:
Gerry
Jeri
Jerry

GERRI GRANGER. See: Jones,
Dean

GERRY. See:
Gerri
Jeri
Jerry
Redigo, Jim (2)
Sterling, Vanessa Dale

GERRY BOOKER. See: Packard,
Jack

GERRY MULLIGAN. See: O'Connor, Father Norman

GERSHWIN, GEORGE. See:
Drew, John

GERSON, BETTY LOU. See:
First Nighter, Mr.

GERTIE. See: Mason, Perry

GERTIE GLUMP. See: Kaltenmeyer, Professor August,
D.U.N.

GERTRUDE246

GERTRUDE. See:
  Benny, Jack
  Morgan, Henry
  Penner, Joe

Gertrude Berg. See: Green,
  Sarah

GERTRUDE STONE. See: Horn,
  Aggie

GERTRUDE WARNER. See:
  Beck, Jackson
  Gregory, Helen

Get It Together. See: Riddle,
  Sam (1)

Get Ready, Nine To. See:
  Bragonier, Dr. J. Robert

Get Smart. See: Smart, Maxwell

Getting Together. See: Conway,
  Bobby

GHETTO MOTHER, THE. See:
  Rowan, Dan

GHOST. See:
  Ghost, The
  Space Ghost

Ghost and Mrs. Muir, The. See:
  Muir, Carolyn

Ghost, Casper, The Friendly. See:
  Casper

Ghost Story. See: Essex, Winston

GHOST, THE. See:
  Ghost
  Muir, Carolyn

Ghost, The Gray. See: Mosby,
  Major John

GHOST, THE GRAY. See: Mosby,
  Major John

GHOSTLEY, ALICE. See:
  Andrews, Julie

GIACOMO, DR. See: Cross,
  Milton (1)

GIANNETTA, CHARLIE. See:

Marshall, Owen

GIANT. See: Hungarian Giant,
  The

Giant Step. See: Parks, Bert
  (3)

Giant Step, Take a. See:
  Marshall, E. G.

Giant, Talking With a. See:
  Marshall, E. G.

Giants, The Land of the. See:
  Lockridge, Barry

Giants, The World of. See:
  Hunter, Mel

GIBBONS, FLOYD. See: Thomas,
  Lowell (1)

GIBBONS, MYRNA. See: Martin,
  Doris

GIBBONS, SALLY. See: Marlin,
  Mary

GIBBS
  FINNEY, residents of New England village
  Gibbs and Finney, General Delivery (R) (Drama)

Gibbs and Finney, General Delivery.
  See: Gibbs

GIBBS, GEORGIA (1), singer, star
  of the program (herself)
  MANY GUEST SINGERS
  EDDIE SAFRANSKI, orchestra
  leader (himself)
  HIS ORCHESTRA
  Georgia Gibbs (TV) (Popular
  songs) (also known as The Million Record Show) (TV)

GIBBS, GEORGIA (2)
  MARTHA TILTON
  VIRGINIA REES, vocalists, fea-
  tured on the program (them-
  selves)
  THE MERRY MACS, vocal group,
  featured on the program
  PAUL WHITEMAN, orchestra
  leader (himself)
  HIS ORCHESTRA

Radio Hall of Fame (R) (Music)

GIBBS, GEORGIA. See also: Ross,
Lanny

GIBBS, MRS. See: Penny

GIBSON, DOT
SALLY GIBSON
BOBBY GIBSON
MOTHER
FATHER
AWFUL, butler, characters ap-
pearing in the drama
DONALD VORHEES, orchestra
leader (himself)
HIS ORCHESTRA
The Gibson Family (R) (Drama)

Gibson Family, The. See: Gibson,
Dot

GIBSON, GEORGE STANLEY. See:
Walleck, Meredith

GIBSON, HENRY. See: Rowan,
Dan

GIBSON, JACK
JILL JOHNSON, heads of com-
peting model agencies
PEARL, Jack's secretary
RICHARD, Jill's secretary
Love That Jill (TV) (Comedy)

GIBSON, PRIVATE. See: Wright,
Conley

GIBSON, STEVE. See: Whiteman,
Paul

GIBSON, VIRGINIA. See:
Buxton, Frank
Lanson, Snooky

GIDDINGS, ELWOOD. See: Barbour, Henry Wilson

GIDDINGS, TEDDY BARBOUR.
See: Barbour, Henry Wilson

GIDDYAP GOURMET, THE. See:
Nuvo, Arnie

GIDEON. See: Boone, Daniel

Gidget. See: Gidget

GIDGET, teenage girl growing up
in Southern California
RUSS, her father
ANN, her sister
JOHN, Ann's husband, psychia-
trist
JEFF, her boy friend
LARUE, her girl friend
Gidget (TV) (Situation comedy)

GIDLEY, THELMA. See: Johnson, Bess

GIL. See:
Favor, Gil
Gill
Hanley, Lieut. Gil

GIL CASEY. See: Kaufman,
Seymour

GIL HOOLEY. See: Big Jon

GIL KENDAL. See: Warren,
Wendy

GIL WHITNEY. See: Trent,
Helen

GILBERT. See: Hodges, Gilbert

GILBERT GRAU. See: Bernie,
Ben

GILBERT MACK. See: Johnson,
Raymond Edward (1)

GILBREATH, ANDY. See: Wizard,
Mr.

GILDA BOROS. See: Johnson,
Bess

GILDER, MRS. See: Dyke,
Charity Amanda

GILDERSLEEVE, THROCKMORTON
P., bachelor water commissioner
of the town of Summerfield
LEROY FORRESTER, his nephew
MARJORIE FORRESTER, his
niece
BIRDIE LEE COGGINS, maid
PEAVEY, druggist
FLOYD, barber
JUDGE HOOKER, jurist
LEILA RANSOM, Southern belle
OLIVER HONEYWELL

CRAIG BULLARD
BRONCO, residents of Summerfield
The Great Gildersleeve (R) (Situation comedy) (later performed
on TV with many of the same
characters)

GILDERSLEEVE, THROCKMORTON
P. See also: McGee, Fibber

GILES FRENCH. See: Davis,
Uncle Bill

GILES HENNING. See: Marlin,
Mary

GILFORD, JACK. See: Frost,
David (2)

GILL. See also: Gil

GILL AND DEMLING. See: Brown,
Joe E. (1)

GILLESPIE, DR. LEONARD. See:
Kildare, Dr. James

GILLIAM, BYRON. See: Rowan,
Dan

GILLIAN GRAY. See: Drake,
Nora

GILLIGAN, "first mate and crew"
of the charter boat "Minnow"
SKIPPER of the "Minnow"; Gilli-
gan's superior
HOWELL, millionaire
MRS. HOWELL, Howell's wife
BEASLEY
THE PROFESSOR
GINGER
MARY ANN, all castaways
Gilligan's Island (TV) (Comedy)

Gilligan's Island. See: Gilligan

GILLIS. See: Riley, Chester A.

GILLIS, DOBIE, teenage boy
HERBERT, his father, store
keeper
WINIFRED, his mother
DAVEY, his older brother
THALIA MENNINGER, his girl
friend
MAYNARD KREBS, his beatnick

friend
The Many Loves of Dobie Gillis
(TV) (Situation comedy)

GILLIS, WILLIE. See: Ryker,
Lieut. Eddie

GILLMER. See also: Gilmore

GILLMER, CAROL LYNN. See:
Allen, Frederick Lewis

GILMAN, BURTON. See: Gar-
rett, Sam

GILMAN, FRED. See: Garrett,
Sam

GILMAN, GORDON
MRS. GILMAN
STANLEY GILMAN
PHYLLIS GILMAN
AUNT BESSIE
WHEEZY, characters appearing
on the program
Those Happy Gilmans (R)
(Family adventure)

GILMAN, HOBY, Texas ranger
Trackdown (TV) (Western)

GILMAN, RUSSELL. See: Lawton,
Lora

Gilmans, Those Happy. See: Gilman, Gordon

GILMORE. See:
Box, Harvey
Gillmer

GILMORE, VIRGINIA. See:
Brynner, Yul

GINGER. See:
Gilligan
Hillman, India
Pud
Rogers, Ginger

GINGER LEROY. See: Trent,
Helen

GINGER RAYMOND. See: O'Neill,
Mrs.

Ginger Rogers Show, The. See:
Rogers, Ginger

GINNIE. See also:
Ginny
Jinny

GINNIE SAWYERS. See: Fairchild, Kay

GINNY. See:
Ginnie
Jinny
Nelson, Carolyn Kramer
Susan (1)

GINNY PRICE. See: Wayne,
Ruth Evans

GINNY SIMMS. See: Kyser, Kay

GINO. See: Endicott, Professor
Mike

GINO PRATO. See:
March, Hal
Story, Ralph

GINSBURG, BENEDICT. See:
Steel, Richard

GIRAFFE, HERMIONE. See: Pam

GIRARD, CAROL. See: Renfrew,
Inspector Douglas

GIRELLI, JOE, superintendent of
New York tenement-type apart-
ment
FRANCESCA, his wife
ANTHONY
JOANNE, his children
FRANKIE, his brother
The Super (TV) (Situation comedy)

GIRL. See: Armstrong Quaker
Girl, The

Girl Alone. See: Rogers, Patricia

GIRL FRIENDS, THE THREE. See:
Waring, Fred (1)

Girl From U. N. C. L. E. , The. See:
Dancer, April

Girl, Helen Holden: Government.
See: Holden, Helen

Girl Intern, Joyce Jordan. See:
Jordan, Joyce

Girl Marries, When a. See:
Davis, Joan Field

GIRL NEXT DOOR, THE LITTLE.
See: Carson, Jack

Girl, Peck's Bad. See: Peck,
Torey

GIRL REPORTER, THE. See:
Cop, The

GIRL, SLAVE. See: Speaker,
The

Girl, Society. See: Barrington,
Bryn Clark

Girl Talk. See: Graham, Virginia (1)

Girl, That. See: Hollinger, Don

GIRL, THE. See: North, Major
Hugh

GIRL, THE COCA COLA. See:
Vivian

GIRL, THE LITTLE. See: Jones,
Amos

GIRL, THE LITTLE BETSY ROSS.
See: Loveridge, Marion

Girl Variety Program, The Little
Betsy Ross. See: Loveridge,
Marion

Girls, Harry's. See: Harry

Girls, Leave It to the. See:
Connors, Nancy
Landi, Elissa

Girls, My Best. See: Bartlett,
Jill

Girls, N. T. G. and His. See:
Granlund, Nils Thor

GIRLS, THE FLORADORA. See:
Kay, Beatrice

GIRLS, THE OPERATION ENTER-
TAINMENT. See: Shawn, Dick

Girls, Those Whiting. See:

Whiting, Margaret

GISELE. See also: Griesel

GISELE MACKENZIE. See:
Lanson, Snooky
MacKenzie, Gisele

Gisele MacKenzie Show, The. See:
MacKenzie, Gisele

GISH, DOROTHY. See: Soule,
Olan (1)

GITTEL THE WITCH. See: Pam

Give and Take. See: King, John
Reed (2)

GLAD, GLADYS
ILKA CHASE, actresses; hos-
tesses of the program (themselves)
Penthouse Party (R) (Conversation)

GLADYS. See:
Glad, Gladys
Grimm, Arnold
Harding, Karen Adams
Porter, Pete

GLADYS, AUNT. See: Grimm,
Arnold

GLADYS GLOWWORM. See: Cosby,
Bill (1)

GLADYS KRAVITZ. See: Stephens,
Samantha

GLADYS ORMPHBY. See: Rowan,
Dan

GLADYS PENDLETON. See:
Perkins, Ma

Gladys, Pete and. See: Porter,
Pete

GLADYS RICE. See: Roxy

GLADYS SWARTHOUT. See:
Taylor, Deems

GLADYS ZABISCO. See: Benny,
Jack

Glamour Manor. See: Baker,
Kenny

GLASS, BESSIE, Jewish housewife
ELLEN MUDGE, her friend
The House of Glass (R) (Serial
drama)

GLASS, JULIA. See: Roxy

Glass, The House of. See: Glass,
Bessie

GLASSMAN, DR. See: Perkins,
Ma

GLEASON, CHARLIE. See:
Winters, Evelyn

GLEASON, JACKIE (1), actor and
comedian; star of the program
(himself)
JOE THE BARTENDER
REGINALD VAN GLEASON III
FENWICK BABBITT
CHARLIE BRATTON (The Loud-
mouth)
RALPH KRAMDEN, characters
portrayed by Gleason
PERT KELTON, comedienne
(herself)
LARRY STORCH, comedian
(himself)
MANY GUEST STARS
The Cavalcade of Stars (TV)
(Variety)

GLEASON, JACKIE (2), actor and
comedian; star of the program
(himself)
JOE THE BARTENDER
REGINALD VAN GLEASON III
FENWICK BABBITT
CHARLIE BRATTON (The Loud-
mouth), characters portrayed by
Gleason
CRAZY GUGGENHEIM, character
portrayed by Frank Fontaine
MANY GUEST STARS
RAY BLOCH
SAMMY SPEAR, orchestra
leaders
THEIR ORCHESTRAS
THE JUNE TAYLOR DANCERS
The Jackie Gleason Show (TV)
(Variety) (also known as Jackie
Gleason's American Scene Maga-
zine) (TV)

GLEASON, JACKIE. See also:
Kramden, Ralph

GLEASON, NELLIE. See: Solomon, David

GLEASON, RALPH, host of the program (himself)
MANY GUEST JAZZ MUSICIANS
Net Jazz (TV) (Jazz music and discussion)

GLEN. See:
Campbell, Glen
Glenn

Glen Campbell Goodtime Hour, The.
See: Campbell, Glen

GLEN MORLEY. See: Holstrum, Katy

GLENDA. See: Graham, Dr. Bob

GLENN. See:
Barton, Dr. Glenn
Davis, Glenn
Evans, Glenn
Gene
Glen
Gregory, Glenn Garth
Howard, Glenn
Riggs, Glenn

GLENN, COLONEL JOHN, astronaut; narrator of the program (himself)
Here Comes Tomorrow (TV)
(Science)

GLENN HUNTER, JUDGE. See:
Barbour, Henry Wilson

GLENN MILLER. See: Como, Perry (1)

GLENN TURNER. See: Manning, Laura

GLENN WAGNER. See: Sherwood, Grace

Glenn With Jake and Lena, Gene and. See: Gene

GLICK. See: Jiménez, José

GLORIA. See:
Honest Harold
Nelson, Ozzie
Ungar, Felix

GLORIA BLAINE. See: Jordan, Joyce

GLORIA GRAFTON. See: Bowers, Brainy

GLORIA HARDING. See: Cameron

GLORIA LAMBERT. See: Miller, Mitch

GLORIA LOCKERMAN. See:
March, Hal

GLORIA MARSH. See: Carter, Kathryn

GLORIA MULVANEY. See:
Cameron, Barry

GLORIA QUIGLEY DIXON. See:
Dixon, Robert

GLORIA STIVIC. See: Bunker, Archie

Glorious One. See: Bradley, Judith

GLOWWORM, GLADYS. See:
Cosby, Bill (1)

GLUMP, GERTIE. See: Kaltenmeyer, Professor August, D. U. N.

GLUSKIN, LUD. See: Peterson, Irma

Glynis. See: Granville, Glynis

GLYNIS. See: Granville, Glynis

Go, Down You. See: Evans, Bergen (1)

Go-Go, Hollywood A. See: Riddle, Sam (2)

Go, On the. See: Linkletter, Jack (1)

Go, 1, 2, 3. See: Lescoulie, Jack (3)

Go, Stop and. See: Brown, Joe E. (2)

GOBEL, GEORGE, comedian and

entertainer, star of the program
(himself)
ALICE, his wife
PEGGY KING, vocalist (herself)
MARY McCARTHY, comedienne
(herself)
EDDIE FISHER, singer; perma-
nent guest (himself)
MANY GUEST STARS
The George Gobel Show (TV)
(Variety)

GOBEL, GEORGE. See also:
Berman, Shelley
Crosby, Bing (2)
Fisher, Eddie
Kelly, Joe (1)

GODDARD, DON, narrator of the
program (himself)
Medical Horizons (TV) (Medical
education)

GODFREY, ARTHUR (1), master of
ceremonies of the program (him-
self)
JANETTE DAVIS
BILL LAWRENCE
FRANK PARKER
LU ANN SIMMS
JULIUS LA ROSA
HALEOKE, performers appear-
ing on the program (themselves)
THE CHORDETTES
THE MARINERS
THE JUBILAIRES
THE McGUIRE SISTERS, vocal
groups
ARCHIE BLEYER, orchestra
leader (himself)
HIS ORCHESTRA
Arthur Godfrey Time (R) (TV)
(Variety)
Arthur Godfrey and His Friends
(TV) (Variety)

GODFREY, ARTHUR (2), master of
ceremonies of the program (him-
self)
MARION MARLOWE
PEGGY MARSHALL, vocalists
(themselves)
THE HOLIDAYS, vocal group
ARCHIE BLEYER, orchestra
leader (himself)
HIS ORCHESTRA
MANY AMATEUR CONTESTANTS
Arthur Godfrey's Talent Scouts

(R) (TV) (Amateur talent contest)

GODFREY, ARTHUR (3), host of
the program (himself)
GUEST HOSTS
TALENT FROM VARIOUS COL-
LEGES
The College Variety Show (TV)
(Variety)

GODFREY, ARTHUR (4), star of
the program (himself)
Red Godfrey, The Warbling
Banjoist (R) (Music)

GODFREY, ARTHUR. See also:
Funt, Allen (1)

GODFREY CAMBRIDGE. See:
Berman, Shelley

GODOLPHIN, SIDNEY. See:
Churchill, John

GOERING, AL. See: Bernie, Ben

GOGERTY, HANK. See: Carson,
Bob

GOGO DELYS. See: Medbury,
John P.

Going My Way. See: O'Malley,
Father Chuck

Gold, Poet's. See: Ross, David
(3)

Gold, Pot o'. See: Grauer, Ben
(2)

GOLDBERG, MOLLY, Jewish house-
wife
JAKE GOLDBERG, her husband
ROSALIE GOLDBERG, her
daughter
SAMMY GOLDBERG, her son
UNCLE DAVID, her uncle
SYLVIA ALLISON
CHRISTOPHER KEATOR
DEBBIE BANNER
ELI EDWARDS
MR. FOWLER
ESTHER MILLER
MICKEY BLOOM
WALTER JEROME
MARTHA WILBERFORCE

SEYMOUR FINGERHOOD
UNCLE CARLO
MALCOLM
LIBBY
JOYCE
JANE BROWN
SOLLY
MR. MENDALL
MR. SCHNEIDER
MRS. MELENKA, characters ap-
pearing in the drama
The Rise of the Goldbergs (R)
(Serial drama) (later known as
The Goldbergs) (R) (TV)

Goldbergs, The. See: Goldberg,
Molly

Goldbergs, The Rise of the. See:
Goldberg, Molly

Golddiggers, Dean Martin Presents
the. See: Chidsey, Jackie

Golddiggers, The. See: Chidsey,
Jackie

GOLDDIGGERS, THE. See:
Chidsey, Jackie
Martin, Dean (2)

Golden Store, Caroline's. See:
Caroline

GOLDFISH, TITUS THE. See:
Wilson, Flip

GOLDIE. See:
Halliday, Mike
Noble, Mary
Strickland, Goldie

GOLDIE HAWN. See: Rowan, Dan

GOLDSTONE, DR. PETER, physician
DR. SAM MARSH, intern
BOBBE, Marsh's wife
DR. GREGORY PETTIT, intern
DR. POOCH HARDIN, intern
The Interns (TV) (Medical drama)

Golf, The World of. See: Sarazen,
Gene

Golf, World Championship. See:
Crosby, Bob (3)

GOMER PYLE. See:

Pyle, Gomer
Taylor, Andy

Gomer Pyle, U. S. M. C. See:
Pyle, Gomer

GOMEZ. See: Addams, Gomez

GONIFF. See: Garrison, Lieut.
Craig

GOOBER PYLE. See: Jones,
Sam

GOOCH, MORTIMER
BETTY LOU, characters appearing in the drama)
Mortimer Gooch (R) (Comedy
serial drama)

GOOD. See also: Gude

GOOD, ANGEL. See: Rowan, Dan

GOOD, CHESTER. See: Dillon,
Marshal Matt

Good Company. See: Bailey, F.
Lee

Good Guys, The. See: Gramus,
Bert

Good Life, The. See: Miller,
Albert

Good Morning, World. See: Lewis,
Dave

Good News, Hollywood. See:
Stewart, James

Good Ole Nashville Music, That.
See: Ritter, Tex (2)

Good Wife, My. See: Francis,
Arlene (3)

Good Will Court, A. L. Alexander's.
See: Alexander, A. L. (2)

Good Year, It Was a Very. See:
Torme, Mel

GOODFELLOW, MR. See: Lewis,
Shar1

GOODHEART, PHOEBE. See:

Hastings, Bill

GOODHUE, CAPTAIN. See: Lee,
Terry

GOODHUE, TOD. See: Noble,
Mary

GOODMAN ACE. See:
Ace, Goodman
Kaye, Danny

GOODMAN, AL. See:
Allen, Fred
Ross, Lanny
Taylor, Deems

GOODMAN, BENNY. See: Cugat,
Xavier (1)

GOODMAN, DODY. See: Paar,
Jack

GOODMAN, GORDON. See:
Waring, Fred (1)

Goodtime Hour, The Glen Campbell.
See: Campbell, Glen

Goodwill Hour, The. See: Anthony,
Mr.

GOODWIN, ANNE. See: Grimm,
Arnold

GOODWIN, ARCHIE. See: Wolfe,
Nero

GOODWIN, BILL, quizmaster of
the program (himself)
MANY CONTESTANTS
Penny to a Million (TV) (Quiz)

GOODWIN SCHAEFER. See: Fadiman, Clifton (2)

GOOFY. See: Mouse, Mickey

GOOK, VIC, husband
SADE GOOK, his wife
RUSH GOOK, their son
UNCLE FLETCHER
CHUCK BRAINFEEBLE
DOTTIE BRAINFEEBLE
RUSSELL STEMBOTTOM
SMELLY CLARK
BLUE-TOOTH JOHNSON
THE BRICK-MUSH MAN

JAKE GUMPOX
MR. BULLER
ROBERT HINK
SLOBBERT HINK, identical
twins
ISHIGAN FISHIGAN OF SISHIGAN,
MICHIGAN, characters appearing
on the program
Vic and Sade (R) (Comedy serial)

GOOSE, CABOOSE. See: Beany

GORDIE TAPP. See: Owens, Buck

GORDON. See:
Barnes, Gordon
Cookie Monster, The
Gilman, Gordon
MacRae, Gordon
Munro, Gordon

GORDON, ANITA. See: Bergen,
Edgar (2)

GORDON, ARTEMUS. See: West,
Jim (2)

GORDON, BARBARA. See: Batman

GORDON BERGER. See: Waring,
Fred (1)

GORDON DECKER. See: Trent,
Helen

GORDON, DOC. See: Joe (1)

GORDON, DR. See: Hardy, Dr.
Steven

GORDON, DR. ALEC. See: Hargrave-Scott, Joan

GORDON, DOROTHY, hostess of
the program (herself)
MANY ACTORS AND ACTRESSES
Yesterday's Children (R) (Dramatizations of old stories for children)

GORDON ELLIS. See: Rutledge,
Dr. John

GORDON, FLASH, adventurer
DR. ZARKOV, his associate and
fellow-adventurer
DALE ARDEN, his girl friend

MING, his enemy
Flash Gordon (R) (TV) (Science
fiction adventure)

GORDON GOODMAN. See: Waring,
Fred (1)

GORDON HATHAWAY. See: Allen,
Steve (1)

GORDON JENKINS. See:
Haymes, Dick
Lane, Richard

GORDON MATHER, DR. See:
Davis, Dr. Althea

GORDON, MAYME. See: O'Neill,
Mrs.

GORDON, MRS. See: Bradley,
Judith

GORDON, MYRA. See: Hargrave-
Scott, Joan

GORDON, PHYLLIS. See: Rutledge,
Dr. John

GORDON, POLICE COMMISSIONER.
See: Batman

GOREN, CHARLES, writer and
lecturer on bridge; host of the
program (himself)
ALEX DREIER, commentator
(himself)
TWO PAIRS OF BRIDGE PLAYERS
Championship Bridge With Charles
Goren (TV) (Bridge instruction)

GORGEOUS GEORGE. See: James,
Dennis (4)

GORHAM, MARGOT. See: Harding,
Mrs. Rhoda

GORHAM, MR. See: Harding,
Mrs. Rhoda

GORME. See also: Gourmet

GORME, EYDIE. See:
Allen, Steve (3)
Crosby, Bing (2)
Lawrence, Steve (1)

Gorme, Lawrence and. See:

Lawrence, Steve (1)

GORSHIN, FRANK. See: Little,
Rich

GOSFIELD, MAURICE. See:
Morgan, Henry

GOULD, SID. See: Lewis, Robert
Q. (1)

GOURMET. See also: Gorme

Gourmet, The Galloping. See:
Kerr, Graham

GOURMET, THE GIDDYAP. See:
Nuvo, Arnie

Government Girl, Helen Holden.
See: Holden, Helen

Governor and J.J., The. See:
Drinkwater, William

GOVERNOR OF HAWAII, THE.
See: McGarrett, Steve

GOVERNOR, THE. See: Drinkwater, William

GOWDY, CURT. See: Jackson,
Keith (2)

GOWER. See: Champion, Marge

Gower Champion Show, The Marge
and. See: Champion, Marge

GOWER, MATTHEW, deputy police
commissioner
CAPTAIN GUS HONOCHECK
SERGEANT DANNY KELLER,
police officers
The Asphalt Jungle (TV) (Police)

GRACE. See:
Graves, Harry
Sherwood, Grace

GRACE DOBLEN. See: Johnson,
Bess

GRACE DUTTON. See: Miller,
Albert

GRACE FERGUSON. See: Guest,
Edgar A. (2)

GRACE MARSHALL. See: Harper, Linda Emerson

GRACE MOORE. See: Bell, Alexander Graham

GRACE WILSON. See: Hargrave-Scott, Joan

GRACIE. See: Fields, Gracie

GRACIE ALLEN. See: Burns, George (1) (2)

Gracie Fields Show, The. See: Fields, Gracie

GRADY. See also: Brady

GRADY, EDDIE. See: Whiteman, Paul

GRADY, GUS. See: Dallas, Stella

GRADY, INSPECTOR. See: Kelly, Kitty

GRADY, MICKEY, native of Omaha; inherits hotel at Newport Beach, California
NORA, his wife
TIMMY
BUDDY, his sons
SAMMEE LING, hotel manager
LOOPHOLE LING, Sammee's cousin; shyster lawyer
Mickey (TV) (Comedy)

GRADY, MINNIE. See: Dallas, Stella

GRADY, PAT. See: Perry, John

GRAFTON, GLORIA. See: Bowers, Brainy

GRAFTON, HARRY, foreman in small factory; conniver
BRINK
LESTER
ROXY, fellow-workers
The New Phil Silvers Show (TV) (Comedy)

GRAHAM. See:
Kerr, Graham
McNamee, Graham

GRAHAM, BILLY, evangelist; host of the program (himself)
MANY GUEST SINGERS
The Billy Graham Crusade (TV) (Religion)

GRAHAM, BOB. See: Archie

GRAHAM, DR. BOB, physician
RUTH ANN GRAHAM
DR. BRUCE PORTER, physician
DR. MADELYN KELLER, physician
DAVIE LANE
JOE HOUSTON
SAM RYDER
JANET RYDER
SUSAN GRANT
THERESA PECH
MARJORY CARROLL
ALISON RADCLIFFE
MARGARET GARDNER
WILTON COMSTOCK
ELSIE JONES
KATHLEEN CARNEY
NORMA STARR
ELLEN COLLINS
LAWRENCE MITCHELL
MRS. FRED HOPKINS
MISS BENNETT
MICHAEL KENT
GLENDA
MARJORIE, characters appearing in the drama
Bachelor's Children (R) (Serial drama)

GRAHAM, DR. PAUL. See: Bassett, Dr. Theodore

GRAHAM, JUDY. See: Kelly, Joe (2)

GRAHAM McNAMEE. See:
Cowen, Thomas
Fire Chief, The
Johnson, Parks
McNamee, Graham

GRAHAM, MAGGIE. See: Casey, Dr. Ben

GRAHAM, MRS. See: Harding, Mrs. Rhoda

GRAHAM, PRUDENCE. See: Sunday

GRAHAM, ROSS. See:
Dragonette, Jessica (1)
Henry, Captain
Taylor, Deems

GRAHAM, SHEILAH, star of the
program (herself)
MANY INTERVIEWEES
Hollywood Today (TV) (Interviews
dealing with the motion picture
world)

GRAHAM, TRACY. See: Ferguson, Martha

GRAHAM, VIRGINIA (1), hostess of
the program (herself)
MANY CELEBRITY GUESTS
Girl Talk (TV) (Interviews)

GRAHAM, VIRGINIA (2), hostess
of the program (herself)
MANY CELEBRITY GUESTS
The Virginia Graham Show (TV)
(Interviews)

GRAHAM, VIVIAN. See: Sunday

GRAHAME, TAFFY. See: Peters,
Bill

GRAINGER. See also: Granger

GRAINGER, CARL. See: Drake,
Betty

GRAINGER, CLAY. See: Virginian,
The

GRAINGER, ETHEL. See: Drake,
Betty

GRAINGER, MARK. See: Alexander, Nick

GRAINGER, SHARON. See: Rowlands, Hugh

GRAMMIE. See: Dickey, Dan'l

GRAMPA. See:
Grandpa
Grandpappy
McCoy, Grampa

GRAMUS, BERT
CLAUDIA, his wife, operators of
diner co-owned by Bert and Rufus

RUFUS BUTTERWORTH, part-
ner in the diner; also cab driver
The Good Guys (TV) (Comedy)

Grand Central Station. See:
Arthur, Jack (2)

Grand Hotel. See: Ameche, Don
(3)

Grand Marquee. See: Soule,
Olan (2)

Grand Ole Opry, The. See:
Solemn Old Judge, The

Grand, 100. See: Clark, Jack

Grand Slam. See: Beasley,
Irene (1)

Granddaddy, Make Room for. See:
Williams, Danny

GRANDFATHER CLOCK. See:
Kangaroo, Captain

GRANDFATHER GRANT. See:
Waring, Evelyn

GRANDMA, character portrayed by
Hazel Dopheide
Grandma Travels (R) (Serial
drama)

GRANDMA. See also:
Barton, Bud
Hanks, Henrietta
Marlin, Mary
Pride, Ben
Walton, Grandpa

Grandma Travels. See: Grandma

GRANDMAMA. See: Addams,
Gomez

GRANDPA. See:
Burton, Grandpa
Grampa
Grandpappy
Hanks, Henrietta
Harum, David
Hughes, Chris
Munster, Herman
Parker, Richard
Pride, Ben
Walton, Grandpa

GRANDPA ANDY PRUITT. See:
Endicott, Professor Mike

GRANDPA BEASLEY. See:
Peppertag, Aaron

Grandpa Burton. See: Burton,
Grandpa

GRANDPA ELLIS. See: Rutledge,
Dr. John

GRANDPA HUBBELL. See:
O'Neill, Mrs.

GRANDPA JONES. See: Owens,
Buck

GRANDPA SUTTER. See: Brent,
Dr. Jim

GRANDPA TARLTON. See:
Tammy

GRANDPAPPY. See also:
Grampa
Grandpa

GRANDPAPPY SPEARS. See:
Edwards, Lum

GRANDSIR (WILBUR Z. KNOX).
See: Dickey, Dan'l

Grandstand Thrills. See: Soule,
Olan (3)

GRANGER. See also: Grainger

GRANGER, GERRI. See: Jones,
Dean

GRANGER, NANCY. See: Trent,
Helen

GRANIK, THEODORE (1), attorney,
host of the program (himself)
MANY PARTICIPANTS
The American Forum of the Air
(R) (Public service discussion)

GRANIK, THEODORE (2), attorney,
host of the program (himself)
Law For the Layman (R) (Legal
advice)

GRANLUND. See also: Grantland

GRANLUND, NILS THOR, master of
ceremonies of the program (him-
self)
HARRY SALTER, orchestra
leader (himself)
HIS ORCHESTRA
GUEST CHORUS GIRLS
N. T. G. and His Girls (R)
(Variety)

GRANNY. See:
Clampett, Jed
Perry, John

GRANNY HEWITT. See: Jordan,
Joyce

GRANNY T. V. See: Pam

GRANT. See: Cummings, Brenda

GRANT, BART, police lieutenant
City Detective (TV) (Detective)

GRANT, BEN. See: Hillman,
India

GRANT, CARY. See:
Carroll, Madeleine
Frees, Paul

GRANT, DAVID. See: Hillman,
India

GRANT, DR. DICK. See:
Bauer, Bertha

GRANT, ELLEN. See: Hillman,
India

GRANT FRASIER, DR. See:
Brent, Dr. Jim

GRANT, GRANDFATHER. See:
Waring, Evelyn

GRANT, HARRY, owner-bartender
of Grant's Toomb, New York
tavern
JOE, cook at the tavern
FRED COSTELLO
PHIL BRACKEN
PETER PANAMA
MEYER SHAPIRO, habitues of
the tavern
The Corner Bar (TV) (Comedy)

GRANT, JILL. See: Hillman, India

GRANT, KATY. See: August, Dan

GRANT, KEVIN. See: Bracken,
John

GRANT, LOU. See: Richards,
Mary

GRANT, MARIE. See: Bauer,
Bertha

GRANT, MARJORIE. See: Bracken,
John

GRANT, PETER. See: Jostyn,
Jay (1)

GRANT, PHINEAS T. See: Waring,
Evelyn

GRANT, SUSAN. See: Graham,
Dr. Bob

GRANT THURSDAY. See: Kelly,
Kitty

GRANTLAND. See also: Granlund

GRANTLAND RICE. See: Cowan,
Thomas

GRANVILLE, GLYNIS, novice mystery story writer and amateur detective
KEITH, her husband, attorney
CHICK ROGERS, retired policeman
Glynis (TV) (Comedy)

GRAU, GILBERT. See: Bernie,
Ben

GRAUBART, JUDY. See:
Cosby, Bill (1)
Klein, Robert

GRAUER, BEN (1), narrator of the
program (himself)
GUEST ACTORS AND ACTRESSES
The Big Story (TV) (dramatizations
of real-life stories about news-
papermen)

GRAUER, BEN (2)
RUSH HUGHES, quizmasters on
the program (themselves)
HORACE HEIDT
TOMMY TUCKER, orchestra

leaders (themselves)
THEIR ORCHESTRAS
MANY CONTESTANTS
Pot o' Gold (R) (Quiz)

GRAUER, BEN (3), master of
ceremonies of the program (him-
self)
MANY ACTORS AND ACTRESSES
MANY CONTESTANTS
What Would You Have Done? (R)
(Drama/quiz)

GRAVES, HARRY, lawyer
GRACE, his wife
LOIS, his sixteen-year-old
daughter
JUDY, his thirteen-year-old
daughter
FUFFY ADAMS, thirteen-year-
old friend of Judy Graves
HILDA, maid
Junior Miss (R) (Situation comedy)

GRAVES, LEONARD, narrator of
the program (himself)
WORLD WAR II NEWSREEL
FILMS
Victory at Sea (TV) (News/
history)

GRAVES, TERESA. See:
Kelly, Gene
Rowan, Dan

GRAY. See also: Grey

GRAY, BARRY (1)
JOHN K. M. McCAFFERY, mod-
erators of the program (them-
selves)
VARIOUS LITERARY CRITICS
VARIOUS AUTHORS
The Author Meets the Critics
(R) (Literary discussion)

GRAY, BARRY (2), moderator of
the program (himself)
MANY PARTICIPANTS
Barry Gray on Broadway (R)
(Discussion)

GRAY, DR. LLOYD. See: Welles,
Orson (3)

GRAY, EDIE. See: Young, Larry
"Pepper"

Gray Ghost, The. See: Mosby, Major John

GRAY GHOST, THE. See: Mosby, Major John

GRAY, GILLIAN. See: Drake, Nora

GRAY, JERRY. See: Crosby, Bob (2)

GRAYCO, HELEN. See: Jones, Spike (1) (2)

GRAHAM, ABBY. See: Banyon, Miles C.

GRAYLING. See: Dennis, Liz

GRAYSON, BARBARA. See: O'Neill, Mrs.

GRAYSON, CARL. See: Jones, Spike (1)

GRAYSON, DICK. See:
Batman
Kent, Clark

GRAZIANO, ROCKY. See: Raye, Martha (2)

Great Adventure, The. See: Heflin, Van

Great American Dream Machine, The. See: Efron, Marshall

Great Gildersleeve, The. See: Gildersleeve, Throckmorton P.

Great Life, It's a. See:
Morgan, Mrs. Amy
O'Shea, Michael

GREAT McGONIGLE, THE. See: O'Brien, Daniel J.

Great Mysteries, The Dow Hour of. See: Welch, Joseph N.

GREAT VOODINI, THE. See: Nye, Louis

Greatest Bands, America's. See: Whiteman, Paul

Greatest Show on Earth, The. See: Slate, Johnny

Greatest Story Ever Told, The. See: Jesus

GREATGUY, COACH. See: Daring, Dick

GREB, INSPECTOR MATT. See: Guthrie, Lieut. Ben

GRECO, BUDDY
GEORGE CARLIN
BUDDY RICH, hosts of the program (themselves)
THE BUDDY RICH ORCHESTRA
MANY GUEST STARS
Away We Go (TV) (Variety)

GREELEY. See: Monroe, John

Green Acres. See: Douglas, Oliver

GREEN, ALAN. See: Perry, John

GREEN, BERNIE. See: Morgan, Henry

GREEN, BILLY, young boy, resident of Spring City
HIS SISTER
BELINDA BOYD
JEEP, his friends, also residents of Spring City
Those Websters (R) (Situation comedy)

Green Hornet, The. See: Reid, Britt

GREEN HORNET, THE. See: Reid, Britt

GREEN, JOHNNY. See:
Benny, Jack
Clayton, Margie
Johnny
Ross, Lanny

GREEN, LORNE. See: Cookie Monster, The

GREEN, REUBEN. See: Prescott, Kate Hathaway

GREEN, SARAH, housewife, enrolls
in college
PROFESSOR CRAYON, Cambridge
don, on loan to the college she
attends
Mrs. G. Goes to College (TV)
(Comedy) (later known as Gertrude
Berg) (TV)

Green Valley, U.S.A. See: Ortega,
Santos

GREEN, W.C. See: Rogers,
Patricia

GREENE, BILLY M. See: Kay,
Beatrice

GREENE, LAURA. See: Klein,
Robert

GREENE, SHECKY. See: Martindale, Wink (2)

GREENJEANS, MR. See: Kangaroo,
Captain

GREENMAN, EDWARD. See: Rutledge, Dr. John

GREENMAN, NORMA. See: Rutledge, Dr. John

GREENSPRING, RANDY. See:
Myrt

GREENWOOD, CHARLOTTE, come-
dienne and actress; star of the
program (herself)
MANY GUEST STARS
The Charlotte Greenwood Show
(R) (Comedy/variety)

GREER, CAPTAIN ADAM. See:
Hayes, Linc

GREG. See: Brady, Mike

GREG MARTIN. See: Burton,
Terry

GREG PETERS, DR. See: Horton,
Dr. Tom

GREGG, CAPTAIN. See: Muir,
Carolyn

GREGG, CLAYMORE. See:

Muir, Carolyn

GREGG, UNCLE BENTLEY,
Beverly Hills lothario; attorney
KELLY, his niece
PETER, his Chinese houseboy
Bachelor Father (TV) (Situation
comedy)

GREGG, VIRGINIA. See: Soule,
Olan (4)

GREGORY. See:
Hood, Gregory
Smith, Gregory

GREGORY ALDEN. See: O'Farrell, Packy

GREGORY, BEN, magazine writer
ERIC JASON, newspaper re-
porter
Follow the Sun (TV) (Adventure/
drama)

GREGORY, CAPTAIN KEITH. See:
Adams, Lieut. Price

GREGORY, GLENN GARTH, government research expert; has photo-
graphic memory
SYBIL VAN LOWEEN, Washington hostess
The Delphi Bureau (The Men)
(TV) (Crime adventure)

GREGORY, HELEN, narrator of
the program, portrayed by
Gertrude Warner
Modern Romances (R) (Serial
drama)

Gregory Hood, The Case Book of.
See: Hood, Gregory

GREGORY IVANOFF. See:
Perkins, Ma

GREGORY, MICHAEL. See:
Carter, Kathryn

GREGORY, MR. See: Ames,
Peter

GREGORY OGDEN. See: Jordan,
Joyce

GREGORY PEARSON. See:

Worthington, Nora

GREGORY PETTIT, DR. See:
Goldstone, Dr. Peter

GRESS, LOUIS. See: Cantor,
Eddie (2)

GRETA. See:
Christopher, Peter
Perkins, Ma

GRETA JACKSON. See: Jones,
Loco

GRETA POWERS. See: Davis,
Dr. Althea

GRETCHEN WYLER. See: Crosby,
Bob (1)

GREY. See:
Gray
Holden, Grey

GREY, BILL. See: Johnson, Bess

GREY, CAPTAIN. See: Ballinger,
Lieut. Frank

GREY, DR. ALEXANDER. See:
Jordan, Joyce

GREY, MRS. See: Harding,
Karen Adams

GREYSTOKE, LORD. See: Tarzan

GRIEF, CAPTAIN DAVID, adventurer; commander of the sailing
ship "Rattler"
Captain David Grief (TV) (South
Seas adventure)

GRIER, JIMMIE. See: Medbury,
John P.

GRIESEL. See also: Gisele

GRIESEL, BERNARD. See: Kelly,
Joe (2)

GRIFF KING. See: Cartwright,
Ben

GRIFFIN, ASA. See: Wayne,
Ruth Evans

GRIFFIN, MEG. See: Manning,
Portia Blake

GRIFFIN, MERV (1), entertainer
and singer, host of the program
(himself)
ARTHUR TREACHER, comedian
appearing on the program (him-
self)
MORT LINDSEY, orchestra
leader (himself)
HIS ORCHESTRA
MANY GUESTS
The Merv Griffin Show (TV)
(Talk/interview)

GRIFFIN, MERV (2), quizmaster
of the program (himself)
TWO HUSBAND-AND-WIFE
TEAMS OF CONTESTANTS
Play Your Hunch (TV) (Quiz)

GRIFFIN, MERV (3), host of the
program (himself)
MANY MUSICIANS AS GUESTS
BOBBY VINTOR, orchestra
leader (himself)
HIS ORCHESTRA
Saturday Prom (TV) (Popular
music)

GRIFFIN, MERV. See also:
Lewis, Robert Q. (2)
Reiner, Carl

GRIFFIN, TONY. See: Trent,
Helen

GRIFFITH, ANDY. See:
Sawyer, Andy
Taylor, Andy
Thompson, Andy

GRIFFITH, D. W. See: Drew,
John

GRIM. See also: Grimm

GRIM, SAM. See: Perkins, Ma

GRIMES, BILL, master of ceremonies of the program (himself)
AMATEUR TALENT
Stars of Tomorrow (TV) (Amateur entertainment)

GRIMES, JACK. See: Halop,
Billy

GRIMM. See also: Grim

GRIMM, ARNOLD, the father
CONSTANCE, his daughter
MRS. GRIMM
GLADYS GRIMM
TOM GRIMM
MARIAN MOORE
LOUIE STERLING
SONIA KIRKOFF
MR. TREMAINE
MRS. TREMAINE
MR. TWEEDY
MR. DUFFY
JIM KENT
MEREDITH JONES
BUNNY SHAPIRO
KIRBY WILLOUGHBY
DR. DAVID McKENZIE, physician
DR. MILBURN, physician
MRS. HIGSBY-SMITH
DAL TREMAINE
PAUL MARTEL
MARIE MARTEL
ARTHUR HALL
ANNE GOODWIN
BILL HARTLEY
STANLEY WESTLAND
BERNICE FARRADAY
PAT PATTERSON
STEPHANIE SUMMERS
JEFF CORBETT
JUDY, maid
AUNT GLADYS
LILY
BABY DAL
THELMA
MADAME BABETTE, characters
appearing in the drama
Arnold Grimm's Daughter (R)
(Serial drama)

GRIMSLEY, WINSTON. See: Karr,
Mike

Grindl. See: Grindl

GRINDL, "maid of all trades," perpetually seeking employment
ANSON FOSTER, manager of
employment agency
Grindl (TV) (Comedy)

GRISWOLD, AGATHA. See:
Dallas, Stella

GROFE, FERDE. See: Allen,
Fred

GRONK. See: Mac

Groom, Bride and. See: Nelson,
John

GROOVIE. See: Holiday, Laurel

GROSS. See also: Cross

GROSS, DR. MASON. See:
Shriner, Herb (3)

GROSVENOR, DICK. See:
Dallas, Stella

GROSVENOR, LAUREL DALLAS.
See: Dallas, Stella

GROSVENOR, MRS. See: Dallas,
Stella

Grouch Club, The. See: Lescoulie,
Jack (2)

GROUCHO MARX. See:
Carroll, Madeleine
Marx, Groucho (1) (2) (3)
Raye, Martha (1)

Groucho, Tell It to. See: Marx,
Groucho (2)

Groucho, The Best of. See: Marx,
Groucho (3)

GROUNDHOG, WOODROW THE.
See: Pam

GROVE, BETTY ANN. See:
Parks, Bert (6)

GROVER, CHRISTOPHER ROBIN.
See: Cameron

GROVER COURTNEY. See:
Farrell, David

GROVER, MILLIE, airline steward-
ess
MAGGIE RALSTON, her friend,
also a stewardess
MR. BEAUCHAMP, supervisor
of stewardesses for airline
From a Bird's Eye View (TV)
(Comedy)

GROVER, MRS. See: Spencer,
Jeff

GROVER, SERGEANT. See:
Bilko, Sergeant Ernest

GROWNUP, JULIA. See: Cosby,
Bill (1)

GRUBB, WAYNE. See: Barbour,
Henry Wilson

GRUBER, LESTER. See: McHale,
Lieut. Commander Quinton

GRUNECKER, MAHALIA MAY.
See: Wivenhoe, Commander

GUDE. See also: Good

GUDE, ERIK. See: Bergen, Edgar
(1)

GUDE, HELENA. See: Bergen,
Edgar (1)

GUERCIO, JOE. See: Lawrence,
Steve (2)

Guerrillas, Garrison's. See:
Garrison, Lieut. Craig

Guest, Be Our. See: Brasselle,
Keefe

GUEST, EDGAR A. (1), poet; host
of the program (himself)
MANY GUEST STARS
MANY ACTORS AND ACTRESSES
It Can Be Done (R) (Drama)

GUEST, EDGAR A. (2), poet; host
of the program (himself)
EMMY FERGUSON
ESTHER FERGUSON
GRACE FERGUSON
SHERIFF LUKE FERGUSON
DOLORES DUMONT
DR. HAINES, physician
BOB DRAINARD
BILL SUTTER
JEFFREY BARKER
MATHILDA BARKER
TEENIE, characters appearing in
the drama
Welcome Valley (R) (Serial
drama)

GUEST, MYSTERY. See: Daly,
John (3)

Guest of Honor. See: Nielsen,
Leslie (2)

Guestward Ho! See: Hooton, Babs

GUFFY, MR. See: Cantor,
Eddie (2)

GUGGENHEIM, CRAZY. See:
Gleason, Jackie (2)

GUGGENHEIM, MAX. See:
Nebb, Rudolph

Guide to Love, The Amateur's.
See: Rayburn, Gene (1)

Guiding Light, The. See:
Bauer, Bertha
Rutledge, Dr. John

Guild of the Air, The Theater.
See: Langner, Lawrence

Guild Theater, Screen. See:
Pryor, Roger

GUINEVERE, QUEEN. See: Sir
Lancelot

Guitar, Folk. See: Weber,
Laura

Guitar, Playing the. See: Noad,
Frederick

Guitar Plus, Folk. See: Weber,
Laura

GUIZAR, TITO. See: Archie

GUMM, COLONEL. See: Batman

GUMP, ANDY, head of the house
MIN, his wife
CHESTER, their son
TILDA, maid
The Gumps (R) (Comedy/drama)

GUMP, DRIZ. See: Brent, Portia

GUMPOX, JAKE. See: Gook, Vic

Gumps, The. See: Gump, Andy

GUN. See also:
Gunn
Guns

Gun, Man Without a. See: McLean,
  Adam

Gun, Restless. See: Bonner, Vint

Gun, The Man Behind the. See:
  McCormick, Myron

Gun, The Quill and the. See:
  Drum, Jefferson

GUNGA RAM. See: Devine, Andy

GUNILLA HUTTON. See: Owens,
  Buck

GUNN. See also:
  Gun
  Guns

GUNN, PETER, detective
  LIEUT. JACOBY, police officer
  MOTHER, saloon keeper
  EDIE HART, singer, friend of
  Jacoby
  Peter Gunn (TV) (Detective drama)

GUNNER. See: Welles, Orson (3)

GUNS. See also:
  Gun
  Gunn

Guns of Will Sonnett, The. See:
  Sonnett, Will

Gunslinger. See: Cord

Gunsmoke. See: Dillon, Marshal
  Matt

GUNTHER, DAVID. See: Hansen,
  Dean Eric

GUNTHER HOLLANDER. See:
  Kelly, Joe (2)

GUNTHER, JOHN, narrator of the
  program (himself)
  John Gunther's High Road (TV)
  (Travel/adventure) (also known as
  High Road) (TV)

GUNTHER TOODY. See: Muldoon,
  Francis

GURNEY, MRS. See: Peepers,
  Robinson J.

GUS. See:
  Angel, Gus
  Holiday, Laurel

GUS ARNHEIM. See: Medbury,
  John P.

GUS, AUNT. See: Miller,
  Socrates

GUS GRADY. See: Dallas, Stella

GUS HONOCHECK, CAPTAIN. See:
  Gower, Matthew

GUS VAN. See: Arnold, Gene

GUSTAVE HAENSCHEN. See:
  Dragonette, Jessica (3)
  Munn, Frank (1)

GUTHRIE, LIEUT. BEN
  INSPECTOR MATT GREB
  INSPECTOR FRED ASHER,
  police officials
  SANDY McALLISTER, police-
  woman
  PETER LARKINS, policeman
  The Lineup (TV) (Crime drama)
  (also called San Francisco Beat)
  (TV)

GUTHRIE, MITCH, champion rodeo
  rider
  ANDY, his younger brother
  The Wide Country (TV) (Western)

GUY. See:
  Lombardo, Guy
  Mitchell, Guy
  Sorel, Guy

GUY ALDIS. See: Cameron,
  Christy Allen

GUY ENGLISH. See: Welk,
  Lawrence

GUY LOMBARDO. See:
  Basie, Count
  Burns, George (2)
  Lombardo, Guy

Guy Lombardo and His Royal
  Canadians. See: Lombardo,
  Guy

Guy Lombardo Show, The. See:
  Lombardo, Guy

GUY MITCHELL. See:
Miller, Mitch
Mitchell, Guy

Guy Mitchell Show, The. See:
Mitchell, Guy

Guys, The Good. See: Gramus,
Bert

GWEN. See also:
Gwenn
Gwinn
Gwyn

GWEN BARRY. See: Johnson,
Bess

GWEN DAVIES. See: Halop, Billy

GWEN PARKER. See: Nona

GWENDOLYN DEVOL. See: Armstrong, Jack

GWENN. See:
Gwen
Gwinn
Gwyn
Ungar, Felix

GWINN. See also:
Gwen
Gwenn
Gwyn

GWINN, BILL. See: Williamson,
Dud

GWYN. See also:
Gwen
Gwenn
Gwinn

GWYN JENNINGS. See: Horn,
Aggie

GYNT, HAMLYN "HAM." See:
Strange, Adam

GYP MENDOZA. See: Solomon,
David

Gypsies, The A. & P. See:
Parker, Frank

GYPSY. See:
Harrigan, James, Sr.

Lee, Gypsy Rose

Gypsy Rose Lee. See: Lee,
Gypsy Rose

GYPSY ROSE LEE. See:
Lee, Gypsy Rose
Stokey, Mike

"GYPSY VIOLINS" ORCHESTRA,
THE. See: Ross, David (1)

H. M. "STAFF" STAFFORD. See:
Ryan, Paul

H. NORMAN SCHWARTZKOPF,
COLONEL. See: Lord, Phillips
H.

H. R. See: Pufnstuf, H. R.

H. R. Pufnstuf. See: Pufnstuf, H. R.

HACK. See also: Huck

HACK, HARRY THE. See: Wilson,
Steve

HACKETT, CHARLEY. See:
Cooper, Dick

HACKETT, DOC, country druggist
DR. ABERNATHY, physician
DR. GEORGE PRIESTLEY,
physician
BILLY MOOREHEAD
JERRY WHIPPLE
SARAH WHIPPLE
LAURA PAIGE, characters appear-
ing in the drama
County Seat (R) (Serial drama)

HACKETT, JOHN. See: Davis,
Joan Field

HACKETT, LOVEY. See: Cooper,
Dick

HADJI. See: Quest, Jonny

HADLEY, ARCH. See: Wilbur,
Judy

HAENSCHEN, GUSTAVE. See:
Dragonette, Jessica (3)
Munn, Frank (1)

HAGEN. See also: Haggen

HAGEN, DR. HARRY
EDDIE DUNN
BILL SLATER, quizmasters of
the program (themselves)
MANY CONTESTANTS
True or False (R) (Quiz)

HAGEN, JAMES. See: Daly, John
(4)

HAGEN, MIKE. See: Hargrave-

Scott, Joan

HAGERS. See: Owens, Buck

HAGGEN. See also: Hagen

HAGGEN, FESTUS. See: Dillon,
Marshal Matt

Haggis Baggis. See: Robbins,
Fred

HAINES, DR. See: Guest, Edgar
A. (2)

HAINES, LARRY. See: McCormick, Myron

HAINES, LIEUT. MIKE
DETECTIVE JEFF WARD
DETECTIVE JOHNNY CORSO,
members of New York Police
Department
N. Y. P. D. (TV) (Police drama)

HAINES, LOBO. See: Karr,
Mike

HAIRY. See:
Hari
Harry
Kangaroo, Captain

HAIZLIP, ELLIS. See: Butler,
Jerry

HAL
TOM, bumbling World War II
soldiers
The Soldiers (TV) (Comedy)

HAL. See also:
Beamish, Stanley
Everett, Professor
Falvey, Hal
Kemp, Hal
Lambert, Louise
March, Hal
Sharp, Hal
Towne, Hal
Williams, Dr.

HAL BLOCK. See: Daly, John
(3)

HAL McINTYRE. See: Whiteman,
Paul

HAL MARCH. See:
March, Hal
Sweeney, Bob

HAL O'HALLORAN. See: Kelly,
Joe (1)

Hal Peary Show, The. See:
Honest Harold

HAL RUGG. See: Wilburn, Doyle

HAL SMITH. See: Paulsen, Pat

HAL, THE MUSIC MAIDS AND.
See: Crosby, Bing (3)

HALE. See: Sparks, Hale

HALE, ALAN. See: Featherstone,
Mrs.

HALE, ANTHONY. See: James,
Nancy

HALE, ARTHUR, newscaster (himself)
Confidentially Yours (R) (News)

HALE, FLINT. See: Adams,
Major Seth

HALE, INSPECTOR. See: Penny

HALE, LUCRETIA. See: Cameron,
Christy Allen

HALE, MARTHA. See: Hennesey,
Lieut. Chick

HALE, MRS. See: Malone, Dr.
Jerry

HALEOKE. See: Godfrey, Arthur
(1)

HALEY. See also:
Healey
Healy
Holly

HALEY, JACK. See:
Henry, Captain
Owner

Half a Comedy Hour, Pat Paulsen's.
See: Paulsen, Pat

HALL, ARTHUR. See: Grimm,
Arnold

HALL, CHARLOTTE. See: Welk,
Lawrence

HALL, COLONEL. See: Bilko,
Sergeant Ernest

HALL, DR. WILLIAM TODHUNTER,
educator
VICKY HALL, his wife
PENNY, the maid
CLARENCE WELLMAN
MR. MERRIWEATHER, charac-
ters appearing in the drama
The Halls of Ivy (R) (TV)
(Drama)

HALL, LYNN. See: Burnley,
Walter

HALL, MRS. See: Bilko, Sergeant Ernest

HALL, MONTY (1), host and narrator of the program (himself)
MANY OLD WESTERN FILMS
Cowboy Theater (TV) (Western
motion pictures)

HALL, MONTY (2), host of the
program (himself)
AUDIENCE PARTICIPANTS
Let's Make a Deal (TV) (Audience participation)

HALL, MONTY (3), host and
"mayor" of the program (himself)
EILEEN BARTON, co-host and
"assistant mayor" of the program
(herself)
KEN WILLIAMS, "town crier" of
the program (himself)
Video Village, Jr. (TV) (Children's game show)

HALL, MONTY. See also:
Reiner, Carl

Hall, Music. See: O'Connor, Des

Hall of Fame, Radio. See:
Gibbs, Georgia (2)

Hall of Fame, The Hallmark Radio.
See: Hilton, James

Hall of Fun. See: Lane, Richard

HALL, PEG. See: Dane, Prudence

HALL, PETER. See: Manning, Laura

HALL, SANDRA. See: Allen, Joan Houston

HALL, SYLVIA. See: Trent, Helen

Hall, The Kraft Music. See:
  Como, Perry (2)
  Crosby, Bing (3)

HALL, TONY, host of the program (himself)
MANY GUEST MUSICIANS
Oh, Boy! (TV) (Rock music)

HALLET, SONNY. See: Perkins, Ma

HALLIDAY. See also:
  Holiday
  Holliday

HALLIDAY, DR. See: Chandler, Dr. Susan

HALLIDAY, LARRY. See: West, Michael

HALLIDAY, MIKE, adventurer in the Klondike
KATHY O'HARA, Klondike hotel proprietress
JEFF DURAIN, confidence man and opportunist
GOLDIE, Durain's accomplice
Klondike (TV) (Adventure)

HALLIGAN. See: Dillon, Marshal Matt

Hallmark Playhouse, The. See: Hilton, James

Hallmark Radio Hall of Fame, The. See: Hilton, James

HALLORAN, DETECTIVE JIM. See: Parker, Lieut. Mike

Halls of Ivy, The. See: Hall, Dr. William Todhunter

HALOP, BILLY
FLORENCE HALOP
PATRICIA RYAN
MIRIAM WOLFE
JACK GRIMES
BILL LIPTON
MICHAEL O'DAY
ARTHUR ANDERSON
LESTER JAY
ALBERT ALEY
JACK JORDAN
MARILYN ERSKINE
DONALD HUGHES
KINGSLEY COLTON
EDDIE RYAN, JR.
ROBERT LEE
VIVIAN BLOCK
SIDNEY LUMET
MAURY BENKOIL
BILLY MAUCH
BOBBY MAUCH
PATRICIA PEARDON
JIMSEY SOMMERS
RONALD LISS
ELAINE ENGLER
GWEN DAVIES
RITA LLOYD
JULIAN ALTMAN
SYBIL TRENT
WALTER TETLEY
BOB READICK, child actors and actresses featured on the program (themselves)
UNCLE BILL, character on the program portrayed by Bill Adams
MAURICE BROWN, orchestra leader (himself)
HIS ORCHESTRA
Let's Pretend (R) (Children's drama) (originally known as The Adventures of Helen and Mary) (R)

HALOP, BILLY. See also: Cross, Milton (2)

HALOP, FLORENCE. See:
  Cross, Milton (2)
  Halop, Billy

HALPER. See also: Helper

HALPER, CHARLEY. See: Williams, Danny

HALSEY, JACK. See: Allen, Dr. Kate

HALVORSEN. See: Falvey, Hal

"HAM" GYNT, HAMLYN. See:
Strange, Adam

HAMBURG, GERALDINE. See:
Kelly, Joe (2)

HAMILTON, BARBARA. See:
Sunday

HAMILTON, BETTY. See:
Lockridge, Barry

HAMILTON BURGER. See: Mason,
Perry

HAMILTON CAMP. See: Martindale, Wink (2)

HAMILTON, CLAYTON. See:
Beck, Jackson

HAMILTON, CLIPPER. See:
Ross, Scott

HAMILTON, DICK. See: Shayne,
Michael

HAMILTON, DR. PHILIP. See:
Gentry, Dr. Anne

HAMILTON FAMILY, THE. See:
Bryson, Dr. Lyman (2)

HAMILTON, GENE. See: Cross,
Milton (1)

HAMILTON, GEORGE, singer and
entertainer; star of the program
(himself)
JAN CROCKETT
JO DAVIS
MARY KLICK
ALEC HOUSTON, singers and
entertainers (themselves)
THE TEXAS WILDCATS
THE COUNTRY LADS, musical
groups
MANY GUEST STARS
George Hamilton IV (TV) (Variety)

HAMILTON, GEORGE. See also:
Jones, Jack

HAMILTON, KATY. See: Noble,
Mary

HAMILTON, LIEUT. See: Sterling,
Vanessa Dale

HAMILTON, LUCY. See: Shayne,
Michael

HAMILTON MAJORS, JR. See:
Nuvo, Arnie

HAMILTON, STEPHEN. See:
Solomon, David

HAMILTON TRIO, THE. See:
Caesar, Sid (3)

HAMLYN "HAM" GYNT. See:
Strange, Adam

HAMMER, MIKE, detective
Mike Hammer (R) (TV) (Detective)

HAMMILL, ZEKE. See: Perkins,
Ma

HAMMOND, BRIGADIER GENERAL.
See: Pierce, Captain Hawkeye

HAMMOND, HELEN. See: Hut-
ton, Ina Ray

HAMMOND, LIZA, widowed novelist
JENNY
MARY, her twin daughters
NORA, her mother
GEORGE HOWELL, her literary
agent
The Eve Arden Show (TV) (Situ-
ation comedy)

HAMMOND, SHELAH. See:
Horton, Dr. Tom

HAMPDEN, BURFORD. See:
Marais, Josef

HAMPTON, LIONEL. See:
Basie, Count
O'Connor, Father Norman

Hand, Helping. See: Anthony,
John J.

HAND, ROLLIN. See: Phelps,
Jim

HANEY. See: Douglas, Oliver

Hank. See: Hank

HANK, high school dropout, takes

courses under various aliases at
Western State University
DR. LEWIS ROYAL, registrar
of the university
DORIS ROYAL
TINA ROYAL, his daughters
COACH WEISS, athletic coach at
the university
Hank (TV) (Comedy)

HANK. See also:
Brackett, Hank
Dillon, Marshal Matt
Norby, Pearson
Young, Larry "Pepper"

HANK BLOOMGARDEN. See:
Narz, Jack (2)

HANK BRISTOW. See: Solomon,
David

HANK GOGERTY. See: Carson,
Bob

"HANK" HERBERT, HENRY BAR-
BOUR. See: Barbour, Henry
Wilson

HANK KIMBALL. See: Douglas,
Oliver

HANK McCLURE. See: Bell,
Mike

HANK MILLER. See: Nash, Jim

HANK O'HOOLIHAN. See: Solo-
man, David

HANKS, HENRIETTA, citizen of
Western town of Wretched
LUCY, her daughter
GRANDMA, her mother
GRANDPA, her father
HAROLD SYKES, sheriff
DAISY FROGG, local character
KITTY, her pet wildcat
BOWSER, her pet timber wolf
Pistols 'n' Petticoats (TV)
(Comedy Western)

HANLEY, LIEUT. GIL
SERGEANT CHIP SAUNDERS
PRIVATE BRADDOCK
PRIVATE CAJE, World War II
soldiers
Combat! (TV) (Drama)

HANLEY, MRS. See: Garrison,
Spencer

HANLEY, PAUL. See: Peyton,
Martin

HANLEY, PETER. See: Kovacs,
Ernie (1)

HANNAH. See: O'Leary, Hannah

HANNAH CORD. See:
Hughes, Chris
Peyton, Martin

Hannah, Houseboat. See: O'Leary,
Hannah

HANNIBAL. See:
Calhoun, Ben
Cobb, Hannibal
Heyes, Hannibal

Hannibal Cobb. See: Cobb, Hannibal

HANOVER, PETER. See: Roxy

HANS. See: Horwitz, Hans

HANS CONRIED. See: Kovacs,
Ernie (1)

HANS DIETRICH, CAPTAIN. See:
Troy, Sergeant Sam

HANS HOLBEIN. See: Henry
VIII, King of England

HANS SCHMIDT. See: James,
Dennis (4)

HANS SIMONS, DR. See: Jordan,
Joyce

HANSEN. See also: Hanson

HANSEN DANCERS, THE TOM.
See: Junior

HANSEN, DAVID
GABRIEL KAYE
DEBORAH SULLIVAN, lawyers,
operate N. L. S. (Neighborhood
Legal Service) in Los Angeles
The Store Front Lawyers (TV)
(Courtroom drama) (later called
Men at Law) (TV)

DEVLIN McNEIL, lawyer, senior
partner, associated with Hansen,
Kaye and Sullivan in N. L. S.
BUMP, McNeil's chauffeur
Men at Law (TV)

HANSEN, DEAN ERIC, Dean of
Students at university
COREY LEHMAN, his secretary
CHARLOTTE MARLEYBONE
HESTER MARLEYBONE
IVAN JONES
LIZA ARNOLD
DAVID GUNTHER
STEPHANIE COLE
TOMMY, characters appearing in
the drama
The Open Door (R) (Serial drama)

HANSEN, DR. See: Davis, Dr.
Althea

HANSEN, MAMA, head of Nor-
wegian/American family in San
Francisco
PAPA HANSEN, her husband
KATRIN
NELS
DAGMAR, their children
Mama (TV) (Family serial drama)

HANSHAW, ANNETTE. See: Henry,
Captain

HANSI. See: Nielson, Torwald

HANSON. See also: Hansen

HANSON, MAL. See: Arnold,
Eddy

HANSON, PRIVATE. See: Wright,
Conley

HAP. See: Holiday, Laurel

Happiness Boys, The. See: Happiness Boys, The

HAPPINESS BOYS, THE, vocal duet
composed of singers Billy Jones
and Ernie Hare
The Happiness Boys (R) (Music)

Happiness Exchange, The. See:
Rosenfield, Joe, Jr.

Happiness, Pursuit of. See:

Meredith, Burgess

Happiness, The Right to. See:
Nelson, Carolyn Kramer

Happy. See: Day, Chris

HAPPY. See:
Day, Chris
Felton, Happy
McHale, Lieut. Commander
Quinton
Templar, Simon

Happy Birthday, Your. See:
Birthday Man, The

Happy Days Are Here Again. See:
Nye, Louis

HAPPY DAYS SINGERS, THE.
See: Nye, Louis

Happy Family, One. See: Cooper,
Dick

HAPPY FELTON. See:
Felton, Happy
Parks, Bert (6)

Happy Felton's Spotlight Gang.
See: Felton, Happy

Happy Gilmans, Those. See:
Gilman, Gordon

Happy Herb Presents. See:
Isaacs, Herb

Happy Hollow. See: Peppertag,
Aaron

Happy Island. See: Bubbles, King

HAPPY MACMANN. See: Kane,
Martin

HAPPY POSTMAN, THE. See:
Burns, George (1)

Happy Returns, Many. See:
Burnley, Walter

HAPPY RICHMAN. See: Lindsey,
Peter

HAPPY, UNCLE. See: Ryan,
Tim

Harbor Command. See: Baxter,
Captain Ralph

Harbourmaster. See: Scott, David

Hardart Children's Hour, The Horn
and. See: Edwards, Ralph (1)

HARDESTY, VIRGINIA. See:
Rogers, Patricia

HARDIE. See also: Hardy

HARDIE, JIM, trouble-shooting
Wells Fargo agent
BEAU McCLOUD, his assistant
JEB GAINE, ranch foreman
OVIE, widow; Hardie's neighbor
MARY GEE
TINA, Ovie's daughters
Tales of Wells Fargo (TV)
(Western adventure)

HARDIN, DR. POOCH. See:
Goldstone, Dr. Peter

HARDING, DAVID, counterspy, member of "United States Counterspies"
during World War II
SPECIAL AGENT PETERS, his
assistant
Counterspy (R) (Adventure) (also
known as David Harding, Counterspy) (R)

HARDING, GLORIA. See: Cameron

HARDING, KAREN ADAMS (The
Woman in White), nurse
JOHN ADAMS
BETTY ADAMS
DR. LEE MARKHAM
DR. KIRK HARDING
DR. PURDY
DR. WILTON
DR. TORRANCE
DR. PAUL BURTON, physicians
JANET MUNSON ADAMS
BOB BANNING
ROSEMARY HEMINGWAY
UNCLE BILL
TIM BARNES
ROY PALMER
DR. JONATHAN McNEILL
ALICE DAY
FRANK FENTON
CRANDALL BOONE
ALICE CRAIG

KENNETH CRAIG
MR. MUNSON
DR. JACK LANDIS, physician
SISTER ELAINE
DAVE TALBOT
ALICE HENDRICKS
LEONARD HUNTLEY
EILEEN HOLMES
LINDA MUNSON
ANNIE MARIE TEMPLETON
AMELIA JAMESON
DAD MUNSON
BRYANT CHANDLER
THOMAS HAWKINS
MRS. GREY
GLADYS
SYBELLA MAYFIELD
RUTH CRAIG
MYRA WALKER
DR. BRADLEY, physician
ANNA
HELEN BRADLEY
AUNT HELEN SPALDING, char-
acters appearing in the drama
The Woman in White (R) (Serial
drama)

HARDING, MRS. RHODA, widow of
Dan Harding
DONNA HARDING
DEAN HARDING
MRS. GRAHAM
EULA SHERMAN
ARNIE TOPPER
MR. GORHAM
MR. TILLER
MARGOT GORHAM
MABEL KLOONER
REX KRAMER
STOOGE LOWE
PENNY LATHAM
JACK GARLAND
RALPH FRASER
FOWLER
EVA FOSTER, characters appear-
ing in the story
Dan Harding's Wife (R) (Serial
drama)

HARDWICKE, SIR CEDRIC. See:
Wallace, Mike (5)

HARDY. See also: Hardie

HARDY, ANDY, sixteen-year-old
boy
JUDGE HARDY, his father
MRS. HARDY, his mother

BEASEY, his friend
The Hardy Family (R) (Situation comedy)

HARDY, COACH. See: Armstrong, Jack

HARDY, DR. STEVEN
AUDREY BALDWIN
DIANA TAYLOR
MARY BRIGGS
LUCILLE WALL
ANN HELM
TONY CAMPO
CHASE MURDOCH
JUDGE BENNETT
JESSIE BREWER
DR. PHIL BREWER
DR. PETER TAYLOR
MR. BARKER
DR. MacINTOSH
DR. TOM BALDWIN
TRACY TAYLOR
KAREN
MARGARET
LIEUTENANT
STEVIE NELSON
DR. DAVIDSON
MR. MICHAELS
AL WEEKS
HOWIE DAWSON
JEAN DAWSON
JANE DAWSON
SHARON PINKHAM
DR. PINKHAM
DR. SIMMONS
DR. GORDON
LEE BALDWIN
MRS. NELSON, characters appearing in the drama
General Hospital (TV) (Serial drama)

Hardy Family, The. See: Hardy, Andy

HARE, ERNIE. See:
Happiness Boys, The
Jones, Billy

HARGATE, PAUL. See: Myrt

HARGRAVE-SCOTT, JOAN (The Valiant Lady)
DR. TRUMAN "TUBBY" SCOTT, her husband, physician
JIM BARRETT, her father
MRS. SCOTT, Dr. Truman's

mother
CARLA SCOTT
MONICA BREWSTER
LAFE SIMMS
NORMAN PRICE
PAMELA STANLEY
JUDGE KRUGER, jurist
MILDRED FARRELL
EMMA "STEVIE" STEVENS
AGNES WESTCOTT
MARGIE COOK
ABBEY TROWBRIDGE
DUDLEY TROWBRIDGE
LESTER BRENNAN
PIXIE JEFFERYS
NORMAN PRICE, SR.
DR. ABENDROTH, physician
DR. ALEC GORDON, physician
JEFFREY CLARK
CLARISSA CLARK
MIKE HAGEN
THOMAS R. CLARK
ELEANOR RICHARDS
DR. LILIENTHAL, physicial
DR. LANSON, physician
EDWARD CURRAN
MR. WRIGHT
MYRA GORDON
COLIN KIRBY
AMY BINGHAM
MR. CARSON
DR. CHRISTOPHER ELLERBE, physician
MR. TRENT
PAUL MORRISON
JOLLY ROGERS
EMILIO
MRS. EVANS
MR. COLLINS
MR. BARCLAY
GRACE WILSON
BILLY
MR. RICHARDS
NELSON, butler
OLIVER
ESTELLE CUMMINGS, characters appearing in the drama
Valiant Lady (R) (TV) (Serial drama)

HARI. See also:
Hairy
Harry

HARI, MATA AND. See: Caesar, Sid (3)

HARKA. See: Benson, Bobby

HARKER, TONY. See: Drake,
Betty

HARKNESS, DETECTIVE, investi-
gator for the National Surety
Company
JAKE, his friend and associate;
store keeper
National Surety's Secret Cases
(R) (Detective drama)

HARLAN. See: Day, Clarence

HARLEY, ROBERT. See: Churchill,
John

HARMON, ARTHUR. See: Findlay,
Maude

HARMON, PATTY. See: Marx,
Groucho (2)

HARMONY. See: Bizarre, Benita

Harmony, Hearts in. See: Penny

HAROLD. See:
Buell, Mrs. Harold C.
Cosby, Bill (3)
Honest Harold
Teen, Harold

HAROLD BAXTER. See: Hazel

HAROLD CRAIG. See: Barry,
Jack (9)

Harold, Honest. See: Honest
Harold

HAROLD LEVEY. See: Langner,
Lawrence

HAROLD SYKES. See: Hanks,
Henrietta

Harold Teen. See: Teen, Harold

HAROLD VAN DUZEE. See: Roxy

HAROLD VERMILYEA. See: Soule,
Olan (1)

HAROLD WILKINSON. See: O'Neill,
Mrs.

HARPER. See also:
Hooper
Hopper

HARPER, ELLIE. See: Tate,
Joanne

HARPER, JESS
SLIM SHERMAN
JONESEY, operators of Sherman
ranch and stagecoach station
near Laramie, Wyoming
Laramie (TV) (Western)

HARPER, LEFTIE. See: Brewster, Joey

HARPER, LINDA EMERSON
STEVE HARPER
CLYDE MARSHALL
GRACE MARSHALL
GEORGE EMERSON
IRENE EMERSON
HOLLY EMERSON, characters
appearing in the drama
Helpmate (R) (Serial drama)

HARPER, MRS. See: McGovern,
Dan

HARRIET. See:
Bumstead, Blondie
Harriot
Taylor, Andy

HARRIET, AUNT. See:
Aldrich, Henry
Batman
Endicott, Professor Mike

HARRIET BLACKBURN. See:
Hutton, Ina Ray

HARRIET BROOKS. See: Allen,
Joan Houston

HARRIET CONKLIN. See:
Brooks, Connie

HARRIET COOPER. See: Batman

HARRIET DURANT. See: Wayne,
Ruth Evans

HARRIET EAGLE. See: Trent,
Helen

HARRIET HILLIARD. See:
Murray, Feg
Penner, Joe

HARRIET HILLIARD NELSON.
See: Nelson, Ozzie

Harriet, The Adventures of Ozzie
and. See: Nelson, Ozzie

HARRIET'S MOTHER. See: Nelson, Ozzie

Harrigan and Son. See: Harrigan, James, Sr.

HARRIGAN, HOP, World War I flyer, afterwards civilian free lance pilot
GAIL NOLAN, his girl friend
TANK TINKER, his mechanic and part-time gunner
Hop Harrigan, America's Ace of the Airways (R) (Aviation adventure)

HARRIGAN, JAMES, SR., lawyer
JAMES HARRIGAN, JR., his son, also a lawyer
GYPSY, Harrigan, Sr.'s secretary
MISS CLARIDGE, Harrigan, Jr.'s secretary
Harrigan and Son (TV) (Drama)

HARRIMAN. See: Nelson, Admiral Harriman

HARRINGTON. See:
District Attorney, Mr.
Peters, Bill

HARRINGTON, BETTY ANDERSON. See: Peyton, Martin

HARRINGTON, BILL. See: Ross, Lanny

HARRINGTON, CLEVE. See: Winters, Evelyn

HARRINGTON, J. W. See: Miller, Johnny

HARRINGTON, LESLIE. See: Peyton, Martin

HARRINGTON, MADGE. See: Bradley, Judith

HARRINGTON, NORMAN. See: Peyton, Martin

HARRINGTON, PAT, JR., master of ceremonies of the program

(himself)
DIANA DORS
SEBASTIAN CABOT
BEVERLY GARLAND
ROSS MARTIN
MICKEY MANNERS
JAN CLAYTON, contestants on the program (themselves)
TWO GUEST CELEBRITIES
Stump the Stars (TV) (Charades) (originally called Pantomime Quiz Time) (TV)

HARRINGTON, RITA JACKS. See: Peyton, Martin

HARRINGTON, RODNEY. See: Peyton, Martin

HARRIOT. See also: Harriet

HARRIOT, ELINOR. See: Soule, Olan (1)

Harris Against the World. See: Harris, Alan

HARRIS, ALAN, Hollywood studio executive; resident of apartment complex in Southern California
KATE, his wife
DEE DEE
BILLY, their children
Harris Against the World (TV) (Comedy) (Segment of Ninety Bristol Court) (TV)

HARRIS, ALICE FAYE. See: Harris, Phil

HARRIS, BILL, music publisher
PAT BAKER, his daughter and partner
STEVE BAKER, Pat's husband
STUBBY WILSON, song plugger; employee of Harris
SOPHIE, Harris' secretary
Love and Marriage (TV) (Situation comedy/music)

HARRIS, CHARLIE. See: Dyke, Charity Amanda

HARRIS, DR. ADRIENNE. See: Prescott, Kate Hathaway

HARRIS, PAULINE. See: Ames, Peter

HARRIS, PHIL, singer and orchestra
leader (himself)
ALICE FAYE HARRIS, his wife
(herself)
LITTLE ALICE, their daughter
ALICE FAYE HARRIS' mother
FRANK REMLEY, "the left-
handed guitar player"
WAMOND WADCLIFFE
JULIUS ABRUZIO, "the grocery
boy"
EMILY WILLIAMS, comedians and
characters appearing on the pro-
gram
The Fitch Bandwagon (R) (Music/
variety)

HARRIS, PHIL. See also:
Benny, Jack
Crosby, Bing (2)

HARRIS, ST. JOHN. See: Sunday

HARRIS, SILKY
RENO McKEE, prospectors in
Alaska in the late 1890s
ROCKY SHAW, singer and enter-
tainer
The Alaskans (TV) (Adventure)

HARRIS, TOM. See: Kirkwood,
Jack

HARRISON. See:
Carter, Lucy
Holloway, Harrison

HARRISON, ARLINE. See:
Manning, Portia Blake

HARRISON, BETTY. See: Arden,
Jane

HARRISON, DOC. See: Malone,
Dr. Jerry

HARRISON, FRANK. See: Peters,
Bill

HARRISON, GENERAL. See:
Nelson, Sergeant

HARRISON, GEORGE. See: Jackson, Martha

HARRISON, RITA. See: Trent,
Helen

HARRON, DON. See: Owens,
Buck

HARRY, song-and-dance man,
leader of three-girl vaudeville
act
RUSTY
LOIS
TERRY, members of his act
Harry's Girls (TV) (Comedy)

HARRY. See also:
Barrett, Timothy "Spud"
Bell, Harry
Blackstone, Harry
Davis, Joan Field
Dickens, Harry
Elders, Harry
Fosdick, Rev. Harry Emerson
Grafton, Harry
Grant, Harry
Graves, Harry
Hagen, Dr. Harry
Hairy
Hari
Hollister, Dick
Lime, Harry
Overstreet, Buddy
Reasoner, Harry
Reser, Harry
Rule, Harry
Tom

HARRY BABBITT. See: Kyser,
Kay

HARRY BACKSTAGE. See:
Ballew, Wally

HARRY BLAKE. See: Falvey,
Hal

HARRY, BROADWAY. See: Kay,
Beatrice

HARRY FRANKEL. See: Singin'
Sam

HARRY HENDERSON. See:
Beulah

HARRY HERSHFIELD. See:
Bower, Roger
Wilson, Ward

HARRY HOLCOMBE. See: Jostyn,
Jay (1)

HARRY HORLICK. See: Parker,
Frank

HARRY HYAMS. See: Welk,
Lawrence

HARRY JAMES. See:
Basie, Count
Kaye, Danny
Whiteman, Paul

HARRY LANG. See: Bolger, Ray

HARRY McDONALD. See: Welles,
Orson (3)

HARRY McGIL. See: Brooks,
Cameron

HARRY McNAUGHTON. See:
Howard, Tom (1)

HARRY MILLIKEN. See: Crane,
Betty

HARRY MORTON. See: Burns,
George (1)

HARRY PRICE. See: Burnley,
Walter

HARRY REASONER. See:
Reasoner, Harry
Smith, Howard K. (1)
Wallace, Mike (4)

HARRY RESER. See:
Kaye, Sammy (1)
Reser, Harry

HARRY SALTER. See:
Elman, Dave (2)
Granlund, Nils Thor
Parks, Bert (6)

HARRY SOSNIK. See:
Brown, Joe E. (1)
Elman, Dave (2)
Hildegarde (1)
Levenson, Sam

HARRY THE HACK. See: Wilson,
Steve

HARRY, TOM, DICK AND. See:
Duke of Paducah, The
Skelton, Red
Uncle Walter

HARRY, UNCLE. See: Carter,
Lucy

HARRY VON ZELL. See:
Burns, George (1)
Husing, Ted
Pitcher, The

HARRY ZIMMERMAN. See:
Shore, Dinah (2)

Harry's Girls. See: Harry

HART. See also:
Harte
Heart

HART, DOROTHY. See: Stokey,
Mike

HART, EDIE. See: Gunn, Peter

HART, JASON. See: Fuller,
Ward

HART, JOHN. See: Benti,
Joseph

HART, LES. See: Burke, Amos

HART, SERGEANT. See: King,
Rocky

HART, TED. See: Young, Larry
"Pepper"

HARTE. See also:
Hart
Heart

HARTE, MADGE. See: Dallas,
Stella

HARTFORD, JANE. See: Drake,
Betty

HARTFORD, JOHN. See: Crosby,
Bing (2)

HARTLEY, BILL. See: Grimm,
Arnold

HARTLEY, DR. ROBERT, Chicago
psychologist
EMILY, his wife, substitute
teacher
HOWARD BORDEN, his neighbor,
747 navigator

MARGARET HOOVER, his neigh-
bor, housewife
MARGARET'S TWO CHILDREN
JERRY ROBINSON, his friend;
orthodontist
CAROL KESTER, his receptionist
The Bob Newhart Show (TV) (Situ-
ation comedy)

HARTLEY, JUDGE. See: Perkins,
Ma

HARTLEY KNOWLTON. See:
Brent, Dr. Jim

HARTLEY, LORRAINE. See:
Drake, Nora

HARTLINE, MARY. See:
Kirchener, Claude (2)

HARUM, DAVID, horse trader and
banker
AUNT POLLY BENSON, his sister
LISH HARUM
DEACON PERKINS
CLARISSA OAKLEY
SUSAN PRICE WELLS
CHARLIE CULLOM
JOHN LENNOX
TESS TERWILLIGER
JAMES BENSON
ZEKE SWINNEY
MARK CARTER
ELSIE ANDERSON
BRIAN WELLS
HENRY LONGACRE
MR. FINKE
WILLY
GRANDPA, his friends and
neighbors
XANTHIPPE, renamed TOWN
TALK, his horse
David Harum (R) (Serial drama)

HARVE. See also: Harvey

HARVE ANDERS. See: Varner,
Will

HARVE FISCHMAN. See: Kelly,
Joe (2)

Harvest of Stars. See: Melton,
James (2)

HARVEY. See:
Booth, Martha

Box, Harvey
Clayton, Margie
Harve
Hays, Harvey

HARVEY BLACKWELL, COLONEL.
See: McKeever, Cadet Gary

HARVEY, CAPTAIN. See: Wing,
Howie

HARVEY KORMAN. See: Burnett,
Carol

HARVEY, MISS. See: Novak,
John

HARVEY, PAUL (1), commentator
and newscaster (himself)
Paul Harvey Comments (TV)
(News and comment)

HARVEY, PAUL (2), commentator
and newscaster (himself)
Paul Harvey News (R) (News
and comment)

HARVEY, PAUL. See also:
Shadel, Bill

HARVEY, PETER. See: Dawson,
Rosemary

HARVEY STONE. See: Lewis,
Robert Q. (1)

HARVEY STOVALL, MAJOR. See:
Savage, Brigadier General Frank

HARVEY WESKIT. See: Peepers,
Robinson J.

HARWOOD, PAULA. See: Brent,
Dr. Jim

HASKELL, JACK. See: Garroway,
Dave (2) (3)

HASKELL, JOE. See: Collins,
Barnabas

HASSIE. See: McCoy, Grampa

HASTINGS. See: Young, Larry
"Pepper"

HASTINGS, BILL, former college
professor, takes job on Los

Angeles paper as advice
columnist using the penname
Phoebe Goodheart
MICKEY RILEY, sports writer
MR. FOSDICK, managing editor
HUMPHREY, copy boy
Dear Phoebe (TV) (Comedy)

HASTINGS, BOB
CHARLIE DYER, characters appearing in the drama
This Life Is Mine (R) (Serial
drama)

HASTINGS, BOB. See also: Kelly,
Joe (1)

HASTINGS, JEFFREY. See:
Carlyle, Baylor

HASTINGS, NORMAN. See: Trent,
Helen

HASTINGS, PHILIP. See: Carlyle,
Baylor

HASTINGS, TRACY CARLYLE. See:
Carlyle, Baylor

HATFIELD, EMMIE. See: Dane,
Prudence

HATHAWAY, DANIEL. See: Prescott, Kate Hathaway

HATHAWAY, ED. See: Prescott,
Kate Hathaway

HATHAWAY, ELINOR
WALTER HATHAWAY, her hus-
band; owners of three chimpanzees
CHARLIE
ENOCH
CANDY, their pet chimpanzees
The Hathaways (TV) (Comedy)

HATHAWAY, GORDON. See: Allen,
Steve (1)

HATHAWAY, LILLIAN. See:
Prescott, Kate Hathaway

HATHAWAY, MARY. See: Prescott,
Kate Hathaway

HATHAWAY, MICHAEL. See:
Prescott, Kate Hathaway

HATHAWAY, PROFESSOR JULIAN.
See: Prescott, Kate Hathaway

HATHAWAY, STELLA. See:
Prescott, Kate Hathaway

HATHAWAY, VICKI. See:
Prescott, Kate Hathaway

Hathaways, The. See: Hathaway,
Elinor

HATTEN, BOB. See: Conrad,
Jim

HATTER, THE MAD. See: Batman

HATTIE. See: Dickey, Dan'l

Hattie, Miss. See: Barrymore,
Ethel

HATTIE WILLIAMS. See: Young,
Larry "Pepper"

HAUSER, DON. See: Wagoner,
Porter

HAUSER, JOHNNY. See: Ross,
Lanny

Have Gun, Will Travel. See:
Paladin

HAVEN. See: MacQuarrie, Haven
(1) (2)

HAVEN, BOB. See: Welk,
Lawrence

HAVENS, NICK. See: Young,
Larry "Pepper"

HAVILLAND. See: Carella

Haw Haw, Lord. See: Joyce,
William

HAW HAW, LORD. See: Joyce,
William

Hawaii Calls. See: Edwards,
Webley

Hawaii Five-0. See: McGarrett,
Steve

HAWAII, THE GOVERNOR OF. See:
McGarrett, Steve

Hawaiian Eye. See: Steele, Tracy

Hawk. See: Hawk, John

HAWK. See:
Black Hawk
Hawkes
Hawks

Hawk, Black. See: Black Hawk

HAWK, BLACK. See also: Blackhawk

HAWK, BOB (1), quizmaster of the
program (himself)
MANY STUDIO CONTESTANTS
The Bob Hawk Show (R) (Quiz)

HAWK, BOB (2), quizmaster of
the program (himself)
MANY CONTESTANTS
Thanks to the Yanks (R) (Quiz)

HAWK, BOB. See also: Baker,
Phil (3)

HAWK, HENRY. See: Bunny, Bugs

HAWK, JOHN, Iroquois Indian
detective; works out of New York
district attorney's office
Hawk (TV) (Crime drama)

HAWK, THE. See: Mallory, Lieut.
Col. Spencer

Hawk, The Sparrow and the. See:
Mallory, Lieut. Col. Spencer

HAWKES. See also:
Hawk
Hawks

HAWKES, JEB. See: Collins,
Barnabas

HAWKEYE, Indian, employed by
British in Colonial America
CHINGACHGOOK, Indian, the Last
of the Mohicans; also employed
by the British
Hawkeye and the Last of the
Mohicans (TV) (Adventure)

HAWKEYE. See also:
Hooton, Babs
Pierce, Captain Hawkeye

Hawkeye and the Last of the Mohicans. See: Hawkeye

HAWKINS, COLEMAN. See: O'Connor, Father Norman

HAWKINS, MARIA. See: Brown,
Ellen

HAWKINS, THOMAS. See:
Harding, Karen Adams

HAWKS. See also:
Hawk
Hawkes

HAWKS, FRANK, flying ace, featured on the program (himself)
Time Flies (R) (Adventure)

HAWLEY, MARK, narrator of the
program (himself)
MANY ACTORS AND ACTRESSES
Famous Fortunes (R) (Drama)

HAWN, GOLDIE. See: Rowan,
Dan

HAWTHORN, CAPTAIN, O. S. S.
officer
O. S. S. (TV) (Adventure)

Hawthorne Hotel. See: Liston,
Lois

HAYDON, CHARLES. See: Steel,
Richard

HAYES. See also:
Hays
Heyes

Hayes and Henderson. See: Hayes,
Bill

HAYES, BILL
FLORENCE HENDERSON, singers
and entertainers (themselves)
MANY ACTORS AND ACTRESSES
Hayes and Henderson (TV)
(Dramas with music)

HAYES, BILL. See also: Caesar,
Sid (3)

HAYES, BUDDY. See: Welk,
Lawrence

HAYES, DEXTER. See: Barrington, Bryn Clark

HAYES, GABBY, Western actor,
host of the program (himself)
MANY WESTERN ACTORS AND
MUSICIANS
The Gabby Hayes Show (TV)
(Western drama/music)

HAYES, HELEN (1), actress;
hostess of the program (herself)
MANY ACTORS AND ACTRESSES
The Helen Hayes Theater (R)
(Drama)

HAYES, HELEN (2), actress; star
of the program (herself)
JOSEPH BELL, actor, featured
on the program (himself)
MANY ACTORS AND ACTRESSES
A New Penny (R) (Drama)

HAYES, LINC
JULIE BARNES
PETE COCHRAN, youthful crime
fighters; undercover agents for
Los Angeles police
CAPTAIN ADAM GREER, police
captain
The Mod Squad (TV) (Crime
drama)

HAYES, PETER LIND (1), quiz-
master of the program (himself)
MANY PROMINENT UNIVERSITY
ALUMNI
Alumni Fun (TV) (Quiz)

HAYES, PETER LIND (2), comedian;
star of the program (himself)
MARY HEALY, his wife; comedienne, co-star of the program
(herself)
MANY GUEST STARS
Inside U.S.A. (TV) (Variety/
talk)

HAYES, PETER LIND (3), comedian,
featured on the program (himself)
MARY HEALY, his wife, come-
dienne, also featured (herself)
MANY GUEST STARS
The Peter Lind Hayes Show (TV)
(Variety)

HAYES, PETER LIND (4), comedian; interviewer on the program
MARY HEALY, his wife; comedienne; co-interviewer
SHERMAN BILLINGSLEY, nightclub owner; co-interviewer (all
themselves)
MANY GUEST INTERVIEWEES
The Stork Club (TV) (Interviews)

HAYES, WING COMMANDER,
African rancher
JIM SINCLAIR, champion rodeo
rider, brought to Africa by
Hayes
JOHN HENRY, Navaho friend of
Sinclair
SAMSON, African boy, friend of
Sinclair
Cowboy in Africa (TV) (African
adventure)

HAYFIELD, FRANCIS. See: Myrt

HAYMAN, LILLIAN. See: Uggams,
Leslie

HAYMES, DICK, singer, star of
the program (himself)
MARTHA TILTON
HELEN FORREST
HITS AND A MISS, vocalists
and vocal group featured on the
program (themselves)
MRS. WILSON, comic character
portrayed by Cliff Arquette
GORDON JENKINS, orchestra
leader (himself)
HIS ORCHESTRA
The Dick Haymes Show (R)
(Music)

HAYS. See:
Hayes
Heyes
Stowe, Senator Hays

HAYS, ANDY. See: Alcala,
Thomas Jefferson

HAYS, HARVEY, narrator of the
program (himself)
Words and Music (R) (Music)

HAYTON, LENNIE. See:
Allen, Fred
Ross, Lanny

HAYWARD, JONATHAN. See:
Trent, Helen

HAYWORTH, LUELLA. See: Fairchild, Kay

HAYWORTH, PHIL. See: Brewster, Joey

Hazel. See: Hazel

HAZEL, maid and housekeeper
GEORGE BAXTER, her employer
DOROTHY BAXTER, George's
wife
HAROLD BAXTER, son of George
and Dorothy
STEVE BAXTER, George's
brother
Hazel (TV) (Comedy)

HAZEL. See also:
Driggs, Karleton King
Johnson, Bess

HAZEL BARBOUR HERBERT. See:
Barbour, Henry Wilson

HAZEL BIRD. See: Rogers,
Patricia

HAZEL DOPHEIDE. See: Grandma

HAZEL NORRIS. See: McGee,
Fibber

HAZY, MISS. See: Wiggs, Mrs.

He and She. See: Hollister, Dick

He Said! She Said! See:
Garagiola, Joe (1)

Headline. See: Wilson, Steve

Headline Hunters. See: Thomas,
Lowell (1)

HEADLINERS ORCHESTRA, THE.
See: Boyd, Tom

Headmaster. See: Thompson, Andy

HEALEY. See also:
Haley
Healy
Holly

HEALEY, MAJOR ROGER. See:
Nelson, Major Tony

HEALY. See also:
Haley
Healey
Holly

HEALY, MARY. See: Hayes,
Peter Lind (2) (3) (4)

HEAR. See also: Here

Hear It Now. See: Murrow, Edward R. (2)

HEARN, SAM. See: Henry,
Captain

HEART. See also:
Hart
Harte

Heart Is, Where the. See:
Prescott, Kate Hathaway

Heart of the City, The. See:
Wilson, Steve

HEARTBURN, MRS. SARAH.
See: Baker, Phil (2)

HEARTHSTONE, INSPECTOR.
See: Lenrow, Bernard

Hearthstone of the Death Squad.
See: Lenrow, Bernard

Heart's Desire. See: Alexander,
Ben (3)

Hearts in Harmony. See: Penny

HEATH. See: Barkley, Victoria

HEATH, SERGEANT ERNEST.
See: Vance, Philo

HEATHER FINCH. See: Walker,
Eddie

HEATHERTON, JOEY. See:
Edwards, Ralph (1)

HEATHERTON, RAY, host of the
program (himself)
MANY JUVENILE GUESTS
Merry Mailman (TV) (Children's
program)

HEATTER, GABRIEL, host of the
program (himself)
We, The People (R) (TV) (Human
interest stories)
MILO BOULTON
BURGESS MEREDITH
DWIGHT WEIST
EDDIE DOWLING, hosts of the
program (themselves)
OSCAR BRADLEY, orchestra
leader (himself)
HIS ORCHESTRA
We, The People (R)

"HEC." See: Ramsey, Hector
"Hec"

Hec Ramsey. See: Ramsey,
Hector "Hec"

HECK MARTIN. See: Caine, Frank

HECKLE
JECKLE, magpies (cartoon characters)
Heckle and Jeckle (TV) (Children's program)

HECTOR. See:
Mac
Ramsey, Hector "Hec"

HECTOR SMITH. See: Anderson,
Jim

HEDDA. See: Tell, William

HEDGEROW, CHESTER. See:
Jordan, Joyce

HEDGEROW, DR. MOLLY. See:
Jordan, Joyce

Hee Haw. See: Owens, Buck

HEFLIN, VAN, narrator of the
program (himself)
MANY ACTORS AND ACTRESSES
The Great Adventure (TV) (Dramatizations of American historical
events)

HEFNER, HUGH, publisher of Playboy Magazine; host of the program
(himself)
MANY GUEST CELEBRITIES
Playboy After Dark (TV) (Variety/
conversation) (also known as

Playboy's Penthouse) (TV)

HEIDT, HORACE (1), orchestra
leader, moderator of the program
(himself)
HIS ORCHESTRA
AMATEUR TALENT
GUEST STARS
INTERVIEWEES
Horace Heidt's Show Wagon (TV)
(Music/variety)

HEIDT, HORACE (2), orchestra
leader; host of the program (him-
self)
HIS ORCHESTRA
MANY CONTESTANTS
A Night With Horace Heidt (R)
(Amateur talent contest)

HEIDT, HORACE. See also:
Bower, Roger
Grauer, Ben (2)

HEIFETZ, JASCHA. See: Bell,
Alexander Graham

HEINSIUS. See: Churchill, John

Heinz Magazine of the Air, The.
See: Edmondson, Delmar

Heirs, The Court of Missing. See:
Waters, Jim

HEJAK, ANNA. See: Keene, Kitty

HELEN. See:
Carey, Dr. Philip
Dallas, Stella
Gregory, Helen
Hayes, Helen (1) (2)
Holden, Helen
Judd, Clinton
Kimble, Dr. Richard
Larimore, Marilyn
Lee, Jim
Morrison, Mother
Norby, Pearson
O'Connell, Helen
Trent, Helen
Wilson, Dr. Thomas

Helen and Mary, The Adventures of.
See: Halop, Billy

HELEN BEHMILLER. See: Caine,
Betty

HELEN BRADLEY. See: Harding, Karen Adams

HELEN CLAIRE. See: Twin Stars, The

HELEN ELDRIDGE. See: Hughes, Lisa

HELEN ELLIOTT DONNELLY. See: Garrison, Spencer

HELEN FORREST. See: Haymes, Dick

HELEN GOWAN STEPHENSON. See: Brent, Dr. Jim

HELEN GRAYCO. See: Jones, Spike (1) (2)

HELEN HAMMOND. See: Hutton, Ina Ray

Helen Hayes Theater, The. See: Hayes, Helen (1)

Helen Holden: Government Girl. See: Holden, Helen

HELEN HUNT. See: Sterling, Vanessa Dale

HELEN KAYE. See: Sharp, Hal

HELEN MARSHALL. See: Carter, Kathryn

HELEN MILLIKEN. See: Crane, Betty

Helen O'Connell. See: O'Connell, Helen

HELEN O'CONNELL. See:
Birthday Man, The
Morgan, Russ
O'Connell, Helen

HELEN SMITH. See: Hutton, Ina Ray

HELEN SPALDING, AUNT. See: Harding, Karen Adams

HELEN TRAUBEL. See: Bell, Alexander Graham

Helen Trent, The Romance of. See: Trent, Helen

HELEN WARD. See: Archie

HELEN WOOLEY. See: Hutton, Ina Ray

HELENA GUDE. See: Bergen, Edgar (1)

HELENE HUDSON. See: Lawton, Lora

HELLER, LITTLE JACKIE. See: Bernie, Ben

Hello, Pea Pickers. See: Ford, Tennessee Ernie (3)

Hello, Peggy. See: Hopkins, Peggy

HELM, ANN. See: Hardy, Dr. Steven

HELMI. See: Myrt

HELPER. See also: Halper

HELPER, JERRY. See: Petrie, Rob

HELPER, MILLIE. See: Petrie, Rob

Helping Hand. See: Anthony, John J.

Helpmate. See: Harper, Linda Emerson

HEMINGWAY, MR. See: Canova, Judy

HEMINGWAY, ROSEMARY. See: Harding, Karen Adams

HEMPSTEAD, MRS. See: Waring, Evelyn

HENDERSON, ALICE. See: Beulah

HENDERSON, CHARLIE. See: Ballard, Pat

HENDERSON, CHUCK. See: Hughes, Chris

HENDERSON, DR. MYRON. See:

Solomon, David

HENDERSON, DONNIE. See:
Beulah

HENDERSON, FAY PERKINS. See:
Perkins, Ma

HENDERSON, FLORENCE. See:
Hayes, Bill

HENDERSON, HARRY. See:
Beulah

Henderson, Hayes and. See:
Hayes, Bill

HENDERSON, LUTHER, JR. See:
Bergen, Polly

HENDERSON, MARY ANN. See:
Kelly, Joe (2)

HENDERSON, PAUL. See:
Perkins, Ma

HENDERSON, PAULETTE. See:
Perkins, Ma

HENDERSON, SKITCH. See:
Allen, Steve (3)
Carson, Johnny (1)

HENDRA, TONY. See: DeLuise,
Dom (2)

HENDRICKS, ALICE. See:
Harding, Karen Adams

HENDRICKS, NEVER-FAIL. See:
Marlin, Mary

HENDRIX, BURNETT. See:
Sharp, Hal

HENDRIX, MRS. See: Drake,
Betty

Hennesey. See: Hennesey, Lieut.
Chick

HENNESEY, LIEUT. CHICK, naval
doctor
MARTHA HALE, naval nurse;
his girl friend
CAPTAIN SHAFER, his commanding officer
MAX BRONSKY, corpsman

SHATZ, seaman
Hennesey (TV) (Military comedy)

HENNESSY. See: Marlin, Mary

HENNING, GILES. See: Marlin,
Mary

HENNY. See also: Henry

HENNY YOUNGMAN. See: Lewis,
Robert Q. (1)

HENPECKED HUSBAND, THE.
See: Junior

HENRIETTA. See:
Hanks, Henrietta
Topper, Cosmo

HENRIETTA, AUNT. See:
Everett, Professor

HENRIETTA DORNE. See:
Marlin, Mary

HENRY. See:
Aldrich, Henry
Barbour, Henry Wilson
Burbig, Henry
Burke, Amos
Douglas, Steve
Foster, Henry
Henny
Hull, Henry
Larimore, Marilyn
Mitchell, Dennis
Morgan, Henry
Phyfe, Henry
Sam
Sloan, Holly

HENRY VIII, King of England
CATHERINE OF ARAGON
ANNE BOLEYN
JANE SEYMOUR
ANNE OF CLEVES
CATHERINE HOWARD
CATHERINE PARR, his six
wives
EDWARD VI, his son
PRINCESS MARY, his daughter
CARDINAL WOLSEY
MARIA
DUKE OF NORFOLK
CHAPUYS
CARDINAL CAMPEGGIO
THOMAS CROMWELL
LADY ROCHFORD

ARCHBISHOP THOMAS CRANMER
MARK SMEATON
THOMAS SEYMOUR
HANS HOLBEIN
ROBERT BARNES
THOMAS CULPEPPER
FRANCIS DEREHAM
DOWAGER DUCHESS OF NORFOLK
BISHOP GARDINER
LORD HERTFORD
THOMAS WRIOTHESELEY, his-
torical characters appearing in
the drama
The Six Wives of Henry VIII (TV)
(Historical drama)

Henry Aldrich. See: Aldrich, Henry

HENRY BARBOUR "HANK" HER-
BERT. See: Barbour, Henry
Wilson

HENRY BLAKE, LIEUT. COL.
See: Pierce, Captain Hawkeye

HENRY BRINTHROPE, LORD. See:
Sunday

HENRY BURR. See: Kelly, Joe
(1)

HENRY, CAPTAIN, proprietor of
show boat; host of the program
CAPTAIN BARNET BARNETT
AUNT MARIA
MARY LOU
MOLASSES AND JANUARY
MAMMY
THE SHOW BOAT FOUR, char-
acters appearing on the program
CONRAD THIBAULT
WINIFRED CECIL
EDMUND "TINY" RUFFNER
JACK HALEY
ROSS GRAHAM
VIRGINIA VERRILL
NADINE CONNOR
SAM HEARN
JULES BLEDSOE
WARREN HULL
DICK TODD
FRANK WILLOUGHBY
LANNY ROSS
ANNETTE HANSHAW, singers
and comedians appearing on the
program (themselves)
Show Boat (R) (Variety) (also
known as The Maxwell House
Show Boat) (R)

HENRY GARTH, JUDGE. See:
Virginian, The

HENRY GIBSON. See: Rowan,
Dan

HENRY HAWK. See: Bunny, Bugs

HENRY, JOHN. See: Hayes,
Wing Commander

HENRY LEVINE. See: Cross,
Milton (1)

HENRY LONGACRE. See: Harum,
David

HENRY MANCINI. See: Pam

HENRY MATTHEWS. See:
Carter, Kathryn
Marlin, Mary

HENRY MORGAN. See:
Moore, Garry (4)
Morgan, Henry

Henry Morgan Show, The. See:
Morgan, Henry

HENRY NEWMAN. See: Bennett,
Nita

HENRY, O., American short story
writer, portrayed by Thomas
Mitchell
MANY ACTORS AND ACTRESSES
The O. Henry Playhouse (TV)
(Dramatizations of stories by
O. Henry)

Henry Phyfe, The Double Life of.
See: Phyfe, Henry

HENRY RUSSELL CHORUS, THE.
See: Borge, Victor

HENRY ST. JOHN. See: Churchill,
John

Henry, Sam 'n.' See: Sam

HENRY SENRICH. See: Rogers,
Patricia

HENRY THAYER, MRS. See:
Jones, Lorenzo

HENRY VAN PORTER. See:
Jones, Amos

HENSHAW, MATT. See: Ruskin,
Lily

HENSHAW, RUTH. See: Ruskin,
Lily

Her Honor, Nancy James. See:
James, Nancy

HERB. See:
Isaacs, Herb
Shriner, Herb (1) (2) (3)

HERB HUBBARD. See: Buell,
Roger

HERB POLESIE. See: Slater,
Bill (2)

HERB SHELDON. See: Kirkwood,
Jack

Herb Shriner Show, The. See:
Shriner, Herb (2)

HERB WOODLEY. See: Bum-
stead, Blondie

HERBERT. See:
Gillis, Dobie
Maris, Herbert L.
Philbrick, Herbert

HERBERT CLARK. See: Brewster,
Joey

HERBERT, DON. See: Wizard,
Mr.

HERBERT DUNSTAN. See: Banks,
Stanley

HERBERT, HAZEL BARBOUR. See:
Barbour, Henry Wilson

HERBERT, HENRY BARBOUR
"HANK." See: Barbour, Henry
Wilson

HERBERT HULSE. See: Barry,
Jack (9)

HERBERT KENWROTH. See:
Barrett, Timothy "Spud"

HERBERT M. STEMPEL. See:
Barry, Jack (9)

HERBERT, MARGARET. See:
Barbour, Henry Wilson

HERBERT MARSHALL. See:
Powell, Dick (3)

HERBERT PEABODY. See: Carson, Jack

HERBERT TEMPLE. See: Brown,
Ellen

HERBERT, WILLIAM "BILL."
See: Barbour, Henry Wilson

HERBERT, WILLIAM MARTIN
"PINKY." See: Barbour,
Henry Wilson

HERBERT WILSON. See: Andrews,
Walter

HERBIE. See: Bell, Harry

HERE. See also: Hear

Here Come the Brides. See:
Bolt, Jason

Here Come the Double Deckers.
See: Brains

Here Come the Stars. See:
Jessel, George (2)

Here Comes Tomorrow. See:
Glenn, Colonel John

Here, Look! See: Agronsky,
Martin

Here, Look Who's. See: Boyd,
Tom

Here's Babe Ruth. See: Ruth,
Babe

Here's Lucy. See: Carter, Lucy

HERK LAMSON. See: Fry,
Marshal Simon

HERLIHY, ED, master of ceremonies of the program (himself)
MANY GUEST STARS

The Army Hour (R) (Army/variety)

HERLIHY, ED. See also: Edwards,
Ralph (1)

HERMAN. See:
Herrmann
Munster, Herman

HERMAN, BERNIE, host of the pro-
gram (himself)
GUEST SPEAKERS
Contact (TV) (Discussion)

HERMAN BRANCH. See: Barton,
Bud

HERMAN, GEORGE. See: Schoumacher, David

HERMAN THE DUCK. See: Burns,
George (1)

HERMAN, WOODY, orchestra
leader (himself)
HIS ORCHESTRA, featured on
the program
The Woody Herman Show (R)
(Music)

HERMIONE GIRAFFE. See: Pam

HERMIT, THE, story teller and
host of the program
The Hermit's Cave (R) (Fantasy
story program)

Hermit's Cave, The. See: Hermit,
The

HERNANDEZ, JUANO. See:
Marais, Josef

Hero, My. See: Beanblossom,
Robert S.

Hero, The. See: Garrett, Sam

Heroes, Hogan's. See: Hogan,
Colonel Robert

HERRICK, CAP'N JOHN, captain of
the tug boat "Cheryl Ann"
MAY, his wife
Waterfront (TV) (Adventure)

HERRINGBONE, FLOSSIE. See:
Perkins, Ma

HERRINGBONE, JESSICA. See:
Perkins, Ma

HERRINGBONE, PHINEAS. See:
Perkins, Ma

HERRINGBONE, TWEETSIE. See:
Perkins, Ma

HERRMANN. See also: Herman

HERRMANN, BERNARD, symphony
orchestra conductor (himself)
THE COLUMBIA BROADCASTING
SYMPHONY ORCHESTRA
Gateway to Music (R) (Symphony
orchestra)

HERSHFIELD, HARRY. See:
Bower, Roger
Wilson, Ward

HERTFORD, LORD. See: Henry
VIII, King of England

HESTER MARLEYBONE. See:
Hansen, Dean Eric

HEWITT, GRANNY. See: Jordan,
Joyce

HEWITT, MRS. See: Randolph,
Alice

HEY BOY. See: Paladin

Hey Jeannie! See: MacLennon,
Jeannie

Hey Landlord! See: Banner,
Woody

Hey, Mulligan! See: Mulligan,
Mickey

HEYES. See also:
Hayes
Hays

HEYES, HANNIBAL, alias Joshua
Smith, former safe cracker
JED "KID" CURRY, alias Thaddeus Jones, former gun toter,
both outlaws trying to earn
amnesty by going straight for
a year
Alias Smith and Jones (TV)
(Western)

HEYWOOD BOTTS. See: Clayton,
Margie

HICKOCK, WILD BILL, Western
law enforcement officer
JINGLES, his friend and companion
Wild Bill Hickock (TV) (Western
adventure)

Hide, No Need to. See: Linkletter, Art (3)

HIGBY, MARY JANE, played the
part of a blind pianist (herself)
PETER CAPELL, also star of the
program (himself)
AUNT AGATHA
CHINESE HOUSEBOY
THE AMAH, characters appearing
in the drama
Thanks For Tomorrow (R)
(Serial drama)

HIGGENBOTTOM, SERGEANT. See:
Crooke, Lennie

HIGGINS, English butler
DUNCAN MacROBERTS, his
employer
ALICE MacROBERTS, Duncan's
wife
TOMMY MacROBERTS
DINGHY MacROBERTS
JOANIE MacROBERTS, children
of Duncan and Alice
Our Man Higgins (TV) (Comedy)

HIGGINS, CLARABELLE. See:
Barclay, Doc

HIGGINS, DADDY. See:
Baby Snooks
Dragonette, Jessica (2)
Morgan, Frank (2)

HIGGINS, JOE. See: Everly,
Don

HIGGINS, LEFTY. See: Dawson,
Rosemary

HIGH. See also: Hy

High Adventure. See: Thomas,
Lowell (2)

High Chaparral, The. See: Cannon, John

High Finance. See: James, Dennis (2)

High Low. See: Barry, Jack (3)

High Road. See: Gunther, John

High Road, John Gunther's. See:
Gunther, John

High Street, The House on. See:
Abbott, Philip

High, Twelve O'Clock. See:
Savage, Brigadier General Frank

Highway, Lincoln. See: McIntire,
John

Highway Patrol. See:
Matthews, Dan
Taylor, Corporal Steve

HIGSBY-SMITH, MRS. See:
Grimm, Arnold

HILARY. See:
Hillery
Stockton, Sandy (2)

HILDA. See:
Abbott, John
Graves, Harry
Hope, Hilda
Hulda
Ruskin, Lily

HILDA CROCKER. See: Porter,
Pete

Hilda Hope, M.D. See: Hope,
Hilda

HILDA MARSHALL. See: Sunday

HILDEGARDE (1), (The Incompar-
able Hildegarde), hostess of the
program (herself)
MARVEL MAXWELL
MARILYN THORNE, featured
vocalists (themselves)
TED WEEMS
HARRY SOSNIK, orchestra
leaders (themselves)
THEIR ORCHESTRAS
Beat the Band (R) (Musical
quiz)

HILDEGARDE (2), (The Incomparable Hildegarde), featured vocalist on the program (herself)
The Raleigh Room (R) (Music)

HILDEGARDE, THE INCOMPARABLE. See: Hildegarde (1) (2)

HILDRETH, DICK, host of the program (himself)
MANY JAZZ-ROCK MUSICAL GROUPS
The Session (TV) (Music)

HILGEMEIER, EDWARD, JR. See: Narz, Jack (2)

Hill, Amanda of Honeymoon. See: Dyke, Charity Amanda

HILL, ANNE. See: Jordan, Joyce

HILL, EDWARD. See: Allen, Frederick Lewis

HILL, RUANE
JON TUSKA, hosts of the program (themselves)
They Went That 'a Way (TV)
(Biographies of old Western motion picture actors and clips from their films)

HILL TOPPERS, THE. See: Kelly, Joe (1)

Hillbillies, The Beverly. See: Clampett, Jed

HILLBILLY, THE PARK AVENUE. See: Jones, Spike (2)

HILLERY, JONATHAN. See: Davidson, Bill

HILLEY, JOHN C. See: Lord, Phillips H.

HILLIARD, HARRIET. See: Murray, Feg
Penner, Joe

HILLMAN, INDIA
CHUCK HILLMAN
REX COOPER
LAURA COOPER
TONY COOPER
BEN GRANT

ELLEN GRANT
DAVID GRANT
JILL GRANT
PAMMY DAVIS
RANDOLPH BUCHANAN
GINGER
BILL
MITCHELL FARMER
MR. MENEFEE
DR. KURTZ
MRS. PAULSEN
LORRAINE ADAMS
MARGARET
MR. MURCHISON
MRS. MURCHISON, characters appearing in the drama
Somerset (TV) (Serial drama)

Hilltop House. See: Johnson, Bess

HILLYER FIELD, LIZ. See: Karr, Mike

HILLYER, JULIE. See: Karr, Mike

HILLYER, ORRIN. See: Karr, Mike

HILTON. See also: Holton

HILTON, JAMES, author; narrator of the program (himself)
MANY ACTORS AND ACTRESSES
LYN MURRAY, orchestra leader (himself)
HIS ORCHESTRA
The Hallmark Playhouse (R)
(Drama) (Afterwards known as The Hallmark Radio Hall of Fame) (R)

HILTON, MARK. See: Randolph, Ellen

HIMBER, RICHARD, orchestra leader, host of the program (himself)
HIS ORCHESTRA
JOEY NASH, featured vocalist on the program (himself)
Studebaker Champions (R) (Music)

HIMBER, RICHARD. See also: Ross, Lanny
Whiteman, Paul

HINES, JEROME. See: Barlow,
Howard

HINK, ROBERT. See: Gook, Vic

HINK, SLOBBERT. See: Gook, Vic

HINNANT, SKIP. See: Cosby,
Bill (1)

HINSHAW, ERNIE. See: Beamer,
John

HIPPITY HOPPER. See: Bunny,
Bugs

HIPPO, FLIP THE. See: Pam

HIPPOCRATES BROWN. See:
Baines, Scattergood

HIRAM. See: Holliday, Hiram

Hiram Holliday, The Adventures of.
See: Holliday, Hiram

HIRAM NEVILLE. See: Dickey,
Dan'l

HIRAM WEATHERBEE. See:
Trent, Helen

Hire, Not For. See: Dekker,
Steve

HIRT, AL (1), trumpeter; star of
the program (himself)
MANY GUEST STARS
THE DON McKAYLE DANCERS
MORT LINDSEY, orchestra
leader (himself)
HIS ORCHESTRA
Al Hirt (TV) (Variety)

HIRT, AL (2)
THE CARPENTERS
PATCHETT AND TARSES
THE NEW DOODLETOWN PIPERS,
musicians, singers and enter-
tainers appearing on the program
(themselves)
MORT LINDSEY, orchestra lead-
er (himself)
HIS ORCHESTRA
MANY GUEST STARS
Make Your Own Kind of Music (TV)
(Music/variety)

His Honor, the Barber. See:
Fitz, Judge

History, Burbig's Syncopated. See:
Burbig, Henry

Hit, It's a. See: Felton, Happy

HIT PARADE DANCERS, THE.
See: Lanson, Snooky

HIT PARADE SINGERS, THE. See:
Lanson, Snooky

Hit Parade, Your. See:
Lanson, Snooky
Ross, Lanny

Hit the Jackpot. See: Cullen, Bill
(2)

HITCHCOCK, ALFRED, motion pic-
ture director and host of the
program (himself)
MANY ACTORS AND ACTRESSES
Alfred Hitchcock Presents (TV)
(Suspense drama) (later known as
The Alfred Hitchcock Hour) (TV)

HITCHCOCK, PRIVATE MARK.
See: Troy, Sergeant Sam

HITLER, ADOLF. See: Husing,
Ted

HITS AND A MISS. See:
Haymes, Dick
Hope, Bob (2)

Hits, Bits of. See: King, Jean
Paul

HOBART. See:
Crackerby, O.K.
Hubert

HOBBY. See also: Hoby

Hobby Lobby. See:
Elman, Dave (2)
Weaver, Charley

Hobby, Murder Is My. See: Drake,
Barton

Hobo, The Littlest. See: London

HOBY. See:

Gilman, Hoby
Hobby

HODES, ART, jazz musician; host
of the program (himself)
MANY GUEST MUSICIANS
Jazz Alley (TV) (Music)

HODGES, GILBERT
FRANK REYNOLDS, narrators of
the program (themselves)
OTHER NARRATORS
Directions (TV) (Current events)

HODGES, JOY. See: Kirby,
Durward

HODGES, VERN. See: Macauley,
Wes

HOFF, CARL. See: Crosby, Bob
(1)

HOFFA, PORTLAND. See: Allen,
Fred

HOFFMAN, DR. OSWALD J., host
of the program (himself)
The International Lutheran Hour
(R) (Religion)

HOFFMAN, DR. TED. See: Casey,
Dr. Ben

HOFFMAN, JULIA. See: Collins,
Barnabas

HOGAN, BARNEY. See: Cooper,
Dick

HOGAN, COLONEL ROBERT, U.S.
prisoner of war of Germans
NEWKIRK
KINCHLOE
LeBEAU
CARTER
BAKER, American prisoners of
war, with Hogan in Stalag 13
SCHULTZ, German sergeant
KLINK, commandant of Stalag 13;
Schultz' commanding officer
GENERAL BURKHALTER, Ameri-
can general officer
Hogan's Heroes (TV) (Comedy)

HOGAN, LIZZIE. See: Alexander,
Nick

HOGAN, MILDRED. See: Cooper,
Dick

HOGAN, SERGEANT JOAN. See:
Bilko, Sergeant Ernest

HOGAN, SNAKE. See: Edwards,
Lum

Hogan's Heroes. See: Hogan,
Colonel Robert

HOLBEIN, HANS. See: Henry
VIII, King of England

HOLBROOK, CAPTAIN MATT
LIEUT. JOHNNY RUSSO, police
detectives
The Detectives (TV) (Crime
fighting)

HOLBROOK, LINDA. See: Perry,
John

HOLCOMBE, HARRY. See:
Jostyn, Jay (1)

HOLDEN, GREY, captain of the
river boat "Enterprise"
BEN FRASER, his mate
BLAKE
CARNEY, members of his crew
Riverboat (TV) (Adventure)

HOLDEN, HELEN, "government
girl"
Helen Holden: Government Girl
(R) (Serial drama)

HOLDEN, MARK. See: Bauer,
Bertha

HOLDEN, NED. See: Rutledge,
Dr. John

HOLDEN, TORCHY REYNOLDS.
See: Rutledge, Dr. John

HOLIDAY. See also:
Halliday
Holliday

HOLIDAY, DAN, adventurer
Box 13 (R) (Adventure)

HOLIDAY, LAUREL, matron of
ancient Rome
GUS, her husband

HAP, her son
PRECOCIA, her daughter
GROOVIE, Hap's girl friend
BRUTUS, their pet lion
CLEO, lioness
EVICTOR, the Holidays' landlord;
all cartoon characters
The Roman Holidays (TV) (Cartoon)

Holiday Lodge. See: Miller,
Johnny

HOLIDAYS, THE. See: Godfrey,
Arthur (2)

Holidays, The Roman. See: Holiday, Laurel

HOLLANDER, GUNTHER. See:
Kelly, Joe (2)

HOLLIDAY. See also:
Halliday
Holiday

HOLLIDAY, ALICE, pre-teen age
girl
HER FATHER
HER MOTHER
SOAPY, her friend
This Is Alice (TV) (Situation
comedy)

HOLLIDAY, DOC. See: Earp,
Wyatt

HOLLIDAY, HIRAM, newspaper
proofreader, becomes adventurer
JOEL SMITH, reporter, his
friend and fellow-adventurer
The Adventures of Hiram Holliday (TV) (Adventure/comedy)

HOLLINGER, DON, magazine writer
ANN MARIE, his girl friend,
later his wife
ANN'S FATHER, restaurant owner
HER MOTHER
That Girl (TV) (Comedy)

HOLLISTER, AMBER. See: Cord

HOLLISTER, CLAY, sheriff of
Tombstone Territory
Tombstone Territory (TV) (Western)

HOLLISTER, DICK, cartoonist
PAULA, his wife
HARRY, fireman
OSCAR NORTH, actor; star of
television's "Jetman" program,
based on Hollister's comic strip
ANDREW HUMMEL, apartment
superintendent
He and She (TV) (Comedy)

Hollow, Happy. See: Peppertag,
Aaron

HOLLOWAY, DICK, host and commentator of the program (himself)
House Detective (TV) (Advice for
home buyers)

HOLLOWAY, HARRISON, master of
ceremonies of the program (himself)
VERA VAGUE
REGINALD CHEERILY
YAHBUT
FRANK WATANABE
OTHERS, entertainers featured
on the program
MANY GUEST STARS
OWEN SWEETEN, orchestra
leader (himself)
HIS ORCHESTRA
Blue Monday Jamboree (R)
(Variety)

HOLLY. See:
Carr, Alison
Forsyte, Soames
Haley
Healey
Healy
Sloan, Holly

HOLLY, BETH. See: Barbour,
Henry Wilson

HOLLY EMERSON. See: Harper,
Linda Emerson

HOLLY NORRIS. See: Bauer,
Bertha

Holly Sloan. See: Sloan, Holly

Holly Sloan, The Story of. See:
Sloan, Holly

HOLLY THORPE. See: Bauer,
Bertha

Hollywood A-Go-Go. See: Riddle,
Sam (2)

Hollywood and the Stars. See:
Cotten, Joseph (1)

Hollywood, Breakfast in. See:
Breneman, Tom (2)

Hollywood Calling. See: Murphy,
George

Hollywood Good News. See:
Stewart, James

Hollywood Hotel. See: Powell,
Dick (3)

Hollywood Jackpot. See: Delmar,
Kenny

Hollywood, Little Ol'. See: Alexander, Ben (4)

Hollywood, Man About. See:
McCall, George

Hollywood Movie, Rona Barrett's.
See: Barrett, Rona

Hollywood Palace, The. See:
Crosby, Bing (2)

Hollywood Playhouse. See: Ameche,
Jim

Hollywood, So This Is. See:
Dugan, Queenie

Hollywood Squares, The. See:
Marshall, Peter

Hollywood: The Dream Factory.
See: Cavett, Dick (2)

Hollywood Today. See: Graham,
Sheilah

HOLM. See also: Home

HOLM, CELESTE. See: Wallace,
Mike (5)

HOLMES, EILEEN. See: Harding,
Karen Adams

HOLMES, PATRICIA. See:
Templar, Simon

HOLMES, SHERLOCK, famous
British private detective
DR. JOHN WATSON, his friend
and associate
PROFESSOR MORIARTY, his
enemy, "the Napoleon of Crime"
The Adventures of Sherlock
Holmes (R) (Detective drama)

HOLSTRUM, KATY, Minnesota
farm girl, employed by Glen
Morley as governess to his
children
GLEN MORLEY, widowed con-
gressman
STEVE MORLEY
DANNY MORLEY, Glen's children
MRS. MORLEY, Glen's widowed
mother
The Farmer's Daughter (TV)
(Situation comedy)

HOLT, MARY. See: Brent, Dr.
Jim

HOLT, RACHEL. See: Bracken,
John

HOLTON. See also: Hilton

HOLTON, DR. STANLEY. See:
Manning, Portia Blake

HOME. See also: Holm

Home, Dorothy Dix at. See: Dix,
Dorothy (1)

Home Hour, The National Farm and.
See: Mitchell, Everett

Home of the Brave. See: Joe (1)

Home Sweet Home. See: Kent,
Fred

Home, The Soldier Who Came.
See: Cameron, Barry

Homemaker's Exchange, Eleanor
Howe's. See: Howe, Eleanor

HOMER BROWN. See: Aldrich,
Henry

HOMER NELSON, CHIEF PETTY
OFFICER. See: O'Toole,
Ensign

HOMER SMITH. See: Peters,
Lowell

Hondo. See: Lane, Hondo

HONDO. See: Lane, Hondo

Honest Harold. See: Honest Harold

HONEST HAROLD, radio commentator
GLORIA, his girl friend
The Hal Peary Show (R) (Situation
comedy) (also known as Honest
Harold) (R)

HONEY. See: West, Honey

HONEY AND THE BEES. See:
Waring, Fred (1)

HONEY CHILE. See: Hope, Bob
(2)

"HONEY" JOHNSON, MARGARET.
See: Butterworth, Wally

HONEY ROBINSON. See: Bratter,
Paul

Honey West. See: West, Honey

HONEYBEE. See: Riley, Chester
A.

Honeymoon Hill, Amanda of. See:
Dyke, Charity Amanda

Honeymoon in New York. See:
Kirby, Durward

Honeymoon, Second. See: Parks,
Bert (5)

Honeymooners, The. See: Kramden, Ralph

Honeysuckle, Moonshine and. See:
Gaddis, Cracker

HONEYWELL, OLIVER. See:
Gildersleeve, Throckmorton P.

Hong Kong. See: Evans, Glenn

HONOCHECK, CAPTAIN GUS. See:
Gower, Matthew

Honolulu Bound. See: Baker, Phil
(1)

Honor, Guest of. See: Nielsen,
Leslie (2)

Honor, Nancy James, Her. See:
James, Nancy

Honor, Radio's Court of. See:
Towne, Don

HOOD, GREGORY, detective
SANDY, his associate
The Case Book of Gregory Hood
(R) (Mystery)

HOOD, ROBIN, medieval outlaw
living in Sherwood Forest with
his followers
FRIAR TUCK
WILL SCARLETT
LITTLE JOHN, his followers
MAID MARIAN, his friend
SIR PETER MARSTON
SIR SIMON
THE SHERIFF OF NOTTINGHAM,
his enemies
Robin Hood (TV) (Adventure)
(also called The Adventures of
Robin Hood) (TV)

Hood, The Black. See: Cop, The

HOODOO, HORATIO J., evil magi-
cian
MARK, teenage boy, visits Lids-
ville
GENII, Mark's friend
INHABITANTS OF LIDSVILLE
Lidsville (TV) (Children's fan-
tasy/comedy)

HOOK, CAPTAIN. See: Pan,
Peter

Hook 'n' Ladder Follies. See:
Walt, Captain

HOOKER, JUDGE. See: Gildersleeve, Throckmorton P.

HOOKEY, BOBBY. See:
Edwards, Ralph (1)
Loveridge, Marion

HOOKSTRATTEN, CHUCK. See:
Banner, Woody

HOOLEY, GIL. See: Big Jon

HOOPER. See also:
Harper
Hopper

HOOPER, LARRY. See: Welk,
Lawrence

HOOPER, MR. See: Cookie
Monster, The

HOOPES, NED, educator; host of
the program (himself)
PANEL OF CHILDREN
Reading Room (TV) (Book discussion by children)

HOOPLE. See also: Hopple

HOOPLE, MAJOR AMOS, loqua-
cious, portly resident of boarding
house
MARTHA, his wife, proprietress
of boarding house
Major Hoople (R) (Comedy)

HOOSIER HOT SHOTS, THE. See:
Kelly, Joe (1)

Hootenanny. See: Linkletter, Jack
(3)

HOOTON, BABS, New York woman,
operating dude ranch in New
Mexico
BILL
BROOK, her sons
MRS. CRAWFORD, her mother
LONESOME, ranch hand
HAWKEYE, Indian storekeeper,
friend of Babs Hooton
Guestward Ho! (TV) (Comedy)

HOOVER, MARGARET. See:
Hartley, Dr. Robert

HOP. See: Harrigan, Hop

Hop Harrigan, America's Ace of
the Airways. See: Harrigan,
Hop

HOP SING. See: Cartwright, Ben

HOPALONG. See: Cassidy, Hopalong

Hopalong Cassidy. See: Cassidy,
Hopalong

HOPE. See:
Bauer, Bertha
Carter, Hope
Winslow, Hope

HOPE ALISON. See: Jordan,
Joyce

HOPE, BOB (1), master of cere-
monies of the program (himself)
OTHER MASTERS OF CERE-
MONY
MANY ACTOR AND ACTRESS
AWARD WINNERS
The Academy Awards (TV)
(Motion picture awards)

HOPE, BOB (2), comedian; star
of the program (himself)
THE PROFESSOR
VERA VAGUE
BRENDA
COBINA
HONEY CHILE
JOHN L. C. SIVONEY
MIRIAM, characters appearing
on the program
HITS AND A MISS, vocal group
SKINNAY ENNIS
LES BROWN, orchestra leaders
(themselves)
THEIR ORCHESTRAS
MANY GUEST STARS
The Bob Hope Show (R) (Comedy)

HOPE, BOB (3), host of the pro-
gram (himself)
VARIOUS MOTION PICTURES
Bob Hope Theater (TV) (Motion
pictures) (also known as Bob
Hope Presents the Chrysler
Theater) (TV) (later reissued as
The N.B.C. Adventure Theater)
(TV)

HOPE, BOB. See also: Martin,
Dean (1)

HOPE, HILDA, physician
Hilda Hope, M.D. (R) (Drama)

HOPE MELTON EVANS. See:
Wayne, Ruth Evans

HOPE WAYNE MUNKS. See:
Brown, Ellen

HOPEWELL, ALLISON. See:
Ames, Peter

HOPKINS, KATE
TOM HOPKINS
DIANE PERS
ROBERT ATWOOD
JESSIE ATWOOD
TRUDY
ELISE
LOUISE, characters appearing in
the drama
Kate Hopkins, Angel of Mercy (R)
(Serial drama)

HOPKINS, MRS. See: Marlin, Mary

HOPKINS, MRS. FRED. See:
Graham, Dr. Bob

HOPKINS, PEGGY
TED HOPKINS
BELLBOYS, characters appearing
in the drama
Hello, Peggy (R) (Serial drama)

HOPPER. See also:
Harper
Hooper

HOPPER, DeWOLF, actor
ELIZABETH LOVE, actress, fea-
tured on the program (themselves)
MANY OTHER ACTORS AND
ACTRESSES
Roses and Drums (R) (Historical
dramas)

HOPPER, HIPPITY. See: Bunny,
Bugs

HOPPLE. See also: Hoople

HOPPLE, MARY. See: Weems,
Ambrose J.

HORACE. See:
Heidt, Horace (1) (2)
Horse
Hoss

HORACE CAPP, SERGEANT. See:
Rice, Lieut. Bill

HORACE HEIDT. See:
Bower, Roger
Grauer, Ben (2)
Heidt, Horace (1) (2)

Horace Heidt, A Night With. See:
Heidt, Horace (2)

Horace Heidt's Show Wagon. See:
Heidt, Horace (1)

HORACE SUTTON. See: Malone,
Dr. Jerry

HORACE TRENT. See: Young,
Larry "Pepper"

HORATIO. See: Hoodoo, Horatio
J.

HORATIO BULLWINKLE. See:
Brennan, Tugboat Annie

HORATIO K. BOOMER. See:
McGee, Fibber

Horizon, Bright. See: West,
Michael

Horizons, Medical. See: Goddard,
Don

HORLICK, HARRY. See: Parker,
Frank

HORN, AGGIE
GERTRUDE STONE
EDGAR LEE
MONICA LEE
MARTIN LEE
GWYN JENNINGS
BALDY
BEANIE
WILLIAMS, characters appear-
ing in the drama
In Care of Aggie Horn (R)
(Serial drama)

Horn and Hardart Children's Hour,
The. See: Edwards, Ralph (1)

HORNE, LENA. See: Cross,
Milton (1)

HORNEIGH, TYRONE. See: Rowan,
Dan

Hornet, The Green. See: Reid,
Britt

HORNET, THE GREEN. See:
Reid, Britt

HOROWITZ. See:
Horwitz
Luigi

HORRIBLY, CLAUDE. See: Allen,
Steve (2)

HORSE. See also:
Horace
Hoss

HORSE, CHARLIE. See: Lewis,
Shari

HORSE, CRAZY. See: Custer,
George Armstrong

HORSE OF THE WORLD, THE
WONDER. See: Mix, Tom

Horse, The Iron. See: Calhoun,
Ben

HORSE, THE IRON. See: Calhoun,
Ben

HORTENSE. See: Morgan, Henry

HORTON, CAPTAIN. See: Rango

HORTON, DR. TOM, physician
DR. LAURA HORTON
MICKEY HORTON
MICHAEL HORTON
ALICE HORTON
MARIE HORTON
PHILIP HORTON
DR. MARK BROOKS
JOHN McGUIRE
ELLEN McGUIRE
DR. WILLIAM HORTON
SUSAN MARTIN
DR. GREG PETERS
DR. DOUG WILLIAMS
MARY ANDREWS
SCOTT BANNING
LOGAN SCHMIDT
RICK
SHELAH HAMMOND
RUTHIE
KITTY
SARAH, characters appearing in
the drama
Days of Our Lives (TV) (Serial
drama)

HORTON, DOT, wife
WILL HORTON, her husband
MOTHER ALDRIDGE, her mother
MOTHER HORTON, Will's mother
PROFESSOR KNAPP
MADGE

JULIA
ROGER
DULCY
ROSIE
CORINNE
PETE SLOAN
MARIETTA, characters appear-
ing in the drama
Dot and Will (R) (Serial drama)

HORTON, EDWARD EVERETT.
See: Jolson, Al

HORWICH, DR. FRANCES, educator; moderator of the program (herself)
MANY JUVENILE STUDENTS
Ding Dong School (TV) (Education)

HORWITZ. See also: Horowitz

HORWITZ, HANS
ADAM GARNER
FRANK MITTLER
GEORGE ROBERT
EDWARD EDSON
VEE PADWA, classical pianists,
featured on the program (them-
selves)
The First Piano Quartet (R)
(Classical music, arranged for
four pianos)

HOSKINS, JELLY. See: Lancer,
Murdoch

Hospital, General. See: Hardy,
Dr. Steven

HOSS. See:
Cartwright, Ben
Horace
Horse

HOST, YOUR. See: Raymond

Hostess, Your. See: Wright,
Cobina

Hot Dog. See: Worley, Jo Anne

Hot Hour, The Jerry Reed When
You're Hot You're. See: Reed,
Jerry

Hot Line, Dial. See: Lincoln,
Dr. Matt

"HOT LIPS" HOULIHAN, MAJOR.
See: Pierce, Captain Hawkeye

HOT, MARY. See: Brent, Dr.
Jim

HOT SHOTS, THE HOOSIER. See:
Kelly, Joe (1)

Hot Summer, The Long. See:
Varner, Will

HOTBREATH HOULIHAN. See:
Durante, Jimmy

Hotel Cosmopolitan. See: Woods,
Donald

Hotel de Paree. See: Sundance

Hotel For Pets. See: Jolly, Mr.

Hotel, Grand. See: Ameche, Don
(3)

Hotel, Hawthorne. See: Liston,
Lois

Hotel, Hollywood. See: Powell,
Dick (3)

HOTSHOT CHARLIE. See: Lee,
Terry

HOULIHAN, HOTBREATH. See:
Durante, Jimmy

HOULIHAN, MAJOR "HOT LIPS."
See: Pierce, Captain Hawkeye

HOUND. See: Huckleberry Hound

Hound, The Sea. See: Silver,
Captain

Houndcats, The. See: Houndcats,
The

HOUNDCATS, THE, cartoon char-
acters
The Houndcats (TV) (Comedy
Western cartoon)

Hour, America's. See: Welles,
Orson (1)

Hour, Caesar's. See: Caesar,
Sid (2)

Hour, Jimmy Durante Presents the
Lennon Sisters. See: Lennon,
Janet

Hour, Major Bowes and His Original Amateur. See: Bowes,
Major Edward (2)

Hour of Charm, The. See: Spitalny,
Phil

Hour of Great Mysteries, The Dow.
See: Welch, Joseph N.

Hour of Smiles, The. See: Allen,
Fred

Hour, Pat Paulsen's Half a Comedy.
See: Paulsen, Pat

Hour, Ted Mack's Amateur. See:
Mack, Ted

Hour, The Army. See: Herlihy,
Ed

Hour, The Capitol Family. See:
Bowes, Major Edward (1)

Hour, The Carnation Contented.
See: Faith, Percy

Hour, The Chase and Sanborn.
See:
Ameche, Don (1)
Cantor, Eddie (2)

Hour, The Children's. See:
Cross, Milton (2)

Hour, The Colgate Comedy. See:
Martin, Dean (1)

Hour, The Contented. See: Faith,
Percy

Hour, The Cuckoo. See: Weems,
Ambrose J.

Hour, The Electric. See: Eddy,
Nelson (1)

Hour, The Eleventh. See: Bassett,
Dr. Theodore

Hour, The Eveready. See: Drew,
John

Hour, The Family. See: Bowes,
Major Edward (1)

Hour, The Fleischmann's. See:
Vallee, Rudy (2)

Hour, The Flintstone Comedy.
See: Flintstone, Fred

Hour, The Ford Summer. See:
Melton, James (1)

Hour, The Glen Campbell Goodtime.
See: Campbell, Glen

Hour, The Goodwill. See: Anthony,
Mr.

Hour, The Horn and Hardart Children's. See: Edwards Ralph (1)

Hour, The International Lutheran.
See: Hoffman, Dr. Oswald J.

Hour, The Jerry Reed When You're
Hot You're Hot. See: Reed,
Jerry

Hour, The Jim Nabors. See:
Nabors, Jim

Hour, The John Byner Comedy.
See: Byner, John (1)

Hour, The Julie Andrews. See:
Andrews, Julie

Hour, The Kate Smith. See:
Smith, Kate (1)

Hour, The Majestic Theater. See:
Two Black Crows, The (1)

Hour, The Major Bowes Family.
See: Bowes, Major Edward (1)

Hour, The National Farm and Home.
See: Mitchell, Everett

Hour, The Old-Fashioned Revival.
See: Fuller, Rev. Charles E.

Hour, The Prudential Family. See:
Taylor, Deems

Hour, The Railroad. See: Mac-
Rae, Gordon (2)

Hour, The Red Skelton. See:
Junior

Hour, The Sealtest. See: Vallee,
Rudy (2)

Hour, The Smothers Brothers
Comedy. See: Smothers, Tom
(1)

Hour, The Sonny and Cher Comedy.
See: Bono, Salvatore

Hour, The Ted Mack Family. See:
Bowes, Major Edward (1)

Hour, The Telephone. See: Bell,
Alexander Graham

Hour, The Tim Conway Comedy.
See: Conway, Tim

Hour, The United States Steel.
See: Langner, Lawrence

Hour With Mary and Bob, The True
Story. See: Mary

House, Broadway Open. See:
Lester, Jerry

House Coffee Time, Maxwell. See:
Morgan, Frank (2)

House Detective. See: Holloway,
Dick

House, Doctor in the. See: Upton,
Michael

House, Hilltop. See: Johnson,
Bess

House in the Country, The. See:
Husband

House of Glass, The. See: Glass,
Bessie

House of Mystery, The. See:
Elliott, Roger

House of Squibb, Music From the.
See: Ives, Burl (2)

House on High Street, The. See:
Abbott, Philip

House Party. See: Linkletter, Art
(1)

House, Rainbow. See: Emery,
Bob

House, Trouble. See: Booth,
Martha

House, Uncle Walter's Dog. See:
Uncle Walter

House, Woman in My. See:
Carter, James

Houseboat Hannah. See: O'Leary,
Hannah

HOUSEBOY, CHINESE. See:
Higby, Mary Jane

HOUSEMAN, DAVID. See: Fairchild, Kay

HOUSTON, ALEC. See: Hamilton,
George

HOUSTON, BILLY. See: Allen,
Joan Houston

HOUSTON, CLYDE. See: Law-
ton, Lora

HOUSTON, DOT. See: Allen,
Joan Houston

HOUSTON, IRIS. See: Lawton,
Lora

HOUSTON, JOE. See: Graham,
Dr. Bob

HOUSTON, ROBERT. See: Allen,
Joan Houston

HOUSTON, TEMPLE, lawyer; son
of Sam Houston
GEORGE TAGGART, gunslinger
turned lawman
Temple Houston (TV) (Western)

HOVIS. See also: Novis

HOVIS, LARRY. See:
Martindale, Wink (2)
Rowan, Dan

How Do You Rate? See: Reddy,
Tom

How to Marry a Millionaire. See:
Jones, Loco

HOWARD. See:
Adams, Howard
Barlow, Howard
Finucane, Lieut. Howard
Miller, Howard
Smith, Howard K. (1) (2)
Thurston, Howard

HOWARD, ANN. See: Peyton,
Martin

HOWARD BARLOW. See:
Barlow, Howard
Mary
Melton, James (2)

HOWARD, BOB. See: Seymour,
Dan

HOWARD BORDEN. See: Hartley,
Dr. Robert

HOWARD, CATHERINE. See:
Henry VIII, King of England

HOWARD CHANDLER, DR. See:
Chandler, Dr. Susan

HOWARD, CLAY. See: Welk,
Lawrence

HOWARD COSELL. See:
Jackson, Keith (2)
McKay, Jim (1)

HOWARD, EDDIE. See: Whiteman,
Paul

HOWARD, GLENN, magazine pub-
lisher
DAVE COREY
JEFF DILLON
DAN FARRELL, reporter/writers
PEGGY MAXWELL, researcher
The Name of the Game (TV)
(Crime adventure)

HOWARD, JIM, professor of
anthropology at college
MARTHA, his wife
TEDDY, his eight-year-old son
P.J., his married son
WENDY, P.J.'s wife
JAKE, eight-year-old son of
P.J. and Wendy

LUTHER QUINCE, Jim Howard's colleague
The Jimmy Stewart Show (TV) (Family comedy)

HOWARD, JOE. See: Kay, Beatrice

HOWARD, MRS. See: Farrell, David

HOWARD MORRIS. See: Caesar, Sid (2) (3) Stokey, Mike

HOWARD, MORTY. See: Moylan, Marianne

HOWARD ROBERTS SINGERS, THE. See: Uggams, Leslie

HOWARD, SPENCER. See: Joe (1)

HOWARD SPRAGUE. See: Jones, Sam

Howard Thurston, the Magician. See: Thurston, Howard

HOWARD, TINA COLE. See: Driggs, Karleton King

HOWARD, TOM (1), moderator of the program (himself)
LULU McCONNELL
HARRY McNAUGHTON
GEORGE SHELTON, panelists (themselves)
GUEST PANELISTS
It Pays To Be Ignorant (R) (TV) (Comedy quiz)

HOWARD, TOM (2)
GEORGE SHELTON, comedians, starred on the program (themselves)
THE ETON BOYS, vocal group, featured on the program
MANY GUEST STARS
RAY BLOCH, orchestra leader (himself)
HIS ORCHESTRA
Model Minstrels (R) (Music/comedy)

HOWARD, WILLIE
EUGENE HOWARD, his brother,

comedians featured on the program (themselves)
MANY GUEST STARS
The Folies Bergere of the Air (R) (Variety)

HOWDY. See: Doody, Howdy

Howdy Doody. See: Doody, Howdy

HOWDY LEWIS. See: Jones, Ben

HOWE, ANN. See: Palooka, Joe

HOWE, ELEANOR, homemaking expert
Eleanor Howe's Homemaker's Exchange (R) (Homemaking)

HOWE, JOSEPH. See: Baker, Dean Fred

HOWE, QUINCY. See: Shadel, Bill

HOWELL. See: Gilligan

HOWELL, GEORGE. See: Hammond, Liza

HOWELL, MRS. See: Gilligan

HOWELL, WAYNE. See: Lester, Jerry

HOWETH, EVIE. See: Hutton, Ina Ray

HOWIE. See:
Dillon, Marshal Matt
Macauley, Wes
Wing, Howie

HOWIE DAWSON. See: Hardy, Dr. Steven

HOWIE DICKERSON. See: Simms, Paul

Howie Wing. See: Wing, Howie

How's Your Mother-in-Law? See: Martindale, Wink (2)

HOYT, ANDY. See: Young, Larry "Pepper"

HOYT, VIKKI ADAMS, housewife

ROGER HOYT, her husband
HER FATHER
HER MOTHER
AUNT DEBBIE, Roger's aunt
PAMELA TOWERS, Roger's old
girl friend
LORETTA, Vikki's matron of
honor
MIKE, Loretta's husband
Marriage For Two (R) (Serial
drama)

HUBBARD, EVE. See: Buell,
Roger

HUBBARD, HERB. See: Buell,
Roger

HUBBELL, GRANDPA. See:
O'Neill, Mrs.

HUBERT. See also: Hobart

HUBERT UPDYKE. See: Young,
Alan

HUBIE DODD. See: Dugan, Queenie

HUCK. See:
Finn, Huck
Hack

Huck Finn, The New Adventures of.
See: Finn, Huck

HUCKLEBERRY. See: Finn,
Huckleberry

Huckleberry Finn, The Adventures
of. See: Finn, Huckleberry

Huckleberry Hound. See: Huckleberry Hound

HUCKLEBERRY HOUND, dog; cartoon character
Huckleberry Hound (TV) (Cartoon)

HUCKO, PEANUTS. See: Welk,
Lawrence

HUDDLES, ED, star quarterback
MARGE, his wife
POM POM, their daughter
BUBBA McCOY, football center
PENNY, Bubba's wife
CLAUDE PERTWEE, coach
FREIGHT TRAIN, football player

SLIPPERY CHARLIE, football
player, all cartoon characters
Where's Huddles? (TV) (Cartoon feature)

HUDDLESTON, DICK. See:
Edwards, Lum

HUDDLESTON, JOE. See: Adams,
Lieut. Price

HUDSON, DR. WAYNE, physician
KATHY, his daughter
Dr. Hudson's Secret Journal (TV)
(Medical drama)

HUDSON, DORIS. See: Coffee,
Dr. Daniel

HUDSON, EDGAR. See: Davidson,
Bill

HUDSON, HELENE. See: Lawton,
Lora

HUDSON, JIM. See: Prescott,
Kate Hathaway

HUDSON, NANCY SMITH, daughter
of President of the United States
DR. ADAM HUDSON, her husband,
veterinarian
ABBY, her chaperone
UNCLE EVERETT, Dr. Adam
Hudson's uncle
TURNER
RODRIGUEZ, secret service
men guarding Nancy
Nancy (TV) (Comedy)

HUER, DR. See: Rogers, Buck

HUGH. See:
Downs, Hugh
Drummond, Captain Hugh
Hefner, Hugh
North, Major Hugh
Reilly, Hugh
Rowlands, Hugh

HUGH CLAYBORN. See: Ames,
Peter

HUGH DOWNS. See:
Clayton, Bob (1)
Downs, Hugh
Paar, Jack

HUGH FARR. See: Nolan, Bob

HUGH JESSUP, DR. See: Prescott,
Kate Hathaway

HUGHES, ALICE. See: Malone,
Dr. Jerry

HUGHES, CAPTAIN. See: Armstrong, Jack

HUGHES, CHRIS, attorney
  NANCY HUGHES, his wife
  PENNY HUGHES
  DON HUGHES
  BOB HUGHES, their children
  GRANDPA HUGHES, Chris' father
  EDITH HUGHES, Chris' spinster
  sister; paramour of Jim Lowell
  JEFF BAKER, marries Penny
  Hughes
  JIM LOWELL, attorney; Chris'
  law partner, Edith's lover; dies
  CLAIRE LOWELL, Jim's wife
  ELLEN LOWELL, teenage daugh-
  ter of Jim and Claire
  JUDGE LOWELL, Jim's father
  MARK RYDELL
  LISA SHEA
  HANNAH CORD
  CHUCK HENDERSON
  EMMA
  ELIZABETH STUART
  PAUL STUART
  DAN STUART
  JULIA STUART
  SUSAN STUART
  BARBARA RYAN
  JENNY RYAN
  EMILY STUART
  TOM HUGHES
  CAROL DENNING
  DR. DAVID STUART
  ELLEN STUART
  BETSY STUART
  DR. JOHN DICKSON
  JANE WILEY
  JERRY SMITH
  PEGGY REGAN
  DR. LONSBERRY
  MRS. MILLER
  DR. TIM COLE
  LOUISE COLE
  DR. DOUGLAS CASSEN
  LARRY WINTERS
  TOM POPE, characters appear-
  ing in the drama
  As the World Turns (TV) (Serial
  drama)

HUGHES, DONALD. See: Halop,
Billy

HUGHES, LISA, divorcee
  DR. BOB HUGHES, her husband
  HELEN ELDRIDGE, society
  matron
  JOHN ELDRIDGE
  TOM ELDRIDGE, Helen's sons
  EVE ELDRIDGE, Helen's daugh-
  ter, Lisa's girl friend
  DAVID STEWART
  SANDY LARSON
  DR. TONY LARSON
  BRAD ROBINSON, characters
  appearing in the drama
  Our Private World (TV) (Serial
  drama)

HUGHES, MRS. JESSIE. See:
Malone, Dr. Jerry

HUGHES, ROBBIE. See: Malone,
Dr. Jerry

HUGHES, RUSH. See:
Grauer, Ben (2)
Kaye, Danny

HUGHES, TOM. See: Jordan,
Joyce

HUGHES, TOMMY. See: Wilson,
Steve

HUGHEY, BARBARA. See:
O'Leary, Hannah

HUGHEY, BOSS. See: O'Leary,
Hannah

HUJAZ, PETER. See: Marlin,
Mary

HULDA. See:
Brown, Ellen
Hilda

HULICK, WILBUR BUDD
  FRED UTTAL
  ARLENE FRANCIS, quizmasters
  and quizmistress on the program
  (themselves)
  MANY CONTESTANTS
  What's My Name? (R) (Quiz)

HULICK, WILBUR BUDD. See
also:

Pitcher, The
Stoopnagle, Colonel Lemuel Q.
(2)

HULL, HENRY, actor, featured on
the program (himself)
True Story Theater (R) (Drama)

HULL, SHERMAN. See: Farrell,
Charlie

HULL, WARREN (1), quizmaster
of the program (himself)
MANY CONTESTANTS
Spin to Win (R) (Quiz)

HULL, WARREN (2), master of
ceremonies of the program (himself)
MANY AUDIENCE PARTICIPANTS
Strike It Rich (R) (TV) (Financial
aid)
TODD RUSSELL, master of
ceremonies of the program (himself)
Strike It Rich (R)

HULL, WARREN (3), interviewer on
the program (himself)
MANY NEWSWORTHY INTER-
VIEWEES
Who In the World? (TV) (Interviews of persons recently in the
headlines)

HULL, WARREN. See also:
Fields, Arthur
Henry, Captain
Johnson, Parks

Hullabaloo. See: Jones, Jack

HULSE, HERBERT. See: Barry,
Jack (9)

Human Bondage, Of. See: Carey,
Dr. Philip

HUMAN CHATTERBOX, THE. See:
Blurt, Elmer

Human Relations, The Court of.
See: Alexander, A.L. (3)

HUMBARD, REX, evangelist; host
of the program (himself)
MAUDE AIMEE HUMBARD, his
wife, gospel singer (herself)

Rex Humbard (TV) (Religion)

HUME CRONYN. See: Arthur,
Jack (2)

HUMMEL, ANDREW. See:
Hollister, Dick

HUMPERDINCK, ENGELBERT,
singer; host of the program
(himself)
MANY GUEST STARS
The Engelbert Humperdinck
Show (TV) (Music/variety)

HUMPERDINCK, ENGELBERT.
See also: Crosby, Bing (2)

HUMPHREY. See:
Flack, Colonel Humphrey
Hastings, Bill

HUMPHREY, DALE. See:
Brent, Dr. Jim

HUMPHREY MANNERS. See:
Keene, Kitty

HUMPHRIES, MRS. See: Jackson, Martha

Hunch, Play Your. See: Griffin,
Merv (2)

Hundred, Cain's. See: Cain,
Nicholas

Hundred Years, The Second. See:
Carpenter, Luke

HUNGARIAN GIANT, THE
IMPY THE MIDGET, characters
appearing on the program
Cloak and Dagger (R) (Drama)

HUNK MARRINER. See: Rogers,
Major Robert

HUNKINS. See: Perkins, Ma

HUNNICUT, CLAY. See: Miller,
Socrates

Hunt Club, The Fish and. See:
Bickart, Sanford

HUNT, ELLA. See: Waring,
Evelyn

HUNT, FRANCES. See: Lane,
Richard

HUNT, HELEN. See: Sterling,
Vanessa Dale

Hunt, Melody Treasure. See:
Ballard, Pat

HUNT, MR. See: Waring, Evelyn

HUNT, ROSE. See: Sunday

Hunt, Sea. See: Nelson, Mike

HUNT, TEDDY. See: Waring,
Evelyn

Hunt, Treasure. See: Murray,
Jan (4)

HUNTER BARBOUR, ELAINE. See:
Barbour, Henry Wilson

HUNTER, DR. PAUL, chief of
medicine at Benjamin Craig
Institute of New Medicine
DR. DAVID CRAIG, physician
DR. TED STUART, surgeon
The Bold Ones (The Doctors) (TV)
(Medical drama)

HUNTER, JUDGE GLENN. See:
Barbour, Henry Wilson

HUNTER, MEL, government agent,
6 inches tall
BILL WINTERS, his normal sized
partner
The World of Giants (TV) (Adventure)

Hunters, Headline. See: Thomas,
Lowell (1)

Hunting Club of the Air, The Fishing
and. See: Begley, Martin

Huntley-Brinkley Report, The. See:
Huntley, Chet (1)

HUNTLEY, CHET (1)
DAVID BRINKLEY, newscasters
(themselves)
The Huntley-Brinkley Report
(TV) (News)

HUNTLEY, CHET (2), newscaster;

commentator of the program (himself)
Outlook (TV) (News/commentary)

HUNTLEY, CHET (3), newscaster;
commentator of the program
(himself)
Time: Present (TV) (News
analysis)

HUNTLEY, LEONARD. See:
Harding, Karen Adams

HUNTLEY, LLOYD. See:
Winchell, Walter (1)

HURLEY, GEORGE. See:
Brent, Dr. Jim

HURLEY, JIM. See: Begley,
Martin

HURLEY, MRS. See: Brent,
Dr. Jim

HUSBAND
WIFE
PLUMBER
SHOPKEEPER
TELEPHONE OPERATOR, char-
acters appearing on the program
The House in the Country (R)
(Serial drama)

Husband, My Favorite. See:
Cooper, Liz

Husband, Second. See: Cummings,
Brenda

HUSBAND, THE HENPECKED.
See: Junior

Husbands and Wives. See: Miles,
Allie Lowe

HUSH PUPPY. See: Lewis,
Shari

HUSING, TED
WESTBROOK VAN VOORHIS
HARRY VON ZELL, narrators
on the program (themselves)
FRANKLIN D. ROOSEVELT,
President of the United States
ELEANOR ROOSEVELT, his
wife
ADOLF HITLER

JOSEF STALIN
BENITO MUSSOLINI
NEVILLE CHAMBERLAIN
WINSTON CHURCHILL
KING FAROUK, international
political figures portrayed on
the program
The March of Time (R) (Documentary)

HUTCHINSON, MA
JEAN CARTER
TEX, circus performers
SALLY, trapeze artist
RUTH, knife thrower
The Mighty Show (R) (Circus
drama)

HUTCHINSON, MRS. See: Tena

HUTCHINSON, PAUL. See: Johnson, Bess

HUTSON, TOM. See: Bracken,
John

HUTTON, GUNILLA. See: Owens,
Buck

HUTTON, INA RAY, leader of all-
girl orchestra and hostess of the
program (herself)
DEE DEE BALL
HELEN SMITH
MARGARET RINKER
JANIE DAVIS
HARRIET BLACKBURN
JUDY VAN EUER
MICKEY ANDERSON
EVIE HOWETH
HELEN WOOLEY
LOIS CRONEN
PEGGY FAIRBANKS
HELEN HAMMOND
ZOE ANN WILLY, featured
musicians in the orchestra (them-
selves)
The Ina Ray Hutton Show (TV)
(Popular music)

HUTTON, ROLAND B., JR. See:
Lewis, Dave

HUXLEY, CAPTAIN. See:
Pomeroy, Susanna

HY. See also: High

HY GARDNER. See:
James, Dennis (3)
Johnson, Van
Moore, Garry (5)

HYAMS, HARRY. See: Welk,
Lawrence

HYATT, PROFESSOR CARL.
See: Corey, Don

I Am the Law. See: Kirby, Lieut.

I Deal in Crime. See: Gargan,
    William (1)

I Dream of Jeannie. See: Nelson,
    Major Tony

I Led Three Lives. See: Phil-
    brick, Herbert

I Love a Mystery. See: Packard,
    Jack

I Love Linda Dale. See: Dale,
    Linda

I Love Lucy. See: Ricardo, Ricky

I. Magination, Mr. See: Tripp,
    Paul

I Married Joan. See: Stevens,
    Joan

I.Q. BUGALOO. See: Bizarre,
    Benita

I.Q., DR. (The Mental Banker),
    quizmaster of the program, por-
    trayed by Lew Valentine
    MANY AUDIENCE CONTESTANTS
    Dr. I.Q. (R) (Quiz)

I.Q. JR., DR., quizmaster of the
    program, portrayed by Lew
    Valentine
    MANY AUDIENCE CONTESTANTS
    Dr. I.Q., Jr. (R) (Children's
    quiz)

I Search for Adventure. See:
    Douglas, Jack (1)

I Spy. See: Scott, Alexander

IAN. See: Keith, Ian

Ice, Music on. See: Desmond,
    Johnny

Ice Palace. See: Davidson, John
    (1)

ICHABOD ADAMS. See: Major,
    Bob

Ichabod and Me. See: Major, Bob

ICHABOD "ICHY" MUDD. See:
    Midnight, Captain

"ICHY" MUDD, ICHABOD. See:
    Midnight, Captain

IDA. See: Allen, Ida Bailey

Ida Bailey Allen. See: Allen,
    Ida Bailey

IDA, IDAHO. See: Wallet,
    Skeezix

IDA LUPINO. See:
    Boyer, Charles
    Frees, Paul

IDAHO IDA. See: Wallet,
    Skeezix

If You Had a Million. See:
    Anthony, Michael

Ignorant, It Pays To Be. See:
    Howard, Tom (1)

IKE DAWSON. See: Taylor,
    Danny

IKE, UKULELE. See: Lane,
    Richard

ILKA CHASE. See:
    Donald, Peter
    Glad, Gladys

I'll Bet. See: Narz, Jack (3)

I'll Never Forget. See: Luther,
    Frank (1)

ILLYA KURYAKIN. See: Solo,
    Napoleon

I'm Dickens--He's Fenster. See:
    Dickens, Harry

IMEL, JACK. See: Welk,
    Lawrence

Immortal, The. See: Richards,
    Ben

IMMORTAL, THE. See: Richards,
    Ben

IMOGENE COCA. See:

Caesar, Sid (3)
Crosby, Bing (2)

Imogene Coca Show, The. See:
  Crane, Betty

Impossible, Mission. See: Phelps,
  Jim

Impression, Your First. See:
  Leyden, Bill (2)

IMPY THE MIDGET. See:
  Hungarian Giant, The

In Care of Aggie Horn. See:
  Horn, Aggie

INA. See: Hutton, Ina Ray

Ina Ray Hutton Show, The. See:
  Hutton, Ina Ray

INCOMPARABLE HILDEGARDE,
  THE. See: Hildegarde (1) (2)

INDIA. See: Hillman, India

INDIAN. See also: Injun

INDIAN CHIEF. See: Tennessee
  Jed

Information, For Your. See:
  Allison, Fran

Information, Please! See: Fadiman, Clifton (1)

INGRAM, DAN
  JOSEPH JULIAN, narrators of
  the program (themselves)
  The World We Live In (TV)
  (Science)

INGRID. See: Malone, Dr. Jerry

INJUN. See also: Indian

INJUN JOE. See: Finn, Huck

Inner Sanctum. See: Raymond

Inner Sanctum Mysteries. See:
  Raymond

Inside Story. See: Sullivan, Fred

Inside U. S. A. See: Hayes, Peter
  Lind (2)

Insight. See: Kieser, Father
  Elwood

INSPECTOR. See:
  Burke, Inspector
  Derek, Inspector
  Erskine, Inspector Louis
  Fabian, Inspector
  Novak, Pat
  Queen, Ellery
  Renfrew, Inspector Douglas
  White, Inspector

INSPECTOR ARGYLE. See: West,
  Jim (1)

Inspector Burke, Scotland Yard's.
  See: Burke, Inspector

INSPECTOR CALLAHAN. See:
  Wilson, Steve

INSPECTOR CARSON. See:
  Jordan Joyce

INSPECTOR CHESTER. See:
  Saber, Mark

INSPECTOR CLAUDE EUSTACE
  TEAL. See: Templar, Simon

INSPECTOR CORDONA. See:
  Cranston, Lamont

INSPECTOR FARADAY. See:
  Boston Blackie

INSPECTOR FRED ASHER. See:
  Guthrie, Lieut. Ben

INSPECTOR GRADY. See: Kelly,
  Kitty

INSPECTOR HALE. See: Penny

INSPECTOR HEARTHSTONE. See:
  Lenrow, Bernard

INSPECTOR MATT GREB. See:
  Guthrie, Lieut. Ben

INSPECTOR, THE. See: Preston,
  Sergeant

Inspector White of Scotland Yard.

See: White, Inspector

INTERIOR, SECRETARY OF THE.
See: Welles, Orson (3)

Intern, Joyce Jordan, Girl. See:
Jordan, Joyce

International Airport, San Francisco.
See: Conrad, Jim

International Lutheran Hour, The.
See: Hoffman, Dr. Oswald J.

International Show Time. See:
Ameche, Don (4)

Interns, The. See: Goldstone,
Dr. Peter

Interpol, Man From. See: Smith,
Anthony

Interviews, Mike Wallace. See:
Wallace, Mike (2)

Interviews, Sidewalk. See: Johnson, Parks

Intrigue. See: Powers, Michael

Intrigue, Foreign. See: Storm,
Christopher

Invaders, The. See: Vincent,
David

Invasion From Mars, The. See:
Welles, Orson (3)

Investigator, The. See: Prior,
Jeff

Investigators, The. See: Andrews,
Russ

Invisible Man, The. See: Brady,
Peter

INZA. See: Merriwell, Frank

Ipana Troubadours, The. See:
Lanin, Sam

IREENE. See also: Irene

IREENE WICKER. See:
Lovejoy, Frank (2)

Singing Lady, The

IRELAND, QUEEN OF. See:
Sir Lancelot

IRENE. See:
Beasley, Irene (1) (2)
Bordoni, Irene
Forsyte, Soames
Ireene
McDonald, Bob
Noble, Mary
Rich, Irene

IRENE BRADY. See: Potter, Tom

IRENE EMERSON. See: Harper,
Linda Emerson

IRENE FRANKLIN BARBOUR. See:
Barbour, Henry Wilson

IRENE GALWAY. See: Sunday

IRENE MILLER. See: Dyke,
Charity Amanda

IRENE NOBLETTE. See: Ryan,
Tim

Irene Rich Dramas. See: Rich,
Irene

Irene Show, The Tim and. See:
Ryan, Tim

IRENE, TIM AND. See: Cook,
Joe

IRINA TROYER. See: Marlin,
Mary

IRIS BLAKELY. See: Jordan,
Joyce

IRIS DONNELLY GARRISON. See:
Garrison, Spencer

IRIS FLOWER. See: Buddy

IRIS HOUSTON. See: Lawton,
Lora

IRIS MARSH. See: Rutledge,
Dr. John

Irish Rose, Abie's. See: Levy,
Abie

IRMA. See: Peterson, Irma

IRMA BARKER. See: Jones,
Lorenzo

IRMA CAMERON. See: Davis,
Joan Field

IRMA MIZZNICK. See: Meyer

Irma, My Friend. See: Peterson,
Irma

IRMA WALLACE. See: Cummings,
Brenda

Iron Horse, The. See: Calhoun,
Ben

IRON HORSE, THE. See: Calhoun, Ben

Ironside. See: Ironside, Chief
Robert

IRONSIDE, CHIEF ROBERT, San
Francisco police detective, con-
fined to a wheelchair
MARK SANGER, his Negro valet,
associate and friend
SERGEANT ED BROWN, police
detective
SERGEANT EVE WHITFIELD
SERGEANT FRAN BELDING,
police officers, associates of
Ironside
Ironside (TV) (Police drama)

IRVIN. See also:
Erwin
Irving

IRVIN S. COBB. See:
Drew, John
Old Southern Colonel, The

IRVING. See:
Erwin
Irvin
Monroe, John

IRVING AARONSON. See: Winchell,
Walter (1)

IRVING CUMMINGS. See: De-
Mille, Cecil B.

IRVING, GEORGE. See: Frost,
David (2)

IRVING MILLER. See: Sweeney,
Bob

IRWIN. See:
Erwin
Irvin
Irving

ISAACS. See also: Isak

ISAACS, HERB, host of the pro-
gram (himself)
MANY CARTOONS
Happy Herb Presents (TV)
(Children's cartoon)

ISABEL. See:
Isobel
Red Lantern

ISABEL ANDREWS. See: Kelly,
Kitty

ISABEL KENYON. See: Abbott,
John

ISAK. See also: Isaacs

ISAK POOLE. See: Larkin,
Jeremy

ISH KABIBBLE. See: Kyser, Kay

ISHIGAN FISHIGAN OF SISHIGAN,
MICHIGAN. See: Gook, Vic

Island, Gilligan's. See: Gilligan

Island, Happy. See: Bubbles, King

ISLAND PRINCESS, THE. See:
Bailey, Sam

Islanders, The. See: Wade, Sandy

Islands in the Sun. See: Burrud,
Bill (2)

ISOBEL. See also: Isabel

ISOBEL DALEY. See: Brent, Dr.
Jim

ISOLT. See: Sir Lancelot

ISRAEL. See: Boone, Daniel

Issues and Answers. See: Peterson, Roger

IT. See also: Itt

It Can Be Done. See: Guest,
Edgar A. (1)

It Could Be You. See: Leydon,
Bill (1)

It Pays To Be Ignorant. See:
Howard, Tom (1)

It Takes a Thief. See: Mundy,
Alexander

It Takes a Woman. See: Scott,
Frances

It Takes Two. See: Scully, Vin

It Was a Very Good Year. See:
Torme, Mel

ITALO LAGORRO. See: Carter,
Kathryn

Italy, Little. See: Nick

It's a Great Life. See:
Morgan, Mrs. Amy
O'Shea, Michael

It's a Hit. See: Felton, Happy

It's a Man's World. See:
Macauley, Wes

It's About Time. See: Mac

It's Always Jan. See: Stewart,
Jan

It's Your Bet. See: Waggoner,
Lyle

ITT. See also: It

ITT, COUSIN. See: Addams,
Gomez

ITURBI, JOSE. See: Bell,
Alexander Graham

IVA. See: d'Aquino, Iva Ikuko
Toguri

IVAN JONES. See: Hansen, Dean
Eric

IVAN SHARK. See: Midnight,
Captain

Ivanhoe. See: Ivanhoe

IVANHOE, medieval knight
Ivanhoe (TV) (Adventure)

IVANHOE. See also: Wivenhoe

IVANOFF, GREGORY. See:
Perkins, Ma

I've Got a Secret. See: Moore,
Garry (4)

IVERS, NURSE JENNIFER. See:
Peyton, Martin

IVERSON, DR. See: Davis, Dr.
Althea

IVES, BURL (1), guitarist and
folk-singer; star of the program
(himself)
The Burl Ives Show (R) (Music)

IVES, BURL (2)
JAN PEERCE
REGINA RESNIK
RICHARD TUCKER, singers fea-
tured on the program (themselves)
LYN MURRAY, orchestra leader
(himself)
HIS ORCHESTRA
Music From the House of Squibb
(R) (Music)

Ivy, The Halls of. See: Hall,
Dr. William Todhunter

IVY TRENT. See: Young, Larry
"Pepper"

IZZY FINKELSTEIN. See: Kaltenmeyer, Professor August, D. U. N.

J. See:
  Bragonier, Dr. J. Robert
  Jay
  Jaye

J. BLASINGAME BOND. See:
  Kaye, Sammy (1)

J. C. DITHERS. See: Bumstead,
  Blondie

J. D. SMITH. See: Marshal, The

J. E. SNODGRASS. See: Barry,
  Jack (9)

J. H. PHILLIPS. See: Karr, Mike

J. J. See: Drinkwater, William

J. J. JACKSON. See: Cade, Sam

J. J. McNISH. See: Simms, Paul

J. J., The Governor and. See:
  Drinkwater, William

J. L. FOX. See: Burnley, Walter

J. NEWTON NUMBSKULL. See:
  Junior

J. W. HARRINGTON. See: Miller,
  Johnny

J. WELLINGTON KEATS. See:
  Baines, Scattergood

JACE. See: Pearson, Jace

JACK. See:
  Abbott, John
  Armstrong, Jack
  Arthur, Jack (1) (2) (3)
  Bailey, Jack
  Barbour, Henry Wilson
  Barry, Jack (1) (2) (3) (4) (5)
  (6) (7) (8) (9) (10)
  Benny, Jack
  Brennan, Jack
  Carson, Jack
  Clark, Jack
  Dallas, Stella
  Douglas, Jack (1) (2) (3)
  Gibson, Jack
  Jackson, Jarrin' Jack
  Jacques
  Jake

Jones, Jack
King
Kirkwood, Jack
LaLanne, Jack
Lescoulie, Jack (1) (2) (3) (4)
Linkletter, Art (2)
Linkletter, Jack (1) (2) (3)
Little, Little Jack
Narz, Jack (1) (2) (3) (4) (5)
  (6)
Paar, Jack
Packard, Jack
Rogers, Patricia
Roseleigh, Jack
Smilin' Jack
Smith, Jack
Sterling, Jack
Sunday
Webb, Jack
Winters, Jack
Wyatt, Jack

JACK ANDREWS. See: Sterling,
  Vanessa Dale

Jack Armstrong, The All-American
Boy. See: Armstrong, Jack

JACK ARNOLD. See: Myrt

JACK ARTHUR. See:
  Arthur, Jack (1) (2) (3)
  Weems, Ambrose J.

JACK BAILEY. See:
  Bailey, Jack
  Edwards, Ralph (3)
  Elliott, Win (1)

JACK BECKMAN. See: Kelly,
  Joe (2)

JACK BENNY. See:
  Benny, Jack
  Crosby, Bing (2)
  Lundigan, Bill (2)

JACK BENNY, MRS. See:
  Benny, Jack

Jack Benny Program, The. See:
  Benny, Jack

JACK BRINKLEY. See: Soule,
  Olan (1)

JACK BURNS. See:
  DeLuise, Dom (2)
  Nye, Louis

JACK, CAPTAIN. See: Story
Lady, The

Jack Carson Show, The. See:
Carson, Jack

JACK CHANDLER. See: Peyton,
Martin

JACK CRANDALL. See: Lari-
more, Marilyn

JACK DENNY. See: Winchell,
Walter (1)

JACK DOTY. See: First Nighter,
Mr.

JACK E. LEONARD. See: Clark,
Dick (3)

JACK ELLENHORN. See: Banner,
Woody

JACK FASCINATO. See: Ford,
Tennessee Ernie (4)

JACK FELZER. See: Brent, Dr.
Jim

JACK FORBES. See: Murphy,
Peter

JACK FRASER. See: Arden,
Jane

JACK FRENCH. See: Kelly, Joe
(2)

JACK GALLOWAY. See: Arden,
Jane

JACK GARLAND. See: Harding,
Mrs. Rhoda

JACK GILFORD. See: Frost,
David (2)

JACK GRIMES. See: Halop,
Billy

JACK HALEY. See:
Henry, Captain
Owner

JACK HALSEY. See: Allen, Dr.
Kate

JACK HASKELL. See: Garroway,
Dave (2) (3)

JACK IMEL. See: Welk,
Lawrence

JACK JORDAN. See: Halop,
Billy

Jack LaLanne Show, The. See:
LaLanne, Jack

JACK LANDIS, DR. See: Harding,
Karen Adams

JACK LEMMON. See: Ryan,
Robert (1)

JACK LESCOULIE. See:
Davis, Fred
Lescoulie, Jack (1) (2) (3) (4)

JACK LINKLETTER. See:
Linkletter, Art (2)
Linkletter, Jack (1) (2) (3)
Robbins, Fred

JACK LUCAL. See: Kelly, Joe
(2)

JACK McCARTHY. See: Cross,
Milton (1)

JACK McELROY. See: Brene-
man, Tom (2)

JACK McGIVERN. See: Patrick,
Dion

JACK MARSH. See: Carter,
Kathryn

JACK MARTIN. See: Welk,
Lawrence

JACK MEAKIN. See: Marx,
Groucho (3)

JACK MILLER. See: Smith,
Kate (2)

JACK MOFFITT, SERGEANT.
See: Troy, Sergeant Sam

JACK PAAR. See:
Baker, Phil (3)
Bruner, Wally (1)
Paar, Jack

Jack Paar Show, The. See:
Paar, Jack

JACK PARNELL. See:
Berman, Shelley
Chidsey, Jackie
Davidson, John (2)
Doonican, Val

Jack Pearl Show, The. See:
Munchausen, Baron

JACK ROONEY. See: Kelly,
Joe (2)

JACK SMART. See: Welles,
Orson (2)

JACK SMITH. See:
Smith, Jack
Taylor, Deems

JACK TEAGARDEN. See: Crosby,
Bing (3)

JACK VAN ORPINGTON. See:
Kelly, Kitty

JACK VERNON. See: O'Neill,
Mrs.

JACK WHEELER. See: Marx,
Groucho (2)

JACK WHITING. See: Champion,
Marge

JACKIE. See:
Chidsey, Jackie
Coogan, Jackie
Erwin, Stu
Gleason, Jackie (1) (2)
Sunday

Jackie Gleason Show, The. See:
Gleason, Jackie (2)
Kramden, Ralph

Jackie Gleason's American Scene
Magazine. See: Gleason,
Jackie (2)

JACKIE HELLER, LITTLE. See:
Bernie, Ben

JACKMAN, LEWIS. See: Peyton,
Martin

Jackpot Bowling Starring Milton
Berle. See: Berle, Milton (1)

Jackpot, Hit the. See: Cullen,
Bill (2)

Jackpot, Hollywood. See: Delmar, Kenny

JACKS, ADA. See: Peyton,
Martin

JACKS, EDDIE. See: Peyton,
Martin

JACK'S PRESS AGENT. See:
Carson, Jack

JACKSON BECK. See:
Beck, Jackson
Roberts, Ken

JACKSON, BILL. See: Beulah

JACKSON, CALEB. See: Dane,
Prudence

JACKSON, DR. STEVE. See:
Bauer, Bertha

JACKSON, DOROTHY. See:
. Miller, Johnny

JACKSON, EDDIE. See: Durante,
Jimmy

JACKSON, GRETA. See: Jones,
Loco

JACKSON, J. J. See: Cade, Sam

JACKSON, JARRIN' JACK, former
athlete; still sports-minded
ALICE, his wife
JUNIOR, his bookworm son
That's My Boy (TV) (Comedy)

JACKSON, JAY. See:
Barry, Jack (8)
Slater, Bill (2)

Jackson, Jet. See: Midnight,
Captain

JACKSON, KEITH (1)
BILL BURNETTA, hosts of the
program (themselves)
GUEST BOWLERS

The Best of Bowling (TV) (Sports)

JACKSON, KEITH (2)
DON MEREDITH
HOWARD COSELL
CURT GOWDY, sports announcers
(themselves)
N. F. L. Monday Night Football
(TV) (Sports)

JACKSON, KEITH. See also:
McKay, Jim (1)

JACKSON, MARTHA, The Woman
of Courage
JIM JACKSON
LUCY JACKSON
TOMMY JACKSON
JOSEPH BENEDICT
SUSAN BENEDICT
LILLIAN BURKE
TOMMY LEWIS
GEORGE HARRISON
MRS. HUMPHRIES
MRS. SULLIVAN
CORA
RED, characters appearing in
the drama
Woman of Courage (R) (Serial
drama)

JACKSON, MAYBELLE. See:
Clayton, Margie

JACKSON, "SELDOM." See:
Jones, Kenneth Yarborough

JACKSON, SHERIFF. See: Tennessee Jed

JACKSON, UNCLE ED. See:
Noble, Mary

JACOB. See: Tarshish, Jacob

JACOB KRANSKY. See: Rutledge,
Dr. John

JACOBY, LIEUT. See: Gunn,
Peter

JACQUELINE DuBIEF. See:
Desmond, Johnny

JACQUELINE, SR. See: Bertrille,
Sr.

JACQUELINE SUSAN. See:

Kidder, Margot

JACQUES. See:
Carr, Alison
Cousteau, Jacques
Jack
Jake

Jacques Cousteau, The Undersea
World of. See: Cousteau,
Jacques

JACQUES RENARD. See: Cantor,
Eddie (2)

JAGGER, DON, deputy chief; law
enforcement officer
Border Patrol (TV) (Adventure)
(also known as U.S. Border
Patrol) (TV)

JAI. See: Tarzan

JAIME. See also:
Jaimie
Jamie

JAIME ROGERS DANCERS, THE.
See: Berry, Ken

JAIMIE. See:
Cartwright, Ben
Jaime
Jamie
McPheeters, Dr. Sardinius

Jaimie McPheeters, The Travels of.
See: McPheeters, Dr. Sardinius

JAKE. See:
Bradley, Judith
Gene
Goldberg, Molly
Harkness, Detective
Howard, Jim
Jack
Jacques
Webster, Jake

JAKE GUMPOX. See: Gook, Vic

Jake and Lena, Gene and Glenn
With. See: Gene

Jambo. See: Thompson, Marshall

Jamboree, Blue Monday. See:
Holloway, Harrison

JAMES. See:
Carter, James
Harrigan, James, Sr.
Hilton, James
Kildare, Dr. James
Kirk, Captain James
MacAndrew, James
Mason, James
Melton, James (1) (2)
O'Hara, James
Peterson, Dr. James
Sonnett, Will
Stewart, James
Whitman, Dr. James

JAMES II. See: Churchill, John

JAMES ANDERSON, LIEUT. See:
Mason, Perry

JAMES, ART (1), moderator of the
program (himself)
MANY CONTESTANTS
Say When (TV) (Game)

JAMES, ART (2), moderator of the
program (himself)
GUEST CONTESTANTS
The Who, What or Where Game
(TV) (Game)

JAMES BENSON. See: Harum,
David

JAMES, BOB. See: Dallas, Stella

JAMES BUSTARD, SERGEANT.
See: Custer, George Armstrong

JAMES CRAIG, DR. See: Walleck,
Meredith

JAMES, DENNIS (1), master of
ceremonies of the program (him-
self)
NANCY WRIGHT
MIKE DOUGLAS, singers fea-
tured on the program (them-
selves)
THE MELLO-LARKS QUARTET
JOE GALLICCHIO, orchestra
leader (himself)
HIS ORCHESTRA
Club 60 (TV) (Variety)

JAMES, DENNIS (2), quizmaster of
the program (himself)
MANY CONTESTANTS

High Finance (TV) (Quiz)

JAMES, DENNIS (3)
BOB AND RAY, moderators of
the program (themselves)
BESS MYERSON
JOAN ALEXANDER
GENE RAYBURN
ROGER PRICE
AUDREY MEADOWS
HY GARDNER
WALTER SLEZAK, panelists
(themselves)
OTHER PANELISTS
GUEST CONTESTANTS
The Name's the Same (TV)
(Game)

JAMES, DENNIS (4), announcer of
the program (himself)
DICK THE BRUISER
VERNE GAGNE
WILBUR SNYDER
GORGEOUS GEORGE
MR. AMERICA
HANS SCHMIDT
THE SWEDISH ANGEL
THE ZEBRA KID
RICKI STARR
ANTONINO ROCCA
MANY OTHERS, professional
wrestlers (themselves)
Wrestling (TV) (Sports)

JAMES, DENNIS. See also:
Leyden, Bill (2)

JAMES, DR. See: Flipper

JAMES EARL JONES. See:
Cookie Monster, The

JAMES FIELD, DR. See: Karr,
Mike

James Garner as Nichols. See:
Nichols

JAMES HAGEN. See: Daly, John
(4)

JAMES HARRIGAN, JR. See:
Harrigan, James, Sr.

JAMES, HARRY. See:
Basie, Count
Kaye, Danny
Whiteman, Paul

JAMES, JESSE, American outlaw
FRANK, his brother, also an out-
law
The Legend of Jesse James (TV)
(Western)

JAMES MELTON. See:
Bell, Alexander Graham
Melton, James (1) (2)
Roxy

JAMES, NANCY, judge
RICHARD WHARTON, mayor
EVELYN WHARTON, wife of
the mayor
ANTHONY HALE, district attorney
DR. BAXTER, physician
ELLEN CLARK
STAN ADAMIK
CARRIE DEAN
MADGE KELLER
GEORGE NOVACK
LAURA
TRIXIE, characters appearing in
the drama
Her Honor, Nancy James (R)
(Serial drama)

JAMESON. See also: Jamison

JAMESON, AMELIA. See: Harding,
Karen Adams

JAMIE. See:
Driggs, Karleton King
Jaime
Jaimie

JAMIE DAVIS. See: Randolph,
Alice

JAMIE O'CONNOR. See: Fairchild,
Kay

JAMISON. See also: Jameson

JAMISON, ALICE. See: Brent,
Dr. Jim

JAMISON, DR. SEAN, pediatrician,
practicing in Honolulu
ANNE, his daughter and partner;
recent medical school graduate
PUNI, their Hawaiian nurse
RONNIE, handyman
The Little People (TV) (Medical
comedy)

JAN. See:
Brady, Mike
Jane
Jayne
Joan
Joanne
John
June
Murray, Jan (1) (2) (3) (4)
Stewart, Jan

JAN CLAYTON. See: Harrington,
Pat, Jr.

JAN CROCKETT. See: Hamilton,
George

JAN GARBER. See: Basie, Count

Jan, It's Always. See: Stewart,
Jan

Jan Murray Show, The. See: Murray, Jan (2)

JAN PEERCE. See:
Ives, Burl (2)
Roxy

JANAC, MR. See: Malone, Dr.
Jerry

JANE. See:
Ace, Goodman
Arden, Jane
Brent, Portia
Brewster, Joey
Brown, Ellen
Froman, Jane (1) (2)
Jan
Jayne
Jetson, George
Joan
Joanne
June
Lee, Jim
Miller, Albert
Mix, Tom
Parker, Seth
Starrett, Dick
Wyman, Jane

JANE ALLEN. See: Williams,
Emily

Jane Arden. See: Arden, Jane

JANE BELLE. See: Jordan, Joyce

JANE BROWN. See: Goldberg,
Molly

JANE BROWNING. See: Nelson,
Carolyn Kramer

JANE, CALAMITY. See: Buffalo
Bill, Jr.

JANE COLLINS. See: Davis, Dr.
Althea

JANE CONNELL. See: Caesar,
Sid (1)

JANE COWL. See: Kaye, Danny

JANE DALY. See: Anthony

JANE DAWSON. See: Hardy,
Dr. Steven

JANE ELLIOTT. See: Dean,
Spencer

Jane Froman Show, The. See:
Froman, Jane (1)

JANE HARTFORD. See: Drake,
Betty

Jane, Judy and. See: Judy

JANE KAYE. See: Kelly, Joe
(1)

JANE LEE. See: Judy

Jane, Mr. Ace and. See: Ace,
Goodman

JANE PICKENS. See: Cross,
Milton (1)

JANE PORTER. See: Tarzan

JANE POWELL. See: Ryan,
Robert (1)

JANE SEYMOUR. See: Henry VIII,
King of England

JANE STACY. See: Peterson,
Irma

JANE WILEY. See: Hughes,
Chris

JANE WILSON. See: Waring,
Fred (1)

JANE, WRANGLER. See: Par-
menter, Captain Wilton

Jane Wyman Theater, The. See:
Wyman, Jane

JANET BLAIR. See:
Blair, Janet
Caesar, Sid (2)

JANET CRAIG, DR. See: Carson,
Uncle Joe

JANET DIONCHECK. See: Perry,
John

JANET LENNON. See:
Lennon, Janet
Welk, Lawrence

JANET MASON NORRIS. See:
Bauer, Bertha

JANET MERCER. See: Brent,
Dr. Jim

JANET MUNSON ADAMS. See:
Harding, Karen Adams

JANET RYDER. See: Graham,
Dr. Bob

JANET WALTON. See: Tate,
Joanne

JANETTE DAVIS. See: Godfrey,
Arthur (1)

JANEY. See also:
Janie
Janney
Johnny
Jonny

JANEY BROWN. See: Brewster,
Joey

JANICE. See:
Collins, Bing
Janis
Janos
O'Neill, Mrs.

JANICE CRAIG, DR. See: Walleck, Meredith

JANICE KING. See: Winters, Evelyn

JANIE. See:
Janey
Janney
Johnny
Jonny
Robinson, Don

JANIE AND CONNIE. See: Kelly,
Joe (1)

JANIE DAVIS. See: Hutton, Ina
Ray

JANIE JONES. See: Kaye,
Sammy (1)

JANIS. See also:
Janice
Janos

JANIS, ELSIE. See: Drew, John

JANITOR, POP THE. See: Junior

JANITOR, SONNY THE. See:
Wilson, Flip

JANNEY. See also:
Janey
Janie
Johnny
Jonny

JANNEY, LEON. See: Cross,
Mason

JANOS. See also:
Janice
Janis

JANOS PROHASKA. See: Williams,
Andy (2)

JANSON. See: Jensen

JANUARY, DR. BEN, physician
RICK JANUARY, brothers; keep
law and order in the frontier
town of Gunnison
Two Faces West (TV) (Western)

JANUARY, MOLASSES AND. See:
Henry, Captain

JARRIN' JACK. See: Jackson,
Jarrin' Jack

JARROD. See: Barkley, Victoria

JARVIS, EDGAR. See: Jordan,
Joyce

JASCHA HEIFETZ. See: Bell,
Alexander Graham

JASON. See:
Bolt, Jason
McCord, Jason
Walton, Grandpa

JASON ALLEN. See: Kaufman,
Seymour

JASON, ERIC. See: Gregory,
Ben

JASON HART. See: Fuller, Ward

JASON McKINLEY ALLEN, PRO-
FESSOR. See: Cameron,
Christy Allen

JASON NICHOLS. See: Randall,
Josh

JAY. See:
Brent, Portia
J.
Jaye
Jostyn, Jay (1) (2)
Reynolds, Jay
Stewart, Jay (1) (2)

JAY C. FLIPPEN. See:
Bower, Roger
Bowes, Major Edward (2)
Crumit, Frank (1)

JAY JACKSON. See:
Barry, Jack (8)
Slater, Bill (2)

JAY JOSTYN. See:
Jostyn, Jay (1) (2)
Judge (2)

JAY, LESTER. See: Halop, Billy

Jay Stewart's Fun Fair. See:
Stewart, Jay (1)

JAY STONE TONEY. See: Peters,
Lowell

JAYE. See:

J.
Jay
Morgan, Jaye P.

Jaye P. Morgan Show, The. See:
Morgan, Jaye P.

JAYNE. See also:
Jan
Jane
Joan
Joanne
June

JAYNE MEADOWS. See: Moore,
Garry (4)

Jazz Alley. See: Hodes, Art

JAZZ BAND, THE CIRCUSEVEN.
See: Kirchener, Claude (1)

Jazz, Net. See: Gleason, Ralph

Jazz, People in. See: Rockwell,
Jim

JEAN. See:
Bennett, Nita
Garrison, Spencer
Gene
King, Jean Paul
Lambert, Louise
O'Neill, Mrs.

JEAN ADAIR. See: Johnson, Bess

Jean Arthur Show, The. See:
Marshall, Patricia

JEAN BAKER. See: Noble, Mary

JEAN CARTER. See: Hutchinson,
Ma

JEAN CURTIS. See: Dyke,
Charity Amanda

JEAN DAWSON. See: Hardy, Dr.
Steven

JEAN DICKENSON. See: Munn,
Frank (1)

JEAN-GASTON ANDRE. See:
Sheppard, Franklin

JEAN McKEAN. See: Kirkwood,

Jack

JEAN OSBORNE. See: Malone,
Dr. Jerry

JEAN PAGANO. See: Novak,
John

JEAN PAGE. See: Bannister,
Clay

JEAN PAUL DESMOND. See:
Carr, Alison

JEAN PAUL KING. See:
Judge, The
King, Jean Paul

JEAN REED. See: Malloy,
Officer Pete

JEANETTE McNEILL. See:
Trent, Helen

JEANETTE NOLAN. See:
Reed, Alan
Welles, Orson (2)

JEANNIE. See:
Jennie
Jenny
MacLennon, Jeannie
Nelson, Major Tony
Spitalney, Phil

Jeannie, Hey! See: MacLennon,
Jeannie

Jeannie, I Dream of. See: Nelson, Major Tony

JEANNINE RILEY. See: Owens,
Buck

JEB GAINE. See: Hardie, Jim

JEB HAWKES. See: Collins,
Barnabas

JECKLE. See: Heckle

Jeckle, Heckle and. See: Heckle

JED. See:
Clampett, Jed
Tennessee Jed

JED CLAYTON. See: Garrett,
Sam

JED COLBY. See: Favor, Gil

JED "KID" CURRY. See: Heyes, Hannibal

JED SILLS. See: Corey, Don

JEEP. See: Green, Billy

JEFF. See:
Canfield, Ben
Carter, James
Gidget
Prior, Jeff
Rose, George
Sonnett, Will
Spencer, Jeff
Stone, Dr. Alex
Thompson, Jeff

JEFF BAKER. See: Hughes, Chris

JEFF BRADY. See: Trent, Helen

JEFF CLARK. See: Ross, Lanny

JEFF CONWAY. See: Burns, George (3)

JEFF CORBETT. See: Grimm, Arnold

JEFF DILLON. See: Howard, Glenn

JEFF DURAIN. See: Halliday, Mike

JEFF KITTREDGE. See: Scott, David

JEFF MARTIN. See: Davis, Ann Tyler

JEFF MILLER. See: Lassie

JEFF RYDER. See: Collier, Tim

JEFF SPENCER. See:
Bailey, Stuart
Spencer, Jeff

JEFF WARD, DETECTIVE. See: Haines, Lieut. Mike

JEFFERS, DAVID. See: Johnson, Bess

JEFFERSON. See:
Drum, Jefferson
Keyes, Jefferson

Jefferson Drum. See: Drum, Jefferson

JEFFERSON FOWLEY. See: Keene, Kitty

JEFFERYS. See also: Jeffries

JEFFERYS, PIXIE. See: Hargrave-Scott, Joan

JEFFORDS, TOM, Indian agent
COCHISE
KOTOY, Apache Indian chiefs
Broken Arrow (TV) (Western)

JEFFREY. See also: Geoffrey

JEFFREY BARKER. See: Guest, Edgar A. (2)

JEFFREY BARTON. See: Johnson, Bess

JEFFREY CLARK. See: Hargrave-Scott, Joan

JEFFREY HASTINGS. See: Carlyle, Baylor

JEFFRIES. See also: Jefferys

JEFFRIES, PRENTISS. See: Sloan, Holly

Jeff's Collie. See: Lassie

JELLY HOSKINS. See: Lancer, Murdoch

JEMAL, DAVID. See: Corey, Earl

JEN BURTON. See: Carter, Kathryn

JENIFER. See also: Jennifer

JENIFER BISHOP. See: Owens, Buck

JENKINS, BILL. See: Sunday

JENKINS, DAVID. See: Kelly, Joe (2)

JENKINS, GORDON. See:
Haymes, Dick
Lane, Richard

JENKINS, MR. See: Beulah

JENKS, BEEZIE. See: Teen,
Harold

JENKS, FRANK. See: Lane,
Richard

JENKS, POP. See: Teen,
Harold

JENNA McMAHON. See:
Jones, Dean
Kelly, Gene

JENNIE. See:
Fox, Jennie
Jeannie
Jenny

JENNIE OAKSBERRY. See:
Peppertag, Aaron

JENNIFER. See:
Conway, Bobby
Driggs, Karleton King
Jenifer

JENNIFER DAVIS. See: Noble,
Mary

JENNIFER IVERS, NURSE. See:
Peyton, Martin

JENNIFER JO. See: Drinkwater,
William

JENNINGS, AMY. See: Collins,
Barnabas

JENNINGS, CHRIS. See: Collins,
Barnabas

JENNINGS, GWYN. See: Horn,
Aggie

JENNINGS, MARION. See: Cummings, Brenda

JENNINGS, SENATOR. See:
Carlyle, Baylor

JENNY. See:
Aunt Jenny (Aunt Lucy)
Hammond, Liza
Jeannie
Jennie
Peabody, Jenny
Preston, Dick

Jenny Peabody. See: Peabody,
Jenny

JENNY RYAN. See: Hughes, Chris

JENSEN, SANDI. See: Welk,
Lawrence

Jeopardy! See: Fleming, Art

JEREMY. See:
Bolt, Jason
Larkin, Jeremy

JEREMY LLOYD. See: Rowan,
Dan

Jergens Journal. See: Winchell,
Walter (3)

JERI. See also:
Gerri
Gerry
Jerry

JERI SULLAVAN. See: Bolger,
Ray

Jericho. See: Sheppard, Franklin

JEROME BROOKS. See: Randolph,
Ellen

JEROME, EDWIN. See: Welles,
Orson (2)

JEROME HINES. See: Barlow,
Howard

JEROME, JERRY. See: Kirby,
Durward

JEROME, MR. See: Young,
Larry "Pepper"

JEROME SANDERS. See: Sothern,
Mary

JEROME, WALTER. See: Goldberg, Molly

JERROD, BEN, attorney

Ben Jerrod: Attorney at Law (TV)
(Serial drama)

JERRY. See:
Buell, Roger
Butler, Jerry
Carmichael, Lucy
Crane, Betty
Dallas, Stella
Dennis, Liz
Gerri
Gerry
Jeri
Lester, Jerry
Lewis, Jerry
Malone, Dr. Jerry
Nipper
North, Jerry
Offstein, Jerry
Reed, Jerry
Silver, Captain
Webster, Jerry

JERRY ADAIR. See: Johnson,
Bess

JERRY ALLEN. See: Novak, John

JERRY AUSTIN. See: Malone,
Mike

JERRY BELCHER. See: John-
son, Parks

JERRY BROWNELL. See: Thompson, Andy

JERRY BURKE. See: Welk,
Lawrence

JERRY COLONNA. See: Olsen,
Ole

JERRY GRAY. See: Crosby, Bob
(2)

JERRY HELPER. See: Petrie,
Rob

JERRY JEROME. See: Kirby,
Durward

JERRY LACY. See: Klein,
Robert

JERRY LEE LEWIS. See: Owens,
Buck

JERRY LESTER. See:
Crosby, Bing (3)
Lester, Jerry

JERRY LEWIS. See:
Lewis, Jerry
Martin, Dean (1) (3)

Jerry Lewis Show, The. See:
Lewis, Jerry

JERRY MAHONEY. See:
Olsen, Ole
Winchell, Paul (1) (2) (3) (4)
(5) (6) (7)

JERRY MANN VOICES, THE. See:
Thomas, Thomas L.

JERRY MARVIN. See: Perry,
John

JERRY MILLER. See: Wayne,
Ruth Evans

JERRY NOLAND, DR. See:
Campanelli, Dr. Vincent

JERRY PAYNE. See: Marshall,
John

Jerry Reed When You're Hot You're
Hot Hour, The. See: Reed,
Jerry

JERRY ROBINSON. See: Hartley,
Dr. Robert

JERRY RYAN. See: Carter,
Kathryn

JERRY SEARS. See: Fields,
Arthur

JERRY SMITH. See: Hughes,
Chris

JERRY STULIR. See: Rogers,
Patricia

JERRY TREMAINE. See: Liston,
Lois

JERRY VALE. See: Miller,
Mitch

JERRY WHIPPLE. See: Hackett,
Doc

JESS. See:
Carter, Mr.
Harper, Jess
Jesse
Jessie

JESS BRANDON. See: Marshall,
Owen

JESS KIRKPATRICK. See: Story
Lady, The

JESSE. See:
James, Jesse
Jess
Jessie

Jesse James, The Legend of. See:
James, Jesse

JESSEL, GEORGE (1), monologist
and entertainer; star of the pro-
gram (himself)
MANY GUEST STARS
The George Jessel Show (R)
(Comedy/variety)

JESSEL, GEORGE (2), monologist
and entertainer; host of the pro-
gram (himself)
MANY GUEST STARS
Here Come the Stars (TV)
(Variety)

JESSICA. See:
Dawson, Rosemary
Dragonette, Jessica (1) (2) (3)

JESSICA HERRINGBONE. See:
Perkins, Ma

JESSICA MORRISON. See: Davis,
Dr. Althea

JESSIE. See:
Carter, James
Charlie
Jess
Jesse

JESSIE ATWOOD. See: Hopkins,
Kate

JESSIE BREWER. See: Hardy,
Dr. Steven

Jessie, Charlie and. See:
Charlie

JESSIE HUGHES, MRS. See:
Malone, Dr. Jerry

JESSIE KING, MRS. See: Bennett, Nita

JESSIE WARD. See: Aunt Mary

JESSUP, ALLISON HATHAWAY.
See: Prescott, Kate Hathaway

JESSUP, CHRIS. See: Prescott,
Kate Hathaway

JESSUP, DR. HUGH. See: Prescott, Kate Hathaway

JESSUP, SIMON. See: Karr,
Mike

JESUS, portrayed by Warren
Parker
The Greatest Story Ever Told (R)
(Religion)

Jet Jackson. See: Midnight,
Captain

JETHRO. See: Clampett, Jed

JETMAN. See: Hollister, Dick

JETSON, GEORGE
JANE, his wife
JUDY, his daughter
ELROY, his son
ASTRO, his dog, all cartoon
characters
The Jetsons (TV) (Cartoons;
space age satire)

Jetsons, The. See: Jetson,
George

JEWETT, TED. See: Welles,
Orson (2)

JIGGS, wealthy "diamond in the
rough" head of the house
MAGGIE, his domineering wife
NORA, their daughter
DINTY MOORE, friend of Jiggs
Bringing up Father (R) (Situa-
tion comedy)

Jigsaw. See: Dain, Lieut. Frank

JILL. See:

Bartlett, Jill
Keene, Kitty
Malone, Dr. Jerry

JILL CLAYBORN. See: Ames,
Peter

JILL COREY. See:
Lanson, Snooky
Lewis, Robert Q. (2)

JILL DANKO. See: Ryker, Lieut.
Eddie

JILL GRANT. See: Hillman, India

JILL JOHNSON. See: Gibson,
Jack

Jill, Love That. See: Gibson,
Jack

JILL THROPP. See: Perry, John

JILLSON. See: Barnes, Joey

JIM. See:
Ameche, Don
Ameche, Jim
Ames, Peter
Anderson, Jim
Bailey, Sam
Bishop, Jim
Bowie, Jim
Brent, Dr. Jim
Brewster, Joey
Bronson, Jim
Chandler, Jim
Chaplain Jim
Chase, Dennis
Conrad, Jim
Crown, Jim
Curtis, Brenda
Davis, Jim
Fairchild, Kay
Finn, Huckleberry
Flagg, Captain Jim
Hardie, Jim
Howard, Jim
Jackson, Martha
Jordan, Jim (1) (2)
Jungle Jim
Lange, Jim
Lee, Jim
McKay, Jim (1) (2)
McKenna, Jim
McWilliams, Jim (1) (2)
Monroe, Clayt

Nabors, Jim
Nash, Jim
Newton, Jim
Phelps, Jim
Prentiss, Jim
Redigo, Jim (1) (2)
Rockwell, Jim
Silver, Long John
Skipper Jim
Slattery, Jim
Taylor, Jim
Thompson, Jim
Uncle Jim
Waters, Jim
West, Jim (1) (2)

JIM AMECHE. See:
Ameche, Don (3)
Ameche, Jim
Arthur, Jack (2)

JIM ANDERSON. See:
Anderson, Jim
Burton, Terry

JIM BACKUS. See:
Kaye, Danny
Marshall, Peter

Jim Backus Show, The. See:
O'Toole, John Michael

JIM BARETT. See: Hargrave-
Scott, Joan

JIM BARKER. See: Jones,
Lorenzo

JIM BARNETT. See: Myrt

JIM BENEDICT, CAPTAIN. See:
Wright, Conley

JIM BISHOP. See:
Allison, Fran
Bishop, Jim

JIM-BOB. See: Walton, Grandpa

JIM BOLES. See: Morrison,
Bret

Jim Bowie. See: Bowie, Jim

Jim Bowie, The Adventures of.
See: Bowie, Jim

JIM BRIGGS. See: Stone, Sam

JIM BRITT. See: Cowan, Thomas

JIM BUCKLEY. See: McKeever, Ted

JIM CARROLL. See: Webster, Martha

JIM CATUSI. See: Frost, David (2)

JIM CONKLING. See: Driggs, Karleton King

JIM COTTER, DR. See: Dawson, Rosemary

JIM DOOLEY. See: Caesar, Sid (1)

JIM ED LOVE. See: Jones, Ben

JIM EGAN. See: March, Hal

JIM FAIRFIELD, UNCLE. See: Armstrong, Jack

JIM FARRELL. See: Malone, Dr. Jerry

JIM FOWLER. See: Perkins, Marlin

JIM HALLORAN, DETECTIVE. See: Parker, Lieut. Mike

JIM HUDSON. See: Prescott, Kate Hathaway

JIM HURLEY. See: Begley, Martin

Jim, Jungle. See: Jungle Jim

JIM KENT. See: Grimm, Arnold

JIM LANGE. See: Lange, Jim Shawn, Dick

JIM LOVERING. See: Skippy

JIM LOWELL. See: Hughes, Chris

JIM McKINNON. See: Tate, Joanne

JIM MATTHEWS. See: Bennett, Nita

JIM NABORS. See: Cookie Monster, The Nabors, Jim

Jim Nabors Hour, The. See: Nabors, Jim

JIM NICHOLS. See: O'Leary, Hannah

JIM, PREACHER. See: Keene, Kitty

JIM REED, OFFICER. See: Malloy, Officer Pete

JIM RHODES. See: Erskine, Inspector Louis

JIM ROBERTS. See: Welk, Lawrence

JIM SARGENT. See: Judy

JIM SINCLAIR. See: Hayes, Wing Commander

Jim, Skipper. See: Skipper Jim

JIM TOLLIVER. See: Dyke, Charity Amanda

JIMENEZ, JOSE, bellboy at plush hotel
EDDIE, bellboy
PHILLIPS, hotel manager
GLICK, house detective
The Bill Dana Show (TV) (Comedy)

JIMENEZ, JOSE. See also: Jones, Spike (2)

JIMMIE. See:
Allen, Jimmie
Dodd, Jimmie
Dugan, Jimmie
Fidler, Jimmie
Jimmy
Jimsey
Rodgers, Jimmie

Jimmie Allen, The Air Adventures of. See: Allen, Jimmie

Jimmie Fidler. See: Fidler, Jimmie

JIMMIE GRIER. See: Medbury,
John P.

JIMMIE KENT. See: Myrt

Jimmie Rodgers Show, The. See:
Rodgers, Jimmie

JIMMIE THOMPSON, UNCLE. See:
Solemn Old Judge, The

JIMMY. See:
Baines, Scattergood
Dean, Jimmy
Dorsey, Tommy
Durante, Jimmy
Jimmie
Jimsey
Lincoln, Dr. Matt
Mix, Tom
O'Neill, Jimmy
Ruskin, Lily
Scribner, Jimmy
Shields, Jimmy
Stewart, Jimmy
Valentine, Jimmy

JIMMY BRIERLY. See: Reser,
Harry

JIMMY CLARK. See: Erwin, Stu

JIMMY DALE. See:
Berry, Ken
Bono, Salvatore
Stevens, Ray

JIMMY DAVIS. See: Brown,
Ellen

JIMMY DEAN. See:
Dean, Jimmy
Shawn, Dick

Jimmy Dean Show, The. See:
Dean, Jimmy

JIMMY DORSEY. See:
Birthday Man, The
Crosby, Bing (3)
Dorsey, Tommy

JIMMY DURANTE. See:
Bowers, Brainy
Durante, Jimmy
Lennon, Janet
Martin, Dean (1)
Raye, Martha (1)

Jimmy Durante Presents the Lennon Sisters Hour. See: Lennon,
Janet

Jimmy Durante Show, The. See:
Durante, Jimmy

JIMMY FLUTE. See: Pufnstuf,
H. R.

JIMMY GALE. See: Carter, Hope

JIMMY JOYCE. See: Junior

JIMMY McCALLION. See: Cross,
Milton (2)

JIMMY MALONE. See: Jordan,
Joyce

JIMMY MINTER. See: Myrt

JIMMY OLSEN. See: Kent, Clark

Jimmy Stewart Show, The. See:
Howard, Jim

Jimmy Valentine, Alias. See:
Valentine, Jimmy

JIMSEY. See also:
Jimmie
Jimmy

JIMSEY SOMMERS. See: Halop,
Billy

JINGLES. See: Hickock, Wild
Bill

JINKS, MR. See: Pixie

JINKY. See: Brown, Robinson,
Jr.

JINNY. See:
Ginnie
Ginny
Powell, Dick (3)

JINNY ROBERTS. See: Winters,
Evelyn

JINNY STOREY. See: Meredith,
Charles

JINX FALKENBURG. See: Mc-
Crary, Tex

Jinx Show, The Tex and. See:
McCrary, Tex

"JITCHY" VASS, VIRGINIA. See:
Vass, Fran

JO. See:
Joe
José
March, Mrs.

JO ANN CASTLE. See: Welk,
Lawrence

JO ANNE WORLEY. See:
Rowan, Dan
Worley, Jo Anne

JO DAVIS. See:
Dean, Jimmy
Hamilton, George

JO, JENNIFER. See: Drinkwater,
William

JO STAFFORD. See:
Como, Perry (1)
Crosby, Bob (2)

JOAN
KERMIT, characters appearing
in the drama
Joan and Kermit (R) (Serial
drama)

JOAN. See also:
Allen, Joan Houston
Baez, Joan
Davis, Joan
Davis, Joan Field
Dixon, Wesley
Hargrave-Scott, Joan
Jan
Jane
Jayne
Joanne
June
Nash, Jim
Rivers, Joan
Stevens, Joan
Worthington, Nora

JOAN ALEXANDER. See:
James, Dennis (3)
Roberts, Ken

Joan and Kermit. See: Joan

JOAN BANKS. See: Lovejoy,
Frank (1) (2)

JOAN BISHOP. See: Kelly, Joe
(2)

JOAN BROOKS. See: Marlowe,
Sylvia

JOAN DAVIS. See:
Davis, Joan
Owner

JOAN EDWARDS. See:
Kaye, Danny
Ross, Lanny

JOAN HOGAN, SERGEANT. See:
Bilko, Sergeant Ernest

Joan, I Married. See: Stevens,
Joan

Joan, Leave It to. See: Davis,
Joan

JOAN O'BRIEN. See: Crosby,
Bob (1)

JOAN RANDALL. See: Burnley,
Walter

JOAN ROBERTS FARNSWORTH.
See: Barbour, Henry Wilson

JOAN WARD. See: Manning,
Portia Blake

JOAN WELDON. See: Palmer,
Byron

JOAN WESTON. See: Brasuhn,
Tuffy

JOAN YOUNG. See: Carter,
Kathryn

JOANIE. See:
Cade, Sam
Junie

JOANIE MacROBERTS. See:
Higgins

JOANNA. See: Foster, Major
John

JOANNA MORRISON. See: Ames,
Peter

JOANNE. See:
    Girelli, Joe
    Jan
    Jane
    Jayne
    Joan
    June
    Tate, Joanne

JOANNE WHEATLEY. See:
    Waring, Fred (1)

JOB. See: Dyke, Charity Amanda

JOCELYN. See: Brent, Dr. Jim

JOCKO. See: Novak, Pat

JODY. See:
    Davis, Uncle Bill
    Dodd, Jimmie
    Judy
    O'Connell, Jody

JOE (1)
    SPENCER HOWARD
    DOC GORDON
    LOIS FARMER
    LOIS DAVISSON
    NEIL DAVISSON
    PATRICK MULVANEY
    CASINO, characters appearing
    in the drama
    Home of the Brave (R) (Serial
    drama)

JOE (2), big city cab driver
    MABEL STOOLER, manicurist, in
    love with Joe, wishes to marry
    him
    SHOIMAN STOOLER, Mabel's
    brother
    MRS. STOOLER, Mabel's
    mother
    MIKE
    DOLLY
    M.C., at local beer parlor;
    characters appearing on the pro-
    gram
    Joe and Mabel (R) (Situation
    comedy) (originally called Women
    and Children First) (R) (later
    broadcast in revised form as
    Joe and Mabel) (TV)

JOE (3), head of the house
    VI, his wife
    Mr. and Mrs. (R) (Comedy)

JOE. See also:
    Ames, Joe
    Barton, Joe
    Brown, Joe E. (1) (2)
    Carson, Uncle Joe
    Cook, Joe
    DiMaggio, Joe
    Franklin, Joe
    Friday, Sergeant Joe
    Garagiola, Joe (1) (2) (3)
    Girelli, Joe
    Grant, Harry
    Jo
    José
    Kelly, Joe (1) (2)
    Leighton, Linda
    Lincoln, Joe
    Mannix, Joe
    Marlin, Mary
    Michaels, Joe
    Palooka, Joe
    Penner, Joe
    Pyne, Joe
    Rosenfield, Joe, Jr.
    Shannon, Joe
    Turp, Joe

Joe and Ethel Turp. See: Turp,
    Joe

Joe and Mabel. See: Joe (2)

JOE BAKER. See: Little, Rich

JOE BIDEAUX. See: West, Jim
    (1)

JOE, BIG. See: Rosenfield, Joe,
    Jr.

JOE BILLINGS. See: Waring,
    Evelyn

JOE BINNEY. See: Noble,
    Mary

JOE BUCKLEY. See: Brent,
    Dr. Jim

JOE CHERNAK. See: Peyton,
    Martin

JOE, CHOPSTICK. See: Lee,
    Terry

JOE COBB, MAJOR. See: Savage,
    Brigadier General Frank

JOE CORELLI, DR.   See: Sterling,
Vanessa Dale

JOE CORNTASSLE.   See: Little
Orphan Annie

JOE CRUNCHMILLER.   See:
Canova, Judy

Joe DiMaggio Show, The.   See:
DiMaggio, Joe

Joe E. Brown.   See: Brown, Joe
E. (1)

JOE EARLY, DR.   See: Gage,
John

JOE EDWARDS.   See: Brent,
Portia

JOE FEENEY.   See: Welk,
Lawrence

JOE FOLEY.   See: Burnley,
Walter

JOE FRANCIS.   See: King

Joe Franklin Show, The.   See:
Franklin, Joe

Joe Franklin's Memory Lane.   See:
Franklin, Joe

JOE GALLICCHIO.   See: James,
Dennis (1)

Joe Garagiola's Memory Game.
See: Garagiola, Joe (2)

JOE GUERCIO.   See: Lawrence,
Steve (2)

JOE HASKELL.   See: Collins,
Barnabas

JOE HIGGINS.   See: Everly, Don

JOE HOUSTON.   See: Graham,
Dr. Bob

JOE HOWARD.   See: Kay,
Beatrice

JOE HUDDLESTON.   See: Adams,
Lieut. Price

JOE, INJUN.   See: Finn, Huck

JOE LAURIE, JR.   See: Wilson,
Ward

JOE LAVOTI.   See: Welk,
Lawrence

JOE, LITTLE.   See: Cartwright,
Ben

JOE MACCHIAVERNA.   See: Kaye,
Sammy (1)

JOE MAPHIS.   See: Ritter, Tex
(1)

JOE MARKHAM.   See: Rogers,
Patricia

JOE MARTIN, DR.   See: Davis,
Ann Tyler

JOE MILNER, CALIFORNIA.   See:
Custer, George Armstrong

JOE MULHOLLAND.   See: Ames,
Peter

Joe Palooka.   See: Palooka, Joe

JOE PARSONS.   See: Kelly,
Joe (1)

Joe Penner Show, The.   See:
Penner, Joe

JOE POST.   See: Marlin, Mary

JOE PRESCOTT, DR.   See: Prescott, Kate Hathaway

Joe Pyne Show, The.   See: Pyne,
Joe

JOE RILEY.   See:
Parmalee, Ranger Captain
Walleck, Meredith

JOE RIVERA.   See: August, Dan

JOE ROSSI.   See: Peyton, Martin

JOE SMITH, DETECTIVE.   See:
Friday, Sergeant Joe

JOE SULLIVAN.   See: Ames,
Peter

JOE TAYLOR. See: Garrison,
Spencer

JOE TEX. See: Butler, Jerry

JOE THE BARTENDER. See:
Gleason, Jackie (1) (2)

JOE VENUTI. See:
Archie
Crosby, Bing (3)

JOE WARNER, DR. See: Bauer,
Bertha

JOEL. See: Nash, Jim

JOEL KUPPERMAN. See: Kelly,
Joe (2)

JOEL McCREA. See: Boyer,
Charles

JOEL SMITH. See: Holliday,
Hiram

JOEY. See:
Adams, Joey (1) (2)
Barnes, Joey
Bishop, Joey
Brewster, Joey
Drum, Jefferson
Mitchell, Dennis
Newton, Jim

JOEY BISHOP. See:
Bishop, Joey
Reiner, Carl

Joey Bishop Show, The. See:
Barnes, Joey
Bishop, Joey

JOEY HEATHERTON. See:
Edwards, Ralph (1)

JOEY NASH. See: Himber,
Richard

JOEY STARRETT. See: Shane

JOEY THE CLOWN. See: Corky

JOHN. See:
Abbott, John
Anthony, John J.
Beamer, John
Bickerson, John

Booth, Martha
Bracken, John
Byner, John (1) (2)
Cannon, John
Chancellor, John
Churchill, John
Ciardi, John
Craig, Colonel John B.
Crosby, John
Daly, John (1) (2) (3) (4)
Dane, Prudence
Davidson, John (1) (2)
Day, Clarence
Dix, Dorothy (1)
Douglas, Steve
Drake, John
Drew, John
Driggs, Karleton King
Fairchild, Kay
Foster, Major John
Gage, John
Gidget
Glenn, Colonel John
Gunther, John
Hawk, John
Herrick, Cap'n John
Jan
John's
Jon
Karr, Mike
King, John
King, John Reed (1) (2)
Lackland, John
Lane, Rebecca
Lassie
McCaffery, John K. M. (1) (2)
McIntire, John
McKeever, Dr. John
Mannering, John
Marshall, John
Medbury, John P.
Monroe, John
Morrison, Mother
Mosby, Major John
Nelson, John
Nesbit, John (1) (2)
Newland, John
Novak, John
O'Toole, John Michael
Parker, Seth
Perkins, Ma
Perry, John
Randolph, Alice
Rutledge, Dr. John
Shuttleworth, John
Silver, Long John
Smith, Angel
Steed, John

Stephenson, John
Swayze, John Cameron
Walton, Grandpa
Wayne, John
Wincholl, John

JOHN ADAM DRAYTON. See:
Perkins, Ma

JOHN ADAMS. See: Harding,
Karen Adams

JOHN AMOS. See: Kelly, Gene

JOHN BARRY, CAPTAIN. See:
Johnson, Bess

JOHN BARTLETT. See: Carter,
Kathryn

JOHN BENSON, DR. See: Sothern,
Mary

JOHN BERRESFORD TIPTON. See:
Anthony, Michael

JOHN BICKERSON. See:
Bergen, Edgar (2)
Bickerson, John

JOHN-BOY. See: Walton, Grandpa

JOHN BRENT. See: Tammy

JOHN BRITTON. See: Davidson,
Bill

JOHN BROWN. See: Cantor,
Eddie (2)

John Byner Comedy Hour, The.
See: Byner, John (1)

JOHN C. HILLEY. See: Lord,
Phillips H.

JOHN CHANCELLOR. See:
Chancellor, John
Downs, Hugh

JOHN CONTE. See: Francis,
Arlene (3)

John Daly and the News. See:
Daly, John (1)

JOHN DARLING. See: Pan,
Peter

JOHN DAVIDSON. See:
Davidson, John (1) (2)
DeLuise, Dom (2)

John Davidson Show, The. See:
Davidson, John (2)

John, Dear. See: Chandler,
Faith

JOHN DICKSON, DR. See:
Hughes, Chris

JOE DOE. See: Allen, Fred

JOHN EGAN. See: Anderson,
Sergeant Nick

JOHN ELDRIDGE. See: Hughes,
Lisa

JOHN ELLIOTT. See: Meredith,
Charles

JOHN FLETCHER, DR. See:
Bauer, Bertha

John Forsythe Show, The. See:
Foster, Major John

JOHN FOWLER. See: Peyton,
Martin

John Gunther's High Road. See:
Gunther, John

JOHN HACKETT. See: Davis,
Joan Field

JOHN HART. See: Benti, Joseph

JOHN HARTFORD. See: Crosby,
Bing (2)

JOHN HENRY. See: Hayes,
Wing Commander

JOHN J. ANTHONY. See: Anthony,
Mr.

JOHN K. M. McCAFFERY. See:
Gray, Barry (1)
McCaffery, John K. M. (1) (2)

JOHN KIERAN. See: Fadiman,
Clifton (1)

JOHN KNIGHT. See: Rogers,
Patricia

JOHN L. C. SIVONEY.   See:
Benny, Jack
Hope, Bob (2)

JOHN LARDNER.   See: Cross,
Mason

JOHN LARSEN.   See: Morgan,
Paul

JOHN LENNOX.   See: Harum,
David

JOHN, LITTLE.   See: Hood, Robin

JOHN McGUIRE.   See: Horton,
Dr. Tom

JOHN McINTIRE.   See: Welles,
Orson (2)

JOHN McINTYRE, TRAPPER.
See: Pierce, Captain Hawkeye

JOHN MASON BROWN.   See:
Evans, Bergen (2)

JOHN MONKS.   See: Welles,
Orson (1)

JOHN MORRISON, DR.   See:
Davis, Dr. Althea

JOHN MURRAY.   See:
Carter, Kathryn
Larimore, Marilyn

JOHN NELSON.   See:
Cameron, Barry
Nelson, John

JOHN P. MULCAHY, FATHER.
See: Pierce, Captain Hawkeye

JOHN PARKER.   See: Manning,
Portia Blake

JOHN POLLACK.   See: Kelly,
Joe (2)

JOHN RAINEY.   See: Prescott,
Kate Hathaway

JOHN RAITT.   See: Blair, Janet

JOHN REED KING.   See:
Compton, Walter
King, John Reed (1) (2)

Parks, Bert (1)

JOHN REID.   See: Lone Ranger,
The

JOHN RICHMAN, DR.   See:
Rogers, Patricia

JOHN ROBINSON, PROFESSOR.
See: Smith, Colonel Zachary

JOHN ROLFSON.   See: Shadel,
Bill

JOHN SCALI.   See:
Peterson, Roger
Smith, Howard K. (2)

JOHN SCOTT TROTTER.   See:
Crosby, Bing (1)

John Silver, Long.   See: Silver,
Long John

JOHN TWOMEY.   See: Reed,
Jerry

JOHN WATSON, DR.   See:
Holmes, Sherlock

JOHN WAYNE, DR.   See: Wayne,
Ruth Evans

JOHN WILSON.   See: Mitchell,
Dennis

JOHNNY, Philip Morris Cigarettes
page boy, portrayed by Johnny
Roventini and Freddy (Buddy)
Douglas
MANY ACTORS, ACTRESSES
AND VOCALISTS
JOHNNY GREEN, orchestra
leader (himself)
HIS ORCHESTRA
Johnny Presents (R) (Drama)

JOHNNY.   See also:
Ace, Goodman
Blake, Tom
Carson, Johnny (1) (2)
Cash, Johnny
Dane, Prudence
Desmond, Johnny
Dollar, Johnny
Dotty
Janey
Janie

Janney
Jonny
Madero, Johnny
Mann, Johnny
Midnight, Johnny
Miller, Johnny
O'Connor, Katy
Olsen, Johnny (1) (2)
Ringo, Johnny
Slate, Johnny
Staccato, Johnny
Sterling, Vanessa Dale
Wayne, Johnny (1) (2)
Yohnny
Yuma, Johnny

JOHNNY AMOROSO. See:
Kaye, Sammy (1)
Lopez, Vincent

JOHNNY BOONE, JR. See:
Bronson, Millie

JOHNNY BOONE, SR. See:
Bronson, Millie

JOHNNY BROWN. See:
Rowan, Dan
Uggams, Leslie

JOHNNY CASH. See:
Cash, Johnny
Ritter, Tex (1)

Johnny Cash Presents the Everly
Brothers. See: Everly, Don

Johnny Cash Show, The. See:
Cash, Johnny

JOHNNY CORSO, DETECTIVE.
See: Haines, Lieut. Mike

Johnny Dollar, Yours Truly. See:
Dollar, Johnny

JOHNNY DOW. See: Lane, Hondo

JOHNNY GREEN. See:
Benny, Jack
Clayton, Margie
Johnny
Ross, Lanny

JOHNNY HAUSER. See: Ross,
Lanny

JOHNNY JOHNSON. See: Elliott,
Win (2)

JOHNNY JOHNSTON. See:
Donald, Peter
Moore, Garry (1)

JOHNNY KLEIN. See: Welk,
Lawrence

JOHNNY LONG. See: Whiteman,
Paul

JOHNNY McAFEE. See: Kaye,
Sammy (1)

JOHNNY McKAY. See: Troop,
Marshal Dan

Johnny Madero, Pier 23. See:
Madero, Johnny

JOHNNY MADRID. See: Lancer,
Murdoch

JOHNNY MANN. See:
Bishop, Joey
Mann, Johnny

JOHNNY MANN SINGERS, THE.
See: Mann, Johnny

Johnny Mann: Stand Up and Cheer.
See: Mann, Johnny

JOHNNY MERCER. See: Crosby,
Bing (3)

Johnny Midnight. See: Midnight,
Johnny

JOHNNY OLSEN. See:
Moore, Tom (1)
Olsen, Johnny (1) (2)

Johnny Presents. See: Johnny

JOHNNY RAMOS. See: Slattery,
Jim

JOHNNY REACH. See: Brackett,
Hank

Johnny Ringo. See: Ringo,
Johnny

JOHNNY ROBERTS. See: Barbour,
Henry Wilson

JOHNNY ROVENTINI. See:
Johnny

JOHNNY RUSSO, LIEUT.   See: Holbrook, Captain Matt

JOHNNY "SCAT" DAVIS.   See:
Waring, Fred (1)

JOHNNY STARR.   See: Sloan,
Holly

JOHNNY WARD.   See: Allen,
Joan Houston

JOHN'S.   See also:
John
Jon

John's Other Wife.   See: Perry,
John

JOHNSON.   See:
Johnston
Johnstone
Kimble, Dr. Richard
Yohnson

JOHNSON, ALICE.   See: Kaufman,
Seymour

JOHNSON, ARTE.   See: Rowan,
Dan

JOHNSON, BAYN.   See: Jones,
Dean

JOHNSON, BESS, matron at
orphanage, later superintendent
of a boarding school
DR. ROBBY CLARK, physician
GRACE DOBLEN, superintendent
DR. BOROS, physician
JERRY ADAIR
JEAN ADAIR
JULIE ERICKSON
GILDA BOROS
PAUL HUTCHINSON
TULIP VALENTINE ELSON
TINY TIM
POKEY
DAVID JEFFERS
JEFFREY BARTON
THELMA GIDLEY
STELLA RUDNICK
STEVE CORTLAND
BILL GREY
CAPTAIN JOHN BARRY
GWEN BARRY
ROY BARRY

MICHAEL PATERNO
DANIEL FINDLAY
LINDA CLARK
ED CROWLEY
CLEMENTINE
DUKE
LANA
MARNY
HAZEL
SHIRLEY, characters appearing
in the drama
Hilltop House (R) (Serial drama)
(later known as The Story of
Bess Johnson) (R)

JOHNSON, BESS.   See also: Lady
Esther

JOHNSON, BLUE-TOOTH.   See:
Gook, Vic

JOHNSON, CHICK.   See: Olsen,
Ole

Johnson Family, The.   See:
Scribner, Jimmy

JOHNSON, JILL.   See: Gibson,
Jack

JOHNSON, JOHNNY.   See: Elliott,
Win (2)

JOHNSON, JUDY.   See: Caesar,
Sid (3)

JOHNSON, JULIE.   See: Carter,
Kathryn

JOHNSON, LEWIS.   See: Dallas,
Stella

JOHNSON, MALCOLM.   See:
Malone, Dr. Jerry

JOHNSON, MARGARET "HONEY."
See: Butterworth, Wally

JOHNSON, MRS.   See:
Collins, Barnabas
Young, Alan

JOHNSON, PARKS
JERRY BELCHER
WALLY BUTTERWORTH
WARREN HULL
GRAHAM McNAMEE, interviewers
and quizmasters on the program

(themselves)
Sidewalk Interviews (R) (Quiz and
interviews) (later known as Vox
Pop) (R) (TV)

JOHNSON, POLICE LIEUT. See:
Midnight, Captain

JOHNSON, RAYMOND EDWARD (1)
BETTY CAINE
BILL LIPTON
LUIS VAN ROOTEN
ANN SHEPHERD
GILBERT MACK, actors and
actresses featured on the pro-
gram (themselves)
MANY GUEST ACTORS AND
ACTRESSES
Everyman's Theater (R) (Drama)

JOHNSON, RAYMOND EDWARD (2)
BETTY CAINE, featured on the
program (themselves)
MANY ACTORS AND ACTRESSES
There Was a Woman (R) (Drama)

JOHNSON, RAYMOND EDWARD.
See also:
Ameche, Don (3)
Bell, Alexander Graham
First Nighter, Mr.
Judge, The
Raymond
Roberts, Ken
Welles, Orson (2)
Winkler, Betty

JOHNSON, VAN, actor; host of the
program (himself)
HY GARDNER, columnist; inter-
view personality guest (himself)
MANY INTERVIEWEES AND
ENTERTAINERS
The Van Johnson Show (TV)
(Variety/interview)

JOHNSON, VAN. See also:
Crosby, Bing (2)

JOHNSON, VERA. See: Dallas,
Stella

JOHNSTON. See also:
Johnson
Johnstone
Yohnson

JOHNSTON, JOHNNY. See:

Donald, Peter
Moore, Garry (1)

JOHNSTON, MERLE. See:
Reser, Harry

JOHNSTONE. See also:
Johnson
Johnston
Yohnson

JOHNSTONE, BILL. See: Welles,
Orson (2)

JOKER, THE. See: Batman

Joker's Wild, The. See: Barry,
Jack (4)

JOLLY. See: Forsyte, Soames

JOLLY, MR., former postman,
now operator of animal shelter
DOC, veterinarian
Hotel for Pets (R) (Serial
drama)

JOLLY ROGERS. See: Hargrave-
Scott, Joan

JOLSON, AL
SMITH BALLEW
WALLACE BEERY
EDWARD EVERETT HORTON,
hosts of the program (themselves)
NADINE CONNOR, featured
vocalist (herself)
MANY GUEST STARS
VICTOR YOUNG, orchestra
leader (himself)
HIS ORCHESTRA
Shell Chateau (R) (Variety)

JOLSON, AL. See also: Crosby,
Bing (3)

JOLYON, OLD. See: Forsyte,
Soames

JOLYON, YOUNG. See: Forsyte,
Soames

JON. See:
Big Jon
Forsyte, Soames
John
John's

Jon and Sparky, Big. See: Big
  Jon

JON TUSKA. See: Hill, Ruane

JONAH. See: Crowell, Jonah

JONATHAN. See:
  Carlyle, Baylor
  Croft, Jonathan
  Driggs, Karleton King
  Kegg, Jonathan
  Marlin, Mary
  Speaker, The
  Trimble, Jonathan
  Winters, Jonathan

JONATHAN HAYWARD. See:
  Trent, Helen

JONATHAN HILLERY. See:
  Davidson, Bill

Jonathan Kegg. See: Kegg,
  Jonathan

JONATHAN McNEILL, DR. See:
  Harding, Karen Adams
  Rutledge, Dr. John

Jonathan Trimble, Esq. See:
  Trimble, Jonathan

JONATHAN WINTERS. See:
  Winters, Jonathan
  Worley, Jo Anne

Jonathan Winters Show, The. See:
  Winters, Jonathan

JONES, ABRAHAM LINCOLN,
  crusading attorney
  MARSHA SPEAR, his secretary
  C. E. CARRUTHERS, his law
  clerk
  The Law and Mr. Jones (TV)
  (Courtroom drama)

Jones, Alias Smith and. See:
  Heyes, Hannibal

JONES, AMOS
  ANDREW H. BROWN (Andy),
  partners; proprietors of the
  Fresh Air Taxicab Company
  GEORGE STEVENS (Kingfish),
  official of the lodge, The Mystic
  Knights of the Sea

SAPPHIRE STEVENS, wife of
  Kingfish
LIGHTNIN', handyman
HENRY VAN PORTER, wealthy
  friend of Amos and Andy
RUBY TAYLOR, Amos' girl
  friend
MADAME QUEEN, Andy's girl
  friend, manicurist
ARBADELLA, "The Little Girl"
SHORTY, barber
STONEWALL, lawyer
MISS GENEVIEVE BLUE, friend
  of Andy
Amos 'n' Andy (R) (TV) (Black-
  face situation comedy)

JONES' ANSWERING SERVICE,
  MR. See: Pam

JONES, BEN, cowhand
  HOWDY LEWIS, his friend; cow-
  hand
  JIM ED LOVE, owner of the
  J. L. ranch
  OLD FOOLER, horse
  The Rounders (TV) (Western)

JONES, BILLY
  ERNIE HARE, singers and
  entertainers featured on the
  program (themselves)
  Community Sing (R) (Music)

JONES, BILLY. See also:
  Happiness, Boys, The

JONES, BOB. See: Keene, Kitty

JONES, CASEY (1), engineer of
  the Wabash Cannonball
  CASEY, JR., his son
  Casey Jones (TV) (Railroad
  adventure)

JONES, CASEY (2), New York
  policewoman
  Decoy (TV) (Police drama)

JONES, CHUCK. See: Pam

JONES, DAVY
  MICKY DOLENZ
  MIKE NESMITH
  PETER TORK, members of
  "The Monkees," rock and roll
  singing group
  MANY GUEST MUSICIANS

The Monkees (TV) (Music/
variety)

JONES, DEAN, host of the program
(himself)
DENNIS ALLEN
MAUREEN ARTHUR
DICK CLAIR
JENNA McMAHON
GERRI GRANGER
BAYN JOHNSON
SCOEY MITCHILL
RON PRINCE
ALEX DREIER, entertainers ap-
pearing on the program (them-
selves)
MANY GUEST STARS
What's It All About, World? (TV)
(Comedy/satire)

JONES, DEAN. See also:
Jones, Jack
Shawn, Dick

JONES, EDGAR ALLAN, JR.,
presiding judge of traffic court
(himself)
Traffic Court (TV) (Actual court
cases)

JONES, ELSIE. See: Graham,
Dr. Bob

JONES, FIVE STAR. See: Jones,
Tom (1)

JONES, GERALDINE. See: Wilson, Flip

JONES, GRANDPA. See: Owens,
Buck

JONES, IVAN. See: Hansen,
Dean Eric

JONES, JACK
MICHAEL LANDON
PAUL ANKA
GEORGE HAMILTON
GARY CROSBY
FRANK SINATRA, JR.
FRANKIE AVALON
ANNETTE FUNICELLO
SAMMY DAVIS, JR.
TRINI LOPEZ
BOBBY VINTON
DEAN JONES
OTHERS, hosts of the program

(themselves)
MANY GUEST STARS
PETER MATZ, orchestra
leader (himself)
HIS ORCHESTRA
Hullabaloo (TV) (Variety)

JONES, JAMES EARL. See:
Cookie Monster, The

JONES, JANIE. See: Kaye,
Sammy (1)

JONES, JUGHEAD. See: Andrews,
Archie

JONES, KENNETH YARBOROUGH
(Kentucky), horse trainer and
veterinarian
"SELDOM" JACKSON, his
assistant
DWIGHT EISENHOWER WONG,
Chinese boy, escapee from Red
China; Jones' foster son
Kentucky Jones (TV) (Comedy)

Jones, Kentucky. See: Jones,
Kenneth Yarborough

JONES, LOCO
MIKE McCALL
GRETA JACKSON, golddiggers;
hope to marry rich men
How to Marry a Millionaire
(TV) (Comedy)

Jones, Lorenzo. See: Jones,
Lorenzo

JONES, LORENZO, automobile
mechanic and inventor of use-
less gadgets
BELLE, his wife
JIM BARKER, garage owner;
Lorenzo Jones' employer
IRMA BARKER, wife of Jim
Barker
ABBY MATSON
SANDY MATSON
CLARENCE J. MUGGINS
CHESTER VAN DYNE
MRS. HENRY THAYER
JUDY
NICK
FRANCES
MILLIE
WALTER
ANGUS

MARGARET, characters appearing in the drama
Lorenzo Jones (R) (Serial comedy/drama)

JONES, MEREDITH. See: Grimm, Arnold

JONES, MICKEY. See: Rogers, Kenny

JONES, MR. See: Dillon, Marshal Matt

JONES, QUINCY. See: Cosby, Bill (2)

JONES, ROCKY, trouble-shooter for the United Worlds of the Solar System
Rocky Jones, Space Ranger (TV) (Science fiction adventure)

JONES, SAM, farmer, widower and resident of Mayberry
MIKE, his 13-year-old son
COUSIN ALICE
AUNT BEE, his housekeepers
HOWARD SPRAGUE, "a minor functionary at City Hall"
EMMETT CLARK, town fix-it man
MARTHA CLARK, Emmett's wife
GOOBER PYLE, gasoline station operator
MILLIE SWANSON, Sam Jones's girl friend
Mayberry R.F.D. (TV) (Situation comedy)

JONES, SPEARCHUCKER. See: Pierce, Captain Hawkeye

JONES, SPIKE (1), drummer and orchestra leader, featured on the program (himself)
GEORGE ROCK
DOODLES WEAVER
CARL FORTINA
LEN CARRIE
KEN CAPPS
CARL GRAYSON
WILLIE SPICER
HELEN GRAYCO, musicians and comedians featured on the program (themselves); members of the "City Slickers" orchestra
MANY GUEST STARS

Club Oasis (TV) (Music/slapstick comedy)

JONES, SPIKE (2), drummer and orchestra leader; star of the program (himself)
The Spike Jones Show (R) (TV) (Music/comedy)
THE CITY SLICKERS, orchestra
DOROTHY SHAY (The Park Avenue Hillbilly), featured vocalist (herself)
The Spike Jones Show (R)
HIS ORCHESTRA
HELEN GRAYCO, featured vocalist (herself)
BILL DANA (José Jiménez)
LEN WEINRIB, comedians featured on the program (themselves)
MANY GUEST STARS
The Spike Jones Show (TV)

JONES, THADDEUS. See: Heyes, Hannibal

JONES, TOM (1), (Five Star Jones), newspaper reporter
SALLY JONES, his wife
CITY EDITOR of "The Register"
MA MORAN, Jones' friend
Five Star Jones (R) (Serial drama)

JONES, TOM (2), singer and entertainer, host of the program (himself)
MANY GUEST STARS
This Is Tom Jones (TV) (Variety)

JONES, WASHINGTON. See: Dugan, Jimmie

JONESEY. See: Harper, Jess

JONNY. See:
Janey
Janie
Janney
Johnny
Quest, Jonny
Yohnny

Jonny Quest. See: Quest, Jonny

JORDAN BOYLE. See: Stowe, Senator Hays

JORDAN BRADDOCK. See:
Richards, Ben

JORDAN, JACK. See: Halop, Billy

JORDAN, JIM, comedian (1)
MARION JORDAN, comedienne;
featured on the program (themselves)
The Smackouts (R) (Comedy)

JORDAN, JIM (2), comedian, fea-
tured on the program
MARION JORDAN, comedienne;
featured on the program (them-
selves)
THEIR TWO MARRIAGEABLE
DAUGHTERS
THEIR DAUGHTERS' BOY
FRIENDS
The Smith Family (R) (Situation
comedy)

JORDAN, JOYCE, intern and
physician in the town of Preston
DR. HANS SIMONS
DR. THOMAS WEBSTER
DR. MOLLY HEDGEROW
DR. ANDREWS
DR. TRACY
DR. ALEXANDER GREY
DR. ALAN WEBSTER
DR. CLIFFORD REED
DR. REINHARDT
DR. DAVID MORGAN
DR. MILDERMAUL, physicians
PAUL SHERWOOD
EDGAR JARVIS
DORIA VAN DORN
VIC MANION
INSPECTOR CARSON
HOPE ALISON
DORIE WINTERS
OLLIE
MARGOT SHERWOOD
DIANE OGDEN
JIMMY MALONE
CHESTER HEDGEROW
BILL WINTERS
MYRA LEE
ROGER WALTON
ANNE HILL
DEAN RUSSELL
MIKE MALONE
GRANNY HEWITT
IRIS BLAKELY
CAPTAIN CLAYTON
GREGORY OGDEN

LYDIA DRAKE
SHEILA BRAND
COURTNEY LEE
WILLIAM WALTER
DAWSON BLAKELY
TOM HUGHES
ERNEST EDEN
CELIA
STEVE WELLES
MARTIN SPARROWHILL
JANE BELLE
GLORIA BLAINE
ADA MANION, characters ap-
pearing in the drama
Joyce Jordan, Girl Intern (R)
(Serial drama) (later known as
Joyce Jordan, M.D.) (R)

JORDAN, NED, railroad detective
Ned Jordan, Secret Agent (R)
(Detective adventure)

JOSE. See also:
Jo
Joe

JOSE ITURBI. See: Bell, Alexander Graham

JOSE JIMENEZ. See:
Jiménez, José
Jones, Spike (2)

JOSE MELIS. See: Paar, Jack

JOSEF. See:
Joseph
Marais, Josef

JOSEF PASTERNACK. See: Faith,
Percy

JOSEF STALIN. See: Husing, Ted

JOSEPH. See:
Benti, Joseph
Cotten, Joseph (1) (2)
Dunninger, Joseph
Dyke, Charity Amanda
Josef
Perkins, Ma
Welch, Joseph N.

JOSEPH BELL. See: Hayes,
Helen (2)

JOSEPH BENEDICT. See: Jackson, Martha

JOSEPH COTTEN. See:
Cotten, Joseph (1) (2)
Welles, Orson (1) (2)

JOSEPH DUNNINGER. See:
Dunninger, Joseph
Winchell, Paul (1)

JOSEPH GANNON, DR. See:
Lochner, Dr. Paul

JOSEPH HOWE. See: Baker,
Dean Fred

JOSEPH JULIAN. See: Ingram,
Dan

JOSEPHINE ANTOINE. See:
Faith, Percy

JOSEPHINE WHITFIELD. See:
Cameron, Barry

JOSH. See:
Chandler, Faith
Joshua
Randall, Josh

JOSH, UNCLE. See: Brown,
Ellen

JOSH VINDUC. See: Sterling,
Vanessa Dale

JOSHUA. See:
Bolt, Jason
Josh

JOSHUA SMITH. See: Heyes,
Hannibal

JOSIAH. See: Speaker, The

JOSIE
MELODY
ALEXANDRIA, members of the
"Pussycats," rock music group
VALERIE
ALEC
ALAN
SEBASTIAN, cat; all cartoon
characters
Josie and the Pussycats (TV)
(Cartoon) (later renamed Josie
and the Pussycats In Outer Space)
(TV)

JOSIE. See also:

Perkins, Ma
Stewart, Jan
Teen, Harold

Josie and the Pussycats. See:
Josie

Josie and the Pussycats in Outer
Space. See: Josie

JOSTYN, JAY (1)
CHARLES WOODS
HARRY HOLCOMBE
PETER GRANT
DON DOWD
PALMER WARD, narrators on
the program (themselves)
Moon River (R) (Poetry and
music)

JOSTYN, JAY (2), narrator and
host of the program (himself)
VARIOUS ACTORS AND AC-
TRESSES
The Mystery Man (R) (Dramatizations of popular suspense
novels)

JOSTYN, JAY. See also: Judge
(2)

Journal, Black. See: Brown,
Tony

Journal, David Brinkley's. See:
Brinkley, David

Journal, Dr. Hudson's Secret.
See: Hudson, Dr. Wayne

Journal, Jergens. See: Winchell,
Walter (3)

Journey, Bold. See: Stephenson,
John

Journey, Lone. See: Bennett,
Nita

JOY. See: Bazarre, Benita

JOY, DAVID. See: Welk,
Lawrence

JOY HODGES. See: Kirby, Durward

JOY WYNN. See: Barton, Bud

JOYCE. See:
Brothers, Dr. Joyce
Collins, Bing
Goldberg, Molly
Jordan, Joyce

JOYCE BROTHERS, DR. See:
Brothers, Dr. Joyce
March, Hal
Story, Ralph
Walleck, Meredith

JOYCE CARRAWAY. See: Drake,
Bradley

JOYCE CLARK. See: Erwin, Stu

JOYCE, JIMMY. See: Junior

Joyce Jordan, Girl Intern. See:
Jordan, Joyce

Joyce Jordan, M. D. See: Jordan,
Joyce

JOYCE MILLER. See: Dawson,
Rosemary

JOYCE RYAN. See: Midnight,
Captain

JOYCE TURNER. See: Brown,
Ellen

JOYCE, WILLIAM, Nazi propaganda
broadcaster in World War II
(himself); known as Lord Haw Haw
Lord Haw Haw (R) (Nazi war
propaganda)

JUANO HERNANDEZ. See: Marais,
Josef

JUBILAIRES, THE. See: Godfrey,
Arthur (1)

Jubilee, U. S. A. See: Foley, Red

JUD STRUNK. See: Rowan, Dan

JUDD, CLINTON, prominent Houston
trial lawyer
BENJAMIN CALDWELL, his young
law partner
HELEN, his secretary
Judd For the Defense (TV)
(Courtroom drama)

Judd For the Defense. See: Judd,
Clinton

JUDE FAWLEY. See: Cooke,
Alistaire (1)

Jude the Obscure. See: Cooke,
Alistaire (1)

JUDGE (1), presiding in divorce
court, portrayed by Voltaire
Perkins
MANY COUPLES SEEKING
DIVORCES
Divorce Court (TV) (Courtroom
drama)

JUDGE (2), character portrayed
by Jay Jostyn
MANY DEFENDANTS
COURT OFFICIALS
Night Court (TV) (Courtroom
drama)

JUDGE. See also:
Bean, Judge Roy
Fitz, Judge
Hardy, Andy
Judge, The
Solemn Old Judge, The

JUDGE BALDWIN. See: Walleck,
Meredith

JUDGE BENNETT. See: Hardy,
Dr. Steven

JUDGE CARTER COLBY. See:
Larimore, Marilyn

JUDGE CHESTER. See: Peyton,
Martin

JUDGE COLBY. See: Carter,
Kathryn

JUDGE GLENN HUNTER. See:
Barbour, Henry Wilson

JUDGE HARTLEY. See: Perkins,
Ma

JUDGE HENRY GARTH. See:
Virginian, The

JUDGE HOOKER. See: Gildersleeve, Throckmorton P.

JUDGE KRUGER. See: Hargrave-
Scott, Joan

JUDGE LOWELL. See: Hughes,
Chris

JUDGE PARSONS. See: Mix, Tom

Judge Roy Bean. See: Bean, Judge
Roy

JUDGE SCOTT. See: O'Neill, Mrs.

JUDGE SUMMERFIELD. See:
Barton, Bud

JUDGE, THE, jurist, portrayed by
Maurice Franklin
DeWITT McBRIDE
ROGER DeKOVEN, narrators of
the program (themselves)
JEAN PAUL KING
MANDEL KRAMER
RAYMOND EDWARD JOHNSON
BYRON KANE
TRUE BOARDMAN
FRANK READICK, actors appear-
ing on the program (themselves)
Famous Jury Trials (R) (Court-
room drama)

JUDGE, THE. See also:
Dale, Linda
Judge
Mason, Perry

JUDGE WATSON. See: Burton,
Terry

JUDGE WILEY. See: Buffalo Bill,
Jr.

Judgment, Snap. See: McMahon,
Ed (2)

JUDITH. See: Bradley, Judith

JUDITH ADAMS. See: Brown,
Ellen

JUDITH CLARK. See: Larimore,
Marilyn

JUDITH EVANS. See: Larimore,
Marilyn

JUDITH MERRITT. See: Noble,
Mary

JUDSON. See: McKay, Judson

JUDY
JANE LEE
JIM SARGENT, characters ap-
pearing in the drama
Judy and Jane (R) (Serial drama)

JUDY. See also:
Canova, Judy
Foster, Judy
Garland, Judy
Graves, Harry
Grimm, Arnold
Jetson, George
Jody
Jones, Lorenzo
Massey, Christine
Perry, John
Sterling, Vanessa Dale
Tracy, Dr. Marsh
Wilbur, Judy

Judy, A Date With. See: Foster,
Judy

Judy and Jane. See: Judy

Judy Canova Show, The. See:
Canova, Judy

JUDY CARNE. See: Rowan, Dan

Judy Garland Show, The. See:
Garland, Judy

JUDY GRAHAM. See: Kelly, Joe
(2)

JUDY GRAUBART. See:
Cosby, Bill (1)
Klein, Robert

JUDY JOHNSON. See: Caesar,
Sid (3)

JUDY LYNN. See: Lopez, Vincent

JUDY PRICE. See: Christian,
Dr. Paul

JUDY ROBINSON. See: Smith,
Colonel Zachary

JUDY SPLINTERS. See:
Cantor, Eddie (2)
Dinsdale, Shirley

Judy Splinters, Shirley Dinsdale and.
See: Dinsdale, Shirley

JUDY TYLER. See: Stokey, Mike

JUDY VAN EUER. See: Hutton,
Ina Ray

JUGHEAD JONES. See: Andrews,
Archie

JULES BLEDSOE. See: Henry,
Captain

JULES CARLSHORN. See: Chandler, Faith

Julia. See: Baker, Julia

JULIA. See:
Baker, Julia
Brent, Dr. Jim
Child, Julia
Horton, Dot
Julius
Meredith, Charles

JULIA GLASS. See: Roxy

JULIA GROWNUP. See: Cosby,
Bill (1)

JULIA HOFFMAN. See: Collins,
Barnabas

JULIA MARLOWE. See: Drew,
John

JULIA MEADE. See: Sullivan,
Ed

JULIA SANDERSON. See:
Crumit, Frank (1) (2) (3)

Julia Sanderson, Frank Crumit and.
See: Crumit, Frank (3)

JULIA STUART. See: Hughes,
Chris

JULIAN ALTMAN. See: Halop,
Billy

JULIAN HATHAWAY, PROFESSOR.
See: Prescott, Kate Hathaway

JULIAN, JOSEPH. See: Ingram,
Dan

JULIE. See:
Andrews, Julie
Blair, Timothy
Brown, Robinson, Jr.
McCray, Linc
Palmer, Dan
Willis, David

JULIE ANDERSON. See: Peyton,
Martin

Julie Andrews Hour, The. See:
Andrews, Julie

JULIE BARNES. See: Hayes,
Linc

JULIE COLLINS. See: Rutledge,
Dr. John

JULIE ERICKSON. See: Johnson,
Bess

JULIE HILLYER. See: Karr,
Mike

JULIE JOHNSON. See: Carter,
Kathryn

JULIE McWHIRTER. See: Nye,
Louis

JULIE STEVENS. See: Roberts,
Ken

JULIET. See: Worthington, Nora

JULIET PROWSE. See: Berman,
Shelley

JULIKAK, ANTON. See: Perkins,
Ma

JULIUS. See:
Julie
La Rosa, Julius
Nuvo, Arnie

JULIUS ABBRUZIO. See: Harris,
Phil

JULIUS LA ROSA. See:
Godfrey, Arthur (1)
La Rosa, Julius

Julius La Rosa Show, The. See:
La Rosa, Julius.

Jumbo. See: Bowers, Brainy

Junction, Petticoat. See: Carson, Uncle Joe

JUNE. See:
Allyson, June
Cleaver, Ward
Conrad, Jim
Erwin, Stu
Forsyte, Soames
Jan
Jane
Jayne
Joan
Joanne

June Allyson Show, The. See: Allyson, June

June Allyson, The DuPont Show With. See: Allyson, June

JUNE CARTER. See: Cash, Johnny

JUNE MEREDITH. See: First Nighter, Mr.

JUNE TAYLOR DANCERS, THE. See:
DeLuise, Dom (1)
Dorsey, Tommy
Ford, Tennessee Ernie (2)
Gleason, Jackie (2)

JUNE VALLI. See: Williams, Andy (1)

June Valli, Andy Williams and. See: Williams, Andy (1)

Jungle Jim. See: Jungle Jim

JUNGLE JIM, adventurer-explorer
KOLU, his servant
KIMBA, his pet chimpanzee
SHANGHAI LIL
TIGER LIL, "women in his life"
Jungle Jim (R) (TV) (Adventure)
SKIPPER, his friend
Jungle Jim (TV)

Jungle, Ramar of the. See: Reynolds, Dr. Tom

Jungle, Sheena, Queen of the. See: Sheena

Jungle, The Asphalt. See: Gower, Matthew

JUNIE. See:
Allen, Steve (2)
Joanie

JUNIOR, "The Mean Widdle Kid"
BOLIVAR SHAGNASTY
CLEM KADIDDLEHOPPER
J. NEWTON NUMBSKULL
WILLY LUMP-LUMP
FREDDIE THE FREELOADER
SAN FERNANDO RED
COLOSSAL MAN
LUDWIG VON HUMPERDOO,
characters portrayed by Red
Skelton on the program
MANY GUEST STARS AND
ENTERTAINERS
The Red Skelton Show (R) (TV)
(Comedy/variety)
OZZIE NELSON
DAVID ROSE, orchestra leaders
THEIR ORCHESTRAS
The Red Skelton Show (R) (Comedy/variety)
CAULIFLOWER McPUGG
POP THE JANITOR
THE DRUNK
GEORGE APPLEBY
THE HENPECKED HUSBAND
COOKIE THE SAILOR
DEADEYE THE COWBOY, characters portrayed by Red Skelton
THE TOM HANSEN DANCERS
JIMMY JOYCE, orchestra leader
(himself)
HIS ORCHESTRA
The Red Skelton Hour (TV) (Comedy/variety)

JUNIOR. See also:
Jackson, Jarrin' Jack
Nebb, Rudolph
Riley, Chester A.
Tracy, Dick

JUNIOR DEVERE. See: Overstreet, Buddy

JUNIOR FITZ. See: Perkins, Ma

JUNIOR MATTHEWS. See: Carter, Kathryn

Junior Miss. See: Graves, Harry

JUNIOR, NICHOLAS "NICKY" LACEY.
See: Barbour, Henry Wilson

Junior Nurse Corps. See: Barton,
Clara

JUNIOR SAMPLES. See: Owens,
Buck

JUNIOR STEPHENSON. See:
Brent, Dr. Jim

Jury, American Woman's. See:
Williams, Emily

Jury, Juvenile. See: Barry, Jack
(5)

Jury Trials, Famous. See: Judge,
The

Just Generation, The. See: Miller,
Howard

Just Men, The Four. See: Collier, Tim

Just Neighbors. See: Caine,
Betty

Just Plain Bill. See: Davidson,
Bill

Justice, Frontier. See: Ayres,
Lew

Juvenile Jury. See: Barry, Jack
(5)

KABIBBLE, ISH. See: Kyser, Kay

KADIDDLEHOPPER, CLEM. See:
Junior

KAHN, MADELINE. See: Klein,
Robert

KAISER. See also:
Kieser
Kyser

KAISER, MAJOR "DOC." See:
Savage, Brigadier General Frank

KALB, BERNARD. See: Benti,
Joseph

KALBER, FLOYD, newscaster (himself)
N.B.C. News (TV) (News)

KALTENMEYER, PROFESSOR
AUGUST, D.U.N. (Doctor of
Utter Nonsense), schoolteacher
PROFESSOR ULYSSES S. APPLE-
GATE, schoolteacher
IZZY FINKELSTEIN
YOHNNY YOHNSON
GERTIE GLUMP
MICKEY DONOVAN
PERCY VAN SCHUYLER
CHAUNCEY, the bum
DAISY DEAN
TOUGH GUY CORNELIUS CAL-
LAHAN, members of kinder-
garten class
Kaltenmeyer's Kindergarten (R)
(Children's program) (later known
as Kindergarten Kapers) (R)

Kaltenmeyer's Kindergarten. See:
Kaltenmeyer, Professor August,
D.U.N.

KAM CHANG. See: Garlund,
Frank

KAMEN, MILT. See: Stokey,
Mike

KANAVARAS, NICK. See: Casey,
Dr. Ben

KANE. See also:
Cain
Caine
Cane

KANE, BYRON. See: Judge, The

KANE, CANDY. See: Nash,
Carter

KANE, DAVID. See: Perry, Luke

KANE, KILLER. See: Rogers,
Buck

KANE, MARTIN, private detective
HAPPY MACMANN, his associate
Martin Kane, Private Eye (R)
(Detective); The New Adventures
of Martin Kane (TV)

KANE, MARTIN. See also: Rutledge, Dr. John

KANE, RUFUS. See: Marlin,
Mary

KANE, SARAH JANE. See:
Marlin, Mary

KANE, SIMON. See: Perry, Luke

KANE, THOMAS. See:
March, Hal
Story, Ralph

KANGAROO, CAPTAIN, character
portrayed by Bob Keeshan
MR. GREENJEANS
BUNNY RABBIT
GRANDFATHER CLOCK
GARUMPH
HAIRY
FUMBLE
BIRD
MIKE
NICOLA, cartoon characters
and puppets appearing on the
program
MANY LIVE ANIMALS
Captain Kangaroo (TV) (Chil-
dren's educational program)

Kapers, Kindergarten. See:
Kaltenmeyer, Professor August,
D.U.N.

KARAM, EDDIE. See:
Darin, Bobby
Miller, Roger

KARAMENEH. See: Fu Manchu

Karen. See: Scott, Karen

KAREN. See:
Dodd, Jimmie
Harding, Karen Adams
Hardy, Dr. Steven
Nabors, Jim
Scott, Karen

KAREN MARTIN. See: Davis,
Ann Tyler

KAREN WELLS. See: Diamond,
Richard

KAREN WERNER, DR. See:
Davis, Dr. Althea

KARIN O'BRIEN. See: Cullen,
Bill (3)

KARL. See:
Carl
Carle
Darl
Edman, Karl
Manning, Laura

KARL FARR. See: Nolan, Bob

KARLETON. See:
Carleton
Carlton
Driggs, Karleton King
Tarlton

KARLOFF, BORIS (1), host of the
program (himself)
MANY ACTORS AND ACTRESSES
Boris Karloff Presents Thriller
(TV) (Dramatizations of suspense
stories)

KARLOFF, BORIS (2), actor por-
traying "horror" roles (himself)
MANY ACTORS AND ACTRESSES
Starring Boris Karloff (R)
(Mystery drama)

KARLOFF, BORIS. See also:
Munster, Herman

KARNAC, DR., detective
HIS ASSISTANT
The Strange Dr. Karnac (R)
(Detective)

KARR. See also: Carr

KARR, MIKE, detective, later
attorney
NANCY KARR, his wife
LORY ANN CARR
SARAH KARR, his daughters
COOKIE CHRISTOPHER, Nancy's
sister
RON CHRISTOPHER, Nancy's
brother
VIC LAMONT, lawyer in Karr's
law office
BETTY CORCORAN (CORKY),
Karr's receptionist
ORRIN HILLYER, invalid mil-
lionaire
JULIE HILLYER, dead wife of
Orrin Hillyer
LIZ HILLYER FIELD, Hillyer's
daughter
DR. JAMES FIELD, husband
of Liz
ADAM DRAKE, attorney
NICOLE TRAVIS, Drake's
secretary
FRANK SLOAN, dope peddler,
deceased
KATE SLOAN, wife of Frank
BILL MARCEAU, chief of police
at Monticello
MARTHA MARCEAU, wife of
Bill
LIEUT. BLAINE, police officer
TRUDY, cook
JOHN, butler
SIMON JESSUP, spiritualist
FRED BURNS
CELIA BURNS, wife of Fred
ERIC MORGAN
LOBO HAINES
AL BUTLER
GERALDINE WHITNEY
J. H. PHILLIPS
PETER DALTON
WINSTON GRIMSLEY
MATTIE LANE
BEBE SPODE
MARTIN SPODE, characters ap-
pearing in the drama
The Edge of Night (TV) (Serial
drama)

KAT. See also: Cat

KAT, KITTY. See: Addams,
Gomez

KATE. See:
Allen, Dr. Kate

Dickens, Harry
Harris, Alan
Hopkins, Kate
McCoy, Grampa
Prescott, Kate Hathaway
Smith, Kate (1) (2) (3)
Stockton, Sandy (1)

KATE, AUNT. See: Rogers,
Patricia

KATE BRADLEY. See: Carson,
Uncle Joe

Kate, Dr. See: Allen, Dr. Kate

KATE, FIDDLING. See: Ritter,
Tex (1)

Kate Hopkins, Angel of Mercy.
See: Hopkins, Kate

KATE MARTIN. See: Davis,
Ann Tyler

KATE NOLAN. See: Walleck,
Meredith

KATE PHILLIPS. See: Sterling,
Vanessa Dale

KATE SLOAN. See: Karr, Mike

Kate Smith Hour, The. See: Smith,
Kate (1)

Kate Smith Show, The. See:
Smith, Kate (2)

Kate Smith Speaks. See: Smith,
Kate (3)

KATE WELLS. See: Evans, Dean

KATHARINE. See also:
Caterina
Catherine
Katherine
Kathryn
Katrin

KATHARINE MONROE. See:
Noble, Mary

KATHARINE SMITH. See:
Spitalny, Phil

KATHERINE. See also:

Caterina
Catherine
Katharine
Kathryn
Katrin

KATHERINE NORTON. See:
Carter, Kathryn

KATHIE. See:
Cathie
Cathy
Kathy

KATHLEEN. See:
Monroe, Clayt
Norris, Kathleen

KATHLEEN ANDERSON. See:
Aldrich, Henry

KATHLEEN CARNEY. See:
Graham, Dr. Bob

KATHLEEN CHATTON. See:
Davidson, Bill

KATHLEEN CONWAY. See:
Randolph, Ellen

Kathleen Norris, By. See: Norris,
Kathleen

KATHRYN. See:
Carter, Kathryn
Caterina
Catherine
Katharine
Katherine
Katrin
Murray, Kathryn

KATHRYN CARD. See: Caine,
Betty

KATHY. See:
Anderson, Jim
Bauer, Bertha
Cathie
Cathy
Hudson, Dr. Wayne
Marshall, John
Morgan, Mrs. Amy
Sunday
Williams, Danny

KATHY CAHILL. See: Darin,
Bobby

KATHY CAMERON. See: Davis,
Joan Field

KATHY LENNON. See:
Lennon, Janet
Welk, Lawrence

KATHY MARSH. See: Manning,
Portia Blake

KATHY O'HARA. See: Halliday,
Mike

KATHY PARKER. See: Tate,
Joanne

KATHY PRENTICE. See: Kennedy,
Carol

KATHY REIMER. See: Cameron,
Christy Allen

KATHY STONE. See: Drake,
Betty

KATIE. See:
Brown, Robinson, Jr.
Cooper, Liz
Douglas, Steve
Katy
O'Brien, Daniel J.

KATO. See: Reid, Britt

KATRIN. See:
Caterina
Catherine
Hansen, Mama
Katharine
Katherine
Kathryn

KATY. See:
Holstrum, Katy
Katie
O'Connor, Katy

KATY BENSON. See: Ryan,
Paul

KATY GRANT. See: August,
Dan

KATY HAMILTON. See: Noble,
Mary

KATZMAN, LOU. See: Allen,
Fred

KAUFMAN, SEYMOUR, principal
of Whitman High School, Los
Angeles
GIL CASEY, vice principal
PETE DIXON, history teacher
LIZ McINTYRE, counsellor
ALICE JOHNSON, student teacher
JASON ALLEN, Japanese student
RICHIE LANE, student
Room 222 (TV) (Situation drama)

KAY. See:
Banks, Stanley
Fairchild, Kay
Kaye
Kyser, Kay
Moynihan, Mother
Sterling, Vanessa Dale

KAY ADDISON. See: Post, Wilbur

KAY ARMEN. See: Parks, Bert
(6)

KAY BARNETT. See: Farrell,
David

KAY, BEATRICE
BILLY M. GREENE
JOE HOWARD, entertainers fea-
tured on the program (them-
selves)
BROADWAY HARRY
DANNY DONOVAN, characters
appearing on the program
THE ELM CITY FOUR
THE FOUR CLUBMEN, vocal
groups
THE FLORADORA GIRLS, dance
group
RAY BLOCH, orchestra leader
(himself)
HIS ORCHESTRA
The Gay Nineties Revue (R)
(Music/variety)

KAY CRANE. See: Carter,
Kathryn

KAY, EVELYN. See: Spitalny,
Phil

KAY FOX. See: Stockton, Sandy
(2)

Kay Kyser's Kollege of Musical
Knowledge. See:
College of Musical Knowledge, The.
Kyser, Kay

KAY LORRAINE. See: Ross,
Lanny

KAY MEDFORD. See: Martin,
Dean (2)

KAY, SIR. See: Sir Lancelot

KAY SMITH. See: Webster,
Martha

KAY STARR. See: Como, Perry
(1)

KAY THOMPSON. See:
Martin, Tony (2)
Ross, Lanny
Waring, Fred (1)

KAY THOMPSON'S RHYTHM
SINGERS. See: Martin, Tony
(2)

KAYDEN, MRS. See: O'Neill,
Mrs.

KAYDEN, MONTE. See: O'Neill,
Mrs.

KAYDEN, PEGGY O'NEILL. See:
O'Neill, Mrs.

KAYE. See:
Buell, Roger
Kay

KAYE, DANNY, comedian and
entertainer; star of the program
(himself)
MANY GUEST STARS
The Danny Kaye Show (R) (TV)
(Comedy/variety)
GOODMAN ACE
EVE ARDEN
JOAN EDWARDS
EVERETT CLARK
EVERETT SLOANE
JIM BACKUS
BUTTERFLY McQUEEN
JANE COWL
LIONEL STANDER
RUSH HUGHES, entertainers
appearing on the program (them-
selves)
MR. AVERAGE RADIO LISTENER,
character portrayed by Kenny
Delmar
HARRY JAMES

DAVID TERRY
LYN MURRAY, orchestra
leaders (themselves)
THEIR ORCHESTRAS
THE FOUR CLUBMEN, vocal
group
The Danny Kaye Show (R)
(Comedy/variety)

KAYE, GABRIEL. See: Hansen,
David

KAYE, HELEN. See: Sharp, Hal

KAYE, JANE. See: Kelly, Joe
(1)

KAYE, SAMMY (1), orchestra
leader; host of the program
(himself)
HIS ORCHESTRA
RAY MICHAELS
JOHNNY AMOROSO
JOHNNY McAFEE
HARRY RESER
LARRY ELLIS
J. BLASINGAME BOND
LYNN ROBERTS
JOE MACCHIAVERNA
TOBY WRIGHT
LARRY O'BRIEN
JANIE JONES, singers and
musicians featured on the pro-
gram (themselves)
The Sammy Kaye Show (TV)
(Music)

KAYE, SAMMY (2), orchestra
leader (himself)
HIS ORCHESTRA
AUDIENCE PARTICIPANTS
So You Want To Lead a Band?
(R) (Music)

KAYE, SAMMY (3), orchestra
leader, featured on the program
(himself)
HIS ORCHESTRA
Sunday Serenade (R) (Popular
music and poetry)

KAYE, SAMMY. See also:
Basie, Count
Como, Perry (1)
Whiteman, Paul

KAYE, STUBBY. See: Stokey,
Mike

KAZAN, DR. See: Bauer, Bertha

Kazootie, Rootie. See: Russell, Todd

KAZOOTIE, ROOTIE. See: Russell, Todd

KEANE. See also:
Keen
Keene

KEANE, MARTHA. See: Andrews, Walter

KEATING, LARRY. See: Daley, Cass

KEATOR, CHRISTOPHER. See: Goldberg, Molly

KEATS, J. WELLINGTON. See: Baines, Scattergood

KEE, OLIVER. See: Troy, Adam

KEEFE. See: Brasselle, Keefe

KEEN. See also:
Keane
Keene

KEEN, BOBBY. See: Old Ranger, The

KEEN, MR., detective
MIKE CLANCY, his partner and assistant
MISS ELLIS, his secretary
Mr. Keen, Tracer of Lost Persons (R) (Mystery/adventure)

KEENA. See: Brave Eagle

KEENE. See also:
Keane
Keen

KEENE, KITTY
JEFFERSON FOWLEY
LEDDY FOWLEY
BOB JONES
CLARA LUND
BUZZER WILLIAMS
CHARLES WILLIAMS
NORMA VERNACK
PEARL DAVIS
PREACHER JIM

ANNA HEJAK
HUMPHREY MANNERS
NEIL PERRY
MISS BRANCH
JILL
DIMPLES, characters appearing in the drama
Kitty Keene, Inc. (R) (Serial drama)

Keep Talking. See: Reiner, Carl

KEEPER OF THE OLD CURIOSITY SHOP, THE, merchant
HIS DAUGHTER
The Old Curiosity Shop (R) (Drama)

KEESHAN, BOB. See:
Doody, Howdy
Kangaroo, Captain

KEGG, JONATHAN, Amicus Curiae (Friend of the Court), attorney
Jonathan Kegg (R) (Courtroom drama)

KEIGHLEY, WILLIAM. See: DeMille, Cecil B.

KEITH. See:
Granville, Glynis
Jackson, Keith (1) (2)
Partridge, Connie

KEITH ARMOUR. See: Carter, Kathryn

KEITH BERGMAN. See: Tate, Joanne

KEITH, DR. See: Randolph, Ellen

KEITH GREGORY, CAPTAIN. See: Adams, Lieut. Price

KEITH, IAN, master of ceremonies of the program (himself)
MANY AUDIENCE PARTICIPANTS
Your Dream Has Come True (R) (Audience participation)

KEITH JACKSON. See:
Jackson, Keith (1) (2)
McKay, Jim (1)

KEITH RICHARDS. See: West, Michael

KEL MURRAY. See: Cugat,
  Xavier (1)

KELLER, DETECTIVE STEVE.
  See: Stone, Detective Lieut.
  Mike

KELLER, DR. MADELYN. See:
  Graham, Dr. Bob

KELLER, MADGE. See: James,
  Nancy

KELLER, SERGEANT DANNY.
  See: Gower, Matthew

KELLOGG, MAUDE. See:
  Solomon, David

Kellogg's Presents the Banana
  Splits Adventure Hour. See:
  Fleegle

KELLY. See:
  Gregg, Uncle Bentley
  Troy, Adam

KELLY BRACKETT, DR. See:
  Gage, John

KELLY, CHIN HO. See: Mc-
  Garrett, Steve

KELLY, EMMETT. See: Crosby,
  Bob (1)

KELLY, FREDERICK THOMAS,
  superintendent of overland stage
  line running from Missouri to
  California
  FRANK "FLIP" FLIPPEN, his
  assistant and trouble shooter
  Overland Trail (TV) (Western
  adventure)

KELLY, GENE, host of the program
  (himself)
  WARREN BERLINGER
  PAT FINLEY (The Blue-Collar
  Couple)
  DICK CLAIR
  JENNA McMAHON (The Sophisti-
  cates)
  JOHN AMOS
  TERESA GRAVES (The Black
  Couple)
  MICHAEL LEMBECK
  CINDY WILLIAMS (The Teen-agers)

BURT MUSTIN
QUEENIE SMITH (The Senior
  Citizens), appearing on the
  program (themselves)
The Funny Side (TV) (Comedy/
  satire)

KELLY, JOE (1), master of
  ceremonies of the program (him-
  self)
  UNCLE EZRA
  THE MAPLE CITY FOUR
  LOUISE MASSEY AND THE
  WESTERNERS
  ARKIE, THE ARKANSAS WOOD-
  CHOPPER
  THE DINNING SISTERS
  THE HOOSIER HOT SHOTS
  LULUBELLE AND SCOTTY
  THE CUMBERLAND RIDGE RUN-
  NERS
  SPARE RIBS
  THE VERNE, LEE AND MARY
  TRIO
  POKEY MARTIN
  TOM AND DON
  CAPTAIN STUBBY AND THE
  BUCCANEERS
  PAT BUTTRAM
  OTTO AND HIS NOVELODIANS
  LINDA PARKER
  SALLY FOSTER
  BOB ATCHER
  EDDIE PEABODY
  BOB HASTINGS
  GEORGE GOBEL
  DANNY DUNCAN
  BILL O'CONNOR
  HAL O'HALLORAN
  HENRY BURR
  THE TUNE TWISTERS
  BOB BALLANTINE
  SKIP FARRELL
  TINY STOKES
  JANE KAYE
  THE HILL TOPPERS
  FLORENCE FOLSOM
  JANIE AND CONNIE
  RED BLANCHARD
  LUCILLE LONG
  JOE PARSONS
  THE DEAN BROTHERS, musicians
  and performers appearing on the
  program
  The National Barn Dance (R)
  (Country and Western music)

KELLY, JOE (2), quizmaster of

the program (himself)
ANDRE AERNE
BOBBY BURNS
JACK LUCAL
JACK FRENCH
RUTHIE DUSKIN
NOREEN NOVICK
HARVE FISCHMAN
SPARKY FISCHMAN
STORMY BARRY
JOEL KUPPERMAN
SHEILA CONLON
LONNIE LUNDE
JOAN BISHOP
RICHARD WILLIAMS
DARICE RICHMAN
GERALDINE HAMBURG
MARK MULLIN
CHARLES SCHWARTZ
MARY CLARE McHUGH
GUNTHER HOLLANDER
SANDRA BAGUS
JACK BECKMAN
MARY ANN HENDERSON
BETTY SWANSON
DAVID JENKINS
GERARD DARROW
VANESSA BROWN
DANNY MARTIN
JUDY GRAHAM
RICHARD WEIXLER
CYNTHIA CLINE
DAVID FREIFELDER
PATRICK CONLON
VIRGINIA RODES
NAOMI COOKS
DICK CRAVENS
CLAUDE BRENNER
ROCHELL LIEBLING
JACK ROONEY
JOHN POLLACK
DAVE PROCHASKA
CORINNE TEMPLETON
DICK SEDLACK
MARGARET MARY DOUGHERTY
MARGARET MERRICK
VAN DYKE TIERS
DIANNE MATHRE
BERNARD GRIESEL, panelists
on the program; all under the
age of 16 (themselves)
The Quiz Kids (R) (Quiz)

KELLY, KITTY
JACK VAN ORPINGTON
BUNNY WILSON
PATRICK CONWAY
THE DOCTOR

KYRON WELBY
MR. ASTRAKHAN
MRS. MURGER
MR. WELBY
MRS. WELBY
DENNIE PIERCE
GRANT THURSDAY
ISABEL ANDREWS
DR. ORBO, physician
INSPECTOR GRADY, police
official
MICHAEL CONWAY
MRS. MOGRAM
SLIM, characters appearing in
the drama
Pretty Kitty Kelly (R) (Serial
drama)

KELLY, MISS. See: Smith,
Eugene

KELLY, PETE, jazz band leader
and trumpet player in the 1920s
SAVANNAH BROWN, singer
Pete Kelly's Blues (TV) (Jazz
music/drama)

KELLY ROBINSON. See: Scott,
Alexander

KELLY, TIM
TOUBO SMITH, adventurers
Soldiers of Fortune (TV) (Ad-
venture)

KELLY, WALTER C. See: Drew,
John

KELTON, PERT. See: Gleason,
Jackie (1)

KELVIN. See also:
Calvin
Kevin

KELVIN, MR. See: Trent, Helen

KELVIN, MRS. See: Trent,
Helen

KEMP, HAL, orchestra leader,
featured on the program (him-
self)
HIS ORCHESTRA
NAN WYNN
BOB ALLEN, vocalists (them-
selves)
THE SMOOTHIES, vocal group

Time to Shine (R) (Music)

KEN. See:
Berry, Ken
Carpenter, Luke
Kin
McLaughlin, Ken
Murray, Ken (1) (2) (3) (4)
Roberts, Ken
Thurston, Ken
Wilbur, Judy

Ken Berry Wow Show, The. See:
Berry, Ken

KEN CAPPS. See: Jones, Spike
(1)

KEN DELO. See: Welk,
Lawrence

KEN LANE. See: Martin, Dean
(2)

KEN LANE CHORUS, THE. See:
Ross, Lanny

KEN MARTINSON, DR. See:
Drake, Nora

Ken Murray Program, The. See:
Murray, Ken (2)

Ken Murray Show, The. See:
Murray, Ken (3)

KEN NORRIS. See: Bauer, Bertha

KEN WILLIAMS. See: Hall,
Monty (3)

KENDAL, GIL. See: Warren,
Wendy

KENDALL. See: Lassie

KENDRICK, ALEXANDER. See:
Ciardi, John

KENDRICKS. See: Bratter, Paul

KENJI TAKICHI. See: Cavanaugh,
Father Samuel Patrick

KENMORE, LEONA. See: Sunday

KENNEDY, BOB (1), host of the
program (himself)

WILLIAM A. WOOD, referee of
the program (himself)
MANY CONTESTANTS
Window Shopping (TV) (Game)

KENNEDY, BOB (2), quizmaster
of the program (himself)
MANY CONTESTANTS
Wingo (TV) (Quiz)

KENNEDY, CAROL
GARY CRANDALL
KATHY PRENTICE
DR. OWEN CRAIG, physician
PETER CLARKE
RANDY, characters appearing
in the drama
Carol Kennedy's Romance (R)
(Serial drama)

KENNEDY, PAT. See: Bernie,
Ben

KENNEDY, SARAH. See: Rowan,
Dan

KENNEDY, TOM (1), quizmaster
of the program (himself)
MANY CONTESTANTS
The Big Game (TV) (Quiz)

KENNEDY, TOM (2), quizmaster
of the program (himself)
MANY CONTESTANTS
Split Second (TV) (Quiz)

KENNEDY, TOM. See also: Narz,
Jack (6)

KENNEDY, VINCE. See: Randolph,
Ellen

KENNETH. See:
Clark, Lord Kenneth
Jones, Kenneth Yarborough
Lane, Patty
Preston, Lawrence

KENNETH CRAIG. See: Harding,
Karen Adams

KENNICOTT, MARY. See: Davis,
Ann Tyler

KENNY. See:
Baker, Kenny
Delmar, Kenny
Madison, Kenny
Rogers, Kenny

KENNY BAKER. See:
Baker, Kenny
Benny, Jack
Marx, Groucho (1)

KENNY DELMAR. See:
Delmar, Kenny
Kaye, Danny

KENNY GARDNER. See: Steele,
Ted

Kenny Rogers and the First Edition,
Rollin' on the River With. See:
Rogers, Kenny

KENNY TRIMBLE. See: Welk,
Lawrence

KENNY WOODMAN. See: Doonican,
Val

KENRAD. See also:
Conrad
Conried
Konrad

KENRAD, DR., detective
Dr. Kenrad's Unsolved Mysteries
(R) (Mystery)

KENT, CLARK, mild-mannered
reporter on staff of the "Daily
Planet," alias Superman (The
Man of Steel), crime fighter
LOIS LANE, his girl friend, re-
porter
JIMMIE OLSEN, office boy
PERRY WHITE, editor of the
"Daily Planet"
The Adventures of Superman (R)
(Crime adventure) (later revised
and released as cartoon series
under the title Superman (TV) and
as filmed performance of live
actors under the title Superman)
(TV)
BEANIE, office boy
MILLIONAIRE BRUCE WAYNE
(Batman), masked crime fighter
DICK GRAYSON (Robin), Wayne's
ward; young masked crime
fighter
The Adventures of Superman (R)

KENT DAVIS. See: Vance, Connie

KENT, FRED, head of the house

LUCY, his wife
DICK, their son
UNCLE WILL, Fred's uncle
Home Sweet Home (R) (Serial
drama)

KENT, JIM. See: Grimm, Arnold

KENT, JIMMIE. See: Myrt

KENT LARSEN. See: Driggs,
Karleton King

KENT, MICHAEL. See: Graham,
Dr. Bob

KENTON, STAN, orchestra leader,
host of the program (himself)
HIS ORCHESTRA
MANY GUEST STARS
Music '55 (TV) (Popular music)

KENTON, STAN. See also:
Basie, Count
O'Connor, Father Norman
Whiteman, Paul

KENTUCKY. See: Jones, Kenneth
Yarborough

Kentucky Jones. See: Jones,
Kenneth Yarborough

KENTURAH. See: Sloan, Holly

KENWROTH, HERBERT. See:
Barrett, Timothy "Spud"

KENYON. See also: Canyon

KENYON, ISABEL. See: Abbott,
John

KENYON, MRS. See: Dawson,
Rosemary

KEOGH, CAPTAIN MYLES. See:
Custer, George Armstrong

KERBY. See also: Kirby

KERBY, GEORGE. See: Topper,
Cosmo

KERBY, MARION. See: Topper,
Cosmo

KERMIT. See: Joan

Kermit, Joan and. See: Joan

KERR, GRAHAM, cookery expert,
host of the program (himself)
GUEST COOKING EXPERTS
The Galloping Gourmet (TV)
(Cookery)

KERRY DONOVAN. See: Davidson, Bill

KESNER, DICK. See: Welk,
Lawrence

KESTER, CAROL. See: Hartley,
Dr. Robert

KETCHAM. See: Nichols

KETCHAM, MA. See: Nichols

KEVIN. See:
Calvin
Kelvin
Lincoln, Dr. Matt
O'Leary, Hannah

KEVIN GRANT. See: Bracken,
John

KEVIN KINCAID. See: Ames,
Peter

Key of R.C.A., The Magic. See:
Stoopnagle, Colonel Lemuel Q.
(1)

Key to the Ages. See: Low,
Theodore

KEYES. See also: Keys

KEYES, JEFFERSON, private detective; accepts only cases
paying one million dollars in
advance
Cool Million (TV) (Crime drama)

Keyhole. See: Douglas, Jack (2)

KEYS. See also: Keyes

Keys, Seven. See: Narz, Jack
(4)

KEYSTONE KOPS. See: Russell,
Todd

KID. See:
Billy the Kid
Cisco Kid, The
Kids

"KID" CURRY, JED. See: Hayes,
Hannibal

Kid Power. See: Nipper

Kid Talk. See: Adler, Bill

Kid, The Cisco. See: Cisco Kid,
The

KID, THE MEAN WIDDLE. See:
Junior

KID, THE ZEBRA. See: James,
Dennis (4)

KIDDER, DR. ALFRED. See:
Rainey, Dr. Froelich

KIDDER, MARGOT
MEREDITH MACRAE
SUZANNE SOMMERS
JACQUELINE SUSANN
ANNA CAMERON
OTHERS, panelists of the pro-
gram (themselves)
GUEST AUTHORS AND EXPERTS
Mantrap (TV) (Discussion)

KIDS. See also: Kid

Kids, Fat Albert and the Cosby.
See: Cosby, Bill (3)

KIDS, THE NABORS. See:
Nabors, Jim

Kids, The Quiz. See:
Fadiman, Clifton (2)
Kelly, Joe (2)

KIERAN, JOHN. See: Fadiman,
Clifton (1)

KIERNAN, WALTER. See: Allen,
Frederick Lewis

KIESER. See also:
Kaiser
Kyser

KIESER, FATHER ELWOOD,
Paulist educator and theologian;

host of the program (himself)
MANY ACTORS AND ACTRESSES
Insight (TV) (Religious drama
anthology)

KILBOURNE, LORELEI. See:
Wilson, Steve

KILDARE, DR. JAMES, physician
on staff of Blair General Hospital
DR. LEONARD GILLESPIE,
senior staff physician at the
hospital
Dr. Kildare (TV) (Medical drama)

KILEY, DR. STEVEN. See:
Welby, Dr. Marcus

KILEY, PHIL "COO COO. " See:
Kirchener, Claude (1)

KILGALLEN, DOROTHY (1), newspaper woman and television personality (herself)
DICK KOLLMAR, her husband,
actor and television personality
(himself)
Breakfast With Dorothy and Dick
(R) (Breakfast conversation)

KILGALLEN, DOROTHY (2), news-
paper woman (herself)
The Voice of Broadway (R)
(Broadway gossip)

KILGALLEN, DOROTHY. See also:
Daly, John (3)
Landi, Elissa

KILGORE, LILE. See: Marshall,
John

KILGORE, RODNEY. See:
Marshall, John

KILGORE, ROGER, lawyer
Roger Kilgore, Public Defender
(R) (Courtroom drama)

KILLER KANE. See: Rogers,
Buck

KILPATRICK, PROFESSOR. See:
Davis, Joan Field

KIM. See:
Carter, Lucy
Randolph, Walt
Steele, Tracy

KIM SCHUSTER. See: Peyton,
Martin

KIM TRACY. See: Dugan, Queenie

KIMBA. See: Jungle Jim

KIMBALL, HANK. See: Douglas,
Oliver

KIMBALL, MR. See: Omar

KIMBALL, MRS. See: Omar

KIMBALL, NURSE. See: Solomon,
David

KIMBALL, Y. See: Narz, Jack
(2)

KIMBLE, DR. RICHARD, unjustly
accused of murdering his wife;
fleeing punishment and seeking
the murderer
HELEN KIMBLE, his murdered
wife
LIEUT. PHILIP GERARD, police
detective, pursuing Kimble
JOHNSON, one-armed murderer
of Helen Kimble
The Fugitive (TV) (Crime drama)

KIMBRO, LIEUT. See: Wright,
Conley

KIN. See also: Ken

KIN VASSEY. See: Rogers,
Kenny

KINCAID, CHET, Negro physical
education instructor and occasion-
al substitute teacher at Richard
Allen Holmes High School
MRS. KINCAID, his mother
BRIAN, his brother
VERNA, his sister-in-law
MISS FISK, gym teacher at the
high school
LEONARD LILLYBRIDGE, chair-
man of art department at the
high school
MARSHA PATTERSON, counselor
at the high school
The Bill Cosby Show (TV)
(Comedy)

KINCAID, DAN. See: Ames, Peter

KINCAID, KEVIN. See: Ames, Peter

KINCAID, REUBEN. See: Partridge, Connie

KINCHLOE. See: Hogan, Colonel Robert

Kindergarten, Kaltenmeyer's. See: Kaltenmeyer, Professor August, D. U. N.

Kindergarten Kapers. See: Kaltenmeyer, Professor August, D. U. N.

KING
JOE FRANCIS
MIKE
STEVE
JACK
KIP
FINCH, members of crew of the ship "Endeavor" exploring Great Barrier Reef off the coast of Australia
SUSAN PRESCOTT
TRACEY, girls associated with the exploration
Barrier Reef (TV) (Underwater adventure)

KING. See also:
Brown, Velvet
Bubbles, King
Cole, Nat "King"
King's

KING, ANDREW. See: Drake, Nora

King, Anna and the. See: Owens, Anna

KING ARTHUR. See: Sir Lancelot

KING, CISSY. See: Welk, Lawrence

"King" Cole Show, The Nat. See: Cole, Nat "King"

KING, DAVE (1), star and host of the program (himself)
MANY GUEST STARS
The Dave King Show (TV) (Variety)

KING, DAVE (2), comedian; host of the program (himself)
MANY GUEST STARS
THE BILL FOSTER DANCERS
VIC SCHOEN, orchestra leader (himself)
HIS ORCHESTRA
England's Dave King (TV) (Variety)

KING, DOLORES. See: Webster, Martha

KING, DONNA. See: Driggs, Karleton King

King Family, The. See: Driggs, Karleton King

KING FAROUK. See: Husing, Ted

KING, GRIFF. See: Cartwright, Ben

KING, JANICE. See: Winters, Evelyn

KING, JEAN PAUL, host of the program (himself)
Bits of Hits (R) (Music)

KING, JEAN PAUL. See also: Judge, The

KING, JOHN, security agent, deals with traffic in diamonds
King of Diamonds (TV) (Police drama)

KING, JOHN REED (1), quizmaster of the program (himself)
MANY CONTESTANTS
Chance of a Lifetime (R) (Quiz)

KING, JOHN REED (2), moderator of the program (himself)
AUDIENCE PARTICIPANTS
Give and Take (R) (Game)

KING, JOHN REED. See also:
Compton, Walter
Parks, Bert (1)

KING, KYLE. See: Bennett, Nita

KING, LUISE. See: Driggs, Karleton King

KING, MARILYN. See: Driggs, Karleton King

KING, MAXINE. See: Driggs, Karleton King

KING, MRS. JESSIE. See: Bennett, Nita

KING OF BRITAIN. See: Sir Lancelot

King of Diamonds. See: King, John

KING OF ENGLAND. See: Churchill, John Henry VIII, King of England

KING OF FRANCE. See: Churchill, John

KING OF SIAM, THE. See: Owens, Anna

KING OF THE COWBOYS. See: Rogers, Roy

KING, OTTO. See: Slate, Johnny

KING, PEGGY. See: Gobel, George

KING, PHILIP. See: Trent, Helen

KING, ROCKY, private detective
SERGEANT HART, police officer
Rocky King (TV) (Detective)

KING, SCHYLER "SKY," aviator and owner of the Flying Crown Ranch
PENNY, his niece
CLIPPER, his nephew
SKY KING'S FOREMAN, employee
DR. SHADE, his enemy
Sky King (R) (TV) (Aviation/ Western adventure)

KING, SERGEANT. See: Stockdale, Will

KING SISTERS, THE. See: Kyser, Kay

King, Sky. See: King, Schyler "Sky"

KING, SYLVIA. See: Noble, Mary

KING, TARA. See: Steed, John

KING, THE CLOCK. See: Batman

KING TUT. See: Batman

KING, WAYNE. See: Lady Esther

KING, YUKON. See: Preston, Sergeant

KING, YVONNE. See: Driggs, Karleton King

Kingdom, Wild. See: Perkins, Marlin

KINGFISH. See: Jones, Amos

KINGMAN, ADELE. See: Sloan, Holly

KINGMAN, CHARLIE. See: Primus, Carter

KING'S. See also: King

KING'S MEN QUARTET, THE. See: McGee, Fibber

KINGSLEY COLTON. See: Halop, Billy

KINGSLEY, DR. BRUCE. See: O'Neill, Mrs.

KINGSLEY MAYO. See: Perry, John

KIP. See:
King
Pride, Ben

KIP RYSDALE. See: Ames, Peter

KIP TYLER. See: Cameron, Christy Allen

KIRBY. See:
Anderson, Sergeant Nick
Kerby

KIRBY, COLIN. See: Hargrave-Scott, Joan

KIRBY, DURWARD, master of
ceremonies of the program (him-
self)
JOY HODGES, mistress of cere-
monies of the program (herself)
MANY AUDIENCE PARTICIPANTS
JERRY JEROME, orchestra
leader (himself)
HIS ORCHESTRA
Honeymoon in New York (R)
(Game)

KIRBY, DURWARD. See also:
Funt, Allen (1)
Moore, Garry (1) (3) (5)
Morgan, Henry

KIRBY, GEORGE. See: Little,
Rich

KIRBY, LEE. See: Myrt

KIRBY, LIEUT., police officer
I Am the Law (TV) (Crime
fighting)

KIRBY, LIEUT. See also: Flagg,
Captain Jim

KIRBY, PAULA. See: Myrt

KIRBY STONE FOUR, THE. See:
Rodgers, Jimmie

KIRBY WILLOUGHBY. See:
Grimm, Arnold

KIRCHENER, CLAUDE (1), "ring-
master" of the program (him-
self)
BONNIE LEE, baton twirler,
herself
DOUGLAS "MR. DOCUS" ANDER-
SON
BILL "BOOM BOOM" BAILEY
PHIL "COO COO" KILEY, circus
clowns (themselves)
THE CIRCUSEVEN JAZZ BAND
OTHER CIRCUS ACTS
Magic Midway (TV) (Children's
circus)

KIRCHENER, CLAUDE (2), "ring-
master" of the program (himself)
MARY HARTLINE, circus band-
leader (herself)
NICKY
CLIFFY

SCAMPY, clowns
MANY CIRCUS ACTS
Super Circus (TV) (Circus)

KIRGO, GEORGE. See: Leyden,
Bill (2)

KIRK, CAPTAIN JAMES, com-
mander of the space ship
"Enterprise"
MR. SPOCK, Vulcan, second
in command
DR. McCOY, physician aboard
the "Enterprise"
MR. SCOTT (Scotty), chief
engineer of the "Enterprise"
MR. SULU, helmsman
LIEUT. UHURA, female com-
munications officer
TONIA BARROWS, yeoman
Star Trek (TV) (Science fiction/
adventure)

KIRK, GENERAL WOODY. See:
Newman, Tony

KIRK HARDING, DR. See:
Harding, Karen Adams

KIRK RODER. See: Manning,
Portia Blake

KIRKLAND, STEVE. See: Talbot,
Commander Dan

KIRKOFF, SONIA. See: Grimm,
Arnold

KIRKPATRICK, JESS. See:
Story Lady, The

KIRKWOOD, JACK
DON REID
TOM HARRIS
RANSOM SHERMAN
LEE BRODIE
HERB SHELDON
JEAN McKEAN
MIKE McTOOCH
LILLIAN LEE, entertainers
featured on the program (them-
selves)
Mirth and Madness (R) (Comedy/
variety)

KIRKWOOD, MARGO. See: Wayne,
Ruth Evans

KIRKWOOD, PETE. See: Wayne, Ruth Evans

KIT. See:
Carson, Kit
Marshall, John
Wilson, Dr. Thomas

Kit Carson. See: Carson, Kit

KIT COLLINS. See: Peters, Bill

KIT FARRELL. See: Bauer, Bertha

Kitchen Quiz. See: East, Ed (1)

KITTINGER, STRINGBEAN. See: Aldrich, Henry

KITTREDGE, JEFF. See: Scott, David

KITTY. See:
Bell, Harry
Carlisle, Kitty
Foyle, Kitty
Hanks, Henrietta
Horton, Dr. Tom
Keene, Kitty
Kelly, Kitty
Michael
Reynolds, Dr. Mike

KITTY CARLISLE. See:
Carlisle, Kitty
Moore, Garry (4) (5)

Kitty Foyle. See: Foyle, Kitty

KITTY KAT. See: Addams, Gomez

Kitty Keene, Inc. See: Keene, Kitty

Kitty Kelly, Pretty. See: Kelly, Kitty

KITTY MARSHALL. See: Noble, Mary

Kitty, Michael and. See: Michael

KITTY RUSSELL. See: Dillon, Marshal Matt

KITTY SHEA. See: Davis, Ann Tyler

KITZEL, MR. See:
Benny, Jack
Blurt, Elmer

KIWI, THE. See: Butcher, Major Simon

KLAVAN, GENE. See: Wallace, Mike (5)

KLEIN. See also: Cline

KLEIN, JOHNNY. See: Welk, Lawrence

KLEIN, ROBERT, host of the program (himself)
BONI ENTEN
PETER BOYLE
MARTY BARRIS
BARBARA CASON
MACINTYRE DIXON
JUDY GRAUBART
LAURA GREENE
MADELINE KAHN
JERRY LACY
LYNN LIPTON, entertainers appearing on the program (themselves)
MANY GUEST STARS
Comedy Tonight (TV) (Comedy/variety)

KLICK, MARY. See:
Dean, Jimmy
Hamilton, George

KLING. See: Carella

KLINK. See:
Clink
Hogan, Colonel Robert

KLINKER, EFFIE. See:
Ameche, Don (1)
Bergen, Edgar (1) (2)

Klondike. See: Halliday, Mike

KLOONER, MABEL. See: Harding, Mrs. Rhoda

KLOSE, WOODY
VIRGINIA KLOSE, featured on the program (themselves)
Red Hook-31 (R) (Farm)

KLUGIE. See: Alexander, Nick

KNAPP, PROFESSOR. See:
Horton, Dot

Knickerbocker Playhouse. See:
Lewis, Elliott

KNIGHT, EVELYN. See: Crosby,
Bob (2)

KNIGHT, FELIX. See: Marlowe,
Sylvia

KNIGHT, FRANK, host of the pro-
gram (himself)
MISCHEL PIASTRO, orchestra
leader (himself)
HIS ORCHESTRA
The Longines Symphonette (R)
(Music)

KNIGHT, JOHN. See: Rogers,
Patricia

KNIGHT, RAYMOND. See:
Reser, Harry
Weems, Ambrose J.

Knitter, The Busy. See: Zimmermann, Elizabeth

KNOBBY WALSH. See: Palooka,
Joe

KNOTTS, DON, comedian, host of
the program (himself)
MANY GUEST STARS
NICK PERITO, orchestra leader
HIS ORCHESTRA
The Don Knotts Show (TV)
(Variety)

KNOTTS, DON. See also:
Allen, Steve (1) (3)
Berman, Shelley

Knowledge, The College of Musical.
See:
Ford, Tennessee Ernie (1)
Kay Kyser's Kollege of Musical
Knowledge

KNOWLTON, HARTLEY. See:
Brent, Dr. Jim

KNOX, WILBUR Z. (GRANDSIR).
See: Dickey, Dan'l

KNUCKLEHEAD SMIFF. See:

Winchell, Paul (3)

KOBICK. See: Lockridge, Barry

KODIAK. See: Dugan

KOKUA, BEN. See: McGarrett,
Steve

Kollege of Musical Knowledge, Kay
Kyser's. See:
College of Musical Knowledge, The
Kyser, Kay

KOLLMAR, DICK. See: Kilgallen,
Dorothy (1)

KOLTANOWSKI, GEORGE, chess
expert, narrator of the program
(himself)
Koltanowski on Chess (TV) (Dis-
cussions of famous chess games)

Koltanowski on Chess. See:
Koltanowski, George

KOLU. See: Jungle Jim

KONO. See: McGarrett, Steve

KONRAD. See:
Conrad
Conried
Kenrad
Styner, Dr. Konrad

KOOKIE. See: Bailey, Stuart

KOOKSON, GERALD LLOYD, III.
See: Bailey, Stuart

KOPS, KEYSTONE. See: Russell,
Todd

Kopykats, The (The A.B.C. Comedy
Hour). See: Little, Rich

KORMAN, HARVEY. See: Burnett,
Carol

KOSTELANETZ, ANDRE. See:
Martin, Tony (2)

KOSTER, DAVID, assistant district
attorney
PHYLLIS, his wife
CELESE, his assistant
For the People (TV) (Drama)

KOTOY. See: Jeffords, Tom

KOVACS, ERNIE (1), comedian;
star of the program (himself)
PERCY DOVETONSILS
MOTHER RUSTIC
EUGENE, characters portrayed
by Kovacs
EDIE ADAMS
PETER HANLEY
MAUREEN ARTHUR
HANS CONRIED
CESAR ROMERO
PEGGY CONNOLLY, entertainers
appearing on the program (them-
selves)
MANY GUEST STARS
The Ernie Kovacs Show (TV)
(Humor/variety)

KOVACS, ERNIE (2), host and commentator of the program (himself)
MANY OLD SILENT MOTION
PICTURES
Silents, Please (TV) (Old motion
pictures)

KOVACS, MIKE, free lance pho-
tographer
The Man With a Camera (TV)
(Adventure/drama)

KOWALSKI. See:
Morgan, Lieut. Anne
Nelson
Nelson, Admiral Harriman

Kraft Music Hall, The. See:
Como, Perry (2)
Crosby, Bing (3)

KRALAHOME. See: Owens, Anna

KRAMDEN, RALPH, Brooklyn bus
driver, portrayed by Jackie
Gleason
ALICE KRAMDEN, his wife
ED NORTON, his neighbor and
friend; sewer worker
TRIXIE NORTON, Ed's wife
SAMMY SPEAR, orchestra leader
(himself)
HIS ORCHESTRA
The Honeymooners (TV) (Situation
comedy) (Segment of The Jackie
Gleason Show) (TV) (also segment
of The Cavalcade of Stars) (TV)

except for the Sammy Spear
orchestra)

KRAMDEN, RALPH. See also:
Gleason, Jackie (1)

KRAMER, DWIGHT. See: Nelson,
Carolyn Kramer

KRAMER, MANDEL. See:
Judge, The
Roberts, Ken

KRAMER, MR. See: Nelson,
Carolyn Kramer

KRAMER, MRS. See: Nelson,
Carolyn Kramer

KRAMER, PHIL. See: Lescoulie,
Jack (2)

KRAMER, REX. See: Harding,
Mrs. Rhoda

KRAMER, SUSANNAH. See:
Webster, Jerry

KRAMER, TRACY. See: Webster,
Jerry

KRANSKY, JACOB. See: Rutledge,
Dr. John

KRANSKY, MRS. See: Rutledge,
Dr. John

KRANSKY, ROSE. See:
Nelson, Carolyn Kramer
Rutledge, Dr. John

KRAUSE, FRIEDA. See: Marshall,
Owen

KRAVITZ, ABNER. See: Stephens,
Samantha

KRAVITZ, GLADYS. See: Stephens,
Samantha

KREBS, MAYNARD. See: Gillis,
Dobie

KREITZER, MRS. CATHERINE.
See: March, Hal

KRESKIN, illusionist and mind-
reader; host of the program

(himself)
The Amazing World of Kreskin
(TV) (Magic/mind reading)

KROPOTKIN, PROFESSOR. See:
Peterson, Irma

KRUGER, JUDGE. See: Hargrave-
Scott, Joan

KRUMP, NORMAN. See: Pruitt,
Mrs. Phyllis Poindexter

KRUPA. See also: Cooper

KRUPA, GENE. See:
O'Connor, Father Norman
Whiteman, Paul

KUKAI. See: Silver, Captain

KUKLA
    OLLIE, dragon
    MADAME OGLEPUSS
    BEULAH THE WITCH
    CECIL BILL
    COLONEL CRACKLE
    DOLORES DRAGON
    MERCEDES RABBITT
    FLETCHER RABBITT, puppets
    operated by Burr Tillstrom
    FRAN ALLISON, actress (her-
    self)
    Kukla, Fran and Ollie (TV)
    (Children's puppets)

Kukla, Fran and Ollie. See: Kukla

KUMMER, ELOISE
    CHARLOTTE MANSON, nar-
    rators of the program (them-
    selves)
    American Women (R) (War re-
    cruitment program)

Kung Fu. See: Caine

KUODA. See: Cameron

KUPPERMAN, JOEL. See: Kelly,
Joe (2)

KURT. See also:
Cort
Curt

KURT, ANITA. See: Riggs,
Tommy

KURTZ, DR. See: Hillman,
India

KURYAKIN, ILLYA. See: Solo,
Napoleon

KWAN, DR. See: Malone, Dr.
Jerry

KYLE. See: Nash, Jim

KYLE KING. See: Bennett, Nita

KYRON. See also: Byron

KYRON WELBY. See: Kelly,
Kitty

KYSER. See also:
Kaiser
Kieser

KYSER, KAY, orchestra leader
and quizmaster; host of the
program (himself)
HIS ORCHESTRA
ISH KABIBBLE, character por-
trayed by Mervyn Bogue,
trumpeter with the orchestra
TRUDY ERWIN
SULLY MASON
GINNY SIMMS
HARRY BABBITT
GEORGIA CARROLL
SHIRLEY MITCHELL, vocalists
appearing on the program (them-
selves)
THE KING SISTERS
THE TOWN CRIERS, vocal
groups
MANY CONTESTANTS
Kay Kyser's Kollege of Musical
Knowledge (R) (Music/quiz)

LAARA LACEY. See: Nye, Louis

LABOR, MANUEL. See: Allen,
Steve (2)

Lace, Lavender and New. See:
Marlowe, Sylvia

Lace, Lavender and Old. See:
Scheff, Fritzi

LA CENTRA, PEG. See: Cook,
Joe

LACEY. See also: Lacy

LACEY, CAPTAIN NICHOLAS
"NICKY." See: Barbour,
Henry Wilson

LACEY, CLAUDIA BARBOUR
ROBERTS. See: Barbour,
Henry Wilson

LACEY, JR., NICHOLAS "NICKY."
See: Barbour, Henry Wilson

LACEY, LAARA. See: Nye,
Louis

LACEY, PENNY. See: Barbour,
Henry Wilson

LACKLAND, JOHN, San Francisco
advertising man; becomes beachcomber in the South Seas
Beachcomber (TV) (Adventure)

LACY. See also: Lacey

LACY, JERRY. See: Klein,
Robert

LADADOG. See: Nash, Jim

Ladies Be Seated. See: Moore,
Tom (1)

Ladies Fair. See: Moore, Tom
(2)

LADS, THE COUNTRY. See:
Dean, Jimmy
Hamilton, George

LADY. See:
Leddy
Lyddie

Singing Lady, The
Story Lady, The

LADY CLARA. See: Noble, Mary

LADY ESTHER, personification,
portrayed by Bess Johnson
WAYNE KING, orchestra leader
(himself)
HIS ORCHESTRA
The Lady Esther Serenade (R)
(Music)

Lady Esther Serenade, The. See:
Lady Esther

LADY FITZHARDING. See:
Churchill, John

LADY NEXT DOOR, THE. See:
Conductor, The

Lady of Millions. See: Robson,
May

LADY PENELOPE PEASOUP. See:
Batman

LADY ROCHFORD. See: Henry
VIII, King of England

LADY, THE DRAGON. See: Lee,
Terry

LADY, THE LAUGHING. See:
Blurt, Elmer

LADY, THE LULLABY. See:
Faith, Percy

Lady, The Singing. See: Singing
Lady, The

LADY, THE VALIANT. See:
Hargrave-Scott, Joan

LADY THIANG. See: Owens,
Anna

Lady, Valiant. See: Hargrave-
Scott, Joan

LADY VERE-DE-VERE. See:
McGee, Fibber

LADY WHEEDLEDUCK, OLD. See:
McGee, Fibber

LAFAYETTE, GENERAL. See:
Larkin, Jeremy

LAFE SIMMS. See: Hargrave-
Scott, Joan

LAGORRO, DAVID. See: Carter,
Kathryn

LAGORRO, ITALO. See: Carter,
Kathryn

LAHR, LARRY. See: Andrews,
Drake

LAINE. See also:
Lane
Layne

LAINE, FRANKIE, singer and
entertainer; star of the program
(himself)
MANY GUEST STARS
The Frankie Laine Show (TV)
(Variety)

LAITH PETTINGAL. See: Parker,
Seth

LAKALE, EDWARD DUKE. See:
McGarrett, Steve

LAKE, MYRA. See: Ames, Peter

LaLANNE, JACK, physical culturist,
host of the program (himself)
The Jack LaLanne Show (TV)
(Exercise)

LA LING. See: Randolph, Ellen

LAMB CHOP. See: Lewis, Shari

LAMBERT. See: Manning, Portia
Blake

LAMBERT, GLORIA. See: Miller,
Mitch

LAMBERT, LOUISE
MARTY LAMBERT
JEAN LAMBERT
HAL LAMBERT
WHIT DAVIS
PHIL BARNES
BRAD FORBES, characters ap-
pearing in the drama
Brave Tomorrow (R) (Serial
drama)

LAMONT. See:
Cranston, Lamont
Sanford, Fred

LAMONT, VIC. See: Karr, Mike

LAMOUR, DOROTHY, singer and
actress; star of the program
(herself)
MANY GUEST STARS
The Dorothy Lamour Program
(R) (Variety)

LAMOUR, DOROTHY. See also:
Ameche, Don (1)

Lamplighter, The. See: Tarshish,
Jacob

LAMSON. See also: Lanson

LAMSON, HERK. See: Fry,
Marshal Simon

LANA. See:
Johnson, Bess
Lina

LANCE. See also: Lange

LANCE DUDLEY. See: Brent,
Portia

LANCE McKENZIE. See: Bennett,
Nita

LANCELOT. See:
Link, Lancelot
Sir Lancelot

Lancelot Link, Secret Chimp. See:
Link, Lancelot

Lancer. See: Lancer, Murdoch

LANCER. See also:
Langer
Langner

LANCER, MURDOCH, rancher
SCOTT LANCER, his son
JOHNNY MADRID, his son,
Scott's half brother
JELLY HOSKINS, ranch hand
Lancer (TV) (Western)

Lancers, Tales of the 77th Bengal.
See: Storm, Lieut.

Lancers, The Bengal. See: Storm, Lieut.

Land of Allakazam, The Magic. See: Wilson, Mark

Land of the Giants, The. See: Lockridge, Barry

Land of the Lost, The. See: Red Lantern

LANDESBERG, STEVE. See: Darin, Bobby

LANDI, ELISSA
PAULA STONE
MAGGI McNELLIS, moderators of the program (themselves)
BINNIE BARNES
CONSTANCE BENNETT
LUCILLE BALL
ROBIN CHANDLER
DOROTHY KILGALLEN
ELOISE McELHONE
FLORENCE PRICHETT, panelists (themselves)
Leave It to the Girls (R) (Panel discussion)

LANDIS, DR. JACK. See: Harding, Karen Adams

Landlord, Hey! See: Banner, Woody

LANDON. See also: London

LANDON, MICHAEL. See: Cookie Monster, The
Jones, Jack

LANE. See also:
Laine
Layne

LANE, ABBE. See: Cugat, Xavier (2)

LANE CHORUS, THE KEN. See: Ross, Lanny

LANE, DAVIE. See: Graham, Dr. Bob

LANE, HONDO, ex-Civil War cavalry scout; widower, trouble-shooter for U.S. Army

BUFFALO BAKER, his friend
ANGIE DOW, widow
JOHNNY DOW, Angie's young son
Hondo (TV) (Western)

Lane, Joe Franklin's Memory. See: Franklin, Joe

LANE, KEN. See: Martin, Dean (2)

LANE, LOIS. See: Kent, Clark

LANE, MARGO. See: Cranston, Lamont

LANE, MATTIE. See: Karr, Mike

LANE, PATTY, modern American teenage girl
KENNETH, her father, managing editor
NATALIE, her mother
ROSS, her twelve-year-old brother
CATHY, her look-alike English cousin
MARTIN, Cathy's father
RICHARD, Patty's boy friend
The Patty Duke Show (TV) (Comedy)

LANE, REBECCA
DAVID
JOHN, characters appearing in the drama
Beyond These Valleys (R) (Serial drama)

LANE, RICHARD
FRANK JENKS
CLIFF EDWARDS (Ukulele Ike)
FRANCES HUNT, entertainers and singers appearing on the program (themselves)
GORDON JENKINS, orchestra leader (himself)
HIS ORCHESTRA
Hall of Fun (R) (Variety)

LANE, RICHIE. See: Kaufman, Seymour

LANE, SHERMAN. See: Dix, Dorothy (1)

LANE SISTERS, THE. See:
Waring, Fred (1)

LANE TEMPLE. See: Rockford,
Matthew

LANETTE. See: Sunday

LANG, ADELE. See: Warren,
Wendy

LANG, CHARLES. See: Warren,
Wendy

LANG, FREDERICKA. See:
Rutledge, Dr. John

LANG, HARRY. See: Bolger, Ray

LANG, LUCIA. See: Trent, Helen

LANGDON TOWNE. See: Rogers,
Major Robert

LANGE. See also: Lance

LANGE, JIM, host of the program
(himself)
GUEST PARTICIPANTS
The Dating Game (TV) (Intro-
duction game)

LANGE, JIM. See also: Shawn,
Dick

LANGER. See also:
Lancer
Langner

LANGER, ROY. See: Edwards,
Ralph (1)

LANGNER. See also:
Lancer
Langer

LANGNER, LAWRENCE, host of
the program (himself)
MANY ACTORS AND ACTRESSES
HAROLD LEVEY, orchestra
leader (himself)
HIS ORCHESTRA
The Theater Guild of the Air (R)
(Drama) (also known as The
United States Steel Hour) (R)

LANIER, NURSE. See: Brent,
Dr. Jim

LANIN, SAM, orchestra leader
(himself)
THE IPANA TROUBADOURS,
his orchestra
The Ipana Troubadours (R)
(Dance music)

LANNY. See:
Lennie
Lenny
Lonnie
Perry, John
Ross, Lanny

LANNY ROSS. See:
Henry, Captain
Ross, Lanny

LANSING, CAPTAIN. See:
Welles, Orson (3)

LANSING, CURT. See: Perry,
John

LANSING McKENZIE. See:
Bennett, Nita

LANSING, ROBERTA. See:
Perry, John

LANSING, STEVE. See: Sunday

LANSING, VIRGINIA. See: Noble,
Mary

LANSON. See also: Lamson

LANSON, DR. See: Hargrave-
Scott, Joan

LANSON, SNOOKY
DOROTHY COLLINS
GISELE MACKENZIE
RUSSELL ARMS
JILL COREY
TOMMY LEONETTI
VIRGINIA GIBSON
ALAN COPELAND, singers
appearing on the program (them-
selves)
THE HIT PARADE SINGERS,
musical group
THE HIT PARADE DANCERS,
dance group
RAYMOND SCOTT, orchestra
leader (himself)
Your Hit Parade (TV) (Drama-
tizations of popular music)

LANTERN. See: Red Lantern

Lantern, The Orange. See: Botak

LANYARD, MICHAEL, adventurer;
called the "Lone Wolf"
The Lone Wolf (TV) (Adventure)

Laramie. See: Harper, Jess

LARDNER, JOHN. See: Cross,
Mason

LARDNER, RUTH. See: Rogers,
Patricia

Laredo. See: Parmalee, Ranger
Captain

Large, Garroway at. See: Garroway, Dave (2)

LARIMORE, MARILYN
JACK CRANDALL
EDITH CRANDALL
VIRGINIA MARSHALL
MRS. SCHULTZ
MR. SCHULTZ
GEORGE BARTLETT
JUDGE CARTER COLBY
MRS. CARTER COLBY
JOHN MURRAY
JUDITH CLARK
LAURA RICHARDSON
MR. CONWAY
JUDITH EVANS
BERTHA SCHULTZ
HENRY
PEGGY
NORA
HELEN, characters appearing in
the drama
Lonely Woman (R) (Serial drama)
(also known as Today's Children)
(R)

LARKIN, JEREMY, young leader of
the Yankee Doodle Society,
American revolutionary guerrilla
band
ISAK POOLE, Negro blacksmith
and former slave; member of the
band
ELIZABETH COATES, member of
the band
GENERAL LAFAYETTE, French
officer, assisting the Americans
The Young Rebels (TV) (Historical
drama)

LARKINS, PETER. See: Guthrie,
Lieut. Ben

LARKS QUARTET, THE MELLO.
See: James, Dennis (1)

LA ROSA, JULIUS, singer and
entertainer; host of the program
(himself)
MANY CELEBRITY GUESTS
MITCHELL AYRES, orchestra
leader (himself)
HIS ORCHESTRA
The Julius La Rosa Show (TV)
(Variety)

LA ROSA, JULIUS. See also:
Godfrey, Arthur (1)

LARRY. See:
Blyden, Larry (1) (2)
Lori
Lorre
Lory
Noble, Mary
Sterling, Vanessa Dale
Walker, Eddie
Walleck, Meredith
Young, Larry "Pepper"

LARRY BLYDEN. See:
Blyden, Larry (1) (2)
Fox, Sonny

LARRY BURTON. See: Carter,
Hope

LARRY CLARK. See: Lewis,
Dave

LARRY CLINTON. See: Whiteman, Paul

LARRY CRANDALL. See: Boyd,
Tom

LARRY DEAN. See: Welk,
Lawrence

LARRY ELLIS. See: Kaye,
Sammy (1)

LARRY HAINES. See: Mc-
Cormick, Myron

LARRY HALLIDAY. See: West,
Michael

LARRY HOOPER. See: Welk, Lawrence

LARRY HOVIS. See: Martindale, Wink (2)
Rowan, Dan

LARRY, JR. See: Noble, Mary

LARRY KEATING. See: Daley, Cass

LARRY LAHR. See: Andrews, Drake

LARRY O'BRIEN. See: Kaye, Sammy (1)

LARRY STEVENS. See: Benny, Jack

LARRY STORCH. See: Gleason, Jackie (1)

LARRY WINTERS. See: Hughes, Chris

LARSEN, JOHN. See: Morgan, Paul

LARSEN, KENT. See: Driggs, Karleton King

LARSEN, MARILYN DRIGGS. See: Driggs, Karleton King

LARSEN, SAM, chief investigator for the Court of Last Resort The Court of Last Resort (TV) (Crime drama)

LARSON, DR. TONY. See: Hughes, Lisa

LARSON, SANDY. See: Hughes, Lisa

LARUE. See: Gidget

LASAGNE, LOLA. See: Batman

LASH, RUFUS. See: Carter, Chick

Lassie. See: Lassie

LASSIE, collie dog, star of the program (herself)

SCOTT
JEFF MILLER
BOB
JOHN
REED
TIMMIE
KENDALL
CHARLIE
COREY STUART
OTHERS, characters appearing on the program
Lassie (TV) (Animal adventure) (Some units later re-released under the title Jeff's Collie) (TV) (appeared originally in different form under title Lassie) (R)

Last of the Mohicans, Hawkeye and the. See: Hawkeye

Last Resort, The Court of. See: Larsen, Sam

Last Word, The. See: Evans, Bergen (2)

LATHAM, PENNY. See: Harding, Mrs. Rhoda

LATHROP. See: Dillon, Marshal Matt

Latitude Zero. See: McKenzie, Captain Craig

LA TRIVIA, MAYOR. See: McGee, Fibber

LATTIMER, BARBARA. See: Sterling, Vanessa Dale

LATTIMER, RICKEY. See: Sterling, Vanessa Dale

LATTIMER, STACY. See: Sterling, Vanessa Dale

LATZI, UNCLE. See: McCray, Linc

Laugh Doctors. See: Pratt, Russell

Laugh-In. See: Rowan, Dan

Laugh-In, Letters to. See: Owens, Gary

Laugh-In, Rowan and Martin's. See: Rowan, Dan

Laugh Line. See: Van Dyke, Dick (1)

Laugh, Make Me. See: Lewis, Robert Q. (1)

LAUGHING LADY, THE. See: Blurt, Elmer

LAURA. See:
Ace, Goodman
James, Nancy
Laurie
Lora
Manning, Laura
Petrie, Rob
Weber, Laura

LAURA COOPER. See: Hillman, India

LAURA DEANE. See: Bracken, John

LAURA ELLIOTT. See: Garrison, Spencer

LAURA GREENE. See: Klein, Robert

LAURA HORTON, DR. See: Horton, Dr. Tom

LAURA MARTIN. See: Rutledge, Dr. John

LAURA PAIGE. See: Hackett, Doc

LAURA PUTNAM. See: Wilbur, Judy

LAURA RICHARDSON. See: Larimore, Marilyn

LAURA WEATHERBY. See: Mallory, Lieut. Col. Spencer

LAURALEE McWILLIAMS. See: Sloan, Holly

LAUREL. See: Holiday, Laurel

LAUREL DALLAS GROSVENOR. See: Dallas, Stella

LAURENCE. See: Lawrence

LAURETTE. See: Driggs, Karleton King

LAURIE. See:
Beamer, John
Laura
Lora
Partridge, Connie
Rose, George

LAURIE ANDERS. See: Murray, Ken (3)

LAURIE, JOE, JR. See: Wilson, Ward

LAURIE PHILIPS. See: Tate, Joanne

LAURIE, PIPER. See: Crosby, John

LAURIE RANDALL. See: Burnley, Walter

LAVALLE, PAUL. See:
Cross, Milton (1)
Dragonette, Jessica (1)

LAVARN THOMAS. See: Driggs, Karleton King

Lavender and New Lace. See: Marlowe, Sylvia

Lavender and Old Lace. See: Scheff, Fritzi

LAVINIA TATE. See: Tammy

LA VOLTA, DIANNE, "international chanteuse"
Time For Love (R) (Drama)

LAVOTI, JOE. See: Welk, Lawrence

Law and Mr. Jones, The. See: Jones, Abraham Lincoln

Law, Attorney at. See: Regan, Terry

Law, Ben Jerrod, Attorney at. See: Jerrod, Ben

Law, Burke's. See: Burke, Amos

Law For the Layman. See:
Granik, Theodore (2)

Law, I Am the. See: Kirby,
Lieut.

Law, Men at. See: Hansen, David

Law of the Plainsman, The. See:
Buckhart, Sam

Law, Owen Marshall, Counselor at.
See: Marshall, Owen

Law, Terry Regan, Attorney at.
See: Regan, Terry

Lawbreaker. See: Marvin, Lee

LAWES, LEWIS E., warden of Sing
Sing Prison (himself)
MR. STARK, interviewer
Twenty Thousand Years in Sing
Sing (R) (Crime stories)

LAWLESS, RICHARD, 17th century
English adventurer
Richard Lawless (R) (Adventure)

Lawless Years, The. See:
Ruditsky, Barney

Lawman. See: Troop, Marshal
Dan

LAWRENCE. See:
Langner, Lawrence
Preston, Lawrence
Welk, Lawrence

Lawrence and Gorme. See:
Lawrence, Steve (1)

LAWRENCE, BILL. See:
Como, Perry (1)
Godfrey, Arthur (1)

LAWRENCE, CAROL. See:
Damone, Vic (2)
Davidson, John (1)

LAWRENCE, ELLIOT. See:
Dixon, Bobby

LAWRENCE FECHTENBERGER.
See: Ballew, Wally

LAWRENCE, LEOTA. See: Myrt

LAWRENCE, LUCILE. See: Ross,
Lanny

LAWRENCE MITCHELL. See:
Graham, Dr. Bob

LAWRENCE SHIEFFIELD. See:
Sunday

LAWRENCE SPIVAK. See:
Rountree, Martha

LAWRENCE, STEVE (1)
EYDIE GORME, singers and
entertainers; co-stars of the
program (themselves)
MANY GUEST STARS
Lawrence and Gorme (TV)
(Variety)

LAWRENCE, STEVE (2), singer
and entertainer; star of the pro-
gram (himself)
MANY GUEST STARS
JOE GUERCIO, orchestra leader
(himself)
HIS ORCHESTRA
The Steve Lawrence Show (TV)
(Variety)

LAWRENCE, STEVE. See also:
Allen, Steve (3)
Crosby, Bing (2)

LAWRENCE, VICKI. See:
Burnett, Carol

Lawrence Welk Show, The. See:
Welk, Lawrence

Lawrence Welk's Top Tunes and
New Talent. See: Welk,
Lawrence

LAWSON, AGNES. See: Aldrich,
Henry

LAWTON, LORA, housekeeper
PETER CARVER, her employer;
shipbuilder
MAY CASE, secretary
CLYDE HOUSTON
IRIS HOUSTON
RUSSELL GILMAN
REX LAWTON
ANGUS MacDONALD

HELENE HUDSON
GAIL CARVER, characters ap-
pearing in the drama
Lora Lawton (R) (Serial drama)

LAWYER FELDMAN. See: Meyer

LAWYER, THE. See: Malone,
Dr. Jerry

Lawyers, The (The Bold Ones).
See: Nichols, Walter

Lawyers, The Store Front. See:
Hansen, David

Lawyers, The Young. See: Barrett, David

Layman, Law For the. See:
Granik, Theodore (2)

LAYNE. See also:
Laine
Lane

LAYNE, BRONCO, Ex-Confederate
army officer
Bronco (TV) (Western)

LAYTON. See: Leighton

LAZYFOOT. See: Parmalee,
Ranger Captain

LEACE, DONAL. See: Walsh,
Bob

Lead a Band, So You Want To?
See: Kaye, Sammy (2)

LEADBOTTOM, OLD. See:
McHale, Lieut. Commander
Quinton

LEADER, MR. See: Pip the
Piper

LEAF. See: Leif

LEAHY, FRANK. See: Anthony,
Ray

Learn to Smile. See: Cantor,
Eddie (2)

Learn, We Love and. See:
Peters, Bill

Learning, What's New in? See:
Sparks, Hale

Leave It, Take It or. See:
Baker, Phil (3)

Leave It to Beaver. See: Cleaver,
Ward

Leave It to Joan. See: Davis,
Joan

Leave It to Mike. See: Mike

Leave It to the Girls. See:
Connors, Nancy
Landi, Elissa

LeBEAU. See: Hogan, Colonel
Robert

LECUONA CUBAN BOYS, THE.
See: Whiteman, Paul

LEDDY. See also:
Lady
Lyddie

LEDDY FOWLEY. See: Keene,
Kitty

LEE. See:
Cochran, Lee
Leigh
Marvin, Lee
Sawyer, Andy
Taylor, Andy

LEE AND MARY TRIO, THE
VERNE. See: Kelly, Joe (1)

LEE BALDWIN. See: Hardy,
Dr. Steven

LEE BLAIR. See: Marshall, E.G.

LEE, BOB. See: Susan (1)

LEE, BONNIE. See: Kirchener,
Claude (1)

LEE BOWMAN. See: Donald,
Peter

LEE BRODIE. See: Kirkwood,
Jack

LEE CASTLE. See: Basie, Count

LEE CHAMBERLIN. See: Cosby,
Bill (1)

LEE, COURTNEY. See: Jordan,
Joyce

LEE CRANE, COMMANDER. See:
Nelson, Admiral Harriman

LEE, EDGAR. See: Horn, Aggie

LEE, GYPSY ROSE, entertainer;
hostess of the program (herself)
MANY CELEBRITY INTER-
VIEWEES
Gypsy Rose Lee (TV) (Interviews)

LEE, GYPSY ROSE. See also:
Stokey, Mike

LEE, JANE. See: Judy

LEE, JIM, head of the family
HELEN LEE, his wife
ANNE LEE, his daughter, high
school student
MARJORIE LEE, his daughter,
receptionist
JANE LEE, his daughter,
neophyte lawyer
BARBARA LEE, his daughter,
employed in advertising agency
MARY LEE WALDON, his
daughter, married
DON WALDON, Mary's husband,
junior executive
Our Five Daughters (TV) (Family
situation comedy)

LEE KIRBY. See: Myrt

LEE, LILLIAN. See: Kirkwood,
Jack

LEE, LINDA. See: Ripley,
Robert L.

LEE LOO. See: Mix, Tom

LEE MARKHAM, DR. See:
Harding, Karen Adams

LEE, MARTIN. See: Horn, Aggie

LEE, MONICA. See: Horn, Aggie

LEE, MYRA. See: Jordan, Joyce

LEE, PEGGY. See:
Crosby, Bing (3)
Parkyakarkas, Nick

LEE, PINKY (1), host of the pro-
gram (himself)
MOLLY BEE, vocalist (herself)
The Pinky Lee Show (TV)
(Children)

LEE, PINKY (2), comedian
VIVIAN BLAINE, comedienne
(themselves)
MANY GUEST STARS
The Two of Us (TV) (Music/
variety)

LEE, ROBERT. See: Halop,
Billy

LEE, TERRY, young soldier of
fortune in the Orient
THE DRAGON LADY, Chinese
pirate
BURMA, his friend
HOTSHOT CHARLIE, aviator
Terry and the Pirates (R) (TV)
(Adventure)
PATRICK RYAN, soldier of
fortune; Lee's mentor
FLIP CORKIN
CAPTAIN GOODHUE, aviators
CONNIE, Lee's friend
Terry and the Pirates (R)
CHOPSTICK JOE, Chinese friend
of Lee
Terry and the Pirates (TV)

LEE WEBBER. See: Peyton,
Martin

LE FAVE TRIO, THE CARMEN.
See: Edwards, Frank

LEFKOWITZ, CORPORAL. See:
McKay, Judson

LEFTIE HARPER. See: Brew-
ster, Joey

LEFTY. See: McCray, Linc

LEFTY HIGGINS. See: Dawson,
Rosemary

Legend of Jesse James, The. See:
James, Jesse

Legend of Wyatt Earp, The Life and.
See: Earp, Wyatt

Legion, Assignment Foreign. See:
Oberon, Merle

Legion, Captain Gallant of the
Foreign. See: Gallant, Captain

Legion Time, Safety. See: Story
Lady, The

LEHMAN, COREY. See: Hansen,
Dean Eric

LEHR, LEW. See: Uttal, Fred
(1)

LEICESTER. See also: Lester

LEICESTER, R. See: Barry,
Jack (9)

LEIF
FINN, Vikings
Tales of the Vikings (TV) (Ad-
venture)

LEIGH. See also: Lee

LEIGH, TARA. See: Chidsey,
Jackie

LEIGHTON, COLONEL. See:
Dyke, Charity Amanda

LEIGHTON, EDWARD. See:
Dyke, Charity Amanda

LEIGHTON, LINDA
THORNTON DREXEL
TOM FIELD
JOE, characters appearing in
the drama
Masquerade (R) (Serial drama)

LEIGHTON, MARION. See: Dyke,
Charity Amanda

LEIGHTON, MRS. See: Dyke,
Charity Amanda

LEIGHTON, SUSAN. See: Dyke,
Charity Amanda

LEILA RANSOM. See: Gildersleeve, Throckmorton P.

LELA WALLINGFORD. See: Dix,
Dorothy (1)

LELIA MATTHEWS. See: Ben-
nett, Nita

LEM STACEY. See: Wilbur,
Judy

LEMBECK, MICHAEL. See:
Kelly, Gene

LEMMON, JACK. See: Ryan,
Robert (1)

LEMUEL. See: Stoopnagle,
Colonel Lemuel Q. (1) (2)

LEMUEL CARP, PROFESSOR.
See: Bergen, Edgar (2)

LEN CARRIE. See: Jones, Spike
(1)

LEN REYNOLDS. See: Tate,
Joanne

LEN WEINRIB. See: Jones,
Spike (2)

LENA. See:
Gene
McGee, Fibber

Lena, Gene and Glenn With Jake
and. See: Gene

LENA HORNE. See: Cross,
Milton (1)

LENNIE. See:
Crooke, Lennie
Lanny
Lenny
Lonnie

LENNIE HAYTON. See:
Allen, Fred
Ross, Lanny

LENNON, DIANNE. See:
Lennon, Janet
Welk, Lawrence

LENNON, JANET
DIANNE LENNON
KATHY LENNON
PEGGY LENNON (The Lennon

Sisters), singers, featured on the
program (themselves)
JIMMY DURANTE, comedian,
singer and pianist, also featured
on the program (himself)
MANY GUEST STARS
Jimmy Durante Presents the
Lennon Sisters Hour (TV) (Variety)

LENNON, JANET. See also:
Welk, Lawrence

LENNON, KATHY. See:
Lennon, Janet
Welk, Lawrence

LENNON, PEGGY. See:
Lennon, Janet
Welk, Lawrence

Lennon Sisters Hour, Jimmy
Durante Presents the. See:
Lennon, Janet

LENNON SISTERS, THE. See:
Lennon, Janet
Welk, Lawrence

LENNOX, ELIZABETH. See:
Munn, Frank (1)

LENNOX, JOHN. See: Harum,
David

LENNY. See also:
Lanny
Lennie
Lonnie

LENNY ROSS. See:
Barry, Jack (1)
Story, Ralph

LENORD. See also: Leonard

LENORD, MR. See: Dyke,
Charity Amanda

LENORD, MRS. See: Dyke,
Charity Amanda

LENORE. See: Randolph, Alice

LENORE CASE. See: Reid, Britt

LENROW, BERNARD, host of the
program (himself)
MANY ACTORS AND ACTRESSES

The Mollé Mystery Theater (R)
(Detective mystery drama)
(later called Mystery Theater
(R) and Hearthstone of the Death
Squad) (R)
INSPECTOR HEARTHSTONE "of
the Death Squad," police officer
Hearthstone of the Death Squad
(R)

LENYA, RICKI. See: Wayne,
Ruth Evans

LEO REISMAN. See: Ross, Lanny

LEO WARNER. See: Rogers,
Patricia

LEON JANNEY. See: Cross,
Mason

LEON LEONARDI. See: Lescoulie,
Jack (2)

LEONA KENMORE. See: Sunday

LEONARD. See:
Bernstein, Leonard
Graves, Leonard
Lenord

LEONARD, BILL, host of the pro-
gram (himself)
Eye on New York (TV) (New
York life)

LEONARD CLARK. See: Fairchild, Kay

LEONARD GILLESPIE, DR. See:
Kildare, Dr. James

LEONARD HUNTLEY. See:
Harding, Karen Adams

LEONARD, JACK E. See: Clark,
Dick (3)

LEONARD LILLYBRIDGE. See:
Kincaid, Chet

LEONARD, SHELDON. See:
Benny, Jack

LEONARD WARREN. See: Roxy

LEONARDI, LEON. See: Lescoulie, Jack (2)

LEONETTI, TOMMY. See: Lanson, Snooky

LEOTA LAWRENCE. See: Myrt

LEPRECHAUN MARCHING BAND, HIS. See: Big Jon

LERNER, DAVID. See: Levy, Abie

LEROY. See: Martin, Doris

LEROY FORRESTER. See: Gildersleeve, Throckmorton P.

LEROY, GINGER. See: Trent, Helen

LEROY, REVEREND. See: Wilson, Flip

LES. See:
Crane, Les
Paul, Les

LES BROWN. See:
Damone, Vic (2)
Hope, Bob (2)
Martin, Dean (2)
Whiteman, Paul

Les Crane Show, The. See:
Crane, Les

LES ELGART. See: Whiteman, Paul

LES HART. See: Burke, Amos

LES PAUL. See:
Paul, Les
Waring, Fred (1)

Les Paul and Mary Ford. See:
Paul, Les

LES TREMAYNE. See: First Nighter, Mr.

LESCOULIE, JACK (1), host of the program (himself)
MANY GUEST STARS
Doin' Their Thing (TV) (Variety)

LESCOULIE, JACK (2), master of ceremonies on the program (himself)

ARTHUR Q. BRYAN
PHIL KRAMER
EMERY PARNELL
WALTER TETLEY
BETH WILSON, entertainers appearing on the program (themselves)
LEON LEONARDI, orchestra leader (himself)
HIS ORCHESTRA
The Grouch Club (R) (Comedy)

LESCOULIE, JACK (3), host of the program (himself)
RICHARD THOMAS, his protege (himself)
1, 2, 3, Go! (TV) (Children's education)

LESCOULIE, JACK (4), host of the program (himself)
BOB CONSIDINE, newscaster (himself)
GUEST VOCALISTS
MUSICAL GROUPS
GOSSIP COLUMN INTERVIEWERS
INTERVIEWEES
Tonight! (TV) (New York City night life) (also known as America After Dark) (TV)

LESCOULIE, JACK. See also:
Davis, Fred

LESLIE. See:
Lindsey, Peter
Manning, Laura
Nielsen, Leslie (1) (2)
Uggams, Leslie

LESLIE FOSTER, DR. See:
Marshall, John

LESLIE HARRINGTON. See:
Peyton, Martin

LESLIE JACKSON BAUER. See:
Bauer, Bertha

LESLIE PALMER. See: Manning, Portia Blake

LESLIE UGGAMS. See:
Davidson, John (1)
Miller, Mitch
Uggams, Leslie

Leslie Uggams Show, The. See:
Uggams, Leslie

LESTER. See:
Grafton, Harry
Leicester
Rowan, Dan

LESTER BRENNAN. See: Har-
grave-Scott, Joan

LESTER, BUDDY. See: Lewis,
Robert Q. (1)

LESTER GRUBER. See: McHale,
Lieut. Commander Quinton

LESTER JAY. See: Halop, Billy

LESTER, JERRY
MOREY AMSTERDAM, comedians;
hosts of the program (themselves)
DAGMAR, comedienne (herself)
DAVE STREET
WAYNE HOWELL, entertainers
(themselves)
MILTON DeLUGG, accordionist
and orchestra leader (himself)
HIS ORCHESTRA
MANY GUEST CELEBRITIES
Broadway Open House (TV)
(Conversation/variety)

LESTER, JERRY. See also:
Crosby, Bing (3)

LESTER LEWIS. See: O'Neill,
Mrs.

LESTER WILLIAMS DANCERS, THE.
See: Davis, Sammy, Jr.

Let George Do It. See: Soule,
Olan (4)

LETA POWELL DRAKE. See:
Bragonier, Dr. J. Robert

Let's Dance. See: Cugat, Xavier
(1)

Let's Make a Deal. See: Hall,
Monty (2)

Let's Pretend. See: Halop, Billy

Let's Take a Trip. See: Pud

Letter to Loretta, A. See: Young,
Loretta (1)

Letters to Laugh-In. See: Owens,
Gary

LETTERS, WALKING. See:
Cookie Monster, The

LETTVIN, MAGGIE, physical cul-
turist, hostess of the program
(herself)
GUEST EXERCISERS
Maggie and the Beautiful Machine
(TV) (Physical culture)

LEVANG, NEIL. See: Welk,
Lawrence

LEVANT, OSCAR. See:
Crosby, Bing (3)
Fadiman, Clifton (1)

LEVENSON. See also: Levinson

LEVENSON, SAM, host of the pro-
gram (himself)
MANY CELEBRITY GUESTS
MANY AMATEUR CONTESTANTS,
discovered and introduced by the
celebrities
HARRY SOSNIK, orchestra leader
(himself)
HIS ORCHESTRA
Celebrity Talent Scouts (TV)
(Amateur talent contest)

LEVENSON, SAM. See also:
Donald, Peter
Shriner, Herb (3)

LEVEY. See also: Levy

LEVEY, HAROLD. See: Langner,
Lawrence

LEVI. See:
Levey
Levy

LEVINE, HENRY. See: Cross,
Milton (1)

LEVINSON. See also: Levenson

LEVINSON, LIEUT. See: Diamond,
Richard

LEVITT, PERRY. See: Raven,
Dan

LEVY. See also: Levey

LEVY, ABIE, Jewish youth
ROSEMARY LEVY, his Irish wife
THE TWINS, their children
SOLOMON LEVY, Abie's father
PATRICK JOSEPH MURPHY, Rosemary's father
MR. COHEN, Jewish working man
MRS. COHEN, Cohen's wife
FATHER WHELAN, Catholic priest
DAVID LERNER
MRS. BROWN, friends of the Levys
DR. MUELLER, physician
MRS. MUELLER, Dr. Mueller's wife
CASEY, secretary
Abie's Irish Rose (R) (Situation comedy)

LEVY, MORRIS. See: O'Neill, Mrs.

LEW. See:
Ayres, Lew
Loo
Lou
Lu

LEW LEHR. See: Uttal, Fred (1)

LEW MILES. See: Peyton, Martin

LEW VALENTINE. See:
I.Q., Dr.
I.Q. Jr., Dr.

LEWANDOWSKI, BOB, host of the program (himself)
CAROLYN DeZURIK, vocalist (herself)
THE POLKA ROUNDERS, musical group
THE CAIN DANCERS
MANY GUEST STARS
LOU PROHUT, orchestra leader (himself)
HIS ORCHESTRA
Polka-Go-Round (TV) (Polka music/variety)

LEWIS. See:
Lawes, Lewis E.
Lois
Louie

Louis
Louisa
Louise
Luis
Luise
Rogers, Patricia
Yablonsky, Lewis

LEWIS, ARTHUR Q. See:
Edwards, Ralph (1)

LEWIS, BROOK. See: Cameron, Christy Allen

LEWIS, DAVE, disc jockey
LINDA, his wife
LARRY CLARK, disc jockey
SANDY, neighbor of the Lewis family
ROLAND B. HUTTON, JR., television station owner
Good Morning, World (TV) (Comedy)

LEWIS, DR. See: Randolph, Ellen

LEWIS, ELLIOTT, featured on the program (himself)
MANY ACTORS AND ACTRESSES
Knickerbocker Playhouse (R) (Drama)

LEWIS, HOWDY. See: Jones, Ben

LEWIS J. VALENTINE. See:
Lord, Phillips H.

LEWIS JACKMAN. See: Peyton, Martin

LEWIS, JERRY, comedian; host of the program (himself)
THE NUTTY PROFESSOR
THE SHOESHINE BOY, characters portrayed by Lewis
THE NICK CASTLE DANCERS
THE GEORGE WYLE SINGERS
LOU BROWN, orchestra leader (himself)
HIS ORCHESTRA
MANY GUESTS
The Jerry Lewis Show (TV) (Comedy/variety)

LEWIS, JERRY. See also: Martin, Dean (1) (3)

LEWIS, JERRY LEE. See:
Owens, Buck

LEWIS JOHNSON. See: Dallas,
Stella

LEWIS, LESTER. See: O'Neill,
Mrs.

LEWIS, ROBERT Q. (1), comedian;
master of ceremonies of the
program (himself)
SID GOULD
BUDDY LESTER
HENNY YOUNGMAN
GENE BAYLOS
HARVEY STONE
OTHERS, comedians on the pro-
gram (themselves)
CELEBRITY CONTESTANTS
GUEST CONTESTANTS
Make Me Laugh (TV) (Game)

LEWIS, ROBERT Q. (2), comedian;
host of the program (himself)
MERV GRIFFIN
JILL COREY, vocalists (them-
selves)
MANY GUEST STARS
The Robert Q. Lewis Show (TV)
(Variety)

LEWIS ROYAL, DR. See: Hank

LEWIS, SHARI, ventriloquist;
hostess of the program (herself)
LAMB CHOP
HUSH PUPPY
CHARLIE HORSE, her puppets
MR. GOODFELLOW, her next
door neighbor
MANY GUEST STARS
The Shari Lewis Show (TV)
(Ventriloquism/variety)

Lewis Show, The Martin and. See:
Martin, Dean (3)

LEWIS, TOMMY. See: Jackson,
Martha

LEWIS, WELCOME (1), featured
vocalist on the program (herself)
Singing Bee (R) (Music)

LEWIS, WELCOME (2)
ART GENTRY, vocalists on the
program (themselves)

Singo (R) (Musical quiz)

LEX. See: Rogers, Lex

LEX DE AZEVDO. See: Driggs,
Karleton King

LEYDEN, BILL (1)
RALPH EDWARDS, quizmasters
of the program (themselves)
MANY CONTESTANTS
It Could Be You (TV) (Quiz)

LEYDEN, BILL (2), moderator of
the program (himself)
DENNIS JAMES
GEORGE KIRGO, panelists
(themselves)
ONE GUEST STAR PANELIST
Your First Impression (TV)
(Game)

LIBBY. See:
Farrow, Valentine
Goldberg, Molly
Parker, Lieut. Mike

LIBERACE, pianist; host of the
program (himself)
GEORGE LIBERACE, his brother,
violinist (himself)
MANY GUEST STARS
The Liberace Show (TV) (Music/
variety)

LIBERACE. See also: Berman,
Shelley

Liberace Show, The. See: Liberace

LIBERTINI, DICK. See: Moore,
Melba

LIDDELL, BARNEY. See: Welk,
Lawrence

LIDO, BOB. See: Welk, Lawrence

Lidsville. See: Hoodoo, Horatio
J.

LIEBLING, ROCHELL. See:
Kelly, Joe (2)

LIEUT. See:
Adams, Lieut. Price
Ballinger, Lieut. Frank

LIEUT. SNEDIGAR, POLICE. See: Madison, Kenny

Lieutenant, The. See: Rice, Lieut. Bill

LIEUT. UHURA. See: Kirk, Captain James

LIEUT. VOUGHT. See: Welles, Orson (3)

Life and Legend of Wyatt Earp, The. See: Earp, Wyatt

Life and Loves of Dr. Susan, The. See: Chandler, Dr. Susan

Life Begins. See: Webster, Martha

Life Begins at Eighty. See: Barry, Jack (6)

Life Can Be Beautiful. See: Solomon, David

Life, Food For. See: Cederquist, Dena

Life Is Mine, This. See: Hastings, Bob

Life Is Worth Living. See: Sheen, Bishop Fulton J.

Life, It's a Great. See: Morgan, Mrs. Amy
O'Shea, Michael

Life, Love of. See: Sterling, Vanessa Dale

Life of Dennis Day, A Day in the. See: Day, Dennis

Life of Henry Phyfe, The Double. See: Phyfe, Henry

Life of Mary Sothern, The. See: Sothern, Mary

Life of Riley, The. See: Riley, Chester A.

Life, Portia Faccs. See: Manning, Portia Blake

Life, Road of. See: Brent, Dr. Jim

Life, Run for Your. See: Bryan, Paul

Life, That's. See: Dixon, Bobby

Life, The Good. See: Miller, Albert

Life, This Is Your. See: Edwards, Ralph (2)

Life to Live, One. See: Walleck, Meredith

Life With Elizabeth. See: Elizabeth

Life With Father. See: Day, Clarence

Life With Linkletter. See: Linkletter, Art (2)

Life With Luigi. See: Luigi

Life, You Bet Your. See: Marx, Groucho (3)

Lifetime, Chance of a. See: King, John Reed (1)

Light of the World, The. See: Speaker, The

Light, The Blue. See: March, David

Light, The Guiding. See: Bauer, Bertha
Rutledge, Dr. John

LIGHTNIN'. See: Jones, Amos

Lights Out. See: Winkler, Betty

Like Young. See: McKenna, Jim

LIL. See: Nuvo, Arnie

LI'L. See also: Little

Li'l Abner. See: Yokum, Li'l Abner

LI'L ABNER. See: Yokum, Li'l Abner

LIL, AUNT. See: Peepers,
Robinson J.

LIL, SHANGHAI. See: Jungle Jim

LIL, TIGER. See: Jungle Jim

LILA NORTH. See: Runyon, Brad

LILAC, LOUIE THE. See: Batman

Lilac Time. See: Murray, Arthur

LILE. See also: Lyle

LILE FLORENZE. See: Sunday

LILE KILGORE. See: Marshall,
John

LILIAS. See:
Folan, Lilias
Lilli
Lillie
Lily

Lilias, Yoga and You. See:
Folan, Lilias

LILIENTHAL, DR. See: Hargrave-
Scott, Joan

LILLI. See:
Lilias
Lillie
Lily
Manning, Portia Blake

LILLIAN. See: Bradley, Judith

LILLIAN ANDERSON. See:
Burton, Terry

LILLIAN BURKE. See: Jackson,
Martha

LILLIAN HATHAWAY. See:
Prescott, Kate Hathaway

LILLIAN HAYMAN. See: Uggams,
Leslie

LILLIAN LEE. See: Kirkwood,
Jack

LILLIAN, SISTER. See: Rutledge,
Dr. John

LILLIE. See:
Davis, Joan Field
Lilias
Lilli
Lily

LILLUMS. See: Teen, Harold

LILLYBRIDGE, LEONARD. See:
Kincaid, Chet

LILY. See:
Grimm, Arnold
Lilias
Lilli
Lillie
Meek, Mortimer
Munster, Herman
Ruskin, Lily
West, Michael

LILY BOHEME MONTAGUE. See:
Montague, Edwin

LILY MERRILL. See: Troop,
Marshal Dan

LILY PONS. See: Bell, Alexander Graham

LILY, TIGER. See: Pan, Peter

LILY TOMLIN. See: Rowan, Dan

LIME, HARRY, investigator and
adventurer
WEBSTER, his friend and
associate
The Third Man (TV) (Mystery)

LINA. See also: Lana

LINA TROYER. See: Marlin,
Mary

LINC. See:
Hayes, Linc
Link
McCray, Linc
Sterling, Vanessa Dale

LINC CASE. See: Murdock, Buz

LINCOLN. See: Vail, Lincoln

LINCOLN, DR. MATT, psychiatrist
TAG
KEVIN

ANN
JIMMY, his young aides
Matt Lincoln (TV) (Medical drama)
(formerly known as Dial Hot Line)
(TV)

Lincoln Highway. See: McIntire,
John

LINCOLN, JOE, chief agent for
U. S. Treasury
Treasury Agent (R) (Drama)

LINDA, character appearing in the
drama
Linda's First Love (R) (Serial
drama)

LINDA. See also:
Abbott, John
Bartlett, Jill
Dale, Linda
Dane, Prudence
Dodd, Jimmie
Driggs, Karleton King
Harper, Linda Emerson
Leighton, Linda
Lewis, Dave
Redigo, Jim (2)
Williams, Danny

LINDA BENTON. See: Young,
Larry "Pepper"

LINDA CLARK. See: Johnson,
Bess

Linda Dale, I Love. See: Dale,
Linda

LINDA HOLBROOK. See: Perry,
John

LINDA LEE. See: Ripley, Robert
L.

LINDA MUNSON. See: Harding,
Karen Adams

LINDA PARKER. See: Kelly,
Joe (1)

LINDA SUBLETTE. See: Byner,
John (1)

LINDA, THE LUCKY. See: Barrett, Timothy "Spud"

LINDA WEBSTER. See: Winters,
Jack

Linda's First Love. See: Linda

LINDEN WAKE. See: Brent, Dr.
Jim

LINDSEY, MORT. See:
Griffin, Merv (1)
Hirt, Al (1) (2)

LINDSEY, PETER
MARY, his wife; members of
nightclub act
LESLIE
STEVE, their children
WILMA, their housekeeper
HAPPY RICHMAN, their the-
atrical agent
Peter Loves Mary (TV) (Situa-
tion comedy)

LINDSTROM, BESS. See: Richards,
Mary

LINDSTROM, PHYLLIS. See:
Richards, Mary

Line, Battle. See: Bishop, Jim

LINE DANCERS, THE LONDON.
See: Berman, Shelley

Line, Dial Hot. See: Lincoln,
Dr. Matt

Line, Firing. See: Buckley,
William F.

Line, Laugh. See: Van Dyke, Dick
(1)

Line-Up, The. See:
Guthrie, Lieut. Ben
Police Lieutenant

Line, What's My? See: Daly,
John (3)

LING, LA. See: Randolph, Ellen

LING, LOOPHOLE. See: Grady,
Mickey

LING, SAMMEE. See: Grady,
Mickey

LING WEE. See: Wallet, Skeezix

LINK. See:
Coffee, Dr. Daniel
Linc

LINK, ANTHONY. See: Myrt

LINK, LANCELOT, cartoon char-
acter
Lancelot Link, Secret Chimp (TV)
(Cartoon)

LINKLETTER, ART (1), host of the
program (himself)
MANY GUESTS
House Party (R) (TV) (Audience
participation) (later known as The
Linkletter Show) (TV)

LINKLETTER, ART (2), host of the
program (himself)
JACK LINKLETTER, his son, co-
host of the program (himself)
MANY GUESTS (adult and children)
Life With Linkletter (TV) (Discussion)

LINKLETTER, ART (3), host of
the program (himself)
MANY GUEST INTERVIEWEES
No Need to Hide (TV) (Interview)

LINKLETTER, ART (4), host of the
program (himself)
MANY CONTESTANTS
People Are Funny (R) (TV)
(Audience participation)

LINKLETTER, JACK (1), host of
the program (himself)
MANY INTERVIEWEES
On the Go (TV) (Interviews)

LINKLETTER, JACK (2), host of
the program (himself)
MANY CONTESTANTS
Rebus (TV) (Game)

LINKLETTER, JACK (3), host of
the program (himself)
MANY GUESTS
Hootenanny (TV) (Music/dancing)

LINKLETTER, JACK. See also:
Linkletter, Art (2)
Robbins, Fred

Linkletter, Life With. See: Linkletter, Art (2)

Linkletter Show, The. See: Linkletter, Art (1)

LINN. See:
Lyn
Lynn
Lynne

LINUS, timid lion
SO-HI, his Chinese boy friend
RORY, raccoon
LOVEABLE TRULY, postman,
all cartoon characters
Linus the Lionhearted (TV)
(Cartoon)

Linus the Lionhearted. See: Linus

LIONEL. See:
Bunker, Archie
Carson, Bob

LIONEL HAMPTON. See:
Basie, Count
O'Connor, Father Norman

LIONEL POINDEXTER. See:
Conway, Bobby

LIONEL STANDER. See: Kaye,
Danny

Lionhearted, Linus the. See:
Linus

LIPP, DAVID. See: Rowan, Dan

LIPTON, BILL. See:
Halop, Billy
Johnson, Raymond Edward (1)

LIPTON, LYNN. See:
Frost, David (2)
Klein, Robert

LISA. See:
Douglas, Oliver
Hughes, Lisa
Liza

LISA BRITTON. See: Ames,
Peter

LISA DE BECK. See: Cameron,
Christy Allen

LISA SHEA. See: Hughes, Chris

LISA VALENTINE. See: Trent, Helen

LISAGOR, PETER. See: Mac-Neil, Robert

LISH. See: Harum, David

LISH, TIZZIE. See: Blurt, Elmer

LISS, RONALD. See: Halop, Billy

Listen to This. See: Dotty

LISTENER, MR. AVERAGE RADIO. See: Kaye, Danny

LISTON, LOIS
JERRY TREMAINE, characters appearing in the drama
Hawthorne Hotel (R) (Serial drama)

LITTLE. See also: Li'l

LITTLE ALICE. See: Harris, Phil

LITTLE BEAVER. See: Ryder, Red

LITTLE BETSY ROSS GIRL, THE. See: Loveridge, Marion

Little Betsy Ross Girl Variety Program, The. See: Loveridge, Marion

LITTLE, BIG TINY. See: Welk, Lawrence

LITTLE DOUGLAS BUTTERNUT. See: Peppertag, Aaron

LITTLE FRENCH PRINCESS. See: Marie

Little French Princess, Marie the. See: Marie

LITTLE, FLORA. See: Allen, Joan Houston

LITTLE GIRL NEXT DOOR, THE. See: Carson, Jack

LITTLE GIRL, THE. See: Jones, Amos

Little Italy. See: Nick

Little Jack Little. See: Little, Little Jack

LITTLE JACKIE HELLER. See: Bernie, Ben

LITTLE JOE. See: Cartwright, Ben

LITTLE JOHN. See: Hood, Robin

LITTLE, LITTLE JACK, pianist and singer, featured on the program (himself)
Little Jack Little (R) (Music)

LITTLE LUKE. See: McCoy, Grampa

Little Margie, My. See: Albright, Margie

LITTLE NED "NEDDIE" EVANS. See: Wayne, Ruth Evans

Little Ol' Hollywood. See: Alexander, Ben (4)

Little Old New York. See: Arthur, Jack (3)

LITTLE ORPHAN ANNIE, perpetually eight-year-old orphan
OLIVER "DADDY" WARBUCKS, her guardian
MR. SILO
MRS. SILO, his wife, Annie's parents by adoption
JOE CORNTASSLE, neighbor boy, Annie's friend
SANDY, Annie's dog
PUNJAB
ASP, confidential employees of Warbucks
CLAY COLLIER, decoder inventor
AHA, Chinese cook
CAPTAIN SPARKS, aviator
Little Orphan Annie (R) (Adventure)

Little People, The. See: Jamison, Dr. Sean

LITTLE RAYMOND. See: Archer,
Corliss

LITTLE, RICH
FRANK GORSHIN
GEORGE KIRBY
MARILYN MICHAELS
CHARLIE CALLAS
JOE BAKER, impressionists fea-
tured on the program (themselves)
MANY GUEST CELEBRITIES,
HOSTS AND HOSTESSES
The Kopykats (The A.B.C. Com-
edy Hour) (TV) (Comedy impres-
sions)

LITTLE, RICH. See also:
Andrews, Julie
Davidson, John (2)

LITTLE RUDY CAMERON. See:
Davis, Joan Field

LITTLE TWIN. See: Monroe,
Clayt

Little Women. See: March, Mrs.

Littlest Hobo, The. See: London

Live, One Life to. See: Walleck,
Meredith

LIVELY. See: Sunday

Lively Arts, The Seven. See:
Crosby, John

Lively Ones, The. See: Damone,
Vic (1)

Lives, Days of Our. See: Horton,
Dr. Tom

Lives, I Led Three. See: Philbrick, Herbert

Living Doll, My. See: McDonald,
Bob

Living For the Sixties. See:
Furness, Betty

Living Should Be Fun. See:
Fredericks, Carlton

LIVINGSTON GEARHART. See:
Waring, Fred (1)

LIVINGSTON, MRS. See: Corbett,
Tom (1)

LIVINGSTONE, MARY. See:
Benny, Jack

LIVVY, AUNT. See: Major, Bob

LIZ. See:
Cooper, Liz
Dennis, Liz
Fraser, Ben
Reynolds, Dr. Mike
Thorpe, Liz

LIZ ALLISON. See: Davis, Dr.
Althea

LIZ ANDREWS. See: Slattery,
Jim

LIZ FORSYTHE. See: Garrett,
Susan

LIZ HILLYER FIELD. See: Karr,
Mike

LIZ McINTYRE. See: Kaufman,
Seymour

LIZ MURRAY. See: MacLennon,
Jeannie

LIZ TORRES. See: Moore, Melba

LIZA. See:
Carter, Kathryn
Driggs, Karleton King
Hammond, Liza
Lisa

LIZA ARNOLD. See: Hansen,
Dean Eric

LIZETTE. See: Farrell, David

LIZZIE HOGAN. See: Alexander,
Nick

LIZZIE LUMP. See: Myrt

LIZZIE PETERS. See: Parker,
Seth

LLOYD. See: Thaxton, Lloyd
(1) (2) (3)

LLOYD, ADAM. See: Driggs,
Karleton King

Lloyd Bridges Show, The.   See:
Shepherd, Adam

LLOYD GRAY, DR.   See:
Welles, Orson (3)

LLOYD HUNTLEY.   See: Winchell,
Walter (1)

LLOYD, JEREMY.   See: Rowan,
Dan

LLOYD PERRYMAN.   See: Nolan,
Bob

LLOYD RAMSEY.   See: Brooks,
Cameron

LLOYD, RITA.   See: Halop, Billy

LLOYD SCHAEFER.   See: Como,
Perry (1)

LLOYD, SHIRLEY.   See: Penner,
Joe

LLOYD, SUE.   See: Mannering,
John

LLOYD, SUSANNAH.   See: Driggs,
Karleton King

Lobby, Hobby.   See:
Elman, Dave (2)
Weaver, Charley

LOBO.   See also: Loco

LOBO HAINES.   See: Karr, Mike

LOCHNER, DR. PAUL, chief of
staff at medical center
DR. JOSEPH GANNON, physician
on medical center staff
DR. BARTLETT, psychiatrist
on medical center staff
NURSE WILCOX, nurse
Medical Center (TV) (Hospital
drama)

Lock Up.   See: Maris, Herbert L.

LOCKE, DR. SIMON (1), country
physician
DR. ANDREW SELLERS, physician;
his associate
MRS. WYNN, office nurse employed by Locke and Sellers

Dr. Simon Locke (TV) (Medical
drama)

LOCKE, DR. SIMON (2), head of
city police department medical
emergency unit
LIEUT. DAN PALMER, police
officer
Police Surgeon (TV) (Medical/
crime drama)

LOCKE, PATRICIA, "The Manhattan Mother"
HER FAMILY
Manhattan Mother (R) (Serial
drama)

LOCKERMAN, GLORIA.   See:
March, Hal

LOCKRIDGE, BARRY, tycoon
CAPTAIN STEVE BURTON,
pilot of space ship
DAN ERICKSON, co-pilot
BETTY HAMILTON, stewardess
VALERIE
MARK
FITZHUGH, Earthlings cast
away on planet populated by
giants in the year 1983
ZARKIN
KOBICK
BOLGAR, giants
The Land of the Giants (TV)
(Science fiction/adventure)

LOCKWOOD.   See: Cameron

LOCO.   See:
Jones, Loco
Lobo

Lodge, Holiday.   See: Miller,
Johnny

LODGE, MR.   See: Andrews,
Archie

LODGE, ROBERT.   See: Shadel,
Bill

LODGE, SULLIVAN.   See: Armstrong, Jack

LODGE, VERONICA.   See:
Andrews, Archie

LOFTHOUSE, PETE.   See: Welk,
Lawrence

LOFTUS, PROFESSOR. See: Upton, Michael

LOGAN, ARNY. See: Brooks, Cameron

LOGAN, CHRIS. See: Brooks, Cameron

LOGAN, POLICE CAPTAIN. See: Casey

LOGAN, SAM, investigator for Blackhawk Insurance Co. in the 1870s
The Man From Blackhawk (TV) (Drama)

LOGAN SCHMIDT. See: Horton, Dr. Tom

LOGAN, SHIRLEY, roving photographer-reporter
DENNIS CROFT, her editor and boss
Shirley's World (TV) (Comedy/ adventure)

LOGAN SMITH. See: Solomon, David

LOHMAN, AL
ROGER BARKLEY, co-hosts of the program (themselves)
PANEL OF CELEBRITY GUESTS
AUDIENCE PARTICIPANTS
Name Droppers (TV) (Game)

LOIS. See:
Graves, Harry
Harry
Lewis
Liston, Lois
Louie
Louis
Louisa
Louise
Luis
Luise

LOIS COLTON. See: Trent, Helen

LOIS CRONEN. See: Hutton, Ina Ray

LOIS DAVISSON. See: Joe (1)

LOIS FARMER. See: Joe (1)

LOIS LANE. See: Kent, Clark

LOLA. See:
Chase, Dennis
Davis, Joan Field
Lula
Lulu

LOLA FALANA. See: Cosby, Bill (2)

LOLA LASAGNE. See: Batman

LOLA MITCHELL. See: Wayne, Ruth Evans

LOLLY BABY. See: Dallas, Stella

LOMBARD, CAROLE. See: Carroll, Madeleine

LOMBARDO, GUY, orchestra leader (himself)
HIS ROYAL CANADIANS ORCHESTRA
MANY GUEST STARS
The Guy Lombardo Show (TV) (Music/variety) (also known as Guy Lombardo and His Royal Canadians) (TV)

LOMBARDO, GUY. See also:
Basie, Count
Burns, George (2)

LON, ALICE. See: Welk, Lawrence

LONDON, German sheep dog; "roams the world helping people out of predicaments"
The Littlest Hobo (TV) (Animal adventure)

LONDON. See also: Landon

LONDON LINE DANCERS, THE. See: Berman, Shelley

London, Saber of. See: Saber, Mark

Lone Journey. See: Bennett, Nita

Lone Ranger, The. See: Lone
Ranger, The

LONE RANGER, THE (John Reid),
masked crime fighter of the Old
West
SILVER, his horse
TONTO, his Indian friend and
associate
SCOUT, Tonto's horse
The Lone Ranger (R) (TV) (West-
ern adventure)
DAN REID, his nephew
The Lone Ranger (R)

Lone Wolf, The. See: Lanyard,
Michael

LONE WOLF, THE. See: Lanyard,
Michael

Lonely Woman. See: Larimore,
Marilyn

Loner, The. See: Colton,
William

LONESOME. See: Hooton, Babs

LONESOME COWBOY, THE. See:
Old Ranger, The

LONG, DOC. See: Packard, Jack

Long, Hot Summer, The. See:
Varner, Will

LONG JOHN. See: Silver, Long
John

Long John Silver. See: Silver,
Long John

LONG, JOHNNY. See: Whiteman,
Paul

LONG, LUCILLE. See: Kelly,
Joe (1)

LONG PAN, ONE. See: Allen,
Fred

LONGACRE, HENRY. See: Harum,
David

LONGFELLOW. See: Deeds, Longfellow

Longines Symphonette, The. See:
Knight, Frank

LONGLEY, BILL, foreman of
telegraph work crew
The Texan (TV) (Western adventure)

Longstreet. See: Longstreet,
Mike

LONGSTREET, MIKE, blind New
Orleans insurance investigator;
widower
NIKKI BELL, his assistant
DUKE PAIGE, his friend and
business associate
PAX, his white German shepherd
guide dog
Longstreet (TV) (Crime detection
adventure)

LONNIE. See:
Dodd, Jimmie
Lanny
Lennie
Lenny
Sunday

LONNIE LUNDE. See: Kelly,
Joe (2)

LONSBERRY, DR. See: Hughes,
Chris

LOO. See also:
Lew
Lou
Lu

LOO, LEE. See: Mix, Tom

Look Here! See: Agronsky,
Martin

Look Who's Here. See: Boyd,
Tom

Look Your Best. See: Charm
Expert

LOOMIS, CONNIE. See: Sterling,
Vanessa Dale

LOOMIS, WILLIE. See: Collins,
Barnabas

LOOPHOLE LING. See: Grady,
Mickey

LOPAKA, TOM. See: Steele,
Tracy

LOPEZ, CONSUELO. See: Welby,
Dr. Marcus

LOPEZ, TRINI. See: Jones, Jack

LOPEZ, VINCENT, pianist and
orchestra leader, star of the
program (himself)
HIS ORCHESTRA
TEDDY NORMAN
JUDY LYNN
DANNY DAVIS
EDDIE O'CONNOR
JOHNNY AMOROSO, entertainers
and musicians featured on the
program (themselves)
THE LOPEZIANS, vocal group
Vincent Lopez (TV) (Popular
music)

LOPEZ, VINCENT. See also:
Whiteman, Paul

LOPEZIANS, THE. See: Lopez,
Vincent

LOR, DENISE. See: Paige, Bob

LORA. See:
Laura
Laurie
Lawton, Lora

Lora Lawton. See: Lawton, Lora

LORD. See: Clark, Lord Kenneth

LORD BILGEWATER. See: Blurt,
Elmer

LORD BRETT SINCLAIR. See:
Wilde, Danny

LORD GREYSTOKE. See: Tarzan

Lord Haw Haw. See: Joyce,
William

LORD HAW HAW. See: Joyce,
William

LORD HENRY BRINTHROPE.

See: Sunday

LORD HERTFORD. See: Henry
VIII, King of England

LORD MARMADUKE FFOGG.
See: Batman

LORD, MR. See: Walleck,
Meredith

LORD PERCY. See: Sunday

LORD, PHIL. See: Ameche,
Don (3)

LORD, PHILLIPS H.
COLONEL H. NORMAN
SCHWARTZKOPF
LEWIS J. VALENTINE
JOHN C. HILLEY, hosts and
narrators of the program (them-
selves)
MANY RADIO AND TELEVISION
ACTORS
Gangbusters (R) (TV) (Crime
detection drama) (originally
known as G-Men) (R)

LORD ROCHESTER. See:
Churchill, John

LORD SHAFTSBURY. See:
Churchill, John

LORELEI CIRCE. See: Batman

LORELEI KILBOURNE. See:
Wilson, Steve

LOREN. See: Eiseley, Loren C.

LORENZO. See: Jones, Lorenzo

Lorenzo Jones. See: Jones,
Lorenzo

LORETTA. See:
Hoyt, Vikki Adams
Young, Loretta (1) (2)

Loretta, A Letter to. See:
Young, Loretta (1)

LORETTA ALLEN. See: Sterling,
Vanessa Dale

LORETTA LYNN. See: Wilburn,
Doyle

LORETTA McLEAN. See: Prescott, Kate Hathaway

Loretta Young Show, The. See: Young, Loretta (2)

Loretta Young Show, The New. See: Massey, Christine

LORI. See:
Larry
Lorre
Lory
Sawyer, Andy
Taylor, Andy

LORINDA. See: Baines, Scattergood

LORING, DR. ANTHONY. See: Brown, Ellen

LORING, VICTORIA. See: Brown, Ellen

LORNE GREEN. See: Cookie Monster, The

LORNE, MARION. See: Moore, Garry (3)

LORRAINE ADAMS. See: Hillman, India

LORRAINE HARTLEY. See: Drake, Nora

LORRAINE, KAY. See: Ross, Lanny

LORRE. See also:
Larry
Lori
Lory

LORRE, PETER, featured on the program (himself)
STONEWALL SCOTT
TEX, characters appearing on the program
Mystery in the Air (R) (Mystery)

LORY. See also:
Larry
Lori
Lorre

LORY ANN KARR. See: Karr, Mike

Lost in Space. See: Smith, Colonel Zachary

Lost Persons, Mr. Keen, Tracer of. See: Keen, Mr.

Lost, The Land of the. See: Red Lantern

LOTHAR. See: Mandrake

LOTTIE. See: Bolt, Jason

LOTUS. See: Winslow, Don

LOU. See:
Clara
Lew
Loo
Lu
Parker, Lou

LOU, BETTY. See:
Gooch, Mortimer
Riggs, Tommy

LOU BROWN. See: Lewis, Jerry

LOU COSTELLO. See:
Abbott, Bud (1) (2)
Martin, Dean (1)

LOU, EMMY. See: Nelson, Ozzie

LOU GRANT. See: Richards, Mary

LOU KATZMAN. See: Allen, Fred

LOU, MARY. See:
Barbour, Henry Wilson
Henry, Captain

LOU MERRILL. See: Winkler, Betty

LOU PROHUT. See: Lewandowski, Bob

LOU RAWLS. See: Steinberg, David (2)

LOU SCOTT. See: Young, Larry "Pepper"

LOU SHELDON. See: Taylor, Danny

LOU, THELMA. See: Taylor,
Andy

LOUDMOUTH, THE. See: Gleason,
Jackie (1) (2)

LOUDON, DOROTHY. See: Van
Dyke, Dick (1)

LOUELLA PARSONS. See:
Parsons, Louella
Powell, Dick (3)

Louella Parsons Show, The. See:
Parsons, Louella

LOUIE. See:
Lewis
Lois
Louis
Louisa
Louise
Luis
Luise
Meek, Mortimer
Templar, Simon

LOUIE PALLUCCI. See: Martin,
Doris

LOUIE STERLING. See: Grimm,
Arnold

LOUIE THE LILAC. See: Batman

LOUIS. See:
Erskine, Inspector Louis
Lewis
Lois
Louie
Louisa
Louise
Luis
Luise
Nye, Louis
Owens, Anna
Rukeyser, Louis

LOUIS XIV. See: Churchill,
John

LOUIS ARMSTRONG. See: Whiteman, Paul

LOUIS BELLSON. See: Bailey,
Pearl

LOUIS DA PRON DANCERS, THE.
See: Como, Perry (1) (3)

LOUIS GRESS. See: Cantor,
Eddie (2)

LOUIS NYE. See:
Allen, Steve (1) (3)
Martindale, Wink (2)
Nye, Louis

LOUIS PHEETERS. See: Dillon,
Marshal Matt

LOUIS UNTERMEYER. See: Daly,
John (3)

LOUISA. See:
Carey, Dr. Philip
Lewis
Lois
Louie
Louis
Louise
Luis
Luise

LOUISE. See:
Baker, Biff
Burton, Terry
Hopkins, Kate
Lambert, Louise
Lewis
Lois
Louie
Louis
Louisa
Luis
Luise

LOUISE COLE. See: Hughes,
Chris

LOUISE McPHERSON. See:
Cummings, Brenda

LOUISE MASSEY AND THE
WESTERNERS. See:
Duke of Paducah, The
Kelly, Joe (1)

LOUISE O'BRIEN. See: Miller,
Mitch

LOUISE SIMS. See: Nelson,
Carolyn Kramer

LOUISE STULIR. See: Rogers,
Patricia

LOUISE "WEEZY" VASS. See:
Vass, Fran

LOUISE WEST. See: Arden, Jane

Love. See: Endicott, Professor
Mike

LOVE. See: Morgan, Lieut.
Anne

Love a Mystery, I. See: Packard,
Jack

Love and Learn, We. See:
Peters, Bill

Love and Marriage. See: Harris,
Bill

LOVE, ELIZABETH. See:
Hopper, DeWolf

Love Is a Many Splendored Thing.
See: Garrison, Spencer

LOVE, JIM ED. See: Jones, Ben

Love Linda Dale, I. See: Dale,
Linda

Love, Linda's First. See: Linda

Love Lucy, I. See: Ricardo, Ricky

Love of Life. See: Sterling,
Vanessa Dale

Love on a Rooftop. See: Willis,
David

Love That Bob. See: Collins, Bob

Love That Jill. See: Gibson, Jack

Love, The Amateur's Guide to.
See: Rayburn, Gene (1)

Love, Those We. See: Marshall,
John

Love, Time For. See: La Volta,
Dianne

Love, To Rome With. See:

Endicott, Professor Mike

LOVEABLE TRULY. See: Linus

LOVEJOY, FRANK (1)
JOAN BANKS
SANTOS ORTEGA, featured on
the program (themselves)
Blue Playhouse (R) (Drama)

LOVEJOY, FRANK (2)
JOAN BANKS
IREENE WICKER
BOB WHITE, featured on the
program (themselves)
Deadline Drama (R) (Drama)

LOVEJOY, FRANK. See also:
McCormick, Myron

LOVELESS, DR. MIGUELITO.
See: West, Jim (2)

Lover, Your. See: Luther, Frank
(2)

LOVERIDGE, MARION (The Little
Betsy Ross Girl)
BOBBY HOOKEY
"TERMITE" DANIELS
BILLY DANIELS, child actors
and actresses appearing on the
program (themselves)
The Little Betsy Ross Girl
Variety Program (R) (Children's
variety)

LOVERIDGE, MARION. See also:
Edwards, Ralph (1)

LOVERING, JIM. See: Skippy

Loves Mary, Peter. See: Lindsey,
Peter

Loves of Dobie Gillis, The Many.
See: Gillis, Dobie

Loves of Dr. Susan, The Life and.
See: Chandler, Dr. Susan

LOVE'S VOCAL GROUP, ANDY.
See: Dunninger, Joseph

LOVEY HACKETT. See: Cooper,
Dick

Low, High. See: Barry, Jack (3)

LOW, THEODORE
PHOEBE STANTON, moderators
of the program (themselves)
GUEST MODERATORS
MANY INTERVIEWEES
Key to the Ages (TV) (Interview/
discussion)

LOWE, GERALD. See: Fairchild,
Kay

LOWE, STOOGE. See: Harding,
Mrs. Rhoda

LOWELL. See:
Peters, Lowell
Thomas, Lowell (1) (2)

LOWELL, CLAIRE. See: Hughes,
Chris

LOWELL, ELLEN. See: Hughes,
Chris

LOWELL, JIM. See: Hughes,
Chris

LOWELL, JUDGE. See: Hughes,
Chris

LOWELL, MAGGIE. See: Brent,
Dr. Jim

Lower Basin Street, The Chamber
Music Society of. See: Cross,
Milton (1)

LOWERY. See also: Lowry

LOWERY, ANN. See: Booth,
Martha

LOWN, BERT. See: Winchell,
Walter (1)

LOWRY. See also: Lowery

LOWRY, ED. See: Reid, Britt

LU. See also:
Lew
Loo
Lou

LU ANN SIMMS. See: Godfrey,
Arthur (1)

LUCAL, JACK. See: Kelly, Joe (2)

LUCAS. See:
McCain, Lucas
Preston, Dick

LUCAS, GAIL. See: Thorpe, Liz

LUCAS TANEY. See: Varner,
Will

LUCAVICH, PRIVATE. See:
Wright, Conley

LUCIA. See also: Lucius

LUCIA GARRETT. See: Redigo,
Jim (1)

LUCIA LANG. See: Trent, Helen

LUCIA STANDISH. See: Malone,
Dr. Jerry

LUCILE LAWRENCE. See: Ross,
Lanny

LUCILLE. See: Rivers, Lucille

LUCILLE BALL. See:
Carmichael, Lucy
Carter, Lucy
Frees, Paul
Landi, Elissa
Ricardo, Ricky

Lucille Ball Show, The. See:
Carmichael, Lucy

LUCILLE CRAWFORD. See:
Malone, Dr. Jerry

LUCILLE LONG. See: Kelly,
Joe (1)

LUCILLE MANNERS. See:
Dragonette, Jessica (1)

Lucille Rivers Show, The--Fashions
in Sewing. See: Rivers, Lucille

LUCILLE WALL. See: Hardy,
Dr. Steven

LUCINDA SKINFLINT, AUNT.
See: Peppertag, Aaron

LUCIUS. See also: Lucia

LUCIUS, UNCLE. See: Tammy

LUCKY. See:
Smith, Lucky
Stone, Lucky

LUCKY LINDA, THE. See:
Barrett, Timothy "Spud"

LUCKY, MR., honest gambler,
owner of gambling ship "Fortuna"
ANDAMO, his friend and associate
Mr. Lucky (TV) (Adventure)

Lucky Partners. See: Cordell, Carl

Lucky Pup. See: Lucky Pup

LUCKY PUP
PINHEAD
FOODINI, puppets
Lucky Pup (TV) (Children)

Lucky Smith. See: Smith, Lucky

Lucky Strike Magic Carpet, The.
See: Winchell, Walter (1)

Lucky Strike Theater. See: Montgomery, Robert

LUCRETIA. See: McKenzie,
Captain Craig

LUCRETIA HALE. See: Cameron,
Christy Allen

LUCY. See:
Carmichael, Lucy
Carter, Lucy
Hanks, Henrietta
Jackson, Martha
Kent, Fred
Ricardo, Ricky

Lucy, Aunt. See: Aunt Jenny
(Aunt Lucy)

LUCY, AUNT. See: Aunt Jenny
(Aunt Lucy)

LUCY BEGGS. See: Farrell, David

LUCY CRAIG. See: Webster,
Martha

LUCY HAMILTON. See: Shayne,
Michael

Lucy, Here's. See: Carter, Lucy

Lucy, I Love. See: Ricardo,
Ricky

LUCY MONROE. See: Cook, Joe

LUCY MORAN. See: Carter,
Kathryn

Lucy Show, The. See: Carmichael,
Lucy

LUD GLUSKIN. See: Peterson,
Irma

LUDA BARCLAY. See: Davis,
Red

LUDDEN, ALLEN, quizmaster of
the program (himself)
TWO CELEBRITY PANELISTS
GUEST PANELISTS
Password (TV) (Quiz)

LUDDY, BARBARA. See:
Ameche, Don (3)
First Nighter, Mr.

LUDWIG, PROFESSOR DONALD,
host of the program (himself)
First Aid (TV) (Education)

LUDWIG VON HUMPERDOO. See:
Junior

LUELLA HAYWORTH. See: Fairchild, Kay

LUIGI, Italian
ROSA, his wife
PASQUALE
HOROWITZ
MISS SPALDING, his friends
Life With Luigi (R) (Situation
comedy)

Luigi, Life With. See: Luigi.

LUIS. See also:
Lewis
Lois
Louie
Louis
Louisa
Louise
Luise

LUIS VAN ROOTEN. See:
Johnson, Raymond Edward (1)

Welles, Orson (2)

LUISE. See also:
Lewis
Lois
Louie
Louis
Louisa
Louise
Luis

LUISE DRIGGS McBURNEY. See:
Driggs, Karleton King

LUISE KING. See: Driggs,
Karleton King

LUKE. See:
Carpenter, Luke
McCoy, Grampa
Perry, Luke

LUKE BAXTER. See: Brown,
Ellen

LUKE FERGUSON, SHERIFF. See:
Guest, Edgar A. (2)

LUKE, LITTLE. See: McCoy,
Grampa

LULA. See:
Lola
Lulu
Perkins, Ma

LULLABY LADY, THE. See:
Faith, Percy

LULU. See:
Lola
Lula
Stevens, Ray

LULU McCONNELL. See: Howard,
Tom (1)

LULU ROMAN. See: Owens,
Buck

LULUBELLE AND SCOTTY. See:
Kelly, Joe (1)

LUM. See: Edwards, Lum

Lum and Abner. See: Edwards,
Lum

LUMET, SIDNEY. See: Halop,
Billy

LUMP, LIZZIE. See: Myrt

LUMP-LUMP, WILLY. See:
Junior

LUMPY BRANNUM. See: Waring,
Fred (1)

Luncheon at Sardi's. See: Slater,
Bill (1)

LUND, CLARA. See: Keene, Kitty

LUND, DR. See: Marshall, John

LUND, SUSAN. See: Chidsey,
Jackie

LUNDE, LONNIE. See: Kelly,
Joe (2)

LUNDIGAN, BILL (1), host of the
program (himself)
MANY ACTORS AND ACTRESSES
Climax (TV) (Drama anthology)

LUNDIGAN, BILL (2), host of the
program (himself)
JACK BENNY, featured on the
program (himself)
MANY GUEST STARS
Shower of Stars (TV) (Musical
revue)

LUPINO, IDA. See:
Boyer, Charles
Frees, Paul

LURCH. See: Addams, Gomez

LURENE TUTTLE. See: Coogan,
Jackie

LUSTGARDEN, EDGAR, narrator
of the program (himself)
MANY ACTORS AND ACTRESSES
Scotland Yard (TV) (Dramatizations of Scotland Yard cases)

LUTHER, FRANK, singer (1),
featured on the program (himself)
I'll Never Forget (R) (Drama)

LUTHER, FRANK (2), singer, featured on the program (himself) Your Lover (R) (Music/talk)

LUTHER HENDERSON, JR. See: Bergen, Polly

LUTHER, PAUL. See: McCormick, Myron

LUTHER QUINCE. See: Howard, Jim

LUTHER WARREN. See: Farrell, David

Lutheran Hour, The International. See: Hoffman, Dr. Oswald J.

Lux Radio Theater, The. See: DeMille, Cecil B.

Lux Video Theater. See: MacRae, Gordon (1)

LYDDIE. See also: Lady Leddy

LYDDIE BENSON. See: Fraser, Ben

LYDIA. See: Monroe, John Perera, Lydia Trent, Helen Webster, Nancy

LYDIA DENNISON. See: Marshall, John

LYDIA DRAKE. See: Jordan, Joyce

LYLE WAGGONER. See: Burnett, Carol Waggoner, Lyle

LYMAN. See: Bryson, Dr. Lyman (1) (2)

LYMAN, ABE. See: Munn, Frank (2) Winchell, Walter (1)

LYN. See also: Lynn Lynne

LYN MURRAY. See: Baker, Phil (1) Hilton, James Ives, Burl (2) Kaye, Danny

LYN MURRAY SINGERS, THE. See: Ross, Lanny

LYNCH, PEG. See: Soule, Olan (1)

LYNDE, PAUL. See: Marshall, Peter

LYNN. See also: Lyn Lynne

LYNN ANDERSON. See: Welk, Lawrence

LYNN, BAMBI. See: Caesar, Sid (3)

LYNN DOLLAR. See: March, Hal

LYNN HALL. See: Burnley, Walter

LYNN, JUDY. See: Lopez, Vincent

LYNN LIPTON. See: Frost, David (2) Klein, Robert

LYNN, LORETTA. See: Wilburn, Doyle

LYNN REED. See: Chandler, Faith

LYNN ROBERTS. See: Kaye, Sammy (1)

LYNN ROYCE. See: Marshall, John

LYNNE. See also: Lyn Lynn

LYNNE ALEXANDER. See: Bennett, Nita

LYNNE DINEEN. See: Malone, Dr. Jerry

LYNNE, EVELYN. See: Moore,
Garry (1)

LYTELL, BERT (1), actor; host
and sometimes star of the program (himself)
MANY ACTORS AND ACTRESSES
Philco Playhouse (TV) (Drama)

LYTELL, BERT (2), actor, host
of the program (himself)
RAYMOND PAIGE, orchestra
leader
HIS ORCHESTRA
MANY GUESTS
Stage Door Canteen (R) (Variety)

M*A*S*H. See: Pierce, Captain
Hawkeye

M.C. See: Joe (2)

M.C., THE SINGING. See:
Morgan, Frank (2)

M For Music, Dial. See: O'Connor, Father Norman

M.G.M. Screen Test. See:
Murphy, Dean

M.J.B. Demitasse Revue, The.
See: Medbury, John P.

M-Squad. See: Ballinger, Lieut.
Frank

MA
PA, conversationalists
Ma and Pa (R) (Comedy dialogue)

MA. See also:
Hutchinson, Ma
Parker, Seth
Perkins, Ma

Ma and Pa. See: Ma

MA KETCHAM. See: Nichols

MA MORAN. See: Jones, Tom (1)

MA PARKER. See: Batman

Ma Perkins. See: Perkins, Ma

MA SMALLEY. See: Dillon,
Marshal Matt

MABEL. See:
Benny, Jack
Maybelle

Mabel, Joe and. See: Joe (2)

MABEL KLOONER. See: Harding,
Mrs. Rhoda

MABEL (MAMA). See: Bratter,
Paul

MABEL STOOLER. See: Joe (2)

MAC
HECTOR, astronauts, break

through sound barrier, discover
race of cave people
SHAD
GRONK
MLOR
BREER
BOSS
CLON, cave people
It's About Time (TV) (Comedy)

MAC. See also:
Mack
McMillan, Stuart
Tillie

MAC PERRON. See: Waring,
Fred (1)

McAFEE, JOHNNY. See: Kaye,
Sammy (1)

McALLISTER, SANDY. See:
Guthrie, Lieut. Ben

MACANDREW, JAMES, host of
the program (himself)
MANY GUEST EXPERTS
Camera Three (TV) (Documentary/
discussion)

McARTHUR, REVEREND. See:
Barbour, Henry Wilson

MACAULAY, MR. See: O'Connor, Katy

MACAULAY, MRS. See: O'Connor, Katy

MACAULEY, WES, college student,
living in houseboat in Ohio River,
near town of Cordelia
HOWIE, his younger brother,
college student
TOM-TOM DEWITT, college student
VERN HODGES, footloose young
man, living in the houseboat
with the others
It's a Man's World (TV) (Comedy)

McBOING-BOING, GERALD, cartoon
character
The Boing-Boing Show (TV)
(Cartoon)

McBRIDE, DeWITT. See: Judge,
The

McBRIDE, MARY MARGARET,
hostess of the program (herself)
MANY CELEBRITIES AND GUESTS
Mary Margaret McBride (R)
(Interview)

McBRIDE, MARY MARGARET.
See also: Deane, Martha

McBURNEY, AL. See: Driggs,
Karleton King

McBURNEY, LUISE DRIGGS. See:
Driggs, Karleton King

McCAFFERY, JOHN K. M. , (1),
moderator of the program (himself)
TWO GUEST EXPERTS
The Nation's Future (TV) (Current events discussion)

McCAFFERY, JOHN K. M. (2),
quizmaster of the program (him-
self)
STUDIO CONTESTANTS
TWO PROFESSIONAL PSY-
CHOLOGISTS
What Makes You Tick? (R)
(Psychological quiz)

McCAFFERY, JOHN K. M. See
also: Gray, Barry (1)

McCAIN, LUCAS, widowed rancher
in the Old West
MARK, his son
The Rifleman (TV) (Western)

McCALL, DIXIE. See: Gage,
John

McCALL, GEORGE, Hollywood commentator, host of the program
(himself)
MANY HOLLYWOOD PERSON-
ALITIES
Man About Hollywood (R) (Interviews)

McCALL, MIKE. See: Jones,
Loco

McCALLION, JIMMY. See: Cross,
Milton (2)

McCALLISTER, CAPTAIN. See:
Cat, Thomas Hewitt Edward

McCANN, CHUCK. See: Nye,
Louis

McCANN, DR. NOAH, veterinarian
SAM, his assistant
Noah's Ark (TV) (Drama)

McCAREY, CHARLES. See:
West, Michael

McCAREY, MARGARET ANDERSON.
See: West, Michael

McCARTHY, CHARLIE. See:
Ameche, Don (1)
Bergen, Edgar (1) (2)

McCARTHY, JACK. See: Cross,
Milton (1)

McCARTHY, MARY. See: Gobel,
George

McCARTHY'S SCHOOL PRINCIPAL,
CHARLIE. See: Bergen, Edgar
(2)

McCASKEY, SERGEANT. See:
Young, Captain David

McCAULEY, COLONEL EDWARD,
astronaut
Men Into Space (TV) (Adventure)

MACCHIAVERNA, JOE. See:
Kaye, Sammy (1)

McCLELLAND, BART, railroad
detective
Union Pacific (TV) (Adventure)

McCLINTOCK, POLEY. See:
Waring, Fred (1)

McCLINTOCK, ROYAL. See:
Calhoun, Ben

McCloud. See: McCloud, Sam

McCLOUD, BEAU. See: Hardie,
Jim

McCLOUD, SAM, deputy marshal
from Taos, N.M., training in
metropolitan police work in New
York
DETECTIVE BROADHURST
CHIEF CLIFFORD, New York

police officials
McCloud (TV) (Crime drama)

McCLURE, HANK. See: Bell,
Mike

McCLUSKEY, MONA, highly paid
motion picture star
SERGEANT MIKE McCLUSKEY,
her husband, air force non-commissioned officer
GENERAL CRONE, officer
Mona McCluskey (TV) (Situation
comedy)

McCONNELL, ED, host and storyteller of the program (himself)
Smilin' Ed's Gang (TV) (Children's stories)

McCONNELL, LULU. See: Howard,
Tom (1)

McCORD, CLAY. See: Fry,
Marshal Simon

McCORD, FRAN. See: Fry,
Marshal Simon

McCORD, JASON, former Civil War
cavalry captain; drummed out of
the army for cowardice
Branded (TV) (Western)

McCORMICK, MYRON
FRANK LOVEJOY
ELIZABETH RELLER
PAUL LUTHER
LARRY HAINES
WILLIAM QUINN, featured on the
program (themselves)
The Man Behind the Gun (R)
(Wartime adventure drama)

McCOY. See: Wild, Charlie

McCOY, BUBBA. See: Huddles,
Ed

McCOY, CLYDE. See: Whiteman,
Paul

McCOY, DR. See: Kirk, Captain
James

McCOY, GRAMPA, head of the family
LUKE, his son
KATE, Luke's wife

HASSIE
LITTLE LUKE, his grandchildren;
all West Virginia hillbillies living
in San Fernando, California
The Real McCoys (TV) (Situation
comedy)

McCOY, MARY. See: Weems,
Ambrose J.

McCOY, PENNY. See: Huddles,
Ed

McCoys, The Real. See: McCoy,
Grampa

McCRARY, TEX
JINX FALKENBURG, his wife,
host and hostess of the program
(themselves)
The Tex and Jinx Show (R)
(Breakfast conversation)

McCRAY. See also:
McCrea
MacRae

McCRAY, LINC, Chicago speakeasy
operator in 1920's
BIG NICK MARR, his cousin,
racketeer
MARVIN, his cousin, accountant
UNCLE LATZI, his Hungarian
uncle; partner in the speakeasy
JULIE, his bodyguard
DUTCH
DUKE
LEFTY, hoodlums, associates of
Big Nick Marr
The Chicago Teddy Bears (TV)
(Comedy)

McCREA. See also:
McCray
MacRae

McCREA, DR. VIDO. See: Davis,
Dr. Althea

McCREA, JOEL. See: Boyer,
Charles

McCREA, MARGARET. See:
Brown, Joe E. (1)
Ross, Lanny

McCULLOUGH, FLINT. See:
Adams, Major Seth

McCUTCHEON, BILL.
See: DeLuise, Dom (1)

McCUTCHEON, CAPTAIN EDWARD.
See:
March, Hal
Story, Ralph

McDANIELS, BILLIE. See:
Sothern, Mary

McDEVITT, RUTH. See: Everly,
Don

MACDONALD, AIMI. See: Davidson, John (2)

MacDONALD, ANGUS. See:
Lawton, Lora

McDONALD, BETTY. See: Davis,
Joan Field

McDONALD, BOB, bachelor psy-
chiatrist
IRENE, his sister
RHODA THE ROBOT, mechanical
being
PETER ROBINSON, physicist
My Living Doll (TV) (Comedy)

MACDONALD CAREY. See: First
Nighter, Mr.

MACDONALD, CHUCK. See:
Collins, Bob

MACDONALD, ELEANOR
PAT CURTIS
CURTIS CURTIS
FRANK ALLISON
CATHERINE ALLISON
EUGENE SNELL
MISS FARNSWORTH
MRS. SIMPSON
WONG, characters appearing in
the drama
This Day Is Ours (R) (Serial
drama)

McDONALD, HARRY. See:
Welles, Orson (3)

MACDONALD, MARGARET. See:
Collins, Bob

MacDONALD, RUSS. See: Scott,
Captain

McELHONE, ELOISE. See:
Cross, Mason
Landi, Elissa

McELROY, JACK. See: Breneman, Tom (2)

McELROY, WILLIAM OMAHA.
See: Batman

McEVOY, OLIVIA. See: Brown,
Ellen

McFARLAND TWINS, THE. See:
Waring, Fred (1)

McGARRETT, STEVE, detective,
head of Five-O, law enforcement
agency in Hawaii
DAN WILLIAMS, detective, his
assistant
KONO
CHIN HO KELLY
BEN KOKUA, investigators on
his staff
EDWARD DUKE LAKALE, policeman on his staff
WO FAT, Chinese criminal, his
enemy
THE GOVERNOR OF HAWAII,
his superior
Hawaii Five-O (TV) (Detective
drama)

McGarry and His Mouse. See:
McGarry, Dan

McGARRY, DAN, detective
KITTY ARCHER (The Mouse), his
friend and companion
MOM ARCHER, Kitty's mother
UNCLE MATTHEW
SAM
BERNICE, characters appearing
on the program
PETER VAN STEEDEN, orchestra
leader (himself)
HIS ORCHESTRA
McGarry and His Mouse (R)
(Comedy detective)

McGEE, FIBBER, henpecked husband
MOLLY McGEE, his wife
Fibber McGee and Molly (R)
(TV) (Comedy)
THROCKMORTON P. GILDER-
SLEEVE
DOC GAMBLE

WALLACE WIMPLE
BEULAH, maid
LENA, maid
MAYOR LA TRIVIA
THE OLD TIMER
ALICE DARLING
NICK DEPOPOLOUS
TEENY
GERALDINE
SIS
UNCLE DENNIS
MORT TOOPS
SILLY WATSON
MRS. UPPINGTON
HORATIO K. BOOMER
VODKA
OLD LADY WHEEDLEDUCK
LADY VERE-DE-VERE
MRS. WEARYBOTTOM, McGee's
friends and neighbors
THE KING'S MEN QUARTET,
vocal group
RICO MARCHIELLI
BILLY MILLS, orchestra leaders
(themselves)
THEIR ORCHESTRAS
Fibber McGee and Molly (R)
HAZEL NORRIS, neighbor of the
McGees
ROY NORRIS, her husband
Fibber McGee and Molly (TV)

McGEE, FIBBER. See also: Mc-
Neill, Don

McGEE, FRANK, host of the pro-
gram (himself)
GUEST REPORTERS
The Frank McGee Report (TV)
(News)

McGEE, FRANK. See also:
Chancellor, John
Downs, Hugh

McGEEHAN, PATRICK. See: Whitman, Gayne

McGIL, HARRY. See: Brooks,
Cameron

McGILL, private investigator
Man in a Suitcase (TV) (Mystery)

McGIVERN, JACK. See: Patrick,
Dion

McGIVERN, MARTHA. See: Patrick,
Dion

McGLOIN, MAHATMA. See:
North, Jerry

McGLONE, MICKI. See: Chidsey,
Jackie

McGONIGLE. See: Bumstead,
Blondie

McGONIGLE, THE GREAT. See:
O'Brien, Daniel J.

McGOVERN, DAN, widower; Holly-
wood writer
NAN, his second wife; Broadway
star
NANCY
BUDDY, his children
MRS. HARPER, his housekeeper
Yes, Yes, Nanette (TV) (Situa-
tion comedy)

McGRAW, "adverturesome character, accepts dangerous assign-
ments for a fee"
Meet McGraw (TV) (Crime/ad-
venture)

McGRAW, QUICK DRAW, horse
SNOOPER
BLABBER, detective team
AUGIE DOGGIE, dog; all cartoon
characters
Quick Draw McGraw (TV) (Car-
toon)

McGRAW, WALTER, narrator of
the program (himself)
Wanted (TV) (Descriptions of persons sought by police)

McGREGOR, DR. RAY. See:
Newman, Tony

McGREGOR, FRANK. See: Crown,
Jim

McGUIRE. See: Morgan, Lieut.
Anne

McGUIRE, ELLEN. See: Horton,
Dr. Tom

McGUIRE, JOHN. See: Horton,
Dr. Tom

McGUIRE, PICO. See: Cord

McGUIRE SISTERS, THE. See:
Godfrey, Arthur (1)

McHALE. See also: McKayle

McHALE, LIEUT. COMMANDER
QUINTON, American naval offi-
cer; commander of PT 73
ENSIGN CHARLES "CHUCK"
PARKER, his bumbling second
in command
HAPPY
CHRISTY
VIRGIL
WILLY
TINKER BELL
LESTER GRUBER, members of
crew of PT 73
FUJI, Japanese prisoner of war
CAPTAIN WALLACE BINGHAMP-
TON (Old Leadbottom), American
naval officer; McHale's command-
ing officer and enemy
LIEUT. ELROY CARPENTER,
Binghampton's aide
MOLLY TURNER, naval nurse;
McHale's friend
McHale's Navy (TV) (Comedy)

McHale's Navy. See: McHale,
Lieut. Commander Quinton

Machine, Maggie and the Beautiful.
See: Lettvin, Maggie

Machine, The Great American Dream.
See: Efron, Marshall

Machine, The Marty Feldman
Comedy. See: Feldman, Marty

MACHITO. See: Whiteman, Paul

McHUGH, MARY CLARE. See:
Kelly, Joe (2)

MACINERNEY, MILDRED. See:
Campanelli, Dr. Vincent

McINTIRE. See also:
MacIntyre
McIntyre

McINTIRE, JOHN, narrator of the
program (himself)
MANY ACTORS AND ACTRESSES
Lincoln Highway (R) (Drama)

McINTIRE, JOHN. See also:
Welles, Orson (2)

MacINTOSH, DR. See: Hardy,
Dr. Steven

MACINTYRE. See also:
McIntire
McIntyre

MACINTYRE DIXON. See: Klein,
Robert

McINTYRE. See also:
McIntire
MacIntyre

McINTYRE, DR. SARAH. See:
Bauer, Bertha

McINTYRE, HAL. See: Whiteman, Paul

McINTYRE, LIZ. See: Kaufman,
Seymour

McINTYRE, MRS. See: Riggs,
Tommy

McINTYRE, TRAPPER JOHN.
See: Pierce, Captain Hawkeye

MACK. See also: Mac

MACK, CHARLIE. See: Two
Black Crows, The (1) (2)

MACK, DOTTY. See: Van Dyke,
Dick (2)

MACK, GILBERT. See: Johnson,
Raymond Edward (1)

MACK, MORAN AND. See:
Drew, John
Two Black Crows, The (1) (2)

MACK, "PROFESSOR" TOMMY.
See: Skelton, Red

MACK, TED, master of ceremonies
of the program (himself)
Ted Mack's Amateur Hour (TV)
(Amateur talent)

MACK, TED. See also: Bowes,
Major Edward (1) (2)

McKAY, JIM (1)
BILL FLEMMING
CHRIS SCHENKEL
KEITH JACKSON
HOWARD COSELL
VIN SCULLY
RAY SCOTT, sportscasters, hosts
of the programs (themselves)
A.B.C.'s Wide World of Sports
(TV) (Sports)

McKAY, JIM (2)
BILL STOUT, hosts of the pro-
gram (themselves)
MANY ACTORS AND ACTRESSES
JURY SELECTED FROM STUDIO
AUDIENCE
The Verdict Is Yours (TV)
(Simulated court trials)

McKAY, JOHNNY. See: Troop,
Marshal Dan

McKAY, JUDSON, veterinarian
stationed in Paris with the U.S.
Army
COLONEL U. CHARLES BARKER,
his commanding officer
GENERAL STEELE
FIRST SERGEANT WOLZNIAK
CORPORAL LEFKOWITZ, officers
and non-commissioned officers
of U.S. Army
PAT PERRY, General Steele's
secretary
SELMA YOSSARIAN, secretary
MADAME FATIME, concierge
Don't Call Me Charlie (TV)
(Comedy)

McKAY MORRIS. See: Arthur,
Jack (2)

McKAYLE. See also: McHale

McKAYLE DANCERS, THE DON.
See:
Cosby, Bill (2)
Hirt, Al (1)
Uggams, Leslie

McKEAN, JEAN. See: Kirkwood,
Jack

McKEE, RENO. See: Harris,
Silky

McKeever and the Colonel. See:

McKeever, Cadet Gary

McKEEVER, CADET GARY, cadet
at Westfield Academy
COLONEL HARVEY BLACKWELL,
commander of the Academy
SERGEANT BARNES, aide to
Colonel Blackwell
MRS. WARNER, dietician at the
Academy
TUBBY
MONK, friends of Cadet Mc-
Keever
McKeever and the Colonel (TV)
(Situation comedy)

McKEEVER, DR. JOHN, Northern
physician in Kentucky village
PEGGY DALE, daughter of
penniless horse breeder; marries
McKeever
Peggy's Doctor (R) (Serial drama)

McKEEVER, TED
JIM BUCKLEY, partners in Ripcord, Inc.; hire out for para-
chute jumps
Ripcord (TV) (Adventure)

McKENNA, JIM, host of the pro-
gram (himself)
MANY GUEST STARS
Like Young (TV) (Variety)

McKENNA, SERGEANT. See:
Wright, Conley

MACKENZIE, ALLISON. See:
Peyton, Martin

McKENZIE, CAPTAIN CRAIG, sub-
marine captain
BROCK SPENCER
BERT COLLINS
TIBBS CANARD
BABYFACE NELSON
SIMBA
LUCRETIA
MOLOCH, characters appearing
in the drama
Latitude Zero (R) (Submarine
adventure)

MACKENZIE, COLONEL ALAN,
Englishman, owner of the Shiloh
Ranch
TRAMPAS
THE VIRGINIAN

ROY TATE, ranch hands
The Men From Shiloh (TV)
(Western) (formerly called The
Virginian) (TV)

MacKENZIE, COLONEL RONALD S.,
Western border adventurer
MacKenzie's Raiders (TV) (West-
ern)

McKENZIE, DENNIE. See:
Marlin, Mary

McKENZIE, DR. DAVID. See:
Grimm, Arnold

MacKENZIE, GISELE, singer and
entertainer; star of the program
(herself)
MANY GUEST STARS
AXEL STORDAHL, orchestra
leader (himself)
HIS ORCHESTRA
The Gisele MacKenzie Show (TV)
(Variety)

MACKENZIE, GISELE. See also:
Lanson, Snooky

McKENZIE, LANCE. See: Bennett, Nita

McKENZIE, LANSING. See: Bennett, Nita

McKENZIE, SYDNEY SHERWOOD.
See: Bennett, Nita

MacKenzie's Raiders. See: Mac-
Kenzie, Colonel Ronald S.

McKINLEY. See: Thompson, Dr.
McKinley

McKINLEY, BARRY, baritone
HIS SWEETHEART, novelist
RAY SINATRA, orchestra leader
(himself)
HIS ORCHESTRA
Dreams Come True (R) (Serial
drama with music)

McKINLEY, RAY. See: Basie,
Count

McKINNEY, BOSS. See: Fairchild, Kay

McKINNON, JIM. See: Tate,
Joanne

MacKNIGHT, BUFF. See: Sawyer,
Andy

McLAUGHLIN, KEN, young boy
FLICKA, his horse
My Friend Flicka (TV) (Drama)

McLEAN, ADAM, Westerner
MARSHAL TALLMAN, law en-
forcement officer
Man Without a Gun (TV) (Western)

McLEAN, LORETTA. See:
Prescott, Kate Hathaway

McLEAN, MURRAY, featured on
the program (himself)
The Secret Three (R) (Serial
drama)

McLEAN, PETER. See: Prescott,
Kate Hathaway

McLEAN STEVENSON. See: Conway, Tim

MACLENNON, JEANNIE, Scottish
immigrant
AL MURRAY, cab driver,
Jeannie's sponsor
LIZ MURRAY, Al's wife
Hey Jeannie! (TV) (Comedy)

McLEOD, MAGGIE. See: Drinkwater, William

McMAHON, ED (1), host of the
program (himself)
VARIOUS MOTION PICTURES
The N.B.C. Adventure Theater
(TV) (reruns of pictures originally
appearing on Bob Hope Theater)
(TV)

McMAHON, ED (2), moderator of
the program (himself)
MANY GUEST STARS
Snap Judgment (TV) (Game)

McMAHON, ED. See also:
Carson, Johnny (1)
Sterling, Jack

McMAHON, JENNA. See:

Jones, Dean
Kelly, Gene

MACMANN, HAPPY. See: Kane,
Martin

MACMICHAEL, BAYARD. See:
March, Hal
Story, Ralph

McMillan and Wife. See: McMillan,
Stuart

McMILLAN, STUART (Mac), San
Francisco police commissioner
SALLY, his wife
SERGEANT ENRIGHT, police
officer; his aide
MILDRED, maid
McMillan and Wife (TV) (Crime/
comedy)

MacMURRAY, FRED. See: Powell,
Dick (3)

McNAMARA, SUSIE, private secre-
tary
PETER SANDS, her boss
VI, office switchboard operator
Private Secretary (TV) (Situation
comedy)

McNAMEE, GRAHAM, master of
ceremonies of the program (himself)
Behind the Mike (R) (Broadcasting
drama)

McNAMEE, GRAHAM. See also:
Cowen, Thomas
Fire Chief, The
Johnson, Parks

McNAUGHTON, HARRY. See:
Howard, Tom (1)

McNEIL, DEVLIN. See: Hansen,
David

McNEIL, LIEUT. PETE. See:
Banyon, Miles C.

MACNEIL, ROBERT, moderator of
the program (himself)
PETER LISAGOR
NEIL MACNEIL
CHARLES CORDDRY, newsmen,
panelists on the program

(themselves)
Washington Week in Review (TV)
(News analysis)

McNEILL, DR. JONATHAN. See:
Harding, Karen Adams
Rutledge, Dr. John

McNEILL, DON, host of the pro-
gram (himself)
AUNT FANNY
FIBBER McGEE
MOLLY
SAM
MR. WIMPLE
THE THREE ROMEOS, char-
acters appearing on the program
The Breakfast Club (R) (Variety)
(also known as Don McNeill's
Breakfast Club (R) and The
Pepper Pot) (R)

McNEILL, JEANETTE. See:
Trent, Helen

McNELLIS, MAGGI. See: Landi,
Elissa

McNISH, J.J. See: Simms, Paul

McNULTY, PROFESSOR RAY,
small town schoolteacher
PEGGY, his wife
Meet Mr. McNulty (McNutley) (TV)
(Situation comedy) (later called
The Ray Milland Show) (TV)

McPHEETERS, DR. SARDINIUS,
physician
JAIMIE, his twelve-year-old
son; both traveling from Kentucky
to California in 1849
The Travels of Jaimie McPheeters
(TV) (Drama)

McPHERSON, LOUISE. See:
Cummings, Brenda

McPUGG, CAULIFLOWER. See:
Junior

MACQUARRIE, HAVEN (1), master
of ceremonies of the program
(himself)
MANY AUDIENCE PARTICIPANTS
Marriage Club (R) (Audience
participation)

MACQUARRIE, HAVEN (2), quizmaster of the program (himself)
MANY CONTESTANTS
Noah Webster Says (R) (Diction-
ary quiz)

McQUEEN, BUTTERFLY. See:
Kaye, Danny

MACRAE. See also:
McCray
McCrea

MACRAE, ALLAN. See: Marshall,
John

MACRAE, GORDON (1), host of
the program (himself)
MANY ACTORS AND ACTRESSES
Lux Video Theater (TV)
(Dramas)

MACRAE, GORDON (2), singer,
featured on the program (himself)
The Railroad Hour (R) (Music)

MACRAE, MEREDITH. See:
Kidder, Margot

MACREADY, SHARRON. See:
Stirling, Craig

MacROBERTS, ALICE. See:
Higgins

MacROBERTS, DINGHY. See:
Higgins

MacROBERTS, DUNCAN. See:
Higgins

MacROBERTS, JOANIE. See:
Higgins

MacROBERTS, TOMMY. See:
Higgins

MACS, THE MERRY. See:
Gibbs, Georgia (2)
Ross, Lanny

McTOOCH, MIKE. See: Kirkwood,
Jack

McVICKER, DR. CARSON. See:
Brent, Dr. Jim

McWHIRTER, JULIE. See: Nye,
Louis

McWILLIAMS, JIM (1)
ED EAST, quizmasters of the
program (themselves)
MANY CONTESTANTS
The Ask-it Basket (R) (Quiz)

McWILLIAMS, JIM (2), quizmaster
of the program (himself)
MANY CONTESTANTS
Correction, Please (R) (Quiz)

McWILLIAMS, LAURALEE. See:
Sloan, Holly

Macy's Annual Thanksgiving Day
Parade. See: Myerson, Bess

MAD HATTER, THE. See: Batman

MAD RUSSIAN, THE. See: Cantor,
Eddie (2)

MADAME BABETTE. See: Grimm,
Arnold

Madame Courageous. See: Craine,
Betty

MADAME FATIME. See: McKay,
Judson

MADAME OGLEPUSS. See: Kukla

MADAME QUEEN. See: Jones,
Amos

MADAME ROSALIE. See: Cosby,
Bill (1)

MADAME SOPHIE. See: Peters,
Bill

MADELEINE. See:
Carroll, Madeleine
Dane, Prudence

MADELEINE, NURSE. See:
Cameron, Christy Allen

MADELINE. See: Drake, Betty

MADELINE CARTER. See:
Dallas, Stella

MADELINE KAHN. See: Klein,
Robert

MADELYN. See: Abbott, John

MADELYN KELLER, DR. See:
Graham, Dr. Bob

MADELYN TRAVERS. See: Sunday

MADEMOISELLE FIFI. See:
Cantor, Eddie (2)

MADERO, JOHNNY, San Francisco
detective
Johnny Madero, Pier 23 (R)
(Detective/drama)

MADGE. See:
Horton, Dot
Milquetoast, Casper

MADGE HARRINGTON. See:
Bradley, Judith

MADGE HARTE. See: Dallas,
Stella

MADGE KELLER. See: James,
Nancy

Madigan. See: Madigan, Sergeant
Dan

MADIGAN, SERGEANT DAN, New
York City police officer
Madigan (TV) (Crime drama)

MADISON. See:
Davis, Joan Field
Matheson
Mathison
Matson

MADISON, KENNY
SANDY WINFIELD
DAVE THORNE, private investi-
gators in Miami
CHA-CHA O'BRIEN, singer
POLICE LIEUT. SNEDIGAR,
police officer
MOUSIE, waiter
DAPHNE DeWITT DUTTON,
heiress
Surfside Six (TV) (Crime drama)

MADISON, MIKE. See: Andrews,
Drake

MADISON, OSCAR. See: Ungar,
Felix

Madness, Mirth and. See: Kirkwood, Jack

MADRID, JOHNNY. See: Lancer,
Murdoch

MADRIGUERA, ENRIC. See:
Whiteman, Paul

MAE. See:
Drake, Betty
May

MAE, DAISY. See: Yokum, Li'l
Abner

MAEN. See also:
Man
Mann
Men

MAEN DANCERS, THE NORMAN.
See: Doonican, Val

MAESTRO, THE OLD. See:
Bernie, Ben

Magazine, Jackie Gleason's American Scene. See: Gleason,
Jackie (2)

Magazine of the Air, The Heinz.
See: Edmondson, Delmar

MAGGI McNELLIS. See: Landi,
Elissa

MAGGIE. See:
Jiggs
Lettvin, Maggie
Myrt
Randolph, Walt
Sterling, Vanessa Dale
Winters, Evelyn

Maggie and the Beautiful Machine.
See: Lettvin, Maggie

MAGGIE EVANS. See: Collins,
Barnabas

MAGGIE GRAHAM. See: Casey,
Dr. Ben

MAGGIE LOWELL. See: Brent,
Dr. Jim

MAGGIE McLEOD. See: Drinkwater, William

MAGGIE PETERS. See: Andrews,
Russ

MAGGIE POWERS, DR. See:
Davis, Dr. Althea

MAGGIE RALSTON. See: Grover,
Millie

MAGGIE SPRAGUE. See: Brown,
Ellen

Magic Carpet, The Lucky Strike.
See: Winchell, Walter (1)

Magic Clown, The. See: Bonomo

Magic Cottage, The. See: Meikle,
Pat

Magic Detective, Blackstone the.
See: Blackstone, Harry

Magic Key of R. C. A. , The. See:
Stoopnagle, Colonel Lemuel Q.
(1)

Magic Land of Allakazam, The.
See: Wilson, Mark

Magic Midway. See: Kirchener,
Claude (1)

Magic Ranch. See: Alan, Don

MAGICIAN. See: Chandu the
Magician

Magician, Chandu the. See:
Chandu the Magician

Magician, Howard Thurston The.
See: Thurston, Howard

Magician, Mandrake the. See:
Mandrake

Magician, Thurston the. See:
Thurston, Howard

Magnificent Montague, The. See:
Montague, Edwin

Magnolia, Miracles of. See:
Baldridge, Fanny May

MAGOO, MR. , nearsighted elderly
gentleman
CHARLEY, his Chinese servant
Mr. Magoo (TV) (Cartoons)
(also called The Famous Adventures of Mr. Magoo) (TV)

MAGOON, MARY. See: Ballew,
Wally

MAGUIRE, FRANCESCA. See:
Bennett, Nita

MAHALIA MAY GRUNECKER. See:
Wivenhoe, Commander

MAHATMA McGLOIN. See: North,
Jerry

MAHER, WALLY. See: Roseleigh,
Jack

MAHLON CLARK. See: Welk,
Lawrence

MAHONEY, BETTY. See: Bracken,
Eddie

MAHONEY, DOTTIE. See: Allen,
Fred

MAHONEY, JERRY. See:
Olsen, Ole
Winchell, Paul (1) (2) (3) (4)
(5) (6) (7)

MAID MARIAN. See: Hood, Robin

MAIDA. See: Noble, Mary

MAIDS AND HAL, THE MUSIC.
See: Crosby, Bing (3)

MAIDS, THE MOON. See: Monroe,
Vaughn

MAIDS, THE MUSIC. See: Powell,
Dick (1)

MAIDSTONE, VICTOR. See:
Sunday

Mailman, Merry. See: Heatherton,
Ray

MAILMEN, THE SINGING. See:
Wincholl, John

MAIMIE. See:
  Mammy
  Mickey
  Mommy

Main Event. See: Marciano, Rocky

Main Street, Window on. See:
  Brooks, Cameron

Maisie. See: Maisie

MAISIE
  BILL, characters appearing on
  the program
  Maisie (R) (Situation comedy)

MAISIE. See also: Maizie

MAITLAND. See: Richards, Ben

MAIZIE. See also: Maisie

MAIZIE, AUNT. See: Dyke,
  Charity Amanda

Majestic Theater Hour, The. See:
  Two Black Crows, The (1)

MAJOR. See:
  Adams, Major Seth
  Bowes, Major Edward
  Butcher, Major Simon
  Foster, Major John
  Hoople, Major Amos
  Majors
  Morgan, Major
  Mosby, Major John
  Nelson, Major Tony
  North, Major Hugh
  Rogers, Major Robert

Major Adams. See: Adams, Major
  Seth

MAJOR BARNEY CALDWELL. See:
  Webster, Jake

MAJOR, BOB, widower; publisher
  of small newspaper in New
  England town of Phippsboro
  BENJIE, his son
  ICHABOD ADAMS, former owner
  of the newspaper; now traffic
  commissioner of Phippsboro
  ABBY, Ichabod's daughter
  AUNT LIVVY, Major's house-
  keeper

Ichabod and Me (TV) (Situation
comedy)

Major Bowes and His Original
  Amateur Hour. See: Bowes,
  Major Edward (2)

Major Bowes Family Hour, The.
  See: Bowes, Major Edward (1)

MAJOR "DOC" KAISER. See:
  Savage, Brigadier General Frank

MAJOR DONALD WEST. See:
  Smith, Colonel Zachary

MAJOR DRUCKER. See: Barton,
  Clara

MAJOR FELLOWES. See: Falvey,
  Hal

MAJOR FRANK BURNS. See:
  Pierce, Captain Hawkeye

MAJOR FRANK WHITTAKER.
  See: Young, Captain David

MAJOR GENERAL WILEY CROWE.
  See: Savage, Brigadier General
  Frank

MAJOR HARVEY STOVALL. See:
  Savage, Brigadier General Frank

Major Hoople. See: Hoople, Major
  Amos

MAJOR "HOT LIPS" HOULIHAN.
  See: Pierce, Captain Hawkeye

MAJOR JOE COBB. See: Savage,
  Brigadier General Frank

MAJOR MAPOY. See: Monroe,
  Clayt

MAJOR ROGER HEALEY. See:
  Nelson, Major Tony

MAJOR STEEL. See: Midnight,
  Captain

MAJORETTE, DRUM. See: Ross,
  Arthur

MAJORS. See also: Major

MAJORS, HAMILTON, JR. See:
Nuvo, Arnie

Make a Face. See: Clayton, Bob (2)

Make a Wish. See: Chapin, Tom

Make-Believe Ballroom, The. See:
Block, Martin

Make Me Laugh. See: Lewis,
Robert Q. (1)

Make Room For Daddy. See:
Williams, Danny

Make Room For Granddaddy. See:
Williams, Danny

Make That Spare. See: Elliott,
Win (2)

Make Your Own Kind of Music.
See: Hirt, Al (2)

Makes You Tick, What? See:
McCaffery, John K. M. (2)

MAL. See also: Mel

MAL HANSON. See: Arnold, Eddie

MAL TANNER. See: Bennett, Nita

MALCOLM. See: Goldberg, Molly

Malcolm Claire. See: Old Witch,
The

MALCOLM CLAIRE. See: Old
Witch, The

MALCOLM JOHNSON. See: Malone,
Dr. Jerry

MALE QUARTET, THE ROXY. See:
Roxy

Malibu Run. See: Andrews, Drake

MALIK. See: Fu Manchu

MALLORY, LIEUT. COL. SPENCER
(The Hawk), former air corps
flying officer
HIS MOTHER
BARNEY MALLORY (The Sparrow),
his nephew

LAURA WEATHERBY
TONY, their friends
The Sparrow and the Hawk (R)
(Adventure)

MALLOY, OFFICER PETE
OFFICER JIM REED, prowl car
police officers in Los Angeles,
Calif.
JEAN REED, Jim's wife
Adam-12 (TV) (Police drama)

MALLOY, ROBERT. See: Marlin,
Mary

MALLOY, ZACK. See: Wade,
Sandy

MALNECK, MATTY. See: Powell,
Dick (1)

MALONE, DR. JERRY, physician;
associated with the Three Oaks
Medical Center
ANN RICHARDS MALONE
DR. COPP
DR. DUNHAM
DR. AXLAND
DR. KWAN
DR. SEWALL CRAWFORD,
physicians
DAVID CRAWFORD
LUCILLE CRAWFORD
DOC HARRISON, physician
ALICE HUGHES
MRS. JESSIE HUGHES
ROBBIE HUGHES
CHRISTINE TAYLOR
JEAN OSBORNE
DAISY MATTHEWS
TRACY MALONE
BUN DAWSON
BUN DAWSON'S FRIEND
MRS. DAWSON
GENE WILLIAMS
JILL MALONE
LYNNE DINEEN
HORACE SUTTON
VERONICA FERRAL
MIRA DUNHAM
MALCOLM JOHNSON
FRANK PALMER
JIM FARRELL
ROGER DINEEN
PHYLLIS DINEEN
EDDIE BLOMFIELD
CARL WARD
MARIE DUNCAN

LUCIA STANDISH
DR. RALPH MUNSON, physician
MISS BURNS
MR. WRIGHT
DR. DAVID MALONE, physician
GEORGE FREDERICKS
SANDY
MOTHER
MOLLY
MRS. PENNY
RUBY
SAM
MRS. HALE
MRS. MORRISON
SHARI
INGRID
MARSHA
TONY
MR. JANAC
THE LAWYER, characters appear-
ing in the drama
Young Dr. Malone (R) (TV)
(Serial drama)

MALONE, FLIP. See: Bauer,
Bertha

MALONE, JIMMY. See: Jordan,
Joyce

MALONE, MIKE, trucker driving
between U. S. and Canada
JERRY AUSTIN, his driving
partner
Cannonball (TV) (Adventure)

MALONE, MIKE. See also:
Jordan, Joyce

MALONE, MR., detective
Murder and Mr. Malone (R)
(Detective adventure) (also known
as The Amazing Mr. Malone) (R)

MALONE, MR. See also: Ames,
Peter

MALONE, POLICE LIEUT. BOB.
See: Dante, Willy

MALONE, SANFORD. See: Myrt

MALONE, TED (1), master of ceremonies on the program (himself)
Between the Bookends (R) (Con-
versation/poetry)

MALONE, TED (2), quizmaster of

the program (himself)
MANY CONTESTANTS
Yankee Doodle Quiz (R) (Quiz)

MALOOF, DICK. See: Welk,
Lawrence

MALTBY, RICHARD. See:
Whiteman, Paul

Mama. See: Hansen, Mama

MAMA. See:
Bronson, Millie
Hansen, Mama
Mamma

MAMA (MABEL). See: Bratter,
Paul

MAMA VITALE. See: Endicott,
Professor Mike

MAME. See: Mayme

MAMMA. See also: Mama

MAMMA CASS ELLIOT. See:
Riddle, Sam (1)
Stevens, Ray

MAMMY. See:
Henry, Captain
Maimie
Mommy
Yokum, Li'l Abner

MAN. See:
Answer Man, The
Birthday Man, The
Maen
Mann
Men
Spider Man

Man About Hollywood. See: Mc-
Call, George

Man Against Crime. See: Barnett,
Mike

Man and the Challenge, The. See:
Barton, Dr. Glenn

Man and the City, The. See:
Alcala, Thomas Jefferson

Man Behind the Gun, The. See:
McCormick, Myron

Man Called Shenandoah, A. See:
Shenandoah

Man Called X, A. See: Thurston,
Ken

MAN, COLOSSAL. See: Junior

Man, Danger. See: Drake, John

Man Dawson, This. See: Dawson

Man, Follow That. See: Barnett,
Mike

Man From Blackhawk, The. See:
Logan, Sam

Man From G-2, The. See: North,
Major Hugh

Man From Interpol. See: Smith,
Anthony

Man From U. N. C. L. E., The. See:
Solo, Napoleon

Man Higgins, Our. See: Higgins

Man I Married, The. See: Waring,
Evelyn

Man in a Suitcase. See: McGill

MAN IN BLACK, THE. See:
Frees, Paul

MAN OF STEEL, THE. See:
Kent, Clark

MAN ON THE STREET, NORMAN
NEAT. See: Cosby, Bill (1)

Man, Spider. See: Spider Man

Man, T. See: Treasury Agent

Man, The Answer. See: Answer
Man, The

MAN, THE BRICK MUSH. See:
Gook, Vic

Man, The D. A. 's. See: Shannon

Man, The Fat. See: Runyon,
Brad

MAN, THE FAT. See: Runyon,
Brad

Man, The Invisible. See: Brady,
Peter

Man, The Mystery. See: Jostyn,
Jay (2)

MAN, THE MYSTERY. See:
Elliott, Roger

MAN, THE OLD. See: Old Witch,
The

Man, The Tall. See: Billy the
Kid

Man, The Thin. See: Charles,
Nick

Man, The Third. See: Lime,
Harry

Man Who Never Was, The. See:
Murphy, Peter

Man With a Camera, The. See:
Kovacs, Mike

Man Without a Gun. See: Mc-
Lean, Adam

MANAGER, THE. See: Archie

MANCHU. See: Fu Manchu

Manchu, Fu. See: Fu Manchu

MANCINI, HENRY. See: Pam

MANDEL KRAMER. See:
Judge, The
Roberts, Ken

MANDRAKE, magician and adven-
turer
LOTHAR, his giant Negro ser-
vant and friend
NARDA, his girl friend
Mandrake the Magician (R)
(Adventure)

Mandrake the Magician. See:
Mandrake

MANDY. See: Miller, Socrates

MANFRED, BEN. See: Collier,
Tim

Manhattan at Midnight. See: Reed,
Alan

MANHATTAN CHORUS, THE. See:
Munn, Frank (2)

Manhattan Merry-Go-Round, The.
See: Thomas, Thomas L.

Manhattan Mother. See: Locke,
Patricia

Manhunt. See: Finucane, Lieut.
Howard

MANION, ADA. See: Jordan,
Joyce

MANION, VIC. See: Jordan,
Joyce

MANN. See also:
Maen
Man
Men

MANN, AL. See: Shadel, Bill

MANN, JOHNNY, musician, host of
the program (himself)
THE JOHNNY MANN SINGERS,
vocal group
MANY GUEST STARS
Johnny Mann: Stand Up and
Cheer (TV) (Music) (also known
as Stand Up and Cheer) (TV)

MANN, JOHNNY. See also:
Bishop, Joey

MANN SINGERS, THE JOHNNY.
See: Mann, Johnny

MANN VOICES, THE JERRY. See:
Thomas, Thomas L.

MANNA, CHARLIE. See: Martindale, Wink (2)

MANNERING, JOHN (The Baron),
American antique shop owner and
undercover agent
SUE LLOYD, his fellow-agent
The Baron (TV) (Suspense drama)

MANNERING, MARCIA. See:
Noble, Mary

MANNERS, HUMPHREY. See:
Keene, Kitty

MANNERS, LUCILLE. See:
Dragonette, Jessica (1)

MANNERS, MICKEY. See: Harrington, Pat, Jr.

MANNERS, MRS. See: Perry,
John

MANNING, LAURA, assistant
school principal
NICK MANNING
KARL MANNING
LESLIE MANNING
GLENN TURNER
ELLEN WILSON
PETER HALL, characters ap-
pearing in the drama
Today Is Ours (TV) (Serial
drama)

MANNING, PORTIA BLAKE, lawyer
ARLINE MANNING
BILL BAKER
ERIC WATSON
AMELIA BLAKE
DICKIE BLAKE
WALTER MANNING
KATHY MARSH
SUSAN PETERS
ELBERT GALLO
DR. STANLEY HOLTON
JOAN WARD
CLINT MORLEY
ARLINE HARRISON
JOHN PARKER
MARK RANDALL
MEG GRIFFIN
KIRK RODER
DR. BYRON
PHILLIP COOLIDGE
LESLIE PALMER
MISS DAISY
LILLI
LAMBERT
BUCK, characters appearing in
the drama
Portia Faces Life (R) (TV)
(Serial drama)

MANNING, ROGER. See: Dyke,
Charity Amanda

Mannix. See: Mannix, Joe

MANNIX, JOE, private detective
PEGGY THAYER, his Negro
secretary
Mannix (TV) (Detective drama)

MANNO, PETER. See: Rutledge,
Dr. John

MANNY PRAEGER, COLONEL.
See: Bernie, Ben

MANOLITO. See: Cannon, John

Manor, Glamour. See: Baker,
Kenny

Man's Darling, Rich. See: O'Farrell, Packy

Man's World, It's a. See:
Macauley, Wes

MANSON, CHARLOTTE, actress,
star of the program (herself)
MANY ACTORS AND ACTRESSES
Parade of Progress (R) (Drama)

MANSON, CHARLOTTE. See also:
Kummer, Eloise
Murphy, Dean

MANTLE, REGGIE. See: Andrews,
Archie

Mantovani. See: Mantovani

MANTOVANI, orchestra conductor
(himself)
HIS CONCERT ORCHESTRA
Mantovani (TV) (Music)

Mantrap. See: Kidder, Margot

MANUEL LABOR. See: Allen,
Steve (2)

MANUEL SANDOVAL. See:
Cameron, Christy Allen

Many Happy Returns. See:
Burnley, Walter

Many Loves of Dobie Gillis, The.
See: Gillis, Dobie

Many Splendored Thing, Love Is a.

See: Garrison, Spencer

MANZINI, CAPTAIN. See: Crabtree, Dave

MAPHIS, JOE. See: Ritter, Tex
(1)

MAPLE CITY FOUR, THE. See:
Kelly, Joe (1)

MAPOY, MAJOR. See: Monroe,
Clayt

MARAINE. See also:
Marian
Marianne
Marion
Mary Ann

MARAINE CLARK. See: Cameron,
Barry

MARAIS, JOSEF, host of the program (himself)
JUANO HERNANDEZ
BURFORD HAMPDEN, featured
on the program (themselves)
African Trek (R) (Stories and
songs of Africa)

MARATHON DANCE ANNOUNCER.
See: Nye, Louis

MARCEAU, BILL. See: Karr,
Mike

MARCEAU, MARTHA. See: Karr,
Mike

MARCEL ST. CLAIR. See:
Fleming, Tony

MARCELLA THE MENACE. See:
Young, Larry "Pepper"

MARCELLE BERTRAND. See:
Noble, Mary

MARCH. See also: Marsh

MARCH, COLONEL, British Scot-
land Yard detective
Colonel March of Scotland Yard
(TV) (Detective)

MARCH, DAVID, American foreign
correspondent and espionage

agent; poses as traitor
The Blue Light (TV) (Espionage
drama)

MARCH, FREDERIC, actor; narrator of the program (himself)
This Is War (R) (Discussion of
issues of World War II)

MARCH, HAL, quizmaster of the
program (himself)
LYNN DOLLAR, March's assistant
on the program (herself)
BILLY PEARSON
CAPTAIN EDWARD McCUTCHEON
BAYARD MACMICHAEL
REDMOND O'HANLON
DR. JOYCE BROTHERS
MRS. CATHERINE KREITZER
GLORIA LOCKERMAN
GINO PRATO
MERT POWER
ROBERT STROMM
MICHAEL DELLA ROCCA
THOMAS KANE
PETER FREUCHEN
TEDDY NADLER
JIM EGAN
BILL EGAN
DR. ALEXANDER SAS-JAWORSKY,
contestants on the program (them-
selves)
MANY OTHER CONTESTANTS
The $64,000 Question (TV) (Quiz)

MARCH, HAL. See also: Sweeney,
Bob

MARCH, MRS., head of the family
JO
MEG
BETH
AMY, her daughters
Little Women (R) (Serial drama)

March of Games, The. See: Ross,
Arthur

March of Time, The. See: Husing,
Ted

March, Sweeney and. See:
Sweeney, Bob

MARCHIELLI, RICO. See: McGee,
Fibber

MARCIA. See:

Brady, Mike
Cummings, Brenda
Drake, Betty
Marcie
Trent, Helen

MARCIA ADAMS. See: Ames,
Peter

MARCIA MANNERING. See:
Noble, Mary

MARCIA RODD. See: Frost,
David (2)

MARCIANO, ROCKY, professional
pugilist; host of the program
(himself)
MANY GUESTS
FILMS OF FAMOUS PRIZE
FIGHTS
Main Event (TV) (Sports)

MARCIE. See also: Marcia

MARCIE WADE. See: Walleck,
Meredith

MARCUS. See:
Mark
Welby, Dr. Marcus

Marcus Welby, M.D. See: Welby,
Dr. Marcus

MARGARET. See:
Anderson, Jim
Arlen, Margaret
Hardy, Dr. Steven
Hillman, India
Jones, Lorenzo
Marguerite
Mitchell, Dennis
Munro, Gordon
O'Brien, Daniel J.
Thompson, Andy
Whiting, Margaret

MARGARET ALLEN, MRS. See:
Cameron, Christy Allen

MARGARET ANDERSON McCAREY.
See: West, Michael

Margaret Arlen. See: Arlen,
Margaret

MARGARET, AUNT. See: Fleming,
Tony

MARGARET BURNS. See: Davidson, Bill

MARGARET GARDNER. See:
Graham, Dr. Bob

MARGARET HERBERT. See:
Barbour, Henry Wilson

MARGARET "HONEY" JOHNSON.
See: Butterworth, Wally

MARGARET HOOVER. See:
Hartley, Dr. Robert

MARGARET McCREA. See:
Brown, Joe E. (1)
Ross, Lanny

MARGARET MACDONALD. See:
Collins, Bob

MARGARET MARY DOUGHERTY.
See: Kelly, Joe (2)

MARGARET MERRICK. See:
Kelly, Joe (2)

MARGARET RINKER. See: Hutton,
Ina Ray

MARGARET ST. CLAIR. See:
Fleming, Tony

MARGARET SPEAKS. See:
Barlow, Howard

MARGARET WHITING. See:
Cantor, Eddie (2)
Crosby, Bob (2)
Whiting, Margaret

MARGE. See:
Ace, Goodman
Barclay, Doc
Champion, Marge
Huddles, Ed
Margie
Myrt

MARGE ADAMS. See: Marlin,
Mary

Marge and Gower Champion Show,
The. See: Champion, Marge

MARGE BERGMAN. See: Tate,
Joanne

Marge, Myrt and. See: Myrt

MARGE WESKIT. See: Peepers,
Robinson J.

MARGERY. See also:
Marjorie
Marjory

MARGERY DAVIS. See: O'Leary,
Hannah

Margie. See: Clayton, Margie

MARGIE. See:
Albright, Margie
Baines, Scattergood
Clayton, Margie
Dickey, Dan'l
Marge
Uncle Walter

MARGIE COOK. See: Hargrave-
Scott, Joan

Margie, My Little. See: Albright,
Margie

MARGO. See:
Carver, Margo
Whiteman, Margo

MARGO KIRKWOOD. See: Wayne,
Ruth Evans

MARGO LANE. See: Cranston,
Lamont

Margo of Castlewood. See: Carver,
Margo

MARGOT. See:
Kidder, Margot
Noble, Mary

MARGOT BURKHART. See:
Trent, Helen

MARGOT GORHAM. See: Harding,
Mrs. Rhoda

MARGOT SHERWOOD. See:
Jordan, Joyce

MARGUERITE. See also:
Margaret

MARGUERITE PIAZZA. See:

Caesar, Sid (3)

MARIA. See:
Henry VIII, King of England
Marie
Marlin, Mary
Mary
Massey, Christine
Merie

MARIA, AUNT. See: Henry,
Captain

MARIA GAMBARELLI. See:
Roxy

MARIA HAWKINS. See: Brown,
Ellen

MARIAN. See:
Burnett, Carol
Maraine
Marianne
Marion
Mary Ann

MARIAN ANDERSON. See: Bell,
Alexander Graham

MARIAN CRANE. See: Alcala,
Thomas Jefferson

MARIAN, MAID. See: Hood,
Robin

MARIAN MERCER. See:
DeLuise, Dom (1)
Martin, Dean (2)

MARIAN MOORE. See: Grimm,
Arnold

MARIAN STARRETT. See: Shane

MARIAN SULLIVAN. See: Burton,
Terry

MARIANNE. See:
Maraine
Marian
Marion
Mary Ann
Moylan, Marianne

MARIE, princess, runs away from
home to become a commoner
RICHARD COLLINS, her friend
Marie, The Little French

Princess (R) (Serial drama)

MARIE. See also:
Horton, Dr. Tom
Maria
Mary
Merie

MARIE, ANN. See: Hollinger,
Don

MARIE DUNCAN. See: Malone,
Dr. Jerry

MARIE GRANT. See: Bauer,
Bertha

MARIE MARTEL. See: Grimm,
Arnold

MARIE, ROSE. See: Marshall,
Peter

Marie, The Little French Princess.
See: Marie

MARIE WAGGEDORN. See: Baker,
Julia

MARIETTA. See: Horton, Dot

MARILLY. See:
Mary Lee
Russell, Mayor

MARILYN. See:
Carter, Kathryn
Chandler, Dr. Susan
Larimore, Marilyn
Munster, Herman

MARILYN DAY. See: Dunninger,
Joseph

MARILYN DRIGGS LARSEN. See:
Driggs, Karleton King

MARILYN ERSKINE. See: Halop,
Billy

MARILYN KING. See: Driggs,
Karleton King

MARILYN MICHAELS. See:
Little, Rich

MARILYN SCOTT. See: Novak,
John

MARILYN THORNE. See: Hildegarde (1)

MARILYN VAN DERBUR. See:
Funt, Allen (1)
Myerson, Bess

MARINA. See also: Marino

MARINA MARINOFF. See: Perry,
John

MARINERS, THE. See: Godfrey,
Arthur (1)

MARINO. See also: Marina

MARINO, MRS. See: Nick

MARINO, PAPA. See: Nick

MARINOFF, MARINA. See: Perry,
John

MARION. See:
Burton, Terry
Jordan, Jim (1) (2)
Loveridge, Marion
Maraine
Marian
Marianne
Mary Ann

MARION BAXTER. See: Brent,
Dr. Jim

MARION BOTNIK. See: Morgan,
Lieut. Anne

MARION EVANS. See: O'Connell,
Helen

MARION JENNINGS. See: Cummings, Brenda

MARION KERBY. See: Topper,
Cosmo

MARION LEIGHTON. See: Dyke,
Charity Amanda

MARION LORNE. See: Moore,
Garry (3)

MARION LOVERIDGE. See:
Edwards, Ralph (1)
Loveridge, Marion

MARION MARLOWE. See: God-
frey, Arthur (2)

MARION SAYLE TAYLOR, DR.
See: Voice of Experience, The

MARION WINTERS. See: Bauer,
Bertha

MARION YOUNG TAYLOR. See:
Deane, Martha

MARIS, HERBERT L., attorney
Lock Up (TV) (Crime drama)

MARITZ, CARL. See: Webster,
Nancy

MARJORIE. See:
Graham, Dr. Bob
Lee, Lim
Margery
Marjory

MARJORIE CLAIBORNE. See:
Trent, Helen

MARJORIE FORRESTER. See:
Gildersleeve, Throckmorton P.

MARJORIE GRANT. See: Bracken,
John

MARJORIE WILLIAMS. See:
Brown, Ellen

MARJORY. See also:
Margery
Marjorie

MARJORY CARROLL. See:
Graham, Dr. Bob

MARK. See:
Brown, Ellen
Hawley, Mark
Hoodoo, Horatio J.
Lockridge, Barry
McCain, Lucas
Marcus
Saber, Mark
Trail, Mark
Wedloe, Tom
Wilson, Mark

MARK BROOKS, DR. See:
Horton, Dr. Tom

MARK BROWN.   See: Brewster,
Joey

MARK CARTER.   See: Harum,
David

MARK CHASE, SHERIFF.   See:
Old Ranger, The

MARK CHRISTIAN, DR.   See:
Christian, Dr. Paul

MARK DOUGLAS.   See: Warren,
Wendy

MARK ELLIOTT.   See: Garrison,
Spencer

MARK GRAINGER.   See: Alexander, Nick

MARK HILTON.   See: Randolph,
Ellen

MARK HITCHCOCK, PRIVATE.
See: Troy, Sergeant Sam

MARK HOLDEN.   See: Bauer,
Bertha

MARK MATTHEWS.   See: Perkins,
Ma

MARK MULLIN.   See: Kelly, Joe
(2)

MARK PHILLIPS, DR.   See:
Cummings, Brenda

MARK RANDALL.   See: Manning,
Portia Blake

MARK RYDELL.   See: Hughes,
Chris

MARK SANGER.   See: Ironside,
Chief Robert

MARK SCOTT.   See: Cameron,
Christy Allen

MARK SLATE.   See: Dancer,
April

MARK SMEATON.   See: Henry VIII,
King of England

Mark Trail.   See: Trail, Mark

MARK VENABLE.   See: Randolph,
Alice

MARK WAINWRIGHT.   See:
Murphy, Peter

MARK WARNOW.   See: Ross,
Lanny

Markham.   See: Markham, Roy

MARKHAM.   See: Vance, Philo

MARKHAM, BARRY.   See: Solomon, David

MARKHAM, DR.   See: Solomon,
David

MARKHAM, DR. LEE.   See:
Harding, Karen Adams

MARKHAM, DR. VINCENT.   See:
Peyton, Martin

MARKHAM, JOE.   See: Rogers,
Patricia

MARKHAM, MRS.   See: Solomon,
David

MARKHAM, ROY, detective
Markham (TV) (Detective)

MARKLEY, STEVEN.   See:
Dennis, Liz

MARLBOROUGH, DUKE OF.   See:
Churchill, John

MARLEY.   See: Morley

MARLEYBONE, CHARLOTTE.
See: Hansen, Dean Eric

MARLEYBONE, HESTER.   See:
Hansen, Dean Eric

MARLIN.   See:
Martin
Merlin
Perkins, Marlin

MARLIN, MARY, senator
SARAH JANE KANE
PHILO "SANDY" SANDS
SALLY GIBBONS
DOC SHARPE

MICHAEL DORNE
NEVER-FAIL HENDRICKS
ABNER PEABODY
BILL TAYLOR
CYNTHIA ADAMS
MARGE ADAMS
ARNOLD, butler
ANNIE, maid
FRANCES MORAN MATTHEWS
HENRIETTA DORNE
BARBARA CRAYLEY
JOE MARLIN
DAVID POST
DAVEY MARLIN
HENRY MATTHEWS
PETER HUJAZ
PETER FORTUNE
CAMPBELL E. CAMPBELL
BUNNY MITCHELL
FRAZIER MITCHELL
ARTHUR ADAMS
DENNIE McKENZIE
JOE POST
GEORGE CRABBE
IRINA TROYER
LINA TROYER
FRANKLIN ADAMS
RUFUS KANE
HENNESSY, head nurse
DANIEL BURKE
GILES HENNING
MRS. HOPKINS
OSWALD CHING
TANYA
TIMOTHY
MARIA
MISS WOOD
ROBERT MALLOY
OLGA
EVE UNDERWOOD
JONATHAN
GRANDMA
TOOTIE
PENNY
PARKER, characters appearing
in the drama
The Story of Mary Marlin (R)
(Serial drama)

Marlowe, Concerning Miss. See:
Marlowe, Miss

MARLOWE, DR. See: Wayne,
Ruth Evans

MARLOWE, JULIA. See: Drew,
John

MARLOWE, MARION. See: Godfrey, Arthur (2)

MARLOWE, MAUDE. See: Noble,
Mary

MARLOWE, MISS, "famous but
over-40 actress"
Concerning Miss Marlowe (TV)
(Serial drama)

MARLOWE, PHILIP, detective
The Adventures of Philip Mar-
lowe (R) (Crime/adventure);
Philip Marlowe (TV)

MARLOWE, SYLVIA, harpsichordist
(herself)
JOAN BROOKS
FELIX KNIGHT, vocalists, fea-
tured on the program (them-
selves)
Lavender and New Lace (R)
(Variety)

MARLOWE, VAL. See: Stewart,
Jan

MARMADUKE FFOGG, LORD.
See: Batman

MARNIE. See: Massey, Christine

MARNY. See: Johnson, Bess

Marquee, Grand. See: Soule,
Olan (2)

MARR, BIG NICK. See: McCray,
Linc

Marriage Club. See: MacQuarrie,
Haven (1)

Marriage For Two. See: Hoyt,
Vikki Adams

Marriage, Love and. See: Harris,
Bill

Marriage, The Trouble With. See:
Barry

Married Joan, I. See: Stevens,
Joan

Married, The Man I. See:
Waring, Evelyn

Marrieds, The Young. See: Garrett, Susan

Marries, When a Girl. See: Davis,
Joan Field

MARRINER, HUNK. See: Rogers,
Major Robert

Marry a Millionaire, How to. See:
Jones, Loco

Mars, The Invasion From. See:
Welles, Orson (3)

MARSH. See:
March
Tracy, Dr. Marsh

MARSH, BOBBE. See: Goldstone,
Dr. Peter

MARSH, DR. SAM. See: Goldstone,
Dr. Peter

MARSH, GLORIA. See: Carter,
Kathryn

MARSH, IRIS. See: Rutledge, Dr.
John

MARSH, JACK. See: Carter,
Kathryn

MARSH, KATHY. See: Manning,
Portia Blake

MARSH, MRS. See: Ace, Goodman

MARSH, NONA. See: Warren,
Wendy

MARSHA. See: Malone, Dr. Jerry

MARSHA PATTERSON. See: Kincaid, Chet

MARSHA RUSSELL. See: Peyton,
Martin

MARSHA SPEAR. See: Jones,
Abraham Lincoln

MARSHAL. See:
Dillon, Marshal Matt
Fry, Marshal Simon
Morgan, Marshal
Troop, Marshal Dan

Wayne, Marshal Matt

Marshal Dillon. See: Dillon,
Marshal Matt

MARSHAL TALLMAN. See:
McLean, Adam

MARSHAL, THE, law enforcement
officer
J. D. SMITH, his deputy
The Dakotas (TV) (Western)

Marshal, U. S. See: Morgan,
Marshal

MARSHALL. See:
Dodge, Marshall "Mike"
Efron, Marshall
Thompson, Marshall

MARSHALL, CLYDE. See: Harper,
Linda Emerson

MARSHALL, E. G.
TANIA SOLNICK
MEREDITH FOX
DAMARIS COLON
LEE BLAIR
PHYLLIS NEWMAN
DENNIS WEAVER
BARBARA WALTERS
MICHAEL J. POLLARD
OTHERS, hosts of the program
(themselves)
FOUR TEENAGE PANELISTS
MANY POPULAR MUSICIANS
Take a Giant Step (TV) (Juvenile
discussion) (later retitled Talking
With a Giant) (TV)

MARSHALL, ELIZABETH. See:
Carr, Alison

MARSHALL, GERALD. See:
Noble, Mary

MARSHALL, GRACE. See:
Harper, Linda Emerson

MARSHALL, HELEN. See: Carter,
Kathryn

MARSHALL, HERBERT. See:
Powell, Dick (3)

MARSHALL, HILDA. See: Sunday

MARSHALL, JOHN
  KATHY MARSHALL
  KIT MARSHALL, Kathy's twin
  AMY FOSTER
  ALLAN MacRAE
  PEGGY EDWARDS
  LYDIA DENNISON
  LILE KILGORE
  RODNEY KILGORE
  ED NEELY
  ELAINE DASCOMB
  ROY MEADOWS
  MARTHA NEWBURY, cook
  DAVID ADAIR
  LYNN ROYCE
  MRS. EMMETT
  DR. LUND
  AUNT EMILY MAYFIELD
  STEVE BLACKMAN
  DR. LESLIE FOSTER
  JERRY PAYNE
  ABNER
  ELLIS
  RAGS, the dog, characters appearing in the drama
  Those We Love (R) (Serial drama)

MARSHALL, KITTY. See: Noble, Mary

MARSHALL, OWEN, widower; attorney
  MELISSA, his adolescent daughter
  JESS BRANDON, his junior partner
  FRIEDA KRAUSE, his secretary
  CHARLIE GIANNETTA, district attorney
  Owen Marshall: Counselor at Law (TV) (Courtroom drama)

MARSHALL, PATRICIA, female lawyer
  PAUL, her son, also a lawyer
  The Jean Arthur Show (TV) (Comedy)

MARSHALL, PEGGY. See: Godfrey, Arthur (2)

MARSHALL, PETER, moderator of the program (himself)
  PAUL LYNDE
  CLIFF ARQUETTE (Charley Weaver)
  WALLY COX
  NANETTE FABRAY
  ROSE MARIE

JIM BACKUS, panelists on the program (themselves)
OTHER STARS as guest panelists
TWO CONTESTANTS on each program
The Hollywood Squares (TV) (Game)

MARSHALL, ROBERT. See: Carter, Kathryn

MARSHALL, VIRGINIA. See: Larimore, Marilyn

MARSHALL, WILLIE. See: Aldrich, Henry

MARSHALL, WOODY. See: Wilbur, Judy

MARSTON, SIR PETER. See: Hood, Robin

MARTEL, MARIE. See: Grimm, Arnold

MARTEL, PAUL. See: Grimm, Arnold

MARTHA. See:
  Bishop, Neil
  Booth, Martha
  Brown, Ellen
  Deane, Martha
  Ferguson, Martha
  Hoople, Major Amos
  Howard, Jim
  Jackson, Martha
  Muir, Carolyn
  Raye, Martha (1) (2)
  Rountree, Martha
  Scott, Martha
  Simms, Paul
  Webster, Martha

MARTHA ANN ASHLEY. See: Ames, Peter

MARTHA, AUNT. See: Carter, Kathryn

MARTHA CLARK. See: Jones, Sam

MARTHA CURTIS. See: Perry, John

Martha Deane. See: Deane, Martha

MARTHA HALE. See: Hennesey,
Lieut. Chick

MARTHA KEANE. See: Andrews,
Walter

MARTHA McGIVERN. See:
Patrick, Dion

MARTHA MARCEAU. See: Karr,
Mike

MARTHA MEARS. See: Penner,
Joe

MARTHA NEWBURY. See:
Marshall, John

MARTHA RAYE. See:
Bizarre, Benita
Raye, Martha (1) (2)

Martha Raye Show, The. See:
Raye, Martha (2)

MARTHA STEVENSON. See:
Cameron, Barry

MARTHA TILTON. See:
Gibbs, Georgia (2)
Haymes, Dick

Martha Webster. See: Webster,
Martha

MARTHA WILBERFORCE. See:
Goldberg, Molly

MARTHA WILSON. See: Mitchell,
Dennis

MARTHA YOUNG DUDLEY. See:
Brent, Portia

Martian, My Favorite. See:
Uncle Martin

MARTIN. See:
Agronsky, Martin
Begley, Martin
Block, Martin
Kane, Martin
Lane, Patty
Marlin
Merlin
Morton
Norton
Peyton, Martin

Uncle Martin

Martin and Lewis Show, The. See:
Martin, Dean (3)

MARTIN, BEATRICE. See: Dallas,
Stella

MARTIN, BERNARD. See: Murray,
Jan (1)

MARTIN, CAROL EVANS. See:
Brent, Dr. Jim

MARTIN, CHARLIE. See: Dallas,
Stella

MARTIN, CHERRY. See: Trent,
Helen

MARTIN, DANNY. See: Kelly,
Joe (2)

MARTIN, DEAN (1)
JERRY LEWIS
DONALD O'CONNOR
FRED ALLEN
EDDIE CANTOR
JIMMY DURANTE
BOB HOPE
BUD ABBOTT
LOU COSTELLO, hosts of the
program on a rotating basis
(themselves)
OTHER HOSTS
MANY GUEST STARS
The Colgate Comedy Hour (TV)
(Variety/comedy)

MARTIN, DEAN (2), star of the
program (himself)
KAY MEDFORD
KEN LANE
RODNEY DANGERFIELD
DOM DeLUISE
MARIAN MERCER
TOM BOSLEY
NIPSEY RUSSELL, entertainers
appearing on the program (them-
selves)
THE GOLDDIGGERS, singing
and dancing group
THE DING-A-LINGS, singing
group
LES BROWN, orchestra leader
(himself)
HIS ORCHESTRA
MANY GUEST STARS

The Dean Martin Show (TV)
(Variety)

MARTIN, DEAN (3), singer
JERRY LEWIS, comedian, co-
stars of the program (themselves)
MANY GUEST STARS
The Martin and Lewis Show (R)
(Comedy/variety)

MARTIN, DICK. See:
Allen, Joan Houston
Rowan, Dan

MARTIN, DR. JOE. See: Davis,
Ann Tyler

MARTIN, DORIS, widow, secretary,
works for magazine publisher
TOBY
BILL, her sons
BUCK, her father
MYRNA GIBBONS, her friend and
fellow-secretary
LEROY, hired hand
MICHAEL NICHOLSON, her boss;
magazine editor
ANGIE PALLUCCI
LOUIE PALLUCCI, neighbors,
operate Italian restaurant
The Doris Day Show (TV) (Comedy)

MARTIN, DOUG. See: Tate,
Joanne

MARTIN DOUGLAS. See: Dyke,
Charity Amanda

MARTIN, EB. See: Perkins, Ma

MARTIN, ERICA. See: Davis,
Ann Tyler

MARTIN, EUNICE. See: Tate,
Joanne

MARTIN FLAHERTY. See:
Winchell, Walter (2)

MARTIN, FREDDY. See: Daley,
Cass

MARTIN, GAIL. See: Damone,
Vic (2)

MARTIN, GREG. See: Burton,
Terry

MARTIN, HECK. See: Caine,
Frank

MARTIN, JACK. See: Welk,
Lawrence

MARTIN, JEFF. See: Davis,
Ann Tyler

MARTIN KANE. See:
Kane, Martin
Rutledge, Dr. John

Martin Kane, Private Eye. See:
Kane, Martin

Martin Kane, The New Adventures
of. See: Kane, Martin

MARTIN, KAREN. See: Davis,
Ann Tyler

MARTIN, KATE. See: Davis,
Ann Tyler

MARTIN, LAURA. See: Rutledge,
Dr. John

MARTIN LEE. See: Horn, Aggie

MARTIN, MARY. See: Crosby,
Bing (3)

MARTIN, MICHELE. See: Porter,
Pete

MARTIN, MILLICENT, comedienne
and singer; hostess of the program (herself)
MANY GUEST STARS
Piccadilly Palace (TV) (Variety)

MARTIN, MR. See:
Baines, Scattergood
Dawson, Rosemary

MARTIN, NORA. See: Cantor,
Eddie (2)

MARTIN, PAUL. See: Davis,
Ann Tyler

MARTIN, PHIL. See: Porter,
Pete

MARTIN, POKEY. See: Kelly,
Joe (1)

MARTIN, ROSS. See: Harrington, Pat, Jr.

MARTIN, RUTH. See: Davis, Ann Tyler

MARTIN, SHELLY. See: Waring, Evelyn

MARTIN, SKIP. See: O'Neill, Mrs.

MARTIN SPARROWHILL. See: Jordan, Joyce

MARTIN SPODE. See: Karr, Mike

MARTIN, SUSAN. See: Horton, Dr. Tom

MARTIN, TONY (1), singer and actor; star of program (himself)
DAVID ROSE, orch. leader (self)
HIS ORCHESTRA; GUEST STARS
Tony Martin (TV) (Music/variety)
[(2) host of program (self): Kay Thompson singer (self); Kay Thompson's Rhythm Singers mus. gp.;
André Kostelanetz, orch. ldr. (self);
His Orchestra; Tune-Up Time (R) (Music).]

MARTIN, TONY. See also: Crosby, Bing (2)

MARTIERE, RALPH. See: Basie, Count
Whiteman, Paul

MARTINDALE, WINK (1), moderator of the program (himself)
TWO PAIRS OF MARRIED COUPLES AS CONTESTANTS
Gambit (TV) (Game)

MARTINDALE, WINK (2)
SANDY BARRON
LARRY HOVIS
LOUIS NYE
SHECKY GREENE
CHARLIE MANNA
HAMILTON CAMP
RICHARD DAWSON
OTHERS, "comic counselors" of the program (themselves)
How's Your Mother-in-Law? (TV) (Game)

MARTINSON, CAPTAIN. See: Stockdale, Will

MARTINSON, DR. KEN. See: Drake, Nora

MARTINSON, PEG. See: Drake, Nora

MARTY. See:
Feldman, Marty
Lambert, Louise
Morty
Salem, Peter

MARTY BARRIS. See: Klein, Robert

MARTY FELDMAN. See:
Chidsey, Jackie
Feldman, Marty

Marty Feldman Comedy Machine, The. See: Feldman, Marty

MARTY RUFUS. See: Noble, Mary

MARVEL MAXWELL. See: Hildegarde (1)

MARVIN. See:
McCray, Linc
Mervyn

MARVIN, JERRY. See: Perry, John

MARVIN, LEE, narrator/commentator of the program (himself)
MANY ACTORS AND ACTRESSES
Lawbreaker (TV) (Dramatizations of true crime stories)

MARVIN, REX. See: Myrt

MARX, CHICO. See: Carroll, Madeleine

MARX, GROUCHO (1)
VIRGINIA O'BRIEN
KENNY BAKER
DONALD DIXON, comedians, actors and singers featured on the program (themselves)
ROBERT ARMBRUSTER, orchestra leader (himself)
HIS ORCHESTRA
Blue Ribbon Town (R) (Comedy/variety)

MARX, GROUCHO (2), comedian
and actor, star of the program
(himself)
JACK WHEELER
PATTY HARMON, entertainers on
the program (themselves)
MANY CONTESTANTS
Tell It to Groucho (TV) (Inter-
view/game)

MARX, GROUCHO (3), comedian
and actor; interviewer and quiz-
master of the program (himself)
GEORGE FENNEMAN, his an-
nouncer and assistant (himself)
MANY INTERVIEWEE/CONTES-
TANTS
JACK MEAKIN, orchestra leader
(himself)
HIS ORCHESTRA
You Bet Your Life (R) (TV)
(Comedy interview/quiz) (Some
units later re-released under the
title The Best of Groucho) (TV)

MARX, GROUCHO. See also:
Carroll, Madeleine
Raye, Martha (1)

MARY, wife
BOB, husband, characters ap-
pearing in the dramas
HOWARD BARLOW, orchestra
leader (himself)
HIS ORCHESTRA
The True Story Hour With Mary
and Bob (R) (Drama)

MARY. See also:
Aldrich, Henry
Andrews, Archie
Aunt Mary
Blake, Tom
Boston Blackie
Carter, Kathryn
Crowell, Jonah
Foster, Henry
Gentry, Tom
Hammond, Liza
Higby, Mary Jane
Lindsey, Peter
McBride, Mary Margaret
Maria
Marie
Marlin, Mary
Maury
Merie
Nelson, Carolyn Kramer

Noble, Mary
Richards, Mary
Rose, George
Rutledge, Dr. John
Sothern, Mary
Stone, Dr. Alex
Young, Larry "Pepper"

Mary and Bob, The True Story
Hour With. See: Mary

MARY ANDREWS. See: Horton,
Dr. Tom

MARY ANN. See:
Gilligan
Maraine
Marian
Marianne
Marion

MARY ANN HENDERSON. See:
Kelly, Joe (2)

MARY ANN RANDOLPH. See:
Randolph, Alice

MARY ARNOLD. See: Rogers,
Kenny

MARY ASHWORTH. See: Como,
Perry (1)

Mary, Aunt. See: Aunt Mary

MARY BACKSTAGE, NOBLE WIFE.
See: Ballew, Wally

MARY BOWER. See: Wincholl,
John

MARY BRIGGS. See: Hardy,
Dr. Steven

MARY CASTLE. See: Davis,
Jim

MARY CLARE McHUGH. See:
Kelly, Joe (2)

MARY ELLEN. See: Walton,
Grandpa

MARY ELLEN TERRY. See:
ZaBach, Florian

MARY FICKETT. See: Reasoner,
Harry

MARY FORD. See: Paul, Les

Mary Ford, Les Paul and. See:
Paul, Les

Mary Foster, The Editor's Daughter.
See: Foster, Henry

MARY GARDNER. See: Brasuhn,
Tuffy

MARY GEE. See: Hardie, Jim

MARY HARTLINE. See: Kirchener,
Claude (2)

MARY HATHAWAY. See: Prescott,
Ann Hathaway

MARY HEALY. See: Hayes, Peter
Lind (2) (3) (4)

MARY HOLT. See: Brent, Dr.
Jim

MARY HOPPLE. See: Weems,
Ambrose J.

MARY HOT. See: Brent, Dr.
Jim

MARY KAY BROWN. See: Packard,
Jack

MARY KENNICOTT. See: Davis,
Ann Tyler

MARY KLICK. See:
Dean, Jimmy
Hamilton, George

MARY LEE. See also: Marilly

MARY LEE WALDON. See: Lee,
Jim

MARY LIVINGSTONE. See: Benny,
Jack

MARY LOU. See:
Barbour, Henry Wilson
Henry, Captain

MARY McCARTHY. See: Gobel,
George

MARY McCOY. See: Weems,
Ambrose J.

MARY MAGOON. See: Ballew,
Wally

Mary Margaret McBride. See:
McBride, Mary Margaret

MARY MARGARET McBRIDE.
See: Deane, Martha

Mary Marlin, The Story of. See:
Marlin, Mary

MARY MARTIN. See: Crosby,
Bing (3)

MARY MASON. See: Arthur,
Jack (2)

Mary Noble, Backstage Wife. See:
Noble, Mary

Mary, Peter Loves. See: Lindsey, Peter

MARY, PRINCESS. See: Henry
VIII, King of England

MARY ROSE SPENCER VANCE.
See: Drake, Betty

MARY SMALL. See: Bernie, Ben

Mary Sothern, The Life of. See:
Sothern, Mary

Mary, The Adventures of Helen
and. See: Halop, Billy

Mary, Tom, Dick and. See:
Gentry, Tom

MARY TRIO, THE VERNE, LEE
AND. See: Kelly, Joe (1)

MARY TYLER. See: Wayne,
Ruth Evans

Mary Tyler Moore. See: Richards,
Mary

Mary Tyler Moore Show, The. See:
Richards, Mary

MARYBELLE OWENS. See:
Solomon, David

M*A*S*H. See: Pierce, Captain
Hawkeye

MASON. See: Cross, Mason

MASON, BUCK. See: Benson, Bobby

MASON GROSS, DR. See: Shriner, Herb (3)

MASON, JAMES, actor; host of the program (himself)
MANY ACTORS AND ACTRESSES
Video Theater (TV) (Dramas)

MASON, MARY. See: Arthur, Jack (2)

MASON, MAUDIE
DAVY DILLON
PAULY, characters appearing on the program
Maudie's Diary (R) (Situation comedy)

MASON, NINA. See: Trent, Helen

MASON, PERRY, Los Angeles criminal lawyer; solves murder mysteries
DELLA STREET, his confidential secretary
PAUL DRAKE, private detective employed by him
LIEUTENANT ARTHUR TRAGG, Los Angeles police officer
HAMILTON BURGER, district attorney for Los Angeles
Perry Mason (R) (TV) (Courtroom mystery drama)
SERGEANT DORSET, Los Angeles police officer
THE JUDGE, jurist
Perry Mason (R)
LIEUTENANT JAMES ANDERSON, Los Angeles police officer
GERTIE, Mason's switchboard operator
Perry Mason (TV)

MASON, SULLY. See: Kyser, Kay

MASON, TEX. See: Benson, Bobby

Masquerade. See: Leighton, Linda

Masquerade Party. See: Donald, Peter

MASSEY AND THE WESTERNERS,

LOUISE. See:
Duke of Paducah, The
Kelly, Joe (1)

MASSEY, CHRISTINE, widow, free-lance magazine writer
JUDY
MARNIE
DACK
DIRK
MARIA
BINKIE
VICKIE, her children
PAUL BELZER, magazine editor
The New Loretta Young Show (TV) (Drama)

MASSEY, CURT. See: Skelton, Red

Master Detective, Nick Carter. See: Carter, Nick

MASTER MENTALIST, THE. See: Dunninger, Joseph

MASTERS. See: Tennessee Jed

MASTERS, THE WAGON. See: Wagoner, Porter

MASTERSON. See: Deeds, Long-fellow

MASTERSON, BAT, American frontier Indian fighter, scout, gambler and U.S. marshal
Bat Masterson (TV) (Frontier adventure)

MASTERSON, BAT. See also: Earp, Wyatt

MATA AND HARI. See: Caesar, Sid (3)

Match Game, The. See: Rayburn, Gene (2)

Match, Three on a. See: Cullen, Bill (4)

Mate, Rate Your. See: Adams, Joey (2)

MATEY. See: Popeye

MATHER, DR. GORDON. See:

Davis, Dr. Althea

MATHESON. See also:
Madison
Mathison
Matson

MATHESON, BEN. See: Dunbar,
Mike

MATHIEU, MIREILLE. See:
Davidson, John (2)

MATHILDA BARKER. See: Guest,
Edgar A. (2)

MATHILDA PENDLETON. See:
Perkins, Ma

MATHISON. See also:
Madison
Matheson
Matson

MATHISON, SERGEANT (MATTY).
See: Carter, Nick

MATHRE, DIANNE. See: Kelly,
Joe (2)

Matinee, Club. See: Moore, Garry (1)

Matinee, Milkman's. See: Shaw,
Stan

MATSON. See also:
Madison
Matheson
Mathison

MATSON, ABBY. See: Jones,
Lorenzo

MATSON, SANDY. See: Jones,
Lorenzo

MATT. See:
Anders, Matt
Dillon, Marshal Matt
Holbrook, Captain Matt
Lincoln, Dr. Matt
Wayne, Marshal Matt

MATT, AUNT. See: Waring,
Evelyn

MATT CRANE. See: Garrett,
Susan

MATT DAWSON. See: Carr,
Alison

MATT GREB, INSPECTOR. See:
Guthrie, Lieut. Ben

MATT HENSHAW. See: Ruskin,
Lily

Matt Lincoln. See: Lincoln, Dr.
Matt

MATT POWERS, DR. See: Davis,
Dr. Althea

MATT SWAIN, UNCLE. See:
Peyton, Martin

MATTHEW. See:
Gower, Matthew
Rockford, Matthew
Wilbur, Judy

MATTHEW, UNCLE. See: Mc-
Garry, Dan

MATTHEWS, CARL. See: Weems,
Ambrose J.

MATTHEWS, DAISY. See: Malone,
Dr. Jerry

MATTHEWS, DAN, California highway patrol officer
Highway Patrol (TV) (Crime
drama) (also called Ten-4) (TV)

MATTHEWS, DEBORAH. See:
Perkins, Ma

MATTHEWS, DR. CHARLES. See:
Rutledge, Dr. John

MATTHEWS, FRANCES MORAN.
See:
Carter, Kathryn
Marlin, Mary

MATTHEWS, HENRY. See:
Carter, Kathryn
Marlin, Mary

MATTHEWS, JIM. See: Bennett,
Nita

MATTHEWS, JUNIOR. See:
Carter, Kathryn

MATTHEWS, LELIA. See:
Bennett, Nita

MATTHEWS, MARK. See: Perkins,
Ma

MATTHEWS, MRS. See: Randolph,
Ellen

MATTHEWS, RUSS. See: Randolph,
Alice

MATTIE. See: Fairchild, Kay

MATTIE LANE. See: Karr, Mike

MATTY
SISTERBELLE, cartoon characters
Matty's Funday Funnies (TV)
(Cartoon)

MATTY MALNECK. See: Powell,
Dick (1)

MATTY (SERGEANT MATHISON).
See: Carter, Nick

Matty's Funday Funnies. See:
Matty

MATZ, PETER. See:
Burnett, Carol
Jones, Jack

MAUCH, BILLY. See:
Cross, Milton (2)
Halop, Billy

MAUCH, BOBBY. See:
Cross, Milton (2)
Halop, Billy

MAUD
BILL, conversationalists
Maud and Cousin Bill (R) (Com-
edy dialogue)

Maud and Cousin Bill. See: Maud

Maude. See: Findlay, Maude

MAUDE. See: Findlay, Maude

MAUDE AIMEE HUMBARD. See:
Humbard, Rex

MAUDE DAVIS. See: Cantor,
Eddie (2)

MAUDE FRICKERT. See: Winters,
Jonathan

MAUDE KELLOGG. See: Solomon,
David

MAUDE MARLOWE. See: Noble,
Mary

MAUDE-ROXBY, RODDY. See:
Rowan, Dan

MAUDIE. See: Mason, Maudie

Maudie's Diary. See: Mason,
Maudie

MAUPIN, REX. See: Moore,
Garry (1)

MAUREEN ARTHUR. See:
Jones, Dean
Kovacs, Ernie (1)

MAUREEN ROBINSON. See:
Smith, Colonel Zachary

MAURICE BROWN. See: Halop,
Billy

MAURICE FRANKLIN. See:
Judge, The

MAURICE GOSFIELD. See:
Morgan, Henry

MAURICE PEARSON. See: Welk,
Lawrence

MAURICE TARPLIN. See: Weird,
Dr.

MAURIOS. See: Brennan, Jack

MAURY. See also: Mary

MAURY BENKOIL. See: Halop,
Billy

Maverick. See: Maverick, Bret

MAVERICK, BRET
BART MAVERICK
BEAU MAVERICK
BRENT MAVERICK, Western
gamblers
Maverick (TV) (Western adven-
ture)

MAWSON, NORA. See: Brent,
Portia

MAX. See:
Morath, Max
Nelson

MAX BRONSKY. See: Hennesey,
Lieut. Chick

MAX CANFIELD. See: Dennis,
Liz

MAX GUGGENHEIM. See: Nebb,
Rudolph

MAX TILLEY. See: Sothern, Mary

MAX WOODARD. See: Myrt

MAXINE. See: Spitalny, Phil

MAXINE DRIGGS THOMAS. See:
Driggs, Karleton King

MAXINE KING. See: Driggs,
Karleton King

MAXWELL. See: Smart, Maxwell

Maxwell House Coffee Time. See:
Morgan, Frank (2)

Maxwell House Show Boat, The.
See: Henry, Captain

MAXWELL, MARVEL. See: Hildegarde (1)

MAXWELL, MR. See: Davis,
Ann Tyler

MAXWELL, PEGGY. See: Howard,
Glenn

MAXWELL, RICHARD, singer-
philosopher, star of the program
(himself)
MANY GUEST STARS
Friend in Deed (R) (Variety)

MAXWELL, TED. See: Winkler,
Betty

MAXWELL TROTTER, LIEUT.
See: Morgan, Lieut. Anne

MAY. See:

Breen, May Singhi
Herrick, Cap'n John
Mae
Robson, May

MAY, BILLY. See:
Coogan, Jackie
Whiteman, Paul

MAY CASE. See: Lawton, Lora

MAY, ELAINE. See:
Ames, Nancy
Van Dyke, Dick (1)

MAY, ELLY. See: Clampett, Jed

Maya. See: Bowen, Terry

MAYA. See: Bowen, Terry

MAYBELLE. See also: Mabel

MAYBELLE JACKSON. See:
Clayton, Margie

Mayberry, Andy of. See: Taylor,
Andy

Mayberry R. F. D. See: Jones,
Sam

MAYBERRY, WILL. See: Sherwood, Grace

MAYFIELD, AUNT EMILY. See:
Marshall, John

MAYFIELD, CURTIS. See: Butler,
Jerry

MAYFIELD, SYBELLA. See:
Harding, Karen Adams

MAYME GORDON. See: O'Neill,
Mrs.

MAYNARD KREBS. See: Gillis,
Dobie

MAYO, KINGSLEY. See: Perry,
John

MAYO, SHEILA. See: Perry,
John

MAYOR. See: Russell, Mayor

MAYOR LA TRIVIA. See: McGee,
  Fibber

MAYOR MIZZNICK. See: Meyer

Mayor of the Town, The. See:
  Russell, Mayor

MAYOR PEOPLES. See: Miller,
  Socrates

MAYOR POTTS. See: Carson,
  Uncle Joe

Me and the Chimp. See: Reynolds,
  Dr. Mike

Me, Ichabod and. See: Major,
  Bob

Me, Wendy and. See: Burns,
  George (3)

MEADE, JULIA. See: Sullivan,
  Ed

MEADOWS, AUDREY. See:
  Donald, Peter
  James, Dennis (3)

MEADOWS, JAYNE. See: Moore,
  Garry (4)

MEADOWS, ROY. See: Marshall,
  John

MEADOWS, SYLVIA. See: Dyke,
  Charity Amanda

MEAKIN, JACK. See: Marx,
  Groucho (3)

MEAN WIDDLE KID, THE. See:
  Junior

MEARS, MARTHA. See: Penner,
  Joe

"MEATHEAD." See: Bunker,
  Archie

MED FLORY. See: Anthony, Ray

MEDBURY, JOHN P., comedian and
  host of the program (himself)
  GOGO DELYS, featured vocalist
  (herself)
  MUTTER

MUMBLE
ELSIE (The Dumb Dame), char-
  acters appearing on the program
TED FIORITO
GUS ARNHEIM
ANSON WEEKS
JIMMIE GRIER, orchestra leaders
  (themselves)
THEIR ORCHESTRAS
The M. J. B. Demitasse Revue
(R) (Music /comedy)

MEDFORD, KAY. See: Martin,
  Dean (2)

Mediation Board, A. L. Alexander
  and His. See: Alexander, A. L.
  (1)

Medic. See: Styner, Dr. Konrad

Medical Center. See: Lochner,
  Dr. Paul

Medical Horizons. See: Goddard,
  Don

MEEK, MORTIMER, head of the
  house
  AGATHA MEEK, his wife
  PEGGY MEEK, their daughter
  PEGGY'S BOYFRIEND
  LOUIE, Agatha's brother
  LILY, maid
  MR. BARKER
  MRS. BARKER
  MR. APPLE, characters appear-
  ing on the program
  The Adventures of Mr. Meek (R)
  (Situation comedy)

Meet Corliss Archer. See:
  Archer, Corliss

Meet McGraw. See: McGraw

Meet Me at Parky's. See:
  Parkyakarkas, Nick

Meet Millie. See: Bronson,
  Millie

Meet Mr. McNulty (McNutley).
  See: McNulty, Professor Ray

Meet the Dixons. See: Dixon,
  Wesley

Meet the Press. See: Rountree, Martha

Meeting, America's Town. See: Murrow, Edward R. (1)

Meeting of the Air, America's Town. See: Denny, George V., Jr.

Meets the Critics, The Author. See: Gray, Barry (1)

MEG. See: March, Mrs.

MEG, AUNT. See: West, Honey

MEG DALE ANDREWS. See: Sterling, Vanessa Dale

MEG GRIFFIN. See: Manning, Portia Blake

MEIKLE, PAT, hostess and teacher of the program (herself) MANY CHILDREN PARTICIPANTS The Magic Cottage (TV) (Children's education)

MEL. See:
Blanc, Mel
Hunter, Mel
Mal
Torme, Mel

MEL ALLEN. See: Cowan, Thomas

Mel Blanc Show, The. See: Blanc, Mel

Mel Blanc's Fix-it Shop. See: Blanc, Mel

MEL COOLEY. See: Petrie, Rob

MEL MOUNDS. See: Cosby, Bill (1)

MEL WARSHAW. See: Dickens, Harry

MELBA. See: Moore, Melba

Melba Moore-Clifton Davis Show, The. See: Moore, Melba

MELENKA, MRS. See: Goldberg, Molly

MELIS, JOSE. See: Paar, Jack

MELISSA. See: Marshall, Owen

MELLISH, MUGG. See: Ballew, Wally

MELLO-LARKS QUARTET, THE. See: James, Dennis (1)

Melodies, Enna Jettick. See: Shields, Jimmy

MELODY. See: Josie

MELODY LEE MERCER. See: Randolph, Rex

Melody Puzzles. See: Uttal, Fred (2)

Melody Ranch, Gene Autry's. See: Autry, Gene

Melody Treasure Hunt. See: Ballard, Pat

MELTON. See also: Milton

MELTON, JAMES (1), singer, featured on the program (himself) FRANCIA WHITE, singer (herself) THE ROUGE REPORTER, news analyist DONALD VOORHEES, orchestra leader (himself) HIS ORCHESTRA The Ford Summer Hour (R) (Music/news)

MELTON, JAMES (2), singer, featured on the program (himself) FRANK BLACK HOWARD BARLOW, orchestra leaders (themselves) THEIR ORCHESTRAS Harvest of Stars (R) (Music)

MELTON, JAMES. See also: Bell, Alexander Graham Roxy

MELVIN CASTLEBURY. See: White, Billy

MELVYN. See: Foster, Judy

MELVYN DOUGLAS. See: Ayres,
Lew

Memory Game, Joe Garagiola's.
See: Garagiola, Joe (2)

Memory Lane, Joe Franklin's. See:
Franklin, Joe

MEN. See also:
Maen
Man
Mann

Men at Law. See: Hansen, David

Men From Shiloh, The. See:
MacKenzie, Colonel Alan
Virginian, The

Men, G. See: Lord, Phillips H.

Men In Action, Treasury. See:
Chief, The

Men In Crisis. See: O'Brien,
Edmond

Men Into Space. See: McCauley,
Colonel Edward

Men, The (Assignment: Vienna).
See: Webster, Jake

Men, The (Jigsaw). See: Dain,
Lieut. Frank

Men, The (The Delphi Bureau). See:
Gregory, Glenn Garth

Men, The Four Just. See: Collier, Tim

Men, The Gallant. See: Wright,
Conley

Men, 26. See: Travis, Clint

Menace, Dennis the. See: Mitchell,
Dennis

MENACE, DENNIS THE. See:
Mitchell, Dennis

MENACE, MARCELLA THE. See:
Young, Larry "Pepper"

MENCKEN, CHARLOTTE. See:

Ames, Peter

MENDALL, MR. See: Goldberg,
Molly

MENDOZA, GYP. See: Solomon,
David

MENEFEE, MR. See: Hillman,
India

MENJOU, ADOLPHE, actor; host
and narrator of the program
(himself)
MANY ACTORS AND ACTRESSES
Target (TV) (Suspense drama)

Mennen Shave Time. See: Parker,
Lou

MENNINGER, THALIA. See:
Gillis, Dobie

MENTAL BANKER, THE. See:
I.Q., Dr.

MENTALIST, THE MASTER. See:
Dunninger, Joseph

MERCEDES COLBY. See:
Winslow, Don

MERCEDES RABBITT. See: Kukla

MERCER, JANET. See: Brent,
Dr. Jim

MERCER, JOHNNY. See: Crosby,
Bing (3)

MERCER, MARIAN. See:
DeLuise, Dom (1)
Martin, Dean (2)

MERCER, MELODY LEE. See:
Randolph, Rex

MERCY. See: Noble, Mary

Mercy, Kate Hopkins, Angel of.
See: Hopkins, Kate

MEREDITH. See: Walleck,
Meredith

MEREDITH, BURGESS, master of
ceremonies of the program
(himself)

MANY GUEST STARS
Pursuit of Happiness (R) (Variety)

MEREDITH, BURGESS. See also:
Heatter, Gabriel

MEREDITH, CHARLES
JULIA MEREDITH
DAVID MEREDITH
MIDGE
JINNY STOREY
TIMOTHY STOREY
MEREDITH CONWAY
STANLEY BARTLETT
RUTH ANDREWS
AMY GORDON BARTLETT
JOHN ELLIOTT
SANDY SANDERSON
BERTHA, characters appearing
in the drama
Midstream (R) (Serial drama)

MEREDITH CONWAY. See:
Meredith, Charles

MEREDITH, DON. See: Jackson,
Keith (2)

MEREDITH FOX. See: Marshall,
E. G.

MEREDITH JONES. See: Grimm,
Arnold

MEREDITH, JUNE. See: First
Nighter, Mr.

MEREDITH MACRAE. See: Kidder,
Margot

MEREDITH WILLSON. See:
Bankhead, Tallulah
Morgan, Frank (2)

MERIE. See also:
Maria
Marie
Mary

MERIE EARLE. See: Reed, Jerry

MERLE. See: Oberon, Merle

MERLE CHATWIN. See: Dallas,
Stella

MERLE JOHNSTON. See: Reser,
Harry

MERLE TRAVIS. See: Ritter,
Tex (1)

MERLIN. See:
Marlin
Martin
Sir Lancelot

MERMAN, ETHEL, singer and
actress; star of the program
(herself)
MANY GUEST STARS
The Ethel Merman Show (R)
(Music/variety)

MERRICK, MARGARET. See:
Kelly, Joe (2)

MERRILL, BUDDY. See: Welk,
Lawrence

MERRILL, LILY. See: Troop,
Marshal Dan

MERRILL, LOU. See: Winkler,
Betty

MERRIMAN, RANDY. See: Paige,
Bob

MERRITT, JUDITH. See: Noble,
Mary

MERRIWEATHER, MR. See:
Hall, Dr. William Todhunter

MERRIWELL, FRANK
BART
INZA, characters appearing on
the program
Frank Merriwell (R) (Adventure)

Merry-Go-Round, The College. See:
Sharp, Hal

Merry-Go-Round, The Manhattan.
See: Thomas, Thomas L.

MERRY MACS, THE. See:
Gibbs, Georgia (2)
Ross, Lanny

Merry Mailman. See: Heatherton,
Ray

MERRYNOTE, MISS. See: Pip
the Piper

MERT. See also: Myrt

MERT POWER. See: March, Hal

MERTZ, ETHEL. See: Ricardo,
Ricky

MERTZ, FRED. See: Ricardo,
Ricky

MERV GRIFFIN. See:
Griffin, Merv (1) (2) (3)
Lewis, Robert Q. (2)
Reiner, Carl

Merv Griffin Show, The. See:
Griffin, Merv (1)

MERVYN. See also: Marvin

MERVYN BOGUE. See: Kyser, Kay

META BAUER. See: Rutledge,
Dr. John

META BAUER ROBERTS. See:
Bauer, Bertha

METCALF, BERT. See: Slattery,
Jim

METRANO, ART. See: Conway,
Tim

Metropolitan Opera Broadcasts.
See: Cross, Milton (3)

MEYER, Jewish businessman
MAYOR MIZZNICK, politician
IRMA MIZZNICK, his wife
MILTON MIZZNICK, his son
LAWYER FELDMAN, attorney
BEATRICE
MOLLIE
UNCLE BEN, characters appearing
on the program
Meyer the Buyer (R) (Comedy)

MEYER. See also: Carella

MEYER SHAPIRO. See: Grant,
Harry

Meyer the Buyer. See: Meyer

MI. See:
Brown, Velvet
Do

Miami Undercover. See: Thompson,
Jeff

MICHAEL
KITTY, amateur detectives
Michael and Kitty (R) (Mystery)

MICHAEL. See also:
Alden, Michael
Anthony, Michael
Armstrong, Jack
Bauer, Bertha
Brent, Portia
Fitzmaurice, Michael
Horton, Dr. Tom
Lanyard, Michael
Miguel
O'Shea, Michael
Packard, Jack
Powers, Michael
Randolph, Alice
Rhodes, Dr. Michael
Shayne, Michael
Upton, Michael
West, Michael
Williams, Danny
Worthington, Nora

Michael and Kitty. See: Michael

MICHAEL AXFORD. See: Reid,
Britt

MICHAEL BARTLETT. See:
Benny, Jack

MICHAEL CONWAY. See: Kelly,
Kitty

MICHAEL DARLING. See: Pan,
Peter

MICHAEL DELLA ROCCA. See:
March, Hal
Story, Ralph

MICHAEL DENBY. See: Allen,
Joan Houston

MICHAEL DORNE. See: Marlin,
Mary

MICHAEL FRANCIS O'CASEY.
See: Douglas, Steve

MICHAEL GREGORY. See:
Carter, Kathryn

MICHAEL HATHAWAY. See: Prescott, Kate Hathaway

MICHAEL J. POLLARD. See: Marshall, E. G.

MICHAEL KENT. See: Graham, Dr. Bob

MICHAEL LANDON. See:
Cookie Monster, The
Jones, Jack

MICHAEL LEMBECK. See: Kelly, Gene

MICHAEL, MR. See: Walleck, Meredith

MICHAEL MONT. See: Forsyte, Soames

MICHAEL MURRY. See: Chandler, Faith

MICHAEL NICHOLSON. See: Martin, Doris

MICHAEL O'DAY. See: Halop, Billy

MICHAEL PATERNO. See: Johnson, Bess

MICHAEL PORATH. See: Narz, Jack (2)

MICHAEL ROSSI, DR. See: Peyton, Martin

Michael Shayne, Private Detective. See: Shayne, Michael

MICHAEL WEST. See:
Wayne, Ruth Evans
West, Michael

MICHAELS, JOE, interviewer, host of the program (himself)
MANY INTERVIEWEES
As Others See Us (TV) (Interviews)

MICHAELS, MARILYN. See: Little, Rich

MICHAELS, MR. See: Hardy, Dr. Steven

MICHAELS, RAY. See: Kaye, Sammy (1)

MICHELE MARTIN. See: Porter, Pete

MICHELLE DELLA FAVE. See: Chidsey, Jackie

Mickey. See: Grady, Mickey

MICKEY
CLARA GAINES
MAIMIE, characters appearing in the drama
Mickey of the Circus (R) (Drama)

MICKEY. See also:
Grady, Mickey
Horton, Dr. Tom
Mouse, Mickey
Mulligan, Mickey
Spencer, Jeff

MICKEY ANDERSON. See: Hutton, Ina Ray

MICKEY BLOOM. See: Goldberg, Molly

MICKEY DONOVAN. See: Kaltenmeyer, Professor August, D. U. N.

MICKEY JONES. See: Rogers, Kenny

MICKEY MANNERS. See: Harrington, Pat, Jr.

Mickey Mouse Club, The. See: Dodd, Jimmie

Mickey Mouse Theater of the Air, The. See: Mouse, Mickey

Mickey of the Circus. See: Mickey

MICKEY, PATRICIA. See: Chidsey, Jackie

MICKEY RILEY. See: Hastings, Bill

Mickey Rooney. See: Mulligan, Mickey

MICKI McGLONE. See: Chidsey, Jackie

Mickie Finn. See: Finn, Fred

MICKY DOLENZ. See: Jones, Davy

Microphone, Candid. See: Funt,
Allen (2)

MIDGE. See:
Beamer, John
Meredith, Charles
Pride, Ben

MIDGET, IMPY THE. See: Hungarian Giant, The

MIDGET, THE. See: Spencer, Jeff

MIDGIE. See: Myrt

MIDNIGHT, CAPTAIN, SS-1, flyer,
commander of government under-
cover agency known as the
Secret Squadron
MAJOR STEEL, his commanding
officer
CHUCK RAMSEY, SS-2
JOYCE RYAN, SS-3, his chief
assistants
ICHABOD "ICHY" MUDD, his
mechanic
SS-11, member of the Secret
Squadron
IVAN SHARK, his enemy
FURY SHARK, Ivan's ugly daugh-
ter, also his enemy
FANG, accomplice of the Sharks
Captain Midnight (R) (TV) (Ad-
venture) (later re-issued on TV
under the title Jet Jackson)
POLICE LIEUT. JOHNSON, police
officer
Captain Midnight (TV)

MIDNIGHT, JOHNNY, private detective
Johnny Midnight (TV) (Crime
drama)

Midnight, Manhattan at. See: Reed,
Alan

Midstream. See: Meredith,
Charles

Midway, Magic. See: Kirchener,
Claude (1)

Mighty Mouse. See: Mighty Mouse

MIGHTY MOUSE, cartoon character
Mighty Mouse (TV) (Cartoon)

Mighty Show, The. See: Hutchinson, Ma

Mighty Thor, The. See: Mighty
Thor, The

MIGHTY THOR, THE, crime
fighter; cartoon character
The Mighty Thor (TV) (Cartoon)

MIGUEL. See also: Michael

MIGUEL SANTERRA. See: Carlyle,
Baylor

MIGUELITO LOVELESS, DR. See:
West, Jim (2)

MIKE
HIS SWEETHEART
MR. BERKELEY, his boss
Leave It To Mike (R) (Comedy)

MIKE. See also:
Barnett, Mike
Bell, Mike
Brady, Mike
Brannagan, Mike
Connors, Mike
Dodge, Marshall "Mike"
Douglas, Mike
Dunbar, Mike
Endicott, Professor Mike
Fitzgerald, Bridget Theresa
Mary Coleen
Haines, Lieut. Mike
Halliday, Mike
Hammer, Mike
Hoyt, Vikki Adams
Joe (2)
Jones, Sam
Kangaroo, Captain
Karr, Mike
King
Kovacs, Mike
Longstreet, Mike
Malone, Mike
Nelson, Mike
Parker, Lieut. Mike
Preston, Dick
Redigo, Jim (2)
Reynolds, Dr. Mike
Roy, Mike
Stokey, Mike
Stone, Detective Lieut. Mike

Tracy, Dr. Marsh
Wallace, Mike (1) (2) (3) (4) (5)
Waring, Mike
Wilson, Mike

MIKE BARLOW. See: Rogers,
Patricia

Mike, Behind the. See: McNamee,
Graham

MIKE CLANCY. See: Keen, Mr.

MIKE DANKO. See: Ryker, Lieut.
Eddie

MIKE DOUGLAS. See:
Douglas, Mike
James, Dennis (1)

Mike Douglas Show, The. See:
Douglas, Mike

MIKE HAGEN. See: Hargrave-
Scott, Joan

Mike Hammer. See: Hammer,
Mike

Mike, Leave It to. See: Mike

MIKE McCALL. See: Jones, Loco

MIKE McCLUSKEY, SERGEANT.
See: McCluskey, Mona

MIKE McTOOCH. See: Kirkwood,
Jack

MIKE MADISON. See: Andrews,
Drake

MIKE MALONE. See:
Jordan, Joyce
Malone, Mike

MIKE NESMITH. See: Jones, Davy

MIKE NICHOLS. See:
Ames, Nancy
Van Dyke, Dick (1)

MIKE POST. See: Williams, Andy
(2)

MIKE POWERS, DR. See: Davis,
Dr. Althea

Mike Roy's Cooking Thing. See:
Roy, Mike

MIKE SAMMES SINGERS, THE.
See:
Berman, Shelley
Doonican, Val
O'Connor, Des

MIKE SHAW, SHERIFF. See:
Mix, Tom

MIKE STIVIC. See: Bunker,
Archie

MIKE VALERA. See: Slattery,
Jim

MIKE WALLACE. See:
Barry, Jack (1)
Wallace, Mike (1) (2) (3) (4) (5)

Mike Wallace Interviews. See:
Wallace, Mike (2)

MILBURN, DR. See: Grimm,
Arnold

MILBURN DRYSDALE. See:
Clampett, Jed

MILDERMAUL, DR. See: Jordan,
Joyce

MILDRED. See:
McMillan, Stuart
Sisk, Mildred Elizabeth
Trimble, Jonathan

MILDRED ANDERSON. See: Day,
Dennis

MILDRED CARTER RANDOLPH.
See: Carter, Mr.

MILDRED FARELL. See: Har-
grave-Scott, Joan

MILDRED HOGAN. See: Cooper,
Dick

MILDRED MACINERNEY. See:
Campanelli, Dr. Vincent

MILDRED ROGERS. See: Carey,
Dr. Philip

MILES. See:
Banyon, Miles C.
Mills
Myles
Nelson, Carolyn Kramer

MILES, ALLIE LOWE
SEDLEY BROWN, interviewers of
the program (themselves)
MANY INTERVIEWEES
Husbands and Wives (R) (Interview)

MILES, DR. See: Peyton, Martin

MILES, LEW. See: Peyton, Martin

MILES NOVAK. See: Chandler,
Faith

MILES, SHERRY. See: Paulsen,
Pat

Milkman's Matinee. See: Shaw,
Stan

MILLER. See:
Anderson, Sergeant Nick
Ordway, Dr. Benjamin
Wilson, Steve

MILLER, ALBERT
JANE, his wife, take position as
"experienced" butler and cook with
Charles Dutton
CHARLES DUTTON, their wealthy
employer
NICK DUTTON, Dutton's hippie son
GRACE DUTTON, Dutton's maiden
sister
The Good Life (TV) (Situation
comedy)

MILLER, CHIEF. See: Butcher,
Major Simon

MILLER, DAN. See: Evans, Dean

MILLER, DOC. See: Edwards,
Lum

MILLER, DR. See: Trent, Dr.
Jim

MILLER, ESTHER. See: Goldberg, Molly

MILLER, GLENN. See: Como,
Perry (1)

MILLER, HANK. See: Nash, Jim

MILLER, HOWARD, host of the
program (himself)
The Just Generation (TV)
(Legal instruction)

MILLER, IRENE. See: Dyke,
Charity Amanda

MILLER, IRVING. See: Sweeney,
Bob

MILLER, JACK. See: Smith,
Kate (2)

MILLER, JEFF. See: Lassie

MILLER, JERRY. See: Wayne,
Ruth Evans

MILLER, JOHNNY
FRANK BOONE, social directors
at vacation resort
DOROTHY JACKSON, hotel re-
ceptionist
J. W. HARRINGTON, hotel
manager
WOODROW, bellhop
Holiday Lodge (TV) (Comedy)

MILLER, JOYCE. See: Dawson,
Rosemary

MILLER, MISS EDITH. See:
District Attorney, Mr.

MILLER, MRS. See:
Burton, Terry
Carey, Dr. Philip
Hughes, Chris
Tate, Joanne

MILLER, MITCH, oboeist and singer;
host of the program (himself)
LESLIE UGGAMS
GUY MITCHELL
DIANA TRASK
GLORIA LAMBERT
EARL ROGERS
LOUISE O'BRIEN
JERRY VALE
SANDY STEWART
THE SINGALONGERS, vocalists
appearing on the program (them-
selves)
Sing Along With Mitch (TV)
(Group singing)

MILLER, MITCH. See also:
Whiteman, Paul

MILLER, ROGER, star of the pro-
gram (himself)
MANY GUEST STARS
THE DOODLETOWN PIPERS,
musical group
EDDIE KARAM, orchestra leader
(himself)
HIS ORCHESTRA
The Roger Miller Show (TV)
(Variety)

MILLER, ROGER. See also: Shawn,
Dick

MILLER, RUSSELL. See: Gook,
Vic

MILLER, SOCRATES, councilman;
lives in a trailer
MANDY, his wife
MAYOR PEOPLES, Mandy's father
AUNT GUS, his aunt
CLAY HUNNICUT, his friend
CLEO, his basset hound
The People's Choice (TV) (Comedy)

MILLER, SUE EVANS. See: Wayne,
Ruth Evans

MILLETTE, BOBBY. See: Welles,
Orson (3)

MILLICENT. See: Martin, Millicent

MILLICENT PENNINGTON. See:
Wilbur, Judy

MILLICENT STARR. See: Sloan,
Holly

MILLIE. See:
Bronson, Millie
Grover, Millie
Jones, Lorenzo
Milly

MILLIE BAXTER. See: Brown,
Ellen

MILLIE CHERNAK. See: Garrison,
Spencer

MILLIE HELPER. See: Petrie,
Rob

Millie, Meet. See: Bronson,
Millie

MILLIE SWANSON. See: Jones,
Sam

MILLIGAN. See also: Mulligan

Milligan and Milligan. See:
Detective

MILLIKEN, HARRY. See: Crane,
Betty

MILLIKEN, HELEN. See: Crane,
Betty

Million, Cool. See: Keyes, Jefferson

Million, If You Had a. See:
Anthony, Michael

Million, Penny to a. See: Goodwin, Bill

Million Record Show, The. See:
Gibbs, Georgia (1)

MILLIONAIRE BRUCE WAYNE.
See:
Batman
Kent, Clark

Millionaire, How to Marry a. See:
Jones, Loco

Millionaire, The. See: Anthony,
Michael

MILLIONAIRE, THE. See:
Anthony, Michael

Millions, Lady of. See: Robson,
May

MILLS. See also:
Miles
Myles

MILLS, ALLISON. See: Uggams,
Leslie

MILLS, BILLY. See:
Borge, Victor
McGee, Fibber

MILLS, VERLYE. See: Ross,
Lanny

MILLY. See also: Millie

MILLY ANDERSON. See: Stockdale, Will

MILNER, CALIFORNIA JOE. See:
Custer, George Armstrong

MILO BOULTON. See: Heatter,
Gabriel

MILQUETOAST, CASPER (The Timid
Soul), feeble, hen-pecked and
afraid to face the world
MADGE, his wife
THE DRUGGIST, merchant
The Timid Soul (R) (Comedy)

MILT KAMEN. See: Stokey, Mike

MILTON. See:
Berle, Milton (1) (2) (3)
Cross, Milton (1) (2) (3) (4)
Melton

MILTON BERLE. See:
Berle, Milton (1) (2) (3)
Bower, Roger
Crosby, Bing (2)

Milton Berle, Jackpot Bowling
Starring. See: Berle, Milton
(1)

Milton Berle Show, The. See:
Berle, Milton (2)

MILTON BROWNSPUN. See:
Cummings, Brenda

MILTON DeLUGG. See:
Lester, Jerry
Winchell, Paul (3)

MILTON MIZZNICK. See: Meyer

MILTON RETTENBERG. See:
Dragonette, Jessica (1)

Milton the Monster. See: Milton
the Monster

MILTON THE MONSTER, cartoon
character
Milton the Monster (TV) (Cartoon)

MIMI. See:
Barclay, Doc
Scott, Karen

MIMI DAVIS. See: Phelps, Jim

MIN. See: Gump, Andy

Mine, This Life Is. See:
Hastings, Bob

MINERVA. See:
Batman
Brewster, Joey

MINERVA PIOUS. See: Morgan,
Henry

MING. See: Gordon, Flash

MINGO. See: Boone, Daniel

MINISTER, THE. See: Peters,
Bill

MINIVER, MRS. , English house-
wife during World War II
MR. MINIVER, her husband
Mrs. Miniver (R) (Drama)

MINNIE. See: Varner, Will

MINNIE GRADY. See: Dallas,
Stella

MINNIE MOUSE. See: Mouse,
Mickey

MINNIE PEARL, COUSIN. See:
Owens, Buck
Solemn Old Judge, The

MINNOW, THE. See: Gilligan

MINSTREL MEN, THE SINCLAIR.
See: Arnold, Gene

Minstrel Show, The Sinclair. See:
Arnold, Gene

MINSTREL, THE. See: Batman

Minstrels, Model. See: Howard,
Tom (2)

Minstrels, The New Christy. See:
Sparks, Randy

MINTA OWENS, AUNT. See:
Vance, Connie

MINTER, JIMMY. See: Myrt

MINTURN, FRED. See: Nelson,
Carolyn Kramer

Minutes, 60. See: Wallace, Mike
(4)

MIRA DUNHAM. See: Malone, Dr.
Jerry

Miracles of Magnolia. See: Baldridge, Fanny May

MIRANDA. See: Chandler, Dr.
Susan

MIRANDY. See: Baines, Scattergood

MIREILLE MATHIEU. See: Davidson, John (2)

MIRIAM. See:
Hope, Bob (2)
Ungar, Felix

MIRIAM WOLFE. See: Halop,
Billy

Mirth and Madness. See: Kirkwood, Jack

MISHEL PIASTRO. See: Knight,
Frank

MISS. See: Marlowe, Miss

MISS ADAMS. See: Perkins, Ma

Miss America Contest, The. See:
Parks, Bert (4)

MISS BEAN. See: Winters,
Evelyn

MISS BENNETT. See: Graham,
Dr. Bob

MISS BOYLE. See: Brent, Dr.
Jim

MISS BRADLEY. See: Brent,
Dr. Jim

MISS BRANCH. See: Keene, Kitty

MISS BRIGGS. See: Bauer, Bertha

Miss Brooks, Our. See: Brooks,
Connie

MISS BURNS. See: Malone, Dr.
Jerry

MISS CLARIDGE. See: Harrigan,
James, Sr.

MISS CULVER. See: Foster,
Major John

MISS DAISY. See: Manning, Portia
Blake

MISS DUFFY. See: Archie

MISS EDITH MILLER. See:
District Attorney, Mr.

MISS ELLIS. See: Keen, Mr.

MISS FARNSWORTH. See: Mac-
Donald, Eleanor

MISS FISK. See: Kincaid, Chet

MISS FOSTER. See: Wilson, Steve

MISS G. See: O'Brien, Daniel J.

MISS GENEVIEVE BLUE. See:
Jones, Amos

MISS HARVEY. See: Novak, John

Miss Hattie. See: Barrymore, Ethel

MISS HAZY. See: Wiggs, Mrs.

MISS, HITS AND A. See:
Haymes, Dick
Hope, Bob (2)

Miss, Junior. See: Graves, Harry

MISS KELLY. See: Smith, Eugene

MISS MARLOWE. See: Marlowe,
Miss

Miss Marlowe, Concerning. See:
Marlowe, Miss

MISS MERRYNOTE. See: Pip
the Piper

MISS RADCLIFF. See: Brent,
Dr. Jim

MISS RAND. See: District
Attorney, Mr.

MISS SPALDING. See: Luigi

MISS THOMAS. See: Ace, Goodman

MISS TODD. See:
Brent, Dr. Jim
Brown, Ellen

MISS WILSON. See:
Bridges, Cara
Foster, Major John

MISS WITCHIE-POO. See: Pufnstuf, H. R.

MISS WOOD. See: Marlin, Mary

Missing Heirs, The Court of. See:
Waters, Jim

Mission: Impossible. See: Phelps, Jim

MR. See:
Abbott, Mr.
Anthony, Mr.
Arden, Jane
Brent, Dr. Jim
Brown, Velvet
Carter, Mr.
Chameleon, Mr.
District Attorney, Mr.
First Nighter, Mr.
Fix-It, Mr.
Jolly, Mr.
Keen, Mr.
Lucky, Mr.
Magoo, Mr.
Malone, Mr.
Miniver, Mrs.
Murgatroyd, Mr.
Parker, Richard
Wizard, Mr.

Mr. Ace and Jane. See: Ace, Goodman

Mr. Adams and Eve. See: Adams, Howard

MR. AMERICA. See: James, Dennis (4)

Mr. and Mrs. See:
Brynner, Yul
Joe (3)

Mr. and Mrs. North. See: North, Jerry

MR. ANDERSON. See: Day, Dennis

MR. APPLE. See: Meek, Mortimer

MR. ARCANE. See: Croft, Jonathan

MR. ARCHER. See: Archer, Corliss

MR. ARNOLD. See: Myrt

MR. ASTRAKHAN. See: Kelly, Kitty

MR. AVERAGE RADIO LISTENER. See: Kaye, Danny

MR. BANNISTER. See: Dickens, Harry

MR. BARCLAY. See: Hargrave-Scott, Joan

MR. BARKER. See:
Hardy, Dr. Steven
Meek, Mortimer

MR. BARRETT. See: Randolph, Ellen

MR. BEAUCHAMP. See: Grover, Millie

MR. BERKELEY. See: Mike

MR. BOB. See: Wiggs, Mrs.

MR. BODKIN. See: Dillon, Marshal Matt

Mr. Broadway. See: Bell, Mike

MR. BRUCE. See: Dallas, Stella

MR. BULLER. See: Gook, Vic

MR. BUNDY. See: Burns, George (3)

MR. BURNS. See: Uncle Martin

MR. CAMERON. See:

Cameron, Christy Allen
Davis, Joan Field

MR. CARSON. See: Hargrave-
Scott, Joan

Mr. Chameleon. See: Chameleon,
Mr.

MR. CHERNAK. See: Garrison,
Spencer

Mr. Citizen. See: Edwards, Allyn

MR. CLYDE. See: Peterson,
Irma

MR. COHEN. See: Levy, Abie

MR. COLBY. See: Blanc, Mel

MR. COLEMAN. See: O'Neill,
Mrs.

MR. COLLINS. See:
Hargrave-Scott, Joan
O'Neill, Mrs.

MR. CONWAY. See: Larimore,
Marilyn

MR. CUSHING. See: Blanc, Mel

MR. D. See: Overstreet, Buddy

MR. DARLING. See: Pan, Peter

Mr. Deeds Goes to Town. See:
Deeds, Longfellow

MR. DENNIS. See: Dawson,
Rosemary

MR. DEVERY. See: O'Connor,
Katy

Mr. District Attorney. See:
District Attorney, Mr.

"MR. DOCUS" (DOUGLAS ANDER-
SON). See: Kirchener, Claude
(1)

MR. DUFFY. See: Grimm,
Arnold

Mr. Ed. See: Post, Wilbur

MR. ED. See: Post, Wilbur

Mr. Ed, Wilbur and. See: Post,
Wilbur

MR. ERP. See: Perkins, Ma

MR. FARNUM. See: Perkins,
Ma

MR. FIELDING. See: O'Neill,
Mrs.

MR. FINKE. See: Harum, David

Mr. Fix-It. See: Fix-It, Mr.

MR. FOLEY. See: Taylor, Andy

MR. FOSDICK. See: Hastings,
Bill

MR. FOWLER. See: Goldberg,
Molly

MR. FREEZE. See: Batman

MR. FULLERTON. See: Cameron,
Christy Allen

Mr. Garlund. See: Garlund,
Frank

MR. GARRETT. See: Perkins,
Ma

MR. GODFELLOW. See: Lewis,
Shari

MR. GORHAM. See: Harding,
Mrs. Rhoda

MR. GREENJEANS. See: Kangaroo,
Captain

MR. GREGORY. See: Ames,
Peter

MR. GUFFY. See: Cantor,
Eddie (2)

MR. HEMINGWAY. See: Canova,
Judy

MR. HOOPER. See: Cookie
Monster, The

MR. HUNT. See: Waring, Evelyn

Mr. I. Magination. See: Tripp,
Paul

MR. JANAC. See: Malone, Dr.
Jerry

MR. JENKINS. See: Beulah

MR. JEROME. See: Young,
Larry "Pepper"

MR. JINKS. See: Pixie

MR. JONES. See: Dillon,
Marshal Matt

MR. JONES' ANSWERING SERVICE.
See: Pam

Mr. Jones, The Law and. See:
Jones, Abraham Lincoln

Mr. Keen, Tracer of Lost Persons.
See: Keen, Mr.

MR. KELVIN. See: Trent, Helen

MR. KIMBALL. See: Omar

MR. KITZEL. See:
Benny, Jack
Blurt, Elmer

MR. KRAMER. See: Nelson,
Carolyn Kramer

MR. LEADER. See: Pip the
Piper

MR. LENORD. See: Dyke,
Charity Amanda

MR. LODGE. See: Andrews,
Archie

MR. LORD. See: Walleck,
Meredith

Mr. Lucky. See: Lucky, Mr.

MR. MACAULEY. See: O'Con-
nor, Katy

Mr. McNulty (McNutley), Meet.
See: McNulty, Professor Ray

Mr. Magoo. See: Magoo, Mr.

Mr. Magoo, The Famous Adventures of. See: Magoo, Mr.

MR. MALONE. See:
Ames, Peter
Malone, Mr.

Mr. Malone, Murder and. See:
Malone, Mr.

Mr. Malone, The Amazing. See:
Malone, Mr.

MR. MARTIN. See:
Baines, Scattergood
Dawson, Rosemary

MR. MAXWELL. See: Davis,
Ann Tyler

Mr. Meek, The Adventures of.
See: Meek, Mortimer

MR. MENDALL. See: Goldberg,
Molly

MR. MENEFEE. See: Hillman,
India

MR. MERRIWEATHER. See:
Hall, Dr. William Todhunter

MR. MICHAEL. See: Walleck,
Meredith

MR. MICHAELS. See: Hardy,
Dr. Steven

MR. MORTIMER. See: Perkins,
Ma

MR. MUNSON. See: Harding,
Karen Adams

MR. MURCHISON. See: Hillman,
India

MR. MURPHY. See: Ames, Peter

MR. NERVOUS. See: Allen,
Steve (1)

MR. NOBODY FROM NOWHERE.
See: Rutledge, Dr. John

Mr. Novak. See: Novak, John

MR. OVERTON. See: Brent, Dr.
Jim

MR. PECK. See: Peck, Torey

Mr. Peepers. See: Peepers,
Robinson J.

MR. PINKBAUM. See: Allen,
Fred

Mr. President. See: President,
The

MR. QUIGLEY. See: Dixon,
Bobby

MR. REMINGTON. See: Peepers,
Robinson J.

MR. RICHARDS. See: Hargrave-
Scott, Joan

Mr. Roberts. See: Roberts, Doug

MR. SCHNEIDER. See: Goldberg,
Molly

MR. SCHULTZ. See:
Carter, Kathryn
Dyke, Charity Amanda
Larimore, Marilyn

MR. SCOTT. See: Kirk, Captain
James

MR. SELKIRK. See: Erwin, Stu

MR. SILO. See: Little Orphan
Annie

MR. SILVUS. See: Perkins, Ma

MR. SIMPKINS. See: Tillie

MR. SLOCUM. See: Bell, Harry

Mr. Smith Goes to Washington.
See: Smith, Eugene

Mr. Smith, The Amazing. See:
Smith, Gregory

MR. SPOCK. See: Kirk, Captain
James

MR. STARK. See: Lawes, Lewis
E.

MR. STEBBINS. See: Wiggs, Mrs.

MR. SULU. See: Kirk, Captain
James

Mr. Sweeney, The World of. See:
Sweeney, Cicero P.

Mr. Terrific. See: Beamish,
Stanley

MR. TERRIFIC. See: Beamish,
Stanley

MR. THACKERAY. See: Bean-
blossom, Robert S.

MR. TILLER. See: Harding, Mrs.
Rhoda

MR. TRASK. See: O'Neill, Mrs.

MR. TREMAINE. See: Grimm,
Arnold

MR. TRENT. See: Hargrave-
Scott, Joan

MR. TURNER. See: O'Neill,
Mrs.

MR. TWEEDY. See: Grimm,
Arnold

MR. WARSHAW. See: Bauer,
Bertha

MR. WELBY. See: Kelly, Kitty

MR. WILLOUGHBY. See: Day,
Dennis

MR. WILMUTH. See: Welles,
Orson (3)

MR. WILSON. See: Mitchell,
Dennis

MR. WIMPLE. See: McNeill,
Don

Mr. Wizard. See: Wizard, Mr.

Mr. Wizard, Watch. See: Wizard,
Mr.

MR. WOLPER. See: Sterling,
Vanessa Dale

MR. WRIGHT. See:
Hargrave-Scott, Joan
Malone, Dr. Jerry

Misterogers Neighborhood.   See:
Rogers, Fred

MRS. See:
Abbott, Mr.
Archer, Corliss
Arden, Jane
Brent, Dr. Jim
Brown, Velvet
Buell, Mrs. Harold C.
Burton, Terry
Carter, Mr.
Featherstone, Mrs.
Gilman, Gordon
Grimm, Arnold
Harding, Mrs. Rhoda
Hardy, Andy
Kincaid, Chet
March, Mrs.
Miniver, Mrs.
Morgan, Mrs. Amy
Murgatroyd, Mr.
Nash, Carter
O'Connell, Jody
O'Neill, Mrs.
Parker, Richard
Peck, Torey
Pruitt, Mrs. Phyllis Poindexter
Stephens, Samantha
Stowe, Senator Hays
Wiggs, Mrs.

MRS. ANDERSON. See:
Aldrich, Henry
Day, Dennis
West, Michael

MRS. ANNA NIELSON. See:
Nielson, Torwald

MRS. ARMSTRONG. See: Myrt

MRS. ARNE ANDERS. See: Nielson, Torwald

MRS. ARNOLD. See: Myrt

MRS. BARKER. See: Meek,
Mortimer

MRS. BARNETT. See: Prescott,
Kate Hathaway

MRS. BARRETT. See: Randolph,
Ellen

MRS. BEETHOVEN. See: Morgan,
Henry

MRS. BELLOWS. See: Nelson,
Major Tony

MRS. BIDDLE. See: Baker,
Kenny

MRS. BILLINGSLEY. See: Burns,
George (1)

MRS. BLACK. See: Baines,
Scattergood

MRS. BOONE. See: Bronson,
Millie

MRS. BRAHMS. See: Christopher,
Peter

MRS. BROWN. See:
Aldrich, Henry
Levy, Abie
Naughton, Claudia
Uncle Martin

MRS. BURTON, THE FIRST. See:
Burton, Terry

Mrs. Burton, The Second.   See:
Burton, Terry

MRS. CALABASH. See: Durante,
Jimmy

MRS. CAMERON. See: Winters,
Jack

MRS. CAREY. See: Drake,
Betty

MRS. CARSON. See: O'Neill,
Mrs.

MRS. CARTER COLBY. See:
Larimore, Marilyn

MRS. CARVELL. See: Wayne,
Ruth Evans

MRS. CATHERINE KREITZER.
See: March, Hal

MRS. CHAPMAN. See: Brent,
Dr. Jim

MRS. CHARLOTTE BROWN. See:
Brown, Ellen

MRS. CHEGLEY. See: Baker,
Julia

MRS. CHERNAK. See: Garrison,
Spencer

MRS. COHEN. See: Levy, Abie

MRS. COLLINS. See: O'Neill,
Mrs.

MRS. CRAWFORD. See:
Barrett, Timothy "Spud"
Hooton, Babs

MRS. CUNNINGHAM. See: Rutledge, Dr. John

MRS. CURT BRADLEY. See:
Young, Larry "Pepper"

MRS. DARLING. See: Pan, Peter

MRS. DAVIS. See: Brooks, Connie

MRS. DAWSON. See: Malone, Dr.
Jerry

MRS. DIAMOND. See: Diamond,
Captain

MRS. DRYSDALE. See: Clampett,
Jed

MRS. DUBOIS. See: Noble, Mary

MRS. EDLIN. See: Cooke,
Alistaire (1)

MRS. EMMA PEEL. See: Steed,
John

MRS. EMMETT. See: Marshall,
John

MRS. EVANS. See: Hargrave-
Scott, Joan

MRS. FARNUM. See: Perkins,
Ma

MRS. FEATHERSTONE. See:
Featherstone, Mrs.
O'Malley, Father Chuck

Mrs. Featherstone, The Gay. See:
Featherstone, Mrs.

MRS. FLETCHER. See: Fair-
child, Kay

MRS. FOSTER. See:
Carson, Jack
Foster, Henry

MRS. FRED ALLEN. See: Allen,
Fred

MRS. FRED HOPKINS. See:
Graham, Dr. Bob

Mrs. G. Goes to College. See:
Green, Sarah

MRS. GARVIN. See: Brown,
Ellen

MRS. GEORGE T. PENNYFEATHER.
See: Weems, Ambrose J.

MRS. GIBBS. See: Penny

MRS. GILDER. See: Dyke,
Charity Amanda

MRS. GORDON. See: Bradley,
Judith

MRS. GRAHAM. See: Harding,
Mrs. Rhoda

MRS. GREY. See: Harding,
Karen Adams

MRS. GROSVENOR. See: Dallas,
Stella

MRS. GROVER. See: Spencer,
Jeff

MRS. GURNEY. See: Peepers,
Robinson J.

MRS. HALE. See: Malone, Dr.
Jerry

MRS. HALL. See: Bilko, Sergeant
Ernest

MRS. HANLEY. See: Garrison,
Spencer

MRS. HARPER. See: McGovern,
Dan

MRS. MORRISON. See: Malone,
Dr. Jerry

MRS. MUELLER. See: Levy, Abie

Mrs. Muir, The Ghost and. See:
Muir, Carolyn

MRS. MURCHISON. See: Hillman,
India

MRS. MURGER. See: Kelly, Kitty

MRS. MYRTLE BANFORD. See:
Truesdale, Sally

MRS. NELSON. See: Hardy, Dr.
Steven

Mrs. North, Mr. and. See:
North, Jerry

MRS. OFRA BIKEL. See: Barry,
Jack (1)

MRS. O'REILLY. See: Peterson,
Irma

MRS. OVERTON. See: Brent,
Dr. Jim

MRS. PANGBORN. See: Prescott,
Kate Hathaway

MRS. PANSY NUSSBAUM. See:
Allen, Fred

MRS. PAULSEN. See: Hillman,
India

MRS. PEG RILEY. See: Riley,
Chester A.

MRS. PENDLETON. See: Perkins,
Ma

MRS. PENNY. See: Malone, Dr.
Jerry

MRS. PRINGLE. See: Bracken,
Eddie

MRS. QUIGLEY. See: Dixon,
Bobby

MRS. REMINGTON. See: Peepers,
Robinson J.

MRS. RHINELANDER. See:
Peterson, Irma

MRS. RILEY. See:
Riley, Chester A.
Webster, Martha

MRS. S. KENT WADSWORTH.
See: Solomon, David

MRS. SARAH HEARTBURN. See:
Baker, Phil (2)

MRS. SCHULTZ. See: Larimore,
Marilyn

MRS. SCOTT. See:
Cameron, Christy Allen
Hargrave-Scott, Joan
O'Neill, Mrs.

MRS. SEDGEWICK. See: Sunday

MRS. SHERWOOD. See: Prescott,
Kate Hathaway

MRS. SILO. See: Little Orphan
Annie

MRS. SIMPSON. See: Mac-
Donald, Eleanor

MRS. STANFIELD. See: Bell,
Harry

MRS. STANLEY. See: Davis,
Joan Field

MRS. STOOLER. See: Joe (2)

MRS. SULLIVAN. See: Jackson,
Martha

MRS. SWANSON. See: Sterling,
Vanessa Dale

MRS. TAYLOR. See: Garrison,
Spencer

MRS. TRASK. See: O'Neill, Mrs.

MRS. TREMAINE. See: Grimm,
Arnold

MRS. TRUDY BAILEY. See:
O'Neill, Mrs.

MRS. TURNER. See: O'Neill, Mrs.

MRS. TYRRELL. See: Ames,
Peter

MRS. TYSON. See: Brown, Ellen

MRS. UPPINGTON. See: McGee,
Fibber

MRS. VAN ATWATER. See:
Canova, Judy

MRS. VAN CLEVE. See: Peters,
Bill

MRS. VENTO. See: Sterling,
Vanessa Dale

MRS. WADDINGTON. See:
Nelson, Ozzie

MRS. WARD SMITH. See: Trent,
Helen

MRS. WARNER. See: McKeever,
Cadet Gary

MRS. WARREN. See: Wayne,
Ruth Evans

MRS. WEARYBOTTOM. See:
McGee, Fibber

MRS. WELBY. See: Kelly, Kitty

MRS. WESTON. See: Tate,
Joanne

Mrs. Wiggs of the Cabbage Patch.
See: Wiggs, Mrs.

MRS. WILSON. See:
Baker, Kenny
Haymes, Dick

MRS. WOLFE BENNETT, SR.
See: Bennett, Nita

MRS. WYNN. See: Locke, Dr.
Simon (1)

MRS. ZIFFEL. See: Douglas,
Oliver

MISTY. See: Winslow, Don

MITCH. See:

Guthrie, Mitch
Miller, Mitch

MITCH BROWNING. See: Ames,
Peter

MITCH MILLER. See:
Miller, Mitch
Whiteman, Paul

Mitch, Sing Along With. See:
Miller, Mitch

MITCHELL. See: Nichols

MITCHELL AYRES. See:
Como, Perry (1) (2) (3)
Crosby, Bing (2)
Dunninger, Joseph
La Rosa, Julius

MITCHELL, BUNNY. See:
Marlin, Mary

MITCHELL, DENNIS (Dennis the
Menace), precocious five-year-
old boy
HENRY, his father
ALICE, his mother
GEORGE WILSON (Mr. Wilson),
neighbor of the Mitchell family
MARTHA WILSON, George Wil-
son's wife
JOHN WILSON, George Wilson's
brother
TOMMY
MARGARET
SEYMOUR
JOEY, young friends of Dennis
Mitchell
Dennis the Menace (TV) (Family
situation comedy)

MITCHELL, DR. See: Bauer,
Bertha

MITCHELL, EVERETT, master of
ceremonies on the program (himself)
FOREST RANGER, character on
the program
The National Farm and Home
Hour (R) (Variety)

MITCHELL FARMER. See: Hillman, India

MITCHELL, FRAZIER. See:

Marlin, Mary

MITCHELL, GUY, singer and
entertainer; star of the program
(himself)
MANY GUEST STARS
The Guy Mitchell Show (TV)
(Variety)

MITCHELL, GUY. See also:
Miller, Mitch

MITCHELL, LAWRENCE. See:
Graham, Dr. Bob

MITCHELL, LOLA. See: Wayne,
Ruth Evans

MITCHELL, MRS. See:
Cameron, Barry
O'Neill, Mrs.

MITCHELL, MOOSE. See: Nelson

MITCHELL, SHIRLEY. See:
Kyser, Kay

MITCHELL, STEVE, U.S. espionage
agent
Dangerous Assignment (R) (TV)
(Adventure)

MITCHELL, THOMAS. See: Henry,
O.

MITCHILL, SCOEY. See: Jones,
Dean

MITTLER, FRANK. See: Horwitz,
Hans

MITZI. See: Foster, Judy

MIX, TOM (The Ralston Straight
Shooter), cowboy and owner of the
T-M Bar Ranch in Dobie Township
JIMMY
JANE, his young wards
PECOS WILLIAMS
SHERIFF MIKE SHAW, his friends
WASH, his Negro cook
LEE LOO, Chinese cook
TONY (The Wonder Horse of the
World), his horse
AMOS Q. SNOOD, miserly owner
of the Cozy Rest Hotel
WILLIAM SNOOD, Amos' son
JUDGE PARSONS, jurist

THE OLD WRANGLER, Mix's friend
CALAMITY
CHRIS ACROPOLOUS
BERTIE
FOGHORN
PAT CURTIS
PROFESSOR WALLACE
THE RANCH BOYS, characters
appearing on the program
Tom Mix and His Ralston
Straight Shooters (R) (Western
adventure) (Also known as The
Adventures of Tom Mix) (R)

MIZZNICK, IRMA. See: Meyer

MIZZNICK, MAYOR. See: Meyer

MIZZNICK, MILTON. See: Meyer

MLOR. See: Mac

Mod Squad, The. See: Hayes,
Linc

Model Minstrels. See: Howard,
Tom (2)

Modern Cinderella. See: Carter,
Hope

Modern Romances. See:
Gregory, Helen
Scott, Martha

MODERNAIRES, THE. See:
Crosby, Bob (1) (2)

MODOC, MUGGSY. See: Rogers,
Patricia

MOE PLOTNIK, UNCLE. See:
Fitzgerald, Bridget Theresa Mary
Coleen

MOE SHREVNITZ. See: Cranston,
Lamont

MOFFITT, SERGEANT JACK. See:
Troy, Sergeant Sam

MOGRAM, MRS. See: Kelly,
Kitty

Mohicans, Hawkeye and the Last of
the. See: Hawkeye

MOLASSES AND JANUARY. See:
Henry, Captain

Mollé Mystery Theater, The. See:
  Lenrow, Bernard

MOLLIE. See: Meyer

MOLLY, motion picture actress
  Molly of the Movies (R) (Serial
  drama)

MOLLY. See also:
  Burnett, Carol
  Goldberg, Molly
  McGee, Fibber
  McNeill, Don
  Malone, Dr. Jerry
  Perry, John

MOLLY BEE. See:
  Ford, Tennessee Ernie (4)
  Lee, Pinky (1)

Molly, Fibber McGee and. See:
  McGee, Fibber

MOLLY HEDGEROW, DR. See:
  Jordan, Joyce

Molly of the Movies. See: Molly

MOLLY O'HARA. See: Young,
  Larry "Pepper"

MOLLY TURNER. See: McHale,
  Lieut. Commander Quinton

MOLLY WOOD. See: Virginian,
  The

MOLOCH. See: McKenzie, Captain
  Craig

MOM ARCHER. See: McGarry,
  Dan

Moment, Big. See: Palmer, Bud

MOMMY. See:
  Baby Snooks
  Maimie
  Mammy

MONA. See: McCluskey, Mona

Mona McCluskey. See: McCluskey,
  Mona

MONASTARIO, CAPTAIN. See:
  Vega, Don Diego

MONDAY. See also: Mundy

Monday Jamboree, Blue. See:
  Holloway, Harrison

Monday Night Football, N.F.L.
  See: Jackson, Keith (2)

MONET, DORIS. See: Wayne,
  Ruth Evans

MONEY. See also: Mooney

Money, For Love or. See: Nimmo,
  Bill

Money, More For Your. See:
  Pletcher, Doug

Money, Two For the. See:
  Shriner, Herb (3)

MONICA BREWSTER. See: Hargrave-Scott, Joan

MONICA LEE. See: Horn, Aggie

MONICA WARD SMITH. See:
  Trent, Helen

MONK. See: McKeever, Cadet
  Gary

Monkees, The. See: Jones, Davy

MONKS. See also: Munks

MONKS, JOHN. See: Welles,
  Orson (1)

MONROE. See also: Munro

MONROE, CLAYT
  KATHLEEN MONROE
  BIG TWIN
  LITTLE TWIN
  AMY MONROE, brothers and
  sisters; orphans struggling to
  make a life for themselves in
  Wyoming Territory
  JIM, friendly Indian
  MAJOR MAPOY, land baron
  The Monroes (TV) (Western
  saga)

MONROE, JOHN, cartoonist on
  "The Manhattanite" magazine
  ELLEN, his wife

LYDIA, his 10-year-old daughter
GREELEY, his boss
CHRISTABEL
IRVING, his two dogs
O'MALLEY, bartender
My World and Welcome to It (TV)
(Comedy)

MONROE, KATHARINE. See:
Noble, Mary

MONROE, LUCY. See: Cook, Joe

MONROE, RALPH. See: Douglas,
Oliver

MONROE, TESSIE. See: Rogers,
Patricia

MONROE, VAUGHN, orchestra
leader and singer, featured on
the program (himself)
HIS ORCHESTRA
ZIGGY TALENT, comedian (him-
self)
THE MOON MAIDS, vocal group
MANY GUEST STARS
The Camel Caravan (R) (TV)
(Music/variety)

MONROE, VAUGHN. See also:
Basie, Count
Whiteman, Paul

Monroes, The. See: Monroe,
Clayt

MONSTER. See:
Cookie Monster, The
Milton the Monster
Munster

Monster, Milton the. See: Milton
the Monster

MONSTER, THE FRANKENSTEIN.
See: Munster, Herman

MONT, MICHAEL. See: Forsyte,
Soames

MONTAGUE DARTIE. See:
Forsyte, Soames

MONTAGUE, EDWIN, former
Shakespearian actor
LILY BOHEME MONTAGUE, his
wife

AGNES, maid
The Magnificent Montague (R)
(Situation comedy)

Montague, The Magnificent. See:
Montague, Edwin

MONTE. See also: Monty

MONTE CRISTO, THE COUNT OF,
adventurer
RENE, his friend
The Count of Monte Cristo (R)
(TV) (Adventure)

MONTE DEVOL. See: Armstrong,
Jack

MONTE KAYDEN. See: O'Neill,
Mrs.

MONTGOMERY, ROBERT, actor;
host of the program (himself)
MANY PROMINENT ACTORS
AND ACTRESSES
Robert Montgomery Presents (TV)
(Dramatic presentations) (origin-
ally called Lucky Strike Theater)
(TV)

MONTGOMERY SMITH, BRIGA-
DIER GENERAL. See: Welles,
Orson (3)

MONTY. See:
Hall, Monty (1) (2) (3)
Monte
Nash, Monty

MONTY HALL. See:
Hall, Monty (1) (2) (3)
Reiner, Carl

Monty Nash. See: Nash, Monty

MOOCHIE. See: Dodd, Jimmie

MOODY, TITUS. See: Allen, Fred

MOOKERJI, DR. MOTILAL. See:
Coffee, Dr. Daniel

Moon, Follow the. See: Bannister, Clay

MOON MAIDS, THE. See:
Monroe, Vaughn

Moon River. See: Jostyn, Jay (1)

MOONEY. See also: Money

MOONEY, ART. See:
Basie, Count
Whiteman, Paul

MOONEY, THEODORE. See:
Carmichael, Lucy

Moonshine and Honeysuckle. See:
Gaddis, Cracker

MOORE, BETTY, decorating expert
Betty Moore (R) (Home decorating)

MOORE, COLLEEN. See: Story
Lady, The

MOORE, DARRELL. See: Myrt

MOORE, DINTY. See: Jiggs

MOORE, GARRY (1), featured on
the program (himself)
BILL SHORT
DURWARD KIRBY
RANSOM SHERMAN
JOHNNY JOHNSTON
PHIL SHUKIN
EVELYN LYNNE, vocalists fea-
tured on the program (themselves)
THE THREE ROMEOS, vocal
group
MANY GUEST STARS
REX MAUPIN, orchestra leader
(himself)
HIS ORCHESTRA
Club Matinee (R) (Variety)

MOORE, GARRY (2) (Garry Morfit),
host of the program (himself)
MANY YOUNG DANCE ORCHES-
TRA LEADERS
THEIR ORCHESTRAS
The Fitch Bandwagon (R) (Popular
music)

MOORE, GARRY (3), entertainer;
host of the program (himself)
CAROL BURNETT
MARION LORNE
DURWARD KIRBY
ALLEN FUNT, entertainers appear-
ing on the program (themselves)
MANY GUEST STARS
The Garry Moore Show (TV)

(Comedy/variety)

MOORE, GARRY (4)
STEVE ALLEN, moderators of
the program (themselves)
CHESTER MORRIS
HENRY MORGAN
KITTY CARLISLE
BETSY PALMER
BESS MYERSON
BILL CULLEN
JAYNE MEADOWS
FAYE EMERSON
OTHERS, panelists on the pro-
gram (themselves)
MANY GUEST CONTESTANTS
I've Got a Secret (TV) (Panel
quiz game)

MOORE, GARRY (5)
CLAYTON "BUD" COLLYER
BILL CULLEN
WALLY BRUNER, moderators of
the program (themselves)
KITTY CARLISLE
PEGGY CASS
DURWARD KIRBY
TOM POSTON
ORSON BEAN
POLLY BERGEN
RALPH BELLAMY
HY GARDNER, panelists
OTHER GUEST PANELISTS
(themselves)
TRIO OF PERSONS ONE OF
WHOM IS TELLING THE TRUTH
To Tell the Truth (TV) (Panel
quiz) (also known as Nothing But
the Truth) (TV)

MOORE, GARRY. See also:
Baker, Phil (3)
Durante, Jimmy

MOORE, GRACE. See: Bell,
Alexander Graham

MOORE, MARIAN. See: Grimm,
Arnold

MOORE, MELBA
CLIFTON DAVIS, singers and
entertainers; co-stars of the
program (themselves)
TIMMIE RODGERS
RON CAREY
DICK LIBERTINI
LIZ TORRES, entertainers

on the program (themselves)
MANY GUEST STARS
CHARLES COLEMAN, orchestra
leader (himself)
HIS ORCHESTRA
The Melba Moore-Clifton Davis
Show (TV) (Variety)

MOORE, NICOLETTE. See: Barbour, Henry Wilson

MOORE, STELLA. See: Rogers,
Patricia

MOORE, TOM (1)
JOHNNY OLSEN
PENNY OLSEN, moderators of
the program (themselves)
MANY AUDIENCE PARTICIPANTS
Ladies Be Seated (R) (Audience
participation)

MOORE, TOM (2), master of ceremonies of the program (himself)
MANY AUDIENCE PARTICIPANTS
Ladies Fair (R) (Audience participation)

MOOREHEAD, AGNES. See:
Frees, Paul
Welles, Orson (1) (2)

MOOREHEAD, BILLY. See:
Hackett, Doc

MOOSE MITCHELL. See: Nelson

MOOSIE DRIER. See: Rowan, Dan

MORAN AND MACK. See:
Drew, John
Two Black Crows, The (1) (2)

MORAN, BOBBY. See: Carter,
Kathryn

MORAN, DOROTHY. See: Carter,
Kathryn

MORAN, EILEEN. See: Carter,
Kathryn

MORAN, GEORGE. See: Two
Black Crows, The (1) (2)

MORAN, LUCY. See: Carter,
Kathryn

MORAN, MA. See: Jones, Tom
(1)

MORAN, MOTHER. See: Carter,
Kathryn

MORAN, PATTY. See: Carter,
Kathryn

MORAN, TERRY. See: Carter,
Kathryn

MORATH. See also: Porath

MORATH, MAX, pianist and lecturer on jazz/folk music (himself)
The Ragtime Era (TV) (Educa-
tion/music)

MORDENTE DANCERS, THE TONY.
See: Bono, Salvatore

More For Your Money. See:
Pletcher, Doug

MORENO, RITA. See: Cosby,
Bill (1)

MOREY. See also: Morley

MOREY AMSTERDAM. See:
Amsterdam, Morey
Lester, Jerry
Reiner, Carl

MORFIT, GARRY. See: Moore,
Garry (2)

MORGAN, CLAY. See: Pearson,
Jace

MORGAN, DR. DAVID. See:
Jordan, Joyce

MORGAN, EDWARD P. See:
Shadel, Bill

MORGAN, ERIC. See: Karr,
Mike

MORGAN, FRANK (1), comedian;
star of the program (himself)
ERIC BLORE
CASS DALEY
ROBERT YOUNG, comedians
and actors, featured on the program (themselves)

OTHER GUEST STARS
CARLOS RAMIREZ, featured
vocalist (himself)
ALBERT SACK, orchestra leader
(himself)
HIS ORCHESTRA
The Frank Morgan Show (R)
(Variety)

MORGAN, FRANK (2), comedian,
star of the program (himself)
HIS NIECE
THE SINGING M. C.
BABY SNOOKS, precocious young
child
DADDY HIGGINS, Snooks' father
MEREDITH WILLSON, orchestra
leader (himself)
HIS ORCHESTRA
Maxwell House Coffee Time (R)
(Comedy/variety)

MORGAN FREEMAN. See: Cosby,
Bill (1)

MORGAN, HENRY, comedian, star
of the program (himself)
GERARD
HORTENSE
THE ATHLETE
MRS. BEETHOVEN
GERTRUDE
DAPHNE, characters appearing on
the program
BETTY GARDE
DURWARD KIRBY
MINERVA PIOUS
MAURICE GOSFIELD, actors
and actresses appearing on the
program (themselves)
BERNIE GREEN, orchestra leader
(himself)
HIS ORCHESTRA
The Henry Morgan Show (R)
(Comedy)

MORGAN, HENRY. See also:
Moore, Garry (4)

MORGAN, JAYE P., singer; star
of the program (herself)
CHARLIE
BOB
DICK
DUKE, her brothers; singers
(themselves)
The Jaye P. Morgan Show (TV)
(Popular music)

MORGAN, LIEUT. ANNE, WAVE
officer
LOVE
McGUIRE
KOWALSKI, WAVES, assigned to
Pacific island
COMMANDER ADRIAN, com-
manding officer
LIEUT. MAXWELL TROTTER,
naval officer
MARION BOTNIK, "a male
WAVE by clerical error"
Broadside (TV) (Comedy)

MORGAN, MAJOR, espionage agent
Secret File, U. S. A. (TV)
(Drama)

Morgan Manner, Music in the.
See: Morgan, Russ

MORGAN, MARSHAL, law enforcement officer
U. S. Marshal (TV) (Western)

MORGAN, MRS. AMY, widow
KATHY, her daughter
DENNY
STEVE
EARL, her friends
It's a Great Life (TV) (Comedy)

MORGAN, PAUL, creator of comic
strip called "Bachelor at Large"
PETER FAIRFIELD III, his play-
boy buddy
JOHN LARSEN, proprietor of
Comics, Inc.
The Tab Hunter Show (TV)
(Comedy)

Morgan, Russ. See: Morgan, Russ

MORGAN, RUSS, orchestra leader,
host of the program (himself)
HIS ORCHESTRA
HELEN O'CONNELL, featured
vocalist
MANY GUEST STARS
Russ Morgan (TV) (Music) (also
known as Music in the Morgan
Manner) (TV)

MORGAN, RUSS. See also: Whiteman, Paul

MORGAN, SHERIFF, law enforcement
officer

The Sheriff of Cochise (TV) (Contemporary Western)

MORGAN, TESS. See: Noble,
Mary

MORGENSTERN, RHODA. See:
Richards, Mary

MORIARTY, PROFESSOR. See:
Holmes, Sherlock

MORLEY. See also: Morey

MORLEY, CLINT. See: Manning,
Portia Blake

MORLEY, DANNY. See: Holstrum,
Katy

MORLEY, GLEN. See: Holstrum,
Katy

MORLEY, MRS. See: Holstrum,
Katy

MORLEY SAFER. See: Wallace,
Mike (4)

MORLEY, STEVE. See: Holstrum,
Katy

MORLEY, TOM. See: Drake, Nora

MORLEY, VIRGINIA. See: Waring,
Fred (1)

Morning News, The C.B.S. See:
Benti, Joseph

Morning Show, The. See: Bruner,
Wally (1)

MORNING STAR. See: Brave Eagle

Morning, This. See: Cavett, Dick
(3)

MORRIS, CHESTER. See: Moore,
Garry (4)

MORRIS, HOWARD. See:
Caesar, Sid (2) (3)
Stokey, Mike

MORRIS LEVY. See: O'Neill,
Mrs.

MORRIS, McKAY. See: Arthur,
Jack (2)

MORRISON, BRET, host and nar-
rator of the program (himself)
JIM BOLES, featured on the pro-
gram (himself)
MANY OTHER ACTORS AND
ACTRESSES
Best Seller (R) (Drama)

MORRISON, DR. JOHN. See:
Davis, Dr. Althea

MORRISON, JESSICA. See:
Davis, Dr. Althea

MORRISON, JOANNA. See:
Ames, Peter

MORRISON, MRS. See: Malone,
Dr. Jerry

MORRISON, MOTHER
ANNE
HELEN
JOHN
PETE
PAUL STRONG
POP WHITEHOUSE, characters
appearing in the drama
Mother o' Mine (R) (Serial
drama)

MORRISON, PAUL. See: Har-
grave-Scott, Joan

MORROW. See also: Murrow

MORROW, BUDDY. See: Rodgers,
Jimmie

MORROW, DON, moderator of the
program (himself)
MANY CONTESTANTS
Camouflage (TV) (Game)

MORROW, KAREN. See: Nabors,
Jim

MORROW, RUTH. See: Falvey,
Hal

MORSE, PROFESSOR. See:
Welles, Orson (3)

MORT LINDSEY. See:

Griffin, Merv (1)
Hirt, Al (1) (2)

MORT TOOPS. See: McGee,
Fibber

MORTICIA. See: Addams, Gomez

MORTIMER. See:
Gooch, Mortimer
Meek, Mortimer

Mortimer Gooch. See: Gooch,
Mortimer

MORTIMER, MR. See: Perkins,
Ma

MORTIMER SNERD. See:
Ameche, Don (1)
Bergen, Edgar (1) (2)

MORTON. See:
Martin
Nelson, Admiral Harriman
Norton

MORTON BLAIR. See: Brent,
Dr. Jim

MORTON, BLANCHE. See: Burns,
George (1)

MORTON, CAPTAIN. See:
Roberts, Doug

MORTON CHEGLEY, DR. See:
Baker, Julia

MORTON, DR. CLAIRE. See:
Peyton, Martin

MORTON, HARRY. See: Burns,
George (1)

MORTY. See also: Marty

MORTY HOWARD. See: Moylan,
Marianne

MOSBY, MAJOR JOHN, Civil War
officer, leader of Mosby's Rangers; called the "Gray Ghost"
The Gray Ghost (TV) (Adventure)

MOSS, ARNOLD. See: Arthur,
Jack (2)

Most Deadly Game, The. See:
Croft, Jonathan

MOTHER
DAD, family couple
Mother and Dad (R) (Comedy
dialogue)

MOTHER. See also:
Anderson, Jim
Davis, Red
Dawson, Rosemary
Day, Clarence
Fairchild, Kay
Gibson, Dot
Gunn, Peter
Horton, Dot
Malone, Dr. Jerry
Morrison, Mother
Moynihan, Mother
Steed, John
Uncle Walter

MOTHER ALDRIDGE. See:
Horton, Dot

Mother and Dad. See: Mother

MOTHER BUTCHER. See: Ballew,
Wally

MOTHER DAVIS (ANNE DAVIS).
See: Davis, Joan Field

MOTHER, DENNIS DAY'S. See:
Benny, Jack

MOTHER FIELD. See: Davis,
Joan Field

MOTHER, HARRIET'S. See: Nelson, Ozzie

Mother-in-Law, How's Your? See:
Martindale, Wink (2)

MOTHER-IN-LAW, THE. See:
Curtis, Brenda

Mother, Manhattan. See: Locke,
Patricia

MOTHER MORAN. See: Carter,
Kathryn

Mother o' Mine. See: Morrison,
Mother

MOTHER, REVEREND. See:
Bertrille, Sr.

MOTHER RUSTIC. See: Kovacs,
Ernie (1)

Mother the Car, My. See: Crabtree, Dave

MOTHER, THE GHETTO. See:
Rowan, Dan

Mother's Day. See: Van Dyke,
Dick (2)

Mothers-in-Law, The. See: Buell,
Roger

MOTHERS, THREE. See: Van
Dyke, Dick (2)

MOTILAL MOOKERJI, DR. See:
Coffee, Dr. Daniel

MOULAN, FRANK. See: Roxy

MOUNDS, MEL. See: Cosby,
Bill (1)

Mounted, Renfrew of the. See:
Renfrew, Inspector Douglas

Mountie, Silver Eagle. See: West,
Jim (1)

MOUSE. See: Mighty Mouse

MOUSE, EEEEK A. See: Pam

MOUSE, EL SQUEEKO. See:
Russell, Todd

Mouse, McGarry and His. See:
McGarry, Dan

MOUSE, MICKEY
DONALD DUCK
MINNIE MOUSE
GOOFY
CLARA, cartoon characters
created by Walt Disney
The Mickey Mouse Theater of the
Air (R) (Children's program)

Mouse, Mighty. See: Mighty Mouse

MOUSE, MINNIE. See: Mouse,
Mickey

MOUSE, THE. See: McGarry, Dan

MOUSIE. See: Madison, Kenny

Mousketeers, The. See: Dodd,
Jimmie

Movie Game, The. See: Fox,
Sonny

Movie, Rona Barrett's Hollywood.
See: Barrett, Rona

Movies, Molly of the. See: Molly

Movies, The New Scooby Doo.
See: Scooby Doo

MOYERS, BILL, host of the pro-
gram (himself)
MANY INTERVIEWEES
This Week (TV) (News feature)

MOYLAN, MARIANNE
PEGGY JOAN MOYLAN, singers,
featured on the program (themselves)
MORTY HOWARD, pianist, their
accompanist (himself)
The Moylan Sisters (R) (Music)

Moylan Sisters, The. See: Moylan, Marianne

MOYNIHAN, MOTHER, proprietress
of boarding house
EILEEN, her own daughter
KAY, orphan, her adopted daughter
Painted Dreams (R) (Serial
drama)

MOZART. See: Wilson, Steve

MR. Items so prefixed are indexed
as though spelled "Mister"

MRS. Items so prefixed are indexed as though spelled "Mistress"

MUDD, ICHABOD "ICHY." See:
Midnight, Captain

MUDGE, ELLEN. See: Glass,
Bessie

MUELLER, DR. See: Levy,
Abie

MUELLER, MRS. See: Levy,
Abie

MUGG MELLISH. See: Ballew,
Wally

MUGGINS, CLARENCE J. See:
Jones, Lorenzo

MUGGS. See: Downs, Hugh

MUGGSY, ghost of Revolutionary
War soldier
BOO, his cat, also a ghost
AUGIE
SKIP
APRIL, his live friends
ELMO, live bulldog (all cartoon
characters)
The Funky Phantom (TV) (Car-
toon)

MUGGSY MODOC. See: Rogers,
Patricia

MUIR, CAROLYN, youthful widow,
lives in Gull Cottage
MARTHA
CANDY, her daughters
UNCLE ARNOLD, her uncle
CAPTAIN GREGG (The Ghost),
ghost of sea captain
CLAYMORE GREGG, Captain
Gregg's nephew, Mrs. Muir's
landlord
The Ghost and Mrs. Muir (TV)
(Comedy)

MULCAHY, FATHER JOHN P.
See: Pierce, Captain Hawkeye

MULDOON, DETECTIVE LIEUT.
DAN. See: Parker, Lieut. Mike

MULDOON, FRANCIS
GUNTHER TOODY, prowl car
policemen
CAPTAIN BLOCK
SERGEANT SOL ABRAMS, police
officers
SCHNAUZER
O'HARA
NICHOLSON
RODRIGUEZ, police patrolmen
Car 54, Where Are You? (TV)
(Comedy)

MULHOLLAND, FLORENCE.

See: Roxy

MULHOLLAND, JOE. See: Ames,
Peter

MULLIGAN. See:
Dickens, Harry
Milligan

MULLIGAN, GERRY. See: O'Connor, Father Norman

Mulligan, Hey! See: Mulligan,
Mickey

MULLIGAN, MICKEY, messenger
boy
FREDDIE, his friend
BOBO, his girl friend
Hey, Mulligan! (TV) (Comedy)
(Also known as Mickey Rooney)
(TV)

MULLIGAN, SOCRATES. See:
Allen, Fred

MULLIN, MARK. See: Kelly,
Joe (2)

MULLINS, SERGEANT. See:
North, Jerry

MULVANEY, GLORIA. See:
Cameron, Barry

MULVANEY, PATRICK. See:
Joe (1)

MUMBLE. See: Medbury, John P.

MUMSY PIG. See: Conductor,
The

MUNCHAUSEN, BARON, teller of
tall tales
SHARLIE, his friend, challenges
the truth of his tales
The Jack Pearl Show (R) (Comedy)

MUNDY. See also: Monday

MUNDY, ALEXANDER, "respect-
able cat burglar," works for
S. I. A.
ALISTER, his father, master
thief
NOAH BAIN, S. I. A. chief, his
superior

It Takes a Thief (TV) (Crime
drama)

MUNKS. See also: Monks

MUNKS, HOPE WAYNE. See:
Brown, Ellen

MUNN, ED. See: Dallas, Stella

MUNN, FRANK (1)
JEAN DICKENSON
ELIZABETH LENNOX
VIVIEN DELLA CHIESA, featured
vocalists on the program (them-
selves)
GUSTAVE HAENSCHEN, orchestra
leader (himself)
HIS CONCERT ORCHESTRA
The American Album of Familiar
Music (R) (Music)

MUNN, FRANK (2), tenor, featured
on the program (himself)
THE MANHATTAN CHORUS, vocal
group
ABE LYMAN, orchestra leader
(himself)
HIS ORCHESTRA
Waltz Time (R) (Music)

MUNRO. See also: Monroe

MUNRO, GORDON, head of the
family
MARGARET, his wife
The Munros (R) (Family dialogue)

Munros, The. See: Munro, Gordon

MUNSEL, PATRICE, hostess of the
program (herself)
MANY GUEST STARS
The Patrice Munsel Show (TV)
(Music/variety)

MUNSEL, PATRICE. See also:
Barlow, Howard

MUNSON, DAD. See: Harding,
Karen Adams

MUNSON, DR. RALPH. See:
Malone, Dr. Jerry

MUNSON, LINDA. See: Harding,
Karen Adams

MUNSON, MR. See: Harding,
Karen Adams

MUNSTER. See also: Monster

MUNSTER, HERMAN, head of the
family, resembles the Franken-
stein Monster as played by Boris
Karloff
LILY, his wife
EDDIE, their six-year-old son
MARILYN, niece of Herman
Munster
GRANDPA, vampire
SPOT, pet monster belonging
to the family
The Munsters (TV) (Family situ-
ation comedy/horror drama
satire)

Munsters, The. See: Munster,
Herman

MURCHISON, MR. See: Hillman,
India

MURCHISON, MRS. See: Hillman,
India

Murder and Mr. Malone. See:
Malone, Mr.

Murder Is My Hobby. See: Drake,
Barton

Murder Will Out. See: Gargan,
William (2)

MURDOCH. See: Lancer, Murdoch

MURDOCH, CHASE. See: Hardy,
Dr. Steven

MURDOCK, BUZ
TOD STILES
LINC CASE, adventurers
"wandering about the United States
seeking activity and romance"
Route 66 (TV) (Adventure)

MURGATROYD, MR., husband
MRS. MURGATROYD, his wife
The Don Ameche Show (R)
(Comedy skits)

MURGER, MRS. See: Kelly,
Kitty

MURIEL. See: Burns, George (1)

MURPHY, DEAN, master of cere-
monies of the program (himself)
CHARLOTTE MANSON, featured
vocalist (herself)
TED STEELE, orchestra leader
(himself)
HIS ORCHESTRA
MANY CONTESTANTS
M.G.M. Screen Test (R) (Talent
show)

MURPHY, GEORGE, quizmaster of
the program (himself)
MANY CONTESTANTS
Hollywood Calling (R) (Quiz)

MURPHY, GEORGE. See also:
Crosby, Bing (3)

MURPHY, MR. See: Ames, Peter

MURPHY, NANCY. See: Rhodes,
Dr. Michael

MURPHY, PAT. See: Stewart, Jan

MURPHY, PATRICK JOSEPH.
See: Levy, Abie

MURPHY, PETER, American
espionage agent; assumes the
identity of deceased look-alike
wealthy playboy Mark Wainwright
EVA WAINWRIGHT, Mark's widow
ROGER WAINWRIGHT, Mark's
ambitious half brother
JACK FORBES, intelligence chief
The Man Who Never Was (TV)
(Espionage drama)

MURRAY. See:
McLean, Murray
Murry
Ungar, Felix

MURRAY, AL. See: MacLennon,
Jeannie

MURRAY, ARTHUR, dance instructor
and host of the program (himself)
CARL OXFORD, featured vocalist
(himself)
Lilac Time (R) (Dance instruction)

MURRAY, ARTHUR. See also:
Murray, Kathryn

MURRAY, BILL. See: Barton, Bud

MURRAY, FEG, newspaper cartoonist; star of the program
(himself)
HARRIET HILLIARD, vocalist
OZZIE NELSON, orchestra
leader (themselves)
HIS ORCHESTRA
The Feg Murray Show (R) (Hollywood gossip)

MURRAY, GANN. See: Sunday

MURRAY, JAN (1), quizmaster of
the program
PAT WHITE, hostess of the
program
BERNARD MARTIN, "stunt man"
(themselves)
MANY CONTESTANTS
Dollar a Second (TV) (Quiz)

MURRAY, JAN (2), host of the
program; moderator of game
called "Charge Account"
MANY CONTESTANTS
The Jan Murray Show (TV)
(Game)

MURRAY, JAN (3), master of
ceremonies of the program (him-
self)
AMATEUR SONG WRITERS
PROFESSIONAL MUSICIANS
Songs For Sale (R) (Music)

MURRAY, JAN (4), quizmaster of
the program (himself)
MANY CONTESTANTS
Treasure Hunt (TV) (Quiz)

MURRAY, JOHN. See:
Carter, Kathryn
Larimore, Marilyn

MURRAY, KATHRYN, hostess of
the program (herself)
ARTHUR MURRAY, her husband,
dance instructor (himself)
MANY CELEBRITY GUESTS,
dance contestants
DANCE INSTRUCTORS FROM
THE MURRAY STUDIOS
RAY CARTER, orchestra leader
(himself)
HIS ORCHESTRA
The Arthur Murray Party (TV)
(Ballroom dancing/contest)

MURRAY, KEL. See: Cugat,
Xavier (1)

MURRAY, KEN (1), entertainer;
host of the program (himself)
VARIOUS GUEST PERSONALITIES
Where Were You? (TV) (Game)

MURRAY, KEN (2), entertainer;
star of the program (himself)
The Ken Murray Program (R)
(Comedy)

MURRAY, KEN (3), entertainer;
host of the program (himself)
LAURIE ANDERS, cowgirl, his
assistant (herself)
MANY GUEST STARS
The Ken Murray Show (TV)
(Variety/extravaganza)

MURRAY, KEN (4), quizmaster of
the program (himself)
MANY CONTESTANTS
Which Is Which? (R) (Quiz)

MURRAY, LIZ. See: MacLennon,
Jeannie

MURRAY, LYN. See:
Baker, Phil (1)
Hilton, James
Ives, Burl (2)
Kaye, Danny

MURRAY SINGERS, THE LYN.
See: Ross, Lanny

MURRAY SLAUGHTER. See:
Richards, Mary

MURROW. See also: Morrow

MURROW, EDWARD R. (1), news-
caster, moderator of the pro-
gram (himself)
MANY INTERVIEWEES
America's Town Meeting (TV)
(Discussion)

MURROW, EDWARD R. (2), newscaster (himself)
Hear It Now (R) (News commentary)

MURROW, EDWARD R. (3), newscaster; interviewer on the program (himself)

MANY INTERVIEWEES
Person to Person (TV) (Interviews)

MURROW, EDWARD R. (4)
CHARLES COLLINGWOOD, news-
casters; interviewers of the pro-
gram (themselves)
MANY PROMINENT INTER-
VIEWEES
See It Now (TV) (Interviews)

MURROW, EDWARD R. (5)
FRED W. FRIENDLY, news-
casters; interviewers on the pro-
gram (themselves)
MANY PROMINENT INTER-
VIEWEES
Small World (TV) (Interviews)

MURRY. See also: Murray

MURRY, MICHAEL. See: Chandler, Faith

MUSH MAN, THE BRICK. See:
Gook, Vic

MUSHMOUTH. See: Cosby, Bill
(3)

MUSHY. See: Favor, Gil

Music Appreciation Hour, The.
See: Damrosch, Walter

Music Box, Bob Ralston's. See:
Ralston, Bob

Music, Dial M for. See: O'Connor, Father Norman

Music '55. See: Kenton, Stan

Music From the House of Squibb.
See: Ives, Burl (2)

Music, Gateway to. See: Herrmann, Bernard

Music Hall. See: O'Connor, Des

Music Hall, The Kraft. See:
Como, Perry (2)
Crosby, Bing (3)

Music in the Morgan Manner.
See: Morgan, Russ

MUSIC MAIDS AND HAL, THE.
See: Crosby, Bing (3)

MUSIC MAIDS, THE. See:
Powell, Dick (1)

Music, Make Your Own Kind of.
See: Hirt, Al (2)

Music on Ice. See: Desmond,
Johnny

Music Scene, The. See: Steinberg, David (2)

Music Shop. See: Bregman,
Buddy

Music Society of Lower Basin
Street, The Chamber. See:
Cross, Milton (1)

Music, Stop the. See: Parks,
Bert (6)

Music, That Good Ole Nashville.
See: Ritter, Tex (2)

Music, The American Album of
Familiar. See: Munn, Frank
(1)

Music, This Is Your. See: Palmer,
Byron

Music, Words and. See: Hays,
Harvey

Musical Comedy Hour, The. See:
Vivian

Musical Knowledge, The College of.
See:
Ford, Tennessee Ernie (1)
Kay Kyser's Kollege of Musical
Knowledge

Musical Steelmakers, The. See:
Wincholl, John

MUSKIE. See: Dawg, Deputy

MUSSOLINI, BENITO. See:
Husing, Ted

MUSTIN, BURT. See: Kelly,
Gene

MUTTER. See: Medbury, John P.

My Best Girls. See: Bartlett,
Jill

My Boy, That's. See: Jackson,
Jarrin' Jack

My Favorite Husband. See:
Cooper, Liz

My Favorite Martian. See: Uncle
Martin

My Friend Flicka. See: Mc-
Laughlin, Ken

My Friend Irma. See: Peterson,
Irma.

My Friend Tony. See: Woodruff,
Professor

My Good Wife. See: Francis,
Arlene (3)

My Hero. See: Beanblossom,
Robert S.

My Little Margie. See: Albright,
Margie

My Living Doll. See: McDonald,
Bob

My Mother the Car. See: Crabtree, Dave

My Sister Eileen. See: Sherwood,
Ruth

My Son and I. See: Vance,
Connie

My Three Sons. See: Douglas,
Steve

My True Story. See: Riggs,
Glenn

My World and Welcome to It.
See: Monroe, John

MYERSON, BESS
ARLENE FRANCIS
DAVE GARROWAY
DOUGLAS EDWARDS
MARILYN VAN DERBUR

OTHERS, hosts of the program
(themselves)
Macy's Annual Thanksgiving Day
Parade (TV) (Parade narration/
description)

MYERSON, BESS. See also:
James, Dennis (3)
Moore, Garry (4)
Paige, Bob

MYLES. See also:
Miles
Mills

MYLES KEOGH, CAPTAIN. See:
Custer, George Armstrong

MYRA GORDON. See: Hargrave-
Scott, Joan

MYRA LAKE. See: Ames, Peter

MYRA LEE. See: Jordan, Joyce

MYRA SHERWOOD. See: Welby,
Dr. Marcus

MYRA WALKER. See: Harding,
Karen Adams

MYRNA FAHEY. See: Peyton,
Martin

MYRNA GIBBONS. See: Martin,
Doris

MYRON. See: McCormick, Myron

MYRON FLOREN. See: Welk,
Lawrence

MYRON HENDERSON, DR. See:
Solomon, David

MYRT, actress; "a hard-boiled
trouper"
MARGE, her sister, new to the
acting profession
EDNA SEYMOUR
JACK ARNOLD
MR. and MRS. ARNOLD
BILLIE DE VERE
BRELLERTON WHITE
LIZZIE LUMP
PAULA KIRBY
BILL BOYLE
LEE KIRBY

DARRELL MOORE
REX MARVIN
BIDDY
CLARENCE TIFFINGTUFFER
JIMMY MINTER
JIMMIE KENT
THADDEUS CORNFELDER
AGATHA FOLSOM
JIM BARNETT
PAUL HARGATE
MAX WOODARD
FRANCIS HAYFIELD
ANTHONY LINK
PETE VANESSI
SANFORD MALONE
MRS. ARMSTRONG
POP NUNALLY
BARNEY BELZER
TAD SMITH
PHYLLIS ROGERS
DR. BURR, physician
LEOTA LAWRENCE
MIDGIE
BRAD
MAGGIE
HELMI
CHRIS
RANDY GREENSPRING, char-
acters appearing in the drama
Myrt and Marge (R) (Serial
drama)

MYRT. See also: Mert

Myrt and Marge. See: Myrt

MYRTLE BANFORD, MRS. See:
Truesdale, Sally

Mysteries, Dr. Kenrad's Unsolved.
See: Kenrad, Dr.

Mysteries, Inner Sanctum. See:
Raymond

Mysteries, The Dow Hour of Great.
See: Welch, Joseph N.

Mysteries, True Detective. See:
Shuttleworth, John

Mysterious Traveler, The. See:
Mysterious Traveler, The

MYSTERIOUS TRAVELER, THE,
adventurer
The Mysterious Traveler (R)
(Adventure)

MYSTERY GUEST. See: Daly,
    John (3)

Mystery, I Love a. See: Packard,
    Jack

Mystery in the Air. See: Lorre,
    Peter

Mystery Man, The. See: Jostyn,
    Jay (2)

MYSTERY MAN, THE. See:
    Elliott, Roger

Mystery Show. See: Slezak,
    Walter

Mystery, The House of. See:
    Elliott, Roger

Mystery Theater. See: Lenrow,
    Bernard

Mystery Theater, The George
    Sanders. See: Sanders, George

Mystery Theater, The Mollé. See:
    Lenro, Bernard

Mystic, Omar the. See: Omar

N. B. C. Adventure Theater. See:
Hope, Bob (3)
McMahon, Ed (1)

N. B. C. Evening News, The. See:
Chancellor, John

N. B. C. News. See: Kalber,
Floyd

N. F. L. Monday Night Football.
See: Jackson, Keith (2)

N. T. G. and His Girls. See:
Granlund, Nils Thor

N. Y. P. D. See: Haines, Lieut.
Mike

NABORS. See also: Neighbors

NABORS, JIM, actor and singer,
star of the program (himself)
FRANK SUTTON
KAREN MORROW
RONNIE SCHELL, entertainers
appearing on the program (them-
selves)
THE NABORS KIDS, singing group
MANY GUEST STARS
PAUL WESTON, orchestra leader
(himself)
HIS ORCHESTRA
The Jim Nabors Hour (TV)
(Variety)

NABORS, JIM. See also: Cookie
Monster, The

NAD. See: Og

NADINE. See: Randolph, Ellen

NADINE CONNOR. See:
Henry, Captain
Jolson, Al

NADLER, TEDDY. See:
March, Hal
Story, Ralph

NAGEL, CONRAD, actor; host of
the program (himself)
MANY ACTORS AND ACTRESSES
Silver Theater (R) (Drama)

NAGURSKI. See: Butcher, Major
Simon

NAGY, PRIVATE. See: Bilko,
Sergeant Ernest

Naked City. See: Parker, Lieut.
Mike

Name Droppers. See: Lohman,
Al

Name of That Song, What's the?
See: Williamson, Dud

Name of the Game, The. See:
Howard, Glenn

Name That Tune. See: DeWitt,
George

Name, What's My? See: Hulick,
Wilbur Budd

Name's the Same, The. See:
James, Dennis (3)

NAN. See:
McGovern, Dan
Prescott, Kate Hathaway

NAN RAE. See: Cantor, Eddie
(2)

NAN WYNN. See: Kemp, Hal

NANA. See:
Nani
Nanny
Pan, Peter

NANCIE PHILLIPS. See: Rowan,
Dan

Nancy. See: Hudson, Nancy
Smith

NANCY. See:
Ames, Nancy
Ames, Peter
Booth, Martha
Brent, Portia
Brewster, Joey
Chandler, Dr. Susan
Connors, Nancy
Dodd, Jimmie
Hudson, Nancy Smith
Hughes, Chris
James, Nancy
Karr, Mike
McGovern, Dan

Parker, Richard
Peepers, Robinson J.
Randolph, Walt
Trent, Helen
Ungar, Felix
Waring, Mike
Webster, Nancy

NANCY COLEMAN. See: Arthur, Jack (2)

NANCY DONOVAN. See: Davidson, Bill

NANCY GRANGER. See: Trent, Helen

Nancy James, Her Honor. See: James, Nancy

NANCY MURPHY. See: Rhodes, Dr. Michael

NANCY, OLD. See: Cole, Alonzo Dean

NANCY STEWART. See: Rutledge, Dr. John

NANCY WRIGHT. See: James, Dennis (1)

NANETTE FABRAY. See: Caesar, Sid (2)
Marshall, Peter

Nanette, Yes, Yes. See: McGovern, Dan

NANI. See also:
Nana
Nanny

NANI DARNELL. See: Wilson, Mark

NANNY. See:
Cameron, Christy Allen
Everett, Professor
Nana
Nani

Nanny and the Professor. See: Everett, Professor

NAOMI. See: Carter, Kathryn

NAOMI COOKS. See: Kelly, Joe (2)

NAPOLEON. See: Solo, Napoleon

NAPOLEON OF CRIME, THE. See: Holmes, Sherlock

NAPOLEON, PHIL. See: Whiteman, Paul

NARDA. See: Mandrake

NARŻ, JACK (1)
CLAYTON "BUD" COLLYER
ROXANNE, moderators of the program (themselves)
GUEST STARS
AUDIENCE PARTICIPANTS
Beat the Clock (TV) (Game)

NARZ, JACK (2), quizmaster of the program (himself)
HANK BLOOMGARDEN
SERGEANT FRANK BURKE
EDWARD HILGEMEIER, JR.
Y. KIMBALL
MICHAEL PORATH, contestants on the program (themselves)
MANY OTHER CONTESTANTS
Dotto (TV) (Quiz)

NARZ, JACK (3), moderator of the program (himself)
MANY CONTESTANTS
I'll Bet (TV) (Game)

NARZ, JACK (4), host of the program (himself)
MANY CONTESTANTS
Seven Keys (TV) (Game)

NARZ, JACK (5), quizmaster of the program (himself)
MANY CONTESTANTS
Video Village (TV) (Quiz)

NARZ, JACK (6)
TOM KENNEDY, moderators of the program (themselves)
GUEST STARS
GUEST PARTICIPANTS
You Don't Say! (TV) (Game)

NASH, CARTER, police chemist; doubles as Captain Nice, caped crime fighter
MRS. NASH, his mother
CANDY KANE, his police sergeant girl friend
Captain Nice (TV) (Crime fighting satire)

NASH, DOROTHY. See: Davidson, Bill

NASH, JIM, head of the family
JOAN, his wife
JOEL, their son
KYLE
TREVOR, their identical twin children
HANK MILLER, friend of Joel
LADADOG, their dog
Please Don't Eat the Daisies (TV) (Family situation comedy)

NASH, JOEY. See: Himber, Richard

NASH, MONTY, special investigator for the U. S. government
Monty Nash (TV) (Crime detection)

NASH, OGDEN. See: Donald, Peter

Nashville Music, That Good Ole. See: Ritter, Tex (2)

NAT. See:
Cole, Nat "King"
Dyke, Charity Amanda

Nat "King" Cole Show, The. See: Cole, Nat "King"

NAT SHILKRET. See: Stoopnagle, Colonel Lemuel Q. (1)

NATALIE. See:
Bruner, Wally (1) (2)
Lane, Patty

NATALIE NEVINS. See: Welk, Lawrence

NATASHA, BORIS. See: Bullwinkle

NATHAN. See: Cameron, Christy Allen

NATHAN BURKE. See: Dillon, Marshal Matt

Nation, Face the. See: Schoumacher, David

National Amateur Night. See: Perkins, Ray

National Barn Dance, The. See: Kelly, Joe (1)

National Church of the Air, The. See: Fosdick, Rev. Harry Emerson

National Farm and Home Hour, The. See: Mitchell, Everett

National Radio Pulpit, The. See: Cadman, Rev. S. Parkes

National Spelling Bee, The. See: Wing, Paul

National Surety's Secret Cases. See: Harkness, Detective

National Velvet. See: Brown, Velvet

National Vespers. See: Fosdick, Rev. Harry Emerson

Nation's Future, The. See: McCaffery, John K. M. (1)

NATTILY ATTIRED. See: Ballew, Wally

NAUGHTON, CLAUDIA, young married woman, "reluctant to grow to full stature as a wife"
DAVID, her husband
MRS. BROWN, her mother
Claudia (also known as Claudia and David) (R) (Drama)

Navy, Don Winslow of the. See: Winslow, Don

Navy, McHale's. See: McHale, Lieut. Commander Quinton

NAYLAND SMITH. See: Fu Manchu

NEAL. See: Neil

NEARING, VIVIENNE. See: Barry, Jack (9)

NEAT, NORMAN, MAN ON THE STREET. See: Cosby, Bill (1)

NEBB, RUDOLPH, husband and

father
FANNY, his wife
BETSY, his daughter
JUNIOR, his son
MAX GUGGENHEIM, his friend
The Nebbs (R) (Situation comedy)

Nebbs, The. See: Nebb, Rudolph

NEBUCHADNEZZAR. See:
Speaker, The

NED. See:
Hoopes, Ned
Jordan, Ned

NED BROOKS. See: Rountree,
Martha

NED HOLDEN. See: Rutledge,
Dr. John

Ned Jordan, Secret Agent. See:
Jordan, Ned

NED "NEDDIE" EVANS, LITTLE.
See: Wayne, Ruth Evans

NED SHEPHERD. See: Davidson,
Bill

NED, UNCLE. See: Pruitt, Mrs.
Phyllis Poindexter

"NEDDIE" EVANS, LITTLE NED.
See: Wayne, Ruth Evans

NEELY, ED. See: Marshall,
John

NEIGHBOR. See: Canova, Judy

Neighborhood, Misterogers. See:
Rogers, Fred

NEIGHBORS. See also: Nabors

Neighbors, Just. See: Caine,
Betty

NEIGHBORS, PAUL. See: Whiteman, Paul

NEIL. See:
Bishop, Neil
MacNeil, Robert
Nell
Topper, Cosmo

NEIL CAMPBELL. See: Evans,
Glenn

NEIL DARRELL. See: Nichols,
Walter

NEIL DAVISSON. See: Joe (1)

NEIL FOWLER. See: Robin

NEIL LEVANG. See: Welk,
Lawrence

NEIL OGILVIE. See: Nuvo,
Arnie

NEIL PERRY. See: Keene, Kitty

NEIL RAWSON. See: Bauer,
Bertha

NELL. See:
Do-Right, Dudley
Neil

NELLIE CONRAD. See: Solomon,
David

NELLIE ELLIS. See: Dallas,
Stella

NELLIE GLEASON. See: Solomon,
David

NELS. See: Hansen, Mama

NELSON, captain of the steamer
"Queen"
DUFFY, sailor, his rival
MOOSE MITCHELL
MAX
OZZIE, crew members
KOWALSKI
BECKER
BARNEY, characters appearing
on the program
The Queen and I (TV) (Comedy)

NELSON. See also:
Eddy, Nelson (1) (2)
Hargrave-Scott, Joan
Olmstead, Nelson

NELSON, ADMIRAL HARRIMAN,
director of Nelson Oceanographic
Institute
COMMANDER LEE CRANE, cap-
tain of the submarine "Seaview"

CHIEF SHARKEY
MORTON
PATTERSON
KOWALSKI, members of crew of
"Seaview"
Voyage to the Bottom of the Sea
(TV) (Undersea adventure)

NELSON, BABYFACE. See:
McKenzie, Captain Craig

NELSON BENTON. See: Benti,
Joseph

NELSON, CAROLYN KRAMER
FRED MINTURN
MR. KRAMER
MRS. KRAMER
DWIGHT KRAMER
DR. RICHARD CAMPBELL,
   physician
DORIS CAMERON
CONSTANCE WAKEFIELD
SUSAN WAKEFIELD
TED WAKEFIELD
BILL WALKER
ED NORTON
EMILY NORTON
LOUISE SIMS
ADELE CARMODY
MILES NELSON
JANE BROWNING
ROSE KRANSKY
ALEX DELAVAN
TERRY BURKE
GINNY
MARY, characters appearing in
the drama
The Right to Happiness (R) (Serial
drama)

NELSON, CHIEF PETTY OFFICER
HOMER. See: O'Toole, Ensign

NELSON DAVIS. See: Brown,
Ellen

NELSON EDDY. See:
Ameche, Don (1)
Bell, Alexander Graham
Eddy, Nelson (1) (2)

Nelson Eddy Show, The. See:
Eddy, Nelson (2)

Nelson Family, The. See: Nelson,
Ozzie

NELSON, FRANK. See: Benny,
Jack

NELSON, FREDERICK. See:
Brown, Ellen

NELSON, JOHN, master of cere-
monies of the program (himself)
COUPLES, MARRIED ON THE
PROGRAM
Bride and Groom (R) (Audience
participation)

NELSON, JOHN. See also:
Cameron, Barry

NELSON, MAJOR TONY, astronaut,
employed by N. A. S. A.
JEANNIE, his wife, a djinn or
genii
MAJOR ROGER HEALEY, astro-
naut, pal of Tony
DR. BELLOWS, physician, friend
of the Nelsons
MRS. BELLOWS, wife of Dr.
Bellows
DJINN-DJINN, Jeannie's dog, a
genii
I Dream of Jeannie (TV) (Comedy)

NELSON, MIKE, professional scuba
diver
Sea Hunt (TV) (Underwater adventure)

NELSON, MRS. See: Hardy, Dr.
Steven

NELSON, OZZIE, head of the house
HARRIET HILLIARD NELSON, his
wife
DAVID NELSON
RICKY NELSON, their sons
(themselves)
HARRIET'S MOTHER
THORNY, their neighbor
ROGER WADDINGTON
MRS. WADDINGTON
GLORIA, maid
EMMY LOU, characters appear-
ing on the program
The Adventures of Ozzie and
Harriet (R) (TV) (Situation com-
edy) (also called The Nelson
Family) (TV)

NELSON, OZZIE. See also:
Junior

Murray, Feg
Penner, Joe

NELSON RIDDLE. See:
Andrews, Julie
Cole, Nat "King"
Rogers, Ginger
Smothers, Tom (1)

NELSON, SERGEANT, World War
II soldier stationed in North
Africa
GENERAL HARRISON, American
officer
NONO, Algiers restaurant pro-
prietress
Combat Sergeant (TV) (War ad-
venture)

NELSON, STEVIE. See: Hardy,
Dr. Steven

NELSON, SUSAN. See: Noble,
Mary

NELSON, TOBY. See: Solomon,
David

NERO. See: Wolfe, Nero

Nero Wolfe, The Adventures of.
See: Wolfe, Nero

NERVOUS, MR. See: Allen,
Steve (1)

NESBIT, JOHN (1), narrator of the
program (himself)
The Passing Parade (R) (Documentary)

NESBIT, JOHN (2)
FRANK BAXTER, narrators of
the program (themselves)
MANY ACTORS AND ACTRESSES
Telephone Time (TV) (Dramatiza-
tions of true stories)

NESMITH, MIKE. See: Jones,
Davy

NESS, ELIOT. See: Winchell,
Walter (2)

Net Jazz. See: Gleason, Ralph

NEVER-FAIL HENDRICKS. See:
Marlin, Mary

Never Forget, I'll. See: Luther,
Frank (1)

Never Was, The Man Who. See:
Murphy, Peter

NEVILLE CHAMBERLAIN. See:
Husing, Ted

NEVILLE FINCH. See: Walker,
Eddie

NEVILLE, HIRAM. See: Dickey,
Dan'l

NEVILS, LIEUT. See: Sunday

NEVINS, NATALIE. See: Welk,
Lawrence

New Adventure of Huck Finn, The.
See: Finn, Huck

New Adventures of Martin Kane,
The. See: Kane, Martin

New Andy Griffith Show, The. See:
Sawyer, Andy

New Ann Sothern Show, The. See:
O'Connor, Katy

New Bill Cosby Show, The. See:
Cosby, Bill (2)

New Breed, The. See: Adams,
Lieut. Price

New Christy Minstrels, The. See:
Sparks, Randy

New Dick Van Dyke Show, The.
See: Preston, Dick

NEW DOODLETOWN PIPERS, THE.
See: Hirt, Al (2)

New in Learning, What's? See:
Sparks, Hale

New Lace, Lavender and. See:
Marlowe, Sylvia

New Loretta Young Show, The.
See: Massey, Christine

New Penny, A. See: Hayes,
Helen (2)

New People, The. See: Susan (1)

New Phil Silvers Show, The. See:
Grafton, Harry

New Price Is Right, The. See:
Barker, Bob

New Scooby Doo Movies, The. See:
Scooby Doo

NEW SEEKERS, THE. See: Berry,
Ken

New Talent, Lawrence Welk's Top
Tunes and. See: Welk,
Lawrence

New, What's? See: Binford, Al

NEW YEAR, THE. See: Benny,
Jack

New York Confidential. See:
Cochran, Lee

New York, Eye on. See: Leonard,
Bill

New York, Honeymoon in. See:
Kirby, Durward

New York, Little Old. See:
Arthur, Jack (3)

NEW YORK PHILHARMONIC
ORCHESTRA, THE. See:
Bernstein, Leonard

NEW YORK SYMPHONY ORCHESTRA,
THE. See: Damrosch, Walter

NEWBURY, MARTHA. See:
Marshall, John

Newcomers, The C.B.S. See:
Garroway, Dave (1)

NEWELL, DAVE. See: Begley,
Martin

NEWHART, BOB, actor, monologist
and entertainer; host of the program (himself)
MANY GUEST STARS
PAUL WESTON, orchestra leader
(himself)
HIS ORCHESTRA

The Bob Newhart Show (TV)
(Humor/variety)

NEWHART, BOB. See also:
DeLuise, Dom (2)

NEWKIRK. See: Hogan, Colonel
Robert

NEWLAND, JOHN, host of the
program (himself)
MANY ACTORS AND ACTRESSES
One Step Beyond (TV) (Mystery
drama)

Newlywed Game, The. See:
Eubanks, Bob

NEWMAN, EDWIN (1), moderator
of the program (himself)
MANY GUESTS
Comment! (TV) (Interview)

NEWMAN, EDWIN (2), host of the
program (himself)
MANY GUESTS
Speaking Freely (TV) (Interview/
discussion)

NEWMAN, EDWIN. See also:
Rountree, Martha

NEWMAN, HENRY. See: Bennett,
Nita

NEWMAN, PHYLLIS. See:
Marshall, E.G.

NEWMAN, TONY
DOUG PHILLIPS, scientists, visit
various times in history via the
Time Tunnel
GENERAL WOODY KIRK, officer
in charge of the Time Tunnel
operation
DR. RAY McGREGOR, scientist
working with the Time Tunnel
DR. ANN SWENK, technical
assistant, working with the Time
Tunnel
The Time Tunnel (TV) (Science-
fiction/adventure)

News Club, Animal. See: Straight,
Clarence

News, Douglas Edwards With the.
See: Edwards, Douglas

News, Hollywood Good. See:
Stewart, James

News, John Daly and the. See:
Daly, John (1)

News, N.B.C. See: Kalber, Floyd

News of Youth. See: Scoop

News, Paul Harvey. See: Harvey,
Paul (2)

News, Science in the. See:
Soule, Olan (5)

News, The A.B.C. Evening. See:
Smith, Howard K. (1)

News, The C.B.S. Morning. See:
Benti, Joseph

News, Wendy Warren and the. See:
Warren, Wendy

News With Walter Cronkite, The
C.B.S. Evening. See: Cronkite,
Walter (2)

NEWSCASTER. See: Warren,
Wendy

NEWSPAPER REPORTER, nameless
journalist
Final Edition (R) (Drama)

Newsreel, Bill Stern's Colgate
Sports. See: Stern, Bill

Newsreel Starring Bill Stern, The
Colgate Sports. See: Stern,
Bill

NEWTON, JIM, widowed rancher
JOEY, young orphan boy, adopted
by Newton
FURY, black stallion
Fury (TV) (Western drama)
(later reissued under the title
Brave Stallion) (TV)

Next, Dave Garroway. See: Garroway, Dave (3)

Next Door, The Couple. See:
Soule, Olan (1)

NEXT DOOR, THE LADY. See:

Conductor, The

NEXT DOOR, THE LITTLE GIRL.
See: Carson, Jack

NIC. See also: Nick

NIC ULLETT. See: DeLuise,
Dom (2)

Nice, Captain. See: Nash,
Carter

NICE, CAPTAIN. See: Nash,
Carter

NICHOLAS. See:
Cain, Nicholas
Nichols
Niklos

NICHOLAS BROTHERS, THE.
See: Edwards, Ralph (1)

NICHOLAS GAGE. See: Sheppard,
Franklin

NICHOLAS "NICKY" LACEY,
CAPTAIN. See: Barbour,
Henry Wilson

NICHOLAS "NICKY" LACEY, JR.
See: Barbour, Henry Wilson

Nichols. See: Nichols

NICHOLS, sheriff of Arizona town
in 1914
MA KETCHAM, rancher
KETCHAM, her son
MITCHELL, treacherous deputy
sheriff
RUTH, barmaid
Nichols (TV) (Western) (later
titled James Garner as Nichols)
(TV)

NICHOLS. See also:
Nicholas
Niklos

Nichols, James Garner as. See:
Nichols

NICHOLS, JASON. See: Randall,
Josh

NICHOLS, JIM. See: O'Leary,
Hannah

NICHOLS, MIKE.   See:
Ames, Nancy
Van Dyke, Dick (1)

NICHOLS, WALTER, Los Angeles
attorney
NEIL DARRELL
BRIAN DARRELL, brothers;
associates of Nichols in law firm
The Bold Ones (The Lawyers)
(TV) (Courtroom drama)

NICHOLSON. See: Muldoon,
Francis

NICHOLSON, MICHAEL.   See:
Martin, Doris

NICK, Italian
BEATRICE
PAPA MARINO
MRS. MARINO, his wife
TONY, characters appearing in
the drama
Little Italy (R) (Serial drama)

NICK.   See also:
Alexander, Nick
Anderson, Sergeant Nick
Barkley, Victoria
Carter, Chick
Carter, Nick
Charles, Nick
Davis, Ann Tyler
Farrell, David
Jones, Lorenzo
Manning, Laura
Nic
Parkyakarkas, Nick

NICK BELLINI, DR. See: Davis,
Dr. Althea

NICK BIANCO. See: Cameron

NICK CASTLE DANCERS, THE.
See: Lewis, Jerry

NICK COLLINS. See: Trent,
Helen

NICK DEPOPOLOUS.   See:
McGee, Fibber

NICK DUTTON. See: Miller,
Albert

NICK HAVENS. See: Young,
Larry "Pepper"

NICK KANAVARAS. See: Casey,
Dr. Ben

NICK MARR, BIG. See: McCray,
Linc

NICK PERITO. See: Knotts, Don

NICKERSON, PETE. See: Young,
Larry "Pepper"

NICKIE. See also:
Nicky
Nikki

NICKIE SMITH. See: Walleck,
Meredith

NICKY. See:
Kirchener, Claude (2)
Nickie
Nikki
Strickland, Goldie

"NICKY" LACEY, CAPTAIN
NICHOLAS. See: Barbour,
Henry Wilson

"NICKY" LACEY, JR., NICHOLAS.
See: Barbour, Henry Wilson

NICOLA. See: Kangaroo, Captain

NICOLE ALLISON CHERNAK. See:
Garrison, Spencer

NICOLE SCOTT. See: Cameron,
Christy Allen

NICOLE TRAVIS. See: Karr,
Mike

NICOLETTE MOORE. See: Barbour, Henry Wilson

NIECE, HIS. See: Morgan, Frank
(2)

NIELSEN, LESLIE (1), host of the
program (himself)
The Explorers (TV) (Modern
day adventure)

NIELSEN, LESLIE (2), interviewer
of famous historical characters
(himself)

MANY GUEST STARS portraying historical characters
Guest of Honor (TV) (Simulated interviews)

NIELSON, TORWALD, settler in Minnesota
MRS. ANNA NIELSON, his wife
ADAM BASSETT
CURTIS BASSETT
ARNE ANDERS
MRS. ARNE ANDERS
ELDORA WILKINS
HANSI
SMILEY, characters appearing in the drama
Prairie Folks (R) (Serial drama)

Night Beat. See: Stone, Lucky

Night, Circus. See: Cook, Joe

Night Court. See: Judge (2)

Night Football, N. F. L. Monday. See: Jackson, Keith (2)

Night Gallery. See: Serling, Rod (1)

Night Gallery, Rod Serling's. See: Serling, Rod (1)

Night, National Amateur. See: Perkins, Ray

Night, Opening. See: Dahl, Arlene

Night Serenade, Saturday. See: Dragonette, Jessica (3)

Night Shift With Rayburn and Finch. See: Rayburn, Gene (3)

Night, The Edge of. See: Karr, Mike

Night With Horace Heidt, A. See: Heidt, Horace (2)

NIGHTER. See: First Nighter, Mr.

Nighter, First. See: First Nighter, Mr.

NIKKI. See also:

Nickie
Nicky

NIKKI BELL. See: Longstreet, Mike

NIKKI PORTER. See: Queen, Ellery

NIKLOS. See:
Gallant, Captain
Nicholas
Nichols

NILS. See: Granlund, Nils Thor

NILS TORVALD. See: Calhoun, Ben

NIMMO, BILL, quizmaster of the program (himself)
MANY CONTESTANTS
For Love or Money (TV) (Quiz)

NINA CLOCK. See: Wallet, Skeezix

NINA MASON. See: Trent, Helen

9, Coronado. See: Adams, Don

Nine To Get Ready. See: Bragonier, Dr. J. Robert

Nineties Revue, The Gay. See: Kay, Beatrice

Ninety Bristol Court. See:
Gentry, Tom
Harris, Alan
Scott, Karen

99, AGENT. See: Smart, Maxwell

NIPPER
ROCKY
SYBIL
OLIVER
ALBERT
GEORGE
JERRY
RALPH
CONNIE, children; members of the Rainbow Club; all cartoon characters
Kid Power (TV) (Cartoon)

NIPSEY RUSSELL. See: Martin,
Dean (2)

NITA. See:
Anita
Bennett, Nita

NITTI, FRANK. See: Winchell,
Walter (2)

NIVEN, DAVID, actor; host of the
program (himself)
MANY ACTORS AND ACTRESSES
The David Niven Show (TV)
(Drama)

NIVEN, DAVID. See also:
Boyer, Charles
Ryan, Robert (1)

NO. Items so prefixed are indexed
as though spelled "Number" when
abbreviating this word.

No Need to Hide. See: Linkletter,
Art (3)

No Time for Sergeants. See:
Stockdale, Will

No Warning! See: Van Voorhis,
Westbrook (2)

NOAD, FREDERICK, guitarist and
teacher, host of the program
(himself)
Playing the Guitar (TV) (Music
education)

NOAH. See: McCann, Dr. Noah

NOAH BAIN. See: Mundy, Alexander

Noah Webster Says. See: Mac-
Quarrie, Haven (2)

Noah's Ark. See: McCann, Dr.
Noah

NOBLE, MARY, Iowa stenographer,
marries Larry Noble
LARRY NOBLE, her husband,
Broadway matinee idol
LARRY JR., Larry's son
LADY CLARA, Larry Noble's
mother
TESS MORGAN

KITTY MARSHALL
VIRGINIA LANSING
POP, stage doorman
ARNOLD CAREY, stage manager
WARD ELMOND
MAUDE MARLOWE
MARCELLE BERTRAND
TOD GOODHUE
GERALD MARSHALL
TOM BLAKE
REGINA RAWLINGS
TOM BRYSON
JOE BINNEY
SANDRA CAREY
MARTY RUFUS
PETER DARNELL
JENNIFER DAVIS
BETTY BURNS
DENNIS CONROY
ALICE DUFFY
VI WATERS
KATHARINE MONROE
SYLVIA KING
UNCLE ED JACKSON
SANDRA BARCLAY
CLIFF CALDWELL
SUSAN NELSON
DORIS DEE
MRS. DUBOIS
JUDITH MERRITT
KATY HAMILTON
MARCIA MANNERING
JEAN BAKER
ADA, maid
IRENE
MARGOT
OCKO
GOLDIE
MERCY
SAGO
COSMO
CALLAHAN
TAYLOR
CHRISTINE
MAIDA, characters appearing in
the drama
Backstage Wife (R) (Serial
drama) (Also called Mary Noble,
Backstage Wife) (R)

NOBLE, RAY. See:
Ameche, Don (1)
Bergen, Edgar (2)
Burns, George (1)

NOBLE WIFE, MARY BACKSTAGE.
See: Ballew, Wally

NOBLETTE, IRENE. See: Ryan,
Tim

NOBODY FROM NOWHERE, MR.
See: Rutledge, Dr. John

NOEL. See: Chandler, Faith

NOEL PENN. See: Sterling,
Vanessa Dale

NOLAN, BOB, composer; leader
of "The Sons of the Pioneers,"
musical group (himself)
PAT BRADY
HUGH FARR
KARL FARR
LLOYD PERRYMAN, musicians,
members of the group (themselves)
The Sons of the Pioneers (R)
(Western music)

NOLAN, GAIL. See: Harrigan, Hop

NOLAN, JEANETTE. See:
Reed, Alan
Welles, Orson (2)

NOLAN, KATE. See: Walleck,
Meredith

NOLAN, PETE. See: Favor, Gil

NOLAND, DR. JERRY. See:
Campanelli, Dr. Vincent

NONA
GWEN PARKER
THELMA POWELL
PAT BRADY
VERNON DUTELL, characters
appearing in the drama
Nona From Nowhere (R) (Serial
drama)

Nona From Nowhere. See: Nona

NONA MARSH. See: Warren,
Wendy

NONO. See: Nelson, Sergeant

NORA. See:
Charles, Nick
Clayton, Margie
Drake, Nora
Grady, Mickey
Hammond, Liza

Jiggs
Larimore, Marilyn
Randolph, Alice
Sawyer, Andy
Taylor, Andy
Worthington, Nora

Nora Drake, This Is. See:
Drake, Nora

NORA MARTIN. See: Cantor,
Eddie (2)

NORA MAWSON. See: Brent,
Portia

Norby. See: Norby, Pearson

NORBY, PEARSON, banker living
in Pearl River, N. Y.
HELEN, his wife
DIANE
HANK, his children
Norby (TV) (Comedy)

NOREEN NOVICK. See: Kelly,
Joe (2)

NORFOLK, DR. See: Brent,
Portia

NORFOLK, DOWAGER DUCHESS
OF. See: Henry VIII, King of
England

NORFOLK, DUKE OF. See:
Henry VIII, King of England

NORINE TEMPLE. See: Brown,
Ellen

NORM CROSBY. See: Diller,
Phyllis

NORMA. See: Stowe, Senator
Hays

NORMA DOUGLAS. See: Caesar,
Sid (1)

NORMA GREENMAN. See: Rutledge,
Dr. John

NORMA PRICE. See: Hargrave-
Scott, Joan

NORMA STARR. See: Graham,
Dr. Bob

NORMA VERNACK. See: Keene,
Kitty

NORMA ZIMMER. See: Welk,
Lawrence

NORMAN. See:
Corbett, Tom (1)
O'Connor, Father Norman
Peale, Norman Vincent

NORMAN ANDREWS. See: Reed,
Jerry

NORMAN BAILEY. See: Welk,
Lawrence

NORMAN, DOUGLAS. See:
Solomon, David

NORMAN HARRINGTON. See:
Peyton, Martin

NORMAN HASTINGS. See: Trent,
Helen

NORMAN KRUMP. See: Pruitt,
Mrs. Phyllis Poindexter

NORMAN MAEN DANCERS, THE.
See: Doonican, Val

NORMAN NEAT, MAN ON THE
STREET. See: Cosby, Bill (1)

NORMAN PARIS TRIO, THE.
See: Francis, Arlene (1)

NORMAN PRICE. See: Hargrave-
Scott, Joan

NORMAN PRICE, SR. See: Hargrave-Scott, Joan

NORMAN, TEDDY. See: Lopez,
Vincent

NORRIS, BARBARA. See: Bauer,
Bertha

NORRIS, CHICK. See: Davis,
Joan Field

NORRIS, HAZEL. See: McGee,
Fibber

NORRIS, HOLLY. See: Bauer,
Bertha

NORRIS, JANET MASON. See:
Bauer, Bertha

NORRIS, KATHLEEN, author;
portrayed on the program by
Ethel Everett
MANY ACTORS AND ACTRESSES
By Kathleen Norris (R) (Drama-
tizations of stories authored by
Kathleen Norris)

NORRIS, KEN. See: Bauer,
Bertha

NORRIS, ROY. See: McGee,
Fibber

NORRIS, SCOTT. See: Garrison,
Pat

NORSEMEN QUARTET, THE. See:
Shields, Jimmy

NORTH, DECODER, FARGO. See:
Cosby, Bill (1)

NORTH, DICK. See: Trent,
Helen

NORTH, JERRY, book publisher
and amateur detective
PAMELA, his wife, also an
amateur detective
SUSAN, their niece
BILL WEIGAND, chief detective
SERGEANT MULLINS, police
officer
MAHATMA McGLOIN, driver
Mr. and Mrs. North (R) (TV)
(Detective/drama)

NORTH, LILA. See: Runyon,
Brad

NORTH, MAJOR HUGH, officer
and international spy
THE GIRL, his associate
The Man From G-2 (R) (Spy
adventure)

NORTH, OSCAR. See: Hollister,
Dick

Northwest Passage. See: Rogers,
Major Robert

NORTON. See also:

Martin
Morton

NORTON CHEGLEY. See: Baker,
Julia

NORTON, CLIFF. See: Garroway,
Dave (2)

NORTON, ED. See:
Kramden, Ralph
Nelson, Carolyn Kramer

NORTON, EMILY. See: Nelson,
Carolyn Kramer

NORTON, KATHERINE. See:
Carter, Kathryn

NORTON, TRIXIE. See: Kramden,
Ralph

NOSTALGIA THE ELEPHANT. See:
Pam

Not For Hire. See: Dekker, Steve

Not For Women Only. See:
Walters, Barbara

Nothing But the Truth. See:
Moore, Garry (5)

Nothing, Double or. See: Compton,
Walter

NOTTINGHAM, THE SHERIFF OF.
See: Hood, Robin

NOVACK, GEORGE. See: James,
Nancy

NOVAK, JOHN, high school teacher
ALBERT VANE, principal of the
high school
MISS HARVEY
EVELYN ROSE
JEAN PAGANO
JERRY ALLEN
MARILYN SCOTT, teachers and
students
Mr. Novak (TV) (Drama)

NOVAK, MILES. See: Chandler,
Faith

NOVAK, PAT, detective
JOCKO, his friend

INSPECTOR, police officer
Pat Novak, For Hire (R) (Detective adventure)

NOVELODIANS, OTTO AND HIS.
See: Kelly, Joe (1)

NOVICK, NOREEN. See: Kelly,
Joe (2)

NOVIS. See also: Hovis

NOVIS, DONALD. See: Bowers,
Brainy

Now, Hear It. See: Murrow,
Edward R. (2)

Now, See It. See: Murrow, Edward R. (4)

NOWHERE, MR. NOBODY FROM.
See: Rutledge, Dr. John

Nowhere, Nona From. See: Nona

NUGENT, NUGEY. See: Pomeroy,
Susanna

NUGEY NUGENT. See: Pomeroy,
Susanna

No. 1, R. F. D. See: Beasley,
Irene (2)

NUMBER ONE SON. See: Chan,
Charlie

Number, Please. See: Collyer,
Clayton "Bud"

NO. 6. See: Prisoner, The

Number, Take a. See: Benson,
Red

NUMBSKULL, J. NEWTON. See:
Junior

Nun, The Flying. See: Bertrille,
Sr.

NUNALLY, POP. See: Myrt

NURSE BURTON. See: Wayne,
Ruth Evans

NURSE CHOATE. See: Peyton,
Martin

Nurse Corps, Junior. See:
Barton, Clara

NURSE JENNIFER IVERS. See:
Peyton, Martin

NURSE KIMBALL. See: Solomon,
David

NURSE LANIER. See: Brent,
Dr. Jim

NURSE MADELEINE. See: Cameron,
Christy Allen

NURSE WILCOX. See: Lochner,
Dr. Paul

NURSE WILLS. See: Casey, Dr.
Ben

Nurses, The. See: Thorpe, Liz

NUSSBAUM, MRS. PANSY. See:
Allen, Fred

NUSSBAUM, PIERRE. See: Allen,
Fred

NUTTY PROFESSOR, THE. See:
Lewis, Jerry

NUVO, ARNIE, loading-dock fore-
man, promoted to vice president
LIL, his wife
RICHARD, his son
ANDREA, his daughter
HAMILTON MAJORS, JR., his
polo-playing boss
FELICIA FARFUS, his extremely
overweight secretary
JULIUS, his friend, loading dock
worker
NEIL OGILVIE, his business rival
at the office
FRANCES, his neighbor
RANDY ROBINSON, "The Giddyap
Gourmet," television actor, his
neighbor
Arnie (TV) (Family situation
comedy)

NYE, LOUIS
CLIVE CLERK
JULIE McWHIRTER
ALAN COPELAND
BOB AND RAY
LAARA LACEY

JACK BURNS
CHUCK McCANN, comedians and
entertainers appearing on the
program (themselves)
THE GREAT VOODINI, escape
artist
SUPERMAN, characters por-
trayed by Chuck McCann
MARATHON DANCE ANNOUNCER,
character portrayed by Jack
Burns
MANY GUEST ORCHESTRA
LEADERS AND VOCALISTS
OF THE 1930's and 1940's
THE HAPPY DAYS SINGERS,
vocal group
THE WISA D'ORSO DANCERS
Happy Days Are Here Again (TV)
(Music/variety of the 1930's
and 1940's)

NYE, LOUIS. See also:
Allen, Steve (1) (3)
Martindale, Wink (2)

O.   See: Henry, O.

O. Henry Playhouse, The.   See:
Henry, O.

O.K.   See: Crackerby, O.K.

O.K. Crackerby!   See: Crackerby,
O.K.

O.K., JR.   See: Crackerby, O.K.

O.S.S.   See: Hawthorn, Captain

OAKLEY, ANNIE, sharpshooter and
performer
TAGG, her young brother
Annie Oakley (TV) (Western
drama)

OAKLEY, CLARISSA.   See: Harum,
David

OAKSBERRY, JENNIE.   See: Peppertag, Aaron

Oasis, Club.   See: Jones, Spike
(1)

OATES.   See also: Otis

OATES, TITUS.   See: Churchill,
John

OBERON, MERLE, narrator of the
program; plays part of newspaper
correspondent (herself)
MANY ACTORS AND ACTRESSES
Assignment Foreign Legion (TV)
(Dramatizations)

O'BRIEN, CHA-CHA.   See: Madison, Kenny

O'BRIEN, DANIEL J., lawyer,
"legal con man"
KATIE, his ex-wife
MARGARET, his former mother-
in-law
MISS G., his secretary
THE GREAT McGONIGLE, his
partner
Trials of O'Brien (TV) (Drama)

O'BRIEN, EDMOND, narrator of
the program (himself)
Men in Crisis (TV) (Documenta-
ries about international figures)

O'BRIEN, JOAN.   See: Crosby,
Bob (1)

O'BRIEN, KARIN.   See: Cullen,
Bill (3)

O'BRIEN, LARRY.   See: Kaye,
Sammy (1)

O'BRIEN, LOUISE.   See: Miller,
Mitch

O'Brien, Trials of.   See: O'Brien,
Daniel J.

O'BRIEN, VIRGINIA.   See: Marx,
Groucho (1)

Obscure, Jude the.   See: Cooke,
Alistaire (1)

O'CASEY, MICHAEL FRANCIS.
See: Douglas, Steve

Occasional Wife.   See: Christopher,
Peter

OCEAN QUEEN, THE.   See:
Pomeroy, Susanna

OCHRIS.   See: Driggs, Karleton
King

OCKO.   See: Noble, Mary

O'CONNELL, HELEN, singer; star
of the program (herself)
MARION EVANS, orchestra
leader
HIS ORCHESTRA
Helen O'Connell (TV) (Songs)

O'CONNELL, HELEN.   See also:
Birthday Man, The
Morgan, Russ

O'CONNELL, JODY, 12-year-old
boy
MRS. O'CONNELL, his widowed
mother, operates hotel on Mon-
tana frontier
Buckskin (TV) (Western)

O'CONNOR, BILL.   See: Kelly,
Joe (1)

O'CONNOR, DES, singer and
entertainer; star of the program
(himself)

THE MIKE SAMMES SINGERS
MANY GUEST STARS
Music Hall (TV) (Variety) (also
called The Des O'Connor Show) (TV)

O'CONNOR, DONALD, actor, dancer
and entertainer; host of the pro-
gram (himself)
MANY GUEST STARS
The Donald O'Connor Show (TV)
(Variety)

O'CONNOR, DONALD. See also:
Crosby, Bing (2); Martin, Dean (1)

O'CONNOR, ED. See: Dillon,
Marshal Matt

O'CONNOR, EDDIE. See: Lopez,
Vincent

O'CONNOR, FATHER NORMAN, host
of the program (himself)
STAN KENTON
COUNT BASIE
LIONEL HAMPTON
GENE KRUPA
GERRY MULLIGAN
DAVE BRUBECK
COLEMAN HAWKINS, orchestra
leaders (themselves)
THEIR ORCHESTRAS
OTHER JAZZ ORCHESTRAS AND
MUSICAL GROUPS
Dial M for Music (TV) (Jazz music)

O'CONNOR, JAMIE. See: Fairchild, Kay

O'CONNOR, KATY, assistant man-
ager of the Bartley House,
luxury hotel
OLIVE, her roommate
MR. MACAULAY, her boss
MRS. MACAULAY, Macaulay's wife
MR. DEVERY, owner of the
Bartley House
DONALD CARPENTER, resident
of the Bartley House
JOHNNY, bellboy
PAUL, desk clerk
The New Ann Sothern Show (TV)
(Situation comedy)

O'DAY, MICHAEL. See: Halop, Billy

Odd Couple, The. See: Ungar, Felix

O'DELL, DIGGER. See: Riley,
Chester A.

O'DONOVAN, TIM. See: Farrell,
David

Odyssey. See: Collingwood,
Charles (2)

Of Human Bondage. See: Carey,
Dr. Philip

O'FARRELL, PACKY
PEGGY O'FARRELL
GREGORY ALDEN
CLAIRE VAN ROON
Rich Man's Darling (R) (Serial
drama)

OFFICER. See:
Malloy, Officer Pete
Welles, Orson (3)

OFFICER BILL GANNON. See:
Friday, Sergeant Joe

OFFICER JIM REED. See: Malloy,
Officer Pete

Official Detective. See:
Britt, Dan
Sloane, Everett

OFFSTEIN, JERRY, karate expert;
host of the program (himself)
Self-Defense for Women (TV)
(Karate instruction)

O'FLYNN, CAPTAIN FLYNN,
officer
The O'Flynns (R) (Serial drama)

O'Flynns, The. See: O'Flynn,
Captain Flynn

OFRA BIKEL, MRS. See: Barry,
Jack (1)

OG
NAD
RU
BIG TOOTH, cavemen and
women
Og, Son of Fire (R) (Prehistoric
adventure)

Og, Son of Fire. See: Og

OGDEN, DIANE. See: Jordan,
Joyce

OGDEN, GREGORY. See: Jordan,
Joyce

OGDEN NASH. See: Donald, Peter

OGILVIE, NEIL. See: Nuvo, Arnie

OGLEPUSS, MADAME. See: Kukla

Oh, Boy! See: Hall, Tony

Oh! Susanna. See: Pomeroy,
Susanna

Oh, Those Bells! See: Bell,
Harry

O'HALLORAN, HAL. See: Kelly,
Joe (1)

O'HANLON, REDMOND. See:
March, Hal
Story, Ralph

O'HARA. See:
Cane, Vic
Muldoon, Francis

O'HARA, JAMES, special agent for
U.S. Treasury
O'Hara, United States Treasury
(TV) (Adventure)

O'HARA, KATHY. See: Halliday,
Mike

O'HARA, MOLLY. See: Young,
Larry "Pepper"

O'HARA, POLICE CHIEF. See:
Batman

O'HARA, SERGEANT. See: Runyon, Brad

O'HARA, TIM. See: Uncle Martin

O'Hara, United States Treasury.
See: O'Hara, James

O'HARE, DETECTIVE. See:
Benny, Jack

O'HOOLIHAN, HANK. See:
Solomon, David

OIL. See: Oyl

O'KEEFE, WALTER. See:
Compton, Walter
Crumit, Frank (1)
Shriner, Herb (3)

OL'. See also:
Old
Ole

Ol' Hollywood, Little. See:
Alexander, Ben (4)

OLAN SOULE. See:
Ameche, Don (3)
First Nighter, Mr.
Soule, Olan (1) (2) (3) (4) (5)

OLD. See also:
Ol'
Ole

Old Curiosity Shop, The. See:
Keeper of the Old Curiosity
Shop, The

OLD CURIOSITY SHOP. See:
Keeper of the Old Curiosity Shop,
The

Old-Fashioned Revival Hour, The.
See: Fuller, Rev. Charles E.

OLD FOOLER. See: Jones, Ben

OLD JOLYON. See: Forsyte,
Soames

Old Lace, Lavender and. See:
Scheff, Fritzi

OLD LADY WHEEDLEDUCK. See:
McGee, Fibber

OLD LEADBOTTOM. See: Mc-
Hale, Lieut. Commander Quinton

OLD MAESTRO, THE. See:
Bernie, Ben

OLD MAN, THE. See: Old Witch,
The

OLD NANCY. See: Cole, Alonzo
Dean

Old New York, Little. See:

Arthur, Jack (3)

OLD PROSPECTOR, THE. See:
Old Ranger, The

OLD RANGER, THE, narrator of
the program
THE OLD PROSPECTOR
THE LONESOME COWBOY
SHERIFF MARK CHASE
BOBBY KEEN
CASSANDRA DRINKWATER
(Cousin Cassie), residents of
Death Valley, California
Death Valley Days (R) (TV)
(Western adventure) (also called
Death Valley Sheriff (R) and The
Sheriff) (R)

Old Skipper, The. See: Old
Skipper, The

OLD SKIPPER, THE, sailor
The Old Skipper (R) (Children's
program)

OLD SOUTHERN COLONEL, THE,
character portrayed by Irvin S.
Cobb
MANY GUEST STARS
Paducah Plantation (R) (Variety)

OLD TIMER, THE. See: McGee,
Fibber

OLD WITCH, THE
WHITEWASH
SPARE RIBS
THE OLD MAN, characters in
stories told by Malcolm Claire
Malcolm Claire (R) (Children's
stories)

OLD WRANGLER, THE. See:
Mix, Tom

OLE. See:
Ol'
Old
Olsen, Ole

Ole Nashville Music, That Good.
See: Ritter, Tex (2)

Ole Opry, The Grand. See:
Solemn Old Judge, The

O'LEARY, HANNAH

DAN O'LEARY
ABE FINKELSTEIN
BECKY FINKELSTEIN
P. WALLACE CARVER
BARBARA HUGHEY
BOSS HUGHEY
JIM NICHOLS
ALEC FERGUSON
MARGERY DAVIS
ELLEN SMITH
KEVIN
SHAMUS
CLEM, characters appearing in
the drama
Houseboat Hannah (R) (Serial
drama)

OLGA. See: Marlin, Mary

OLIVE. See: O'Connor, Katy

OLIVE COURTLEIGH. See: Dyke,
Charity Amanda

OLIVE OYL. See: Popeye

OLIVER. See:
Douglas, Oliver
Hargrave-Scott, Joan
Nipper

OLIVER "DADDY" WARBUCKS.
See: Little Orphan Annie

OLIVER DREXTON. See: Sunday

OLIVER HONEYWELL. See:
Gildersleeve, Throckmorton P.

OLIVER KEE. See: Troy, Adam

OLIVER STAMP, CHIEF. See:
Ramsey, Hector "Hec"

OLIVIA. See: Walton, Grandpa

OLIVIA McEVOY. See: Brown,
Ellen

OLIVIO. See: Santoro, Olivio

Olivio Santoro. See: Santoro,
Olivio

OLLIE. See:
Jordan, Joyce
Kukla

OLMSTEAD, NELSON, story teller
of the program; played parts of
all characters (himself)
Stories by Olmstead (R) (Drama)

OLSEN, GEORGE. See:
Benny, Jack
Winchell, Walter (1)

OLSEN, JIMMY. See: Kent,
Clark

OLSEN, JOHNNY (1), master of
ceremonies of the program (himself)
MANY AUDIENCE PARTICIPANTS
Rumpus Room (R) (Audience participation)

OLSEN, JOHNNY (2), quizmaster
of the program (himself)
MANY CONTESTANTS
Whiz Quiz (R) (Quiz)

OLSEN, JOHNNY. See also:
Moore, Tom (1)

OLSEN, OLE
CHICK JOHNSON
PAUL WINCHELL
JERRY MAHONEY
BEN BLUE
JERRY COLONNA
SEÑOR WENCES
OTHERS, hosts of the program
(themselves)
MANY GUEST STARS
Five Star Comedy (TV) (Comedy/
variety)

OLSEN, PENNY. See: Moore,
Tom (1)

OLSON, EMILY
ROBERT SHALLENBERGER,
characters appearing in the drama
Central City (R) (Drama)

O'MALLEY. See: Monroe, John

O'MALLEY, FATHER CHUCK,
young Catholic priest
FATHER FITZGIBBONS, Catholic
priest
MRS. FEATHERSTONE, their
housekeeper
TOM COLWELL, Protestant minister, friend of Father O'Malley

Going My Way (TV) (Drama)

OMAR, the mystic
MR. KIMBALL
MRS. KIMBALL
THE KIMBALLS' DAUGHTER
ZAIDDA, characters appearing
on the program
Omar the Mystic (R) (Adventure)

Omar the Mystic. See: Omar

Omnibus. See: Cooke, Alistaire
(2)

On Broadway Tonight. See: Vallee,
Rudy (1)

On the Go. See: Linkletter, Jack
(1)

On Trial. See: Cotten, Joseph (2)

On Your Own, You're. See:
Dunne, Steve

ONE. See: Rogers, Buck

One, Glorious. See: Bradley,
Judith

One Happy Family. See: Cooper,
Dick

100 Grand. See: Clark, Jack

One Life to Live. See: Walleck,
Meredith

ONE LONG PAN. See: Allen,
Fred

One Man's Family. See: Barbour,
Henry Wilson

One More, Room For. See: Rose,
George

1, R. F. D. No. See: Beasley,
Irene (2)

One Step Beyond. See: Newland,
John

1, 2, 3, Go! See: Lescoulie,
Jack (3)

O'NEILL, JIMMY, host of the

program (himself)
MANY GUEST STARS
THE SHINDIG DANCERS
RAY POHLMAN, orchestra
leader (himself)
HIS ORCHESTRA
Shindig! (TV) (Music/variety)

O'NEILL, MRS.
EDDIE COLLINS O'NEILL
SALLY SCOTT O'NEILL
JANICE COLLINS O'NEILL
DANNY O'NEILL
PEGGY O'NEILL KAYDEN
BARBARA GRAYSON
MR. TURNER
MRS. TURNER
MRS. SCOTT
GINGER RAYMOND
MR. COLLINS
MONTE KAYDEN
MAYME GORDON
EILEEN TURNER
MRS. TRUDY BAILEY
DR. BRUCE KINGSLEY, physician
MR. TRASK
MRS. TRASK
MRS. KAYDEN
JUDGE SCOTT, jurist
MR. FIELDING
HAROLD WILKINSON
BOB WINTON
JEAN
MRS. MITCHELL
MORRIS LEVY
MRS. CARSON
SKIP MARTIN
TILLIE
GRANDPA HUBBELL
JACK VERNON
BASIL
LESTER LEWIS
MRS. COLLINS
MR. COLEMAN, characters appearing in the drama
The O'Neills (R) (Serial drama)

O'Neills, The. See: O'Neill, Mrs.

Ones, The Lively. See: Damone, Vic (1)

OOGIE PRINGLE. See: Foster, Judy

OOGLE. See: Pam

Open Door, The. See: Hansen,

Dean Eric

Open End. See: Susskind, David

Open House, Broadway. See: Lester, Jerry

Opening Night. See: Dahl, Arlene

OPENSHAW, FALSTAFF. See: Allen, Fred

OPERA. See also: Opry

Opera Broadcasts, Metropolitan. See: Cross, Milton (3)

Operation: Entertainment. See: Shawn, Dick

OPERATION ENTERTAINMENT GIRLS, THE. See: Shawn, Dick

OPERATOR, TELEPHONE. See: Husband
Powell, Dick (3)

OPHELIA. See: Addams, Gomez

OPIE. See: Taylor, Andy

OPIE CATES. See: Parkyakarkas, Nick

OPRY. See also: Opera

Opry, The Grand Ole. See: Solemn Old Judge, The

ORAL. See: Roberts, Oral

Oral Roberts Presents. See: Roberts, Oral

Orange Lantern, The. See: Botak

ORBO, DR. See: Kelly, Kitty

ORCHESTRA, THE BOSTON POPS. See: Fiedler, Arthur

ORCHESTRA, THE COLUMBIA BROADCASTING SYMPHONY. See: Herrmann, Bernard

ORCHESTRA, THE CONNECTICUT YANKEES. See: Vallee, Rudy (2) (3)

ORCHESTRA, THE "GYPSY
VIOLINS." See: Ross, David
(1)

ORCHESTRA, THE NEW YORK
PHILHARMONIC. See: Bern-
stein, Leonard

ORCHESTRA, THE PENNSYLVAN-
IANS. See: Waring, Fred (2)

ORCHESTRA, THE ROYAL CANADI-
ANS. See:
Burns, George (2)
Lombardo, Guy

Order, Story to. See: Perera,
Lydia

ORDWAY, DR. BENJAMIN, detective
MILLER, district attorney
ROSS, police inspector
Crime Doctor (R) (Detective/
drama)

O'REILLY, CORPORAL RADAR.
See: Pierce, Captain Hawkeye

O'REILLY, MRS. See: Peterson,
Irma

ORIE AMODEO. See: Welk,
Lawrence

Orient, Echoes of the. See: Von
Hallberg, Gene

Original Amateur Hour, Major
Bowes and His. See: Bowes,
Major Edward (2)

ORIOLE. See: Beulah

ORMANDY, EUGENE. See:
Bordoni, Irene

ORMPHBY, GLADYS. See:
Rowan, Dan

O'ROURKE, ROCKET. See:
Batman

O'ROURKE, SERGEANT. See:
Parmenter, Captain Wilton

ORPHAN ANNIE. See: Little
Orphan Annie

Orphan Annie, Little. See: Little
Orphan Annie

Orphans of Divorce. See: Worthington, Nora

ORRIN HILLYER. See: Karr,
Mike

ORRIN TUCKER. See: Ross,
Lanny

ORSON BEAN. See:
Moore, Garry (5)
Reiner, Carl

ORSON WELLES. See:
Frees, Paul
Welles, Orson (1) (2) (3)

ORTEGA, SANTOS, narrator of the
program (himself)
MANY ACTORS AND ACTRESSES
Green Valley, U.S.A. (R)
(Drama)

ORTEGA, SANTOS. See also:
Lovejoy, Frank (1)
Roberts, Ken

ORVILLE SHARP. See: Parkyakarkas, Nick

OSBORNE, JEAN. See: Malone,
Dr. Jerry

OSCAR. See: Brand, Oscar

OSCAR BRADLEY. See:
Heatter, Gabriel
Pryor, Roger

OSCAR DeGRUY. See: Cosby,
Bill (2)

OSCAR FINCH. See: Solomon,
David

OSCAR LEVANT. See:
Crosby, Bing (3)
Fadiman, Clifton (1)

OSCAR MADISON. See: Ungar,
Felix

OSCAR NORTH. See: Hollister,
Dick

OSGOOD, CHARLES, host of the
program (himself)
Profile (R) (Current events)

OSGOOD CONKLIN. See: Brooks,
Connie

O'SHAUGHNESSEY, SHARON. See:
Arkansas Traveler, The

O'SHEA, MICHAEL, host of the
program (himself)
SUPPORTING CAST AND GUESTS
It's a Great Life (TV) (Comedy)

O'SHEA, TESSIE. See: DeLuise,
Dom (2)

Osmond Brothers, The. See:
Osmond Brothers, The

OSMOND BROTHERS, THE, cartoon
reproduction of popular music
group
The Osmond Brothers (TV) (Cartoon)

OSWALD. See: Hoffman, Dr.
Oswald J.

OSWALD CHING. See: Marlin,
Mary

Other Wife, John's. See: Perry,
John

Others See Us, As. See:
Michaels, Joe

OTIS. See also: Oates

OTIS FOSTER. See: Fitzgerald,
Bridget Theresa Mary Coleen

O'TOOLE, BUGGSY. See: Trent,
Helen

O'TOOLE, ENSIGN, U. S. naval
officer, assigned to the U. S. S.
"Appleby"
LIEUT. COMMANDER VIRGIL
STONER, his commanding officer
LIEUT. J. G. REX ST. JOHN,
supply officer
CHIEF PETTY OFFICER HOMER
NELSON
GABBY DI JULIO
SPICER

WHITE, seamen on the "Appleby"
Ensign O'Toole (TV) (Comedy)

O'TOOLE, JOHN MICHAEL, editor
The Jim Backus Show (TV)
(Comedy)

OTTO AND HIS NOVELODIANS.
See: Kelly, Joe (1)

OTTO KING. See: Slate, Johnny

Our Five Daughters. See: Lee,
Jim

Our Gal Sunday. See: Sunday

Our Lives, Days of Our. See:
Horton, Dr. Tom

Our Man Higgins. See: Higgins

Our Miss Brooks. See: Brooks,
Connie

Our Private World. See: Hughes,
Lisa

Ours, This Day Is. See: Mac-
Donald, Eleanor

Ours, Today Is. See: Manning,
Laura

Out, Murder Will. See: Gargan,
William (2)

Outcasts, The. See: Corey, Earl

Outer Space, Josie and the Pussycats in. See: Josie

Outlaws, The. See: Caine, Frank

Outlook. See: Huntley, Chet (2)

Outsider, The. See: Ross, David
(2)

Overland Trail. See: Kelly,
Frederick Thomas

OVERSTREET, BUDDY, accountant,
overhears mobsters plotting a
murder
DEVERE (Mr. D.), syndicate
boss
JUNIOR DEVERE, Devere's son

WENDELL
HARRY, mobsters, pursuing Over-
street in effort to silence him
Run, Buddy, Run (TV) (Drama)

OVERTON, MR. See: Brent, Dr.
Jim

OVERTON, MRS. See: Brent, Dr.
Jim

OVIE. See: Hardie, Jim

OWEN. See: Marshall, Owen

OWEN CRAIG, DR. See: Kennedy,
Carol

OWEN, ETHEL. See: Arthur,
Jack (1)

Owen Marshall: Counselor at Law.
See: Marshall, Owen

OWEN SWEETEN. See: Holloway,
Harrison

OWENS, ANNA, widowed American
schoolteacher; employed by King
of Siam to educate his children
LOUIS, her 12-year-old son
THE KING OF SIAM, her em-
ployer
LADY THIANG, one of the King's
wives
PRINCE CHULALONGKORN, 12-
year-old Crown Prince of Siam
THE KING'S OTHER CHILDREN
KRALAHOME, the King's Prime
Minister
Anna and the King (TV) (Comedy)

OWENS, AUNT MINTA. See:
Vance, Connie

OWENS, BUCK
ROY CLARK
GRANDPA JONES
JUNIOR SAMPLES
COUSIN MINNIE PEARL
JEANNINE RILEY
DIANNA SCOTT
DAVE AKEMAN
LULU ROMAN
CATHY BAKER
ARCHIE CAMPBELL
SHEB WOOLEY
GORDIE TAPP

STRINGBEAM
DON HARRON
HAGERS
GUNILLA HUTTON
SUSAN RAYE
JENIFER BISHOP
JERRY LEE LEWIS
CONWAY TWITTY, comedians,
musicians and entertainers
appearing on the program (them-
selves)
Hee Haw (TV) (Country variety
and music)

OWENS, GARY, host of the pro-
gram (himself)
MANY GUEST STARS
Letters to Laugh-In (TV) (Game)

OWENS, GARY. See also:
Blyden, Larry (2)
Rowan, Dan

OWENS, MARYBELLE. See:
Solomon, David

Own Kind of Music, Make Your.
See: Hirt, Al (2)

OWNER of the Village Store, por-
trayed by Jack Haley
JOAN DAVIS
EVE ARDEN, actresses appear-
ing on the program (themselves)
DAVE STREET, vocalist appear-
ing on the program (himself)
PENELOPE "PENNY" CART-
WRIGHT
BLOSSOM BLIMP, characters
appearing on the program
Village Store (R) (Variety) (also
known as At the Village Store
(R) and Sealtest Village Store)
(R)

OXFORD, CARL. See: Murray,
Arthur

OYL, OLIVE. See: Popeye

OZZIE. See: Nelson

Ozzie and Harriet, The Adventures
of. See: Nelson, Ozzie

OZZIE NELSON. See:
Junior
Murray, Feg
Nelson, Ozzie
Penner, Joe

P. J.   See: Howard, Jim

P. M.   See: Wallace, Mike (3)

P. T.   See: Chuck

P. WALLACE CARVER.   See:
O'Leary, Hannah

PA.   See:
Barton, Bud
Canfield, Ben
Ma
Wiggs, Mrs.

Pa, Ma and.   See: Ma

PAAR.   See also:
Baar
Parr

PAAR, JACK, host of the program
(himself)
MANY GUEST HOSTS
DODY GOODMAN, singer (her-
self)
HUGH DOWNS, announcer (him-
self)
JOSE MELIS, orchestra leader
(himself)
HIS ORCHESTRA
MANY GUEST CELEBRITIES
The Tonight Show (TV) (Talk/
interview) (also known as The
Jack Paar Show) (TV)

PAAR, JACK.   See also:
Baker, Phil (3)
Bruner, Wally (1)

Package, Surprise.   See: Stewart,
Jay (2)

PACKARD, JACK
DOC LONG
REGGIE YORKE, operators of
the A-1 Detective Agency, Los
Angeles, Calif.
GERRY BOOKER, Packard's
secretary and traveling companion
TERRY BURKE
MICHAEL
SWEN, operatives with the A-1
Detective Agency
MARY KAY BROWN, secretary
I Love a Mystery (R) (Adven-
ture)

PACKY.   See: O'Farrell, Packy

Paducah Plantation.   See: Old
Southern Colonel, The

PADUCAH, THE DUKE OF.   See:
Duke of Paducah, The
Solemn Old Judge, The

PADWA, VEE.   See: Horwitz,
Hans

PAGANO, JEAN.   See: Novak,
John

PAGE.   See also: Paige

PAGE, BILL.   See: Welk,
Lawrence

PAGE, FRONT.   See: Farrell,
David

PAGE, GALE.   See: Ameche, Jim

PAGE, JEAN.   See: Bannister,
Clay

PAGE, PATTI (1), singer and
entertainer; hostess of the pro-
gram (herself)
MANY GUEST RECORDING
ARTISTS
VIC SCHOEN, orchestra leader
(himself)
HIS ORCHESTRA
The Big Record (TV) (Music)

PAGE, PATTI (2), singer and
entertainer; star of the program
(herself)
MANY GUEST STARS
VIC SCHOEN, orchestra leader
(himself)
HIS ORCHESTRA
The Patti Page Show (TV)
(Variety)

PAHOO-KA-TA-WHA.   See: Derringer, Yancy

PAIGE.   See also: Page

PAIGE, BOB
RANDY MERRIMAN, quizmasters
of the program (themselves)
DENISE LOR, assistant quizmaster (herself)

BESS MYERSON, model on the
program (herself)
MANY CONTESTANTS
The Big Payoff (TV) (Quiz)

PAIGE, DUKE. See: Longstreet,
Mike

PAIGE, LAURA. See: Hackett,
Doc

PAIGE, RAYMOND. See:
Lytell, Bert (2)
Powell, Dick (3)

Painted Dreams. See: Moynihan,
Mother

PAINTER, VES. See: Burke,
Stoney

Palace, Ice. See: Davidson, John
(1)

Palace, Piccadilly. See: Martin,
Millicent

Palace, The Hollywood. See:
Crosby, Bing (2)

PALADIN, former U.S. army
officer, now gunfighter in the
Old West
HEY BOY, Chinese servant
Have Gun, Will Travel (TV)
(Western drama)

PALLUCCI, ANGIE. See: Martin,
Doris

PALLUCCI, LOUIE. See: Martin,
Doris

PALMER, BETSY. See:
Donald, Peter
Moore, Garry (4)

PALMER, BUD, host of the program
(himself)
FILMS OF "GREAT MOMENTS
IN SPORTS"
Big Moment (TV) (Sports)

PALMER, BYRON
JOAN WELDON, singers featured
on the program (themselves)
THE PIED PIPERS, vocal group
This Is Your Music (TV) (Songs)

PALMER, DAN
JULIE, characters appearing in
the drama
The Doctor's Wife (R) (Serial
drama)

PALMER, EVERETT. See:
Walleck, Meredith

PALMER, FRANK. See: Malone,
Dr. Jerry

PALMER, LESLIE. See: Manning,
Portia Blake

PALMER, LIEUT. DAN. See:
Locke, Dr. Simon (2)

PALMER, ROY. See: Harding,
Karen Adams

PALMER WARD. See: Jostyn,
Jay (1)

PALMIERI, VICTOR, host of the
program (himself)
GUEST PANELISTS
STUDIO AUDIENCE PARTICI-
PANTS
The Advocates (TV) (Discussion)

Palmolive Beauty Box Theater, The.
See: Dragonette, Jessica (2)

PALOOKA, JOE, professional
heavyweight boxer
ANN HOWE, his girl friend
KNOBBY WALSH, his manager
Joe Palooka (R) (Comedy/drama)

PAM
CINDY
RALPH
GERARD, children appearing on
the program
GITTEL THE WITCH, character
appearing on the program
CHUCK JONES, creator and pro-
ducer of the program, appears in
audio only as "Mr. Jones' Answer-
ing Service"
GRANNY T.V., television set
showing old film clips
FLIP THE HIPPO
OOGLE
NOSTALGIA THE ELEPHANT
EEEEK A. MOUSE
HERMIONE GIRAFFE

WOODROW THE GROUNDHOG,
puppets appearing on the program
HENRY MANCINI, orchestra
leader (himself)
HIS ORCHESTRA
MANY CARTOONS
Curiosity Shop (TV) (Children's
education)

PAM. See also: Blake, Tom

PAMELA. See:
Chandler, Faith
North, Jerry

PAMELA RODGERS. See:
Rowan, Dan
Winters, Jonathan

PAMELA STANLEY. See: Har-
grave-Scott, Joan

PAMELA TOWERS. See: Hoyt,
Vikki Adams

PAMMY. See also:
Sammy
Tammy

PAMMY DAVIS. See: Hillman,
India

PAN, ONE LONG. See: Allen,
Fred

PAN, PETER, young boy "who
refused to grow up"
MR. DARLING
MRS. DARLING
MICHAEL DARLING
JOHN DARLING
WENDY DARLING, visited by
Peter Pan
NANA, dog, nurse to the Darling
children
CAPTAIN HOOK, pirate
CAPTAIN HOOK'S CREW
FIRST TWIN
SECOND TWIN, members of
Peter Pan's band
TINKER BELL, fairy
TIGER LILY, Indian maid
THE CROCODILE, swallows
alarm clock
Peter Pan (TV) (Musical fantasy)

PANAMA. See: Randall, Josh

PANAMA, PETER. See: Grant,
Harry

Panatela Program, The Robert
Burns. See: Burns, George
(2)

PANCHO. See: Cisco Kid, The

PANGBORN, MRS. See: Pres-
cott, Kate Hathaway

Panic! See: Van Voorhis, Westbrook (2)

Panorama 15. See: Sterling, Dick

PANOSIAN, LIEUT. SAMUEL. See:
Rice, Lieut. Bill

PANSY NUSSBAUM, MRS. See:
Allen, Fred

Pantomime Quiz Time. See:
Harrington, Pat, Jr.
Stokey, Mike

PAP. See:
Dodger, Willy
Pip
Pop
Pup

PAPA. See:
Bauer, Bertha
Hansen, Mama
Pappy
Poppa

PAPA DAVID. See: Solomon,
David

PAPA DITTENFEFFER. See:
Young, Alan

PAPA MARINO. See: Nick

PAPARELLI, PRIVATE. See:
Bilko, Sergeant Ernest

PAPPY. See:
Papa
Poppa
Yokum, Li'l Abner

Parade, Game. See: Elmer,
Arthur

Parade, Macy's Annual Thanksgiving Day. See: Myerson, Bess

Parade of Progress. See: Manson, Charlotte

Parade, Soldier. See: Francis, Arlene (4)

Parade, The Passing. See: Nesbit, John (1)

Parade, The Sunbrite Smile. See: Sherman, Ransom (2)

Parade, Your Hit. See:
Lanson, Snooky
Ross, Lanny

PARADINE. See: Drake, Bradley

Paradise, Adventures in. See: Troy, Adam

Paradise, Dangerous. See: Brewster, Gail

Paradise, Strange. See: Carr, Alison

Paree, Hotel de. See: Sundance

Parent Game, The. See: Race, Clark

Parents, Raising Your. See: Cross, Milton (4)

PARIS. See: Phelps, Jim

Paris Cavalcade of Fashions. See: Emerson, Faye (2)

Paris 7000. See: Brennan, Jack

PARIS TRIO, THE NORMAN. See: Francis, Arlene (1)

PARK AVENUE HILLBILLY, THE. See: Jones, Spike (2)

Park, Barefoot in the. See: Bratter, Paul

PARKER. See: Marlin, Mary

PARKER, CAROL. See: Willis, David

PARKER, ELLEN. See: Caesar, Sid (2)

PARKER, ENSIGN CHARLES "CHUCK." See: McHale, Lieut. Commander Quinton

Parker Family, The. See: Parker, Richard

PARKER, FRANK, featured vocalist on the program (himself)
HARRY HORLICK, orchestra leader (himself)
HIS ORCHESTRA
The A&P Gypsies (R) (Music)

PARKER, FRANK. See also:
Benny, Jack
Donald, Peter
Godfrey, Arthur (1)

PARKER, GWEN. See: Nona

PARKER, JOHN. See: Manning, Portia Blake

PARKER, KATHY. See: Tate, Joanne

PARKER, LIEUT. MIKE
DETECTIVE ADAM FLINT
DETECTIVE FRANK ARCARO
DETECTIVE JIM HALLORAN
DETECTIVE LIEUT. DAN MULDOON, police officers
LIBBY, Flint's girl friend
Naked City (TV) (Crime drama)

PARKER, LINDA. See: Kelly, Joe (1)

PARKER, LOU
ANN THOMAS, featured on the program (themselves)
Mennen Shave Time (R) (comedy)

PARKER, MA. See: Batman; Parker, Seth

PARKER, RICHARD
MR. PARKER
MRS. PARKER
NANCY PARKER
GRANDPA PARKER
ELLY, characters appearing on the program
The Parker Family (R) (Situation comedy)

PARKER, SETH, patriarch of Jones-
port, Maine
MA PARKER, his wife
LIZZIE PETERS
CEFUS PETERS
JANE
CAPTAIN BANG
GEORGE, the captain's brother
LAITH PETTINGAL
DR. TANNER
JOHN, Parker's friends and
neighbors
Seth Parker (R) (Religious music/
drama)

PARKER, STAN. See: Willis,
David

PARKER, SUSIE. See: Perkins,
Ma

PARKER, WARREN. See: Jesus

PARKS. See: Johnson, Parks

PARKS, BERT (1)
JOHN REED KING
CLAYTON "BUD" COLLYER,
quizmasters on the program
(themselves)
Break the Bank (R) (TV) (Quiz)
(later known as Break the
$250,000 Bank) (TV)

PARKS, BERT (2), host of the program (himself)
MANY CIRCUS ACTS
Circus! (TV) (European circus
performances)

PARKS, BERT (3), quizmaster of
the program (himself)
MANY CONTESTANTS, 7 to 17
years of age
Giant Step (TV) (Children's quiz)

PARKS, BERT (4), host of the pro-
gram (himself)
MANY "MISS AMERICA" CON-
TESTANTS
The Miss America Contest (TV)
(Beauty contest)

PARKS, BERT (5)
DICK TODD, masters of ceremony of the program (themselves)
MANY AUDIENCE PARTICIPANTS

Second Honeymoon (R) (Audience
participation)

PARKS, BERT (6)
KAY ARMEN
DICK BROWN, quizmasters on the
program (themselves)
BETTY ANN GROVE, featured
vocalist (herself)
HARRY SALTER
HAPPY FELTON, orchestra
leaders (themselves)
THEIR ORCHESTRAS
MANY CONTESTANTS
Stop the Music (R) (TV) (Musical
quiz)

PARKS, BERT (7), host of the
program (himself)
MANY CONTESTANTS
Yours For a Song (TV) (Musical
game)

PARKYAKARKAS. See: Cantor,
Eddie (2)

PARKYAKARKAS, NICK, restaurant
proprietor
CASHIER at the restaurant
PRUDENCE ROCKBOTTOM
ORVILLE SHARP, patrons of
the restaurant
PATTY BOLTON
DAVE STREET
PEGGY LEE
BETTY JANE RHODES, vocalists
featured on the program (them-
selves)
OPIE CATES, orchestra leader
(himself)
HIS ORCHESTRA
Meet Me at Parky's (R) (Comedy)

Parky's, Meet Me at. See:
Parkyakarkas, Nick

PARMALEE, RANGER CAPTAIN,
Texas Ranger
THE VIRGINIAN
TRAMPAS
REESE BENNETT
CHAD COOPER
JOE RILEY
ERIC
LAZYFOOT, characters appear-
ing in the drama
Laredo (TV) (Western) (later re-
issued in revised form under

the title The Virginian (TV)

PARMENTER, CAPTAIN WILTON,
head of F Troop, assigned to
Fort Courage on Western frontier
SERGEANT O'ROURKE
CORPORAL AGARN
DUFFY
DOBBS, soldiers; members of
F Troop
WRANGLER JANE, Parmenter's
girl friend
CRAZY CAT
SMOKEY BEAR
WILD EAGLE
ROARING CHICKEN, Indians
F Troop (TV) (Comedy/Western)

PARNELL, EMERY. See: Les-
coulie, Jack (2)

PARNELL, JACK. See:
Berman, Shelley
Chidsey, Jackie
Davidson, John (2)
Doonican, Val

PARR. See also:
Baar
Paar

PARR, CATHERINE. See: Henry
VIII, King of England

PARSON, THE. See: Brewster,
Gail

PARSONS, DR. REGINALD. See:
Brent, Dr. Jim

PARSONS, GEORGE. See: Prescott, Kate Hathaway

PARSONS, JOE. See: Kelly,
Joe (1)

PARSONS, JUDGE. See: Mix,
Tom

PARSONS, LOUELLA, Hollywood
columnist; hostess of the program (herself)
The Louella Parsons Show (R)
(Hollywood gossip)

PARSONS, LOUELLA. See also:
Powell, Dick (3)

PARTENON PROTEUS, PROFESSOR.
See: Allen, Jimmie

Partners, Lucky. See: Cordell,
Carl

Partners, The. See: Crooke,
Lennie

PARTON, DOLLY. See: Wagoner,
Porter

Partridge Family, The. See:
Partridge, Connie

PARTRIDGE, CONNIE, widow,
heads family rock singing group
KEITH
DANNY
LAURIE
CHRIS
TRACY, her children
REUBEN KINCAID, their busi-
ness manager
The Partridge Family (TV)
(Family situation comedy/music)

Party, House. See: Linkletter,
Art (1)

Party, Masquerade. See: Donald,
Peter

Party, Penthouse. See: Glad,
Gladys

Party, Plantation. See: Duke of
Paducah, The

Party, Ranch. See: Ritter, Tex
(1)

Party, Surprise. See: Wilson,
Stu

Party, The Arthur Murray. See:
Murray, Kathryn

Party, Western Ranch. See: Ritter, Tex (1)

PASCAL TYLER. See: Cameron,
Christy Allen

PASQUALE. See:
Bergen, Edgar (2)
Luigi

Passage, Northwest. See: Roberts,
Major Robert

Passing Parade, The. See: Nesbit,
John (1)

Passport for Adams. See: Adams,
Doug

Password. See: Ludden, Allen

PASTERNACK, JOSEF. See:
Faith, Percy

PASTOR, TONY. See: Whiteman,
Paul

PAT. See:
Ballard, Pat
Barry
Boone, Pat
Garrison, Pat
Harrington, Pat, Jr.
Meikle, Pat
Novak, Pat
Paulsen, Pat
Smith, Eugene
Stevens, Joan
Stockton, Sandy (1)
Strickland, Goldie
Webster, Nancy

PAT BAKER. See: Harris, Bill

Pat Boone Show, The. See: Boone,
Pat

PAT BRADY. See:
Nolan, Bob
Nona
Rogers, Roy

PAT BURNS. See: Andrews,
Walter

PAT BUTTRAM. See:
Autry, Gene
Kelly, Joe (1)
Rogers, Roy

PAT CARROLL. See:
Caesar, Sid (2)
Daly, John (4)
Reiner, Carl

PAT CURTIS. See:
MacDonald, Eleanor
Mix, Tom

PAT FINLEY. See: Kelly, Gene

PAT FRIDAY SINGERS, THE.
See: Borge, Victor

PAT GARRETT. See: Billy the
Kid

PAT GRADY. See: Perry, John

PAT KENNEDY. See: Bernie,
Ben

PAT MURPHY. See: Stewart,
Jan

Pat Novak, For Hire. See:
Novak, Pat

PAT PATTERSON. See: Grimm,
Arnold

PAT PATTON. See: Tracy, Dick

PAT PAULSEN. See:
Cookie Monster, The
Paulsen, Pat
Paulson, Pete
Smothers, Tom (1) (3)

Pat Paulsen's Half a Comedy Hour.
See: Paulsen, Pat

PAT PERRY. See: McKay,
Judson

PAT RORITY. See: Fairchild,
Kay

PAT WALTERS. See: Barrett,
David

PAT WHITE. See: Murray, Jan
(1)

PAT WILLIAMS. See: Steinberg,
David (2)

PATCHETT AND TARSES. See:
Hirt, Al (2)

PATERNO, MICHAEL. See:
Johnson, Bess

PATRICE MUNSEL. See:
Barlow, Howard
Munsel, Patrice

Patrice Munsel Show, The. See:
Munsel, Patrice

PATRICIA. See:
Locke, Patricia
Marshall, Patricia
Randolph, Alice
Rogers, Patricia

PATRICIA BOWMAN. See: Roxy

PATRICIA HOLMES. See:
Templar, Simon

PATRICIA MICKEY. See:
Chidsey, Jackie

PATRICIA PEARDON. See:
Halop, Billy

PATRICIA RYAN. See: Halop,
Billy

PATRICK. See: Peyton, Father
Patrick

PATRICK CONLON. See: Kelly,
Joe (2)

PATRICK CONWAY. See: Kelly,
Kitty

PATRICK, DION, Irishman living
in San Francisco in 1851
JACK McGIVERN, storekeeper;
his friend
MARTHA McGIVERN, Jack's
wife
STEVE THOMPSON, Dion's
friend and partner
The Californians (TV) (Western
adventure)

PATRICK JOSEPH MURPHY. See:
Levy, Abie

PATRICK McGEEHAN. See:
Whitman, Gayne

PATRICK MULVANEY. See:
Joe (1)

PATRICK RYAN. See: Lee,
Terry

Patrol, African. See: Derek,
Inspector

Patrol, Border. See: Jagger,
Don

Patrol, Flying. See: Rowlands,
Hugh

Patrol, Highway. See:
Matthews, Dan
Taylor, Corporal Steve

Patrol, The Rat. See: Troy,
Sergeant Sam

Patrol, U. S. Border. See: Jagger, Don

PATSY. See:
Dennis, Liz
Patti
Patty

PATSY BOLTON. See: Sweeney,
Bob

PATSY BOWEN. See: Carter,
Nick

PATSY CLINE. See: Ritter,
Tex (1)

PATSY PIERCE. See: Canova,
Judy

PATTERSON. See: Nelson,
Admiral Harriman

PATTERSON, MARSHA. See:
Kincaid, Chet

PATTERSON, PAT. See: Grimm,
Arnold

PATTI. See:
Dawson, Rosemary
Page, Patti (1) (2)
Patsy
Patty
Roberts, Oral

PATTI CLAYTON. See: Seymour,
Dan

PATTI DEUTSCH. See:
Byner, John (1)
Rowan, Dan

Patti Page Show, The. See: Page,
Patti (2)

Les Paul and Mary Ford (TV)
(Music)

PAUL, LES. See also: Waring,
Fred (1)

PAUL LUTHER. See: McCormick,
Myron

PAUL LYNDE. See: Marshall,
Peter

Paul Lynde Show, The. See:
Simms, Paul

PAUL MARTEL. See: Grimm,
Arnold

PAUL MARTIN. See: Davis, Ann
Tyler

PAUL MORRISON. See: Har-
grave-Scott, Joan

PAUL NEIGHBORS. See: Whiteman, Paul

PAUL SAND. See: Caesar, Sid
(1)

PAUL SHERWOOD. See: Jordan,
Joyce

PAUL STEWART. See: Welles,
Orson (2)

PAUL STRONG. See: Morrison,
Mother

PAUL STUART. See: Hughes,
Chris

PAUL WESTON. See:
Nabors, Jim
Newhart, Bob
Winters, Jonathan

PAUL WHITEMAN. See:
Burns, George (1)
Gibbs, Georgia (2)
Whiteman, Paul

PAUL WINCHELL. See:
Olsen, Ole
Reiner, Carl
Winchell, Paul (1) (2) (3) (4)
(5) (6) (7)

Paul Winchell Show, The. See:
Winchell, Paul (3)

PAULA. See:
Hollister, Dick
Randolph, Alice

PAULA CINKO. See: Chidsey,
Jackie

PAULA HARWOOD. See: Brent,
Dr. Jim

PAULA KIRBY. See: Myrt

PAULA STONE. See: Landi,
Elissa

PAULETTE DOUGLAS. See:
Bracken, John

PAULETTE HENDERSON. See:
Perkins, Ma

PAULINE ANTONY. See: Chidsey,
Jackie

PAULINE HARRIS. See: Ames,
Peter

PAULSEN, MRS. See: Hillman,
India

PAULSEN, PAT, comedian; star
of the program (himself)
HAL SMITH
SHERRY MILES
PEDRO RAGAS
BOB EINSTEIN, entertainers
appearing on the program (them-
selves)
MANY GUEST STARS
Pat Paulsen's Half a Comedy
Hour (TV) (Variety)

PAULSEN, PAT. See also:
Cookie Monster, The
Smothers, Tom (1) (3)

PAULSON, PETE. See: Saber,
Mark

PAULY. See: Mason, Maudie

PAX. See: Longstreet, Mike

PAYNE, JERRY. See: Marshall,
John

PAYNE, WALTER. See: Perkins,
Ma

Payoff, The Big. See: Paige,
Bob

Pays To Be Ignorant, It. See:
Howard, Tom (1)

Pays, Who? See: Wallace, Mike
(5)

PEA. See also: Pee

Pea Pickers, Hello. See: Ford,
Tennessee Ernie (3)

PEABODY, ABNER. See:
Edwards, Lum
Marlin, Mary

PEABODY, EDDIE. See: Kelly,
Joe (1)

PEABODY, HERBERT. See: Carson, Jack

PEABODY, JENNY, postmistress
and general store proprietor at
Hillsdale
Jenny Peabody (R) (Serial drama)

Peace and War, The F.B.I. in.
See: Sheppard, F.B.I. Field
Agent

PEALE. See also: Peel

PEALE, NORMAN VINCENT, host of
the program (himself)
What's Your Trouble? (TV)
(Discussion of marital problems)

PEANUTS HUCKO. See: Welk,
Lawrence

PEARDON, PATRICIA. See: Halop,
Billy

PEARL. See:
Bailey, Pearl
Gibson, Jack

Pearl Bailey Show, The. See:
Bailey, Pearl

PEARL, COUSIN MINNIE. See:

Owens, Buck
Solemn Old Judge, The

PEARL DAVIS. See: Keene,
Kitty

PEARL TAGGART. See: Sunday

PEARSON. See:
Norby, Pearson
Pierson

PEARSON, BILLY. See:
March, Hal
Story, Ralph

PEARSON, DREW, columnist and
newsman (himself)
Drew Pearson (TV) (News)

PEARSON, GREGORY. See:
Worthington, Nora

PEARSON, JACE
CLAY MORGAN, Texas Rangers
The Texas Rangers (TV) (West-
ern)

PEARSON, MAURICE. See:
Welk, Lawrence

PEASOUP, LADY PENELOPE.
See: Batman

PEAVEY. See: Gildersleeve,
Throckmorton P.

PECH, THERESA. See: Graham,
Dr. Bob

PECK, DR. See: Sterling,
Vanessa Dale

PECK, TOREY, 12-year-old girl
MR. PECK, her father, physicist
MRS. PECK, her mother
ROGER, her younger brother
Peck's Bad Girl (TV) (Family
situation comedy)

Peck's Bad Girl. See: Peck,
Torey

PECOS WILLIAMS. See: Mix,
Tom

PEDRO. See: Canova, Judy

PEDRO RAGAS. See: Paulsen,
Pat

PEE. See also: Pea

PEE WEE. See:
Brewster, Joey
Peewee

PEEL. See also: Peale

PEEL, MRS. EMMA. See: Steed,
John

PEEPERS, ROBINSON J., science
teacher at Jefferson City Junior
High School
NANCY PEEPERS, his wife;
school nurse
AUNT LIL, their aunt
MR. REMINGTON
MRS. REMINGTON, Nancy's
parents
HARVEY WESKIT, Peepers' best
friend
MARGE WESKIT, Harvey's wife
MRS. GURNEY, English teacher
at the high school
Mr. Peepers (TV) (Comedy)

PEERCE. See also: Pierce

PEERCE, JAN. See:
Ives, Burl (2)
Roxy

PEEWEE
WINDY, young sailors on shore
leave
Peewee and Windy (R) (Comedy)

PEEWEE. See also: Pee Wee

Peewee and Windy. See: Peewee

PEG HALL. See: Dane, Prudence

PEG LA CENTRA. See: Cook,
Joe

PEG LYNCH. See: Soule, Olan
(1)

PEG MARTINSON. See: Drake,
Nora

PEG RILEY, MRS. See: Riley,
Chester A.

PEGASUS. See: Susan (2)

PEGEEN. See: Fitzgerald, Ed

PEGGY. See:
Fairchild, Kay
Hopkins, Peggy
Larimore, Marilyn
McNulty, Professor Ray
Meek, Mortimer
O'Farrell, Packy
Taylor, Andy
Young, Larry "Pepper"

PEGGY BANNING. See: Benton,
Steve

PEGGY CASS. See:
Blyden, Larry (2)
Moore, Garry (5)
Reiner, Carl

PEGGY CONNOLLY. See: Kovacs,
Ernie (1)

PEGGY DALE. See: McKeever,
Dr. John

PEGGY DEVLIN. See: Randolph,
Alice

PEGGY DILLON. See: Bauer,
Bertha

PEGGY EDWARDS. See: Marshall,
John

PEGGY FAIRBANKS. See: Hutton,
Ina Ray

PEGGY GAYLORD. See: Rutledge,
Dr. John

Peggy, Hello. See: Hopkins,
Peggy

PEGGY JOAN MOYLAN. See:
Moylan, Marianne

PEGGY KING. See: Gobel,
George

PEGGY LEE. See:
Crosby, Bing (3)
Parkyakarkas, Nick

PEGGY LENNON. See:

Lennon, Janet
Welk, Lawrence

PEGGY MARSHALL. See: God-
frey, Arthur (2)

PEGGY MAXWELL. See: Howard,
Glenn

PEGGY O'NEILL KAYDEN. See:
O'Neill, Mrs.

PEGGY REGAN. See: Hughes,
Chris

PEGGY REVERE. See: Banyon,
Miles C.

PEGGY SMITHGIRL. See:
Webster, Martha

PEGGY THAYER. See: Mannix,
Joe

Peggy's Doctor. See: McKeever,
Dr. John

PELLETIER, VINCENT. See:
Wordmaster, The

PENDLETON, AUGUSTUS. See:
Perkins, Ma

PENDLETON, GLADYS. See:
Perkins, Ma

PENDLETON, MATHILDA. See:
Perkins, Ma

PENDLETON, MRS. See:
Perkins, Ma

PENELOPE PEASOUP, LADY.
See: Batman

PENELOPE "PENNY" CARTWRIGHT.
See: Owner

PENGUIN, CAESAR P. See:
Susan (2)

PENGUIN, THE. See: Batman

PENN, NOEL. See: Sterling,
Vanessa Dale

PENNER JOE
ROBERT L. RIPLEY, hosts of

the program (themselves)
SUSABELLE
GERTRUDE
STOOGE, characters appearing
on the program
HARRIET HILLIARD
MARTHA MEARS
SHIRLEY LLOYD, featured
vocalists (themselves)
OZZIE NELSON, orchestra
leader and vocalist (himself)
HIS ORCHESTRA
MANY GUEST STARS
The Baker's Broadcast (R)
(Comedy/variety) (later known
as The Joe Penner Show) (R)

PENNINGTON, MILLICENT. See:
Wilbur, Judy

PENNINGTON, RED. See:
Winslow, Don

PENNSYLVANIANS ORCHESTRA,
THE. See: Waring, Fred (2)

PENNSYLVANIANS, WARING'S.
See: Waring, Fred (2)

PENNY, volunteer entertainer at
U. S. O.
HER AUNT
HER G. I. FRIENDS
MRS. GIBBS
INSPECTOR HALE, characters
appearing on the program
Hearts in Harmony (R) (Drama)

PENNY. See also:
Bartlett, Jill
Cameron, Christy Allen
Cooper, Dick
Dale, Linda
Endicott, Professor Mike
Hall, Dr. William Todhunter
Hughes, Chris
King, Schyler "Sky"
Marlin, Mary
West, Michael

Penny, A New. See: Hayes,
Helen (2)

"PENNY" CARTWRIGHT (PENEL-
OPE). See: Owner

PENNY LACEY. See: Barbour,
Henry Wilson

PENNY LATHAM. See: Harding,
Mrs. Rhoda

PENNY McCOY. See: Huddles, Ed

PENNY, MRS. See: Malone, Dr.
Jerry

PENNY OLSEN. See: Moore, Tom
(1)

PENNY ROBINSON. See: Smith,
Colonel Zachary

Penny to a Million. See: Goodwin,
Bill

PENNYFEATHER, MRS. GEORGE T.
See: Weems, Ambrose J.

PENROSE, TRADER. See: Troy,
Adam

Penthouse Party. See: Glad,
Gladys

Penthouse, Playboy's. See:
Hefner, Hugh

People Are Funny. See: Linkletter,
Art (4)

People, For the. See: Koster,
David

People in Jazz. See: Rockwell,
Jim

People, Slattery's. See: Slattery,
Jim

People, The Little. See: Jamison,
Dr. Sean

People, The New. See: Susan (1)

People, We, the. See: Heatter,
Gabriel

People's Choice, The. See:
Miller, Socrates

People's Conference, Young. See:
Poling, Rev. Daniel

PEOPLES, MAYOR. See: Miller,
Socrates

People's Platform. See: Bryson,
Dr. Lyman (1)

PEPE. See:
Cade, Sam
Cat, Thomas Hewitt Edward

"PEPPER." See: Young, Larry
"Pepper"

Pepper Pot, The. See: McNeill,
Don

Pepper Young's Family. See:
Davis, Red
Young, Larry "Pepper"

PEPPERTAG, AARON
SARAH PEPPERTAG
JENNIE OAKSBERRY
GRANDPA BEASLEY
UNCLE EZRA BUTTERNUT
LITTLE DOUGLAS BUTTERNUT
AUNT LUCINDA SKINFLINT,
characters appearing in the
drama
Happy Hollow (R) (Drama)

PERCY. See:
Blakeney, Sir Percy
Faith, Percy

PERCY BLIVENS. See: Davidson,
Bill

PERCY CRUMP. See: Dillon,
Marshal Matt

PERCY DOVETONSILS. See:
Kovacs, Ernie (1)

PERCY FAITH. See:
Faith, Percy
Whiteman, Paul

PERCY, LORD. See: Sunday

PERCY VAN SCHUYLER. See:
Kaltenmeyer, Professor August,
D. U. N.

PERERA, LYDIA, narrator on the
program (herself)
Story to Order (R) (Children's
stories)

PEREZ PRADO. See:

Basie, Count
Whiteman, Paul

PERITO, NICK. See: Knotts, Don

PERKINS, CARL. See:
Cash, Johnny
Ritter, Tex (1)

PERKINS, DEACON. See: Harum,
David

PERKINS, MA, proprietress of
lumberyard in the town of Rush-
ville Center
FAY PERKINS HENDERSON, her
daughter
PAUL HENDERSON, Fay's hus-
band
EVEY PERKINS FITZ, her
daughter
WILLIE FITZ
JUNIOR FITZ, Evey's sons
JOHN PERKINS
GRETA, maid
MR. FARNUM
MRS. FARNUM
CATHERINE SHAUGHNESSEY
C. PEMBERTON TOOHEY
JOHN ADAM DRAYTON
ZENITH SAMBRINI
SHUFFLE SHOBER
ANTON JULIKAK
BURTON WILEY
DR. GLASSMAN, physician
EB MARTIN
JESSICA HERRINGBONE
FLOSSIE HERRINGBONE
TWEETSIE HERRINGBONE
PHINEAS HERRINGBONE
SAM GRIM
DORA
JOSIE
FRANK FENTON
WALTER PAYNE
JUDGE HARTLEY, jurist
GREGORY IVANOFF
BESSIE FLOUNCE
TOMMY TAYLOR
SONNY HALLET
MR. MORTIMER
BURT CARLON
STELLA CARLON CURTIS
LULA
SUSIE PARKER
MISS ADAMS
AUGUSTUS PENDLETON
MATHILDA PENDLETON

MR. GARRETT
JOSEPH
HUNKINS
ESTHER
MR. SILVUS
RUFUS
RUSSELL
DR. STEVENS, physician
GARY ST. DENIS
MARK MATTHEWS
MR. ERP
DR. ANDREW WHITE, physician
MRS. PENDLETON
DEBORAH MATTHEWS
ZEKE HAMMILL
DORIS FAIRCHILD
CHARLEY BROWN
PAULETTE HENDERSON
GLADYS PENDLETON
GARY CURTIS
TIMOTHY GALLAGHER, char-
acters appearing in the drama
Ma Perkins (R) (Serial drama)

PERKINS, MARLIN
JIM FOWLER, naturalists; co-
hosts of the program
Wild Kingdom (TV) (Wild animal lore)

PERKINS, RAY, moderator of the
program (himself)
AMATEUR TALENT CONTES-
TANTS
National Amateur Night (R) (Ama-
teur talent)

PERKINS, VOLTAIRE. See: Judge
(1)

PERRON, MAC. See: Waring,
Fred (1)

PERRY. See:
Como, Perry (1) (2) (3)
Mason, Perry
Ward, Perry

PERRY, BILL. See: Dragonette,
Jessica (3)

PERRY COMO. See:
Como, Perry (1) (2) (3)
Crosby, Bing (2)

Perry Como Show, The. See:
Como, Perry (3)

PERRY, JOHN, store owner
ELIZABETH PERRY, his wife
MARTHA CURTIS, his secretary
and "other wife"
ALAN GREEN
DR. TONY CHALMERS
ANNETTE ROGERS SULLIVAN
CAROLYN PRINCE
PAT GRADY
ROBERTA LANSING
JILL THROPP
SHEILA MAYO
KINGSLEY MAYO
LINDA HOLBROOK
JANET DIONCHECK
BALLARD BRANDON
JERRY MARVIN
RIDGEWAY TEARLE
YVONNE CLAIRE
MRS. MANNERS
DOLORES WINTERS
CURT LANSING
MARINA MARINOFF
MOLLY
GRANNY
EVELYN
LANNY
ROBIN
JUDY, characters appearing in
the drama
John's Other Wife (R) (Serial
drama)

PERRY LEVITT. See: Raven,
Dan

PERRY, LUKE
SIMON KANE, stagecoach drivers
DAVID KANE, son of Simon
Stagecoach West (TV) (Western)

Perry Mason. See: Mason, Perry

PERRY, NEIL. See: Keene,
Kitty

PERRY, PAT. See: McKay,
Judson

PERRY "QUIZ" QUISINBERRY.
See: Adams, Doug

PERRY WHITE. See: Kent,
Clark

PERRYMAN, LLOYD. See: Nolan,
Bob

PERS, DIANE. See: Hopkins,
Kate

Person, The Creative. See:
Baez, Joan

Person to Person. See: Murrow,
Edward R. (3)

Personality. See: Blyden, Larry
(1)

Personality, Split. See: Poston,
Tom

Persuaders, The. See: Wilde,
Danny

PERT KELTON. See: Gleason,
Jackie (1)

PERTWEE, CLAUDE. See:
Huddles, Ed

Pet Set, Betty White's. See:
White, Betty (2)

Pet Set, The. See: White, Betty
(2)

PETE. See:
Armstrong, Jack
Flipper
Kelly, Pete
Malloy, Officer Pete
Morrison, Mother
Porter, Pete
Randolph, Walt
Ruskin, Lily

Pete and Gladys. See: Porter,
Pete

PETE COCHRAN. See: Hayes,
Linc

PETE DIXON. See: Kaufman,
Seymour

PETE FOUNTAIN. See: Welk,
Lawrence

PETE GARCIA. See: Adams,
Lieut. Price

Pete Kelly's Blues. See: Kelly,
Pete

PETE KIRKWOOD. See: Wayne, Ruth Evans

PETE LOFTHOUSE. See: Welk, Lawrence

PETE McNEIL, LIEUT. See: Banyon, Miles C.

PETE NICKERSON. See: Young, Larry "Pepper"

PETE NOLAN. See: Favor, Gil

PETE PAULSON. See:
Paulsen, Pat
Saber, Mark

PETE SLOAN. See: Horton, Dot

PETE STONE. See: Wayne, Ruth Evans

PETE VANESSI. See: Myrt

PETER. See:
Ames, Peter
Black, Peter
Brady, Mike
Brady, Peter
Brent, Portia
Brown, Ellen
Cameron, Christy Allen
Christopher, Peter
Cummings, Brenda
Donald, Peter
Goldstone, Dr. Peter
Gregg, Uncle Bentley
Gunn, Peter
Hayes, Peter Lind (1) (2) (3) (4)
Lindsey, Peter
Lorre, Peter
Marshall, Peter
Murphy, Peter
Pan, Peter
Potomas, Peter
Salem, Peter
Weston, Sam

PETER BOYLE. See: Klein, Robert

PETER CAPELL. See: Higby, Mary Jane

PETER CARVER. See: Lawton, Lora

PETER CHANG. See: Randolph, Ellen

PETER CHERNAK, DR. See: Garrison, Spencer

PETER CLARKE. See: Kennedy, Carol

PETER DALTON. See: Karr, Mike

PETER DARNELL. See: Noble, Mary

PETER DeROSE. See: Breen, May Singhi

PETER DONALD. See:
Cross, Milton (2)
Donald, Peter
Wilson, Ward

PETER FAIRFIELD III. See: Morgan, Paul

PETER FORTUNE. See: Marlin, Mary

PETER FREUCHEN. See:
March, Hal
Story, Ralph

PETER GALWAY. See: Sunday

PETER GRANT. See: Jostyn, Jay (1)

Peter Gunn. See: Gunn, Peter

PETER HALL. See: Manning, Laura

PETER HANLEY. See: Kovacs, Ernie (1)

PETER HANOVER. See: Roxy

PETER HARVEY. See: Dawson, Rosemary

PETER HUJAZ. See: Marlin, Mary

PETER LARKINS. See: Guthrie, Lieut. Ben

Peter Lind Hayes Show, The. See:
Hayes, Peter Lind (3)

PETER LISAGOR. See: MacNeil,
Robert

Peter Loves Mary. See: Lindsey,
Peter

PETER McLEAN. See: Prescott,
Kate Hathaway

PETER MANNO. See: Rutledge,
Dr. John

PETER MARSTON, SIR. See:
Hood, Robin

PETER MATZ. See:
Burnett, Carol
Jones, Jack

Peter Pan. See: Pan, Peter

PETER PANAMA. See: Grant,
Harry

PETER PIPER. See: Carter,
Kathryn

Peter Potomas. See: Potomas,
Peter

PETER ROBINSON. See: Mc-
Donald, Bob

Peter Salem, The Affairs of.
See: Salem, Peter

PETER SANDS. See: McNamara,
Susie

PETER STANDISH. See: Drake,
Betty

PETER TAYLOR, DR. See:
Hardy, Dr. Steven

PETER TORK. See: Jones, Davy

PETER TURNER. See: Brown,
Ellen

PETER VAN STEEDEN. See:
Allen, Fred
McGarry, Dan

PETER WEXLER. See: Bauer,
Bertha

PETERS, BILL
MRS. VAN CLEVE
ABRAHAM LINCOLN WATTS
KIT COLLINS
MADAME SOPHIE
FRANK HARRISON
ANDREA REYNOLDS
HARRINGTON, butler
TAFFY GRAHAME
DIXIE
THE MINISTER, characters
appearing in the drama
We Love and Learn (R) (Serial
drama) (previously known as
As the Twig is Bent) (R)

PETERS, CAROL. See: Farrell,
David

PETERS, CEFUS. See: Parker,
Seth

PETERS, DR. GREG. See:
Horton, Dr. Tom

PETERS, GEORGE. See:
Finucane, Lieut. Howard

PETERS, LIZZIE. See: Parker,
Seth

PETERS, LOWELL
WILLIAM EDMONDSON
HOMER SMITH
JAY STONE TONEY, singers;
members of the Southernaires
Quartet (themselves)
The Southernaires (R) (Negro
spirituals)'

PETERS, MAGGIE. See: Andrews,
Russ

PETERS, SPECIAL AGENT. See:
Harding, David

PETERS, SUSAN. See: Manning,
Portia Blake

PETERSON, DR. JAMES, marriage
counselor and professor of
sociology; host of the program
(himself)
MANY ACTORS AND ACTRESSES
For Better or Worse (TV)
(Dramatizations of case histories
of marital difficulties)

PETERSON, IRMA, secretary
JANE STACY
PROFESSOR KROPOTKIN
RICHARD RINELANDER III
MRS. RHINELANDER
MRS. O'REILLY
MR. CLYDE
AL, characters appearing on the
program
THE SPORTSMEN QUARTET,
featured vocal group
LUD GLUSKIN, orchestra leader
(himself)
HIS ORCHESTRA
My Friend Irma (R) (TV) (Situ-
ation comedy)

PETERSON, ROGER
JOHN SCALI, newscasters;
moderators of the program (themselves)
MANY INTERVIEWEES
Issues and Answers (TV) (Inter-
views/current events)

PETOFI, COUNT. See: Collins,
Barnabas

PETRIE, DR. See: Fu Manchu

PETRIE, ROB, head television script
writer for the Alan Brady show
LAURA, his wife
RITCHIE, his son
JERRY HELPER, his neighbor,
dentist
MILLIE HELPER, Jerry's wife
SALLY ROGERS
BUDDY SORRELL, writers for
the Alan Brady show
PICKLES, Buddy's wife
MEL COOLEY, producer for the
Alan Brady show
ALAN BRADY, television star
The Dick Van Dyke Show (TV)
(Situation comedy)

PETRILLO, CAESAR. See: First
Nighter, Mr.

Pets, Hotel for. See: Jolly, Mr.

Petticoat Junction. See: Carson,
Uncle Joe

Petticoats, Pistols 'n'. See:
Hanks, Henrietta

PETTIGREW, PRIVATE TULLY.
See: Troy, Sergeant Sam

PETTINGAL, LAITH. See:
Parker, Seth

PETTIT, DR. GREGORY. See:
Goldstone, Dr. Peter

PETTY OFFICER HOMER NELSON,
CHIEF. See: O'Toole, Ensign

PEYTON, FATHER PATRICK, host
of the program (himself)
MANY ACTORS AND ACTRESSES
The Family Theater (R) (Drama)

PEYTON, MARTIN, head of the
Peyton family
JOE CHERNAK
JOE ROSSI
DR. MICHAEL ROSSI
DR. MILES
JUDGE CHESTER
MYRNA FAHEY
SERGEANT WALKER
DR. CLAIRE MORTON
MARSHA RUSSELL
NORMAN HARRINGTON
RITA JACKS HARRINGTON
ADA JACKS
EDDIE JACKS
TOM WINTER
SUSAN WINTER
ELI CARSON
BETTY ANDERSON HARRINGTON
CAROLYN RUSSELL
ANN HOWARD
PAUL HANLEY
ALLISON MACKENZIE
CONSTANCE MACKENZIE CAR-
SON
LEWIS JACKMAN
ROBERTA CARTER
NURSE JENNIFER IVERS
NURSE CHOATE
JULIE ANDERSON
LESLIE HARRINGTON
RODNEY HARRINGTON
LEW MILES
UNCLE MATT SWAIN
JACK CHANDLER
HANNAH CORD
JOHN FOWLER
KIM SCHUSTER
FRED RUSSELL
MARSHA RUSSELL
ELLIOT CARSON

RACHEL WELLES
SANDY WEBBER
CHRIS WEBBER
LEE WEBBER
CATHERINE PEYTON
DR. VINCENT MARKHAM
STEVEN CORD
ADRIENNE, characters appearing
in the drama
Peyton Place (TV) (Serial drama)
(later revived as Return to
Peyton Place) (TV)

Peyton Place. See: Peyton,
Martin

Peyton Place, Return to. See:
Peyton, Martin

Phantom, The Funky. See:
Muggsy

PHEETERS, LOUIS. See: Dillon,
Marshal Matt

PHELPS, JIM
DAN BRIGGS, leaders of Impos-
sible Missions Force law enforce-
ment team
CINNAMON CARTER
BARNEY
ROLLIN HAND
WILLY
DANA
CASEY
PARIS
MIMI DAVIS, associates;
members of the team
Mission: Impossible (TV) (Crime
fighting drama)

PHIL. See:
Baker, Phil (1) (2) (3)
Conroy, Phil
Cook, Phil
Donahue, Phil
Everly, Phil
Harris, Phil
Spitalny, Phil

Phil Baker Show, The. See:
Baker, Phil (2)

PHIL BARNES. See: Lambert,
Louise

PHIL BRACKEN. See: Grant,
Harry

PHIL BREWER, DR. See: Hardy,
Dr. Steven

PHIL "COO COO" KILEY. See:
Kirchener, Claude (1)

Phil Cook. See: Cook, Phil

Phil Donahue Show, The. See:
Donahue, Phil

PHIL FORRESTER. See: Ames,
Peter

PHIL HARRIS. See:
Benny, Jack
Crosby, Bing (2)
Harris, Phil

PHIL HAYWORTH. See: Brewster,
Joey

PHIL KRAMER. See: Lescoulie,
Jack (2)

PHIL LORD. See: Ameche, Don
(3)

PHIL MARTIN. See: Porter,
Pete

PHIL NAPOLEON. See: Whiteman,
Paul

PHIL SHUKIN. See: Moore,
Garry (1)

PHIL SILVERS. See:
Crosby, Bing (2)
Donald, Peter

Phil Silvers Show, The. See:
Bilko, Sergeant Ernest

Phil Silvers Show, The New. See:
Grafton, Harry

PHIL SPITALNY. See:
Spitalny, Phil
Whiteman, Paul

PHIL STANLEY. See: Davis,
Joan Field

PHILBIN, DR. See: Randolph,
Alice

PHILBIN, REGIS. See: Bishop,
Joey

PHILBRICK, HERBERT, businessman, family man and U. S. undercover counterintelligence agent
I Led Three Lives (TV) (Espionage drama)

Philco Playhouse. See: Lytell,
Bert (1)

PHILHARMONIC ORCHESTRA, THE
NEW YORK. See: Bernstein,
Leonard

PHILIP. See:
Abbott, Philip
Cameron, Christy Allen
Carey, Dr. Philip
Collins, Barnabas
Findlay, Maude
Horton, Dr. Tom
Marlowe, Philip
Phillip

PHILIP BARTON. See: Steele,
Tracy

PHILIP BAXTER. See: Dallas,
Stella

PHILIP BOSINNEY. See:
Forsyte, Soames

PHILIP BOYNTON. See: Brooks,
Connie

PHILIP BRENT. See: Davis,
Ann Tyler

PHILIP GERARD, LIEUT. See:
Kimble, Dr. Richard

PHILIP HAMILTON, DR. See:
Gentry, Dr. Anne

PHILIP HASTINGS. See: Carlyle,
Baylor

PHILIP KING. See: Trent, Helen

Philip Marlowe. See: Marlowe,
Philip

Philip Marlowe, The Adventures of.
See: Marlowe, Philip

PHILIP WEST. See: Brent,
Portia

PHILIPS. See also: Phillips

PHILIPS, ERIC. See: Tate,
Joanne

PHILIPS, LAURIE. See: Tate,
Joanne

PHILIPS, SCOTT. See: Tate,
Joanne

PHILLIP. See also: Philip

PHILLIP COOLIDGE. See:
Manning, Portia Blake

PHILLIPS. See:
Jiménez, José
Lord, Phillips H.
Philips

PHILLIPS, CARL. See: Welles,
Orson (3)

PHILLIPS, DAVE, moderator of
the program (himself)
GUEST PANELISTS
What Am I Doing? (TV) (Panel
game)

PHILLIPS, DICK. See: Dawson,
Rosemary

PHILLIPS, DR. DAN. See:
Sterling, Vanessa Dale

PHILLIPS, DR. MARK. See:
Cummings, Brenda

PHILLIPS, DOUG. See: Newman,
Tony

PHILLIPS, J. H. See: Karr,
Mike

PHILLIPS, KATE. See: Sterling,
Vanessa Dale

PHILLIPS, NANCIE. See: Rowan,
Dan

PHILLOTSON. See: Cooke,
Alistaire (1)

PHILO. See: Vance, Philo

PHILO "SANDY" SANDS. See:
Marlin, Mary

Philo Vance. See: Vance, Philo

PHINEAS HERRINGBONE. See:
Perkins, Ma

PHINEAS T. BLUSTER. See:
Doody, Howdy

PHINEAS T. GRANT. See:
Waring, Evelyn

PHOEBE. See:
Baby Snooks
Booth, Martha

PHOEBE, AUNT. See: Clayton,
Margie

Phoebe, Dear. See: Hastings,
Bill

PHOEBE FIGALILLY. See:
Everett, Professor

PHOEBE GOODHEART. See:
Hastings, Bill

PHOEBE STANTON. See: Low,
Theodore

PHOEBE TYLER. See: Davis,
Ann Tyler

PHYFE. See also: Fife

PHYFE, HENRY, mild-mannered
accountant working as secret
agent
The Double Life of Henry Phyfe
(TV) (Espionage satire)

PHYLLIS. See:
Diller, Phyllis
Driggs, Karleton King
Gilman, Gordon
Koster, David
Pruitt, Mrs. Phyllis Poindexter

PHYLLIS DILLER. See:
Berman, Shelley
Crosby, Bing (2)
Diller, Phyllis

Phyllis Diller Show, The. See:
Pruitt, Mrs. Phyllis Poindexter

Phyllis Diller Show, The Beautiful.
See: Diller, Phyllis

PHYLLIS DINEEN. See: Malone,
Dr. Jerry

PHYLLIS GORDON. See: Rutledge,
Dr. John

PHYLLIS LINDSTROM. See:
Richards, Mary

PHYLLIS NEWMAN. See:
Marshall, E. G.

PHYLLIS ROGERS. See: Myrt

PHYLLIS STRATFORD. See:
Sothern, Mary

Piano Quartet, The First. See:
Horwitz, Hans

PIASTRO, MISCHEL. See: Knight,
Frank

PIAZZA, MARGUERITE. See:
Caesar, Sid (3)

Piccadilly Palace. See: Martin,
Millicent

PICKENS, JANE. See: Cross,
Milton (1)

Pickers, Hello Pea. See: Ford,
Tennessee Ernie (3)

PICKETT, PLINY. See: Baines,
Scattergood

PICKETT, WILSON. See: Butler,
Jerry

PICKLES SORRELL. See: Petrie,
Rob

PICO McGUIRE. See: Cord

PIED PIPERS, THE. See:
Como, Perry (1)
Palmer, Byron

Pier 23, Johnny Madero. See:
Madero, Johnny

PIERCE. See also: Peerce

PIERCE, CAPTAIN HAWKEYE
TRAPPER JOHN McINTYRE
LIEUT. COL. HENRY BLAKE

MAJOR FRANK BURNS
MAJOR "HOT LIPS" HOULIHAN,
nurse
LIEUT. DISH, nurse
SPEARCHUCKER JONES
CORPORAL RADAR O'REILLY
FATHER JOHN P. MULCAHY,
chaplain
BRIGADIER GENERAL HAMMOND,
officers, nurses and non-commis-
sioned officers attached to the
4077th Mobile Army Surgical
Hospital serving in Korea
M*A*S*H (TV) (Comedy)

PIERCE, DENNIE. See: Kelly,
Kitty

PIERCE, PATSY. See: Canova,
Judy

PIERCE, WEBB, host of the pro-
gram (himself)
MANY COUNTRY AND WESTERN
MUSICIANS
Country Show (TV) (Western
music)

PIERRE. See: Vernay, Pierre

PIERRE NUSSBAUM. See: Allen,
Fred

PIERSON. See also: Pearson

PIERSON, PROFESSOR RICHARD.
See: Welles, Orson (3)

PIG, MUMSY. See: Conductor,
The

PIG, PORKY. See: Bunny, Bugs

Pimpernel, The Scarlet. See:
Blakeney, Sir Percy

PIMPERNEL, THE SCARLET. See:
Blakeney, Sir Percy

PINE. See:
Anderson, Sergeant Nick
Pyne

PINHEAD. See: Lucky Pup

PINK CLOUD. See: Rango

PINKBAUM, MR. See: Allen, Fred

PINKHAM, DR. See: Hardy, Dr.
Steven

PINKHAM, PINKY. See: Garrison,
Pat

PINKHAM, SHARON. See: Hardy,
Dr. Steven

PINKY. See: Lee, Pinky (1) (2)

"PINKY" HERBERT, WILLIAM
MARTIN. See: Barbour, Henry
Wilson

Pinky Lee Show, The. See: Lee,
Pinky (1)

PINKY PINKHAM. See: Garrison,
Pat

PINTO. See: Brennan, Tugboat
Annie

PINZA, EZIO. See: Bell, Alexander Graham

Pioneers, The Sons of the. See:
Nolan, Bob

PIONEERS, THE SONS OF THE.
See:
Nolan, Bob
Rogers, Roy

PIOUS, MINERVA. See: Morgan,
Henry

PIP. See also:
Pap
Pop
Pup

PIP THE PIPER
MISS MERRYNOTE
MR. LEADER, fairy tale char-
acters
Pip the Piper (TV) (Children)

PIPER. See: Pip the Piper

PIPER LAURIE. See: Crosby,
John

PIPER, PETER. See: Carter,
Kathryn

PIPERS, THE DOODLETOWN.

See: Miller, Roger

PIPERS, THE NEW DOODLETOWN.
See: Hirt, Al (2)

PIPERS, THE PIED. See:
Como, Perry (1)
Palmer, Byron

Pirates, Terry and the. See:
Lee, Terry

Pistols 'n' Petticoats. See: Hanks,
Henrietta

PITCAIRN, roving cowboy
Wrangler (TV) (Western)

PITCHER, THE, character por-
trayed by Wilbur Budd Hulick
THE UMPIRE, character por-
trayed by Harry Von Zell
MANY CONTESTANTS
Quizzer Baseball (R) (Quiz)

PIXIE
DIXIE, mice
MR. JINKS, cat, cartoon char-
acters
Pixie and Dixie (TV) (Cartoon)

PIXIE. See also:
Dixie
Trixie

Pixie and Dixie. See: Pixie

PIXIE JEFFERYS. See: Hargrave-
Scott, Joan

Place, Dinah's. See: Shore,
Dinah (3)

Place, Peyton. See: Peyton,
Martin

Place, Return to Peyton. See:
Peyton, Martin

Plain Bill, Just. See: Davidson,
Bill

Plainsman, The. See: Buckhart,
Sam

Plainsman, The Law of the. See:
Buchhart, Sam

Plantation, Blackstone. See:
Crumit, Frank (2)

Plantation, Paducah. See: Old
Southern Colonel, The

Plantation Party. See: Duke of
Paducah, The

Platform, People's. See: Bryson,
Dr. Lyman (1)

Play, Anybody Can. See: Fenneman, George

Play Your Hunch. See: Griffin,
Merv (2)

Playboy After Dark. See: Hefner,
Hugh

Playboy's Penthouse. See: Hefner,
Hugh

Playgirl, The Coty. See: Bordoni,
Irene

Playhouse, Blue. See: Lovejoy,
Frank (1)

Playhouse, Don Ameche's. See:
Ameche, Don (2)

Playhouse, Four Star. See:
Boyer, Charles

Playhouse, Hollywood. See:
Ameche, Jim

Playhouse, Knickerbocker. See:
Lewis, Elliott

Playhouse, Philco. See: Lytell,
Bert (1)

Playhouse, Radio City. See:
Collins, Fred (1)

Playhouse, The Hallmark. See:
Hilton, James

Playhouse, The O. Henry. See:
Henry, O.

Playing the Guitar. See: Noad,
Frederick

Please, Correction. See: Mc-
Williams, Jim (2)

Please Don't Eat the Daisies. See:
Nash, Jim

Please, Information. See: Fadiman, Clifton (1)

Please, Number. See: Collyer,
Clayton "Bud"

Please, Quiet. See: Chappell,
Ernest (2)

Please, Silents. See: Kovacs,
Ernie (2)

Pleasure Time. See: Waring,
Fred (2)

PLETCHER. See also: Fletcher

PLETCHER, DOUG, host of the pro-
gram (himself)
More For Your Money (TV)
(Financial advice)

PLINY PICKETT. See: Baines,
Scattergood

PLOTNIK, UNCLE MOE. See:
Fitzgerald, Bridget Theresa
Mary Coleen

PLUMBER. See: Husband

PO CHANG. See: Garlund, Frank

POCCARI, RICCO. See: Collier,
Tim

Poet's Gold. See: Ross, David (3)

POHLMAN, RAY. See: O'Neill,
Jimmy

POINDEXTER BRICE. See:
Chandler, Faith

POINDEXTER, LIONEL. See:
Conway, Bobby

POKEY. See:
Endicott, Professor Mike
Johnson, Bess
Pookie
Porky

POKEY MARTIN. See: Kelly,
Joe (1)

POLATTA, CHARLIE. See: Welk,
Lawrence

POLESIE, HERB. See: Slater,
Bill (2)

POLEY. See also: Polly

POLEY McCLINTOCK. See:
Waring, Fred (1)

Police, Call the. See: Bill

POLICE CAPTAIN LOGAN. See:
Casey

POLICE CHIEF O'HARA. See:
Batman

POLICE COMMISSIONER GORDON.
See: Batman

POLICE LIEUTENANT
POLICE SERGEANT, officers
The Line-Up (R) (Crime drama)

POLICE LIEUT. BOB MALONE.
See: Dante, Willy

POLICE LIEUT. JOHNSON. See:
Midnight, Captain

POLICE LIEUT. SNEDIGAR. See:
Madison, Kenny

POLICE SERGEANT. See:
Britt, Dan
Police Lieutenant

POLICE SERGEANT, THE. See:
Bill

Police Surgeon. See: Locke, Dr.
Simon (2)

POLICEMAN. See: District
Attorney, Mr.

POLICEMEN. See: Welles,
Orson (3)

Policewoman. See: Policewoman,
The

POLICEWOMAN, THE, law

enforcement officer
Policewoman (R) (Crime adventure)

POLING, REV. DANIEL, minister;
host of the program (himself)
Young People's Conference (R)
(Discussion)

POLK, DR. See: Walleck,
Meredith

POLKA DOTTIE. See: Russell,
Todd

Polka-Go-Round. See: Lewandowski, Bob

POLKA ROUNDERS, THE. See:
Lewandowski, Bob

POLLACK, JOHN. See: Kelly,
Joe (2)

POLLARD, MICHAEL J. See:
Marshall, E. G.

POLLY. See:
Bergen, Polly
Douglas, Steve
East, Ed (1)
Poley

POLLY ARMSTEAD. See: Ben-
son, Bobby

POLLY BENSON, AUNT. See:
Harum, David

POLLY BERGEN. See:
Bergen, Polly
Moore, Garry (5)

Polly Bergen Show, The. See:
Bergen, Polly

POLLY WALTERS. See: Andrews,
Russ

POM POM. See: Huddles, Ed

POMEROY, SUSANNA, social
director of the cruise ship
"Ocean Queen"
NUGEY NUGENT, her friend,
operator of ship's beauty salon
CAPTAIN HUXLEY, commander
of the "Ocean Queen"
Oh! Susanna (TV) (Situation

comedy) (later known as The
Gale Storm Show) (TV)

Ponderosa. See: Cartwright, Ben

Pond's Program. See: Roosevelt,
Eleanor

PONS, LILY. See: Bell, Alexander Graham

POOCH HARDIN, DR. See:
Goldstone, Dr. Peter

POOCHIE, GALA. See: Russell,
Todd

POOKIE. See:
Pokey
Porky
Sales, Soupy

POOLE, ISAK. See: Larkin,
Jeremy

POP. See:
Fairchild, Kay
Noble, Mary
Pap
Pip
Pup

POP JENKS. See: Teen, Harold

POP NUNALLY. See: Myrt

POP THE JANITOR. See: Junior

POP WHITEHOUSE. See:
Morrison, Mother

POPE, CARMELITA. See:
Arnold, Eddy

POPE, TOM. See: Hughes, Chris

POPEYE, sailor, gains great
strength by eating spinach
OLIVE OYL, his girl friend
Popeye the Sailor (R) (Children)
Popeye Cartoons (TV) (Cartoon)
MATEY, his adopted son; former
newsboy
WIMPY, his friend, loves ham-
burgers
Popeye the Sailor (R)
BRUTUS, his rival for Olive
Oyl's affections
Popeye Cartoons (TV)

Popeye Cartoons. See: Popeye

Popeye the Sailor. See: Popeye

POPPA. See also:
Papa
Pappy

"POPPA" DENNIS, RICHARD. See:
Dennis, Liz

Pops, Evening With. See: Fiedler,
Arthur

PORATH. See also: Morath

PORATH, MICHAEL. See: Narz,
Jack (2)

PORKY. See also:
Pokey
Pookie

PORKY PIG. See: Bunny, Bugs

PORTER. See: Wagoner, Porter

PORTER, BEN. See: Cummings,
Brenda

PORTER, CORNELIUS. See:
Wayne, Ruth Evans

PORTER, DR. BRUCE. See:
Dale, Linda
Graham, Dr. Bob

PORTER, GENEVIEVE. See:
Fairchild, Kay

PORTER, JANE. See: Tarzan

PORTER, NIKKI. See: Queen,
Ellery

PORTER, PETE, husband
GLADYS PORTER, his wife
HILDA CROCKER, their friend
PHIL MARTIN, their neighbor
MICHELE MARTIN, Phil's wife
Pete and Gladys (TV) (Comedy)

PORTER RICKS. See: Flipper

Porter Wagoner Show, The. See:
Wagoner, Porter

PORTIA. See:

Brent, Portia
Manning, Portia Blake

Portia Faces Life. See: Manning,
Portia Blake

PORTLAND HOFFA. See: Allen,
Fred

PORTNOY, ALICE. See: Burnett,
Carol

POST, DAVID. See: Marlin, Mary

POST, JOE. See: Marlin, Mary

POST, MIKE. See: Williams,
Andy (2)

POST, WILBUR, owner of Mr. Ed,
talking horse
CAROL, his wife
ROGER ADDISON, his next-door
neighbor
KAY ADDISON, Roger's wife
MR. ED, talking horse; talks
only to Wilbur
Mr. Ed (TV) (Comedy) (also
known as Wilbur and Mr. Ed)
(TV)

POSTMAN, THE HAPPY. See:
Burns, George (1)

POSTON, TOM, moderator of the
program (himself)
MANY CONTESTANTS
Split Personality (TV) (Game)

POSTON, TOM. See also:
Allen, Steve (1) (3)
Moore, Garry (5)
Stokey, Mike

Pot o' Gold. See: Grauer, Ben
(2)

Pot, The Pepper. See: McNeill,
Don

POTOMAS, PETER, cartoon character
Peter Potomas (TV) (Cartoon)

POTTER, TOM, real estate operator
FRANCES, his wife
CAROL
DEBBIE

CISSY, his three daughters
IRENE BRADY, his mother-in-
law
The Tom Ewell Show (TV)
(Comedy)

POTTS, CLARA. See: Baines,
Scattergood

POTTS, ED. See: Baines, Scattergood

POTTS, MAYOR. See: Carson,
Uncle Joe

POWELL, DICK (1), singer and
actor, star of the program (him-
self)
THE MUSIC MAIDS, vocal group
MATTY MALNECK, orchestra
leader (himself)
HIS ORCHESTRA
The Campana Serenade (R)
(Music)

POWELL, DICK (2), singer and
actor, host of the program and
leading actor in the dramas
(himself)
GUEST ACTORS AND ACTRESSES
The Dick Powell Theater (TV)
(Drama) (Dick Powell's Zane
Grey Theater) (TV) (Western
dramas)

POWELL, DICK (3)
WILLIAM POWELL
FRED MacMURRAY
HERBERT MARSHALL, actors,
hosts of the program (themselves)
LOUELLA PARSONS, gossip
columnist, hostess of the pro-
gram (herself)
TELEPHONE OPERATOR at the
hotel
JINNY, soprano
TED FIORITO
RAYMOND PAIGE, orchestra
leaders (themselves)
THEIR ORCHESTRAS
MANY GUEST STARS
Hollywood Hotel (R) (Drama)

POWELL, DICK (4), host of the
program (himself)
MANY ACTORS AND ACTRESSES
Zane Grey Theater (TV) (Western dramas)

POWELL, DICK. See also:
Ayres, Lew
Boyer, Charles

POWELL, JANE. See: Ryan,
Robert (1)

POWELL, THELMA. See: Nona

POWELL, WILLIAM. See: Powell,
Dick (3)

Power, Air. See: Cronkite,
Walter (1)

Power, Kid. See: Nipper

POWER, MERT. See: March, Hal

POWER, ROGER. See: Brown,
Ellen

POWERS, DR. MAGGIE. See:
Davis, Dr. Althea

POWERS, DR. MATT. See:
Davis, Dr. Althea

POWERS, DR. MIKE. See: Davis,
Dr. Althea

POWERS, GRETA. See: Davis,
Dr. Althea

POWERS, MICHAEL, reporter
Intrigue (TV) (Adventure)

POWERS, SYLVIA. See: Davidson,
Bill

PRADO. See also: Prato

PRADO, PEREZ. See:
Basie, Count
Whiteman, Paul

PRAEGER, COLONEL MANNY.
See: Bernie, Ben

Prairie Folks. See: Nielson,
Torwald

PRATO. See also: Prado

PRATO, GINO. See:
March, Hal
Story, Ralph

PRATT, ALEX. See: Worthington, Nora

PRATT, RUSSELL
RANSOM SHERMAN, comedians, featured on the program (themselves)
Laugh Doctors (R) (Comedy)

PREACHER JIM. See: Keene, Kitty

Precinct, Eighty-Seventh. See: Carella

PRECOCIA. See: Holiday, Laurel

Premiere, Alcoa. See: Astaire, Fred (1)

PRENTICE, KATHY. See: Kennedy, Carol

PRENTISS JEFFRIES. See: Sloan, Holly

PRENTISS, JIM, public defender
The Public Defender (TV) (Police drama)

PRESCOTT, ALLEN (1), quizmaster of the program (himself)
MANY CONTESTANTS
Crossword Quiz (R) (Quiz)

PRESCOTT, ALLEN (2), host of the program (himself)
Wife Saver (R) (Homemaking)

PRESCOTT, KATE HATHAWAY
STEVE PRESCOTT
MICHAEL HATHAWAY
GEOFFREY SCOTT
VICKI HATHAWAY
ELIZABETH RAINEY
JOHN RAINEY
DR. ADRIENNE HARRIS
DR. HUGH JESSUP
CHRIS JESSUP
CAROL GAULT
PETER McLEAN
AMY SNOWDEN
MARY HATHAWAY
PROFESSOR JULIAN HATHAWAY
DANIEL HATHAWAY
JIM HUDSON
RACHEL RAYBURN
MRS. SHERWOOD

ED HATHAWAY
DR. JOE PRESCOTT
NAN PRESCOTT
ALLISON HATHAWAY JESSUP
STELLA HATHAWAY
LILLIAN HATHAWAY
MRS. PANGBORN
DR. RAYBURN
LORETTA McLEAN
MRS. BARNETT
BRYAN
REUBEN GREEN
GEORGE PARSONS, characters appearing in the drama
Where the Heart Is (TV) (Serial drama)

PRESCOTT, SUSAN. See: King

Present, Time. See: Huntley, Chet (3)

PRESIDENT. See: Super President

President, Mr. See: President, The

President, Super. See: Super President

PRESIDENT, THE, President of the United States
MANY ACTORS AND ACTRESSES
Mr. President (R) (Drama)

PRESS AGENT, JACK'S. See: Carson, Jack

Press, Meet the. See: Rountree, Martha

PRESTON, AL. See: Garrison, Spencer

PRESTON, DICK, host of Arizona television talk show
JENNY, his wife
ANNIE, his 8-year-old daughter
LUCAS, his son, college student
CHRISTY, his baby daughter
MIKE, his sister and secretary; divorcee
BERNIE DAVIS, his manager
CAROL DAVIS, Bernie's wife
The New Dick Van Dyke Show (TV) (Situation comedy)

PRESTON, DR. DOUG. See:
Garrison, Spencer

PRESTON, LAWRENCE, attorney
KENNETH, his son and law partner, also an attorney
The Defenders (TV) (Courtroom
drama)

PRESTON, SERGEANT, of the
Northwest Mounted Police
THE INSPECTOR, his superior
YUKON KING, his dog
BLACKIE
REX, his horses
The Challenge of the Yukon (R)
(Adventure) (also known as
Sergeant Preston) (R) (and as
Sergeant Preston of the Yukon)
(TV)

Pretty Kitty Kelly. See: Kelly,
Kitty

PRICE. See: Adams, Lieut. Price

PRICE, ADDIE. See: Wayne,
Ruth Evans

PRICE, GINNY. See: Wayne,
Ruth Evans

PRICE, HARRY. See: Burnley,
Walter

Price Is Right, The. See: Cullen,
Bill (3)

Price Is Right, The New. See:
Barker, Bob

PRICE, JUDY. See: Christian,
Dr. Paul

PRICE, NORMA. See: Hargrave-
Scott, Joan

PRICE, NORMAN. See: Hargrave-
Scott, Joan

PRICE, NORMAN, SR. See:
Hargrave-Scott, Joan

PRICE, RAY. See: Ritter, Tex
(1)

PRICE, ROGER. See: James,
Dennis (3)

PRICE TRAINOR. See: Walleck,
Meredith

PRICE, VINCENT, actor; modera-
tor of the program (himself)
MANY CONTESTANTS
E. S. P. (TV) (Game)

PRICE, VINCENT. See also:
Story, Ralph

PRICHETT, FLORENCE. See:
Landi, Elissa

PRIDE, BEN, widower; head of
pioneer family traveling to Kansas
in the 1880s
GRANDPA, his father
GRANDMA, his mother
TIM
MIDGE
KIP, his children
CHANCE REYNOLDS, home-
steader
ELIZABETH REYNOLDS, Chance's
sister, marries Ben Pride
The Road West (TV) (Western)

PRIESTLEY, DR. GEORGE. See:
Hackett, Doc

PRIETO, EMILIO. See: Dane,
Prudence

Primus. See: Primus, Carter

PRIMUS, CARTER, scuba diver
CHARLIE KINGMAN, his com-
panion, also a scuba diver
Primus (TV) (Undersea adventure)

PRINCE, CAROLYN. See:
Perry, John

PRINCE CHULALONGKORN. See:
Owens, Anna

PRINCE, FRANK. See: Bernie,
Ben

PRINCE, RON. See: Jones, Dean

PRINCESS ANNE. See: Churchill,
John

PRINCESS, LITTLE FRENCH.
See: Marie

Princess, Marie the Little French.
See: Marie

PRINCESS MARY. See: Henry
VIII, King of England

PRINCESS SUMMERFALL WINTER-
SPRING. See: Doody, Howdy

PRINCESS, THE ISLAND. See:
Bailey, Sam

PRINCIPAL. See: Andrews,
Archie

PRINCIPAL, CHARLIE McCARTHY'S
SCHOOL. See: Bergen, Edgar
(2)

PRINGLE, MRS. See: Bracken,
Eddie

PRINGLE, OOGIE. See: Foster,
Judy

PRIOR, JEFF, New York private
detective
FLOYD PRIOR, his father, retired newspaper man
The Investigator (TV) (Crime
drama)

PRISCILLA. See: Webster, Nancy

PRISONER, THE (No. 6) "in the
Village"
BUTLER, silent characterization
The Prisoner (TV) (Drama)

PRITCHARD, ARLO. See: Cade,
Sam

PRITCHARD, FLORENCE, hostess
of the program (herself)
MANY GUESTS
Florence Pritchard (R) (Interviews)

PRIVATE BRADDOCK. See: Hanley, Lieut. Gil

PRIVATE CAJE. See: Hanley,
Lieut. Gil

PRIVATE D'ANGELO. See:
Wright, Conley

Private Detective, Michael Shayne.
See: Shayne, Michael

Private Detective, Richard Diamond.
See: Diamond, Richard

PRIVATE DOBERMAN. See: Bilko,
Sergeant Ernest

Private Eye, Charlie Wild. See:
Wild, Charlie

Private Eye, Martin Kane. See:
Kane, Martin

PRIVATE GIBSON. See: Wright,
Conley

PRIVATE HANSON. See: Wright,
Conley

PRIVATE LUCAVICH. See: Wright,
Conley

PRIVATE MARK HITCHCOCK. See:
Troy, Sergeant Sam

PRIVATE NAGY. See: Bilko,
Sergeant Ernest

PRIVATE PAPARELLI. See:
Bilko, Sergeant Ernest

Private Secretary. See: Mc-
Namara, Susie

PRIVATE TULLY PETTIGREW.
See: Troy, Sergeant Sam

Private World, Our. See: Hughes,
Lisa

PRIVATE ZIMMERMAN. See:
Bilko, Sergeant Ernest

Probe. See: Cameron

PROCHASKA, DAVE. See: Kelly,
Joe (2)

Professional Father. See: Wilson,
Dr. Thomas

PROFESSOR. See:
Endicott, Professor Mike
Everett, Professor
Kaltenmeyer, Professor August
D. U. N.
Ludwig, Professor Donald

Professor, The
Woodruff, Professor

PROFESSOR CARL HYATT. See:
Corey, Don

PROFESSOR CRAYON. See: Green,
Sarah

PROFESSOR FARRELL. See:
Welles, Orson (3)

PROFESSOR JASON McKINLEY
ALLEN. See: Cameron, Christy
Allen

PROFESSOR JOHN ROBINSON.
See: Smith, Colonel Zachary

PROFESSOR JULIAN HATHAWAY.
See: Prescott, Kate Hathaway

PROFESSOR KILPATRICK. See:
Davis, Joan Field

PROFESSOR KNAPP. See:
Horton, Dot

PROFESSOR KROPOTKIN. See:
Peterson, Irma

PROFESSOR LEMUEL CARP.
See: Bergen, Edgar (2)

PROFESSOR LOFTUS. See:
Upton, Michael

PROFESSOR MORIARTY. See:
Holmes, Sherlock

PROFESSOR MORSE. See: Welles,
Orson (3)

Professor, Nanny and the. See:
Everett, Professor

PROFESSOR PARTENON PROTEUS.
See: Allen, Jimmie

Professor Quiz. See: Professor
Quiz

PROFESSOR QUIZ, quizmaster of
the program, portrayed by Craig
Earl
MANY CONTESTANTS
Professor Quiz (R) (Quiz)

PROFESSOR RICHARD PIERSON.
See: Welles, Orson (3)

PROFESSOR, THE. See:
Gilligan
Hope, Bob (2)
Professor
Spencer, Jeff

PROFESSOR, THE NUTTY. See:
Lewis, Jerry

"PROFESSOR" TOMMY MACK.
See: Skelton, Red

PROFESSOR ULYSSES S. APPLE-
GATE. See: Kaltenmeyer,
Professor August, D. U. N.

PROFESSOR WALLACE. See:
Mix, Tom

Profile. See: Osgood, Charles

PROFOND, PROSPER. See:
Forsyte, Soames

Progress, Parade of. See: Manson, Charlotte

PROHASKA, JANOS. See: Williams, Andy (2)

PROHUT, LOU. See: Lewandowski, Bob

Prom, Saturday. See: Griffin,
Merv (3)

Promise, Bright. See: Ferguson,
Martha

Pros, See the. See: Davis, Glenn

PROSPECTOR, THE OLD. See:
Old Ranger, The

PROSPER PROFOND. See: Forsyte, Soames

Protectors, The. See: Rule,
Harry

Protectors, The (The Bold Ones).
See: Washburn, William

PROTEUS, PROFESSOR PARTENON.
See: Allen, Jimmie

PROWSE, JULIET. See: Berman, Shelley

PRUDENCE. See:
Dane, Prudence
Everett, Professor

PRUDENCE GRAHAM. See: Sunday

PRUDENCE ROCKBOTTOM. See: Parkyakarkas, Nick

Prudential Family Hour, The. See: Taylor, Deems

PRUETT. See: Wivenhoe, Commander

PRUITT, CANDY. See: Bolt, Jason

PRUITT, GRANDPA ANDY. See: Endicott, Professor Mike

PRUITT, MRS. PHYLLIS POINDEXTER, society woman
RUDY PRUITT, her husband
UNCLE NED
THE BUTLER
NORMAN KRUMP, handy man
The Phyllis Diller Show (TV) (Situation comedy) (originally called The Pruitts of Southampton) (TV)

Pruitts of Southampton, The. See: Pruitt, Mrs. Phyllis Poindexter

PRYOR, ROGER, host of the program (himself)
MANY HOLLYWOOD STARS
OSCAR BRADLEY, orchestra leader (himself)
HIS ORCHESTRA
Screen Guild Theater (R) (Adaptations of motion picture plays)

Psychiatrist, The. See: Whitman, Dr. James

Public Defender, Roger Kilgore. See: Kilgore, Roger

Public Defender, The. See: Prentiss, Jim

PUD
GINGER

SONNY, children, visit odd and unusual places
Let's Take a Trip (TV) (Children's education)

PUDDINHEAD DUFFY. See: Dugan, Jimmie

PUFNSTUF, H. R., dragon-mayor of magic island
JIMMY FLUTE, young boy, has adventures on the island
FREDDY FLUTE, Jimmy's alter ego
MISS WITCHIE-POO, arch villainess
DR. BLINKY, friend of Miss Witchie-Poo
H. R. Pufnstuf (TV) (Children's program)

PUGSLEY. See: Addams, Gomez

PULLEN, WHISTLIN'. See: Bernie, Ben

Pulpit, The National Radio. See: Cadman, Rev. S. Parkes

PULVER, ENSIGN. See: Roberts, Doug

PUNI. See: Jamison, Dr. Sean

Punishment, Crime and. See: Roberts, Clete

PUNJAB. See: Little Orphan Annie

PUP. See:
Lucky Pup
Pap
Pip
Pop

Pup, Lucky. See: Lucky Pup

PUPI CAMPO. See: Whiteman, Paul

PUPPY, HUSH. See: Lewis, Shari

PUPS, DAISY'S FIVE. See: Bumstead, Blondie

PURCELL, BETH. See: Rockford, Matthew

PURDY. See: Thompson, Andy

PURDY, DR. See: Harding, Karen
Adams

PURITY. See: Silver, Long John

Pursuit. See: Black, Peter

Pursuit of Happiness. See:
Meredith, Burgess

Pussycats in Outer Space, Josie
and the. See: Josie

Pussycats, Josie and the. See:
Josie

PUSSYCATS, THE. See: Josie

PUTNAM, BARBARA. See:
Wilbur, Judy

PUTNAM, DONALD. See: Wilbur,
Judy

PUTNAM, LAURA. See: Wilbur,
Judy

Putting Me On, You're. See:
Blyden, Larry (2)

PUZZLER, THE. See: Batman

Puzzles, Melody. See: Uttal,
Fred (2)

PYLE, GOMER, bumbling U.S.
Marine private
SERGEANT CARTER, his mili-
tary superior
DUKE, his friend, Marine
LIEUT. ANDERSON, his com-
manding officer
Gomer Pyle, U.S.M.C. (TV)
(Military situation comedy)

PYLE, GOMER. See also: Taylor, Andy

PYLE, GOOBER. See: Jones,
Sam

PYNE. See also: Pine

PYNE, JOE, host of the program;
specialist in "dissecting" guests

MANY GUESTS
The Joe Pyne Show (TV) (Interview)

QUAKER GIRL. See: Armstrong
Quaker Girl, The

Quality Twins, The. See: East,
Ed (2)

QUARTET, THE BILLY WILLIAMS.
See: Caesar, Sid (3)

QUARTET, THE CAVALIERS.
See: Dragonette, Jessica (1)

QUARTET, THE CONTINENTALS.
See: Faith, Percy

Quartet, The First Piano. See:
Horowitz, Hans

QUARTET, THE FLONZALEY
STRING. See: Drew, John

QUARTET, THE KING'S MEN.
See: McGee, Fibber

QUARTET, THE MELLO-LARKS.
See: James, Dennis (1)

QUARTET, THE NORSEMEN. See:
Shields, Jimmy

QUARTET, THE ROXY MALE.
See: Roxy

QUARTET, THE SINCLAIR. See:
Arnold, Gene

QUARTET, THE SOUTHERNAIRES.
See: Peters, Lowell

QUARTET, THE SPORTSMEN.
See:
Benny, Jack
Canova, Judy
Peterson, Irma

QUARTET, THE TOWN HALL.
See: Allen, Fred

Queen and I, The. See: Nelson

QUEEN ANNE. See: Churchill,
John

QUEEN, ELLERY, detective
INSPECTOR QUEEN, his father,
police officer
SERGEANT VELIE, police officer
NIKKI PORTER, Ellery Queen's

secretary and girl friend
Ellery Queen (R) (TV) (Detective drama)

Queen For a Day. See: Bailey,
Jack

QUEEN GUINEVERE. See: Sir
Lancelot

QUEEN, MADAME. See: Jones,
Amos

QUEEN OF BRITAIN. See: Sir
Lancelot

QUEEN OF ENGLAND. See:
Drake, Sir Francis

QUEEN OF IRELAND. See: Sir
Lancelot

Queen of the Jungle, Sheena. See:
Sheena

QUEEN, THE OCEAN. See:
Pomeroy, Susanna

QUEENIE. See: Dugan, Queenie

QUEENIE SMITH. See: Kelly,
Gene

QUENTIN. See:
Collins, Barnabas
Quinton

QUEST, JONNY, young boy
DR. BENTON QUEST, his father;
scientist
HADJI, Hindu boy, his friend
ROGER "RACE" BANNON, avi-
ator; associate of Dr. Quest
BANDIT, Jonny's dog; all car-
toon characters
Jonny Quest (TV) (Cartoon)

Question Bee, Uncle Jim's. See:
Uncle Jim

Question, The Sixty-Four Dollar.
See: Baker, Phil (3)

Question, The $64,000. See:
March, Hal

Questions, Twenty. See: Slater,
Bill (2)

Quick as a Flash. See: Roberts, Ken

QUICK, BEN. See: Varner, Will

QUICK DRAW. See: McGraw, Quick Draw

Quick Draw McGraw. See: McGraw, Quick Draw

QUICKIES, THE BURBANK. See: Rowan, Dan

Quicksilver. See: Sherman, Ransom (1)

Quiet, Please. See: Chappell, Ernest (2)

QUIGLEY, MR. See: Dixon, Bobby

QUIGLEY, MRS. See: Dixon, Bobby

Quill and the Gun, The. See: Drum, Jefferson

QUIN. See also: Quinn

QUIN RYAN. See: Cowan, Thomas

QUINCE, LUTHER. See: Howard, Jim

QUINCY HOWE. See: Shadel, Bill

QUINCY JONES. See: Cosby, Bill (2)

QUINCY, ST. JOHN. See: Crackerby, O.K.

QUINLAN, ROBERTA, pianist and singer; star of the program (herself)
Especially For You (TV) (Music)

QUINN. See also: Quin

QUINN, BERT. See: Stockton, Sandy (2)

QUINN, SPENCER. See: Reed, Jerry

QUINN, WILLIAM. See: McCormick, Myron

QUINT. See: Dillon, Marshal Matt

QUINTET, THE ART VAN DAMME. See: Garroway, Dave (3)

QUINTON. See: McHale, Lieut. Commander Quinton Quentin

QUINTON, GERALDINE. See: Baines, Scattergood

Quirt, Captain Flagg and Sergeant. See: Flagg, Captain

QUIRT, SERGEANT. See: Flagg, Captain

QUISINBERRY, PERRY "QUIZ." See: Adams, Doug

QUITO. See: Carr, Alison

QUIZ. See: Professor Quiz

Quiz, Crossword. See: Prescott, Allen (1)

Quiz Kids, The. See: Fadiman, Clifton (2) Kelly, Joe (2)

Quiz, Kitchen. See: East, Ed (1)

Quiz of Two Cities, The. See: Fitzmaurice, Michael

Quiz, Professor. See: Professor Quiz

"QUIZ" QUISINBERRY, PERRY. See: Adams, Doug

Quiz Time, Pantomime. See: Harrington, Pat, Jr. Stokey, Mike

Quiz, Whiz. See: Olsen, Johnny (2)

Quiz, Yankee Doodle. See: Malone, Ted (2)

Quizzer Baseball. See: Pitcher, The

R. C. A. , The Magic Key of. See:
Stoopnagle, Colonel Lemuel Q.
(1)

R. C. M. P. See: Scott, Constable
Frank

R. F. D. America. See: Bottcher,
Ed

R. F. D. , Mayberry. See: Jones,
Sam

R. F. D. #1. See: Beasley, Irene
(2)

R. G. BROWN. See: Byner, John
(1)

R. LEICESTER. See: Barry,
Jack (9)

RABBIT, BUNNY. See: Kangaroo,
Captain

RABBITT, FLETCHER. See:
Kukla

RABBITT, MERCEDES. See:
Kukla

"RACE" BANNON, ROGER. See:
Quest, Jonny

RACE, CLARK, moderator of the
program (himself)
THREE PAIRS OF HUSBAND
AND WIFE PANELISTS
The Parent Game (TV) (Game)

RACHEL BEALE. See: Sterling,
Vanessa Dale

RACHEL CARLAY. See: Thomas,
Thomas L.

RACHEL CLARK DAVIS. See:
Randolph, Alice

RACHEL HOLT. See: Bracken,
John

RACHEL RAYBURN. See: Prescott, Kate Hathaway

RACHEL WELLES. See: Peyton,
Martin

Racket Squad. See: Braddock,
Captain

RADAR O'REILLY, CORPORAL.
See: Pierce, Captain Hawkeye

RADCLIFF, MISS. See: Brent,
Dr. Jim

RADCLIFFE, ALISON. See:
Graham, Dr. Bob

RADCLIFFE, FRANK. See:
Slattery, Jim

RADIO ANNOUNCERS. See:
Welles, Orson (3)

Radio City Playhouse. See:
Collins, Fred (1)

Radio Hall of Fame. See: Gibbs,
Georgia (2)

RADIO LISTENER, MR. AVERAGE.
See: Kaye, Danny

Radio Pulpit, The National. See:
Cadman, Rev. S. Parkes

Radio Theater, The Lux. See:
DeMille, Cecil B.

Radio's Court of Honor. See:
Towne, Don

RAE. See also:
Ray
Raye
Rey
Roy

RAE, NAN. See: Cantor, Eddie
(2)

RAGAS, PEDRO. See: Paulsen,
Pat

RAGS. See: Marshall, John

Ragtime Era, The. See: Morath,
Max

Raiders, MacKenzie's. See: Mac-
Kenzie, Colonel Ronald S.

Railroad Hour, The. See: Mac-
Rae, Gordon (2)

Rainbow, End of the. See: Baker,
Art (1)

Rainbow House. See: Emery, Bob

RAINEY, DR. FROELICH, modera-
tor of the program (himself)
DR. CARLETON COON
DR. ALFRED KIDDER, panelists
of the program (themselves)
GUEST PANELISTS
What In the World? (TV) (Panel
quiz)

RAINEY, ELIZABETH. See:
Prescott, Kate Hathaway

RAINEY, JOHN. See: Prescott,
Kate Hathaway

Raising Your Parents. See:
Cross, Milton (4)

RAITT, JOHN. See: Blair, Janet

RAJI. See: Bowen, Terry

Raleigh Room, The. See: Hildegarde (2)

RALNA ENGLISH. See: Welk,
Lawrence

RALPH. See:
Baxter, Captain Ralph
Edwards, Ralph (1) (2) (3)
Flanagan, Ralph
Gleason, Ralph
Kramden, Ralph
Nipper
Pam
Story, Ralph

RALPH BELL. See: Voice of
Superstition, The

RALPH BELLAMY. See: Moore,
Garry (5)

RALPH CARMICHAEL. See:
Driggs, Karleton King
Rogers, Roy

RALPH DALY. See: Dyke,
Charity Amanda

RALPH DUMKE. See: East, Ed
(2) (3)

RALPH EDWARDS. See:
Edwards, Ralph (1) (2) (3)
Leyden, Bill (1)

Ralph Flanagan. See: Flanagan,
Ralph

RALPH FLANAGAN. See:
Basie, Count
Flanagan, Ralph

RALPH FONT. See: Whiteman,
Paul

RALPH FRASER. See: Harding,
Mrs. Rhoda

RALPH KRAMDEN. See:
Gleason, Jackie (1)
Kramden, Ralph

RALPH MARTIERE. See:
Basie, Count
Whiteman, Paul

RALPH MONROE. See: Douglas,
Oliver

RALPH MUNSON, DR. See:
Malone, Dr. Jerry

RALPH SANTO. See: Carter,
Kathryn

RALPH STEVENS, DR. See:
Bradley, Judith

RALPH THOMPSON, DR. See:
Brent, Dr. Jim

RALSTON, BOB, organist and
pianist; host of the program
(himself)
MANY GUEST MUSICIANS
Bob Ralston's Music Box (TV)
(Music)

RALSTON, BOB. See also:
Welk, Lawrence

RALSTON, MAGGIE. See:
Grover, Millie

RALSTON STRAIGHT SHOOTER,
THE. See: Mix, Tom

Ralston Straight Shooters, Tom Mix
and His. See: Mix, Tom

RAM, GUNGA. See: Devine, Andy

RAMAGE, WILBUR. See: Sloan,
Holly

RAMAR. See: Reynolds, Dr. Tom

Ramar of the Jungle. See:
Reynolds, Dr. Tom

RAMBRIDGE, CAPTAIN RAYMOND.
See: Rice, Lieut. Bill

RAMEY, DR. See: Dallas, Stella

RAMIREZ, BOB. See: Stafford,
Paul

RAMIREZ, CARLOS. See:
Bertrille, Sr.
Morgan, Frank (1)

RAMON RAQUELLO. See: Welles,
Orson (3)

RAMONA. See: Crosby, Bing (3)

RAMOS, JOHNNY. See: Slattery,
Jim

RAMSEY, CHUCK. See: Mid-
night, Captain

RAMSEY, CURT. See: Welk,
Lawrence

RAMSEY, DIANE CARVELL. See:
Wayne, Ruth Evans

RAMSEY, ERIC. See: Wayne,
Ruth Evans

RAMSEY, HECTOR "HEC," former
gunfighter, now deputy sheriff
in small Oklahoma town at turn
of the century
CHIEF OLIVER STAMP, sheriff,
his superior
Hec Ramsey (TV) (Western)

RAMSEY, LLOYD. See: Brooks,
Cameron

RANCH BOYS, THE. See: Mix,
Tom

Ranch, Gene Autry's Melody.
See: Autry, Gene

Ranch, Magic. See: Alan, Don

Ranch Party. See: Ritter, Tex
(1)

Ranch Party, Western. See:
Ritter, Tex (1)

RAND, MISS. See: District
Attorney, Mr.

RANDALL, ALABAMA. See:
Arden, Jane

RANDALL, ALICE. See: Brent,
Dr. Jim

RANDALL, BETTY. See: Steele,
Ted

RANDALL, BOB. See: Burnley,
Walter

RANDALL, JOAN. See: Burnley,
Walter

RANDALL, JOSH, professional
bounty hunter
JASON NICHOLS, deputy sheriff
PANAMA, Randall's friend
Wanted--Dead or Alive (TV)
(Western)

RANDALL, LAURIE. See: Burnley, Walter

RANDALL, MARK. See: Manning,
Portia Blake

RANDELL, RON, host of the pro-
gram (himself)
MANY ACTORS AND ACTRESSES
The Vise (TV) (Suspense dramas)

RANDOLPH. See: Foster, Judy

RANDOLPH, ALICE
JOHN RANDOLPH
PATRICIA RANDOLPH
MARY ANN RANDOLPH
MICHAEL RANDOLPH
STEVEN FRAME
BERNICE ROBBINS
ADA DOWNS
ERNIE DOWNS
TED DAVIS
RACHEL CLARK DAVIS
JAMIE DAVIS

GERALD DAVIS
WALTER CURTIN
WILLIS FRAME
RUSS MATTHEWS
CINDY CLARK
TED CLARK
DR. RUSS SCOTT
PEGGY DEVLIN
RAY
DR. PHILBIN
MRS. HEWITT
LENORE
MARK VENABLE
PAULA
NORA
CAROLINE, characters appearing in the drama
Another World (TV) (Serial drama)

RANDOLPH BUCHANAN. See: Hillman, India

RANDOLPH, ELLEN
GEORGE RANDOLPH
ROBERT RANDOLPH
ANDY BARRETT
MRS. BARRETT
DR. KEITH, physician
CARL RICHMOND
MARK HILTON
DR. LEWIS, physician
PETER CHANG
KATHLEEN CONWAY
CLAIRE CLAYTON
AGNES FOY
LA LING
TED CLAYTON
JEROME BROOKS
AMY BROWN
VINCE KENNEDY
MR. BARRETT
RENA FLETCHER
MRS. MATTHEWS
SKIPPER
NADINE
DAKIM, characters appearing in the drama
Ellen Randolph (R) (Serial drama)

RANDOLPH, MILDRED CARTER. See: Carter, Mr.

RANDOLPH, REX
CAL CALHOUN, private investigators in New Orleans
MELODY LEE MERCER, their

secretary
Bourbon Street Beat (TV) (Detective drama)

RANDOLPH, SID. See: Carter, Mr.

RANDOLPH, WALT, widower
NANCY
KIM
CHARLIE, his daughters
DEMPSTER
TRACY
WILLOW
PETE
MAGGIE, characters appearing on the program
The Best Years (TV) (Family comedy)

RANDY. See:
Carter, Mr.
Crabtree, Dave
Kennedy, Carol
Sparks, Randy

RANDY GREENSPRING. See: Myrt

RANDY MERRIMAN. See: Paige, Bob

RANDY ROBINSON. See: Nuvo, Arnie

RANDY VAN HORN CHORAL GROUP. See: Cole, Nat "King"

RANGER. See:
Lone Ranger, The
Old Ranger, The
Yogi Bear

RANGER CAPTAIN. See: Parmalee, Ranger Captain

RANGER, FOREST. See: Mitchell, Everett

Ranger, The Lone. See: Lone Ranger, The

RANGER, VIDEO. See: Video, Captain

Rangers, The Texas. See: Pearson, Jace

Rango. See: Rango

RANGO, Texas Ranger, nephew of
commandant of Texas Rangers
PINK CLOUD, his Indian friend
CAPTAIN HORTON, Texas Ranger
Rango (TV) (Comedy)

RANSOM. See: Sherman, Ransom
(1) (2)

RANSOM, LEILA. See: Gildersleeve, Throckmorton P.

RANSOM SHERMAN. See:
Kirkwood, Jack
Moore, Garry (1)
Pratt, Russell
Sherman, Ransom (1) (2)

RAQUELLO, RAMON. See: Welles,
Orson (3)

RASPUTIN X. DELMAROFF. See:
Delmar, Kenny

Rat Patrol, The. See: Troy,
Sergeant Sam

Rate, How Do You? See: Reddy,
Tom

Rate Your Mate. See: Adams,
Joey (2)

RATHBONE, BASIL, narrator and
star of the program (himself)
Tales of Fatima (R) (Adventure)

RATHBONE, BASIL. See also:
Carroll, Madeleine

RATTLER, THE. See:
Carter, Chick
Grief, Captain David

RAVEN, DAN, detective lieutenant
with West Hollywood sheriff's
office
SERGEANT BURKE, detective
sergeant; his partner
PERRY LEVITT, photographer;
also his partner
Dan Raven (TV) (Crime drama)

Rawhide. See: Favor, Gil

RAWLINGS, REGINA. See:

Noble, Mary

RAWLS, LOU. See: Steinberg,
David (2)

RAWSON, NEIL. See: Bauer,
Bertha

RAXL. See: Carr, Alison

RAY. See:
Anthony, Ray
Bolger, Ray
Driggs, Karleton King
Heatherton, Ray
McNulty, Professor Ray
Perkins, Ray
Rae
Randolph, Alice
Raye
Rey
Rogers, Patricia
Roy
Stevens, Ray

RAY ANTHONY. See:
Anthony, Ray
Whiteman, Paul

Ray Anthony Show, The. See:
Anthony, Ray

RAY BLOCH. See:
Gleason, Jackie (2)
Howard, Tom (2)
Kay, Beatrice
Seymour, Dan

Ray, Bob and. See: Ballew,
Wally

RAY, BOB AND. See:
James, Dennis (3)
Nye, Louis

RAY BOLGER. See:
Bolger, Ray
Crosby, Bing (2)
Rogers, Ginger

Ray Bolger Show, The. See:
Bolger, Ray

RAY CARTER. See: Murray,
Kathryn

RAY CHARLES SINGERS, THE.
See:

Como, Perry (1) (2) (3)
Fisher, Eddie

RAY COLLINS. See: Welles,
Orson (1) (2)

RAY McGREGOR, DR. See:
Newman, Tony

RAY McKINLEY. See: Basie,
Count

RAY MICHAELS. See: Kaye,
Sammy (1)

Ray Milland Show, The. See:
McNulty, Professor Ray

RAY NOBLE. See:
Ameche, Don (1)
Bergen, Edgar (2)
Burns, George (1)

RAY POHLMAN. See: O'Neill,
Jimmy

RAY PRICE. See: Ritter, Tex
(1)

RAY SAWYER. See: Brent, Dr.
Jim

RAY SCOTT. See: McKay, Jim
(1)

RAY SINATRA. See: McKinley,
Barry

Ray Stevens Show, The. See:
Stevens, Ray

Rayburn and Finch, Night Shift With.
See: Rayburn, Gene (3)

RAYBURN, DR. See: Prescott,
Kate Hathaway

RAYBURN, GENE (1), host of the
program (himself)
THREE CELEBRITY PANELISTS
AUDIENCE INTERVIEWEES
INTERVIEWERS
The Amateur's Guide to Love (TV)
(Game)

RAYBURN, GENE (2), host of the
program (himself)
MANY GUEST STARS

The Match Game (TV) (Game)

RAYBURN, GENE (3)
DEE FINCH, hosts of the pro-
gram (themselves)
RECORDED MUSIC
Night Shift With Rayburn and
Finch (R) (Talk and recorded
music)

RAYBURN, GENE. See also:
James, Dennis (3)

RAYBURN, RACHEL. See: Prescott, Kate Hathaway

RAYE. See also:
Rae
Ray
Rey
Roy

RAYE, MARTHA (1)
JIMMY DURANTE
GROUCHO MARX, comedians
and entertainers, hosts of the
program (themselves)
MANY GUEST STARS
The All Star Revue (TV) (Com-
edy/variety)

RAYE, MARTHA (2), comedienne;
star of the program (herself)
ROCKY GRAZIANO, former
boxing star; featured on the pro-
gram (himself)
MANY GUEST STARS
The Martha Raye Show (TV)
(Variety)

RAYE, MARTHA. See also:
Bizarre, Benita

RAYE, SUSAN. See: Owens, Buck

RAYMER, DR. WILLIAM. See:
Thompson, Dr. McKinley

RAYMOND, "your host," introduced
each episode of the series; por-
trayed by Raymond Edward John-
son
MANY GUEST ACTORS AND
ACTRESSES
Inner Sanctum (R) (Mystery
drama) (originally The Squeaking
Door) (R) (also known as Inner
Sanctum Mysteries) (R)

RAYMOND. See also:
Johnson, Raymond Edward (1) (2)
Scott, Raymond
Wamond

RAYMOND EDWARD JOHNSON. See:
Ameche, Don (3)
Bell, Alexander Graham
First Nighter, Mr.
Johnson, Raymond Edward (1) (2)
Judge, The
Raymond
Roberts, Ken
Welles, Orson (2)
Winkler, Betty

RAYMOND, GINGER. See: O'Neill,
Mrs.

RAYMOND KNIGHT. See:
Reser, Harry
Weems, Ambrose J.

RAYMOND, LITTLE. See: Archer,
Corliss

RAYMOND PAIGE. See:
Lytell, Bert (2)
Powell, Dick (3)

RAYMOND RAMBRIDGE, CAPTAIN.
See: Rice, Lieut. Bill

RAYMOND SCOTT. See:
Lanson, Snooky
Ross, Lanny
Scott, Raymond

RE. See: Do

REACH, JOHNNY. See: Brackett,
Hank

Reader's Digest, T. V. See: Reilly,
Hugh

READICK, BOB. See: Halop,
Billy

READICK, FRANK. See:
Judge, The
Welles, Orson (1) (2)

Reading Room. See: Hoopes, Ned

READS, ARTHUR. See: Brent,
Dr. Jim

READS, DOROTHY. See: Brent,
Dr. Jim

REAGAN, investigator
Tracer (TV) (Mystery)

REAGAN. See also: Regan

REAGAN, RONALD, star, later
host of the program (himself)
MANY PROMINENT ACTORS
AND ACTRESSES
General Electric Theater (TV)
(Drama series)

REAL. See also: Reel

Real McCoys, The. See: McCoy,
Grampa

REAR ADMIRAL. See: Zacharias,
Rear Admiral Ellis M.

REASONER, HARRY
MARY FICKETT, co-interviewers
on the program (themselves)
MANY INTERVIEWEES
Calendar (TV) (Interviews)

REASONER, HARRY. See also:
Smith, Howard K. (1)
Wallace, Mike (4)

REBA BRITTON. See: Davidson,
Bill

REBECCA. See:
Boone, Daniel
Lane, Rebecca

Rebel, The. See: Yuma, Johnny

Rebels, The Young. See: Larkin,
Jeremy

Rebus. See: Linkletter, Jack (2)

Record Show, The Million. See:
Gibbs, Georgia (1)

Record, The Big. See: Page,
Patti (1)

RED. See:
Benson, Red
Cassidy, Hopalong
Davis, Red
Foley, Red

Jackson, Martha
Ryder, Red
Skelton, Red

Red Adams. See: Davis, Red

RED BARBER. See: Cowan,
Thomas

RED BLANCHARD. See: Kelly,
Joe (1)

Red Cross Course. See: Buell,
Mrs. Harold C.

Red Davis. See: Davis, Red

Red Godfrey, The Warbling Banjoist.
See: Godfrey, Arthur (4)

RED-HEADED ANGEL, THE. See:
Wilbur, Judy

Red Hook-31. See: Klose, Woody

RED LANTERN, big red fish which
glowed under water; acted as
guide for children on each adventure
ISABEL
BILLY, children, enjoyed many
adventures
The Land of the Lost (R) (Children's adventure)

RED PENNINGTON. See: Winslow, Don

Red Ryder. See: Ryder, Red

RED, SAN FERNANDO. See:
Junior

RED SKELTON. See:
Junior
Skelton, Red

Red Skelton Hour, The. See:
Junior

Red Skelton Show, The. See:
Junior

REDCAPS, THE. See: White-
man, Paul

REDDY, TOM, quizmaster of the
program (himself)

MALE VS. FEMALE CONTES-
TANTS
How Do You Rate? (TV) (Quiz)

REDIGO, JIM (1), ranch foreman
LUCIA GARRETT, ranch owner;
his employer
TAL GARRETT
CONNIE GARRETT, Lucia's
children
Empire (TV) (Western)

REDIGO, JIM (2), ranch foreman
TAL GARRETT, cowboy
MIKE
FRANK, ranch hands
LINDA, Frank's wife, ranch
cook
GERRY, assistant hotel man-
ager in town of Mesa
Redigo (TV) (Western)

Redigo. See: Redigo, Jim (2)

REDMOND O'HANLON. See:
March, Hal
Story, Ralph

REED. See:
Lassie
Reid

REED, ALAN
TED DE CORSIA
JEANETTE NOLAN, featured
on the program (themselves)
MANY ACTORS AND ACTRESSES
Manhattan at Midnight (R)
(Drama)

REED BANNISTER, DR. See:
Wayne, Ruth Evans

REED, BARTON J. See:
Beamish, Stanley

REED, BETH. See: Baines,
Scattergood

REED, DR. CLIFFORD. See:
Jordan, Joyce

REED, ELLIOT. See: Ames,
Nancy

REED, JEAN. See: Malloy,
Officer Pete

REED, JERRY, singer and enter-
tainer; host of the program (him-
self)
MERIE EARLE
JOHN TWOMEY
SPENCER QUINN
CAL WILSON
NORMAN ANDREWS, comedians
and entertainers appearing on the
program (themselves)
MANY GUEST STARS
GEORGE WYLE, orchestra leader
(himself)
HIS ORCHESTRA
The Jerry Reed When You're
Hot You're Hot Hour (TV)
(Variety)

REED, LYNN. See: Chandler,
Faith

REED, OFFICER JIM. See:
Malloy, Officer Pete

REED, TOBY, quizmaster of the
program (himself)
MANY CONTESTANTS
Top Dollar (TV) (Quiz)

Reef, Barrier. See: King

REEL. See also: Real

Reel Game, The. See: Barry,
Jack (7)

REES, VIRGINIA. See: Gibbs,
Georgia (2)

REESE BENNETT. See: Parmalee,
Ranger Captain

REET VEET REEVES. See:
Archie

REEVES, REET VEET. See:
Archie

REGAN. See also: Reagan

REGAN, PEGGY. See: Hughes,
Chris

REGAN, TERRY, attorney
HIS FATHER
HIS MOTHER
HIS SISTER
SALLY DUNLAP, his secretary

DOROTHY WALLACE WEBB, his
friend
Attorney-at-Law (R) (Serial
drama) (also known as Terry
Regan: Attorney-at-Law) (R)

REGGIE MANTLE. See: Andrews,
Archie

REGGIE YORKE. See: Packard,
Jack

REGINA COLBERT. See:
Wincholl, John

REGINA RAWLINGS. See: Noble,
Mary

REGINA RESNIK. See: Ives,
Burl (2)

REGINALD CHEERILY. See:
Blurt, Elmer
Holloway, Harrison

REGINALD PARSONS, DR. See:
Brent, Dr. Jim

REGINALD VAN GLEASON III.
See: Gleason, Jackie (1) (2)

REGIS PHILBIN. See: Bishop,
Joey

Reg'lar Fellers. See: Dugan,
Jimmie

REID. See also: Reed

REID, BRITT (The Green Hornet),
young publisher and masked
crime fighter
KATO, his Japanese valet and
assistant
LENORE CASE (Casey), his
secretary
BLACK BEAUTY, his super-
powered automobile
MICHAEL AXFORD
ED LOWRY, reporters
The Green Hornet (R) (TV)
(Mystery/adventure)

REID, DAN. See: Lone Ranger,
The

REID, DON. See: Kirkwood,
Jack

REID, JOHN. See: Lone Ranger,
The

REID WILSON. See: Cameron,
Christy Allen

REILLY. See:
Ames, Peter
Riley

REILLY, CHARLES NELSON. See:
Chidsey, Jackie

REILLY, HUGH, host of the pro-
gram (himself)
MANY ACTORS AND ACTRESSES
T. V. Reader's Digest (TV)
(Dramatizations of "Reader's
Digest" stories and articles)

REIMER, DR. See: Cameron,
Christy Allen

REIMER, KATHY. See: Cameron,
Christy Allen

REIMER, TORBEN. See: Cameron,
Christy Allen

REINER, CARL
MERV GRIFFIN
MONTY HALL, moderators of
the program (themselves)
JOEY BISHOP
ORSON BEAN
PAT CARROLL
PAUL WINCHELL
MOREY AMSTERDAM
PEGGY CASS
DANNY DAYTON, panelists on
the program, divided into two
teams, "Chatterboxes" and
"Gabbers" (themselves)
Keep Talking (TV) (Panel game)

REINER, CARL. See also:
Caesar, Sid (2) (3)

REINHARDT, DR. See: Jordan,
Joyce

REINHOLD SCHMIDT. See:
Faith, Percy

REISMAN, LEO. See: Ross,
Lanny

Relations, The Court of Human.

See: Alexander, A. L. (3)

RELLER, ELIZABETH. See:
McCormick, Myron

RELUCTANT, THE. See:
Roberts, Doug

REMINGTON, MR. See: Peepers,
Robinson J.

REMINGTON, MRS. See: Peepers,
Robinson J.

REMLEY, FRANK. See:
Benny, Jack
Harris, Phil

REMUS. See: Uncle Remus

Remus, Uncle. See: Uncle Remus

RENA FLETCHER. See: Randolph,
Ellen

RENARD, JACQUES. See: Cantor,
Eddie (2)

RENATA TEBALDI. See: Barlow,
Howard

RENE. See: Monte Cristo, The
Count of

RENEE. See: Waring, Mike

RENFREW, INSPECTOR DOUGLAS,
of the Royal Canadian Mounted
Police
CAROL GIRARD, his friend
Renfrew of the Mounted (R)
(Adventure)

Renfrew of the Mounted. See:
Renfrew, Inspector Douglas

RENICH. See: Ames, Peter

RENO McKEE. See: Harris,
Silky

Report, Strange. See: Strange,
Adam

Report, The Frank McGee. See:
McGee, Frank

Report, The Huntley-Brinkley.

See: Huntley, Chet (1)

REPORTER. See: Newspaper
Reporter

Reporter, Dick Steele, Boy. See:
Steele, Dick

Reporter, The. See: Taylor,
Danny

REPORTER, THE GIRL. See:
Cop, The

REPORTER, THE ROUGE. See:
Melton, James (1)

Reporting, Walter Cronkite. See:
Cronkite, Walter (5)

Rescue 8. See: Skip

RESER, HARRY, banjo virtuoso and
orchestra leader (himself)
HIS ORCHESTRA
RAYMOND KNIGHT
MERLE JOHNSTON
JIMMY BRIERLY
EVERETT CLARK, performers
featured on the program (them-
selves)
The Cliquot Club Eskimos (R)
(Music)

RESER, HARRY. See also: Kaye,
Sammy (1)

Reserved for Garroway. See: Garroway, Dave (3)

RESNIK, REGINA. See: Ives,
Burl (2)

Restless Gun. See: Bonner, Vint

RETTENBERG, MILTON. See:
Dragonette, Jessica (1)

Return to Peyton Place. See:
Peyton, Martin

Returns, Many Happy. See: Burnley, Walter

REUBEN GREEN. See: Prescott,
Kate Hathaway

REUBEN KINCAID. See:

Partridge, Connie

REVERE, PEGGY. See: Banyon,
Miles C.

REVEREND. See:
Atkins, Reverend C. E.
Cadman, Rev. S. Parkes
Fosdick, Rev. Harry Emerson
Fuller, Rev. Charles E.
Poling, Rev. Daniel

REVEREND LEROY. See: Wilson,
Flip

REVEREND McARTHUR. See:
Barbour, Henry Wilson

REVEREND MOTHER. See:
Bertrille, Sr.

REVEREND TOM BANNION. See:
Rutledge, Dr. John

REVIEW. See also: Revue

Review, Washington Week In.
See: MacNeil, Robert

Revival Hour, The Old-Fashioned.
See: Fuller, Rev. Charles E.

REVUE. See also: Review

Revue, The All Star. See: Raye,
Martha (1)

Revue, The David Frost. See:
Frost, David (2)

Revue, The Gay Nineties. See:
Kay, Beatrice

Revue, The M. J. B. Demitasse.
See: Medbury, John P.

Revue, The Salad Bowl. See:
Allen, Fred

Revue, Your Show of Shows, Admiral Broadway. See: Caesar,
Sid (3)

REX. See:
Humbard, Rex
Lawton, Lora
Preston, Sergeant
Randolph, Rex

REX COOPER. See: Hillman,
India

Rex Humbard. See: Humbard, Rex

REX KRAMER. See: Harding,
Mrs. Rhoda

REX MARVIN. See: Myrt

REX MAUPIN. See: Moore, Garry
(1)

REX ST. JOHN, LIEUT. J. G.
See: O'Toole, Ensign

REX TWINING. See: Tate,
Joanne

REY. See also:
Rae
Ray
Raye
Roy

REY, ALVINO. See: Driggs,
Karleton King

REYES, EMILIO. See: Whiteman,
Paul

REYNOLDS, ANDREA. See:
Peters, Bill

REYNOLDS, CHANCE. See:
Pride, Ben

REYNOLDS, DR. MIKE, dentist
LIZ, his wife
SCOTT, their son, age 9
KITTY, their daughter, age 6
BUTTONS, chimpanzee, adopted
by Scott and Kitty
Me and the Chimp (TV) (Family
situation comedy)

REYNOLDS, DR. TOM, researcher,
called Ramar
Ramar of the Jungle (TV) (Jungle
adventure)

REYNOLDS, ELIZABETH. See:
Pride, Ben

REYNOLDS, FRANK. See:
Hodges, Gilbert

REYNOLDS, JAY, host of the pro-

gram (himself)
MANY GUEST MUSICIANS
Scene Seventy (TV) (Music)

REYNOLDS, LEN. See: Tate,
Joanne

REYNOLDS, SAM. See: Tate,
Joanne

RHINELANDER, MRS. See:
Peterson, Irma

RHINELANDER III, RICHARD.
See: Peterson, Irma

RHODA. See: Harding, Mrs.
Rhoda

RHODA MORGENSTERN. See:
Richards, Mary

RHODA THE ROBOT. See: Mc-
Donald, Bob

RHODES. See also: Rodes

RHODES, BETTY JANE. See:
Parkyakarkas, Nick

RHODES, DR. MICHAEL, para-
psychologist
NANCY MURPHY, his assistant
The Sixth Sense (TV) (Drama)

RHODES, GENE. See: Davis,
Sammy, Jr.

RHODES, JIM. See: Erskine,
Inspector Louis

RHODES, LIEUT. See: Storm,
Lieut.

RHODES, SPECK. See: Wagoner,
Porter

Rhythm, Concert in. See: Scott,
Raymond

RHYTHM SINGERS, KAY THOMP-
SON'S. See: Martin, Tony (2)

Rhythm, Universal. See: Crumit,
Frank (4)

Rhythms, Rosa Rio. See: Rio,
Rosa

RIAKOS, ANTAEUS. See: Carlyle,
Baylor

Ribbon Town, Blue. See: Marx,
Groucho (1)

RIBS, SPARE. See:
Arnold, Gene
Kelly, Joe (1)
Old Witch, The

RIC DE AZEVDO. See: Driggs,
Karleton King

RICARDO, RICKY, band leader and
night club performer
LUCY, his wife, portrayed by
Lucille Ball
ETHEL MERTZ, Lucy's girl
friend and neighbor
FRED MERTZ, Ethel's husband
I Love Lucy (TV) (Comedy)

RICCO. See also: Rico

RICCO POCCARI. See: Collier,
Tim

RICE, GLADYS. See: Roxy

RICE, GRANTLAND. See: Cowan,
Thomas

RICE, LIEUT. BILL, new marine
officer, assigned to Camp Pendleton, Calif., marine base
CAPTAIN RAYMOND RAMBRIDGE
LIEUT. SAMUEL PANOSIAN,
marine officers
SERGEANT HORACE CAPP,
marine non-commissioned officer
The Lieutenant (TV) (Military
drama)

RICH. See: Little, Rich

RICH, BUDDY. See: Greco, Buddy

RICH, FREDDIE. See: Ross,
Lanny

RICH, IRENE, actress, star of the
program (herself)
MANY ACTORS AND ACTRESSES
Irene Rich Dramas (R) (Drama)

RICH LITTLE. See:
Andrews, Julie

Davidson, John (2)
Little, Rich

Rich Man's Darling. See: O'Farrell, Packy

Rich, Strike It. See: Hull,
Warren (2)

RICHARD. See:
Boone, Richard
Diamond, Richard
Gibson, Jack
Himber, Richard
Kimble, Dr. Richard
Lane, Patty
Lane, Richard
Lawless, Richard
Maxwell, Richard
Nuvo, Arnie
Parker, Richard
Rickard
Roberts, Oral
Rogue, Richard
Steel, Richard
Wayne, Ruth Evans

RICHARD BARRETT. See:
Stirling, Craig

Richard Boone Show, The. See:
Boone, Richard

RICHARD C. RIDDLE. See:
Butcher, Major Simon

RICHARD CAMPBELL, DR. See:
Nelson, Carolyn Kramer

RICHARD COLES. See: Carter,
Kathryn

RICHARD COLLINS. See: Marie

RICHARD CRAIG. See: Webster,
Martha

RICHARD CROOKS. See: Barlow,
Howard

RICHARD CUTLER. See: Fadiman, Clifton (2)

RICHARD DAWSON. See:
Martindale, Wink (2)
Rowan, Dan

Richard Diamond, Private Detective.

See: Diamond, Richard

RICHARD HIMBER. See:
Himber, Richard
Ross, Lanny
Whiteman, Paul

Richard Lawless. See: Lawless,
Richard

RICHARD MALTBY. See: Whiteman, Paul

RICHARD PIERSON, PROFESSOR.
See: Welles, Orson (3)

RICHARD "POPPA" DENNIS. See:
Dennis, Liz

RICHARD RHINELANDER III.
See: Peterson, Irma

RICHARD THOMAS. See: Les-
coulie, Jack (3)

RICHARD TUCKER. See: Ives,
Burl (2)

RICHARD WEIXLER. See: Kelly,
Joe (2)

RICHARD WHARTON. See:
James, Nancy

RICHARD WILLIAMS. See: Kelly,
Joe (2)

RICHARD WILLIS. See: Charm
Expert

RICHARDS, BEN (The Immortal),
"a rare human being whose blood
contains antibodies which make
him immune to all diseases in-
cluding the aging process"
MAITLAND
JORDAN BRADDOCK, billionaires,
wish Richards' gift of immortality
for themselves
FLETCHER, employee of Maitland, pursues Richards
The Immortal (TV) (Adventure)

RICHARDS, CAROL. See: Crosby,
Bob (1)

RICHARDS, ELEANOR. See:
Hargrave-Scott, Joan

RICHARDS, FAITH. See: Brent,
Dr. Jim

RICHARDS, KEITH. See: West,
Michael

RICHARDS, MARY, thirtyish single
career girl; associate producer
of newscast television show in
Minneapolis
RHODA MORGENSTERN
PHYLLIS LINDSTROM, her
neighbors and friends
BESS LINDSTROM, Phyllis'
11-year-old daughter
TED BAXTER, newscaster
MURRAY SLAUGHTER, news
writer
LOU GRANT, producer of news-
cast; Mary's boss
Mary Tyler Moore (TV) (Comedy)
(also known as The Mary Tyler
Moore Show) (TV)

RICHARDS, MR. See: Hargrave-
Scott, Joan

RICHARDSON, LAURA. See:
Larimore, Marilyn

Riches, Gags to. See: Adams,
Joey (1)

RICHIE. See also: Ritchie

RICHIE LANE. See: Kaufman,
Seymour

RICHMAN, DARICE. See: Kelly,
Joe (2)

RICHMAN, DR. JOHN. See:
Rogers, Patricia

RICHMAN, HAPPY. See: Lindsey, Peter

RICHMOND, CARL. See: Randolph,
Ellen

RICK. See:
January, Dr. Ben
Horton, Dr. Tom

RICKARD. See also: Richard

RICKARD, CONNIE. See: Davis,
Red

RICKEY.   See also:
  Ricki
  Ricky

RICKEY LATTIMER.   See: Sterling,
  Vanessa Dale

RICKI.   See also:
  Rickey
  Ricky

RICKI LENYA.   See: Wayne, Ruth
  Evans

RICKI STARR.   See: James,
  Dennis (4)

RICKLES, TINA.   See: Corbett,
  Tom (1)

RICKS, BUD.   See: Flipper

RICKS, PORTER.   See: Flipper

RICKS, SANDY.   See: Flipper

RICKY.   See:
  Nelson, Ozzie
  Ricardo, Ricky
  Rickey
  Ricki

RICKY DONNELLY.   See: Garrison, Spencer

RICO.   See also: Ricco

RICO MARCHIELLI.   See: Mc-
  Gee, Fibber

RIDDLE, NELSON.   See:
  Andrews, Julie
  Cole, Nat "King"
  Rogers, Ginger
  Smothers, Tom (1)

RIDDLE, RICHARD C.   See:
  Butcher, Major Simon

RIDDLE, SAM (1), disc jockey,
  host of the program (himself)
  MAMMA CASS ELLIOT, co-host
  of the program (herself)
  CELEBRITY GUEST STARS
  POPULAR MUSIC GROUPS
  Get It Together (TV) (Popular
  music)

RIDDLE, SAM (2), host of the
  program (himself)
  TEENAGE MUSIC STARS AND
  GROUPS
  THE GAZZARI DANCERS
  THE SINNERS, vocal group
  Hollywood A-Go-Go (TV) (Music)

RIDDLER, THE.   See: Batman

RIDDLERS, THE.   See: Seymour,
  Dan

RIDER, EASY.   See: Cosby, Bill
  (1)

Riders, Rough.   See: Flagg, Captain Jim

RIDGE RUNNERS, THE CUMBER-
  LAND.   See: Kelly, Joe (1)

RIDGEWAY TEARLE.   See: Perry,
  John

Rifleman, The.   See: McCain,
  Lucas

RIGGS, GLENN, announcer of the
  program (himself)
  MANY ACTORS AND ACTRESSES
  My True Story (R) (Drama)

RIGGS, TOMMY, ventriloquist
  (himself)
  BETTY LOU, his dummy; his
  niece in skits
  WILBUR, Betty Lou's boy friend
  MRS. McINTYRE, character on
  the program
  ANITA KURT, vocalist (herself)
  Tommy Riggs and Betty Lou (R)
  (Comedy)

RIGHT, GENERAL BULL.   See:
  Rowan, Dan

Right, The New Price Is.   See:
  Barker, Bob

Right, The Price Is.   See: Cullen,
  Bill (3)

Right to Happiness, The.   See:
  Nelson, Carolyn Kramer

RILEY.   See also: Reilly

RILEY, AGGIE. See: Dugan,
Jimmie

RILEY, CHESTER A., head of the
house
MRS. PEG RILEY, his wife
JUNIOR RILEY, his son
BABS RILEY, his daughter
DIGGER O'DELL (The Friendly
Undertaker), his friend
WALDO BINNEY
UNCLE BUCKLEY
UNCLE BAXTER, characters
appearing on the program
The Life of Riley (R) (TV) (Situ-
ation comedy)
GILLIS
HONEYBEE, their neighbors
The Life of Riley (TV)

RILEY, JEANNINE. See: Owens,
Buck

RILEY, JOE. See:
Parmalee, Ranger Captain
Walleck, Meredith

RILEY, MICKEY. See: Hastings,
Bill

RILEY, MRS. See:
Riley, Chester A.
Webster, Martha

Riley, The Life of. See: Riley,
Chester A.

RILEY, VICTORIA LORD. See:
Walleck, Meredith

Rin-Tin-Tin. See: Rin-Tin-Tin

RIN-TIN-TIN (Rinty) (The Wonder
Dog), living on Western army
post in the 1880s
RUSTY, orphan boy, his owner
Rin-Tin-Tin (R) (Animal adven-
ture)
The Adventures of Rin-Tin-Tin
(TV)

Rin-Tin-Tin, The Adventures of.
See: Rin-Tin-Tin

RINARD, FLORENCE. See: Slater,
Bill (2)

RINGO, JOHNNY, gunfighter; be-

comes Arizona sheriff
Johnny Ringo (TV) (Western)

RINKER, MARGARET. See: Hutton, Ina Ray

RINTY. See: Rin-Tin-Tin

RIO, ROSA, organist, featured on
the program (herself)
Rosa Rio Rhythms (R) (Organ
music)

RIP TAYLOR. See: Darin,
Bobby

Ripcord. See: McKeever, Ted

RIPLEY, ROBERT L., host of the
program (himself)
LINDA LEE, vocalist (herself)
B. A. ROLFE, orchestra leader
(himself)
HIS ORCHESTRA
Believe It or Not (R) (Strange
and unusual facts)

RIPLEY, ROBERT L. See also:
Penner, Joe

Rise of the Goldbergs, The. See:
Goldberg, Molly

RISE STEVENS. See: Cross,
Milton (2)

Rising, Temperatures. See:
Campanelli, Dr. Vincent

RITA ELLIS. See: Drake, Galen

RITA HARRISON. See: Trent,
Helen

RITA JACKS HARRINGTON. See:
Peyton, Martin

RITA LLOYD. See: Halop, Billy

RITA LOUISE ZUCCA. See:
Sisk, Mildred Elizabeth

RITA MORENO. See: Cosby,
Bill (1)

RITA SIMON. See: Conway,
Bobby

RITA YATES. See: Solomon, David

RITCHIE. See:
Petrie, Rob
Richie

RITTER, LIEUT. See: Coffee,
Dr. Daniel

RITTER, TEX (1), Western singer
and entertainer; host of the pro-
gram (himself)
JOE MAPHIS
FIDDLING KATE
MERLE TRAVIS
EDDIE DEAN
TEX WILLIAMS
RAY PRICE
JOHNNY CASH
PATSY CLINE
CARL PERKINS
SMILEY BURNETTE
OTHERS, Country/Western
musicians and entertainers (them-
selves)
Ranch Party (TV) (Western/
country music) (also known as
Western Ranch Party) (TV)

RITTER, TEX (2), Western singer
and entertainer; host of the pro-
gram (himself)
MANY COUNTRY AND WESTERN
MUSICIANS
That Good Ole Nashville Music
(TV) (Western/country music)

RITZIK, EMMA. See: Bilko,
Sergeant Ernest

RITZIK, SERGEANT RUPERT. See:
Bilko, Sergeant Ernest

River, Moon. See: Jostyn, Jay
(1)

River, Rollin' on the. See: Rogers,
Kenny

River, Rollin' on the, With Kenny
Rogers and the First Edition.
See: Rogers, Kenny

RIVERA, JOE. See: August, Dan

Riverboat. See: Holden, Grey

RIVERS, JOAN, comedienne, hostess
of the program (herself)
MANY GUESTS (celebrities and
people with unusual hobbies and
vocations)
That Show (TV) (Interviews)

RIVERS, LUCILLE, home economist,
hostess of the program (herself)
The Lucille Rivers Show--Fash-
ions in Sewing (TV) (Sewing instruction)

Road, High. See: Gunther, John

Road, John Gunther's High. See:
Gunther, John

Road of Life. See: Brent, Dr.
Jim

Road West, The. See: Pride,
Ben

Road, Wilderness. See: Weston,
Sam

ROADRUNNER. See: Bunny, Bugs

ROARING CHICKEN. See: Parmenter, Captain Wilton

Roaring Twenties, The. See:
Garrison, Pat

ROB. See: Petrie, Rob

ROBBIE. See:
Douglas, Steve
Robby
Robi

ROBBIE DeHAVEN. See: Winters,
Evelyn

ROBBIE HUGHES. See: Malone,
Dr. Jerry

ROBBINS, BERNICE. See:
Randolph, Alice

ROBBINS, FRED
JACK LINKLETTER, quizmasters
of the program (themselves)
MANY CONTESTANTS
Haggis Baggis (TV) (Quiz)

ROBBINS, ROSEY. See: Williams,
Danny

ROBBINS, SERGEANT ED.   See:
Foster, Major John

ROBBY.   See also:
Bobby
Robbie
Robi

ROBBY CLARK, DR.   See: Johnson, Bess

ROBERT.   See:
Alba, Robert
Beanblossom, Robert S.
Dixon, Bobby
Earle, Robert
Hartley, Dr. Robert
Hogan, Colonel Robert
Ironside, Chief Robert
Klein, Robert
Lewis, Robert Q. (1) (2)
MacNeil, Robert
Montgomery, Robert
Randolph, Ellen
Ripley, Robert L.
Rogers, Major Robert
Ryan, Robert (1) (2)
Sloane, Robert
Trout, Robert

ROBERT ARMBRUSTER.   See:
Ameche, Don (1)
Bergen, Edgar (2)
Eddy, Nelson (1)
Marx, Groucho (1)
Weems, Ambrose J.

ROBERT ATWOOD.   See: Hopkins,
Kate

ROBERT BARNES.   See: Henry
VIII, King of England

Robert Burns Panatela Program,
The.   See: Burns, George (2)

ROBERT CASADESUS.   See: Bell,
Alexander Graham

ROBERT COULTER.   See: Williams, Emily

ROBERT GARDNER, DR.   See:
Allen, Joan Houston

ROBERT, GEORGE.   See: Horwitz,
Hans

ROBERT HARLEY.   See: Churchill,
John

ROBERT HINK.   See: Gook, Vic

ROBERT HOUSTON.   See: Allen,
Joan Houston

ROBERT L. RIPLEY.   See:
Penner, Joe
Ripley, Robert L.

ROBERT LEE.   See: Halop, Billy

ROBERT LODGE.   See: Shadel,
Bill

ROBERT MALLOY.   See: Marlin,
Mary

ROBERT MARSHALL.   See:
Carter, Kathryn

Robert Montgomery Presents.   See:
Montgomery, Robert

Robert Q. Lewis Show, The.   See:
Lewis, Robert Q. (2)

ROBERT SHALLENBERGER.   See:
Olson, Emily

ROBERT SHAW.   See: Waring,
Fred (1)

ROBERT STROMM.   See:
Fadiman, Clifton (2)
March, Hal

ROBERT WEEDE.   See: Froman,
Jane (2)

ROBERT YOUNG.   See:
Morgan, Frank (1)
Stewart, James

ROBERTA.   See: Quinlan, Roberta

ROBERTA CARTER.   See: Peyton, Martin

ROBERTA FLACK.   See: Fiedler,
Arthur

ROBERTA LANSING.   See: Perry,
John

ROBERTS, AUDREY. See: Dawson, Rosemary

ROBERTS, BILL. See: Dawson, Rosemary

ROBERTS, CLETE, interviewer on the program (himself)
INMATES OF CALIFORNIA PRISONS, interviewees
Crime and Punishment (TV) (Interviews)

ROBERTS, DOUG, cargo officer of U. S. supply ship "Reluctant"
CAPTAIN MORTON, captain of the "Reluctant"
DOC
ENSIGN PULVER, officers of the "Reluctant"
Mr. Roberts (TV) (Comedy)

ROBERTS FARNSWORTH, JOAN. See: Barbour, Henry Wilson

ROBERTS, FRANK. See: Brent, Dr. Jim

ROBERTS, JIM. See: Welk, Lawrence

ROBERTS, JINNY. See: Winters, Evelyn

ROBERTS, JOHNNY. See: Barbour, Henry Wilson

ROBERTS, KEN
BILL CULLEN
WIN ELLIOTT, quizmasters of the program (themselves)
JACKSON BECK
JOAN ALEXANDER
MANDEL KRAMER
SANTOS ORTEGA
JULIE STEVENS
ELSPETH ERIC
RAYMOND EDWARD JOHNSON
CHARLES WEBSTER, performers in dramatic portion of the program (themselves)
MANY STUDIO CONTESTANTS
Quick as a Flash (R) (Quiz)

ROBERTS LACEY, CLAUDIA BARBOUR. See: Barbour, Henry Wilson

ROBERTS, LYNN. See: Kaye, Sammy (1)

ROBERTS, META BAUER. See: Bauer, Bertha

ROBERTS, ORAL, evangelist, host of the program (himself)
RICHARD ROBERTS, his son (himself)
PATTI ROBERTS (herself)
THE WORLD ACTION SINGERS, vocal group appearing on the program
GUEST SINGERS
Oral Roberts Presents (R) (TV) (Religion)

ROBERTS SINGERS, THE HOWARD. See: Uggams, Leslie

ROBERTS, VERNA. See: Brent, Dr. Jim

ROBERTSON, DALE, narrator of the program (himself)
MANY GUEST ACTORS AND ACTRESSES
Death Valley Days (TV) (Western adventure)

ROBERTSON, SPEED. See: Allen, Jimmie

ROBESPIERRE. See: Baby Snooks

ROBI. See:
Driggs, Karleton King
Robby

ROBIN, narrator of the program
NEIL FOWLER, detective
TOBY, his assistant
Calling All Detectives (R) (Mystery)

ROBIN. See also:
Batman
Bauer, Bertha
Fraser, Ben
Hood, Robin
Kent, Clark
Perry, John
Robyn
Scott, Robin

ROBIN CHANDLER. See: Landi, Elissa

Robin, Dangerous. See: Scott,
Robin

Robin Hood. See: Hood, Robin

Robin Hood, The Adventures of.
See: Hood, Robin

ROBINSON. See:
Brown, Robinson, Jr.
Peepers, Robinson J.

ROBINSON, BRAD. See: Hughes,
Lisa

ROBINSON, CAROL. See: Stevens,
Ray

Robinson Crusoe, Jr. See: Brown,
Robinson, Jr.

ROBINSON, DON, advertising
executive
BARBARA, his wife
JANIE, his daughter
TYLER BENEDICT, his friend
The Don Rickles Show (TV) (Situ-
ation comedy)

ROBINSON, GEORGE. See: Crooke,
Lennie

ROBINSON, HONEY. See: Bratter,
Paul

ROBINSON, JERRY. See: Hartley,
Dr. Robert

ROBINSON, JUDY. See: Smith,
Colonel Zachary

ROBINSON, KELLY. See: Scott,
Alexander

ROBINSON, MAUREEN. See:
Smith, Colonel Zachary

ROBINSON, PENNY. See: Smith,
Colonel Zachary

ROBINSON, PETER. See: Mc-
Donald, Bob

ROBINSON, PROFESSOR JOHN.
See: Smith, Colonel Zachary

ROBINSON, RANDY. See: Nuvo,
Arnie

ROBINSON, SUSAN. See: Sunday

ROBINSON, WILL. See: Smith,
Colonel Zachary

ROBOT, RHODA THE. See:
McDonald, Bob

ROBOT, THE. See: Smith,
Colonel Zachary

ROBSON, MAY, actress, featured
on the program (herself)
MANY ACTORS AND ACTRESSES
Lady of Millions (R) (Drama)

ROBYN. See also: Robin

ROBYN, WILLIAM. See: Roxy

ROCCA, ANTONINO. See: James,
Dennis (4)

ROCCA, MICHAEL DELLA. See:
March, Hal
Story, Ralph

ROCHELL LIEBLING. See: Kelly,
Joe (2)

ROCHESTER. See: Benny, Jack

ROCHESTER, LORD. See:
Churchill, John

ROCHFORD. See also: Rockford

ROCHFORD, LADY. See: Henry
VIII, King of England

ROCK, GEORGE. See: Jones,
Spike (1)

ROCKBOTTOM, PRUDENCE. See:
Parkyakarkas, Nick

ROCKET O'ROURKE. See: Batman

ROCKFORD. See also: Rochford

ROCKFORD, MATTHEW, mayor
of Cimarron City
BETH PURCELL, his friend
LANE TEMPLE, deputy
Cimarron City (TV) (Western)

ROCKWELL, JIM, disc jockey,

host of the program (himself)
VARIOUS JAZZ MUSICIANS
People in Jazz (TV) (Music)

ROCKWELL, ROCKY. See: Welk,
Lawrence

ROCKWELL SIN. See: Farrow,
Valentine

ROCKY. See:
Jones, Rocky
King, Rocky
Marciano, Rocky
Nipper

ROCKY GRAZIANO. See: Raye,
Martha (2)

Rocky Jones, Space Ranger. See:
Jones, Rocky

Rocky King. See: King, Rocky

ROCKY ROCKWELL. See: Welk,
Lawrence

ROCKY SHAW. See: Harris, Silky

ROCKY SQUIRREL. See: Bullwinkle

Rocky, The Adventures of Bullwinkle and. See: Bullwinkle

ROD. See:
Blake, Rod
Serling, Rod (1) (2)

ROD ALEXANDER. See: Caesar,
Sid (3)

ROD SERLING. See:
Cousteau, Jacques
Serling, Rod (1) (2)

Rod Serling's Night Gallery. See:
Serling, Rod (1)

RODD, MARCIA. See: Frost,
David (2)

RODDY MAUDE-ROXBY. See:
Rowan, Dan

RODER, KIRK. See: Manning,
Portia Blake

RODES. See also: Rhodes

RODES, VIRGINIA. See: Kelly,
Joe (2)

RODGERS. See also: Rogers

RODGERS, JIMMIE, singer and
entertainer; host of the program
(himself)
CONNIE FRANCIS, featured
vocalist (herself)
THE KIRBY STONE FOUR,
musical group
MANY GUEST STARS
BUDDY MORROW, orchestra
leader (himself)
HIS ORCHESTRA
The Jimmie Rodgers Show (TV)
(Variety)

RODGERS, PAMELA. See:
Rowan, Dan
Winters, Jonathan

RODGERS SISTERS, THE. See:
Stoopnagle, Colonel Lemuel Q.
(1)

RODNEY DANGERFIELD. See:
Martin, Dean (2)

RODNEY HARRINGTON. See:
Peyton, Martin

RODNEY KILGORE. See:
Marshall, John

RODRIGUEZ. See:
Hudson, Nancy Smith
Muldoon, Francis

RODRIGUEZ, TITO. See: Whiteman, Paul

ROGER. See:
Baby Snooks
Barkley, Arnie
Bower, Roger
Buell, Roger
Burnett, Carol
Collins, Barnabas
Elliott, Roger
Horton, Dot
Hoyt, Vikki Adams
Kilgore, Roger
Miller, Roger
Peck, Torey

Peterson, Roger
Pryor, Roger

ROGER ADDISON. See: Post,
Wilbur

ROGER ALLEN. See: Wayne,
Ruth Evans

ROGER BARKLEY. See: Lohman,
Al

ROGER COLLINS. See: Rutledge,
Dr. John

ROGER DeKOVEN. See: Judge,
The

ROGER DINEEN. See: Malone,
Dr. Jerry

ROGER HEALEY, MAJOR. See:
Nelson, Major Tony

Roger Kilgore, Public Defender.
See: Kilgore, Roger

ROGER MANNING. See: Dyke,
Charity Amanda

ROGER MILLER. See:
Miller, Roger
Shawn, Dick

Roger Miller Show, The. See:
Miller, Roger

ROGER POWER. See: Brown,
Ellen

ROGER PRICE. See: James,
Dennis (3)

ROGER "RACE" BANNON. See:
Quest, Jonny

ROGER THORPE. See: Bauer,
Bertha

ROGER WADDINGTON. See:
Nelson, Ozzie

ROGER WAINWRIGHT. See:
Murphy, Peter

ROGER WALTON. See: Jordan,
Joyce

ROGERS. See also: Rodgers

ROGERS, ALICE. See: Allen,
Frederick Lewis

ROGERS, BARNABAS. See:
Calhoun, Ben

ROGERS, BUCK, twenty-fifth
century adventurer
WILMA DEERING, his girl
friend and fellow-adventurer
DR. HUER, his associate; in-
ventor
ONE, robot, also his associate
KILLER KANE
ARDALA VALMAR
BLACK BARNEY, his enemies
WILLIE, Black Barney's child
protege
Buck Rogers in the Twenty-
Fifth Century A.D. (R) (Science
fiction adventure)

ROGERS, BUDDY. See: Whiteman, Paul

ROGERS, CHICK. See: Gran-
ville, Glynis

ROGERS DANCERS, THE JAIME.
See: Berry, Ken

ROGERS, DR. BOB. See: Tate,
Joanne

ROGERS, EARL. See: Miller,
Mitch

ROGERS, FRED, host of the
program (himself)
Misterogers Neighborhood (TV)
(Children's education)

ROGERS, GINGER, actress and
entertainer; hostess of the pro-
gram (herself)
RAY BOLGER, dancer, featured
on the program (himself)
MANY GUEST STARS
NELSON RIDDLE, orchestra
leader (himself)
HIS ORCHESTRA
The Ginger Rogers Show (TV)
(Variety)

ROGERS, JOLLY. See: Har-
grave-Scott, Joan

ROGERS, KENNY
  TERRY WILLIAMS
  KIN VASSEY
  MICKEY JONES
  MARY ARNOLD, musicians com-
  posing the First Edition, musical
  group featured on the program
  (themselves)
  MANY GUEST STARS
  Rollin' on the River (TV) (Music/
  variety) (later retitled Rollin' on
  the River With Kenny Rogers and
  the First Edition) (TV)

ROGERS, LEX, special agent for
  Florida Sheriff's Bureau
  Tallahassee 7000 (TV) (Police
  adventure)

ROGERS, MAJOR ROBERT, fron-
  tiersman; leader of Rogers'
  Rangers
  HUNK MARRINER
  LANGDON TOWNE, Rangers
  Northwest Passage (TV) (Frontier
  adventure)

ROGERS, MILDRED. See: Carey,
  Dr. Philip

ROGERS, PATRICIA (The Girl Alone)
  SCOOP CURTIS
  ALICE AMES WARNER
  LEO WARNER
  VIRGINIA HARDESTY
  HENRY SENRICH
  LIEUTENANT CUSTER
  ARTHUR COOK
  DR. WARREN DOUGLAS, physician
  DICK SHERIDAN
  STELLA MOORE
  HAZEL BIRD
  JERRY STULIR
  LOUISE STULIR
  CLARA SCHEND
  MIKE BARLOW
  MUGGSY MODOC
  JOHN KNIGHT
  TY DeYOE
  RUTH LARDNER
  JACK ROGERS
  SCOTSON WEBB
  DR. JOHN RICHMAN, physician
  W.C. GREEN
  STORMY WILSON CURTIS
  TESSIE MONROE
  AUNT KATE
  EMMETT DAYTON

JOE MARKHAM
DICK CONOVER
LEWIS
RAY
JACK
ZIEHM
CHUPRIN, characters appearing
  in the drama
  Girl Alone (R) (Serial drama)

ROGERS, PHYLLIS. See: Myrt

ROGERS, ROY, "King of the Cow-
  boys," singer and entertainer
  (himself)
  DALE EVANS, his wife, singer
  and cowgirl (herself)
  The Roy Rogers Show (R) (TV)
  (Western adventure)
  The Roy Rogers-Dale Evans Show
  (TV) (Variety)
  TRIGGER, Rogers' horse
  PAT BUTTRAM, comedian fea-
  tured on the program (himself)
  The Roy Rogers Show (R) (TV)
  CHARLIE WEAVER
  PAT BRADY, comedians featured
  on the program (themselves)
  THE SONS OF THE PIONEERS,
  musical group
  RALPH CARMICHAEL, orchestra
  leader (himself)
  HIS ORCHESTRA
  The Roy Rogers-Dale Evans
  Show (TV)

ROGERS, ROY. See also: Crosby,
  Bing (2)

ROGERS, SALLY. See: Petrie,
  Rob

ROGERS, TIMMIE. See: Moore,
  Melba

ROGERS, WILL. See: Drew, John

ROGUE, RICHARD, detective
  Rogue's Gallery (R) (Detective
  drama)

Rogue's Gallery. See: Rogue,
  Richard

Rogues, The. See: Fleming,
  Tony

ROLAND. See also:

Rollin
Rollins
Rowlands

ROLAND B. HUTTON, JR. See:
Lewis, Dave

ROLAND WINTERS. See: Begley,
Martin

ROLFE, B. A. See:
Edmondson, Delmar
Ripley, Robert L.

ROLFSON, JOHN. See: Shadel,
Bill

Roller Derby, The. See: Brasuhn,
Tuffy

ROLLIN. See also:
Roland
Rollins
Rowlands

ROLLIN HAND. See: Phelps,
Jim

Rollin' on the River. See: Rogers,
Kenny

Rollin' on the River With Kenny
Rogers and the First Edition.
See: Rogers, Kenny

ROLLINS. See also:
Roland
Rollin
Rowlands

ROLLINS, SALLY. See: Sterling,
Vanessa Dale

ROLLO. See: Daddy

Rollo, Daddy and. See: Daddy

ROLLO ST. CLOUD. See: Bennett, Nita

Roman Holidays, The. See: Holiday, Laurel

ROMAN, LULU. See: Owens,
Buck

Romance. See: Voice of Romance,
The

ROMANCE. See: Voice of Romance, The

Romance, Carol Kennedy's. See:
Kennedy, Carol

Romance, Chance for. See:
Swayze, John Cameron

Romance of Evelyn Winters, The
Strange. See: Winters, Evelyn

Romance of Helen Trent, The.
See: Trent, Helen

Romances, Modern. See:
Gregory, Helen
Scott, Martha

Rome With Love, To. See: Endicott, Professor Mike

ROMEOS, THE THREE. See:
McNeill, Don
Moore, Garry (1)

ROMERO, CESAR. See: Kovacs,
Ernie (1)

ROMERO, SERGEANT BEN. See:
Friday, Sergeant Joe

RON. See:
Cochran, Ron
Randell, Ron

RON CAREY. See: Moore, Melba

RON CHRISTOPHER. See: Karr,
Mike

RON PRINCE. See: Jones, Dean

RONA. See: Barrett, Rona

Rona Barrett's Hollywood Movie.
See: Barrett, Rona

RONALD. See:
MacKenzie, Colonel Ronald S.
Reagan, Ronald

RONALD COLMAN. See: Carroll,
Madeleine

RONALD FIELD DANCERS, THE.
See: Damone, Vic (2)

RONALD LISS. See: Halop, Billy

RONNIE. See:
Burns, George (1)
Jamison, Dr. Sean

RONNIE CRAWFORD. See: Barrett, Timothy "Spud"

RONNIE SCHELL. See: Nabors, Jim

Rooftop, Love on a. See:
Willis, David

Rookies, The. See: Ryker, Lieut.
Eddie

Room For Daddy, Make. See:
Williams, Danny

Room For Granddaddy, Make. See:
Williams, Danny

Room For One More. See: Rose,
George

Room, Reading. See: Hoopes, Ned

Room, Rumpus. See: Olsen,
Johnny (1)

Room, The Raleigh. See: Hildegarde (2)

Room 222. See: Kaufman, Seymour

ROONEY, JACK. See: Kelly,
Joe (2)

Rooney, Mickey. See: Mulligan,
Mickey

ROOSEVELT, ELEANOR, featured
on the program (herself)
Pond's Program (R) (Talk)

ROOSEVELT, ELEANOR. See
also: Husing, Ted

ROOSEVELT, FRANKLIN D.,
President of the United States
(himself)
Fireside Chats (R) (Political
reports)

ROOSEVELT, FRANKLIN D. See:

also: Husing, Ted

ROOSTY, aviator
Roosty of the A.A.F. (R)
(Adventure)

ROOSTY. See also: Rusty

Rootie Kazootie. See: Russell,
Todd

ROOTIE KAZOOTIE. See: Russell,
Todd

Roots, From These. See: Fraser,
Ben

RORITY, PAT. See: Fairchild,
Kay

RORY. See: Linus

RORY APPLEGATE. See: Farrell,
David

ROSA. See:
Luigi
Rio, Rosa

Rosa Rio Rhythms. See: Rio,
Rosa

ROSALIE. See: Goldberg, Molly

ROSALIE, MADAME. See: Cosby,
Bill (1)

ROSALIND RUSSELL. See:
Boyer, Charles

ROSARIO BORDON. See:
Dragonette, Jessica (1)

ROSCOE. See:
Bailey, Stuart
Turner, Colonel Roscoe

ROSCOE WORTLE. See: Canova,
Judy

ROSE, character appearing in the
drama
Rose of My Dreams (R) (Serial
drama)

Rose, Abie's Irish. See: Levy,
Abie

ROSE CORELLI FRASER. See:
Fraser, Ben

ROSE, DAVID. See:
Junior
Martin, Tony (1)

ROSE, EVELYN. See: Novak,
John

ROSE FULLER. See: Drake,
Nora

ROSE, GEORGE, head of the
family
ANNA, his wife
FLIP
LAURIE, their children
MARY
JEFF, their adopted children
TRAMP, their dog
Room For One More (TV)
(Family situation comedy)

ROSE HUNT. See: Sunday

ROSE KRANSKY. See:
Nelson, Carolyn Kramer
Rutledge, Dr. John

ROSE MARIE. See:
Marshall, Peter
Rosemarie
Rosemary

Rose of My Dreams. See: Rose

Rose, Tokyo. See: d'Aquino, Iva
Ikuko Toguri

ROSELEIGH, JACK
ELIZABETH COUNCIL
BRUCE EVANS
WALLY MAHER, featured in the
drama (themselves)
Circus Days (R) (Drama)

ROSEMARIE. See also:
Rose Marie
Rosemary

ROSEMARIE BRONCATO. See:
Twin Stars, The

Rosemary. See: Dawson, Rosemary

ROSEMARY. See:

Dawson, Rosemary
Levy, Abie
Rose Marie
Rosemarie

ROSEMARY HEMINGWAY. See:
Harding, Karen Adams

ROSENFIELD, JOE, JR. (Big Joe),
host of the program (himself)
MANY GUEST CELEBRITIES
The Happiness Exchange (R)
(Advice and assistance)

ROSENGARDEN, BOB. See:
Cavett, Dick (1) (3)

Roses and Drums. See: Hopper,
DeWolf

ROSETTA COX. See: Chidsey,
Jackie

ROSEY ROBBINS. See: Williams,
Danny

ROSIE. See: Horton, Dot

ROSS. See:
Lane, Patty
Ordway, Dr. Benjamin

ROSS, ARTHUR, quizmaster of
the program (himself)
DRUM MAJORETTE, character
appearing on the program
MANY CONTESTANTS
The March of Games (R) (Quiz)

ROSS, DAVID (1), narrator of the
program (himself)
ACHMED, Arab chieftain
THE CAPTAIN, characters ap-
pearing on the program
EMERY DEUTSCH, orchestra
leader (himself)
HIS "GYPSY VIOLINS" ORCHES-
TRA
Arabesque (R) (Drama)

ROSS, DAVID (2), Los Angeles
private investigator
The Outsider (TV) (Crime drama)

ROSS, DAVID (3), narrator of the
program (himself)
Poet's Gold (R) (Poetry)

ROSS, DIANA. See: Crosby, Bing
(2)

ROSS FARNSWORTH. See: Barbour, Henry Wilson

ROSS GIRL, THE LITTLE BETSY.
See: Loveridge, Marion

ROSS GRAHAM. See:
Dragonette, Jessica (1)
Henry, Captain
Taylor, Deems

ROSS, LANNY
DOROTHY COLLINS
BUDDY CLARK
JOAN EDWARDS
GEORGIA GIBBS
ANDY RUSSELL
BARRY WOOD
DORIS DAY
EILEEN WILSON
KAY THOMPSON
BONNIE BAKER
JOHNNY HAUSER
DINAH SHORE
KAY LORRAINE
MARGARET McCREA
JEFF CLARK
BEA WAYNE
FRANK SINATRA
BILL HARRINGTON
OTHERS, vocalists featured on
the program (themselves)
RAYMOND SCOTT
MARK WARNOW
AXEL STORDAHL
JOHNNY GREEN
LENNIE HAYTON
ORRIN TUCKER
FREDDIE RICH
LEO REISMAN
AL GOODMAN
RICHARD HIMBER
OTHERS, orchestra leaders fea-
tured on the program together
with their orchestras (themselves)
LUCILE LAWRENCE
VERLYE MILLS, harpists (them-
selves)
FRED ASTAIRE, singer and
dancer (himself)
ETHEL SMITH, organist
THE KEN LANE CHORUS
THE LYN MURRAY SINGERS
THE MERRY MACS, vocal groups
Your Hit Parade (R) (Popular
music)

ROSS, LANNY. See also: Henry,
Captain

ROSS, LENNY. See:
Barry, Jack (1)
Story, Ralph

ROSS MARTIN. See: Harrington,
Pat, Jr.

ROSS, SCOTT
CLIPPER HAMILTON, owners
of Straightaway Garage where
they build and service racing
cars
Straightaway (TV) (Racing
adventure)

ROSSI, DR. MICHAEL. See:
Peyton, Martin

ROSSI, ENRICO. See: Winchell,
Walter (2)

ROSSI, JOE. See: Peyton,
Martin

ROTH, ALLEN. See: Berle,
Milton

ROTHAFEL, SAMUEL L. See:
Roxy

ROUGE REPORTER, THE. See:
Melton, James (1)

Rough Riders. See: Flagg,
Captain Jim

Rounders, The. See: Jones, Ben

ROUNDERS, THE POLKA. See:
Lewandowski, Bob

Roundup U.S.A. See: Shadel,
Bill

ROUNTREE, MARTHA
NED BROOKS
LAWRENCE SPIVAK
EDWIN NEWMAN
OTHERS, moderators of the
program (themselves)
PROMINENT POLITICAL FIG-
URES, interviewees (themselves)
PANEL OF GUEST NEWSPAPER-
MEN
Meet the Press (R) (TV)

(Political discussion/interview)

ROURKE, TIM. See: Shayne,
   Michael

Route 66. See: Murdock, Buz

ROVENTINI, JOHNNY. See:
   Johnny

Rowan and Martin's Laugh-In. See:
   Rowan, Dan

ROWAN, DAN
   DICK MARTIN, co-hosts of the
   program (themselves)
   GOLDIE HAWN
   CHELSEA BROWN
   JO ANNE WORLEY
   JUDY CARNE
   TERESA GRAVES
   BARBARA SHARMAN
   LILY TOMLIN
   RUTH BUZZI
   TINY TIM
   ARTE JOHNSON
   ALAN SUES
   PAMELA RODGERS
   GARY OWENS
   HENRY GIBSON
   JOHNNY BROWN
   JEREMY LLOYD
   ANN ELDER
   NANCIE PHILLIPS
   LARRY HOVIS
   BYRON GILLIAM
   JUD STRUNK
   PATTI DEUTSCH
   EILEEN BRENNAN
   DAVID LIPP
   RODDY MAUDE-ROXBY
   BRIAN BRESSLER
   SARAH KENNEDY
   DONNA JEAN YOUNG
   TODD BASS
   RICHARD DAWSON
   MOOSIE DRIER, entertainers
   featured on the program (them-
   selves)
   WILLIE TYLER, ventriloquist
   (himself)
   LESTER, Tyler's dummy
   TYRONE HORNEIGH, character
   portrayed by Arte Johnson
   GENERAL BULL RIGHT, char-
   acter portrayed by Dan Rowan
   GLADYS ORMPHBY, character
   portrayed by Ruth Buzzi

ERNESTINE, telephone operator
THE GHETTO MOTHER
ANGEL GOOD, characters por-
trayed by Lily Tomlin
THE BURBANK QUICKIES,
musical group
THE BEAUTIFUL DOWNTOWN
BEAUTIES, chorus
MANY GUEST STARS
Laugh-In (TV) (Comedy) (also
known as Rowan and Martin's
Laugh-In) (TV)

ROWDY YATES. See: Favor, Gil

ROWLANDS. See also:
   Roland
   Rollin
   Rollins

ROWLANDS, HUGH
   SHARON GRAINGER, featured on
   the program (themselves)
   MANY ACTORS AND ACTRESSES
   Flying Patrol (R) (Dramatiza-
   tions of stories concerning Coast
   Guard flyers)

ROXANNE. See: Narz, Jack (1)

ROXANNE WALLINGFORD. See:
   Dix, Dorothy (1)

ROXY (Samuel L. Rothafel), impre-
sario, featured on the program
(himself)
   FLORENCE MULHOLLAND
   LEONARD WARREN
   WILLIAM ROBYN
   DOUGLAS STANBURY
   PATRICIA BOWMAN
   JULIA GLASS
   JAMES MELTON
   FRANK MOULAN
   HAROLD VAN DUZEE
   JAN PEERCE
   CAROLINE ANDREWS
   BEATRICE BELKIN
   ADELAIDE DE LOCA
   MARIA GAMBARELLI
   BETSY AYRES
   YASHA GAMBARELLI
   PETER HANOVER
   GLADYS RICE
   ALVA BOMBERGER
   THE ROXY MALE QUARTET,
   singers, musicians and enter-
   tainers featured on the program

Roxy's Gang (R) (Music)

ROXY. See also: Grafton, Harry

ROXY MALE QUARTET, THE. See:
Roxy

Roxy's Gang. See: Roxy

ROY. See:
Bean, Judge Roy
Brenner, Roy
Douglas, Steve
Markham, Roy
Rae
Ray
Raye
Rey
Rogers, Roy
Strickland, Goldie
Ungar, Felix

ROY BARGY. See:
Bolger, Ray
Crosby, Bing (3)

ROY BARRY. See: Johnson, Bess

Roy Bean, Judge. See: Bean,
Judge Roy

ROY CALVERT. See: Dyke,
Charity Amanda

ROY CLARK. See:
Crosby, Bing (2)
Owens, Buck

ROY DeSOTO. See: Gage, John

ROY FENCHER. See: Rutledge,
Dr. John

ROY GABLER. See: Trent,
Helen

ROY LANGER. See: Edwards,
Ralph (1)

ROY MEADOWS. See: Marshall,
John

ROY, MIKE
DENNIS BRACKEN, hosts of the
program (themselves)
Mike Roy's Cooking Thing (R)
(Cookery)

ROY NORRIS. See: McGee,
Fibber

ROY PALMER. See: Harding,
Karen Adams

ROY ROGERS. See:
Crosby, Bing (2)
Rogers, Roy

Roy Rogers-Dale Evans Show, The.
See: Rogers, Roy

Roy Rogers Show, The. See:
Rogers, Roy

ROY SHIELD. See: Sullivan,
Fred

ROY TATE. See: MacKenzie,
Colonel Alan

Royal Canadians, Guy Lombardo
and His. See: Lombardo, Guy

ROYAL CANADIANS ORCHESTRA,
THE. See:
Burns, George (2)
Lombardo, Guy

ROYAL, DR. LEWIS. See: Hank

ROYAL, DORIS. See: Hank

ROYAL McCLINTOCK. See: Calhoun, Ben

ROYAL, TINA. See: Hank

ROYCE, DAPHNE. See: Brent,
Portia

ROYCE, LYNN. See: Marshall,
John

RU. See: Og

RUANE. See: Hill, Ruane

RUBBLE, BARNEY. See: Flintstone, Fred

RUBBLE, BETTY. See: Flintstone, Fred

RUBINOFF, DAVE. See: Cantor,
Eddie (2)

RUBY. See:
Malone, Dr. Jerry
Valentine, Ruby

RUBY TAYLOR. See: Jones,
Amos

Ruby Valentine. See: Valentine,
Ruby

Ruby Valentine, The Story of.
See: Valentine, Ruby

RUBY WAGNER. See: Benny,
Jack

RUDITSKY, BARNEY, New York
detective in the 1920s
The Lawless Years (TV) (Crime
drama)

RUDNICK, STELLA. See: Johnson, Bess

RUDOLPH. See: Nebb, Rudolph

RUDOLPH ATTERBURY. See:
Cooper, Liz

RUDY. See:
Cade, Sam
Conway, Bobby
Cosby, Bill (3)
Pruitt, Mrs. Phyllis Poindexter
Vallee, Rudy (1) (2) (3)

RUDY CAMERON, LITTLE. See:
Davis, Joan Field

RUDY, ERNIE. See: Whiteman,
Paul

RUDY VALLEE. See:
Vallee, Rudy (1) (2) (3)
Whiteman, Paul

Rudy Vallee Show, The. See:
Vallee, Rudy (2)

RUFE RYKER. See: Shane

RUFFNER, EDMUND "TINY." See:
Birthday Man, The
Henry, Captain

RUFUS. See: Perkins, Ma

RUFUS BUTTERWORTH. See:

Gramus, Bert

RUFUS KANE. See: Marlin, Mary

RUFUS LASH. See: Carter, Chick

RUFUS, MARTY. See: Noble,
Mary

RUGG, HAL. See: Wilburn,
Doyle

RUKEYSER, LOUIS, financial expert, host of the program (himself)
MANY GUEST FINANCIAL EX-
PERTS
Wall Street Week (TV) (Finance
discussion)

RULE, HARRY
CAROLINE, CONTESSA DI CON-
TINI
PAUL BUCHET, operators of
international detective agency
The Protectors (TV) (Crime
adventure)

Rumpus Room. See: Olsen,
Johnny (1)

Run Around. See: Winchell, Paul
(7)

Run, Buddy, Run. See: Overstreet, Buddy

Run For Your Life. See: Bryan,
Paul

Run, Malibu. See: Andrews, Drake

Runamuck, Camp. See: Wivenhoe,
Commander

Runaround. See: Winchell, Paul
(4)

RUNNERS, THE CUMBERLAND
RIDGE. See: Kelly, Joe (1)

RUNYON, BRAD (The Fat Man),
private detective
LILA NORTH, his friend and
secretary
SERGEANT O'HARA, police officer
The Fat Man (R) (Detective
drama)

RUPERT RITZIK, SERGEANT. See:
Bilko, Sergeant Ernest

RUSH. See: Gook, Vic

RUSH HUGHES. See:
Grauer, Ben (2)
Kaye, Danny

RUSKIN, LILY, widow
RUTH HENSHAW, her daughter
MATT HENSHAW, Ruth's husband
JIMMY, her nephew
PETE, friend of Jimmy
HILDA, her friend
December Bride (TV) (Situation
comedy)

RUSS. See:
Andrews, Russ
Barrington, Bryn Clark
Gidget
Morgan, Russ

RUSS, CAPTAIN. See: Falvey,
Hal

RUSS CLINE. See: Welk,
Lawrence

RUSS MacDONALD. See: Scott,
Captain

RUSS MATTHEWS. See: Randolph,
Alice

Russ Morgan. See: Morgan, Russ

RUSS MORGAN. See:
Morgan, Russ
Whiteman, Paul

RUSS SCOTT, DR. See: Randolph,
Alice

RUSSELL. See:
Bartlett, Jill
Cosby, Bill (3)
Perkins, Ma
Pratt, Russell

RUSSELL, ANDY. See: Ross,
Lanny

RUSSELL ARMS. See: Lanson,
Snooky

RUSSELL, BOB, moderator of the
program (himself)
INDIVIDUALS WITH PERSONAL
PROBLEMS
STUDIO AUDIENCE MEMBERS
VOLUNTEERING PROBLEM
SOLUTIONS
Stand Up and Be Counted (TV)
(Advice)

RUSSELL, CAROLYN. See: Peyton, Martin

RUSSELL CHORUS, THE HENRY.
See: Borge, Victor

RUSSELL, CONNIE. See: Garroway, Dave (2) (3)

RUSSELL, DEAN. See: Jordan,
Joyce

RUSSELL, FRED. See: Peyton,
Martin

RUSSELL GILMAN. See: Lawton,
Lora

RUSSELL, KITTY. See: Dillon,
Marshal Matt

RUSSELL, MARSHA. See: Peyton, Martin

RUSSELL, MAYOR, of Springdale,
Illinois
BUTCH, his nephew
MARILLY, his housekeeper
VARIOUS CITIZENS OF THE
TOWN
The Mayor of the Town (R) (TV)
(Comedy/drama)

RUSSELL MILLER. See: Gook,
Vic

RUSSELL, NIPSEY. See: Martin,
Dean (2)

RUSSELL, ROSALIND. See:
Boyer, Charles

RUSSELL, TODD, puppeteer; host
of the program (himself)
ROOTIE KAZOOTIE
EL SQUEEKO MOUSE
GALA POOCHIE
POLKA DOTTIE, puppets
operated by Russell

KEYSTONE KOPS MOTION PIC-
TURES
Rootie Kazootie (TV) (Children)

RUSSELL, TODD. See also:
Compton, Walter
Hull, Warren (2)

RUSSIAN, THE MAD. See:
Cantor, Eddie (2)

RUSSO, LIEUT. JOHNNY. See:
Holbrook, Captain Matt

RUSTIC, MOTHER. See: Kovacs,
Ernie (1)

RUSTY. See:
Donovan, Steve
Harry
Rin-Tin-Tin
Roosty
Susan (2)
Williams, Danny

RUTH. See:
Garrett, Sam
Hutchinson, Ma
Nichols
Sherwood, Ruth
Wayne, Ruth Evans

RUTH ANDREWS. See: Meredith,
Charles

RUTH ANN GRAHAM. See:
Graham, Dr. Bob

RUTH, BABE, American professional baseball player (himself)
Here's Babe Ruth (R) (Sports)

RUTH BUZZI. See: Rowan, Dan

RUTH CRAIG. See:
Harding, Karen Adams
Rutledge, Dr. John

RUTH HENSHAW. See: Ruskin,
Lily

RUTH LARDNER. See: Rogers,
Patricia

RUTH McDEVITT. See: Everly,
Don

RUTH MARTIN. See: Davis,

Ann Tyler

RUTH MORROW. See: Falvey,
Hal

RUTH WAYNE. See: West,
Michael

RUTHIE. See: Horton, Dr. Tom

RUTHIE DUSKIN. See: Kelly,
Joe (2)

RUTHIE STEMBOTTOM. See:
Gook, Vic

RUTLEDGE, DR. JOHN, minister
MARY RUTLEDGE, his wife
IRIS MARSH
NANCY STEWART
RUTH CRAIG
NED HOLDEN
ROSE KRANSKY
SISTER ADA
SISTER LILLIAN
NORMA GREENMAN
CHARLOTTE BRANDON
META BAUER
SPIKE WILSON
ELLIS SMITH
DR. JONATHAN McNEILL
EDWARD GREENMAN
TORCHY REYNOLDS HOLDEN
TRUDY BAUER
JACOB KRANSKY
PEGGY GAYLORD
CELESTE CUNNINGHAM
LAURA MARTIN
TED WHITE
MRS. KRANSKY
REV. TOM BANNION
GORDON ELLIS
JULIE COLLINS
ROGER COLLINS
CHARLES CUNNINGHAM
MRS. CUNNINGHAM
ELLEN
ROY FENCHER
CLIFFORD FOSTER
MARTIN KANE
FREDERICKA LANG
DR. CHARLES MATTHEWS
MR. NOBODY FROM NOWHERE
GRANDPA ELLIS
PHYLLIS GORDON
ETHEL FOSTER
PETER MANNO, characters
appearing in the drama

The Guiding Light (R) (Serial drama)

RUTLEDGE, DR. JOHN. See also: Bauer, Bertha

RYAN, BARBARA. See: Hughes, Chris

RYAN, EDDIE, JR. See: Halop, Billy

RYAN, JENNY. See: Hughes, Chris

RYAN, JERRY. See: Carter, Kathryn

RYAN, JOYCE. See: Midnight, Captain

RYAN, PATRICIA. See: Halop, Billy

RYAN, PATRICK. See: Lee, Terry

RYAN, PAUL, district attorney
H.M. "STAFF" STAFFORD, his chief deputy
BOB RAMIREZ, investigator
KATY BENSON, deputy public defender
The D.A. (TV) (Courtroom drama)

RYAN, QUIN. See: Cowan, Thomas

RYAN, ROBERT (1)
DAVID NIVEN
JANE POWELL
CHARLES BOYER
JACK LEMMON, actors and actresses starred in the dramas (themselves)
VARIOUS SUPPORTING ACTORS AND ACTRESSES
Turn of Fate (TV) (Drama anthology)

RYAN, ROBERT (2), narrator of the program (himself)
WORLD WAR I FILMS
World War I (TV) (World War I documentary)

RYAN, TIM
IRENE NOBLETTE, featured on

the program (themselves)
UNCLE HAPPY, character portrayed by Teddy Bergman
The Tim and Irene Show (R) (Variety)

RYDELL, MARK. See: Hughes, Chris

RYDER, JANET. See: Graham, Dr. Bob

RYDER, JEFF. See: Collier, Tim

RYDER, RED, cowboy
LITTLE BEAVER, Indian boy, his friend
Red Ryder (R) (Western adventure)

RYDER, SAM. See: Graham, Dr. Bob

RYKER, CATHIE. See: Davis, Dr. Althea

RYKER, CORT. See: Scott, Captain

RYKER, LIEUT. EDDIE, police officer
WILLIE GILLIS
TERRY WEBSTER
MIKE DANKO, young rookie non-violence policemen
JILL DANKO, Mike's wife, nurse
The Rookies (TV) (Police drama)

RYKER, RUFE. See: Shane

RYSDALE, KIP. See: Ames, Peter

S. See: Cadman, Rev. S. Parkes

S. A. 7. See: Conroy, Phil

S. KENT WADSWORTH, MRS.
See: Solomon, David

SABER, MARK, British detective-
investigator
PETE PAULSON, his assistant
INSPECTOR CHESTER, Scotland
Yard official
Saber of London (TV) (Detective)
(also known as Detective Diary
(TV) and Uncovered) (TV)

Saber of London. See: Saber,
Mark

SABRINA. See: Collins, Barnabas

SACK. See: Sad Sack, The

SACK, ALBERT. See: Morgan,
Frank (1)

Sack, The Sad. See: Sad Sack,
The

Sad Sack, The. See: Sad Sack,
The

SAD SACK, THE, perpetually un-
lucky ex-soldier
The Sad Sack (R) (Comedy)

Saddle, Black. See: Culhane,
Clay

Saddles, Boots and. See: Adams,
Captain

SADE. See: Gook, Vic

Sade, Vic and. See: Gook, Vic

SAFER, MORLEY. See: Wallace,
Mike (4)

Safety Legion Time. See: Story
Lady, The

SAFRANSKI, EDDIE. See: Gibbs,
Georgia (1)

Saga, The Forsyte. See: Forsyte,
Soames

SAGERQUIST, ERIC. See: First
Nighter, Mr.

SAGO. See: Noble, Mary

SAILOR, COOKIE THE. See:
Junior

Sailor, Popeye the. See: Popeye

ST. CLAIR, MARCEL. See:
Fleming, Tony

ST. CLAIR, MARGARET. See:
Fleming, Tony

ST. CLAIR, TIMMY. See:
Fleming, Tony

ST. CLOUD, ROLLO. See: Bennett, Nita

ST. DENIS, GARY. See: Perkins,
Ma

ST. JOHN. See: Churchill, John

ST. JOHN HARRIS. See: Sunday

ST. JOHN, HENRY. See:
Churchill, John

ST. JOHN, LIEUT. J. G. REX.
See: O'Toole, Ensign

ST. JOHN QUINCY. See:
Crackerby, O. K.

Saint, The. See: Templar, Simon

SAINT, THE. See: Templar,
Simon

Saints and Sinners. See: Alexander, Nick

Sal Hepatica Revue, The. See:
Allen, Fred

Salad Bowl Revue, The. See:
Allen, Fred

Sale of the Century. See:
Garagiola, Joe (3)

Sale, Songs For. See: Murray,
Jan (3)

SALEM, PETER, detective
MARTY, his assistant
The Affairs of Peter Salem (R)
(Detective drama)

SALES, SOUPY, comedian; host of
the program (himself)
WHITE FANG
BLACK TOOTH, dogs
WILLIE THE WORM
POOKIE, characters appearing on
the program
FILM CLIPS FROM OLD SILENT
MOTION PICTURES
Soupy Sales (TV) (Children)

SALES, SOUPY. See also: Daly,
John (3)

SALLI FLYNN. See: Welk,
Lawrence

SALLIE BELLE COX. See: Weems,
Ambrose J.

Sally. See: Truesdale, Sally

SALLY. See:
Allen, Joan Houston
Day, Chris
Farrell, David
Gibson, Dot
Hutchinson, Ma
Jones, Tom (1)
McMillan, Stuart
O'Neill, Mrs.
Simms, Paul
Sloan, Holly
Stevens, Joan
Truesdale, Sally
Vass, Fran
Young, Larry "Pepper"

SALLY ATHELNEY. See: Carey,
Dr. Philip

SALLY, AUNT. See: Carson,
Jack

Sally, Axis. See: Sisk, Mildred
Elizabeth

SALLY BARNETT. See: Brent,
Dr. Jim

SALLY DUNLAP. See: Regan,
Terry

SALLY FOSTER. See: Kelly,
Joe (1)

SALLY GIBBONS. See: Marlin,
Mary

SALLY ROGERS. See: Petrie,
Rob

SALLY ROLLINS. See: Sterling,
Vanessa Dale

SALLY STRUTHERS. See:
Conway, Tim
Smothers, Tom (3)

SALTER, HARRY. See:
Elman, Dave (2)
Granlund, Nils Thor
Parks, Bert (6)

SALTZMAN, DR. See: Sterling,
Vanessa Dale

SALVATORE. See: Bono, Salvatore

SAM
HENRY, blackface entertainers
Sam 'n' Henry (R) (Comedy)

SAM. See also:
Aldrich, Henry
Bailey, Sam
Benedict, Sam
Buckhart, Sam
Cade, Sam
Cannon, John
Davis, Red
Diamond, Richard
Dillon, Marshal Matt
Dodsworth, Sam
Garrett, Sam
Houston, Temple
Jones, Sam
Lanin, Sam
Larsen, Sam
Levenson, Sam
Logan, Sam
McCann, Dr. Noah
McCloud, Sam
McGarry, Dan
McNeill, Don
Malone, Dr. Jerry
Riddle, Sam (1) (2)
Singin' Sam
Spade, Sam
Stone, Sam

Troy, Sergeant Sam
Warren, Wendy
Weston, Sam
Young, Larry "Pepper"

Sam Benedict. See: Benedict, Sam

SAM BOLT. See: West, Honey

SAM DANFORTH. See: Washburn,
William

SAM DONOHUE. See: Basie,
Count

SAM DRUCKER. See:
Carson, Uncle Joe
Douglas, Oliver

SAM ELLIS. See: Dallas, Stella

SAM GRIM. See: Perkins, Ma

SAM HEARN. See: Henry, Captain

SAM LEVENSON. See:
Donald, Peter
Levenson, Sam
Shriner, Herb (3)

SAM MARSH, DR. See: Goldstone,
Dr. Peter

Sam 'n' Henry. See: Sam

SAM REYNOLDS. See: Tate,
Joanne

SAM RYDER. See: Graham, Dr.
Bob

Sam Spade, Detective. See:
Spade, Sam

Sam Spade, The Adventures of.
See: Spade, Sam

SAM STEINBERG. See: Fitzgerald,
Bridget Theresa Mary Coleen

SAM WESTON. See:
Garrison, Spencer
Weston, Sam

SAMANTHA. See: Stephens,
Samantha

SAMBRINI, ZENITH. See: Perkins,
Ma

Same, The Name's the. See:
James, Dennis (3)

SAMMEE. See also: Sammy

SAMMEE LING. See: Grady,
Mickey

SAMMES SINGERS, THE MIKE.
See:
Berman, Shelley
Doonican, Val
O'Connor, Des

SAMMY. See:
Davis, Joan Field
Davis, Sammy, Jr.
Goldberg, Molly
Kaye, Sammy (1) (2) (3)
Sammee
Tammy

SAMMY DAVIS, JR. See:
Crosby, Bing (2)
Davis, Sammy, Jr.
Jones, Jack

Sammy Davis, Jr. Show, The.
See: Davis, Sammy, Jr.

SAMMY KAYE. See:
Basie, Count
Como, Perry (1)
Kaye, Sammy (1) (2) (3)
Whiteman, Paul

Sammy Kaye Show, The. See:
Kaye, Sammy (1)

SAMMY SPEAR. See:
DeLuise, Dom (1)
Gleason, Jackie (2)
Kramden, Ralph

SAMMY WARNER. See: Farrell,
David

SAMPLES, JUNIOR. See: Owens,
Buck

SAMSON. See:
Hayes, Wing Commander
Wayne, Ruth Evans

SAMUEL. See: Cavanaugh, Father
Samuel Patrick

SAMUEL L. ROTHAFEL. See:
Roxy

SAMUEL PANOSIAN, LIEUT. See:
Rice, Lieut. Bill

SAMUEL TILDEN FIELD, DR.
See: Davis, Joan Field

SAN FERNANDO RED. See:
Junior

San Francisco Beat. See: Guthrie,
Lieut. Ben

San Francisco International Airport.
See: Conrad, Jim

San Francisco, The Streets of.
See: Stone, Detective Lieut. Mike

Sanborn Hour, The Chase and. See:
Ameche, Don (1)
Cantor, Eddie (2)

Sanctum, Inner. See: Raymond

Sanctum Mysteries, Inner. See:
Raymond

SAND. See also: Sands

SAND, PAUL. See: Caesar, Sid
(1)

SANDER. See: Vanocur, Sander

SANDERS, ALICE. See: Sothern,
Mary

SANDERS, CUFFY. See: Gallant,
Captain

SANDERS, GEORGE, actor; host
of the program (himself)
MANY ACTORS AND ACTRESSES
The George Sanders Mystery
Theater (TV) (Drama; adapta-
tions of suspense stories)

SANDERS, JEROME. See: Sothern,
Mary

SANDERS, VERNE. See: Baines,
Scattergood

SANDERSON, JULIA. See: Crumit,
Frank (1) (2) (3)

SANDERSON, SANDY. See:
Meredith, Charles

SANDI. See also:
Sandy
Sondi

SANDI JENSEN. See: Welk,
Lawrence

SANDMAN, THE. See: Batman

SANDOVAL, MANUEL. See:
Cameron, Christy Allen

SANDRA. See: Ferguson, Martha

SANDRA BAGUS. See: Kelly, Joe
(2)

SANDRA BARCLAY. See: Noble,
Mary

SANDRA CAREY. See: Noble,
Mary

SANDRA HALL. See: Allen,
Joan Houston

SANDRA TALBOT. See: Dennis,
Liz

SANDS. See also: Sand

SANDS, PETER. See: McNamara,
Susie

SANDS, PHILO "SANDY." See:
Marlin, Mary

SANDY. See:
Becker, Sandy
Hood, Gregory
Lewis, Dave
Little Orphan Annie
Malone, Dr. Jerry
Sandi
Sondi
Stockton, Sandy (1) (2)
Wade, Sandy
Webster, Jerry

SANDY BARRON. See: Martindale, Wink (2)

Sandy Duncan Show, The. See:
Stockton, Sandy (2)

SANDY LARSON. See: Hughes,
Lisa

SANDY McALLISTER. See:
Guthrie, Lieut. Ben

SANDY MATSON. See: Jones,
Lorenzo

SANDY RICKS. See: Flipper

SANDY SANDERSON. See: Meredith, Charles

"SANDY" SANDS, PHILO. See:
Marlin, Mary

SANDY STEWART. See: Miller,
Mitch

SANDY WEBBER. See: Peyton,
Martin

SANDY WINFIELD. See: Madison,
Kenny

SANFORD. See: Bickart, Sanford

Sanford and Son. See: Sanford,
Fred

SANFORD, FRED, Negro junk dealer;
widower
LAMONT, his son, associated
with him in the business
Sanford and Son (TV) (Situation
comedy) (broadcast in England
as Steptoe and Son) (TV)

SANFORD MALONE. See: Myrt

SANGER, MARK. See: Ironside,
Chief Robert

SANTERRA, MIGUEL. See:
Carlyle, Baylor

SANTO, RALPH. See: Carter,
Kathryn

SANTORO, OLIVIO, boy singer,
guitarist and yodeler
Olivio Santoro (R) (Music)

SANTOS ORTEGA. See:
Lovejoy, Frank (1)
Ortega, Santos
Roberts, Ken

SAPPHIRE STEVENS. See:
Jones, Amos

SARA. See:
Drinkwater, William
Sarah
Sari

SARAH. See:
Fraser, Ben
Green, Sarah
Horton, Dr. Tom
Karr, Mike
Peppertag, Aaron
Sara
Sari

SARAH DALE. See: Sterling,
Vanessa Dale

SARAH FANKBONER. See:
Darin, Bobby

SARAH HEARTBURN, MRS. See:
Baker, Phil (2)

SARAH JANE KANE. See: Marlin,
Mary

SARAH JENNINGS CHURCHILL.
See: Churchill, John

SARAH KENNEDY. See: Rowan,
Dan

SARAH McINTYRE, DR. See:
Bauer, Bertha

SARAH TUTTLE. See: Allen,
Dr. Kate

SARAH WHIPPLE. See: Hackett,
Doc

SARAZEN, GENE, professional
golfer, host of the program
(himself)
OUTSTANDING GOLFER INTER-
VIEWEES
The World of Golf (TV) (Sports
interviews)

SARDINIUS. See: McPheeters,
Dr. Sardinius

Sardi's, Breakfast at. See:
Breneman, Tom (1)

Sardi's, Luncheon at. See: Slater,
Bill (1)

Sarge. See: Cavanaugh, Father
Samuel Patrick

SARGE. See:
Cavanaugh, Father Samuel
Patrick
Towne, Hal

SARGENT. See also: Sergeant

SARGENT, JIM. See: Judy

SARI. See:
Adams, Crunch
Sara
Sarah

SAS-JAWORSKY, DR. ALEXANDER.
See: March, Hal

SATISFIERS, THE. See: Como,
Perry (1)

Saturday Night Serenade. See:
Dragonette, Jessica (3)

Saturday Night Swing Club, The.
See: Douglas, Paul

Saturday Prom. See: Griffin,
Merv (3)

Saturday's Child. See: Cooper,
Ann

SAUNDERS, SERGEANT CHIP.
See: Hanley, Lieut. Gil

SAUTER, EDDIE. See: Whiteman,
Paul

SAVAGE, BRIGADIER GENERAL
FRANK, commander of Air Force
bomber group stationed near
World War II London
MAJOR GENERAL WILEY CROWE
MAJOR HARVEY STOVALL
MAJOR JOE COBB
MAJOR "DOC" KAISER, officers
Twelve O'Clock High (TV) (World
War II drama)

SAVANNAH BROWN. See: Kelly,
Pete

Saver, Wife. See: Prescott, Allen
(2)

SAVILLE, DAVID, song writer;
host of the program (himself)
ALVIN
SIMON
THEODORE, chipmunks; cartoon
characters
The Alvin Cartoon Show (TV)
(Children's program)

SAWYER, ANDY, acting mayor of
small North Carolina town, por-
trayed by Andy Griffith
LEE, his wife
LORI, his daughter
T.J., his son
NORA, Lee's spinster sister
BUFF MacKNIGHT, councilman
The New Andy Griffith Show (TV)
(Comedy)

SAWYER, RAY. See: Brent,
Dr. Jim

SAWYER, TOM. See: Finn, Huck

SAWYERS, GINNIE. See: Fairchild, Kay

Say When. See: James, Art

Say, You Don't! See: Narz, Jack
(6)

SCALI, JOHN. See:
Peterson, Roger
Smith, Howard K. (2)

SCAMPY. See: Kirchener, Claude
(2)

Scarlet Pimpernel, The. See:
Blakeney, Sir Percy

SCARLET PIMPERNEL, THE.
See: Blakeney, Sir Percy

SCARLETT, WILL. See: Hood,
Robin

"SCAT" DAVIS, JOHNNY. See:
Waring, Fred (1)

SCATTERGOOD. See: Baines,
Scattergood

Scattergood Baines. See: Baines,
Scattergood

Scene Magazine, Jackie Gleason's American. See: Gleason, Jackie (2)

Scene Seventy. See: Reynolds, Jay

Scene, The Music. See: Steinberg, David (2)

SCHAEFER. See also: Shafer

SCHAEFER, GOODWIN. See: Fadiman, Clifton (2)

SCHAEFER, LLOYD. See: Como, Perry (1)

SCHEFF, FRITZI, singer and actress, featured on the program (herself) Lavender and Old Lace (R) (Music)

SCHEIBER, STANLEY. See: Stewart, Jan

SCHELL, RONNIE. See: Nabors, Jim

SCHENCK, VAN AND. See: Drew, John

SCHEND, CLARA. See: Rogers, Patricia

SCHENKEL, CHRIS. See: McKay, Jim (1)

SCHLEPPERMAN. See: Baker, Kenny Benny, Jack

SCHMIDT, HANS. See: James, Dennis (4)

SCHMIDT, LOGAN. See: Horton, Dr. Tom

SCHMIDT, REINHOLD. See: Faith, Percy

SCHMIDT, VIOLA. See: Spitalny, Phil

SCHNAUZER. See: Muldoon, Francis

SCHNEIDER, MR. See: Goldberg, Molly

SCHOEN, VIC. See: King, Dave (2) Page, Patti (1) (2)

School, Ding Dong. See: Horwich, Dr. Frances

School of the Air of the Americas. See: Bryson, Dr. Lyman (2)

School of the Air, The American. See: Bryson, Dr. Lyman (2)

SCHOOL PRINCIPAL, CHARLIE McCARTHY'S. See: Bergen, Edgar (2)

SCHOUMACHER, DAVID GEORGE HERMAN DAVID S. BRODER, newscasters; interviewers on the program (themselves) PROMINENT POLITICAL FIGURES AS INTERVIEWEES Face the Nation (TV) (Interview)

SCHULTZ. See: Hogan, Colonel Robert

SCHULTZ, BERTHA. See: Carter, Kathryn Larimore, Marilyn

SCHULTZ, MR. See: Carter, Kathryn Dyke, Charity Amanda Larimore, Marilyn

SCHULTZ, MRS. See: Larimore, Marilyn

SCHULTZIE. See: Collins, Bob

SCHUMANN, THE VOICES OF WALTER. See: Ford, Tennessee Ernie (2)

SCHUSTER, FRANK. See: Wayne, Johnny (1) (2)

SCHUSTER, KIM. See: Peyton, Martin

Schuster Show, The Wayne and. See: Wayne, Johnny (2)

Schuster, Wayne and. See: Wayne, Johnny (1)

SCHUYLER. See also: Schyler

SCHUYLER, LIEUT. GEORGE.
See: Dawson, Rosemary

SCHWARTZ, CHARLES. See:
Kelly, Joe (2)

SCHWARTZKOPF, COLONEL H.
NORMAN. See: Lord, Phillips
H.

SCHYLER. See:
King, Schyler "Sky"
Schuyler

Science Fiction Theater. See:
Bradley, Truman

Science in the News. See: Soule,
Olan (5)

SCOEY MITCHILL. See: Jones,
Dean

Scooby Doo. See: Scooby Doo

SCOOBY DOO, cowardly great Dane
DAPHNE
VELMA
FRED
SHAGGY, all cartoon characters
Scooby Doo (TV) (Cartoon)
(later retitled The New Scooby
Doo Movies) (TV)

Scooby Doo Movies, The New.
See: Scooby Doo

SCOOP, newscaster
News of Youth (R) (Dramatized
news)

SCOOP CURTIS. See: Rogers,
Patricia

SCOOPER. See: Brains

Scope, A.B.C. See: Smith,
Howard K. (2)

Scotland Yard. See: Lustgarden,
Edgar

Scotland Yard, Colonel March of.
See: March, Colonel

Scotland Yard, Fabian of. See:

Fabian, Inspector

Scotland Yard, Inspector White of.
See: White, Inspector

Scotland Yard's Inspector Burke.
See: Burke, Inspector

SCOTSON WEBB. See: Rogers,
Patricia

SCOTT. See:
Lancer, Murdoch
Lassie
Reynolds, Dr. Mike
Ross, Scott

SCOTT, ALEXANDER
KELLY ROBINSON, tennis
players and secret agents
I Spy (TV) (Crime drama)

SCOTT BANNING. See: Horton,
Dr. Tom

SCOTT, CAPTAIN
CORT RYKER
RUSS MacDONALD
BERTELLI, flyers
Blue Angels (TV) (Aviation ad-
venture)

SCOTT, CARLA. See: Hargrave-
Scott, Joan

SCOTT, CONSTABLE FRANK,
officer of the Royal Canadian
Mounted Police
R.C.M.P. (TV) (Adventure)

SCOTT, DAVID, harbor master of
New England port
JEFF KITTREDGE, his partner
Harbourmaster (TV) (Sailing ad-
venture) (also known as Adventure
at Scott Island) (TV)

SCOTT, DIANNA. See: Owens,
Buck

SCOTT, DR. RUSS. See: Randolph,
Alice

SCOTT, DR. TRUMAN "TUBBY."
See: Hargrave-Scott, Joan

SCOTT, FRANCES, hostess of
the program (herself)

It Takes a Woman (R) (Women's
program)

SCOTT, FRANK. See: Welk,
Lawrence

SCOTT, GEOFFREY. See: Prescott, Kate Hathaway

SCOTT, GEORGE C., star of the
program (himself)
MANY SUPPORTING ACTORS
AND ACTRESSES
East Side/West Side (TV)
(Topical social problems drama)

Scott Island, Adventure at. See:
Scott, David

SCOTT, JUDGE. See: O'Neill,
Mrs.

SCOTT, KAREN, teenage girl
living in apartment complex in
Southern California
STEVE, her father
BARBARA, her mother
MIMI, her younger sister
Karen (TV) (Comedy) (Segment
of Ninety Bristol Court) (TV)

SCOTT, LOU. See: Young,
Larry "Pepper"

SCOTT, MARILYN. See: Novak,
John

SCOTT, MARK. See: Cameron,
Christy Allen

SCOTT, MARTHA, hostess of the
program (herself)
MANY ACTORS AND ACTRESSES
Modern Romances (TV) (Drama)

SCOTT, MR. See: Kirk, Captain
James

SCOTT, MRS. See:
Cameron, Christy Allen
Hargrave-Scott, Joan
O'Neill, Mrs.

SCOTT, NICOLE. See: Cameron,
Christy Allen

SCOTT NORRIS. See: Garrison,
Pat

SCOTT PHILIPS. See: Tate,
Joanne

SCOTT, RAY. See: McKay, Jim
(1)

SCOTT, RAYMOND, orchestra
leader (himself)
HIS ORCHESTRA
Concert in Rhythm (R) (Music)

SCOTT, RAYMOND. See also:
Lanson, Snooky
Ross, Lanny

SCOTT, ROBIN, insurance investigator
Dangerous Robin (TV) (Mystery
drama)

SCOTT, STONEWALL. See:
Lorre, Peter

SCOTTY. See:
Kirk, Captain James
Spotty
Trail, Mark

SCOTTY, LULUBELLE AND.
See: Kelly, Joe (1)

SCOUT. See: Lone Ranger, The

Scouts, Arthur Godfrey's Talent.
See: Godfrey, Arthur (2)

Scouts, Celebrity Talent. See:
Levenson, Sam

Scramby Amby. See: Ward,
Perry

Scrapbook, Tony Wons'. See:
Wons, Tony

Screen Guild Theater. See:
Pryor, Roger

Screen Test, M.G.M. See:
Murphy, Dean

SCRIBNER, JIMMY, star of the
program; played parts of all 21
characters in the drama (himself)
The Johnson Family (R) (Ethnic
comedy/drama)

SCUBBY. See: Carter, Nick

SCULLY, VIN, sportscaster; host
of the program (himself)
MANY GUEST STARS (husbands
and wives)
It Takes Two (TV) (Game)

SCULLY, VIN. See also: McKay,
Jim (1)

Sea, Davy Adams, Son of the.
See: Adams, Franklin P.

Sea Hound, The. See: Silver,
Captain

Sea Hunt. See: Nelson, Mike

Sea, Victory at. See: Graves,
Leonard

Sea, Voyage to the Bottom of the.
See: Nelson, Admiral Harriman

SEABROOK, DR. See: Wayne,
Ruth Evans

Sealab 2020. See: Williams, Dr.

Sealtest Hour, The. See: Vallee,
Rudy (2)

Sealtest Village Store. See:
Owner

SEAN. See: Jamison, Dr. Sean

Search. See: Cameron

Search for Tomorrow. See: Tate,
Joanne

SEARS, JERRY. See: Fields,
Arthur

Seat, County. See: Hackett, Doc

Seated, Ladies Be. See: Moore,
Tom (1)

SEAVIEW, THE. See: Nelson,
Admiral Harriman

SEBASTIAN. See: Josie

SEBASTIAN CABOT. See: Harrington, Pat, Jr.

SEBASTIAN, CLIFF. See: Dennis,
Liz

SEBASTIAN, DON. See: Cannon,
John

SEBASTIAN, VICTOR
SIMONE GENET, counterintelligence agents
Five Fingers (TV) (Mystery/
adventure)

Second, Dollar a. See: Murray,
Jan (1)

Second Honeymoon. See: Parks,
Bert (5)

Second Hundred Years, The. See:
Carpenter, Luke

Second Husband. See: Cummings,
Brenda

Second Mrs. Burton, The. See:
Burton, Terry

Second, Split. See: Kennedy,
Tom (2)

SECOND TWIN. See: Pan, Peter

Second Wife. See: Burton, Terry

Secret Agent. See: Drake, John

Secret Agent, Amos Burke. See:
Burke, Amos

Secret Agent, Ned Jordan. See:
Jordan, Ned

Secret Cases, National Surety's.
See: Harkness, Detective

Secret Chimp, Lancelot Link.
See: Link, Lancelot

Secret City. See: Clark, Ben

Secret File, U.S.A. See: Morgan,
Major

Secret, I've Got a. See: Moore,
Garry (4)

Secret Journal, Dr. Hudson's. See:
Hudson, Dr. Wayne

Secret Squirrel. See: Secret
Squirrel

SECRET SQUIRREL, cartoon character
Secret Squirrel (TV) (Cartoon)

Secret Storm, The. See: Ames,
Peter

Secret Three, The. See: McLean,
Murray

SECRETARY OF THE INTERIOR.
See: Welles, Orson (3)

Secretary, Private. See: Mc-
Namara, Susie

Secrets, Animal. See: Eiseley,
Loren C.

SEDGEWICK, MRS. See: Sunday

SEDLACK, DICK. See: Kelly,
Joe (2)

SEDLEY BROWN. See: Miles,
Allie Lowe

See It Now. See: Murrow, Edward
R. (4)

See the Pros. See: Davis, Glenn

SEEADLER. See: Von Luckner,
Count Felix

SEEKERS, THE NEW. See:
Berry, Ken

"SELDOM" JACKSON. See: Jones,
Kenneth Yarborough

Self-Defense for Women. See:
Offstein, Jerry

SELKIRK, MR. See: Erwin, Stu

Seller, Best. See: Morrison, Bret

SELLERS, DR. ANDREW. See:
Locke, Dr. Simon (1)

SELMA YOSSARIAN. See: McKay,
Judson

SENATOR. See: Stowe, Senator
Hays

SENATOR BEAUREGARD CLAG-
HORN. See: Allen, Fred

SENATOR BLOAT. See: Allen,
Fred

SENATOR ED FORD. See: Wilson, Ward

SENATOR JENNINGS. See:
Carlyle, Baylor

Senator, The (The Bold Ones).
See: Stowe, Senator Hays

SENIOR CITIZENS, THE. See:
Kelly, Gene

SEÑOR WENCES. See: Olsen,
Ole

SENRAM, FRANK. See: Sharp,
Hal

SENRICH, HENRY. See: Rogers,
Patricia

Sense, The Sixth. See: Rhodes,
Dr. Michael

SERENA. See: Stephens,
Samantha

Serenade, Saturday Night. See:
Dragonette, Jessica (3)

Serenade, Sunday. See: Kaye,
Sammy (3)

Serenade, The Campana. See:
Powell, Dick (1)

Serenade, The Lady Esther. See:
Lady Esther

SERGEANT. See:
Anderson, Sergeant Nick
Bilko, Sergeant Ernest
Friday, Sergeant Joe
Madigan, Sergeant Dan
Nelson, Sergeant
Preston, Sergeant
Sargent
Troy, Sergeant Sam

SERGEANT BARNES. See: Mc-
Keever, Cadet Gary

SERGEANT BEN ROMERO. See:

Friday, Sergeant Joe

Sergeant Bilko Show, The.   See:
    Bilko, Sergeant Ernest

SERGEANT BUCK SINCLAIR.   See:
    Flagg, Captain Jim

SERGEANT BURKE.   See: Raven,
    Dan

SERGEANT CARTER.   See: Pyle,
    Gomer

SERGEANT CHIP SAUNDERS.   See:
    Hanley, Lieut. Gil

Sergeant, Combat.   See: Nelson,
    Sergeant

SERGEANT CORNELIUS TRUMBULL.
    See: Spencer, Jeff

SERGEANT DANNY KELLER.   See:
    Gower, Matthew

SERGEANT, DR.   See: Drake,
    Nora

SERGEANT DORSET.   See: Mason,
    Perry

SERGEANT ED BROWN.   See:
    Ironside, Chief Robert

SERGEANT ED ROBBINS.   See:
    Foster, Major John

SERGEANT ENRIGHT.   See: Mc-
    Millan, Stuart

SERGEANT ERNEST HEATH.   See:
    Vance, Philo

SERGEANT EVE WHITFIELD.
    See: Ironside, Chief Robert

SERGEANT FRAN BELDING.   See:
    Ironside, Chief Robert

SERGEANT FRANK BURKE.   See:
    Narz, Jack (2)

SERGEANT GARCIA.   See: Vega,
    Don Diego

SERGEANT GROVER.   See: Bilko,
    Sergeant Ernest

SERGEANT HART.   See: King,
    Rocky

SERGEANT HIGGENBOTTOM.   See:
    Crooke, Lennie

SERGEANT HORACE CAPP.   See:
    Rice, Lieut. Bill

SERGEANT JACK MOFFITT.   See:
    Troy, Sergeant Sam

SERGEANT JAMES BUSTARD.   See:
    Custer, George Armstrong

SERGEANT JOAN HOGAN.   See:
    Bilko, Sergeant Ernest

SERGEANT KING.   See: Stock-
    dale, Will

SERGEANT McCASKEY.   See:
    Young, Captain David

SERGEANT McKENNA.   See:
    Wright, Conley

SERGEANT MATHISON (MATTY).
    See: Carter, Nick

SERGEANT MIKE McCLUSKEY.
    See: McCluskey, Mona

SERGEANT MULLINS.   See:
    North, Jerry

SERGEANT O'HARA.   See: Run-
    yon, Brad

SERGEANT O'ROURKE.   See:
    Parmenter, Captain Wilton

SERGEANT, POLICE.   See:
    Britt, Dan
    Police Lieutenant

Sergeant Preston.   See: Preston,
    Sergeant

Sergeant Preston of the Yukon.
    See: Preston, Sergeant

SERGEANT QUIRT.   See: Flagg,
    Captain

Sergeant Quirt, Captain Flagg and.
    See: Flagg, Captain

SERGEANT RUPERT RITZIK.
See: Bilko, Sergeant Ernest

SERGEANT SOL ABRAMS. See:
Muldoon, Francis

SERGEANT, THE POLICE. See:
Bill

SERGEANT VELIE. See: Queen,
Ellery

SERGEANT VINCE CAVELLI.
See: Adams, Lieut. Price

SERGEANT WALKER. See: Peyton, Martin

SERGEANT WOLZNIAK, FIRST.
See: McKay, Judson

Sergeants, No Time for. See:
Stockdale, Will

Series, The World. See: Cowan,
Thomas

SERLING. See also:
Sterling
Stirling

SERLING, ROD (1), author and host
of the program (himself)
MANY ACTORS AND ACTRESSES
Night Gallery (TV) (Drama) (also
known as Rod Serling's Night
Gallery) (TV)

SERLING, ROD (2), author and
host of the program (himself)
MANY ACTORS AND ACTRESSES
Twilight Zone (TV) (Suspense
drama)

SERLING, ROD. See also:
Cousteau, Jacques

Service Concert, The Cities.
See: Dragonette, Jessica (1)

SERVICE, MR. JONES' ANSWERING.
See: Pam

Service, Wire. See: Evans, Dean

Sesame Street. See: Cookie
Monster, The

Session, The. See: Hildreth, Dick

Set, Betty White's Pet. See:
White, Betty (2)

Set, The Pet. See: White,
Betty (2)

SETH. See:
Adams, Major Seth
Parker, Seth

Seth Parker. See: Parker, Seth

SEVAREID, ERIC, newscaster,
host of the program (himself)
MANY GUEST SCIENTISTS
Conquest (TV) (Discussion of
recent scientific advances)

SEVAREID, ERIC. See also:
Cronkite, Walter (2)

714, Badge. See: Friday, Sergeant
Joe

Seven Keys. See: Narz, Jack (4)

Seven League Boots. See: Douglas, Jack (3)

Seven Lively Arts, The. See:
Crosby, John

7, S. A. See: Conroy, Phil

7, Special Agent. See: Conroy,
Phil

7000, Paris. See: Brennan, Jack

7000, Tallahassee. See: Rogers,
Lex

Seventy, Scene. See: Reynolds,
Jay

77 Sunset Strip. See: Bailey,
Stuart

SEVERINSEN, DOC. See:
Carson, Johnny (1)
Fiedler, Arthur

SEWALL CRAWFORD, DR. See:
Malone, Dr. Jerry

Sexes, The Battle of the. See:
Crumit, Frank (1)

SEYMOUR. See:
Kaufman, Seymour
Mitchell, Dennis

SEYMOUR, ANNE. See: Ameche,
Don (3)

SEYMOUR, DAN, master of cere-
monies and quizmaster of the
program (himself)
PATTI CLAYTON
BOB HOWARD
ALAN DALE, featured vocalists
on the program (themselves)
THE RIDDLERS, vocal group
MANY CONTESTANTS
RAY BLOCH, orchestra leader
(himself)
HIS ORCHESTRA
Sing It Again (R) (Music/quiz)

SEYMOUR, EDNA. See: Myrt

SEYMOUR FINGERHOOD. See:
Goldberg, Molly

SEYMOUR, JANE. See: Henry
VIII, King of England

SEYMOUR, THOMAS. See: Henry
VIII, King of England

SHAD. See: Mac

SHADE, DR. See: King, Schyler
"Sky"

SHADEL, BILL
QUINCY HOWE
EDWARD P. MORGAN
PAUL HARVEY
AL MANN
JOHN ROLFSON
WILLIAM WINTER
ROBERT LODGE, newscasters
(themselves)
Roundup U.S.A. (TV) (News)

SHADOW. See: Teen, Harold

Shadow, The. See: Cranston,
Lamont

SHADOW, THE. See: Cranston,
Lamont

Shadows, Dark. See: Collins,
Barnabas

SHAFER. See also: Schaefer

SHAFER, CAPTAIN. See: Hennesey, Lieut. Chick

SHAFTSBURY, LORD. See:
Churchill, John

SHAGGY. See: Scooby Doo

SHAGNASTY, BOLIVAR. See:
Junior

SHALLENBERGER, ROBERT. See:
Olson, Emily

SHALLUM. See: Speaker, The

SHAME. See:
Batman
Shane
Shayne

SHAMUS. See: O'Leary, Hannah

Shane. See: Shane

SHANE, cowboy, employed by the
Starretts
MARIAN STARRETT, widow
JOEY STARRETT, Marian's
eight-year-old son
TOM STARRETT, Joey's grand-
father
RUFE RYKER, cattle man,
Shane's enemy
Shane (TV) (Western)

SHANE. See also:
Shame
Shayne

SHANE, VIOLET. See: Chandler,
Faith

SHANGHAI LIL. See: Jungle Jim

Shannon. See: Shannon, Joe

SHANNON, confidential investigator
for District Attorney
AL BONACORSI, his contact with
the District Attorney's office
The D.A.'s Man (TV) (Detective
drama)

SHANNON, JOE, insurance investigator for Transport Bonding and Surety Company
BILL COCHRAN, his boss
Shannon (TV) (Drama)

SHANNON, SLATE, Westerner
Bold Venture (TV) (Western)

SHAPIRO, BUNNY. See: Grimm, Arnold

SHAPIRO, CONCHITA. See: Vallee, Rudy (2)

SHAPIRO, MEYER. See: Grant, Harry

SHARI. See:
Lewis, Shari
Malone, Dr. Jerry
Sherry

Shari Lewis Show, The. See: Lewis, Shari

SHARK, FURY. See: Midnight, Captain

SHARK, IVAN. See: Midnight, Captain

SHARKEY, CHIEF. See: Nelson, Admiral Harriman

SHARLIE. See:
Charley
Charlie
Munchausen, Baron

SHARMAN. See also:
Sherman
Shoiman

SHARMAN, BARBARA. See: Rowan, Dan

SHARON. See:
Dodd, Jimmie
Sharron

SHARON GRAINGER. See: Rowlands, Hugh

SHARON O'SHAUGHNESSEY. See: Arkansas Traveler, The

SHARON PINKHAM. See: Hardy, Dr. Steven

SHARP, HAL, pianist and orchestra leader, featured on the program (himself)
BOB CARTER
CORWIN TUTTLE
BERNIE WEIL
BOB WAGNER
VINCE DUCKLES
CASEY FLANNIGAN
BURNETT HENDRIX
FRANK SENRAM
SKIPPER COOK
HELEN KAYE, musicians and entertainers (themselves)
MANY STUDENT GUEST PERFORMERS
The College Merry-Go-Round (R) (College variety)

SHARP, ORVILLE. See: Parkyakarkas, Nick

SHARPE, DOC. See: Marlin, Mary

SHARRON. See also: Sharon

SHARRON MACREADY. See: Stirling, Craig

SHATZ. See: Hennesey, Lieut. Chick

SHAUGHNESSEY, CATHERINE. See: Perkins, Ma

Shave Time, Mennen. See: Parker, Lou

SHAW, ROBERT. See: Waring, Fred (1)

SHAW, ROCKY. See: Harris, Silky

SHAW, SHERIFF MIKE. See: Mix, Tom

SHAW, STAN
ART FORD, disk jockeys; hosts of the program (themselves)
Milkman's Matinee (R) (Phonograph recordings)

SHAWN, DICK
FLIP WILSON
GEORGE CARLIN
TIM CONWAY

DEAN JONES
DICK CAVETT
ROGER MILLER
JIM LANGE
JIMMY DEAN
OTHERS, masters of ceremony of
the program (themselves)
MANY SOLDIER PARTICIPANTS
MANY GUEST STARS AND
ENTERTAINERS
THE OPERATION ENTERTAIN-
MENT GIRLS, themselves
Operation: Entertainment (TV)
(Military entertainment)

SHAY. See also: Shea

SHAY, DOROTHY. See: Jones,
Spike (2)

SHAYNE. See also:
Shame
Shane

SHAYNE, MICHAEL, detective
LUCY HAMILTON, his girl Friday
DICK HAMILTON, Lucy's brother
TIM ROURKE, newspaperman
WILL GENTRY, police chief
Michael Shayne, Private Detective
(R) (TV) (Detective drama)

She, He and. See: Hollister, Dick

SHEA. See also: Shay

SHEA, KITTY. See: Davis, Ann
Tyler

SHEA, LISA. See: Hughes, Chris

SHEB WOOLEY. See: Owens, Buck

SHECKY GREENE. See: Martindale, Wink (2)

SHEEN, BISHOP FULTON J.,
churchman, host of the program
(himself)
Life is Worth Living (TV) (Religious discussion)

SHEENA, a "female Tarzan"
Sheena, Queen of the Jungle (TV)
(Jungle adventure)

Sheets to the Wind, Three. See:
Wayne, John

SHEFFIELD. See: Shieffield

SHEILA BARRETT. See: Stoopnagle, Colonel Lemuel Q. (1)

SHEILA BLADE. See: Dale,
Linda

SHEILA BRAND. See: Jordan,
Joyce

SHEILA CONLON. See: Kelly,
Joe (2)

SHEILA MAYO. See: Perry,
John

SHEILAH. See: Graham, Sheilah

SHELAH HAMMOND. See: Horton,
Dr. Tom

SHELDON. See also: Shelton

SHELDON, HERB. See: Kirk-
wood, Jack

SHELDON LEONARD. See: Benny, Jack

SHELDON, LOU. See: Taylor,
Danny

Shell Chateau. See: Jolson, Al

SHELLEY. See:
Berman, Shelley
Shelly
Shirley

SHELLY. See also:
Shelley
Shirley

SHELLY MARTIN. See: Waring,
Evelyn

SHELTON. See also: Sheldon

SHELTON, GEORGE. See: Howard,
Tom (1) (2)

SHENANDOAH, amnesia victim
seeking his identity
A Man Called Shenandoah (TV)
(Western)

SHEPHERD, ADAM, journalist

MANY ACTORS AND ACTRESSES
The Lloyd Bridges Show (TV)
(Drama)

SHEPHERD, ANN. See: Johnson,
Raymond Edward (1)

SHEPHERD, GARY, host of the
program (himself)
Today in Business (R) (Financial
advice)

SHEPHERD, NED. See: Davidson,
Bill

SHEPPARD, F.B.I. FIELD AGENT,
agent of Federal Bureau of
Investigation
The F.B.I. in Peace and War (R)
(Adventure)

SHEPPARD, FRANKLIN, American
expert on psychological warfare
NICHOLAS GAGE, English demo-
lition and underwater work
specialist
JEAN-GASTON ANDRE, French
specialist in "arms, armaments
and armour"
Jericho (TV) (World War II
drama)

SHERIDAN, DICK. See: Rogers,
Patricia

SHERIFF. See:
Morgan, Sheriff
Sheriff, The

Sheriff, Death Valley. See: Old
Ranger, The

SHERIFF JACKSON. See: Tennessee Jed

SHERIFF LUKE FERGUSON. See:
Guest, Edgar A. (2)

SHERIFF MARK CHASE. See:
Old Ranger, The

SHERIFF MIKE SHAW. See: Mix,
Tom

Sheriff of Cochise, The. See:
Morgan, Sheriff

SHERIFF OF NOTTINGHAM, THE.

See: Hood, Robin

Sheriff, The. See: Old Ranger,
The

SHERIFF, THE. See:
Dawg, Deputy
Sheriff

SHERLOCK. See: Holmes, Sherlock

Sherlock Holmes, The Adventures
of. See: Holmes, Sherlock

SHERMAN. See:
Barrett, Timothy "Spud"
Carmichael, Lucy
Sharman
Shoiman

SHERMAN BILLINGSLEY. See:
Hayes, Peter Lind (4)

SHERMAN, BOBBY. See: Steinberg, David (2)

SHERMAN, EULA. See: Harding,
Mrs. Rhoda

SHERMAN HULL. See: Farrell,
Charlie

SHERMAN LANE. See: Dix,
Dorothy (1)

SHERMAN, RANSOM (1)
BOB BROWN, quizmasters of
the program (themselves)
MANY CONTESTANTS
Quicksilver (R) (Quiz)

SHERMAN, RANSOM (2), host of
the program (himself)
BILL THOMPSON, featured on
the program (himself)
MANY GUESTS
The Sunbrite Smile Parade (R)
(Variety)

SHERMAN, RANSOM. See also:
Kirkwood, Jack
Moore, Garry (1)
Pratt, Russell

SHERMAN, SLIM. See: Harper,
Jess

SHERRY. See:
Cherry
Farrell, David
Shari

SHERRY MILES. See: Paulsen, Pat

SHERWOOD, BOBBY. See:
Donald, Peter

SHERWOOD, GRACE, proprietor of
diner in small town of Sunrise,
Colorado
WILL MAYBERRY, sheriff
ELMA GAHRINGER, waitress
GLENN WAGNER, district at-
torney
Bus Stop (TV) (Drama)

SHERWOOD, MARGOT. See:
Jordan, Joyce

SHERWOOD, MRS. See: Prescott,
Kate Hathaway

SHERWOOD, MYRA. See: Welby,
Dr. Marcus

SHERWOOD, PAUL. See: Jordan,
Joyce

SHERWOOD, RUTH, aspiring author;
Ohio girl living in Greenwich
Village, New York, with her
sister
EILEEN SHERWOOD, her sister,
aspiring actress
APPOPOLOUS, their landlord;
aspiring painter
BERTHA BRINSKY
CHUCK ADAMS, their friends
My Sister Eileen (TV) (Situation
comedy)

SHIEFFIELD, LAWRENCE. See:
Sunday

SHIELD, ROY. See: Sullivan,
Fred

SHIELDS, JIMMY, singer, featured
on the program (himself)
THE NORSEMEN QUARTET,
singing group
D'ARTEGA, orchestra leader
(himself)
HIS ORCHESTRA
Enna Jettick Melodies (R) (Music)

Shift With Rayburn and Finch, Night.
See: Rayburn, Gene (3)

SHILKRET, NAT. See: Stoopnagle,
Colonel Lemuel Q. (1)

Shiloh, The Men From. See:
MacKenzie, Colonel Alan
Virginian, The

Shindig! See: O'Neill, Jimmy

SHINDIG DANCERS, THE. See:
O'Neill, Jimmy

Shine, Time to. See: Kemp, Hal

Ship in the Army, The Wackiest.
See: Butcher, Major Simon

SHIRA. See: Smith, China

SHIRLEY. See:
Dinsdale, Shirley
Johnson, Bess
Logan, Shirley
Shelley
Shelly
Temple, Shirley

SHIRLEY DINSDALE. See:
Cantor, Eddie (2)
Dinsdale, Shirley

Shirley Dinsdale and Judy Splinters.
See: Dinsdale, Shirley

SHIRLEY LLOYD. See: Penner,
Joe

SHIRLEY MITCHELL. See: Kyser,
Kay

SHIRLEY SWANSON. See: Collins,
Bob

Shirley Temple Show, The. See:
Temple, Shirley

Shirley Temple's Story Book. See:
Temple, Shirley

Shirley's World. See: Logan,
Shirley

SHOBER, SHUFFLE. See: Perkins,
Ma

SHOEMAKER. See: Schoumacher

SHOESHINE BOY, THE. See:
Lewis, Jerry

SHOIMAN. See also:
Sharman
Sherman

SHOIMAN STOOLER. See: Joe (2)

SHOOTER, THE RALSTON STRAIGHT.
See: Mix, Tom

Shooters, Tom Mix and His Ralston
Straight. See: Mix, Tom

SHOP. See: Keeper of the Old
Curiosity Shop, The

Shop, Curiosity. See: Pam

Shop, Mel Blanc's Fix-It. See:
Blanc, Mel

Shop, Music. See: Bregman, Buddy

Shop, The Fix-It. See: Blanc, Mel

Shop, The Old Curiosity. See:
Keeper of the Old Curiosity Shop,
The

Shop, The Song. See: Carlisle,
Kitty

SHOPKEEPER. See: Husband

Shopping, Window. See: Kennedy,
Bob (1)

SHORE, DINAH (1), singer; star of
the program (herself)
MANY GUEST STARS
The Chevy Show Starring Dinah
Shore (TV) (Music)

SHORE, DINAH (2), singer, hostess
of the program (herself)
THE SKYLARKS, vocal group
MANY GUEST STARS
HARRY ZIMMERMAN, orchestra
leader (himself)
HIS ORCHESTRA
The Dinah Shore Show (TV)
(Variety)

SHORE, DINAH (3), singer, hostess

of the program (herself)
MANY GUESTS
Dinah's Place (TV) (Interviews)

SHORE, DINAH. See also:
Cantor, Eddie (2)
Cross, Milton (1)
Ross, Lanny

SHORT, BILL. See: Moore,
Garry (1)

SHORTY. See:
Boston Blackie
Jones, Amos

SHOTGUN. See: Slade, Shotgun

Shotgun Slade. See: Slade, Shotgun

SHOTS, THE HOOSIER HOT. See:
Kelly, Joe (1)

Show Boat. See: Henry, Captain

SHOW BOAT FOUR, THE. See:
Henry, Captain

Show Boat, The Maxwell House.
See: Henry, Captain

Show Business, Inc. See: Winchell,
Paul (5)

Show of Shows, Admiral Broadway
Revue, Your. See: Caesar, Sid
(3)

Show of Shows, Your. See:
Caesar, Sid (3)

Show on Earth, The Greatest. See:
Slate, Johnny

Show, The. See: Walsh, Bob

Show, The Big. See: Bankhead,
Tallulah

SHOW TIME. See also: Showtime

Show Time, International. See:
Ameche, Don (4)

Show Wagon, Horace Heidt's. See:
Heidt, Horace (1)

Showcase 68. See: Thaxton, Lloyd
(3)

Shower of Stars. See: Lundigan,
Bill (2)

Shows, Admiral Broadway Revue,
Your Show of. See: Caesar,
Sid (3)

Shows, Your Show of. See:
Caesar, Sid (3)

Showtime. See: Berman, Shelley

SHOWTIME. See also: Show Time

SHREVIE. See: Cranston, Lamont

SHREVNITZ, MOE. See: Cranston,
Lamont

SHREWSBURY. See: Churchill,
John

SHRINER, HERB (1), star of the
program (himself)
Alka Seltzer Time (R) (Humor)

SHRINER, HERB (2), host of the
program (himself)
MANY GUEST STARS
The Herb Shriner Show (TV)
(Variety)

SHRINER, HERB (3), quizmaster of
the program (himself)
MANY CONTESTANTS
Two For the Money (Quiz) (R)
(TV)
WALTER O'KEEFE, quizmaster
of the program (himself)
Two For the Money (R)
SAM LEVENSON, quizmaster of
the program (himself)
DR. MASON GROSS, referee of
the program (himself)
Two For the Money (TV)

SHUFFLE SHOBER. See: Perkins,
Ma

SHUKIN, PHIL. See: Moore,
Garry (1)

SHUTTA, ETHEL. See: Benny,
Jack

SHUTTLEWORTH, JOHN, editor of
True Detective Magazine (him-
self)
MANY ACTORS AND ACTRESSES
True Detective Mysteries (R)
(Detective drama)

SI ZENTNER. See: Basie, Count

SIAM, THE KING OF. See:
Owens, Anna

SID. See also: Cyd

SID CAESAR. See:
Caesar, Sid (1) (2) (3)
Crosby, Bing (2)

SID GOULD. See: Lewis, Robert
Q. (1)

SID RANDOLPH. See: Carter,
Mr.

Side, The Funny. See: Kelly,
Gene

Sidewalk Interviews. See: Johnson, Parks

SIDNEY. See also: Sydney

SIDNEY DANCERS, THE BOB.
See: Bailey, Pearl

SIDNEY ELLSTROM. See: Winkler,
Betty

SIDNEY GODOLPHIN. See:
Churchill, John

SIDNEY LUMET. See: Halop,
Billy

SIEGEL, DAVID. See: Walleck,
Meredith

SIEGEL, EILEEN MARGARET.
See: Walleck, Meredith

SIGMUND. See: Spaeth, Sigmund

SILAS DRAKE. See: Wilbur,
Judy

SILENCE. See: Silents

Silent Force, The. See: Fuller,
Ward

Silents, Please. See: Kovacs,
Ernie (2)

SILKY. See: Harris, Silky

SILLS, JED. See: Corey, Don

SILLY WATSON. See: McGee,
Fibber

SILO, MR. See: Little Orphan
Annie

SILO, MRS. See: Little Orphan
Annie

SILVER. See: Lone Ranger, The

SILVER ALBATROSS, THE. See:
Armstrong, Jack

SILVER, CAPTAIN
CAROL ANDERSON
JERRY
KUKAI
TEX, characters appearing on
the program
The Sea Hound (R) (Adventure)

Silver Eagle, Mountie. See: West,
Jim (1)

SILVER, LONG JOHN, skipper of
pirate ship
JIM
PURITY, characters appearing
on the program
Long John Silver (TV) (Adventure)

Silver Theater. See: Nagel,
Conrad

SILVERMAN, AARON. See: Barrett, David

SILVERS, PHIL. See:
Crosby, Bing (2)
Donald, Peter

SILVUS, MR. See: Perkins, Ma

SIMBA. See: McKenzie, Captain
Craig

SIMMONS, CORNELIA. See:

Tate, Joanne

SIMMONS, DR. See: Hardy,
Dr. Steven

SIMMS. See also: Sims

SIMMS, DR. ALAN. See: Dallas,
Stella

SIMMS, GINNY. See: Kyser, Kay

SIMMS, LAFE. See: Hargrave-
Scott, Joan

SIMMS, LU ANN. See: Godfrey,
Arthur (1)

SIMMS, PAUL, lawyer; head of
the house
MARTHA, his wife
BARBARA DICKERSON, his
daughter
HOWIE DICKERSON, his unem-
ployed genius son-in-law
SALLY, his teen-age daughter
The Paul Lynde Show (TV)
(Family situation comedy)

SIMON. See:
Butcher, Major Simon
Fry, Marshal Simon
Locke, Dr. Simon
Saville, David
Templar, Simon

SIMON JESSUP. See: Karr, Mike

SIMON KANE. See: Perry, Luke

Simon Locke, Dr. See: Locke,
Dr. Simon (1)

SIMON LOCKE, DR. See: Locke,
Dr. Simon (1) (2)

SIMON, RITA. See: Conway,
Bobby

SIMON, SIR. See: Hood, Robin

SIMON, UNCLE. See: Ward,
Tammy

SIMONE GENET. See: Sebastian,
Victor

SIMONS, DR. HANS. See:

Jordan, Joyce

SIMPKINS, MR. See: Tillie

Simpson Boys of Sprucehead Bay,
The. See: Simpson Boys, The

SIMPSON BOYS, THE, residents of
rural New England
The Simpson Boys of Sprucehead
Bay (R) (Drama)

SIMPSON, CORA LEE. See: Davis,
Dr. Althea

SIMPSON, EMMA. See: Davis,
Dr. Althea

SIMPSON, MRS. See: MacDonald,
Eleanor

SIMS. See also: Simms

SIMS, LOUISE. See: Nelson,
Carolyn Kramer

SIN, ROCKWELL. See: Farrow,
Valentine

SINATRA, FRANK, singer and actor;
star of the program (himself)
MANY GUEST STARS
The Frank Sinatra Show (R) (TV)
(Variety)
AXEL STORDAHL, orchestra
leader (himself)
HIS ORCHESTRA
The Frank Sinatra Show (R)

SINATRA, FRANK. See also:
Ross, Lanny

SINATRA, FRANK, JR. See:
Jones, Jack

SINATRA, RAY. See: McKinley,
Barry

SINCLAIR, DREW. See: Trent,
Helen

SINCLAIR, JIM. See: Hayes,
Wing Commander

SINCLAIR, LORD BRETT. See:
Wilde, Danny

SINCLAIR MINSTREL MEN, THE.

See: Arnold, Gene

Sinclair Minstrel Show, The. See:
Arnold, Gene

SINCLAIR QUARTET, THE. See:
Arnold, Gene

SINCLAIR, SERGEANT BUCK. See:
Flagg, Captain Jim

Sing Along With Mitch. See:
Miller, Mitch

Sing, Community. See: Jones,
Billy

SING, HOP. See: Cartwright,
Ben

Sing It Again. See: Seymour,
Dan

Sing Sing, Twenty Thousand Years
in. See: Lawes, Lewis E.

SINGALONGERS, THE. See:
Miller, Mitch

Singer, The Street. See: Tracy,
Arthur

SINGERS, KAY THOMPSON'S
RHYTHM. See: Martin, Tony
(2)

SINGERS, THE CLAY WARNICK.
See: Crosby, Bob (1)

SINGERS, THE DICK WILLIAMS.
See: Andrews, Julie

SINGERS, THE EARL BROWN. See:
Bono, Salvatore

SINGERS, THE GEORGE WYLE.
See: Lewis, Jerry

SINGERS, THE HAPPY DAYS. See:
Nye, Louis

SINGERS, THE HIT PARADE. See:
Lanson, Snooky

SINGERS, THE HOWARD ROBERTS.
See: Uggams, Leslie

SINGERS, THE JOHNNY MANN.

See: Mann, Johnny

SINGERS, THE LYN MURRAY.
See: Ross, Lanny

SINGERS, THE MIKE SAMMES.
See:
Berman, Shelley
Doonican, Val
O'Connor, Des

SINGERS, THE PAT FRIDAY. See:
Borge, Victor

SINGERS, THE RAY CHARLES.
See:
Como, Perry (1) (2) (3)
Fisher, Eddie

SINGERS, THE WORLD ACTION.
See: Roberts, Oral

SINGIN' SAM, vocalist, portrayed
by Harry Frankel
Singin' Sam, The Barbasol Man
(R) (Music)

Singing Bee. See: Lewis, Welcome

Singing Lady, The. See: Singing
Lady, The

SINGING LADY, THE, vocalist,
portrayed by Ireene Wicker
The Singing Lady (R) (Children's
stories and songs)

SINGING M.C., THE. See:
Morgan, Frank (2)

SINGING MAILMEN, THE. See:
Wincholl, John

SINGLETON, BUCK. See: Bailey,
Sam

Singo. See: Lewis, Welcome

Sinners, Saints and. See: Alexander, Nick

SINNERS, THE. See: Riddle,
Sam (2)

SIR CEDRIC HARDWICKE. See:
Wallace, Mike (5)

SIR FRANCIS. See: Drake, Sir
Francis

Sir Francis Drake. See: Drake,
Sir Francis

SIR GAWAIN. See: Sir Lancelot

SIR KAY. See: Sir Lancelot

SIR LANCELOT, knight of the
Round Table
BRIAN, his squire
KING ARTHUR, King of Britain
QUEEN GUINEVERE, Queen of
Britain
ELAINE THE FAIR, Sir Lance-
lot's sweetheart
SIR GAWAIN
SIR KAY, knights of the Round
Table
MERLIN, magician
ISOLT, Queen of Ireland
The Adventures of Sir Lancelot
(TV) (Adventure)

Sir Lancelot, The Adventures of.
See: Sir Lancelot

SIR PERCY. See: Blakeney, Sir
Percy

SIR PETER MARSTON. See:
Hood, Robin

SIR SIMON. See: Hood, Robin

SIREN, THE. See: Batman

SIRI ALLEN. See: Cameron,
Christy Allen

SIS. See: McGee, Fibber

SISK, MILDRED ELIZABETH
RITA LOUISE ZUCCA, Nazi
propaganda broadcasters in
World War II (themselves)
Axis Sally (R) (Nazi war propa-
ganda)

SR. See: Bertrille, Sr.

SR. ADA. See: Rutledge, Dr.
John

SR. ANA. See: Bertrille, Sr.

Sister, Big. See: Wayne, Ruth
Evans

Sister Eileen, My. See: Sherwood, Ruth

SR. ELAINE. See: Harding, Karen Adams

SR. JACQUELINE. See: Bertrille, Sr.

SR. LILLIAN. See: Rutledge, Dr. John

SR. SIXTO. See: Bertrille, Sr.

SISTER, THE BIG. See: Wayne, Ruth Evans

SISTERBELLE. See: Matty

Sisters Hour, Jimmy Durante Presents the Lennon. See: Lennon, Janet

Sisters of the Skillet. See: East, Ed (3)

SISTERS, THE ANDREWS. See: Baker, Phil (1) Crosby, Bob (2)

SISTERS, THE DEMARCO. See: Allen, Fred

SISTERS, THE DINNING. See: Kelly, Joe (1)

SISTERS, THE FONTANE. See: Como, Perry (1)

SISTERS, THE KING. See: Kyser, Kay

SISTERS, THE LANE. See: Waring, Fred (1)

SISTERS, THE LENNON. See: Lennon, Janet Welk, Lawrence

SISTERS, THE McGUIRE. See: Godfrey, Arthur (1)

Sisters, The Moylan. See: Moylan, Marianne

SISTERS, THE RODGERS. See: Stoopnagle, Colonel Lemuel Q. (1)

SISTERS, THE STEELE. See: Wincholl, John

SIVONEY, JOHN L. C. See: Benny, Jack Hope, Bob (2)

6, NO. See: Prisoner, The

Six-Shooter, The. See: Stewart, Jimmy

Six, Surfside. See: Madison, Kenny

Six Wives of Henry VIII, The. See: Henry VIII, King of England

Sixth Sense, The. See: Rhodes, Dr. Michael

Sixties, Living For the. See: Furness, Betty

SIXTO, SR. See: Bertrille, Sr.

60, Club. See: James, Dennis (1)

68, Showcase. See: Thaxton, Lloyd (3)

Sixty-Four Dollar Question, The. See: Baker, Phil (3)

$64,000 Challenge, The. See: Story, Ralph

$64,000 Question, The. See: March, Hal

60 Minutes. See: Wallace, Mike (4)

66, Route. See: Murdock, Buz

SKEEZIX. See: Wallet, Skeezix

SKELLY, BERT. See: Walleck, Meredith

SKELTON, RED, comedian; star of the program (himself) CURT MASSEY, baritone (himself) "PROFESSOR" TOMMY MACK, entertainer (himself)

TOM, DICK AND HARRY, vocal
group
BOB STRONG, orchestra leader
(himself)
HIS ORCHESTRA
Avalon Time (R) (Variety)

SKELTON, RED. See also: Junior

SKIDMORE, BETTY. See: Davis,
Joan Field

SKIDMORE, STEVE. See: Davis,
Joan Field

Skillet, Sisters of the. See: East,
Ed (3)

SKIMP, SQUIRE. See: Edwards,
Lum

SKINFLINT, AUNT LUCINDA.
See: Peppertag, Aaron

SKINNAY ENNIS. See: Hope, Bob
(2)

SKIP
WES, firemen
Rescue 8 (TV) (Fire fighting
adventure)

SKIP. See also: Muggsy

SKIP FARRELL. See:
Ford, Tennessee Ernie (4)
Kelly, Joe (1)

SKIP HINNANT. See: Cosby,
Bill (1)

SKIP-JACKS, THE. See: Desmond,
Johnny

SKIP MARTIN. See: O'Neill, Mrs.

SKIPPER. See:
Gilligan
Jungle Jim
Old Skipper, The
Randolph, Ellen

"SKIPPER" BARBOUR, ANDREW.
See: Barbour, Henry Wilson

SKIPPER COOK. See: Sharp, Hal

Skipper Jim. See: Skipper Jim

SKIPPER JIM, sailor
Skipper Jim (R) (Children's program)

Skipper, The Old. See: Old
Skipper, The

SKIPPY
SOOKY
JIM LOVERING, characters
appearing on the program
Skippy (R) (Children's program)

SKITCH HENDERSON. See:
Allen, Steve (3)
Carson, Johnny (1)

"SKY." See: King, Schyler "Sky"

Sky Blazers. See: Turner,
Colonel Roscoe

Sky King. See: King, Schyler
"Sky"

SKY KING'S FOREMAN. See:
King, Schyler "Sky"

SKYLARKS, THE. See: Shore,
Dinah (2)

SLADE, SHOTGUN, law enforcement officer
Shotgun Slade (TV) (Western)

Slam, Grand. See: Beasley,
Irene (1)

SLATE. See: Shannon, Slate

SLATE, JOHNNY, circus boss
OTTO KING, treasurer of circus
MANY CIRCUS ACTS
The Greatest Show on Earth (TV)
(Circus)

SLATE, MARK. See: Dancer,
April

SLATER, BILL (1)
TOM SLATER, interviewers
(themselves)
MANY INTERVIEWEES
Luncheon at Sardi's (R) (Inter-
view)

SLATER, BILL (2)
JAY JACKSON, quizmasters of

the program (themselves)
BOBBY VANDERVENTER
FRED VANDERVENTER
HERB POLESIE
FLORENCE RINARD, panelists on
the program (themselves)
Twenty Questions (R) (Panel
quiz)

SLATER, BILL. See also:
Cowan, Thomas
Dunninger, Joseph
Hagen, Dr. Harry

SLATTERY, JIM, crusading state
legislator
MIKE VALERA, his aide
WENDY WENDKOSKI, his secre-
tary
LIZ ANDREWS, his girl friend
BERT METCALF
B. J. CLAWSON
JOHNNY RAMOS
FRANK RADCLIFFE, politicians
Slattery's People (TV) (Drama)

Slattery's People. See: Slattery,
Jim

SLAUGHTER, MURRAY. See:
Richards, Mary

SLAVE GIRL. See: Speaker, The

SLEZAK, WALTER, host of the
program (himself)
MANY ACTORS AND ACTRESSES
Mystery Show (TV) (Suspense
dramas)

SLEZAK, WALTER. See also:
James, Dennis (3)

SLICKERS, THE CITY. See:
Jones, Spike (2)

SLIM. See:
Caine, Frank
Kelly, Kitty

SLIM DELANEY. See: Sunday

SLIM SHERMAN. See: Harper,
Jess

SLIM STARK. See: Dane,
Prudence

SLIM WILSON. See: Foley, Red

SLIPPERY CHARLIE. See: Huddles, Ed

SLOAN, FRANK. See: Karr, Mike

SLOAN, HOLLY
HENRY SLOAN
JOHNNY STARR
MILLICENT STARR
WILBUR RAMAGE
PRENTISS JEFFRIES
CLAY BROWN
LAURALEE McWILLIAMS
ADELE KINGMAN
KENTURAH
SALLY, characters appearing in
the drama
Holly Sloan (R) (Serial drama)
(also called The Story of Holly
Sloan) (R)

SLOAN, KATE. See: Karr, Mike

SLOAN, PETE. See: Horton,
Dot

SLOANE, EVERETT, host of the
program (himself)
MANY ACTORS AND ACTRESSES
Official Detective (TV) (Dramatizations of true detective stories)

SLOANE, EVERETT. See also:
Kaye, Danny
Welles, Orson (2)

SLOANE, ROBERT, narrator of
the program (himself)
MANY ACTORS AND ACTRESSES
The Big Story (R) (Newspaper
reporting drama)

SLOBBERT HINK. See: Gook,
Vic

SLOCUM, MR. See: Bell, Harry

Smackouts, The. See: Jordan,
Jim (1)

SMALE, BOB. See: Welk,
Lawrence

SMALL, MARY. See: Bernie,
Ben

Small World. See: Murrow,
Edward R. (5)

SMALLEY, MA. See: Dillon,
Marshal Matt

SMART, JACK. See: Welles,
Orson (2)

SMART, MAXWELL (Agent 86),
investigator, represents
CONTROL, opposing KAOS
AGENT 99, his wife, also an
investigator
CHIEF, their supervisor
Get Smart (TV) (Comedy)

SMEATON, MARK. See: Henry
VIII, King of England

SMELLY CLARK. See: Gook, Vic

SMIFF. See also: Smith

SMIFF, KNUCKLEHEAD. See:
Winchell, Paul (3)

Smile-In, Downeast. See: Dodge,
Marshall "Mike"

Smile, Learn to. See: Cantor,
Eddie (2)

Smile Parade, The Sunbrite. See:
Sherman, Ransom (2)

Smile Time. See: Allen, Steve
(2)

Smiles, The Hour of. See: Allen,
Fred

SMILEY. See: Nielson, Torwald

SMILEY BURNETTE. See:
Ritter, Tex (1)

Smilin' Ed's Gang. See: McConnell, Ed

Smilin' Jack. See: Smilin' Jack

SMILIN' JACK, aviator-adventurer
Smilin' Jack (R) (Aviation adventure)

SMITH. See also: Smiff

Smith and Jones, Alias. See:
Heyes, Hannibal

SMITH, ANGEL, French girl,
marries American
JOHN SMITH, her husband;
architect
SUSY
GEORGE, their neighbors
Angel (TV) (Comedy)

SMITH, ANTHONY, International
Police Organization agent and
Scotland Yard official
Man From Interpol (TV) (Adven-
ture)

SMITH BALLEW. See: Jolson, Al

SMITH, BILLY. See: Anderson,
Jim

SMITH, BRIGADIER GENERAL
MONTGOMERY. See: Welles,
Orson (3)

SMITH, BUFFALO BOB. See:
Doody, Howdy

SMITH, CHAD, detective sergeant,
25 years on the force
BETTY, his wife
CINDY, his daughter
BRIAN
BOB, his sons
The Smith Family (TV) (Comedy
drama)

SMITH, CHINA, adventurer in the
Orient
SHIRA, his assistant
China Smith (TV) (Adventure)

SMITH, COLONEL ZACHARY,
enemy agent
PROFESSOR JOHN ROBINSON,
astro-physicist
MAUREEN ROBINSON, his wife
JUDY ROBINSON
WILL ROBINSON
PENNY ROBINSON, children of
John and Maureen; members of
family stranded on unknown
planet in the year 1997
MAJOR DONALD WEST, geologist
THE ROBOT, mechanical being
Lost in Space (TV) (Science
fiction/drama)

SMITH, COOPER. See: Adams,
Major Seth

SMITH, DESPERATE. See: Adams,
Crunch

SMITH, DETECTIVE JOE. See:
Friday, Sergeant Joe

SMITH, DON. See: Warren, Wendy

SMITH, ELIZABETH. See: Anderson, Jim

SMITH, ELLEN. See: O'Leary,
Hannah

SMITH, ELLIS. See: Rutledge,
Dr. John

SMITH, ETHEL. See: Ross, Lanny

SMITH, EUGENE, newly-elected
U. S. Senator
PAT, his wife
ARNIE, his chauffeur
MISS KELLY, his secretary
UNCLE COOTER, "guitar-playing
rural philosopher"
Mr. Smith Goes to Washington
(TV) (Comedy)

Smith Family, The. See:
Jordan, Jim (2)
Smith, Chad

SMITH, GREGORY, comic detective
HIS VALET
The Amazing Mr. Smith (R)
(Comedy/mystery)

SMITH, HAL. See: Paulsen, Pat

SMITH, HECTOR. See: Anderson,
Jim

SMITH, HELEN. See: Hutton,
Ina Ray

SMITH, HOMER. See: Peters,
Lowell

SMITH, HOWARD K. (1)
HARRY REASONER, newscasters
(themselves)
The A. B. C. Evening News (TV)
(News)

SMITH, HOWARD K. (2)
JOHN SCALI, newscasters (them-
selves)
VARIOUS INTERVIEWEES
A. B. C. Scope (TV) (Coverage of
Vietnam War)

SMITH, J. D. See: Marshal, The

SMITH, JACK, singer; host of the
program (himself)
The American West (TV) (Travel
in Western America)

SMITH, JACK. See also: Taylor,
Deems

SMITH, JERRY. See: Hughes,
Chris

SMITH, JOEL. See: Holliday,
Hiram

SMITH, JOSHUA. See: Heyes,
Hannibal

SMITH, KATE (1), singer, star
of the program (herself)
TED COLLINS, host of the pro-
gram (himself)
MANY GUEST STARS
The Kate Smith Hour (TV)
(Music/variety)

SMITH, KATE (2), singer, star of
the program (herself)
TED COLLINS, host of the program (himself)
JACK MILLER, orchestra
leader (himself)
HIS ORCHESTRA
MANY GUEST STARS
The Kate Smith Show (R) (Variety)
(also known as The A. &P. Bandwagon) (R)

SMITH, KATE (3), hostess of the
program (herself)
MANY GUEST CELEBRITIES
Kate Smith Speaks (R) (Interview/
talk)

SMITH, KATHARINE. See:
Spitalny, Phil

SMITH, KAY. See: Webster,
Martha

SMITH, LOGAN. See: Solomon,
David

SMITH, LUCKY, detective
Lucky Smith (R) (Detective adventure)

SMITH, MRS. WARD. See:
Trent, Helen

SMITH, MONICA WARD. See:
Trent, Helen

SMITH, NAYLAND. See: Fu
Manchu

SMITH, NICKIE. See: Walleck,
Meredith

SMITH, QUEENIE. See: Kelly,
Gene

SMITH, STEVE. See: Welk,
Lawrence

SMITH, TAD. See: Myrt

SMITH, TAO. See: Bennett, Nita

SMITH, TOBY. See: Aldrich,
Henry

SMITH, TOUBO. See: Kelly,
Tim

SMITH, VANESSA. See: Croft,
Jonathan

SMITH, ZERO. See: Wing,
Howie

SMITHGIRL, PEGGY. See: Webster, Martha

Smokey Bear. See: Smokey Bear

SMOKEY BEAR, cartoon character,
advocate of fire prevention
Smokey Bear (TV) (Children's
program)

SMOKEY BEAR. See also: Parmenter, Captain Wilton

SMOOTHIES, THE. See: Kemp,
Hal

Smothers Brothers Comedy Hour,

The. See: Smothers, Tom (1)

Smothers Brothers Show, The. See:
Smothers, Tom (2)

Smothers Brothers Summer Show,
The. See: Smothers, Tom (3)

SMOTHERS, TOM (1)
DICK SMOTHERS, brothers;
singers and comedians, co-hosts
of the program (themselves)
PAT PAULSEN, comedian ap-
pearing on the program (himself)
MANY GUEST STARS
NELSON RIDDLE, orchestra
leader (himself)
HIS ORCHESTRA
The Smothers Brothers Comedy
Hour (TV) (Comedy/variety)

SMOTHERS, TOM (2), recently de-
ceased, returns as an apprentice
angel (himself)
DICK, his brother (himself)
The Smothers Brothers Show (TV)
(Comedy/fantasy)

SMOTHERS, TOM (3)
DICK SMOTHERS, brothers;
singers and comedians, hosts of
the program (themselves)
PAT PAULSEN, comedian appear-
ing on the program (himself)
SALLY STRUTHERS, comedienne
appearing on the program (her-
self)
MANY GUEST STARS
The Smothers Brothers Summer
Show (TV) (Comedy/variety)

SNAFFLE, DOLLY. See: Archie

SNAKE HOGAN. See: Edwards,
Lum

Snap Judgment. See: McMahon,
Ed (2)

SNEDIGAR, POLICE LIEUT. See:
Madison, Kenny

SNELL, EUGENE. See: Mac-
Donald, Eleanor

SNERD, MORTIMER. See:
Ameche, Don (1)
Bergen, Edgar (1) (2)

SNIDELY WHIPLASH. See: Do-
Right, Dudley

SNODGRASS, J. E. See: Barry,
Jack (9)

SNOOD, AMOS Q. See: Mix, Tom

SNOOD, WILLIAM. See: Mix,
Tom

SNOOKS, BABY. See:
Baby Snooks
Dragonette, Jessica (2)
Morgan, Frank (2)

SNOOKY. See: Lanson, Snooky

SNOOPER. See: McGraw, Quick
Draw

SNORKY. See: Fleegle

Snow Village. See: Dickey, Dan'l

SNOWDEN, AMY. See: Prescott,
Kate Hathaway

SNYDER. See: Anderson, Sergeant
Nick

SNYDER, WILBUR. See: James,
Dennis (4)

SO-HI. See: Linus

So This Is Hollywood. See: Dugan,
Queenie

So You Want To Lead a Band?
See: Kaye, Sammy (2)

SOAMES. See: Forsyte, Soames

SOAPY. See:
Holliday, Alice
Soupy

Society Girl. See: Barrington,
Bryn Clark

Society of Lower Basin Street,
The Chamber Music. See:
Cross, Milton (1)

SOCRATES. See: Miller, Socrates

SOCRATES MULLIGAN. See: Allen,
Fred

SOL ABRAMS, SERGEANT. See:
Muldoon, Francis

SOLARI AND CARR. See: Stevens,
Ray

Soldier Parade. See: Francis,
Arlene (4)

Soldier Who Came Home, The. See:
Cameron, Barry

Soldiers of Fortune. See: Kelly,
Tim

Soldiers, The. See: Hal

SOLEMN OLD JUDGE, THE
COUSIN MINNIE PEARL
THE DUKE OF PADUCAH
UNCLE JIMMIE THOMPSON,
musicians and entertainers
appearing on the program
MANY COUNTRY-WESTERN
MUSICIANS AND ENTERTAINERS
The Grand Ole Opry (R)
(Country music and variety)

SOLLY. See:
Goldberg, Molly
Soule
Sully

SOLNICK, TANIA. See: Marshall,
E. G.

SOLO, NAPOLEON
ILLYA KURYAKIN, crime fighters,
represent U. N. C. L. E. opposing
THRUSH
ALEXANDER WAVERLY, their
supervisor
The Man from U. N. C. L. E. (TV)
(Crime drama)

SOLOMON. See: Levy, Abie

SOLOMON, DAVID (Papa David),
proprietor of the Slightly Read
Book Shop
CAROL "CHICHI" CONRAD, his
adopted daughter
STEPHEN HAMILTON, Carol's
invalid husband
BARRY MARKHAM
RITA YATES
OSCAR FINCH
TOBY NELSON

AL DOUGLAS
GYP MENDOZA
DR. MYRON HENDERSON, physician
NURSE KIMBALL
MARYBELLE OWENS
LOGAN SMITH
MRS. S. KENT WADSWORTH
MRS. MARKHAM
DR. MARKHAM, physician
DOUGLAS NORMAN
HANK BRISTOW
NELLIE GLEASON
NELLIE CONRAD
MAUDE KELLOGG
HANK O'HOOLIHAN, characters
appearing in the drama
Life Can Be Beautiful (R) (Serial
drama) (also known as Elsie
Beebe) (R)

SOMERS. See:
Churchill, John
Sommers
Summers

Somerset. See: Hillman, India

SOMERVILLE, DAVID. See:
Conway, Tim

Something Else. See: Byner,
John (2)

SOMMERS. See also:
Somers
Summers

SOMMERS, JIMSEY. See: Halop,
Billy

SOMMERS, SUZANNE. See:
Kidder, Margot

SON. See also:
Sons
Sun

Son and I, My. See: Vance,
Connie

Son, Harrigan and. See: Harrigan,
James, Sr.

SON, NUMBER ONE. See: Chan,
Charlie

Son of Fire, Og. See: Og

Son of the Sea, Davy Adams. See:
Adams, Franklin P.

Son, Sanford and. See: Sanford,
Fred

Son, Steptoe and. See: Sanford,
Fred

SONDI. See:
Sandi
Sandy
Troy, Adam

Song of a Stranger, The. See:
Vernay, Pierre

Song Shop, The. See: Carlisle,
Kitty

Song, What's the Name of That?
See: Williamson, Dud

Song, Yours For a. See:
Froman, Jane (2)
Parks, Bert (7)

Songs For Sale. See: Murray,
Jan (3)

Songs of the B-Bar-B. See:
Benson, Bobby

SONIA KIRKOFF. See: Grimm,
Arnold

SONNETT, WILL, former gun-
slinger, now sheepman
JAMES, his son
JEFF, son of James
The Guns of Will Sonnett (TV)
(Western)

SONNY. See:
Boni, Salvatore
Fox, Sonny
Pud

Sonny and Cher Comedy Hour, The.
See: Bono, Salvatore

Sonny and Cher Show, The. See:
Bono, Salvatore

SONNY FOX. See:
Fox, Sonny
Story, Ralph

SONNY HALLET. See: Perkins, Ma

SONNY THE JANITOR. See: Wilson, Flip

SONS. See also:
Son
Sun

Sons, My Three. See: Douglas, Steve

Sons of the Pioneers, The. See: Nolan, Bob

SONS OF THE PIONEERS, THE.
See:
Nolan, Bob
Rogers, Roy

SOOKY. See: Skippy

SOPHIE. See: Harris, Bill

SOPHIE, MADAME. See: Peters, Bill

SOPHIE STEINBERG. See: Fitzgerald, Bridget Theresa Mary Coleen

SOPHISTICATES, THE. See:
Kelly, Gene

SOREL, GUY, announcer, host of the program (himself)
VARIOUS RADIO ANNOUNCERS AND INTERVIEWERS
GUEST ACTORS AND ACTRESSES
You are There (R) (Historical drama) (originally titled C. B. S. Is There) (R)

SORRELL, BUDDY. See: Petrie, Rob

SORRELL, PICKLES. See:
Petrie, Rob

SOSNIK, HARRY. See:
Brown, Joe E. (1)
Elman, Dave (2)
Hildegarde (1)
Levenson, Sam

SOTHERN. See also: Southern

SOTHERN, MARY

MAX TILLEY
DR. JOHN BENSON, physician
BILLIE McDANIELS
JEROME SANDERS
ALICE SANDERS
DADDY STRATFORD
PHYLLIS STRATFORD
DANNY STRATFORD, characters appearing in the drama
The Life of Mary Sothern (R) (Serial drama)

SOUBIER, CLIFF. See:
First Nighter, Mr.
Thurston, Howard

Soul! See: Butler, Jerry

Soul, The Timid. See: Milquetoast, Casper

SOUL, THE TIMID. See: Milquetoast, Casper

SOULE. See also:
Solly
Sully

SOULE, OLAN (1)
JACK BRINKLEY
HAROLD VERMILYEA
DOROTHY GISH
ELINOR HARRIOT
PEG LYNCH
ALAN BUNCE
DONNA CREED, actors and actresses featured on the program (themselves)
The Couple Next Door (R) (Serial drama)

SOULE, OLAN (2)
BERYL VAUGHN, featured on the program (themselves)
MANY OTHER ACTORS AND ACTRESSES
Grand Marquee (R) (Drama)

SOULE, OLAN (3), narrator of the program (himself)
Grandstand Thrills (R) (Sports)

SOULE, OLAN (4)
BOB BAILEY
VIRGINIA GREGG, featured on the program (themselves)
MANY ACTORS AND ACTRESSES
Let George Do It (R) (Drama)

SOULE, OLAN (5), narrator of the program (himself)
Science in the News (R) (Science)

SOULE, OLAN. See also:
Ameche, Don (3)
First Nighter, Mr.

SOUPY. See also: Soapy

Soupy Sales. See: Sales, Soupy

SOUPY SALES. See:
Daly, John (3)
Sales, Soupy

Southampton, The Pruitts of. See:
Pruitt, Mrs. Phyllis Poindexter

SOUTHERN. See also: Sothern

SOUTHERN COLONEL. See: Old
Southern Colonel, The

SOUTHERNAIRES QUARTET, THE.
See: Peters, Lowell

Southernaires, The. See: Peters,
Lowell

Space Cadet. See: Corbett, Tom
(2)

Space Cadet, Tom Corbett. See:
Corbett, Tom (2)

Space Ghost. See: Space Ghost

SPACE GHOST, crime fighter; cartoon character
Space Ghost (TV) (Cartoon)

Space, Josie and the Pussycats in
Outer. See: Josie

Space, Lost in. See: Smith,
Colonel Zachary

Space, Men Into. See: McCauley,
Colonel Edward

Space Ranger, Rocky Jones. See:
Jones, Rocky

SPADE, SAM, private detective,
license No. 137596
EFFIE, his secretary
The Adventures of Sam Spade (R)

(Detective drama) (also known as
Sam Spade, Detective) (R)

SPAETH, SIGMUND, musicologist;
master of ceremonies of the program (himself)
The Tune Detective (R) (Music)

SPALDING, AUNT HELEN. See:
Harding, Karen Adams

SPALDING, ED. See: Waring,
Evelyn

SPALDING, MISS. See: Luigi

SPARE. See also: Spear

Spare, Make That. See: Elliott,
Win (2)

SPARE RIBS. See:
Arnold, Gene
Kelly, Joe (1)
Old Witch, The

SPARKS. See: Williams, Dr.

SPARKS, CAPTAIN. See: Little
Orphan Annie

SPARKS, HALE, host of the program (himself)
What's New in Learning? (R)
(Education)

SPARKS, RANDY, leader of the
group (himself)
CHORUS OF VOCALISTS/INSTRU-
MENTALISTS
The New Christy Minstrels
(TV) (group singing)

SPARKY. See:
Big Jon
Bizarre, Benita

Sparky, Big Jon and. See: Big
Jon

SPARKY FISCHMAN. See: Kelly,
Joe (2)

Sparrow and the Hawk, The. See:
Mallory, Lieut. Col. Spencer

SPARROW, THE. See: Mallory,
Lieut. Col. Spencer

SPARROWHILL, MARTIN. See:
Jordan, Joyce

Speak Up, America. See: Wordmaster, The

SPEAKER, THE, host of the pro-
gram
ARAM
NEBUCHADNEZZAR
JOSIAH
SHALLUM
JONATHAN
DANIEL
SLAVE GIRL
ELONA, characters appearing
on the program
MANY GUEST STARS
The Light of the World (R)
(Dramatizations of Bible stories)

Speaking Freely. See: Newman,
Edwin (2)

Speaks, Kate Smith. See: Smith,
Kate (3)

SPEAKS, MARGARET. See: Barlow, Howard

SPEAR. See also: Spare

SPEAR, MARSHA. See: Jones,
Abraham Lincoln

SPEAR, SAMMY. See:
DeLuise, Dom (1)
Gleason, Jackie (2)
Kramden, Ralph

SPEARCHUCKER JONES. See:
Pierce, Captain Hawkeye

SPEARS, GRANDPAPPY. See:
Edwards, Lum

Special Agent. See: Drake, Alan

SPECIAL AGENT PETERS. See:
Harding, David

Special Agent 7. See: Conroy,
Phil

SPECIAL, THE BLUE BIRD. See:
Allen, Jimmie

SPECK RHODES. See: Wagoner,

PORTER

SPEED. See: Ungar, Felix

SPEED ROBERTSON. See: Allen,
Jimmie

Speidel Show, The. See: Winchell,
Paul (6)

SPELL-A-PHONE. See: Cookie
Monster, The

Spelling Bee, The National. See:
Wing, Paul

SPENCER. See:
Dean, Spencer
Garrison, Spencer
Mallory, Lieut. Col. Spencer

SPENCER, BROCK. See: Mc-
Kenzie, Captain Craig

SPENCER, CHARLES. See:
Churchill, John

SPENCER HOWARD. See: Joe (1)

SPENCER, JEFF
DEBBY SPENCER, his wife
SERGEANT CORNELIUS TRUM-
BULL
MRS. GROVER
MICKEY
THE MIDGET
THE PROFESSOR, characters
appearing on the program
Two On a Clue (R) (Mystery)

SPENCER, JEFF. See also:
Bailey, Stuart

SPENCER QUINN. See: Reed,
Jerry

SPICER. See: O'Toole, Ensign

SPICER, WILLIE. See: Jones,
Spike (1)

Spider Man. See: Spider Man

SPIDER MAN, crime fighter;
cartoon character
Spider Man (TV) (Cartoon)

SPIFFY, COUNSELOR. See:

Wivenhoe, Commander

SPIKE. See: Jones, Spike (1) (2)

Spike Jones Show, The. See:
Jones, Spike (2)

SPIKE WILSON. See: Rutledge,
Dr. John

Spin to Win. See: Hull, Warren
(1)

Spirit of '41, The. See: Daly,
John (2)

SPITALNY, PHIL, conductor of
all-girl orchestra (himself)
EVELYN KAY (Evelyn and Her
Magic Violin)
KATHARINE SMITH, cornetist
VIOLA SCHMIDT, drummer
MAXINE, vocalist
JEANNIE, vocalist, featured
performers on the program
(themselves)
The Hour of Charm (R) (Music)

SPITALNY, PHIL. See also:
Whiteman, Paul

SPIVAK, LAWRENCE. See:
Rountree, Martha

SPLINTERS, JUDY. See:
Cantor, Eddie (2)
Dinsdale, Shirley

Split Personality. See: Poston,
Tom

Split Second. See: Kennedy, Tom
(2)

Splits Adventure Hour, Kellogg's
Presents the Banana. See:
Fleegle

Splits, The Banana. See: Fleegle

SPOCK, DR. BENJAMIN M.,
physician; authority on child
care
MANY GUEST PARENTS
Dr. Spock (TV) (Child care)

SPOCK, MR. See: Kirk, Captain
James

SPODE, BEBE. See: Karr, Mike

SPODE, MARTIN. See: Karr,
Mike

SPOOK. See: Top Cat

Sports, A.B.C.'s Wide World of
See: McKay, Jim (1)

Sports Newsreel, Bill Stern's Colgate. See: Stern, Bill

Sports Newsreel Starring Bill
Stern, The Colgate. See: Stern,
Bill

Sportsman's Club, T.V. See:
Wylber, Darl

SPORTSMEN QUARTET, THE.
See:
Benny, Jack
Canova, Judy
Peterson, Irma

SPOT. See: Munster, Herman

Spotlight Gang, Happy Felton's.
See: Felton, Happy

SPOTTY. See:
Baines, Scattergood
Scotty

SPRAGUE. See: Falvey, Hal

SPRAGUE, HOWARD. See: Jones,
Sam

SPRAGUE, MAGGIE. See: Brown,
Ellen

SPRAY. See: Flipper

SPRING. See: Brains

Spring Festival. See: Crosby,
John

Sprucehead Bay, The Simpson Boys
of. See: Simpson Boys, The

"SPUD." See: Barrett, Timothy
"Spud"

Squad, Hearthstone of the Death.
See: Lenrow, Bernard

Squad, Racket. See: Braddock,
Captain

Squad, The Felony. See: Stone,
Sam

Squad, The Mod. See: Hayes,
Linc

Squares, The Hollywood. See:
Marshall, Peter

Squeaking Door, The. See: Raymond

SQUEEKO MOUSE, EL. See:
Russell, Todd

Squibb, Music From the House of.
See: Ives, Burl (2)

SQUIRE SKIMP. See: Edwards,
Lum

SQUIRREL. See: Secret Squirrel

SQUIRREL, ROCKY. See: Bullwinkle

SR. Items so prefixed are indexed
as though spelled "Sister"

SS-11. See: Midnight, Captain

ST. Items so prefixed are indexed
as though spelled "Saint"

STAATS COTSWORTH. See:
Welles, Orson (2)

STABILE, DICK. See: Bernie,
Ben

Staccato. See: Staccato, Johnny

STACCATO, JOHNNY, jazz pianist
and private detective
Staccato (TV) (Detective)

STACEY, LEM. See: Wilbur,
Judy

STACY, JANE. See: Peterson,
Irma

STACY LATTIMER. See: Sterling,
Vanessa Dale

"STAFF" STAFFORD, H. M. See:
Ryan, Paul

STAFFORD. See also:
Strafford
Stratford

STAFFORD, H. M. "STAFF." See:
Ryan, Paul

STAFFORD, JO. See:
Como, Perry (1)
Crosby, Bob (2)

Stage Door Canteen. See: Lytell,
Bert (2)

Stage Show. See: Dorsey, Tommy

Stagecoach West. See: Perry,
Luke

STAGWELL, TOOTSIE. See:
Burns, George (1)

STALIN, JOSEF. See: Husing,
Ted

Stallion, Brave. See: Newton,
Jim

STAMP, CHIEF OLIVER. See:
Ramsey, Hector "Hec"

STAN. See:
Burton, Terry
Kenton, Stan
Shaw, Stan

STAN ADAMIK. See: James,
Nancy

STAN KENTON. See:
Basie, Count
Kenton, Stan
O'Connor, Father Norman
Whiteman, Paul

STAN PARKER. See: Willis,
David

STANBURY, DOUGLAS. See:
Roxy

Stand Up and Be Counted. See:
Russell, Bob

Stand Up and Cheer. See:

Mann, Johnny

Stand Up and Cheer: Johnny Mann.
See: Mann, Johnny

Stand, Youth Takes a. See:
Cochran, Ron

STANDER, LIONEL. See: Kaye,
Danny

STANDISH, LUCIA. See: Malone,
Dr. Jerry

STANDISH, PETER. See: Drake,
Betty

STANFIELD, MRS. See: Bell,
Harry

STANG, ARNOLD. See: Edwards,
Ralph (1)

Stanley. See: Stanley

STANLEY, newspaper and cigar
clerk in hotel lobby
CELIA, his girl friend
Stanley (TV) (Situation comedy)

STANLEY. See also:
Banks, Stanley
Beamish, Stanley
Burton, Terry
Gilman, Gordon
Susan (1)

STANLEY BARTLETT. See:
Meredith, Charles

STANLEY, EVE TOPPING. See:
Davis, Joan Field

STANLEY HOLTON, DR. See:
Manning, Portia Blake

STANLEY, MRS. See: Davis,
Joan Field

STANLEY, PAMELA. See: Hargrave-Scott, Joan

STANLEY, PHIL. See: Davis,
Joan Field

STANLEY SCHEIBER. See:
Stewart, Jan

STANLEY WESTLAND. See:
Grimm, Arnold

STANTON, PHOEBE. See: Low,
Theodore

STANWYCK, BARBARA, hostess
of the program (herself)
MANY GUEST ACTORS AND
ACTRESSES
The Barbara Stanwyck Show (TV)
(Drama)

STAR. See also:
Starr
Stars

Star Comedy, Five. See: Olsen,
Ole

Star Jones, Five. See: Jones,
Tom (1)

STAR JONES, FIVE. See: Jones,
Tom (1)

STAR, MORNING. See: Brave
Eagle

Star Playhouse, Four. See:
Boyer, Charles

Star Revue, The All. See: Raye,
Martha (1)

Star Theater, The Texaco. See:
Berle, Milton (3)

STAR TRAVIS. See: Barton, Joe

Star Trek. See: Kirk, Captain
James

STARK, MR. See: Lawes, Lewis
E.

STARK, SLIM. See: Dane, Prudence

STARR. See also:
Star
Stars

STARR, JOHNNY. See: Sloan,
Holly

STARR, KAY. See: Como,
Perry (1)

STARR, MILLICENT. See: Sloan,
Holly

STARR, NORMA. See: Graham,
Dr. Bob

STARR, RICKI. See: James,
Dennis (4)

STARRETT, DICK, American in-
surance claims adjuster in
London
JANE, his wife, British duchess
Dick and the Duchess (TV) (Situ-
ation comedy)

STARRETT, JOEY. See: Shane

STARRETT, MARIAN. See:
Shane

STARRETT, TOM. See: Shane

Starring Boris Karloff. See: Karloff, Boris (2)

STARS. See:
Star
Starr
Twin Stars, The

Stars, Festival of. See: Young,
Loretta (2)

Stars, Harvest of. See: Melton,
James (2)

Stars, Here Come the. See:
Jessel, George (2)

Stars, Hollywood and the. See:
Cotten, Joseph (1)

Stars of Tomorrow. See: Grimes,
Bill

Stars Show, The Twin. See: Twin
Stars, The

Stars, Shower of. See: Lundigan,
Bill (2)

Stars, Stump the. See:
Harrington, Pat, Jr.
Stokey, Mike

Stars, The Cavalcade of. See:

Gleason, Jackie (1)
Kramden, Ralph

State Trooper. See: Blake, Rod

Station, Grand Central. See:
Arthur, Jack (2)

STATLER BROTHERS, THE. See:
Cash, Johnny

STEAMBOAT WILLIE VANDEVEER.
See: Wade, Sandy

STEBBINS, MR. See: Wiggs, Mrs.

STEED, JOHN, secret agent
MRS. EMMA PEEL
TARA KING, his judo expert
assistants
MOTHER, character appearing in
the drama
The Avengers (TV) (Adventure)

Steel Hour, The United States.
See: Langner, Lawrence

STEEL, MAJOR. See: Midnight,
Captain

STEEL, RICHARD
WILLIAM F. X. GEOGHAN, JR.
CHARLES HAYDON
BENEDICT GINSBURG, attorneys
(themselves)
ACTORS AND ACTRESSES POR-
TRAYING CRIMINALS
The Witness (TV) (Crime drama)

STEEL, THE MAN OF. See:
Kent, Clark

STEELE, DICK, young newspaper
reporter
Dick Steele, Boy Reporter (R)
(Adventure)

STEELE, GENERAL. See: Mc-
Kay, Judson

STEELE SISTERS, THE. See:
Wincholl, John

STEELE, TED, master of cere-
monies of the program (himself)
KENNY GARDNER
BETTY RANDALL, vocalists
(themselves)
Easy Does It (R) (Music)

STEELE, TED. See also:
Como, Perry (1)
Murphy, Dean

STEELE, TRACY
TOM LOPAKA, detectives in
Hawaii
CRICKET BLAKE
KIM, their associates
PHILIP BARTON, hotel social
director
Hawaiian Eye (TV) (Crime
drama)

Steelmakers, The Musical. See:
Wincholl, John

STEINBERG, BERNIE. See: Fitzgerald, Bridget Theresa Mary
Coleen

STEINBERG, DAVID (1), star of
the program (himself)
MANY GUEST STARS
The David Steinberg Show (TV)
(Music/variety)

STEINBERG, DAVID (2)
PAT WILLIAMS
BOBBY SHERMAN
STEVE ALLEN
LOU RAWLS
OTHERS, hosts of the program
(themselves)
MANY GUEST MUSICIANS
The Music Scene (TV) (Contem-
porary music)

STEINBERG, SAM. See: Fitzgerald,
Bridget Theresa Mary Coleen

STEINBERG, SOPHIE. See: Fitzgerald, Bridget Theresa Mary
Coleen

STELLA. See: Dallas, Stella

STELLA AND THE FELLAS. See:
Waring, Fred (1)

STELLA CARLON CURTIS. See:
Perkins, Ma

Stella Dallas. See: Dallas, Stella

STELLA FIELD. See: Davis,
Joan Field

STELLA HATHAWAY. See: Prescott, Kate Hathaway

STELLA MOORE. See: Rogers,
Patricia

STELLA RUDNICK. See: Johnson, Bess

STEMBOTTOM, RUTHIE. See:
Gook, Vic

STEMPEL, AARON. See: Bolt,
Jason

STEMPEL, HERBERT M. See:
Barry, Jack (9)

Step, Giant. See: Parks, Bert
(3)

Step, Take a Giant. See: Marshall,
E. G.

STEPHANIE COLE. See: Hansen,
Dean Eric

STEPHANIE SUMMERS. See:
Grimm, Arnold

STEPHEN. See:
Carey, Dr. Philip
Dallas, Stella
Steven

STEPHEN HAMILTON. See:
Solomon, David

STEPHENS. See also: Stevens

STEPHENS, SAMANTHA, witch
DARRIN, her husband, advertising
man
TABITHA, their daughter, witch
ENDORA, Samantha's mother,
witch
SERENA, Samantha's look-alike
cousin, witch
MRS. STEPHENS, Darrin's
mother
ESMERALDA, the Stephens'
maid
UNCLE ARTHUR, Samantha's
uncle
AUNT CLARA, Samantha's aunt
GLADYS KRAVITZ, neighbor of
the Stephens
ABNER KRAVITZ, Gladys'

husband
Bewitched (TV) (Family situation comedy)

STEPHENSON. See also: Stevenson

STEPHENSON, HELEN GOWAN.
See: Brent, Dr. Jim

STEPHENSON, JOHN, narrator and host of the program (himself)
Bold Journey (TV) (Travel)

STEPHENSON, JUNIOR. See: Brent, Dr. Jim

STEPHENSON, TOM. See: Brent, Dr. Jim

Stepmother. See: Fairchild, Kay

Steptoe and Son. See: Sanford, Fred

STERLING. See also:
Serling
Stirling

STERLING, DICK, newscaster; host of the program (himself)
Panorama 15 (TV) (News)

STERLING, JACK
GENE CRANE, hosts and ringmasters of the program (themselves)
ED McMAHON, appearing as clown on the program (himself)
MANY CIRCUS ACTS
The Big Top (TV) (Circus)

STERLING, LOUIE. See: Grimm, Arnold

STERLING, VANESSA DALE
SARAH DALE
MEG DALE ANDREWS
DR. TARLIFF
STACY LATTIMER
BARBARA LATTIMER
LARRY
GERRY
JOSH VINDUC
BRUCE STERLING
KATE PHILLIPS
ALEX CALDWELL
RICKEY LATTIMER
DR. DAN PHILLIPS

RACHEL BEALE
DR. PECK
DR. JOE CORELLI
LORETTA ALLEN
DR. WESTHEIMER
TESS
SALLY ROLLINS
CYNTHIA AGAR
MRS. SWANSON
MR. WOLPER
JUDY
HELEN HUNT
TODD
JOHNNY
JACK ANDREWS
TOM CRAYTHORNE
NOEL PENN
TAMMY FOREST
CONNIE LOOMIS
ALAN STERLING
TONY VENTO
MRS. VENTO
DR. SALTZMAN
MAGGIE
KAY
LINC
LIEUT. HAMILTON, characters appearing in the drama
Love of Life (TV) (Serial drama)

STERN, BILL, sportscaster, narrator of the program (himself)
The Colgate Sports Newsreel Starring Bill Stern (R) (Sports) (also known as Bill Stern's Colgate Sports Newsreel) (R)

STEVE. See:
Allen, Steve (1) (2) (3)
Benton, Steve
Dekker, Steve
Donovan, Steve
Douglas, Steve
Drake, Bradley
Driggs, Karleton King
Dunne, Steve
Harper, Linda Emerson
King
Lawrence, Steve (1) (2)
Lindsey, Peter
McGarrett, Steve
Mitchell, Steve
Morgan, Mrs. Amy
Prescott, Kate Hathaway
Scott, Karen
Taylor, Corporal Steve
Virginian, The
Wilson, Steve

STEVE ADAMS. See: Straight
Arrow

STEVE ALDRICH, DR. See:
Davis, Dr. Althea

STEVE ALLEN. See:
Allen, Steve (1) (2) (3)
Berman, Shelley
Daly, John (3)
Moore, Garry (4)
Steinberg, David (2)

Steve Allen Show, The. See: Allen,
Steve (1)

STEVE BAKER. See: Harris, Bill

STEVE BANKS. See: Andrews,
Russ

STEVE BAXTER. See: Hazel

STEVE BLACKMAN. See:
Marshall, John

STEVE BOSCO. See: Ballew,
Wally

STEVE BRIGGS. See: Edman,
Karl

STEVE BRUCE. See: Baker,
Julia

STEVE BURTON, CAPTAIN. See:
Lockridge, Barry

Steve Canyon. See: Canyon,
Stevenson B.

STEVE CORTLAND. See: Johnson, Bess

STEVE DIRK. See: Brent, Portia

STEVE, DR. See: Arden, Jane

Steve Donovan. See: Donovan,
Steve

STEVE ELLIOTT. See: Carson,
Uncle Joe

STEVE GIBSON. See: Whiteman,
Paul

STEVE JACKSON, DR. See:

Bauer, Bertha

STEVE KELLER, DETECTIVE.
See: Stone, Detective Lieut.
Mike

STEVE KIRKLAND. See: Talbot,
Commander Dan

STEVE LANDESBERG. See:
Darin, Bobby

STEVE LANSING. See: Sunday

STEVE LAWRENCE. See:
Allen, Steve (3)
Crosby, Bing (2)
Lawrence, Steve (1) (2)

Steve Lawrence Show, The. See:
Lawrence, Steve (2)

STEVE MORLEY. See: Hol-
strum, Katy

STEVE SKIDMORE. See: Davis,
Joan Field

STEVE SMITH. See: Welk,
Lawrence

STEVE THOMPSON. See: Patrick,
Dion

STEVE WATSON. See: Berry,
Ken

STEVE WELLES. See: Jordan,
Joyce

STEVEN. See:
Hardy, Dr. Steven
Stephen

STEVEN BURKE. See: Walleck,
Meredith

STEVEN CORD. See: Peyton,
Martin

STEVEN FRAME. See: Randolph,
Alice

STEVEN FROHLICH. See: Story,
Ralph

STEVEN KILEY, DR. See:
Welby, Dr. Marcus

STEVEN MARKLEY. See: Dennis, Liz

STEVENS. See:
Brennan, Jack
Stephens

STEVENS, DIZZY. See: Aldrich, Henry

STEVENS, DR. See: Perkins, Ma

STEVENS, DR. RALPH. See: Bradley, Judith

STEVENS, EMMA "STEVIE." See: Hargrave-Scott, Joan

STEVENS, GEORGE. See: Jones, Amos

STEVENS, JOAN, wife
BRAD STEVENS, her husband, judge
PAT, Joan's younger sister
WALLY, their friend
SALLY, Wally's wife
I Married Joan (TV) (Situation comedy)

STEVENS, JULIE. See: Roberts, Ken

STEVENS, LARRY. See: Benny, Jack

STEVENS, RAY, singer and composer, star of the program (himself)
BILLY VAN
LULU
MAMMA CASS ELLIOT
DICK CURTIS
SOLARI AND CARR
CAROL ROBINSON, singers and entertainers appearing on the program (themselves)
MANY GUEST STARS
JIMMY DALE, orchestra leader (himself)
HIS ORCHESTRA
The Ray Stevens Show (TV) (Music/variety)

STEVENS, RISE. See: Cross, Milton (2)

STEVENS, SAPPHIRE. See: Jones, Amos

STEVENSON. See:
Canyon, Stevenson B.
Stephenson

STEVENSON, McLEAN. See: Conway, Tim

STEVENSON, MARTHA. See: Cameron, Barry

STEVENSON, WILL. See: Cameron, Barry

STEVIE NELSON. See: Hardy, Dr. Steven

"STEVIE" STEVENS, EMMA. See: Hargrave-Scott, Joan

STEWART. See also: Stuart

STEWART, BLANCHE. See: Benny, Jack

STEWART, DAVID. See: Hughes, Lisa

STEWART, DOROTHY. See: Drake, Nora

STEWART, GEORGE. See: Drake, Nora

STEWART, JAMES
ROBERT YOUNG, actors, featured on the program (themselves)
Hollywood Good News (R) (Variety)

STEWART, JAN, widowed nightclub entertainer
JOSIE, her ten-year-old daughter
PAT MURPHY
VAL MARLOWE, her friends
STANLEY SCHEIBER, delicatessen errand boy
It's Always Jan (TV) (Comedy)

STEWART, JAY (1), moderator of the program (himself)
MANY AUDIENCE PARTICIPANTS
Jay Stewart's Fun Fair (R) (Audience participation)

STEWART, JAY (2), moderator of
the program (himself)
MANY AUDIENCE PARTICIPANTS
Surprise Package (R) (Audience
participation)

STEWART, JIMMY, actor, featured
on the program (himself)
The Six-Shooter (R) (Western
adventure)

STEWART, NANCY. See: Rutledge,
Dr. John

STEWART, PAUL. See: Welles,
Orson (2)

STEWART, SANDY. See: Miller,
Mitch

STEWART STYLES. See: Dante,
Willy

STILES, TOD. See: Murdock, Buz

STIRLING. See also:
Serling
Sterling

STIRLING, CRAIG
SHARRON MACREADY
RICHARD BARRETT, secret
agents working for Nemesis,
British crime fighting agency
TREMAYNE, head of Nemesis
The Champions (TV) (Adventure)

STIVIC, GLORIA. See: Bunker,
Archie

STIVIC, MIKE. See: Bunker,
Archie

STOCKDALE, WILL, Southern boy,
inducted into the army
MILLY ANDERSON, his girl
friend
BEN WHITLEDGE, his friend,
fellow-inductee
SERGEANT KING, non-commis-
sioned officer
CAPTAIN MARTINSON, officer
No Time For Sergeants (TV)
(Comedy)

STOCKER, E. J. See: Burke,
Stoney

STOCKTON, SANDY (1), student
teacher and actress on TV com-
mercials
ALICE, her neighbor
KATE, her landlady
PAT, Kate's husband
Funny Face (TV) (Comedy)

STOCKTON, SANDY (2), secretary
at talent agent's office, television
actress and student at U. C. L. A.
BERT QUINN, talent agent; her
employer and agent
HILARY, co-worker at the agency
KAY FOX, Sandy's neighbor
BEN, handyman at Sandy's apart-
ment house
ALEX, motorcycle officer, Sandy's
friend
The Sandy Duncan Show (TV)
(Situation comedy)

STODDARD, CAROLYN. See:
Collins, Barnabas

STODDARD, ELIZABETH COLLINS.
See: Collins, Barnabas

STOKES, T. ELIOT. See: Collins,
Barnabas

STOKES, TINY. See: Kelly, Joe
(1)

STOKEY, MIKE, moderator of the
program (himself)
HOWARD MORRIS
CAROL BURNETT
STUBBY KAYE
DENICE DARCEL
DOROTHY HART
TOM POSTON
MILT KAMEN
GYPSY ROSE LEE
JUDY TYLER
OTHERS, contestants on the
program (themselves)
Pantomime Quiz Time (TV)
(Charades) (later known as
Stump the Stars) (TV)

STOLL, GEORGIE. See: Cantor,
Eddie (2)

STONE, DETECTIVE LIEUT. MIKE,
San Francisco police officer
DETECTIVE STEVE KELLER,
his partner

The Streets of San Francisco (TV)
(Crime drama)

STONE, DR. ALEX, small town
pediatrician
DONNA, his wife
MARY
JEFF, their children
The Donna Reed Show (TV)
(Family situation comedy)

STONE FOUR, THE KIRBY. See:
Rodgers, Jimmie

STONE, GERTRUDE. See: Horn,
Aggie

STONE, HARVEY. See: Lewis,
Robert Q. (1)

STONE, KATHY. See: Drake,
Betty

STONE, LUCKY, Chicago newspaper columnist
Night Beat (R) (Adventure)

STONE, PAULA. See: Landi,
Elissa

STONE, PETE. See: Wayne,
Ruth Evans

STONE, SAM, detective sergeant;
head of Felony Squad
DAN BRIGGS, police sergeant
JIM BRIGGS, Dan's son; police
detective
The Felony Squad (TV) (Detective)

STONER, LIEUT. COMMANDER
VIRGIL. See: O'Toole, Ensign

STONEWALL. See: Jones, Amos

STONEWALL SCOTT. See: Lorre,
Peter

STONEY. See: Burke, Stoney

Stoney Burke. See: Burke, Stoney

STOOGE. See: Penner, Joe

STOOGE LOWE. See: Harding,
Mrs. Rhoda

STOOLER, MABEL. See: Joe (2)

STOOLER, MRS. See: Joe (2)

STOOLER, SHOIMAN. See: Joe
(2)

Stoopnagle and Budd. See: Stoopnagle, Colonel Lemuel Q. (2)

STOOPNAGLE, COLONEL LEMUEL
Q. (1), comedian; host of the
program
SHEILA BARRETT (herself)
THE RODGERS SISTERS, fea-
tured entertainers on the pro-
gram (themselves)
NAT SHILKRET, orchestra
leader (himself)
HIS ORCHESTRA
MANY GUEST STARS
The Magic Key of R. C. A. (R)
(Variety)

STOOPNAGLE, COLONEL LEMUEL
Q. (2), comedian; host of the
program
WILBUR BUDD HULICK, fea-
tured on the program (himself)
Stoopnagle and Budd (R) (Comedy)

Stop and Go. See: Brown, Joe E.
(2)

Stop, Bus. See: Sherwood, Grace

Stop Me If You've Heard This One.
See: Bower, Roger

Stop the Music. See: Parks, Bert
(6)

STORCH, LARRY. See: Gleason,
Jackie (1)

STORDAHL, AXEL. See:
MacKenzie, Gisele
Ross, Lanny
Sinatra, Frank

Store, At the Village. See: Owner

Store, Caroline's Golden. See:
Caroline

Store Front Lawyers, The. See:
Hansen, David

Store, Sealtest Village. See:
Owner

Store, Village. See: Owner

STOREY. See also:
Stories
Story

STOREY, JINNY. See: Meredith,
Charles

STOREY, TIMOTHY. See: Meredith,
Charles

STORIES. See also:
Storey
Story

Stories by Olmstead. See: Olmstead, Nelson

Stories of the Black Chamber. See:
Drake, Bradley

Stories of the Century. See:
Davis, Jim

Stork Club, The. See: Hayes,
Peter Lind (4)

STORM. See also: Stromm

Storm, Against the. See: Cameron,
Christy Allen

STORM, BARBARA. See: Brown,
Ellen

STORM, CHRISTOPHER, American
owner of hotel in Vienna
Foreign Intrigue (TV) (Drama

STORM, DEBI. See: Winters,
Jonathan

STORM, LIEUT.
LIEUT. RHODES
COLONEL BEAMISH, Bengal
lancers
Tales of the 77th Bengal Lancers
(TV) (Adventure) (also known as
The Bengal Lancers) (TV)

Storm, The Secret. See: Ames,
Peter

STORMY BARRY. See: Kelly,
Joe (2)

STORMY WILSON CURTIS. See:

Rogers, Patricia

STORY. See also:
Storey
Stories

Story Book, Shirley Temple's.
See: Temple, Shirley

Story Ever Told, The Greatest.
See: Jesus

Story, Ghost. See: Essex, Winston

Story Hour With Mary and Bob,
The True. See: Mary

Story, Inside. See: Sullivan,
Fred

STORY LADY, THE, portrayed
by Colleen Moore
CAPTAIN JACK, portrayed by
Jess Kirkpatrick
Safety Legion Time (R) (Chil-
dren's program)

Story, My True. See: Riggs,
Glenn

Story of Bess Johnson, The. See:
Johnson, Bess

Story of Bud Barton, The. See:
Barton, Bud

Story of Holly Sloan, The. See:
Sloan, Holly

Story of Mary Marlin, The. See:
Marlin, Mary

Story of Ruby Valentine, The.
See: Valentine, Ruby

STORY, RALPH
SONNY FOX, quizmasters of the
program (themselves)
BAYARD MACMICHAEL
VINCENT PRICE
BILLY PEARSON
STEVEN FROHLICH
FLOYD YEOMANS
CAPTAIN EDWARD McCUTCHEON
TEDDY NADLER
THOMAS KANE
DR. JOYCE BROTHERS

PETER FREUCHEN
MICHAEL DELLA ROCCA
LENNY ROSS
REDMOND O'HANLON
GINO PRATO, contestants on the
program (themselves)
MANY OTHER CONTESTANTS
The $64,000 Challenge (TV)
(Quiz)

Story, The Big. See:
   Grauer, Ben (1)
   Sloane, Robert

Story Theater, True. See: Hull,
   Henry

Story to Order. See: Perera,
   Lydia

STOUT, BILL. See: McKay,
   Jim (2)

STOVALL, MAJOR HARVEY. See:
   Savage, Brigadier General Frank

STOWE, SENATOR HAYS, "a pro-
   gressive politician"
   MRS. STOWE, his wife
   NORMA, his daughter
   JORDAN BOYLE, his aide
   The Bold Ones (The Senator)
   (TV) (Drama)

STOWELL, ERIC. See: Trent,
   Helen

STRAFFORD. See also:
   Stafford
   Stratford

STRAFFORD, WYN. See: Foyle,
   Kitty

Straight Arrow. See: Straight
   Arrow

STRAIGHT ARROW, actually Steve
   Adams, Western rancher who
   assumed the role of Straight
   Arrow, Indian, when necessary
   COMANCHE, his horse
   Straight Arrow (R) (Western ad-
   venture)

STRAIGHT, CLARENCE, animal
   imitator (himself)
   Animal News Club (R) (Children's
   program)

STRAIGHT SHOOTER, THE RAL-
   STON. See: Mix, Tom

Straight Shooters, Tom Mix and
   His Ralston. See: Mix, Tom

Straightaway. See: Ross, Scott

STRANGE, ADAM, English master
   scientific criminologist
   HAMLYN "HAM" GYNT, American assistant to Strange
   EVELYN, American artist and
   assistant to Gynt
   Strange Report (TV) (Crime
   drama)

Strange As It Seems. See: Whitman, Gayne

Strange Dr. Karnac, The. See:
   Karnac, Dr.

Strange Dr. Weird, The. See:
   Weird, Dr.

Strange Paradise. See: Carr,
   Alison

Strange Report. See: Strange,
   Adam

Strange Romance of Evelyn Winters,
   The. See: Winters, Evelyn

STRANGER. See: Welles, Orson
   (3)

Stranger, The. See: Stranger,
   The

STRANGER, THE, nameless adventurer
   The Stranger (TV) (Drama)

STRANGER, THE. See also:
   Vernay, Pierre

Stranger, The Song of a. See:
   Vernay, Pierre

STRATFORD. See also:
   Stafford
   Strafford

STRATFORD, DADDY. See:
   Sothern, Mary

STRATFORD, DANNY. See:
    Sothern, Mary

STRATFORD, PHYLLIS. See:
    Sothern, Mary

Streamliner's Show. See: Fields,
    Arthur

Street Beat, Bourbon. See:
    Randolph, Rex

STREET, DAVE. See:
    Lester, Jerry
    Owner
    Parkyakarkas, Nick

STREET, DELLA. See: Mason,
    Perry

STREET, MAN ON THE, NORMAN
    NEAT. See: Cosby, Bill (1)

Street, Sesame. See: Cookie
    Monster, The

Street Singer, The. See: Tracy,
    Arthur

Street, The Chamber Music Society
    of Lower Basin. See: Cross,
    Milton (1)

Street, The House on High. See:
    Abbott, Philip

Street, Window on Main. See:
    Brooks, Cameron

Streets of San Francisco, The.
    See: Stone, Detective Lieut. Mike

Streets, Whispering. See: Winslow,
    Hope

STRICKLAND, GOLDIE, former
    manicurist and showgirl; guardian
    of her late husband's children
    by a previous marriage
    PAT STRICKLAND
    NICKY STRICKLAND
    ROY STRICKLAND, her wards
    The Betty Hutton Show (TV)
    (Situation comedy)

Strike It Rich. See: Hull, War-
    ren (2)

STRING QUARTET, THE FLON-
    ZALEY. See: Drew, John

STRINGBEAN. See: Owens, Buck

STRINGBEAN CRACHET. See:
    Walt, Captain

STRINGBEAN KITTINGER. See:
    Aldrich, Henry

Strip, Cimarron. See: Crown,
    Jim

Strip, 77 Sunset. See: Bailey,
    Stuart

STROMM. See also: Storm

STROMM, ROBERT. See:
    Fadiman, Clifton (2)
    March, Hal

STRONG, BOB. See:
    Skelton, Red
    Uncle Walter

STRONG, PAUL. See: Morrison,
    Mother

STRUNK, JUD. See: Rowan, Dan

STRUTHERS, SALLY. See:
    Conway, Tim
    Smothers, Tom (3)

STU. See:
    Erwin, Stu
    Wilson, Stu

STU BERGMAN. See: Tate,
    Joanne

STUART. See:
    Bailey, Stuart
    Ferguson, Martha
    McMillan, Stuart
    Stewart

STUART, BETSY. See: Hughes,
    Chris

STUART CHURCHILL. See:
    Waring, Fred (1)

STUART-CLARK, DICK. See:
    Upton, Michael

STUART, COREY. See: Lassie

STUART, DAN. See: Hughes,
Chris

STUART, DR. DAVID. See:
Hughes, Chris

STUART, DR. TED. See: Hunter,
Dr. Paul

STUART, ELIZABETH. See:
Hughes, Chris

STUART, ELLEN. See: Hughes,
Chris

STUART, EMILY. See: Hughes,
Chris

STUART FOSTER. See: Drake,
Galen

STUART, JULIA. See: Hughes,
Chris

STUART, PAUL. See: Hughes,
Chris

STUART, SUSAN. See: Hughes,
Chris

STUBBY AND THE BUCCANEERS,
CAPTAIN. See: Kelly, Joe (1)

STUBBY KAYE. See: Stokey, Mike

STUBBY WILSON. See: Harris,
Bill

Studebaker Champions. See: Himber, Richard

STUDS TERKEL. See: Efron,
Marshall

STULIR, JERRY. See: Rogers,
Patricia

STULIR, LOUISE. See: Rogers,
Patricia

Stump the Stars. See:
Harrington, Pat, Jr.
Stokey, Mike

STYLES, STEWART. See: Dante,
Willy

STYNER, DR. KONRAD, physician
MANY ACTORS AND ACTRESSES
Medic (TV) (Medical drama)

SUBLETTE, LINDA. See: Byner,
John (1)

Submariner. See: Submariner

SUBMARINER, crime fighter; cartoon character
Submariner (TV) (Cartoon)

SUE. See:
Carter, Chick
Falvey, Hal

SUE, BARBARA. See: Trent,
Helen

SUE BRIDEHEAD. See: Cooke,
Alistaire (1)

SUE EVANS MILLER. See:
Wayne, Ruth Evans

SUE LLOYD. See: Mannering,
John

SUES, ALAN. See: Rowan, Dan

Sugarfoot. See: Brewster, Tom

SUGARFOOT. See: Brewster, Tom

Suitcase, Man in a. See: McGill

SULLAVAN, JERI. See: Bolger,
Ray

SULLIVAN, ANNETTE ROGERS.
See: Perry, John

SULLIVAN, DEBORAH. See:
Hansen, David

SULLIVAN, ED, newspaper
columnist and host of the pro-
gram (himself)
MANY GUEST PERFORMERS
The Ed Sullivan Show (R) (TV)
(also known as The Toast of the
Town) (TV)
JULIA MEADE, co-hostess of
the program (herself)
The Ed Sullivan Show (TV)

SULLIVAN, FRED, master of

ceremonies of the program (him-
self)
MANY ACTORS AND ACTRESSES
ROY SHIELD, orchestra leader
HIS ORCHESTRA
Inside Story (R) (Dramatization
of "news behind the headlines")

SULLIVAN, JOE. See: Ames,
Peter

SULLIVAN LODGE. See: Arm-
strong, Jack

SULLIVAN, MARIAN. See: Burton,
Terry

SULLIVAN, MRS. See: Jackson,
Martha

SULLY. See also:
Solly
Soule

SULLY MASON. See: Kyser, Kay

SULTANA, THE. See: Tempest,
Dan

SULU, MR. See: Kirk, Captain
James

Summer Hour, The Ford. See:
Melton, James (1)

Summer Show, The Smothers
Brothers. See: Smothers, Tom
(3)

Summer, The Long Hot. See:
Varner, Will

SUMMERFALL WINTERSPRING,
PRINCESS. See: Doody, Howdy

SUMMERFIELD, JUDGE. See:
Barton, Bud

SUMMERS. See also:
Somers
Sommers

SUMMERS, STEPHANIE. See:
Grimm, Arnold

SUN. See also:
Son
Sons

Sun, Follow the. See: Gregory,
Ben

Sun, Islands in the. See: Burrud,
Bill (2)

Sunbrite Smile Parade, The. See:
Sherman, Ransom (2)

SUNDANCE, Western character
Hotel de Paree (TV) (Western)

SUNDAY, American orphan girl,
marries Lord Henry Brinthrope
LORD HENRY BRINTHROPE, her
husband, wealthy English noble-
man
MRS. SEDGEWICK
ROSE HUNT
FRED DAVIS
BARBARA HAMILTON
FRED CASTLESON
LAWRENCE SHIEFFIELD
ST. JOHN HARRIS
LEONA KENMORE
BILL JENKINS
OLIVER DREXTON
LORD PERCY
PEARL TAGGART
SLIM DELANEY
PETER GALWAY
IRENE GALWAY
VIVIAN GRAHAM
GANN MURRAY
CHARLOTTE ABBOTT
PRUDENCE GRAHAM
LILE FLORENZE
STEVE LANSING
AUNT ALICE
HILDA MARSHALL
VICTOR MAIDSTONE
COUNTESS FLORENZE
MADELYN TRAVERS
SUSAN ROBINSON
ANNA
KATHY
JACKIE
LIVELY
DWIGHT
LONNIE
JACK
LANETTE
LIEUT. NEVILS
ELAINE, characters in the drama
Our Gal Sunday (R) (Serial
drama)

Sunday, Chicken Every. See:

Burke, Billie (2)

Sunday Serenade. See: Kaye,
   Sammy (3)

SUNDERLAND. See: Churchill,
   John

SUNDOWN, BETTY ANN. See:
   Cade, Sam

Sunset Strip, 77. See: Bailey,
   Stuart

Super Circus. See: Kirchener,
   Claude (2)

Super President. See: Super
   President

SUPER PRESIDENT, crime fighter;
   cartoon character
   Super President (TV) (Cartoon)

Super, The. See: Girelli, Joe

Superman. See: Kent, Clark

SUPERMAN. See:
   Kent, Clark
   Nye, Louis

Superman, The Adventures of.
   See: Kent, Clark

Superstition. See: Voice of Superstition, The

SUPERSTITION. See: Voice of
   Superstition, The

Supper Club, The Chesterfield.
   See: Como, Perry (1)

Surfside Six. See: Madison, Kenny

Surgeon, Police. See: Locke, Dr.
   Simon (2)

Surprise Package. See: Stewart,
   Jay (2)

Surprise Party. See: Wilson, Stu

Surprise, The Big. See: Barry,
   Jack (1)

Survivors, The. See: Carlyle,
   Baylor

SUSABELLE. See: Penner, Joe

SUSAN (1)
   GEORGE
   WASHINGTON
   GINNY
   BOB LEE
   STANLEY, group of young people
   who crash land on remote Pacific
   island; "must start creating a
   new civilization from scratch"
   The New People (TV) (Social
   discussion/drama)

SUSAN (2), young girl
   RUSTY, her dog
   CAESAR P. PENGUIN, stuffed
   animal
   PEGASUS, talking table
   MANY CARTOONS
   Susan's Show (TV) (Children's
   program)

SUSAN. See also:
   Anthony
   Bradley, Judith
   Chandler, Dr. Susan
   Cookie Monster, The
   Garrett, Susan
   North, Jerry
   Susanna
   Susannah
   Suzanne
   Williams, Danny

SUSAN BENEDICT. See: Jackson,
   Martha

SUSAN CARVER. See: Ames,
   Peter

SUSAN GRANT. See: Graham,
   Dr. Bob

SUSAN, JACQUELINE. See:
   Kidder, Margot

SUSAN LEIGHTON. See: Dyke,
   Charity Amanda

SUSAN LUND. See: Chidsey,
   Jackie

SUSAN MARTIN. See: Horton,
   Dr. Tom

SUSAN NELSON. See: Noble,
   Mary

SUSAN PETERS. See: Manning,
Portia Blake

SUSAN PRESCOTT. See: King

SUSAN PRICE WELLS. See:
Harum, David

SUSAN RAYE. See: Owens, Buck

SUSAN ROBINSON. See: Sunday

SUSAN STUART. See: Hughes,
Chris

SUSAN TOLSKY. See: Cosby, Bill
(2)

SUSAN WAKEFIELD. See: Nelson,
Carolyn Kramer

SUSAN WINTER. See: Peyton,
Martin

SUSANNA. See:
Pomeroy, Susanna
Susan
Susannah
Suzanne

Susanna, Oh! See: Pomeroy,
Susanna

SUSANNAH. See also:
Susan
Susanna
Suzanne

SUSANNAH KRAMER. See: Webster, Jerry

SUSANNAH LLOYD. See: Driggs,
Karleton King

Susan's Show. See: Susan (2)

SUSIE. See:
McNamara, Susie
Susy
Suzie

SUSIE PARKER. See: Perkins,
Ma

Suspense. See: Frees, Paul

Suspicion. See: Abel, Walter

SUSSKIND, DAVID, host of the pro-
gram (himself)
MANY GUESTS
The David Susskind Show (TV)
(Panel discussion) (also called
Open End) (TV)

SUSY. See:
Smith, Angel
Susie
Suzie

SUSY, BABY. See: Ethel

SUTHERLAND, WEBB. See:
Davis, Dr. Althea

SUTTER, BILL. See: Guest,
Edgar A. (2)

SUTTER, GRANDPA. See: Brent,
Dr. Jim

SUTTON, DAVID. See: Virginian,
The

SUTTON, FRANK. See: Nabors,
Jim

SUTTON, HORACE. See: Malone,
Dr. Jerry

SUZANNE. See:
Bailey, Stuart
Susan
Susanna
Susannah

SUZANNE SOMMERS. See:
Kidder, Margot

SUZANNE TURRIE. See: Drake,
Nora

SUZIE. See:
Buell, Roger
Conrad, Jim
Susie
Susy

SVEN. See:
Swen
Von Hallberg, Gene

SWAIN, UNCLE MATT. See:
Peyton, Martin

SWANSON, BETTY. See: Kelly,
Joe (2)

SWANSON, MILLIE. See: Jones,
Sam

SWANSON, MRS. See: Sterling,
Vanessa Dale

SWANSON, SHIRLEY. See: Collins, Bob

SWARTHOUT, GLADYS. See:
Taylor, Deems

SWAYZE, JOHN CAMERON, host of
the program (himself)
THREE MALE INTERVIEWEES
THREE FEMALE INTERVIEWEES
Chance for Romance (TV) (Intro-
ductions/interviews)

SWEDISH ANGEL, THE. See:
James, Dennis (4)

Sweeney and March. See: Sweeney,
Bob

SWEENEY, BOB
HAL MARCH, comedians, fea-
tured on the program (themselves)
PATSY BOLTON, vocalist, fea-
tured on the program (herself)
IRVING MILLER, orchestra leader
(himself)
HIS ORCHESTRA
Sweeney and March (R) (Comedy)

SWEENEY, CICERO P., widowed
proprietor of general store
The World of Mr. Sweeney (TV)
(Serial drama)

SWEET ADELINE. See: Uncle
Walter

SWEETEN, OWEN. See: Holloway, Harrison

SWEN. See:
Packard, Jack
Sven

SWENK, DR. ANN. See: Newman, Tony

Swing Club, The Saturday Night.
See: Douglas, Paul

SWINGER, FREDDIE THE. See:
Wilson, Flip

SWINNEY, ZEKE. See: Harum,
David

SYBELLA MAYFIELD. See:
Harding, Karen Adams

SYBIL. See: Nipper

SYBIL FINCH. See: Walker,
Eddie

SYBIL TRENT. See: Halop, Billy

SYBIL VAN LOWEEN. See:
Gregory, Glenn Garth

SYDNEY. See also: Sidney

SYDNEY SHERWOOD McKENZIE.
See: Bennett, Nita

SYKES, HAROLD. See: Hanks,
Henrietta

SYLVESTER. See: Bell, Harry

SYLVESTER THE CAT. See:
Bunny, Bugs

SYLVIA. See:
Chase, Sylvia
Dane, Prudence
Marlowe, Sylvia

SYLVIA ALLISON. See: Goldberg,
Molly

SYLVIA BARDINE. See: Davidson, Bill

SYLVIA BARTRAM. See: Brent,
Dr. Jim

SYLVIA CALDWELL. See:
Bracken, John

SYLVIA FIELD. See: Davis,
Joan Field

SYLVIA HALL. See: Trent,
Helen

SYLVIA KING. See: Noble, Mary

SYLVIA MEADOWS. See: Dyke,
Charity Amanda

SYLVIA POWERS. See:

Davidson, Bill

Symphonette, The Longines. See:
Knight, Frank

Syncopated History, Burbig's. See:
Burbig, Henry

T. ELIOT STOKES. See: Collins,
Barnabas

T. H. E. Cat. See: Cat, Thomas
Hewitt Edward

T. J. See: Sawyer, Andy

T. J. THISTLE. See: Corbett,
Tom (2)

T-Man. See: Treasury Agent

T. V., GRANNY. See: Pam

T. V. Reader's Digest. See:
Reilly, Hugh

T. V. Sportsman's Club. See:
Wylber, Darl

T. W. 3. See: Ames, Nancy

Tab Hunter Show, The. See:
Morgan, Paul

TABAK, DAVE. See: Alexander,
Nick

TABITHA. See: Stephens,
Samantha

TAD. See also: Ted

TAD SMITH. See: Myrt

TAFFY. See: Tempest, Dan

TAFFY GRAHAME. See: Peters,
Bill

TAG. See: Lincoln, Dr. Matt

TAGG. See: Oakley, Annie

TAGGART, GEORGE. See:
Houston, Temple

TAGGART, PEARL. See:
Sunday

TAIT. See: Tate

Take a Card. See: Butterworth,
Wally

Take a Giant Step. See: Marshall,
E. G.

Take a Number. See: Benson,
Red

Take All, Winner. See: Cullen,
Bill (5)

Take, Give and. See: King,
John Reed (2)

Take It or Leave It. See: Baker,
Phil (3)

Takes a Thief, It. See: Mundy,
Alexander

TAKICHI, KENJI. See: Cavanaugh,
Father Samuel Patrick

TAL GARRETT. See: Redigo,
Jim (1) (2)

TALBOT, COMMANDER DAN, cap-
tain of destroyer escort DD181
CAPTAIN BEN FOSTER, captain
of freighter flagship
STEVE KIRKLAND, chief officer
Convoy (TV) (World War II drama)

TALBOT, DAVE. See: Harding,
Karen Adams

TALBOT, SANDRA. See: Dennis,
Liz

TALE. See also: Tales

Tale of Today, A. See: Allen,
Joan Houston

Tale, The Witch's. See: Cole,
Alonzo Dean

TALEB. See: Gallant, Captain

Talent, Lawrence Welk's Top Tunes
and New. See: Welk, Lawrence

Talent Scouts, Arthur Godfrey's.
See: Godfrey, Arthur (2)

Talent Scouts, Celebrity. See:
Levenson, Sam

Talent, The World of. See:
Clark, Dick (3)

TALENT, ZIGGY. See: Monroe,
Vaughn

TALES. See also: Tale

Tales of Fatima. See: Rathbone,
Basil

Tales of the 77th Bengal Lancers.
See: Storm, Lieut.

Tales of the Vikings. See: Leif

Tales of Wells Fargo. See: Hardie,
Jim

Talk, Girl. See: Graham,
Virginia (1)

Talk, Kid. See: Adler, Bill

TALK, TOWN. See: Harum,
David

Talking, Everybody's. See:
Thaxton, Lloyd (1)

Talking, Keep. See: Reiner,
Carl

Talking With a Giant. See:
Marshall, E. G.

TALL MAN. See also: Tallman

Tall Man, The. See: Billy the
Kid

Tallahassee 7000. See: Rogers,
Lex

TALLMAN. See also: Tall Man

TALLMAN, MARSHAL. See:
McLean, Adam

TALLULAH. See: Bankhead,
Tallulah

Tammy. See: Tammy

TAMMY, backwoods girl, becomes
secretary
JOHN BRENT, her employer,
plantation owner
GRANDPA TARLTON
UNCLE LUCIUS
DWAYNE WITT
LAVINIA TATE, friends and
neighbors
Tammy (TV) (Drama)

TAMMY. See also:
Pammy
Sammy
Tommy
Ward, Tammy

TAMMY FOREST. See: Sterling,
Vanessa Dale

Tammy Grimes Show, The. See:
Ward, Tammy

TANEY, LUCAS. See: Varner,
Will

TANIA. See also: Tanya

TANIA SOLNICK. See: Marshall,
E. G.

TANK TINKER. See: Harrigan,
Hop

TANNER, DR. See: Parker,
Seth

TANNER, MAL. See: Bennett,
Nita

TANYA. See:
Marlin, Mary
Tania

TANYA FALAN WELK. See:
Welk, Lawrence

TAO SMITH. See: Bennett, Nita

TAPP, GORDIE. See: Owens,
Buck

TARA KING. See: Steed, John

TARA LEIGH. See: Chidsey,
Jackie

TARE, CHARLES DELAWARE.
See: Collins, Barnabas

Target. See: Menjou, Adolphe

TARLIFF, DR. See: Sterling,
Vanessa Dale

TARLTON. See also:
Carleton
Carlton
Karleton

TARLTON, GRANDPA. See:
Tammy

TARPLIN, MAURICE. See: Weird,
Dr.

TARRANT, DAVE. See: Calhoun,
Ben

TARSES, PATCHETT AND. See:
Hirt, Al (2)

TARSHISH, JACOB, host of the
program (himself)
The Lamplighter (R) (Talk)

TARZAN, son of Lord Greystoke,
English nobleman; raised by
apes in Africa
JANE PORTER, his girl friend
Tarzan (R) (TV) (Jungle adven-
ture)
JAI, young native boy, his friend
CHEETAH, his chimpanzee
Tarzan (TV)

TARZAN. See also: Sheena

Tate. See: Tate

TATE, "one-armed, Bible-quoting
gunfighter"
Tate (TV) (Western)

TATE, JOANNE
PATTI WHITING
SAM REYNOLDS
LEN REYNOLDS
EUNICE MARTIN
CHRISTOPHER WHITING
SCOTT PHILIPS
KATHY PARKER
LAURIE PHILIPS
ERIC PHILIPS
MARGE BERGMAN
KEITH BERGMAN
STU BERGMAN
ELLIE HARPER
DAN BERGMAN
DR. TONY VINCENTE
DR. BOB ROGERS
ANDREA WHITING
DOUG MARTIN
JIM McKINNON
MRS. WESTON
DR. WADE COLLINS
MRS. MILLER
JANET WALTON

GARY WALTON
ARTHUR TATE
EUNICE WEBSTER
REX TWINING
CORNELIA SIMMONS
DUNCAN ERIC TATE
BUD GARDNER, characters ap-
pearing in the drama
Search for Tomorrow (TV)
(Serial drama)

TATE, LAVINIA. See: Tammy

TATE, ROY. See: MacKenzie,
Colonel Alan

Tavern, Cimarron. See: Barton,
Joe

Tavern, Duffy's. See: Archie

TAYLOR. See:
Baylor
Noble, Mary

TAYLOR, ANDY, sheriff of May-
berry, portrayed by Andy
Griffith
BARNEY FIFE, deputy
GOMER PYLE
WILBUR FINCH
AUNT BEE
THELMA LOU
PEGGY
OPIE
DON
ELLIE
NORA
HARRIET
WARREN
LEE
LORI
FLOYD
MR. FOLEY, characters appear-
ing on the program
The Andy Griffith Show (TV)
(Situation comedy) (episodes
later re-released under the title
Andy of Mayberry) (TV)

TAYLOR, BILL. See:
Carter, Kathryn
Marlin, Mary

TAYLOR, CHRISTINE. See:
Malone, Dr. Jerry

TAYLOR, CORPORAL STEVE, state

trooper
HIS FELLOW TROOPER
Highway Patrol (R) (Adventure)

TAYLOR DANCERS, THE JUNE.
See:
DeLuise, Dom (1)
Dorsey, Tommy
Ford, Tennessee Ernie (2)
Gleason, Jackie (2)

TAYLOR, DANNY, New York news-
paperman
LOU SHELDON, city editor;
Taylor's mentor
ARTIE BURNS, cab driver,
Taylor's friend
IKE DAWSON, bartender
The Reporter (TV) (Newspaper
drama)

TAYLOR, DEEMS, host and com-
mentator of the program (himself)
ROSS GRAHAM
JACK SMITH
GLADYS SWARTHOUT, featured
singers (themselves)
AL GOODMAN, orchestra leader
(himself)
HIS ORCHESTRA
The Prudential Family Hour (R)
(Music)

TAYLOR, DIANA. See: Hardy,
Dr. Steven

TAYLOR, DR. MARION SAYLE.
See: Voice of Experience, The

TAYLOR, DR. PETER. See:
Hardy, Dr. Steven

TAYLOR, JIM, F.B.I. agent
This Is Your F.B.I. (R) (Drama)

TAYLOR, JOE. See: Garrison,
Spencer

TAYLOR, MARION YOUNG. See:
Deane, Martha

TAYLOR, MRS. See: Garrison,
Spencer

TAYLOR, RIP. See: Darin, Bobby

TAYLOR, RUBY. See: Jones,
Amos

TAYLOR, TOMMY. See:
Dawson, Rosemary
Perkins, Ma

TAYLOR, TRACY. See: Hardy,
Dr. Steven

TEACHER. See also: Treacher

TEACHER, ENGLISH. See:
Brewster, Joey

TEACHER, VIOLIN. See: Benny,
Jack

TEAGARDEN, JACK. See:
Crosby, Bing (3)

TEAL, INSPECTOR CLAUDE
EUSTACE. See: Templar,
Simon

TEARLE, RIDGEWAY. See:
Perry, John

TEBALDI, RENATA. See: Barlow, Howard

TED. See:
Booth, Martha
Hopkins, Peggy
Husing, Ted
Mack, Ted
McKeever, Ted
Malone, Ted (1) (2)
Steele, Ted
Tad
Terry
West, Michael

TED BAXTER. See: Richards,
Mary

TED BLADES. See: Winters,
Evelyn

TED BLAKE. See: Dennis, Liz

TED CLARK. See: Randolph,
Alice

TED CLAYTON. See: Randolph,
Ellen

TED COLLINS. See: Smith, Kate
(1) (2)

TED DAVIS. See: Randolph, Alice

TED DE CORSIA. See:
Reed, Alan
Welles, Orson (2)

TED FIORITO. See:
Powell, Dick
Medbury, John P.

TED HART. See: Young, Larry
"Pepper"

TED HOFFMAN, DR. See: Casey,
Dr. Ben

TED JEWETT. See: Welles,
Orson (2)

TED MACK. See:
Bowes, Major Edward (1) (2)
Mack, Ted

Ted Mack Family Hour, The. See:
Bowes, Major Edward (1)

Ted Mack's Amateur Hour. See:
Mack, Ted

TED MAXWELL. See: Winkler,
Betty

TED STEELE. See:
Como, Perry (1)
Murphy, Dean
Steele, Ted

TED STUART, DR. See: Hunter,
Dr. Paul

Ted, Terry and. See: Terry

TED WAKEFIELD. See: Nelson,
Carolyn Kramer

TED WEEMS. See:
Benny, Jack
Hildegarde (1)
Whiteman, Paul

TED WHITE. See: Rutledge, Dr.
John

TEDDY. See:
Howard, Jim
Wilburn, Doyle

TEDDY BARBOUR GIDDINGS. See:
Barbour, Henry Wilson

Teddy Bears, The Chicago. See:
McCray, Linc

TEDDY BERGMAN. See: Ryan,
Tim

TEDDY HUNT. See: Waring,
Evelyn

TEDDY NADLER. See:
March, Hal
Story, Ralph

TEDDY NORMAN. See: Lopez,
Vincent

TEEN-AGERS, THE. See: Kelly,
Gene

TEEN, HAROLD, young high school
boy
HAROLD'S FATHER
JOSIE, his younger sister
LILLUMS, his girl friend
SHADOW
CYNTHIA, his friends
POP JENKS, proprietor of local
soda fountain
BEEZIE JENKS, Pop Jenks' son
Harold Teen (R) (Situation
comedy)

TEENIE. See:
Guest, Edgar A. (2)
Teeny
Tina
Tinney
Tiny

TEENY. See:
McGee, Fibber
Teenie
Tina
Tinney
Tiny

TEICHER, FERRANTE AND.
See: Fiedler, Arthur

Telephone Hour, The. See: Bell,
Alexander Graham

TELEPHONE OPERATOR. See:
Husband
Powell, Dick (3)

Telephone Time. See: Nesbit,
John (2)

Tell It to Groucho. See: Marx,
  Groucho (2)

Tell the Truth, To. See: Moore,
  Garry (5)

TELL, WILLIAM, Swiss national
  hero and archer
  HEDDA TELL, his wife
  William Tell (TV) (Adventure)

TEMBER ADAMS. See: Trent,
  Helen

Temperatures Rising. See: Campanelli, Dr. Vincent

TEMPEST, DAN, 18th century
  former pirate; captain of the
  "Sultana"
  ANNE BONNY, female pirate
  LIEUT. BEAMISH, officer;
  governor of New Providence
  GAFF
  TAFFY
  DICKON, members of Tempest's
  crew
  The Buccaneers (TV) (Adventure)

TEMPLAR, SIMON (The Saint),
  gentleman thief and adventurer
  INSPECTOR CLAUDE EUSTACE
    TEAL, British detective
  The Saint (R) (TV) (Crime ad-
  venture
  PATRICIA HOLMES
  LOUIE
  HAPPY, characters appearing in
  the drama
  The Saint (R)

TEMPLE. See: Houston, Temple

TEMPLE, HERBERT. See: Brown,
  Ellen

Temple Houston. See: Houston,
  Temple

TEMPLE, LANE. See: Rockford,
  Matthew

TEMPLE, NORINE. See: Brown,
  Ellen

TEMPLE, SHIRLEY, actress and
  former child star; hostess of the
  program (herself)

MANY GUEST ACTORS AND
  ACTRESSES
  The Shirley Temple Show (TV)
  (Drama) (also known as Shirley
  Temple's Story Book) (TV)

TEMPLETON, ALEC, pianist, singer
  and entertainer; host of the program (himself)
  Alec Templeton Time (R) (Music)

TEMPLETON, ANNIE MARIE. See:
  Harding, Karen Adams

TEMPLETON, CORINNE. See:
  Kelly, Joe (2)

TEMPLETON FOX. See: Winkler,
  Betty

Ten-4. See: Matthews, Dan

TENA, wife
  TIM, her husband
  MRS. HUTCHINSON, character
  appearing on the program
  Tena and Tim (R) (Comedy)

Tena and Tim. See: Tena

TENNESSEE ERNIE. See: Ford,
  Tennessee Ernie (1) (2) (3) (4)

Tennessee Ernie Show, The. See:
  Ford, Tennessee Ernie (4)

Tennessee Jed. See: Tennessee
  Jed

TENNESSEE JED, Westerner
  MASTERS, gambler
  INDIAN CHIEF
  SHERIFF JACKSON
  THE DEPUTY, characters
  appearing on the program
  Tennessee Jed (R) (Western ad-
  venture)

TENNESSEE THREE, THE. See:
  Cash, Johnny

Tent Show, Uncle Charlie's. See:
  Uncle Charlie

TERENCE. See: Ward, Tammy

TERESA. See also:
  Theresa
  Therese

TERESA GRAVES. See:
Kelly, Gene
Rowan, Dan

TERI. See also: Terry

TERI GARR. See: Barry, Ken

TERKEL, STUDS. See: Efron,
Marshall

"TERMITE" DANIELS. See:
Edwards, Ralph (1)
Loveridge, Marion

Terrific, Mr. See: Beamish,
Stanley

TERRIFIC, MR. See: Beamish,
Stanley

Territory, Tombstone. See:
Hollister, Clay

TERRY
TED
CHICO, characters appearing in
the drama
Terry and Ted (R) (Children's
adventure)

TERRY. See also:
Barkley, Arnie
Bowen, Terry
Burton, Terry
Harry
Lee, Terry
Regan, Terry
Teri
Williams, Danny

Terry and Ted. See: Terry

Terry and the Pirates. See: Lee,
Terry

TERRY BURKE. See:
Nelson, Carolyn Kramer
Packard, Jack

TERRY, DAVID. See: Kaye,
Danny

TERRY, MARY ELLEN. See:
ZaBach, Florian

TERRY MORAN. See: Carter,
Kathryn

Terry Regan: Attorney at Law.
See: Regan, Terry

TERRY-THOMAS. See: Berman,
Shelley

TERRY WEBSTER. See: Ryker,
Lieut. Eddie

TERRY WILLIAMS. See: Rogers,
Kenny

TERWILLIGER, TESS. See:
Harum, David

TESS. See: Sterling, Vanessa
Dale

TESS MORGAN. See: Noble,
Mary

TESS TERWILLIGER. See:
Harum, David

TESS TRUEHEART. See: Tracy,
Dick

TESSIE MONROE. See: Rogers,
Patricia

TESSIE O'SHEA. See: DeLuise,
Dom (2)

TETLEY, WALTER. See:
Cross, Milton (2)
Halop, Billy
Lescoulie, Jack (2)

TETLOW. See: Bannister, Clay

TEX. See:
Ames, Peter
Carter, Chick
Hutchinson, Ma
Lorre, Peter
McCrary, Tex
Ritter, Tex (1) (2)
Silver, Captain

Tex and Jinx Show, The. See:
McCrary, Tex

TEX BENEKE. See:
Basie, Count
Whiteman, Paul

TEX BLAISDELL. See: Ballew,
Wally

TEX, JOE. See: Butler, Jerry

TEX MASON. See: Benson, Bobby

TEX WILLIAMS. See: Ritter, Tex
(1)

Texaco Star Theater, The. See:
Berle, Milton (3)

Texaco Theater, The. See: Allen,
Fred

Texan, The. See: Longley, Bill

Texas Rangers, The. See: Pearson, Jace

TEXAS WILDCATS, THE. See:
Dean, Jimmy
Hamilton, George

THACKERAY, MR. See: Bean-
blossom, Robert S.

THADDEUS CORNFELDER. See:
Myrt

THADDEUS JONES. See: Heyes,
Hannibal

THALIA MENNINGER. See: Gillis,
Dobie

Thanks For Tomorrow. See: Higby, Mary Jane

Thanks to the Yanks. See: Hawk,
Bob (2)

Thanksgiving Day Parade, Macy's
Annual. See: Myerson, Bess

That Brewster Boy. See: Brewster,
Joey

That Girl. See: Hollinger, Don

That Good Ole Nashville Music.
See: Ritter, Tex (2)

That Show. See: Rivers, Joan

That Was the Week That Was. See:
Ames, Nancy

That, Who Said? See:

Daly, John (4)
Trout, Robert

THATCHER. See: Colt, Thatcher

THATCHER, BECKY. See: Finn,
Huck

Thatcher Colt. See: Colt, Thatcher

That's Life. See: Dixon, Bobby

That's My Boy. See: Jackson,
Jarrin' Jack

THAXTON, LLOYD (1), moderator
of the program (himself)
MANY CELEBRITY GUESTS
Everybody's Talking (TV) (Game)

THAXTON, LLOYD (2), moderator
of the program (himself)
MANY GUESTS
Funny You Should Ask (TV)
(Game)

THAXTON, LLOYD (3), moderator
of the program (himself)
GUEST CELEBRITY JUDGES
AMATEUR TALENT CONTESTANTS
Showcase 68 (TV) (Amateur
talent contest)

THAYER, MRS. HENRY. See:
Jones, Lorenzo

THAYER, PEGGY. See: Mannix,
Joe

Theater, Bob Hope. See:
Hope, Bob (3)
McMahon, Ed (1)

Theater, Bob Hope Presents the
Chrysler. See: Hope, Bob (3)

Theater, Brownstone. See: Beck,
Jackson

Theater, Cowboy. See: Hall,
Monty (1)

Theater, Dick Powell's Zane Grey.
See: Powell, Dick (2)

Theater, Everyman's. See: Johnson, Raymond Edward (1)

Theater, General Electric. See:
Reagan, Ronald

Theater Guild of the Air, The.
See: Langner, Lawrence

Theater Hour, The Majestic. See:
Two Black Crows, The (1)

Theater, Lucky Strike. See:
Montgomery, Robert

Theater, Lux Video. See: Mac-
Rae, Gordon (1)

Theater, Mystery. See: Lenrow,
Bernard

Theater of the Air, The Mickey
Mouse. See: Mouse, Mickey

Theater of Today, The Armstrong.
See: Armstrong Quaker Girl,
The

Theater, Science Fiction. See:
Bradley, Truman

Theater, Screen Guild. See:
Pryor, Roger

Theater, Silver. See: Nagel,
Conrad

Theater, The Dick Powell. See:
Powell, Dick (2)

Theater, The Eddie Cantor Comedy.
See: Cantor, Eddie (1)

Theater, The Family. See: Peyton, Father Patrick

Theater, The George Sanders
Mystery. See: Sanders, George

Theater, The Helen Hayes. See:
Hayes, Helen (1)

Theater, The Jane Wyman. See:
Wyman, Jane

Theater, The Lux Radio. See:
DeMille, Cecil B.

Theater, The Mollé Mystery. See:
Lenrow, Bernard

Theater, The N. B. C. Adventure.
See:
Hope, Bob (3)
McMahon, Ed (1)

Theater, The Palmolive Beauty
Box. See: Dragonette, Jessica
(2)

Theater, The Texaco. See: Allen,
Fred

Theater, The Texaco Star. See:
Berle, Milton (3)

Theater, True Story. See: Hull,
Henry

Theater, Video. See: Mason,
James

Theater, Zane Grey. See:
Ayres, Lew
Powell, Dick (4)

THELMA. See: Grimm, Arnold

THELMA GIDLEY. See: John-
son, Bess

THELMA LOU. See: Taylor,
Andy

THELMA POWELL. See: Nona

Then Came Bronson. See: Bronson, Jim

THEODORE. See:
Bassett, Dr. Theodore
Granik, Theodore (1) (2)
Low, Theodore
Saville, David

THEODORE "BEAVER" CLEAVER.
See: Cleaver, Ward

THEODORE MOONEY. See:
Carmichael, Lucy

There Was a Woman. See: Johnson, Raymond Edward (2)

There, You Are. See:
Cronkite, Walter (6)
Sorel, Guy

THERESA. See also:

Teresa
Therese

THERESA PECH. See: Graham,
Dr. Bob

THERESE. See:
Carter, Kathryn
Teresa
Theresa

They Went That 'a Way. See:
Hill, Ruane

THIANG, LADY. See: Owens,
Anna

THIBAULT, CONRAD. See:
Henry, Captain

Thief, It Takes a. See: Mundy,
Alexander

Thin Man, The. See: Charles,
Nick

THING. See: Addams, Gomez

Thing, Doin' Their. See: Lescoulie, Jack (1)

Thing, Mike Roy's Cooking. See:
Roy, Mike

Think Fast. See: Cross, Mason

Third Man, The. See: Lime,
Harry

13, Box. See: Holiday, Dan

31, Red Hook. See: Klose, Woody

This Changing World. See:
Bishop, Neil

This Day Is Ours. See: Mac-
Donald, Eleanor

This Is Alice. See: Holliday,
Alice

This Is Nora Drake. See: Drake,
Nora

This Is Tom Jones. See: Jones,
Tom (2)

This Is War. See: March, Frederic

This Is Your F.B.I. See: Taylor,
Jim

This Is Your Life. See: Edwards,
Ralph (2)

This Is Your Music. See: Palmer,
Byron

This Life Is Mine. See: Hastings,
Bob

This, Listen to. See: Dotty

This Man Dawson. See: Dawson

This Morning. See: Cavett, Dick
(3)

This Week. See: Moyers, Bill

THISTLE, T.J. See: Corbett,
Tom (2)

THOMAS. See:
Alcala, Thomas Jefferson
Banacek, Thomas
Cat, Thomas Hewitt Edward
Cowan, Thomas
Dallas, Stella
Wilson, Dr. Thomas

THOMAS, ANN. See: Parker,
Lou

THOMAS BOSWELL. See: Ferguson, Martha

THOMAS, CARLA. See: Butler,
Jerry

THOMAS CRANMER, ARCHBISHOP.
See: Henry VIII, King of England

THOMAS CROMWELL. See:
Henry VIII, King of England

THOMAS CULPEPPER. See:
Henry VIII, King of England

THOMAS HAWKINS. See: Harding,
Karen Adams

THOMAS KANE. See:
March, Hal
Story, Ralph

THOMAS, LAVARN. See: Driggs, Karleton King

THOMAS, LOWELL (1)
FLOYD GIBBONS, newscasters (themselves)
Headline Hunters (R) (News)

THOMAS, LOWELL (2), narrator and host of the program (himself)
High Adventure (TV) (Travel/adventure)

THOMAS, MAXINE DRIGGS. See: Driggs, Karleton King

THOMAS, MISS. See: Ace, Goodman

THOMAS MITCHELL. See: Henry, O.

THOMAS R. CLARK. See: Hargrave-Scott, Joan

THOMAS, RICHARD. See: Lescoulie, Jack (3)

THOMAS SEYMOUR. See: Henry VIII, King of England

THOMAS, TERRY. See: Berman, Shelley

THOMAS, THOMAS L.
RACHEL CARLAY, singers, featured on the program (themselves)
THE JERRY MANN VOICES, choral group
The Manhattan Merry-Go-Round (R) (Music)

THOMAS WEBSTER, DR. See: Jordan, Joyce

THOMAS WRIOTHESELEY. See: Henry VIII, King of England

THOMASON, ADELINA. See: Weems, Ambrose J.

THOMPSON, ANDY, headmaster of coeducational school in California, portrayed by Andy Griffith
MARGARET, his wife, teacher at the school
JERRY BROWNELL, coach at the school
PURDY, caretaker at the school
Headmaster (TV) (Comedy)

THOMPSON, BILL. See: Sherman, Ransom (2)

THOMPSON, COLONEL CASEY, owner of one-ring circus in the 1880s
BEN TRAVIS, his partner
TONY GENTRY, trail scout
MANY CIRCUS PERFORMERS
Frontier Circus (TV) (Circus/adventure)

THOMPSON, DR. FRED. See: Barbour, Henry Wilson

THOMPSON, DR. McKINLEY, hospital staff psychiatrist
DR. WILLIAM RAYMER, his supervisor
Breaking Point (TV) (Medical drama)

THOMPSON, DR. RALPH. See: Brent, Dr. Jim

THOMPSON, JEFF, Miami man-about-town
Miami Undercover (TV) (Mystery/adventure)

THOMPSON, JIM, sports columnist
DEBBIE, his wife
CHARLOTTE, Debbie's sister
BOB, Charlotte's husband
BRUCE, 11-year-old son of Charlotte and Bob; editor of neighborhood gossip sheet
The Debbie Reynolds Show (TV) (Family situation comedy)

THOMPSON, KAY. See:
Martin, Tony (2)
Ross, Lanny
Waring, Fred (1)

THOMPSON, MARSHALL, storyteller of the program (himself)
Jambo (TV) (Children's program)

THOMPSON, STEVE. See: Patrick, Dion

THOMPSON, UNCLE JIMMIE. See: Solemn Old Judge, The

THOMPSON'S RHYTHM SINGERS,
KAY. See: Martin, Tony (2)

THOR. See: Mighty Thor, The

Thor, The Mighty. See: Mighty
Thor, The

THORNE. See also: Thorny

THORNE, DAVE. See: Madison,
Kenny

THORNE, MARILYN. See: Hildegarde (1)

THORNHILL, CLAUDE. See:
Whiteman, Paul

THORNTON DREXEL. See: Leighton, Linda

THORNY. See:
Nelson, Ozzie
Thorne

THORPE, ADAM. See: Bauer,
Bertha

THORPE, HOLLY. See: Bauer,
Bertha

THORPE, LIZ, nurse at metropolitan hospital
GAIL LUCAS, student nurse at
the hospital
The Nurses (TV) (Medical drama)

THORPE, ROGER. See: Bauer,
Bertha

Those Bartons. See: Barton, Bud

Those Bells, Oh! See: Bell, Harry

Those Happy Gilmans. See: Gilman, Gordon

Those We Love. See: Marshall,
John

Those Websters. See: Green, Billy

Those Whiting Girls. See: Whiting,
Margaret

THOW, GEORGE. See: Welk,
Lawrence

Three, Camera. See: Macandrew,
James

Three Flats, The. See: Caine,
Betty

THREE GIRL FRIENDS, THE.
See: Waring, Fred (1)

Three Lives, I Led. See: Philbrick, Herbert

THREE MOTHERS. See: Van
Dyke, Dick (2)

Three on a Match. See: Cullen,
Bill (4)

THREE ROMEOS, THE. See:
McNeill, Don
Moore, Garry (1)

Three Sheets to the Wind. See:
Wayne, John

Three Sons, My. See: Douglas,
Steve

3, T. W. See: Ames, Nancy

Three, The Secret. See: McLean,
Murray

THREE, THE TENNESSEE. See:
Cash, Johnny

Thriller, Boris Karloff Presents.
See: Karloff, Boris (1)

Thrills, Grandstand. See: Soule,
Olan (3)

THROCKMORTON P. GILDER-
SLEEVE. See:
Gildersleeve, Throckmorton P.
McGee, Fibber

THROPP, JILL. See: Perry,
John

THUNDERTHUD, CHIEF. See:
Doody, Howdy

THURSDAY, GRANT. See: Kelly,
Kitty

THURSTON, HOWARD. magician,
star of the program (himself)

CLIFF SOUBIER
CARLTON BRICKERT, featured
on the program (themselves)
Thurston the Magician (R) (Adventure) (also known as Howard
Thurston, the Magician) (R)

Thurston, Howard, The Magician.
See: Thurston, Howard

THURSTON, KEN, detective
HIS GIRL FRIEND
HIS SIDE KICK
A Man Called X (R) (TV) (Detective adventure)

Thurston the Magician. See:
Thurston, Howard

TIBBS CANARD. See: McKenzie,
Captain Craig

Tic-Tac-Dough. See: Barry, Jack
(8)

Tick, What Makes You? See: McCaffery, John K. M. (2)

TIERS, VAN DYKE. See: Kelly,
Joe (2)

TIFFINGSTUFFER, CLARENCE.
See: Myrt

TIGE. See: Brown, Buster

TIGER. See:
Brady, Mike
Brains

TIGER LIL. See: Jungle Jim

TIGER LILY. See: Pan, Peter

Tightrope! See: Connors, Mike

TIKI, THE. See: Troy, Adam

TILDA. See: Gump, Andy

TILLER, MR. See: Harding,
Mrs. Rhoda

TILLEY, MAX. See: Sothern,
Mary

TILLIE, stenographer and working
girl

HER MOTHER
MAC, her fellow-employee and
occasional boy friend
MR. SIMPKINS, her employer
Tillie the Toiler (R) (Situation
comedy)

TILLIE. See also: O'Neill, Mrs.

Tillie the Toiler. See: Tillie

TILLSTROM, BURR. See: Kukla

TILSON, TIM. See: Burke, Amos

TILTON, MARTHA. See:
Gibbs, Georgia (2)
Haymes, Dick

TIM. See:
Carr, Alison
Collier, Tim
Conway, Tim
Kelly, Tim
Pride, Ben
Ryan, Tim
Tena
Tom

TIM AND IRENE. See: Cook, Joe

Tim and Irene Show, The. See:
Ryan, Tim

TIM BARNES. See: Harding,
Karen Adams

TIM BENSON. See: Fraser, Ben

TIM CHAMPION, BIG. See:
Corky

TIM COLE, DR. See: Hughes,
Chris

TIM CONWAY. See:
Conway, Tim
Shawn, Dick

Tim Conway Comedy Hour, The.
See: Conway, Tim

Tim Conway Show, The. See:
Barrett, Timothy "Spud"

TIM O'DONOVAN. See: Farrell,
David

TIM O'HARA. See: Uncle Martin

TIM ROURKE. See: Shayne,
Michael

Tim, Tena and. See: Tena

TIM TILSON. See: Burke, Amos

TIM, TINY. See:
Johnson, Bess
Rowan, Dan

TIMBER. See: Tember

Time, Alec Templeton. See:
Templeton, Alec

Time, Alka Seltzer. See: Shriner,
Herb (1)

Time, Arthur Godfrey. See: Godfrey, Arthur (1)

Time, Avalon. See: Skelton, Red

Time, Circus. See: Winchell,
Paul (2)

Time, Curtain. See: Elders,
Harry

Time Flies. See: Hawks, Frank

Time, Flying. See: Falvey, Hal

Time For Beany. See: Beany

Time For Betty Crocker. See:
Crocker, Betty

Time For Love. See: La Volta,
Dianne

Time For Sergeants, No. See:
Stockdale, Will

Time, International Show. See:
Ameche, Don (4)

Time, It's About. See: Mac

Time, Lilac. See: Murray, Arthur

Time, Maxwell House Coffee. See:
Morgan, Frank (2)

Time, Mennen Shave. See:

Parker, Lou

Time, Pantomime Quiz. See:
Harrington, Pat, Jr.
Stokey, Mike

Time, Pleasure. See: Waring,
Fred (2)

Time: Present. See: Huntley,
Chet (3)

Time, Safety Legion. See: Story
Lady, The

Time, Smile. See: Allen, Steve
(2)

Time, Telephone. See: Nesbit,
John (2)

Time, The March of. See:
Husing, Ted

Time to Shine. See: Kemp, Hal

Time, Tune-Up. See: Martin,
Tony (2)

Time Tunnel, The. See: Newman,
Tony

Time, Waltz. See: Munn, Frank
(2)

TIMER, THE OLD. See: McGee,
Fibber

Timid Soul, The. See: Milquetoast, Casper

TIMID SOUL, THE. See: Milquetoast, Casper

TIMMIE. See:
Lassie
Timmy
Tommy

TIMMIE ROGERS. See: Moore,
Melba

TIMMY. See:
Blair, Timothy
Grady, Mickey
Timmie
Tommy

TIMMY ST. CLAIR. See: Fleming,
Tony

TIMOTHY. See:
Barrett, Timothy "Spud"
Blair, Timothy
Forsyte, Soames
Marlin, Mary

TIMOTHY GALLAGHER. See:
Perkins, Ma

TIMOTHY STOREY. See:
Meredith, Charles

TINA. See:
Hardie, Jim
Teenie
Teeny
Tena
Tinney
Tiny

TINA COLE HOWARD. See:
Driggs, Karleton King

TINA RICKLES. See: Corbett,
Tom (1)

TINA ROYAL. See: Hank

TINKER BELL. See:
McHale, Lieut. Commander
Quinton
Pan, Peter

TINKER, TANK. See: Harrigan,
Hop

TINNEY. See also:
Teenie
Teeny
Tina
Tiny

TINNEY, CAL, quizmaster of the
program (himself)
MANY CONTESTANTS
Youth Vs. Age (R) (Quiz)

TINY. See also:
Teenie
Teeny
Tina
Tinney

TINY LITTLE, BIG. See: Welk,
Lawrence

"TINY" RUFFNER, EDMUND. See:
Birthday Man, The
Henry, Captain

TINY STOKES. See: Kelly, Joe
(1)

TINY TIM. See:
Johnson, Bess
Rowan, Dan

TIPPY. See: Waring, Evelyn

TIPTON, JOHN BERRESFORD.
See: Anthony, Michael

TITO GUIZAR. See: Archie

TITO RODRIGUEZ. See: Whiteman, Paul

TITUS MOODY. See: Allen, Fred

TITUS OATES. See: Churchill,
John

TITUS THE GOLDFISH. See:
Wilson, Flip

TIZZIE LISH. See: Blurt, Elmer

To Rome With Love. See: Endicott, Professor Mike

To Tell the Truth. See: Moore,
Garry (5)

Toast of the Town, The. See:
Sullivan, Ed

TOBIN, DAN. See: Winters, Jack

TOBY. See:
Martin, Doris
Reed, Toby
Robin
Wilson, Steve

TOBY NELSON. See: Solomon,
David

TOBY SMITH. See: Aldrich,
Henry

TOBY WRIGHT. See: Kaye,
Sammy (1)

TOD. See also: Todd

TOD GOODHUE. See: Noble, Mary

TOD STILES. See: Murdock, Buz

Today. See: Downs, Hugh

Today, A Tale of. See: Allen,
    Joan Houston

Today, Hollywood. See: Graham,
    Sheilah

Today in Business. See: Shepherd,
    Gary

Today Is Ours. See: Manning,
    Laura

Today On the Farm. See: Arnold,
    Eddy

Today, The Armstrong Theater of.
    See: Armstrong Quaker Girl,
    The

Today's Children. See:
    Carter, Kathryn
    Larimore, Marilyn

Today's Woman. See: Chase,
    Sylvia

TODD. See:
    Russell, Todd
    Sterling, Vanessa Dale
    Tod

TODD BASS. See: Rowan, Dan

TODD, BOB. See: Doonican, Val

TODD, DICK. See:
    Henry, Captain
    Parks, Bert (5)

TODD, MISS. See:
    Brent, Dr. Jim
    Brown, Ellen

TODD RUSSELL. See:
    Compton, Walter
    Hull, Warren (2)
    Russell, Todd

Toiler, Tillie the. See: Tillie

TOKI. See: Bell, Mike

Tokyo Rose. See: d'Aquino, Iva
    Ikuko Toguri

TOLLIVER, JIM. See: Dyke,
    Charity Amanda

TOLSKY, SUSAN. See: Cosby,
    Bill (2)

TOM
    DICK
    HARRY, characters appearing in
    the drama
    The Affairs of Tom, Dick and
    Harry (R) (Serial drama)

TOM. See also:
    Barkley, Victoria
    Blake, Tom
    Boyd, Tom
    Breneman, Tom (1) (2)
    Brewster, Tom
    Chapin, Tom
    Corbett, Tom (1) (2)
    Davis, Joan Field
    Driggs, Karleton King
    Gentry, Tom
    Grimm, Arnold
    Hal
    Hopkins, Kate
    Horton, Dr. Tom
    Howard, Tom (1) (2)
    Hughes, Chris
    Jeffords, Tom
    Jones, Tom (1) (2)
    Kennedy, Tom (1) (2)
    Mix, Tom
    Moore, Tom (1) (2)
    Poston, Tom
    Potter, Tom
    Reddy, Tom
    Reynolds, Dr. Tom
    Slater, Bill (1)
    Smothers, Tom (1) (2) (3)
    Tim
    Waring, Fred (1)
    Wedloe, Tom

TOM AMES. See: Dyke, Charity
    Amanda

TOM AND DON. See: Kelly,
    Joe (1)

TOM BALDWIN, DR. See: Hardy,
    Dr. Steven

TOM BANNION, REV.   See: Rut-
    ledge, Dr. John

TOM BLAKE.   See:
    Blake, Tom
    Noble, Mary

TOM BOSLEY.   See: Martin, Dean
    (2)

TOM BRYSON.   See: Noble, Mary

TOM CLARK.   See: Barclay, Doc

TOM COAKLEY.   See: Winchell,
    Walter (1)

TOM COLBY.   See: Erskine, In-
    spector Louis

TOM COLWELL.   See: O'Malley,
    Father Chuck

Tom Corbett, Space Cadet.   See:
    Corbett, Tom (2)

TOM CRAYTHORNE.   See:
    Sterling, Vanessa Dale

TOM, DICK AND HARRY.   See:
    Duke of Paducah, The
    Skelton, Red
    Uncle Walter

Tom, Dick and Harry, The Affairs
    of.   See: Tom

Tom, Dick and Mary.   See:
    Gentry, Tom

TOM DONNELLY.   See: Garrison,
    Spencer

TOM ELDRIDGE.   See: Hughes,
    Lisa

Tom Ewell Show, The.   See:
    Potter, Tom

TOM FIELD.   See: Leighton,
    Linda

TOM HANSEN DANCERS, THE.
    See: Junior

TOM HARRIS.   See: Kirkwood,
    Jack

TOM HUGHES.   See: Jordan,
    Joyce

TOM HUTSON.   See: Bracken,
    John

Tom Jones, This Is.   See: Jones,
    Tom (2)

TOM KENNEDY.   See:
    Kennedy, Tom (1) (2)
    Narz, Jack (6)

TOM LOPAKA.   See: Steele,
    Tracy

Tom Mix and His Ralston Straight
    Shooters.   See: Mix, Tom

Tom Mix, The Adventures of.   See:
    Mix, Tom

TOM MORLEY.   See: Drake, Nora

TOM POPE.   See: Hughes, Chris

TOM POSTON.   See:
    Allen, Steve (1) (3)
    Moore, Garry (5)
    Poston, Tom
    Stokey, Mike

TOM SAWYER.   See: Finn, Huck

TOM STARRETT.   See: Shane

TOM STEPHENSON.   See: Brent,
    Dr. Jim

TOM-TOM DEWITT.   See:
    Macauley, Wes

TOM WARING.   See: Waring, Fred
    (1)

TOM WINTER.   See: Peyton,
    Martin

Tombstone Territory.   See: Hollis-
    ter, Clay

TOMLIN, LILY.   See: Rowan, Dan

TOMMY.   See:
    Bartlett, Tommy
    Dane, Prudence
    Dorsey, Tommy
    Hansen, Dean Eric

Jackson, Martha
Mitchell, Dennis
Riggs, Tommy
Tammy
Timmie
Timmy

TOMMY DORSEY. See:
Crosby, Bing (3)
Dorsey, Tommy

TOMMY FINCH. See: Walker,
Eddie

TOMMY HUGHES. See: Wilson,
Steve

TOMMY LEONETTI. See: Lanson,
Snooky

TOMMY LEWIS. See: Jackson,
Martha

TOMMY MACK, "PROFESSOR."
See: Skelton, Red

TOMMY MacROBERTS. See:
Higgins

Tommy Riggs and Betty Lou. See:
Riggs, Tommy

TOMMY TAYLOR. See:
Dawson, Rosemary
Perkins, Ma

TOMMY TUCKER. See: Grauer,
Ben (2)

TOMMY TUNE. See: Chidsey,
Jackie

Tomorrow, Brave. See: Lambert,
Louise

Tomorrow, Here Comes. See:
Glenn, Colonel John

Tomorrow, Search for. See: Tate,
Joanne

Tomorrow, Stars of. See: Grimes,
Bill

Tomorrow, Thanks For. See:
Higby, Mary Jane

Tomorrow's Tops. See:

Whiteman, Margo

TONEY. See also: Tony

TONEY, JAY STONE. See:
Peters, Lowell

TONIA BARROWS. See: Kirk,
Captain James

Tonight! See: Lescoulie, Jack (4)

Tonight, Comedy. See: Klein,
Robert

Tonight, On Broadway. See:
Vallee, Rudy (1)

Tonight Show, The. See:
Allen, Steve (3)
Carson, Johnny (1)
Paar, Jack

Tonight, Town Hall. See: Allen,
Fred

TONOOSE, UNCLE. See: Williams,
Danny

TONTO. See: Lone Ranger, The

TONY. See:
Bennett, Tony
Brown, Tony
Carter, Kathryn
Deeds, Longfellow
Falvey, Hal
Fleming, Tony
Hall, Tony
Mallory, Lieut. Col. Spencer
Malone, Dr. Jerry
Martin, Tony (1) (2)
Mix, Tom
Nelson, Major Tony
Newman, Tony
Nick
Toney
Webster, Nancy
Wons, Tony
Woodruff, Professor

TONY AMATO. See: Darin,
Bobby

Tony Bennett. See: Bennett, Tony

TONY CAMPO. See: Hardy,
Dr. Steven

TONY CHALMERS, DR. See:
Perry, John

TONY CHARMOLI DANCERS, THE.
See: Andrews, Julie

TONY COOPER. See: Hillman,
India

TONY GENTRY. See: Thompson,
Colonel Casey

TONY GRIFFIN. See: Trent,
Helen

TONY HARKER. See: Drake,
Betty

TONY HENDRA. See: DeLuise,
Dom (2)

TONY LARSON, DR. See: Hughes,
Lisa

Tony Martin. See: Martin, Tony
(1)

TONY MARTIN. See:
Crosby, Bing (2)
Martin, Tony (1) (2)

TONY MORDENTE DANCERS, THE.
See: Bono, Salvatore

Tony, My Friend. See: Woodruff,
Professor

TONY PASTOR. See: Whiteman,
Paul

TONY VENTO. See: Sterling,
Vanessa Dale

TONY VINCENTE, DR. See: Tate,
Joanne

Tony Wons' Scrapbook. See: Wons,
Tony

Too Young to Go Steady. See:
Blake, Tom

TOODY, GUNTHER. See: Muldoon,
Francis

TOOHEY, C. PEMBERTON. See:
Perkins, Ma

TOOPS, MORT. See: McGee,
Fibber

TOOTH, BIG. See: Og

TOOTH, BLACK. See: Sales,
Soupy

TOOTIE. See: Marlin, Mary

TOOTSIE STAGWELL. See:
Burns, George (1)

TOOTSIE WOODLEY. See: Bumstead, Blondie

TOP CAT
DIBBLE
BENNY
CHOO CHOO
SPOOK
THE BRAIN
FANCY-FANCY
BILL BAILEY, cartoon charac-
ters
Top Cat (TV) (Cartoon)

Top Dollar. See: Reed, Toby

Top, The Big. See: Sterling,
Jack

Top This, Can You? See:
Amsterdam, Morey
Wilson, Ward

Top Tunes and New Talent,
Lawrence Welk's. See: Welk,
Lawrence

Topper. See: Topper, Cosmo

TOPPER, ARNIE. See: Harding,
Mrs. Rhoda

TOPPER, COSMO, banker
HENRIETTA TOPPER, his wife
GEORGE KERBY, ghost, friend
of Cosmo Topper
MARION KERBY, George's wife,
ghost; also friend of Cosmo
Topper
NEIL, ghost of dog, pet of the
Kerbys
The Adventures of Topper (R)
(Comedy/fantasy); Topper (TV)

Topper, The Adventures of. See:
Topper, Cosmo

TOPPERS, THE HILL. See:
Kelly, Joe (1)

Tops, Tomorrow's. See: Whiteman, Margo

TORBEN REIMER. See:
Cameron, Christy Allen

TORCHY REYNOLDS HOLDEN.
See: Rutledge, Dr. John

TOREY. See: Peck, Torey

TORK, PETER. See: Jones, Davy

TORME, MEL, singer and enter-
tainer, host of the program
(himself)
MOTION PICTURE CLIPS OF
HISTORICAL EVENTS AND
PERSONALITIES
MANY GUEST STARS
It Was a Very Good Year (TV)
(History)

TORO, EL. See: Carson, Kit

TORRANCE, DR. See: Harding,
Karen Adams

TORRES, LIZ. See: Moore,
Melba

TORVALD, NILS. See: Calhoun,
Ben

TORWALD. See: Nielson, Torwald

TOUBO SMITH. See: Kelly, Tim

TOUGH. See also: Tuffy

TOUGH GUY CORNELIUS CALLA-
HAN. See: Kaltenmeyer, Professor August, D. U. N.

TOWERS, PAMELA. See: Hoyt,
Vikki Adams

Town, Big. See: Wilson, Steve

Town, Blue Ribbon. See: Marx,
Groucho (1)

Town Crier, The. See: Woollcott,
Alexander

TOWN CRIER, THE. See: Woollcott, Alexander

TOWN CRIERS, THE. See:
Kyser, Kay

TOWN HALL QUARTET, THE.
See: Allen, Fred

Town Hall Tonight. See: Allen,
Fred

Town, Mayor of the. See:
Russell, Mayor

Town Meeting, America's. See:
Murrow, Edward R. (1)

Town Meeting of the Air, America's.
See: Denny, George V., Jr.

Town, Mr. Deeds Goes to. See:
Deeds, Longfellow

TOWN TALK. See: Harum,
David

Town, The Mayor of the. See:
Russell, Mayor

Town, The Toast of the. See:
Sullivan, Ed

Town, The Ugliest Girl in. See:
Blair, Timothy

Town, Wichita. See: Dunbar,
Mike

TOWNE, DON, character appear-
ing on the program
Radio's Court of Honor (R)
(Drama)

TOWNE, HAL, roving newspaper
reporter
SARGE, his housekeeper
The Dennis O'Keefe Show (TV)
(Situation comedy)

TOWNE, LANGDON. See: Rogers,
Major Robert

Tracer. See: Reagan

Tracer of Lost Persons, Mr. Keen.
See: Keen, Mr.

Tracer, The. See: Chandler, Jim

TRACER, THE. See: Chandler,
Jim

TRACEY. See:
King
Tracy

TRACEY ENDICOTT. See: Winters,
Evelyn

Trackdown. See: Gilman, Hoby

TRACY. See:
Malone, Dr. Jerry
Partridge, Connie
Randolph, Walt
Steele, Tracy
Tracey

TRACY, ARTHUR, accordionist
and singer, star of the program
(himself)
The Street Singer (R) (Music)

TRACY BAKER. See: Barbour,
Henry Wilson

TRACY CARLYLE HASTINGS. See:
Carlyle, Baylor

TRACY DELMAR. See: Bauer,
Bertha

TRACY, DICK, police officer
JUNIOR TRACY, his adopted son
PAT PATTON, police officer,
Tracy's associate
CHIEF BRANDON, police chief,
Tracy's superior
TESS TRUEHEART, Tracy's girl
friend
Dick Tracy (R) (Crime adventure)

TRACY, DR. See: Jordan, Joyce

TRACY, DR. MARSH, scientist
MIKE, Negro zoologist
JUDY, chimpanzee
Daktari (TV) (African adventure)

TRACY GRAHAM. See: Ferguson,
Martha

TRACY, KIM. See: Dugan,
Queenie

TRACY KRAMER. See: Webster,
Jerry

TRACY TAYLOR. See: Hardy,
Dr. Steven

TRADER PENROSE. See: Troy,
Adam

Traffic Court. See: Jones,
Edgar Allan, Jr.

TRAGG, LIEUT. ARTHUR. See:
Mason, Perry

TRAIL, MARK, outdoorsman and
woodsman
SCOTTY
CHERRY, his friends
Mark Trail (R) (Outdoor adven-
venture)

Trail, Overland. See: Kelly,
Frederick Thomas

Trailmaster. See: Adams, Major
Seth

TRAIN, FREIGHT. See: Huddles,
Ed

Train, Wagon. See: Adams,
Major Seth

TRAINOR, PRICE. See: Walleck,
Meredith

TRAMP. See: Rose, George

TRAMPAS. See:
MacKenzie, Colonel Alan
Parmalee, Ranger Captain
Virginian, The

TRAPPER JOHN McINTYRE.
See: Pierce, Captain Hawkeye

TRASK, DIANA. See: Miller,
Mitch

TRASK, MR. See: O'Neill, Mrs.

TRASK, MRS. See: O'Neill, Mrs.

TRAUBEL, HELEN. See: Bell,
Alexander Graham

TRAVELER. See:
Arkansas Traveler, The
Mysterious Traveler, The

Traveler, The Mysterious. See:
Mysterious Traveler, The

Traveler, Welcome. See: Bartlett, Tommy

Travels, Grandma. See: Grandma

Travels of Jaimie McPheeters, The.
See: McPheeters, Dr. Sardinius

TRAVERS, MADELYN. See:
Sunday

TRAVIS, BEN. See: Thompson,
Colonel Casey

TRAVIS, CLINT, Arizona ranger
26 Men (TV) (Western)

TRAVIS, MERLE. See: Ritter,
Tex (1)

TRAVIS, NICOLE. See: Karr,
Mike

TRAVIS, STAR. See: Barton,
Joe

TRAVIS, WALTER. See: Garrison,
Spencer

Trawlers, Forty Fathom. See:
Forty Fathom

TREACHER. See also: Teacher

TREACHER, ARTHUR. See:
Griffin, Merv (1)

Treasure. See: Burrud, Bill (3)

Treasure Hunt. See: Murray, Jan
(4)

Treasure Hunt, Melody. See:
Ballard, Pat

Treasury Agent. See: Lincoln,
Joe

TREASURY AGENT, employee of
U.S. Treasury Department
T-Man (R) (Adventure)

Treasury Men in Action. See:
Chief, The

Treasury, O'Hara, United States.
See: O'Hara, James

Trek, African. See: Marias,
Josef

Trek, Star. See: Kirk, Captain
James

TREMAINE. See also: Tremayne

TREMAINE, DAL. See: Grimm,
Arnold

TREMAINE, JERRY. See: Liston,
Lois

TREMAINE, MR. See: Grimm,
Arnold

TREMAINE, MRS. See: Grimm,
Arnold

TREMAN. See also: Truman

TREMAN, CLAIRE. See: Dyke,
Charity Amanda

TREMAYNE. See:
Stirling, Craig
Tremaine

TREMAYNE, LES. See: First
Nighter, Mr.

TRENIERS, THE. See: Whiteman,
Paul

TRENT, CARTER. See: Young,
Larry "Pepper"

TRENT, HELEN, fashion designer
AGATHA ANTHONY
ROY GABLER
CHERRY MARTIN
CURTIS BANCROFT
ERIC STOWELL
CHUCK BLAIR
SYLVIA HALL
NICK COLLINS
CLARA BLAKE

RITA HARRISON
BUGGSY O'TOOLE
GIL WHITNEY
ALICE CARROLL
MRS. WARD SMITH
MONICA WARD SMITH
GINGER LEROY
LUCIA LANG
MARJORIE CLAIBORNE
JONATHAN HAYWARD
LISA VALENTINE
HIRAM WEATHERBEE
NORMAN HASTINGS
DR. FLEMING
HARRIET EAGLE
TEMBER ADAMS
LOIS COLTON
JEFF BRADY
BARBARA SUE
DREW SINCLAIR
TONY GRIFFIN
PHILIP KING
MARGOT BURKHART
JEANETTE McNEILL
DICK NORTH
NANCY GRANGER
CHRIS WILSON
GORDON DECKER
FRANK CHASE
NINA MASON
CYNTHIA CARTER
BROOK FORRESTER
MR. KELVIN
MRS. KELVIN
MARCIA
DOUGLAS
NANCY
BUD
LYDIA
AGNES, characters appearing in
the drama
The Romance of Helen Trent (R)
(Serial drama)

TRENT, HORACE. See: Young,
Larry "Pepper"

TRENT, IVY. See: Young, Larry
"Pepper"

TRENT, MR. See: Hargrave-
Scott, Joan

TRENT, SYBIL. See: Halop, Billy

TREVOR. See: Nash, Jim

Trial, Arrest and. See:

Anderson, Sergeant Nick

Trial, On. See: Cotten, Joseph
(2)

Trials, Famous Jury. See:
Judge, The

Trials of O'Brien. See: O'Brien,
Daniel J.

TRIGGER. See: Rogers, Roy

TRIMBLE. See also: Trumbull

TRIMBLE, JONATHAN
ALICE TRIMBLE
MILDRED, characters appearing
in the drama
Jonathan Trimble, Esq. (R)
(Serial drama)

TRIMBLE, KENNY. See: Welk,
Lawrence

TRINI LOPEZ. See: Jones, Jack

TRIO, THE CARMEN LE FAVE.
See: Edwards, Frank

TRIO, THE HAMILTON. See:
Caesar, Sid (3)

TRIO, THE NORMAN PARIS. See:
Francis, Arlene (1)

TRIO, THE VERNE, LEE AND
MARY. See: Kelly, Joe (1)

Trip, Let's Take a. See: Pud

TRIPP, PAUL, host of the program
(himself)
Mr. I. Magination (TV) (Children's program)

TRIXIE. See:
Dixie
James, Nancy
Pixie

TRIXIE NORTON. See: Kramden,
Ralph

Troop, F. See: Parmenter,
Captain Wilton

TROOP, MARSHAL DAN, law

enforcement official at Laramie,
Wyoming
JOHNNY McKAY, his deputy
LILY MERRILL, saloon keeper
Lawman (TV) (Western)

Trooper, State. See: Blake, Rod

TROTTER, JOHN SCOTT. See:
Crosby, Bing (1)

TROTTER, LIEUT. MAXWELL.
See: Morgan, Lieut. Anne

Troubadours, The Ipana. See:
Lanin, Sam

Trouble House. See: Booth,
Martha

Trouble, What's Your? See:
Peale, Norman Vincent

Trouble With Father. See: Erwin,
Stu

Trouble With Marriage, The. See:
Barry

Troubleshooters. See: Dugan

TROUT, ROBERT, quizmaster of
the program (himself)
MANY CONTESTANTS
Who Said That? (R) (Quiz)

TROWBRIDGE, ABBEY. See:
Hargrave-Scott, Joan

TROWBRIDGE, DUDLEY. See:
Hargrave-Scott, Joan

TROY, ADAM, captain of the
schooner "Tiki"
OLIVER KEE, his Chinese part-
ner
CLAY BAKER, his first mate
TRADER PENROSE, hotel
operator
SONDI
KELLY, young Tahitians
Adventures in Paradise (TV)
(Tropic adventure)

TROY, SERGEANT SAM
SERGEANT JACK MOFFITT
PRIVATE MARK HITCHCOCK
PRIVATE TULLY PETTIGREW,

members of Rat Patrol, Allied
military desert unit
CAPTAIN HANS DIETRICH, head
of German troop
The Rat Patrol (TV) (Adventure)

TROYER, IRINA. See: Marlin,
Mary

TROYER, LINA. See: Marlin,
Mary

TRUDY. See:
Hopkins, Kate
Karr, Mike

TRUDY BAILEY, MRS. See:
O'Neill, Mrs.

TRUDY BAUER. See: Rutledge,
Dr. John

TRUDY ERWIN. See: Kyser, Kay

TRUE BOARDMAN. See: Judge,
The

True Detective Mysteries. See:
Shuttleworth, John

True, Dreams Come. See: Mc-
Kinley, Barry

True, G. E. See: Webb, Jack

True Life Stories, Aunt Jennie's.
See: Aunt Jenny (Aunt Lucy)

True or False. See: Hagen, Dr.
Harry

True Story Hour With Mary and
Bob, The. See: Mary

True Story, My. See: Riggs,
Glenn

True Story Theater, The. See:
Hull, Henry

True, Your Dream Has Come.
See: Keith, Ian

TRUEHEART, TESS. See: Tracy,
Dick

TRUESDALE, SALLY, traveling
companion

MRS. MYRTLE BANFORD, her wealthy globe-trotting employer
Sally (TV) (Situation comedy)

TRULY, LOVEABLE. See: Linus

TRUMAN. See:
Bradley, Truman
Treman

TRUMAN "TUBBY" SCOTT, DR. See: Hargrave-Scott, Joan

TRUMBULL. See also: Trimble

TRUMBULL, SERGEANT CORNELIUS. See: Spencer, Jeff

Trust, Who Do You? See: Carson, Johnny (2)

Trust Your Wife, Do You? See: Bergen, Edgar (1)

Truth, Nothing But the. See: Moore, Garry (5)

Truth or Consequences. See: Edwards, Ralph (3)

Truth, To Tell the. See: Moore, Garry (5)

TUBBY. See: McKeever, Cadet Gary

"TUBBY" SCOTT, DR. TRUMAN. See: Hargrave-Scott, Joan

TUCK, FRIAR. See: Hood, Robin

TUCKER, ORRIN. See: Ross, Lanny

TUCKER, RICHARD. See: Ives, Burl (2)

TUCKER, TOMMY. See: Grauer, Ben (2)

Tuesday, First. See: Vanocur, Sander

TUFFY. See:
Brasuhn, Tuffy
Tough

TUG BAXTER. See: Brown, Ellen

TUGBOAT. See: Brennan, Tugboat Annie

Tugboat Annie. See: Brennan, Tugboat Annie

TUGWELL. See: Carson, Jack

TULIP VALENTINE ELSON. See: Johnson, Bess

TULLY. See: Evans, Glenn

TULLY PETTIGREW, PRIVATE. See: Troy, Sergeant Sam

Tune Detective, The. See: Spaeth, Sigmund

Tune, Name That. See: DeWitt, George

TUNE, TOMMY. See: Chidsey, Jackie

TUNE TWISTERS, THE. See: Kelly, Joe (1)

Tune-Up Time. See: Martin, Tony (2)

Tunes and New Talent, Lawrence Welk's Top. See: Welk, Lawrence

Tunnel, The Time. See: Newman, Tony

Turn of Fate. See: Ryan, Robert (1)

TURNER. See: Hudson, Nancy Smith

TURNER, COLONEL ROSCOE, air pioneer and aviator; narrator of the program (himself)
Sky Blazers (R) (Aviation adventure)

TURNER, EILEEN. See: O'Neill, Mrs.

TURNER, ELLEN. See: Campanelli, Dr. Vincent

TURNER, GLENN. See: Manning,
Laura

TURNER, JOYCE. See: Brown,
Ellen

TURNER, MR. See: O'Neill, Mrs.

TURNER, MRS. See: O'Neill,
Mrs.

TURNER, MOLLY. See: McHale,
Lieut. Commander Quinton

TURNER, PETER. See: Brown,
Ellen

Turns, As the World. See:
Hughes, Chris

TURP, JOE, head of the house
ETHEL, his wife
UNCLE BEN, his uncle
Joe and Ethel Turp (R) (Situa-
tion comedy)

TURRIE, SUZANNE. See: Drake,
Nora

TUSKA, JON. See: Hill, Ruane

TUT, KING. See: Batman

TUTTLE, CORWIN. See: Sharp,
Hal

TUTTLE, LURENE. See: Coogan,
Jackie

TUTTLE, SARAH. See: Allen,
Dr. Kate

TWEEDY, MR. See: Grimm,
Arnold

TWEETSIE HERRINGBONE. See:
Perkins, Ma

TWEETY THE BIRD. See: Bunny,
Bugs

12, Adam. See: Malloy, Officer
Pete

Twelve O'Clock High. See:
Savage, Brigadier General Frank

Twenties, The Roaring. See:
Garrison, Pat

Twentieth Century, The. See:
Cronkite, Walter (3)

Twenty-Fifth Century A.D., Buck
Rogers in the. See: Rogers,
Buck

21st Century, The. See: Cronkite,
Walter (4)

Twenty-One. See: Barry, Jack
(9)

21 Beacon Street. See: Chase,
Dennis

Twenty Questions. See: Slater,
Bill (2)

26 Men. See: Travis, Clint

Twenty Thousand Years in Sing Sing.
See: Lawes, Lewis E.

23, Johnny Madero, Pier. See:
Madero, Johnny

2020, Sealab. See: Williams, Dr.

TWIG. See: Wilson, Dr. Thomas

Twig Is Bent, As the. See:
Peters, Bill

Twilight Zone. See: Serling, Rod
(2)

TWIN. See also: Twins, The

TWIN, BIG. See: Monroe, Clayt

TWIN, FIRST. See: Pan, Peter

TWIN, LITTLE. See: Monroe,
Clayt

TWIN, SECOND. See: Pan, Peter

Twin Stars Show, The. See: Twin
Stars, The

TWIN STARS, THE, portrayed by
Rosemarie Broncato and Helen
Claire
The Twin Stars Show (R) (Variety)

TWING, ERSEL. See: Bergen,
Edgar (2)

TWINING, REX. See: Tate,
Joanne

TWINS, THE. See:
Brown, Robinson, Jr.
Levy, Abie
Twin

TWINS, THE BLACKSTONE. See:
Edwards, Ralph (1)

TWINS, THE McFARLAND. See:
Waring, Fred (1)

Twins, The Quality. See: East,
Ed (2)

TWISTERS, THE TUNE. See:
Kelly, Joe (1)

TWITTY, CONWAY. See: Owens,
Buck

TWO BLACK CROWS, THE (Moran
and Mack) (1), blackface comedy
act consisting of George Moran
and Charlie Mack
MANY GUEST STARS
The Majestic Theater Hour (R)
(Variety)

TWO BLACK CROWS, THE (Moran
and Mack) (2), blackface comedy
act consisting of George Moran
and Charlie Mack
The Two Black Crows (R)
(Comedy)

Two Cities, The Quiz of. See:
Fitzmaurice, Michael

Two Faces West. See: January,
Dr. Ben

Two For the Money. See:
Shriner, Herb (3)

$250,000 Bank, Break the. See:
Parks, Bert (1)

Two, It Takes. See: Scully, Vin

Two, Marriage For. See: Hoyt,
Vikki Adams

Two of Us, The. See: Lee, Pinky
(2)

Two On a Clue. See: Spencer,
Jeff

2, The Man from G. See: North,
Major Hugh

222, Room. See: Kaufman, Seymour

TWOMEY, JOHN. See: Reed,
Jerry

TY COON. See:
Dawg, Deputy
Tycoon

TY DeYOE. See: Rogers,
Patricia

TYCOON. See also: Ty Coon

Tycoon, The. See: Andrews,
Walter

TYLER. See: Butcher, Major
Simon

TYLER BENEDICT. See: Robinson, Don

TYLER, CHUCK. See: Davis,
Ann Tyler

TYLER, DR. CHARLES. See:
Davis, Ann Tyler

TYLER, JUDY. See: Stokey,
Mike

TYLER, KIP. See: Cameron,
Christy Allen

TYLER, MARY. See: Wayne,
Ruth Evans

TYLER, PASCAL. See: Cameron,
Christy Allen

TYLER, PHOEBE. See: Davis,
Ann Tyler

TYLER, WILLIE. See: Rowan,
Dan

TYPHOON. See: Wing, Howie

TYRONE HORNEIGH. See: Rowan,
Dan

TYRRELL, MRS. See: Ames,
Peter

TYSON, MRS. See: Brown, Ellen

U. CHARLES BARKER, COLONEL.
See: McKay, Judson

U. N. C. L. E. See also: Uncle

U. N. C. L. E. , The Girl From. See:
Dancer, April

U. N. C. L. E. , The Man From. See:
Solo, Napoleon

U. S. A. , Four Corners. See:
Crowell, Jonah

U. S. A. , Green Valley. See:
Ortega, Santos

U. S. A. , Inside. See: Hayes,
Peter Lind (2)

U. S. A. , Jubilee. See: Foley, Red

U. S. A. , Roundup. See: Shadel,
Bill

U. S. A. , Secret File. See: Morgan, Major

U. S. Border Patrol. See: Jagger,
Don

U. S. Canteen Show, The. See:
Froman, Jane (1)

U. S. M. C. , Gomer Pyle. See:
Pyle, Gomer

U. S. Marshal. See: Morgan,
Marshal

UGGAMS, LESLIE, singer; star of
the program (herself)
LILLIAN HAYMAN
JOHNNY BROWN
ALLISON MILLS, entertainers
appearing on the program (them-
selves)
THE DON McKAYLE DANCERS
THE HOWARD ROBERTS SINGERS
ERNIE FREEMAN, orchestra
leader (himself)
HIS ORCHESTRA
MANY GUEST STARS
The Leslie Uggams Show (TV)
(Variety)

UGGAMS, LESLIE. See also:

Davidson, John (1)
Miller, Mitch

Ugliest Girl in Town, The. See:
Blair, Timothy

UHURA, LIEUT. See: Kirk,
Captain James

UKULELE IKE. See: Lane,
Richard

ULLETT, NIC. See: DeLuise,
Dom (2)

ULYSSES. See: Calhoun, Ben

ULYSSES S. APPLEGATE, PROFES-
SOR. See: Kaltenmeyer, Professor August, D. U. N.

UMBRIAGO. See: Durante, Jimmy

UMPIRE, THE. See: Pitcher,
The

UNA FIELDS. See: Andrews,
Walter

UNCLE. See:
Carson, Uncle Joe
Gregg, Uncle Bentley
U. N. C. L. E.

UNCLE ABE
DAVID, characters appearing in
the drama
Uncle Abe and David (R) (Serial
drama)

Uncle Abe and David. See: Uncle
Abe

UNCLE ARNOLD. See: Muir,
Carolyn

UNCLE ARTHUR. See: Stephens,
Samantha

UNCLE BAXTER. See: Riley,
Chester A.

UNCLE BEN. See:
Meyer
Turp, Joe

UNCLE BILL. See:
Davis, Dr. Althea

Davis, Uncle Bill
Halop, Billy
Harding, Karen Adams

UNCLE BUCKLEY. See: Riley,
Chester A.

UNCLE CARLO. See: Goldberg,
Molly

UNCLE CHARLEY. See: Douglas,
Steve

UNCLE CHARLIE, proprietor of
tent show
Uncle Charlie's Tent Show (R)
(Music and variety)

UNCLE CHARLIE DOOLEY. See:
Day, Chris

Uncle Charlie's Tent Show. See:
Uncle Charlie

UNCLE COOTER. See: Smith,
Eugene

UNCLE DAVID. See: Goldberg,
Molly

UNCLE DENNIS. See: McGee,
Fibber

Uncle Don. See: Uncle Don

UNCLE DON, master of ceremonies
on program
Uncle Don (R) (Children's program)

UNCLE ED JACKSON. See:
Noble, Mary

UNCLE EVERETT. See: Hudson,
Nancy Smith

UNCLE EZRA. See: Kelly, Joe
(1)

UNCLE EZRA BUTTERNUT. See:
Peppertag, Aaron

UNCLE FESTER. See: Addams,
Gomez

UNCLE FLETCHER. See: Gook,
Vic

UNCLE HAPPY. See: Ryan, Tim

UNCLE HARRY. See: Carter,
Lucy

UNCLE JIM, quizmaster of the
program
MANY CONTESTANTS
Uncle Jim's Question Bee (R)
(Quiz)

UNCLE JIM FAIRFIELD. See:
Armstrong, Jack

UNCLE JIMMIE THOMPSON. See:
Solemn Old Judge, The

Uncle Jim's Question Bee. See:
Uncle Jim

UNCLE JOSH. See: Brown, Ellen

UNCLE LATZI. See: McCray, Linc

UNCLE LUCIUS. See: Tammy

UNCLE MARTIN, Martian, stranded
on Earth after crash landing
TIM O'HARA, newspaper re-
porter, his roommate
MRS. BROWN, their landlady
MR. BURNS, Tim's boss
My Favorite Martian (TV)
(Comedy)

UNCLE MATT SWAIN. See:
Peyton, Martin

UNCLE MATTHEW. See: Mc-
Garry, Dan

UNCLE MOE PLOTNIK. See:
Fitzgerald, Bridget Theresa
Mary Coleen

UNCLE NED. See: Pruitt, Mrs.
Phyllis Poindexter

Uncle Remus. See: Uncle Remus

UNCLE REMUS, story teller
Uncle Remus (R) (Children's
program)

UNCLE SIMON. See: Ward,
Tammy

UNCLE SIP, AUNT SAP AND.
See: Foley, Red

UNCLE TONOOSE. See: Williams, Danny

UNCLE WALTER
FATHER
MOTHER
MARGIE
SWEET ADELINE, characters appearing on the program
TOM, DICK AND HARRY, musical group (themselves)
BOB STRONG, orchestra leader (himself)
HIS ORCHESTRA
Uncle Walter's Dog House (R) (Family situation comedy)

Uncle Walter's Dog House. See: Uncle Walter

UNCLE WILL. See: Kent, Fred

Uncovered. See: Saber, Mark

Under Arrest. See: Drake, Captain

Undercover, Miami. See: Thompson, Jeff

Underdog. See: Underdog

UNDERDOG, cartoon character
Underdog (TV) (Cartoon)

Undersea World of Jacques Cousteau, The. See: Cousteau, Jacques

UNDERTAKER, THE FRIENDLY. See: Riley, Chester A.

UNDERWOOD, EVE. See: Marlin, Mary

UNGAR, FELIX, photographer, divorced; prissy and overly neat
OSCAR MADISON, his roommate, sports writer; divorced; "a slob"
SPEED
ROY
VINNIE, poker playing friends of Ungar and Madison
MURRAY, policeman, also poker playing friend of Ungar and Madison
GLORIA, Ungar's ex-wife
BLANCHE, Madison's ex-wife
GWENN

CECILY
NANCY
MIRIAM, girl friends of Ungar and Madison
The Odd Couple (TV) (Situation comedy)

Union Pacific. See: McClelland, Bart

United States Steel Hour, The. See: Langner, Lawrence

United States Treasury, O'Hara. See: O'Hara, James

Universal Rhythm. See: Crumit, Frank (4)

Unknown, Diagnosis. See: Coffee, Dr. Daniel

Unsolved Mysteries, Dr. Kenrad's. See: Kenrad, Dr.

UNTERMEYER, CHIEF GEORGE. See: August, Dan

UNTERMEYER, LOUIS. See: Daly, John (3)

Untouchables, The. See: Winchell, Walter (2)

UPDYKE, HUBERT. See: Young, Alan

UPPINGTON, MRS. See: McGee, Fibber

UPTON, MICHAEL
DICK STUART-CLARK
DUNCAN WARING, students at St. Swithin's Medical College
PROFESSOR LOFTUS, faculty member of the College
DEAN of the College
Doctor in the House (TV) (Comedy)

URCHIN, BILLY. See: Cord

URSULA WINTHROP. See: Ames, Peter

UTTAL, FRED (1)
WENDY BARRY
LEN LEHR, quizmasters of the

program (themselves)
MANY CONTESTANTS
Detect and Collect (R) (Quiz)

UTTAL, FRED (2), quizmaster of
the program (himself)
MANY CONTESTANTS
Melody Puzzles (R) (Quiz)

UTTAL, FRED. See also:
Hulick, Wilbur Budd

Vagabond. See: Burrud, Bill (4)

VAGUE, VERA. See:
Bergen, Edgar (2)
Durante, Jimmy
Holloway, Harrison
Hope, Bob (2)

VAIL, LINCOLN, law enforcement
officer in southern Florida
marshes
The Everglades (TV) (Crime)

VAL. See: Doonican, Val

VAL DARTIE. See: Forsyte,
Soames

Val Doonican. See: Doonican,
Val

VAL MARLOWE. See: Stewart,
Jan

VALE, JERRY. See: Miller,
Mitch

VALENTE, CATERINA. See:
DeLuise, Dom (2)

VALENTINE. See: Farrow,
Valentine

VALENTINE, JIMMY, notorious
safe-cracker
Alias Jimmy Valentine (R)
(Adventure)

VALENTINE, LEW. See:
I. Q., Dr.
I. Q. Jr., Dr.

VALENTINE, LEWIS J. See:
Lord, Phillips H.

VALENTINE, LISA. See: Trent,
Helen

VALENTINE, RUBY, operator of
metropolitan beauty shop
The Story of Ruby Valentine (R)
(Serial drama) (also known as
Ruby Valentine) (R)

Valentine's Day. See: Farrow,
Valentine

VALERA, MIKE. See: Slattery,
Jim

VALERIE. See:
Cavanaugh, Father Samuel
Patrick
Josie
Lockridge, Barry

VALERIE WELLES. See: Cum-
mings, Brenda

Valiant Lady. See: Hargrave-
Scott, Joan

VALIANT LADY, THE. See:
Hargrave-Scott, Joan

VALLEE, RUDY (1), host of the
program (himself)
MANY CELEBRITY GUESTS
YOUNG PROFESSIONAL ENTER-
TAINERS
On Broadway Tonight (TV)
(Music/variety)

VALLEE, RUDY (2), orchestra
leader and singer; host of the
program (himself)
HIS CONNECTICUT YANKEES
ORCHESTRA
CONCHITA SHAPIRO, comedienne
MANY GUEST STARS
The Rudy Vallee Show (R) (Varie-
ty) (also known as The Fleisch-
mann's Hour and The Sealtest
Hour) (R)

VALLEE, RUDY (3), orchestra
leader and singer; host of the
program (himself)
HIS CONNECTICUT YANKEES
ORCHESTRA
MANY GUEST STARS
Vallee Varieties (R) (Variety)

VALLEE, RUDY. See also:
Whiteman, Paul

Vallee Varieties. See: Vallee,
Rudy (3)

Valley, The Big. See: Barkley,
Victoria

Valley, U.S. A., Green. See:
Ortega, Santos

Valley, Welcome. See: Guest,
Edgar A. (2)

Valleys, Beyond These. See: Lane,
Rebecca

VALLI, JUNE. See: Williams,
Andy (1)

VALMAR, ARDALA. See:
Rogers, Buck

VAN. See:
Heflin, Van
Johnson, Van
Von

VAN ALEXANDER. See: Arthur,
Jack (1)

VAN AND SCHENCK. See:
Drew, John

VAN ATWATER, MRS. See:
Canova, Judy

VAN, BILLY. See:
Berry, Ken
Stevens, Ray

VAN BUREN, ABIGAIL, newspaper
columnist; hostess of the program (herself)
Dear Abbie (R) (Personal advice)

VAN CLEVE, MRS. See: Peters,
Bill

VAN DAMME QUINTET, THE ART.
See: Garroway, Dave (3)

VAN DERBUR, MARILYN. See:
Funt, Allen (1)
Myerson, Bess

VAN DOREN, CHARLES. See:
Barry, Jack (9)

VAN DORN, DORIA. See: Jordan,
Joyce

VAN DUZEE, HAROLD. See:
Roxy

VAN DYKE, DICK (1), moderator
of the program (himself)
MIKE NICHOLS
ELAINE MAY
DOROTHY LOUDON, panelists of
the program (themselves)
GUEST PANELISTS

Laugh Line (TV) (Comedy panel)

VAN DYKE, DICK (2), host of the
program (himself)
BETTY ANDREWS
DOTTY MACK, models (them-
selves)
THREE MOTHERS, guests/con-
testants
Mother's Day (TV) (Game)

VAN DYKE TIERS. See: Kelly,
Joe (2)

VAN DYNE, CHESTER. See:
Jones, Lorenzo

VAN EUER, JUDY. See: Hutton,
Ina Ray

VAN GLEASON III, REGINALD.
See: Gleason, Jackie (1) (2)

VAN GOPHER, VINCENT. See:
Dawg, Deputy

VAN, GUS. See: Arnold, Gene

VAN HORN CHORAL GROUP,
RANDY. See: Cole, Nat "King"

VAN JOHNSON. See:
Crosby, Bing (2)
Johnson, Van

Van Johnson Show, The. See:
Johnson, Van

VAN LOWEEN, SYBIL. See:
Gregory, Glenn Garth

VAN ORPINGTON, JACK. See:
Kelly, Kitty

VAN PATTEN, DICKIE. See:
Barrymore, Ethel

VAN PORTER, HENRY. See:
Jones, Amos

VAN ROON, CLAIRE. See:
O'Farrell, Packy

VAN ROOTEN, LUIS. See:
Johnson, Raymond Edward (1)
Welles, Orson (2)

VAN SCHYLER, PERCY. See:

Kaltenmeyer, Professor August,
D. U. N.

VAN STEEDEN, PETER. See:
Allen, Fred
McGarry, Dan

VAN VLIET. See: Burton, Terry

VAN VOORHIS, WESTBROOK (1),
narrator of the program (himself)
Crusade in Europe (TV) (Documentary series)

VAN VOORHIS, WESTBROOK (2),
narrator of the program (himself)
MANY ACTORS AND ACTRESSES
Panic! (TV) (Suspense drama)
(later called No Warning!) (TV)

VAN VOORHIS, WESTBROOK. See
also: Husing, Ted

VANCE, CONNIE, widow
BUDDY WATSON, her son
KENT DAVIS
AUNT MINTA OWENS, charac-
ters appearing in the drama
My Son and I (R) (Serial drama)

VANCE, MARY ROSE SPENCER.
See: Drake, Betty

VANCE, PHILO, detective and man-
about-town
MARKHAM, district attorney
SERGEANT ERNEST HEATH,
police officer
Philo Vance (R) (Detective drama)

VANDEVEER, STEAMBOAT WILLIE.
See: Wade, Sandy

VANDERVENTER, BOBBY. See:
Slater, Bill (2)

VANDERVENTER, FRED. See:
Slater, Bill (2)

VANE, ALBERT. See: Novak,
John

VANESSA. See: Sterling, Vanessa
Dale

VANESSA BROWN. See: Kelly,
Joe (2)

VANESSA SMITH. See: Croft,
Jonathan

VANESSI, PETE. See: Myrt

VANGIE. See: Carr, Alison

VANOCUR, SANDER, newscaster;
host of the program (himself)
First Tuesday (TV) (News magazine) (later called Chronolog)
(TV) and Fourth Friday (TV)

Varieties, Vallee. See: Vallee,
Rudy (3)

Variety Program, The Little Betsy
Ross Girl. See: Loveridge,
Marion

Variety Show, The College. See:
Godfrey, Arthur (3)

VARNER, WILL, ruthless dictator
of Frenchman's Bend, southern
town
CLARA, his daughter
BEN QUICK, drifter, challenges
Varner's power
HARVE ANDERS
DUANE GALLOWAY
LUCAS TANEY
MINNIE
AGNES, residents of Frenchman's
Bend
The Long, Hot Summer (TV)
(Drama)

Vass Family, The. See: Vass,
Fran

VASS, FRAN
LOUISE "WEEZY" VASS
VIRGINIA "JITCHY" VASS
EMILY VASS
SALLY VASS, featured on the
program (themselves)
The Vass Family (R) (Variety)

VASSEY, KIN. See: Rogers, Kenny

VAUGHN, BERYL. See:
Elders, Harry
Soule, Olan (2)

VAUGHN MONROE. See:
Basie, Count
Monroe, Vaughn
Whiteman, Paul

VEE PADWA. See: Horwitz, Hans

VEGA, DON DIEGO, Spanish noble-
man; fop by day, masked rider
at night under the name of Zorro
HIS FATHER, Spanish nobleman
CAPTAIN MONASTARIO, com-
mander of Spanish fort in old
California; Zorro's enemy
SERGEANT GARCIA, Spanish
soldier
BERNARDO, Zorro's deaf mute
servant
Zorro (TV) (Adventure)

VELIE, SERGEANT. See: Queen,
Ellery

VELMA. See: Scooby Doo

VELVET. See: Brown, Velvet

Velvet, National. See: Brown,
Velvet

VENABLE, MARK. See: Randolph,
Alice

VENTO, MRS. See: Sterling,
Vanessa Dale

VENTO, TONY. See: Sterling,
Vanessa Dale

Venture, Bold. See: Shannon,
Slate

VENUTA, BENAY. See: Archie

VENUTI, JOE. See:
Archie
Crosby, Bing (3)

VERA. See: Wayne, Ruth Evans

VERA JOHNSON. See: Dallas,
Stella

VERA VAGUE. See:
Bergen, Edgar (2)
Durante, Jimmy
Holloway, Harrison
Hope, Bob (2)

Verdict Is Yours, The. See:
McKay, Jim (2)

VERE, BILLIE DE. See: Myrt

VERE-DE-VERE, LADY. See:
McGee, Fibber

VERGIL. See: Virgil

VERICK, BARNEY. See:
Cavanaugh, Father Samuel
Patrick

VERLYE MILLS. See: Ross,
Lanny

VERMILYEA, HAROLD. See:
Soule, Olan (1)

VERN. See:
Albright, Margie
Verne

VERN HODGES. See: Macauley,
Wes

VERNA. See: Kincaid, Chet

VERNA FELTON. See: Bolger,
Ray

VERNA ROBERTS. See: Brent,
Dr. Jim

VERNACK, NORMA. See: Keene,
Kitty

VERNAY, PIERRE (The Stranger)
The Song of a Stranger (R)
(Adventure)

VERNE. See also: Vern

VERNE GAGNE. See: James,
Dennis (4)

VERNE, LEE AND MARY TRIO,
THE. See: Kelly, Joe (1)

VERNE SANDERS. See: Baines,
Scattergood

VERNON DUTELL. See: Nona

VERNON, JACK. See: O'Neill,
Mrs.

VERONICA FERRAL. See:
Malone, Dr. Jerry

VERONICA LODGE. See: Andrews,
Archie

VERRILL, VIRGINIA. See: Henry,
Captain

Very Good Year, It Was a. See:
Torme, Mel

VES. See also: Wes

VES PAINTER. See: Burke,
Stoney

Vespers, National. See: Fosdick,
Rev. Harry Emerson

VI. See:
Joe (3)
McNamara, Susie

VI WATERS. See: Noble, Mary

VIC. See:
Ames, Joe
Cane, Vic
Damone, Vic (1) (2)
Gook, Vic

Vic and Sade. See: Gook, Vic

VIC CORELLI. See: Ames, Peter

Vic Damone. See: Damone, Vic
(2)

VIC LAMONT. See: Karr, Mike

VIC MANION. See: Jordan, Joyce

VIC SCHOEN. See:
King, Dave (2)
Page, Patti (1) (2)

VICKI. See also:
Vickie
Vicky
Vikki

VICKI HATHAWAY. See: Prescott, Kate Hathaway

VICKI LAWRENCE. See: Burnett,
Carol

VICKIE. See:
Angel, Gus
Massey, Christine
Vicki
Vicky
Vikki

VICKY. See:
Hall, Dr. William Todhunter
Vicki
Vickie
Vikki

VICTOR. See:
Borge, Victor
Dugan, Jimmie
Palmieri, Victor
Sebastian, Victor

VICTOR BORGE. See:
Borge, Victor
Crosby, Bing (3)

Victor Borge Show, The. See:
Borge, Victor

VICTOR MAIDSTONE. See: Sunday

VICTOR YOUNG. See: Jolson, Al

VICTORIA. See:
Barkley, Victoria
Cannon, John

VICTORIA LORD RILEY. See:
Walleck, Meredith

VICTORIA LORING. See: Brown,
Ellen

VICTORIA WINTERS. See: Collins,
Barnabas

Victory at Sea. See: Graves,
Leonard

Victory Volunteers. See: Fadiman, Clifton (3)

VIDEO, CAPTAIN, crime fighter;
"guardian of the safety of the
world"
VIDEO RANGER, his associate
Captain Video (TV) (Crime
fighting)

Video Theater. See: Mason,
James

Video Theater, Lux. See: Mac-
Rae, Gordon (1)

Video Village. See: Narz, Jack
(5)

Video Village, Jr. See: Hall,
  Monty (3)

VIDO McCREA, DR. See: Davis,
  Dr. Althea

Vienna, Assignment. See: Webster, Jake

View, From a Bird's Eye. See:
  Grover, Millie

Vikings, Tales of the. See: Leif

VIKKI. See:
  Hoyt, Vikki Adams
  Vicki
  Vickie
  Vicky

VIKKI CARR. See: Davidson,
  John (1)

Village, Snow. See: Dickey, Dan'l

Village Store. See: Owner

Village Store, At the. See: Owner

Village Store, Sealtest. See:
  Owner

Village, Video. See: Narz, Jack
  (5)

Village, Video, Jr. See: Hall,
  Monty (3)

VIN SCULLY. See:
  McKay, Jim (1)
  Scully, Vin

VINCE. See: Walleck, Meredith

VINCE CAVELLI, SERGEANT.
  See: Adams, Lieut. Price

VINCE DUCKLES. See: Sharp,
  Hal

VINCE KENNEDY. See: Randolph,
  Ellen

VINCENT. See:
  Campanelli, Dr. Vincent
  First Nighter, Mr.
  Lopez, Vincent
  Price, Vincent

VINCENT, DAVID, architect, "engaged in battle to save the world
  from alien beings from another
  galaxy he alone recognized"
  The Invaders (TV) (Drama)

Vincent Lopez. See: Lopez,
  Vincent

VINCENT LOPEZ. See:
  Lopez, Vincent
  Whiteman, Paul

VINCENT MARKHAM, DR. See:
  Peyton, Martin

VINCENT PELLETIER. See:
  Wordmaster, The

VINCENT PRICE. See:
  Price, Vincent
  Story, Ralph

VINCENT VAN GOPHER. See:
  Dawg, Deputy

VINCENTE, DR. TONY. See:
  Tate, Joanne

VINDUC, JOSH. See: Sterling,
  Vanessa Dale

VINNIE. See:
  Cameron, Barry
  Day, Clarence
  Ungar, Felix

VINT. See: Bonner, Vint

VINTON, BOBBY. See: Jones,
  Jack

VINTOR, BOBBY. See: Griffin,
  Merv (3)

VIOLA SCHMIDT. See: Spitalny,
  Phil

VIOLET FLOWER. See: Buddy

VIOLET SHANE. See: Chandler,
  Faith

VIOLIN TEACHER. See: Benny,
  Jack

VIOLINS ORCHESTRA, THE
  GYPSY. See: Ross, David (1)

VIRGIL. See: McHale, Lieut.
Commander Quinton

VIRGIL STONER, LIEUT. COM-
MANDER. See: O'Toole, Ensign

VIRGINIA. See:
Carter, James
Graham, Virginia (1) (2)
Klose, Woody

VIRGINIA CRAIG. See: Webster,
Martha

VIRGINIA CURTIS. See: Caesar,
Sid (2)

VIRGINIA GIBSON. See:
Buxton, Frank
Lanson, Snooky

VIRGINIA GILMORE. See:
Brynner, Yul

Virginia Graham Show, The. See:
Graham, Virginia (2)

VIRGINIA GREGG. See: Soule,
Olan (4)

VIRGINIA HARDESTY. See:
Rogers, Patricia

VIRGINIA "JITCHY" VASS. See:
Vass, Fran

VIRGINIA LANSING. See: Noble,
Mary

VIRGINIA MARSHALL. See:
Larimore, Marilyn

VIRGINIA MORLEY. See: Waring,
Fred (1)

VIRGINIA O'BRIEN. See: Marx,
Groucho (1)

VIRGINIA REES. See: Gibbs,
Georgia (2)

VIRGINIA RODES. See: Kelly,
Joe (2)

VIRGINIA VERRILL. See:
Henry, Captain

VIRGINIAN, THE

TRAMPAS
CLAY GRAINGER
DAVID SUTTON, cowboys and
ranch hands at Shiloh Ranch
JUDGE HENRY GARTH, jurist
BETSEY GARTH, daughter of
Judge Garth
MOLLY WOOD, newspaper pub-
lisher
STEVE, friend of the Virginian
The Virginian (TV) (Western)
(later called The Men From
Shiloh) (TV)

Virginian, The. See:
MacKenzie, Colonel Alan
Parmalee, Ranger Captain
Virginian, The

Vise, The. See: Randell, Ron

VITALE, MAMA. See: Endicott,
Professor Mike

VIV. See: Carmichael, Lucy

VIVIAN, "The Coca-Cola Girl"
The Musical Comedy Hour (R)
(Music/comedy)

VIVIAN BLAINE. See: Lee,
Pinky (2)

VIVIAN BLOCK. See: Halop,
Billy

VIVIAN GRAHAM. See: Sunday

VIVIEN DELLA CHIESA. See:
Munn, Frank (1)

VIVIENNE NEARING. See: Barry,
Jack (9)

VODKA. See: McGee, Fibber

Voice of Broadway, The. See:
Kilgallen, Dorothy (2)

Voice of Experience, The. See:
Voice of Experience, The

VOICE OF EXPERIENCE, THE,
portrayed by Dr. Marion Sayle
Taylor; giver of advice
The Voice of Experience (R)
(Advice)

Voice of Firestone, The. See:
    Barlow, Howard

VOICE OF ROMANCE, THE, per-
    sonification
    Romance (R) (Serial drama)

VOICE OF SUPERSTITION, THE,
    personification, portrayed by
    Ralph Bell
    Superstition (R) (Fantasy/drama)

VOICES OF WALTER SCHUMANN,
    THE. See: Ford, Tennessee
    Ernie (2)

VOICES, THE JERRY MANN. See:
    Thomas, Thomas L.

VOLTAIRE PERKINS. See: Judge
    (1)

Volunteers, Victory. See: Fadi-
    man, Clifton (3)

VON. See also: Van

VON HALLBERG, GENE
    SVEN VON HALLBERG, his
    brother; both composers and
    performers of Near East music
    (themselves)
    Echoes of the Orient (R) (Music)

VON HUMPERDOO, LUDWIG. See:
    Junior

VON LUCKNER, COUNT FELIX,
    German naval officer; commander
    of the raider "Seeadler" in
    World War I
    Count Von Luckner's Adventures
    (R) (Adventure)

VON NARDROFF, ELFRIDA. See:
    Barry, Jack (9)

VON ZELL, HARRY. See:
    Burns, George (1)
    Husing, Ted
    Pitcher, The

VOODINI, THE GREAT. See:
    Nye, Louis

VOORHEES, DONALD. See:
    Bell, Alexander Graham
    Gibson, Dot

Melton, James (1)
Welles, Orson (2)

VOUGHT, LIEUT. See: Welles,
    Orson (3)

Vox Pop. See: Johnson, Parks

Voyage to the Bottom of the Sea.
    See: Nelson, Admiral Harri-
    man

W. C. FIELDS. See: Ameche, Don
(1)

W. C. GREEN. See: Rogers,
Patricia

WABASH CANNONBALL, THE.
See: Jones, Casey

Wackiest Ship in the Army, The.
See: Butcher, Major Simon

WADCLIFFE, WAMOND. See:
Harris, Phil

WADDINGTON, MRS. See:
Nelson, Ozzie

WADDINGTON, ROGER. See:
Nelson, Ozzie

WADE COLLINS, DR. See: Tate,
Joanne

WADE, DAVID, author and gourmet cook; host of the program
(himself)
Dining With David Wade (TV)
(Cookery)

WADE DOUGLAS. See: Dane,
Prudence

WADE, MARCIE. See: Walleck,
Meredith

WADE, SANDY
ZACK MALLOY, pilots and
proprietors of one-plane airline
in the Spice Islands
STEAMBOAT WILLIE VANDEVEER,
their firm's business manager
The Islanders (TV) (Adventure)

WADSWORTH, MRS. S. KENT.
See: Solomon, David

WAGGEDORN. See: Baker, Julia

WAGGEDORN, EARL. See: Baker,
Julia

WAGGEDORN, MARIE. See: Baker,
Julia

WAGGONER. See also:
Wagner
Wagoner

WAGGONER, LYLE, host of the
program (himself)
MANY CONTESTANTS
It's Your Bet (TV) (Game)

WAGGONER, LYLE. See also:
Burnett, Carol

WAGNER. See also:
Waggoner
Wagoner

WAGNER, BOB. See: Sharp, Hal

WAGNER, GLENN. See: Sher-
wood, Grace

WAGNER, RUBY. See: Benny,
Jack

Wagon, Horace Heidt's Show. See:
Heidt, Horace (1)

WAGON MASTERS, THE. See:
Wagoner, Porter

Wagon Train. See: Adams,
Major Seth

WAGONER. See also:
Waggoner
Wagner

WAGONER, PORTER, guitarist and
singer; star of the program
(himself)
DOLLY PARTON
SPECK RHODES
DON HAUSER, featured singers
on the program (themselves)
THE WAGON MASTERS, orchestra
GUEST SINGERS
The Porter Wagoner Show (TV)
(Country music)

WAINWRIGHT, EVA. See: Murphy,
Peter

WAINWRIGHT, MARK. See:
Murphy, Peter

WAINWRIGHT, ROGER. See:
Murphy, Peter

WAITE BARBOUR, ANN. See:
Barbour, Henry Wilson

WAKE, LINDEN. See: Brent, Dr.
Jim

WAKEFIELD, CONSTANCE. See:
Nelson, Carolyn Kramer

WAKEFIELD, SUSAN. See: Nelson, Carolyn Kramer

WAKEFIELD, TED. See: Nelson,
Carolyn Kramer

WALDO. See:
Burns, George (1)
Everett, Professor

WALDO BINNEY. See: Riley,
Chester A.

WALDO BRIGGS. See: Wayne,
Ruth Evans

WALDON, DON. See: Lee, Jim

WALDON, MARY LEE. See:
Lee, Jim

WALES, WINDY. See: Benson,
Bobby

WALKER. See: Ames, Peter

WALKER, BILL. See: Nelson,
Carolyn Kramer

WALKER, E.J. See: Arden,
Jane

WALKER, EDDIE, American father
DOROTHY WALKER, his wife
LARRY WALKER, his son
PATTY WALKER, his teenage
daughter, living with the Finch
family
TOMMY FINCH, English father
SYBIL FINCH, Tommy's wife
NEVILLE FINCH, Tommy's son
HEATHER FINCH, Tommy's
teenage daughter, living with the
Walker family
Fair Exchange (TV) (Comedy)

WALKER, GEORGE. See: Farrell,
David

WALKER, MYRA. See: Harding,
Karen Adams

WALKER, SERGEANT. See:
Peyton, Martin

WALKING LETTERS. See: Cookie
Monster, The

WALL, LUCILLE. See: Hardy,
Dr. Steven

Wall Street Week. See: Rukeyser,
Louis

WALLACE BEERY. See: Jolson,
Al

WALLACE BINGHAMPTON, CAP-
TAIN. See: McHale, Lieut.
Commander Quinton

WALLACE, IRMA. See: Cum-
mings, Brenda

WALLACE, MIKE (1), interviewer
of the program (himself)
MANY PROMINENT INTERVIEW-
EES
Biography (TV) (Interviews with
prominent persons)

WALLACE, MIKE (2), interviewer
of the program (himself)
MANY PROMINENT INTERVIEW-
EES
Mike Wallace Interviews (TV)
(Interviews)

WALLACE, MIKE (3), interviewer
of the program (himself)
MANY INTERVIEWEES
P.M. (TV) (Interviews)

WALLACE, MIKE (4)
HARRY REASONER
MORLEY SAFER, newscasters,
hosts of the program (themselves)
60 Minutes (TV) (News magazine)

WALLACE, MIKE (5), moderator
of the program (himself)
CELESTE HOLM
SIR CEDRIC HARDWICKE
GENE KLAVAN, panelists (them-
selves)
MANY GUEST PARTICIPANTS
Who Pays? (TV) (Panel game)

WALLACE, MIKE. See also:
Barry, Jack (1)

WALLACE, PROFESSOR. See:
Mix, Tom

WALLACE WIMPLE. See: Mc-
Gee, Fibber

WALLECK, MEREDITH
VICTORIA LORD RILEY
NICKIE SMITH
MARCIE WADE
MR. LORD
JOE RILEY
DAVID SIEGEL
EILEEN MARGARET SIEGEL
STEVEN BURKE
EVERETT PALMER
JUDGE BALDWIN
DR. JOYCE BROTHERS (herself)
DR. JANICE CRAIG
DR. JAMES CRAIG
CARLA BENARI
KATE NOLAN
PRICE TRAINOR
BERT SKELLY
LARRY WALLECK
DICK CHANDLER
GEORGE STANLEY GIBSON
VINCE WALLECK
DANNY WALLECK
DR. MICHAEL
DR. POLK, characters appearing
in the drama
One Life to Live (TV) (Serial
drama)

WALLENSTEIN, ALFRED. See:
Barlow, Howard

WALLET, SKEEZIX, young man
NINA CLOCK, his girl friend
WUMPLE, his employer
IDAHO IDA, his friend
LING WEE, Chinese waiter
Gasoline Alley (R) (Drama)

WALLINGFORD, LELA. See: Dix,
Dorothy (1)

WALLINGFORD, ROXANNE. See:
Dix, Dorothy (1)

WALLY. See:
Ballew, Wally
Bruner, Wally (1) (2)
Butterworth, Wally
Christopher, Peter
Cleaver, Ward
Stevens, Joan

WALLY BRUNER. See:
Bruner, Wally (1) (2)
Daly, John (3)
Moore, Garry (5)

WALLY BUTTERWORTH. See:
Butterworth, Wally
Johnson, Parks

WALLY COX. See: Marshall,
Peter

WALLY MAHER. See: Roseleigh,
Jack

Wally's Workshop. See: Bruner,
Wally (2)

WALSH, BOB
DONAL LEACE, co-hosts of the
program (themselves)
MANY GUESTS
The Show (TV) (Variety)

WALSH, KNOBBY. See: Palooka,
Joe

WALT. See: Randolph, Walt

WALT, CAPTAIN, fireman
STRINGBEAN CRACHET, come-
dian
Hook 'n' Ladder Follies (R)
(Variety)

WALTER. See:
Abel, Walter
Andrews, Walter
Burnley, Walter
Compton, Walter
Coy, Walter
Cronkite, Walter (1) (2) (3) (4)
(5) (6)
Damrosch, Walter
Dodger, Willy
Findlay, Maude
Fitzgerald, Bridget Theresa
Mary Coleen
Hathaway, Elinor
Jones, Lorenzo
McGraw, Walter
Manning, Portia Blake
Nichols, Walter
Slezak, Walter
Uncle Walter
Winchell, Walter (1) (2) (3) (4)
(5)

WALTER C. KELLY   664

WALTER C. KELLY. See: Drew,
John

WALTER CARLIN. See: Dane,
Prudence

WALTER COURTLEIGH. See:
Dyke, Charity Amanda

Walter Cronkite Reporting. See:
Cronkite, Walter (5)

Walter Cronkite, The C. B. S.
Evening News With. See:
Cronkite, Walter (2)

WALTER CURTIN. See: Randolph,
Alice

WALTER DENTON. See: Brooks,
Connie

WALTER DRAKE. See: Carter,
Kathryn

WALTER JEROME. See: Gold-
berg, Molly

WALTER KIERNAN. See: Allen,
Frederick Lewis

WALTER O'KEEFE. See:
Compton, Walter
Crumit, Frank (1)
Shriner, Herb (3)

WALTER PAYNE. See: Perkins,
Ma

WALTER SCHUMANN, THE VOICES
OF. See: Ford, Tennessee
Ernie (2)

WALTER SLEZAK. See:
James, Dennis (3)
Slezak, Walter

WALTER TETLEY. See:
Cross, Milton (2)
Halop, Billy
Lescoulie, Jack (2)

WALTER TRAVIS. See: Garrison,
Spencer

WALTER, WILLIAM. See: Jordan,
Joyce

Walter Winchell. See: Winchell,
Walter (3)

Walter Winchell File, The. See:
Winchell, Walter (4)

Walter Winchell Show, The. See:
Winchell, Walter (5)

WALTERS, BARBARA, hostess of
the program (herself)
MANY INTERVIEWEES
Not For Women Only (TV)
(Interviews)

WALTERS, BARBARA. See also:
Downs, Hugh
Marshall, E. G.

Walter's Dog House, Uncle. See:
Uncle Walter

WALTERS, PAT. See: Barrett,
David

WALTERS, POLLY. See:
Andrews, Russ

WALTERS, WILLY. See: Collins,
Bing

WALTON, GARY. See: Tate,
Joanne

WALTON, GRANDPA, patriarch of
Blue Ridge Mountain family in the
1930s
GRANDMA WALTON, his wife
OLIVIA, mother of the family
JOHN, father of the family
JOHN-BOY
MARY ELLEN
JIM-BOB
ELIZABETH
JASON
BEN
ERIN, their seven children
The Waltons (TV) (Family drama)

WALTON, JANET. See: Tate,
Joanne

WALTON, ROGER. See: Jordan,
Joyce

Waltons, The. See: Walton,
Grandpa

Waltz Time. See: Munn, Frank
(2)

WAMOND. See also: Raymond

WAMOND WADCLIFFE. See:
Harris, Phil

WANDA BAILEY. See: Chidsey,
Jackie

WANDA WEREWULF. See:
Baker, Kenny

Want To Lead a Band?, So You
See: Kaye, Sammy (2)

Wanted. See:
Collins, Fred (2)
McGraw, Walter

Wanted- Dead or Alive. See:
Randall, Josh

War I, World. See: Ryan,
Robert (2)

War, The F.B.I. in Peace and.
See: Sheppard, F.B.I. Field
Agent

War, This Is. See: March,
Frederic

Warbling Banjoist, Red Godfrey, The.
See: Godfrey, Arthur (4)

WARBUCKS, OLIVER "DADDY."
See: Little Orphan Annie

WARD. See:
Cleaver, Ward
Fuller, Ward
Wilson, Ward

WARD ARCHER. See: Bernie, Ben

WARD, ARTHUR. See: Erskine,
Inspector Louis

WARD, CARL. See: Malone,
Dr. Jerry

WARD, DETECTIVE JEFF. See:
Haines, Lieut. Mike

WARD ELMOND. See: Noble,
Mary

WARD, HELEN. See: Archie

WARD, JESSIE. See: Aunt Mary

WARD, JOAN. See: Manning,
Portia Blake

WARD, JOHNNY. See: Allen,
Joan Houston

WARD, PALMER. See: Jostyn,
Jay (1)

WARD, PERRY, quizmaster of the
program (himself)
MANY CONTESTANTS
CHARLES DANT, orchestra
leader (himself)
HIS ORCHESTRA
Scramby Amby (R) (Quiz)

WARD SMITH, MRS. See: Trent,
Helen

WARD, TAMMY, "madcap heiress"
TERENCE, her twin brother,
"symmetrical square"
UNCLE SIMON, their skinflint
uncle
The Tammy Grimes Show (TV)
(Comedy)

WARD WILSON. See:
Cullen, Bill (5)
Weems, Ambrose J.
Wilson, Ward

WARING, DIANE. See: Bracken,
John

WARING, DUNCAN. See: Upton,
Michael

WARING, EVELYN, wife
ADAM WARING, her husband
ELLA HUNT
MR. HUNT
TEDDY HUNT
GRANDFATHER GRANT
PHINEAS T. GRANT
MRS. HEMPSTEAD
JOE BILLINGS
AUNT MATT
SHELLY MARTIN
FLORENCE WESTON
ED SPALDING
FRANK FLIPPIN
TIPPY

BROOKS, characters appearing in the drama
The Man I Married (R) (Serial drama)

WARING, FRED (1), orchestra leader and star of the program (himself)
STELLA AND THE FELLAS
THE LANE SISTERS
THE THREE GIRL FRIENDS
HONEY AND THE BEES
BABS AND HER BROTHERS
STUART CHURCHILL
JANE WILSON
GORDON GOODMAN
DONNA DAE
ROBERT SHAW
GORDON BERGER
JOANNE WHEATLEY
TOM WARING
JOHNNY "SCAT" DAVIS
MAC PERRON
KAY THOMPSON
LES PAUL
VIRGINIA MORLEY
LIVINGSTON GEARHART
LUMPY BRANNUM
THE McFARLAND TWINS
POLEY McCLINTOCK, musicians and entertainers featured on the program (themselves)
The Fred Waring Show (R) (Music)

WARING, FRED (2), orchestra leader and star of the program (himself)
HIS PENNSYLVANIANS ORCHES-TRA (Waring's Pennsylvanians)
MANY ENTERTAINERS
Pleasure Time (R) (Music)

WARING, FRED. See also: Como, Perry (1)

WARING, MIKE (The Falcon), de-tective-adventurer
NANCY
RENEE, his friends
The Falcon (R) (Mystery/adven-ture)

WARING, TOM. See: Waring, Fred (1)

WARING'S PENNSYLVANIANS. See: Waring, Fred (2)

WARNER. See also: Werner

WARNER, ALICE AMES. See: Rogers, Patricia

WARNER, DR. JOE. See: Bauer, Bertha

WARNER, GERTRUDE. See: Beck, Jackson
Gregory, Helen

WARNER, LEO. See: Rogers, Patricia

WARNER, MRS. See: McKeever, Cadet Gary

WARNER, SAMMY. See: Farrell, David

WARNICK SINGERS, THE CLAY. See: Crosby, Bob (1)

Warning, No. See: Van Voorhis, Westbrook (2)

WARNOW, MARK. See: Ross, Lanny

WARREN. See:
Hull, Warren (1) (2) (3)
Taylor, Andy

WARREN BERLINGER. See: Kelly, Gene

WARREN DOUGLAS, DR. See: Rogers, Patricia

WARREN HULL. See:
Fields, Arthur
Henry, Captain
Hull, Warren (1) (2) (3)
Johnson, Parks

WARREN, LEONARD. See: Roxy

WARREN, LUTHER. See: Farrell, David

WARREN, MRS. See: Wayne, Ruth Evans

WARREN PARKER. See: Jesus

WARREN, WENDY, newspaper-woman

NEWSCASTER
MARK DOUGLAS
BILL FLOOD, announcer
GIL KENDAL
SAM WARREN
CHARLES LANG
ADELE LANG
NONA MARSH
AUNT DORRIE
DON SMITH, characters appear-
ing in the drama
Wendy Warren (R) (Serial drama)
(also known as Wendy Warren and
the News) (R)

WARSHAW, MEL. See: Dickens,
Harry

WARSHAW, MR. See: Bauer,
Bertha

WASH. See: Mix, Tom

WASHBURN, WILLIAM, Negro
district attorney
SAM DANFORTH, White deputy
police chief
The Bold Ones (The Protectors)
(TV) (Crime drama)

WASHINGTON. See: Susan (1)

WASHINGTON JONES. See:
Dugan, Jimmie

Washington, Mr. Smith Goes to.
See: Smith, Eugene

Washington Week in Review. See:
MacNeil, Robert

WATANABE, FRANK. See: Holloway, Harrison

Watch Mr. Wizard. See: Wizard,
Mr.

Watch the Fords Go By. See:
Blurt, Elmer

Waterfront. See: Herrick, Cap'n
John

WATERS, ETHEL, Negro singer
and actress, star of the program
(herself)
MANY ENTERTAINERS

The Borden Show (TV) (Variety)

WATERS, JIM, master of cere-
monies of the program (himself)
The Court of Missing Heirs (R)
(Human interest)

WATERS, VI. See: Noble, Mary

WATSON, BUDDY. See: Vance,
Connie

WATSON, DR. JOHN. See:
Holmes, Sherlock

WATSON, ERIC. See: Manning,
Portia Blake

WATSON, JUDGE. See: Burton,
Terry

WATSON, SILLY. See: McGee,
Fibber

WATSON, STEVE. See: Berry,
Ken

WATTS, ABRAHAM LINCOLN.
See: Peters, Bill

WAVERLY, ALEXANDER. See:
Dancer, April
Solo, Napoleon

WAYNE. See: Hudson, Dr.
Wayne

Wayne and Schuster. See: Wayne,
Johnny (1)

Wayne and Schuster Show, The.
See: Wayne, Johnny (2)

WAYNE, BEA. See:
Edwards, Ralph (1)
Ross, Lanny

WAYNE, DON. See: Berry, Ken

WAYNE GARDNER. See: Brown,
Ellen

WAYNE GRUBB. See: Barbour,
Henry Wilson

WAYNE HOWELL. See: Lester,
Jerry

WAYNE, JOHN, "he-man" type hero
(himself)
Three Sheets to the Wind (R)
(Adventure)

WAYNE, JOHNNY (1)
FRANK SCHUSTER, comedians;
narrators and commentators of
the program (themselves)
CLIPS OF OLD MOTION PIC-
TURES
Wayne and Schuster (TV) (Old
motion pictures)

WAYNE, JOHNNY (2)
FRANK SCHUSTER, comedians
featured on the program (them-
selves)
GEORGIA DAY, featured vocalist
(herself)
MANY GUEST STARS
The Wayne and Schuster Show (R)
(Comedy/variety)

WAYNE KING. See: Lady Esther

WAYNE, MARSHAL MATT, Cali-
fornia law enforcement officer
The Californians (TV) (Historical
Western drama)

WAYNE, MILLIONAIRE BRUCE.
See:
Batman
Kent, Clark

WAYNE, RUTH. See: West,
Michael

WAYNE, RUTH EVANS (The Big
Sister)
SUE EVANS MILLER, her sister
DR. JOHN WAYNE, physician
DR. DUNCAN CARVELL, physician
MRS. CARVELL
ERNEST BANNING
ELSA BANNING
ADDIE PRICE
GINNY PRICE
HOPE MELTON EVANS
DR. MARLOWE, physician
DR. SEABROOK, physician
DAVID BREWSTER
FRANK WAYNE
PAUL GEROND
NURSE BURTON
LOLA MITCHELL
LITTLE NED "NEDDIE" EVANS

HARRIET DURANT
DORIS MONET
WALDO BRIGGS
DR. REED BANNISTER, physician
MARY TYLER
MARGO KIRKWOOD
RICHARD WAYNE
JERRY MILLER
PETE STONE
WELLINGTON DURANT
ERIC RAMSEY
ASA GRIFFIN
CHARLES DANIELS
MICHAEL WEST
VERA WAYNE
CORNELIUS PORTER
RICKI LENYA
MRS. WARREN
RODGER ALLEN
PETE KIRKWOOD
DIANE CARVELL RAMSEY
EUNICE
SAMSON, characters appearing in
the drama
Big Sister (R) (Serial drama)

We Are Four. See: Webster,
Nancy

We Love and Learn. See: Peters,
Bill

We, The Abbotts. See: Abbott,
John

We, The People. See: Heatter,
Gabriel

WEARYBOTTOM, MRS. See:
McGee, Fibber

Weather, Weekend. See: Barnes,
Gordon

WEATHERBEE, HIRAM. See:
Trent, Helen

WEATHERBY, LAURA. See:
Mallory, Lieut. Col. Spencer

WEAVER, CHARLEY, master of
ceremonies of the program (him-
self)
CELEBRITY HOBBYISTS
GUEST HOBBYISTS
Hobby Lobby (TV) (Hobbies) (also
known as The Charley Weaver
Show) (TV)

WEAVER, CHARLEY. See also:
Marshall, Peter
Rogers, Roy
Winters, Jonathan

WEAVER, DENNIS. See: Marshall,
E. G.

WEAVER, DOODLES. See: Jones,
Spike (1)

WEBB. See: Pierce, Webb

WEBB, DOROTHY WALLACE. See:
Regan, Terry

WEBB, JACK, narrator and host
of the program (himself)
MANY ACTORS AND ACTRESSES
G. E. True (TV) (Dramatizations
of stories from "True" Magazine)

WEBB, SCOTSON. See: Rogers,
Patricia

WEBB SUTHERLAND. See:
Davis, Dr. Althea

WEBBER, CHRIS. See: Peyton,
Martin

WEBBER, LEE. See: Peyton,
Martin

WEBBER, SANDY. See: Peyton,
Martin

WEBER AND FIELDS. See:
Drew, John

WEBER, LAURA, guitarist and
teacher, hostess of the program
(herself)
Folk Guitar (TV) (Music education)
(also known as Folk Guitar Plus)
(TV)

WEBLEY. See:
Edwards, Webley
Welby

WEBSTER. See: Lime, Harry

WEBSTER, CHARLES. See:
Roberts, Ken

WEBSTER, DR. ALAN. See:

Jordan, Joyce

WEBSTER, DR. THOMAS. See:
Jordan, Joyce

WEBSTER, EUNICE. See: Tate,
Joanne

WEBSTER, JAKE, owner of bar in
Vienna; investigator for U. S.
Intelligence
MAJOR BARNEY CALDWELL,
U. S. Intelligence officer
Assignment: Vienna (The Men)
(TV) (Crime adventure)

WEBSTER, JERRY, widower; former
Las Vegas comic, now farmer
SANDY WEBSTER, his son
SUSANNAH KRAMER, divorcee;
farmer
TRACY KRAMER, Susannah's
daughter
Accidental Family (TV) (Situa-
tion comedy)

WEBSTER, LINDA. See: Winters,
Jack

WEBSTER, MARTHA
DICK YOUNG
KAY SMITH
LUCY CRAIG
RICHARD CRAIG
VIRGINIA CRAIG
WINFIELD CRAIG
ALVIN CRAIG
PEGGY SMITHGIRL
DOLORES KING
JIM CARROLL
AUNT ETHEL
DON CAVANAUGH
MRS. RILEY
WILBUR, characters appearing in
the drama
Life Begins (R) (Serial drama)
(later known as Martha Webster)
(R)

WEBSTER, NANCY
LYDIA WEBSTER
TONY WEBSTER
CARL MARITZ
ARTHUR BLAINE
PAT
PRISCILLA, characters appearing
in the drama
We Are Four (R) (Serial drama)

Webster Says, Noah. See: Mac-
Quarrie, Haven (2)

WEBSTER, TERRY. See: Ryker,
Lieut. Eddie

Websters, Those. See: Green,
Billy

WEDLOE, TOM, game warden
MARK, his son
ELLEN, his wife
GENTLE BEN, his pet bear
BOOMHAUER, rancher
Gentle Ben (TV) (Animal/ad-
venture)

WEDNESDAY. See: Addams,
Gomez

WEE, LING. See: Wallet, Skeezix

WEEDE, ROBERT. See: Froman,
Jane (2)

Week in Review, Washington.
See: MacNeil, Robert

Week That Was, That Was the.
See: Ames, Nancy

Week, This. See: Moyers, Bill

Week, Wall Street. See: Rukeyser,
Louis

Weekend Weather. See: Barnes,
Gordon

WEEKS, AL. See: Hardy, Dr.
Steven

WEEKS, ANSON. See:
Medbury, John P.
Winchell, Walter (1)

WEEMS, AMBROSE J., host of the
program, portrayed by Raymond
Knight
MRS. GEORGE T. PENNY-
FEATHER, homemaker, charac-
ter portrayed by Adelina Thoma-
son
JACK ARTHUR
MARY McCOY
SALLIE BELLE COX
MARY HOPPLE
CARL MATTHEWS

WARD WILSON, singers and
entertainers appearing on the
program (themselves)
ROBERT ARMBRUSTER, orchestra leader (himself)
HIS ORCHESTRA
The Cuckoo Hour (R) (Comedy)

WEEMS, TED. See:
Benny, Jack
Hildegarde (1)
Whiteman, Paul

WEEP, WILLIE THE. See: Wilson, Steve

"WEEZY." See also: Wheezy

"WEEZY" VASS, LOUISE. See:
Vass, Fran

WEHUNT, CEDRIC. See: Edwards,
Lum

WEIGAND, BILL. See: North,
Jerry

WEIL, BERNIE. See: Sharp, Hal

WEINRIB, LEN. See: Jones,
Spike (2)

WEIRD, DR., character portrayed
by Maurice Tarplin
MANY ACTORS AND ACTRESSES
The Strange Dr. Weird (R) (Suspense drama)

WEIRDOS, THE WILLIAMS. See:
Williams, Andy (2)

WEISS, COACH. See: Hank

WEISSLEDER, WOLFGANG. See:
Barry, Jack (9)

WEISSOUL. See: Armstrong, Jack

WEIST, DWIGHT. See: Heatter,
Gabriel

WEIXLER, RICHARD. See:
Kelly, Joe (2)

WELBY. See also: Webley

WELBY, DR. MARCUS, physician;
general practitioner

DR. STEVEN KILEY, physician;
G. P. ; his associate
MYRA SHERWOOD, "the lady in
Welby's life"
CONSUELO LOPEZ, office nurse
for Welby and Kiley
Marcus Welby, M. D. (TV) (Medi-
cal drama)

WELBY, KYRON. See: Kelly,
Kitty

WELBY, MR. See: Kelly, Kitty

WELBY, MRS. See: Kelly, Kitty

WELCH, COLONEL FRANCIS. See:
Barton, Bud

WELCH, FRANCIS, JR. See:
Barton, Bud

WELCH, JOSEPH N. , host of the
program (himself)
MANY ACTORS AND ACTRESSES
The Dow Hour of Great Mysteries
(TV) (Suspense drama)

WELCOME. See: Lewis, Welcome

Welcome to It, My World and.
See: Monroe, John

Welcome, Traveler. See: Bartlett,
Tommy

Welcome Valley. See: Guest,
Edgar A. (2)

WELDON, JOAN. See: Palmer,
Byron

WELK, LAWRENCE, orchestra
leader and accordionist; host of
the program (himself)
MYRON FLOREN
BUDDY MERRILL
NEIL LEVANG
JERRY BURKE
BOB SMALE
BOB RALSTON
FRANK SCOTT
LARRY HOOPER
ALADDIN
BOB LIDO
JOE LAVOTI
DICK CATHCART
CHARLIE POLATTA

RUSS CLINE
NATALIE NEVINS
GEORGE THOW
NORMAN BAILEY
KENNY TRIMBLE
BOB HAVEN
BARNEY LIDDELL
DICK DALE
BILL PAGE
CHARLOTTE HALL
JOHNNY KLEIN
JACK IMEL
BUDDY HAYES
ORIE AMODEO
PETE FOUNTAIN
DAVID JOY
STEVE SMITH
LARRY DEAN
LYNN ANDERSON
PEANUTS HUCKO
JO ANN CASTLE
DICK MALOOF
BIG TINY LITTLE
ALICE LON
NORMA ZIMMER
BARBARA BOYLAN
CISSY KING
BOBBY BURGESS
ARTHUR DUNCAN
CLAY HOWARD
SANDI JENSEN
SALLI FLYNN
ANDRA WILLIS
GAIL FARRELL
DICK KESNER
PETE LOFTHOUSE
JACK MARTIN
CURT RAMSEY
GEORGE AUBRY
MAURICE PEARSON
ROCKY ROCKWELL
HARRY HYAMS
MAHLON CLARK
JOE FEENEY
JIM ROBERTS
GUY ENGLISH
RALNA ENGLISH
KEN DELO
TANYA FALAN WELK
DIANE LENNON
JANET LENNON
KATHY LENNON
PEGGY LENNON (The Lennon
Sisters), musicians and enter-
tainers appearing on the program
(themselves)
MANY GUEST ENTERTAINERS
AND MUSICIANS

The Lawrence Welk Show (TV)
(Music/variety) (Many of these
musicians/entertainers also
appeared on Lawrence Welk's Top
Tunes and New Talent) (TV)

WELK, TANYA FALAN. See:
Welk, Lawrence

WELLES. See also:
Wells
Willis
Wills

WELLES, ORSON (1)
JOSEPH COTTEN
FRANK READICK
RAY COLLINS
JOHN MONKS
BETTY GARDE
AGNES MOOREHEAD (all them-
selves), featured on the program
America's Hour (R) (Documentary)

WELLES, ORSON (2)
JEANETTE NOLAN
BILL ADAMS
JOSEPH COTTEN
RAY COLLINS
RAYMOND EDWARD JOHNSON
JACK SMART
BILL JOHNSTONE
LUIS VAN ROOTEN
FRANK READICK
AGNES MOOREHEAD
PAUL STEWART
EVERETT SLOANE
STAATS COTSWORTH
EDWIN JEROME
TED JEWETT
JOHN McINTIRE
TED DE CORSIA, actors and
actresses appearing on the pro-
gram (themselves)
DONALD VORHEES, orchestra
leader (himself)
HIS ORCHESTRA
Cavalcade of America (R) (His-
torical drama)

WELLES, ORSON (3), host of the
program (himself) and portrayer
of the character Professor
Richard Pierson
PROFESSOR RICHARD PIERSON,
astronomer at Princeton University
RAMON RAQUELLO, orchestra

leader
HIS ORCHESTRA, playing at the
Meridian Room, Hotel Park Plaza,
New York City
PROFESSOR FARRELL, astron-
omer
CARL PHILLIPS, radio com-
mentator
DR. LLOYD GRAY, astronomer
PROFESSOR MORSE, astronomer
BOBBY MILLETTE, orchestra
leader
HIS ORCHESTRA, playing at the
Hotel Martinet, Brooklyn, N.Y.
POLICEMEN
MR. WILMUTH, farmer
RADIO ANNOUNCERS
BRIGADIER GENERAL MONT-
GOMERY SMITH, commander of
State Militia, Trenton, N.J.
HARRY McDONALD, radio net-
work vice president, in charge of
operations
CAPTAIN LANSING, Signal Corps
officer, New Jersey State Militia
SECRETARY OF THE INTERIOR,
U.S. Cabinet officer
OFFICER of field artillery
GUNNER of field artillery
LIEUT. VOUGHT, aviator,
bomber commander
COMMANDER FAIRFAX, of
Langham Field, Virginia
STRANGER, former artilleryman,
survivor of Martian invasion
The Invasion From Mars (R)
(Dramatic adaptation of H. G.
Wells' "The War of the Worlds")

WELLES, ORSON. See also:
Frees, Paul

WELLES, RACHEL. See: Peyton,
Martin

WELLES, STEVE. See: Jordan,
Joyce

WELLES, VALERIE. See: Cummings, Brenda

WELLINGTON DURANT. See:
Wayne, Ruth Evans

WELLMAN, CLARENCE. See:
Hall, Dr. William Todhunter

WELLS. See also:

Welles
Willis
Wills

WELLS, BRIAN. See: Harum,
David

WELLS, CHRISTOPHER, newspaper
reporter
HIS ASSISTANT
The Adventures of Christopher
Wells (R) (Drama)

Wells Fargo, Tales of. See:
Hardie, Jim

WELLS, KAREN. See: Diamond,
Richard

WELLS, KATE. See: Evans, Dean

WELLS, SUSAN PRICE. See:
Harum, David

WENCES, SEÑOR. See: Olsen,
Ole

WENDELL. See: Overstreet,
Buddy

WENDELL, BILL. See: Barry,
Jack (8)

WENDOWSKI, WENDY. See:
Slattery, Jim

WENDY. See:
Howard, Jim
Warren, Wendy

Wendy and Me. See: Burns,
George (3)

WENDY BARRY. See: Uttal,
Fred (1)

WENDY CONWAY. See: Burns,
George (3)

WENDY DARLING. See: Pan,
Peter

Wendy Warren. See: Warren,
Wendy

Wendy Warren and the News.
See: Warren, Wendy

WENDY WENDOWSKI. See: Slattery,
Jim

WEREWULF, WANDA. See: Baker,
Kenny

WERNER. See also: Warner

WERNER, DR. See: Bauer,
Bertha

WERNER, DR. KAREN. See:
Davis, Dr. Althea

WES. See:
Macauley, Wes
Skip
Ves

WESKIT, HARVEY. See: Peepers,
Robinson J.

WESKIT, MARGE. See: Peepers,
Robinson J.

WESLEY. See: Dixon, Wesley

WEST, ALVY. See: Williams,
Andy (1)

WEST, HONEY, female detective
and judo expert
SAM BOLT, her right-hand man
AUNT MEG, her aunt
BRUCE, her pet ocelot
Honey West (TV) (Crime drama
satire)

WEST, JIM (1), Northwest Mounted
Police officer
JOE BIDEAUX, French-Canadian
INSPECTOR ARGYLE of the
Northwest Mounted Police
DOC, physician
MANY OTHERS
Silver Eagle, Mountie (R)
(Adventure)

WEST, JIM (2)
ARTEMUS GORDON, American
underground intelligence agents
in the 1870s
DR. MIGUELITO LOVELESS,
"diminutive master of crime"
The Wild, Wild West (TV)
(Western/espionage)

WEST, LOUISE. See: Arden, Jane

WEST, MAJOR DONALD. See:
Smith, Colonel Zachary

WEST, MICHAEL
CAROL WEST
RUTH WAYNE
MARGARET ANDERSON McCAREY
CEZAR BENEDICT
LARRY HALLIDAY
CHARLES McCAREY
MRS. ANDERSON
KEITH RICHARDS
BOBBY
BARBARA
BONNIE
PENNY
LILY
TED, characters appearing in
the drama
Bright Horizon (R) (Serial drama)

WEST, MICHAEL. See also:
Wayne, Ruth Evans

WEST, PHILIP. See: Brent, Portia

West, Stagecoach. See: Perry,
Luke

West, The American. See: Smith,
Jack

West, The Road. See: Pride, Ben

West, The Wild, Wild. See: West,
Jim (2)

West, Two Faces. See: January,
Dr. Ben

WESTBROOK VAN VOORHIS. See:
Husing, Ted
Van Voorhis, Westbrook (1) (2)

WESTCOTT, AGNES. See: Hargrave-Scott, Joan

Western Ranch Party. See: Ritter,
Tex (1)

Westerner, The. See: Blassingame, Dave

WESTERNERS, LOUISE MASSEY
AND THE. See:

Duke of Paducah, The
Kelly, Joe (1)

WESTHEIMER, DR. See: Sterling,
Vanessa Dale

WESTLAND, STANLEY. See:
Grimm, Arnold

WESTON, BERT. See: Fair-
child, Kay

WESTON, COMMISSIONER. See:
Cranston, Lamont

WESTON, FLORENCE. See:
Waring, Evelyn

WESTON, JOAN. See: Brasuhn,
Tuffy

WESTON, MRS. See: Tate,
Joanne

WESTON, PAUL. See:
Nabors, Jim
Newhart, Bob
Winters, Jonathan

WESTON, SAM
PETER WESTON
ANN WESTON, characters appear-
ing in the drama
Wilderness Road (R) (Serial
drama)

WESTON, SAM. See also: Garrison, Spencer

WEXLER, PETER. See: Bauer,
Bertha

WHARTON, EVELYN. See:
James, Nancy

WHARTON, RICHARD. See:
James, Nancy

What Am I Doing? See: Philips,
Dave

What In the World? See: Rainey,
Dr. Froelich

What Makes You Tick? See: Mc-
Caffery, John K. M. (2)

What or Where Game, The Who.
  See: James, Art

What Would You Have Done? See:
  Grauer, Ben (3)

What's It All About, World? See:
  Jones, Dean

What's My Line? See: Daly, John
  (3)

What's My Name? See: Hulick,
  Wilbur Budd

What's New. See: Binford, Al

What's New in Learning? See:
  Sparks, Hale

What's the Name of That Song?
  See: Williamson, Dud

What's Your Trouble? See: Peale,
  Norman Vincent

WHEATLEY, JOANNE. See:
  Waring, Fred (1)

WHEEDLEDUCK, OLD LADY. See:
  McGee, Fibber

WHEELER, JACK. See: Marx,
  Groucho (2)

WHEEZY. See:
  Gilman, Gordon
  "Weezy"

WHELAN, FATHER. See: Levy,
  Abie

When a Girl Marries. See: Davis,
  Joan Field

When You're Hot You're Hot Hour,
  The Jerry Reed. See: Reed,
  Jerry

Where Are You, Car 54? See:
  Muldoon, Francis

Where Game, The Who, What or.
  See: James, Art

Where the Heart Is. See: Prescott,
  Kate Hathaway

Where Were You? See: Murray,
  Ken (1)

Where's Huddles? See: Huddles,
  Ed

Which Is Which? See: Murray,
  Ken (4)

WHIPLASH, SNIDELY. See: Do-
  Right, Dudley

WHIPPLE, JERRY. See: Hackett,
  Doc

WHIPPLE, SARAH. See: Hackett,
  Doc

Whirlybirds. See: Chuck

Whispering Streets. See: Winslow,
  Hope

Whistler, The. See: Whistler,
  The

WHISTLER, THE, observed and
  commented on "many strange tales
  hidden in the hearts of men and
  women"
  MANY ACTORS AND ACTRESSES
  The Whistler (R) (TV) (Mystery
  drama)

WHISTLIN' PULLEN. See: Bernie,
  Ben

WHISTLING CANARY, HER. See:
  Aunt Jenny (Aunt Lucy)

WHIT DAVIS. See: Lambert,
  Louise

WHITE. See: O'Toole, Ensign

WHITE, BETTY (1), star and
  hostess of the program (herself)
  MANY GUEST STARS
  The Betty White Show (TV)
  (Variety)

WHITE, BETTY (2), hostess of
  the program (herself)
  GUEST CELEBRITIES, pet owners
  OTHER PET OWNERS
  The Pet Set (TV) (Interviews with
  pet owners) (also called Betty
  White's Pet Set) (TV)

WHITE, BILLY, child
BETTY WHITE, his sister
MELVIN CASTLEBURY, their
friend
Billy and Betty (R) (Children's
adventures)

WHITE, BOB. See:
Detective
Lovejoy, Frank (2)

WHITE, BRELLERTON. See:
Myrt

WHITE, DR. ANDREW. See:
Perkins, Ma

WHITE FANG. See: Sales, Soupy

WHITE, FRANCIA. See: Melton,
James (1)

WHITE, INSPECTOR, British
detective
Inspector White of Scotland Yard
(R) (Crime fighting)

WHITE, PAT. See: Murray, Jan
(1)

WHITE, PATTY. See: Davis,
Ann Tyler

WHITE, PERRY. See: Kent,
Clark

WHITE, TED. See: Rutledge,
Dr. John

White, The Woman in. See:
Harding, Karen Adams

WHITEHOUSE, POP. See:
Morrison, Mother

WHITEMAN. See also: Whitman

WHITEMAN, MARGO, hostess of
the program (herself)
MANY TEEN-AGE AMATEUR
PERFORMERS
Tomorrow's Tops (R) (Teen-age
talent)

WHITEMAN, PAUL, host of the
program (himself)
LES ELGART
RUSS MORGAN

HARRY JAMES
EDDIE HOWARD
HAL McINTYRE
MACHITO
STEVE GIBSON
THE REDCAPS
TITO RODRIGUEZ
GENE KRUPA
PERCY FAITH
JOHNNY LONG
BILLY MAY
RICHARD HIMBER
CLAUDE THORNHILL
STAN KENTON
RICHARD MALTBY
CLYDE McCOY
RALPH MARTIERE
THE TRENIERS
BUDDY ROGERS
THE LECUONA CUBAN BOYS
LES BROWN
VAUGHN MONROE
EDDIE GRADY
PUPI CAMPO
PHIL NAPOLEON
RAY ANTHONY
ENRIC MADRIGUERA
ART MOONEY
RUDY VALLEE
COUNT BASIE
XAVIER CUGAT
TED WEEMS
RALPH FONT
TONY PASTOR
CHARLIE BARNETT
EMILIO REYES
MITCH MILLER
VINCENT LOPEZ
PAUL NEIGHBORS
LARRY CLINTON
BOB CROSBY
EDDIE SAUTER
BILL FINEGAN
SAMMY KAYE
TEX BENEKE
LOUIS ARMSTRONG
PEREZ PRADO
PHIL SPITALNY
DUKE ELLINGTON
ERNIE RUDY, dance orchestra
leaders (themselves)
THEIR ORCHESTRAS AND FEA-
TURED VOCALISTS
America's Greatest Bands (TV)
(Dance music)

WHITEMAN, PAUL. See also:
Burns, George (1)

Gibbs, Georgia (2)

WHITEWASH. See: Old Witch,
The

WHITEY. See: Davis, Joan Field

WHITEY FORD. See: Duke of
Paducah, The

WHITFIELD, JOSEPHINE. See:
Cameron, Barry

WHITFIELD, SERGEANT EVE.
See: Ironside, Chief Robert

WHITING, ANDREA. See: Tate,
Joanne

WHITING, CHRISTOPHER. See:
Tate, Joanne

Whiting Girls, Those. See:
Whiting, Margaret

WHITING, JACK. See: Champion,
Marge

WHITING, MARGARET, singer
BARBARA WHITING, her sister,
also singer; featured on the
program (themselves)
MANY ACTORS AND ACTRESSES
Those Whiting Girls (TV) (Drama)

WHITING, MARGARET. See also:
Cantor, Eddie (2)
Crosby, Bob (2)

WHITING, PATTI. See: Tate,
Joanne

WHITLEDGE, BEN. See: Stockdale, Will

WHITMAN. See also: Whiteman

WHITMAN, DR. JAMES, psychiatrist
DR. BERNARD ALTMAN, his
"supervisor and father figure"
The Psychiatrist (TV) (Medical
drama)

WHITMAN, GAYNE
PATRICK McGEEHAN, narrators
of the program (themselves)
Strange As It Seems (R) (Dramatizations of strange and unusual
facts)

WHITNEY. See: Day, Clarence

WHITNEY, GERALDINE. See:
Karr, Mike

WHITNEY, GIL. See: Trent,
Helen

WHITTAKER, MAJOR FRANK.
See: Young, Captain David

Whiz Quiz. See: Olsen, Johnny
(2)

Who Do You Trust? See: Carson,
Johnny (2)

Who In the World? See: Hull,
Warren (3)

Who Pays? See: Wallace, Mike
(5)

Who Said That? See:
Daly, John (4)
Trout, Robert

Who, What or Where Game, The.
See: James, Art

Wichita Town. See: Dunbar, Mike

WICKER, IREENE. See:
Lovejoy, Frank (2)
Singing Lady, The

Widder Brown, Young. See:
Brown, Ellen

WIDDLE KID, THE MEAN. See:
Junior

Wide Country, The. See: Guthrie,
Mitch

Wide, Wide World. See: Garroway, Dave (4)

Wide World of Sports, A.B.C.'s.
See: McKay, Jim (1)

WIDOW, THE BLACK. See:
Batman

WIFE. See: Husband

Wife, Backstage. See: Noble,
Mary

Wife, Dan Harding's. See:
  Harding, Mrs. Rhoda

Wife, Do You Trust Your? See:
  Bergen, Edgar (1)

Wife, John's Other. See: Perry,
  John

Wife, McMillan and. See: Mc-
  Millan, Stuart

WIFE, MARY BACKSTAGE, NOBLE.
  See: Ballew, Wally

Wife, Mary Noble, Backstage.
  See: Noble, Mary

Wife, My Good. See: Francis,
  Arlene (3)

Wife, Occasional. See: Christopher,
  Peter

Wife Saver. See: Prescott, Allen
  (2)

Wife, Second. See: Burton, Terry

Wife, The Doctor's. See: Palmer,
  Dan

WIGGINS, DR. See: Davis, Joan
  Field

WIGGS, MRS.
  PA WIGGS, her father
  BILLY WIGGS, her husband
  MR. BOB
  MR. STEBBINS
  MISS HAZY, characters appearing
  in the drama
  Mrs. Wiggs of the Cabbage Patch
  (R) (Serial drama)

WIKI. See: Davidson, Bill

WILBERFORCE, MARTHA. See:
  Goldberg, Molly

WILBUR. See:
  Dickey, Dan'l
  Hulick, Wilbur Budd
  Post, Wilbur
  Riggs, Tommy
  Webster, Martha
  Wylber

Wilbur and Mr. Ed. See: Post,
  Wilbur

WILBUR BUDD HULICK. See:
  Hulick, Wilbur Budd
  Pitcher, The
  Stoopnagle, Colonel Lemuel Q.
  (2)

WILBUR FINCH. See: Taylor,
  Andy

WILBUR, JUDY (The Red-headed
  Angel)
  WOODY MARSHALL
  BARBARA PUTNAM
  LAURA PUTNAM
  DONALD PUTNAM
  SILAS DRAKE
  DICK BURGESS
  MATTHEW WILBUR
  ARCH HADLEY
  WINIFRED WILBUR
  KEN WILBUR
  MILLICENT PENNINGTON
  LEM STACEY, characters ap-
  pearing in the drama
  Your Family and Mine (R)
  (Serial drama)

WILBUR RAMAGE. See: Sloan,
  Holly

WILBUR SNYDER. See: James,
  Dennis (4)

WILBUR Z. KNOX (GRANDSIR).
  See: Dickey, Dan'l

Wilburn Brothers Show, The. See:
  Wilburn, Doyle

WILBURN, DOYLE
  TEDDY WILBURN, guitarists and
  singers; co-hosts of the program
  (themselves)
  LORETTA LYNN, featured singer
  on the program (herself)
  HAL RUGG, steel guitarist and
  orchestra leader
  HIS ORCHESTRA
  GUEST SINGERS
  The Wilburn Brothers Show (TV)
  (Country music)

WILCOX, NURSE. See: Lochner,
  Dr. Paul

WILD. See also: Wilde

WILD BILL. See: Hickock, Wild
Bill

Wild Bill Hickock. See: Hickock,
Wild Bill

WILD, CHARLIE, private detective
McCOY, his assistant
Charlie Wild, Private Eye (R)
(Detective)

WILD EAGLE. See: Parmenter,
Captain Wilton

Wild Kingdom. See: Perkins,
Marlin

Wild, The Joker's. See: Barry,
Jack (4)

Wild, Wild West, The. See:
West, Jim (2)

WILDCATS, THE TEXAS. See:
Dean, Jimmy
Hamilton, George

WILDE. See also: Wild

WILDE, DANNY, American adven-
turer
LORD BRETT SINCLAIR, his
British fellow-adventurer
The Persuaders (TV) (Adventure)

WILDE, FRANCIS. See: Crown,
Jim

Wilderness Road. See: Weston,
Sam

WILENTZ, CHARLES. See:
August, Dan

WILER. See: Wyler

WILEY. See also: Wyle

WILEY, BURTON. See: Perkins,
Ma

WILEY CROWE, MAJOR GENERAL.
See: Savage, Brigadier General
Frank

WILEY, JANE. See: Hughes, Chris

WILEY, JUDGE. See: Buffalo
Bill, Jr.

WILFRED FINNEGAN. See:
Archie

WILGUS, BILL. See: Bernie,
Ben

WILKINS, ELDORA. See: Nielson, Torwald

WILKINSON, HAROLD. See:
O'Neill, Mrs.

WILL. See:
Horton, Dot
Sonnett, Will
Stockdale, Will
Varner, Will

WILL BROWN. See: Aldrich,
Henry

WILL DONNELLY, DR. See:
Garrison, Spencer

Will, Dot and. See: Horton, Dot

WILL FOREMAN. See: Caine,
Frank

WILL GENTRY. See: Shane,
Michael

WILL MAYBERRY. See: Sher-
wood, Grace

WILL ROBINSON. See: Smith,
Colonel Zachary

WILL ROGERS. See: Drew, John

WILL SCARLETT. See: Hood,
Robin

Will Sonnett, The Guns of. See:
Sonnett, Will

WILL STEVENSON. See: Cam-
eron, Barry

WILL, UNCLE. See: Kent, Fred

WILLIAM. See:
Buckley, William F., Jr.
Carey, Dr. Philip
Colton, William

Drinkwater, William
Gargan, William (1) (2)
Hall, Dr. William Todhunter
Joyce, William
Powell, Dick (3)
Tell, William
Washburn, William

WILLIAM A. WOOD. See: Kennedy,
Bob (1)

WILLIAM "BILL" HERBERT. See:
Barbour, Henry Wilson

WILLIAM BOSWELL. See:
Canova, Judy

WILLIAM BOYD. See: Cassidy,
Hopalong

WILLIAM EDMONDSON. See:
Peters, Lowell

WILLIAM F. X. GEOGHAN, JR.
See: Steel, Richard

WILLIAM HORTON, DR. See:
Horton, Dr. Tom

WILLIAM KEIGHLEY. See:
DeMille, Cecil B.

WILLIAM KING DRIGGS, JR.
See: Driggs, Karleton King

WILLIAM MARTIN "PINKY" HER-
BERT. See: Barbour, Henry
Wilson

WILLIAM OMAHA McELROY. See:
Batman

WILLIAM POWELL. See: Powell,
Dick (3)

WILLIAM QUINN. See: Mc-
Cormick, Myron

WILLIAM RAYMER, DR. See:
Thompson, Dr. McKinley

WILLIAM ROBYN. See: Roxy

WILLIAM SNOOD. See: Mix,
Tom

William Tell. See: Tell, William

WILLIAM WALTER. See: Jordan,
Joyce

WILLIAM WINTER. See: Shadel,
Bill

WILLIAM YOUNGFELLOW. See:
Winchell, Walter (2)

WILLIAMS. See: Horn, Aggie

WILLIAMS, ANDY (1)
JUNE VALLI, singers and enter-
tainers; stars of the program
(themselves)
ALVY WEST, orchestra leader
HIS ORCHESTRA
Andy Williams and June Valli
(TV) (Songs)

WILLIAMS, ANDY (2), singer and
entertainer, host of the program
(himself)
JANOS PROHASKA
CHARLIE CALLAS
THE WILLIAMS WEIRDOS, enter-
tainers appearing on the program
(themselves)
MANY GUEST STARS
MIKE POST, orchestra leader
(himself)
HIS ORCHESTRA
The Andy Williams Show (TV)
(Variety)

WILLIAMS, ANN. See: Casey

WILLIAMS, BUZZER. See: Keene,
Kitty

WILLIAMS, CHARLES. See: Keene,
Kitty

WILLIAMS, CINDY. See: Kelly,
Gene

WILLIAMS, DAN. See: McGarrett,
Steve

WILLIAMS DANCERS, THE LESTER.
See: Davis, Sammy, Jr.

WILLIAMS, DANNY, entertainer at
the Copa
KATHY, his wife
RUSTY, his son
LINDA, his daughter

UNCLE TONOOSE, his Lebanese
uncle
CHARLIE HALPER, his buddy and
employer; owner of the Copa
Make Room for Daddy (TV)
(Family situation comedy) (later
known as The Danny Thomas Show)
(TV) and Make Room for Grand-
daddy) (TV)
TERRY, his daughter
Make Room for Daddy (TV) (The
Danny Thomas Show) (TV)
SUSAN, Rusty's wife
MICHAEL, his six-year-old grand-
son, son of Terry
ROSEY ROBBINS, his accompanist
Make Room for Grandaddy (TV)

WILLIAMS, DR., scientist in under-
sea complex in the year 2020
SPARKS
PAUL
GAIL
ED
HAL
CARLSON, his associates; all
cartoon characters
Sealab 2020 (TV) (Cartoon)

WILLIAMS, DR. DOUG. See:
Horton, Dr. Tom

WILLIAMS, EBENEZER. See:
Charles, Nick

WILLIAMS, EMILY, judge
JANE ALLEN, defense attorney
ROBERT COULTER, prosecutor
TWELVE HOUSEWIVES ACTING
AS JURORS (themselves)
American Woman's Jury (R)
(Courtroom drama)

WILLIAMS, EMILY. See also:
Harris, Phil

WILLIAMS, GENE. See: Malone,
Dr. Jerry

WILLIAMS, HATTIE. See:
Young, Larry "Pepper"

WILLIAMS, KEN. See: Hall,
Monty (3)

WILLIAMS, MARJORIE. See:
Brown, Ellen

WILLIAMS, PAT. See: Steinberg,
David (2)

WILLIAMS, PECOS. See: Mix,
Tom

WILLIAMS QUARTET, THE BILLY.
See: Caesar, Sid (3)

WILLIAMS, RICHARD. See: Kelly,
Joe (2)

WILLIAMS SINGERS, THE DICK.
See: Andrews, Julie

WILLIAMS, TERRY. See: Rogers,
Kenny

WILLIAMS, TEX. See: Ritter,
Tex (1)

WILLIAMS WEIRDOS, THE. See:
Williams, Andy (2)

WILLIAMSON, DUD
BILL GWINN, quizmasters of the
program (themselves)
MANY CONTESTANTS
What's the Name of That Song?
(R) (Musical quiz)

WILLIE. See:
Erwin, Stu
Howard, Willie
Rogers, Buck
Willy

WILLIE FITZ. See: Perkins, Ma

WILLIE GILLIS. See: Ryker,
Lieut. Eddie

WILLIE LOOMIS. See: Collins,
Barnabas

WILLIE MARSHALL. See: Aldrich,
Henry

WILLIE SPICER. See: Jones,
Spike (1)

WILLIE THE WEEP. See: Wilson,
Steve

WILLIE THE WORM. See: Sales,
Soupy

WILLIE TYLER. See: Rowan, Dan

WILLIE VANDEVEER, STEAMBOAT.
See: Wade, Sandy

WILLIS. See also:
Welles
Wells
Wills

WILLIS, ANDRA. See: Welk,
Lawrence

WILLIS, DAVID, newlywed
JULIE WILLIS, his wife
JULIE'S FATHER
STAN PARKER, Willis' neighbor
CAROL PARKER, Stan's wife
Love on a Rooftop (TV) (Situa-
tion comedy)

WILLIS FRAME. See: Randolph,
Alice

WILLIS, RICHARD. See: Charm
Expert

WILLOUGHBY, FRANK. See:
Henry, Captain

WILLOUGHBY, KIRBY. See:
Grimm, Arnold

WILLOUGHBY, MR. See: Day,
Dennis

WILLOW. See: Randolph, Walt

WILLS. See also:
Welles
Wells
Willis

WILLS, NURSE. See: Casey,
Dr. Ben

WILLSON. See also: Wilson

WILLSON, MEREDITH. See:
Bankhead, Tallulah
Morgan, Frank (2)

Willy. See: Dodger, Willy

WILLY. See:
Dante, Willy
Dodger, Willy
Harum, David
McHale, Lieut. Commander
Quinton

Phelps, Jim
Willie

WILLY LUMP-LUMP. See:
Junior

WILLY WALTERS. See: Collins,
Bing

WILLY, ZOE ANN. See: Hutton,
Ina Ray

WILMA. See:
Flintstone, Fred
Lindsey, Peter

WILMA CLEMSON. See: Angel,
Gus

WILMA DEERING. See: Rogers,
Buck

WILMA FRITTER. See: Burnley,
Walter

WILMUTH, MR. See: Welles,
Orson (3)

WILSON. See also: Willson

WILSON, BETH. See: Lescoulie,
Jack (2)

WILSON, BOB. See: Driggs,
Karleton King

WILSON, BUNNY. See: Kelly,
Kitty

WILSON, CAL. See: Reed, Jerry

WILSON, CANDY CONKLING. See:
Driggs, Karleton King

WILSON, CHRIS. See: Trent,
Helen

WILSON, CLAUDIA. See: Brent,
Dr. Jim

WILSON, DIMPLES. See: Bumstead, Blondie

WILSON, DR. THOMAS, child
psychologist
HELEN, his wife
TWIG
KIT, his children

Professional Father (TV) (Comedy)

WILSON, EILEEN. See: Ross,
Lanny

WILSON, ELLEN. See: Manning,
Laura

WILSON, FLIP, comedian; star of
the program (himself)
GERALDINE JONES
REVEREND LeROY
SONNY THE JANITOR
FREDDIE THE SWINGER, char-
acters portrayed by Wilson
TITUS THE GOLDFISH, charac-
ter appearing on the program
GEORGE WYLE, orchestra leader
(himself)
HIS ORCHESTRA
MANY GUEST STARS
The Flip Wilson Show (TV)
(Comedy/variety)

WILSON, FLIP. See also: Shawn,
Dick

WILSON, GEORGE. See: Mitchell,
Dennis

WILSON, GRACE. See: Hargrave-
Scott, Joan

WILSON, HERBERT. See:
Andrews, Walter

WILSON, JANE. See: Waring,
Fred (1)

WILSON, JOHN. See: Mitchell,
Dennis

WILSON, MARK, illusionist (him-
self)
NANI DARNELL, his wife (herself)
MIKE, their son (himself)
CARTOONS
Allakazam (TV) (Children's magic/
cartoon) (also called The Magic
Land of Allakazam) (TV)

WILSON, MARTHA. See: Mitchell,
Dennis

WILSON, MISS. See:
Bridges, Cara
Foster, Major John

WILSON, MR. See: Mitchell,
Dennis

WILSON, MRS. See:
Baker, Kenny
Haymes, Dick

WILSON PICKETT. See: Butler,
Jerry

WILSON, REID. See: Cameron,
Christy Allen

WILSON, SLIM. See: Foley, Red

WILSON, SPIKE. See: Rutledge,
Dr. John

WILSON, STEVE, editor of the
"Illustrated Press"
LORELEI KILBOURNE, society
editor
MILLER, district attorney
TOBY, photographer
INSPECTOR CALLAHAN, police
officer
EDDIE, cab driver
HARRY THE HACK
WILLIE THE WEEP
MISS FOSTER
TOMMY HUGHES
DANNY
FLETCHER
MOZART, characters appearing in
the drama
Big Town (R) (Newspaper adven-
ture) (later produced in modified
form under the title The Heart of
the City (TV) and Headline) (TV)

WILSON, STU, master of ceremonies of the program (himself)
MANY AUDIENCE PARTICIPANTS
Surprise Party (R) (Audience
participation)

WILSON, STUBBY. See: Harris,
Bill

WILSON, WARD, host of the pro-
gram (himself)
PETER DONALD, joke teller
(himself)
HARRY HERSHFIELD
SENATOR ED FORD
JOE LAURIE, JR., members of
panel (themselves)
Can You Top This? (R) (Comedy
panel)

WILSON, WARD. See also:
Cullen, Bill (5)
Weems, Ambrose J.

WILTON. See: Parmenter, Captain
Wilton

WILTON COMSTOCK. See:
Graham, Dr. Bob

WILTON, DR. See: Harding,
Karen Adams

WIMPLE. See also: Wumple

WIMPLE, MR. See: McNeill,
Don

WIMPLE, WALLACE. See: Mc-
Gee, Fibber

WIMPY. See: Popeye

WIN. See also:
Wyn
Wynn

WIN ELLIOTT. See:
Elliott, Win (1) (2)
Roberts, Ken

Win, Spin to. See: Hull, Warren
(1)

Win With a Winner. See: Becker,
Sandy

WINCHELL, PAUL (1), ventriloquist,
star of the program (himself)
JERRY MAHONEY, his dummy
JOSEPH DUNNINGER, mentalist,
co-star of the program (himself)
The Bigelow Show (TV) (Ventrilo-
quism/mind reading)

WINCHELL, PAUL (2), ventriloquist
JERRY MAHONEY, his dummy;
co-hosts of the program (them-
selves)
MANY CIRCUS ACTS
Circus Time (TV) (Circus)

WINCHELL, PAUL (3), ventriloquist;
host of the program (himself)
JERRY MAHONEY
KNUCKLEHEAD SMIFF, his dum-
mies
MANY GUEST STARS

MILTON DeLUGG, orchestra
leader (himself)
HIS ORCHESTRA
The Paul Winchell Show (TV)
(Variety/ventriloquism)

WINCHELL, PAUL (4), ventriloquist;
quizmaster of the program (him-
self)
JERRY MAHONEY, his dummy
MANY JUVENILE CONTESTANTS
Runaround (TV) (Children's quiz)

WINCHELL, PAUL (5), ventriloquist,
host of the program (himself)
JERRY MAHONEY, his dummy
MANY GUEST STARS
Show Business, Inc. (TV) (Vari-
ety/ventriloquism)

WINCHELL, PAUL (6), ventriloquist;
host of the program (himself)
JERRY MAHONEY, his dummy
The Speidel Show (TV) (Ventrilo-
quism)

WINCHELL, PAUL (7), ventriloquist;
host of the program (himself)
JERRY MAHONEY, his dummy
NINE CHILDREN
GUEST STARS
Run Around (TV) (Children's
game)

WINCHELL, PAUL. See also:
Olsen, Ole
Reiner, Carl

WINCHELL, WALTER (1), gossip
columnist and host of the program
(himself)
JACK DENNY
GEORGE OLSEN
ABE LYMAN
TOM COAKLEY
ANSON WEEKS
LLOYD HUNTLEY
IRVING AARONSON
BERT LOWN, dance orchestra
leaders (themselves)
THEIR ORCHESTRAS
MANY OTHER DANCE ORCHES-
TRAS
The Lucky Strike Magic Carpet
(R) (Dance music)

WINCHELL, WALTER (2), gossip
columnist, narrator of the pro-

gram (himself)
ELIOT NESS, U. S. Treasury
agent in prohibition era
ENRICO ROSSI
MARTIN FLAHERTY
WILLIAM YOUNGFELLOW
CAM ALLISON, enforcement
agents on Ness' staff
AL CAPONE
FRANK NITTI, gangsters
OTHER GANGSTERS
The Untouchables (TV) (Crime
drama)

WINCHELL, WALTER (3), gossip
columnist, featured on the program (himself)
Walter Winchell (R) (News) (also
known as Jergens Journal) (R)

WINCHELL, WALTER (4), gossip
columnist, narrator of the pro-
gram (himself)
MANY ACTORS AND ACTRESSES
The Walter Winchell File (TV)
(Suspense drama)

WINCHELL, WALTER (5), gossip
columnist, master of ceremonies
of the program (himself)
MANY GUEST STARS AND ACTS
JURY OF CELEBRITIES
The Walter Winchell Show (TV)
(Variety)

WINCHOLL, JOHN, master of cere-
monies of the program (himself)
THE SINGING MAILMEN
THE STEELE SISTERS, vocal
groups
REGINA COLBERT, vocalist
(herself)
MARY BOWER, harpist (herself)
The Musical Steelmakers (R)
(Music)

Wind, Three Sheets to the. See:
Wayne, John

Window on Main Street. See:
Brooks, Cameron

Window Shopping. See: Kennedy,
Bob (1)

WINDY. See: Peewee

Windy, Peewee and. See: Peewee

WINDY WALES. See: Benson,
Bobby

WINFIELD CRAIG. See: Webster,
Martha

WINFIELD, SANDY. See: Madison,
Kenny

WING COMMANDER. See: Hayes,
Wing Commander

WING, HOWIE, aviator
DONNA CAVENDISH
CAPTAIN HARVEY
ZERO SMITH
TYPHOON
THE CHIEF
BURTON YORK, characters
appearing on the program
Howie Wing (R) (Aviation adven-
ture)

WING, PAUL, spelling master of
the program (himself)
MANY CONTESTANTS
The National Spelling Bee (R)
(Education)

WINGATE, CAPTAIN ZACHARY.
See: Cord

Wingo. See: Kennedy, Bob (2)

Wings of Destiny. See: Benton,
Steve

WINIFRED. See:
Gillis, Dobie
Wilbur, Judy

WINIFRED CECIL. See: Henry,
Captain

WINIFRED DARTIE. See:
Forsyte, Soames

WINK. See: Martindale, Wink
(1) (2)

WINKLER, BETTY
TED MAXWELL
RAYMOND EDWARD JOHNSON
LOU MERRILL
SIDNEY ELLSTROM
TEMPLETON FOX
MANY OTHERS, actors and
actresses appearing on the

program (themselves)
Lights Out (R) (Suspense drama)

WINKLER, BETTY. See also:
Ameche, Don (3)

WINKY-DINK. See: Barry, Jack
(10)

Winky-Dink and You. See: Barry,
Jack (10)

Winner Take All. See: Cullen,
Bill (5)

Winner, Win With a. See: Becker,
Sandy

WINSLOW, DR. See: Brent, Dr.
Jim

WINSLOW, DON, American naval
officer; member of the Squadron
of Peace
RED PENNINGTON, fellow-officer
MERCEDES COLBY, Winslow's
girl friend
LOTUS
MISTY, friends of Winslow
Don Winslow of the Navy (R)
(Adventure)

WINSLOW, HOPE, narrator of the
program
MANY ACTORS AND ACTRESSES
Whispering Streets (R) (Drama)

WINSTON. See: Essex, Winston

WINSTON, ADELLA. See: Fairchild, Kay

WINSTON BURDETTE. See:
Ciardi, John

WINSTON CHURCHILL. See:
Husing, Ted

WINSTON GRIMSLEY. See: Karr,
Mike

WINTER, SUSAN. See: Peyton,
Martin

WINTER, TOM. See: Peyton,
Martin

WINTER, WILLIAM. See:

Shadel, Bill

WINTERS, ANDREW. See: Davis,
Dr. Althea

WINTERS, BILL. See:
Hunter, Mel
Jordan, Joyce

WINTERS, DOLORES. See:
Perry, John

WINTERS, DORIE. See: Jordan,
Joyce

WINTERS, EVELYN
TED BLADES
ROBBIE DeHAVEN
GARY BENNETT
CHARLIE GLEASON
JANICE KING
TRACEY ENDICOTT
JINNY ROBERTS
MISS BEAN
EDITH WINTERS ELKINS
CLEVE HARRINGTON
MAGGIE, characters appearing in
the drama
Evelyn Winters (R) (Serial drama)
(also known as The Strange Ro-
mance of Evelyn Winters) (R)

WINTERS, JACK
LINDA WEBSTER
DAN TOBIN
MRS. CAMERON
CARUSO, characters appearing in
the drama
City Desk (R) (Drama)

WINTERS, JONATHAN, comedian,
star of the program (himself)
MAUDE FRICKERT, character
portrayed by Winters
CLIFF ARQUETTE, comedian
(himself)
CHARLEY WEAVER, character
portrayed by Arquette
PAMELA RODGERS
DICK CURTIS
DEBI STORM
DIANE DAVIS, entertainers ap-
pearing on the program (them-
selves)
PAUL WESTON, orchestra leader
(himself)
HIS ORCHESTRA
The Jonathan Winters Show (TV)
(Comedy/variety)

WINTERS, JONATHAN. See also:
Worley, Jo Anne

WINTERS, LARRY. See: Hughes,
Chris

WINTERS, MARION. See: Bauer,
Bertha

WINTERS, ROLAND. See: Begley,
Martin

WINTERS, VICTORIA. See:
Collins, Barnabas

WINTERSPRING, PRINCESS SUM-
MERFALL. See: Doody, Howdy

WINTHROP, BARBARA. See:
Dix, Dorothy (2)

WINTHROP, DOUGLAS. See:
Ames, Peter

WINTHROP, URSULA. See: Ames,
Peter

WINTON, BOB. See: O'Neill,
Mrs.

Wire Service. See: Evans, Dean

WISA D'ORSO DANCERS, THE.
See: Nye, Louis

Wish, Make a. See: Chapin, Tom

WISHBONE. See: Favor, Gil

WITCH. See: Old Witch, The

WITCH, BEULAH THE. See:
Kukla

WITCH, GITTEL THE. See:
Pam

WITCHIE-POO, MISS. See:
Pufnstuf, H. R.

Witch's Tale, The. See: Cole,
Alonzo Dean

Without a Gun, Man. See: Mc-
Lean, Adam

Witness, The. See: Steel,
Richard

WITT, DWAYNE. See: Tammy

WIVENHOE. See also: Ivanhoe

WIVENHOE, COMMANDER, director
of boys' summer camp; hates
children
COUNSELOR SPIFFY
PRUETT, camp staff members
MAHALIA MAY GRUNECKER,
head counselor at the camp
CAPRICE YEUDLEMAN, coun-
selor at girls' camp
Camp Runamuck (TV) (Comedy)

Wives, Husbands and. See: Miles,
Allie Lowe

Wives of Henry VIII, The Six. See:
Henry VIII, King of England

WIZARD, MR., science teacher,
portrayed by Don Herbert
ANDY GILBREATH, his pupil
(himself)
OTHER PUPILS
Mr. Wizard (TV) (Children's
science) (also called Watch Mr.
Wizard) (TV)

WO FAT. See: McGarrett, Steve

WOLF. See also: Wolfe

Wolf, The Lone. See: Lanyard,
Michael

WOLF, THE LONE. See: Lanyard,
Michael

WOLFE. See:
Bennett, Nita
Wolf

WOLFE BENNETT SR., MRS.
See: Bennett, Nita

WOLFE, MIRIAM. See: Halop,
Billy

WOLFE, NERO, private detective
ARCHIE GOODWIN, his assistant
The Adventures of Nero Wolfe
(R) (Crime/adventure)

WOLFGANG WEISSLEDER. See:
Barry, Jack (9)

WOLPER, MR. See: Sterling, Vanessa Dale

WOLSEY, CARDINAL. See: Henry VIII, King of England

WOLZNIAK, FIRST SERGEANT. See: McKay, Judson

Woman in My House. See: Carter, James

Woman in White, The. See: Harding, Karen Adams

Woman, It Takes a. See: Scott, Frances

Woman, Lonely. See: Larimore, Marilyn

Woman of America, A. See: Dane, Prudence

Woman of Courage. See: Jackson, Martha

WOMAN, THE CAT. See: Batman

Woman, There Was a. See: Johnson, Raymond Edward (2)

Woman, Today's. See: Chase, Sylvia

Woman's Jury, American. See: Williams, Emily

Women, American. See: Kummer, Eloise

Women and Children First. See: Joe (2)

Women, Little. See: March, Mrs.

Women Only, Not For. See: Walters, Barbara

Women, Self-Defense For. See: Offstein, Jerry

WONDER DOG, THE. See: Rin-Tin-Tin

WONDER HORSE OF THE WORLD, THE. See: Mix, Tom

WONDER, THE BOY. See: Batman

WONG. See: MacDonald, Eleanor

WONG, DWIGHT EISENHOWER. See: Jones, Kenneth Yarborough

WONS, TONY, reader of poetry (himself)
Tony Wons' Scrapbook (R) (Poetry)

WOOD, BARRY. See: Ross, Lanny

WOOD, EDITH. See: Fairchild, Kay

WOOD, MISS. See: Marlin, Mary

WOOD, MOLLY. See: Virginian, The

WOOD, WILLIAM A. See: Kennedy, Bob (1)

WOODARD, MAX. See: Myrt

WOODCHOPPER, ARKIE THE ARKANSAS. See: Kelly, Joe (1)

WOODLEY, HERB. See: Bumstead, Blondie

WOODLEY, TOOTSIE. See: Bumstead, Blondie

WOODMAN, KENNY. See: Doonican, Val

WOODPECKER. See: Woody Woodpecker

Woodpecker, Woody. See: Woody Woodpecker

WOODROW. See: Miller, Johnny

WOODROW THE GROUNDHOG. See: Pam

WOODRUFF, PROFESSOR TONY, investigators
My Friend Tony (TV) (Crime drama)

WOODS, CHARLES. See: Jostyn,
Jay (1)

WOODS, DONALD, actor; resident
of swank Hotel Cosmopolitan in
New York (himself)
MANY ACTORS AND ACTRESSES
Hotel Cosmopolitan (TV) (Drama)

WOODY. See:
Banner, Woody
Herman, Woody
Klose, Woody

WOODY ALLEN. See: Worley,
Jo Anne

Woody Herman Show, The. See:
Herman, Woody

WOODY KIRK, GENERAL. See:
Newman, Tony

WOODY MARSHALL. See: Wilbur,
Judy

Woody Woodpecker. See: Woody
Woodpecker

WOODY WOODPECKER, cartoon
character
Woody Woodpecker (TV) (Cartoon)

WOOLEY, HELEN. See: Hutton,
Ina Ray

WOOLEY, SHEB. See: Owens,
Buck

WOOLLCOTT, ALEXANDER (The
Town Crier), host of the pro-
gram (himself)
MANY INTERVIEWEES
The Town Crier (R) (Interviews)

WORD CARR. See: Ballew, Wally

Word, The Last. See: Evans,
Bergen (2)

WORDMASTER, THE, portrayed by
Vincent Pelletier
MANY CONTESTANTS
Speak Up, America (R) (Educa-
tional quiz)

Words and Music. See: Hays,
Harvey

Workshop, Wally's. See: Bruner,
Wally (2)

WORLD ACTION SINGERS, THE.
See: Roberts, Oral

World and Welcome to It, My.
See: Monroe, John

World, Animal. See: Burrud, Bill
(1)

World, Another. See: Randolph,
Alice

World, Bracken's. See: Bracken,
John

World Championship Golf. See:
Crosby, Bob (3)

World, Good Morning. See:
Lewis, Dave

World, Harris Against the. See:
Harris, Alan

World, It's a Man's. See: Macauley,
Wes

World of Giants, The. See: Hunter,
Mel

World of Golf, The. See: Sarazen, Gene

World of Jacques Cousteau, The
Undersea. See: Cousteau,
Jacques

World of Kreskin, The Amazing.
See: Kreskin

World of Mr. Sweeney, The. See:
Sweeney, Cicero P.

World of Sports, A.B.C.'s Wide.
See: McKay, Jim (1)

World of Talent, The. See: Clark,
Dick (3)

World, Our Private. See: Hughes,
Lisa

World Series, The. See: Cowan,
Thomas

World, Shirley's. See: Logan,
Shirley

World, Small. See: Murrow,
Edward R. (5)

World, The Light of the. See:
Speaker, The

WORLD, THE WONDER HORSE OF
THE. See: Mix, Tom

World, This Changing. See:
Bishop, Neil

World Turns, As the. See: Hughes,
Chris

World War I. See: Ryan, Robert
(2)

World We Live In, The. See:
Ingram, Dan

World, What In the? See: Rainey,
Dr. Froelich

World, What's It All About? See:
Jones, Dean

World, Who In the? See: Hull,
Warren (3)

World, Wide, Wide. See: Garroway, Dave (4)

WORLEY, JO ANNE
JONATHAN WINTERS
WOODY ALLEN, hosts of the
program (themselves)
MANY GUESTS
Hot Dog (TV) (Children's educa-
tional program)

WORLEY, JO ANNE. See also:
Rowan, Dan

WORM, WILLIE THE. See:
Sales, Soupy

Worse, For Better or. See:
Peterson, Dr. James

WORTH, FRANK. See: First
Nighter, Mr.

WORTHINGTON, NORA
CYRIL WORTHINGTON

JULIET WORTHINGTON
JOAN WORTHINGTON
DICK WORTHINGTON
BARBARA WORTHINGTON
GREGORY PEARSON
ALEX PRATT
MICHAEL
ANNIE, characters appearing in
the drama
Orphans of Divorce (R) (Serial
drama)

WORTLE, ROSCOE. See:
Canova, Judy

Wow Show, The Ken Berry. See:
Berry, Ken

Wrangler. See: Pitcairn

WRANGLER JANE. See: Par-
menter, Captain Wilton

WRANGLER, THE OLD. See:
Mix, Tom

WRATISLAW. See: Churchill,
John

Wrestling. See: James, Dennis
(4)

WRIGHT, COBINA, hostess of the
program (herself)
MANY INTERVIEWEES
Your Hostess (R) (Interview/
conversation)

WRIGHT, CONLEY, war corres-
pondent assigned to 5th Army in
World War II Italian Campaign
CAPTAIN JIM BENEDICT
LIEUT. KIMBRO
SERGEANT McKENNA
PRIVATE D'ANGELO
PRIVATE LUCAVICH
PRIVATE HANSON
PRIVATE GIBSON, officers and
soldiers of 5th Army
The Gallant Men (TV) (World
War II drama)

WRIGHT, MR. See:
Hargrave-Scott, Joan
Malone, Dr. Jerry

WRIGHT, NANCY. See: James,
Dennis (1)

WRIGHT, TOBY. See: Kaye,
  Sammy (1)

WRIOTHESELEY, THOMAS. See:
  Henry VIII, King of England

WUMPLE. See:
  Wallet, Skeezix
  Wimple

WYATT. See: Earp, Wyatt

Wyatt Earp, The Life and Legend of.
  See: Earp, Wyatt

WYATT, JACK, interviewer (him-
  self)
  CONVICTED CRIMINAL INTER-
  VIEWEES
  PANEL of clergymen, lawyers,
  psychiatrists, psychologists,
  penologists and/or sociologists
  Confession (TV) (Interview)

WYLBER. See also: Wilbur

WYLBER, DARL, host of the pro-
  gram (himself)
  MANY GUEST SPORTSMEN
  T. V. Sportsman's Club (TV)
  (Sports discussion)

WYLE. See also: Wiley

WYLE, GEORGE. See:
  Reed, Jerry
  Wilson, Flip

WYLE SINGERS, THE GEORGE.
  See: Lewis, Jerry

WYLER, GRETCHER. See: Crosby,
  Bob (1)

WYMAN, JANE, actress; hostess of
  the program (herself)
  MANY ACTORS AND ACTRESSES
  The Jane Wyman Theater (TV)
  (Play anthology)

WYN. See also:
  Win
  Wynn

WYN STRAFFORD. See: Foyle,
  Kitty

WYNN. See also:

Win
Wyn

WYNN, ED, comedian; host of the
  program (himself)
  MANY GUEST STARS
  The Ed Wynn Show (TV) (Comedy/
  variety)

WYNN, ED. See also:
  Beamer, John
  Bubbles, King
  Fire Chief, The

WYNN, JOY. See: Barton, Bud

WYNN, MRS. See: Locke, Dr.
  Simon (1)

WYNN, NAN. See: Kemp, Hal

WYNTOON, BARBARA. See:
  Bailey, Sam

WYNTOON, CECIL. See: Bailey,
  Sam

X, A Man Called. See: Thurston,
   Ken

XAN. See: Driggs, Karleton
   King

XANTHIPPE. See: Harum, David

Xavier Cugat. See: Cugat, Xavier
   (2)

XAVIER CUGAT. See:
   Cugat, Xavier (1) (2)
   Durante, Jimmy
   Whiteman, Paul

Y. KIMBALL. See: Narz, Jack
(2)

YABLONSKY, LEWIS, moderator
of the program (himself)
MANY ASSORTED PANELISTS
The Family Game (TV) (Discussion of family problems)

YAHBUT. See:
Blurt, Elmer
Cheerily, Reginald

YANCY. See: Derringer, Yancy

Yancy Derringer. See: Derringer,
Yancy

Yankee Doodle Quiz. See: Malone,
Ted (2)

YANKEES ORCHESTRA, THE CON-
NECTICUT. See: Vallee, Rudy
(2) (3)

Yanks, Thanks to the. See:
Hawk, Bob (2)

YASHA GAMBARELLI. See: Roxy

YATES, DR. See: Brent, Dr.
Jim

YATES, RITA. See: Solomon,
David

YATES, ROWDY. See: Favor,
Gil

Year, It Was a Very Good. See:
Torme, Mel

YEAR, THE NEW. See: Benny,
Jack

Years, The Best. See: Randolph,
Walt

Years, The Lawless. See: Ruditsky, Barney

Years, The Second Hundred. See:
Carpenter, Luke

YEOMANS, FLOYD. See: Story,
Ralph

Yes, Yes, Nanette. See:

McGovern, Dan

Yesterday's Children. See: Gordon,
Dorothy

YEUDLEMAN, CAPRICE. See:
Wivenhoe, Commander

Yoga and You, Lilias. See:
Folan, Lilias

Yogi Bear. See: Yogi Bear

YOGI BEAR, stealer of "pickinick
baskets"
BOO-BOO, bear, his friend
RANGER, at Jellystone Park;
all cartoon characters
Yogi Bear (TV) (Cartoon)

YOGI YORGESON. See: Blurt,
Elmer

YOHNNY. See also:
Johnny
Jonny

YOHNNY YOHNSON. See: Kaltenmeyer, Professor August, D. U. N.

YOHNSON. See also:
Johnson
Johnston
Johnstone

YOHNSON, YOHNNY. See: Kaltenmeyer, Professor August, D. U. N.

YOKUM, LI'L ABNER, young hill-
billy
MAMMY YOKUM, his mother
PAPPY YOKUM, his father
DAISY MAE, his sweetheart
Li'l Abner (R) (TV) (Comedy)

YORGESON, YOGI. See: Blurt,
Elmer

YORK, BURTON. See: Wing,
Howie

YORK, THE DUKE OF. See:
Churchill, John

YORKE, REGGIE. See: Packard,
Jack

YOSSARIAN, SELMA. See:

McKay, Judson

You Are There. See:
  Cronkite, Walter (6)
  Sorel, Guy

You Asked for It. See: Baker,
  Art (2)

You Bet Your Life. See: Marx,
  Groucho (3)

You Don't Say! See: Narz, Jack
  (6)

You, Especially For. See: Quinlan, Roberta

You, It Could Be. See: Leyden,
  Bill (1)

You Tick?, What Makes. See:
  McCaffery, John K. M. (2)

You Want To Lead a Band?, So.
  See: Kaye, Sammy (2)

You?, Where Were. See: Murray,
  Ken (1)

You, Winky-Dink and. See:
  Barry, Jack (10)

You'll Never Get Rich. See:
  Bilko, Sergeant Ernest

YOUNG, ALAN, comedian, star of
  the program (himself)
  MANY GUEST STARS
  The Alan Young Show (R) (TV)
  (Comedy/variety)
  MRS. JOHNSON
  PAPA DITTENFEFFER
  HUBERT UPDYKE
  ZERO
  BETTY, comedians and char-
  acters appearing on the program
  The Alan Young Show (R)

YOUNG, CAPTAIN DAVID
  MAJOR FRANK WHITTAKER,
  attorneys in military service;
  attached to J. A. G. office in
  Europe
  SERGEANT McCASKEY, non-
  commissioned officer
  Courtmartial (TV) (Military
  drama)

YOUNG, DICK. See: Webster,
  Martha

Young Dr. Malone. See: Malone,
  Dr. Jerry

YOUNG, DONNA JEAN. See:
  Rowan, Dan

Young, Forever. See: Davis,
  Red

YOUNG, JOAN. See: Carter,
  Kathryn

YOUNG JOLYON. See: Forsyte,
  Soames

YOUNG, LARRY "PEPPER," resi-
  dent of Elmwood
  PEGGY, his sister
  MARY YOUNG
  SAM YOUNG
  TED HART, football coach
  CURT BRADLEY
  MRS. CURT BRADLEY
  BIFF BRADLEY
  MARCELLA THE MENACE
  CARTER TRENT
  IVY TRENT
  HORACE TRENT
  LINDA BENTON
  HATTIE WILLIAMS, maid
  MR. JEROME
  EDIE GRAY
  MOLLY O'HARA
  PETE NICKERSON
  ANDY HOYT
  LOU SCOTT
  NICK HAVENS
  SALLY
  ANNA
  HANK
  HASTINGS
  BUTCH, characters appearing in
  the drama
  Pepper Young's Family (R)
  (Serial drama)

Young Lawyers, The. See: Bar-
  ret, David

Young, Like. See: McKenna,
  Jim

YOUNG, LORETTA (1), actress;
  hostess and star of the program
  (herself)

MANY SUPPORTING ACTORS
AND ACTRESSES
A Letter to Loretta (TV) (Drama)

YOUNG, LORETTA (2), actress;
hostess of the program (herself)
MANY SUPPORTING ACTORS AND
ACTRESSES
The Loretta Young Show (TV)
(Drama) (later reissued as
Festival of Stars) (TV)

Young Marrieds, The. See: Garrett, Susan

Young People's Concerts. See:
Bernstein, Leonard

Young People's Conference. See:
Poling, Rev. Daniel

Young Rebels, The. See: Larkin,
Jeremy

YOUNG, ROBERT. See:
Morgan, Frank (1)
Stewart, James

YOUNG, VICTOR. See: Jolson,
Al

Young Widder Brown. See:
Brown, Ellen

YOUNGFELLOW, WILLIAM. See:
Winchell, Walter (2)

YOUNGMAN, HENNY. See:
Lewis, Robert Q. (1)

Your Bet, It's. See: Waggoner,
Lyle

Your Dream Has Come True.
See: Keith, Ian

Your F.B.I., This Is. See:
Taylor, Jim

Your Family and Mine. See:
Wilbur, Judy

Your First Impression. See:
Leyden, Bill (2)

Your Happy Birthday. See: Birthday Man, The

Your Hit Parade. See:
Lanson, Snooky
Ross, Lanny

YOUR HOST. See: Raymond

Your Hostess. See: Wright, Cobina

Your Life, This Is. See: Edwards,
Ralph (2)

Your Life, You Bet. See: Marx,
Groucho (3)

Your Lover. See: Luther, Frank (2)

Your Music, This Is. See:
Palmer, Byron

Your Show of Shows. See: Caesar,
Sid (3)

Your Show of Shows, Admiral
Broadway Revue. See: Caesar,
Sid (3)

Your Trouble?, What's. See: Peale,
Norman Vincent

You're On Your Own. See:
Dunne, Steve

You're Putting Me On. See:
Blyden, Larry (2)

Yours For a Song. See:
Froman, Jane (2)
Parks, Bert (7)

Yours, The Verdict Is. See:
McKay, Jim (2)

Yours Truly, Johnny Dollar. See:
Dollar, Johnny

Youth, News of. See: Scoop

Youth Takes a Stand. See: Cochran, Ron

Youth Vs. Age. See: Tinney, Cal

YUKON KING. See: Preston,
Sergeant

Yukon, Sergeant Preston of the.
See: Preston, Sergeant

Yukon, The Challenge of the. See:
   Preston, Sergeant

YUL. See: Brynner, Yul

YUMA, JOHNNY, post Civil War
   cowboy and gunman
   The Rebel (TV) (Western)

YVONNE. See: Brown, Ellen

YVONNE CLAIRE. See: Perry,
   John

YVONNE DRIGGS BURCH. See:
   Driggs, Karleton King

YVONNE KING. See: Driggs,
   Karleton King

ZA BACH, FLORIAN, violinist; star
of the program (himself)
MARY ELLEN TERRY, dancer,
featured on the program (herself)
MANY GUEST STARS
The Florian ZaBach Show (TV)
(Music)

ZABISCO, GLADYS. See: Benny,
Jack

ZACHARIAS, REAR ADMIRAL
ELLIS M., American naval
officer
MANY ACTORS AND ACTRESSES
Behind Closed Doors (TV)
(Dramatizations of espionage
cases)

ZACHARY. See: Smith, Colonel
Zachary

ZACHARY WINGATE, CAPTAIN.
See: Cord

ZACK MALLOY. See: Wade,
Sandy

ZAIDDA. See: Omar

Zane Grey Theater. See:
Ayres, Lew
Powell, Dick (4)

Zane Grey Theater, Dick Powell's.
See: Powell, Dick (2)

ZARKIN. See: Lockridge, Barry

ZARKOV, DR. See: Gordon,
Flash

ZEB. See: Blurt, Elmer

ZEBRA KID, THE. See: James,
Dennis (4)

ZEKE HAMMILL. See: Perkins,
Ma

ZEKE SWINNEY. See: Harum,
David

ZELDA. See: Batman

ZENITH SAMBRINI. See: Perkins,
Ma

ZENTNER, SI. See: Basie, Count

ZERO. See: Young, Alan

Zero, Latitude. See: McKenzie,
Captain Craig

ZERO SMITH. See: Wing, Howie

ZIEHM. See: Rogers, Patricia

ZIFFEL. See: Douglas, Oliver

ZIFFEL, MRS. See: Douglas,
Oliver

ZIGGY TALENT. See: Monroe,
Vaughn

Zigzag. See: Croft, Jonathan

ZIMMER, NORMA. See: Welk,
Lawrence

ZIMMERMAN, HARRY. See:
Shore, Dinah (2)

ZIMMERMAN, PRIVATE. See:
Bilko, Sergeant Ernest

ZIMMERMANN, ELIZABETH,
hostess of the program (herself)
The Busy Knitter (TV) (Knitting
instruction)

ZOE ANN WILLY. See: Hutton,
Ina Ray

Zone, Twilight. See: Serling,
Rod (2)

ZORBA, DR. DAVID. See: Casey,
Dr. Ben

Zorro. See: Vega, Don Diego

ZORRO. See: Vega, Don Diego

ZUCCA, RITA LOUISE. See:
Sisk, Mildred Elizabeth